GENERAL PRINCIPLES AND EMPIRICALLY SUPPORTED TECHNIQUES OF COGNITIVE BEHAVIOR THERAPY

GENERAL PRINCIPLES AND EMPIRICALLY SUPPORTED TECHNIQUES OF COGNITIVE BEHAVIOR THERAPY

Edited by

William O'Donohue

Jane E. Fisher

WILEY

John Wiley & Sons, Inc.

Copyright © 2009 by John Wiley & Sons, Inc. All rights reserved.

Published by John Wiley & Sons, Inc., Hoboken, New Jersey.
Published simultaneously in Canada.

Library of Congress Cataloging-in-Publication Data:

General principles and empirically supported techniques of cognitive behavior therapy / edited by William O'Donohue, Jane E. Fisher.
    p. ; cm.
  Includes bibliographical references and index.
  ISBN 978-0-470-22777-0 (cloth : alk. paper)
  1. Cognitive therapy. I. O'Donohue, William T. II. Fisher, Jane E. (Jane Ellen), 1957-
  [DNLM: 1. Cognitive Therapy–methods. WM 425.5.C6 G326 2009]
  RC489.C63G46 2009
  616.89′142–dc22

          2008036138

Printed in the United States of America

10 9 8 7 6 5

CONTENTS

PREFACE

This book includes introductory material (the first five chapters) so that the reader can gain both a general overview of CBT as well as gain a general understanding of some of the basics of cognitive behavior therapy. The first chapter provides a brief history of cognitive behavior therapy and presents some of its current and future challenges. A key problem is that cognitive behavior therapy was based on learning research and other research in experimental psychology, but now the ties to this research are much looser and indirect. This might have certain costs that are not properly realized. The second chapter covers assessment issues in cognitive behavior therapy, focusing on functional analysis. This chapter introduces and explains much of the basic terminology that the student needs to understand to properly understand CBT, such as contingency, schedule of reinforcement, functional relationship, and so forth. The third chapter provides an overview of some of the evidence base for CBT. CBT is different than many other forms of psychotherapy in that its appeal is not based solely on its conceptual attractiveness but upon scientific studies of its outcomes. This puts CBT in the camp of "evidenced based practice," an important quality improvement development in healthcare. This is not to say CBT is a "done deal"; there is always more evidence to collect regarding outcomes and processes involved in CBT. We are at the beginnings of our research agenda, not at the end. The next chapter covers cultural issues in the implementation of CBT. CBT attempts to develop regularities but countenances the fact that each client has a unique history and present circumstance and thus it is part of the clinician's job to understand the relevance of this and make appropriate adaptations to assessment and treatment plans. Finally, the last chapter in this section covers some of the new developments in CBT. Dialectical Behavior Therapy, Mindfulness, and Acceptance and Commitment Therapy have been gaining a lot of attention in the last few decades and the promise and problems of these are discussed.

Over the last three decades there has been a significant increase in interest in cognitive behavior therapy. This has occurred for several reasons: 1) Mounting experimental evidence supports the effectiveness of cognitive behavioral therapy for certain psychological problems including high incidence problems such as depression and the anxiety disorders. The well-known Chambless report, for example, identifies many cognitive behavioral therapies as being empirically supported. In fact, cognitive behavioral techniques comprise most of the list. 2) Cognitive behavior therapy tends to be relatively brief and often can be delivered in groups. Therefore it can be more cost-effective than some alternatives and be seen to offer good value. These qualities have become particularly important in the era of managed care with its emphasis upon cost containment. 3) Cognitive behavior therapy has been applied with varying success to a wide variety of problems (see Fisher and O'Donohue, 2006 for over 70 behavioral health problems in which CBT can be considered an evidence based treatment. Thus, it has considerable scope and utility for the practitioner in general practice or the professional involved in the training of therapists. 4) Cognitive behavior therapy is a relatively straight forward and clearly operationalized approach to psychotherapy. This does not mean that case formulation or implementing these techniques is easy. However, CBT is more learnable that techniques such as psychoanalysis or Gestalt therapy. 5) Cognitive behavioral therapy is a therapy system comprised of many individual techniques, with researchers and practitioners constantly adding to this inventory. A given behavior therapist, because of his or her specialty, may know or use only a small subset of these. A clinician or clinical researcher may want to creatively combine individual techniques to treat some intransigent problem or an unfamiliar or complicated clinical presentation.

This volume attempts to bring together all of the specific techniques of cognitive behavior therapy. It does this in an ecumenical fashion. Historically, and currently, there are divisions inside behavior therapy that this book attempts to ignore. For example, cognitive and more traditionally behavioral techniques are included. This offended some prospective authors who were clearly warriors in the cognitive-behavioral battle. We wanted to be inclusive, particularly because pragmatically the outcome research favors both sides of this particular battle.

Our major interest in compiling this book was twofold: First we noted the lack of a volume that provides detailed descriptions of the techniques of cognitive behavioral therapy. Many books mentioned these but few described the techniques in detail. The absence of a comprehensive collection of the methods of cognitive-behavior therapy creates a gap in the training of students and in the faithful practice of cognitive behavior therapy. Second, with the increased interest in cognitive behavior therapy, particularly by the payers in managed care, there has been an increasing bastardization of behavior therapy. Some therapists are claiming they are administering some technique (e.g., relapse prevention or contingency management) when they clearly are not. This phenomenon, in our experience, rarely involves intentional deception but instead reflects an ignorance of the complexities of faith-fully implementing these techniques. This book is aimed at reducing this problem.

There is an important question regarding the extent to which a clinician can faithfully implement these techniques without a deeper understanding of behavior therapy. The evidence is not clear and of course the question is actually more complicated. Perhaps a generically skilled therapist with certain kinds of clients and certain kinds of techniques can implement the techniques well. On the other hand, a less skilled therapist dealing with a complicated clinical presentation utilizing a more subtle technique might not do so well. There is certainly a Gordon Paul type ultimate question lurking here. Something like: "What kind of therapist, with what type of problem, using what kind of cognitive behavior therapy technique, with what kind of training, can have what kinds of effects. . ." With the risk of being seen as self-promoting, the reader can learn about the learning and conditioning underpinnings of many of thes techniques in O'Donohue (1998); and more of the theories associated with these techniques in O'Donohue and Krasner (1995). Fisher and O'Donohue (2006) provide a description of particular problems that these techniques can be used with.

References

Fisher, J.E.,& O'Donohue, W.T. (2006) Practitioner's guide to evidence based psychotherapy. New York: Springer
O'Donohue, W., & Krasner, L. (Eds.). (1995). Theories of behavior therapy. Washington: APA Books
O'Donohue, W. (Ed.). (1998). Learning and behavior therapy. Boston: Allyn & Bacon.

ACKNOWLEDGMENTS

We wish to thank all the chapter authors. They uniformly wrote excellent chapters and completed these quickly.

We'd also like to thank our editor at John Wiley & Sons, Patricia Rossi. She shared our vision for this book, gave us some excellent suggestions for improvement, and has been wonderful to work with.

We'd also like to thank Linda Goddard for all her secretarial skills and expert assistance in all aspects of the manuscript preparation; she was invaluable.

Finally, we'd like to thank our families for their support, and especially our children, Katie and Annie, for their enthusiasm and delightfulness.

CONTRIBUTORS

Jonathan S. Abramowitz
University of North Carolina
Chapel Hill, NC

Dean T. Acheson
University at Albany, SUNY
Albany, NY

Jennifer H. Adams
University of Colorado at Denver
Denver, CO

Mark A. Adams, Ph.D., B.C.B.A
Best Consulting, Inc.
Fresno, CA

K. Angeleque Akin-Little
Massey University
Auckland, NZ

Mark Alavosius, Ph.D.
University of Nevada, Reno
Reno, NV

Claudia Avina, Ph.D.
University of Nevada, Reno
Reno, NV

Jenna L. Baddeley, M.A.
The University of Texas at Austin
Austin, TX

Anjali Barretto, Ph.D.
Gonzaga University
Spokane, WA

Wendy K. Berg, M.A.
University of Iowa
Iowa City, IA

Jennifer L. Best, Ph.D.
University of North Carolina
Charlotte, NC

Arthur W. Blume, Ph.D.
University of North Carolina
Charlotte, NC

Stephen R. Boggs, Ph.D.
University of Florida
Gainesville, FL

Jordan T. Bonow
University of Nevada, Reno
Reno, NV

John C. Borrero, Ph.D.
University of Maryland
Baltimore, MD

Carrie S. W. Borrero, Ph.D.
Kennedy-Krieger Institute
Baltimore, MD

Stephanie Both, Ph. D.
Leiden University Medical Center
Leiden, Netherlands

J. Annette Brooks, Ph. D.
New Mexico VA Healthcare System
Albuquerque, NM

Jeffery A. Buchanan
Minnesota State University
Mankato, MN

Eric Burkholder
Dublin Unified School District
Department of Special Education
Dublin, CA

James E. Carr, Ph.D.
Western Michigan University
Kalamazoo, MI

Lavina L. Cavasos
New Mexico VA Healthcare System
Albuquerque, NM

Daniel Cervone, Ph.D.
University of Illinois at Chicago
Chicago, IL

Stacey M. Cherup
University of Nevada, Reno
Reno, NV

Kim Christiansen
Carson City, NV

Linda J. Cooper-Brown, Ph.D.
University of Iowa Children's Hospital
Iowa City, IA

Michelle G. Craske, Ph.D.
UCLA
Los Angeles, CA

Dan Crimmins, Ph.D.
The Marcus Institute
Atlanta, GA

Wendy Crook
University of Nevada, Reno
Reno, NV

Jesse M. Crosby
Utah State University
Logan, UT

Joseph Dagen
University of Nevada, Reno
Reno, NV

Sabrina M. Darrow
University of Nevada, Reno
Reno, NV

Gerald C. Davison, Ph.D.
UCLA
Los Angeles, CA

Kim DeRuyk, Ph.D.
Boys' Town
Boys' Town, NE

Sona Dimidjian, Ph.D.
University of Colorado
Boulder, CO

Keith S. Dobson, Ph.D.
University of Calgary
Calgary, Canada

Brad Donohue, Ph.D.
University of Nevada, Las Vegas
Las Vegas, NV

Crissa Draper
University of Nevada, Reno
Reno, NV

Claudia Drossel, Ph.D.
University of Nevada, Reno
Reno, NV

Melanie P. Duckworth, Ph.D.
University of Nevada, Reno
Reno, NV

V. Mark Durand
University of South Florida
St. Petersburg, FL

Anna Edwards, Ph.D.
The Marcus Institute
Atlanta, GA

Albert Ellis, Ph.D.
Deceased

Erica L. England
Drexel University
Philadelphia, PA

Sheila M. Eyberg, Ph.D.
University of Florida
Gainesville, FL

Kyle E. Ferguson, M.A.
Riverview Hospital
Coquitlam, BC, Canada

Jane E. Fisher, Ph.D.
University of Nevada, Reno
Reno, NV

Edna B. Foa, Ph.D.
University of Pennsylvania
Philadelphia, PA

William C. Follette.
University of Nevada, Reno
Reno, NV

Evan M. Forman
Drexel University
Philadelphia, PA

John P. Forsyth, Ph.D.
University at Albany (SUNY)
Albany, NY

Maxwell R. Frank
University of Hawaii at Manoa
Honolulu, HI

Michelle A. Frank
Kennedy-Krieger Institute
Baltimore, MD

Martin E. Franklin, Ph.D.
University of Pennsylvania
Philadelphia, PA

Patrick C. Friman, Ph.D.
Father Flanagan's Boys' Home
Boys' Town, NE

Armida R. Fruzzetti
University of Nevada, Reno
Reno, NV

Alan E. Fruzzetti, Ph.D.
University of Nevada, Reno
Reno, NV

Tiffany Fuse, Ph.D.
National Center for PTSD
Jamaica Plain, MA

Christina G. Garrison-Diehn
University of Nevada, Reno
Reno, NV

Robert J. Gatchel, Ph.D.
University of Texas at Arlington
Arlington, TX

Scott Gaynor, Ph.D.
Western Michigan University
Kalamazoo, MI

Patrick M. Ghezzi, Ph.D.
University of Nevada, Reno
Reno, NV

Elizabeth V. Gifford, Ph.D.
Palo Alto Veterans Administration
Palo Alto, CA

Alan M. Gross
University of Mississippi
University, MI

Kate E. Hamilton
Peter Lougheed Centre
Calgary, Canada

Jay Harding, Ed.S.
University of Iowa
Iowa City, IA

Cathi D. Harris, M.A.
Washington Special Commitment Center
Steilacoom, WA

Nicole L. Hausman
Kennedy-Krieger Institute
Baltimore, MD

Steven C. Hayes
University of Nevada, Reno
Reno, NV

Holly Hazlett-Stevens
University of Nevada, Reno
Reno, NV

Lara S. Head, Ph.D.
University of Wisconsin
Madison, WI

Elaine M. Heiby
University of Hawaii at Manoa
Honolulu, HI

James D. Herbert, Ph.D.
Drexel University
Philadelphia, PA

Ramona Houmanfar, Ph.D.
University of Nevada, Reno
Reno, NV

Kathryn L. Humphreys, Ph.D.
National Center for PTSD,
    VA Boston Healthcare System
Boston, MA

Nicole N. Jacobs, Ph.D.
University of Nevada, Reno
    School of Medicine
Reno, NV

Alyssa H. Kalata, M.A.
Western Michigan University
Kalamazoo, MI

Mary Lou Kelley, Ph.D.
Louisiana State University
Baton Rouge, LA

Brian C. Kersh, Ph.D.
New Mexico VA Healthcare System
Albuquerque, NM

Kelly Koerner
EBP
Seattle, WA

Douglas Kostewicz, Ph.D.
University of Pittsburgh
Pittsburgh, PA

Ellen Laan, Ph.D.
University of Amsterdam
Amsterdam, Netherlands

Arnold A. Lazarus, Ph.D.
Rutgers, The State University of New Jersey
Piscataway, NJ

Linda A. LeBlanc, Ph.D.
Western Michigan University
Kalamazoo, MI

Deborah A. Ledley, Ph.D.
University of Pennsylvania
Penn Valley, PA

Jung Eun Lee
University of Nevada, Reno
Reno, NV

Eric R. Levensky, Ph.D.
New Mexico VA Healthcare System
Albuquerque, NM

Donald J. Levis, Ph.D.
Binghamton University
Binghamton, NY

Jennifer M. Lexington, Ph.D.
University of Massachusetts Amherst
Amherst, MA

Marsha M. Linehan, Ph.D.
University of Washington
Seattle, WA

Steven G. Little, Ph.D.
Massey University
Auckland, New Zealand

Andy Lloyd, Ph.D.
U.S. Army

Jessa R. Love
Western Michigan University
Kalamazoo, MI

Tamara M. Loverich, Ph.D.
Eastern Michigan University
Ypsilanti, MI

Jason B. Luoma, Ph.D.
Portland Psychotherapy Clinic
Portland, OR

John R. Lutzker, Ph.D.
The Marcus Institute
Atlanta, GA

Kenneth R. MacAleese, M.A., B.C.B.A.
Reno, NV

Kristen A. Maglieri
Trinity College
Dublin, Ireland

Christine Maguth Nezu, Ph.D.
Drexel University
Philadelphia, PA

Gayla Margolin, Ph.D.
UCLA
Los Angeles, CA

G. Alan Marlatt, Ph.D.
University of Washington
Seattle, WA

Christopher Martell
Private Practice
Seattle, WA

Brian P. Marx, Ph.D.
National Center for PTSD,
    VA Boston Healthcare System
Boston, MA

Mary McMurran
University of Nottingham
Nottingham, United Kingdom

Donald Meichenbaum, Ph.D.
University of Waterloo
Waterloo, Ontario, Canada

Victoria E. Mercer
University of Nevada, Reno
Reno, NV

Eileen Merges
St. John Fisher College
Rochester, NY

Gerald I. Metalsky, Ph.D.
Lawrence University
Appleton, WI

Raymond G. Miltenberger, Ph.D., B.C.B.A.
University of South Florida
Tampa, FL

Sally A. Moore
University of Washington
Seattle, WA

Kevin J. Moore
Oregon Social Learning Center,
    Community Programs
Eugene, OR

Karen Murphy
University of Nevada, Reno
Reno, NV

Adel C. Najdowski
Center for Autism and Related Disorders, Inc.
Tarzana, CA

Amy E. Naugle, Ph.D.
Western Michigan University
Kalamazoo, MI

Cory F. Newman, Ph.D.
University of Pennsylvania
Philadelphia, PA

Kirk A. B. Newring, Ph.D.
Nebraska Dept. of Correctional Services
Lincoln, NE

William D. Newsome
University of Nevada, Reno
Reno, NV

Arthur M. Nezu, Ph.D.
Drexel University
Philadelphia, PA

Amanda Nicholson-Adams, Ph.D., B.C.B.A.
California State University at Fresno
Fresno, CA

William T. O'Donohue, Ph.D.
University of Nevada, Reno
Reno, NV

Pamella H. Oliver, Ph.D.
California State University, Fullerton
Fullerton, CA

Jennette L. Palcic
Louisiana State University
Baton Rouge, LA

Gerald R. Patterson, Ph.D.
Oregon Social Learning Center
Eugene, OR

James W. Pennebaker
The University of Texas at Austin
Austin, TX

Michael L. Perlis, Ph.D.
University of Rochester
Rochester, NY

Katherine A. Peterson
Utah State University
Logan, UT

Wilfred R. Pigeon, Ph.D.
University of Rochester Medical Center
Rochester, NY

Alan Poling, Ph.D.
Western Michigan University
Kalamazoo, MI

Lisa Regev, Ph.D.
University of Nevada, Reno
Reno, NV

Lynn P. Rehm, Ph.D.
University of Houston
Houston, TX

Jennifer Resetar, Ph.D.
Boys' Town
Boys' Town, NE

Patricia Robinson, Ph.D.
Mountainview Consulting Group, Inc.
Zillah, WA

Richard C. Robertson, Ph.D.
Baylor University Medical Center
Dallas, TX

Frederick Rotgers, Psy.D., ABPP
Philadelphia College of Osteopathic Medicine
Philadelphia, PA

Clair Rummel
University of Nevada, Reno
Reno, NV

Frank R. Rush, Ph.D.
Pennsylvania State University
University Park, PA

Joel Schmidt, Ph.D.
VA Northern California Healthcare System
Oakland, CA

Walter D. Scott, Ph.D.
University of Wyoming
Laramie, WY

Christine Segrin
University of Arizona
Tucson, AZ

Rachel E. Sgambati
Carson City, NV

Deacon Shoenberger
University of Nevada, Reno
Reno, NV

David M. Slagle
University of Washington
Seattle, WA

Rachel S. F. Tarbox
The Chicago School of Professional
    Psychology at Los Angeles
Los Angeles, CA

Kendra Tracy
University of Nevada, Las Vegas
Las Vegas, NV

Michael P. Twohig, Ph.D.
Utah State University
Logan, UT

Timothy R. Vollmer, Ph.D.
University of Florida
Gainesville, FL

David P. Wacker, Ph.D.
University of Iowa Children's Hospital
Iowa City, IA

Michelle D. Wallace, Ph.D.
California State University, Los Angeles
Los Angeles, CA

Todd A. Ward
University of Wellington
Wellington, New Zealand

Jennifer Wheeler, Ph.D.
Private Practice
Seattle, WA

Daniel J. Whitaker, Ph.D.
The Marcus Institute
Atlanta, GA

Larry W. Williams, Ph.D.
University of Nevada, Reno
Reno, NV

Ginger R. Wilson, Ph.D.
The ABRITE Organization
Santa Cruz, CA

J. M. Worrall
University of Nevada, Reno
Reno, NV

Marat Zanov
University of Southern California
Los Angeles, CA

Lori A. Zoellner, Ph.D.
University of Washington
Seattle, WA

1 A BRIEF HISTORY OF COGNITIVE BEHAVIOR THERAPY: ARE THERE TROUBLES AHEAD?

William O'Donohue

In its beginnings, behavior therapy was linked to learning research in an inextricable and unique manner. I will refer to this period in the history of behavior therapy as "first-generation behavior therapy." First-generation behavior therapy was a scientific paradigm that resulted in important solutions to a number of clinical problems (Task Force on Promotion and Dissemination of Psychological Procedures, 1995). For various reasons, however, many behavior therapists and researchers lost touch with developments in conditioning research and theory. Over the last three decades, behavior therapists turned their attention to topics such as therapies based on "clinical experience" (e.g., Goldfried & Davison, 1976), techniques seen independently from underlying behavioral principles (Hayes, Rincover, & Solnick, 1980), cognitive experimental psychology, cognitive accounts not based on experimental cognitive psychology (e.g., Ellis & Harper, 1975), and integrating or borrowing from other therapeutic approaches (Lazarus, 1969; but see O'Donohue & McKelvie, 1993). I will collectively refer to these developments as "second-generation behavior therapy."

Often, the argument in second-generation behavior therapy for this widening of influences was that "some clinical problem has not yielded to a conditioning analysis; therefore, other domains need to be explored for solutions." This is a reasonable argument, as it is imprudent to restrict behavior therapy to conditioning if there are important resources

in other domains. However, there are grounds for concern because second-generation behavior therapists may have relied too heavily on these other domains to the extent that contemporary learning research extends older research, contradicts older research, or has discovered completely new relationships and principles. Clinical problems may be refractory to behavioral treatment simply because the behavior therapist is not using the more powerful regularities uncovered by recent learning research. It is possible that one of the core ideas—extrapolating results from learning research—of first-generation behavior therapy still remains a useful animating principle for contemporary therapy.

However, many contemporary behavior therapists still look to conditioning principles and theory developed in the 1950s and 1960s for solutions to clinical problems. In this chapter, *third-generation behavior therapy* is called for. Third-generation behavior therapists should extrapolate contemporary learning research to understand and treat clinical problems. Third-generation behavior therapy should rely on regularities found in modern accounts of classical conditioning, latent inhibition, two-factor theory, response-deprivation analysis of reinforcement, behavioral regulation, matching law, other models of choice behavior, behavioral momentum, behavioral economics, optimization, adjunctive behavior, rule-governed behavior, stimulus equivalence, and modern accounts of concept learning and causal attribution.

FIRST-GENERATION BEHAVIOR THERAPY

Prior to the 1960s, the founders of behavior therapy extrapolated laboratory learning results to clinical problems. For example, John Watson and Rosalie Rayner (1920) attempted to demonstrate that a child's phobia could be produced by classical conditioning. Mary Cover Jones (1924a, b) showed that a child's fear of an animal could be counterconditioned by the pairing of the feared stimulus with a positive stimulus. O. Hobart Mowrer and Willie Mowrer (1938) developed a bell and pad treatment for enuresis that conditioned stimulus for sphincter control and the inhibition of urination.

Despite the initial promise of these early extrapolations, these efforts were generally ignored in clinical practice. Psychotherapists of the period were largely interested in psychoanalysis, a paradigm with a much different focus. Behavior therapists had to compete with the many offshoots of psychoanalysis. Andrew Salter (1949) shows some of the antipathy that many behavior therapists had toward psychoanalysis:

> It is high time that psychoanalysis, like the elephant of fable, dragged itself off to some distant jungle graveyard and died. Psychoanalysis has outlived its usefulness. Its methods are vague, its treatment is long drawn out, and more often than not, its results are insipid and unimpressive. Every literate non-Freudian in our day knows these accusations to be true. But we may ask ourselves, might it not be that psychotherapy, by its very nature, must always be difficult, time-consuming, and inefficient? I do not think so. I say flatly that psychotherapy can be quite rapid and extremely efficacious. I know so because I have done so. And if the reader will bear with me, I will show him how by building our therapeutic methods on the firm scientific bed rock of Pavlov, we can keep out of the Freudian metaphysical quicksands and help ten persons in the time that the Freudians are getting ready to "help" one. (p. 1)

In the 1950s, Joseph Wolpe (1958) attempted to countercondition anxiety responses by pairing relaxation with the stimuli that usually elicited anxiety. Wolpe's work represents the real beginnings of modern behavior therapy, as his work comprised a sustained research program that affected subsequent clinical practice. The earlier work of Watson, Jones, and others was not as programmatic and for whatever reasons did not disseminate well. Wolpe's desensitization techniques and his learning account of fears generated dozens of research studies and clinical applications over the following decade. The reader is referred to Kazdin's (1978) excellent history of behavior therapy for additional examples of early learning-based therapies.

First-generation behavior therapists not only utilized learning principles to formulate interventions, but also used learning principles to develop accounts of the origins and maintenance of problems in living. Abnormal behavior was judged to develop and be maintained by the same learning principles as normal behavior (e.g., Ullmann & Krasner, 1969). Problems in learning or problems in maintaining conditions resulted in a variety of behavior problems. Ullmann and Krasner's (1969) textbook on abnormal behavior is a useful compendium of first-generation learning-based accounts of the development and maintenance of changeworthy behavior.

Most of the initial behavioral studies were influenced by Pavlovian principles, particularly simultaneous and forward classical conditioning. This is not surprising, as some of these predated Skinner's work on operant conditioning. However, in the 1950s, another stream of behavior therapy emerged: applied behavior analysis or behavior modification. These interventions relied on operant principles. In one of the first studies to explicitly use operant principles, Lindsley, Skinner, and Solomon (1953) initiated this stream when they operantly conditioned responses in schizophrenics, demonstrating that psychotic disorders did not obviate basic conditioning processes. Another important early operant researcher, Sidney Bijou (e.g., Bijou, 1959) investigated the behavior of both normal and developmentally delayed children through the use of functional analyses and schedules of reinforcement. Baer, Wolf, and Risley (1968) in the first issue of the *Journal of Applied Behavior Analysis* highlighted the importance of the systematic and direct application of learning principles for the future of applied behavior analysis:

> The field of applied behavior analysis will probably advance best if the published descriptions of its procedures are not only precise technologically but also strive for relevance to principle. . . . This can have the effect of making a body of technology into a discipline rather than a collection of tricks. Collections of tricks historically have been difficult to expand systematically, and when they were extensive, difficult to learn and teach. (p. 96)

These cases of first-generation behavior therapy exhibit several important commonalities:

- The clinical scientists had extensive backgrounds in basic learning research. They could reasonably be described as learning researchers seeking to understand the generalizability of laboratory research as well as examining the practical value of this research by helping to solve problems involving human suffering.
- They were applying *what was then current learning research* to clinical problems.
- The results of their clinical research were by and large positive, although the methodological adequacy is problematic by today's standards.
- They saw their particular research as illustrating a much wider program of research and therapy. That is, their research did not exhaust the potential for the applicability of learning principles to clinical problems, but merely illustrated a small part of a much wider program.

During this period, behavior therapy was often defined by a direct and explicit reference to learning principles. For example, Ullmann and Krasner (1965) defined behavior modification as "includ[ing] many different techniques, all broadly related to the field of learning, *but learning with a particular intent, namely clinical treatment and change*" (p. 1; italics in the original). Wolpe (1969) stated, "Behavior therapy, or conditioning therapy, is the use of experimentally established principles of learning for the purpose of changing maladaptive behavior"

(p. vii). Eysenck (1964) defined behavior therapy as "the attempt to alter human behavior and emotion in a beneficial manner according to the laws of modern learning theory" (p. 1). Franks (1964) stated, "Behavior therapy may be defined as the systematic application of principles derived from behavior or learning theory and the experimental work in these areas to the rational modification of abnormal or undesirable behavior" (p. 12). Furthermore, Franks (1964) wrote that essential to behavior therapy is a "profound awareness of learning theory" (p. 12).

Although by and large these early behavior therapists agreed that learning principles should serve as the foundation of behavior therapy, the behavior therapy they advocated was not homogeneous. There was a significant heterogeneity in this early research. These researchers did not draw upon the same learning principles, nor did they subscribe to the same theory of learning. Skinner and his students emphasized operant conditioning principles; Watson, Rayner, and Jones, Pavlovian principles; and Wolpe and others, Hullian and Pavlovian. Moreover, within these broad traditions, different regularities were used: Some used extinction procedures, others excitatory classical conditioning; some differential reinforcement of successive approximations, others counterconditioning. However, each of these is a canonical illustration of behavior therapy of this period because each shares a critical family resemblance: an extrapolation of learning principles to clinical problems.

A related but separate movement occurred during this period. This movement did not gather much momentum and has largely died out. It is best represented by the work of Dollard and Miller (1950). In their classic book, *Personality and Psychotherapy*, these authors attempted to provide an explanation of psychoanalytic therapy techniques and principles based on learning principles. Dollard and Miller attempted to explain psychoanalytic techniques by an appeal to Milian learning principles. This movement should be regarded as separate from the first movement described earlier because the connection between conditioning and a therapy technique in this movement is post hoc. That is, first, therapeutic principles are described with no direct connection to learning principles, and this is followed by an attempt to understand these by learning principles. In the first movement, initially learning principles are discovered, and this is followed by the development of treatment procedures.

Today, there is little work that follows the second paradigm. Few are attempting to uncover the learning mechanisms underlying Rogerian and Gestalt techniques, object-relations therapy, and the like. This is probably because today, unlike the 1950s, there is more doubt regarding whether there is anything to explain. This movement attempted to explain, for example, how psychoanalysis worked (the conditioning processes involved). However, if there is little reason to believe that these other therapies are effective, then there is little reason to explain how they work. Moreover, this movement failed to produce any novel treatment techniques. In its emphasis on attempting to understand existing therapy techniques, it produced no useful innovations.

However, the model of moving from the learning laboratory to the clinic proved to be an extraordinarily rich paradigm. In the 1960s, numerous learning principles were shown to be relevant to clinical problems. Learning research quickly proved to be a productive source of ideas for developing treatments or etiological accounts of many problems in living. The development of psychotherapy had been a quasi-mysterious process before this point. Psychotherapies were usually developed by the unique clinical observations of the person who would become the leader of the school. Psychotherapists were no longer dependent on the "revelations" of insightful and creative seers who founded their schools. For the first time, psychotherapists could do Kuhnian (Kuhn, 1970) normal science because it is considerably more straightforward to extrapolate extant learning principles to clinical phenomena than it is to understand how, say, Freud formed and revised his assertions. "Extrapolate learning principles" is a clear and useful heuristic for the context of discovery.

Six books were critically important in extending the learning-based therapy paradigm. Wolpe's (1958) *Psychotherapy by Reciprocal Inhibition*; Eysenck's (1960) *Behavior Therapy*

and the Neuroses; Franks's (1964) *Conditioning Techniques in Clinical Practice and Research*; Eysenck's Experiments in Behavior Therapy (1964); and Krasner and Ullmann's two volumes, *Case Studies in Behavior Modification* (1965) and *Research in Behavior Modification* (1965). All contained an extensive set of case studies, research, and conceptual analyses that greatly extended the paradigm. Conditioned reinforcement, modeling, generalization and discrimination, satiation techniques, punishment, the effects of schedules of reinforcement, and token economies were investigated. Moreover, these principles were applied to a greater number and variety of clinical problems. Eating, compulsive behavior, elective mutism, cooperative responses, disruptive behavior, anorexia, hysterical blindness, posttraumatic anxiety, fetishism, sexual dysfunction, stuttering, tics, school phobia, tantrums, toilet training, social isolation, teaching skills to people with mental retardation, and hyperactive behavior were all addressed by learning-based treatments in these books. The matrix involving the crossing of learning principles by kinds of problematic behavior resulted in a rich research and therapy program.

Due to the initial successes in applying learning principles to clinical problems, another trend emerged. First-generation behavior therapists started working in the other direction: they began with a clinical problem and then attempted see to what extent it yielded to an analysis based on learning principles. Thus, a reciprocal relationship between the clinic and the learning lab emerged. This movement was important because behavior therapists can also be interested in uncovering basic learning processes in humans and can have a useful vantage point for generating and testing hypotheses concerning basic processes.

However, there is some danger with this approach. Unfortunately, it could be quite attractive to the behavior therapist who knew much more about clinical presentation than about learning research. This may have been the beginnings of the reliance of behavior therapists on something other than a thorough and faithful knowledge of current learning theory and research. With the success of behavior therapy came a new kind of professional: one who was first trained to be a clinical behavior therapist rather than a learning researcher.

Care must be taken not to lose sight of another important dimension of first-generation behavior therapy: its commitment to science and research. This scientific commitment, although not unprecedented in the history of psychotherapy, was more thoroughgoing. In 1952, after more than a half-century of the dominance of psychotherapy by psychoanalysis, Eysenck correctly pointed out that there was little properly controlled research that demonstrated it was more effective than a placebo treatment. Part of Eysenck's thesis was that it may be the case that effective therapies had yet to be discovered. However, another part was that existing therapies had not been adequately evaluated with properly controlled designs. Psychotherapists were doing an inadequate job as clinical researchers by not evaluating the efficacy of their therapies.

Admittedly, many of the early reports of behavior therapy were largely uncontrolled case studies that merely demonstrated its potential utility. Behavior therapists, however, quickly began to conduct unprecedentedly well-controlled research. Paul's (1966) study of the effectiveness of systematic desensitization can properly be regarded as the first research in history that was sufficiently well controlled to demonstrate that a form of psychotherapy was more effective than placebo and no treatment.

The research orientation of behavior therapists may have emanated from the school's roots in conditioning theory and research. Many then-extant forms of therapy had a much different heritage: the founder of the particular school made what were taken by some as astute clinical observations (witness Freud, Perls, Rogers; see O'Donohue & Halsey, 1997) and somehow formed this clinical experience into a more or less systematic school of therapy. It is easier to be "looser" when one is not extrapolating from a basic science. In contrast, the learning researchers/behavior therapists who composed the first wave of behavior therapy did not give up their experimental orientation when turning their attention to clinical problems. Behavior therapy from its beginnings valued science. The epistemological principles from

their backgrounds in experimental psychology remained with them and became an important part of the metascience of behavior therapy. Behavior therapists were interested in process research because they had a strong prior set of expectations (i.e., learning principles) of what these process variables might look like.

First-generation behavior therapy resulted in unprecedented progress in psychotherapy. If we somewhat arbitrarily say that the modern era of psychotherapy began in roughly 1900 with Freud, then we can agree with Eysenck (1952) in that the first 50 years of psychotherapy resulted in little progress. No treatments were developed that effectively resolved the problems they attempted to address. In contrast, during the early years of behavior therapy, significant progress was made with enuresis, phobias, other anxiety problems, child management problems, skill deficits of developmentally disabled individuals, self-injurious behavior and stereotypic behavior of autistic and schizophrenic individuals, and social and verbal problems of schizophrenia. These all were no longer completely refractory to ameliorative attempts. Moreover, as Salter (1949) described, behavioral treatment was also much quicker and less costly. In the span of a little over a decade, psychotherapy made progress that it failed to make in the preceding five decades. Surely, any reasonable observer could see that there was something special about this new movement. Today, if one looks at the Task Force on Promotion and Dissemination of Psychological Procedures (1995), this first-generation behavior therapy still accounts for a significant percentage of what are now considered "validated treatments."

The success of early behavior therapy should not have come as a complete surprise. Psychotherapists for the first time began using a strategy that had proved successful in other domains. For nearly a century, physicians had relied on experimental physiology and microbiology, and by extrapolating from the results of the basic biological sciences they had made significant clinical progress. Engineers relied on the basic sciences of physics and chemistry and made remarkable progress solving many applied problems. The strategy used by these groups was enticing: Extrapolate antecedently validated principles from basic research to applied problems.

For the first time in the 1950s and 1960s, psychotherapy began to use the same strategy: first nomothetics were discovered through basic research, and then these were applied to practical problems. In the learning laboratory, learning researchers derived principles applicable to human behavior. The animals used in their research were largely chosen for convenience rather than because of any strong interest in understanding the behavior of that particular species. Evolutionary theory supported some behavioral continuity across species, which further justified the study of infrahuman animals. The laboratory and the animal preparation allow control that is not possible in naturalistic studies of humans. Variables can be controlled and isolated, and thus false hypotheses can more easily be refuted. Regularities emerging from the learning laboratory have relatively good epistemic credentials and a reasonable potential for revealing clinically useful regularities. The epistemic credentials of the laboratory-derived first-generation behavior therapy were far superior to the epistemic credentials of principles or regularities alleged by the clinical observers who initiated competing schools of therapy. The number of possible therapy techniques is, of course, indefinitely large, and therefore it is useful to have antecedent evidence on which to judge which are worthy of investigation (Erwin, 1978).

An additional, somewhat more subtle, factor may also have contributed to the success of first-generation, learning-based therapies. This paradigm may have met with such unprecedented success because of felicitous correspondences between the core objects of both programs. Learning researchers attempt to uncover how experience changes behavior. In fact, a common definition of learning is that learning is experience that results in relatively enduring changes in behavior. This focus precisely addresses the general question involved in the enterprise of psychotherapy: How can therapists structure experience so that relatively enduring changes occur in the client's behavior? Thus, this paradigm might have been successful because of the confluence of the aims of these two pursuits.

Two further confluences might have accounted for the success of operant approaches. Skinner criticized research utilizing group designs. He argued that group averages are a confused and confusing scientific variable. Instead of group comparisons, Skinner argued for the intensive experimental analysis of the behavior of an individual organism. The goal was to find the controlling variables of the individual's behavior by manipulating environmental conditions to see if these were functionally related to subsequent behavior. Again, this emphasis is highly consistent with the clinician's problem situation. The clinician is rarely concerned with group averages, but rather is concerned with the behavior of an individual client. Moreover, clinicians aim to find manipulable conditions to bring about desirable changes in the client's behavior.

A final confluence was that in conducting these single-subject designs, Skinnerians eschewed statistical analysis. They wanted to show that they had identified controlling variables due to the reliable, high-magnitude changes produced in the dependent variable. Although some learning researchers statistically analyzed group designs in order to find "statistically significant" differences, operant researchers wanted to demonstrate differences that would be readily apparent in any graphical display. This is fortuitous because clinicians generally want or need dependent variables to undergo large changes. The work coming out of the operant lab showed that these large changes were possible. Work coming out of group designs showed that with large enough sample sizes, small differences (that were statistically significant but often not clinically significant) were possible.

Despite the considerable advantages provided by this basic science/applied science model, it has one serious disadvantage. The limits of the basic science place limits on the applied science. Learning research was (and still is) unsettled. Pavlovians, Ruffians, and Skinnerians, among others, engaged in debates concerning fundamental issues. Much of the behavior of the organism remained unaccounted for. There was a clear need for further basic research to fill the many lacunae in the learning account. At times, behavior therapists were stymied because they relied on incorrect information, incomplete information, regularities that were weak, and regularities whose initial conditions or boundary conditions were poorly understood.

SECOND-GENERATION BEHAVIOR THERAPY

In the 1970s, behavior therapy's heterogeneity increased. Systematic desensitization, implosion therapy, and two-factor accounts of anxiety disorders were examples of the continuing influence of Pavlov, Hull, and Mowrer, respectively. Those influenced by Skinner sometimes tried to distinguish themselves from those influenced by nonoperant principles and particularly from those influenced by nonconditioning factors. Operantly inclined behavior therapists sometimes called what they did *applied behavior analysis* or *behavior modification*. These terminological distinctions have not always been clear, but at times they function as code words for background allegiances regarding favored learning principles. The increasing diversity of behavior therapy should not be surprising, as the seeds for the growth of a heterogeneous discipline were present from its beginning. For example, Ullmann and Krasner (1965) described behavior therapy as "treatment deducible from the *sociopsychological model* that aims to alter a person's behavior directly through the application of general psychological principles (p. 244, italics added). These prominent, early behavior therapists viewed behavior therapy as also relying on many social–psychological domains such as role theory, small-group research, demand characteristics, labeling, and conformity. Ullmann and Krasner attempted to set a learning-influenced behavior therapy in the larger context of a psychology of behavior influence.

Gerald Patterson (1969), another prominent early behavior therapist, agreed with the emphasis on social–psychological principles:

It seems to me that future trends will of necessity involve a greater reliance upon principles available from social learning. The term social learning as used here refers to the loosely organized body of literature dealing with changes in learning, or

performance, which occur as a function of contingencies which characterize social interaction. ... Many of the mechanisms which have been described as bringing about these changes have been based upon principles from social psychology rather than learning theory: these would include such processes as persuasion, conformity, and modeling. (p. 342)

Arnold Lazarus, a student of Wolpe's, was probably one of the earliest and most significant forces for turning behavior therapists' attention to areas other than learning. Lazarus argued that learning principles were helpful but insufficient. Lazarus (1968) stated:

Why should behavior therapists limit themselves only to "experimentally established principles of learning against the background of physiology" and ignore other areas of experimental psychology such as studies on perception, emotion, cognition, and so forth? And why should behavior therapists avoid using such techniques as self-disclosure, dyadic interactions, and other methods, as long as they can be reconciled with reinforcement principles? Finally, one might inquire to what extent Wolpe's reference to a "stimulus–response model" is a vague and meaningless abstraction. If the current upsurge of interest in behavior therapy is to expand and mature, we must beware of oversimplified notions, limited procedures, and extravagant claims which would conceivably undermine our efforts. (p. 2)

Following this line of thought, Lazarus (1969) stated that the multimodal behavior therapist is "free to employ any technique, derived from any system, without subscribing to any theoretical underpinnings which do not have the benefit of empirical support" (p. 5).

Bandura's description and analysis of modeling and vicarious learning was another important influence on the development of behavior therapy during this period. Bandura (1969) stated that:

... research conducted within the framework of social-learning theory demonstrates that virtually all learning phenomena resulting from direct experiences can occur on a vicarious basis through observation of other persons' behavior and its consequences for them. Thus, for example, one can acquire intricate response patterns merely by observing the performances of appropriate models; emotional responses can be conditioned observationally by witnessing the affective reactions of others undergoing painful or pleasurable experiences; fearful and avoidance behavior can be extinguished vicariously through observation of modeled approach behavior toward feared objects without any adverse consequences accruing to the performer; inhibitions can be induced by witnessing the behavior of others punished; and finally, the expression of well-learned responses can be enhanced and socially regulated through the actions of influential models. Modeling procedures are therefore ideally suited for effecting diverse outcomes including elimination of behavioral deficits, reduction of excessive fears and inhibitions, transmission of self-regulating systems, and social facilitation of behavioral patterns on a groupwide scale. (p. 118)

Together, these authors argued that social psychology and experimental learning psychology were relevant to behavior therapy. It is also fair to say that many of those influenced by the social-learning perspective relied most heavily on learning principles. Growing from these early seeds, in the second generation, behavior therapy became more broadly defined. Instead of defining behavior therapy as the application of learning principles, behavior therapy came to be defined as the application of principles from experimental and social psychology (e.g., Davison & Neale, 1974; Rimm & Masters, 1974; Franks & Wilson, 1975). This, of course, included learning principles, but it also included a lot of other material.

During this period, applied behavior analysts appeared to become less attentive to the underlying learning principles. Hayes, Rincover, and Solnick (1980) found that in early volumes of the *Journal of Applied Behavior Analysis* it was nearly always the case that the articles contained references to behavioral principles. However, in an analysis of later volumes, Hayes et al. found:

Overall the data show that applied behavior analysis is becoming a more purely technical effort,

with less and less interest in conceptual questions. To answer these technical questions we are using relatively simple experimental designs which determine if the technique had a reliable effect, or if it is better than another technique, with little interest in the components producing the effect or the parametric boundaries of the techniques. (p. 281)

THE RISE OF COGNITIVE BEHAVIOR THERAPY

Behavior therapy is not insulated from events happening outside it. The "cognitive revolution" in psychology occurred in the 1960s, and by the 1970s many behavior therapists influenced by it began to call what they did "cognitive behavior therapy." Wilson (1982) stated:

During the 1950s and 1960s, the behaviour therapies developed within the framework of classical and operant conditioning principles that had originally served importantly to distinguish behaviour therapy from other clinical approaches. Over the course of the 1970s, this conceptual commitment to conditioning theory peaked out—some would say even waned. In part this change reflected the shift to more technological considerations governing the increasingly broad application of behavioral techniques that had been developed and refined during the previous period of growth. Moreover, as psychology "went cognitive" during the 1970s, cognitive concepts inevitably were drawn upon to guide and explain treatment strategies. (p. 51)

Mahoney, an early leader in cognitive behavior therapy, stated a similar theme (1984):

By the late 1970s it was clear that cognitive behavior therapy was not a fad; indeed it had its own special interest group in the AABT. It had become a more frequent topic at conventions, in journals, and in research, and it had become more pervasively integrated into behavioral psychotherapies. Behavior therapy, like psychology in general, had "gone cognitive." (p. 9)

Part of this movement argued that learning research was still relevant but the research that should influence second-generation behavior therapy was *human* learning research that examined cognitive mediators of learning. The argument was that conditioning in humans is not automatic and direct, but rather is mediated by the person's verbal and cognitive abilities. Awareness, attention, expectancy, attribution, and linguistic representation were constructs thought to be necessary to account for learning. The argument was that animal conditioning models were inadequate for the study of human learning because these neglected to include the unique abilities of humans such as verbal abilities. Thus, these animal conditioning models needed to be supplemented or replaced by cognitive accounts.

Not all behavior therapists "went cognitive." Most applied behavior analysts continued to practice first-generation behavior therapy. These and others argued that the so-called cognitive revolution was in part a retreat to folk psychology rather than a progressive scientific movement. Critics were quick to point out that the new cognitive techniques generally had, at best, a rather loose connection with experimental cognitive psychology. This was serious epistemically because, to the extent that this criticism was true, no longer were behavior therapists extrapolating antecedently tested principles.

It does appear that during this period, behavior therapists developed treatments that had a looser relationship with conditioning: self-reinforcement, behavioral rehearsal, covert sensitization, and thought stopping all were clinical techniques that were not derived from basic animal learning research. Conditioning principles became more of a rough heuristic during the second generation of behavior therapy. Admittedly, these techniques have a family resemblance to conditioning procedures, but their actual connection is much more ephemeral. Claims that there was a shift in regard for basic animal research have some empirical support. Poling et al. (1981) found through a citation analysis that sources that report work with nonhuman subjects have been referenced increasingly infrequently since 1965 by clinical authors.

It also may have been the case that the success and credentials of behavior therapy attracted many individuals, some of whom were relatively unfamiliar with learning principles. Psychotherapists and clinical researchers trained in other paradigms "converted" to behavior therapy during this period. However, such conversion rarely entailed an extensive training in learning research. Rather, it more typically included training in behavior therapy techniques themselves. This trend could have hastened the view of these techniques as being more autonomous from the basic learning principles. For this group of behavior therapists, when difficulties were encountered, it was more likely that learning principles were not drawn upon. It is easier for the potential of learning principles to be seen as exhausted when one does not have an exhaustive knowledge of them.

I also conjecture that these less faithful, less accurate extrapolations from basic learning research had a higher likelihood of leading to failures. To the extent that these failures were attributed to the inadequacy or insufficiency of learning principles to gird clinical practice, a movement away from learning and toward other domains occurred. Many behavior therapists have had the experience of hearing psychotherapists say that their failed attempts at what they see as behavior therapy support their conclusions that behavior therapy is a bad form of therapy. I recall an avowed eclectic therapist telling me that behavior therapy failed her because she tried to reinforce an academically underperforming adolescent by rewarding him with a minibike at the end of the semester if he received all As and Bs. If she had even a cursory understanding of operant conditioning, she would have known that:

- One does not reinforce organisms, but rather responses.
- Reinforcement of successive approximations is usually a more effective strategy for producing high-magnitude changes.
- A large, distant reinforcer often needs to be supplemented by more proximate reinforcers.
- Receiving a good grade is not a response.
- A more careful functional analysis of competing behaviors and reinforcers needed to be done to understand controlling variables. Too often during this period, people began to

practice "behavior therapy" in a superficial and rather incompetent manner.

This is not to say simply that the growing schism between behavior therapy and basic learning research can be understood entirely by the behavior of behavior therapists. During this period, basic learning research moved on as well. It admittedly became more esoteric, more technical, and thus there were more barriers to entry to those who wanted to acquaint themselves with contemporary learning research. The difficulty of contemporary learning research helps to explain why many behavior therapists failed to keep up. If one picks up a current issue of, for example, *Journal of the Experimental Analysis of Behavior* and attempts to read one of the articles, it is likely that one will understand little. Learning research became more insular as it grew more technical, quantitative, and specialized. Learning researchers stopped writing for general psychologists and wrote increasingly for their scientific microcommunity. Learning researchers began to experience problems in knowledge utilization and dissemination—topics that are of intellectual interest in their own right.

The advent and success of behavior therapy also created certain interpersonal and professional tensions. Behavior therapists were often critical of the lack of evidence for the efficacy of other schools of therapy, of the lack of scientific commitment of these schools, of the lack of evidence that these schools' favored process variables actually were important, and of the way these schools defined *abnormality*. Part of the general ethos of the psychotherapy movement is to have good interpersonal relationships. But behavior therapists were increasingly critical, skeptical, and unaccepting of many of the claims of other schools, and, frankly, claimed to be practicing a superior form of therapy. These tensions were at least partly relieved when behavior therapists became more eclectic, less stridently learning based, and accepting of techniques from other schools. If one looks at some of the external forces on the development of behavior therapy, one problem behavior therapists had to face was this sort of "foreign relations." Some sought appeasement by

compromise. Eclecticism may be understandably more satisfying in certain political and interpersonal contexts.

Probably the most radical critique of first-generation behavior therapy during this period was the criticism that behavior therapy techniques were not derived from basic laboratory principles of learning. For example, Breger and McGaugh (1965) stated, "When we look at the way conditioning principles are applied in the explanation of more complex phenomena, we see that only a rather flimsy analogue bridges the gap between such laboratory defined terms as stimulus, response, and reinforcement and their reference in the case of complex behavior" (p. 344). Erwin (1978) also argued that behavior therapy techniques were not derived from learning principles. For example, the argument was that in systematic desensitization, Wolpe used an imagined scene as a conditioned stimulus but that this conditioned stimulus did not have properties that laboratory conditioned stimuli have—for example, public observability, direct control by the experimenter, and invariance. Thus, the claim was that animal laboratory research often could serve as a heuristic or useful analog but that behavior therapy techniques were not derived from basic animal learning research.

This argument presents a restrictive view of the relationship between basic and applied research. It is an elementary methodological point that laboratory research trades off external validity for internal validity. Laboratory protocols simplify in order to isolate and improve control of independent variables, and to improve the accuracy of measurement of dependent variables. In doing this, the laboratory preparation often becomes idealized and removed from naturalistic phenomena. However, after regularities are discovered in the lab, the next step is to examine whether they can be extrapolated to related (but not identical) variables in the natural environment. Similar relationships can be found in laboratory preparations and naturalistic phenomena in physiology and medicine, for example. Moreover, it is not clear if it is necessary for a logical entailment between laboratory preparations and behavior therapy techniques to exist. Rather, the behavior therapy technique simply needs to be "covered" (Hempel, 1966) by regularities discovered in the lab. Most competent contingency management procedures are subsumed under general operant principles and procedures. A particular behavior therapy technique may represent a widening of laboratory-derived regularities. This may be the case in Wolpe's systematic desensitization.

These factors contrived to create a heterogenous behavior therapy with more tenuous or even often nonexistent roots in animal learning. Kazdin (1978) stated:

> By now [the mid- to late 1970s] behavior modification is so variegated in its conceptualization of behavior, research methods and techniques that no unifying schema or set of assumptions about behavior can incorporate all the extant techniques. Many of the theoretical positions expressed within behavior modification represent opposing views about the nature of human motivation, the mechanisms that influence behavior and the relative influence of such factors, and the most suitable focus of treatment for a given problem. (p. 374)

TOWARD THIRD-GENERATION BEHAVIOR THERAPY

It is clearly legitimate for behavior therapy to explore all areas of experimental and social psychology. However, it seems prudent that behavior therapists do this in a way that preserves the basic science/applied science relation. Extrapolating regularities found by basic researchers has epistemic advantages as described above. As previously mentioned, there is reason to be somewhat pessimistic about the usefulness of certain areas of basic psychology. Some of these areas do not share any of the three important confluences: (1) a shared search to understand how experience changes behavior; (2) a shared use of single-subject methodologies; and (3) a mutual reliance on large, "clinically significant" change.

The potential or actual usefulness of other areas of basic psychology does not reduce the relevance or importance of contemporary learning research. Nothing that occurred during

the second generation of behavior therapy obviated the usefulness of conditioning research. However, learning is not a settled area. *Behavior therapists need to keep up with the evidential status of learning principles.*

An example may provide a clearer idea of what third-generation behavior therapy would look like. Third-generation behavior therapy suggests new ways of analyzing and intervening with clinically relevant behaviors. First-generation behavior therapists would examine individual contingencies to find controlling variables. However, third-generation behavior therapists would not view the behavior of the organism as controlled by a single contingency but rather as under the influence of multiple contingencies. Thus, the behavior therapist needs to understand the organism's behavior as an example of choice behavior, and as being influenced by competing contingencies. The matching law dictates an analysis of multiple sources of reinforcement, not just the simple, single contingency on which the first-generation behavior therapist would focus. McDowell (1982) argued:

> Hernstein's equation is considerably more descriptive of natural human environments than Skinner's earlier view of reinforcement. It is not always easy to isolate Skinnerian response reinforcement units in the natural environment. Hernstein's equation makes efforts to do so unnecessary and, moreover, obsolete. The equation can help clinicians conceptualize cases more effectively and design treatment regimens more efficiently. It also suggests new treatment strategies that may be especially useful in difficult cases. (p. 778)

The matching law would predict that reducing the reinforcement of competing responses should increase responding in the other contingency. Somewhat counterintuitively (at least to first-generation behavior therapists), the frequency of a behavior can be altered not only by manipulating the contingency the behavior is involved in, but also by the contingency of a competing behavior.

As a further example, behavior therapists often wish to identify reinforcers to influence the behavior of their clients. First-generation behavior therapists used Skinner's empirical law of effect, which renders reinforcer identification a post hoc process: Reinforcers are stimuli that, when presented contingently on some response, increase the frequency of that response. Third-generation behavior therapists could rely on response deprivation/free operant analysis (Timberlake, 1995) to more accurately, more fully, and antecedently identify reinforcers. Using a free operant analysis, behaviors that occur within the system can be identified as reinforcers. Further, any behavior that occurs in the situation can be deprived and function as a reinforcer. This more contemporary analysis is useful because it:

- Can *antecedently* identify what will function as a reinforcer
- Can uncover "natural" reinforcers that occur within the system
- Precisely describes the conditions needed to produce a reinforcer (deprivation is transformed from an unclear initial condition in the empirical law of effect to having an explicit and clear role)
- Indicates that there is no special and unique class of reinforcers
- Describes a wider range of reinforcers
- Indicates why something will function as a reinforcer

Moreover, third-generation behavior therapists can rely on further behavioral principles to greatly augment the analysis of client behavior. Staddon's behavioral-regulation account of the preservation of "bliss points" can be used to make point predictions of response change under the influence of constraints such as contingencies. This analysis suggests that the organism attempts to preserve responses in fixed proportions. This can be further augmented by behavioral economics. The notion of elastic versus inelastic demand (or Staddon's defense variable and Rachlin's research on substitutability) is also relevant and potentially important.

It is hoped that learning researchers will be more mindful of dissemination and utilization issues and more frequently write in an accessible manner so that applied psychologists can more routinely access their important work. It is also hoped that learning researchers will conduct basic human conditioning studies to more clearly investigate the relevance to humans of their initial studies with animals. Often, basic researchers are best equipped to understand how protocols may need to be modified or augmented when applied to significant responses of humans. This would greatly aid behavior therapists' extrapolations to clinically significant behaviors.

Part of the excitement and promise of first-generation behavior therapy was that behavior therapists were not simply technicians. They knew how to faithfully execute procedures but also understood the underlying principles on which these were based. The first-generation behavior therapists understood the basic learning principles and could creatively and opportunistically apply them. Their repertoire was complex and led to many innovative and faithful applications. It is hoped that the subsequent chapters in this book will help reinstate this deep and faithful understanding of learning principles. As Kalish (1981) stated:

> The inclination to regard the methods of intervention in behavior modification as a collection of standardized techniques is especially misleading. It tends to obscure one of the most important contributions to the understanding of behavior change made by the advent of behavior modification procedures: namely, that for every so-called technique, there is a more fundamental and more general principle of behavior derived from research with animals and/or humans which can be applied to the solution of a problem in human functioning. This means, among other things, that those who intend to use behavior modification to help solve human problems should be aware of these principles and resourceful enough to propose treatment strategies which fit the case after a thorough analysis of the conditions which initiate and maintain the behavior. (p. 3)

References

Abramson, L. Y., Seligman, M. E. P., & Teasdale, J. D. (1978). Learned helplessness in humans: Critique and reformulation. *Journal of Abnormal Psychology*, *87*, 49–74.

Baer, D. M., Wolf, M., & Risley, T. R. (1968). Some current dimensions of applied behavior analysis. *Journal of Applied Behavior Analysis, 1,* 91–97.

Bandura, A. (1969). *Principles of behavior modification.* New York: Holt, Rinehart & Winston.

Bijou, S. W. (1955). A systematic approach to the experimental analysis of young children. *Child Development, 26,* 161–168.

Bijou, S. W. (1959). Learning in children. *Monographs for the Society for Research in Child Development, 24.*

Breger, L., & McGaugh, J. L. (1965). Critique and reformulation of "learning theory": Approaches to psychotherapy and neurosis. *Psychological Bulletin, 63,* 338–358.

Davison, G., & Neale, J. (1974). *Abnormal psychology: An experimental clinical approach.* New York: John Wiley & Sons.

Dollard, J., & Miller, N. E. (1950). *Personality and psychotherapy.* New York: McGraw-Hill.

Ellis, A., & Harper, R. A. (1975). *A new guide to rational living.* Englewood Cliffs, NJ: Prentice Hall.

Erwin, E. (1978). *Behavior therapy: Scientific, philosophical, & moral foundations.* Cambridge: Cambridge University Press.

Eysenck, H. J. (1952). The effects of psychotherapy: An evaluation. *Journal of Counseling Psychology, 16,* 319–324.

Eysenck, H. J. (Ed.) (1960). *Behavior therapy and the neuroses.* New York: Pergamon.

Eysenck, H. J. (Ed.) (1964). *Experiments in behavior therapy.* Oxford: Pergamon.

Franks, C. M. (Ed.) (1964). *Conditioning techniques in clinical practice and research.* New York: Springer.

Franks, C. M., & Wilson, G. T. (1975). *Annual review of behavior therapy theory and practice.* New York: Brunner/Mazel.

Goldfried, M. R., & Davison, G. C. (1976). *Clinical behavior therapy.* New York: Holt.

Hayes, S. C., Rincover, A., & Solnick, J. V. (1980). The technical drift of applied behavior analysis. *Journal of Applied Behavior Analysis, 13,* 275–285.

Hempel, C. G. (1966). *Philosophy of natural science.* Englewood Cliffs, NJ: Prentice Hall.

Jones, M. C. (1924a). The elimination of children's fears. *Journal of Experimental Psychology, 7,* 383–390.

Jones, M. C. (1924b). A laboratory study of fear: The case of Peter. *Journal of Genetic Psychology, 31,* 308–315.

Kalish, H. I. (1981). *From behavioral science to behavior modification.* New York: McGraw-Hill.

Kanter, F. H., & Phillips, J. S. (1970). *Learning foundations of behavior therapy.* New York: John Wiley & Sons.

Kazdin, A. E. (1978). *History of behavior modification.* Baltimore: University Park Press.

Kuhn, T. S. (1970). *The structure of scientific revolutions.* Chicago: University of Chicago Press.

Lang, P. J. (1977). Imagery in therapy: An information processing analysis. *Behavior Therapy, 8,* 862–886.

Lazarus, A. A. (1968). A plea for technical and theoretical breadth. *AABT Newsletter, 3,* 2.

Lazarus, A. A. (1969). Broad-spectrum behavior therapy. *AABT Newsletter, 4,* 5–6.

Lindsley, O. R, Skinner, B. F., & Solomon, H. C. (1953). *Studies in behavior therapy: Status report 1.* Waltham, MA: Metropolitan State Hospital.

Mahoney, M. J. (1974). *Cognition and behavior modification.* Cambridge, MA: Ballinger.

Mahoney, M. J. (1984). Behaviorism, cognitivism, and human change processes. In M. A. Reda & M. J. Mahoney (Eds.), *Cognitive psychotherapies* (pp. 3–30). Cambridge, Mass. Ballinger.

McDowell, J. J. (1982). The importance of Hermstein's mathematical statement of the law of effect for behavior therapy. *American Psychologist, 37,* 771–779.

Mowrer, O. H., & Mowrer, W. M. (1938). Enuresis: A method for its study and treatment. *American Journal of Orthopsychiatry, 8,* 436–459.

O'Donohue, W., & Halsey, L. (1997). The substance of the scientist-practitioner relation: Freud, Rogers, Skinner, & Ellis. *New Ideas in Psychology, 15,* 35–53.

O'Donohue, W. T., & McKelvie, M. (1993). Problems in the case for psychotherapeutic integration. *Journal of Behavior Therapy and Experimental Psychiatry, 24,* 161–170.

Patterson, G. R. (1969). Behavioral techniques based upon social learning: An additional base for developing behavior modification technologies. In C. M. Franks (Ed.), *Behavior therapy: Appraisal and status* (pp. 341–374). New York: McGraw-Hill.

Paul, G. L. (1966). *Insight vs. desensitization in psychotherapy.* Stanford, CA: Stanford University Press.

Poling, A., Picker, M., Grossett, D., Hall-Johnson, E., & Holbrook, M. (1981). The schism between experimental and applied behavioral analysis: Is it real and who cares? *Behavior Analyst, 4,* 93–02.

Rimm, D. C., & Masters, J. C. (1979). *Behavior therapy: Techniques and findings* (2nd ed.). New York: Academic Press.

Salter, A. (1949). *Conditioned reflex therapy.* New York: Creative Age Press.

Task Force on Promotion and Dissemination of Psychological Procedures (1995). Training in and dissemination of empirically-validated psychological treatments: Report and recommendations. *Clinical Psychologist, 48,* 3–23.

Ullmann, L. P., & Krasner, L. (1969). *A psychological approach to abnormal behavior.* Englewood Cliffs, NJ: Prentice Hall.

Ullmann, L. P., & Krasner, L. (Eds.) (1965). *Case studies in behavior modification.* New York: Holt, Rinehart & Winston.

Watson, J. B., & Rayner, R. (1920). Conditioned emotional reactions. *Journal of Experimental Psychology, 3,* 1–14.

Wilson, G. T. (1982). The relationship of learning theories to the behavioral therapies: Problems, prospects, and preferences. In J. Boulougouris (Ed.), *Learning theory approaches to psychiatry* (pp. 33–56). New York: John Wiley & Sons.

Wolpe, J. (1958). *Psychotherapy by reciprocal inhibition.* Stanford, CA: Stanford University Press.

Wolpe, J. (1969). *The practice of behavior therapy.* New York: Pergamon.

2 ASSESSMENT AND COGNITIVE BEHAVIOR THERAPY: FUNCTIONAL ANALYSIS AS KEY PROCESS

Claudia Drossel, Clair Rummel, and Jane E. Fisher

Understanding a particular client's presenting problem is necessary both to predict future behavior and to determine a suitable and workable intervention strategy. One way to gain an understanding of client affect, behavior, and cognition is through a functional analysis, which historically underlies the development of cognitive behavioral empirically supported strategies (e.g., systematic desensitization, flooding, behavioral activation, etc.). Unfortunately, as entire empirically supported treatment (EST) packages have been tied to specific diagnostic categories within the *Diagnostic and Statistical Manual of Mental Disorders*, 4th edition (APA, 1994) in recent years, the treatment packages themselves have taken on a standard by which clinicians judge the utility of empirically supported methods (Ruscio & Holohan, 2006). Consequently, Abramowitz (2006) pointed out that:

> ... clinicians mistakenly attribute the essence (i.e., active ingredient) of an EST to the particular manual by which it is delivered. Thus, when patients come along with comorbid disorders or other psychological complications, we sometimes encounter a case of the baby thrown out with the bathwater. That is, the clinician decides the manual does not apply and therefore decides not to use it. (pp. 163–164)

Alternatively, Hunter and colleagues (2008) describe a "diagnose and treat" approach, in which clinicians respond to previous treatment failures by resorting to a different diagnosis and applying yet another generic treatment package fitting the new diagnosis. In all of these cases, the lack of flexibility and skill in selecting a suitable and workable cognitive behavioral treatment for *a particular client* is of concern.

To foster flexibility and skill in matching and applying the empirically supported techniques described in O'Donohue and Fisher (2008), and to prevent clinicians from abandoning cognitive behavioral techniques altogether when clinical problems are idiosyncratic, seemingly intractable, or unfamiliar, this chapter will introduce the reader to the principles of functional analyses. It bears repeating that functional analyses of client affect, behavior, and cognition— while rarely taught—are and have been at the core of cognitive behavioral strategies. Thus, thinking about affect, behavior, and cognition from a functional perspective will enable clinicians to "breathe life into manuals" (Kendall, Chu, Gifford, Hayes, & Nauta, 1998) and to implement strategies not only skillfully but also artfully.

WHAT IS A "FUNCTIONAL ANALYSIS"?

Hesse (1919/1970) wrote, "Each human being ... is a unique, very special, by all means important, and extraordinary point at which the world's phenomena intersect, only once and never again in this fashion. For this reason, each person's history is significant, timeless, and marvelous; for this reason, each person ... is wonderful and worthy of all attention" (p. 10). This quote illustrates three fundamental tenets underlying functional analyses:

1. Human affect, cognition, and behavior (hereafter, "behavior" for convenience) are idiosyncratic. Even if they look the same, they

may occur for different reasons. Categorizing behaviors in terms of topographies does not provide information about the relationship between behavior and various historical and current conditions and events for a particular individual. Rather than emphasizing topographical categorizations of behaviors, functional analyses attempt to answer the question, *"Why is this person reliably engaging in this particular behavior?"*

2. Hesse's conceptualization of the person as a "point" or locus at which the world's phenomena intersect implies that behaviors are best understood in the context in which they occur. "Context" broadly refers to a person's history as well as his or her current circumstances, including physiological, social, and cultural conditions.

3. The individual's behavior and context are an inseparable whole, forming the unit of analysis. Chiesa (1994) elaborates:

Persons are defined *in terms of* their behavior with no other entity, no bounded individual standing behind. The person ... is a unity rather than a duality, an interactive part of the environment rather than a thing separate from the environment. The person ... operates *in* rather than *on* an environment. ... Instead of looking at mechanisms or entities that underlie behavior, the interesting question becomes, "How is this person, unity, related to his or her environment?"

From a functional analytic viewpoint, the client's behaviors reliably occur within a certain context and impact it at the same time. Consequently, the first step in a functional analysis is the process of detecting patterns within the reciprocal relationship of behavior and context. The patterns to be detected are termed *functional relations*, as they are of a probabilistic nature rather than "triggers" or "push-pull" mechanisms. The therapist's task is to "discover the functional relations which prevail between [discernable] aspects of behavior and various conditions and events in the [client's] life" (Skinner, 1956/1982, p. 225). Indeed, the therapist is also part of the client's context, and vice versa. Note that, from this perspective, the client's presenting problems are not perceived

as different in kind from any other behavior; that is, one theoretical system accounts for effective repertoires as well as for psychopathology. "Functional relations" apply to everybody—in the same sense that water flows downhill regardless of geographical location.

In its simplest terms, a functional analysis asks, "In general, what happens when ... ?" For example, what happens when the socially anxious client withdraws in session? Does the therapist start to fill in for the client's silence and work harder to engage the client, or does the therapist continue to place demands for social approach on the client? What happens when the client withdraws at home? Do social demands cease, and do family members work harder to meet implicit expectations? To understand the client's behavior in terms of its broader context, it is necessary to steadily attend to the probability of x (particular client affect, behavior, or cognition) given y (aspects of context). The context includes the social impact of the client's behavior (e.g., on therapist responding) as well as antecedents (e.g., different social settings). An answer to the question, "What is the probability of client behavior given certain aspects of the context," becomes evident only over time and cannot be detected in isolated or noncontextual snapshots of behavior. The detection of functional relations enables the clinician to predict how changes in contextual conditions will bring about behavior change. To be able to make these predictions, the clinician must be familiar with functional analytic principles and related research findings (e.g., Catania, 1998). A functional analysis is complete when alteration of the context has resulted in the predicted behavioral change. If the change has not occurred as predicted, then the functional relations are reexamined and the process starts again.

To summarize, a *functional analysis* is the process of detecting patterns or consistencies within the reciprocal relationship of the client's behavior and context; predicting viable change strategies based on functional analytic principles; implementing these strategies; and assessing the effects on the behaviors of interest (individual "target" behaviors, such as thinking, feeling, remembering, reasoning, problem solving, etc.). This chapter will first provide an overview of the basic principles needed to conduct a functional analysis, detail step-by-step considerations involved in functional analyses, discuss functional analyses in the context of the prevailing third-wave cognitive behavior therapies, and finally address methodological issues and challenges.

BEHAVIORAL PRINCIPLES

Functional Relations

Discerning patterns or consistencies present in the therapeutic session and, more generally, in a client's life is a complex task involving a close and repeated examination of the client's behavior within context. The behavior–context unit is conceptualized as consisting of events reliably preceding and following the occurrence of a particular target behavior, for it was at this level of analysis that lawful relations among antecedents (A), behaviors (B), and consequences (C) first emerged and enabled formal scientific prediction and influence (Skinner, 1938/1991). The entire continuous and dynamic interaction of antecedent, behavior, and contingent consequence over time is called the *operant contingency*. This contingency denotes an integrated behavior-context unit, in which particular behaviors are *more likely* to occur in the presence of certain antecedents, and some consequences are *more likely* to occur following particular behaviors (the behaviors are then said to "produce" the consequences). Note the emphasis on a probabilistic relationship: To repeat, neither antecedents nor consequences are related to the behavior in a push–pull, mechanistic fashion. Antecedents are not "triggers" of behavior. Consequences may be dispersed ("intermittent") and thus often not occur at all, or they may be delayed. For this reason, contingency diagrams illustrating antecedents, behavior, and consequences avoid a flowchart style and use "●" (one may think of it as "increase the likelihood") to denote their probabilistic relationship: antecedents ● behaviors ● consequences.

Detecting operant contingencies would be a rather simple task if the terms of the contingency were solely defined by their temporal relation to the other terms (i.e., antecedent event precedes behavior, which precedes the consequence). However, this is not the case: *Each specific term of an operant contingency is defined in relation to its general effects on the other terms.* To explain this *functional* definition of the terms, we start with "consequences," then elaborate on functional classes of behaviors, and finally cover antecedents.

Consequences

Consequences, as a functional class, are defined in relation to their effects on behavior. They categorize the manner in which people "act upon the world, and change it, and are changed in turn by the consequences of their actions" (Skinner, 1957/1992, p. 1). Consequences denote the general social–environmental impact of a person's behavior (i.e., systematic changes in the intensity, magnitude, duration, frequency, or quality of events) as well as any related behavioral changes over time. For analytic purposes, consequences are differentiated by their effect on the frequency of behavior: Do they increase or decrease the rate of the behavior they follow? These relations are illustrated in Figure 2.1: If behavior is reliably followed by certain consequences, then these consequences might—over time—produce changes in the rate of that behavior.

If the frequency of the behavior increases over time, then the consequence is called a "reinforcer;" if the frequency of the behavior decreases over time, then the consequence is called a "punisher." To illustrate these relations, Figure 2.2 assumes that two clients often try to address a particularly difficult topic in session and shows two different therapist responses: (1) acknowledging the topic and (2) immediately changing the topic. The former would be an example of reinforcement (increase in the rate of the client's behavior across sessions), the latter an example of punishment (decrease in the rate of the client's behavior across sessions).

The adjectives *positive* and *negative* distinguish whether access to consequences is given, or whether they are removed, terminated, or postponed. If behavior produces access to consequences (+), they are called "positive." If behavior results in a reduction of the magnitude, duration, or frequency of consequences (e.g., by prevention, termination, or postponement) (–),

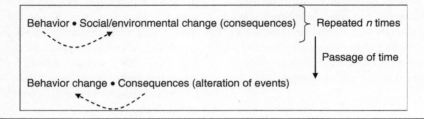

FIGURE 2.1   Consequences and their relationship with behavior.

the consequences are called "negative." Table 2.1 summarizes all possible positive and negative reinforcement and punishment contingencies.

As previously emphasized, behavior consequence patterns emerge over time: Not every behavior produces an outcome (e.g., many of our social behaviors do not have the impact we intended), and the probability with which consequences follow behavior is known as the "schedule" of reinforcement or punishment.

Reinforcement. Reinforcement contingencies always *maintain* behavior or *increase* its frequency in the long run. Rather than by their appearance, reinforcement contingencies are defined by their effect on behavior. The following examples illustrate this distinction.

Example 1: After a client has canceled two appointments in a row, he attends one session. As the client walks through the door, the therapist says to him, "Gee, I am glad you were able to come to session today."

Without knowing how this statement will affect the client's attendance record, we cannot conclude that praise functioned to reinforce session attendance. We would need the following information to determine whether the therapist's response was a reinforcer: Will the frequency of attendance increase over time, and will the client begin to miss sessions if regular praise for attendance is withdrawn?

Example 2: At the beginning of the session, a client engages in emotional recounting

of events that happened to friends and relatives. The therapist attends politely, nods in understanding, does not interrupt, and waits until the client "runs out of steam" before implementing the agenda for the current session. The client's recounting continues and takes up more and more of the session, as time goes by.

As the client's behavior is maintained and increases in duration over time, it is likely that the therapist's behaviors function as reinforcers.

In the vernacular, the terms *reinforcement* and *reward* (or *praise*) are often used interchangeably. A functional approach defines reinforcement by its rate-increasing or -maintaining influence on behavior and thereby sharply distinguishes it from *reward* or *praise*. Moreover, given this functional definition, events that function to maintain or increase the rate of behavior are not necessarily pleasant, and pleasant events do not necessarily maintain behavior—as when engagement in activities for activities' sake does not function to alleviate depression (Martell, Addis, & Jacobson, 2001).

Negative reinforcement is an *increase* in the rate of behavior or the maintenance of behavior as a result of preventing, terminating, or postponing events, or reducing their overall frequency (see Table 2.1). The difference between positively and negatively reinforced behavior can be illustrated with exercise: For some people, exercising has been established as a positive reinforcer that may even be used to maintain other behavior, as when finishing a chore, homework,

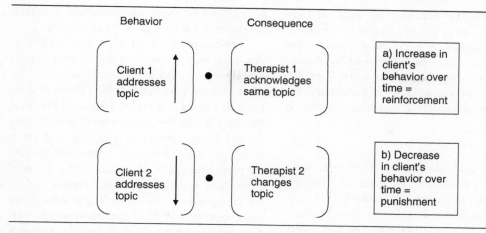

FIGURE 2.2 Illustrations of positive reinforcement and positive punishment.

TABLE 2.1 Reinforcement and Punishment Contingencies

| | | (1) Following behavior, events are | |
		Accessed, presented (+)	Prevented, terminated, postponed, or reduced (frequency, intensity, etc.) (–)
(2) Over time, the frequency of behavior	Increases	Positive reinforcement	Negative reinforcement (avoidance, escape)
	Decreases	Positive punishment	Negative punishment (timeout, penalty)

Adapted from Drossel, Waltz, & Hayes, 2007.

or writing assignment is maintained and followed by access to the gym. For others, exercising is maintained by reducing the dire consequences of a sedentary lifestyle, such as obesity, high blood pressure, or other aches and pains. In those latter cases, exercising is negatively reinforced. Briefly said, "'doing what we want to do' [choice] indicates the operation of positive reinforcement; 'doing what we have to do' [relative absence of choice] specifies negative reinforcement contingencies" (Sidman, 1989, p. 56).

However, negative reinforcement contingencies are frequently not identifiable by the individual whose life they affect: A client who routinely alters the session's agenda by being late, failing to attend, by beginning the session with narratives of "crises" that resemble tempests in a teacup, or by frequently changing topics is not aware of engaging in avoidance behaviors that prevent progression of therapy, just as the therapist may not be aware that he or she negatively

reinforces those behaviors when removing demands and going along with the conversation.

Determining whether behavior is indeed negatively reinforced is also difficult because sociocultural contingencies often reinforce descriptions of escape and avoidance. For example, people are more willing to provide social support when an alcohol-using person speaks of drowning sorrows and not of enjoying the "high" (for the functional properties of drugs, see Poling & Byrne, 2000). For this reason, drug-using clients may represent themselves as having few choices aside from escaping life's troubles. The progressive elimination of choice, however, may be due to the positively reinforcing properties of drugs that come to weaken all other reinforcement contingencies and not due to escape contingencies (Rachlin, 2000). A functional analysis assumes that describing one's own behavior also participates in operant contingencies, and self-descriptions may not necessarily match the actual contingencies operating on the behavior in question (see the section on "Verbal Operants" below). In our example of drug-using clients, the self-description may be maintained by avoidance (i.e., avoiding the loss of social support) while drug use per se may be maintained by positive reinforcement (i.e., obtaining the drug's effects).

Punishment. Parallel to reinforcement contingencies, punishment contingencies always *decrease* the frequency of behavior in the long run (see Table 2.1). Rather than by their appearance, they are also defined by their effect on behavior. As reinforcement is often confused

---

Example 1: An older child teases her younger sibling until the sibling is in tears. Each time the parent observes this behavior, the older child is removed from the situation, is chided, and receives a lecture on how to be a "good older sister." The older child's behavior continues.

*Although it topographically appears as though the child was being "punished," the child's behavior does not decrease in frequency. For this reason, there is **no** punishment contingency in effect. Instead, the parent's exclusive attention may be maintaining (i.e., reinforcing) the problematic teasing behavior. If so, then making parental attention to the older child contingent on behavior other than teasing may reduce its rate.*

Example 2: A therapist rewards a client's self-disclosure by making statements such as, "I am glad you shared these difficult experiences with me, and I feel closer to you as a result." The client's self-disclosures decrease in rate as the sessions continue.

Regardless of the topography of the therapist's behavior: If the client's behavior decreases in rate (and increased if the therapist discontinued these statements), then a punishment contingency is in effect.

---

with *reward* or *praise*, punishment is mistaken for the vernacular *vengeance* or *retribution*.

Therapists should be especially skilled in detecting their inadvertent use of punishment contingencies within session because the disruption of social relationships is one of their most significant side effects (Newsom, Favell, & Rincover, 1983). Punishment contingencies may disrupt other operant responding; and emotional reactions, including aggression toward the punishing agent, are common (Van Houten, 1983). It is not uncommon in Western culture for caregivers to also punish the subsequent emotional responding of their charges (e.g., "I'll give you something to cry about."). If a client's history is such that his or her emotional reactions to punishment procedures were punished, then silent withdrawal may occur in session and the client may not indicate that the therapeutic relationship has been compromised. Kohlenberg and Tsai (1991) suggest that positive feedback and expressions of caring by the therapist may function as positive punishers for many clients. In these cases, establishing these events as positive reinforcers is the therapeutic task.

Because punishment contingencies that work like the proverbial hot stove (immediate, consistent, contingent, brief, and sufficiently yet not excessively intense) have rapid results, they are common in interpersonal interactions (Sidman, 1989). Many couples, for example, want partners to engage in different or novel behavior, yet are punishing the partner's engagement with critical or snide remarks. The rate-reducing effect of punishment is important, for it is—by definition—impossible to build repertoires or to shape novel behaviors by implementing punishment contingencies. Additionally, eliminating ineffective behaviors through punishment procedures may deprive individuals of access to reinforcers.

Example: A client attends therapy for anger management. With the passage of time, the therapist realizes that the client's only social contacts consist of temporary alliances she forms with others against those she accuses of provoking her.

To the extent that the therapist engages in problem solving with the client and speaks with the client about others in her life, the therapist positively reinforces (maintains) the client's pattern. Assuming that the client does not have any other repertoire—other than her angry behavior—to establish and maintain relationships, punishing the client's behavior (e.g., decreasing its rate by commenting or blocking the client's narrative) would deprive her of access to a reinforcer and could possibly harm the therapeutic relationship. Rather than using punishment procedures to reduce ineffective behaviors, it would be advisable to shape an effective repertoire and, with the consent of the client, to shift the therapeutic target from anger management to social skills training. The client's angry behavior would become unnecessary as he or she acquires more effective skills. Note that this scenario parallels that of Yalom's (1995) "help-rejecting complainer," who may access social relationships by seeking help and has no other repertoires to continue social contacts.

Generally, when a reduction of the rate of behavior is considered, establishing alternative, effective repertoires to access the reinforcer may eliminate the need for punishment procedures.

Negative punishment contingencies are known as "time-out" or "penalty" (see Table 2.1). They involve the temporary or permanent loss of access to events dependent on behavior, with the rate of behavior declining over time as a result. One may think of "silent treatment" or "giving somebody the cold shoulder" as examples of negative punishment, if such silent treatment involves the loss of attention contingent on specific behaviors and these behaviors decrease in rate as a result. Like positive punishment, negative punishment also produces emotional reactions—as those know who have received tickets for traffic violations. Later episodes of remembering and self-reprimanding demonstrate the spillover disruption of other ongoing operant behavior as a result of punishment procedures (e.g., I should have . . . could have . . . , etc. disrupts one's focus on work).

Breaking the Contingency. The discontinuation of reinforcement or punishment contingencies is called "extinction." If behavior that used to reliably produce consequences suddenly does not work anymore, the behavior becomes more variable and may also escalate or increase in intensity. Emotional reactions are also common. Operation of a soda machine provides an everyday example: If the machine takes money but does not deliver the usual can of soda, a person may resort to pushing multiple buttons, including the change button, repeatedly (increased variability) and with increasing speed (increased intensity). Then he or she may push or tilt the machine (further increased intensity), and finally kick or punch the machine (emotional responding) before turning away. This sequence is called an **extinction burst**. During extinction bursts, behaviors that were extinguished or occur at a low rate may suddenly reemerge. This phenomenon of "trying all that ever worked before" is called *resurgence* (Podlesnik, Jimenez-Gomez, & Shahan, 2006). Extinction bursts can be prevented by delivering the reinforcer contingent on *other* or *incompatible* behavior (e.g., a parent attends to all appropriate but not to disruptive behavior of a child), or by making the consequence available regardless of behavior (e.g., when a parent provides regular or "noncontingent" attention independent of what the child does).

Extinction is the slow fading or declining in the frequency of behavior after reinforcement has been withdrawn and the extinction burst has passed. If behavior was reinforced intermittently (i.e., it worked once in a while), then extinction will proceed at a slower pace. For this reason, the discontinuation of reinforcement should not be planned and implemented for intervention purposes unless the therapist can be absolutely certain that inadvertent reinforcement of the targeted behavior will not occur.

Example 1: A client has a history of establishing relationships by seeking help. Session after session, the therapist engages in problem solving with the client. The client regularly rejects the suggested solutions as unworkable and leaves them untried. The therapist is slightly irritated and, for a while, tries even harder to develop viable solutions in collaboration with the client. After a few more sessions, the therapist's effort to problem-solve ceases completely.

The client may have extinguished the therapist's problem-solving efforts.

Example 2: After some time, the same client notices that the therapist is reluctant to engage in problem solving. No more suggestions are forthcoming. The client becomes irritated and questions the therapist's expertise and commitment. Subsequently, he fails to attend appointments.

The therapist may have discontinued reinforcement for the client's help-seeking behavior and extinguished it.

Therapists who tackle long-standing and seemingly recalcitrant behavior problems must be especially aware of the effects of extinction on their own behavior. If there is a suspicion that the provision of instrumental assistance, emotional support, and problem solving is being extinguished, this suspicion should prompt a reevaluation of the functional analytic case conceptualization and a discussion with the client about the selection of more appropriate targets for therapy (e.g., social skills building in the preceding example).

The Role of Consequences in Empirically Supported Cognitive Behavioral Strategies. A functional analytic approach is *constructional* in nature (Goldiamond, 1974). The goal of therapy is to enhance psychological flexibility and broaden clients' repertoires by asking the following questions:

• What would the client like to be able to do?

• What are the barriers to engaging in behaviors representative of that chosen lifestyle?

As a general rule, empirically supported interventions (O'Donohue & Fisher, 2008) combine reinforcement and extinction procedures (termed *differential reinforcement*) to build alternative repertoires that compete with and thereby replace life-interfering behaviors. Cognitive restructuring, for example, instructs and differentially reinforces evaluating, testing, and reformulating "What happens when … " statements. Within this process of disputation, the client may contact novel contingencies that then maintain repertoires that compete with the life-interfering behaviors. Similarly, anger management focuses on differentially reinforcing competing repertoires, such as relaxing and problem solving. Mindfulness techniques differentially reinforce pausing, observing, and attending to behavior in its broader context.

When clients engage in avoidance behavior, techniques such as *in vivo* or interoceptive exposure, systematic desensitization, flooding, or acceptance involve rapport building and the concurrent differential reinforcement of the client's approach to previously avoided situations. Interoceptive exposure, for example, involves the client's intentional engagement in behaviors (e.g., hyperventilating, gasping for air, losing one's balance) that the client predicts will be ultimately followed by a loss of control, loss of consciousness, or even death (negative punishment). Clients who have never experienced a dreaded consequence such as a heart attack alter their lives to avoid this negative punishment contingency, plausible or not, and to prevent the behaviors associated with it. Differentially reinforcing approach behaviors, such as breath holding, breathing through a straw, climbing steps, spinning, and the like, serves to demonstrate that the negative punishment contingency is indeed not in effect (i.e., hyperventilating, gasping for air, losing one's balance are not followed by the dreaded event), so that avoidance behaviors—including rules about the significance of physiological cues—become unnecessary. Importantly, for avoidance contingencies to lose their grip on clients' lives, the competing approach behaviors must occur.

Habit reversal explicitly instructs and differentially reinforces behaviors that are incompatible with presenting problems such as tics or chronic hair pulling (Azrin & Nunn, 1973). Regardless of technique, the underlying principles are those of reinforcing or building one repertoire while extinguishing another (e.g., skills training while reducing reason giving or any other barriers to engagement in the therapeutic process). The focus of empirically supported strategies is thus on supporting alternative repertoires, rather than on symptom reduction.

Behaviors

So far, we have focused on the "consequence" end of the antecedent • behavior • consequence unit. We have emphasized that consequences are defined by their effects on the rate of behavior (increase = reinforcement; decrease = punishment). Before we can address the selection of target behaviors within a functional analysis, we also need to define behaviors from a functional perspective. As might be anticipated from the aforementioned examples, in a functional analysis, *behaviors are defined by their impact or dependent on the consequences they produce*, rather than by their topography. For example, if crying, yawning, coughing, blowing one's nose, voicing anger or disappointment about therapy, and distracting function to avoid therapist feedback within session, then all of these behaviors have the same function. They all are part and parcel with the client's avoidance repertoire. From a functional perspective, we can predict that an intervention targeting avoidance will affect all of the behaviors in that class.

The function of behavior is emphasized because its topography can be misleading: A person may claim, for example, that he or she never makes any requests of others. Yet, if utterances such as "I am feeling sad today" or "I am too anxious to attend the party alone" are reliably followed by specific consequences (e.g., social support: friends stop by to ask what they can do, or they offer to be party companions), then these utterances practically function as requests, although they may not have the proper grammatical appearance. Couples that disagree

about the degree to which the partners provide assistance to each other or make requests of each other may have conflicting functional (Partner 1: "I constantly do things for you") versus topographical interpretations (Partner 2: "Yet I never ask anything of you"). For analytic purposes, we can group all utterances that function to produce consistent outcomes (e.g., having one's needs or wants met = positive reinforcement) into one functional category on which to intervene.

All aspects of human behavior may enter into a functional analysis. A functional analysis does not treat a person's thinking, feeling, problem solving, remembering—events that are accessible only to the person engaging in them—any different from observable behaviors. Thinking and feeling do not have any privileged status in the analysis; that is, they are not interpreted as default "reasons" for other behavior. Rather, they are also examined *in terms of their function*. The extent to which a client's effective behavior would be possible if thinking and feeling did not constitute barriers becomes an important aspect of the functional analysis by assessing the context (consequences and antecedents) of particular reported thoughts and emotions. One of the goals of a functional analysis is to decouple the perceived causal link from feelings and thoughts to behavior. *Feeling/thinking* → *behaving* turns into *feeling/thinking/behaving* without a priori causal assumptions (Skinner, 1974). Rather than causing behavior, feeling and thinking are interpreted as things people *do*, events that can be contextualized like any other behavior and that do not have to be altered before behavior changes. Without the perceived causal link, a client may engage in building an environment that supports reengagement and fulfillment without waiting for his or her thinking or feeling to change first. This functional analytic approach to emotions and cognitions is known as "acceptance" (e.g., Hayes, Strosahl, & Wilson 1999; Linehan, 1993a; Martell, Addis, & Jacobson, 2001). Acceptance-based approaches generally alter the extent to which mood and cognition are allowed to function as verbal and socially accepted barriers to effective action (see "Antecedents" below) and provide examples for the role of private events, such as thinking and feeling, in functional analyses.

Antecedents

Antecedents denote the context-appropriate dimension of human behavior, that is, our ability to engage in situation or role-specific repertoires and to "read" social situations properly. We can speak of the influence of antecedents as "knowing when and when not to" do certain things, or as reliable predictors of the consequences of behavior. Antecedents are defined by their common behavioral functions: The set of events that occasions a client's avoidant behavior, for example, may be grouped into one functional class of antecedents, including verbal ("The plane I'm taking is going to crash," "I'll never survive a disagreement with my boss") and nonverbal events (confined seating arrangements, boss's frowning). All context-appropriate behavior relies on a history of reinforcement. This history, however, can be direct (discrimination training or the reinforcement of rule following) or indirect (emergent relations).

Discrimination Training. Antecedents may acquire their behavioral functions through a direct history of discrimination training. *Discrimination training* occurs when some responses are reliably reinforced in the presence of certain antecedents but not in their absence. For example, catchers only catch fly balls if they maintain temporal or spatial constancy while positioning themselves in the path of the ball: Catching is reinforced only in the presence of constancy, the antecedent; otherwise, the catcher misses or chases the ball (Shaffer & McBeath, 2002). Similarly, speaking of "aging" will be appropriate in the presence of some craniofacial changes but not others; that is, these judgments are differentially reinforced in the presence of particular antecedents (Pittenger & Shaw, 1975). This history of reinforcement proceeds without direct instruction, for we are unable to describe the exact nature of "constancy" to the catcher, or the exact nature of the craniofacial changes to the speaker. Behavior becomes context-appropriate even when contextual features cannot be easily characterized.

Correspondingly, if behavior is consistently punished or extinguished in one situation and not in another, the behavior will become less likely in the former situation. "Losing one's accent," for example, may involve extinguishing or punishing the mispronunciation of words, such that the presence of any native speaker comes to set the occasion for careful pronunciation. Similarly, first-generation college students who leave their hometown may find they are speaking a "different language" upon their return. Note that the "discrimination training" lies within the natural interaction of speaker and listener, and that we are not able to give fast and easy rules to describe the antecedents on which a listener may reinforce, extinguish, or punish enunciation, pronunciation, or specific utterances—hence the rule that a second language is best learned in the respective country.

Generally, antecedents that occasion situation-specific repertoires maintained by similar consequences are not static or easily describable. "Tact" and "exquisite social skills," for example, are occasioned by subtle, dynamic cues that we tend to call "gut feelings" in lieu of better descriptions of the shifts in body language and facial expressions that actually occur. Because instructions describing complex antecedents tend to be incomplete, antecedent-behavior relations that have been established through discrimination training rather than instruction often result in a more honed or fine-tuned performance, as when a chef says, "You can follow my recipe, but that doesn't necessarily mean you can cook my dish." Thus, when clients lack subtle social tact, rather than giving instructions, therapists may best monitor the impact of a client's behavior on themselves and discriminate for the client when her or his behavior was skillful (e.g., "I liked what you just did. Do more of *that*," even if therapists cannot describe what *that* was). Again, perfection of a performance involves behavior that is in contact with the actual antecedents and the consequences rather than the instruction.

Instructions. Many verbal antecedents include events that most people, including clients and therapists, have never experienced. For example, pedestrians reach a curb, stop, and look to the left and then to the right so as to yield to traffic, yet a history of having been hit by cars is not necessary to establish a street curb as a functional antecedent. Instructions suffice, for we all share a long history of social reinforcement for following the generic instruction, "If *a*, do *b*." Parents reinforce a match between this verbal antecedent and their children's behavior (*b*) in the appropriate situation (*a*). Reinforcement is gradually faded out as children grow older and are expected to comply. Once a history of rule-following has been established through social reinforcement, this history easily extends to other situations implying "If *a*, do *b*" (e.g., be on time when you have scheduled an appointment).

Example: Clients may not have history of reliable antecedents for rule following (e.g., when "If *a*, do *b*" conflicted with "Do as I say but not as I do"). These clients may not be able to identify the situations that necessitate rule following and, as a result, encounter many social difficulties (*intervention: discrimination training, instruction*). Other clients' rule following may not have been established by positive reinforcement, as when parents expect their child to engage in instructed behavior and punish all other behavior. For these clients, rule following may be maintained by avoidance and thus become rigid and interfere with situational-appropriate behavior (*intervention: identify reinforcers; differentially reinforce approach behavior rather than avoidance*).

Emergent Relations. Verbal antecedents may also emerge because other preexisting relations, such as "if ... then ... ," "larger than," "equal to," etc., provide the context in which novel situations are interpreted (Sidman, 1994; Hayes, Barnes-Holmes, & Roche, 2001). For example, if a person had difficulties conveying her point to one listener, then she might conclude that her

difficulties would be worse were she to speak in the presence of 50 or 100 listeners, even if she has never spoken in front of a larger audience. The preexisting relationship here would be "larger than" (100 > 50 > 1) which, in this context, is also applied to difficulties (difficulties|100 > difficulties|50 > difficulties|1). Correspondingly, relations inherent in instructions ("if *a*, do *b*") may also be extended to different or novel situations, whether plausible or not ("if I am good, I'll go to heaven"; "if I gasp for air, I will die"; "if I feel down, I can't be productive"). Antecedent and consequent functions can "spread" through sets of events that have been linked to each other by their context. These emergent functional relations, relying on a particular history of reinforcement but eliminating the need for discrimination training, account for the generative and creative properties of language.

Important for clinical purposes, emergent functional relations also give an account of how verbal constructs of events never encountered by an individual can exert strong reactions (e.g., heaven and hell, death, ch'i and life energies, or spirits). From an operant standpoint, the processes by which such events acquire antecedent (or consequent) functions are not different in kind from those by which we acquire, maintain, and hone our general language skills. For this reason, client thinking or reasoning is not interpreted as "irrational" or "unreasonable." Rather, as all of the client's behavior, it is understandable within its context.

Multiple Contingencies

As emphasized earlier, operant antecedent • behavior • consequence units are not easily identifiable linear occurrences. Therapists do not have the convenience to observe tidily segmented chains of antecedents, behaviors, and consequences, for behavior is multiply determined: More than one operant contingency is operative at once and multiple interpretations of the client's behavior are possible. Truancy, for example, may be a function of deficient academic skills and a related absence of teacher reinforcement for task completion; peer support for oppositional behavior; and extinction of effective school-related behaviors at home (e.g., a parent is generally indifferent or provides praise regardless of whether the child completed the homework tasks). For this reason, operant contingencies are best thought of as "nested" rather than consecutive units.

Nonverbal and verbal operant contingencies may concurrently operate on one target behavior. Correspondingly, the terms *pliance/counterpliance* and *tracking* identify the degree to which rule following (i.e., verbal antecedents, social consequences) conflicts with adjusting to the demands of changing situations (i.e., nonverbal antecedents and/or consequences).

Pliance. The term *pliance* refers to behavior that is occasioned by verbal antecedents and fails to make contact with the actually prevailing nonverbal contingencies (Zettle & Hayes, 1982). When following rules, advice, or admonitions (whether given by others or self-generated) results in ineffective, rigid, or inflexible behavior, a long history of social reinforcement contingent on "doing what one is supposed to do" may compete with and reduce the influence of actual situational demands.

Counterpliance. Frequently, peers provide social support for behavior that explicitly runs counter to established rules, advice, or admonitions. In these cases, social reinforcers are delivered when one "does what one is *not* supposed to do." As a function of this history of reinforcement, an individual may engage in counterpliant behavior. Note that counterpliant repertoires are not different in kind from pliant ones: Both are governed by rules established by social reinforcement and insensitive to the effects of other contingencies.

Tracking. In contrast to pliance, "tracking" characterizes repertoires that are initially established by verbal antecedents and social reinforcers but later are maintained by contingencies other than those for rule following (or rule rejecting, in the case of counterpliance).

The determination of whether a client tends to engage in pliance, counterpliance, or tracking can be made only over time. No specific agreement with the therapist or failure to comply is

indicative: Pliance, counterpliance, and tracking are *patterns* of behavior–environment interaction and cannot be gauged upon an isolated instance.

In addition to competing contingencies involving one behavior, we are able to choose among a multitude of alternatives each day (multiple contingencies involving multiple behaviors). Functional analyses also include an assessment of choice patterns.

Matching Law. The matching law (Herrnstein, 1961/1997) is a general quantitative description of choice. If two or more contingencies are in effect at the same time, a person's preferences will match the reinforcing effectiveness of the contingencies. The struggle to fulfill concurrent professional and personal demands of daily living illustrates concurrent contingencies. The matching law predicts that, over time, the level of engagement in available alternatives will match the relative reinforcing value of that alternative. It would also predict that, as the quality of an interpersonal relationship deteriorates because of time constraints, even more time will be allocated to other demands—causing a downward spiral if the rate of reinforcement or reinforcer effectiveness of the relationship is not enhanced (see also reinforcement erosion, Jacobson & Christensen, 1996).

The matching law generally applies to all situations in which one behavior is chosen over another. Bulow and Meller (1998) used a matching law analysis to demonstrate a relationship between teenagers' general activity level and sexual behavior; that is, the greater the value of alternative reinforcers, the lower the frequency of sexual risk taking. In general, matching law analyses suggest the enhancement of the reinforcing value of available alternatives rather than interventions to reduce specific target behaviors (see McDowell, 1988, for an elaboration).

Discounting. As an extension of the matching law, the research on "discounting" provides a functional account of impulsive choice, for it describes how reinforcers lose their relative effectiveness when their delivery is delayed or uncertain (Rachlin, 2000). Failures of self-control fall within the purview of discounted reinforcement: Eating french fries or ice cream now rather than fitting into pants later; going out with friends now rather than doing well on an exam later; having the cigarette now rather than having our health later. Note that "fitting into pants," "doing well on an exam," and "having our health" are outcomes most would immediately endorse as desirable. However, the evidence-based discount function shows how the value of these outcomes invariably diminishes when they are pitched against immediate and certain reinforcers (i.e., fat, salt, and sugar; social contact; nicotine). Competing immediate and certain reinforcers may prevent contact with the delayed and uncertain contingency. Applications of discounting to clinical assessment have shown different discount functions (i.e., levels of impulsivity) for individuals who engage in drug use or who have been diagnosed with attention-deficit hyperactivity disorder, for example (see Bickel & Marsch, 2001; Neef & Northup, 2007). Discounting research suggests that delaying the choice (i.e., waiting five minutes to order french fries or ice cream; asking for time to consider before saying "yes" to a request; postponing the cigarette for a little while) and prosthetic reinforcers—serving as "crutches" on the way to the valued outcome—shift choices toward the relatively uncertain or delayed contingency. Evidence-based interventions to reduce impulsivity and enhance self-control utilize these findings (see Critchfield & Kollins, 2001).

Example: Uncertain and delayed reinforcement contingencies can also be conceptualized as overarching characterizations of patterns of behavior. Value statements, such as "being a worthwhile person," "being self-confident," "living a healthy lifestyle," and "being a good parent," are examples of these overarching reinforcement contingencies, and specific behaviors can be evaluated as to their fit into these patterns (e.g., Hayes,

---

Strosahl, & Wilson, 1999). After a period of values identification clients are invited to ask themselves at each behavioral choice point whether their activities contribute to obtaining the uncertain and delayed reinforcer or whether they are indicative of a different, potentially undesirable pattern. As described above, delaying the choice per se might shift the client's behavior toward the uncertain and delayed outcome.

Motivation

In a functional analysis, **motivation** is not thought to "move" or "drive" the person's behavior from the inside. Instead, motivation is found in the context of the person's personal circumstances: To the degree that reinforcers have different relative effectiveness, a person's motivation to engage in behaviors differs. In the context of the matching law, we mentioned that enhancing the effectiveness of alternative reinforcers is often a more useful strategy than reducing a problematic behavior. Such programmed changes in the effectiveness of reinforcers are termed *establishing operations* (Michael, 1993). Although they affect our behavior, we may not be able to identify establishing operations, as when casinos fade the volume of slot machines from loud (low-bet machines) to quiet (high-bet machines) and thereby establish the high-bet area as a reinforcer. Gamblers may be able only to report a liking of high bets and be unaware of escaping the noise of the low-bet area. While many drugs of abuse alter the effectiveness of social reinforcers (e.g., amphetamine; Poling & Byrne, 2000) histories of reinforcement can also establish the reinforcing effectiveness of drugs. Johanson and colleagues (1995), for example, gave differently colored placebo pills to participants before they played video games. Without the participants' knowledge, the experimenters systematically linked the outcome of the video games to the placebo pills' colors, with the result that participants preferred the placebos associated with better outcomes of the game. Generally speaking, any establishing operation produces a shift in preferences and correlated engagement.

Establishing operations in daily life range from the provision of salty food in bars to enhance the reinforcing effectiveness of drinks to motivational utterances ("augmenting"). Augmenting may establish novel or boost existing reinforcers. The statement, "You can exchange this coupon for cash at the end of the week," for example, is an utterance that establishes the coupons as reinforcers, assuming that access to cash already reinforces the person's behavior. Augmenting may also enhance the value of events that have always had a reinforcing function by placing them into a social context and associating them with other reinforcing outcomes (e.g., "Let's go to the gym tomorrow—we'll have fun"). Therapists engage in augmenting to facilitate their client's engagement in an active and fulfilling lifestyle (Martell, Addis, & Jacobson, 2001), for example, via values clarification.

Specific Verbal Operants

From a functional analytic perspective, social interactions are viewed as exercises in rhetoric. Even the smallest social exchange involves a message—an attempt to influence the listener's behavior (e.g., change his/her point of view to the speaker's point of view). It is the therapist's task to decipher this message. For analytic purposes, utterances are organized in terms of stable contextual factors across situations. First, we will discuss invariant antecedent-behavior relations ("tacting") and their effect on sharing and affective meaning in relationships, and then invariant behavior-consequent relations ("manding"). Finally, we will underline the importance of "autoclitic" or self-referential behavior for effective social skills.

Tacting

Tacting can be interpreted as a communicative tool that generates connectedness and understanding between speaker and listener: Specific antecedents reliably occasion the same utterance. In the simplest case, we can think of a child saying "apple" in the presence of an apple and

not in the presence of a pear. A more complex situation would be the description of a sunset or some other complex event. In all of these cases, the speaker's engagement is reinforced by the listener's understanding; that is, the listener's behavior is now occasioned by similar circumstances, regardless of whether he or she experienced them directly. Tacting provides the groundwork for shared meaning between individuals and is thus integral to the therapist's understanding of the client.

The labeling of emotions requires sophisticated tacting repertoires. "I am jealous," for example, communicates a complex social history: the presence of a reinforcing relationship; a history of loss (negative punishment) or self-generated rules about access to social reinforcers (e.g., "If she loved me, she would not spend so much time with friends" and possibly a decrease in the relative frequency of access to the coveted person. In contrast, "I am envious" indicates that others' behavior is being reinforced, a history of relative deprivation (establishing operation), or self-generated rules about access to reinforcers (e.g., "Life's not fair; I should have received the same"). Physiological arousal may be present when either statement is uttered, but "I am x" statements are rarely expressions of "emotion" in the sense of labeling physical stirrings or perturbations (Skinner, 1957/1992, p. 217). Instead, a child's social community shapes emotion talk by carefully observing unfolding complex social events and the child's behavior (e.g., crying, changing intonation or pitch). The child's private events—such as physiological arousal inaccessible to his or her verbal community—may acquire antecedent functions over time by entering equivalence relations with observable aspects of behavior and verbal antecedents (e.g., "jealous," "envious"). Tacting physiological processes (e.g., "I have a tummy ache") is shaped in a similar fashion, with differential reinforcement contingent on the public corollaries (e.g., vomiting, paleness) of the private event. Verbal elaborations of private events may acquire their antecedent function without direct discrimination training and through emergent functional relations (e.g., jealousy as a "green-eyed monster"). To the degree that the child's social environment reinforces talk about private events by responding empathically, the repertoire is further refined and maintained.

Given that the acquisition of tacting relies on careful observation and consistent positive reinforcement within the childhood social environment, many clients present to therapy with deficient tacting repertoires (see also Linehan's (1993a) discussion of "invalidating environments"). Clients may not be able to give descriptions of other people's behaviors. For example, they may respond to the question, "What did he do?," with "He made me mad," and have difficulties describing the actual interaction. Moreover, a history of negative reinforcement may have maintained inaccurate reporting ("lying") or resulted in a general failure to speak about events (Glenn, 1983). To the extent that clients are not observing or tacting their own behavior, they may report moods or events in their life happening "out of the blue" and fail to see the relationship between their own behavior and the consequences it produces. Whether a therapist and a client have agreed to increase the frequency of talk about private events or to enhance the client's understanding of his or her own behavior within the context in which it occurs, shaping of the client's tacting repertoire is required.

Note that tacting is reinforced by the speaker and the listener's ability to be "on the same wavelength." The speaker describes events to which the listener has not had access or has not paid attention, and the listener is then able to behave with respect to them. When the listener's behavior begins to track the contingencies affecting the speaker's behavior, the speaker's behavior is reinforced; that is, the speaker feels understood. Whether a speaker uses figurative speech or poetry to share a complex emotional context with the listener, or whether the speaker simply uses an emotion word such as *jealous* or *envious*, not the form of the tact but the degree to which it generates similar functional antecedents for the subsequent interaction between listener and speaker determines effective tacting.

Manding

Manding describes sets of utterances that serve to get what one wants from others. When a therapist assesses clients' tacting repertoire, he or she may ask, "Has the client assisted me in understanding the situation," or "Is the client speaking of anger in a situation to which others would react similarly?" As outlined above, the focus is on whether the therapist's and the client's behaviors track similar functional antecedents. In contrast, an assessment of clients' manding repertoires requires careful observations of the outcomes of client utterances. Utterances that produce similar functional outcomes are grouped together regardless of their topography. For example, if, "I am jealous," is followed by increased attention from the coveted person, then it falls into the same class as all other utterances that produce this outcome, such as "Please spend more time with me," "I would rather you didn't work so much," or "Would you like to have dinner on Sunday night?". All these utterances are reliably—albeit not always—reinforced by the same class of consequences and, for analytic purposes, constitute mands for attention.

Attention to clients' manding repertoire is important, for frequent manding that does not have the topography of direct requests may be perceived as aversive and manipulative (Glenn, 1983). If a client consistently leaves his or her listeners without the choice to say "no," he or she may become socially isolated as a result. A history of punishment or extinction of direct requests may have led to a pervasive lack of social impact and generated these alternative ("manipulative") strategies.

Autoclitics

Autoclitics are statements whose function is to alter the impact of what is being said on the listener (e.g., to soften criticism or strengthen assertions). Examples are phrases such as "with all due respect," "without wishing to contradict," "of course," "clearly," but also any narrative that weakens or enhances the impact of the tact or mand, such as a descriptions of how one reached a solution, or reasons for asking. Autoclitics provide listeners with additional information about the circumstances under which a speaker makes a statement (e.g., on what evidence an assertion is based) and are thus an integral part of effective social skills.

Example of a Functional Analysis of Verbal Behavior

A therapist, upon asking a simple question, routinely observes that a client gets carried away by discussing tangential circumstances or by focusing on minute details. The therapist formulates four hypotheses concerning the maintenance of the client's behavior:

1. The client may be deprived of social contacts, such that speaking occurs at a higher frequency than otherwise expected (*establishing operation*).
2. The client's social environment may not reinforce the client's utterances contingent on quality (*deficient contingency*).
3. There may be a history of positive or negative reinforcement for weakening one's own impact by extensive reason-giving and elaboration of the circumstances under which one's verbalizations occur (*reinforcement of autoclitics*).
4. The client may fail to identify the situation as one that does not require autoclitic responding.
5. Each of these hypotheses suggests a different intervention:

   - Increasing the frequency of social contact
   - Providing contingent feedback within session
   - Differentially reinforcing concise answers and extinguishing elaborate ones
   - Generating context-appropriate autoclitic responding through discrimination training or instruction.

The outcome of the intervention determines the effectiveness of the functional analysis.

The principles of behavior illustrated here provide the bases for the therapist's predictions and for the resulting change strategies. For functional analyses to be effective, therapists must be very familiar with the theory and application of behavioral principles to verbal and other behavior. Any functional analysis will be limited by the therapist's skillfulness in determining relevant and manipulable contextual conditions.

STEPS TOWARD A FUNCTIONAL ANALYSIS

As described, a functional analysis requires the identification of operant contingencies, that is, entire classes of different behaviors (no two of them exactly the same) that are defined in terms of their social impact or environmental effects. If the social impact or the environmental effects within the class are shifted, we can expect all behaviors in the class to shift, too. Borrowing an example from Wulfert, Greenway, and Dougher (1996), getting drunk, overeating, and gambling may all function to relieve marital stress (negative reinforcement) and, if so, may decrease as a function of marital therapy. Importantly, "a response class is not an operant until its modifiability has been demonstrated" (Catania, 1998, p. 400). This means that the success of the intervention will reveal whether the hypothetical (or "descriptive") operant class proposed by the therapist in collaboration with the client coincides with the actually functioning contingency. To reiterate, a functional analysis tightly links assessment and intervention.

Given the plethora of contextual conditions that affect behavior, specific "how-to" instructions are not available for the determination of functional relations. In general, however, the following guidelines—adapted from Goldiamond (1974) and Hawkins (1986)—may be useful:

1. Consider the DSM a Starting Point

Diagnoses according to the *Diagnostic and Statistical Manual of Mental Disorders*, 4th edition (*DSM*, American Psychiatric Association, 1994) are topographical groupings of covarying behaviors derived from large-N studies that may or may not represent operant classes on an individual level. To the extent that an individual's presentation—categorized according to the *DSM*—coincides with operant classes targeted by cognitive behavioral therapy packages, treatment packages that are selected based on diagnostic criteria will be effective. Drawing an analogy from medicine, abdominal cramping (the topographical category) may be due to chronic stress, food poisoning, or the stomach flu. If an intervention is chosen based upon topography alone, it will be effective to the extent that it matches the actual etiology.

Ferster (1973) describes the DSM as "a good starting point to uncover the actual forms of conduct that describe the way the ... person interacts with his [sic] environment" (p. 857). Correspondingly, Hawkins (1986) proposes a "behavioral assessment funnel" consisting of five phases, progressively narrowing in focus: (1) screening; (2) definition and classification according to DSM criteria; (3) pinpointing specific operant classes that then directly lead to interventions; (4) monitoring progress; and (5) follow-up. Because functional analyses are time and cost-intensive, Wulfert and colleagues (1996) suggest attending to heterogeneity within diagnostic categories and to "use these categories as a point of departure for a functional analysis and refine them by identifying homogeneous subgroups of individuals whose behavior is controlled by common antecedents and consequences" (p. 1141). Applications of this approach to social anxiety and to alcoholism and pedophilia are found in Hayes and Follette (1992) and in Wulfert, Greenway, and Dougher (1996), respectively. Functional analyses thus complement rather than replace the current diagnostic system and provide a problem-solving tool when empirically supported treatment packages do not exist, are not applicable without modification, or have not worked in the past.

As Haynes and O'Brien (2000) recommend, clinicians should be "assessment scholars" and have great familiarity with the *DSM*, the relevant clinical and experimental psychopathological literature, and behavioral principles (e.g., Baum, 1994) before embarking on a functional analysis and formulating hypotheses regarding possible operant classes.

2. Assess Behavior

To facilitate a focus on specific behaviors, Hawkins (1986) recommends the conceptualization of daily living as "multiple, interrelated, and temporally concurrent and overlapping tasks" (p. 338). Therapists assess areas of difficulty and success, and tasks can be grouped by outcome (i.e., consequences), considering different temporal scales (e.g., completing a job assignment versus contributing to society). Special attention may be paid to functional relations involving task completion and communication within session (Kohlenberg & Tsai, 1991). If a client refers to psychological constructs or global self-statements as a barrier to engagement or fulfilled living, these constructs or statements can become part of the functional analysis.

Example: A client states that she would be able to engage in certain activities if she had more self-confidence.

A functional analysis examines the conditions under which the client speaks of "lack of self-confidence" (functional antecedents) and the consequences of such statements (e.g., negative reinforcement). The client is asked to generate a list of specific behaviors that she associates with self-confidence in specific domains (e.g., work, interpersonal relationships). Rather than an internal state, "being self-confident" is conceptualized as an overarching pattern of successful completion of a range of tasks under specific conditions.

---

3. Teach Clients about Functional Relations

The degree to which clients understand and agree with the treatment rationale may affect outcome (Addis & Jacobson, 2000). For this reason, it is recommended to solicit client participation in the ongoing assessment process, examining what the client has tried before, what he or she would like to have happen, discussing the client's priorities, explaining the selected evidence-based treatment strategy in functional terms, and exploring barriers to treatment from a functional analytic viewpoint. Self-monitoring requires clients to record thinking, feeling, and behaving in context. Rather than attending to isolated instances, the focus is on establishing patterns over time. Monitoring acknowledges the client's thoughts and feelings and normalizes them at the same time ("acceptance"). Even if the client's presenting complaints will not be directly targeted by the intervention, the monitoring of antecedent–behavior–consequent relations serves to facilitate active participation as well as the clients' acceptance of the treatment rationale, that is, the building of alternative repertoires (see also Martell, Addis, & Jacobson (2001, Chapter 6) for teaching functional analyses in the context of depression; Linehan (1993a, Chapter 9) for "behavioral chain analyses" in the context of borderline personality disorder; Eifert & Forsyth (2005, Chapters 7 ff.) for monitoring anxiety in context; and McCurry (2006, Chapter 5) for teaching functional analyses to caregivers of individuals with dementia).

4. Develop Hypotheses Concerning the Functions of Current and Potential Alternative Repertoires Using Behavioral Principles

As emphasized repeatedly, operant units can be identified on multiple scales (e.g., within specific aspects of the interaction between therapist and client (Kohlenberg & Tsai, 1991); within general patterns in the client's life, such as discounting delayed or uncertain reinforcers; etc.). Until a functional analysis is complete, as demonstrated by the effectiveness of the intervention, statements about the function of clients' behavior and about its maintenance are working hypotheses. This circumstance should also be shared with the client to foster an atmosphere of collaborative empiricism: Together, client and therapist embark on a journey to discover what works best for the client. Based on these hypotheses and the related behavioral principles, assessment will render multiple points of intervention for the same presenting problem (see the beginning of this chapter for a general introduction to principles of behavior; also Farmer & Nelson-Gray (2005) for an application of behavioral principles to presenting problems).

5. Rather than Reducing or Eliminating Behaviors, Build Alternative Repertoires

The point of intervention that is ultimately chosen depends on practical considerations. Here, we advocate the building of alternative repertoires for four reasons:

1. The therapeutic relationship must be maintained. As the side effects of punishment and extinction may lead to a rupture, it is often more effective to build alternative repertoires than to make the reduction or elimination of repertoires an explicit target. (Note that extinction occurs during differential reinforcement; however, its side effects are buffered or prevented by ensuring alternative access to reinforcers.)
2. Many clients present with already narrow or inflexible repertoires (e.g., clients who engage in avoidance behaviors). As the therapist never has a priori access to all the behaviors that constitute a functional operant class, any extinction procedure that solely targets the reduction or elimination of behaviors may inadvertently narrow adaptive repertoires even further.
3. Adaptive repertoires may be disrupted as a side effect of punishment, or the client's behavior may become more rigid as a function of successfully avoiding aversive consequences.
4. Most if not all clients seek a reengagement in life, which can be accomplished only by contacting contingencies that support and maintain such engagement. Punishment and extinction are, by definition, not suited for this purpose.

6. Shape Repertoires that Allow Contact with Reinforcers Already Available in the Clients' Environment

A second set of pragmatic considerations involves the degree of influence therapists have over a client's environment. As emphasized repeatedly, reinforcement supports and maintains repertoires, and contact with natural reinforcers is the warp and weft of effective therapy. Prosthetic or contrived immediate reinforcers for engaging in novel or previously avoided activities are useful only if natural contingencies are available to keep the client's engagement going once therapy ends. Putting specific activities into the larger context of valued living (e.g., "being a good spouse" or "being self-confident") may provide first social prosthetic and then natural—albeit always delayed and uncertain—reinforcement. Moreover, the larger contingent pattern may continue to evoke engagement even if specific tasks are met with failure (i.e., extinction or punishment). For example, the social reinforcing value of "being a good parent" is not diminished by isolated parent-child interactions that are ineffective; it also is not reduced by engaging in effective behavior (e.g., nobody would say, "I have managed to attend one of my child's baseball games, so now I have met my goal of 'being a good parent.'"). It is more difficult to extinguish *patterns* than it is to extinguish behavior in the service of a narrowly circumscribed goal, such as having a romantic interaction at a specific date and time. Larger patterns prevent discouragement and enable persistence by allowing clients to shift their behavior until it ultimately contacts those reinforcers that are already available in their environment.

Often, ineffective behaviors are maintained by positive or negative reinforcers already available in the clients' environment (e.g., when social attention, such as chiding, reinforces a child's disruptive behavior; or when a client's depressed behavior prevents marital discord). These ineffective behaviors will become unnecessary with the construction of alternative, competing, and novel repertoires that lead to the same outcome ("matching law"). Access to valued reinforcers can thus be maintained (e.g., the child receives attention for academic skills; skilled interpersonal behavior prevents further marital discord).

7. Assess the Effectiveness of the Intervention and Start the Process Again, If Necessary

Functional analyses require that hypotheses are held lightly until practical results have been obtained. Client and therapist work together to test hypotheses. Rather than attributing the failure of an intervention to client variables (e.g., "resistance"), functional analyses require the flexibility to reexamine one's assumptions and to collaborate with the client to enhance or modify the functional case conceptualization. To facilitate this flexibility and to break down the tasks required for expertise in functional analyses, we took over Gambrill's (2005, pp. 427–435) recommendations for clinicians (Table 2.2, column 1) and expanded these recommendations into a therapeutic skill set necessary to develop effective functional analyses for intractable and complex presenting problems (Table 2.2, column 2).

OPERANT CONTINGENCIES AND THIRD-WAVE THERAPIES

In addition to traditional cognitive behavioral therapies developed in the 1960s and 1970s, acceptance-based or "third-wave" therapies of the past two decades are also based on the functional analytic approach outlined above. As described earlier, therapy packages benefit clients to the extent that presenting problems overlap with the functional classes targeted by specific treatment packages. Third-wave therapies are explicitly *contextual*, taking into account antecedent–behavior–consequent relations (e.g., Bach & Moran, 2008). Comprehensive therapies, such as acceptance and commitment therapy (Hayes, Strosahl, & Wilson, 1999), behavioral activation (Martell, Addis, & Jacobson, 2001), dialectical behavioral therapy (Linehan, 1993a), or functional analytic psychotherapy (Kohlenberg & Tsai, 1991) thus share the same philosophical and scientific foundations, yet focus on different repertoires.

The view of thinking, feeling, and behaving as amenable to functional analyses and not necessarily causally related is common to all third-wave approaches. Clients come to report and contextualize their thinking and feeling, and they learn to behave effectively even when negative or disturbing thoughts or feelings are present ("acceptance"). The socially reinforced rule, that self-reports of negative thoughts or emotions must produce certain negative behavioral outcomes (or, in other words, that

TABLE 2.2   Recommended skill sets for functional analyses

Recommendations (*verbatim* from Gambrill, 2005, pp. 427–435)	Tasks (adapted from Gambrill, 2005)
1. Acquire domain-specific knowledge and skills	Become an expert in behavioral principles.
2. Be aware of what you don't know (ignorance as kind of knowledge)	Make sure possible physiological conditions that could lead to the presenting problem are ruled out (e.g., hypothyroidism and depression); note areas of incomplete assessment.
3. Make assumptions explicit	Share your knowledge. Functional analyses are *transparent* and conducted in collaboration with the client. Therefore, introduce the client to the principles of functional analyses; be aware of implicit assumptions that may draw you to assess only certain areas of the client's life.
4. Watch your language	Limit yourself to describing behavior in its context, and avoid labeling the person (e.g., "depressed," "anxious," "dependent"). Normalize the client's behavior in its context.
5. Clearly describe relevant events	Do not use vague terms but formulate clear and detailed descriptions of the client's concerns and wishes; in collaboration with the client, explore specific antecedents and consequences.
6. Watch out for the fundamental attribution error	There is a tendency to attribute our own behavior to environmental circumstances, and others' behavior to unchangeable traits (e.g., "personality disorders," "anxiety"). Make sure not to overlook sources of contextual influence (e.g., financial strain, cultural issues, etc.).
7. Restructure the problem	If clients present with vague problem statements, collaborate to develop concrete and achievable goals. Select alternative repertoires with changeable contextual aspects and focus on reinforcers available in the clients' natural environment.
8. Decrease compartmentalization	To ensure long-term success, identify large patterns: "When small behavioral units (individual responses) resist behavioral analysis—that is, when individual responses have no clear reinforcing consequences . . . take a step backward, and look for reinforcers in the long-term patterns into which the smaller unit fits" (Rachlin, 2000, p. 194).
9. Take advantage of helpful tools	In collaboration with the client, collect data and use graphs illustrating the relationships among antecedents, behavior, and consequences; or use data to show that engagement in preferred activities can change mood and thoughts
10. Be data focused	Do not attach to your ideas about the functions of clients' behaviors; collect data and use them to guide interpretations; document how you made decisions; reconsider hypotheses and interventions when data fail to provide support.
11. Focus on informative data	There is a tendency to believe that "great events need great causes." Do not neglect important data related to a client's daily routine just because they do not stand out. Do not overestimate the importance of isolated, extraordinary events.
12. Assess rather than diagnose/explain rather than name	There is a tendency to engage in circular reasoning (e.g., using behavioral data to confirm a diagnostic label and then using the same label to explain the behavior). Engage in functional analyses of constructs (e.g., speaking of "self-confidence" or "depression") and explore antecedents and consequences to prevent such circular reasoning.
13. Avoid the "single-cause" fallacy	Behavior is multiply determined. Examine multiple contingencies influencing client behavior (e.g., verbal, nonverbal); develop competing hypotheses.
14. Watch out for illusory correlations, pay attention to base rates, enhance your understanding of probabilities	Seek out corrective feedback for your assumptions (e.g., literature on base rates, clinical decision-making); involve the client in the assessment process to receive such feedback. As functional analyses rely on probabilistic relations and ask, "What is the probability of x (particular affect, behavior, or cognition) given y (aspects of context)," familiarize yourself with basic probability theory (e.g., Paulos, 2001).
15. Watch out for sample bias	Beware that the therapeutic context and your properties as the therapist may lead to differential responding on your clients' part, and that some of their behavior may not be representative of what they might do in other contexts. Obtain proxy information or conduct home-based assessments, if possible.
16. Avoid influence by anchoring effects, and search for alternative accounts	Make assessment an ongoing process. Formulate hypotheses about contingencies, derive interventions, test them, and refine the formulation if necessary.

TABLE 2.2   *(Continued)*

17. Watch out for redundant data	Look for disconfirming evidence (e.g., "under what circumstances does the behavior fail to occur," "when doesn't this hypothesis hold?").
18. Be rational (flexible) and use effective troubleshooting skills	As the intervention progresses and the client's circumstances are altered, his or her priorities may shift. Assessment is an ongoing process: Continue to assess; consult, if necessary.
19. Avoid false dilemmas	Explore a range of possible interpretations and interventions.
20. Use multiple metaphors and analogies	Simplify and develop flexible narratives in collaboration with the client to enhance functional understanding.
21. Cultivate positive moods	Be aware that therapists are part of their clients' context. If a client fails to make progress, consider the therapeutic relationship as a factor, and include in-session behaviors in the functional analysis (see Kohlenberg & Tsai, 1991).

thinking something is equivalent to doing it), loses its antecedent power over the person's life. As Jacobson and Christensen (1996) emphasize, "acceptance could be taken to mean grudgingly accepting the status quo. Luckily, this is not what we mean by acceptance. ... Change involves increases or decreases in the frequency or intensity of behavior; acceptance involves a change in [the function of] emotional reactions." While emotional reactions and thoughts are still present, they can be experienced and observed in their own right—without assuming a necessary link to other behavior. This "acceptance" sets apart traditional second-wave from third-wave behavior therapy. As Jacobson and Christensen (1996) assert, " ... acceptance [was the] missing link in traditional behavior therapy" (p. 10). According to the authors, acceptance facilitates the clients' encounter of relevant contingencies in the natural environment—even if the same old thoughts and feelings are present.

Pre-1990 publications on functional analyses (e.g., Kanfer & Saslow, 1969; Kanfer & Grimm, 1977) acknowledged the role of clients' thoughts or feelings as potential barriers to other behavior and the role of verbal operants (e.g., deficient tacting repertoires). Yet, they did not draw explicit attention to the therapist as part of the context for client behavior and to the observation of the clients' behavioral patterns within the therapeutic relationship. They also assumed that a reduction in the *frequency* of life-interfering thoughts or feelings through reconditioning, cognitive restructuring, or thought stopping was always indicated. Today, changing the *antecedent function* of rules related to thoughts and feelings ("acceptance") rather than the frequency

of thinking and feeling per se has become an additional tool for practitioners.

The first explicit step toward a comprehensive functional analytic approach incorporating acceptance was published by Hayes in 1987, followed by Kohlenberg and Tsai in 1991 and Linehan in 1993. While Linehan (1993a) extensively drew from her experience with the Eastern mindfulness practice for clinical work, functional analytic scholars were at the same time devoting conceptual treatises to the parallels between Eastern mysticism and functional analytic philosophy (e.g., Chiesa, 1994; Baum, 1995; see also Watts, 1963, for an early impromptu comparison of Eastern with Skinner's conceptualization of the self). Importantly, "third-wave" behavior therapies do not detract from earlier functional-analytic approaches. Instead, they generate a more complete and flexible approach to human affect, behavior, and cognition, by incorporating research-based principles and ideas into clinical work that were formulated over half a century ago (e.g., Skinner, 1953; 1957/1992).

As one would expect from a functional analytic perspective, depending on the research-practitioners' foci and histories, different third-wave therapies emphasize different aspects of environment-behavior relations. Acceptance and commitment therapy (ACT; Hayes, Strosahl, & Wilson, 1999) assumes that a functional analysis has not revealed any pervasive skill deficits (e.g., social skills, etc.) and that only the client's rules about the causality of thoughts and feelings interfere with a meaningful life. ACT therapists thus explore the client's thinking and feeling within the framework of functional analyses to emphasize that thinking and feeling can be understood in their context (antecedent–behavior–consequence relations). The initial purpose of therapy is to teach clients about the futility of ridding themselves of thinking and feeling in a particular way, that is, the futility of eliminating context-bound private events, without disputing or contradicting the clients' experience. ACT therapists thus emphatically acknowledge the validity of the clients' experience without reinforcing thoughts and feelings as "reasons" for other behavior. At the same time, therapists and clients collaborate to identify valued overarching behavioral patterns. Once these patterns have been established, ACT turns into a "go"/"no-go" therapy: Reason giving involving thoughts or feelings is systematically extinguished, and any activity in accordance with the valued pattern systematically reinforced in the hope that the client will contact reinforcers in the natural environment ("differential reinforcement" and "shaping"). To emphasize, standard ACT protocols assume that a client's rules about the causal role played by thoughts and feelings constitute the main barriers to effective behavior and that further instruction or skills training is not necessary. Note that instruction and skills training could be undertaken from an ACT perspective but that protocols integrating ACT with empirically supported techniques are not currently available.

ACT may be specifically useful for clients with long histories of counterpliance. Given that ACT therapists are trained never to convince or persuade the client and to have the client's experience be the arbiter, ACT extinguishes verbal barriers and establishes the collaboration necessary for other empirically supported techniques (e.g., skills training, exposure). Moreover, clients who have a history of excessive pliance may also benefit, for ACT therapists—based on the assessment that skills deficits are not present, and effective behavior is prevented by rule following—avoid directive problem solving and instruction. Asking for solutions or "fixes" is thus extinguished. As a result of this process, behavioral variability and psychological flexibility increase.

While ACT focuses on extinguishing interfering verbal antecedents, behavioral activation (BA; Martell, Addis, & Jacobson, 2001)—developed to foster engagement in the face of depressed behaviors—puts its emphasis on the consequent end. Increasing access to positive reinforcement and decreasing the influence of punishment, escape, and avoidance contingencies are at the heart of interventions for depressed behavior. BA assumes that clients do not know how daily activities, life events, and affect are related—particularly that engagement in meaningful activities improves mood. For this reason, BA takes a coaching approach, during which clients turn into experts regarding their own behavioral patterns in relation to mood and learn how to effect changes in mood through increased access to reinforcement. Where ACT would assume that a client's rules about thoughts and feelings present barriers to access to reinforcement, BA accommodates a range of barriers, some of which could be private events, others problem-solving deficits. Using the behavioral principles outlined earlier, BA addresses these deficits on an individual basis, consistently shaping engagement over passivity.

Dialectical behavior therapy (DBT; Linehan, 1993a), the third example of "third-wave therapies," was developed for a population with long-standing and pervasive dysfunctional behavior patterns ("personality disorders"). Utilizing both instructional techniques in group settings and differential reinforcement of the instructed material in an individual therapeutic setting, DBT builds a wide range of alternative repertoires (Linehan, 1993b). Among them are mindfulness: observing and tacting as a prerequisite to later functional analyses of contingencies; interpersonal skills training: effective manding and autoclitic repertoires; emotion regulation: tacting private events, recognizing their antecedents and function; and distress tolerance: building preference for effective long-term outcomes over immediate avoidance repertoires ("self-control"). All components of the therapy are implemented within the functional-analytic model described above. While DBT—like all functional analyses—acknowledges potentially biologically based vulnerability, it focuses on the changeable and contextual aspects of the client's behavior.

Functional analytic psychotherapy (FAP; Kohlenberg & Tsai, 1991) differs from other "third-wave" therapies by interpreting anxious, depressed, and other life-interfering behaviors as emerging from clients' dysfunctional social repertoires. FAP assumes that these repertoires interfere with building intimacy and finding fulfillment in relationships. After the therapist has conducted a functional analysis of the client's behavior in session, therapist and client agree on specific within-session treatment goals. Interpersonal deficits and correlated improvements are clearly defined, and this transparency is the background of the collaborative task to improve the therapeutic working relationship. FAP also assumes that, while the client–therapist relationship deepens, the client will begin to bring more and more of his or her typical interpersonal patterns into the session. In other words, the quality of the relationship becomes a functional antecedent for many of the behaviors typically shown with friends, relatives, or partners. The therapeutic relationship then provides a safe and supportive context for the instructing and shaping of social skills using the behavioral principles outlined earlier. Because FAP conceptualizations rely on the therapist–client relationship and challenge the therapist to use his or her own reactions to the benefit of the client within a functional analytic framework using the full range of functional analytic tools, FAP might well be the most difficult of third-wave behavior therapies to learn and implement. Detecting and generating functional patterns in real time, within the client–therapist interaction, are integral skills whose acquisition requires time and practice (e.g., extensive supervision; watching one's own session recordings). This might explain why—as the oldest of the third-wave therapies—FAP has not met with as much interest or adoption as the manualized approaches of ACT and DBT. While FAP connects most explicitly with behavioral principles, all third-wave behavior therapies consist of components that can be further explored in O'Donohue and Fisher (2008), such as "acceptance," "mindfulness," or skills training.

ISSUES AND CHALLENGES

Uncertainty

As described earlier, a functional analysis is a transparent and iterative process: The therapist formulates hypotheses about the functions of the client's behavior and intervenes based on predictions from behavioral principles. If the client's behavior is not affected as would be predicted by the relevant behavioral principles, alternative functions are hypothesized. The hypothesis testing continues until interventions have the predicted influence. This iterative process puts the therapist in a relative position of uncertainty: While grouping client behaviors into clusters based on topography ("depression," "anxiety," "dementia") gives the appearance of explanatory power (particularly when treatment packages have been linked to diagnoses), embarking on a functional analysis with a client makes explicit that the explanation ultimately lies in the relation among hypothesis (verbal antecedent), intervention (therapist/client behavior), and behavior change (consequence). The therapist's role is that of an expert in behavioral principles; their application to the client's situation, however, is an experimental approach that is limited by the degree to which the client participates in the experimental manipulation and contingencies operating on the client's behavior have been accurately characterized. Thus, therapists who begin to utilize functional analyses may experience discomfort about taking an experimental, "let's find out what happens, when ... " stance with their clients. However, anecdotally, clients often express relief about the fact that a recalcitrant problem that has troubled them for years is not easily solved and requires investigation. During therapy, they enjoy participating and engaging in the process of discovering what works.

Reliability of Data

Ideally, a functional analysis would not rely solely on client self reports (see the discussion of tacting on page 28). Instead, it would include observations of the client's behavioral patterns in the natural environment, or proxy reports. Given that many practitioners do not have the time or resources to observe client behavior in the relevant settings, Kohlenberg and Tsai's (1991) suggestion to focus on within-session client behaviors provides a viable alternative: Self-reports and therapist–client interactions are also data from which hypotheses about functional relations can be derived. Consequently, the functional analytic dictum to treat self-reports cautiously and to observe contingencies when possible, turns into the challenge to identify social contingencies as they play out in session, generate interventions from this analysis, and observe the outcome. As an added benefit when concentrating the analysis on within-session behavior patterns, the practitioner also gains direct access to modifiable variables. Again, whether considering in-session data or out-of-session reports, the experimental nature of the functional analysis remains.

Reliability of Functional Units

As described earlier, the analytic carving of environment–behavior relation is a matter of event perception, and antecedent–behavior–consequent relations can be found at multiple scales. Consequently, one functional analysis can render multiple hypotheses and points of intervention, based on the clinician's experience and training, his or her knowledge of the published literature, and client variables (Haynes & O'Brien, 2000). While two independent clinicians conducting functional analyses may start out with different functional units or hypotheses, one may speculate that the experimental approach that is inherent to functional analyses would increase the reliability of functional units with each iteration, that is, result in convergence over time. Functional analyses with widely different starting points would, according to this analysis, produce similar functional end results. Because the selection of functional units has not been sufficiently studied, Haynes and O'Brien (2000) recommend that practitioners document their selection process and the data on which it is based to enable subsequent evaluation and discussion of their assessment strategies.

Validity

Incremental validity hinges on the extent to which a functional analysis delivers more effective interventions than standard topographical assessments (Nelson-Gray, 2003). Unfortunately, clinical treatment utility studies based on functional analyses are still few and far between (see Nelson-Gray, 2003, for a review). In other fields, such as the developmental disabilities, functional analyses have evidenced treatment utility for complex and long-standing behavioral problems (e.g., Iwata et al., 1994). Haynes and O'Brien (2000) conclude that "the value of a complete functional analysis has not been investigated [with clinical populations]. In sum, the functional analysis has a strong conceptual basis. It has promising but undemonstrated treatment validity" (pp. 282–283). Thus, the greatest challenge posed to functional analyses is the current lack of data in the clinical realm.

CONCLUSION

Cognitive behavioral treatments, whether in their second- or third-wave rendition, can be understood using functional analyses of behavior. For this reason, expertise in functional interpretations allows practitioners to track the process and purpose of empirically supported techniques (e.g., O'Donohue & Fisher, 2008) as well as related composite treatment packages (e.g., Hayes, Strosahl, & Wilson, 1999; Linehan, 1993a). Understanding these techniques at the functional level is a complex undertaking: It requires contextual—and thus often countercultural—interpretations of behavior, a review of the functional analytic literature and knowledge of experimental psychopathology. In essence, it invites practitioners to become "assessment scholars" (Haynes & O'Brien, 2000). The rewards of such scholarship are plenty, for practitioners learn to interpret techniques and strategies from one coherent and principled perspective; they learn to integrate topographically different techniques (e.g., from "Gestalt" psychology or "experiential psychology") based on function; consequently, they learn to apply empirically supported strategies flexibly, yet in a goal-directed manner; they learn to analyze behavioral patterns and design interventions for complex presentations and for clients who did not benefit from manualized approaches. In summary, becoming a functional analytic assessment scholar invaluably broadens the range of tools available to practitioners.

Further Reading

Baum, W. M. (1994). *Understanding behaviorism: Science, behavior, and culture.* New York: HarperCollins College Publishers.

Chiesa, M. (1994). *Radical behaviorism: The philosophy and the science.* Sarasota, FL: Authors Co-operative.

Farmer, R. F., & Nelson-Gray, R. O. (2005). *Personality-guided behavior therapy.* Washington, DC: American Psychological Association.

Martell, C. R., Addis, M. E., & Jacobson, N. (2001). *Depression in context: Strategies for guided action.* New York: W. W. Norton & Company.

Rachlin, H. (2000). *The science of self-control.* Cambridge, MA: Harvard University Press.

Sidman, M. (1989). *Coercion and it fallout.* Boston, MA: Authors Cooperative, Inc.

Zettle, R., & Hayes, S. C. (1982). Rule-governed behavior: A potential theoretical framework for cognitive–behavioral therapy. *Advances in Cognitive–Behavioral Research and Therapy, 1,* 73–118.

References

Abramowitz, J. S. (2006). Toward a functional analytic approach to psychologically complex patients: A comment on Ruscio and Holohan (2006). *Clinical Psychology: Science and Practice, 13,* 163–166.

Addis, M. E., & Jacobson, N. S. (2000). A closer look at the treatment rationale and homework compliance in cognitive-behavioral therapy for depression. *Cognitive Therapy and Research, 24*(3), 313–326.

American Psychiatric Association. (1994). *Diagnostic and statistical manual of mental disorders* (4th ed.). Washington, DC: Author.

Azrin, N. H., & Nunn, R. G. (1973). Habit-reversal: A method of eliminating nervous habits and tics. *Behaviour Research and Therapy, 11*(4), 619–628.

Bach, P. A., & Moran, D. J. (2008). *ACT in practice: Case conceptualization in acceptance and commitment therapy.* Oakland, CA: New Harbinger Publications.

Baum, W. M. (1995). Radical behaviorism and the concept of agency. *Behaviorology, 3*(4), 93–106.

Bickel, W., & Marsch, L. A. (2001). Conceptualizing addiction/Toward a behavioral economic understanding of drug addiction: Delay discounting processes. *Addiction, 96,* 73–86.

Bulow, P. J., & Meller, P. J. (1998). Predicting teenage girls' sexual activity and contraception use: An application of matching law. *Journal of Community Psychology, 26*(6), 581–596.

Catania, A. C. (1998). *Learning* (4th ed.). Upper Saddle River, NJ: Prentice Hall.

Critchfield, T. S., & Kollins, S. H. (2001). Temporal discounting: Basic research and the analysis of socially important behavior. *Journal of Applied Behavior Analysis, 34,* 101–122.

Drossel, C., Waltz, T. J., & Hayes, S. C. (2007). An introduction to principles of behavior. In D. W. Woods & J. W. Kanter (Eds.), *Understanding behavior disorders: A contemporary behavioral perspective.* Reno, NV: Context Press.

Eifert, G. H., & Forsyth, J. P. (2005). *Acceptance and commitment therapy for anxiety disorders: A practitioner's guide to using mindfulness, acceptance, and values-based behavior change strategies.* Oakland, CA: New Harbinger Publications.

Ferster, C. B. (1973). A functional analysis of depression. *American Psychologist,* 857–870.

Gambrill, E. (2005). Critical thinking in clinical practice: Improving the quality of judgments and decisions (2nd ed.). Hoboken, NJ: John Wiley & Sons.

Glenn, S. S. (1983). Maladaptive functional relations in client verbal behavior. *Behavior Analyst, 6*(1), 47–56.

Goldiamond, I. (1974). Toward a constructional approach to social problems: Ethical and constitutional issues raised by applied behavior analysis. *Behaviorism, 2,* 1–84.

Hawkins, R. P. (1986). Selection of target behaviors. In R. O. Nelson & S. C. Hayes (Eds.), *Conceptual foundations of behavioral assessment* (pp. 331–385). New York: Guilford.

Hayes, S. C. (1987). A contextual approach to therapeutic change. In N. S. Jacobson (Ed.), *Psychotherapists in clinical practice: Cognitive and behavioral perspectives* (pp. 327–387). New York: The Guilford Press.

Hayes, S. C., & Follette, W. C. (1992). Can functional analysis provide a substitute for syndromal classification? *Behavioral Assessment, 14,* 345-365.

Hayes, S. C., Barnes-Holmes, D., & Roche, B. (Eds.) (2001). *Relational Frame Theory: A post-Skinnerian account of human language and cognition.* New York: Kluwer Academic/Plenum Publishers.

Hayes, S. C., Strosahl, K. D., & Wilson, K. G. (1999). *Acceptance and commitment therapy: An experiential approach to behavior change.* New York: Guilford.

Haynes, S. N., & O'Brien, W. H. (2000). *Principles and practice of behavioral assessment.* New York: Kluwer Academic/Plenum Publishers.

Herrnstein, R. (1961/1997). Relative and absolute strength of response as a function of frequency of reinforcement. In H. Rachlin & D. I. Laibson (Eds.), *The matching law: Papers in psychology and economics—Richard J. Herrnstein* (pp. 15–21). NY/Cambridge, MA: Russell Sage Foundation/Harvard University Press.

Hesse, H. (1919/1970). *Demian: Die Geschichte von Emil Sinclairs Jugend.* Frankfurt am Main: Suhrkamp Verlag.

Hunter, R. H., Gardner, W. I., Wilkness, S., & Silverstein, S. M. (2008). The multimodal functional model: Advancing case formulation beyond the "diagnose and treat" paradigm: Improving outcomes and reducing aggression and the use of control procedures in psychiatric care. *Psychological Services, 5*(1), 11–25.

Iwata, B. A., Pace, G. M., Dorsey, M. F., Zarcone, J. R., Vollmer, B., & Smith, J. (1994). The function of self-injurious behavior: An experimental–epidemiological analysis. *Journal of Applied Behavior Analysis, 27,* 215–240.

Jacobson, N. S., & Christensen, A. (1996). Acceptance and change in couple therapy: A therapist's guide to transforming relationships. New York: W. W. Norton & Company.

Johanson, C.-E., Mattox, A., & Schuster, C. R. (1995). Conditioned reinforcing effects of capsules associated with high versus low monetary payoff. *Psychopharmacology, 120,* 42–48.

Kanfer, F. H., & Grimm, L. G. (1977). Behavioral analysis: Selecting target behaviors in the interview. *Behavior Modification, 1*(1), 7–28.

Kanfer, F. H., & Saslow, G. (1969). Behavioral diagnosis. In C. M. Franks (Ed.), *Behavior therapy: Appraisal and status* (pp. 417–444). New York: McGraw-Hill.

Kendall, P. C., Chu, B., Gifford, A., Hayes, C., & Nauta, M. (1998). Breathing life into a manual: Flexibility and creativity with manual-based treatments. *Cognitive and Behavioral Practice, 5,* 177–198.

Kohlenberg, R. J., & Tsai, M. (1991). Functional analytic psychotherapy: Creating intense and curative therapeutic relationships. New York: Plenum Press.

Linehan, M. M. (1993a). Cognitive-behavioral treatment of borderline personality disorder. New York: Guilford.

Linehan, M. M. (1993b). *Skills training manual for treating borderline personality disorder.* New York: Guilford.

McCurry, S. M. (2006). *When a family member has dementia: Steps to becoming a resilient caregiver.* Westport, CT: Praeger.

McDowell, J. J. (1988). Matching theory in natural human environments. *Behavior Analyst, 11*(2), 95–109.

Michael, J. (1993). Establishing operations. *Behavior Analyst, 16,* 191–206.

Neef, N., & Northup, J. (2007). Attention deficit hyperactivity disorder. In P. Sturmey (Ed.), *Functional analysis in clinical treatment* (pp. 87-110). Burlington, MA: Academic Press.

Nelson-Gray, R. O. (2003). Treatment utility of psychological assessment. *Psychological Assessment, 15*(4), 521–531.

Newsom, C., Favell, J. E., & Rincover, A. (1983). The side effects of punishment. In S. Axelrod & J. Apsche (Eds.), *The effects of punishment on human behavior* (pp. 285–315). New York: Academic Press.

O'Donohue, W., & Fisher, J. E. (Eds.) (2008). *Cognitive behavior therapy: Applying empirically supported techniques in your practice* (2nd ed.). New York: John Wiley & Sons.

Paulos, J. A. (2001). Innumeracy: Mathematical illiteracy and its consequences. New York: Hill and Wang.

Pittenger, J. B., & Shaw, R. E. (1975). Aging faces as viscal-elastic events: Implications for a theory of nonrigid shape perception. *Journal of Experimental Psychology: Human Perception and Performance, 1*(4), 374–382.

Podlesnik, C. A., Jimenez-Gomez, C., & Shahan, T. A. (2006). Resurgence of alcohol-seeking produced by discontinuing non-drug reinforcement as an animal model of drug relapse. *Behavioural Pharmacology, 17*(4), 369–374.

Poling, A., & Byrne, T. (Eds.) (2000). *Behavioral pharmacology.* Reno, NV: Context Press.

Ruscio, A. M., & Holohan, D. R. (2006). Applying empirically supported treatments to complex cases: Ethical, empirical, and practical considerations. *Clinical Psychology: Science and Practice, 13,* 146–162.

Shaffer, D. M., & McBeath, M. K. (2002). Baseball outfielders maintain a linear optical trajectory when tracking uncatchable fly balls. *Journal of Experimental Psychology: Human Perception and Performance, 28*(2), 335-348.

Sidman, M. (1994). *Equivalence relations and behavior: A research story.* Boston, MA: Authors Cooperative, Inc.

Skinner, B. F. (1938/1991). *The behavior of organisms: An experimental analysis.* Acton, MA: Coply Publishing Group.

Skinner, B. F. (1953). *Science and human behavior*. NY: The Free Press: A Division of MacMillan Publishing Co., Inc.

Skinner, B. F. (1956/1982). What is psychotic behavior? In R. Epstein (Ed.), *Skinner for the classroom: Selected papers*. Champaign, IL: Research Press.

Skinner, B. F. (1957/1992). *Verbal behavior*. Acton, MA: Copley Publishing Group.

Skinner, B. F. (1974). *About behaviorism*. New York: Vintage Books.

Van Houten, R. (1983). Punishment: From the animal laboratory to the applied setting. In S. Axelrod & J. Apsche (Eds.), *The effects of punishment on human behavior* (pp. 13–44). New York: Academic Press.

Watts, A. (1963, April 12). The individual as man/world. Social Relations Colloquium, Harvard University.

Wulfert, E., Greenway, D. E., & Dougher, M. J. (1996). A logical functional analysis of reinforcement-based disorders: Alcoholism and pedophilia. *Journal of Consulting and Clinical Psychology, 64*(6), 1140–51.

Yalom, Y. D. (1995). *The theory and practice of group psychotherapy* (4th ed.). New York: Basic Books.

3   COGNITIVE BEHAVIOR THERAPY: A CURRENT APPRAISAL

William C. Follette, Sabrina M. Darrow, and Jordan T. Bonow

In the 30 years since Beck and colleagues presented their treatment for depression (Beck, Rush, Shaw, & Emery, 1979), there have been literally hundreds of studies of cognitive therapy (CT) and cognitive behavior therapy (CBT). Recent research suggests few empirical differences between these two therapies, though philosophical differences remain.

As the CBT literature matures, this seems a good time to remind ourselves about some basic considerations about construct validity and the nomological net described by Cronback and Meehl (1955). In the case of CBT, we consider the basic theory behind CBT, how therapy is designed to produce change, and whether the measurement procedures map onto the relevant psychological variables implicit in the theory, and finally what the evidence is that the therapy change is produced by mechanisms posited.

CBT researchers have attended to developing treatment procedures to assure adherence to the intended interventions. That is a different issue from whether what is done during the treatment produces change in the manner intended by the theory. Internal validity in studies refers to whether the change observed in the dependent variable, treatment outcome, is due to the experimenter's manipulation of the independent variable, therapy delivered with treatment fidelity. One could produce change that results from the manipulations performed in therapy while still not fully or properly understanding the precise way in which the therapy produced observed change. Thus, it is possible for an intervention to have internal validity without necessarily having construct validity.

We will structure our review describing differing views of how CBT is presumed to work.

Following that summary, the chapter will review data on the evidence on whether CBT does in fact produce change. Finally, the chapter will turn to the evidence of whether CBT works according to the mechanisms postulated by the theories. In this effort, we will generally restrict our focus to depressive and anxiety problems since they make up the preponderance of the controlled studies. When CBT is extended to other clinical problems, the theoretical explanations and interventions closely follow the logic for depression and anxiety.

REVIEW OF COGNITIVE THEORY

Beck's Cognitive Theory of Psychological Disorders

Beck provided the dominant theoretical framework underlying traditional CBT (Beck, 1967, 1976, 1983). He postulated that inaccurate cognitions were responsible for the symptoms of psychological disorders, with each disorder associated with specific cognitive content (Beck, 1967; 1976; Table 3.1). The majority of his initial work addressed depression. The pervasive and overgeneralized thoughts common in individuals with this disorder were summarized as the cognitive triad. Specifically, it included "negative evaluations of the self," "negative interpretations of experience," and "negative expectations of the future" (Beck, 1967, p. 273).

Beck's cognitive theory of depression has been widely viewed as a diathesis-stress model: Inaccurate and unrealistic beliefs and faulty logical processes predispose an individual to depression. According to Beck (1967), in many cases depression is immediately precipitated by stressful life events and "psychological

TABLE 3.1 Beck's Initial Outline of Cognitive Content Present in Specific Psychological Syndromes

Syndrome	Idiosyncratic Ideational Content
Depression	Negative view of self, world, and future
Hypomania	Exaggerated positive view of self, world, and future
Anxiety	Personal danger
Phobia	Danger connected with specific, avoidable situations
Hysteria	Motor or sensory abnormality
Paranoia	Abuse, persecution, and injustice
Obsessions	Warning or doubting
Compulsions	Self-commands to perform a specific act to ward off danger and allay obsessive doubting

Adapted from Beck (1967), p. 270; (1976), p. 84.

strain" (p. 281). Depression results when these are interpreted inappropriately. All of the other symptoms of depression (affective, motivational, physical/vegetative) result from the activation of the cognitive triad (Beck, 1967). Furthermore, Beck postulated that these dysfunctional cognitive patterns are involved in a self-reinforcing cycle that exacerbates and maintains depression. Depressed individuals' negative cognitive concepts lead to further negative evaluations, which in turn further support those concepts. This eventually results in the formation of cognitive schemas that pervasively influence the cognitions of an individual.

While emphasizing the role of faulty cognitions in the development and maintenance of emotional disorders, Beck stated that there are many other factors that can contribute to any specific case. There is no single biological or psychological cause of depression (Beck, 1983), but rather it can be the result of many other predisposing and precipitating factors including: heredity, personality type, chemical imbalances, developmental traumas, and failure to learn coping skills. Beck claimed that he was providing a psychological account of depression that should have correlates in other domains (e.g., biology).

Beck (1983) also claimed that two major dimensions of personality were important to depression: sociality, the tendency to readily form relationships, and individuality, the ability to see oneself as distinct. He also claimed that, while each of these two dimensions of personality could dominate in any individual at a given time, one of these typically was more influential in each depressive client. One client's depression may stem from failure to achieve a life goal while another client's depression may stem from the loss of a partner. Thus, there were two general modes or types of depression postulated: autonomous depression (or defeat/failure depression) and dependent depression (or deprivation depression). Beck (1983) then outlined the differences between individuals with these types of depression in premorbid personality, social factors contributing to the depression, maladaptive cognitive schemas, symptom patterns, and the effectiveness of therapeutic techniques.

ALTERNATIVE THEORIES OF DEPRESSION

A number of other theories of the etiology of depression have been critical in the continued development of cognitive behavioral therapy.

Helplessness Theory of Depression

Abramson, Seligman, and Teasdale (1978) developed a theory of depression derived from the learned helplessness literature (Maier & Seligman, 1976). According to this theory, depression is the result of negative expectations about the outcome of situations and feeling hopeless about one's ability to change those outcomes. Experiencing uncontrollable situations leads to decreased motivation, dysfunctional cognitions, and reduced self-esteem. Expectation that undesired outcomes will occur leads to hopelessness and other forms of negative affect.

In this model, the development of depression is initially spurred on by the experience of noncontingency, where one experiences situations in which he or she does not appear to be able to control the outcomes. When this occurs, the individual begins to make attributions about the source of that helplessness. It is the character of these attributions that determines whether or not depression forms.

In an elaboration of this perspective, Abramson and colleagues outlined a subtype of depression resulting from hopelessness (Abramson, Metalsky, & Alloy, 1989). Depression based on a hopelessness model asserted that the most problematic attributions are stable, global, and internal. In such cases, the individual views his or her entire life as hopeless and that it will continue to be filled with negative experiences and void of anything positive. Furthermore, the person attributes these circumstances to some personal failing.

Social Theory of Depression

Brown and Harris (1978) developed a model of depression based on sociological research of women in Camberwell, Greater London, United Kingdom. The survey-based study was designed to determine the social influences of depression. Findings indicated a large effect of social class (as measured by the occupations of the women's husbands) on the development of depression in women with children. Working-class women with children were four times more likely to develop depression than middle-class women with children. In further identifying vulnerability factors, they ultimately identified having greater than three children under the age of 14, being unemployed and at home, early maternal loss, and the lack of a "confiding" relationship as the relevant constellation of conditions increasing vulnerability to depression. In addition, Brown and Harris detected a large impact of "provoking agents" (e.g., losses or threats of loss, long-term difficulties; pp. 158–168) on the development of depression. Of the 114 women identified as having depression, 86 had a clearly identified provoking agent contributing to their depression.

Brown and Harris's (1978, p. 265) model identified three major factors affecting the formation of depression: protective factors, vulnerability factors, and provoking agents in the absence of protective factors. Provoking agents contributed acute and ongoing stress to the individual. This initially leads to grief and hopelessness in the situation. The continued response to this stress is then influenced by the other two factors. Protective factors (e.g., high levels of intimacy with one's husband) lead to higher self-esteem. This allows the initial grief and hopelessness to be resolved as the person finds other sources of meaning in life. As a result, depression does not develop. In contrast, vulnerability factors (e.g., death of one's mother at an early age) lead to low self-esteem. When reacting to provoking agents, an individual with low self-esteem fails to work through his or her grief and generalizes feelings of hopelessness to other life areas. This leads to depression.

Overall, each of these three factors were said to be affected by social class. Low social status leads to increased exposure to vulnerability factors and provoking agents, while high social status leads to increased exposure to protective factors and decreased exposure to provoking agents. In order to explain depression in cases without clear proximal provoking agents and differences in severity of depression, Brown and Harris (1978) added a fourth factor to their model, symptom-formation factors. These susceptibilities to depression included past loss, age, and previous episodes of depression. Brown and Harris hypothesized that these previous encounters with provoking factors could reexperienced, leading to depression. They also hypothesized that symptom-formation factors might result in depressive overreactions to otherwise mundane events. They noted that these factors were similar to Beck's notion of cognitive vulnerabilities. However, they differentiated between the two, noting that Beck's theory claimed that cognitive factors increased the likelihood of depression (making them vulnerability factors) while their theory did not.

Integrative Theory of Depression

Lewinsohn (1974) proposed a primarily behavioral account of depression where depression was either established or maintained by the loss or decrease in the rate of response contingent reinforcement. Over the years Lewinsohn and colleagues (1985) proposed a more integrative theory of depression. They claimed that cognitive models placed too much weight on cognitive vulnerabilities while reinforcement models placed too much weight on situational factors. They instead took the position that environment initiated depression, but that this process was moderated by cognitive factors.

In this model environmental events evoked depression. These events included "macrostressors" such as death of a family member, "microstressors" such as receiving a ticket, and "chronic difficulties" such as poverty (Lewinsohn, et al., 1985, p. 344). These events can lead to the disruption of an individual's normal behavioral patterns. When this occurs, access to reinforcement may decrease and contact with aversive experiences may increase. This results in the experiencing of negative emotions. If an individual is unable to compensate for these changes, that person will begin to focus more on him- or herself. In addition, his or her protective positive self-schemas will begin to deteriorate, leading to an increase in feelings of dysphoria.

As this process progresses, at the behavioral level, the person will withdraw, demonstrate greater social difficulties, reduce effort, and fail to persist in difficult circumstances. At the cognitive level, the individual will become more self-critical, attend more to performance standards, assume more responsibility for the outcome of events, and have more negative expectancies about the outcomes of situations.

Because the entire depressogenic process is moderated by cognitive and behavioral factors, the depressed individual will have increasingly greater adverse reactions (emotional, behavioral, cognitive) to environmental stressors. At this stage, depressed individuals have a decreased ability to protect themselves by compensating for changes in available reinforcement. Consequently, all of these changes will feed into a cycle that perpetuates depression. Throughout his account of depression, Lewinsohn appreciated that one's social milieu was an important factor in ameliorating or enhancing the risk. Members of one's immediate social network could inadvertently reinforce depressive behavior, or conversely not reinforce such behaviors, thereby affecting the likelihood that dysphoric affect might become sustained depression.

Other Theories of Depression

Kwon and Oei (1994) outlined many other models of the development of depression. Before doing this, they distinguished between two levels of cognitions: surface and core. The surface level is the level of cognitive products (e.g., automatic thoughts). The core level is the level of cognitive structures (e.g., schemas, dysfunctional beliefs). As a result, their work focused on models characterizing the role of negative life events, automatic thoughts, and dysfunctional attitudes. In one simple model, these three factors were said to all directly contribute to depression. In an alternative simple model, automatic thoughts mediated the impact of negative life events and dysfunctional attitudes on depression.

Other, more complex models were also reviewed by these authors. In the *linear mediational model*, negative life events lead to the development of dysfunctional attitudes. These in turn result in automatic thoughts, which cause depression. More complex was the *differential activation model*. This model hypothesized that negative life events initially lead to a low level of depression. This depression results in the generation of dysfunctional attitudes. As in many of the other models, these attitudes lead to the automatic thoughts. These automatic thoughts result in more severe depression, perpetuating the disorder. In addition to reviewing these other models, Kwon and Oei (1994) developed an *integrated cognitive model of depression*. They postulated that negative life events, dysfunctional attitudes, and their interaction cause depression. These effects were possibly direct; much of their impact was mediated by automatic thoughts.

TRADITIONAL COGNITIVE BEHAVIOR THERAPY

While Beck (1976) identified irrational cognitive content areas in many psychological disorders, he noted that clients often exhibited rational processes in other content areas. Consequently, he began to explore strategies for correcting irrational processes in order to cure psychological disorders. The results of this exploration led to the traditional form of cognitive behavioral therapy.

Beck (1976) defined cognitive therapy as "all the approaches that alleviate psychological distress through the medium of correcting faulty conceptions and self-signals" (p. 214). These approaches were then categorized into three different method types: intellectual, experiential, and behavioral. Intellectual methods focused on the identification and direct reappraisal of cognitions. Experiential methods focused on exposing clients to psychologically impactful events that would potently contradict inaccurate thoughts. Behavioral methods focused on building patterns of behavior that would lead to more accurate evaluations by having clients directly go out into the environment and test the accuracy of their predictions about behavior and actual outcomes. Thus, all three methods purport to change cognitions in order to alleviate symptoms.

Building on this previous work, Beck outlined a comprehensive cognitive behavioral therapy for depression with his colleagues (Beck, et al., 1979; Rush & Beck, 1978). This treatment, cognitive therapy (CT), was "based on an underlying theoretical rationale that an individual's affect and behavior are largely determined by the way in which he structures the world" (Beck, et al., 1979, p. 3). Depression was a result of the cognitive triad, logical errors, and the formulation of faulty schemas based on these two processes. To combat these issues, CT took the form of "collaborative empiricism" (Beck, et al., 1979, p. 7). The therapist worked to help the client empirically test his or her cognitions. A client's automatic thoughts were elicited, assumptions underlying these thoughts were exposed, and errors in logic were identified. This allowed these thoughts, assumptions, and lines of reasoning to be tested against reality. In Beck's CT for depression (Beck, et al., 1979; Rush & Beck, 1978), two general strategies for enacting this process were promoted. Early in therapy, when clients are typically more severely depressed, behavioral techniques were used to change behavior as well as to elicit automatic thoughts. After this, when "depression lessens, concentration improves, and the intensity of the affect decreases" (Rush & Beck, 1978, p. 207), cognitive techniques were employed.

Ingram and Hollon (1986) identified seven stages typically found in CT and the techniques typically employed during those stages. They also noted that these stages often overlapped; elements of each stage could be found at any time during therapy. The first stage of CT consisted of providing a treatment rationale combating the client's overexpansive explanations for his or her behavior (a cognitive technique). The second stage involved training the client to self-monitor behaviors, events, moods, and cognitions. The third stage, behavioral activation, featured specific techniques, including activity scheduling, graded task assignment, and success therapy. The fourth stage of CT focused on identifying automatic thoughts, the beliefs underlying them, and the process by which those beliefs were formed (i.e., cognitive distortions). Stage five, systematic evaluation of beliefs, began to directly target cognitions for change. This stage included the hallmark of CT, collaborative empiricism. It also included the logical examination of faulty reasoning strategies. The next stage involved the articulation of the assumptions underlying the cognitive triad. This allowed for evaluation of these assumptions. The final stage of CT was preparation for termination. Much of this stage centered on relapse prevention, particularly the promotion of continued use of empirical and logical testing of cognitions.

GENERIC COGNITIVE BEHAVIORAL THEORY FOR PSYCHOLOGICAL DISORDERS

There is a generic cognitive behavioral model of psychological disorders that can be outlined (Brewin, 2006; see Table 3.2). This generic model has been applied to numerous disorders (see Brewin, 2006 for references). It consists of three stages; each of these involves its own causal factors and consequences. The theories and models reviewed above are generally more thorough and identify specific processes thought to be involved in depression. It seems useful, however, to summarize the extensive similarities among these models within the framework of this generic model. Discussions of the efficacy of the cognitive behavioral therapies will be founded on this generic model. Because the most extensive theoretical and empirical work has been conducted in relation to depression, specific focus will be placed on this disorder.

TABLE 3.2   Generic Cognitive Model of Emotional Disorders

Stage	Causal Factors	Consequences
1. Vulnerability	Negative life experiences	Development of latent cognitive content and structures
2. Onset	Negative life experiences	1. Negative affect 2. Activation of dysfunctional cognitive structures 3. Intrusive cognitive content 4. Psychological disorder
3. Maintenance	Interactions between negative affect and dysfunctional cognitive and behavioral processes	Continued negative thoughts, behaviors, and affect

From Brewin (2006), p. 766.

In the generic model, the onset of depression is identified as a diathesis-stress process. An individual first develops a *vulnerability* to depression. In this stage, he or she has life experiences that result in negative affect. From these experiences, the individual develops latent cognitive content and structures related to negative affect. The *onset* of depression occurs when the individual contacts more negative life experiences. These lead to negative affect and activation of dysfunctional cognitive structures (i.e., schemas), which result in intrusive cognitive content (e.g., automatic thoughts, disturbing images, impulses). This process leads to depression. The *maintenance* of depression is driven by an interaction between negative mood and dysfunctional cognitive and behavioral processes. These include: selective attention, selective memory, selective interpretation, reasoning biases, avoidance, safety behaviors, and thought suppression.

MEDIATIONAL THEORIES OF CT

It is clear that the hypothesized mediational mechanism in CT is change in cognitive processes. Ingram and Hollon (1986) noted that theories about cognitive behavioral therapies were becoming very diverse over time, and this was preventing sufficient examination of the mediational processes that had been proposed. Indeed, most discussions of meta-analytic data bemoan the difficulties in defining what is "CBT" and the inherent trouble when comparing across studies. However, there was still much similarity among all of the various theories. Beck and colleagues had claimed that CT alleviated depression because of changes in clients'

cognitions. In an overwhelming majority of cases, CBT theorists at least partially agreed with this claim. As a result, focus was placed on further development of theories regarding the mediational role of changes in cognitions during CBT.

Ingram and Hollon (1986) briefly mentioned three potential models of these changes. These models focused on the changes in schemas thought to be responsible for reduction in depression. The first of these models was the *deactivation* model. This model proposed that therapy served to deactivate the depressive schema currently operating in the depressed individual. In turn, a nondepressive schema was also said to be activated. The second model, *accommodation*, stated that a change in the depressive schema occurred during therapy. It became a nondepressive schema. This model, having been proposed in Beck's theory, was dominant in the literature at the time. The third model proposed that therapy provided *compensation* for the depressive schema. While the depressive schema was unchanged and still active, therapy resulted in the formulation of a new schema that offset the affects of the previously dominant depressive schema.

Ingram and Hollon (1986) attempted to better formulate the cognitive theory underlying CT by using an information processing perspective. They speculatively reviewed how the various specific techniques of CBT might affect the various components of cognitive processing: cognitive structures and their content, cognitive operations, and the products of cognitive processing. In addition, they called for further research to test the three competing, though not mutually exclusive, hypotheses regarding the mechanisms of change in CT.

At the level of *structure*, Ingram and Hollon (1986) predominantly referred to the accommodation model. A simple way to explain the changes resulting from CT is to assume that schemas are being directly changed. However, these authors noted that data unsupportive of this model includes relapse after cognitive interventions, natural remission without cognitive interventions, and the effectiveness of other treatments. Ingram and Hollon also noted that, at a structural level, the development of compensatory schemata could occur. At the level of *process*, deactivation of depressive schemata is the most plausible effect. This might involve a reduction in excessive self-focus. It might also involve a change from automatic to controlled processing modes. The activation of schemata that are incompatible with depressive self-schema may occur at the level of process. Alternatively, a shift from negative information processing to a more positive type of processing might result (i.e., activation and accommodation). At the level of *products*, changes reflect only the changes in the other levels.

Ingram and Hollon (1986) also discussed how the various behavioral and cognitive techniques might effect changes during CT. Generally, behavioral methods provide positive information by having clients directly engage the environment and assess the accuracy of their understanding of actual contingencies. Clients then can directly observe the effect of this activity on their mood. That active behavior can lead to the activation of nondepressive schemata while indirectly leading to the deactivation of depressive schemata (i.e., deactivation). The data may also contradict depressive schemas, leading to their change (i.e., accommodation). Cognitive methods more directly affect cognitions and the cognitive processes underlying them. They directly challenge problematic thoughts and schemas (i.e., accommodation). Nondepressive schemas can be activated as nondepressive thoughts are generated (i.e., deactivation). In addition, cognitive techniques may result in a change from automatic processing to a more controlled processing, potentially lead to development of positive coping schemas (i.e.,

compensation). In summary, Ingram and Hollon (1986) posited that any or all of the three theories may accurately depict what occurs during CT.

Hollon and colleagues (1988) also discussed how these cognitive changes might differentially affect relapse rates. Deactivation would be the most likely to lead to relapse because the problematic schemas were still present in the individual's mind. They could be reactivated by any number of occurrences leading to another depressive episode. In contrast, both accommodation and compensation would prevent relapse by counteracting the effects of the problematic schemas. However, compensation would seemingly provide lesser protection, as these schemas were still present and could become dominant again. Overall, these authors concluded that there was more support for the two latter models, as cognitive therapy had been previously shown to prevent relapse. These authors also called for further longitudinal examination of individuals with recurrent depressive episodes. Evaluation of whether the same schemas were underlying recurrent episodes would aid in the determination of whether accommodation or compensation was the active process in cognitive therapy.

Barber and DeRubeis (1989) claimed that short-term CT works primarily through the teaching of compensatory skills. As evidence for this claim, they cited findings that, while there were no differential effects between CT and pharmacotherapy, CT provided greater relapse prevention. They also claimed that it was likely that compensation led to accommodation over time. Repeated use of skills that compensate for depressive schemas was thought to eventually lead to a change in those schemas.

CURRENT PERSPECTIVES IN CBT

Up to this point, we have been focusing on CT for depression as the most extensive theoretical and empirical work has been conducted in relation to this disorder. Now we loosely refer to cognitive behavior therapy (CBT) as an approach to therapy targeting the behavior and cognitions of a client. There has been a proliferation of specific therapies within this modality. Cognitive behavior Therapy (or some variant of this) is found in abundance in the titles of contemporary therapy manuals and guides. Most often, these words are followed by a name for a disorder (e.g., CBT for obsessive–compulsive disorder, CBT for Asperger's syndrome, etc.). These therapies share a foundation in a generic cognitive behavioral model of psychological disorders explained earlier (Brewin, 2006; Table 2.2).

Second to depression, anxiety disorders have generated the most theoretical and empirical work. The review of the empirical evidence for CBT will include that on generalized anxiety disorder, panic disorder, obsessive–compulsive disorder, and social phobia. Therefore, a brief explanation of the extension of cognitive theory to anxiety disorders is warranted.

Foa and Kozak (1986) provide an analysis of anxiety disorders. Within their theory, fear is a memory structure containing information about feared stimuli and situations, information regarding appropriate responses to those situations, and an interpretation of those two forms of information. These fear structures can result from both firsthand experiences of anxiety-provoking situations and verbally mediated fear-provoking relations. Furthermore, fear structures are typically adaptive in that they allow individuals to escape and avoid danger. Anxiety disorders result when the fear schemas are overactive in some way (e.g., an individual might interpret too many situations as more dangerous than would commonly be reported). They are maintained by a number of factors, including failure to contact the feared situation (i.e., failure to gather contradictory evidence) and impairments in processing information about feared situations (i.e., impairments in interpreting available information).

This brief discussion of extending CT to anxiety disorders is consistent with the same pattern as discussed in the generic model. An extended discussion of the basic thought content and processes purported to operate within each disorder is beyond the scope of this work. However, an understanding of these nuances is not necessary; change in cognitive structures and processes is the common thread.

There has been a continued proliferation of theories regarding CBT in the last 15 years. Some of this work has directly built upon Beck's initial ideas, and some has taken a radically different

approach. The theoretical plethora that is now present cannot be summarized in the limited space available. Following are examples indicative of the current trends.

Modern CT

While Beck has continued to evolve his views about the nature of CBT (see Clark, Beck, & Alford, 1999 for an elaboration), other authors have continued to build on the tradition of Beck's work. Much of this work continues to define and explore the mediational theories of CT by exploring the field of cognitive science. A recent special issue of *Behavior Therapy* is one excellent example. Mathews (2006) summarized the findings of this collection of studies, noting the important conclusion that interpretive biases likely underlie the problematic thought content present during rumination.

Other, more general theories based on cognitive science can be found in the literature. For example, Brewin (2006) provided a *retrieval competition account* of the mechanisms of change involved in CT. It is a modern deactivation–activation model. He argues that there are multiple cognitive structures that compete for activation in a given circumstance. In this account, CT is said to attempt to alter the "accessibility of memory representations containing positive and negative information, particularly when patients are faced with challenging situations" (p. 773).

Third-Wave Therapies

Hayes (2004) identified a number of therapies belonging to what has been dubbed the "third wave" of CBT. This is a theoretical and technological movement founded on functional contextualism. Three third-wave therapies were generated following investigations into traditional CT.

Behavioral activation (BA; Martell, Addis, & Jacobson, 2001) makes use of the behavioral techniques found in traditional CT. Its origins are found in early theoretical work focusing on the environmental causes of depression (e.g., Brown & Harris, 1978; Lewinsohn et al., 1985). More recent interest in this approach was spurred on by research indicating that use of behavioral activation techniques alone is as effective as utilizing them with the other techniques in CT (Jacobson et al., 1996).

Mindfulness-based cognitive therapy (MBCT; Segal, Williams, & Teasdale, 2002) builds on the initial theory and therapy developed by Beck and his colleagues. Many of the novel aspects of MBCT were derived from a model of cognitive vulnerability to depressive relapse. In addition to the use of traditional CT techniques, MBCT also utilizes mindfulness training. It is thought that risk of relapse will be reduced if mindfulness training allows clients to be more aware of and escape depressive cognitive processes. This account fits nicely in the compensation model, where mindfulness builds positive coping schemas.

Early versions of acceptance and commitment therapy (Hayes, Strosahl, & Wilson, 1999) were first developed after component analyses of CT. Currently, ACT focuses on defusion from and acceptance of cognitive content in order to reduce experiential avoidance. This is done in the service of allowing clients to live a life in the service of their values. The changes in this model might also be considered under the compensation model.

SHOW ME THE DATA: EVIDENCE
OF EFFECTIVENESS OF CBT

In general, the evidence from meta-analyses has demonstrated that CBT is effective for a wide range of presenting problems (Butler & Beck, 2001; Butler, Chapman, Forman, & Beck, 2006; Deacon & Abramowitz, 2004). In this section, we will review the meta-analytic data by disorder as an overview of the evidence for CBT. As previously stated, this review will be limited to depression and selected anxiety disorders.

Depression

Meta-analyses for CBT for depression have generally shown treatment to be effective. The within-group effect size comparing change in outcome measures from pre- to posttreatment has been reported to be 2.23 (SD = .78; Westen & Morrison, 2001). Between-group effect sizes

for CBT for depression have demonstrated that CBT is more effective than wait list or control groups (Dobson, 1989; Gaffan, Tsaousis, & Kemp-Wheeler, 1995; Gloaguen, Cottraux, Cucherat, & Blackburn, 1998; Robinson, Berman, & Neimeyer, 1990; Westen & Morrison, 2001). However, this difference has been less pronounced when control groups included active treatments (Wampold, Minami, Baskin, & Tierney, 2002), and these changes do not appear to be clinically significant (Nietzel, Russell, Hemmings, & Gretter, 1987; Westen & Morrison, 2001).

Other meta-analyses that have compared cognitive therapy to behavior therapy or combined treatment have demonstrated less clear trends. Dobson (1989) reported that cognitive therapy was superior to behavior therapy, while three other meta-analyses have supported the idea that cognitive therapy, behavior therapy, and combination treatment are equally effective (Gloaguen et al., 1998; Nietzel et al., 1987; Robinson et al., 1990). Results have been equally mixed with regard to CBT's efficacy compared to pharmacotherapy (Dobson, 1989; Gaffan, Tsaousis, & Kemp-Wheeler, 1995; Gloaguen, Cottraux, Cucherat, & Blackburn, 1998; Robinson, Berman, & Neimeyer, 1990). A mega-analysis by DeRubeis and colleagues (1999) supported the equal efficacy of pharmacotherapy and CBT for depression. (A mega-analysis is a data analysis in which an investigator pulls individual data from similar studies into one large pool of participants.)

Two of the meta-analyses mentioned earlier examined the effects of researcher allegiance and found that outcome for depression treatment was significantly predicted by this factor (Gaffan et al., 1995; Robinson et al., 1990). In the psychotherapy outcome literature, allegiance effects are common. Allegiance effects are assessed by observing a positive correlation between the effect size and the degree of preference the investigator has for the type of treatment being conducted.

Anxiety

Anxiety disorders have also been the subject of a great deal of empirical research. As stated earlier, the general understanding of the etiology of anxiety disorders from a CBT perspective is similar to that of depression, and treatment approaches are often similar. In some specific types of anxiety disorders, more specific behavioral components are also included (e.g., exposure and response prevention).

Generalized Anxiety Disorder

Within-group effect size for treatment of generalized anxiety disorder was reported to be 1.54 (Chambless & Gillis, 1993). Meta-analyses examining the between-group effect sizes have generally supported the superiority of CBT over control groups (Chambless & Gillis, 1993; Covin, Ouimet, Seeds, & Dozois, 2008; Mitte, 2005a). Findings also support improved outcomes when CBT is given as a package versus its cognitive or behavioral components (Gould, Otto, Pollack, & Yap, 1997). Furthermore, analyses of within-group effects for follow-up period show that gains from treatment are maintained up to one year (Chambless & Gillis, 1993; Covin et al., 2008; Gould, Buckminster, Pollack, Otto, & Yap, 1997). Chambless and Gillis (1993) reported conflicting findings regarding whether cognitive components were more effective than behavioral components. However, Borkovec and colleagues (1996) concluded that CBT was more effective than behavior therapy at follow-up.

Mitte (2005a) failed to find a publication bias but did find that effect sizes were greater when CBT was compared to wait list rather than an active control. A few meta-analyses have examined moderators for treatment of GAD. Covin, Ouimet, Seeds, and Dozois (2008) found greater effect sizes for younger patients and for individual versus group therapy. However, Gould and colleagues (1997) failed to find differential effect sizes related to therapy modality.

Panic

Meta-analyses of CBT for panic disorder have also focused on cognitive interventions, exposure, and the combination. Within-group effect sizes have been reported as follows: cognitive therapy 1.16–1.25, exposure .79–1.09, and CBT 1.68 (Bakker, van Balkom, Spinhoven, Blaauw, & van Dyck, 1998; Chambless & Gillis, 1993; van Balkom et al., 1997). Support has generally

been found for CBT's effectiveness when compared with wait list or placebo conditions and for the maintenance of gains through follow-up (Bakker, van Balkom, Spinhoven, Blaauw, & van Dyck, 1998; Chambless & Gillis, 1993; Mitte, 2005b; van Balkom et al., 1997). Results have been mixed regarding the clinical significance of these outcomes (Oei, Llamas, & Devilly, 1999; Westen & Morrison, 2001). Additionally, the data is variable with regard to comparisons between cognitive, behavior, and combination treatments. Combination of exposure and cognitive therapy has been reported more effective than exposure or relaxation alone (Chambless & Gillis, 1993; Gould, Otto, & Pollack, 1995). However, others have reported no differences between cognitive and behavioral techniques (Mitte, 2005b).

Meta-analyses that have examined moderators of CBT for panic disorder have found that presence of agoraphobia does not act as a moderator, while length of disorder and method of assessment do act as moderators (Clum, Clum, & Surls, 1993; Gould, Otto, & Pollack, 1995). Specifically, Clum and colleagues (1993) found greater effect sizes when patients had a history of panic disorder for greater than 10 years and when the experimenters were not blind to condition. Additionally, effect sizes were lower when behavioral assessment methods were employed. Finally, Mitte (2005b) concluded that publication bias did not affect results for CBT treatment for panic disorder.

Obsessive-Compulsive Disorder

Meta-analyses for cognitive behavior therapy for OCD have examined effectiveness of cognitive interventions, exposure, and the combination of the two. Within-group effect sizes have been reported as follows: cognitive therapy 1.09–1.57 (Abramowitz, 1996; van Blakom, van Oppen, Vermeulen, & van Dyck, 1994), exposure 2.36 (Christensen, Hadzi-Pavlovic, Andrews, & Mattick, 1987), and CBT 1.30 (van Blakom, et al., 1994). While generally demonstrated to be more effective than placebo, results comparing within-group effect sizes or examining between-group effect sizes have concluded that no active treatment is more effective than any others in the comparison of active treatments (Abramowitz, 1997; Christensen et al., 1987; van Blakom et al., 1994). Abromowitz and colleagues (1998) examined the clinical significance of improvements with exposure and response prevention and concluded that patients could still be distinguished from normal population after treatment. Two studies examined moderators of CBT and exposure alone for OCD treatment (Abramowitz, 1996; Christensen, et al., 1987). Significant moderators, those variables that led to higher effect sizes, were when therapist supervised exposure, when patients stopped rituals, when compulsions were present, the use of measures other than self-report, longer sessions, longer duration of treatment and shorter history of OCD. The use of self-report measures was associated with lower effect sizes.

Social Phobia

Research on treatment of social phobia has also examined the differences between cognitive therapy, exposure, and the combination. Within-group effect sizes have been reported as follows: exposure 1.08, cognitive restructuring 0.72–0.9, and cognitive behavior therapy 0.84–1.14 (Chambless & Gillis, 1993; Fedoroff & Taylor, 2001; Feske & Chambless, 1995). There is general support for the effectiveness of CBT over placebo and wait list and for the treatment gains to be maintained up to three months' follow-up (Chambless & Gillis, 1993; Fedoroff & Taylor, 2001; Gould, Buckminster et al., 1997; Taylor, 1996). However, there has not been support for CT being more effective than behavior therapy, including exposure (Chambless & Gillis, 1993; Taylor, 1996). Feske and Chambless (1995) reported that longer treatment was associated with better outcomes for the treatment of social phobia.

SUMMARY OF META-ANALYSES

As can be seen from the preceding review, CBT has generally been effective for various disorders. However, the clinical significance of these results is less well established where clinical significance is generally considered a return to functioning indistinguishable from those without a clinical diagnosis or an improvement of two standard deviations on the dependent

measure of primary interest (Jacobson, Follette, & Revenstorf, 1984; Jacobson, Roberts, Berns, & McGlinchey, 1999). Furthermore, comparisons between different studies are made difficult to interpret as the definitions of different treatments vary considerably among studies (Deacon & Abramowitz, 2004). Additionally, the effect sizes decrease as CBT is compared to other active treatments. In recognition of this, Wampold and colleagues (1997) conducted a meta-analysis on studies comparing active treatments. They found that effect sizes were between 0 and 0.21 and concluded that all treatments have the same relative effectiveness.

Researchers have critiqued meta-analytic practices that fail to examine mediators and moderators of treatment and systematic biases involved in these methods (Parker & Fletcher, 2007; Shadish & Sweeney, 1991; Staines & Cleland, 2007). We attempted to highlight the few meta-analyses that have addressed some of these issues. However, the results are equivocal regarding the active ingredients of CBT. As a result, researchers have also turned their attention to mediational modeling and component analyses to better understand what is specifically leading to change.

EVIDENCE OF MEDIATION BY POSITED MECHANISMS

Baron and Kenny (1986) and MacKinnon and colleagues (MacKinnon, Fairchild, & Fritz, 2007; MacKinnon, Lockwood, Hoffman, West, & Sheets, 2002) have outlined mediational methods to examine the mechanism of action operating in treatments that lead to changes in outcome. They also listed criteria that should be met in order to conclude that a variable acts as a mediator of treatment. These criteria, as they have typically been applied to cognitive theory, are as follows:

- Cognitive therapy reduces symptoms more than does the alternative treatment (i.e., a treatment effect on symptom change).
- Cognitive therapy produces greater changes in a cognitive variable than does the alternative treatment (i.e., a treatment effect on cognitive change).

- Change in the cognitive variable covaries with symptom change, even when the variable "treatment" is held constant statistically.
- Inclusion of the cognitive variable as a covariate reduces the treatment effect on symptom change (in complete mediation the relation is reduced to zero).

More extensive discussions of mediational models in CBT can be found elsewhere (Hollon, DeRubeis, & Evans, 1987; S. Kwon & Oei, 1994).

The majority of mediational research tests the generic model of change mentioned above, where vulnerability to depression is caused by development of negative schemas and stressful life events activate these schemas, producing dysfunctional attitudes, negative automatic thoughts, and the like. Thus, these are primarily tests of the activation–deactivation model. In the following sections, we will review the data on cognitive mediation of treatment for depression and anxiety disorders.

MEDIATORS IN DEPRESSION

Mediational research in CBT for depression has examined the Attributional Styles Questionnaire (ASQ; Peterson, 1982), the Automatic Thoughts Questionnaire (ATQ; Hollon & Kendall, 1980), the Dysfunctional Attitudes Scale (DAS; Dobson & Breiter, 1983), and the Hopelessness Scale (HS; Beck, Weissman, Lester, & Trexler, 1974).

The first two steps to examining cognitive mediation are to examine whether cognitive change correlates with changes in depression and whether this change is specific to cognitive interventions. The majority of the research has shown that cognitive changes do co-occur with changes in depression across treatment and within session, precede changes in depression, and result in greater change in depressed mood than cognitive exploration (Garratt et al., 2007; Seligman et al., 1988; Whisman, 1993). Furthermore, regression analyses suggest that belief in automatic thoughts predicts changes in mood and accounts for separate significant portions of the variance from the patient–therapist relationship (Persons & Burns, 1985). However, the specificity of these changes has been questioned by

many studies demonstrating such change across therapy modalities, including psychopharmacology (e.g., Murphy, Simons, Wetzel, & Lustman, 1984; Reda, Carpiniello, Secchiaroli, & Blanco, 1985; Silverman, Silverman, & Eardley, 1984; Simons, Garfield, & Murphy, 1984; Zeiss, Lewinsohn, & Muñoz, 1979). A longitudinal study by Lewinsohn and colleagues (1981) supports the notion that depression-related negative cognitions arise concurrently with depression. Additionally, Beevers and colleagues (2007) found that negative cognitions mediated the prediction that longer history of depression leads to worse outcome across treatments.

Some authors have argued that it is too early to reject the cognitive mediational hypothesis based on this evidence alone. Hollon and colleagues (1987) have argued that study designs did not allow for competing hypotheses. They suggested designs that examine whether cognitive change could be a consequence in treatments other than cognitive therapy. This would not be mutually exclusive to change in cognitions mediating cognitive therapy gains. Additionally, Whisman (1993) suggested that studies have not had sufficient power to detect differences between groups regarding the specificity of cognitive change.

Following this logic, this same research group examined the hypothesis that cognitive change was the mechanism of action for cognitive therapy and a consequence of medication (DeRubeis et al., 1990). They used all four cognitive measures mentioned earlier: Attributional Styles Questionnaire (ASQ; Peterson, 1982), Automatic Thoughts Questionnaire (ATQ; Hollon & Kendall, 1980), Dysfunctional Attitudes Scale (DAS; Dobson & Breiter, 1983), and the Hopelessness Scale (HS; Beck, et al., 1974). Although all four cognitive measures employed demonstrated significant improvement, there were no differences between groups. The ATQ was not a significant predictor of change. However, change in all three other cognitive measures from pre- to midtreatment predicted changes in depression from mid- to posttreatment in the cognitive therapy group and not the medication group. Using hierarchical regression as suggested by Baron and Kenny (1986), they found that early improvement on the ASQ and DAS differentially predicted depression symptoms depending on treatment (i.e., stronger relationship shown in CT group).

Kwon and Oei (2003) found evidence of cognitive mediation in group treatment, although they did not use a control group to examine the specificity of their findings to this treatment modality. They examined the ATQ and DAS and conclude that ATQ might mediate changes between DAS and depression symptoms.

Burns and Spangler (2001) attempted to correct for methodological weaknesses in DeRubeis's study by using structural equation model and examining alternative hypotheses. They examined four causal models using structural equation modeling:

1. Treatment changes dysfunctional attitudes, which leads to changes in depression and anxiety (cognitive mediation hypothesis).
2. Changes in depression and/or anxiety lead to changes in DAs (mood activation hypothesis).
3. DAs and negative emotions have reciprocal causal effects on each other (circular causality hypothesis).
4. No causal links between emotions and DAs; changes in both caused by a third unknown variable.

Their findings lend support for last hypothesis: Changes in depression, anxiety, and dysfunctional attitudes (as measured by the DAS) have no causal links. Finally, they replicated their findings by reanalyzing data from NIMH collaborative depression research study (Elkin, et al., 1989).

Zuroff and colleagues (1999) also analyzed data from the NIMH collaborative depression research study to examine the stability of the DAS. Their structural equation modeling demonstrated that DAS predicted response to treatment and remained relatively stable. They concluded that this is consistent with cognitive theory of depression where dysfunctional attitudes are a vulnerability to depression. However, the fact that DAS remained relatively stable might also explain why it has not functioned well in other tests of mediation.

Additionally, the cognitive mediational model was tested to see if cognitive change mediated relapse prevention in depression (Hollon, Evans, DeRubeis, & Ingram, 1990). Originally, participants received cognitive therapy, antidepressant medication, or both. Following initial treatment, those who received medication where divided into two groups: those who continued antidepressant medication (maintenance group) and those who did not. These researchers examined results in terms of three proposed models of change: accommodation, activation–deactivation, and compensation. Cognitive therapy and continued medication maintenance led to lower relapse/recurrence rates. They concluded that CT is working through accommodation or compensation model. Both the ATQ and HS covaried with depression, but this was not specific to CT. However, the ASQ covaried with depression and was improved when CT was given compared to a medication-alone condition. Also, higher ratings of adherence to the CT protocol predicted better ASQ outcomes. Finally, post-ASQ continued to predict relapse/recurrence. They conclude that the ASQ met all of Baron and Kenny's (1986) criteria for mediation.

However, a study by Teasdale and colleagues (2001) failed to replicate mediation of relapse prevention by the ASQ. They failed to demonstrate that any cognitive variable predicted relapse independent of changes in depression. However, they did find that extreme responding in either direction to items on the ASQ mediated relapse (met all but last criteria of mediation: nonsignificant reduction in prediction when treatment was taken out).

From the preceding summaries, it should be clear that there is no strong evidence for mediation via cognitive change in the treatment of depression. Results are equivocal for all measures of cognition.

MEDIATORS IN ANXIETY

At the time of this review, mediational analyses were not found for generalized anxiety disorder or obsessive–compulsive disorder.

Panic

Smits and colleagues (2004) performed the only mediational analysis of CBT for panic at present. They examined whether fear of fear plays a mediating role as assessed by the Anxiety Sensitivity Index (ASI; Peterson & Reiss, 1987) and the Body Sensations Questionnaire (BSQ; Chambless, Caputo, Bright, & Gallagher, 1984). Participants were assigned to CBT or wait list. Assessments were only given pre and post. They concluded that fear of fear fully mediates effects of treatment on global disability and partially mediates the effects of treatment on panic frequency, anxiety, and agoraphobia. Future research would need to include more assessment points to examine whether change in fear of fear takes place before changes in anxiety as well as whether this mechanism is specific to CBT.

Social Phobia

There have been mixed results for the mediational effects of probability and cost biases in treatment for social anxiety using the Social Probability and Cost Questionnaire (SPCQ; Foa, Franklin, Perry, & Herbert, 1996; Hofmann, 2004; McManus, Clark, & Hackmann, 2000). Smits and colleagues (2006) attempted to improve on previous research by examining alternative variables as mediators, giving assessments throughout treatment (not just pre–post), and doing within-subject analyses for exposure treatments. In addition to examining the SPCQ, they look at fear of fear using the ASI (Peterson & Reiss, 1987) and the BSQ (Chambless et al., 1984) as measures of mediation. The results only support the role of probability bias as a mediator but not other cognitive variables.

Mattick and Peters (1988) were the first to examine the possible mediating role of fear of negative evaluation in the treatment of social phobia. They used the following measures in a multiple, stepwise regression analysis (entered in the following order): the Fear of Negative Evaluation Scale (FNES; Watson & Friend, 1969), the Irrational Beliefs Test (IBT; Jones, 1969), and the Locus of Control of Behavior Scale (LCBS; Craig, Franklin, & Andrews, 1984). The averaged within-exposure habituation of anxiety was entered as outcome measure. The FNES accounted for the most variance (20%), while the other three variables did not add significantly to the accounted-for variance. Additionally, these three variables were significantly associated with end-state functioning at posttreatment and follow-up. Thus, further exploration of the FNES as a mediator might be warranted.

To summarize, ASI and BSQ as measures of fear of fear were shown to mediate CBT in panic disorder but not in social phobia. Additionally, probability biases, as measured by the SPCQ, and fear of negative evaluation, as measured by the FNES, have some support in the mediation of CBT for social phobia.

STATE OF MEDITATIONAL DATA

The preceding results indicate limited and questionable support for the cognitive mediational model. A further caution that we would offer in interpreting the existing data is with regard to the construct validity of the assessments used to measure the hypothesized mediators. In the case of the research reviewed, items on the instruments are the observed variables said to be measuring an underlying construct. Examples of items from these scales are shown in Table 3.3. It is clear that these measures are asking for responses to the same thought content that will be targeted in therapy. Thus, changes in responses to these questionnaires might be artifacts of conflating manipulation checks with outcome, or it could be possible that a third variable is affecting both.

Further support for the inadequacy of some of these measures also exists. The development of the ATQ might bring into question its validity at measuring a construct separate from depression. Hollon and Kendell (1980) selected items that discriminate between depressed and nondepressed. Further research has shown that the ATQ has good sensitivity and specificity in delineating depression (Dobson & Breiter, 1983). Finally, correlations with measures of depression have been found to be as high as 0.87 (Harrell & Ryon, 1983). Together, these findings bring into question the discriminant validity of the ATQ from measures used to identify depression itself.

TABLE 3.3   Sample Items from Measures Examined as Mediators

	Assessment	Sample Items
Depressive cognitions	Dysfunctional Attributions Scale (DAS)	"If I fail partly, it is as bad as being a complete failure"; "If a person asks for help, it is a sign of weakness."
	Automatic Thoughts Questionnaire (ATQ)	"I'm no good"; "I can't stand this anymore"; "Why can't I ever succeed?"
	Attributional Styles Questionnaire (ASQ)	Presented with situations (e.g., you go on a date and it goes badly), must identify the cause of each and rate it on scale of internality, stability, and globality.
	Hopelessness Scale (HS)	"There's no use in really trying to get something I want because I probably won't get it"; "It is very unlikely that I will get any real satisfaction out of the future."
Anxious cognitions	SPCQ (Social Probability and Cost Questionnaire)	Rate likelihood and possible cost of different events, such as "How bad would it be for you to have somebody leave while you are talking to several people?" or "How bad would it be to unexpectedly be called in to see you supervisor at work?"
	ASI fear of fear	"When I am nervous, I worry that I might be mentally ill."
	BSQ fear of fear	Rate how frightening bodily sensations are (e.g., heart palpitations)
	Fear of Negative Evaluation Scale (FNES)	"I worry that others will think I am not worthwhile."

The usefulness of the DAS as a potential mediator is questionable given its stability over time (Zuroff, et al., 1999). Additionally, research has shown that it has poor specificity (Hill, Oei, & Hill, 1989) and that DAS scores increased equally for depressed and nondepressed persons following a sad mood state induction (Brosse, Craighead, & Craighead, 1999).

Although there is more extensive research examining the validity of the ASQ (Peterson, 1982) its use as a mediator is questionable. As a result of low internal consistency and only moderate reliability of the ASQ, the original author expanded this questionnaire (Peterson & Villanova, 1988). However, this more reliable version was not used in the meditational studies. There is also some evidence to suggest that the events listed and amount of information given are related to the types of causes endorsed regardless of attributional style (Higgins & Hay, 2003).

Heimber (1994) reviewed cognitive assessments used in social phobia research. He questioned the use of the FNES (Watson & Friend, 1969) because it confounds the measurement of anxiety and cognition. Although it is beyond the scope of this chapter to review all evidence of the adequacy of cognitive measures, we would like to highlight the need to implement valid and reliable measures in further attempts to examine mediation.

Furthermore, the mediator variables that are examined are not exact tests of cognitive theory. Garratt and colleagues (2007) explain that research on cognitive mediation will never be an exact test of cognitive theory. According to the theory, cognitive schemas are the central mediator but currently, researchers do not know how to measure change in schemas. Rather, they rely on measuring proxy variables such as automatic thoughts, dysfunctional attitudes, negative attribution patterns, and cognitive distortions. As a result of the difficulty in demonstrating cognitive mediation, researchers have investigated different sources of change within CBT.

EVIDENCE FROM COMPONENT ANALYSES

CBT is composed of a number of techniques. This might be a pro for one who subscribes to a "kitchen sink" approach, where the strategy is to use all the known techniques in hopes that one will be useful to a specific individual. However, this is an inefficient strategy. Furthermore, evaluating treatment packages as a whole will not lead to an understanding of the specific mechanisms of action. Component analyses have been employed to explore which techniques are the active ingredients in this approach. Overall, the results have not lent support for the superiority of cognitive components compared to behavioral components (Longmore & Worrell, 2007).

Depression

Component analyses of CBT for depression have followed this same trend, although few such studies have been conducted. As a beginning step, Teasdale and Fennell (1982) examined the effectiveness of thought-change techniques over the nonspecific effect of exploring thoughts in general. They used a within-subject design and measured belief in thoughts and level of depression. They found that greater reduction in belief from thought-change procedures were consistently accompanied by self-reported reductions in depression.

Two early studies that employed within-subject design concluded that components worked in an additive fashion (Jarrett & Nelson, 1987; Zettle & Hayes, 1987). Thus, exposure to all components provided the optimum outcome. Jarrett and Nelson (1987) examined the differential contribution of logical analysis (LA) and hypothesis testing (HT) as well as order effects. They found scores on the Beck Depression Inventory (BDI; Beck, Ward, Mendelson, Mock, & Erbaugh, 1961) and Pleasant Events Schedule (PES; MacPhillamy & Lewinsohn, 1971) were significantly lower when subjects received HT before LA. However, they failed to find significant differences between HT and LA. Finally, they concluded that results suggest exposure to all components was better than exposure to one component. Zettle and Hayes (1987) compared cognitive distancing, cognitive restructuring, and behavioral homework. They found that all three components lead to the best outcomes.

One study found that cognitive intervention did not predict change in depression scores (Hayes, Castonguay, & Goldfried, 1996). These researchers coded session tapes for whether treatment was targeting cognitive, interpersonal, or developmental vulnerabilities to depression and whether these different interventions were associated with symptom reduction. The results from regression analyses suggested that cognitive interventions did not predict better outcomes. Furthermore, targeting interpersonal-related cognitions predicted a worse outcome, whereas actual interpersonal intervention predicted better outcomes.

Finally, three successive studies have lent support for the equal effectiveness of behavior, cognitive, and combination treatment (Dimidjian et al., 2006; Gortner, Gollan, Dobson, & Jacobson, 1998; Jacobson et al., 1996). In the first study, participants were randomly assigned to one of three groups: behavioral activation only, behavioral activation and skills to modify automatic thoughts (excluding focus on core schemas), or full CT (Jacobson, et al., 1996). No significant differences were found on the outcome measures for the total sample or the completer sample or analyses of clinical significance. Follow-up analyses did not demonstrate any significant differences. Also, these researchers looked at mechanisms of change using the PES (measure of behavioral activation), the ATQ (measure of dysfunctional thinking) and the Expanded Attributional Style Questionnaire (measure of cognitive structures). Although all clients showed significant improvement as measured by these assessments, there were no significantly different outcomes as a function of treatment. They also examined the idea that cognitive change could be a consequence in one treatment while a cause in another by calculating change scores at different time points in therapy. Early change in attributional style was associated with later change in depression for BA participants but not CT. Early change in pleasant events was associated with later change in CT but not BA. These findings do not support the cognitive mediational model. Gortner and colleagues (1998) presented two-year follow-up data from this component analysis. No significant differences were reported for 6-, 12-, 18-, and 24-month follow-ups, although all treatment showed substantial ability to prevent relapse.

Finally, the component analysis by Jacobson and colleagues (1996) was replicated and extended (Dimidjian et al., 2006). This research protocol included an extended version of behavioral activation. The results were examined differentially for low- and high-severity-of-depression subsamples. No differences between treatments were found in the low-severity group. However, behavior activation and antidepressants performed better than cognitive therapy for the high-severity subsample.

Anxiety Disorders

Panic

At the time of this review, no component analyses for CBT for panic were found.

Generalized Anxiety Disorder

At the time of this review, only one component analysis of CBT for GAD could be found. Borkovec and colleagues (2002) compared CT alone, applied relaxation combined with self-control desensitization (SCD), and CBT (contained all techniques from both other groups). Quality of therapy was rated "very good" for all three conditions, and there were few "breaks" in therapy where therapist made statements that were proscribed. Clients within each group improved significantly, and 43%–56% made clinically significant improvements. However, there were no significant differences between groups at posttreatment for outcome measures of anxiety or depression. This same trend remained at follow-up assessments up to two years. Furthermore, authors compared effect sizes of all components to those from previous meta-analyses of CBT and results indicated that therapy was at least as effective as previous studies.

Obsessive–Compulsive Disorder

There are a few studies that have added cognitive components of cognitive therapy to exposure as a result of the recognition that exposure is the first-line treatment but has a high refusal and dropout rates. The findings have demonstrated the full range of results, with two studies supporting the improved effectiveness with the addition of cognitive restructuring (Hiss, Foa, & Kozak, 1994; Van Oppen, de Haan, Van Balkom, & Spinhoven, 1995), two studies showing no differences (Emmelkamp & Beens, 1991; Vogel, Stiles, & Götestam, 2004), and one study showing better outcomes with exposure alone (McLean,

et al., 2001). Although their study did not show differential outcome effects, the study by Vogel and colleagues (2004) did show improvement in dropout rates with the addition of cognitive techniques. However, McLean and colleagues (2001) found that more participants in the CBT condition refused treatment compared to those in the exposure group.

Social Phobia

Component analyses of CBT for social phobia have compared exposure and cognitive restructuring elements. In general, findings have not supported differential efficacy between the components (Butler, Cullington, Munby, Amies, & Gelder, 1984; Emmelkamp, Mersch, Vissia, & Van der Helm, 1985; Hope, Heimberg, & Bruch, 1995; Mattick & Peters, 1988; Mattick, Peters, & Clarke, 1989). However, a subsample of these studies has found that combining cognitive restructuring and exposure leads to better outcomes at follow-up (Butler et al., 1984; Mattick & Peters, 1988; Mattick et al., 1989). An interesting finding of Mattick and colleagues (1989) speaks to the need of using different assessments. They found differential results between the cognitive self-report measures and the behavioral avoidance task, but no differences in end-state functioning.

STATE OF THE DATA

Although the evidence does generally support the effectiveness of CBT, it is unclear if it is working the way it should according to cognitive theory. Component and mediational analyses are mixed with regard to this question. The measures used to examine change in cognitions raise questions about construct validity, and we wonder whether these assessments might be reifying the construct. Furthermore, many studies suggest that behavioral components are at least as effective as the cognitive components and question the idea that behavior change occurs as a result of cognitive change.

The most straightforward conclusions at this point are that (1) most forms of CBT produce improvements compared to waitlist or inactive comparison conditions; (2) many treatments produce equivalent results using procedures with reasonable internal consistency; (3) the measure models that would allow proper testing of mediation need to be refined; and (4) the construct validity of our explanations of change in CBT is still in question.

References

Abramowitz, J. S. (1996). Variants of exposure and response prevention in the treatment of obsessive–compulsive disorder: A meta-analysis. *Behavior Therapy, 27*, 583–600.

Abramowitz, J. S. (1997). Effectiveness of psychological and pharmacological treatments for obsessive–compulsive disorder: A quantitative review. *Journal of Consulting and Clinical Psychology, 65*, 44–52.

Abramson, L. Y., Metalsky, G. I., & Alloy, L. B. (1989). Hopelessness depression: A theory-based subtype of depression. *Psychological Review, 96*, 358–372.

Abramson, L. Y., Seligman, M. E. P., & Teasdale, J. D. (1978). Learned helplessness in humans: Critique and reformulation. *Journal of Abnormal Psychology, 87*, 49–74.

Abromowitz, J. S. (1998). Does cognitive–behavioral therapy cure obsessive–compulsive disorder? A meta-analytic evaluation of clinical significance. *Behavior Therapy, 29*, 339–355.

Barber, J. P., & DeRubeis, R. J. (1989). On second thought: Where the action is in cognitive therapy for depression. *Cognitive Therapy and Research, 13*, 441–457.

Baron, R. M., & Kenny, D. A. (1986). The moderator-mediator variable distinction in social psychological research: Conceptual, strategic, and statistical considerations. *Journal of Personality and Social Psychology, 51*, 1173–1182.

Beck, A. T. (1967). Depression: Clinical, experimental, and theoretical aspects. New York: Harper (Hoeber).

Beck, A. T. (1976). *Cognitive therapy and the emotional disorders*. New York: International University Press.

Beck, A. T. (1983). Cognitive therapy of depression: New perspectives. In P. J. Clayton & J. E. Barrett (Eds.), *Treatment of depression: Old controversies and new approaches* (pp. 265–290). New York: Raven Press.

Beck, A. T., Rush, A. J., Shaw, B. F., & Emery, G. (1979). Cognitive therapy of depression. New York: Guilford.

Beck, A. T., Ward, C. H., Mendelson, M., Mock, J., & Erbaugh, J. (1961). An inventory for measuring depression. *Archives of General Psychiatry, 4*, 561–571.

Beck, A. T., Weissman, A., Lester, D., & Trexler, L. (1974). The measurement of pessimism: The Hopelessness Scale. *Journal of Consulting and Clinical Psychology, 42*, 861–865.

Beevers, C. G., Wells, T. T., & Miller, I. W. (2007). Predicting response to depression treatment: The role of negative cognition. *Journal of Consulting and Clinical Psychology, 75*, 422–431.

Borkovec, T. D., Newman, M. G., Pincus, A. L., & Lytle, R. (2002). A component analysis of cognitive-behavioral therapy for generalized anxiety disorder and the role of interpersonal problems. *Journal of Consulting and Clinical Psychology, 70*, 288–298.

Borkovec, T. D., Whisman, M. A., Mavissakalian, M. R., & Prien, R. F. (1996). Psychosocial treatment for generalized anxiety disorder. *Long-term treatments of anxiety disorders*. (pp. 171–199). Washington, DC: American Psychiatric Association.

Brewin, C. R. (2006). Understanding cognitive behaviour therapy: A retrieval competition account. *Behaviour Research and Therapy, 44*, 765–784.

Brosse, A. L., Craighead, L. W., & Craighead, W. E. (1999). Testing the mood-state hypothesis among previously depressed and never-depressed individuals. *Behavior Therapy, 30*, 97–115.

Brown, G. W., & Harris, T. (1978). Social origins of depression: A study of psychiatric disorder in women. New York: Free Press.

Burns, D. D., & Spangler, D. L. (2001). Do changes in dysfunctional attitudes mediate changes in depression and anxiety in cognitive behavioral therapy? *Behavior Therapy, 32*, 337–369.

Butler, G., Cullington, A., Munby, M., Amies, P., & Gelder, M. (1984). Exposure and anxiety management in the treatment of social phobia. *Journal of Consulting and Clinical Psychology, 52*, 642–650.

Chambless, D. L., Caputo, G. C., Bright, P., & Gallagher, R. (1984). Assessment of fear in agoraphobics: The Body Sensations Questionnaire and the Agoraphobic Cognitions Quesitonnaire. *Journal of Consulting and Clinical Psychology, 52*, 1090–1097.

Chambless, D. L., & Gillis, M. M. (1993). Cognitive therapy of anxiety disorders. *Journal of Consulting and Clinical Psychology, 61*, 248–260.

Christensen, H., Hadzi-Pavlovic, D., Andrews, G., & Mattick, R. (1987). Behavior therapy and tricyclic medication in the treatment of obsessive-compulsive disorder: A quantitative review. *Journal of Consulting and Clinical Psychology, 55*, 701–711.

Clark, D. A., Beck, A. T., & Alford, B. A. (1999). *Scientific foundations of cognitive theory and therapy of depression*. New York: John Wiley & Sons.

Clum, G. A., Clum, G. A., & Surls, R. (1993). A meta-analysis of treatments for panic disorder.

Journal of Consulting and Clinical Psychology, 61, 317–326.

Covin, R., Ouimet, A. J., Seeds, P. M., & Dozois, D. J. A. (2008). A meta-analysis of CBT for pathological worry among clients with GAD. *Journal of Anxiety Disorders, 22,* 108–116.

Craig, A. R., Franklin, J. A., & Andrews, G. (1984). A scale to measure locus of control of behaviour. *British Journal of Medical Psychology, 57,* 173–180.

Cronbach, L. J., & Meehl, P. E. (1955). Construct validity in psychological tests. *Psychological Bulletin, 52,* 281–302.

Deacon, B. J., & Abramowitz, J. S. (2004). Cognitive and behavioral treatments for anxiety disorders: A review of meta-analytic findings. *Journal of Clinical Psychology, 60,* 429–441.

DeRubeis, R. J., Evans, M. D., Hollon, S. D., Garvey, M. J., Grove, W. M., & Tuason, V. B. (1990). How does cognitive therapy work? Cognitive change and symptom change in cognitive therapy and pharmacotherapy for depression. *Journal of Consulting and Clinical Psychology, 58,* 862–869.

DeRubeis, R. J., Gelfand, L. A., Tang, T. Z., & Simons, A. D. (1999). Medications versus cognitive behavior therapy for severely depressed outpatients: Mega-analysis of four randomized comparisons. *American Journal of Psychiatry, 156,* 1007–1013.

Dimidjian, S., Hollon, S. D., Dobson, K. S., Schmaling, K. B., Kohlenberg, R. J., Addis, M. E., et al. (2006). Randomized trial of behavioral activation, cognitive therapy, and antidepressant medication in the acute treatment of adults with major depression. *Journal of Consulting and Clinical Psychology, 74,* 658–670.

Dobson, K. S. (1989). A meta-analysis of the efficacy of cognitive therapy for depression. *Journal of Consulting and Clinical Psychology, 57,* 414–419.

Dobson, K. S., & Breiter, H. J. (1983). Cognitive assessment of depression: Reliability and validity of three measures. *Journal of Abnormal Psychology, 92,* 107–109.

Elkin, I., Shea, M. T., Watkins, J. T., Imber, S. D., Sotsky, S. M., Collins, J. F., et al. (1989). National Institute of Mental Health Treatment of Depression Collaborative Research Program: General effectiveness of treatments. *Archives of General Psychiatry, 46,* 971–982.

Emmelkamp, P. M., & Beens, H. (1991). Cognitive therapy with obsessive-compulsive disorder: A comparative evaluation. *Behaviour Research and Therapy, 29,* 293–300.

Emmelkamp, P. M., Mersch, P.-P., Vissia, E., & Van der Helm, M. (1985). Social phobia: A comparative evaluation of cognitive and behavioral interventions. *Behaviour Research and Therapy, 23,* 365–369.

Feske, U., & Chambless, D. L. (1995). Cognitive behavioral versus exposure only treatment for social phobia: A meta-analysis. *Behavior Therapy, 26,* 695–720.

Foa, E. B., Franklin, M. E., Perry, K. J., & Herbert, J. D. (1996). Cognitive biases in generalized social phobia. *Journal of Abnormal Psychology, 105,* 433–439.

Foa, E. B., & Kozak, M. J. (1986). Emotional processing of fear: Exposure to corrective information. *Psychological Bulletin, 99,* 20–35.

Gaffan, E. A., Tsaousis, J., & Kemp-Wheeler, S. M. (1995). Researcher allegiance and meta-analysis: The case of cognitive therapy for depression. *Journal of Consulting and Clinical Psychology, 63,* 966–980.

Garratt, G., Ingram, R. E., Rand, K. L., & Sawalani, G. (2007). Cognitive processes in cognitive therapy: Evaluation of the mechanisms of change in the treatment of depression. *Clinical Psychology: Science and Practice, 14,* 224–239.

Gloaguen, V. R., Cottraux, J., Cucherat, M., & Blackburn, I.-M. (1998). A meta-analysis of the effects of cognitive therapy in depressed patients. *Journal of Affective Disorders, 49,* 59–72.

Gortner, E. T., Gollan, J. K., Dobson, K. S., & Jacobson, N. S. (1998). Cognitive–behavioral treatment for depression: Relapse prevention. *Journal of Consulting and Clinical Psychology, 66,* 377–384.

Gould, R. A., Otto, M. W., & Pollack, M. H. (1995). A meta-analysis of treatment outcome for panic disorder. *Clinical Psychology Review, 15,* 819–844.

Gould, R. A., Otto, M. W., Pollack, M. H., & Yap, L. (1997). Cognitive behavioral and pharmacological treatment of generalized anxiety disorder: A preliminary meta-analyis. *Behavior Therapy, 28,* 285–305.

Harrell, T. H., & Ryon, N. B. (1983). Cognitive-behavioral assessment of depression: Clinical validation of the automatic thoughts questionnaire. *Journal of Consulting and Clinical Psychology, 51,* 721–725.

Hayes, A. M., Castonguay, L. G., & Goldfried, M. R. (1996). Effectiveness of targeting the vulnerability factors of depression in cognitive therapy. *Journal of Consulting and Clinical Psychology, 64,* 623–627.

Hayes, S. C. (2004). Acceptance and commitment therapy, relational frame theory, and the third wave of behavioral and cognitive therapies. *Behavior Therapy, 35,* 639–665.

Hayes, S. C., Strosahl, K. D., & Wilson, K. G. (1999). *Acceptance and commitment therapy: An experiential approach to behavior change.* New York: Guilford.

Heimberg, R. G. (1994). Cognitive assessment strategies and the measurement of outcome of treatment for social phobia. *Behaviour Research and Therapy, 32,* 269–280.

Higgins, N. C., & Hay, J. L. (2003). Attributional style predicts causes of negative life events on the

Attributional Style Questionnaire. *Journal of Social Psychology, 143*, 253–271.

Hill, C. V., Oei, T. P., & Hill, M. A. (1989). An empirical investigation of the specificity and sensitivity of the Automatic Thoughts Questionnaire and Dysfunctional Attitudes Scale. *Journal of Psychopathology and Behavioral Assessment, 11*, 291–311.

Hiss, H., Foa, E. B., & Kozak, M. J. (1994). Relapse prevention program for treatment of obsessive-compulsive disorder. *Journal of Consulting and Clinical Psychology, 62*, 801–808.

Hofmann, S. G. (2004). Cognitive mediation of treatment change in social phobia. *Journal of Consulting and Clinical Psychology, 72*, 392–399.

Hollon, S. D., DeRubeis, R. J., & Evans, M. D. (1987). Causal mediation of change in treatment for depression: Discriminating between nonspecificity and noncausality. *Psychological Bulletin, 102*, 139–149.

Hollon, S. D., Evans, M. D., & DeRubeis, R. J. (1988). Preventing relapse following cognitive treatment for depression: The cognitive pharmacotherapy project. In T. M. Field, P. M. McCabe, & N. Schneiderman (Eds.), *Stress and coping across development* (pp. 227–243). Hillsdale, NJ: Lawrence Erlbaum.

Hollon, S. D., Evans, M. D., DeRubeis, R. J., & Ingram, R. E. (1990). Cognitive mediation of relapse prevention following treatment for depression: Implications of differential risk. *Contemporary psychological approaches to depression: Theory, research, and treatment.* (pp. 117–136). New York: Plenum Press.

Hollon, S. D., & Kendall, P. C. (1980). Cognitive self-statements in depression: Development of an automatic thoughts questionnaire. *Cognitive Therapy and Research, 4*, 383–395.

Hope, D. A., Heimberg, R. G., & Bruch, M. A. (1995). Dismantling cognitive–behavioral group therapy for social phobia. *Behaviour Research and Therapy, 33*, 637–650.

Ingram, R. E., & Hollon, S. D. (1986). Cognitive therapy for depression from an information processing perspective. In R. E. Ingram (Ed.), *Information processing approaches to clinical psychology* (pp. 259–281). San Diego, CA: Academic Press.

Jacobson, N. S., Dobson, K. S., Truax, P. A., Addis, M. E., Koerner, K., Gollan, J. K., et al. (1996). A component analysis of cognitive-behavioral treatment for depression. *Journal of Consulting and Clinical Psychology, 64*, 295–304.

Jacobson, N. S., Follette, W. C., & Revenstorf, D. (1984). Psychotherapy outcome research: Methods for reporting variability and evaluating clinical significance. *Behavior Therapy, 15*, 336–352.

Jacobson, N. S., Roberts, L. J., Berns, S. B., & McGlinchey, J. B. (1999). Methods for defining and determining the clinical significance of treatment effects: Description, application, and alternatives. *Journal of Consulting & Clinical Psychology, 67*, 300–307.

Jarrett, R. B., & Nelson, R. O. (1987). Mechanisms of change in cognitive therapy of depression. *Behavior Therapy, 18*, 227–241.

Jones, R. G. (1969). A factored measure of Ellis's irrational belief system, with personality and maladjustment correlates. *Dissertation Abstracts International, 29* (11-B), p. 4370-4380.

Kwon, S.-M., & Oei, T. P. S. (2003). Cognitive change processes in a group cognitive behavior therapy of depression. *Journal of Behavior Therapy and Experimental Psychiatry, 34*, 73–85.

Kwon, S., & Oei, T. P. S. (1994). The role of two levels of cognitions in the development, maintenance, and treatment of depression. *Clinical Psychology Review, 14*, 331–358.

Lewinsohn, P. M. (1974). A behavioral approach to depression. In R. M. Friedman & M. M. Katz (Eds.), *The psychology of depression: Contemporary theory and research* (pp. 157–185). New York: John Wiley & Sons.

Lewinsohn, P. M., Hoberman, H., Teri, L., & Hautzinger, M. (1985). An integrative theory of depression. In S. Reiss & R. R. Bootzin (Eds.), *Theoretical issues in behavior therapy* (pp. 331–359). Orlando, FL: Academic Press.

Lewinsohn, P. M., Steinmetz, J. L., Larson, D. W., & Franklin, J. (1981). Depression-related cognitions: Antecedent or consequence? *Journal of Abnormal Psychology, 90*, 213–219.

Longmore, R. J., & Worrell, M. (2007). Do we need to challenge thoughts in cognitive behavior therapy? *Clinical Psychology Review, 27*, 173–187.

MacKinnon, D. P., Fairchild, A. J., & Fritz, M. S. (2007). Mediation Analysis. *Annual Review of Psychology, 58*, 593–614.

MacKinnon, D. P., Lockwood, C. M., Hoffman, J. M., West, S. G., & Sheets, V. (2002). A comparison of methods to test mediation and other intervening variable effects. *Psychological Methods, 7*, 83–104.

MacPhillamy, D. J., & Lewinsohn, P. M. (1971). A scale for measurement of positive reinforcement (unpublished manuscript). University of Oregon.

Maier, S. F., & Seligman, M. E. (1976). Learned helplessness: Theory and evidence. *Journal of Experimental Psychology: General, 105*, 3–46.

Martell, C. R., Addis, M. E., & Jacobson, N. S. (2001). *Depression in context: Strategies for guided action.* New York: W. W. Norton.

Mathews, A. (2006). Towards an experimental cognitive science of CBT. *Behavior Therapy, 37*, 314–318.

Mattick, R. P., & Peters, L. (1988). Treatment of severe social phobia: Effects of guided exposure with and without cognitive restructuring. *Journal of Consulting and Clinical Psychology, 56,* 251–260.

Mattick, R. P., Peters, L., & Clarke, J. C. (1989). Exposure and cognitive restructuring for social phobia: A controlled study. *Behavior Therapy, 20,* 3–23.

McLean, P. D., Whittal, M. L., Thordarson, D. S., Taylor, S., Söchting, I., Koch, W. J., et al. (2001). Cognitive versus behavior therapy in the group treatment of obsessive–compulsive disorder. *Journal of Consulting and Clinical Psychology, 69,* 205–214.

McManus, F., Clark, D. M., & Hackmann, A. (2000). Specificity of cognitive biases in social phobia and their role in recovery. *Behavioural and Cognitive Psychotherapy, 28,* 201–209.

Mitte, K. (2005a). Meta-analysis of cognitive-behavioral treatments for generalized anxiety disorder: A comparison with pharmacotherapy. *Psychological Bulletin, 131,* 785–795.

Mitte, K. (2005b). A meta-analysis of the efficacy of psycho- and pharmacotherapy in panic disorder with and without agoraphobia. *Journal of Affective Disorders, 88,* 27–45.

Persons, J. B., & Burns, D. D. (1985). Mechanisms of action of cognitive therapy: The relative contributions of technical and interpersonal interventions. *Cognitive Therapy and Research, 9,* 539–551.

Peterson, C. (1982). The Attributional Style Questionnaire. *Cognitive Therapy and Research, 6,* 287–300.

Peterson, C., & Villanova, P. (1988). An Expanded Attributional Style Questionnaire. *Journal of Abnormal Psychology, 97,* 87–89.

Peterson, R. A., & Reiss, S. (1987). *Anxiety Sensitivity Index.* Palos Heights, IL: International Diagnostic Systems.

Robinson, L. A., Berman, J. S., & Neimeyer, R. A. (1990). Psychotherapy for the treatment of depression: A comprehensive review of controlled outcome research. *Psychological Bulletin, 108,* 30–49.

Rush, A. J., & Beck, A. T. (1978). Cognitive therapy of depression and suicide. *American Journal of Psychotherapy, 32,* 201–219.

Segal, Z. V., Williams, M. G., & Teasdale, J. D. (2002). Mindfulness-based cognitive therapy for depression: A new approach to preventing relapse. New York: Guilford.

Smits, J. A. J., Powers, M. B., Cho, Y., & Telch, M. J. (2004). Mechanism of change in cognitive–behavioral treatment of panic disorder: Evidence for the fear of fear mediational hypothesis. *Journal of Consulting and Clinical Psychology, 72,* 646–652.

Smits, J. A. J., Rosenfield, D., McDonald, R., & Telch, M. J. (2006). Cognitive mechanisms of social anxiety reduction: An examination of specificity and temporality. *Journal of Consulting and Clinical Psychology, 74,* 1203–1212.

Teasdale, J. D., & Fennell, M. J. (1982). Immediate effects on depression of cognitive therapy interventions. *Cognitive Therapy and Research, 6,* 343–352.

Teasdale, J. D., Scott, J., Moore, R. G., Hayhurst, H., Pope, M., & Paykel, E. S. (2001). How does cognitive therapy prevent relapse in residual depression? Evidence from a controlled trial. *Journal of Consulting and Clinical Psychology, 69,* 347–357.

van Blakom, A. J. L. M., van Oppen, P., Vermeulen, A. W. A., & van Dyck, R. (1994). A meta-analysis on the treatment of obsessive compulsive disorder: A comparison of antidepressants, behavior, and cognitive therapy. *Clinical Psychology Review, 14,* 359–381.

Van Oppen, P., de Haan, E., Van Balkom, A. J. L. M., & Spinhoven, P. (1995). Cognitive therapy and exposure in vivo in the treatment of obsessive compulsive disorder. *Behaviour Research and Therapy, 33,* 379–390.

Vogel, P. A., Stiles, T. C., & Götestam, K. G. (2004). Adding cognitive therapy elements to exposure therapy for obsessive compulsive disorder: A controlled study. *Behavioural and Cognitive Psychotherapy, 32,* 275–290.

Wampold, B. E., Minami, T., Baskin, T. W., & Tierney, S. C. (2002). A meta-(re)analysis of the effects of cognitive therapy versus "other therapies" for depression. *Journal of Affective Disorders, 68,* 159–165.

Wampold, B. E., Mondin, G. W., Moody, M., Stich, F., Benson, K., & Ahn, H.-N. (1997). A meta-analysis of outcome studies comparing bona fide psychotherapies: Empirically, "all must have prizes." *Psychological Bulletin, 122,* 203–215.

Watson, D., & Friend, R. (1969). Measurement of social-evaluative anxiety. *Journal of Consulting and Clinical Psychology, 33,* 448–457.

Westen, D., & Morrison, K. (2001). A multidimensional meta-analysis of treatments for depression, panic, and generalized anxiety disorder: An empirical examination of the status of empirically supported therapies. *Journal of Consulting and Clinical Psychology, 69,* 875–899.

Whisman, M. A. (1993). Mediators and moderators of change in cognitive therapy of depression. *Psychological Bulletin, 114,* 248–265.

Zettle, R. D., & Hayes, S. C. (1987). Component and process analysis of cognitive therapy. *Psychological Reports, 61,* 939–953.

Zuroff, D. C., Blatt, S. J., Sanislow, C. A., III, Bondi, C. M., & Pilkonis, P. A. (1999). Vulnerability to depression: Reexamining state dependence and relative stability. *Journal of Abnormal Psychology, 108,* 76–89.

4 CULTURAL AWARENESS AND CULTURALLY COMPETENT PRACTICE

Melanie P. Duckworth

Changing sociodemographic trends within the larger society have resulted in changing demands for the therapeutic process. The therapeutic context increasingly involves the coming together of therapists and clients who represent multiple and diverse cultural factors. This increasing diversity of culture requires that therapists be aware and have knowledge of those cultural factors that are clinically relevant, be prepared to actively engage clients around those cultural factors, and be prepared to effectively manage the influence of cultural factors on the therapeutic process and on therapeutic outcomes. The current chapter outlines strategies for increasing cultural awareness and improving cultural competence in the context of mental health service delivery. The chapter is structured to provide a review of (1) various definitions of culture and related terms; (2) research findings related to the mental health care needs of and disparities in mental health care delivery experienced by culturally diverse populations; (3) strategies to increase cultural awareness and knowledge; (4) strategies to increase cultural competence in the context of mental health care delivery; and (5) key components of culturally competent cognitive behavior therapy (CBT).

DEFINITIONS OF CULTURE AND RELATED TERMS

Draguns (1997) defines *culture* as "the shared social experiences of a group defined on the basis of its origin and/or morphological or "racial" characteristics" (p. 214). Examples of groupings that arise out of this definition of culture include African Americans, Italian Australians, and Finnish Canadians. Culture has also been equated with *ethnic identity*, referring to the historical and cultural patterns and collective identities shared by groups of people from a specific geographic region of the world (Betancourt & Lopez, 1993). Ethnic identity is considered to provide more insight into an individual's heritage and value system than would be provided by knowledge of race (Atkinson, Morten, & Sue, 1993). Hays (1996) defines *culture* as referring to "all the learned behaviors, beliefs, norms, and values that are held by a group of people passed on from older members to newer members, at least in part, to preserve the group" (p. 333), emphasizing the interpersonal and social aspects of culture rather than mere geographic or physical similarities. *Human diversity* refers to group-specific factors salient for the individual (Roysircar, 2004). These include gender, socioeconomic status, age, religion, race, ethnicity, regional/national origin, sexual orientation, and ability status. *Culture competence* would imply knowledge of those factors that render a particular group distinct from other groups, knowledge of the shared interpersonal and social experiences that characterize a particular cultural group, knowledge of the salience of between- and within-group experiences for a given group member, and knowledge of the relevance of salient group experiences to the therapeutic process (Duckworth, 2005). Although these terms are often used interchangeably, it is important that the therapist have an appreciation of the subtle and not-so-subtle differences that exist among these terms. When the therapist–client dyad represents an instance of cultural diversity, the therapist may be required to engage with the client in an active process of defining these terms.

SHIFTING SOCIODEMOGRAPHIC TRENDS AND EXISTING DISPARITIES IN HEALTH CARE DELIVERY

The call for increased attention to cultural factors in the context of mental health service delivery is supported by sociodemographic data that indicate increased representation of persons who are of different national origin, different ethnic groups, and different races among U.S. citizens. According to the U.S. Census Bureau (2008), Caucasians comprise two thirds of the current U.S. population, with African Americans representing 12.8%, Hispanic Americans representing 15.1%, and Asain Americans representing 4.4% of the U.S. population. The U.S. Census Bureau projects that by the year 2050 the Caucasian population will comprise only 46% of the U.S. population and that Hispanic-American and Asian-American populations will double in size from 15% to 30% and 4.4% to 9%, respectively. A relatively small increase of only two percentage points is expected for African Americans. These shifting sociodemographic trends are significant when considered in light of research related to ethnic matching in therapist–client dyads. Research suggests that treatment-seeking behavior, attrition from treatment, treatment benefit, and treatment satisfaction among ethnically diverse clients may all be influenced by the client's perception of the therapist as sharing the client's ethnic identification or as being knowledgeable of and sensitive to the client's experiences as a representative of ethnic diversity. Currently, only 6% of psychologists are of African-American, Hispanic-American, Asian-American, and Native American descent (American Psychological Association, 1997). The increasing ethnic diversity of the U.S. population and the continuing paucity of ethnically diverse mental health providers suggest that the majority of ethnically diverse clients seeking mental health care will continue to be assessed and treated by therapists who are Caucasian and require that those therapists be aware of their

ethnic identification and all that accompanies that identification and knowledgeable of and competent to address issues related to the ethnic identity of clients, as they occur in the therapeutic exchange and in clients' larger life context.

Changes in the political and economic power of previously marginalized groups such as women and persons who represent more diverse sexual orientations are also precipitating an increase in the attention paid to cultural factors in the context of mental health service delivery. The equality of participation of women in all aspects of society has translated to more active examination of women's physical *and* mental health care needs. The increasing open participation of gays, lesbians, bisexuals, and transgendered persons in various aspects of society has resulted in a shift in health care focus that parallels that seen for women. There are an estimated 8.8 million gay, lesbian, and bisexual (GLB) persons in the U.S. Most suggestive of the increased acceptance of persons representing diverse sexual orientations are estimates from the American Community Survey (U.S. Census Bureau, 2006) that suggest a 30% increase in same-sex couples in the U.S. between 2000 and 2005 and an increase in same-sex couples in the Midwest region of the U.S., which is considered to reflect an increased willingness of gays, lesbians, and bisexuals to engage in same-sex relationships and to report the nature of these relationships.

The increasing diversity that characterizes the U.S. population represents a significant challenge when it comes to the provision of effective mental health care. Data published by the U.S. Department of Health and Human Services (DHHS) indicate that, as a consequence of having limited access to health care and as a consequence of receiving health care that is of poorer quality, culturally diverse individuals are likely to suffer greater physical *and* mental disability than representatives of the dominant U.S. culture (DHHS, 2000; New Freedom Commission on Mental Health, 2003). Differences in need for treatment, treatment access, treatment seeking, and treatment benefit have been studied as a function of a number of cultural factors, including age, ethnicity, gender, geographic residence, sexual orientation, and socioeconomic status. Documented disparities in mental health care experienced by ethnically diverse persons and persons with diverse sexual orientations are briefly chronicled.

When the data from the Epidemiological Catchment Area study (Robins & Regier, 1991) and the National Comorbidity Study (Kessler et al., 1996), two of the most referenced epidemiological surveys, are considered together, it can be concluded that the rates of mental illness among African Americans are similar to those of Caucasians. However, significant disparities exist in access to mental health care resources and subsequent utilization of those resources by African Americans (Duckworth, 2005). Utilization of mental health care in the African-American community is characterized by low rates of outpatient care and high rates of emergency services (Baker & Bell, 1999; DHHS, 2001; Snowden, 2001), with the low rates of outpatient care utilization attributable, at least in part, to a lack of access to affordable health care, a reluctance to seek treatment that is out of the stigma associated with psychological distress as well as a documented history of medical abuses. The availability of service providers also affects treatment-seeking behaviors (Holzer et al., 1998). Research indicates that African Americans would prefer to receive services from someone in their community and are more likely to seek treatment from a primary care physician than a mental health specialist (Baker & Bell, 1999). African Americans are less likely to receive are less likely to receive accurate diagnoses when presenting to primary care physicians for psychological help (DHHS, 2001) and are less likely to receive appropriate care when diagnosed with psychological disorders. This history of misdiagnosis and ineffective or inappropriate treatment is related to the fact that African Americans are likely to terminate treatment prematurely (Sue et al., 1994).

The U.S. Census Bureau estimates that 4.1 million American Indians/Alaska Natives (AI/AN) currently reside in the U.S. AI/AN account for 1.5% of the U.S. population and the majority live in urban, suburban, or rural nonreservation areas (DHHS, 2001). The relatively small size of this group is not indicative of the vast diversity within this group. The category of AI/AN includes 561 federally recognized tribes with over 200 indigenous languages spoken. This is simply one indicator of the heterogeneity that exists within this group and another factor that contributes to the challenge of providing mental health services effectively. There are many significant barriers to effectively treating AI/AN for mental disorders. A critical component of this challenge is the dearth of empirical evidence regarding the prevalence of mental disorders in this population. As a result of limitations in collecting adequate sample sizes, epidemiological information is suggestive rather than conclusive. It is estimated that 20%–30% of Native Americans have experienced depression during the course of their lifetime. The suicide rate is 1.5 times greater in the AI/AN population than in the general population (DHHS, 2001). This suggests that there are higher rates of psychological distress than have been previously documented. There is no empirical evidence regarding the phenomenology or prevalence of anxiety disorder. However, it is reasonable to assume given the prevalence of environmental stressors that a significant portion of this population suffers from anxiety-related disorders (DeCoteau, Anderson, & Hope, 2006). Distal factors present within this population that are associated with poor psychological health also suggest the need for further research in this area. The vast diversity of languages that are spoken within this population contributes to the challenges in appropriate assessment and treatment. It is possible that the most salient barrier to treatment is the long history of prejudicial practices and discriminatory treatment at the hands of the U.S. government. This has established deep (and understandable) feelings of mistrust that make it difficult to enter into treatment. This must be carefully considered when working with this population.

The overall prevalence of mental illness among Asian Americans and Pacific Islanders (AAPIs) seems to be similar to other communities in the United States. Despite average rates of mental disorder, AAPIs have historically presented to treatment at much lower rates than all other ethnic groups in the United States. However, when AAPI present to treatment, it is typically with severe symptoms (Chen, Sullivan, Lu, & Shibusawa, 2003). There are several hypotheses that may account for the reluctance on the part of many AAPIs to seek mental health services. Many Eastern traditions assert that the mind and body cannot be separated. This belief is in opposition to most Western philosophies and practices. This conceptualization, which is endorsed by many Asians currently living in the United States, makes seeking the services of any sort of mental health specialist seem unnecessary. Many Asian traditions contend that mental illness is caused by disharmony of emotions or evil spirits; thus, traditional psychotherapy is not the logical step when attempting to resolve these conflicts (Kramer, Kwong, Lee, & Chung, 2002). Alternatively, many AAPIs have had negative experiences with the health care system and are reluctant to seek treatment when they feel that their beliefs will not be respected (Kim, Han, & Kim, 2002). When AAPIs do present for mental health services, there are still potential challenges to overcome in providing effective treatment. Key factors include language, level of acculturation, age, gender, occupational issues, and family structure. Clearly, language is a key component of effective treatment. In people of Asian descent living in the United States, there are over 125 languages and dialects represented (Lin & Cheung, 1999); therefore, it is important to ensure that language is not a barrier to treatment (Duckworth & Iezzi, 2005).

Data from the 1999 Surgeon General's Report (DHHS, 2001) indicate that the rate of mental disorders among Hispanic Americans is comparable to the rates among other members of the U.S. population. A shared set of factors serve to both increase the rate of mental health problems experienced by Hispanic Americans and to limit Hispanic Americans access to health care. These factors include low educational attainment, low per capita income, low rates of health insurance coverage, limited availability of Spanish-speaking health care providers, and a reluctance to seek Western treatment.

The empirical literature documenting the mental health needs of persons of diverse sexual orientation is also woefully lacking. The 2008 report by the American Medical Association Council on Science and Public Health concludes that "gay men and lesbians are confronted with many of the same health issues as their heterosexual counterparts, but in addition have certain unique conditions related either to sexual or other disease risk factors or to use of fewer preventive services." The report also emphasized the importance of considering the influences of stigmatization and societal discrimination, substance use, access to care, and partners' involvement in medical decision making in considering the emotional and mental health concerns experienced by gay men and lesbians. Using a study population drawn from the 1999 Los Angeles Health Survey, Diamant and Wold (2003) assessed and compared the health status of women who self-identified as heterosexual (4023), bisexual (69), and lesbian (43). These researchers determined that bisexual and lesbian women experienced poorer physical and mental health than heterosexual women, with lesbian and bisexual women being significantly more likely to have a diagnosis of heart disease; bisexual women experiencing significantly more days of poor physical health during the 30 days prior to survey participation; and lesbian women experiencing significantly more days of poor mental health during the 30 days prior to survey participation and being more likely to be taking antidepressant medications. Although the empirical literature related to the health care status and health care needs of persons who represent diverse sexual orientations is limited, the existing data suggest that differences in health care status and health care needs that are associated with sexual orientation may be explained by a health care system in which providers place insufficient emphasis on culturally competent health care provision.

The documented disparities in health care status, access and quality between representatives of the dominant culture and persons representing culturally diverse backgrounds may be explained, in part, by hard indicators such as health care affordability and ease of access. However, a more fully explicated model of existing disparities in health care status, access and quality would recognize the contribution of the health care provider's cultural awareness, knowledge, and competency to these differences. The projected population trends that point to increasing cultural diversity and the data reflecting diversity-related disparities in mental health care provision are the strongest arguments for increased emphasis on cultural awareness and cultural competency in the training of mental health care providers.

INCREASING CULTURAL AWARENESS AND KNOWLEDGE

In any therapeutic exchange, therapists and clients bring to the exchange a number of cultural factors that may be relevant to the therapeutic process and to therapeutic outcomes. When cultural differences are present, the therapeutic exchange may be influenced by cultural assumptions and biases that are present but outside of the awareness of the therapist. Hays (1996) developed a helpful approach to becoming aware of the many cultural factors that may influence therapist–client interactions and that may serve as potential sources of bias in providing health care to culturally diverse clients. This approach is designed to aid providers in organizing and systematically recognizing the influence of complex cultural factors on the provider–client relationship. Hays employed the acronym ADRESSING to capture nine therapy-relevant cultural factors, including age, disability, religion, ethnicity, social status, sexual orientation, indigenous heritage, national origin, and gender. Although the model is not exhaustively inclusive, the ADRESSING model does focus on cultural factors that have been recognized as important by the American Psychological Association and other organizations (Hays, 1996, 2008). Hays suggests that beginning with these basic indicators can help to make a health care provider more aware of cultural influences on the psychotherapy relationship. The model can assist the health care provider in identifying his or her own cultural identity and any assumptions or biases that may influence the provider's interactions with members of other cultural groups. The model can also be used by the provider to assist clients in identifying those cultural factors that

are most relevant to their lives and to their therapy goals.

Daniel, Roysircar, Abeles, and Boyd (2004) also emphasize the importance of self-awareness to the provider's delivery of culturally competent mental health care. Although racism, heterosexism, and ageism are the forms of cultural bias that are of primary focus for these researchers, Daniel and colleagues forward suggestions for increasing therapist skill level that apply to other important cultural markers such as disability, religion, social status, and gender. They note that therapists residing in the United States are likely to be exposed to different stereotypes that could lead to biases and unwarranted assumptions about culturally diverse clients—biases and assumptions to which therapists are likely to subscribe, either consciously or unconsciously. It is when biases and assumptions exist outside of awareness that therapists are most vulnerable to enacting such biases and assumptions. Because self-awareness is considered essential to establishing an effective therapeutic alliance, therapists are urged to explicitly examine and acknowledge cultural biases and assumptions that might influence interactions with culturally diverse clients. Sue, Arredondo, and McDavis (1992) define the culturally skilled therapist as "one who is actively engaged in the process of becoming aware of his or her own assumptions about human behavior, values, biases, pre-conceived notions, and personal limitations" (p. 481).

Awareness of culture is a precursor for effective, culturally relevant practice of mental health care. Self-awareness allows for an exploration of barriers to effective, culturally competent mental health care delivery, including defensiveness, anxiety, fear, and guilt. For the practicing mental health care provider, the process of increasing self-awareness might begin with the use of self-report measures of multicultural knowledge and sensitivity (Sodowsky, Taffe, Gutkin, & Wise, 1994), journaling, and the review of clinical notes and critical incidents. Daniel and colleagues also recommend seeking feedback from clients, peers, supervisors, supervisees, and professional and community experts as a means of increasing self-awareness, cultural knowledge, and cultural sensitivity.

In discussing strategies for increasing knowledge of diverse cultures, Daniel and colleagues (2004) entreat providers to recognize that there is a growing literature pertaining to culturally competent health care delivery. It is mental health care providers' responsibility to be active consumers of such information (Duckworth & Iezzi, 2005; Duckworth, Iezzi, Vijay, & Gerber, in press). A good starting point for increasing cultural knowledge is becoming familiar with available ethical guidelines for working with culturally diverse clients. The American Psychological Association has sponsored a number of reports on culture, ethnicity, age, gender, and sexual orientation, including the following: The Guidelines for Multicultural Training, Research, Practice, and Organizational Change for Psychologists (American Psychological Association, 2003a); Guidelines for Providers of Psychological Services to Ethnic, Linguistic, and Culturally Diverse Populations (American Psychological Association, 1993); Guidelines for Psychological Practice with Older Adults (American Psychological Association, 2003b); and Guidelines for Psychotherapy with Lesbian, Gay, and Bisexual Clients (American Psychological Association, 2000). The Council of National Psychological Associations for the Advancement of Ethnic Minority Issues (CNPAAEMI) has published documents related to ethnically diverse populations that are relevant to health care delivery, including Guidelines for Research in Ethnic Minority Communities (CNPAAEMI, 2000) and Psychological Treatment of Ethnic Minority Communities (CNPAAEMI, 2003). Being familiar with these guidelines will not only assist with recognizing biases and assumptions therapists might have about culturally diverse clients, but will also result in clinical practices that are in keeping with the American Psychological Association and other regulatory bodies.

The degree to which increased awareness and knowledge of cultural factors translates to clinical address of such factors depends, in large part, on the philosophical orientation out of which the mental health care provider operates. Although different models exist, there are generally two approaches to conceptualizing the role of culture in defining psychopathology and in guiding the practice of psychotherapy (Draguns, 1997). The *emic* model views culture as permeating all aspects of psychological distress. Culture and psychopathology are viewed as intertwined and as part of a holistic experience. Based on this model, there would be no advantage to comparing psychological distress across cultures because of the uniqueness of each culture. Alternatively, the *etic* model downplays the role of culture in defining psychological experiences. This model emphasizes the examination of common psychological experiences that are present across different cultures.

These two conceptual models have led to the use of two distinct approaches to conducting cross-cultural research. The emic approach favors qualitative and descriptive research that tends to demonstrate the uniqueness of a culture and discourages Western conceptualizations of psychological distress. For example, this type of model would value the role of familism or "familismo" (La Roche, 2002) in the etiology of psychological distress experienced by Hispanic Americans. Although a similar construct may be identified as present in a different culture, the interest would be in how the perception of familism from a Hispanic-American perspective might lead to unique psychological experiences and repercussions. Other culture-specific experiences are presented in the following articles: African-American experiences (Fuertes, Mueller, Chauhan, Walker, & Ladany, 2002); Asian-American experiences (Kim, Yang, Atkinson, Wolfe, & Hong, 2001); and Arab-American experiences (Erickson & Al-Timimi, 2001).

The etic approach to the conduct of psychological research relies on common concepts, methods, and measures that may be applied uniformly to all cultures. Using the etic approach, a researcher would operationalize a construct of interest and then attempt to measure that construct in a standardized manner across different cultures. For example, familism would be conceptualized as those common family-related etiological factors that could be assessed in a consistent manner across Hispanic Americans, African Americans, Asian Americans, European Americans, and other cultural groups. The etic approach is well demonstrated by Wei, Russell, Mallinckrodt, and Zakalik's (2004) cross-cultural examination of attachment. Using the Experiences in Close Relationship Scale (Brennan, Clark, & Shaver, 1998) as a uniform measure of attachment, these researchers compared levels of attachment anxiety and attachment avoidance across African-American, Asian-American, Caucasian, and Hispanic-American college students. Data from the Experiences in Close Relationship Scale indicated that Hispanic-American students displayed greater attachment anxiety than Caucasian students, and that African-American and Asian-American students displayed greater attachment avoidance than their Caucasian peers. In their study of attachment styles, Wei and colleagues provide implicit endorsement of the etic approach to the cross-cultural study of attachment, viewing attachment as a universal phenomenon that can be measured similarly across cultural groups.

Like Wei and colleagues (2004), Robins and Regier's take an etic approach to the study of psychological disorders and their occurrence across cultural groups. In one of the most extensive epidemiological studies of psychological disorders occurring in the United States, Robins and Regier (1991) used the Diagnostic Interview Schedule (Robins, Helzer, Croughan, & Ratcliffe, 1981) to examine rates of anxiety disorders across these African Americans, Caucasians, and Hispanic Americans. Findings indicated higher rates of generalized anxiety disorder and phobias for African Americans and lower rates of generalized anxiety disorder for Hispanic Americans.

The effective application of these conceptual models to mental health care delivery requires that the two models be viewed as complementary, with the emic model suggesting those experiential factors that might be unique to a particular culture, and the etic model suggesting those experiences that may be considered common to the human experience. In the clinical context, the emic approach provides information about abnormal behavior and life experiences that is unique in terms of the historical and sociocultural background of the individual, while the etic approach allows for an appreciation of the shared aspects of human experiences that contribute to and maintain abnormal

behavior. An understanding of these two perspectives helps the therapist to more effectively assess and manage psychological distress in culturally diverse clients. Out of an appreciation for the etic approach and out of an awareness that manifestations of psychological distress remain essentially the same across the world (Draguns, 1997), culturally competent mental health care providers use established diagnostic criteria, base rate data, and clinical outcome data to determine the clinical problem that is to be addressed and the intervention strategies that are most effective for managing that clinical problem. When working with culturally diverse clients, the culturally competent mental health care provider appreciates that an emic approach to cultural influences is most relevant to establishing a workable therapeutic relationship and maximizing the provider's effectiveness as an agent of change in the therapeutic process. The emic model also lends itself well to the single-case research design, an analytic strategy necessary to the process of evaluating the effectiveness of a given therapeutic intervention employed by a given therapist to reduce the distress and improve the function of a given client.

STRATEGIES FOR INCREASING CULTURAL COMPETENCE IN MENTAL HEALTH CARE DELIVERY

Much of the credit for recognizing and valuing cultural competence in psychotherapy is accorded to Stanley Sue. In a seminal position paper, Sue (1998) indicated that the ingredients for culturally competent therapists include: (1) being scientifically minded; (2) having skills in "dynamic sizing;" and (3) acquiring knowledge about a cultural group. Scientifically minded therapists are individuals who apply the scientific method to the therapeutic process. Instead of making premature conclusions based on biases or assumptions about cultural factors, scientifically minded therapists form hypotheses, develop ways to test hypotheses, and try to provide services consistent with the obtained data. Of course, most mental health care providers are versed in the scientific method, but they sometimes forget to apply this methodology to the clinical context, especially when the clinical context is one characterized by limited cultural knowledge and by cultural bias that is either unacknowledged or outside of the awareness of the provider. Sue (1998) defines dynamic sizing as the ability to know when to generalize and be inclusive and when to individualize and be exclusive. Sue recognizes that therapists' perceptions of clients are influenced by stereotypes and these stereotypes can take away from specific characteristics in culturally diverse clients. Dynamic sizing helps the therapist to avoid applying stereotypes to members of a particular cultural group while appreciating the importance of the cultural group. Finally, Sue (1998) emphasizes the need for therapists to acquire knowledge that is relevant to the cultural group of interest. This includes seeking information from the literature, colleagues, community representatives (e.g., translators), and/or previous clients.

While Sue (1998) provides the ingredients for culturally competent mental health care delivery, Sue and colleagues (2007) provide a list of provider behaviors, termed microaggressions, which serve as barriers to effectively assessing and managing mental health problems experienced by culturally diverse clients. They define racial microaggressions as those "brief and commonplace daily verbal, behavioral, or environmental indignities, whether intentional or unintentional, that communicate hostile, derogatory, or negative racial slights and insults toward people of color" (p. 271). Microaggressions are said to occur in three forms: as microassaults, which are defined as "explicit racial derogation characterized primarily by a verbal or nonverbal attack meant to hurt the intended victim through name-calling, avoidant behavior, or purposeful discriminatory actions"; as microinsults, which are characterized by "communications that convey rudeness and insensitivity and demean a person's racial heritage or identity"; and as microinvalidations, which are characterized by "communications that exclude, negate, or nullify the psychological thoughts, feelings, or experiential reality of a person of color" (p. 274). Because these microaggressions are often engaged in without awareness, Sue points to

these microaggressions as the form of ethnic and racial discrimination that is most likely to occur in the context of health care delivery. The therapeutic importance of identifying microaggressions lies in the proposed influence of microaggressions on the health and well-being of persons from ethnically and racially diverse backgrounds and the proposed influence of such behaviors on health care utilization by ethnically and racially diverse persons and on the benefit derived from health care contacts. The unintentional use of such microaggressions by health care providers is thought to create impasses for culturally diverse patients and may partially explain well-documented patterns of therapy underutilization and premature termination of therapy among such patients (Burkard & Knox, 2004; Kearney, Draper, & Baron, 2005).

The mental health care provider's ability to appreciate and benefit from the cultural insights that are laid out in the Sue et al. (2007) article and in other articles that address cultural bias and aggression is a function of the following:

- The provider's ability to approach such information from an open rather than confrontational posture
- The provider's ability to appreciate these cultural insights as forwarded out of generosity rather than rancor
- The provider's ability to take a dualistic approach to the process of reconciling his or her experiences with those of the culturally diverse client

To benefit from such information, the mental health care provider who is a member of the dominant U.S. culture must hold as true the positive intention of the mental health care provider and the culturally diverse client's experience of cultural offense; the mental health care provider's embrace of cultural diversity and the culturally diverse client's experiences of bias and discrimination at the hands of members of the dominant culture; the mental health care provider's experience of cultural aggression and bias as "a thing of the past" and the culturally diverse client's experience of cultural aggression and bias as "what happened to me last night"; and the mental health care provider's experience of feed-back suggesting cultural naiveté, insensitivity, or bias as punishing, to be denied or rational-ized, and suggestive of a therapeutic failure and the culturally diverse client's view of such feed-back as an act of bravery and generosity and as suggestive of a strong therapeutic relationship.

THE PRACTICE OF CULTURALLY COMPETENT MENTAL HEALTH CARE

Everything being equal, obtaining a success-ful therapeutic outcome with culturally diverse clients is likely to be more of a challenge than when working with clients of a similar cul-tural background. It should be understood that therapists working with clients of diverse back-ground need to accept the burden of adjusting to new circumstances. Therapists should not be quick to blame either the client or the cul-ture if psychotherapy does not result in the desired outcome. Instead, modifying the ther-apeutic approach and adapting it to the specific needs of clients will result in a more positive therapeutic outcome and in an overall positive experience throughout the therapeutic process.

It should be understood that no health care provider, no matter how skilled, knows every-thing that there is to know about every cul-ture and cultural influence. However, there are a number of strategies that a skilled clinician can rely on to improve cultural competence practice with patients of culturally diverse back-grounds. Given that health care providers are genuinely invested in the provision of effective health care to all patients, health care providers are motivated to acquire cultural knowledge and skills that will ensure culturally compe-tent health care delivery. Sue (2006) identifies 10 steps that health care providers can take to better ensure effectiveness in treating cultur-ally diverse patients. In addition to steps that are designed to ensure provider self-awareness and the objective assessment of patients' pre-senting symptoms, Sue suggests that providers work to enhance their credibility by demonstrat-ing an understanding of and appreciation for the patient's culture; to understand the nature of their discomfort in dealing with culturally

diverse patients; to understand the patient's perspective; to explore culture-specific explana-tions for patient resistance without blaming the patient or the patient's culture; to engage in ongo-ing assessment of cultural sensitivity, treatment effectiveness, and patient and provider satisfac-tion with treatment outcomes; and to consult cultural experts when necessary.

There are no simple rules about when and how to address cultural differences in the con-text of health care provision. However, 10 clinical considerations in addressing cultural differences have been recommended by La Roche and Maxie. The 10 recommendations are summarized as follows:

1. Providers need to recognize that cultural differences are subjective, complex, and dynamic. The interpretation of cultural differences for patients usually are based on subjective appraisals. The complexity of these subjective appraisals of cultural differ-ences are also magnified by the perception of other variables including gender, age, sexual orientation, and educational level. The perception of these cultural differences by the patient and provider should be viewed as dynamic over the process of treatment rather than fixed over time.
2. The most obvious cultural differences between provider and patient should be addressed first whether it be a difference in race, age, gender, etc.
3. As part of providing a culturally safe ther-apeutic environment, cultural similarities should be addressed before addressing cultural differences.
4. It needs to be recognized that that discussion of cultural differences is easier to have with an emotionally stable and grounded patient. A very emotionally distressed and unstable patient is less likely to benefit from a dis-cussion of cultural differences. In fact, this kind of discussion can frustrate and upset a patient even more when what is being sought is a solution to an overwhelming problem or symptom complaint. Thus, the type and amount of psychological distress can dictate when to have a discussion on cultural differences.

5. Although patients of diverse cultural background have experienced their differences as deficits, cultural differences in patients should be viewed and conceptualized as strengths, which can help move the therapeutic process.

6. Providers need to incorporate the patient's cultural history and racial identity development when assessing and conceptualizing presenting problems and outlining treatment goals.

7. It should be recognized that meaning and saliency of cultural differences are also influenced by ongoing issues that are part of the therapeutic process. The provider must remain alert for concerns related to potential cultural differences when dealing with other issues that superficially might not appear to be related.

8. Providers also need to recognize that the therapeutic relationship is embedded in a broader cultural context (events that occur outside therapy like a potential first African-American president) and can influence the therapeutic process.

9. Without a doubt, cultural competence in the provider will have an impact on how cultural differences will be addressed in therapy. The more culturally competent a provider is, the more likely the discussion of cultural differences will be successful.

10. Successful dialogues about cultural differences between providers and patients will also have an effect on patients' cultural context—most likely a positive effect. In other words, discussions of cultural differences in therapy can empower patients in addressing issues related to cultural differences in the world context.

In addition to the clinical considerations forwarded by LaRoche and Maxie (2003), Cardemil and Battle (2003) have proposed a number of general recommendations for discussing race and ethnicity in the context of health care delivery. Cardemil and Battle encourage therapists to suspend conclusions about the racial and ethnic identity of clients and of clients' family members until confirmed by clients. Making assumptions about race and ethnicity without verification could lead to potential pitfalls in psychotherapy. For example, a client may prefer to be described as an African-American person rather than a black person. When in doubt about the importance of race and ethnicity in treatment, Cardemil and Battle encourage directly asking the client ("How would you describe your racial background?"). The authors encourage therapists to recognize that clients may be quite different from other members of their race and ethnic group. As noted by others (Roysircar, 2004; Sue, 1998), this reduces the likelihood of stereotyping clients. Therapists also need to consider how differences in race and ethnicity between therapist and client might affect psychotherapy. For example, cultural differences between a therapist and client could lead to differences in perception of physical space (e.g., distance between therapist and client) and verbal (e.g., directive versus nondirective statements) and nonverbal (e.g., smiling, hand shaking, or eye contact) behavior. Mismatches in perceptions can lead to awkwardness in the psychotherapeutic relationship. Finally, Cardemil and Battle recommend that Caucasian therapists acknowledge that power, privilege, and racism might affect the therapeutic relationship. Therapists have to recognize that being part of a majority culture has provided them greater power and privilege. This magnifies the power differential already inherent in the therapeutic relationship (i.e., client seeking help from therapist). Again, therapists are encouraged to openly and nondefensively discuss these issues as they come up in therapy or at least to look for opportunities to manage potential barriers to effective therapy.

THE PRACTICE OF CULTURALLY COMPETENT COGNITIVE BEHAVIOR THERAPY

Empirical research aimed at the identification of process variables that characterize culturally competent practice is woefully lacking as is empirical research examining the effectiveness of the many general practice recommendations that have been forwarded to better ensure culturally competent delivery of mental health services. The empirical literature related to the practice of culturally competent CBT is equally limited.

A number of publications aimed at addressing the use of CBT with culturally diverse populations are currently available, including, among others, books, chapters, and research articles that address the use of CBT to treat persons of diverse sexual orientation (Martell, Safren, & Prince, 2003) as well as persons who represent diversity of age, ability, ethnicity, race, and religion (Hays, 2001, 2008; Hays & Iwamasa, 2006; Hinton, Chhean, Pich, Safren, Hofmann, & Pollack, 2005; Lin, 2002).

In the second edition of *Addressing Cultural Complexities in Practice*, Hays (2008) identifies seven key components of culturally responsive cognitive behavior therapy (CR-CBT). The first component requires the therapist to define the client's presenting problem in terms of the "environmental" contributants (including social and cultural contributants) and "internal" or person-specific contributants (i.e., behaviors, cognitions, physiological responses) to the problem. The second component involves therapist validation of the oppressive aspects of the client's environment. The third component encourages the therapist's recognition of cultural influences on the client's affective–physiological, behavioral, and cognitive responses. The fourth component requires the therapist to "work collaboratively to choose goals and interventions that fit the client's cultural context and preferences" (p. 199). The remaining three components specify culturally sensitive strategies for implementing cognitive restructuring that include: an evaluation of the helpfulness of a client's beliefs rather than the rationality of such beliefs, the use of self-talk that references culture related personal strengths and support resources; and the use of homework assignments that are calibrated by the client and aimed at better ensuring successful change and ownership of change.

Although empirical research on culturally competent CBT is limited, CBT serves as an excellent vehicle for delivery of culturally competent mental health care. By its very nature, CBT requires an examination of all the environmental factors that are considered to contribute and maintain behavior. These causal environmental factors necessarily include the sociocultural influences that characterize the client's existence. CBT involves the idiographic application of change strategies, these change strategies selected based on a comprehensive formulation of the specific needs of a given client. The CBT approach to problem identification and treatment ensures that those sociocultural factors that are most relevant to the client are identified and the influence of such sociocultural factors on the process of therapy and on therapy goals and outcomes directly evaluated. Traditionally, models of case formulation that have come out of the behavioral paradigm emphasize direct questioning of all the person and environmental factors that may account for a given behavior. In this context, questioning the role of culture in clients' lives should be routine and should not depend on the presence of "obvious" cultural markers (e.g., age, gender, or race). Similarly, treatment that is out of the behavioral paradigm ensures that proven change strategies are applied to the clients' behaviors. Culturally competent CBT ensures that those proven strategies are applied with recognition of the contextual factors (e.g., ethnic identification, sexual orientation, or socioeconomic status) that are relevant for a given client. CBT is a treatment that is characterized by ongoing assessment of client behaviors, the therapeutic process, and treatment goals and outcomes. As such, CBT allows for the continued reevaluation of all the dynamic, interacting factors that influence mental health care delivery, including the array of cultural factors that are present in the therapist and the client (Daniel et al., 2004).

CONCLUSION

It is almost impossible to be involved in psychotherapy and not have some prominent cultural influence affecting the psychotherapeutic relationship. Even when the cultural backgrounds of clients and therapists are similar, there is still a need to recognize and deal with cultural influences. Becoming a skilled therapist requires an appreciation for the influence of cultural factors on both the client and the therapist, this active appreciation of cultural influences ultimately resulting in culturally competent psychotherapy. Increasing knowledge about cultural influences; increasing self-awareness about cultural biases, assumptions, and beliefs; and open communication about sensitive issues related to culture result in a more positive psychotherapy experience. CBT represents an ideal treatment vehicle for the culturally responsive application of theoretically grounded and empirically supported change strategies to client problems.

References

American Medical Association Council on Science and Public Health. (2008). Optimizing care for gay men and lesbians. Retrieved July 9, 2008, from www.ama-assn.org/ama/pub.

American Psychological Association. (1993). Guidelines for providers of psychological services to ethnic, linguistic, and culturally diverse populations. *American Psychologist, 48*, 45–48.

American Psychological Association. (1997). Commission on ethnic minority recruitment, retention and training in psychology (CEMRATT). Washington DC: Author.

American Psychological Association (2000). Guidelines for psychotherapy with lesbian, gay, and bisexual clients. *American Psychologist, 55*, 1440–1451.

American Psychological Association (2003a). Guidelines and multicultural education, training, research, practice, and organizational change for psychologists. *American Psychologist, 58*, 377–402.

American Psychological Association (2003b). Guidelines for psychological practice with older adults. *Guidelines for psychological practice with older adults*. Washington, DC: Author.

Atkinson, D. R., Morten, G., & Sue, D. W. (1993). *Counseling American minorities: A cross-cultural perspective*. Dubuque, IA: William C. Brown.

Baker, F. M., & Bell, C. C. (1999). Issues in the psychiatric treatment of African Americans. *Psychiatric Services, 50*(3), 362–368.

Betancourt, H., & Lopez, S. R. (1993). The study of culture, ethnicity, and race in American psychology. *American Psychologist, 48*, 629–637.

Brennan, K. A., Clark, C. L., & Shaver, P. R. (1998). Self-report measurement of adult attachment: An integrative overview. In J. A. Simpson & W. S. Rholes (Eds.), *Attachment theory and close relationships* (pp. 46–76). New York: Guilford.

Burkard, A. W., & Knox, S. (2004) Effect of therapist color-blindness on empathy and attributions in cross-cultural counseling. *Journal of Counseling Psychology, 51*, 387–397.

Cardemil, E. C., & Battle, C. L. (2003). Guess who's coming to therapy? Getting comfortable with conversations about race and ethnicity in psychotherapy. *Professional Psychology: Research and Practice, 34*, 278–286.

Chen, S., Sullivan, N. Y., Lu, Y. E., & Shibusawa, T. (2003). Asian Americans and mental health services: A study of utilization patterns in the 1990s. *Journal of Ethnic and Cultural Diversity in Social Work, 12*(2), 19–42.

Council of National Psychological Associations for the Advancement of Ethnic Minority Issues. (2000). *Guidelines for research in ethnic minority communities*. Washington, DC: American Psychological Association.

Council of National Psychological Associations for the Advancement of Ethnic Minority Interests. (2003). *Psychological treatment of ethnic minority populations*. Washington, DC: Association of Black Psychologists.

Daniel, J. H., Roysircar, G., & Abeles, N. (2004). Individual and cultural-diversity competency: Focus on the therapist. *Journal of Clinical Psychology, 60*, 755–770.

DeCoteau, T., Anderson, J., & Hope, D. (2006). Adapting manualized treatments: Treating anxiety disorders among Native Americans. *Cognitive and Behavioral Practice, 13*, 304–309.

Diamant, A. L., & Wold, C. (2003). Sexual orientation and variation in physical and mental health status among women. *Journal of Women's Health, 12*, 41–50.

Draguns, G. (1997). Abnormal behavior patterns across cultures: Implications for counseling and psychotherapy. *International Journal of Intercultural Relations, 21*, 213–248.

Duckworth, M. P. (2005). Behavioral health policy and eliminating disparities through cultural competency. In N. A. Cummings, W. T. O'Donohue, & M. A. Cucciare (Eds.), *Universal healthcare: Readings for mental health professionals*. Reno, NV: Context Press.

Duckworth, M. P., & Iezzi, T. (2005). Recognizing and dealing with cultural influences in psychotherapy. In W. T. O'Donohue (Ed.), *Clinical strategies for becoming a master psychotherapist*. Boston: Elsevier.

Duckworth, M. P., Iezzi, T., Vijay, A., & Gerber, E. (in press). Cultural competency in the primary care setting. In L. James & W. T. O'Donohue & (Eds.), *The primary care consultant toolkit: Tools for behavioral medicine*. New York: Springer.

Erickson, C. D., & Al-Timimi, N. R. (2001). Providing mental health services to Arab-Americans: Recommendations and considerations. *Cultural Diversity in Ethnic Minority Psychology, 7*, 308–327.

Fuertes, J. N., Mueller, L. N., Chauhan, R. V., Walker, J. A., & Ladany, N. (2002). An investigation of European American therapists' approach to counseling African-American clients. *The Counseling Psychologist, 30,* 763–788.

Hays, P. A. (1996). Addressing the complexities of culture and gender in counseling. *Journal of Counseling & Development, 74,* 332–338.

Hays, P. A. (2008). Addressing cultural complexities in practice: A framework for clinicians and counselors (2nd ed.). Washington, DC: American Psychological Association.

Hays, P. A., & Iwamasa, G. Y. (Eds.). (2006). *Culturally responsive cognitive–behavioral therapy: Assessment, practice, and supervision.* Washington, DC: American Psychological Association.

Hinton, D. E., Chhean, D., Pich, V., Safren, S. A., Hofmann, S. G., & Pollack, M. H. (2005). A randomized controlled trial of cognitive-behavior therapy for Cambodian refugees with treatment-resistant PTSD and panic attacks: A cross-over design. *Journal of Traumatic Stress, 18,* 617–629.

Kearney L. K., Draper, M., & Barón, A. (2005). Counseling utilization by ethnic minority college students. *Cultural Diversity and Ethnic Minority Psychology, 11,* 272–285.

Kessler, R. C., Nelson, C. B., McGonagle, K. A., Edlund, M. J., Frank, R. G., & Leaf, P. J. (1996). The epidemiology of co-occurring addictive and mental disorders: Implications for prevention and service utilization. *American Journal of Orthopsychiatry, 66,* 17–31.

Kim, M., Han, H.-R., & Kim, K. B. (2002). The use of traditional and Western medicine among the Korean-American elderly. *Journal of Community Health: The Publication for Health Promotion and Disease Prevention, 27*(2), 109–120.

Kim, B. S. K., Yang, P. H., Atkinson, D. R., Wolfe, M., & Hung, S. (2001). Cultural values similarities and differences among Asian-American ethnic groups. *Cultural Diversity in Ethnic Minority Psychology, 7,* 343–361.

Kramer, E. J., Kwong, K., Lee, E., & Chung, H. (2002). Culture and medicine: Cultural factors influencing the mental health of Asian Americans. *Western Journal of Medicine, 176,* 227–231.

La Roche, M. J. (2002). Psychotherapeutic considerations in treating Latinos. *Harvard Review in Psychiatry, 10,* 115–122.

La Roche, M. J., & Maxie, A. (2003). Ten considerations in addressing cultural differences in psychotherapy. *Professional Psychology: Research and Practice, 34,* 180–186.

Lin, Y., (2002). The application of cognitive–behavioral therapy to counseling Chinese. *American Journal of Psychotherapy, 55,* 46–58.

Lin, K.-M. & Cheung, F. (1999). Mental health issues for Asian Americans. *Psychiatric Services, 50*(6), 774–780.

Martell, C. R., Safren, S. A., & Prince, S. E. (2003). *Cognitive behavioral therapies with lesbian, gay, and bisexual clients.* New York: Guilford.

New Freedom Commission on Mental Health (2003). Achieving the promise: Transforming mental health care in America. Washington, DC: Author. Retrieved July 9, 2008, from www.mentalhealth commission.gov/reports/FinalReport/downloa ds/FinalReport.pdf.

Robins, L. N., Helzer, J. E., Croughan, J., & Ratcliffe, K. (1981). National Institutes of Mental Health Diagnostic Interview Schedule: Its history, characteristics, and validity. *Archives of General Psychiatry, 38,* 381–389.

Robins, L. N., & Regier, D. A. (1991). *Psychiatric disorders in America. The epidemiologic catchment area study.* New York: Free Press.

Roysircar, G. (2004). Cultural self-awareness assessment: Practice examples from psychology training. *Professional Psychology: Research and Practice, 35,* 658–666.

Snowden, L. R. (2001). Barriers to effective mental health services for African Americans. *Mental Health Services Research, 3*(4), 181–187.

Sodowsky, G. R., Taffe, R. C., Gutkin, T. B., & Wise, S. L. (1994). Development of the Multicultural Counseling Inventory: A self-report measure of multicultural competencies. *Journal of Counseling Psychology, 41,* 137–148.

Sue, S. (1998). In search of cultural competence in psychotherapy and counseling. *American Psychologist, 53,* 440–448.

Sue, S. (2006). Cultural competency: From philosophy to research and practice. *Journal of Community Psychology, 34,* 237–245.

Sue, D. W., Arredondo, P., & McDavis, R. J. (1992). Multicultural counseling competencies and standards: A call to the profession. *Journal of Counseling and Development, 70,* 477–486.

Sue, D. W., Capodilupo, C. M., Torino, G. C., Bucceri, J. M., Holder, A. M. B., Nadal, K. L., et al. (2007). Racial microaggressions in everyday life: Implications for clinical practice. *American Psychologist, 62,* 271–286.

Sue, S., Zane, N., & Young, K. (1994. Research on psychotherapy on culturally diverse populations. In A. Bergin & S. Garfield (Eds.), *Handbook of Psychotherapy and Behavior Change* (4th ed., pp. 783–817). New York: John Wiley & Sons.

U.S. Census Bureau. (2001). *2007 Population Estimates and Projections.* Washington, DC: Author. Retrieved September 9, 2008, from www.census.gov/ipc/www/usinterimproj/.

U.S. Census Bureau. (2006). American Community Survey (ACS). Washington, DC: Author. Retrieved July 9, 2008, from factfinder.census.gov.

U.S. Department of Health and Human Services. (2000). *Healthy people 2010: Understanding and improving health* (2nd ed.). Washington, DC: U.S. Government Printing Office. Retrieved July 9, 2008, from www.healthypeople.gov/Publications/.

U.S. Department of Health and Human Services. (2001). *Mental health: Culture, race, and ethnicity—a supplement to mental health: A report of the surgeon general.* Rockville, MD: U.S. Department of Health and Human Services, Substance Abuse and Mental Health Services Administration, Center for Mental Health Services.

Wei, N., Russell, D. W., Mallinckrodt, B., & Zakalik, R. A. (2004). Cultural equivalence of adult attachment across four ethnic groups: Factor structure, structured means, and associations with negative mood. *Journal of Counseling Psychology, 51,* 408–417.

5 NEW DIRECTIONS IN COGNITIVE BEHAVIOR THERAPY: ACCEPTANCE-BASED THERAPIES

Evan M. Forman and James D. Herbert

A new breed of cognitive behavior therapy (CBT), sometimes referred to as "acceptance-based" or "mindfulness-based" therapies, has gained increasing notoriety in recent years. The term *acceptance* refers to psychological acceptance of aversive internal experiences, that is, an openness to experiencing distressing thoughts, images, feelings and sensations without attempts to diminish or avoid them (Cordova, 2001; Hayes, Bissett et al., 1999). Hayes, the developer of one such therapy known as acceptance and commitment therapy (ACT; Hayes, Strosahl, & Wilson, 1999), has argued that these approaches are qualitatively distinct from other, more standard forms of CBT such that they form a new generation of therapies (Hayes, 2004b). A number of scholars associated with both acceptance-based therapies (e.g., Marsha Linehan and Adrienne Wells) and more traditional CBT (e.g., A T. Beck, Michelle Craske, Albert Ellis, Stefan Hofmann) disagree with Hayes's assessment (Arch & Craske, in press; Ellis, 2000, 2005; Hofmann & Asmundson, 2008; Linehan, personal communication, April 16, 2008), and view these new developments as, at most, natural evolutions of traditional CBT rather than something fundamentally new. The rise in profile of acceptance-based therapies, Hayes's conceptualization of these as representing a distinctively new epoch in CBT, and the considerable contention surrounding this assertion raise questions about how acceptance-based models of CBT are different from and similar to traditional CBT. Exploration of these questions, in turn, sheds light on important unresolved issues in the field and points toward needed research efforts.

HISTORY OF THE BEHAVIOR THERAPY MOVEMENT

The notion that acceptance-based approaches to CBT represent a new and distinct phenomenon is born from the view that the history of behavior therapy over the past half century can be divided into three semi-distinct eras (Hayes, 2004b). The first generation of behavior therapy, which crested in the late 1950s and into the 1960s, sought to take an empirical, objective, scientific approach to the understanding and treatment of psychological problems, and developed largely in reaction to the perceived shortcomings of psychoanalytic theory and therapy. The focus was on modifying problematic behavior, broadly defined to include not only overt motor behavior but cognitive and even affective responses, through classical (Wolpe, 1958) and operant (Skinner, 1953) learning principles. The late 1960s through the 1990s represented a second generation of behavior therapy, in which cognitive factors assumed greater importance in both theory and practice. Cognitions were viewed as playing a critical role in individuals' interpretation of, and thus emotional and behavioral responses to, environmental stimuli (Bandura, 1969). Several related psychotherapies combining cognitive and behavioral change strategies were developed, including rational emotive behavior therapy (Ellis, 1962) and cognitive therapy (A. T. Beck, Rush, Shaw, & Emery, 1979). These approaches hold that maladaptive thoughts, schemas, or information-processing styles are responsible for undesirable affect and behavior, and, through psychotherapy, can be modified or eliminated.

Acceptance-based models of CBT generally rose to prominence during and since the 1990s. These approaches span full-fledged models such as mindfulness-based stress reduction, mindfulness-based cognitive therapy (Segal, Williams, & Teasdale, 2002), dialectical behavior therapy (Linehan, 1993), metacognitive therapy (Wells, 2007), and ACT (Hayes, Strosahl et al., 1999); specific applications such as acceptance-based behavior therapy for generalized anxiety disorder (GAD) (Roemer & Orsillo, 2005) and distress tolerance training for smoking cessation (Brown, Lejuez, Kahler, Strong, & Zvolensky, 2005; Brown et al., 2008); and acceptance-influenced modifications of traditional cognitive and behavioral therapies such as behavioral activation (Jacobson, Martell, & Dimidjian, 2001) and panic control treatment (Levitt & Karekla, 2005). Hayes and others (Eifert & Forsyth, 2005; Hayes, 2004b) have argued that these approaches represent a third generation of CBTs because they share a number of features that distinguish them from earlier behavioral therapies. Perhaps the most noteworthy is a shift from the assumption that distressing symptoms, including unwanted thoughts and feelings, must be changed in content or frequency in order to increase overall psychological well-being. Whereas CBT has traditionally focused on reducing or eliminating unwanted symptoms, acceptance-based approaches focus less on symptom reduction per se and more on promoting behavior change and increasing overall quality of life. Instead of attempting to alter the content or frequency of cognitions, ACT, for example, seeks to alter the individual's *psychological relationship* with his or her thoughts, feelings, and sensations (Hayes, Jacobson, Follette, & Dougher, 1994).

COGNITIVE BEHAVIOR THERAPIES

As noted earlier, in terms of its widespread applicability, acceleration of use and training, empirical support, and acceptance by the scientist–practitioner community, CBT has emerged as the predominant model of psychotherapy in North America (Prochaska & Norcross, 1994). Hundreds of controlled clinical trials of the larger family of CBT have been undertaken in recent years (Dobson, 2001; Hollon & Beck, 1994), and a recent review of meta-analyses found multistudy support for the effectiveness of CBT to treat a plethora of psychological conditions, including unipolar and bipolar depression, panic disorder, obsessive–compulsive disorder (OCD), social anxiety disorder, GAD, schizophrenia-linked psychotic symptoms, and bulimia nervosa (Butler, Chapman, Forman, & Beck, 2006). Furthermore, most treatments on lists of empirically supported therapies for specific disorders (Chambless & Hollon, 1998) are CBT in nature. Additionally, CBT is quickly becoming the majority orientation among clinical psychologists, particularly faculty in scientist–practitioner programs (Norcross, Karpiak, & Santoro, 2005; Norcross, Sayette, Mayne, Karg, & Turkson, 1998). Moreover, all residency training programs in psychiatry now offer specific training in CBT (Accreditation Council for Graduate Medical Education, 2004).

CBT, broadly writ, can be described as an active, collaborative, current problem–oriented and relatively short-term treatment that takes its name from the use of both cognitive and behavioral strategies to alleviate distress and reduce clinical symptomatology. It is based on the notion that affect and behavior (and thus psychopathology) are largely determined by in-the-moment cognitive phenomena (e.g., thoughts, images, interpretations, attributions), which, in turn, are influenced by historically developed core beliefs or cognitive schemas (Dobson & Shaw, 1995). Although CBT incorporates some traditional behavioral principles and technologies, what distinguishes it from the larger family of behavioral therapies is the emphasis on cognitive factors as presumed mediators of change, as well as the focus on direct attempts to modify cognitive processes (A. T. Beck, 1993).

A wide array of therapeutic approaches can be considered to fit within the realm of "standard" CBTs. These include models such as rational emotive behavior therapy (Ellis, 1962), stress inoculation training (Meichenbaum & Deffenbacher, 1988) and cognitive therapy (A. T. Beck, 1976). Beck's cognitive therapy

(CT) is the most widely known and practiced model of CBT. The central feature of CT is that problems are conceptualized within a framework of dysfunctional belief systems, and intervention efforts target these beliefs for modification. There are also a number of CBT programs that have been developed for specific psychological problems, including panic control treatment (Barlow, Craske, & Meadows, 2000), exposure with response prevention (Foa & Goldstein, 1978), cognitive processing therapy (Resick & Schnicke, 1993), prolonged exposure (Foa, Hembree, & Rothbaum, 2007), schema therapy (Young & Klosko, 2005), and prevention and relationship enhancement program (Stanley, Blumberg, & Markman, 1999), among others. All of these approaches share an emphasis on identifying and correcting problematic cognitions and behaviors through cognitive change strategies and learning-based behavioral interventions.

ACCEPTANCE-BASED THERAPIES

Mindfulness-Based Stress Reduction

A number of acceptance-based therapies have emerged and taken root in recent years. The development has been spurred, variously, by a recognition that the traditional CBT approaches were not effective with certain types of problems, a skepticism for some of the theoretical underpinnings of CBT, new metacognitive theoretical frameworks, and/or an appreciation of ancient Eastern religious and philosophical practices. One of the acceptance-based approaches to be developed was mindfulness-based stress reduction (MBSR; Kabat-Zinn et al., 1992). MBSR was developed by Jon Kabat-Zinn as a treatment for chronic pain and stress-related medical conditions (Kabat-Zinn, 1982). MBSR emphasizes that all individuals continuously experience a stream of internal experiences and that our reactivity and stress related to these experiences will be markedly decreased through the practice of mindfulness. Mindfulness is a state of moment-by-moment awareness of one's internal experiences that is a skill that will be gradually acquired through training. MBSR involves a variety of exercises to train people to increase mindfulness, including an exercise involving eating a raisin with full attention of moment-by-moment sensory experience, a body scan with systematic attention to sensations coming from each part of the body, and mindfulness while engaging in everyday tasks. MBSR has been used, to good effect, to treat anxiety disorders and medical conditions linked to anxiety, including chronic pain, cancer, and heart disease (Brantley, 2005; Kabat-Zinn, 1982, 2005; Kabat-Zinn et al., 1992).

Mindfulness-Based Cognitive Therapy

Zindel Segal, J. Mark Williams, and John Teasdale created mindfulness-based cognitive therapy (MCBT) in large part by adapting MBSR to serve the purpose of preventing relapse in those who had had previous episodes of major depression (Segal et al., 2002). A central aim of MBCT is to enhance awareness of the present moment such that it is possible to mindfully experience thoughts and feelings without judgment. A premise is that underlying beliefs that make one vulnerable to relapse in depression are neither directly accessible to conscious introspection nor directly modifiable through direct cognitive restructuring techniques such as logical analysis or disputation (Teasdale et al., 2001). Thus, unlike traditional CBT, patients are not instructed to attempt to modify dysfunctional cognitions or emotional reactions; instead, they are taught how to become aware of their internal experiences such that they will not be drawn into automatic reactions such as ruminative spirals.

Dialectical Behavior Therapy

Marsha Linehan developed dialectical behavior therapy (DBT) out of her frustration with the failure of standard CBT protocols for chronically suicidal patients (Linehan & Dimeff, 2001). DBT integrates standard CBT with eastern mindfulness practices. The term *dialectic* is meant to convey, among other things, a tension between the therapist's need to provide validation of the patient's extraordinarily painful internal experience, and also to facilitate changes in attitude and behavior (Linehan, 1993). Therapists encourage the change agenda through psychoeducation, skills training, exposure strategies, direct confrontation, and implicit and explicit contingency management. DBT also teaches core mindfulness skills, including those related to paying attention to the present moment and assuming a nonjudgmental stance. The program is typically delivered across both individual and group modalities.

Metacognitive Therapy

Adrienne Wells developed the self-regulatory executive function theory, which proposes that psychological disorders are linked to the activation of a dysfunctional pattern of cognition called cognitive attentional syndrome (CAS; Wells & Matthews, 1996). This pattern of thinking is characterized by inflexible self-focused attention and perseverative ruminative thinking styles. Beliefs tend to center around metacognitive notions about the usefulness of certain worry-based thinking styles such as "paying attention to every danger will avoid harm." Metacognitive therapy (MT) was developed as a way to counter the CAS and has been applied to GAD, posttraumatic stress disorder (PTSD), OCD, and social anxiety disorder (Fisher & Wells, 2008; Wells, 2005a, 2007; Wells & King, 2006; Wells & Sembi, 2004). Rather than attempting to modify cognitions related to the content of anxious thoughts (which Wells contends are not amenable to conscious cognitive change efforts), MT helps patients to appreciate and modify their higher-level beliefs about the utility and necessity of worrying and other anxious thinking. In addition, the therapy teaches "detached mindfulness," which includes the development of meta-awareness (consciousness of one's thoughts) and cognitive "decentering" (realization that thoughts are mental events and not facts).

Acceptance and Commitment Therapy

Like other third-generation behavior therapies, ACT evolved in part from traditional CBT. In fact, its earliest incarnation was called "comprehensive distancing" because it elaborated and expanded on Beck's notion that patients should be taught to "distance" themselves from their cognitions early in the process of CT (Zettle, 2005b; Zettle & Rains, 1989). Over time, a central unifying goal of ACT was developed and termed *psychological flexibility*, referring to one's ability to choose one's actions from a range of options in order to behave more consistently with personally held values and aspirations rather than having one's behavior constrained by the avoidance of distressing "private events" (thoughts, feelings, sensations, memories, urges, etc.).

ACT makes use of a number of therapeutic strategies—many borrowed and developed from earlier approaches—to promote psychological flexibility. First, the therapy aims to increase psychological acceptance of subjective experiences (e.g., thoughts and feelings) and to decrease unhelpful experiential avoidance. The patient is taught that attempts to control unwanted experiences (e.g., social anxiety, panic sensations, traumatic memories, obsessive thoughts) are likely to be ineffective or even counterproductive, and that these aversive experiences should be accepted fully (without internal or external attempts to eliminate them). Second, ACT works to increase psychological awareness of the present moment, including both external and internal events as they unfold in real time. Third, the treatment teaches patients to "defuse" from subjective experiences, particularly thoughts. Cognitive defusion refers to the ability to step back from or distance oneself from one's thoughts in a manner enabling one to behave independently of the thoughts. These first three aspects of ACT are, in part, borrowed from and implemented through the practice of mindfulness. Fourth, ACT works to decrease excessive focus on and attachment to the "conceptualized self," or personal narrative (e.g., a rape survivor's self-identification as a victim). Fifth, the therapy utilizes "values clarification" to help the patient identify and crystallize key personal values and to translate these values into specific behavioral goals. Finally, ACT promotes the concept of "committed action" to increase action towards goals and values in the context of experiential acceptance.

According to its founders, ACT therapeutic processes emerge from a comprehensive behavioral theory of human language and cognition known as relational frame theory (RFT; Hayes, Barnes-Holmes, & Roche, 2001). RFT argues that human language and cognition, and by extension most psychopathology, is dependent on the human ability to arbitrarily relate events, that these relationships are made up of cognitive networks that can be elaborated but not extinguished, and that direct attempts to change such networks only lead to further elaboration of the network while increasing its functional importance (Hayes, 2004a).

Among the new generation of behavior therapies, ACT in particular has shown signs of rapid growth in the fields of psychotherapy theory and practice. For instance, as of mid-2008, 220 articles and chapters were listed in *PsychLit* with "acceptance and commitment therapy" as a keyword. Moreover, over 20 self-help and clinician–oriented ACT books have been published; one of these, *Get Out of Your Mind and Into Your Life* (Hayes & Smith, 2005), spent time on the *New York Times* and *Amazon.com* bestseller lists. Additionally, there have been several dozen paper presentations, posters, workshops, and panel discussions related to ACT presented at each of the most recent meetings of the Association of Behavioral and Cognitive Therapies (ABCT), more than any other specific therapy. The popularity of the approach does not, of course, necessarily imply that it is effective or that its model is fundamentally correct.

SPECIFIC APPLICATIONS OF ACCEPTANCE-BASED APPROACHES

Several examples exist of applying acceptance-based approaches to the treatment of specific psychological problems. For instance, Brown and colleagues (Brown et al., 2005; Brown et al., 2008) have developed a distress tolerance approach to smoking cessation. In this approach, smokers are helped to enhance their ability to tolerate unpleasant sensations, feelings, and thoughts related to urges to smoke. In addition, several widely used variants of behavior activation for depression can be considered to be acceptance-based approaches as they stress acceptance, rather than change, strategies in relation to internal experiences in the service of behavioral goals (Jacobson et al., 2001; Martell, Addis, & Dimidjian, 2004). Orsillo and Roemer (Roemer & Orsillo, 2007; Roemer, Salters-Pedneault, & Orsillo, 2006)

have combined the approaches of Hayes, Borkovec, and others into an acceptance-based CBT program for GAD. Acceptance-based approaches have also been developed for social anxiety disorder (Dalrymple & Herbert, 2007; Herbert & Cardaciotto, 2005), panic (Levitt & Karekla, 2005), binge eating (Kristeller, Baer, & Quillian-Wolever, 2006), and weight loss (Forman, Butryn, Hoffman, & Herbert, under review). Integrative behavior couples therapy is an acceptance-based approach to couple discord that has shown promising results (Jacobson, Christensen, Prince, Cordova, & Eldridge, 2000).

As described above, there has been a sharp increase over the past decade in acceptance-based applications of CBT. As such, psychological acceptance–linked constructs and techniques are being increasingly incorporated into treatment protocols and descriptions. Whether this trend represents a simple evolution in clinical strategies or a fundamentally new "wave" of CBT continues to be hotly debated (Arch & Craske, in press; Hayes, 2004b, in press; Hofmann & Asmundson, 2008).

COMPARISON OF TWO REPRESENTATIVE APPROACHES

Choice of Specific Approaches to Compare

As is clear from the preceding discussion, there exist a large number of both "standard" CBTs and acceptance-based models of CBTs, and these models themselves differ from one another. As such, comparing the two approaches holistically becomes difficult and not especially informative. A more useful strategy for comparing the two approaches is to pick a representative of each that can serve as a prototype for the sake of comparison. We propose that Beck's cognitive therapy (Beck, 2005) and Hayes and colleagues' acceptance and commitment therapy (Hayes et al., 1999) represent the most prototypical examples of their respective approaches. In addition, these treatments arguably have the best-developed theoretical models, most articulated clinical descriptions, deepest databases of empirical research, and the largest followings among both researchers and practitioners. Moreover, the developers of ACT have stressed its distinctiveness from CT on theoretical, technological, and empirical grounds (Hayes, in press; Hayes, Masuda, & De Mey, 2003). As mentioned, ACT evolved in part directly from CT (Zettle, 2005b). Nevertheless, ACT and CT may differ on key theoretical and technological grounds.

We are fully aware that no model is completely representative of the larger class, and there are ways that both CT and ACT differ from other treatments in their categories. For instance, CT places more emphasis on cognitive change strategies *relative* to behavioral ones compared to some of the other standard CBT approaches, and conversely ACT is a more behaviorally oriented treatment than some other acceptance-based approaches. Also, ACT holds a more purist view that, as a general (but not absolute) rule, direct attempts to modify cognitions are unhelpful, whereas other acceptance-based strategies such as metacognitive therapy and dialectical behavior therapy do incorporate cognitive modification strategies. Similarly, ACT consistently frames the goals of treatment without specifically focusing on symptom reduction, but this is not the case with all other acceptance-based approaches. In a related vein, compared to other acceptance-based treatments, ACT has much greater emphasis on the clarification of, and motivating forces behind, life values. Nevertheless, we believe that CT and ACT share a large number of features with their respective broader approaches to therapy, and certainly enough to justify a comparison of their theoretical models, treatment approaches, and strategies. It is important to clarify that our goal is not to provide a definitive conclusion to the global questions of whether ACT is genuinely distinct from CT or whether acceptance-based approaches represent a new generation of behavior therapies. Rather, by comparing and contrasting the two approaches, we hope to elucidate how the models relate to one another and how they reflect larger issues in the field. Moreover, we also hope that this comparison will point to fruitful research directions.

Basis of Comparison

Our review is based on a sample of representative and descriptive books, chapters, and journal articles describing CT (e.g., Beck, 1976; Beck, Emery, & Greenberg, 1985; Beck, Freeman, & Davis, 2004; Beck et al., 1979; J. S. Beck, 1995, 2005; Dobson, 2001; Dobson & Shaw, 1995; Hollon, Haman, & Brown, 2002; Leahy, 2003a, 2003b; Ledley, Marx, & Heimberg, 2005) and ACT (e.g., Dahl, Wilson, Luciano Soriano, & Hayes, 2005; Dahl, Wilson, & Nilsson, 2004; Eifert & Forsyth, 2005; Gifford et al., 2004; Hayes, 2004a, 2004b; Hayes, Luoma, Bond, Masuda, & Lillis, 2006; Hayes, Strosahl et al., 1999; Hayes & Strosahl, 2005; Herbert & Cardaciotto, 2005; McCracken, Vowles, & Eccleston, 2005; Wilson & Murrell, 2004). The descriptions of the two approaches are based on an integration of these various sources. Thus, specific citations are not provided for every point of comparison between the two approaches. Additionally, given space limitations, our treatment of each approach will necessarily be incomplete.

Comparison of Models

At its most basic level, a psychotherapy model specifies a theory of etiology (i.e., an explanation of how problem behaviors and psychopathology develop and are maintained), intervention technologies (the therapeutic strategies designed to effect change), mechanisms of action (an account of how interventions produce change), and optimal health/functioning (the end goal of the intervention). Each of these model components is considered later in this chapter. In addition, a simplified depiction of the two models is presented in Figure 5.1. The figure depicts the CT view of psychopathology (faulty information processing) as guiding intervention (cognitive restructuring), which enables changes (in cognition) that result in health (symptom reduction). In contrast, the ACT theory of psychopathology (psychological inflexibility) inspires the interventions (e.g., defusion, psychological acceptance) that purportedly work through specific mechanisms (acceptance of and defusion from internal experiences, decreased experiential avoidance) to enable health (living a valued life).

Etiology

Both ACT and CT are members of the larger family of behavior therapies, and thus share

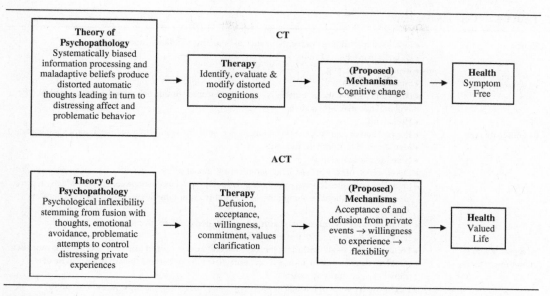

FIGURE 5.1   Simplified Models of Cognitive Therapy (CT) and Acceptance and Commitment (ACT).

several core principles of behavior theory. For instance, both acknowledge the major role played by operant and classical conditioning in learning and strengthening affective and behavioral response tendencies (Beck et al., 1979; Beck, 1995; Hayes, 2004b). Both models would view learning as a core explanation for why someone with battlefield trauma develops intense anxiety and avoidance of situations in which loud sounds are present. Furthermore, both models would view brief exposure to a feared stimulus followed by immediate escape as negatively reinforcing. In the case of CT, emphasis is placed on the role of cognitions in mediating the impact of specific situations. More generally, CT views psychopathology as a result of systematically biased information processing, characterized by maladaptive beliefs and automatic thoughts (J. S. Beck, 1995, 2005; Clark, Beck, & Brown, 1989; Ledley et al., 2005). Thus, the battlefield trauma patient would be theorized to have specific anxiety- and avoidance-provoking cognitions such as "I am not safe" that produce fear and avoidance in relevant situations. ACT, in contrast, views psychopathology as resulting from psychological inflexibility stemming from "fusion" with (overconnection to and literal

belief in) thoughts (such as "I am not safe") and other internal experiences; problematic attempts to control, explain, or even dispute such private events rather than merely experiencing them; emotional avoidance (e.g., attempts to avoid the feeling of anxiety); a lack of clarity about one's core values (e.g., being a good father); and the resulting inability to behave in accordance with those values.

Core Interventions

Core CT strategies include the identification of basic beliefs and associated automatic thoughts, and the restructuring of problematic cognitions so that they are more adaptive and accurate (Beck, 1995; Ledley et al., 2005). Given the popularity and widespread dissemination of cognitive restructuring, the reader is assumed to be familiar with these techniques and we will therefore not pursue them in detail (Table 5.1). For its part, ACT makes use of a number of therapeutic strategies—many borrowed and elaborated from earlier approaches—to promote *psychological flexibility*, which is defined as the ability to select behavior that, in one's current context, will enable movement towards chosen life values (Eifert & Forsyth, 2005; Hayes, Strosahl et al., 1999; Hayes & Strosahl, 2005).

TABLE 5.1   Core Interventions

Shared	• Relationship-building interventions such as empathy, validation, and reflections • Didactic instruction of skills • Experiential learning • Summary statements • Behavioral interventions, especially exposure to feared stimuli, behavioral activation, problem solving, role playing, modeling • Homework
Cognitive therapy	• Presentation of cognitive model (situation → cognitions → affective and behavioral consequences) • Identification of automatic thoughts • Labeling thought errors • Identification of core beliefs, schemas and attributional styles • Cognitive conceptualization recognizing that early experiences shape core beliefs which, in turn, determine conditional assumptions, beliefs and rules, automatic thoughts, and compensatory strategies • Modification of dysfunctional cognitions; generation of alternative responses • Behavioral experiments to test thoughts/beliefs
Acceptance and commitment therapy	• Presentation of model including the idea that attempts to control internal experiences is more of a problem than a solution; induce a necessary state of hopelessness toward doing "more of the same" (i.e., attempts to control). • Increase acceptance of internal experiences (thoughts, feelings, images, sensations, urges) • Increase awareness of present moment experiences • Increase *defusion*, that is, ability to step back from thoughts and other internal experiences in a way that allows seeing them as "just thoughts" that aren't necessarily true • Decrease attachment to *conceptualized self* (i.e., one's personal narrative) • Clarification of core life values • Increased commitment toward values-consistent behavior and a willingness to have difficult internal experiences for the sake of moving toward life values

First, the therapy aims to increase acceptance of distressing subjective experiences (e.g., negative thoughts and feelings) and to decrease unhelpful experiential avoidance. The patient is helped to carefully examine her past attempts to control unwanted experiences and to use her experience to come to a shared view with the therapist that these control attempts have always been, and are likely to continue to be, ineffective or even counterproductive. Thus, a patient with social anxiety would be asked to reflect on the extent to which strategies to reduce or control internal experiences (e.g., thoughts about and fear of negative evaluation, anxiety, blushing) have been successful. This learning exercise is consistent with ACT's emphasis on drawing conclusions on the basis of one's own experiences rather than what other people say or a set of rules. Consistent with ACT's emphasis on experiential learning, the patient would also be asked to attempt, during the session, to prevent herself from having any

thoughts/images/memories of a particular subject (e.g., chocolate cake) for the next 60 seconds. Through this exercise the patient comes to appreciate that we have limited control over internal experiences and, paradoxically, that this is especially true when we are highly motivated to control these experiences. Furthermore, the lack of control over our experiences is less of a problem than our ineffective, resource-wasting, and suffering-inducing attempts to exert control. Helping the patient come to the position that experiential control attempts have not and likely never will result in successful living is sometimes referred to as *creative hopelessness*. ACT relies heavily on metaphors to convey its ideas. For example, a quicksand metaphor is used to communicate the idea that struggles to control internal experiences are usually doomed to fail and only make the problem worse. Someone who has fallen in quicksand and struggles to get out will only sink deeper and deeper into the quicksand, whereas laying back and making full contact with the quicksand, although counterintuitive, enables one to gently slide across the surface to its edge. The purpose of these related sets of teachings is to jolt the patient out of her assumptions about the nature of her problems and how best to address them, and to help her open up to a new way of addressing her problems.

As an alternative to a control orientation, patients are presented with the construct of psychological *acceptance*, which, as described above, refers to the idea that distressing internal experiences can be accepted fully and without defense (Hayes, Strosahl et al., 1999). The idea is to help patients fully embrace all thoughts, no matter how distasteful, all feelings, no matter how painful, and so on. The goal becomes not to feel "better" in the usual sense, but rather to experience the full range of one's thoughts and feelings without struggle. As discussed below, acceptance, or *willingness*, as it is also termed, is not viewed as an end in itself, but as the best means to an end, in the sense that one is willing to have difficult internal experiences in the service of living a valued life. Thus, a patient with social anxiety is helped to become more willing to have subjective feelings of anxiety (including thoughts about humiliation, worry, sweaty palms, and flushed face) in the service of forming social relationships, having a fulfilling job, earning a living, and becoming more autonomous (Herbert & Cardaciotto, 2005).

Acceptance also implies, in part, the need for a sharpened sense of awareness of the present moment, including of both external and internal events, as they unfold in real time. Together, awareness and acceptance are promoted through exercises such as mindful meditation. For instance, patients are trained in an exercise in which they imagine that each of their thoughts, feelings, and sensations are leaves floating down a stream (Hayes, Strosahl et al., 1999). Patients practice becoming aware of each of these experiences, while also accepting each "leaf" no matter whether it is beautiful or ugly and no matter whether it lingers or rushes by quickly; no efforts are made to speed certain leaves along or slow others down.

A critical component of ACT is helping patient to *defuse* from subjective experiences, particularly problematic thoughts (Hayes, 2004a; Wilson & Roberts, 2002). *Cognitive defusion* thus refers to the ability to step back from or distance oneself from one's thoughts in a manner that enables patients to see that their thoughts are "just thoughts" that need not be believed nor disbelieved. Cognitive defusion, when implemented with a perspective of nonjudgmental acceptance, permits one to behave independently of distressing thoughts and feelings. A patient who sees his thought, "she won't want to talk to me; she thinks I'm a loser," as merely a collection of words supplied by his anxious brain is less likely to buy into this thought and more likely to be able to approach another person and initiate a conversation, even while simultaneously having the thought. This process is similar to the notion of challenging the believability of the thought in CT. However, unlike CT, ACT makes no effort to *change* the thought itself or to replace it with some other thought. The metaphor of colored sunglasses is used to help patients understand the concept of defusion. Wearing yellow sunglasses means that the world is experienced as yellow but without a conscious awareness of this fact. In contrast, holding the sunglasses away from the face reveals the process through which the world is being yellowed. A number of ACT exercises exist to help patients learn to defuse from distressing experiences, such as encouraging description of thoughts and feelings in real time and in language that emphasizes the fact that the patient is a person having thoughts and feelings as opposed to simply being immersed in/fused with the experience (e.g., "right now I am having the thought 'she is laughing at me' ").

ACT also works to decrease excessive focus on and attachment to the *conceptualized self*. The conceptualized self is the verbally based narrative that we form about ourselves, including what we are, who we are, and how we came to be that way (Hayes, 2004a; Hayes & Gregg, 2001; Strosahl, 2005). From the perspective of ACT, such stories are viewed as limiting and self-fulfilling. For instance, a story such as "I was treated very badly by other children when I was little, and so now I can't deal well with people" is likely to lead to behavior that is isolating, further strengthening attachment to beliefs of social incompetence.

ACT utilizes *values clarification* to help the patient identify and crystallize key personal values and to translate these values into specific behavioral goals (Hayes, Strosahl et al., 1999; Wilson & Murrell, 2004). Goals are seen as attainable mileposts (e.g., applying for a job), whereas values are directional aspirations (having a fulfilling career). Finally, ACT promotes the concept of "committed action" to increase action towards goal and values in the context of experiential acceptance.

Relationship of ACT/CT Theory with Lay Theory/Folk Culture

A cornerstone of CT is the "cognitive model," which essentially posits that one's cognitive appraisal in a given situation leads directly to affective and behavioral responses (Beck et al., 1979). In this sense, CT theory builds on Western society's generally accepted sequential model of how situations lead to thoughts, and how thoughts, in turn, produce feelings and behavior. CT also implicitly supports the folk culture view that affect itself directly influences behavior (J. S. Beck, 1995, 2005). The notion that behavior is determined by cognition and affect is reflected in CT's emphasis on decreasing problematic thoughts and emotions (e.g., anxiety) in order to reduce problematic behavior (e.g., avoidance; Beck, 1993).

ACT, however, directly challenges the culturally sanctioned view on the relationship between private experiences and overt behavior. Although it views behavior as influenced by cognition and affect, ACT theory emphasizes the possibility of independence between overt behavior on the one hand, and thoughts, feelings, and the like, on the other (Hayes, Strosahl, Bunting, Twohig, & Wilson, 2005). Thus, cognitive or affective change is viewed as unnecessary for behavioral change. ACT, therefore, makes no direct attempt to modify the content or frequency of thoughts or feelings. Where ACT and CT come together is that both posit that verbally mediated cognitive processes play a critical role in the development and maintenance of psychological problems. In the case of ACT, the emphasis is on the problematic role of language in enabling "cognitive fusion" with thoughts and feelings, whereas in CT

it is on the negatively directed cognitive biases generating maladaptive and distorted self-talk.

Comparison of Therapeutic Goals

Specification of Goals

Both CT and ACT are goal-oriented therapies that aim to articulate, actively pursue, and measure progress toward specific goals (Table 5.2). In the case of CT, goals, though individualized, generally stem directly from presenting problems (J. S. Beck, 1995). Presenting complaints often take the form of the experience of distressing affect (anxiety, depression, anger), and stated goals largely focus on the converse (reductions in the frequency and/or intensity of this affect). In contrast, ACT is skeptical of the value of directly targeting symptom reduction per se, and instead places a heavy emphasis on helping individuals discover and clarify their core life values. Goals then become mileposts in the lifelong effort to live consistently with one's values. In this way, there is often less relationship between a patient's initial presenting complaints and therapeutically established goals than is the case in CT. Thus, ACT and CT are at odds with respect to the degree to which they explicitly focus on the reduction of unwanted symptoms. An overt goal of CT is the reduction of unwanted thoughts and negative affect, such as depression and anxiety, and treatment success is in large part determined by the degree to which thought and mood changes occur. In contrast, a fundamental ACT principle is that the very desire to do away with distressing feelings or thoughts is often itself problematic and, furthermore, that it is possible to engage in desired behaviors even while having highly unpleasant subjective experiences (Eifert & Forsyth, 2005; Hayes, 2004b; Hayes et al., 2006; Zettle, 2005a). Therapy, therefore, aims to replace the goal of symptom reduction with one of "living a valued life," which is defined as making one's behavior maximally consistent with one's chosen values. It is worth noting that although ACT and CT do differ in this regard, the difference is really one of degree of emphasis. For example, many CT therapists help their patients identify important personal values

TABLE 5.2   A Comparison of ACT and CT Therapeutic Goals

Issue	Shared	ACT	CT
Specification of goals	Both emphasize clear articulation of goals	Goals are derived from values, which are highly individualistic and not always obvious from presenting symptoms. Hence, values clarification is emphasized.	Goals are logically related to presenting symptoms (e.g., reduction of anxiety, depression), and are individualized based on the patient's specific circumstances.
Symptom reduction	Both allow for symptom reduction when it can be achieved without undue costs	Symptom reduction per se is not an explicit aim; sometimes reduction of symptoms is possible, but often it is not. Instead the goal is to live a valued life.	Symptom reduction is an explicit aim.
Quality of life	Both target improvements in quality of life, which will include success in major life domains	Quality of life is a product of the degree to which someone is living a life consistent with his/her values.	Freedom from bothersome thoughts, feelings, and other symptoms is an important component of quality of life.

and associated goals, and to accept especially intransient thoughts. In the case of ACT, the concern with experiential control is pragmatic rather than philosophical or absolute. ACT's pragmatic focus allows, even advocates, methods of reducing unwanted internal experiences (e.g., exercising, taking medication, progressive muscle relaxation) when they are effective and do not pose undue costs. Nevertheless, the ACT therapist is skeptical of the long-term viability of most direct experiential change efforts, and therefore emphasizes psychological acceptance in the context of behavior change, rather than cognitive change as a necessary precursor to behavioral change.

Quality of Life

Both ACT and CT target quality of life, at least indirectly. However, the two approaches vary in their conceptualization of this construct. ACT views quality of life as primarily reflecting the degree to which someone lives a life consistent with his or her values (Eifert & Forsyth, 2005; Hayes, Follette, & Linehan, 2004; Hayes & Smith, 2005). CT, however, is more likely to conceptualize quality of life as freedom from bothersome thoughts, feelings, and other symptoms (DeRubeis et al., 1990). Yet, CT does recognize that quality of life is tied to success at important life domains (Dobson, 2001).

Comparison of Clinical Strategies

In order to examine further the key similarities and differences between ACT and CT, we now turn to several aspects of the strategies employed by each model. A summary of this discussion is presented in Table 5.3.

Emphasis on the Past versus the Current/Future

Whereas traditional psychodynamic perspectives emphasize past, unresolved conflicts and historical relationships, both ACT and CT tend to focus on the present and future. Both treatments emphasize assessing and improving current functioning, and also encourage patients to try out new ways of behaving in the future. CT views underlying cognitive structures as historically derived, and often a certain degree of insight into these historical origins is believed to be helpful (A. T. Beck, 2005; Beck, 1995). Such insight is not generally viewed as sufficient for change, but may be necessary. ACT also holds that the processes underlying psychopathology are historically determined. However, insight into such processes is not emphasized for several reasons (Eifert & Forsyth, 2005). ACT therapists are skeptical of the accuracy of historical accounts, and question the utility of retrospective reconstructions of etiology. ACT therapists also seek to undermine attachment to a "conceptualized" sense of self, and fear that an historical focus would reinforce precisely such a sense. Most importantly, the ACT model

TABLE 5.3   A Comparison of ACT and CT Strategies

Issue	Shared	ACT	CT
Role of disputation	Both are averse to attempts to directly "control" thoughts.	Skeptical of disputation strategies, and generally avoid.	Disputation is a core strategy of CT.
Characteristic treatment techniques	Both focus on the present and future relative to traditional models of psychotherapy.	Liberal use of metaphors and experiential exercises.	Socratic questioning, cognitive disputation, empirical tests.
Therapeutic focus on private events as related to behavior change	Both emphasize the importance of private experiences (thoughts, feelings, memories, etc.).	Focus on disentangling private experience from behavior, and increasing willingness to experience distressing thoughts/feelings.	Focus on changing content of private experience as precursor to behavior change.
Role of defusion	Both view cognitions as observable by the self.	Defusion is a core strategy to enhance willingness and promote action.	Defusion is a byproduct of cognitive restructuring.
Role of awareness	Both focus on increasing awareness of thoughts, feelings and physiological sensations.	Awareness is a key component of mindfulness training.	Awareness is a key component of recognizing automatic thoughts.
Emphasis on affective expression	Both seek to facilitate emotional expression as a means to an end.	Therapy encourages the expression of difficult affect as part of the goal of reduction of experiential avoidance, leading to greater psychological flexibility.	The depth and permanence of cognitive restructuring is theorized to be enhanced when performed in the context of heightened affect.
Behavioral strategies (exposure, behavioral activation)	Both utilize behavioral strategies.	Behavioral strategies utilized to promote psychological flexibility in the context of increased willingness to experience distressing private experiences	Behavioral strategies utilized in the service of reducing negative affect (e.g., anxiety reduction through exposure) and/or increasing positive affect
Therapeutic relationship	Both emphasize a collaborative relationship.	Greater emphasis on principles applying to therapist & patient alike	Therapist as a benevolent coach, gently leading toward cognitive change

does not hold that historical insight is either necessary or sufficient for behavioral change (Hayes, 2004b; Hayes, 2006).

Therapeutic Focus on Subjective Experiences and Their Relation to Behavior Change

Both ACT and CT interventions are designed to help clients cope with distressing subjective experiences (thoughts, feelings, memories, etc.). The focus of ACT interventions is to increase the degree of acceptance of difficult internal experiences, disentangle such experience from behavior, and increase willingness to experience distressing thoughts and feelings in the service of behavior change (Eifert & Forsyth, 2005; Hayes, 2004b; Hayes et al., 2003; Hayes & Smith, 2005). CT interventions, in contrast, focus on changing

the content and frequency of private experience in order to reduce distress and as a precursor to behavior change (Beck et al., 1985; Beck, 1995; DeRubeis et al., 1990; Dobson & Shaw, 1995).

Role of Disputation

As Beck (1993) has noted, CT "is best viewed as the application of the cognitive model of a particular disorder with the use of a variety of techniques designed to modify dysfunctional beliefs and faulty information processing characteristic of each disorder" (p. 194). Similarly, Clark, in separating CT from other approaches, specified that the goal of the therapy is to "identify distorted cognitions" that are "subjected to logical analysis and empirical hypothesis testing" (D. A. Clark, 1995; p. 155; cited in Longmore

& Worrell, 2007). Thus, CT is fundamentally about disputing, testing, and modifying cognitions. In contrast, ACT takes the position that cognitive disputation is often an inert or even harmful intervention (Hayes, in press). Reasons for this position include the following inter-related assertions: (1) disputation, rather than eliminating unhelpful cognitions, tends, in fact, to elaborate them; (2) patients will only become further "entangled" in the verbal quagmire of their belief systems; and (3) restructuring can act as an attempt at thought control, which, like other forms of experiential control, is likely to fail, especially when the "stakes" are highest (Ciarrochi & Robb, 2005; Hayes, 2005; Hayes et al., 1999). Yet the distinction between ACT and CT lessens when one considers that CT "avoids direct attempts to 'control' thoughts, since such attempts often result in effects opposite to the ones intended" (Alford & Beck, 1997, p. 30). Moreover, ACT formally embraces an explicit "pragmatism" that would call for direct efforts to control cognitions or other private events when there is evidence (presumably rare) that this produces desirable outcomes without undue cost.

Role of Defusion

Inherent in each of the two treatments is the notion that cognitions are observable by and distinguishable from the self, a concept that has been variously termed *metacognitive awareness, distancing,* and *cognitive defusion* (Eifert & Forsyth, 2005; Hayes, Strosahl et al., 1999; Teasdale et al., 2002; Zettle, 2005b). In fact, the enhancement of cognitive defusion is a core strategy within ACT, and a number of exercises and metaphors are employed to help patients grasp and develop this skill (Hayes & Strosahl, 2005). Generally speaking, defusion is more of a by-product of cognitive restructuring (and, in particular, cognitive self-monitoring) rather than an explicit focus in CT, although, as discussed later, some evidence suggests that the positive effects of CT may be largely attributable to defusion (Teasdale et al., 2002). Whereas neither the concept of defusion nor the strategies employed to enhance defusion are central to traditional CT, directly challenging of the believability of specific thoughts is a common CT intervention. In fact, CT patients are often asked "how much do you believe that

thought" (both orally and in written "thought records"), and an oft-repeated reminder from the therapist is "just because you have a thought doesn't make it true" (Beck, 1995). Still, whereas CT has little to say about thoughts that are "true" and functional, ACT takes the position that it is important to recognize that even these thoughts are just a "bunch of words" (Ciarrochi, Robb, & Godsell, 2005).

Role of Awareness

CT and ACT focus on increasing awareness of thoughts, feelings, and physiological sensations. Awareness is a key component of mindfulness training, which is a core therapeutic strategy within ACT (Eifert & Forsyth, 2005; Hayes, 2004a; Hayes et al., 2003). In CT, the development of awareness is viewed as a necessary step in the recognition and eventual restructuring of automatic thoughts (Beck, 1976; Beck et al., 1985).

Role of Psychological Acceptance

It has been argued that mindfulness consists of two core components: awareness and acceptance (Cardaciotto, Herbert, Forman, Moitra, & Farrow, in press; Herbert & Cardaciotto, 2005; Kabat-Zinn, 2005). Within ACT, acceptance refers to the psychological readiness to willingly receive (without "defense") any thoughts, feelings, urges, images, and the like that happen to arise. Whereas awareness is an explicit focus of both treatments, psychological acceptance is a much more central concern of ACT than of CT. Thus, in ACT, there is an explicit and heavy emphasis on the problems inherent in lack of acceptance (i.e., avoidance) of internal experiences, on the advantages of acquiring an accepting stance, and on strategies to enhance psychological acceptance (Eifert & Forsyth, 2005; Hayes & Smith, 2005).

Emphasis on Affective Expression

Given that ACT conceives of experiential avoidance as a critical component of psychopathology and psychological inflexibility, a great deal of emphasis is placed on helping patients experience their affective reactions, especially those that they may habitually avoid, such as anxiety, sadness, and anger (Eifert & Forsyth, 2005; Hayes, 2004a; Hayes & Smith,

2005). This is accomplished through a variety of means, including facilitative, empathic exchanges with a therapist who has worked to create a deep connection with his or her patient, and experiential exercises that evoke strong affect (e.g., vividly role-playing a feared confrontation with a spouse). Although some have stereotyped CT as an emotionless exercise in logical reasoning, this is not accurate. In fact, CT writers have long maintained the importance of emotions in the therapeutic work (Beck et al., 1979), and particularly of facilitating "hot cognitions," that is, "important automatic thoughts and images that arise in the therapy session itself and are associated with a change or increase in emotion" (Beck, 1995, p. 80). According to A.T. Beck, "emotional arousal is a key part of what [cognitive therapists] do" (Beck, 2002, p. 2). In part, this is because cognitive modification is predicted to take place more fundamentally to the extent that it occurs within an affective context. Thus, one recommended experiential exercise for facilitating modification of recalcitrant maladaptive core beliefs is to have clients vividly recall, affectively respond to, and then cognitively reprocess memories of early life in which the core belief was invoked with great intensity (Beck, 1995). Importantly, neither ACT nor CT advocate "cathartic" expression of emotion for its own sake, but rather it is sometimes encouraged as a means to an end. In the case of ACT, the end is psychological flexibility, whereas in the case of CT the end is cognitive modification and symptom reduction.

Behavioral Strategies

ACT and CT are both behavioral therapies, and both utilize behavioral strategies such as exposure to feared stimuli, skills training, and behavioral activation (Beck et al., 1985; Beck, 1995; Hayes, 2004b; Ledley et al., 2005). An interesting difference exists, however, in the context within which the behavioral strategies are employed. Within ACT, behavioral strategies are utilized to promote psychological flexibility in the context of increased willingness to experience distressing private experiences while engaging in value-directed behavior. Within CT, behavioral strategies are utilized primarily in the service of changing dysfunctional beliefs (e.g., through

behavioral experiments) and reducing negative affect (e.g., anxiety reduction through exposure).

Therapeutic Relationship

Both treatment models emphasize a collaborative therapist–patient relationship. ACT, more than CT, emphasizes that principles taught and explored within the therapy apply equally to both patient and therapist (i.e., "we're all in the same soup") (Hayes, Strosahl et al., 1999; Wilson & Murrell, 2004). Consistent with other acceptance-based therapies, many ACT clinicians also emphasize the importance of experiential components to training in ACT (Hayes, Strosahl et al., 1999; Hayes & Strosahl, 2005). For its part, the CT therapist is conceived of as a helpful coach, gently leading the patient toward cognitive change (Beck, 1995).

Empirical Support

Effectiveness

A comprehensive review and critique of the empirical support of CT and ACT is beyond the scope of this chapter. Instead, we briefly summarize the status of research on each approach and refer the reader to recent reviews as a way to gauge the base of empirical support for each model. Hundreds of controlled clinical trials of CT have been conducted in recent years (Dobson, 2001; Hollon & Beck, 1994), enough to form the basis of a number of meta-analyses, nearly all of which have strongly supported the efficacy of CT. In fact, a recent systematic review of 16 meta-analyses (Butler et al., 2006) concluded that the effectiveness of CT has been firmly established to treat a plethora of psychological conditions, including unipolar and bipolar depression, panic disorder, OCD, social anxiety disorder, GAD, schizophrenia-linked psychotic symptoms, and bulimia nervosa. Comprehensive reviews of hundreds of tightly controlled efficacy studies have also been conducted by a task force of the Division of Clinical Psychology of the American Psychological Association. On the basis of these reviews, variants of CT have been labeled as "well established" or "empirically supported" for panic disorder, GAD, OCD, social anxiety disorder, depression, and bulimia (Chambless & Hollon, 1998).

In terms of empirical support, ACT lags far behind CT; evidence for the effectiveness of ACT comes from a relatively small set of studies. In fact, some have criticized the movement behind ACT for "getting ahead of the data" (Corrigan, 2001; but see also Herbert, 2002, for a counterargument). A comprehensive review of ACT outcome studies was conducted by Hayes and colleagues (2006). The authors identified 11 studies comparing ACT to an "active, well-specified" treatment; comparison treatments could generally be identified as psychoeducation, a variant of CT, or psychopharmaceutical (nicotine patch, methadone). The treatment foci were also heterogeneous and consisted of depression, anxiety (social anxiety, work stress, agoraphobia, and math anxiety), distress from cancer, job burnout, substance use (polysubstance abuse, smoking), and diabetes management. Weighted, averaged effect sizes comparing treatment conditions were 0.48 at post and 0.63 at a later follow-up period, in favor of ACT. The authors also computed effect sizes of 0.73 (post) and 0.83 (follow-up) for the four studies that compared ACT to variants of CT. The review cited an additional nine studies demonstrating the effectiveness of ACT (for the treatment of social anxiety, agoraphobia, work stress, trichotillomania, psychosis, borderline personality disorder, chronic pain, and even epilepsy) when compared to wait list, placebo, or treatment as usual (weighted, mean effect size = 0.99 at post and 0.71 at follow-up).

A number of limitations of the Hayes et al. (2006) review are noteworthy. First, the number of comparative trials and participants remains too small to draw definitive conclusions. Second, only a handful of studies compared ACT to a "gold standard" treatment, and these studies had relatively small samples. Of these studies, two (Zettle & Hayes, 1987; Zettle & Rains, 1989) were conducted prior to the full development of ACT. Third, the studies were generally of lower methodological rigor than comparable studies of CT (Öst, 2008), although as discussed later, this is not an entirely fair comparison because research on ACT is at a much younger point and has not yet reached the stage of large, well-funded, multisite trials. Fourth, there have been no dismantling or other component control studies to demonstrate that the distinctive features of ACT contribute to efficacy beyond well-established core behavioral principles. In fact, in the one study comparing ACT to (noncognitive) behavior therapy (Zettle, 2003), outcomes favored behavior therapy (though this advantage disappeared by follow-up). Of course, CT has also not generally fared well against purely behavior therapy across a number of dismantling studies (Longmore & Worrell, 2007). Another limitation of the extant ACT outcome literature is that the majority of studies were conducted by people with an expressed interest in ACT, thus raising the possibility of unintentional experimenter bias.

A more recent meta-analysis, carried out by an independent investigator, examined 13 randomized controlled trials in which ACT was compared to a control group (Öst, 2008). Öst concluded that the research methodology used by ACT studies was less stringent than that used by studies of standard CBT. The calculated mean effect size was 0.68 (i.e., moderate in size) and equivalent to that of Hayes et al. meta-analysis. Öst concluded that the extant empirical support for ACT is sufficient to judge it to be an effective treatment, but called for better-controlled studies. Despite the limitations noted, both the Hayes et al. (2006) and Öst 2008 analyses suggest that ACT is an effective treatment. Moreover, the weaker methodological rigor of many ACT studies relative to those of CT must be understood in the context of ACT's being a much more recent arrival on the therapeutic scene. It takes time for sufficient evidence to accrue to justify the resources to support large-scale efficacy and effectiveness trials. Fortunately, there are signs that these are coming. For instance, both Lappalainen and colleagues (2007) and Forman, Herbert, and colleagues (2007) recently conducted trials comparing ACT and CT for a mixed sample of outpatients, and a larger-scale trial of ACT and CT for anxiety is underway at UCLA.

Postulated Mechanisms of Action

According to cognitive theory, CT operates on outcome variables (e.g., depression, anxiety, avoidance behavior) primarily by modifying distorted thinking and dysfunctional attitudes.

Traditional learning mechanisms are hypothe-sized as well, although we do not elaborate on these because (1) they are common to both ACT and CT, and (2) traditional CT postulates that behavioral interventions ultimately exert their impact through *cognitive* changes (A. T. Beck, 2005).

Several hypotheses emerge from the cognitive framework, including that change in dysfunctional attitudes should mediate change in outcome variables (e.g., depression, anxiety), and that cognitive change should be more pronounced among patients who receive CT than among those who receive alternative treatments such as psychiatric medication. However, as was discussed in Longmore and Worrell's (2007) recent review, the evidence to date does not strongly support the proposed mechanisms of action of CT.

One way to test the assumption that CT effects are mediated by cognitive change is to mea-sure changes in dysfunctional thinking and then attempt to determine whether they mediate out-come. Only a small minority of CT outcome studies have conducted these mediational anal-yses. Of those that have, many have failed to find evidence of cognitive mediation, especially in the case of CT for depression (e.g., Barber & DeRubeis, 1989; Burns & Spangler, 2001; Clark et al., 1989; DeRubeis et al., 1990; Rush, Kovacs, Beck, Weissenburger, & Hollon, 1981; Simons, Garfield, & Murphy, 1984; Teasdale et al., 2001). In the largest of these studies (Burns & Spangler), structural equation modeling revealed no rela-tionship between changes in dysfunctional atti-tudes and decreases in anxiety or depression over a 12-week period among 521 outpatients. How-ever, cognitive changes have been associated with later sudden decreases in depression (Tang, DeRubeis, Beberman, & Pham, 2005). Results from several studies of CT for panic (Casey, Newcombe, & Oei, 2005; D. M. Clark et al., 1994; Hofmann et al., 2007; Kendall & Tread-well, 2007; Michelson, Marchione, Greenwald, Testa, & Marchione, 1996; Prins & Ollendick, 2003; Smits, Powers, Cho, & Telch, 2004; Tread-well & Kendall, 1996) and social anxiety (Foa, Franklin, Perry, & Herbert, 1996; Hofmann, 2004; Hofmann, 2005; Smits, Rosenfield, McDonald, & Telch, 2006) have supported a mediating role for

cognitive change. In two cases, the choices of mediator, that is, fear of fear (Smits et al., 2004) and perception of control over anxiety (Hof-mann, 2005), are noteworthy for their potential interpretation as acceptance-linked constructs. Also, many studies that reported cognitive medi-ation measured cognitive and outcome change contemporaneously and/or did not otherwise meet criteria for formal mediation (Hofmann, 2008; Longmore & Worrell, 2007).

A number of randomized controlled trials comparing CT to medication for depression have tested mediation hypotheses. For the most part, findings suggest that CT produces no more change in maladaptive thoughts than does psychopharmacological intervention (Barber & DeRubeis, 1989; Clark et al., 1989; DeRubeis et al., 1990; Longmore & Worrell, 2007; Rush et al., 1981; Simons et al., 1984; Teasdale et al., 2001). Thus, these findings fail to support the postulated mechanisms of action of CT. However, some findings are explainable within a modified CT theory. For instance, it could be argued that equivalent changes observed in dysfunctional attitudes between CT and medication simply reflect the fact that cognition is a component of the psychobiological system (A. T. Beck, 1984), and also that cognitive variables can be mediators in one treatment and consequences of change in outcome in another (DeRubeis et al., 1990).

An additional challenge to the cognitive medi-ation hypothesis comes from dismantling studies that have compared behavior therapy with and without a cognitive component. For instance, a series of studies have found that exposure-only therapy was at least as effective as an exposure plus cognitive therapy in the treatment of social anxiety disorder (Emmelkamp, Mersch, Vissia, & Van der Helm, 1985; Gelernter, Uhde, Cim-bolic, Arnkoff, & et al., 1991; Hope, Heimberg, & Bruch, 1995; Mattick, Peters, & Clarke, 1989; Scholing & Emmelkamp, 1993) and PTSD (Foa et al., 1999; Foa et al., 2005; Lovell, Marks, Noshir-vani, Thrasher, & Livanou, 2001; Paunovic & Öst, 2001), and that behavioral activation alone was as effective as activation plus cognitive ther-apy in the treatment of depression (Dimidjian et al., 2006; Jacobson et al., 1996). Similarly, meta-analyses have suggested that exposure plus cognitive interventions offer no advantage over exposure-only treatments for GAD (Gould, Otto, Pollack, & Yap, 1997) and OCD (Feske & Chambless, 1995). Hofmann and Admundson (2008) have pointed out that cognitions would logically change from a behavioral intervention (e.g., exposure to a frightening stimulus would change beliefs about the danger of that stimulus). Thus, cognitive change could possibly be a mediator of change in both cognitive and behavioral interventions. Nevertheless, the necessity and efficacy of direct cognitive change strategies are called into question by the extant dismantling research.

The lack of consistent support for postulated mediating mechanisms of CT has led researchers in several related directions. Teasdale and colleagues have presented theoretical and empirical support for the notion that CT "although explicitly focused on changing belief in the *content* of negative thoughts, leads, implicitly, to changes in *relationships* to negative thoughts and feelings, and in particular, to increased metacognitive awareness" (Teasdale et al., 2002, p. 285). Metacognitive awareness, or decentering, "describes a cognitive set in which negative thoughts and feelings are seen as passing events in the mind rather than as inherent aspects of self or as necessarily valid reflections of reality" (Teasdale et al., 2002, p. 285). A related idea was proposed by Barber and DeRubeis (1989, 2001), who have provided evidence that CT operates less by directly impacting troublesome affect or cognition, and more by helping patients develop "compensatory skills" (e.g., generation of alternative explanations or problem solving), many of which are metacognitive in nature, to cope with difficult affect and cognition.

These emerging accounts of the mechanism of action of CT, especially as related to metacognitive awareness, are closely related to theoretical accounts of core ACT processes, especially cognitive defusion. Thus, it is possible that ACT and CT share at least some common mechanisms of action. However, in two studies of depression, evidence across multiple time points was found that early changes in cognitive defusion mediated later decreases in depression for ACT, but not for CT (Hayes, Masuda, Bissett, Luoma, & Guerrero, 2004; Zettle & Hayes, 1986;

Zettle & Rains, 1989). Further, though less specific, evidence for the mediating role of cognitive defusion was found in a pair of studies of ACT for psychosis (Bach & Hayes, 2002; Gaudiano & Herbert, 2006). In each of these studies, ACT was compared to treatment as usual and cognitive defusion was operationalized as the extent to which patients reported that they believed their delusions to be true (which was contrasted to the report of *frequency*). In both cases, findings supported defusion from delusions as a mediator in ACT's superiority, relative to treatment as usual, in decreasing rehospitalization.

ACT is also postulated to influence outcomes by decreasing experiential avoidance (and thereby increasing experiential acceptance). Several outcome studies support this mechanism. Trials of ACT for mathematics and test anxiety (Zettle, 2003), trichotillomania (Woods, Wetterneck, & Flessner, 2006), worksite stress (Bond & Bunce, 2000), chronic pain (McCracken et al., 2005), nicotine addiction (Gifford et al., 2004), and obesity (Forman, Butryn, Hoffman, & Herbert, 2007) have all concluded that experiential avoidance partially mediates the observed treatment effects of ACT. The Zettle (2003) study is noteworthy in that it found that both systematic desensitization and ACT produced substantial decreases in anxiety but that experiential avoidance was a mediator only in the ACT condition. Two randomized controlled trials comparing ACT and CT also produced evidence that experiential avoidance/acceptance is a stronger mediator for ACT (Forman, Herbert, Moitra, Yeomans, & Geller, 2007; Lappalainen et al., 2007). In a unique approach, Hayes, Levin, Yadavaia, and Vilardaga (2007) conducted a meta-analysis of mediational findings in 12 outcome studies of ACT for a variety of conditions. Overall, ACT-consistent variables (e.g., cognitive defusion, experiential avoidance, mindfulness) significantly mediated treatment effects, accounting for a substantial amount of the variance in outcome measures. In addition to clinical trials, a growing number of analog laboratory studies lend support to the mediational role of decreased experiential avoidance in coping with pain (e.g., Hayes, Bissett et al., 1999), panic attacks (e.g., Levitt,

Brown, Orsillo, & Barlow, 2004), anxiety-related distress (e.g., Kashdan, Barrios, Forsyth, & Steger, 2006), and food cravings (Forman, Hoffman et al., 2007).

Except as specifically noted, mediators in the ACT studies cited were assessed at the same time point as outcomes, limiting conclusions about causality. In addition, many of the treatment outcome studies lacked an active comparison condition, so the specificity of mediation remains in question. Even so, the tests of the mechanisms postulated to underlie ACT have thus far been largely supported.

CONCLUSIONS

Over the past four decades CBT, and a particular model of CBT known as cognitive therapy (CT) has been gradually replacing psycho-analysis/psychodynamic psychotherapy as the prevailing model of psychotherapy in clinical practice (A. T. Beck, 2005; Norcross, Hedges, & Castle, 2002; Norcross, Hedges, & Prochaska, 2002). Standard CBT now dominates the psy-chotherapy landscape in terms of demonstrated efficacy, acceleration of usage, and prominence in academic and medical centers. However, a new generation of acceptance-based behavior therapies has emerged and raised challenges to some of the key assumptions behind traditional perspectives on CBT. Our review of CT and ACT, as prototypical representatives of standard CBTs and acceptance-based therapies, respectively, concluded that ACT shares a large number of features with CT, but that the two therapies also differ substantially on both theoretical and technological grounds. There appear to be some important dimensions that distinguish ACT from CT, including the lack of emphasis on symptom reduction, a skepticism of most attempts to directly alter dysfunctional cognitions or other internal experiences, and an emphasis on values clarification. Most fundamentally, and most in concert with other acceptance-based approaches, a bedrock goal of ACT is to facilitate increased acceptance of, and an altered (e.g., metacognitive) rela-tionship with, one's own distressing internal experiences.

In terms of empirical support, CT maintains a distinct advantage on the basis of the sheer number, size, and breadth of clinical trials. The existing ACT outcome literature suggests prelim-inarily, though not yet convincingly, that ACT is a highly efficacious treatment. Research find-ings are equivocal in relation to the theoretically predicted mediating mechanisms of CT. Some findings suggest that CT's positive effects may in fact be largely attributable to the treatment's ability to develop patients' metacognitive aware-ness. Thus far, tests of ACT's mechanisms of action have fared somewhat better, with prelim-inary evidence supporting the mediational role of cognitive defusion and decreased experiential avoidance, although much more work is needed to replicate these findings.

It is still too early to predict the ultimate tra-jectory of acceptance-based behavior therapies in relation to traditional CBT. Certainly, traditional CBT will continue to maintain its preeminent status for some time to come, which appears war-ranted given its vast empirical base. At the same time, data are rapidly accumulating on outcomes and mechanisms of various acceptance-based models of behavior therapy, and ACT in par-ticular. As other commentators have observed (e.g., Arch & Craske, in press), a great deal more research is needed, especially by those without a strong allegiance to these acceptance-based models, to determine if the current promise of these approaches holds up to further scrutiny. Dismantling studies that help to tease apart the active ingredients of both therapies are needed, as are more sophisticated tests of causal medi-ation. If more compelling data supporting the efficacy and especially the proposed mechanisms of acceptance-based interventions emerge in the coming years, these approaches will increasingly present a challenge to traditional CBT.

Already, there are signs that acceptance-based theory, outcome, and mediational data are beginning to influence the practice of traditional CBT. Prime among these is the evolution of standard cognitive and behavioral paradigms to incorporate acceptance-based strategies and theory. Examples include acceptance-based behavioral therapy for GAD (Roemer & Orsillo, 2007; Roemer et al., 2006) and MBCT for preventing depression relapse (Ma & Teasdale,

2004; Teasdale et al., 2000), as well as the theoretical work of leading figures in CBT such as Wells (2005a, 2005b), Barlow (Barlow, 2002; Levitt et al., 2004; Orsillo, Roemer, & Barlow, 2003), Craske (Craske & Barlow, in press; Craske & Mystkowski, 2006) and Borkovec (Borkovec, Alcaine, & Behar, 2004; Borkovec, Ray, & Stober, 1998). Overall, then, irrespective of whether acceptance-based approaches are labeled as a new generation of behavior therapy, aspects of acceptance-based theory appear destined to play an increasing role in cognitive behavioral treatments.

References

Accreditation Council for Graduate Medical Education. (2004). *Program requirements for residency training in psychiatry*. Chicago, IL: Accreditation Council for Graduate Medical Education.

Alford, B. A., & Beck, A. T. (1997). *The integrative power of cognitive therapy*. New York: Guilford.

Arch, J. J., & Craske, M. G. (in press). ACT and CBT for anxiety disorders: Different Treatments, Similar Mechanisms? *Clinical Psychology: Science and Practice*.

Bach, P., & Hayes, S. C. (2002). The use of acceptance and commitment therapy to prevent the rehospitalization of psychotic patients: A randomized controlled trial. *Journal of Consulting & Clinical Psychology, 70*, 1129–1139.

Bandura, A. (1969). *Principles of behavior modification*. Oxford, UK: Holt, Rinehart, & Winston.

Barber, J. P., & DeRubeis, R. J. (1989). On second thought: Where the action is in cognitive therapy for depression. *Cognitive Therapy & Research, 13*, 441–457.

Barber, J. P., & DeRubeis, R. J. (2001). Change in compensatory skills in cognitive therapy for depression. *Journal of Psychotherapy Practice and Research, 10*, 8–13.

Barlow, D. H. (Ed.). (2002). *Anxiety and its disorders: The nature and treatment of anxiety and panic* (2nd ed.). New York: Guilford.

Barlow, D. H., Craske, M. G., & Meadows, E. A. (2000). *Mastery of your anxiety and panic: Therapist's guide to anxiety, panic and agoraphobia*. San Antonio, TX: Graywind Publications/The Psychological Corporation.

Beck, A. T. (1976). *Cognitive therapy and the emotional disorders*. New York: International Universities Press.

Beck, A. T. (1984). Cognition and therapy. *Archives of General Psychiatry, 41*, 1112–1115.

Beck, A. T. (1993). Cognitive therapy: Past, present, and future. *Journal of Consulting and Clinical Psychology, 61*, 194–198.

Beck, A. T. (2002). Emotional arousal in cognitive theory. *Beck Institute Newsletter, 7*, 2.

Beck, A. T. (2005). The current state of cognitive therapy: A 40-year retrospective. *Archives of General Psychiatry, 62*, 953–959.

Beck, A. T., Emery, G., & Greenberg, R. L. (1985). *Anxiety disorders and phobias: A cognitive perspective*. New York: Basic Books.

Beck, A. T., Freeman, A. M., & Davis, D. D. (2004). *Cognitive therapy of personality disorders* (2nd ed.). New York: Guilford Press.

Beck, A. T., Rush, A. J., Shaw, B. F., & Emery, G. (1979). *Cognitive therapy of depression*. New York: Guilford.

Beck, J. S. (1995). *Cognitive therapy: Basics and beyond*. New York: Guilford Press.

Beck, J. S. (2005). *Cognitive therapy for challenging problems: What to do when the basics don't work*. New York: Guilford.

Bond, F. W., & Bunce, D. (2000). Mediators of change in emotion-focused and problem-focused worksite stress management interventions. *Journal of Occupational Health Psychology, 5*, 156–163.

Borkovec, T. D., Alcaine, O. M., & Behar, E. (Eds.). (2004). Avoidance theory of worry and generalized anxiety disorder. In R. G. Heimberg, C. L. Turk, & D. S. Mennin (Eds.), *Generalized anxiety disorder: Advances in research and practice* (pp. 77–108). New York: Guilford.

Borkovec, T. D., Ray, W. J., & Stober, J. (1998). Worry: A cognitive phenomenon intimately linked to affective, physiological, and interpersonal behavioral processes. *Cognitive Therapy and Research, 22*, 561–576.

Brantley, J. (2005). Mindfulness-based stress reduction. [References]. In S. M. Orsillo & L. Roemer (Eds.), *Acceptance and mindfulness-based approaches to anxiety: Conceptualization and treatment* (pp. 131–145). New York, NY: Springer Science+Business Media.

Brown, R. A., Lejuez, C. W., Kahler, C. W., Strong, D. R., & Zvolensky, M. J. (2005). Distress tolerance and early smoking lapse. *Clinical Psychology Review, 25*, 713–733.

Brown, R. A., Palm, K. M., Strong, D. R., Lejuez, C. W., Kahler, C. W., Zvolensky, M. J., et al. (2008). Distress tolerance treatment for early-lapse smokers: Rationale, program description, and preliminary findings. *Behavior Modification, 32*, 302–332.

Burns, D. D., & Spangler, D. L. (2001). Do changes in dysfunctional attitudes mediate changes in depression and anxiety in cognitive behavioral therapy? *Behavior Therapy, 32*, 337–369.

Butler, A. C., Chapman, J. E., Forman, E. M., & Beck, A. T. (2006). The empirical status of cognitive–behavioral therapy: A review of meta-analyses. *Clinical Psychology Review, 26*, 17–31.

Cardaciotto, L., Herbert, J. D., Forman, E. M., Moitra, E., & Farrow, V. (in press). The assessment of present-moment awareness and acceptance: The Philadelphia Mindfulness Scale. *Assessment*.

Casey, L. M., Newcombe, P. A., & Oei, T. P. S. (2005). Cognitive mediation of panic severity: The role of catastrophic misinterpretation of bodily sensations and panic self-efficacy. *Cognitive Therapy and Research, 29*, 187–200.

Chambless, D. L., & Hollon, S. D. (1998). Defining empirically supported therapies. *Journal of Consulting and Clinical Psychology, 66*, 7–18.

Ciarrochi, J., & Robb, H. (2005). Letting a little nonverbal air into the room: Insights from acceptance and commitment therapy: Part 2: Applications. *Journal of Rational–Emotive and Cognitive Behavior Therapy, 23*, 107–130.

Ciarrochi, J., Robb, H., & Godsell, C. (2005). Letting a little nonverbal air into the room: Insights from acceptance and commitment therapy: Part 1: Philosophical and theoretical underpinnings. *Journal of Rational–Emotive and Cognitive Behavior Therapy, 23*, 79–106.

Clark, D. A. (1995). Perceived limitations of standard cognitive therapy: A consideration of efforts to revise Beck's theory and therapy. *Journal of Cognitive Psychotherapy, 9*, 153–172.

Clark, D. A., Beck, A. T., & Brown, G. (1989). Cognitive mediation in general psychiatric outpatients: A test of the content-specificity hypothesis. *Journal of Personality and Social Psychology, 56*, 958–964.

Clark, D. M., Salkovskis, P. M., Hackmann, A., Middleton, H., Anastasiades, P., & Gelder, M. (1994). A comparison of cognitive therapy, applied relaxation and imipramine in the treatment of panic disorder. *British Journal of Psychiatry, 164*, 759–769.

Cordova, J. V. (2001). Acceptance in behavior therapy: Understanding the process of change. *Behavior Analyst, 24*, 213–226.

Corrigan, P. W. (2001). Getting ahead of the data: A threat to some behavior therapies. *Behavior Therapist, 24*, 189–193.

Craske, M. G., & Barlow, D. H. (in press). Panic disorder and agoraphobia. In D. H. Barlow (Ed.), *Clinical handbook of psychological disorders: A step-by-step treatment manual* (4th ed.). New York: Guilford.

Craske, M. G., & Mystkowski, J. L. (2006). Exposure therapy and extinction: Clinical studies. In M. G. Craske, D. Hermans & D. Vansteenwegen (Eds.), *Fear and learning: From basic processes to clinical implications* (1st ed.). Washington, DC: American Psychological Association.

Dahl, J., Wilson, K. G., Luciano Soriano, M., & Hayes, S. C. (2005). *Acceptance and commitment therapy for chronic pain*. Reno, NV: Context Press.

Dahl, J., Wilson, K. G., & Nilsson, A. (2004). Acceptance and commitment therapy and the treatment of persons at risk for long-term disability resulting from stress and pain symptoms: A preliminary randomized trial. *Behavior Therapy, 35*, 785–801.

Dalrymple, K. L., & Herbert, J. D. (2007). Acceptance and commitment therapy for generalized social anxiety disorder: A pilot study. *Behavior Modification, 31*, 543–568.

DeRubeis, R. J., Evans, M. D., Hollon, S. D., Garvey, M. J., Grove, W. M., & Tuason, V. B. (1990). How does cognitive therapy work? Cognitive change and symptom change in cognitive therapy and pharmacotherapy for depression. *Journal of Consulting and Clinical Psychology, 58*, 862–869.

Dimidjian, S., Hollon, S. D., Dobson, K. S., Schmaling, K. B., Kohlenberg, R. J., Addis, M. E., et al. (2006). Randomized trial of behavioral activation, cognitive therapy, and antidepressant medication in the acute treatment of adults with major depression. *Journal of Consulting and Clinical Psychology, 74*, 658–670.

Dobson, K. S. (Ed.). (2001). *Handbook of cognitive-behavioral therapies* (2nd ed.). New York: Guilford.

Dobson, K. S., & Shaw, B. F. (1995). Cognitive therapies in practice. In B. M. Bongar & L. E. Beutler (Eds.), *Comprehensive textbook of psychotherapy: Theory and practice* (Oxford textbooks in clinical psychology) (pp. 159–172). London: Oxford University Press.

Eifert, G. H., & Forsyth, J. P. (2005). *Acceptance and commitment therapy for anxiety disorders: A practitioner's treatment guide to using mindfulness, acceptance, and values-based behavior change strategies*. Oakland, CA: New Harbinger Publications.

Ellis, A. (1962). *Reason and emotion in psychotherapy*. Oxford, UK: Lyle Stuart.

Ellis, A. (2000). The importance of cognitive processes in facilitating accepting in psychotherapy. *Cognitive and Behavioral Practice, 7*, 288–299.

Ellis, A. (2005). Can rational–emotive behavior therapy (REBT) and acceptance and commitment therapy (ACT) resolve their differences and be integrated? *Journal of Rational–Emotive and Cognitive Behavior Therapy, 23*, 153–158.

Emmelkamp, P. M., Mersch, P.-P., Vissia, E., & Van der Helm, M. (1985). Social phobia: A comparative evaluation of cognitive and behavioral interventions. *Behaviour Research and Therapy, 23*, 365–369.

Feske, U., & Chambless, D. L. (1995). Cognitive behavioral versus exposure only treatment for social phobia: A meta-analysis. *Behavior Therapy, 26,* 695–720.

Fisher, P. L., & Wells, A. (2008). Metacognitive therapy for obsessive-compulsive disorder: A case series. *Journal of Behavior Therapy and Experimental Psychiatry, 39,* 117–132.

Foa, E. B., Dancu, C. V., Hembree, E. A., Jaycox, L. H., Meadows, E. A., & Street, G. P. (1999). A comparison of exposure therapy, stress inoculation training, and their combination for reducing posttraumatic stress disorder in female assault victims. *Journal of Consulting and Clinical Psychology, 67,* 194–200.

Foa, E. B., Franklin, M. E., Perry, K. J., & Herbert, J. D. (1996). Cognitive biases in generalized social phobia. *Journal of Abnormal Psychology, 105,* 433–439.

Foa, E. B., & Goldstein, A. (1978). Continuous exposure and complete response prevention in the treatment of obsessive–compulsive neurosis. *Behavior Therapy, 9,* 821–829.

Foa, E. B., Hembree, E. A., Cahill, S. P., Rauch, S. A. M., Riggs, D. S., Feeny, N. C., et al. (2005). Randomized trial of prolonged exposure for posttraumatic stress disorder with and without cognitive restructuring: Outcome at academic and community clinics. *Journal of Consulting and Clinical Psychology, 73,* 953–964.

Foa, E. B., Hembree, E. A., & Rothbaum, B. O. (2007). *Prolonged exposure therapy for PTSD: Emotional processing of traumatic experiences: Therapist guide.* New York: Oxford University Press.

Forman, E. M., Butryn, M. B., Hoffman, K. L., & Herbert, J. D. (2007, November). A pilot study of an acceptance-based behavioral treatment for weight loss. In M. J. Hildebrandt (Chair), *Behavioral demonstrations of distress tolerance: Understanding psychological processes as they apply to clinical outcomes.* Paper presented at the 41st annual convention of the Association for Behavioral and Cognitive Therapies, Philadelphia, PA.

Forman, E. M., Butryn, M. B., Hoffman, K. L., & Herbert, J. D. (under review). An open trial of an acceptance-based behavioral intervention for weight loss.

Forman, E. M., Herbert, J. D., Moitra, E., Yeomans, P. D., & Geller, P. A. (2007). A randomized controlled effectiveness trial of acceptance and commitment therapy and cognitive therapy for anxiety and depression. *Behavior Modification, 31,* 772–799.

Forman, E. M., Hoffman, K. L., McGrath, K. B., Herbert, J. D., Brandsma, L. L., & Lowe, M. R. (2007). A comparison of acceptance- and control-based strategies for coping with food cravings: An analog study. *Behavior Research and Therapy, 45,* 2372–2386.

Gaudiano, B. A., & Herbert, J. D. (2006). Acute treatment of inpatients with psychotic symptoms using acceptance and commitment therapy: Pilot results. *Behavior Research and Therapy, 44,* 415–437.

Gelernter, C. S., Uhde, T. W., Cimbolic, P., Arnkoff, D. B., & et al. (1991). Cognitive-behavioral and pharmacological treatments of social phobia: A controlled study. *Archives of General Psychiatry, 48,* 938–945.

Gifford, E. V., Kohlenberg, B. S., Hayes, S. C., Antonuccio, D. O., Piasecki, M. M., Rasmussen-Hall, M. L., et al. (2004). Acceptance-Based Treatment for Smoking Cessation. *Behavior Therapy, 35,* 689–705.

Gould, R. A., Otto, M. W., Pollack, M. H., & Yap, L. (1997). Cognitive behavioral and pharmacological treatment of generalized anxiety disorder: A preliminary meta-analyis. *Behavior Therapy, 28,* 285–305.

Hayes, S. C. (2004a). Acceptance and commitment therapy and the new behavior therapies: Mindfulness, acceptance, and relationship. In S. C. Hayes, V. M. Follette & M. M. Linehan (Eds.), *Mindfulness and acceptance: Expanding the cognitive-behavioral tradition* (pp. 1–29). New York: Guilford.

Hayes, S. C. (2004b). Acceptance and commitment therapy, relational frame theory, and the third wave of behavioral and cognitive therapies. *Behavior Therapy, 35,* 639–665.

Hayes, S. C. (2005). Stability and change in cognitive behavior therapy: Considering the implications of ACT and RFT. *Journal of Rational–Emotive and Cognitive Behavior Therapy, 23,* 131–151.

Hayes, S. C. (2006). Acceptance and mindfulness at work: Applying acceptance and commitment therapy and relational frame theory to organizational behavior management. New York: Haworth Press.

Hayes, S. C. (in press). Climbing our hills: A beginning conversation on the comparison of ACT and traditional CBT. *Clinical Psychology: Science and Practice.*

Hayes, S. C., Barnes-Holmes, D., & Roche, B. (Eds.). (2001). *Relational frame theory: A post-Skinnerian account of human language and cognition.* New York: Kluwer Academic/Plenum.

Hayes, S. C., Bissett, R. T., Korn, Z., Zettle, R. D., Rosenfarb, I. S., Cooper, L. D., et al. (1999). The impact of acceptance versus control rationales on pain tolerance. *Psychological Record, 49,* 33–47.

Hayes, S. C., Follette, V. M., & Linehan, M. M. (Eds.). (2004). *Mindfulness and acceptance: Expanding the cognitive–behavioral tradition.* New York: Guilford.

Hayes, S. C., & Gregg, J. (2001). Functional contextualism and the self. In J. Muran (Ed.), *Self-relations
in the psychotherapy process* (pp. 291–311). Washington, DC: American Psychological Association.

Hayes, S. C., Jacobson, N. S., Follette, V. M., & Dougher,
M. J. (1994). *Acceptance and change: Content and
context in psychotherapy.* Reno, NV: Context
Press.

Hayes, S. C., Luoma, J. B., Bond, F. W., Masuda, A., &
Lillis, J. (2006). Acceptance and commitment ther-
apy: Model, processes and outcomes. *Behaviour
Research and Therapy, 44,* 1–25.

Hayes, S. C., Masuda, A., Bissett, R., Luoma, J., &
Guerrero, L. (2004). DBT, FAR and ACT: How
empirically oriented are the new behavior therapy
technologies? *Behavior Therapy, 35,* 35–54.

Hayes, S. C., Masuda, A., & De Mey, H. (2003). Acceptance and commitment therapy and the third
wave of behavior therapy. *Gedragstherapie, 36,*
69–96.

Hayes, S. C., & Smith, S. X. (2005). Get out of your mind
and into your life: The new acceptance and commitment therapy. Oakland, CA: New Harbinger
Publications.

Hayes, S. C., Strosahl, K., & Wilson, K. G. (1999).
*Acceptance and commitment therapy: An experiential
approach to behavior change.* New York: Guilford.

Hayes, S. C., & Strosahl, K. D. (Eds.). (2005). *A practical
guide to acceptance and commitment therapy.* New
York: Springer Science.

Hayes, S. C., Strosahl, K. D., Bunting, K., Twohig,
M., & Wilson, K. G. (2005). What is acceptance
and commitment therapy? In S. C. Hayes &
K. D. Strosahl (Eds.), *A practical guide to acceptance
and commitment therapy* (pp. 3–29). New York:
Springer Science.

Herbert, J. D. (2002). The dissemination of novel
psychotherapies: A commentary on Corrigan,
Gaynor, and Hayes. [Comment/Reply]. *The
Behavior Therapist, 25,* 140–144.

Herbert, J. D., & Cardaciotto, L. (2005). An acceptance
and mindfulness-based perspective on social anxiety disorder. In S. M. Orsillo & L. Roemer (Eds.),
*Acceptance and mindfulness-based approaches to anx-
iety: Conceptualization and treatment* (pp. 189–212).
New York: Springer.

Hofmann, S. G. (2004). Cognitive mediation of treatment change in social phobia. *Journal of Consulting
and Clinical Psychology, 72,* 392–399.

Hofmann, S. G. (2005). Perception of control
over anxiety mediates the relation between
catastrophic thinking and social anxiety in
social phobia. *Behaviour Research and Therapy, 43,*
885–895.

Hofmann, S. G. (2008). Common misconceptions
about cognitive mediation of treatment change: A

commentary to to Longmore and Worrell (2007).
Clinical Psychology Review, 28, 67–70.

Hofmann, S. G., & Asmundson, G. J. (2008). Acceptance
and mindfulness-based therapy: New wave or old
hat? *Clinical Psychology Review, 28,* 1–16.

Hofmann, S. G., Meuret, A. E., Rosenfield, D., Suvak,
M. K., Barlow, D. H., Gorman, J. M., et al. (2007).
Preliminary evidence for cognitive mediation
during cognitive-behavioral therapy of panic
disorder. *Journal of Consulting and Clinical
Psychology, 75,* 374–379.

Hollon, S. D., & Beck, A. T. (1994). Cognitive and
cognitive-behavioral therapies. In A. E. Bergin &
S. L. Garfield (Eds.), *Handbook of psychotherapy and
behavior change* (4th ed.) (pp. 428–466). Oxford,
UK: John Wiley & Sons.

Hollon, S. D., Haman, K. L., & Brown, L. L. (2002).
Cognitive-behavioral treatment of depression. In
I. H. Gotlib & C. L. Hammen (Eds.), *Handbook of
depression* (pp. 383–403). New York: Guilford.

Hope, D. A., Heimberg, R. G., & Bruch, M. A. (1995).
Dismantling cognitive-behavioral group therapy
for social phobia. *Behaviour Research and Therapy,
33,* 637–650.

Jacobson, N. S., Christensen, A., Prince, S. E., Cordova,
J., & Eldridge, K. (2000). Integrative behavioral
couple therapy: An acceptance-based, promising
new treatment for couple discord. *Journal of Consulting and Clinical Psychology, 68,* 351–355.

Jacobson, N. S., Dobson, K. S., Truax, P. A., Addis, M. E.,
Koerner, K., Gollan, J. K., et al. (1996). A component analysis of cognitive-behavioral treatment
for depression. *Journal of Consulting and Clinical
Psychology, 64,* 295–304.

Jacobson, N. S., Martell, C. R., & Dimidjian, S. (2001).
Behavioral activation treatment for depression:
Returning to contextual roots. *Clinical Psychology:
Science and Practice, 8,* 255–270.

Kabat-Zinn, J. (1982). An outpatient program in behavioral medicine for chronic pain patients based
on the practice of mindfulness meditation: Theoretical considerations and preliminary results.
General Hospital Psychiatry, 4, 33–47.

Kabat-Zinn, J. (2005). Full catastrophe living: Using the
wisdom of your body and mind to face stress,
pain, and illness. New York: Delta Trade Paperbacks.

Kabat-Zinn, J., Massion, A. O., Kristeller, J., Peterson,
L. G., Fletcher, K. E., Pbert, L., et al. (1992). Effectiveness of a meditation-based stress reduction
program in the treatment of anxiety disorders.
American Journal of Psychiatry, 149, 936–943.

Kashdan, T. B., Barrios, V., Forsyth, J. P., & Steger,
M. F. (2006). Experiential avoidance as a generalized psychological vulnerability: comparisons
with coping and emotion regulation strategies.
Behavior Research and Therapy, 44, 1301–1320.

Kendall, P. C., & Treadwell, K. R. (2007). The role of self-statements as a mediator in treatment for youth with anxiety disorders. *Journal of Consulting and Clinical Psychology, 75*, 380–389.

Kristeller, J. L., Baer, R. A., & Quillian-Wolever, R. (2006). Mindfulness-based approaches to eating disorders. [References]. In R. A. Baer (Ed.), *Mindfulness-based treatment approaches: Clinician's guide to evidence base and applications* (pp. 75–91). San Diego, CA: Elsevier Academic Press.

Lappalainen, R., Lehtonen, T., Skarp, E., Taubert, E., Ojanen, M., & Hayes, S. C. (2007). The impact of CBT and ACT models using psychology trainee therapists: A preliminary controlled effectiveness trial. *Behavior Modification, 31*, 488–511.

Leahy, R. L. (2003a). Cognitive therapy techniques: A practitioner's guide. New York: Guilford.

Leahy, R. L. (2003b). *Roadblocks in cognitive-behavioral therapy: Transforming challenges into opportunities for change.* New York: Guilford.

Ledley, D. R., Marx, B. P., & Heimberg, R. G. (2005). *Making cognitive-behavioral therapy work: Clinical process for new practitioners.* New York: Guilford.

Levitt, J. T., Brown, T. A., Orsillo, S. M., & Barlow, D. H. (2004). The effects of acceptance versus suppression of emotion on subjective and psychophysiological response to carbon dioxide challenge in patients with panic disorder. *Behavior Therapy, 35*, 747–766.

Levitt, J. T., & Karekla, M. (2005). Integrating acceptance and mindfulness with cognitive behavioral treatment for panic disorder. In S. M. Orsillo & L. Roemer (Eds.), *Acceptance and mindfulness-based approaches to anxiety: Conceptualization and treatment* (pp. 165–188). New York: Springer Science+Business Media.

Linehan, M. M. (1993). Cognitive-behavioral treatment of borderline personality disorder. New York: Guilford.

Linehan, M. M., & Dimeff, L. (2001). Dialectical behavior therapy in a nutshell. *California Psychologist, 34*, 10–13.

Longmore, R., & Worrell, M. (2007). Do we need to challenge thoughts in cognitive behavioural therapy? *Clinical Psychology Review, 27*, 173–187.

Lovell, K., Marks, I. M., Noshirvani, H., Thrasher, S., & Livanou, M. (2001). Do cognitive and exposure treatments improve various PTSD symptoms differently? A randomized controlled trial. *Behavioural and Cognitive Psychotherapy, 29*, 107–112.

Ma, S., & Teasdale, J. D. (2004). Mindfulness-based cognitive therapy for depression: Replication and exploration of differential relapse prevention effects. *Journal of Consulting and Clinical Psychology, 72*, 31–40.

Martell, C., Addis, M., & Dimidjian, S. (2004). Finding the action in behavioral activation: The search for empirically supported interventions and mechanisms of change. [References]. In S. C. Hayes, V. M. Follette & M. M. Linehan (Eds.), *Mindfulness and acceptance: Expanding the cognitive-behavioral tradition* (pp. 152–167). New York: Guilford.

Mattick, R. P., Peters, L., & Clarke, J. C. (1989). Exposure and cognitive restructuring for social phobia: A controlled study. *Behavior Therapy, 20*, 3–23.

McCracken, L. M., Vowles, K. E., & Eccleston, C. (2005). Acceptance-based treatment for persons with complex, long standing chronic pain: A preliminary analysis of treatment outcome in comparison to a waiting phase. *Behavior Research and Therapy, 43*, 1335–1346.

Meichenbaum, D. H., & Deffenbacher, J. L. (1988). Stress inoculation training. *Counseling Psychologist, 16*, 69–90.

Michelson, L. K., Marchione, K. E., Greenwald, M., Testa, S., & Marchione, N. J. (1996). A comparative outcome and follow-up investigation of panic disorder with agoraphobia: The relative and combined efficacy of cognitive therapy, relaxation training, and therapist-assisted exposure. *Journal of Anxiety Disorders, 10*, 297–330.

Norcross, J. C., Hedges, M., & Castle, P. H. (2002). Psychologists conducting psychotherapy in 2001: A study of the Division 29 membership. *Psychotherapy: Theory, Research, Practice, and Training, 39*, 97–102.

Norcross, J. C., Hedges, M., & Prochaska, J. O. (2002). The face of 2010: A Delphi poll on the future of psychotherapy. *Professional Psychology: Research and Practice, 33*, 316–322.

Norcross, J. C., Karpiak, C. P., & Santoro, S. O. (2005). Clinical psychologists across the years: The division of clinical psychology from 1960 to 2003. *Journal of Clinical Psychology, 61*, 1467–1483.

Norcross, J. C., Sayette, M. A., Mayne, T. J., Karg, R. S., & Turkson, M. A. (1998). Selecting a doctoral program in professional psychology: Some comparisons among Ph.D. counseling, Ph.D. clinical, and PsyD clinical psychology programs. *Professional Psychology: Research and Practice, 29*, 609–614.

Orsillo, S. M., Roemer, L., & Barlow, D. H. (2003). Integrating acceptance and mindfulness into existing cognitive-behavioral treatment for GAD: A case study. *Cognitive and Behavioral Practice, 10*, 222–230.

Öst, L. (2008). Efficacy of the third wave of behavioral therapies: A systematic review and meta-analysis. *Behaviour Research and Therapy, 46*, 296–321.

Paunovic, N., & Öst, L.-G. (2001). Cognitive-behavior therapy vs exposure therapy in the treatment of

PTSD in refugees. *Behaviour Research and Therapy, 39,* 1183–1197.

Prins, P. J. M., & Ollendick, T. H. (2003). Cognitive change and enhanced coping: Missing mediational links in cognitive behavior therapy with anxiety-disordered children. *Clinical Child and Family Psychology Review, 6,* 87–105.

Prochaska, J. O., & Norcross, J. C. (1994). *Systems of psychotherapy: A transtheoretical analysis* (3rd ed.). Pacific Grove, CA: Brooks/Cole.

Resick, P. A., & Schnicke, M. K. (1993). *Cognitive processing therapy for rape victims: A treatment manual.* Thousand Oaks, CA: Sage Publications.

Roemer, L., & Orsillo, S. M. (2005). An acceptance based behavior therapy for generalized anxiety disorder. In S. M. Orsillo & L. Roemer (Eds.), *Acceptance and mindfulness-based approaches to anxiety: Conceptualization and treatment.* New York: Springer.

Roemer, L., & Orsillo, S. M. (2007). An open trial of an acceptance-based behavior therapy for generalized anxiety disorder. *Behavior Therapy, 38,* 72–85.

Roemer, L., Salters-Pedneault, K., & Orsillo, S. M. (2006). Incorporating mindfulness- and acceptance-based strategies in the treatment of generalized anxiety disorder. [References]. In R. A. Baer (Ed.), *Mindfulness-based treatment approaches: Clinician's guide to evidence base and applications* (pp. 51–74). San Diego, CA: Elsevier Academic Press.

Rush, A. J., Kovacs, M., Beck, A. T., Weissenburger, J., & Hollon, S. D. (1981). Differential effects of cognitive therapy and pharmacotherapy on depressive symptoms. *Journal of Affective Disorders, 3,* 221–229.

Scholing, A., & Emmelkamp, P. M. (1993). Exposure with and without cognitive therapy for generalized social phobia: Effects of individual and group treatment. *Behaviour Research and Therapy, 31,* 667–681.

Segal, Z. V., Williams, J. M. G., & Teasdale, J. D. (2002). *Mindfulness-based cognitive therapy for depression: A new approach to preventing relapse.* New York: Guilford.

Simons, A. D., Garfield, S. L., & Murphy, G. E. (1984). The process of change in cognitive therapy and pharmacotherapy for depression. Changes in mood and cognition. *Archives of General Psychiatry, 41,* 45–51.

Skinner, B. F. (1953). *Science and human behavior.* Oxford, UK: MacMillan.

Smits, J. A., Powers, M. B., Cho, Y., & Telch, M. J. (2004). Mechanism of change in cognitive-behavioral treatment of panic disorder: Evidence for the fear of fear mediational hypothesis. *Journal of Consulting and Clinical Psychology, 72,* 646–652.

Smits, J. A., Rosenfield, D., McDonald, R., & Telch, M. J. (2006). Cognitive mechanisms of social anxiety reduction: An examination of specificity and temporality. *Journal of Consulting and Clinical Psychology, 74,* 1203–1212.

Stanley, S. M., Blumberg, S. L., & Markman, H. J. (1999). Helping couples fight for their marriages: The PREP approach. In R. Berger & M. T. Hannah (Eds.), *Preventive approaches in couples therapy* (pp. 279–303). Philadelphia: Brunner/Mazel.

Strosahl, K. D. (2005). ACT with the multi-problem patient. In S. C. Hayes & K. D. Strosahl (Eds.), *A practical guide to acceptance and commitment therapy* (pp. 209–245). New York: Springer Science.

Tang, T. Z., DeRubeis, R. J., Beberman, R., & Pham, T. (2005). Cognitive changes, critical sessions, and sudden gains in cognitive-behavioral therapy for depression. *Journal of Consulting & Clinical Psychology, 73,* 168–172.

Teasdale, J. D., Moore, R. G., Hayhurst, H., Pope, M., Williams, S., & Segal, Z. V. (2002). Metacognitive awareness and prevention of relapse in depression: Empirical evidence. *Journal of Consulting and Clinical Psychology, 70,* 275–287.

Teasdale, J. D., Scott, J., Moore, R. G., Hayhurst, H., Pope, M., & Paykel, E. S. (2001). How does cognitive therapy prevent relapse in residual depression? Evidence from a controlled trial. *Journal of Consulting and Clinical Psychology, 69,* 347–357.

Teasdale, J. D., Segal, Z. V., Williams, J. G., Ridgeway, V. A., Soulsby, J. M., & Lau, M. A. (2000). Prevention of relapse/recurrence in major depression by mindfulness-based cognitive therapy. *Journal of Consulting and Clinical Psychology, 68,* 615–623.

Treadwell, K. R., & Kendall, P. C. (1996). Self-talk in youth with anxiety disorders: States of mind, specificity, and treatment outcome. *Journal of Consulting and Clinical Psychology, 64.*

Wells, A. (2005a). The metacognitive model of GAD: Assessment of meta-worry and relationship with DSM-IV generalized anxiety disorder. *Cognitive Therapy and Research, 29,* 107–121.

Wells, A. (2005b). Worry, intrusive thoughts, and generalized anxiety disorder: The metacognitive theory and treatment. In D. A. Clark (Ed.), *Intrusive thoughts in clinical disorders: Theory, research, and treatment* (pp. 119–144). New York: Guilford.

Wells, A. (2007). Cognition about cognition: Metacognitive therapy and change in generalized anxiety disorder and social phobia. *Cognitive and Behavioral Practice, 14,* 18–25.

Wells, A., & King, P. (2006). Metacognitive therapy for generalized anxiety disorder: An open trial. *Journal of Behavior Therapy and Experimental Psychiatry, 37,* 206–212.

Wells, A., & Matthews, G. (1996). Modelling cognition in emotional disorder: the S-REF model. *Behavior Research and Therapy, 34,* 881–888.

Wells, A., & Sembi, S. (2004). Metacognitive therapy for PTSD: A core treatment manual. *Cognitive and Behavioral Practice, 11,* 365–377.

Wilson, K. G., & Murrell, A. R. (2004). Values work in acceptance and commitment therapy: Setting a course for behavioral treatment. In S. C. Hayes, V. M. Follette, & M. M. Linehan (Eds.), *Mindfulness and acceptance: Expanding the cognitive-behavioral tradition* (pp. 120–151). New York: Guilford.

Wilson, K. G., & Roberts, M. (2002). Core principles in acceptance and commitment therapy: An application to anorexia. *Cognitive & Behavioral Practice, 9,* 237–243.

Wolpe, J. (1958). *Psychotherapy by reciprocal inhibition.* Pasadena, CA: Stanford University Press.

Woods, D. W., Wetterneck, C. T., & Flessner, C. A. (2006). A controlled evaluation of acceptance and commitment therapy plus habit reversal for trichotillomania. *Behavior Research and Therapy, 44,* 639–656.

Young, J., & Klosko, J. (2005). Schema Therapy. [References]. In J. M. Oldham, A. E. Skodol, & D. S. Bender (Eds.), *The American Psychiatric Publishing textbook of personality disorders* (pp. 289–306). Washington, DC: American Psychiatric Publishing.

Zettle, R. D. (2003). Acceptance and commitment therapy (ACT) vs. systematic desensitization in treatment of mathematics anxiety. *Psychological Record, 53,* 197–215.

Zettle, R. D. (2005a). ACT with affective disorders. In S. C. Hayes & K. D. Strosahl (Eds.), *A practical guide to acceptance and commitment therapy* (pp. 77–102). New York: Springer Science.

Zettle, R. D. (2005b). The evolution of a contextual approach to therapy: From comprehensive distancing to ACT. *International Journal of Behavioral and Consultation Therapy, 1,* 77–89.

Zettle, R. D., & Hayes, S. C. (1986). Dysfunctional control by client verbal behavior: The context of reason giving. *Analysis of Verbal Behavior, 30,* 38.

Zettle, R. D., & Hayes, S. C. (1987). Component and process analysis of cognitive therapy. *Psychological Reports, 61,* 939–953.

Zettle, R. D., & Rains, J. C. (1989). Group cognitive and contextual therapies in treatment of depression. *Journal of Clinical Psychology, 45,* 436–445.

6 PSYCHOLOGICAL ACCEPTANCE

James D. Herbert, Evan M. Forman, and Erica L. England

In one form or another, all psychotherapies seek to produce change. Individuals seek consultation from psychotherapists when they are experiencing emotional pain, struggling with life problems, or when they are not functioning well in school, work, or relationships. The explicit goal is to achieve changes that will reduce pain or suffering, resolve outstanding problems, or enhance functioning. There has also been a longstanding recognition that such change requires some sense of self-acceptance, understood as the ability to respond less self-critically and judgmentally, thereby establishing the context for more effective functioning. Prior to the advent of behavior therapy, psychotherapists traditionally focused less on changing distressing symptoms themselves, concentrating instead on modifying other processes on the assumption that changes in such processes would result in more fundamental, profound, and permanent improvements in distress (Sulloway, 1983). Psychoanalysts sought to increase insight into the developmental origins of unconscious conflicts. By rendering the unconscious conscious, unacceptable drives and fantasies become acceptable to the ego. Humanistic therapists likewise sought to increase congruence between different facets of the self, thereby promoting a sense of self-acceptance. Although the ultimate goal was change, the prevailing clinical wisdom was that targeting distressing thoughts, feelings, or behavior directly would be ineffective at best, and possibly even counterproductive.

Early behavior therapists rejected the idea that change required interventions focusing on processes not directly related to actual presenting problems. Instead, they directly targeted their patients' difficulties. Behavior therapists focused on modifying environmental factors thought to be responsible for problematic behavior, broadly conceived to include distressing thoughts and feelings in addition to overt behavior. Although one might need to accept temporary, short-term distress associated with certain interventions, the overall focus was on changing the form or frequency of distressing behaviors rather than accepting them. This approach was dramatically successful. Effective technologies were developed to increase social skills, desensitize fears, and manage disruptive behavior among children, as well as to address many other problems (Bongar & Beutler, 1995; Goldfried & Davison, 1994). As behavior therapy matured through the last decades of the twentieth century, there evolved an increased focus on changing thoughts and beliefs, and the field itself came to be known by the term *cognitive behavior therapy* (CBT). The various clinical strategies and techniques falling under the rubric of CBT all shared a focus on directly targeting problems using instrumental change strategies. Although acceptance of one's distressing experiences was indirectly targeted in some cases (e.g., acceptance of anxious sensations during exposure-based therapies), even then the ultimate goal was change (e.g., anxiety reduction), and the overall focus of clinical interventions remained squarely on direct change.

THE GROWTH OF PSYCHOLOGICAL ACCEPTANCE IN CBT

It is perhaps ironic, then, that the field of CBT currently finds itself at the forefront of a movement that questions the utility of such direct change strategies under certain circumstances and promotes instead the rather paradoxical idea that more pervasive and enduring improvements in suffering and quality of life may result from accepting, rather than attempting to

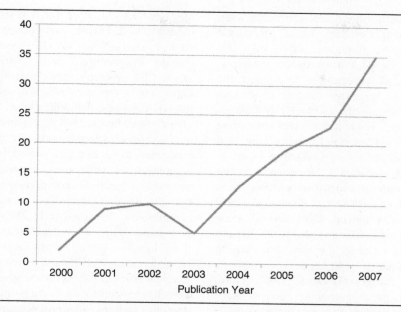

FIGURE 6.1 PsychInfo Citations for Keywords "Experiential Acceptance," "Psychological Acceptance," or "Experiential Avoidance."

change, one's distressing subjective experience. This distinction between direct change efforts and psychological acceptance as a vehicle for change has been described in various ways, including first-order versus second-order change, change in content versus context, and change in form versus function (Hayes, 2001). Regardless of terminology, a number of CBT models have emerged over the past decade that highlight efforts to accept, rather than directly change, distressing experiences, including thoughts, beliefs, feelings, memories, and sensations. These approaches have not abandoned all direct change strategies. Rather, as described later, they suggest that changes in some areas are best facilitated by acceptance in others. It is worth noting that there is no hard-and-fast distinction between traditional change-oriented and acceptance-oriented models of CBT (Orsillo, Roemer, Lerner, & Tull, 2004). A key ultimate goal of both approaches is behavior change (broadly writ), and both draw on technologies that either implicitly or explicitly seek to increase psychological acceptance. Rather, the models differ in the relative degree of emphasis on acceptance versus change processes.

The recent growth of interest in these approaches is undeniable. For example, as illustrated in Figure 6.1, the *PsychInfo* database reveals a steady growth in the hits of the keywords *experiential acceptance*, its synonym *psychological acceptance*, and *experiential avoidance* (which is an antonym for the first two) from 2 in 2000 to 35 in 2007. Parallel increases can be found in related databases (e.g., *Medline*), and in the titles of conference proceedings (e.g., the annual meeting of the Association for Behavioral and Cognitive Therapies).

This increased emphasis on psychological acceptance is the result of several factors (Hayes, 2004; Longmore & Worrell, 2007). First, an accumulating body of experimental research demonstrates that efforts to suppress thoughts generally result in rebound effects in which the frequency and intensity of thoughts increase upon termination of active suppression efforts (Abramowitz, Tolin, & Street, 2001; Wenzlaff & Wegner, 2000). Such findings suggest that CBT interventions such as thought stopping, in which distressing thoughts are deliberately suppressed, might be seriously misguided. In fact, most CBT scholars now disavow this technique (Marks, 1987). Thought suppression studies (in which individuals who deliberately suppress thoughts demonstrate increased rebound of these thoughts relative to those who do not engage in suppression strategies) have been cited as evidence to suspect the advisability of cognitive restructuring, one of the most commonly used CBT techniques (Hayes, in press). The concern is that attempting to restructure distressing thoughts may lead patients to suppress them, resulting in intensification and elaboration. However, it is not clear that cognitive restructuring is analogous to thought suppression (Arch & Craske, in press; Hofmann & Admundson, 2008). Second, some cognitive therapists have recently challenged on theoretical grounds the idea that directly targeting thoughts can produce cognitive or affective changes (Teasdale, 1997). Third, experimental psychopathology studies have found that instructions to accept experimentally induced distress resulted in better outcomes than instructions to control such distress. For example, acceptance-oriented instructions, relative to distraction or control-oriented instructions, have been shown to result in greater pain tolerance in cold pressor tasks (Hayes et al., 1999), in lower behavioral avoidance and fear response following exposure to CO_2 enriched air among high anxiety–sensitivity women (Eifert & Heffner, 2003) and panic disorder patients (Levitt, Brown, Orsillo, & Barlow, 2004), and in reducing chocolate cravings in food-responsive individuals (Forman, Hoffman, et al., 2007). Fourth, psychotherapy process studies often have failed to support the theorized mechanism of cognitive mediation, raising questions about the centrality of cognitive change as a prerequisite for changes in other areas (Longmore & Worrell). Fifth, although standard CBT strategies have been applied to an increasing number of problems and psychological disorders over the past 30 years, outside of a few specific areas (e.g., panic disorder, Craske & Barlow, 2008; social anxiety disorder, Clark et al., 2006, Herbert et al., 2005) progress has slowed or even stalled in many key areas. For example, it is not clear that recent studies of CBT (e.g., DeRubeis et al., 2005; Dimidjian et al., 2006) for depression produced larger effect sizes than studies conducted two or even three decades

ago (see Dobson, 1989, for a review of these older studies). Finally, preliminary component control studies, in which direct cognitive change interventions were extracted from larger CBT protocols, have generally failed to support the incremental effects of such cognitive interventions (e.g., Dimidjian et al., 2006; Hope, Heimberg, & Bruch, 1995; Jacobson et al., 1996).

These observations led several psychotherapy innovators to develop approaches that highlight acceptance of distressing experiences. Such innovations include comprehensive psychotherapy models such as acceptance and commitment therapy (ACT; Hayes, Strosahl, & Wilson, 1999), dialectical behavior therapy (DBT; Linehan, 1993a), mindfulness-based stress reduction (MBSR; 1990) and functional analytic psychotherapy (FAP; Kohlenberg & Tsai, 1991), as well as models focused on a particular clinical domain, such as integrative couples therapy (ICT; Jacobson et al., 2000), mindfulnesss-based cognitive therapy (MBCT; Coelho, Canter, & Ernst, 2007; Segal, Williams, & Teasdale, 2002) for recurrent depression, and the work of leading CBT theorists such as Borkovec (1994), Wells (2000), Marlatt and colleagues (2004), and others.

CONCEPTUALIZATIONS OF ACCEPTANCE

No consensus definition of psychological acceptance has yet emerged, although existing definitions share several common themes. Butler and Ciarrochi (2007) define acceptance as "a willingness to experience psychological events (thoughts, feelings, memories) without having to avoid them or let them unduly influence behavior" (p. 608). These authors also note that acceptance is the mirror image of Hayes and colleagues' (1999) concept of experiential avoidance, which is defined as maladaptive attempts to alter the form or frequency of internal experiences even when doing so causes behavioral harm. Cordova (2001), writing from a behavior analytic perspective, defines acceptance as "allowing, tolerating, embracing, experiencing, or making contact with a source of stimulation that previously provoked escape, avoidance, or aggression" (p. 215), and also as "a change in the behavior evoked by a stimulus from that functioning to avoid, escape, or destroy to behavior functioning to pursue or maintain contact" (p. 215).

These definitions share several common themes. First, they specify that psychological acceptance is relevant in those situations that evoke escape, avoidance, or aggressive behaviors designed to modify or otherwise terminate contact with a stimulus. There is a class of subjective experiences (thoughts, images, feelings, sensations) that are experienced as unpleasant and distressing to the point at which one becomes highly motivated to reduce or eliminate them through either direct mental efforts or through environmental modification such as escape or avoidance. Acceptance is generally not relevant to situations that are not experienced as aversive, which are usually naturally embraced without difficulty. Second, psychological acceptance refers primarily to the internal experience of distress rather than to the situations evoking this distress. In the case of a phobia of heights, for example, acceptance refers to a willingness to experience anxiety—without attempting to control or otherwise change it—in the presence of heights, and not an acceptance that one can never approach heights. Third, the conceptualizations of acceptance implicitly challenge the rule that overt behavior is a direct product of cognition and affect, and that the latter must therefore necessarily be changed in order to produce a change in behavior.

In addition, several additional aspects of psychological acceptance emerge from the literature. On the basis of the literature on thought suppression, experimental psychopathology, and psychotherapy outcome and process described earlier, including the preliminary effectiveness of newer CBT interventions that eschew direct cognitive change, many acceptance-oriented psychotherapists have come to believe that direct efforts to suppress or otherwise change highly distressing internal experiences will often prove ineffective, will result in unacceptable costs, or both (e.g., Eifert & Forsyth, 2005; Segal, Teasdale, & Williams, 2004). This is not to suggest that all such efforts are doomed to failure. DBT, for example, is based on the careful, ongoing balance between acceptance and change and does not abandon the possibility of direct cognitive or affective change efforts.

Likewise, the prohibition against experiential avoidance in ACT is neither absolute nor dogmatic, but rather pragmatic. (In fact, while ACT practitioners are skeptical of experiential avoidance, including many cognitive change strategies, their use is explicitly advised when they work without undue costs.) Second, acceptance is conceptualized as an active process, more akin to an embracing of one's ongoing process of experiencing, rather than as passive resignation. Finally, consistent with the historical focus in CBT on change, psychological acceptance is generally viewed as a means to an end rather than an end in-and-of itself. In fact, this last point is one of the key features that distinguishes psychological acceptance in CBT from acceptance in certain spiritual or religious contexts, and even in popular culture. Meditative practices in Eastern religious traditions view acceptance as part of a desired state of consciousness. Within CBT, the value of acceptance is as a tool to reduce overall suffering and especially to foster behavior change that will lead to better functioning.

CLINICAL INTERVENTIONS TO PROMOTE PSYCHOLOGICAL ACCEPTANCE

A number of techniques have been developed to promote psychological acceptance. Although comprehensive review of such techniques is well beyond the scope of this chapter, we provide representative examples of such strategies below.

Barlow and colleagues (1989) introduced the technique of interoceptive exposure in the context of their treatment of panic disorder. Interoceptive exposure refers to the graduated, systematic exposure to somatic sensations associated with panic attacks. Various exercises are used that reliably elicit panic-like symptoms, including cardiovascular exercises, inhalation of carbon dioxide, spinning in an office chair, breathing through a cocktail straw, and shaking one's head vigorously side to side. The patient is instructed to notice the sensations that arise dispassionately. Although not specifically framed as a technique to promote psychological acceptance, interoceptive exposure is consistent with an acceptance focus.

One of the most common approaches to promoting psychological acceptance is mindfulness meditation. The use of meditation was spearheaded by Jon Kabat-Zinn in the context of MBSR, which was initially introduced in 1979 as a complement to medical treatment of a variety of chronic conditions. MBSR incorporates the practice of mindfulness meditation with certain core principles and "key attitudes," such as acceptance, patience, and the "beginner's mind," that is, viewing experiences as though for the first time (Kabat-Zinn, 1990). The typical format through which MBSR is delivered consists of eight weekly classes (often with 30 or more participants), and a "Day of Mindfulness," a full-day retreat focusing on the practice of meditation and yoga. A key technique used in MBSR is "sitting meditation," in which participants practice nonjudgmental awareness and acceptance of their thoughts and other experiences. In addition to meditation and yoga, participants are taught various techniques designed to promote mindfulness, such as the "body scan," which involves gradually shifting awareness throughout the body, taking notice of any feelings and sensations (Tacon, Caldera, & Ronaghan, 2004). Although similar to the traditional behavior therapy technique of relaxation training, in the case of mindfulness meditation relaxation is not the goal, but rather the adoption of a nonjudgmental stance with respect to one's experience as it occurs in real time. Mindfulness meditation is also contrasted with other meditative traditions in which one attempts to narrow the focus of attention to a specific area (e.g., an image or vocal mantra). By fostering the observation of one's experience without reactively attempting to escape from or otherwise change it, mindfulness meditation is believed to interrupt maladaptive behavioral habits and to set the context for more effective responding.

Mindfulness meditation is also a key feature of DBT, developed by Linehan (1993a) as a comprehensive treatment model for borderline personality disorder. DBT proposes that the change-oriented emphasis in traditional CBT can be perceived as invalidating of the experience of patients with borderline personality disorder. Linehan (1993b) describes modules for teaching four key skill areas: mindfulness skills, emotional regulation skills, interpersonal effectiveness skills, and distress tolerance skills. Each module outlines specific clinical techniques. Mindfulness skills are generally taught first, as they are foundational for the other skill areas. The DBT mindfulness module emphasizes observing and labeling emotional states from a detached, nonjudgmental, accepting perspective. Patients are taught to integrate the "emotional mind" and "reasonable mind" into the "wise mind" that can inform decisions from an informed, balanced, holistic perspective.

A potentially unresolved issue with DBT concerns the reconciliation of experiential acceptance and change. DBT explicitly teaches a number of emotion regulation strategies, such as the principle of "opposite action," which refers to attempting to change an emotional state by behaving in a way that is contrary to its usual behavioral manifestation. For example, a phobic who approaches rather than avoids a fear-inducing stimulus is displaying the principle of opposite action. The emphasis on emotion regulation in DBT highlights the dialectic between acceptance and change that is characteristic of the model. However, as discussed above, there may be situations in which attempting to change one's experience only intensifies it. Thoroughgoing acceptance of distressing thoughts or feelings may be precluded if one remains focused on changing such experiences. An obese individual suffering from episodes of binge eating, for example, may not fully accept distressing emotional states that trigger binges, and therefore may not completely disconnect links between such experiences and her behavior, if in the back of her mind she is still struggling with trying to change her experience. As described below, ACT takes a more radical—although arguably more consistent—stance with respect to efforts to control distressing experiences.

Working from a cognitive perspective, Wells (2000) proposes that psychopathology is related to problematic self-regulation of attentional control, resulting in rumination, increased threat monitoring (including self-focused attention), and coping behaviors that fail to provide corrective experiences. The roots of these self-regulatory attentional problems are dysfunctional metacognitive beliefs, or beliefs about beliefs. For example, a person with generalized anxiety disorder might hold a metabelief such as "if I review things over and over again it will reduce the chances of something bad happening." Wells distinguishes such metacognitions from the conscious, propositional beliefs that are the typical targets of standard cognitive therapy. He suggests intervention efforts to target such metacognitions, while simultaneously accepting the stream of one's ongoing conscious thoughts and feelings. Unlike traditional CBT approaches, such change is not accomplished by questioning the beliefs directly, but by encouraging greater attentional control while simultaneously encouraging a heightened sense of awareness of, and an accepting stance toward, one's thoughts as mere mental events. As part of his metacognitive therapy, Wells describes a procedure known as the attention training technique (ATT), in which various sounds are presented as distractions while subjects remain focused on a visual fixation point, accept whatever thoughts enter consciousness without struggling with them, and attempt to direct their attention in various ways as directed by the therapist. ATT has been shown in preliminary studies to result in changes in distressing thoughts and symptoms, despite not directly targeting them, as well as in increases in metacognitive awareness (for a recent review, see Wells, 2007).

ACT makes use of a variety of metaphors and experiential exercises in order to promote acceptance. A great number of such exercises have been developed, and clinical innovations in this area continue apace. One technique has the patient precede discussions of distressing thoughts or feelings by verbally (and subsequently subvocally) inserting the phrase "I'm having the thought [or feeling] that ... " before thoughts. For example, an individual who imagines that he might suddenly shout out a profanity-laced, heretical statement in church would be highly motivated to suppress the urge to do so as well as the linked thoughts and images. Attempts to suppress thoughts or images of such behavior would likely only increase their salience and intensity, thereby further increasing distress. Instead, this person

could simply observe his urge, and say to himself, "I'm having the thought of shouting out right now. That's an interesting thought." The idea is to help the patient to achieve distance from his experience and to accept the thought as simply a mental event, rather than as necessarily reflecting anything whatsoever about his world.

Another example derived from ACT is the "cards" exercise. In one variation of this exercise, the patient is instructed to carry on a conversation with the therapist. As she does so, the therapist tosses index cards, on each of which is written one of the patient's typical distressing thoughts, one-by-one at the patient, who is then instructed either to deflect them away, or to gather them and stack them neatly together, all while continuing the conversation. Needless-to-say, this is a difficult task, and the conversation is inevitably negatively impacted. The exercise is then repeated, this time with the patient instructed simply to let the cards fall where they may, without trying to catch or organize them. Following the exercise, the therapist and patient note how much more difficult the conversation was to maintain in the first scenario, and the effort to gather and organize the cards is framed as analogous to the effort to control one's distressing thoughts. The ACT model is rich with similar exercises designed to promote psychological acceptance.

Roemer and Orsillo (2002) utilize the ACT framework to develop an acceptance-based intervention for generalized anxiety disorder. Their model draws on the work of Borkovec (1994), who conceptualizes worry as an avoidance method that serves to reduce the perceived likelihood of feared future events, as well as to distract the worrier from distressing internal anxiety. Worry, in turn, is negatively reinforced by the resulting decrease in distress. According to Roemer and Orsillo, by learning to accept unpleasant internal events rather than struggling with them, individuals can reduce their experiential avoidance of perceived future threats. Roemer and Orsillo's treatment incorporates various techniques to promote mindfulness, acceptance, and behavior change. For example, the "mindfulness of sound" exercise, borrowed from Segal and colleagues (2002), encourages patients to notice aspects of sound without labeling and judgment (Orsillo, Roemer, & Holowka, 2005).

Marlatt and colleagues have incorporated mindfulness and acceptance into their work on substance abuse treatment (Leigh, Bowen, & Marlatt, 2005; Marlatt et al., 2004; Witkiewitz, Marlatt, & Walker, 2005). Marlatt's relapse-prevention model involves mindful acceptance of urges and cravings. A key intervention of their program is known as "urge surfing," in which the patient is instructed to imagine a craving as an ocean wave (Larimer, Palmer, & Marlatt, 1999). Rather than allowing urges to overwhelm them, patients are taught that cravings surge to a peak relatively quickly and will then subside. By focusing on the idea that distressing emotions will eventually subside, they are more readily tolerated while at their most intense. The patient is encouraged to observe the craving as though detached from it, and to practice mindful acceptance of the urge until it dissipates.

Regardless of approach, the ultimate goal of each of these techniques is the promotion of acceptance toward one's experience on an ongoing basis in real time.

WHEN IS ACCEPTANCE RECOMMENDED, AND WHEN IS IT LIKELY TO BE LESS EFFECTIVE?

As noted above, efforts to exert direct control over one's experience can be considered adaptive when they work and do not result in excessive costs. Of course, this begs the question of how one might ascertain when direct control efforts are likely to be effective and when psychological acceptance is instead indicated. Several theorists have addressed this question, although a clear consensus has yet to emerge. Cordova (2001) suggests that the decision is a judgment call, made collaboratively by the patient and therapist, on whether aversion behavior (escape, avoidance, or aggression toward a stimulus) is more likely to be effective, or lead to excessive negative consequences, over the long term. Of course, this begs the question of exactly what factors should determine such a judgment. Hayes (2001) distinguishes maladaptive overt behavior from acceptance of one's subjective experiences,

noting that acceptance is rarely appropriate for the former but almost always for the latter. For example, an individual suffering from depression can distance herself from and accept feelings of dysphoria and thoughts of worthlessness and suicide, but without accepting her behavior of staying in bed all day. Historically important memories (e.g., one's memories of a traumatic experience) are especially important to accept, as considerable research suggests that avoidant coping strategies are problematic for such memories (Folette et al., 1998; Hayes et al., 1996). Likewise, one's ongoing stream of thoughts, feelings, and sensations also tend to be appropriate targets for acceptance. For example, Hayes and Pankey (2003) note that a pedophile's sexual behavior toward children should be directly targeted for change, whereas his associated feelings and urges are unlikely to be amenable to direct change, and should therefore be accepted. It is in fact precisely this decoupling of subjective experiences from overt behavior that is at the heart of acceptance-based CBTs.

It is critical to distinguish psychological acceptance of a thought from belief in the literal truth of that thought. Acceptance implies the willingness to experience a thought while simultaneously refraining from evaluating its truth value. This distinction is critical when considering the patient's personal narrative, or what Hayes et al. (1999) term the *self-as-content*. Given the powerful human drive to make sense of one's experience, we inevitably construct narratives that tie together important historical events, and that crystallize into broad personality descriptors. The problem with such narratives is that once formed, they tend to be taken literally and strongly defended from question, which can in turn lead to a narrowing of one's behavioral repertoire. For example, a college student may recall academic successes in school, attribute these to her intelligence and strong work ethic, and develop an identity as an "exceptionally smart, hardworking student." Imagine that she then finds herself in a difficult class and not understanding the lecture material. If she holds strongly to her personal narrative, she may refrain from asking a question because doing so would conflict with her self-identity as an exceptionally bright student. As verbal animals, humans have evolved to seek patterns in the ongoing barrage of sensory input (Shermer, 2002), and as part of this process, we construct stories that weave key details of our lives into a seamless narrative. Once constructed, there is a natural tendency to believe such narratives and to defend them from challenge. Psychological acceptance in this context means accepting one's personal narrative as an inevitable product of an active, pattern-seeking mind without either believing or disbelieving it.

Farmer and Chapman (2008) propose three principles in deciding if psychological acceptance is indicated. First, is acceptance "justified"? A justified response is one that is warranted by the situation, such as a fear response in the presence of a phobic stimulus. If the response is justified, then acceptance is in order; if the response is not justified, then one either attempts to change the response or at least to change the behavior elicited by the response (consistent with the DBT principle of "opposite action"). For example, distressing thoughts about being overweight are justified in an obese individual, but the same thoughts are unjustified in a woman suffering from anorexia. Of course, determination of whether a thought is justified requires at least some degree of analysis of the truth value of the thought, which runs the risk of interfering with attempts to accept it. Second, is the reaction or situation changeable or unchangeable? Obviously, acceptance is indicated for unchangeable experiences. Finally, are the patient's responses effective or ineffective? Effective responses are conceptualized as those that are consistent with valued goals, whereas ineffective responses are inconsistent. When responses are ineffective in this sense, they call for acceptance.

A common rule of thumb among acceptance-oriented CBT clinicians is that psychological acceptance is indicated for any distressing personal experiences, such as painful memories, disturbing thoughts, and difficult feelings or sensations, as well as for personal narratives. By contrast, direct change efforts should be reserved for overt behaviors, that is, things involving one's hands, feet, mouth, and so on. Although superficially appealing, such a distinction becomes more difficult upon closer examination. It assumes that all cognitive and affective control efforts are necessarily doomed to failure, which may not be the case. Some experiences are neither fully voluntary (like hand/feet movements) nor involuntary (such as heart rate). Attention is a prime example. In fact, a number of experiences (e.g., thought contents, muscle tension) are on a continuum of controllability. Psychological acceptance can be understood as gentle attempts to influence such experiences where possible, while acknowledging without struggle the inevitable limitations of this influence.

Consider the case of test anxiety. As with other anxiety disorders, it is easy to appreciate how an accepting stance with respect to catastrophic thoughts and anxious sensations evoked by tests could be beneficial. However, to be successful it is not enough to accept one's subjective distress; one must also focus one's attention in order to orient toward the test itself. Approaches such as Wells' (2000) attentional training technique, in which flexible attentional control is targeted without attempting to change ongoing thoughts or feelings, may provide a useful approach to such cases.

Finally, consistent with Farmer and Chapman's (2008) notion of justified responses, there are situations in which the literal truth of a thought or belief is, in fact, critical to evaluate. A man with tachycardia, shortness of breath, and chest pains needs to know whether he is dying of a heart attack or simply having a panic attack. A woman who believes that she is being stalked by an ex-boyfriend must evaluate the evidence for this belief before simply accepting her feelings dispassionately. In such cases, psychological acceptance becomes relevant after an objective evaluation of the relevant evidence (e.g., a medical workup for the individual with chest pains, consultation with appropriate law enforcement authorities for the woman who believes she is being stalked). In many other cases, however, one may be tempted to evaluate the truth of thoughts when doing so may not be necessary. An individual with public speaking anxiety will almost certainly have thoughts concerning negative evaluation by the audience in anticipation of a speech. An objective evaluation of the evidence for such beliefs would not only be difficult to achieve, but is not necessary. The individual can learn simply to notice his catastrophic thoughts and associated feelings of anxiety and to give the speech anyway. The issue of determining when to evaluate versus when to accept distressing thoughts is discussed further below.

UNRESOLVED ISSUES AND DIRECTIONS FOR FUTURE RESEARCH

Given the relatively recent emphasis of acceptance-based therapies within CBT, there remain a number of unresolved questions and directions for future research and clinical innovations. First, there is a need for new technologies to promote psychological acceptance. Given the pervasiveness of psychological change-oriented strategies in Western culture, the notion of fully accepting one's experience while simultaneously engaging in behavior that is seemingly inconsistent with that experience can be counterintuitive. A range of clinical strategies and techniques are needed to foster psychological acceptance. It is likely that there is untapped clinical wisdom among both practicing cognitive behavior therapists and those from other theoretical orientations that would be helpful in promoting acceptance. Similarly, the best methods of training practitioners in acceptance-based technologies require further development. Many leading innovators, including Kabat-Zinn, Linehan, and Teasdale, all stress the importance of therapists cultivating their own mindfulness practice (Lau & McMain, 2005). Likewise, Hayes incorporates various experiential exercises in his training workshops with the purpose of developing a deeper appreciation of ACT principles. Although there is clear logic to the notion that such efforts will be helpful in therapists' efforts to understand and transmit acceptance-based strategies, the importance of such training strategies is not known empirically.

Second, the development of more explicit guidelines is needed in order to distinguish when psychological acceptance is likely to be helpful, and conversely, when direct change strategies are indicated. As discussed above, there are situations in which a certain level of attentional control and evaluation of the truth value of cognitions is clearly necessary. Although at first glance such efforts may appear incompatible with experiential acceptance, acceptance may actually *enhance* one's efforts along these lines. Many existing acceptance-based innovations have not attended sufficiently to the integration of change and acceptance strategies, and the reconciliation of these apparently inconsistent themes.

It may in fact be the case that even the most staunch acceptance-oriented therapists covertly or implicitly do evaluate the validity of their patients' thoughts, and then promote acceptance only when thoughts are inaccurate. In the case of the man with chest pains described earlier, for example, no acceptance-based therapist would suggest that he simply acknowledge and accept the pain without first referring him for an appropriate medical evaluation to rule out cardiac disease. We propose that the determination of whether acceptance versus engagement with thoughts is indicated is best made on the strength of one's knowledge that (1) one has already systematically evaluated a thought before, and/or (2) one's mind routinely emits this exact thought without good cause. An example of a workable strategy along these lines would be to reach an agreement with patients to undertake a thorough evaluation of a troubling thought once and only once, after which the thought is simply noticed and accepted without further elaboration.

In addition to clinical developments, there remain a number of unresolved conceptual issues. For example, is acceptance best conceptualized as an overt behavior that can be directly assessed, as suggested by Cordova (2001), or as a private experience that is only indirectly reflected in overt behavior? An individual with social anxiety disorder may attend a party but may engage in a variety of covert "safety behaviors" that render her not fully engaged in the experience. A purely behavioral assessment of the topography of her behavior would erroneously conclude that she was highly accepting of her anxiety. The quality of one's experience with respect to a distressing stimulus is also unclear. Cordova (2001) argues that "genuine" acceptance involves a "change in the stimulus function from aversive to more attractive" and similarly as " ... change in stimulus function of a situation toward that which inclines the person to seek or remain in contact" (p. 221). According to this analysis, if one remains in contact with an aversive stimulus without the stimulus losing its aversive properties, one is effectively in a state of hopeless resignation rather than true acceptance. It is noteworthy that this perspective effectively requires that the stimulus be experienced as less aversive to qualify as "genuine" acceptance. Yet it seems entirely plausible that one could learn to remain in psychological contact with an aversive stimulus without requiring that one's reactions to it necessarily change. For example, a patient with chronic pain may learn to accept rather than fight his pain. This may or may not result in a change in his pain perception, but it is not clear that the degree of perceived pain should distinguish "real" acceptance from mere resignation. What seems important instead is his abandoning ineffective struggles with the pain and his simultaneously pursuing other activities that will enrich his life.

There also remains confusion about how the construct of psychological acceptance differs from related constructs such as mindfulness. Some theorists view acceptance as a necessary feature of mindfulness. Brown and Ryan (2003), for example, propose that mindful awareness necessarily involves a nonjudgmental, accepting stance toward one's experience. However, this perspective fails to acknowledge that acceptance does not always accompany awareness, as in the case of heightened awareness of one's physiological arousal in panic disorder. This has led other theorists to deconstruct the concept of mindfulness such that acceptance is only one aspect. For example, Herbert and Cardaciotto (2005) argue that mindfulness is best viewed bidimensionally as consisting of ongoing awareness of one's experience and nonjudgmental acceptance of that experience, and that these two components are in fact conceptually and empirically distinct (Cardaciotto, Herbert, Forman, Moitra, & Farrow, in press). This conceptual and terminological confusion stems in part from the fact that investigators are approaching these questions from diverse theoretical perspectives, resulting in conceptual and terminological confusion (Zvolensky, Feldner, Leen-Feldner, & Yartz, 2005).

A review of the outcome research on acceptance-based CBTs is beyond the scope of this chapter; several reviews of the literature are now available (e.g., Brantley, 2005; Coelho et al., 2007; Hayes et al., 2006; Öst, 2008). In general, the status of this body of evidence can be summarized as preliminary but promising. Acceptance-based methods tend to fare at least as well as traditional change-oriented approaches, although only a handful of direct head-to-head comparisons have been conducted to date (e.g., Forman, Herbert, et al., 2007; Lappalainen et al., 2007). Clearly, more outcome research utilizing larger samples and more sophisticated methodological controls is needed (see Öst, 2008, for a detailed discussion of methodological controls within published studies on ACT and DBT). Likewise, much more psychotherapy process research is needed to evaluate the extent to which psychological acceptance mediates changes in acceptance-based models of CBT, as well as perhaps even in more traditional models of CBT. Although initial studies are encouraging (Hayes, Levin, Yadavaia, & Vilardaga, 2007), much more work remains to be done.

CONCLUSION

The field of CBT has recently witnessed an increased interest in theoretical and technological developments related to psychological acceptance. Acceptance-based models of CBT are quickly growing in popularity. Preliminary data not only support the efficacy of such approaches, but also support the conclusion that changes in psychological acceptance may mediate more general changes produced by psychotherapy, although much more work remains to be done with respect to both outcome and process. In addition, a number of theoretical and practical issues remain outstanding and await further development.

References

Abramowitz, J. S., Tolin, D. F., & Street, G. P. (2001). Paradoxical effects of thought suppression:

A meta-analysis of controlled studies. *Clinical Psychology Review, 21,* 683–703.

Barlow, D. H., Craske, M. G., Cerny, J. A., & Klosko, J. S. (1989). Behavioral treatment of panic disorder. *Behavior Therapy, 20,* 261–282.

Bishop, S. R. (2002). What do we really know about mindfulness-based stress reduction? *Psychosomatic Medicine, 64,* 71–83.

Bongar, B. M., & Beutler, L. E. (Eds.) (1995). *Comprehensive textbook of psychotherapy: Theory and Practice.* New York: Oxford University Press.

Borkovec, T. D. (1994). The nature, functions, and origins of worry. In G. C. L. Davey & F. Tallis (Eds.), *Worrying: Perspectives on theory, assessment, and treatment* (pp. 5–34). New York: Wiley.

Borkovec, T. D., Alcaine, O. M., & Behar, E. (Eds.). (2004). Avoidance theory of worry and generalized anxiety disorder. In R. G. Heimberg, C. L. Turk, & D. S. Mennin (Eds.), *Generalized anxiety disorder: Advances in research and practice* (pp. 77–108). New York: Guilford.

Brantley, J. (2005). Mindfulness-based stress reduction. In S. M. Orsillo & L. Roemer (Eds.), *Acceptance and mindfulness-based approaches to anxiety: Conceptualization and treatment* (pp. 131–145). New York: Springer.

Brown, K. W., & Ryan, R. M. (2003). The benefits of being present: Mindfulness and its role in psychological well-being. *Journal of Personality and Social Psychology, 84,* 822–848.

Cardaciotto, L., Herbert, J. D., Forman, E. M., Moitra, E., & Farrow, V. (in press). The assessment of present-moment awareness and acceptance: The Philadelphia Mindfulness Scale. *Assessment.*

Clark, D. M., Ehlers, A., Hackmann, A., McManus, F., Fennell, M., Grey, N., et al. (2006). Cognitive therapy versus exposure and applied relaxation in social phobia: A randomized controlled trial. *Journal of Consulting and Clinical Psychology, 74,* 568–578.

Coelho, H. F., Canter, P. H., & Ernst, E. (2007). Mindfulness-based cognitive therapy: Evaluating current evidence and informing future research. *Journal of Consulting and Clinical Psychology, 75,* 1000–1005.

Cordova, J. V. (2001). Acceptance in behavior therapy: Understanding the process of change. *The Behavior Analyst, 24,* 213–226.

Craske, M. G., & Barlow, D. H. (2008). Panic disorder and agoraphobia. In D. H. Barlow (Ed.), *Clinical handbook of psychological disorders* (4th ed., pp. 1–64). New York: Guilford.

DeRubeis, R. J., Hollon, S. D., Amsterdam, J. D., Shelton, R. C., Young, P. R., Salomon, R. M., et al. (2005). Cognitive therapy vs. medications in the treatment of moderate to severe depression. *Archives of General Psychiatry, 62,* 409–416.

Dimidjian, S., Hollon, S. D., Dobson, K. S., Schmaling, K. B., Kohlenberg, R. J., Addis, M. E., et al. (2006). Randomized trial of behavioral activation, cognitive therapy, and antidepressant medication in the acute treatment of adults with major depression. *Journal of Consulting & Clinical Psychology, 74,* 658–670.

Dobson, K. S. (1989). A meta-analysis of the efficacy of cognitive therapy for depression. *Journal of Consulting and Clinical Psychology, 57,* 414–419.

Eifert, G. H., & Forsyth, J. P. (2005). *Acceptance and commitment therapy for anxiety disorders.* Oakland, CA: New Harbinger.

Eifert, G. H., & Heffner, M. (2003). The effects of acceptance versus control contexts on avoidance of panic-related symptoms. *Journal of Behavior Therapy & Experimental Psychiatry, 34,* 293–312.

Farmer, R. F., & Champman, A. L. (2008). *Behavioral interventions in cognitive behavior therapy: Practical guidance for putting theory into action* (chapter 10). Washington, DC: American Psychological Associaton.

Forman, E. M., Hebert, J. D., Moitra, E., Yeomans, P. D., & Geller, P. A. (2007). A randomized controlled effectiveness trial of acceptance and commitment therapy and cognitive therapy for anxiety and depression. *Behavior Modification, 31,* 772–799.

Forman, E. M., Hoffman, K. L., McGrath, K. B., Herbert, J. D., Brandsma, L. L., & Lowe, M. R. (2007). A comparison of acceptance- and control-based strategies for coping with food cravings: An analog study. *Behaviour Research and Therapy, 45,* 2372–2386.

Folette, V. M., Ruzek, J. I., Abueg, I. I. (1998). *Cognitive behavioral therapies for trauma.* New York: Guilford.

Goldfried, M. R., & Davison, G. C. (1994). *Clinical behavior therapy.* New York: John Wiley & Sons.

Hayes, S. C. (in press). Climbing our hills: A beginning conversation on the comparison of ACT and traditional CBT. *Clinical Psychology: Science and Practice.*

Hayes, S. C. (2001). Psychology of acceptance and change. In N. J. Smelser & P. W. Baltes (Eds.), *International encyclopedia of the social and behavioral sciences* (pp. 27–30). Oxford, UK: Elsevier Sciences.

Hayes, S. C. (2004). Acceptance and commitment therapy and the new behavior therapies: Mindfulness, acceptance, and relationship. In S. C. Hayes, V. M. Follette, & M. M. Linehan (Eds.), *Mindfulness and acceptance: Expanding the cognitive-behavioral tradition* (pp. 1–29). New York: Guilford.

Hayes, S. C., Bissett, R., Korn, Z., Zettle, R. D., Rosenfarb, I., Cooper, L., et al. (1999). The impact of acceptance versus control rationales on pain tolerance. *The Psychological Record, 49,* 33–47.

Hayes, S. C., Levin, M., Yadavaia, J. E., & Vilardaga, R. V. (2007, November). *ACT: Model and processes of change.* Paper presented at the Association for Behavioral and Cognitive Therapies, Philadelphia.

Hayes, S. C., Luoma, J. B., Bond, F. W., Masuda, A., & Lillis, J. (2006). Acceptance and commitment therapy: Model, processes and outcomes. *Behaviour Research and Therapy, 44,* 1–25.

Hayes, S. C., & Pankey, J. (2003). Acceptance. In W. O'Donohue, J. E. Fisher, & S. C. Hayes (Eds.), *Cognitive behavior therapy: Applying empirically supported treatments in your practice* (pp. 4–9). Hoboken, NJ: John Wiley & Sons.

Hayes, S. C., Strosahl, K., & Wilson, K. G. (1999). *Acceptance and commitment therapy: An experiential approach to behavior change.* New York: Guilford.

Hayes, S. C., & Strosahl, K. D. (Eds.). (2005). *A practical guide to acceptance and commitment therapy.* New York: Springer Science.

Hayes, S. C., Wilson, K. W., Gifford, E. V., Follette, V. M., & Strosahl, K. (1996). Emotional avoidance and behavioral disorders: A functional dimensional approach to diagnosis and treatment. *Journal of Consulting and Clinical Psychology, 64,* 1152–1168.

Herbert, J. D., & Cardaciotto, L. (2005). An acceptance and mindfulness-based perspective on social anxiety disorder. In S. M. Orsillo & L. Roemer (Eds.), *Acceptance and mindfulness-based approaches to anxiety: Conceptualization and treatment* (pp. 189–212). New York: Springer.

Herbert, J. D., Gaudiano, B. A., Rheingold, A., Harwell, V., Dalrymple, K., & Nolan, E. M. (2005). Social skills training augments the effectiveness of cognitive behavior group therapy for social anxiety disorder. *Behavior Therapy, 36,* 125–138.

Hope, D. A., Heimberg, R. G., & Bruch, M. A. (1995). Dismantling cognitive–behavioral group therapy for social phobia. *Behaviour Research and Therapy, 33,* 637–650.

Jacobson, N. S., Christensen, A., Prince, S. E., Cordova, J., & Eldridge, K. (2000). Integrative behavioral couple therapy: An acceptance-based, promising new treatment for couple discord. *Journal of Consulting and Clinical Psychology, 68,* 351–355.

Jacobson, N. S., Dobson, K. S., Truax, P. A., Addis, M. E., Koerner, K., Gollan, J. K., et al. (1996). A component analysis of cognitive-behavioral treatment for depression. *Journal of Consulting and Clinical Psychology, 64,* 295–304.

Kabat-Zinn, J. (1990). Full catastrophe living: Using the wisdom of your body and mind to face stress, pain, and illness. New York: Delacorte Press.

Kohlenberg, R. J., & Tsai, M. (1991). Functional analytic psychotherapy: Creating intense and curative therapeutic relationships. New York: Plenum.

Lappalainen, R., Lehtonen, T., Skarp, E., Taubert, E., Ojanen, M., & Hayes, S. C. (2007). The impact of CBT and ACT models using psychology trainee therapists: A preliminary controlled effectiveness trial. *Behavior Modification, 31,* 488–511.

Larimer, M. E., Palmer, R. S., & Marlatt, G. A. (1999). Relapse prevention: An overview of Marlatt's cognitive–behavioral model. *Alcohol Research & Health, 23,* 151–160.

Leigh, J., Bowen, S., & Marlatt, G. A. (2005). Spirituality, mindfulness and substance abuse. *Addictive Behaviors, 30,* 1335–1341.

Levitt, J. T., Brown, T. A., Orsillo, S. M., & Barlow, D. H. (2004). The effects of acceptance versus suppression of emotion on subjective and psychophysiological response to carbon dioxide challenge in patients with panic disorder. *Behavior Therapy, 35,* 747–766.

Lau, M. A., & McMain, S. F. (2005). Integrating mindfulness meditation with cognitive and behavioural therapies: The challenge of combining acceptance- and changed-based strategies. *Canadian Journal of Psychiatry, 50,* 863–869.

Linehan, M. M. (1993a). Cognitive–behavioral treatment of borderline personality disorder. New York: Guilford.

Linehan, M. M. (1993b). Skills training manual for treating borderline personality disorder. New York: Guilford.

Longmore, R. J., & Worrell, M. (2007). Do we need to challenge thoughts in cognitive behavior therapy? *Clinical Psychology Review, 27,* 173–187.

Marks, I. M., (1987). *Fears, phobias, and rituals: Panic, anxiety, and their disorders.* New York: Oxford University Press.

Marlatt, G. A. Witkiewitz, K., Dillworth, T. M., Bowen, S. W., Parks, G. A., Macpherson, L. M., et al. (2004). Vipassana meditation as a treatment for alcohol and drug use disorders. In S. C. Hayes, V. M. Follette, & M. M. Linehan (Eds.), *Mindfulness and acceptance: Expanding the cognitive–behavioral tradition* (pp. 261–287). New York: Guilford.

Orsillo, S. M., Roemer, L., & Barlow, D. H. (2003). Integrating acceptance and mindfulness into existing cognitive-behavioral treatment for GAD: A case study. *Cognitive and Behavioral Practice, 10,* 222–230.

Orsillo, S. M., Roemer, L., Lerner, J. B., & Tull, M. T. (2004). Acceptance, mindfulness, and cognitive-behavioral therapy: Comparisons, contrasts, and applications to anxiety. In S. C. Hayes, V. M. Follette, & M. M. Linehan (Eds.), *Mindfulness and acceptance: Expanding the cognitive-behavioral tradition* (pp. 66–95). New York: Guilford.

Orsillo, S. M., Roemer, L., & Holowka, D. (2005). Acceptance-based behavioral therapies for anxiety: Using acceptance and mindfulness to enhance traditional cognitive-behavioral approaches. In S. M. Orsillo & L. Roemer (Eds.), *Acceptance- and mindfulness-based approaches to anxiety: Conceptualization and treatment* (pp. 3–35). New York: Springer.

Öst, L. (2008). Efficacy of the third wave of behavioral therapies: A systematic review and meta-analysis. *Behaviour Research and Therapy, 46,* 296–321.

Roemer, L., & Orsillo, S. M. (2002). Expanding our conceptualization of and treatment for generalized anxiety disorder: Integrating mindfulness/acceptance-based approaches with existing cognitive-behavioral models. *Clinical Psychology: Science and Practice, 9,* 54–68.

Segal, Z. V., Teasdale, J. D., & Williams, J. M. G. (2004). Mindfulness-based cognitive therapy: Theoretical rationale and empirical status. In S. C. Hayes, V. M. Follette, & M. M. Linehan (Eds.), *Mindfulness and acceptance: Expanding the cognitive–behavioral tradition* (pp. 45–65). New York: Guilford.

Segal, Z. V., Williams, J. M. G., & Teasdale, J. D. (2002). Mindfulness-based cognitive therapy for depression: A new approach to preventing relapse. New York: Guilford.

Shermer, M. (2002). *Why people believe weird things.* New York: Henry Holt.

Sulloway, F. J. (1983). *Freud: Biologist of the mind.* New York: Basic Books.

Tacon, A. M., Caldera, Y. M., & Ronaghan, C. (2004). Mindfulness-based stress reduction in women with breast cancer. *Families, Systems, & Health, 22,* 193–203.

Teasdale, J. D. (1997). The transformation of meaning: The interacting cognitive subsystems approach. In M. Power & C. R. Brewin (Eds.), *The transformation of meaning in psychological therapies* (pp. 141–156). Chichester, UK: Wiley.

Wells, A. (2000). Emotional disorders and metacognition: Innovative cognitive therapy. Chichester, UK: Wiley.

Wells, A. (2007). The attention training technique: Theory, effects, and a metacognitive hypothesis on auditory hallucinations. *Cognitive and Behavioral Practice, 14,* 134–148.

Wenzlaff, R. M., & Wegner, D. M. (2000). Thought suppression. *Annual Review of Psychology, 51,* 59–91.

Witkiewitz, K., Marlatt, G. A., & Walker, D. (2005). Mindfulness-based relapse prevention for alcohol and substance use disorders. *Journal of Cognitive Psychotherapy, 19,* 211–228.

Zvolensky, M. J., Feldner, M. T., Leen-Feldner, E. W., & Yartz, A. R. (2005). Exploring basic processes underlying acceptance and mindfulness. In S. M. Orsillo & L. Roemer (Eds.), *Acceptance and mindfulness-based approaches to anxiety: Conceptualization and treatment* (pp. 325–357). New York: Springer.

7 ANGER (NEGATIVE IMPULSE) CONTROL

Brad Donohue, Kendra Tracy, and Suzanne Gorney

Anger is an internal affective experience that varies in its intensity and chronicity (Deffenbacher, 1996). It may be experienced as a negative impulsive reaction to a specific stimulus in the environment (e.g., aggression in response to being kicked, swearing consequent of being struck in the thumb with a hammer, urges to use drugs in response to an argument) or may persist over time or across situations. Problem-solving skills deficits, maladaptive withdrawal, child and spousal abuse, and increased risk for health problems such as essential hypertension and cardiovascular disease are all examples of problems often influenced by inappropriate management of anger (see, e.g., Deffenbacher, Demm, & Brandon, 1986; Deffenbacher, Oetting, et al., 1996; Gentry, Chesney, Gary, Hall, & Harburg, 1982; Krantz, Contrada, Hill, & Friedler, 1988; Novaco, 1979; Schneider, Egan, Johnson, Drobny, & Julius, 1996).

To assist in the remediation of anger and other negative impulsive disorders, several cognitive behavioral methods have been developed including thought stopping, relaxation training, problem solving, and self-reward for performance of non-anger-associated behaviors. We will briefly delineate each of these methods, including their rationale and empirical support. We will conclude by describing an urge control intervention that combines these methods in the effective management of negative impulses that are associated with behavioral misconduct and impulsive urges to use illicit drugs.

RESPONSIVE POPULATIONS AND CONTRAINDICATIONS

The state of the literature in anger management does not allow clear guidance for specific populations who might or might not benefit. Anger and aggression can sometimes be a side effect of various biological processes, however, so these factors should be considered before focusing entirely on psychological approaches.

ANGER MEASUREMENT

Anger can be measured via self-report, observation, or physiologically. Widely used self-report measures include the State-Trait Anger Expression Inventory-2 (STAXI-2; Spielberger, 1999) and the Novaco Anger Scale and Provocation Inventory (NAS-PI; Novaco, 2003). The STAXI-2 evaluates state anger, defined as the intensity of anger at a particular point in time; trait anger, defined as the frequency with which anger is experienced; and anger expression and anger control, both of which can be either inwardly or outwardly expressed. A sixth-grade reading level is required to complete the STAXI; however, normative data has been collected only for individuals aged 16 years and older. The psychometric properties of the STAXI-2 and its component subscales have been empirically validated, with the exception of test-retest reliability. The NAS-PI consists of two scales (the Novaco Anger Scale and the Provocation Inventory) that can be administered together or separately, to individuals aged 9 to 84 years, and to individuals with developmental difficulties, although the items may need to be read to the respondent in such a case. The Novaco Anger Scale consists of four subscales: Anger Regulation, defined as one's ability to control angry impulses or thoughts; Behavior, impulsive reactions or expressions of anger; Arousal, the intensity and duration of anger; and Cognitive, factors such as rumination, hostility, or justification of angry thoughts.

A Total anger score is provided, which indicates a person's general predisposition toward anger. The Provocation Inventory is used to identify situations that typically cause anger in a particular individual (e.g., unfairness, disrespect, frustration, etc.). The NAS-PI contains a validity index, to evaluate inconsistent responding, and has demonstrated good internal and predictive validity, as well as reliability. The NAS in particular has been found to discriminate between clinical and nonclinical samples with 94% accuracy (Jones, Thomas-Peter, & Trout; 1999).

Anger is associated with increased autonomic activity, thus physiological measures have been used as more objective evaluations of an individual's level of arousal. Increased blood pressure, heart rate, and skin conductivity are associated with higher levels of anger (Dimsdale, Pierce, Schoenfeld, Brown, Zusman, & Graham, 1986; Everson, 1998; Montoya, Campos, & Schandry, 2005; Suchday & Larkin, 2001) in children as well as adults (Hubbard, Parker, & Ramsden, 2004). Physiological measurement is difficult to implement during in vivo situations that involve anger. However, these measures can be utilized during contrived scenarios in which the participant is prompted to imagine triggers or situations that are emotionally laden with anger or upset. Along these lines, the participant can be taught to identify physiological responses (e.g., heart beating faster) that may precede troublesome behavior (e.g., arguments, fist fights).

THOUGHT STOPPING

Thought stopping is a method that may be utilized to interrupt undesirable or unproductive thoughts that often lead to anger. The method is particularly effective when the level of arousal is relatively weak (i.e., first recognition of the stimulus eliciting anger) (Tyson, 1998). As exemplified by Wolpe (1990), the procedure begins with the patient closing his or her eyes and verbalizing a thought that has been associated with negative arousal or anger. The therapist consequently shouts, "stop!" and then points out to the patient that the thought has actually stopped. After practicing the termination of similar thoughts in separate trials, the patient is encouraged to practice the termination of thoughts subvocally.

Other phrases or visual images (e.g., "cut it out," image of a red stop sign) may be used instead of "stop!" to mentally disrupt anger (Deffenbacher, 1996). Thought stopping is conceptualized to work because thought inhibition is reinforced by the arousal reduction that occurs each time the individual successfully stops an undesirable thought (Tyson, 1998). The procedure has demonstrated effectiveness in decreasing negative thinking (Peden, Rayens, Hall, & Beebe, 2001; Peden, Rayens, & Hall, 2005). However, it is important to note that thought stopping is not a primary method of intervention. Rather, the procedure is used as an initial component (Deffenbacher, 1996) because it does not alter the situation or environment or teach coping skills.

RELAXATION TRAINING

Since anger is accompanied by physiological and emotional arousal (Suinn, 1990), relaxation training may be initiated to teach individuals how to become aware of bodily tensions that often precede anger and may be used as cues to elicit relaxation (Kendall et al., 1991). Relaxation procedures vary, but they usually include some aspect of progressive muscle relaxation to assist in the early recognition of tension and subsequent regulation to a calm state of arousal (see Chapter 53, this volume). In this method, the individual is taught to tense and relax each of the major muscle groups, thus allowing him- or herself to focus on feelings distinguishing tension from relaxation. After reviewing all muscles, the individual is often instructed to imagine a relaxing scenario (i.e., resting on a warm beach; sitting in a remote forest). Tension-releasing exercises (e.g., instructing the individual to imagine tension leaving all the major muscle groups; Cahill, Rauch, Hembree, Foa, 2003) and focused breathing (e.g., practicing slow and rhythmic diaphragmatic breathing; Kendall et al., 1991) are also popular relaxation exercise components that may be used in the reduction of anger. Particularly useful is the administration of this technique in conjunction with an in vivo or visualization exposure intervention in which the client is exposed to an anger provoking situation, implementing relaxation techniques as necessary (Gorenstein, Tager, Shapiro, Monk, Sloan, 2007).

PROBLEM-SOLVING SKILLS TRAINING

Anger can be an intrapersonal problem, an interpersonal problem, a community or societal problem, or some combination of these, and problem solving can be implemented in all these cases (Chapter 49, this volume). Problem solving is a conscious, rational, purposeful activity directed at finding one or more solutions to a specific problem (D'Zurilla & Nezu, 1991). For each problem scenario, the individual is taught to (1) make a brief, summative statement of the problem; (2) generate potential solutions without critique; (3) evaluate the good and bad aspects of each solution; (4) choose one or more of the solutions; and (5) attempt the chosen solution(s). Self-instruction should be considered in the implementation of problem-solving strategies to help the individual initiate, implement, and evaluate potential solutions (Daunic, Smith, Brank, Penfield, 2006; Meichenbaum & Deffenbacher, 1988). Problem-solving skills training is an important component in the prevention of anger and aggression. For instance, both juvenile and adult offenders have been found to evidence problem-solving skills deficits (Biggam & Power, 2002; Bourke & Van Hasselt, 2001). Social problem-solving strategies have demonstrated efficacy in reducing anger (Feindler, 1991; Sukhodolsky, Golub, Stone, Orban, 2005), perhaps because in attempting to review options available, the individual is focused on solving the problem and is thus distracted from thoughts that are associated with anger.

SELF-REINFORCEMENT

Hostile or aggressive individuals experience lower levels of self-reinforcement than nonaggressive individuals (Heiby & Mearig, 2002). Therefore, it follows that individuals who have difficulty in the management of their anger (as well as other negative behaviors) benefit from learning to reinforce themselves consequent to performing behaviors that terminate or reduce anger (negative impulses) or that are incompatible with anger (Meichenbaum & Deffenbacher, 1988). Indeed, positive reinforcement is commonly employed in the management of anger, and self-praise has been shown to improve self-efficacy—that is, belief that anger can be sufficiently reduced (Deffenbacher, 1996; Meichenbaum & Deffenbacher, 1988). Moreover, Bandura, Reese, and Adams (1982) found that self-efficacy was related to physiological arousal such that tasks regarded with high self-efficacy resulted in no visceral reaction. Thus, it follows that if an individual has a strong belief in the ability manage arousal, the physiological arousal will also be controlled.

URGE CONTROL

The urge control procedure employs components of each of the preceding anger control methods in sequence (see Chapter 71). The procedure was originally developed to assist adults and adolescents in preventing urges to use drugs and alcohol (Azrin, McMahon, et al., 1994) and was later modified to address all impulsive behaviors that result in troublesome behavior, including those elicited from anger (Azrin, Donohue, Teichner, Crum, Howell, & Decato, 2001).

A step-by-step guide is presented in Table 7.1. Consistent with the principles of behavioral therapy, a rationale for treatment is provided to the client who is evidencing problems associated with impulsive behaviors or anger. For example, "Earlier you told me you often do things that have resulted in trouble for you, such as getting angry and punching other kids. Many people say they do things like this because they react before they've had a chance to think about how the action will affect themselves or others. They also say anger makes it harder to prevent them from doing impulsive behaviors that will get them in trouble. Tell me some impulsive things you've done that later led to trouble for you or someone else [provide empathy]. The technique you are about to learn is called urge control because you will learn to control impulsive thoughts and feeling, such as anger, that usually lead to trouble for you. You will learn to recognize these feelings and thoughts early, when they are not as strong. This should enable you to do other behaviors that will keep you out of trouble. Do you have any questions?"

TABLE 7.1   Steps in Urge Control

First Session

1. Provide rationale.
   a. "Earlier, you said that you had done some spontaneous things that resulted in trouble for you, such as getting angry and yelling at others. Anger often starts out as a casual thought and grows in intensity. As the intensity of the anger grows, it becomes harder to prevent oneself from acting on negative impulses, such as aggressive behavior. The following technique is called the urge control procedure, and it will help you to learn how to control impulsive thoughts and feelings."
2. Identify the most recent situation involving anger.
3. Model the following components of urge control:
   a. Stop!
   b. State one negative consequence for self and one for others if impulse is acted on.
   c. Relaxation, deep breaths.
   d. State four or more behavioral alternatives that are incompatible with anger.
   e. Imagine doing a behavior that is incompatible with anger.
   f. Imagine telling friends or family about doing the behavior, and imagine their positive responses.
   g. State positive things that will happen because the behavior is performed.
4. Reveal step(s) that helped decrease anger the most.
5. Reveal pre- and post-anger ratings.
6. Instruct client to perform urge control for a recent situation involving anger.
7. Instruct client to identify the component that helped decrease anger the most.
8. Instruct client to provide pre- and post- anger ratings.
9. Instruct client to provide ratings of each of the steps that were role-played.
10. Instruct client to continue to role-play urge control trials, as needed.

Future Sessions

1. Instruct client to use urge control in response to a situation involving anger.
2. Solicit client's pre- and post-anger ratings.
3. Solicit which step was most helpful.
4. Solicit or provide feedback regarding the trial.

The client is informed that recognizing and stopping impulsive thoughts or anger when these thoughts first occur will greatly reduce the likelihood of engaging in negative impulsive behaviors. The client is instructed to disclose a situation in which he or she experienced a negative impulsive behavior subsequent to anger and to identify the first thought associated with anger in that situation. As the following vignette demonstrates, the therapist must sometimes assist the client in determining his or her first thought related to anger.

Therapist: Tell me about the last time your anger led to your doing an impulsive or troublesome behavior. I'm especially interested in the thought that you had before you made plans to engage in the impulsive behavior.

Youth: I was arguing with this guy, and I thought it would feel good to let him have it, so I hit him.

Therapist: You did a good job of identifying a thought that eventually led to hitting the boy in this situation. However, I want you to think hard. I'm sure you had a thought that brought you to the argument.

Youth: I started to think what a jerk he was for asking my girlfriend if she'd like to talk with him on the patio.

Therapist: Excellent!

The therapist then models an urge control. The first step of the urge control procedure is to catch the anger-associated thought or image that preceded the troublesome impulsive behavior early in the response chain, and consequently terminate this thought or image by firmly stating "stop" while muscles are tensed. Background information associated with the situation should be stated with just enough detail to illuminate the situation (e.g., "I'm in front of the mailbox. My friend tells me to give the old man's mailbox a bash with the bat I can feel the hatred for the old man because he got me in trouble last week").

The second step is to state at least one negative consequence for getting angry and/or doing the undesired impulsive behavior, and at least one negative consequence for friends, loved ones, or others who care about the client. Use of perspective-taking skills has been shown to decrease anger arousal (Mohr, Howells, Gerace, Day, Wharton, 2007). Therefore, it makes sense that anger can be decreased after thinking about how negative consequences of anger affect others, especially those who are loved, admired, or respected by the client, Along these lines, negative consequences should be stated with affect reflecting despair, and muscles should remain tense. Consequences may be rotated (or changed) as trials progress. Therapists should prompt detail regarding negative consequences.

Stating the last negative consequence should signal the performance of a muscle review to assure that negative feeling states, and tension in muscles, are not present. Therapeutically, relaxation techniques have been efficacious in producing positive change in the short and long term when dealing with anger (Deffenbacher, Oetting, Huff, & Cornell, 1996). Major muscles should be reviewed from head to toe. During this review, if a muscle is tense, the client should use relaxing cue words until the muscle is no longer tense (e.g., My arms are getting more and more relaxed. I am imagining a band of relaxation around my arms. They feel relaxed, calm, more and more relaxed.") Deep, rhythmic breaths should occur throughout the trial. Body weight should be evenly distributed and positioned in a relaxed state. Statements referring to the relaxed state of the body are acceptable throughout the relaxation period, which should continue until all muscle groups feel relaxed (ideally about 5 to 10 seconds). If no tension or negative feeling states are present, the client may be instructed to only breathe deeply.

The next step involves stating several behaviors that may be performed instead of getting angry or engaging in negative impulsive behaviors. These steps may include (1) stating several alternative actions that do not include anger or negative impulsive behaviors, (2) briefly checking to make sure the response is unlikely to bring about anger or negative impulsive behaviors for self or others, or (3) reviewing positive consequences for self and others that may occur consequent to behaviors that are not associated with anger or negative impulsive behaviors. During this exercise, it is important to provide prompts to the client regarding additional alternative behaviors, how self and others would be positively affected by alternative behaviors, what others would do for the client if alternative behaviors were performed, and how problem behaviors may continue to have negative consequences.

After stating several behaviors that are incompatible with the behaviors associated with anger or impulsiveness, the client is encouraged to choose one option and describe doing the behavior (e.g., I'm imagining walking toward Jackie and telling her I'd like to take her to get something to eat. I'm walking away from the guy and toward the car with Jackie. She is smiling and telling me she'd love to get a big salad and she's glad I didn't start a fight with that guy."). When the client performs this step, the therapist should provide prompts to elicit detail, including questions as to how the client will successfully resolve difficult situations that are likely to occur. Sometimes the client may be instructed to practice getting out of difficult interpersonal situations (e.g., "Show me how you would ask your girlfriend to leave. I'll be her.").

The next step is to imagine telling a friend and/or family member about having performed the trouble-free alternative behavior. The recipient should respond in a favorable manner, and positive feeling should be delineated. For example, "I'm telling my mom that I could have fought the guy at the party, but instead I went to get something to eat with my girlfriend. As I'm telling her this, I feel good about myself. My mom looks at me and tells me I'm doing a great job and that she's proud of me. She also tells me she's been thinking about letting me have a curfew extension because I've been acting very responsible."

The trial concludes when the client describes several pleasant outcomes and positive character attributes. For example, "I'm really proud of myself for going out to eat with my girlfriend instead of fighting that guy. I'm going to have a great time with her and improve our relationship. I also liked how I avoided going near that guy. That says a lot about the kind of person I am. I can usually hold my own in a fight but I can also avoid them when I want. If I can keep my anger under control, I'm going to make my girlfriend and my parents proud, and I'll be able to get more privileges at home and school."

When clients practice the urge control procedure for the first time, it may be necessary to state the situation and prompt the client to subsequently state "stop" (e.g., "You're at the party. You hear the guy at the party ask your girlfriend to go out on the patio. Go ahead and yell 'stop!'"). Similarly, it may be necessary to prompt the client to perform each component initially, and later decrease this assistance.

After the client completes each trial, the therapist asks the client to provide his or her rating (0 = no anger, 100 = completely angry) of anger or desire to engage in the impulsive behavior prior to performing the trial, and after the trial is performed (i.e., pre- and posttrial urge level). The client is prompted to critique his or her performance, and the therapist subsequently praises the client for making statements during the trial that reflected protocol adherence, including suggestions or prompts to client regarding ways to improve performance in future sessions. The number of trials performed depends on the extent of the client's troublesome behavior since last contact. Similarly, poor performance during trials necessitates additional trials per session.

EVIDENCE-BASED APPLICATIONS

The urge control procedure was originally developed to prevent urges to use drugs and has demonstrated efficacy in that area (Azrin, McMahon, & Donohue, 1994). This procedure has also demonstrated efficacy in the prevention of other types of impulsive problem behaviors, such as delinquency (Azrin, Donohue, et al., 2001). The individual components of the urge control procedure; thought stopping, relaxation training, problem-solving skills training, and self-reinforcement, have been applied to a host of

problem behaviors in addition to anger management. For instance, thought stopping has been shown to be effective in reducing the unwanted, intrusive thoughts associated with depression (Peden, Rayens, & Hall, 2005), chronic pain (Degotardi, Klass, & Rosenberg, 2006), posttraumatic stress disorder (PTSD) (Foa, 1997), obsessive–compulsive disorder (OCD) (Lam & Steketee, 2001), primary insomnia (Backhaus, Hohagen, Voderholzer, & Rieman, 2001), eating disorders (Cinciripini, Kornblith, & Turner, 1983), and overeating (Bonato & Boland, 1986). Thought stopping has also been applied in sports psychology to decrease thoughts that negatively influence athletes' performance (Sheard & Golby, 2006). Relaxation training is a key feature in exposure and systematic desensitization interventions targeting a broad range of anxiety-laden problem disorders such as generalized anxiety disorder and anorexia nervosa (Ayers, Sorrell, & Thorp, 2007; Goldfarb, Fuhr, & Tsujimoto, 1987; Stapleton, Taylor, & Asmundson, 2006).

Self-reinforcement is a component of many self-monitoring procedures that have been applied to the treatment of depression (Rehm & Rokke, 1988), social anxiety (Kocovski & Endler, 2000), learning disorders (Graham, Harris, & Olinghouse, 2007), and autism (Newman, Buffington, & Hemmes, 1996) to aid in increasing positive or adaptive behaviors. Poor problem-solving skills have been linked to both externalizing and internalizing disorders (D'Zurilla, Chang, & Sanna, 2003; Londahl, Tverskoy, & D'Zurilla, 2005). Indeed, problem-solving skills training has been shown to be efficacious for a variety of problems in children including, but not limited to, anger and aggression (Kazdin, 2000; Sukhodolsky, Golub, Stone, & Orban, 2005). This technique has also been utilized with adults in the treatment of depression (Biggam & Power, 2002) and negative affect (Sahler, Fairclough, & Phipps, 2005). Although the urge control components are well supported, it should be mentioned that none are stand-alone therapies. Research suggests that when they are combined with other therapeutic techniques, they have an additive effect, leading to more positive outcomes (Deffenbacher, Oetting, & DiGiuseppe, 2002; Tyson, 1998). Thus, the combination of behaviorally based components in the urge control procedure work together to effectively reduce negative impulsive behaviors.

RESOURCES

For the individual concerned about anger problems, there are many resources available, both on the Internet and at the local bookstore. Web sites such as www.apa.org provide basic information about anger and offer links to scholarly articles on the subject, in addition to supplying anger management tips from experts in the field (APA, 2008). The APA Help Center provides simple cognitive-behavioral strategies for preventing violent, angry outbursts in children, adolescents, and adults (APA, 2004). Additionally, e-therapy, in which clients communicate with therapists via e-mail and teleconference, is becoming increasingly popular. A simple internet search will turn up dozens of sites that connect clients with therapists; however, a major caveat is that few e-therapy providers identify the type of degree their therapists possess and whether or not they are licensed (Rabasca, 2000). An alternative resource for professionals in the field of psychology is the National Registry of Evidence-Based Programs and Practices (www.nrepp.samhsa.gov), which can be used to identify evidence-based treatment programs with a focus on violence prevention. This web site includes several evidence-based programs that chiefly target anger and associated negative emotions.

Although evidence supporting the use of bibliotherapy is mixed, the literature suggests that in conjunction with therapy, or for those without significant problems, self-help books can be beneficial (Mains & Scogin, 2003; Marrs, 1995). An advantage of self-help books is that cutting-edge therapies are available to the public in an easily accessible form. Campbell and Smith (2003) offer guidelines for therapists seeking to incorporate self-help books into therapy, including ways to evaluate and select books. Books that are strongly founded in research include: *Act on Life Not on Anger: The New Acceptance and Commitment Therapy* (Eifert, McKay, Forsyth, & Hayes, 2006) and *Anger Management for Dummies* (Gentry, 2006).

CONCLUSIONS

Anger and impulse control problems are highly associated with devastating problem behaviors, including various disorders that are relevant to eating, substance abuse, conduct, and mood. Comprehensive evidence-based intervention programs have been developed to ameliorate these problems, and many of these programs include components to specifically address anger management and impulse control problems. These programs are becoming increasingly sophisticated and better integrated into comprehensive psychological interventions, thus enhancing efficacy.

References

American Psychological Association. (2004). Dealing with anger. Retrieved January 8, 2008 from www.apahelpcenter.org/featuredtopics.

American Psychological Association. (2008). Controlling anger before it controls you. Retrieved January 8, 2008, from www.apa.org/topics/controlanger.html.

Ayers, C. R., Sorrell, J. T. & Thorp, S. R. (2007). Evidence-based psychological treatments for late-life anxiety. *Psychology and Aging, 22*(1), 8–17.

Azrin, N. H., Donohue, B., Teichner, G., Crum, T., Howell, J., & DeCato, L. (2001). A controlled evaluation and description of individual-cognitive problem solving and family-behavioral therapies in conduct-disordered and substance dependent youth. *Journal of Child and Adolescent Substance Abuse, 11*, 1–43.

Azrin, N. H., McMahon, P. T., Donohue, B., Besalel, V., Lapinski, K., & Kogan, E. (1994). Behavior therapy for drug use: A controlled treatment outcome study. *Behaviour Research and Therapy, 32*(8), 857–866.

Backhaus, J., Hohagen, F., Voderholzer, U., & Reimann, D. (2001). Long-term effectiveness of a short-term cognitive-behavioral group treatment for primary insomnia. *European Archives of Psychiatry and Clinical Neuroscience, 251*(1), 35–41.

Bandura, A., Reese, L., & Adams, N. E. (1982). Micro-analysis of action and fear arousal as a function of different levels of perceived self-efficacy. *Journal of Personality and Social Psychology, 43*, 5–21.

Biggam, F. H., & Power, K. G. (2002). A controlled, problem-solving, group-based intervention with vulnerable incarcerated young offenders.

International Journal of Offender Therapy and Comparative Criminology, 46(6), 678–698.

Bonato, D. P., & Boland, F. J. (1986). A comparison of specific strategies for long term maintenance following a behavioural treatment program for obese women. *International Journal of Eating Disorders, 5*(5), 949–958.

Bourke, M. L., & Van Hasselt, V. B. (2001). Social problem-solving skills training for incarcerated offenders: A treatment manual. *Behavior Modification, 25*(2), 163–188.

Cahill, S. P., Rauch, S. A., Hembree, E. A., & Foa, E. B. (2003). Effect of cognitive–behavioral treatments for PTSD on anger. *Journal of Cognitive Psychotherapy: An International Quarterly, 17*(2), 113–131.

Campbell, L. F., & Smith, T. P. (2003). Integrating self-help books into psychotherapy. *Journal of Clinical Psychology, 59*(2), 177–186.

Cinciripini, P. M., Kornblinth, S. J., & Turner, S. M. (1983). A behavioral program for the management of anorexia and bulimia. *Journal of Nervous and Mental Disease, 171*(3), 186–189.

Daunic, A. P., Smith, S. W., Brank, E. M., & Penfield, R. D. (2006). Classroom-based cognitive–behavioral intervention to prevent aggression: Efficacy and social validity. *Journal of School Psychology, 44*(2), 123–139.

Deffenbacher, J. L., Demm, P. M., & Brandon, A. D. (1986). High general anger: Correlates and treatment. *Behavior Research and Therapy, 24*, 481–489.

Deffenbacher, J. L. (1996). Cognitive-behavioral approaches to anger reduction. In K. S. Dobson & K. D. Craig (Eds.), *Advances in cognitive-behavioral therapy*. Thousand Oaks, CA: Sage.

Deffenbacher, J. L., Oetting, E. R., & DiGiuseppe, R. A. (2002). Principles of empirically supported interventions applied to anger management. *Counseling Psychologist, (30)* 2, 262–280.

Deffenbacher, J. L., Oetting, E. R., Huff, M. E., & Cornell, G. R. (1996). Evaluation of two cognitive–behavioral approaches to general anger reduction. *Cognitive Therapy and Research, 20*(6), 551–573.

Deffenbacher, J. L., Oetting, E. R., Thwaites, G. A., Lynch, R. S., Baker, D. A., Stark, R. S., et al. (1996). State-trait theory and the utility of the trait anger scale. *Journal of Counseling Psychology, 43*(2), 131–148.

Degotardi, P. J., Klass, E. S., & Rosenberg, B. S. (2006). Development and evaluation of a cognitive-behavioral intervention for juvenile fibromyalgia. *Journal of Pediatric Psychology, 31*(7), 714–723.

Dimsdale, J. E., Pierce, C., Schoenfeld, D., Brown, A., Zusman, R., & Graham, R. (1986). Suppresses anger and blood pressure: The effects of race, sex, social class, obesity, and age. *Psychosomatic Medicine, 48*(6), 430–436.

D'Zurilla, T. J., Chang, E. C., & Sanna, L. J. (2003). Self-esteem and social problem solving as predictors of aggression in college students. *Journal of Social and Clinical Psychology, 22*, 424–440.

D'Zurilla, T. J., & Nezu, A. M. (1991). Problem-solving therapies. In K. S. Dobson (Ed.), *Handbook of cognitive behavioral therapies* (pp. 211–245). New York: Guilford Press.

Everson, S. A. (1998). Anger expression and incident hypertension. *Psychosomatic Medicine, 60*(6), 730–735.

Feindler, E. L. (1991). Cognitive strategies in anger control interventions for children and adolescents. In P. C. Kendall (Ed.), *Child and adolescent therapy: Cognitive–behavioral procedures* (pp. 67–97). New York: Guilford Press.

Foa, E. B. (1997). Trauma and women: Course, predictors, and treatment. *Journal of Clinical Psychiatry, 58*(9) 25–28.

Gentry, W. (2006). *Anger management for dummies.* Hoboken, NJ: Wiley Publishing, Inc.

Gentry, W., Chesney, A., Gary, H., Hall, R., & Harburg, E. (1982). Habitual anger-coping styles: I. Effect on mean blood pressure and risk for essential hypertension. *Psychosomatic Medicine, 44*, 195–202.

Graham, S., Harris, K. R., & Olinghouse, N. (2007). Addressing executive function problems in writing: An example from the self-regulated strategy development model. In L. Meltzer (Ed.), *Executive function in education: From theory to practice* (pp. 216–236). New York: Guilford Press.

Goldfarb, L. A., Fuhr, R., & Tsujimoto, R. N. (1987). Systematic desensitization and relaxation as adjuncts in the treatment of anorexia nervosa: A preliminary study. *Psychological Reports, 60*(2), 511–518.

Gorenstein, E. E., Tager, F. A., Shapiro, P. A., Monk, C., & Sloan, R. P. (2007). Cognitive–behavior therapy for reduction of persistent anger. *Cognitive and Behavioral Practice, 14*(2), 168–184.

Heiby, E. M., & Mearig, A. (2002). Self-control skills and negative emotional state: A focus on hostility. *Psychological Reports, 90*(2), 627–633.

Hubbard, J. A., Parker, E. H., & Ramsden, S. R. (2004). The relations among observational, physiological, and self-report measures of children's anger. *Social Development, 13*(1), 14–39.

Jones, J. P., Thomas-Peter, B. A., & Trout, A. (1999). Normative data for the Novaco Anger Scale from a non-clinical sample and implications for clinical use. *British Journal of Clinical Psychology, 38*(4), 417–424.

Kazdin, A. E. (2000). Treatments for aggressive and antisocial children. *Child and Adolescent*

Psychiatric Clinics of North America, 9(4), 841–858.

Kendall, P. C., Chansky, T. E., Friedman, M., Kim, R., Kortlander, E., Sessa, F. M., et al. (1991). Treating anxiety disorders in children and adolescents. In P. C. Kendall (Ed.), *Child and adolescent therapy: Cognitive–behavioral procedures* (pp. 67–97). New York: Guilford Press.

Kocovski, N. L., & Endler, N. S. (2000). Social anxiety, self-regulation, and fear of negative evaluation. *European Journal of Personality*, 14(4), 347–358.

Krantz, D., Contrada, R., Hill, D., & Friedler, E. (1988). Environmental stress and biobehavioral antecedents of coronary heart disease. *Journal of Consulting and Clinical Psychology*, 56, 333–341.

Lam, J. N., & Steketee, G. S. (2001). Reducing obsessions and compulsions through behavior therapy. *Psychoanalytic Inquiry*, 21(2), 157–182.

Londahl, E. A., Tverskoy, A., & D'Zurilla, T. J. (2005). The relations of internalizing symptoms to conflict and interpersonal problem solving in close relationships. *Cognitive Therapy and Research*, 29(4), 445–462.

Mains, J. A., & Scogin, F. R. (2003). The effectiveness of self-administered treatments: A practice-friendly review of the research. *Journal of Clinical Psychology*, 59(2), 237–246.

Marrs, R. W. (1995). A meta-analysis of bibliotherapy studies. *American Journal of Community Psychology*, 23(6), 843–870.

Meichenbaum, D. H., & Deffenbacher, J. L. (1988). Stress inoculation training. *The Counseling Psychologist*, 16, 69–90.

Mohr, P., Howells, K., Gerace, A., Day, A., & Wharton, M. (2007). The role of perspective taking in anger arousal. *Personality and Individual Differences*, 43(3), 507–517.

Montoya, P., Campos, J. J., & Schandry, R. (2005). See red? Turn pale? Unveiling emotions through cardiovascular and hemodynamic changes. *Spanish Journal of Psychology*, 8(1), 79–85.

Novaco, R. (1979). The cognitive regulation of anger and stress. In P. C. Kendall & S. Hollon (Eds.), *Cognitive-behavioral interventions: Theory, research, and procedures*. New York: Academic.

Novaco, R. (2003). *Novaco anger scale and provocation inventory*. Los Angeles: Western Psychological Services.

Newman, B., Buffington, D. M., & Hemmes, N. S. (1996). Self-reinforcement used to increase the appropriate conversation of autistic teenagers. *Education and Training in Mental Retardation and Developmental Disabilities*, 31(4), 304–309.

Peden, A. R., Rayens, M. K., & Hall, L. A. (2005). A community-based depression prevention intervention with low-income single mothers. *Journal*

of the American Psychiatric Nurses Association, 11(1), 18–25.

Peden, A. R., Rayens, M. K., Hall, L. A., & Beebe, L. H. (2001). Preventing depression in high risk college women: A report of an 18 month follow-up. *Journal of American College Health*, 49, 299–306.

Rabasca, L. (2000). Self-help sites: A blessing or a bane? *Monitor on Psychology*, 31(4).

Rehm, L. P., & Rokke, P. (1988). Self-management therapies. In K. S. Dobson (Ed.), *Handbook of Cognitive-Behavioral Therapies*. New York: Guilford.

Sahler, O. J., Fairclough, D. L., & Phipps, S. (2005). Using problem-solving skills training to reduce negative affectivity in mothers of children with newly diagnosed cancer: Report of a multisite randomized trial. *Journal of Consulting and Clinical Psychology*, 73(2), 272–283.

Schneider, R. H., Egan, B. M., Johnson, E. H., Drobny, H., & Julius, S. (1996). Anger and anxiety in borderline hypertension. *Psychosomatic Medicine*, 48, 242–248.

Sheard, M., & Golby, J. (2006). Effect of a psychological skills training program on swimming performance and positive psychological development. *International Journal of Sport and Exercise Psychology*, 4(2), 149–169.

Spielberger, C. D. (1999). *State-trait anger expression inventory-2*. Odessa, FL: Psychological Assessment Resource, Inc.

Stapleton, J. A., Taylor, S., & Asmundson, G. J. (2006). Effects of three PTSD treatments on anger and guilt: Exposure therapy, eye movement desensitization and reprocessing, and relaxation training. *Journal of Traumatic Stress*, 19(1), 19–28.

Suchday, S., & Larkin, K. T. (2001). Biobehavioral responses to interpersonal conflict during anger expression among anger-in and anger-out men. *Annals of Behavioral Medicine*, 23(4), 282–290.

Suinn, R. M. (1990). Anxiety management training: A behavior therapy. New York: Plenum.

Sukhodolsky, D. G., Golub, A., Stone, E. C., & Orban, L. (2005). Dismantling anger control training for children: A randomized pilot study of social problem-solving versus social skills training components. *Behavior Therapy*, 36(1), 15–23.

Tyson, P. D. (1998). Physiological arousal, reactive aggression, and the induction of an incompatible relaxation response. *Aggression and Violent Behavior*, 3(2), 143–158.

Wolpe, J. (1990). *The practice of behavior therapy* (4th ed.). Elsmford, NY: Pergamon.

8 ASSERTIVENESS SKILLS AND THE MANAGEMENT OF RELATED FACTORS

Melanie P. Duckworth

Assertive behavior usually centers on making requests of others and refusing requests made by others that have been judged to be unreasonable. Assertive behavior also captures the communication of strong opinions and feelings. Assertive communication of personal opinions, needs, and boundaries has been defined as communication that diminishes none of the individuals involved in the interaction, with emphasis on communication accuracy and respect for all persons engaged in the exchange.

Assertiveness is conceptualized as the behavioral middle ground, lying between ineffective passive and aggressive responses. Passiveness is characterized by an overattention to the opinions and needs of others and the masking or restraining of personal opinions and needs. This overattention to and compliance with the opinions and needs of others may serve as a strategy for conflict avoidance or maintenance of particular sources of social reinforcement. Aggressiveness often involves the imposition of one's opinions and requirements on another individual. Implicit in the discussion of assertiveness is the suggestion that assertive behavior is the universally preferred behavioral alternative, and that assertive behavior necessarily leads to preferred outcomes. The degree to which assertive behaviors are to be considered superior to either a passive or an aggressive stance is determined by the situational context. The success of assertiveness does not always lie in tangible outcomes (e.g., request fulfillment). The success of assertiveness sometimes lies in the degree of personal control and personal respect that is achieved and maintained throughout the assertive exchange.

BEHAVIORAL, COGNITIVE–AFFECTIVE, AND SOCIAL FACTORS INFLUENCING ASSERTIVENESS

Given that assertive behavior occurs as a part of a broader interaction complex, the likelihood that an individual will engage in assertive behavior is a function of skill and performance competencies, reinforcement contingencies, and motivational–affective and cognitive–evaluative factors. Behavioral explanations for the use of passive or aggressive strategies rather than assertive strategies emphasize opportunities for skills acquisition and mastery and reinforcement contingencies that have supported the use of passive or aggressive behaviors over time. Behavioral conceptualizations for passivity often emphasize early learning environments in which passive responding may have been modeled (e.g., caregivers who were themselves anxious, shy, or in some other way less than assertive) or more assertive behavior punished (e.g., overly protective or dominating care givers). In the absence of opportunities for acquisition and reinforcement of other interaction strategies, passive behavior persists.

Important to any complete behavioral conceptualization of passive behavior would be an evaluation of the reinforcement that is associated with current displays of passive behavior, that is, how is passivity currently working for the individual? Behaviors that are reinforced are repeated. Repeated engagement in passive behavior suggests repeated reinforcement of such behavior. Passive responding may be reinforced through the avoidance of responsibility and decision making. With what amount of attention, positive or negative, are passive responses met? The individual employing passive strategies may need to reconcile his or her "active" influence on situations with the alleged passivity.

Aggressive behaviors can be learned through the observation of aggressive models and reinforced through their instrumental effects. Even in the absence of overt goal attainment, aggressive behaviors may be experienced as intrinsically reinforcing by virtue of the autonomic discharge associated with such behaviors. Aggressive behavior may serve as a socially sanctioned interaction style (Tedeschi & Felson, 1994). Aggressive behavior may also be a consequence of the absence of opportunities to acquire alternative social interaction strategies.

Motivational–affective factors are important to patterned displays of passive and aggressive behavior. Although the affective experience of anger is not sufficient to explain aggressive behavior, feelings of anger do increase the likelihood that the actions of others will be experienced as aggressive and, thereby, elicit aggressive behavior. Cognitive explanations for passive and aggressive responding would posit that outcome expectations are primary in determining the passive or aggressive response. The passive individual may look to his or her history of failures in making or refusing requests in deciding whether to attempt the recommended assertive behavior. Outcome expectations may interfere with adoption of the "new" assertiveness. Such outcome expectations must be managed if the likelihood of assertive responding is to increase. The passive individual needs to be cautioned regarding the imperfect relationship between assertive responding and desired outcomes. Initially, assertive responses may not meet with desired outcomes. It is the *persistence* of the assertive response that will ensure that the probability of the desired outcome increases over time. In the short run, then, the measure of successful assertion may not be the occurrence of a desired outcome but the mere assertive communication of one's opinions, needs or limits.

In an effort to assist individuals in discriminating assertive behavior from passive behavior and aggressive behavior, clinicians sometimes present these behaviors as falling into three mutually exclusive categories. Assertive behavior is nuanced behavior, the tone, content, and appearance of which is determined by the perception of the social context and social demands of a given moment. Certain social situations require only gentle assertion of needs and desires while other situations require firm assertion of those needs and desires. On the first occasion of your neighbor's dog's chewing through the dividing fence, a communication that brings the neighbor's attention to the damage might be sufficient to resolve the matter. On the fourth occasion of the dog's chewing through the dividing fence, a communication indicating intent to bring the matter to the attention of the neighborhood association and/or animal control may be warranted.

ASSESSMENT

Assessment of assertiveness skills and performance abilities should be broad enough to capture and distinguish among various explanations for performance failure. Traditionally, a hierarchical task analysis is used to determine the causal variable that accounts for the skill or performance deficit (Dow, 1994). Initially, assertiveness skills are evaluated in a nonthreatening (or less threatening) environment. Given that the client demonstrates adequate assertiveness skill in the nonthreatening environment, assertiveness skills are evaluated in the context of more clinically relevant social situations. Given that skills are adequately demonstrated in clinically relevant social situations, other contributions to response failure are evaluated including affective and cognitive variables that might mediate the skill–performance relation. Behavioral models of depression suggest that the pursuit of social interaction (and, thus, experience of reinforcement) may be limited by negative affective experiences that are present throughout the interaction (Lewinsohn, 1974). For example, anxiety that is experienced during an assertive interaction may be insufficient to impair performance but may be sufficient to render the interaction a punishing rather than reinforcing event.

PRECONDITIONS FOR ASSERTIVENESS

Assertive behaviors presuppose the existence of adequate social skills. An assertive communication is measured not only by the content of the verbalization but also by the accompanying nonverbal behaviors. Appropriate posture and eye contact are essential in executing an appropriately assertive response. An appropriately assertive posture would convey relaxed but focused attention, in contrast to an overly rigid posture, which might convey either anxiety or obstinacy. Other important nonverbal behaviors include facial expression and body movements and gestures. Affective displays should be congruent with the content of the assertive communication, not suggesting anxiety, false gaiety, or anger. Body movements that indicate nervousness and uncertainty (e.g., hand wringing) should be avoided. Movements that convey anger or dominance (e.g., invasion of the other's personal space) should also be avoided. These nonverbal behaviors are included among behaviors identified by Dow (1985) as relevant to socially skilled behaving.

The content of the assertive communication is important in its clarity and form. The tone and fluidity of the request or refusal are also important. Generally, the assertive request is characterized by its reasonableness, its specificity regarding actions required to fulfill the request, and its inclusion of statements that convey the potential impact(s) of request fulfillment for both the individual making the request and the request recipient. The tone in which the request is delivered should convey the importance of the request; however, the tone should not imply some obligation on the part of the request recipient to comply with the request. Dow (1994) suggests that, in the context of a request for behavior change, the potential for a satisfactory outcome is maximized when the assertive communicator refrains from making assumptions about the motivations driving others' behaviors, refrains from questioning others regarding their motives, and interjects something positive about the individual with whom they are interacting. The content and tone of assertive refusals share the quality of being even-handed and unwavering.

ASSESSMENT OF ASSERTIVENESS SKILLS AND PERFORMANCE ABILITIES

Assessment of skill sets and performance competencies is necessary prior to skills training and throughout the skills acquisition and practice process. Skills for behaving assertively are evaluated through the use of self-report instruments as well as behavioral observation in simulated and natural settings.

Questionnaires

Assertiveness skill evaluation and training often occurs in the broader context of social skill and social competence. The self-report instruments that purport to measure assertiveness range from actual measures of assertive behaviors to instruments that assess related constructs such as social avoidance, self-esteem, and locus of control. The most commonly used general measure of assertiveness skills is the Rathus Assertiveness Scale (Rathus, 1973). Other assertiveness questionnaires have been designed to evaluate assertive behavior occurring in various professional (e.g., nursing) and clinical (e.g., date rape prevention, HIV/AIDS prevention, social anxiety treatment, and substance abuse relapse prevention) contexts.

Self-Monitoring Assignments

Self-monitoring of social behaviors performed in the client's natural environment is essential to both assessment and treatment of potential skills and performance deficits. Monitoring instructions usually require that the client describe his or her social interactions with others along a number of dimensions. The client may be instructed to briefly describe interactions with males versus females, acquaintances versus intimate others, peers versus persons in authority, and in structured versus unstructured interactions. Although real-world evaluation of skills is preferable, the office is the most common arena for skills evaluation and practice. Therefore, it is essential that the client provide detailed accounts of problem interactions and that the content and cues of the experimental arena be as consistent with that real world as possible.

BEHAVIORAL OBSERVATION

Behavioral observation is considered the preferred strategy for evaluating assertiveness skills and performance competencies. Usually, observations and evaluations of assertive performances are made in clinical or research settings rather than real-world settings. Clinic and laboratory settings provide contexts for informal observation (waiting room behaviors and behaviors engaged in by the client during the clinical interview) and formal observation (social interaction tasks and role-playing) of an individual's behavior.

Clinical Interview

In the clinical setting, the client's waiting room behavior (i.e., his or her interactions with other persons in the waiting room and with clinic staff) is available for observation. Exchanges during initial assessment sessions also serve as data to be used in establishing the presence or absence of verbal and nonverbal communication skills considered essential to assertive displays as well as contextual factors that may influence the likelihood of assertive behaving and the mastery with which assertive behaviors are performed.

Social Interaction Tasks in Analogue Settings

In evaluating a client's social skill and comfort, the therapist may enlist confederates to engage the client in interactions that test the client's ability to initiate and participate in casual exchanges. These tasks are considered low-demand tasks. Usually, they do not contain any of the elements of identified problematic interactions.

Social Interaction Tasks in Real-World Settings

Of course, the optimal arena for evaluating assertive behavior is the client's natural environment. As often as possible, the real-world context should be captured. For example, a male client reporting difficulty initiating social interactions with female peers might be observed in real world settings that are familiar to him and that present opportunities for contact with female peers (e.g., the college library, an undergraduate seminar, a scheduled, on-campus extracurricular event). Other local contact arenas are also acceptable for evaluation of skills including coffee houses, dance clubs, and the like.

Role-Playing

In the clinical context, a "true" observation of assertive behaviors is made through the use of role-playing. Based on the client's report of difficult interpersonal interactions, interaction opportunities that mimic these difficult interpersonal interactions (to a lesser or greater degree) are engineered and the client's use of assertive behaviors observed. Typically, the therapist serves as the "relevant other" in such role play situations. Research participants or clients are asked to display their skills repertoire in the context of contrived interactions with the researcher/therapist or some confederate. In structuring the role play, the therapist aims to lessen the artificial quality of the exercise and to strengthen the correspondence between the client's performance in artificial and natural settings. This is best achieved through the use of dialogue and contextual cues that closely approximate the naturally occurring problematic interactions. Role playing confederates and scenarios are often selected with relevant contextual factors in mind.

ASSERTIVENESS TRAINING

When it has been established that a skills deficit explains performance failure, it is often useful to begin at the beginning. Table 8.1 presents a detailed, step-by-step guide to the conduct of assertiveness skills training. Assertiveness training usually begins with a didactic presentation of (1) definitions of assertiveness, passiveness and aggressiveness; (2) the rationale for the use of assertive behavior; and (3) the basic content and procedural guidelines that govern assertive behavior. In starting the practice of assertiveness skills, the therapist always begins with a review of the more basic elements of assertive communication and continues along a graded hierarchy

TABLE 8.1   Key Components of an Assertiveness Training Protocol

1. *Presenting the rationale for assertiveness skills training.* Assertive communication of personal opinions, needs and boundaries has been defined as communication that diminishes none of the individuals involved in the interaction, with emphasis placed on communication accuracy and respect for all persons engaged in the exchange. The success of assertiveness does not always lie in tangible outcomes (e.g., request fulfillment). The success of assertiveness sometimes lies in the degree of personal control and personal respect that is achieved and maintained throughout the assertive exchange. Assertive communication maximizes the potential for achievement of relationship goals in both professional and intimate contexts.

2. *Defining aggressive, passive, and assertive behaviors.* The therapist follows the presentation of the rationale with descriptions of each of the three common form of communication: aggressive, passive and assertive communication.

   a. Aggressive communication of needs usually involves the goal of getting one's needs met or having one's opinion endorsed no matter the cost to the other individual or individuals participating in the exchange. Aggressive communication is often characterized by "shoulds" or "musts" or other language that suggests that the recipient is bound or required to meet the expressed need or agree with the expressed opinion. Aggressive communication is also characterized by nonverbal behaviors that are of the "in your face" quality. Aggressive communicators may ignore the boundaries of personal space, standing overly close to another individual. They may speak in loud, angry tones and in a number of other ways convey subtle pressure or even threat to the other individual or individuals participating in the communication exchange.

   b. Passive communication is problematic, not because of obvious demands placed on the recipient, but because passive communications often do not reflect the true needs or preferences of the speaker. Passive communications involve the use of acquiescent language. The passive communicator often responds to others' statements of preferences and opinions with statements such as "if you think so" or "whatever you want is fine" or "no problem, I can take care of that." In the short term, the passive communicator may be seen as ensuring the pleasure and happiness of the recipients of such behavior. The problems with passive communications are usually experienced over time. The passive communicator begins to resent the fact that their true needs and opinions aren't being honored within these relationships. The recipient of passive communications may feel that the passive individual is only half-heartedly participating in the relationship and is avoiding responsibility for making important decisions within the relationship.

   c. Assertive communication ensures that the needs and opinions of the speaker are honestly expressed and owned by the speaker. Opinions are expressed as opinions rather than as statements of inarguable fact. This allows other participants in the exchange to comfortably express similar or opposing opinions. In communicator presents the request in a manner that is at the same time clear but respectful of the recipient's right to refuse such a request. In refusing requests, the assertive communicator states the refusal clearly and unwaveringly while at the same time indicating appreciation for the other individual's circumstances. Again, assertive communication has the goal of mutual respect.

3. *Reviewing content and procedural guidelines governing assertive behavior.* The assertive request is characterized by its reasonableness, its specificity regarding actions required to fulfill the request, and its inclusion of statements that convey the potential impact(s) of request fulfillment for both the individual making the request and the request recipient. Imbedding request for behavior change between impact statements is referred to as "sandwiching." In making a request for behavior change, then, the client would begin with a statement regarding the negative impact of the other's current behavior, then suggest a specific and reasonable behavioral alternative, and end with a statement suggesting the positive impact of the proposed behavioral alternative for both parties. The behavior change request is sandwiched between the two impact statements.

4. *Provision of overview of assertiveness skills training package.* Provide the client with an overview of the skill sets that comprise assertiveness skills training (i.e., nonverbal behavior as communication, giving and receiving compliments, giving and receiving criticism, and making and refusing requests). Suggest that the skill sets lie on a hierarchy, with practice of lower level skill sets being critical to the successful acquisition and performance of higher level skill sets. Explain that these general skills can be successfully applied across a variety of contexts.

5. *Specifying in-session tasks and homework assignments.* In-session tasks will center around the introduction of particular skill sets, modeling of the behaviors import to the particular skill set being targeted, and practice of those skills in the context of role-plays. The client should be informed that self-monitoring of day-to-day interpersonal interactions will continue throughout assertiveness skills training. These real-world interactions will eventually serve as the setting for practice of assertive behavior.

6. *Modeling of assertive behavior.* For the particular skill set being targeted, the verbal content of a sufficiently assertive response is delineated and the appropriately assertive delivery of that verbal communication is modeled by the therapist or confederate.

7. *In-session practice of assertive behavior.* The client practices assertive behaviors in the context of in-session role-plays that are (increasingly) similar to the identified problematic interactions.

TABLE 8.1 *(Continued)*

8. *Providing reinforcement and corrective feedback.* The evaluation of the role-play performance should always begin with the solicitation of comments from the client. This strategy allows the therapist to (a) evaluate the client's understanding of the verbal and nonverbal behaviors that comprise the assertive response, and (b) evaluate the accuracy and objectivity with which the client evaluates his or her performance. The client's efforts and performance successes (however approximate) should be roundly reinforced by the therapist. Corrective feedback is provided by the therapist and/or confederate and instructions for further refinement of the assertive performance are provided. Videotaping role-plays is recommended to reduce recall burden and to provide specific, visual evidence for performance problems and performance gains over time.

9. *Real-world practice of assertive behavior.* Having practiced assertive behavior in the context of role-plays designed to simulate interpersonal interactions occurring in the client's natural environment, the client begins to practice assertive behavior in the context of naturally occurring interpersonal interactions. The client provides a technical and affective evaluation of the assertive performance in the real-world situation.

10. *Establishing realistic performance expectations and acceptable schedules of reinforcement.* Reinforcement and reiteration of reasonable performance goals is essential throughout the assertiveness skills training process. As the natural environment becomes the practice arena, realistic expectations for performance success are outlined and obvious and regular self-reinforcement of successive approximations of the goal performance is mandated.

---

of skill sets essential to assertive communication across contexts. Traditionally, assertiveness training packages have identified several skill sets as essential to assertive behaving, including using nonverbal behavior as communication, giving and receiving compliments, giving and receiving criticism, and making and refusing requests. In addressing each of these skill sets, the therapist wishes to establish three things: (1) the presence and strength of a particular skill in the client's behavioral repertoire; (2) the situations in which the client competently and reliably displays the particular skill; and (3) the situations in which the client may be called upon to competently display the particular skill.

The presence and strength of a particular assertive skill or skill set may be established formally or informally. A client's nonverbal behaviors are immediately observable by the therapist. In the context of the therapeutic exchange, the therapist may observe nonverbal behaviors that are not at all consistent with the goals of assertive communication. This would signal that, at least within the context of the therapeutic exchange, direct training and practice of assertive nonverbal behavior are justified. When nonverbal behaviors have been observed to be sufficient in this context, the therapist may feel uncomfortable reviewing these more basic elements of assertive communication. In such situations the therapist is encouraged to (1) acknowledge the appropriateness of the client's nonverbal behavior

in the therapeutic context and (2) suggest that the display of appropriately assertive nonverbal behavior is sometimes bound by context; that is, assertive nonverbal behaviors sometimes depend on how comfortable the person feels in a given situation or with a given individual. A review of nonverbal behaviors would be completed and instructions would be given that the client monitor and evaluate displays of appropriately assertive nonverbal behaviors in the natural environment.

The skills that characterize each level of the assertiveness hierarchy should be approached in a similar manner. For example, if in the ongoing context of therapy the client has evidenced skill in assertively requesting something of the therapist, this instance would be pointed to by the therapist and reinforced through praise. The therapist would then suggest that the display of even well-established skills can be influenced by situations and persons. The various aspects of request making would be reviewed, real-world instances of successful and unsuccessful request making attempts would be solicited, and the client would be instructed to monitor and practice assertive request making in the natural environment. The therapist will structure in-session role-playing and homework assignments so that both more common and less common request making situations are encountered over the course of such practice.

When the absence of assertive behavior is explained by affective or cognitive factors rather than a skills deficit, other strategies are recommended as adjuncts to behavioral rehearsal of assertive behavior. Examples of such strategies include relaxation training to reduce performance inhibiting anxiety or anger, cognitive restructuring to challenge negative performance predictions and overgeneralizations regarding performance errors, and cognitive reframing with respect to performance goals and measures of performance success.

ASSERTIVENESS IN SPECIFIC CONTEXTS

When assertive behavior is routinely absent in the context of a particular relationship or relationship set, an evaluation of the relationship history and implicit or explicit rules of the relationship is appropriate. This information may provide the therapist with clues as to the habit strength associated with the nonassertive behavior and the extent to which the pattern of habitual responding is reinforced by others. A realistic appraisal of the benefits and deficits of the relationship may need to be delineated along with an emphasis on the sufficiency of the self.

Interactions Involving Intimate Others

In the context of intimate relationships, the greatest challenge to assertive behaving is often the long interaction history that has been established. Nonverbal and verbal components of intimate exchanges may have become habitual and less subject to immediate reinforcement contingencies. Intimate relationships are also unique with respect to the sensitivity of topics that may need to be addressed. The assertiveness skills forwarded for nonintimate interactions are applicable to intimate interactions. Particular attention may need to be given to acknowledging the degree to which a new interaction style is being forwarded. Sensitive behavior change requests (or request refusals) may involve family traditions, sexual behavior, or lifestyle behaviors. Sensitive topics such as changes in the frequency or type of sexual activities should be addressed in a manner that suggests an interest in

experimentation rather than a permanent change to the couple's repertoire. In such situations, the emphasis placed on overt reinforcement of satisfying aspects of current interactions can not be too strong.

Assertiveness appears to be of differential utility in the context of domestic violence. Some research suggests that battered women are potentially at increased risk as a result of assertive behavior in the context of ongoing domestic violence (O'Leary, Curley, Rosenbaum & Clarke, 1985). However, assertiveness training has been found to contribute to a woman's decision to leave a violent relationship (Meyers-Abell, & Jansen, 1980). Research addressing male batterers suggests that batterers have assertiveness deficits that may contribute to there use of aggression and violence to express their needs and manage the needs of their domestic partner (Maiuro, Cahn, & Vitiliano, 1986). In the context of female sexual victimization, assertiveness training appears to empower women and reduce their exposure to violence (Mac Greene & Navarro, 1998).

Interactions Involving Business Associates

Business situations are often replete with individuals skilled in the art of persuasion. Because of the high level of assertiveness that often characterizes business interactions, specific techniques have been forwarded as helpful when making or refusing some business request. These include: the use of self-disclosure (suggestions of similarity in personal experiences or preferences are influential in "selling" an individual); repetition of request or request refusal (assuming a finite number of arguments for or against a given position, simple repetition of one's position suggests commitment to that stance and may wear down the resolve of the other individual); and singular focus (discussion of unrelated or tangentially related topics may serve to distract the participants from the critical topic).

Interactions Involving Health Care Providers

There are obvious and subtle health implications associated with engaging in passive behavior and aggressive behavior. Both forms of behavior can result in unmet health care needs, either through nonarticulation of those needs (passive behavior) or through expression of those needs that is experienced by the health care provider as threatening or offensive (aggressive behavior) and, therefore, refused. Less obvious health implications of passive and aggressive behaviors are those that are associated with the shifts in physiological arousal that often accompanies both passive and aggressive behavior. The deleterious effects of anger in (passive responding) and anger out (aggressive responding) have been documented in the context of certain cancers (Penedo et al, 2006; White et al., 2007), cardiovascular disease (Kop et al., 2008; Smith & MacKenzie, 2006), and chronic pain (Bruehl, Chung, & Burns, 2006; Fernandez & Turk, 1995).

Given both the obvious and subtle health-related effects of passive and aggressive behavior, assertive behavior is rendered essential to both the pursuit of health care and the maintenance of health. In the health care context, individuals present to health care providers to obtain a service. Through the use of assertive behavior, an individual can be effective in requesting health care services, even when the patient's perception of best practice requires more than the health care provider might initially consider necessary.

CONCLUSION

In establishing the effectiveness of an assertive response, we often consider the outcome that is achieved. Although the ultimate goal of assertive communication may be to influence the behavior of others, the measure of assertiveness is the extent to which personal opinions, needs, and boundaries have been accurately and respectfully communicated and received. Competent performance of appropriately assertive behavior is best predicted when sufficient attention has been given to the interpersonal context in which the behavior is planned to occur. Very often, treating professionals fail to acknowledge the consequences of assertive behavior that the client would consider negative (e.g., loss of perceived

control for the formerly aggressive individual and loss of attachment figures for the formerly passive individual). In adopting an assertive stance, individuals are not merely engaging in a simple display of a new behavior set. They are often realigning and reordering relationship priorities.

References

Bruehl, S., Chung, O. Y., & Burns, J. W. (2006). Anger expression and pain: An overview of findings and possible mechanisms. *Journal of Behavioral Medicine, 29,* 593–606.

Dow, M. G. (1985). Peer validation and idiographic analysis of social skill deficits. *Behavior Therapy, 16,* 76–86.

Dow, M. G. (1994). Social inadequacy and social skill. In L. W. Craighead, W. E. Craighead, A. E. Kazdin, and M. J. Mahoney (Eds.). *Cognitive and behavioral interventions: An empirical approach to mental health problems* (pp. 123–140). Boston: Allyn and Bacon.

Fernandez, E., & Turk, D. C. (1995). The scope and significance of anger in the experience of chronic pain. *Pain, 61,* 165–175.

Kop, W. J., Weissman, N. J., Bonsall, R. W., Doyle, M., Sretch, M. R., Glaes, S. B., et al. (2008). *American Journal of Cardiology, 101,* 767–773.

Lewinsohn, P. M. (1974). A behavioral approach to depression. In R. J. Friedman & M. M. Katz, (Eds.). *The psychology of aggression: Contemporary theory and research* (pp. 157–178). Washington, DC: John Wiley & Sons.

MacGreene, D., & Navarro, R. L. (1998). Situation-specific assertiveness in the epidemiology of sexual victimization among university women: A progressive path analysis. *Psychology of Women Quarterly, 22,* 589–604.

Maiuro, R. D., Cahn, T. S., & Vitaliano, P. P. (1986). Assertiveness deficits and hostility in domestically violent men. *Violence & Victims, 1,* 279–289.

Meyers-Abell, J. E. & Jansen, M. A. (1980). Assertiveness therapy for battered women: A case illustration. *Journal of Behavior Therapy & Experimental Psychiatry, 11,* 301–305.

O'Leary, K., Curley, A., Rosenbaum, A. & Clarke, C. (1985). Assertion training for abused wives: A potentially hazardous treatment. *Journal of Marital & Family Therapy, 11,* 319–322.

Penedo, F. J., Dahn, J. R., Kinsinger, D., Antoni, M. H., Molton, I., Gonzalez, J. S., et al. (2006). *Journal of Psychosomatic Research, 60,* 423–427.

Rathus, S. A. (1973). A 30-item schedule for assessing assertive behavior. *Behavior Therapy, 4,* 398–406.

Smith, T. W., & MacKenzie, J. (2006). *Annual Review of Clinical Psychology, 2,* 435–467.

Tedeschi, J. T., & Felson, R. B. (1994). *Violence, aggression, and coercive actions.* Washington, DC: American Psychological Association.

White, V. M., English, D. R., Coates, H., Lagerlund, M., Borland, R., & Giles, G. G. (2007). Is cancer risk associated with anger control and negative affect? Findings from a prospective cohort study. *Psychosomatic Medicine, 69,* 667–674.

9   ATTRIBUTION CHANGE*

Rebecca S. Laird and Gerald I. Metalsky

Since Beck first introduced cognitive behavior therapy (CBT) for depression (1967; Beck, Rush, Shaw, & Emery, 1979), there have been numerous studies demonstrating its efficacy (for reviews see Dobson, 1989; Evans et al., 1992; Hollon, Evans, & DeRubeis, 1990; Jacobson & Hollon, 1996). Beck's CBT is based on the underlying theoretical rationale that an individual's emotions, motivations, and behavior are largely determined by the way in which he or she constructs the world. Subjective thoughts, images, and feelings are rooted in the enduring attitudes and assumptions, or schemas, that the individual develops from prior experience. Human experience is automatically filtered through these cognitive structures, by which input is categorized and evaluated.

According to Beck et al. (1979), some individuals develop maladaptive schemas that serve as vulnerability factors predisposing them to depression and other clinical disorders (Beck, Emery, & Greenberg, 1985). Many subsequent studies have found compelling evidence for attributional style (Abramson, Seligman, & Teasdale, 1978; Metalsky & Abramson, 1981; Nolen-Hoeksema, Girgus, & Seligman, 1992) as one such risk factor for depression in children, adolescents, and adults (for reviews, see Andrews, 1989; Harvey & Galvin, 1984; Metalsky, Laird, Heck, & Joiner, 1995; and Peterson & Seligman, 1984). A depressogenic attributional style is the generalized tendency to attribute negative life events to internal, stable, global factors.

Unfortunately, there is a dearth of research that attempts to dismantle and evaluate the components of a cognitive behavior program in order to identify the active ingredients of successful treatment outcome for depression (Harvey & Galvin, 1984; Whisman, 1993). However, one impressive attempt to do this has been undertaken by Jacobson, Dobson, Gortner, and colleagues (Jacobson et al., 1996; Gortner, Gollan, Dobson, & Jacobson, 1998). These investigators compared behavioral therapy with two cognitive behavior treatment packages that were based on Beck et al.'s (1979) CBT for depression. Their partial CBT program was designed to identify and modify automatic thoughts, including maladaptive attributions for negative life events. The complete CBT program included the techniques utilized in the partial CBT program and added several specific interventions that were designed to identify and modify core schemas underlying the kinds of cognitive distortions that were targeted in the partial CBT condition. This complete CBT condition included interventions designed to modify attributional style (Peterson & Villanova, 1988). Both CBT conditions included a behavioral activation component and consisted of 12 to 20 sessions. Individuals receiving treatment met criteria for major depression according to the *Diagnostic and Statistical Manual of Mental Disorders* (3rd edition, revised [*DSM-III-R*], American Psychiatric Association, 1987).

Upon completion of either CBT condition, depressed participants showed a significant improvement in depressive symptoms. Analyses revealed that clinical improvement was accompanied by a significant decrease in depressogenic attributions as well as a significant change in attributional style. The results persisted at 6-month and 2-year follow-ups (Gortner et al., 1998). It should be noted,

* The authors wish to acknowledge Tina Baeten, Eileen Diller, Marvel Herlache, Holly Husting, Kris Hutchison, and Carolyn Martin-Johnson for their invaluable contributions.

however, that these studies did not include complete tests of whether attributional style served as a mediator of the effect of CBT on improvement in symptoms (see Teasdale et al., 2001, for a discussion of this issue).

WHO MIGHT BENEFIT FROM THIS TECHNIQUE

Cognitive behavior therapy that specifically included an attribution change component has been used successfully to treat depression in both individual and group outpatient settings (Nixon & Singer, 1993), with children (Carlyon, 1997), adolescents (Reynolds & Stark, 1987), adults (Goldberg, Gask, & O'Dowd, 1989), and married couples (Birchler, 1986). It may be used in conjunction with pharmacological treatment.

CONTRAINDICATIONS

Research on therapeutic attribution retraining for depression has not studied the efficacy of this technique with hospital inpatients or thought-disordered individuals. This technique is not recommended for implementation with depressed patients who are actively psychotic.

Interestingly, Addis and Jacobson (1996) found that the number and types of explanations clients gave for their depression were significantly associated with treatment outcome. Depressed subjects who attributed their depression to negative childhood experiences failed to respond to CBT, whereas subjects with external attributions for their depression appeared to benefit from CBT.

HOW TO APPLY ATTRIBUTION CHANGE TECHNIQUES: OVERVIEW

Beck et al. (1979) note that CBT ought to take place in the context of a therapeutic *relationship* characterized by warmth, accurate empathy, and genuineness. Building trust and rapport are crucial ingredients when treating depressed clients with CBT. It is also important to elicit client feedback regularly in order to check the client's understanding of the therapy and to assess for any adverse reactions that may impede the therapy process.

Cognitive behavior therapy for depression is conducted within a framework of collaborative empiricism. The therapist assumes an active, directive stance, joining with the client in a logical and empirical investigation of the client's beliefs, attitudes, inferences, and assumptions. Therapy focuses on the present, examining the client's thoughts and feelings as they occur during the session as well as in the client's everyday life. Therapist and client work together to establish specific treatment goals designed to ameliorate depressive symptoms and any other problems that they agree to address.

The therapist begins treatment by educating the depressed client about the theoretical rationale behind CBT, which Beck notes is a very important foundation for this therapeutic approach (Beck et al., 1979). Early therapy sessions focus on two major areas: (1) teaching the client to recognize and understand the connections between his or her thoughts, feelings, and behavior; and (2) training the client to identify the automatic thoughts that accompany negative feelings and problematic behaviors. In particular, the client begins to observe the kinds of attributions that he or she makes for negative life events.

The next phase of therapy involves teaching the depressed client how to evaluate the evidence for and against these maladaptive attributions and other associated automatic thoughts. The therapist teaches the client how to challenge his or her cognitive distortions, and to substitute more rational and reality-based ways of thinking. In particular, the patient is encouraged to shift from making internal, stable global attributions for negative life events to making more adaptive attributions. The client is encouraged to practice self-observation, hypothesis-testing techniques, and logical challenges to cognitive distortions in daily life, and to bring these data in for further examination during therapy sessions.

The final phase of therapy, conducted over eight sessions, involves helping the depressed client identify the maladaptive assumptions and attitudes (schemas) underlying his or her cognitive distortions. The client and therapist together examine and evaluate his or her depressogenic attributional style. Alternative core beliefs are

TABLE 9.1   Attribution Change Step by Step

1. Perform client assessment.
2. Educate the client about the rationale and techniques of CBT for depression.
3. Teach the client to understand the connections between his or her thoughts, feelings, and behavior.
4. Train the client to identify depressogenic attributions that are associated with negative feelings.
5. Examine the evidence for and against those attributions. Substitute more rational, realistic thoughts for depressogenic attributions and other cognitive distortions.
6. Identify underlying assumptions and core beliefs that compose the client's depressogenic attributional style.
7. Evaluate, challenge, and modify the client's depressogenic attributional style.

considered and the advantages and disadvantages of each are evaluated. The client is encouraged to practice evaluating his or her experience according to the new attributional schemas that have been consciously selected.

STEP-BY-STEP PROCEDURES

Step 1

As can be seen in Table 9.1, the therapist must make a thorough assessment of the client's depressive and other symptoms. Other information gathered may include the client's ability to identify and label feelings, the specific kinds of situations that are problematic, the link between presenting complaints and depressive symptoms, and the kinds of thinking distortions to which the client is subject. In particular, the clinician is attuned to any of the client's statements that illustrate a tendency to blame himself or herself or to assume personal responsibility for adverse events, whether or not those events are under personal control.

Questionnaire data can supplement information gathered in a clinical interview. Jacobson et al., (1996) administered the Beck Depression Inventory (BDI; Beck, 1967; Beck, Steer, & Garbin, 1988), the Automatic Thoughts Questionnaire (ATQ; Hollon & Kendall, 1980), and the Expanded Attributional Style Questionnaire (EASQ; Peterson & Villanova, 1988) to each client before and after treatment. Information is also gathered about the client's understanding of the therapy process and his or her therapy goals.

Step 2

The therapist explains the theoretical rationale behind CBT. The client learns about Beck's (1967)

cognitive theory of depression as well as the way in which CBT will be used to treat it.

Step 3

The client is encouraged to begin to apply the cognitive theory to his or her own situation. The therapist encourages the client to make connections between his or her own thoughts, feelings, and behaviors.

Step 4

The client learns to identify automatic thoughts and images that are associated with negative feelings and depressed behaviors. In particular, the client learns to identify and observe attributions that he or she makes for negative life events. The client is encouraged to keep a daily record of attributions and other automatic thoughts together with the feelings, problematic behaviors, and situations in which they occur outside of therapy. The therapist is active in eliciting client attributions for the negative events he or she experiences.

Step 5

The client learns to evaluate the logical and empirical validity of his or her attributions. Together the therapist and client identify an attribution associated with negative affect. They review the situation that gave rise to this automatic thought, gathering and defining all of the factors associated with that event that would be relevant in making a realistic and accurate attribution of responsibility. These factors may include a review of the relevant information available to the client at the time of the event, the possible role of others in contributing to the adverse occurrence, the controllability of the event, and its significance to the client and others. The client is encouraged to come up with alternative attributions and to consider the evidence for and against each of these competing hypotheses. Homework assignments may be given in order for the client to gather more information and to evaluate the empirical evidence for and against depressogenic and more adaptive attributions.

The therapist may question the client about the types of attributions that he or she would make if someone other than the client were in the client's place. Does the client exhibit a double standard when assigning blame to self, but make more realistic attributions for others? The therapist may also challenge the client to consider whether responsibility in this situation is an absolute 100%, or whether it is more logical to view responsibility as shared or partial (known as *deresponsibilitizing*).

The client is thus enabled to gain a more objective, balanced, and realistic view of his or her own responsibility in causing a negative event. The client is then encouraged to generalize this reattribution process to other negative life situations with the therapist's continued support.

Step 6

The therapist goes on to identify more general patterns in the client's depressogenic attributions, identifying the attributional schemas underlying the client's habitual way of construing negative life events. The downward arrow technique is useful here, wherein the therapist elicits the client's explanations for his or her problems, then generates hypotheses about various kinds of general patterns and concerns, ultimately leading to the identification of the core beliefs comprising the client's depressogenic attributional style. Homework assignments enable the client to see whether these core beliefs do in fact characterize his or her everyday experience.

Therapist and client then consider alternative attributional core beliefs and discuss the immediate and long-term advantages and disadvantages of holding each kind of belief. The client is then encouraged to explore how alternative core attributions might be applied to life situations. The therapist and client also subject these underlying attributional assumptions to the same kind of logical and empirical scrutiny that they did the automatic thoughts and attributions in step 5.

Further Reading

Beck, A. T., Rush, A. J., Shaw, B. F., & Emery, G. (1979). *Cognitive therapy of depression*. New York: Guilford.

Jacobson, N. S., Dobson, K. S., Truax, P. A., Addis, M. E., Koerner, K., Gollan, J. K., et al. (1996). A component analysis of cognitive-behavioral treatment for depression. *Journal of Consulting and Clinical Psychology, 64*, 295–304.

Metalsky, G. I., Laird, R. S., Heck, P. M., & Joiner, T. E. Jr. (1995). Attribution theory: Clinical implications. In W. O'Donohue & L. Krasner (Eds.), *Theories of behavior therapy: Exploring behavior change* (pp. 385–413). Washington, DC: American Psychological Association.

References

Abramson, L. Y., Seligman, M. E. P., & Teasdale, J. (1978). Learned helplessness in humans: Critique and reformulation. *Journal of Abnormal Psychology, 87*, 49–74.

Addis, M. E., & Jacobson, N. S. (1996). Reasons for depression and the process and outcome of cognitive-behavioral psychotherapies. *Journal of Consulting and Clinical Psychology, 64*, 1417–1424.

American Psychiatric Association. (1987). *Diagnostic and statistical manual of mental disorders* (3rd ed., rev.). Washington, DC: Author.

Andrews, J. D. W. (1989). Psychotherapy of depression: A self-confirmation model. *Psychological Review, 96*, 576–607.

Beck, A. T. (1967). Depression: *Clinical, experimental, and theoretical aspects*. New York: Hoeber.

Beck, A. T. (1976). *Cognitive therapy and the emotional disorders*. New York: Meridian.

Beck, A. T., Emery, G., & Greenberg, R. L. (1985). *Anxiety disorders and phobias: A cognitive perspective*. New York: Basic Books.

Beck, A. T., Rush, A. J., Shaw, B. F., & Emery, G. (1979). *Cognitive therapy of depression*. New York: Guilford.

Beck, A. T., Steer, R. A., & Garbin, M. G. (1988). Psychometric properties of the Beck Depression Inventory: Twenty-five years of evaluation. *Clinical Psychology Review, 8*, 77–100.

Birchler, G. R. (1986). Alleviating depression with "marital" intervention. *Journal of Psychotherapy and the Family, 2*, 101–116.

Carlyon, W. D. (1997). Attribution training: Implications for its integration into prescriptive social skills training. *School Psychology Review, 26*, 61–73.

Dobson, K. S. (1989). A meta-analysis of the efficacy of cognitive-behavioral therapy for depression. *Journal of Consulting and Clinical Psychology, 57*, 414–419.

Evans, M. D., Hollon, S. D., DeRubeis, R. J., Piasecki, J. M., Grove, W. M., Garvey, M. J., et al. (1992). Differential relapse following cognitive therapy and pharmacotherapy for depression. *Archives of General Psychiatry, 49*, 802–808.

Goldberg, D., Gask, L., & O'Dowd, T. (1989). The treatment of somatization: Teaching techniques of reattribution. *Journal of Psychosomatic Research, 33*, 689–695.

Gortner, E. T., Gollan, J. K., Dobson, K. S., & Jacobson, N. S. (1998). Cognitive–behavioral treatment for depression: Relapse prevention. *Journal of Consulting and Clinical Psychology, 66*, 377–384.

Harvey, J. H., & Galvin, K. S. (1984). Clinical implications of attribution theory and research. *Clinical Psychology Review, 4*, 15–33.

Hollon, S. D., Evans, M. D., & DeRubeis, R. J. (1990). Cognitive mediation of relapse prevention following treatment for depression: Implications of differential risk. In R. E. Ingram (Ed.), *Contemporary psychological approaches to depression* (pp. 117–136). New York: Guilford.

Hollon, S. D., & Kendall, P. E. (1980). Cognitive self-statements in depression: Development of an automatic thoughts questionnaire. *Cognitive Therapy and Research, 4*, 383–396.

Jacobson, N. S., Dobson, K. S., Truax, P. A., Addis, M. E., Koerner, K., Gollan, J. K., et al. (1996). A component analysis of cognitive-behavioral treatment for depression. *Journal of Consulting and Clinical Psychology, 64*, 295–304.

Jacobson, N. S., & Hollon, S. D. (1996). Cognitive behavior therapy vs. pharmacotherapy: Now that the jury's returned its verdict, it's time to present the rest of the evidence. *Journal of Consulting and Clinical Psychology, 64*, 74–80.

Metalsky, G. I., & Abramson, L. Y. (1981). Attributional style: Toward a framework for conceptualization and assessment. In P. C. Kendall & S. D. Hollon (Eds.), *Assessment strategies for cognitive-behavioral interventions* (pp. 13–58). San Diego, CA: Academic Press.

Metalsky, G. I., Laird, R. S., Heck, P. M., & Joiner, T. E. Jr. (1995). Attribution theory: Clinical implications. In W. O'Donohue & L. Krasner (Eds.), *Theories of behavior therapy: Exploring behavior change* (pp. 385–413). Washington, DC: American Psychological Association.

Nixon, C. D., & Singer, G. H. (1993). Group cognitive behavioral treatment for excessive parental self-blame and guilt. *American Journal on Mental Retardation, 97*, 665–672.

Nolen-Hoeksema, S., Girgus, J. S., & Seligman, M. E. P. (1992). Predictors and consequences of childhood depressive symptoms: A 5-year longitudinal study. *Journal of Abnormal Psychology, 101*, 405–422.

Peterson, C., & Seligman, M. E. P. (1984). Causal explanations as a risk factor for depression: Theory and evidence. *Psychological Review, 91*, 347–374.

Peterson, C., & Villanova, P. (1988). An expanded attributional style questionnaire. *Journal of Abnormal Psychology, 97*, 87–89.

Reynolds, W. M., & Stark, K. D. (1987). School-based intervention strategies for the treatment of depression in children and adolescents. *Special Services in the Schools, 3*, 69–88.

Teasdale, J. D., Scott, J., Moore, R. G., Hayhurst, H., Pope, M., & Paykel, E. (2001). How does cognitive therapy prevent relapse in residual depression? Evidence from a controlled trial. *Journal of Consulting and Clinical Psychology, 69*, 347–357.

Whisman, M. A. (1993). Mediators and moderators of change in cognitive therapy of depression. *Psychological Bulletin, 114*, 248–265.

10 BEHAVIORAL ACTIVATION TREATMENT FOR DEPRESSION

Christopher R. Martell

Over the past 10 years there has been a resurgence of interest in behavioral treatments for depression that were originally proposed in the early 1970s with the theoretical formulations of C. B. Ferster (1973, 1981) and the applied work of Peter Lewinsohn and colleagues (Lewinsohn, 1974; Lewinsohn, Biglan, & Zeiss, 1976; Lewinsohn & Graf, 1973). The basic idea of the behavioral theory of depression was that individuals become depressed when there is an imbalance of punishment to positive reinforcement in their lives. According to Ferster (1981), when an individual responds primarily to deprivation and the removal of an aversive, deprived state, he or she develops behaviors that function primarily as avoidance behaviors and there is little access to positive reinforcement built into the behavioral repertoire of the individual. Treatment for depression would, therefore, consist of a process that would increase the individual's access to positive reinforcers.

Following the analysis of Ferster, Lewinsohn and colleagues focused on increasing pleasant events and pleasurable activities in order to treat depression (Lewinsohn & Graf, 1973). These researchers developed the use of activity logs and activity scheduling to help depressed patients increase positive activities that would combat their lethargy and bring them into contact with positive reinforcers. During this same time, cognitive therapy for depression was also being formulated (Beck, 1976) and utilized the activity scheduling elements of Lewinsohn's approach but focused on changing the negative content of depressed patients' beliefs. Cognitive therapy was studied extensively and empirically validated as a treatment for depression, and the field of behavior therapy took on a distinctively

cognitive profile throughout much of the 1980s and 1990s. The idea of increasing pleasant events alone, without cognitive interventions, was questioned (Hammen & Glass, 1975), and cognitive behavior therapy was seen as a psychosocial treatment of choice for depression.

A recent meta-analysis (Ekers, Richards, & Gilbody, 2007) suggests that behavioral treatments are efficacious for treating depression. A component analysis of cognitive therapy for depression (Jacobson et al., 1996) demonstrated that depressed participants treated with behavioral activation alone improved as well as those subjects treated with a full cognitive therapy treatment. Their results were maintained at follow-up (Gortner, Gollan, Dobson, & Jacobson, 1998). The results of the component analysis study opened the door for a larger study of the treatment of depression, which compared cognitive therapy, behavioral activation, paroxetine, and pill placebo (Dimidjian, Hollon, Dobson, et al., 2006). For moderately to severely depressed clients, behavioral activation performed as well as antidepressant medication and outperformed cognitive therapy in the acute treatment. Both behavioral activation and cognitive therapy were efficacious in the prevention of relapse (Dobson, Hollon, Dimidjian, et al., in press).

Behavioral activation is a structured, behavior analytic approach that borrows heavily from earlier behavioral formulations of depression (Jacobson, Martell, & Dimidjian, 2001; Martell, Addis, & Jacobson, 2001). Through functional analyses, client behavior is understood according to its setting and consequences rather than the particular form it takes. The emphasis is, indeed, on the function of a behavior rather than the form and the treatment is not just about getting depressed clients to be more active. For example, while chatting with a friend on the phone may formally appear to be a positive behavior for a depressed individual, one must understand the contexts and consequences prior to coming to such a conclusion. If chatting with the friend serves to keep the individual from working on a project that is overdue, thus making her or him more depressed, it functions as avoidance and has negative consequences. The treatment is theory driven rather than protocol driven with a focus on targeting avoidance behavior as a primary treatment goal with depressed clients.

WHO MIGHT BENEFIT FROM THIS TECHNIQUE

Behavioral activation (BA) is currently a treatment for depression and has undergone evaluation in that arena. A small pilot study has suggested that BA may be useful in the treatment of veterans with posttraumatic stress disorder (Jakupcak, Roberts, Martell, Mulick, Michael, Reed, et al., 2006). The BA focus on avoidance places it in the realm of other exposure-based treatments that have been used for the treatment of anxiety and other disorders. However, no data are yet available to demonstrate the utility of the approach in these areas. Participants in Jacobson's lab met criteria for major depressive disorder and were screened out only if there was presence of a thought disorder or active substance or chemical dependence. No other comorbid disorders were excluded. Therefore, the participant pool on which the treatment was tested had at least an Axis I major depressive disorder, but could have had comorbid Axis I or Axis II disorders (other than psychosis or substance dependence).

CONTRAINDICATIONS OF THE TREATMENT

Understanding the possible contraindications of this treatment requires clinical hypothesis rather than hard data. The treatment does not seem to be contraindicated for most people suffering from major depression. Although it is a context-based, nonpharmachological treatment that encourages clients to look outward at their life context rather than at hypothesized internal defects, it

has even been used with clients who maintain a need for psychotropic medication (implying a flaw in the machine). We would caution clinicians, however, from using this technique with depressed individuals who may be involved in a domestic violence situation, where activating may expose them to greater harm from an abusive partner. Clinicians should be cautious not to encourage a client to engage in behavior that could result in any such harmful interpersonal interaction.

OTHER DECISIONS IN DECIDING WHETHER TO USE BEHAVIORAL ACTIVATION

The data suggest that BA alone, without evaluation of the content of clients' thinking, works well in the treatment of a major depressive episode. However, outside of the research setting, there is no prohibition against using cognitive restructuring although recent investigations into methods for treating client rumination (see, e.g., Watkins, Scott, Wingrove, Rimes, Bathurst, Steiner, et al., 2007) are more consistent with the behavioral formulation. Some clients maintain strong beliefs that their thinking is the problem. We would recommend that, rather than arguing with a client, therapists incorporate the very behavioral aspects of BA with a cognitive conceptualization. The two treatments are complementary and provide a bridge for some clients (and therapists). For example, the context and consequences of clients' thinking (where and when it occurs, and what effect it has on how the client feels and what he or she does next) can be incorporated into BA without focusing on the content.

HOW DOES THE TECHNIQUE WORK?

At this time, we can only make assumptions about the factors that make BA work. Primarily, the therapist takes the role of a coach, encouraging clients to become active even when they feel as if they cannot possibly complete tasks or get any pleasure from life. Because BA works to help clients establish a regular routine, it breaks the destructive process of routine disruption that often accompanies depression (Ehlers, Frank, &

Kupfer, 1988). Activity in BA means getting engaged rather than just doing something for the sake of being busy or living under a Calvinist work ethic.

STEP-BY-STEP PROCEDURES

The treatment is based on the theory, described earlier, that depression often results from changes in a vulnerable individual's life that decrease the person's access to positive reinforcement. Basically, the treatment consists of strategies that increase activity and block avoidance so that the client can come in contact with natural reinforcers in his or her environment. In order to do this in a manner that is idiographic and not merely applying broad classes of pleasant activities that may or may not actually be reinforcing, the therapist needs to do a good functional analysis.

Conducting a Functional Analysis

Whereas the laboratory provides much control over conditions that can lead to accurate understanding of contingencies at work in the behavior of organisms under study, the clinical setting does not provide the same level of control. When we speak of functional analysis we are speaking of the best hypotheses that the therapist and client can develop about the antecedents, behaviors, and consequences that form elements of the client's repertoire contributing to depression. In BA we are interested in the function of the behavior and not the form of the behavior. Therefore, we are less concerned with what popular opinion may be about a certain behavior (e.g., people may think that going for a run early in the morning is a good and healthy thing to do) that with the function of a particular behavior for particular person (e.g., the runner may actually be out early in the morning because she does not want to remain at home to have a discussion with her partner about having neglected to pay an expensive bill). Functional analysis is the heart of BA, and it will be conducted throughout the treatment. The first step, however, is to develop general case conceptualization from a behavior analytic perspective.

There are several questions that the therapist needs to ask about the depressive episode that the client is experiencing. First, the therapist should understand the client's history and gather information about significant life events, positive or negative, that influence the client's current life context. To do this, the therapist simply need ask the client to recount such events, with questions like "What is your family like? What kinds of things have been good in your life? What has hurt you or has been distressing?" It is also important, second, to understand how the client behavior during a depressive episode is different from his behavior at other times. Asking the client "What is your life like when you are not depressed? Are there things that you are not doing now that you typically do when you are not de pressed? What do you hope to accomplish in you life? Are you taking steps toward accomplishing, these things?" can help to gather a picture of what problems the client may be experiencing.

Gathering this information helps the therapist to develop a case conceptualization of the client's depression. We express the case conceptualization in terms of the life events that may have contributed to the depression by making the client's life less rewarding, and we then look at how the client has tried to cope with the symptoms of depression. Often the client's attempts at coping become problems in themselves, and we refer to these as *secondary problem behaviors*. For example, the runner mentioned earlier might be coping with feelings of hopelessness and inadequacy by engaging in a fervent exercise program the enables her to avoid dealing with issues with her significant other. We would call her exercise regime a secondary problem. Even though we know exercise is good for depressed people in general, with this particular client we would want to help her to address her issues with her partner and then institute exercise that is not avoidance.

Day-by-Day Analysis

Since its earliest conception by Lewinsohn and others, BA has made ample use of activity charts to help therapists understand the level of a client's activity and to schedule pleasant events.

We continue to rely heavily on activity charts in our work. We use activity charts for several reasons. The therapist can use an activity chart to understand the following:

- The client's current level of activity
- Restriction of the client's affect
- Connections between the client's activity and mood
- Mastery and pleasure ratings
- How to help the client monitor avoidance behaviors
- Guided activity
- Steps the client is taking toward stated life goals

It does not matter what type of activity chart a therapist chooses to use with his or her clients. All that is important is that the chart include all the hours in the day and provide room enough for the client to record what he or she did and felt, and the intensity of the feeling, in each hour block.

Techniques for Dealing with Client Avoidance

We find it most important that clients continually be vigilant of their avoidance behaviors. It is also a basic tenet in BA that clients can choose to engage in activities that will possibly help them to feel better, or they can choose to continue to avoid and possibly remain depressed. Although we never tell clients that they are choosing to be depressed, we do indeed suggest to clients that choices made about specific behaviors can lead to certain consequences.

While not required in the treatment, three acronyms illustrate the concept of avoidance to clients and help them to be aware of their patterns and to modify behaviors. Using these acronyms simplifies the explanation of complex ideas. The first is the acronym *ACTION*, which stands for the following:

Assess my behavior: Is my current behavior avoidant? How does this behavior serve me?
Choose whether to activate myself and engage in behaviors that could help my depression in the long run, or to continue to avoid this experience.

Try the behavior that I've chosen.
Integrate any new activity into a regular routine, remembering that trying a new behavior only once is unlikely to lead to significant change.
Observe the outcome of the behavior: Does it affect mood, or does it improve a life situation?
Never give up. Counteracting depression and avoidance takes continued work and tenacity in the face of frequent disappointments.

The second acronym we use is *TRAP*, which stands for *trigger*, or some happening or event; *response*, usually the client's emotional response to the trigger; and *avoidance pattern*, which is the typical avoidance response to the trigger. Once the client has identified a TRAP, we use the third acronym to help him or her get back on *TRAC* (*trigger, response, alternative coping*). The strategies of using activity charts and helping clients to recognize avoidance patterns and modify their behavior make up the bulk of BA treatment.

Conceptualized as a contextual treatment, BA focuses on helping clients to change behavior in such a way as to bring them into contact with positive reinforcers in their natural environment. There is much less emphasis on skills training than in other behavioral therapies. The model in BA is that therapists *may* conduct skills training, but they are not *required* to. Whether to conduct skills training such as problem-solving training will depend on the behavioral analysis of each client. In clinical outcome trials of BA, therapists have used problem-solving training or assertiveness training, but they have done so in a fashion that anchors the training in the context of the client's life. In other words, even in skills training, the BA therapist tries not to teach a broad class of skills that can be applied by following rules; rather, the therapist debriefs specific incidents in the client's life and helps the client understand how he or she might have changed an outcome by behaving differently. In some cases the client may be planning a particular encounter, and the therapist would discuss options for achieving particular outcomes.

FINAL CONSIDERATIONS

The therapeutic stance in BA is always collaborative. The therapist serves as a coach for the client. When the therapist is trying to help a client develop a new skill, the therapist takes the position that his or her suggestions are hypotheses to be tested rather than prescriptions from an authority figure. Behavioral activation therapists are working within a model that is quite different from a medical model. Clients are seen as individuals whose lives have somehow gone awry rather than as patients with some defect or flaw that must be modified. The therapist works to help the client understand the areas of his or her life that are not working and to make adjustments in behavior to enhance the workable aspects of life.

In the treatment outcome studies conducted on BA to date from Jacobson's laboratory, the therapy has consisted of a 16-week protocol, with clients allowed up to 24 therapy sessions. Many clients begin to show improvement in depression scores within the first 10 sessions. However, there are no clear data to suggest an optimal length of treatment. Researchers in a different setting, conducting BA that primarily focused on activity scheduling, had successful results with a 10-session protocol (Lejuez, Hopko, LePage, Hopko, & McNeil, 2001). This would suggest that the treatment may be successful over a shorter time period.

Further Reading

Jacobson, N. S., Martell, C. R., & Dimidjian, S. (2001). Behavioral activation treatment for depression: Returning to contextual roots. *Clinical Psychology: Science and Practice, 8*(3), 255–270.

Martell, C. R., Addis, M. E., & Jacobson, N. S. (2001). *Depression in context: Strategies for guided action.* New York: W. W. Norton.

References

Beck, A. T. (1976). *Cognitive therapy and the emotional disorders.* New York: New American Library.

Dimidjian, S., Hollon, S. D., Dobson, K. S., Schmaling, K. B., Kohlenberg, R. J., Addis, M. E., et al. (2006). Randomized trial of behavioral activation, cognitive therapy, and antidepressant medication in the acute treatment of adults with major depression. *Journal of Consulting and Clinical Psychology, 74*(4), 658–670.

Dobson, K. S., Hollon, S. D., Dimidjian, S., Schmaling, K. B., Kohlenberg, R. J., Gallop, R., et al. (in press). Randomized trial of behavioral activation, cognitive therapy, and antidepressant medication in the prevention of relapse and recurrence in major depression. *Journal of Consulting and Clinical Psychology.*

Ekers, D., Richards, D., & Gilbody, S. (2007, October). A meta-analysis of randomized trials of behavioural treatment of depression. *Psychological Medicine, 1*(13) (forthcoming article, e-publication at http://journals.cambridge.org).

Ferster, C. B. (1973). A functional analysis of depression. *American Psychologist, 28,* 857–870.

Ferster, C. B. (1981). A functional analysis of behavior therapy. In L. P. Rehm (Ed.), *Behavior therapy for depression: Present status and future directions* (pp. 181–196). New York: Academic Press.

Gortner, E. T., Gollan, J. K., Dobson, K. S., & Jacobson, N. S. (1998). Cognitive–behavioral treatment for depression: Relapse prevention. *Journal of Consulting and Clinical Psychology, 66*(2), 377–384.

Hammen, C. L., & Glass, D. R. (1975). Depression, activity, and evaluation of reinforcement. *Journal of Abnormal Psychology, 54*(6), 718–721.

Jacobson, N. S., Dobson, K., Truax, P. A., Addis, M. E., Koerner, K., Gollan, J. K., et al. (1996). A component analysis of cognitive–behavioral treatment for depression. *Journal of Consulting and Clinical Psychology, 64*(2), 295–304.

Jacobson, N. S., Martell, C. R., & Dimidjian, S. (2001). Behavioral activation treatment for depression: Returning to contextual roots. *Clinical Psychology: Science and Practice, 8*(3), 255–270.

Jakupcak, M., Roberts, L. J., Martell, C., Mulick, P., Michael, S., Reed, R., et al. (2006). A pilot study of behavioral activation for veterans with posttraumatic stress disorder. *Journal of Traumatic Stress, 19,* 387–391.

Lejuez, C. W., Hopko, D. R., LePage, J. P., Hopko, S. D., & McNeil, D. W. (2001). A brief behavioral activation treatment for depression. *Cognitive and Behavioral Practice, 8,* 164–175.

Lewinsohn, P. M. (1974). A behavioral approach to depression. In R. M. Friedman & M. M. Katz (Eds.), *The psychology of depression: Contemporary theory and research* (pp. 157–185). New York: John Wiley & Sons.

Lewinsohn, P. M., Biglan, A., & Zeiss, A. S. (1976). Behavioral treatment of depression. In P. O. Davidson (Ed.), *The behavioral management of anxiety, depression and pain* (pp. 91–146). New York: Brunner/Mazel.

Lewinsohn, P. M., & Graf, M. (1973). Pleasant activities and depression. *Journal of Consulting and Clinical Psychology, 41,* 261–268.

Martell, C. R., Addis, M. E., & Jacobson, N. S. (2001). *Depression in context: Strategies for guided action.* New York: W. W. Norton.

Watkins, E., Scott, J., Wingrove, J., Rimes, K., Bathurst, N., Steiner, H., et al. (2007). Rumination-focused cognitive behaviour therapy for residual depression: A case series. *Behavior Research and Therapy, 45,* 2144–2154.

11   RESPONSE CHAINING

W. Larry Williams and Eric Burkholder

Chaining refers to a set of procedures used to teach a task that consists of an ordered series of specific responses that must occur in a predetermined order to produce reinforcement. In the behavioral account, each step of this series produces an outcome that serves both as a reinforcer for the response that produced it and as a discriminative stimulus for the next response in the sequence (Martin & Pear, 2007). The chain terminates with some principal outcome, product, or reinforcer.

Chaining has been used by trainers in a myriad of professions dating back well over 100 years (Crafts, 1929; Mountjoy & Lewandowski, 1984). In the basic literature, chaining has been used to study such fundamental processes as the nature of conditioned reinforcement (Boren, 1969; Boren, & Devine, 1968; Fantino, 1965; Jwaideh, 1973; Kelleher & Fry, 1962; Pisacreta, 1982; Thvedt, Zane, & Walls, 1984; Weiss, 1978). In the applied literature, chaining has been shown to be a procedurally sound method of producing a broad range of complex behaviors in a variety of populations, from teaching college students to play golf (Simek, O'Brien, & Figlerski, 1994) to teaching disabled individuals how to engage in activities of daily living (Spooner, 1984). The literature related to persons with intellectual disabilities is particularly well elaborated, where chaining has been used to teach assembly-line tasks (Martin, Koop, Turner, & Hanel, 1981; Spooner, 1984; Spooner, Spooner, & Ulicny, 1986; Weber, 1978); family-style dining (Wilson, Reid, Phillips, & Burgio, 1984); language acquisition (Buckley & Newchok, 2005); responding to a fire alarm (Cohen, 1984); reducing escape behavior (Lalli, Casey, & Kates, 1995); picture naming (Olenick, & Pear, 1980); and treating total liquid refusal (Hagopian, Farrell, & Amari, 1996), self-injurious behavior (Hagopian, Paclawskyj, & Contrucci-Kuhn, 2005), community skills (McDonnell, & Laughlin, 1989), and other complex skills (McWilliams, Nietupski, & Hamre-Nietupski, 1990). Other issues bearing on chaining have also been examined, including trainer preference for chaining procedures (Walls, Zane, & Thvedt, 1980), effects of conditions of reinforcement on chaining (Talkington, 1971), and teaching the effects of prompting and guiding procedures (Zane, Walls, & Thvedt, 1981).

Three conventional methods have evolved for teaching chains. *Total task presentation* involves teaching all of a chain's component responses on each teaching trial. *Forward chaining* teaches the first response in the chain to some criterion, then the first and second response, then the first three responses, and so on until the total chain is acquired. *Backward chaining* teaches the last response in the sequence first, then the second to last and the last responses, then the third to last, second to last, and the last responses, and so on, until the total chain is acquired. Which one of these three variants has the highest level of efficacy has not been satisfactorily answered, due to contradictory findings (Martin, Koop, Turner, & Hanel, 1981). It does seem clear that all three variants can be effective for teaching skills to a wide range of populations.

WHO MIGHT BENEFIT FROM THIS TECHNIQUE?

Professionals and educators who work with populations that need to learn complex activities or populations that have displayed deficits in their ability to learn may benefit from the systematic application of this technique. As described earlier, this technique has been widely used to teach a variety of skills to people with intellectual disabilities. The use of this technique is appropriate for teaching any task that can be broken into smaller steps such as making coffee, tying shoes, making a bed, assembling electrical components, or engaging in any of a wide variety of crafts, hobbies, sports, exercise, and vocational and habilitation skills. Chaining may also be used for acquisition of complex verbal performances or for generating rules or strategies to guide other performances.

HOW DOES THIS TECHNIQUE WORK?

Chaining works by systematically establishing a specific response in the presence of a specific discriminative stimulus, itself the result of a specific prior response. As specific response units are established, they are put together into an ever-increasing sequence of responses until the complete task is achieved. The completed task is itself associated with a more significant functional reinforcer, typically the functional outcome of the task being taught (e.g., a prepared sandwich, a loaded dishwasher, completion of a preflight check). The arrangement of the responses and their outcomes is determined by a *task analysis*. Before starting the teaching procedure, the task analysis should be validated (walked through and tried) and prompting procedures (additional material; instructional, gestural, or physical aides) determined and specified as well as reinforcement criterion. Chaining works because each link in the chain (i.e., each

discrete response), has a clear discriminative stimulus and is either directly reinforced by the trainer, leads to conditioned reinforcement, or both.

COMPLETING AND VALIDATING A TASK ANALYSIS

A task analysis breaks a complex activity into its component parts or units so that they can be individually shaped if they are not already in the subject's repertoire, or brought under appropriate stimulus control within the chain if they are present already. Any task that results in a typical outcome (e.g., taking a shower, making a bed) can be broken into the essential response components rather easily. Consider, for example, the task analyses in Figures 11.1 and 11.2.

Once a task has been broken into its component parts, it needs to be validated prior to starting the teaching procedure. There are many ways of validating a task analysis (Cooper, Heron, & Heward, 1987), including observing and piloting out the procedure, consulting experts or people who are fluent in performing the task, or performing the task repeatedly. Regardless of what method is used for the validation of the task analysis, each behavior to be taught should be discrete and follow a clear, discriminative stimulus produced by either the initial instruction or by the previous link in the chain.

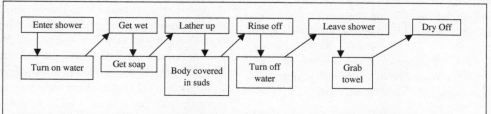

Note that each general response can itself be broken down into smaller responses each of which produce their own specific stimulus outcomes that signal another response. (For example there are many ways to "turn on water" such that some form of "getting wet" is the outcome serving as a prompt to pick up soap, resulting in prompting soap application, etc.) Indeed these are the individual differences in how we shower, but no one applies soap before being wet, nor dries off before turning off the water, etc.

FIGURE 11.1   The sequence of chained responses in taking a shower. Each of the general responses below results in a specific outcome, which signals the next response. The necessary order is also well illustrated. Indeed, because of necessary pre-requisite conditions for some responses (e.g., being wet, being lathered with soap) this chain would best be taught using a forward chaining or whole task presentation method.

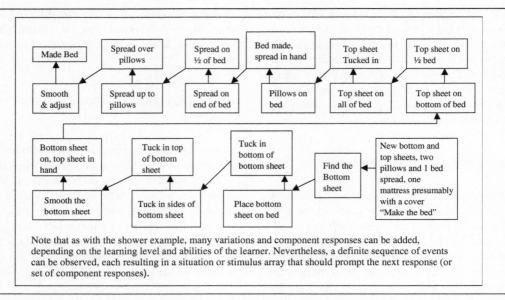

Note that as with the shower example, many variations and component responses can be added, depending on the learning level and abilities of the learner. Nevertheless, a definite sequence of events can be observed, each resulting in a situation or stimulus array that should prompt the next response (or set of component responses).

FIGURE 11.2 Making a bed. Although a certain sequence of responses is involved, this task can be easily arranged to be totally, partially, or not at all complete. As such, it is teachable in a backward chaining format, here the final product of a "made bed" always is the product of a training session. In a backward chaining format training would start with simply smoothing and adjusting the bed spread over the pillows. The rest of the bed would be already made. The rest of the steps would then be introduced one at a time.

The number of steps can be increasingly refined until they are (1) small and easily taught and (2) at the appropriate level for the learner. The ability of the learner, the behavioral characteristics of the learner, and the exact environment the skill will be taught in must be taken into consideration when conducting a task analysis. In the examples shown in the figures, a learner would have to have the ability to use both arms and discriminate bedding materials from other materials, in order to make use of the task analyses presented. For this reason, the exact steps and order of the steps in a task analysis may be different for two different learners, depending on the constraints of the environment and the task.

DETERMINE WHAT CHAINING
PROCEDURE TO USE

The trainer at this point has several different options as to how to chain the behavior. Selecting among the most commonly used chaining procedures depends upon the exact training situation (see Figure 11.3).

Forward Chaining

A forward chaining procedure teaches each component response from the first to the final response in a forward sequential manner. For example, in chaining the skills from the validated task analysis for taking a shower, a learner would be taught to turn on the water and would be reinforced for doing so until he or she displayed mastery (e.g., three consecutive correct responses). Once the learner has demonstrated mastery of step one, the second step of getting oneself all wet would be introduced. Once this second step is introduced, the first step of simply turning on the water would no longer be reinforced; the learner would now have to turn on the water and get appropriately wet to be reinforced by our trainer. The other behaviors in our chain would then be added systematically upon mastery of each, until all steps in our validated task analysis have been performed.

An advantage of forward chaining is that teaching trainers to use a forward chain is relatively simple, and most people are taught to engage in new tasks in a forward manner. These

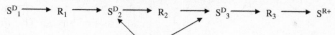

Response Chaining

1. A Chain is an ordered series of specific responses that must occur in a predetermined order to produce its related functional reinforcement.

$$S^D{}_1 \longrightarrow R_1 \longrightarrow S^D{}_2 \longrightarrow R_2 \longrightarrow S^D{}_3 \longrightarrow R_3 \longrightarrow S^{R+}$$

2. Each response produces an outcome that serves as, 1) A conditioned reinforcer for that response, 2) As a discriminative stimulus (S^D) for the next response, and 3) As a discriminative stimulus (S^V) for not engaging in that response.

3. A *Task Analysis* is conducted for the task to be taught which consists of breaking the task down into component response units based on the apparent or natural sequences that make up the task. Once produced it is important to validate the task analysis for accuracy, completeness and detail according to the skill level of the learner to be taught the chain.

Forward chaining teaches the components separately and in the order they occur in the chain. As each response is learned it is added to the others.	R_1 $R_1 \longrightarrow R_2$ $R_1 \longrightarrow R_2 \longrightarrow R_3 \longrightarrow S^{R+}$
Backward Chaining teaches the last response in the chain first, then the second last and so on. Each teaching trial involves the current response being taught and then the rest of the sequence already learned, and ends with the chain's natural reinforcer	$R_3 \longrightarrow S^{R+}$ $R_2 \longrightarrow R_3 \longrightarrow S^{R+}$ $R_1 \longrightarrow R_2 \longrightarrow R_3 \longrightarrow S^{R+}$
Total Task Presentation is a variation of Forward Chaining and teaches all of the component responses on every teaching trial. That is, the whole chain is performed on every trial.	$R_1 \longrightarrow R_2 \longrightarrow R_3 \longrightarrow S^{R+}$

FIGURE 11.3 Response Chaining.

advantages can lead to staff's using forward chaining and can decrease the need for staff supervision with this method of chaining (Wilson et al., 1984).

Backward Chaining

Backward chaining involves teaching a learner the final link in the chain first. For example, from our task analysis of bed making, smoothing the bedspread over the pillows is the final link. The trainer would arrange for the bed to be "made" except for that final link. The learner would then be taught to do that last step. Upon mastery of smoothing the spread over the pillows, the next-to-last step (pulling the spread over the pillows) would be added to the task and both responses would be practiced. The remaining responses would then each be added until the

learner is engaging in the entire task of making the entire bed independently.

One advantage of backward chaining is that right from the beginning of training, the learner's performances result in obtaining or producing the natural reinforcer for engaging in the chain, the made bed in our example. By teaching the last responses first, teaching any given preceding step produces a change in the environment that functions as the discriminative stimulus for the next step, which eventually is the last step that has already been followed by the ultimate reinforcer. Because of this repeated pairing, conditioned reinforcement should occur (Skinner, 1938), and this additional reinforcing function should aid in the acquisition of the chain. There are practical concerns, however, since the learner is initially passive on all steps up to the final link (Cooper, Heron, & Heward, 1987). Staff also sometimes have trouble avoiding confusion in using backward conditioning due to its reverse strategy.

Total Task Presentation

Total task presentation is a variant of forward chaining. This variant has the learner perform every step in the chain on every teaching trial. The trainer assists the learner on any step that he or she cannot perform independently. This training continues until the learner can perform the entire task independently at the mastery criterion. This is accomplished by prespecifying prompts, including time between prompts, prior to the beginning of the training. For example, the trainer would initially use verbal prompts and hand-over-hand assistance for each step in making coffee, waiting 5 seconds between prompts until the learner either independently responds or is prompted to engage in the next behavior in the chain. As the learner begins to perform the task more independently, the prompts are faded until the learner is engaging in the entire task independently. This procedure has been shown to facilitate fast chain acquisition (Martin, et al., 1981; Spooner, 1984). Spooner (1984) suggests that the fast rate of acquisition typically observed with this method may be accounted for by the presentation of every stimulus–response link on every training trial, and may be worth the effort and training time needed to engage in all steps during each teaching trial.

Factors Related to the Effectiveness of Chaining

Research and experience have shown several factors can influence the success of a chaining program.

1. *Conduct a task analysis.* Although there are numerous ways to break down a task into component responses of differing sizes, one should first conduct an analysis that leads to a series of responses that break along natural lines of the task steps and which produce characteristic clear situations or products. Then, depending on the discrimination skill level of the learner (Jackson, Williams &

Biesbrouck, 2006; Martin & Yu, 2000; Yu, Martin, & Williams, 1989) as well as other factors such as motor dexterity, one might further break down component steps into even smaller units. The final components however must maintain clear stimulus and response relationships with no same stimulus presentations controlling different component responses.

2. *Determine the types and arrangement of prompts.* The final response chain must be trained to occur in the presence of a specific instruction or cue and then be performed such that each response sets the occasion for the next, until the entire chain is completed. This requires arranging for the fading of initial interim instructions and prompts as the component responses are acquired as larger and larger units. For learners with language and rule-governed skills (Ellen & Pate, 1986; Hayes, 1989; Skinner, 1953), spoken, written, self-reported, or pictorial aids can effectively guide the learner through the sequence in an independent fashion. For nonverbal learners, interim instructions and prompts (gestural, physical, etc.) may be required to establish component responses and then gradually be eliminated as the main overall instruction gains control over the ever-expanding chain.

3. *Use a modeling demonstration.* Demonstration of the entire task to the learner will often result in much quicker acquisition of a chain, and reduce cumbersome training involving establishment of partial chains and the gradual removal of the interim instructions for them as the appropriate sequence is established.

4. *Training sequence and corrections.* Begin training by providing the final instruction. If the learner errs or stops responding, provide a *momentum* cue such as "keep going" that is not specific to the behavior to be engaged in but that will cue continuing to complete the chain. If an error occurs, intervene with a correction procedure such as modeling the step or instructional or gestural assistance until the learner completes the step. Then proceed to the next step by providing the final chain instruction again.

5. *Reinforcement.* As in any behavior change activity, one should use ample social praise

for progress toward the final target behavior. Praise should be given for completion of individual responses and some larger reinforcer (such as an edible) provided when the whole chain is completed, or when larger units of the final chain are learned. Be cautious to not distract the learner from completing component responses because of well-intentioned but unnecessary reinforcing statements or provision of reinforcers that stop the engagement in completing the task (Gold, 1972). A stimulus preference assessment (see the relevant chapter in this volume) (DeLeong & Iwata, 1996) should be conducted to increase the chance that supposed reinforcers are indeed reinforcers. Choice among several demonstrated reinforcers is a preferred method.

6. *Prompt fading.* Once a learner is engaging in a component response, and especially when component responses are beginning to occur in their desired sequence, it is crucial not to provide unnecessary additional instructions or cues. The objective is to have the naturally occurring cues from the task itself guide performance. Failure to remove instructions and interim prompts or assistance early on in training can result in the learner's "waiting" for assistance and not trying to complete the task independently.

Further Reading

Cooper, J. O., Heron, T. E., and Heward, W. L. (1987). *Applied behavior analysis.* Englewood Cliffs, NJ: Prentice-Hall.

Martin, G., Koop, S., Turner, G., & Hanel, F. (1981). Backward chaining versus total task presentation to teach assembly line tasks to severely retarded persons. *Behavior Research of Severe Developmental Disabilities, 2*, 117–136.

References

Boren, J. (1969). Some variables affecting the superstitious chaining of responses. *Journal of the Experimental Analysis of Behavior, 12*, 959–969.

Boren, J., & Devine, D. (1968). The repeated acquisition of behavior chains. *Journal of the Experimental Analysis of Behavior, 11*, 651–660.

Buckley, S. D., & Newchok, D. B. (2005). Differential impact of response effort within a response chain on use of mands in a student with autism. *Research in Developmental Disabilities, 26*(1), 77–85.

Cohen, I. (1984). Establishment of independent responding to a fire alarm in a blind, profoundly retarded adult. *Journal of Behavior Therapy and Experimental Psychiatry, 15*, 365–367.

Cooper, J. O., Heron, T. E., and Heward, W. L. (1987). *Applied behavior analysis.* Englewood Cliffs, NJ: Prentice Hall.

Crafts, L. (1929). Whole and part methods with non-serial reactions. *American Journal of Psychology, 41*, 543–563.

DeLeong, I. G., & Iwata, B. A. (1996). Evaluation of a multiple stimulus presentation format for assessing reinforcer preferences. *Journal of Applied Behavior Analysis, 29*, 519–533.

Ellen, P., & Pate, J. (1986). Is insight merely chaining?: A reply to Epstein. *The Psychological Record, 36*, 155–160.

Fantino, E. (1965). Some data on the discriminative stimulus hypothesis of secondary reinforcement. *Psychological Record, 15*, 409–415.

Gold, M. (1972). Stimulus factors in skill training of retarded adolescents on a complex assembly task: Acquisition, transfer, and retention. *American Journal on Mental Deficiency, 5*, 517–526.

Hagopian, L., Farrell, D., & Amari, A. (1996). Treating total liquid refusal with backward chaining and fading. *Journal of Applied Behavior Analysis, 29*, 573–575.

Hagopian, L. P., Paclawskyj, T., and Contrucci-Kuhn, S. (2005). The use of conditional probability analysis to identify a response chain leading to the occurrence of eye poking. *Research in Developmental Disabilities, 26*(4), 393–397.

Hayes, S. (1989). Rule governed behavior: Cognition, contingencies and instructional control. New York: Plenum.

Jackson, M, Williams, W.L., & Biesbrouck, J. (2006). Conditional discrimination ability, equivalence formation and mental retardation: Implications for development in children with developmental disabilities. *Journal of Speech Language Pathology and Behavior Analysis, 1*(1), 27–42.

Jwaideh, A. (1973). Responding under chained and tandem fixed-ratio schedules. *Journal of the Experimental Analysis of Behavior, 19*, 259–267.

Kelleher, R., & Fry, W. (1962). Stimulus functions in chained fixed-interval schedules. *Journal of the Experimental Analysis of Behavior, 5*, 167–173.

Lalli, J., Casey, S., & Kates, K. (1995). Reducing escape behavior and increasing task completion with functional communication training, extinction, and response chaining. *Journal of Applied Behavior Analysis, 28*, 261–268.

Martin, G., Koop, S., Turner, G., & Hanel, F. (1981). Backward chaining versus total task presentation to teach assembly line tasks to severely retarded persons. *Behavior Research of Severe Developmental Disabilities, 2,* 117–136.

Martin, G. L., & Pear, J. J. (2007). *Behavior modification: What it is and how to do it* (8th ed). Upper Saddle River, NJ: Prentice Hall.

Martin, G. L., & Yu, D. (2000). Overview of research on the assessment of basic learning abilities. *Journal on Developmental Disabilities 7*(2), 10–36.

Mcdonnell, J., & Laughlin, B. (1989). A comparison of backward and concurrent chaining strategies in teaching community skills. *Education and Training in Mental Retardation,* 230–238.

McWilliams, R., Nietupski, J., & Hamre-Nietupski, S. (1990). Teaching complex activities to students with moderate handicaps through the forward chaining of shorter total cycle response sequences. *Education and Training in Mental Retardation,* 292–298.

Mountjoy, P., Lewandowski, A. (1984). The dancing horse, a learned pig, and muscle twitches. *Psychological Record, 34,* 25–38.

Olenick, D. L., & Pear, J. J. (1980). Differential reinforcement of correct responses to probes and prompts in picture-naming training with severely retarded children. *Journal of Applied Behavior Analysis, 13,* 77–89.

Pisacreta, R. (1982). A comparison of forward and backward procedures for the acquisition of response chains in pigeons. *Bulletin of the Psychometric Society, 20,* 233–236.

Simek, T., O'Brien, R., Figlerski, L. (1994). Contracting and chaining to improve the performance of a college golf team: Improvement and deterioration. *Perceptual and Motor Skills, 78,* 1099–1105.

Skinner, B. F. (1938). *The behavior of organisms.* New York: Appleton-Century-Crofts.

Skinner, B. F. (1953). *Science and human behavior.* New York: Free Press.

Spooner, F. (1984). Comparisons of backward chaining and total task presentation in training severely handicapped persons. *Education and Training of the Mentally Retarded,* 75–21.

Spooner, F., Spooner, D., & Ulicny, G. (1986). Comparisons of modified backward chaining: Backward chaining with leap-aheads and reverse chaining with leap-aheads. *Education and Treatment of Children, 9,* 122–134.

Talkington, L. (1971). Response-chain learning of mentally retarded adolescents under four conditions of reinforcement. *American Journal of Mental Deficiency, 3,* 337–340.

Thvedt, J., Zane, T., Walls, R. (1984). Stimulus functions in response chaining. *American Journal on Mental Deficiency, 88,* 661–667.

Walls, R., Zane, T., Thvedt, J. (1980). Trainers' personal methods compared to two structured training strategies. *American Journal of Mental Deficiency, 3,* 495–507.

Weber, N. (1978). Chaining strategies for teaching sequenced motor tasks to mentally retarded adults. *American Journal of Occupational Therapy, 32,* 385–389.

Weiss, K. (1978). A comparison of forward and backward procedures for the acquisition of response chains in humans. *Journal of the Experimental Analysis of Behavior, 29,* 255–259.

Wilson, P., Reid, D., Phillips, J., & Burgio, L. (1984). Normalization of institutional mealtimes for profoundly retarded persons: Effects and non-effects of teaching family-style dinning. *Journal of Applied Behavior Analysis, 17,* 189–201.

Yu, D., Martin, G., & Williams, W. L. (1989). Expanded assessment for discrimination learning with the mentally retarded. *American Journal on Mental Retardation, 94,* 61–169.

Zane, T., Walls, R., & Thvedt, J. (1981). Prompting and fading guidance procedure: Their effect on chaining and whole task teaching strategies. *Education and Training of the Mentally Retarded,* 125–135.

12 BEHAVIORAL CONTRACTING

Ramona Houmanfar, Kristen A. Maglieri, Horacio R. Roman, and Todd A. Ward

A behavioral contract is a written or oral agreement between a client(s) and a clinician, consultant, or an instructor that specifies expectations, plans, and/or contingencies for the behavior(s) to be changed (Martin & Pear, 2007; Kirschenbaum & Flanery, 1984). In its classic form, behavioral contracts (sometimes also called contingency contracts) are written, and specify a set of terms (i.e., the treatment plan) to be followed by the client, and related positive and/or negative consequences (Kidd & Saudargas, 1988) to be carried out conditionally on compliance or noncompliance with the plan (Homme, 1970; Kidd & Saudargas, 1988; Mann, 1972; Murphy, 1988; Petry, 2000; Welch, & Holborn, 1988). Behavioral contracting has been applied to a wide variety of areas and settings such as classroom behavior problems (Carns & Carns, 1994; De Martini-Scully, Bray, & Kehle, 2000; Homme, 1970; Ruth, 1996), instructional design (Brooks & Ruthvan, 1984), addictive behaviors (Bigelow, Sticker, Liebson, & Griffiths, 1976; Mann, 1972; Vinson, & Devera-Sales, 2000), staff management (Azrin & Pye, 1989; Welch & Holborn, 1988), delinquency (Stuart & Lott, 1972), self-injurious behaviors (Heinssen, Levensky, & Hunter, 1995), family relationships (Blechman, Olson, & Hellman, 1976; Jacobson, 1978), anorexia (Solanto, Jacobson, Heller, Golden, & Hertz, 1994), weight loss programs (Anderson, Mavis, Robinson, & Stoffelmayr, 1993; Kirchenbum, Germann, & Rich, 2005), and bedtime compliance (Robinson, & Sheridan, 2000).

The clear and mutually negotiated guidelines in behavioral contracts serve four primary functions (Martin & Pear, 2007): (1) they provide an agreement of goals; (2) they ensure that all involved individuals have an accessible reference to monitor progress toward goals; (3) they outline specific responsibilities of the individuals involved (e.g., cost of the program to each individual in terms of time, effort, and money); and (4) they ensure that all individuals are committed to the project in that signatures are obtained.

The conceptual foundations of behavioral contracts are based on the basic principles of operant psychology (Murphy, 1988). Most behavioral contracts are based on the A-B-C approach to identify and modifying "antecedents" to the target behavior (A), the target "behaviors" (B), and the "consequences" or reinforcers that shape and maintain behaviors (C). Since behavior is a function of its consequences, behaviors followed by positive or pleasant consequences are more likely to recur than behaviors followed by negative consequences. Behaviors that are influenced by a set of consequences can be changed either by withholding those consequences or imposing a new set of consequences. Accordingly, once problem behaviors (e.g., noncompliance with medication regime, drug or alcohol abuse) and their controlling consequences are identified, additional incentives (e.g., store vouchers, prizes, cash) and loss of privileges can be implemented through behavioral contracting to change the existing contingencies.

Behavioral contracting has particular utility for clinicians in dealing with compliance with treatment plans. Treatment noncompliance poses a major challenge to clinicians. Treatment plans that are more acceptable to clients are more likely to be followed than less acceptable plans (Kolko & Milan, 1983) and thus treatment acceptability is a critical dimension of the efficacy of a treatment plan (Kazdin, 1980; Yeaton & Sechrest, 1981). The negotiation process involved in behavioral contracting can increase treatment acceptability and compliance and for that reason the use of negotiated contingencies and a focus on treatment process, not just outcome, are important participatory factors in design and implementation of behavioral contracts (Kirschenbaum & Flanery, 1984). Since how well the client does is directly related to how well he or she follows the contract related contingencies, behavioral contracts should be viewed as a *tool* (Boudin, 1972) that facilitates treatment compliance and treatment efficacy.

With regard to the consequential aspect of a behavioral contract, the extent to which new consequences compete and prevail over existing consequences is a function of three parameters: relative magnitude or size, schedule of delivery, and latency (Petry, 2000). For instance, a consequence that immediately follows a behavior may be more effective than a delayed consequence. Likewise, consequences that are delivered consistently and in small amounts tend to produce desirable change. Thus, constructing contract terms should be preceded by an identification of reinforcers. Although one can hypothesize about the effectiveness of consequences in advance, change in behavior is the ultimate determinant of their influence. Accordingly, development and implementation of a monitoring system is essential in evaluating compliance with treatment contingencies.

WHO MIGHT BENEFIT FROM THIS TECHNIQUE?

Behavioral contracting is a treatment that is utilized in a variety of settings and for an even greater number of target behaviors, including classroom behavior, family-marital therapy, substance abuse, weight loss, smoking cessation, and physical exercise, to name a few. However, as mentioned earlier, treatment noncompliance poses a major challenge for the success of behavioral contracts and in the selection of clients for use of behavioral contracting variables such as client's skills and repertoire needs to be considered. For example, a developmentally delayed or severely mentally ill client must be able to monitor the relevant contexts and their performances in them to make use of behavioral contracts as a treatment tool. Additionally, clients who exhibit

behaviors that can be monitored directly through observations (e.g., attendance to meetings) or by their permanent products (e.g., urine samples) are better suited to benefit from behavioral contracts.

ASSOCIATED CHALLENGES

According to Miller (1990), difficulties with behavioral contracts develop when contracts (1) are too restrictive or "parental," (2) appear to be punishing or rejecting, (3) substitute for therapy rather than enhance therapy, and (4) are too rigid and do not allow for client determination or client input. Further, variables such as vagueness of the contract and the therapist's lack of vigilance to observe and monitor the client's compliance with the contract and implement the associated contingencies may participate in a contract's ineffective implementation.

STEP-BY-STEP PROCEDURES

This section outlines a scenario that may be experienced by a mental health professional who provides services in the area of family and marriage counseling. The example is used to illustrate the construction of an appropriate contract for a family receiving professional services.

Mr. and Mrs. Philbrick, who have been married for a little over 15 years, have sought out professional advice regarding their marital problems in addition to problems they are experiencing with their daughter. Recently, Mike (the father) has been spending more time at work and less time with the family. Rachel (the mother) feels that Mike isn't home enough and that he would rather be spending time with his friends than with his family on the weekends. Consequently, because Mike is not home during the week, communication between Mike and Rachel has declined considerably. Mike complains that the time he does spend at home is spent arguing about family matters, specifically about money. Rachel feels that she is the only one managing the household and never has time to do things for herself.

Mike and Rachel are also having trouble with their 14-year-old daughter, Katy. She frequently ignores her 10:00 curfew, sometimes coming home around 1:00 in the morning. Katy had always been a good student, but recently her grades have been starting to slip. Mike suspects that Katy may be drinking or, worse, getting into drugs. Mike and Rachel have tried to discipline Katy, but they report that nothing seems to be working. Rachel would like to spend more quality time with Katy and would like to see Mike do the same. Katy complains that her parents are always arguing and she doesn't want to be around them. Both Mike and Rachel would like to improve their marriage and their relationship with their daughter as well.

The first step in suggesting the most appropriate treatment is determining the family's or client's needs. Without a full assessment of the client's needs, determining the most appropriate course of action will be difficult and may result in targeting the wrong problem behaviors. Equally important in determining the appropriate course of treatment is identifying the client's willingness to change his or her behavior (Kirschenbaum & Flanery, 1984). Returning to the preceding example, both Mike and Rachel have expressed an interest in improving their current situation; however, it is unclear whether Katy is committed to change as well. The initial decision to seek professional help is typically a good indicator of willingness to change; however, identifying which behavior the individual is willing to change must be determined during the interview or assessment process.

Once it has been determined that a behavioral contract is an appropriate technique to facilitate treatment, the therapist should begin to construct the written document. A well-written contract must contain several essential pieces of information (See Table 12.1). The necessary components for constructing a behavioral contract are as follows:

- The behavioral contract must clearly specify the goals of the treatment and use language that is geared to the client's reading level. If the client(s) does not understand what is expected of him/her, the treatment will certainly not be followed.

- The behavioral contract should specify short-term as well a long-term goals (Kirschenbaum & Flanery, 1984). The client's participation in setting his/her goals is essential in determining reasonable and obtainable goals (Lock et al., 1981; Ludwig & Geller, 1997). If treatment goals are too difficult, they will not be achieved, and subsequently any attempts to obtain the goal will not be reinforced. This may result in noncompliance with the treatment or termination of services altogether. Thus, providing reinforcing consequences for the completion of each small step toward the end goal will increase treatment success. For those individuals who do not possess the behavioral repertoire that is necessary to complete the end goal, the principle of *shaping* may be utilized (Martin & Pear, 2007; Skinner, 1953). In other words, the contract should specify relatively simple goals, initially ensuring that the client comes into contact with reinforcement. Once the client has achieved the desired level of behavior, systematic increases in goal difficulty should be implemented. For example, it may be better to set a goal for a decrease in the number of arguments between the couple (e.g., decrease by 2) that gradually increases than to start out with a very big goal at the beginning (e.g., decrease by 10).

- The behavioral contract must identify specific target behaviors for change, as well as ones that will be supported in the natural environment once change occurs. It is also important that the contract specifies the conditions under which target behaviors occur, including times and dates. The more specific the contract, the easier it will be to follow. This step is perhaps the most import aspect of the treatment process, but it can also be the most challenging. Identifying target behaviors in some situations may be relatively obvious (e.g., weight loss), but in others, such as family–marital interactions, it may be more difficult to pinpoint critical behaviors that will result treatment success. For example, if the goal is to decrease arguments about money, the defining conditions of that target (topographically and situationally) should be clear.

- Behavioral contracts should include a monitoring system to ensure that the client is meeting his or her goals. Target behaviors that are selected should be objectively quantifiable, that is, sufficiently clear that another individual can verify the completion of assigned goals. The contract should also specify the person responsible for monitoring treatment progress, how often the monitoring should occur, and by what method. Self-monitoring (the client records his or her own behavior) may be utilized in some situations. For instance, Kirchenbum, Germann, and Rich (2005) found that self-monitoring significantly raised the likelihood that participants would benefit from treatment than those that did not self-monitor. Even so, practitioners should be aware that reliability is a known problem, particularly in areas, such as drug addiction, that are difficult to monitor (Petry, 2000). Clients are particularly likely to lie when self-report is linked to important consequences; thus, in these areas, reinforcers should be delivered based on the verification of products of behavior. In the area of drug use, for example, it is better to reward screened clean urinalysis data than to reward claims of abstinence. In some conditions, self-monitoring can be less intrusive, less expensive, and more productive of consistent behavior change than external monitoring, particularly when the goal is personally relevant and important (Kirschenbaum & Flanery, 1984).

- The behavioral contract must specify reward contingencies for compliance with treatment goals in addition to consequences for noncompliance. The contingencies should focus on the positive. That is, the contract should focus on what the client should do rather than on what he or she should avoid doing. The most effective contracts should specify both the reward for compliance and the consequence for noncompliance (Homme, 1970; Clark, Leukefeld, & Godlaski, 1999). Drawing from the example above, an appropriate contract contingency for Katy would be "I agree to come home by my curfew for 3 weeks in a row. In the event that I do come home by my curfew for 3 weeks in a row, I will spend one Saturday a month shopping with my mother. In the event that I do not come home by my curfew, I will not be allowed to go shopping with my mother and I will not be allowed to go out the following weekend." An inappropriate contingency for Katy would be "If I do not come home by my curfew, I will not be able to go out the following weekend and I will not spend one Saturday a month with my Mom shopping."

To maximize the effects of rewards, they should be delivered immediately, in frequent small amounts, and only when the desired behavior is achieved. The delivery of the reward can be systematically faded over time to lessen the amount of effort and any additional monetary costs associated with implementing the contract. For example, a reward may initially be delivered each time the desired behavior occurs and eventually decreased according to a more manageable schedule over time. If the desired behavior has not maintained after the reinforcement schedule has been modified, the therapist should return to a reinforcement schedule that has previously produced successful performance.

- Finally, the negotiated behavioral contract should be agreed upon and signed by all involved parties.

TABLE 12.1   Key Steps in Using Behavioral Contract

1. Clearly specify the goals of the treatment and use language that is geared to the clients reading level.
2. Specify short-term as well as long-term goals.
3. Identify specific target behaviors for change.
4. Include a monitoring system to ensure that the client is meeting his or her goals.
5. Specify reward contingencies for compliance with treatment goals in addition to consequences for noncompliance.
6. Be agreed upon and signed by all involved parties.

Behavioral Contract Example

The example below illustrates a family contract between the Philbrick family and Dr. Evans.

Mike Philbrick (father):

a. I agree to spend one family night a week with the entire family. I agree not to argue with Rachel or Katy during this time.

b. I agree to help Katy with her homework every week on Tuesday and Thursday.

c. I agree to spend 1 hour a week on Sunday nights with Rachel discussing a topic that she chooses that is not related to work, the house, or the kids.

d. I agree to talk to Rachel about financial matters for one hour on Monday nights only.

e. In the event that I do a through d, I will spend one Sunday a month watching football with my friends. In the event that I do not accomplish a through d, I will not be allowed to watch football.

Rachel Philbrick (mother):

a. I agree to spend one family night a week with the entire family. I agree not to argue with Mike or Katy during this time.

b. I agree to take Katy shopping one Saturday afternoon per month. In the event that Katy does not come home by her curfew, she will not be allowed to go shopping.

c. I agree to spend 1 hour a week on Sunday nights with Mike discussing a topic that I choose that is not related to work, the house, or the kids.

d. I agree to talk to Mike about financial matters for 1 hour on Monday nights only.

e. In the event that I do a through d, I will spend one Saturday a month out of the house doing an activity that I choose.

Katy Philbrick (daughter):

a. I agree to come home by my curfew 3 weeks in a row.

b. I agree to spend one family night a week with the entire family. I agree not to argue with my Mom or Dad during this time.

c. I agree to spend the evening two days a week, Tuesday and Thursday, doing my homework with my dad.

d. In the event that I do a through c, I will spend one Saturday a month shopping with my Mom. In the event that I do not do a through c, I will not spend one Saturday a month shopping with my Mom.

By signing below, you indicate that you agree to the terms stated above and agree to monitor the completion of your treatment goals. A written record of accomplished treatment goals must be turned in to Dr. Evans every month during therapy sessions.

The behavioral contract will be monitored and revised by Dr. Evans as treatment goals are achieved.

Date
Family Members   **Negotiator**
Mike Philbrick   Dr. Evans
Rachel Philbrick
Katy Philbrick

The behavioral contracting example utilized in this chapter is designed to build structure and predictability into the family system. Many families tend to highlight the negative behaviors of other family members and are often unclear about the reciprocal interaction of members' behaviors in the family unit. Consequently, behavioral contracting provides initial restructuring of the family behaviors and their antecedents and consequences. In this context, the role of the family therapist is to (1) help the family design, initiate, and negotiate contracts; (2) assist in the identification and monitoring of specific problem behaviors and contingencies that are included in the contract; and (3) eventually facilitate the development of less formal verbal contracts in the later stages of therapy as written formal agreements become less necessary.

Further Reading

Homme, L. (1970). How to use contingency contracting in the classroom (Rev. ed.). Champaign, IL: Research Press.

Kirschenbaum, D. S., & Flanery, R. C. (1984). Toward a psychology of behavioral contracting. *Clinical Psychology Review, 4,* 597–618.

Miller, L. J. (1990). The formal treatment contract in the inpatient management of borderline personality disorder. *Hospital and Community Psychiatry, 41,* 985–987.

References

Anderson, J. V., Mavis, B. E., Robinson, J. I., & Stoffelmayr, B. E. (1993). A work-site weight management program to reinforce behavior. *Journal of Occupational Medicine, 35,* 800–804.

Azrin, N. H., & Pye, G. E. (1989). Staff management by behavioral contracting. *Behavioral Residential Treatment, 4,* 89–98.

Bigelow, G., Sticker, O., Leibson, I., & Griffiths, R. (1976). Maintaining disulfiram ingestion among outpatient alcoholics: A security deposit contingency contracting program. *Behavior Research and Therapy, 14,* 378–580.

Blechman, E. A., Olson, D. H. L., & Hellman, I. D. (1976). Stimulus control over family problem-solving behavior: The family contract game. *Behavior Therapy, 7,* 686–692.

Boudin, H. M. (1972). Contingency contracting as a therapeutic tool in the deceleration of amphetamine use. *Behavior Therapy, 3,* 604–608.

Brooks, R. R., & Ruthven, A. J. (1984). The effects of contingency contracting on student performance in a PSI class. *Teaching of Psychology, 11,* 87–89.

Carns, A. W., & Carns, M. R. (1994). Making behavioral contracts successful. *School Counseling, 42,* 155–160.

Clark, J. J., Leukefeld, C., & Godlaski, T. (1999). Case management and behavioral contracting: Components of rural substance abuse treatment. *Journal of Substance Abuse Treatment, 17,* 293–304.

De Martini-Scully, D., Bray, M. A., & Kehle, T. J. (2000). A packaged intervention to reduce disruptive behaviors in general education students. *Psychology in the Schools, 37,* 149–156.

Heinssen, R. K., Levendusky, P. G., & Hunter, R. H. (1995). Client as colleague: Therapeutic contracting with the seriously mentally ill. *American Psychology, 50,* 522–532.

Homme, L. (1970). How to use contingency contracting in the classroom (Rev. ed.). Champaign, IL.: Research Press.

Jacobson, N. S. (1978). Specific and nonspecific factors in the effectiveness of a behavioral approach to the treatment of marital discord. *Journal of Consulting and Clinical Psychology, 46,* 442–452.

Kazdin, A. E. (1980). Acceptability of alternative treatments for deviant child behavior. *Journal of Applied Behavior Analysis, 13,* 259–273.

Kidd, T. A., & Saudargas, R. A. (1988). Positive and negative consequences in contingency contracts: Their relative effectiveness on arithmetic performance. *Education and Treatment of Children, 11,* 118–126.

Kirchenbum, D.S., Germann, J.N., Rich, B. H. (2005). Treatment of morbid obesity in low-income adolescents: Effects of parental self-monitoring. *Obesity Research, 13,* 1527–1529.

Kirschenbaum, D. S., & Flanery, R. C. (1984). Toward a psychology of behavioral contracting. *Clinical Psychology Review, 4,* 597–618.

Kolko, D. J., & Milan, M. A. (1983). Reframing and paradoxical instruction to overcome "resistance" in the treatment of delinquent youths: A multiple baseline analysis. *Journal of Consulting and Clinical Psychology, 51,* 655–660.

Locke, E. A., Shaw, K. N., Saari, L. M., & Latham, G. P. (1981). Goal setting and task performance 1969–1980. *Psychological Bulletin, 90,* 125–152.

Ludwig, T. D., & Geller, E. S. (1997). Assigned versus participative goal setting and response generalization: Managing injury control among professional pizza deliverers. *Journal of Applied Psychology, 82,* 253–261.

Mann, R. A. (1972). The behavior therapeutic use of contingency contracting to control an adult behavior problem: weight control. *Journal of Applied Behavior Analysis, 5,* 99–109.

Martin, G., & Pear, J. (2007). Behavior modification: What is it and how to do it. (8th ed.) Upper Saddle River, NJ: Prentice Hall.

Miller, L. J. (1990). The formal treatment contract in the inpatient management of borderline personality disorder. *Hospital and Community Psychiatry, 41,* 985–987.

Murphy, J. J. (1988) Contingency contracting in schools: A review. *Education and Treatment of Children, 11,* 257–269.

Petry, N. M. (2000). A comprehensive guide to the application of contingency management procedures in clinical settings. *Drug and Alcohol Dependence, 58,* 9–25.

Robinson, K. E., & Sheridan, S. M. (2000). Using the mystery motivator to improve child bedtime compliance. *Child and Family Behavior Therapy, 22,* 29–49.

Ruth, W. J. (1996). Goal setting and behavior contracting for students with emotional and behavioral difficulties: Analysis of daily, weekly, and total goal attainment. *Psychology in the Schools, 33,* 153–158.

Skinner, B. F. (1953). *Science and human behavior.* New York: Free Press.

Solanto, M. V., Jacobson, M. S., Heller, L., Golden, N. H., & Hertz, S. (1994). Rate of weight gain of inpatients with anorexia nervosa under two behavioral contracts. *Pediatrics, 93,* 989–991.

Stuart, R. B., & Lott, L. A. (1972). Behavioral contracting with delinquents a cautionary note. *Journal of Behavioral Therapy and Experimental Psychiatry, 3,* 161–169.

Vinson, D.C., & Devera-Sales, A. (2000). Computer-generated written behavioral contracts with problem drinkers in primary medical care. *Substance Abuse, 21,* 215–222.

Welch, S. J., & Holborn, S. W. (1988). Contingency contracting with delinquents: Effects of a brief training manual on staff contract negotiation and writing skills. *Journal of Applied Behavior Analysis, 21,* 357–368.

Yeaton, W. H., & Sechrest, L. (1981). Critical dimensions in the choice and maintenance of successful treatments: Strength, integrity, and effectiveness. *Journal of Consulting and Clinical Psychology, 49,* 156–167.

13 BIBLIOTHERAPY UTILIZING COGNITIVE BEHAVIOR THERAPY

Negar Nicole Jacobs

Bibliotherapy is defined in this chapter as the use of written psychotherapeutic self-help materials for the purpose of solving mental health problems. Bibliotherapy originally involved reading fictional or religious stories and identifying with a character as a means of gaining insight and experiencing catharsis (Schrank & Engels, 1981). However, when cognitive behavioral treatments (CBT) were developed and gained popularity in the 1960s, many bibliotherapeutic materials evolved into treatment manuals based on the principles of CBT (Papworth, 2006). Today, bibliotherapeutic materials are widely available to the lay public. The American Psychological Association (1989) has estimated that over 2000 self-help books are published each year, though there is great variability in the quality of these materials.

Delivery of CBT principles in a bibliotherapeutic format has many advantages over traditional psychotherapy. Advantages of bibliotherapy include its demonstrated empirical support across a broad spectrum of problems (see below), cost effectiveness, widespread availability, and potential to reach populations who would otherwise have difficulty accessing traditional psychotherapy (Mains & Scogin, 2003). Readers of bibliotherapeutic materials can take responsibility for their problems and exercise control in managing their symptoms at a self-paced rate. Bibliotherapy can also afford individual readers privacy and help them avoid the stigma that is often associated with seeking mental health services through traditional psychotherapy. Furthermore, bibliotherapy can be utilized in a stepped-care model as a preventive intervention (Papworth, 2006) or for individuals with low levels of symptomatology.

Given these benefits, the use of bibliotherapy by psychologists appears to be very popular. Starker (1988) surveyed 123 psychologists across 36 states to analyze their use of bibliotherapy. He found that the practice of prescribing bibliotherapeutic materials was "widespread," because 97.7% of those surveyed prescribed self-help materials at least regularly.

The present chapter will review the demonstrated range of applicability of bibliotherapies utilizing CBT principles, discuss factors for clinicians to consider in deciding whether to utilize bibliotherapy in their clinical practice, and provide recommendations in the use of bibliotherapy.

EVIDENCE-BASED APPLICATION

The past couple of decades have shown a proliferation of treatment outcome studies involving bibliotherapy. The vast majority of bibliotherapeutic materials that have undergone empirical evaluation are based on CBT techniques. These studies show that bibliotherapy has demonstrated a wide range of applicability across psychological disorders, symptom severities, and levels of therapist assistance. As the scope of this chapter does not allow for a thorough review of the research on bibliotherapy, a brief overview will be provided here and the interested reader will be referred to more detailed reviews of the bibliotherapy outcome literature (i.e., Apodaca & Miller, 2003; Cuijpers, 1997; Den Boer, Wiersma, & Van Den Bosch, 2004; Gould & Clum, 1993; Gregory, Canning, Lee, & Wise, 2004; Hirai & Clum, 2006; Jacobs & Mosco, in press; Mains & Scogin, 2003;

Marrs, 1995; McKendree-Smith, Floyd, & Scogin, 2003; Newman et al., 2003; Papworth, 2006; Scogin, Bynum, Stephens, & Calhoon, 1990).

Bibliotherapeutic approaches for the treatment of depression have been widely investigated. Several meta-analyses have been conducted to examine these numerous research findings, with results that were mostly promising for bibliotherapy. Scogin, Welsh, Hanson, Stump and Coates (2005) conducted a meta-analysis on four treatment studies (Landreville & Bissonnette, 1987; Floyd, Scogin, McKendree-Smith, Floyd, & Rokke, 2004; Scogin, Hamblin, & Beutler, 1987; Scogin, Jamison, & Gochneaur, 1989) employing cognitive bibliotherapy for geriatric depression. Treatments utilized Burns's *Feeling Good* (1980) with minimal therapist contact. Data in all these studies indicated significant improvement in depressive symptoms for bibliotherapy participants. In a meta-analysis of six studies utilizing bibliotherapy to treat depression, Cuijpers (1997) concluded that bibliotherapy was an effective treatment for unipolar depression and that bibliotherapy was as effective as individual or group treatment. In another review of bibliotherapy studies for depression, McKendree-Smith, Floyd, and Scogin (2003) noted that bibliotherapy produced effect sizes that were equivalent to average effect sizes found in traditional psychotherapy studies. A meta-analysis conducted by Gregory, Canning, Lee, and Wise (2004) demonstrated the effectiveness of bibliotherapy across adolescent, adult, and geriatric age groups. Numerous studies have demonstrated that improvements gained from bibliotherapy at posttreatment are maintained at 2-year (Floyd, Rohen, Shackelford, Hubbard, Parnell, Scogin, & Coates, 2006) and even 3-year (Smith, Floyd, Scogin, & Jamison, 1997) follow-ups.

The effectiveness of bibliotherapy for the treatment of a variety of anxiety disorders has also been demonstrated. In a meta-analysis of self-administered treatments for anxiety disorders, Newman, Erickson, Przeworski, and Dzus (2003) noted a medium to large effect size overall. Reeves and Stace (2005) found that adult subjects with mild to moderate anxiety who utilized a cognitive-behavioral bibliotherapy package and had weekly coaching sessions with

a therapist showed significant improvement posttreatment and at a 3-month follow-up. The effectiveness of bibliotherapeutic approaches has also been demonstrated for other anxiety disorders, such as panic attacks (Febbraro, 2005), panic disorder with agoraphobia (Sharp, Power, & Swanson, 2000), and generalized anxiety disorder (Bowman, Scogin, Floyd, Patton, & Gist, 1997). However, bibliotherapy has differential effectiveness for different types of anxiety disorders and levels of therapist contact involved in the treatment package (Mains & Scogin, 2003; Marrs, 1995; Newman et al., 2003).

Bibliotherapy as a treatment modality has also proven to be effective for a number of other psychiatric disorders. In a meta-analysis of 22 studies analyzing the effectiveness of bibliotherapy in the treatment of problem drinking, Apodaca and Miller (2003) found an overall effect size of .80. Studies analyzing the effectiveness of bibliotherapy for the treatment of eating disorders have found moderate effect sizes for bulimia and binge-eating disorder (Bailer, et al., 2004; Carter & Fairburn, 1998; Carter, Olmstead, Kaplan, McCabe, Mills, & Aimé, 2003; Cooper, Coker, & Fleming, 2003; Ghaderi, 2006). A meta-analysis of bibliotherapies for sexual dysfunctions (van Lankveld, 1998) concluded that bibliotherapy for orgasmic disorders was found to be effective at posttreatment but not at follow-up.

LIMITS OF BIBLIOTHERAPY

Despite the evidence base for bibliotherapies described earlier, the vast majority of bibliotherapeutic materials lack empirical support. Concern for the proliferation of self-help materials without empirical evaluation has been addressed by a variety of researchers (i.e., Craighead, McNamara, & Horan, 1984; Glasgow & Rosen, 1978; Riordan and Wilson, 1989; Schrank & Engels, 1981; Stevens & Pfost, 1982). Most notably, Rosen and colleagues have passionately and repeatedly given warning about the massive gap between the number of self-help programs available and the number of such programs evaluated for effectiveness, as well as the potential for iatrogenic effects of such untested materials (i.e., Rosen,

Glasgow, & Moore, 2003). Even when some bibliotherapeutic materials undergo empirical evaluation under research conditions, which involve some level of therapist contact, Rosen (1987) has pointed out that the results do not always hold up under totally self-administered conditions, as when a reader buys a self-help book from a bookstore. Readers may not accurately self-diagnose and they may not properly apply the instructions of the self-help materials (Barrera, Rosen, & Glasgow, 1981). Rosen has criticized psychologists for marketing untested materials and making exaggerated claims of effectiveness of these materials (i.e., Rosen, 1987). Rosen and his colleagues have also provided clear recommendations to address these concerns (i.e., 1978 Task Force on Self-Help Therapies; Rosen, 1981; Rosen, 1987) but they have had to point out repeated failures by psychologists to follow these recommendations (i.e., Rosen, 1993; Rosen, 2004; Rosen, Glasgow & Barrera, 2007).

FACTORS TO CONSIDER WHEN RECOMMENDING BIBLIOTHERAPY

To date, no systematic research has been done on specific indications or contraindications for use of bibliotherapy. Campbell and Smith (2003) have suggested that providers may be able to extrapolate from research matching client characteristics to traditional types of psychotherapies (i.e., Beutler 1991) and they have recommended that cognitive behavioral therapists should exercise their clinical judgment in deciding whether to assign bibliotherapy and how to best match clients with bibliotherapy materials.

Some researchers investigating the effectiveness of self-help materials have discussed client characteristics that they have noted to help or hinder bibliotherapy. For example, in research analyzing matching effects for treatment techniques with various client characteristics, Beutler and colleagues (Beutler, Engle, Mohr, Daldrup, Bergan, Meredith, & Merry, 1991) observed that self-administered treatments such as bibliotherapy produced better treatment outcomes for clients who were high in reactance and resistance. Campbell and Smith (2003) found that

clients with internalizing coping styles more successfully utilized bibliotherapy than those with externalizing coping styles. In the depression literature, some researchers have suggested that bibliotherapy would be the most appropriate treatment for those with mild to moderate levels of depression and for those interested in the self management of chronic depression (i.e., Anderson, Lewis, Araya, Elgie, Harrison, Proudfoot, Schmidt, Sharp, Weightman, & Williams, 2005).

Some studies (i.e., Newman, 2000 and Reeves & Stace, 2005) have suggested that the following client characteristics could be contraindications for use of bibliotherapy: presence of personality disorders, emotional avoidance, high levels of interpersonal distress, comorbid psychological symptoms, and severe symptom severity. In the depression literature, Mains and Scogin (2003) have noted that severe levels of depression, suicidality, defensiveness, lack of learned resourcefulness, and comorbidity are likely to reduce the effectiveness of self-administered treatments. Comorbidity includes factors such as psychosis, alcohol or drug misuse, and high risk of harm to self or others. Clearly, bibliotherapy should not be offered to clients who are not able to read or comprehend the language used in the reading materials.

Several researchers have commented on other factors that should be considered by clinicians when recommending bibliotherapy to their clients. Campbell and Smith (2003) recommend that clinicians should consider both client and therapist characteristics. Client characteristics include reading levels and preferences, ability to understand self-help materials, demographic variables such as ethnicity and culture, and level of symptom severity. They also recommend that clinicians tailor self-help recommendations to specific phases of treatment. They warn clinicians to beware of use of bibliotherapy to intellectualize treatment or otherwise use the materials to divert attention away from the therapy. Therapist considerations include having the clinician be familiar with the self-help materials, ensuring that the recommended reading be related to the client's presenting complaints, and making certain that the recommended exercises in the bibliotherapy materials are feasible for the client in question.

PRACTICE RECOMMENDATIONS

Several researchers have offered a variety of recommendations that should be used by clinicians when assigning self-help books to clients. Katz and Watt (1992) have likened recommendation of bibliotherapy to the prescription of psychotropic medications. As with medications, they have suggested that self-help books be prescribed after considering the patient's problems, individual characteristics of the patient, and the possible effects of the recommended treatment. They hypothesized that, as with medications, compliance to treatment would be most likely in the context of a good therapeutic relationship and when the prescribing provider had a positive attitude toward the treatment. And, similar to the prescription of a drug, they noted that providers recommending bibliotherapy should address patients' expectations of the treatment and discuss the potential problems a patient could encounter when attempting to comply with the treatment.

After reviewing the effectiveness of self-administered treatments, Mains and Scogin (2003) developed a set of practice recommendations for the use of bibliotherapy. First, they suggested that practitioners who recommend bibliotherapy should monitor the client's response to and progress in the treatment, noting that changes in symptomatology could necessitate implementation of higher levels of treatment (as in a stepped-care model). Second, they recommended that maintenance programs should be considered for clients who were progressing in the bibliotherapeutic treatment. Third, they urged clinicians to consider individual characteristics of clients and to only recommend bibliotherapy to clients who would be good candidates (i.e., highly motivated, as discussed earlier). Fourth, they noted that self-administered treatments involving some level of therapist contact were more effective than self-administered treatments alone. However, they also pointed out that even research involving minimal therapist contact would translate into no contact when used by readers who buy the self-help materials in the bookstore. And, as Rosen (1993) has pointed out, bibliotherapy that has demonstrated effectiveness in research conditions, which necessitate at least minimal therapist contact for the purpose of assessment and monitoring, does not always generalize to such effectiveness when self-administered in real-world conditions. Finally, Mains and Scogin (2003) pointed out the variable data on effectiveness of bibliotherapy for different disorders (as discussed above), noting that overall there is good data for bibliotherapeutic treatment of mild alcohol abuse, depression, and many anxiety disorders but unclear data with respect to habit control problems. They suggested that clinicians should recommend bibliotherapies that have undergone rigorous testing for efficacy, such as *Feeling Good* (Burns, 1980) for the treatment of depression. Table 13.1 contains selected examples of excellent bibliotherapy materials, which are either based on empirically supported techniques or have themselves undergone empirical evaluation, for a representative sample of psychiatric disorders.

Because there is mixed data on the effectiveness of bibliotherapies with varying levels of therapist contact, the most conservative recommendation is to utilize bibliotherapy as an adjunctive, as opposed to a totally self-administered, treatment. Some researchers (i.e., Pardeck & Pardeck, 1984) argue that clinicians should offer guidance to clients at every stage of the bibliotherapeutic process, including selection of the reading materials, reading and comprehension of the self-help materials, and tying in the content with the overall therapeutic process. While little is known about the process variables accounting for change in bibliotherapy, some authors (i.e., Hynes & Hynes-Berry, 1986) contend that therapist contact, and not the content of the reading materials, is the essential change agent involved in the effectiveness of bibliotherapy.

CONCLUSION

Bibliotherapy is an excellent means of accessing evidence-based cognitive behavioral techniques for the lay public, including populations who may not otherwise access mental health services due to barriers such as costs, transportation

TABLE 13.1   Sampling of Bibliotherapy Recommendations

Anger Management

- Novaco, R.W. (1975). *Anger Control*. Lexington, MA: Lexington Books.

Anxiety Disorders

- Antony, M. M., Craske, M. G., & Barlow, D. H. (2006). *Mastering your fears and phobias (2nd ed.): Workbook*. New York: Oxford University Press.
- Barlow, D. H., & Craske, M. G. (2007). *Mastery of your anxiety and panic (4th ed.): Workbook*. New York: Oxford University Press.
- Craske, M. G., Barlow, D. H. (2006). *Mastery of your anxiety and worry (2nd ed.): Workbook*. New York: Oxford University Press.
- Foa, E. B., & Wilson, R. (1991). *Stop obsessing!: How to overcome your obsessions and compulsions*. New York: Bantam Books.
- Hazlett-Stevens, H. (2005). *Women who worry too much: How to stop worry and anxiety from ruining relationships, work and fun*. Oakland, CA: New Harbinger.
- Rothbaum, B., Foa, E., & Embree, E. (2007). *Reclaiming your life from a traumatic experience: A prolonged exposure treatment program (workbook)*. New York: Oxford University Press.

Child Management

- Gordon, T. (1975). Parent effectiveness training: The tested way to raise children. New York: New American Library.
- Patterson, G. R., & Gullion, M. E. (1976). Living with children. Champaign, IL: Research Press.
- Webster-Stratton, C. The incredible years series.

Depression

- Burns, D. D. (1980). *Feeling good: The new mood therapy*. New York: Signet.
- Lewinsohn, P. M., Munoz, R. F., Youngren, M. A., & Zeiss, A. M. (1986). *Control your depression*. New York: Prentice Hall.

Eating Disorders

- Agras, W. S., & Apple, R. (2007). Overcoming your eating disorder: A cognitive–behavioral therapy approach for bulimia nervosa and binge-eating disorder, guided self-help workbook. New York: Oxford University Press.

Infertility

- Jacobs, N. N., & O'Donohue, W. T. (2007). Coping with infertility: clinically proven ways of managing the emotional roller coaster. New York: Routledge.

Marital Conflict

- Gottman, J. M., Notarius, C., Gonso, J., & Markman, H. (1979). *A couple's guide to communication*. Champaign, IL: Research Press.

Pain Management

- Lewandowski, M. J. (2006) The chronic pain care workbook: A self-treatment approach to pain relief using the behavioral assessment of pain questionnaire. Oakland, CA: New Harbinger.

Sex Addiction

- Penix-Sbraga, T., & O'Donohue, W. T. (2007). *The sex addiction workbook: Proven strategies to help you regain control of your life*. Oakland, CA: New Harbinger.

Sexual Dysfunction

- Heiman, J., LoPiccolo, J., & Palladini, D. (1987). *Becoming orgasmic: A sexual and personal growth program for women*. New York: Simon Shuster.
- Zilbergeld, B. (1999). *The new male sexuality: The truth about men, sex, and pleasure*. New York: Bantam Books.

TABLE 13.1 *(Continued)*

Sleep Disorders

- Edinger, J. D., & Carney, C. E. (2008). Overcoming insomnia: A cognitive–behavioral therapy approach workbook. New York: Oxford University Press.
- Hauri, P., & Linde, S. (1990). *No more sleepless nights*. New York: John Wiley Sons.

Substance Use Disorders

- Antonuccio, D. O. (1992). Butt out: A compassionate guide to helping yourself quit smoking, with or without a partner. Saratoga, CA: R&E Publishers.
- Daley, D. C., & Marlatt, G. A. (2006). Overcoming your alcohol or drug problem: Effective recovery strategies (2nd ed.). New York: Oxford University Press.
- Miller, W. R., & Munoz, R. F. (1982). How to control your drinking: A practical guide to responsible drinking. Albuquerque, NM: Prentice Hall.

Weight Management

- Beck, J. S. (2007). The Beck diet solution: Train your brain to think like a thin person. Birmingham, AL: Oxmoor House.

TABLE 13.2 Key Points Regarding Bibliotherapy

1. Bibliotherapy is defined as the use of written psychotherapeutic self-help materials for the purpose of solving mental health problems.
2. Delivery of CBT principles in a bibliotherapy format has many advantages over traditional psychotherapy, including cost effectiveness, widespread availability, and potential to reach a broad spectrum of populations.
3. Bibliotherapy has demonstrated empirical support across a wide range of mental health problems. However, the vast majority of bibliotherapy available to the lay public has not undergone empirical evaluation and there is wide variability in the quality of self-help materials.
4. Clinicians wishing to assign self-help materials to their clients should exercise their clinical judgment and follow the practice guidelines discussed in this chapter.

---

problems, and/or stigmas associated with traditional psychotherapy. In addition to accessibility, bibliotherapy offers many advantages over traditional psychotherapy, as described above. Studies evaluating bibliotherapy have demonstrated its empirical support across a broad range of mental health problems, cost effectiveness, and reader satisfaction. Table 13.2 provides a summary of some of the key points regarding bibliotherapy. Given these factors, it behooves health care providers to recommend bibliotherapy as a treatment modality.

References

American Psychological Association (1989). First annual golden fleece awards for do-it-yourself therapies. Presentation at the annual meeting of the American Psychological Association, New Orleans, LA.

American Psychological Association Task Force on Self-Help Therapies (1978). Task force report on self-help therapies. Unpublished manuscript. Washington DC: American Psychological Association.

Anderson, L., Lewis, G., Araya, R., et al. (2005). Self-help books for depression: How can practitioners and patients make the right choice? *British Journal of General Practice, 55,* 387–392.

Apodaca, T. R., & Miller, W. R. (2003). A meta-analysis of the effectiveness of bibliotherapy for alcohol problems. *Journal of Clinical Psychology, 59,* 289–304.

Bailer, U., de Zwaan, M., Leish, F., Strnad, A., Lennkh-Wolfsberg, C., El-Giamal, N., et al. (2004). Guided self-help versus cognitive-behavioral group therapy in the treatment of bulimia nervosa. *American Journal of Psychiatry, 160,* 973–978.

Barrera, M., Rosen, G. M., & Glasgow, R. E. (1981). Rights, risks, and responsibilities in the use of self-help psychotherapy. In J. T. Hannah, R. Clark,

& P. Christian (Eds.), *Preservation of client rights* (pp. 204–220). New York: Free Press.

Beutler, L. E. (1991). Predictors of differential response to cognitive, experiential, and self-directed psychotherapeutic procedures. *Journal of Consulting and Clinical Psychology, 59*, 333–340.

Beutler, L. E., Engle, D., Mohr, D., Daldrup, R. J., Bergan, J., Meredith, K., et al. (1991). Predictors of differential response to cognitive, experiential, and self-directed psychotherapeutic procedures. *Journal of Clinical and Consulting Psychology, 59*, 333–340.

Bowman, D., Scogin, F., Floyd, M., Patton, E., & Gist, L. (1997). Efficacy of self examination therapy in the treatment of generalized anxiety disorder. *Journal of Counseling Psychology, 44*, 267–273.

Burns, D. D. (1980). *Feeling good: The new mood therapy.* New York: Signet.

Campbell, L. F., & Smith, T. P. (2003). Integrating self-help books into psychotherapy. *Journal of Clinical Psychology, 59*, 177–186.

Carter, J. C., & Fairburn, C. G. (1998). Cognitive–behavioral self-help for binge-eatingdisorder: A controlled effectiveness study. *Journal of Consulting and Clinical Psychology, 66*, 616–623.

Carter, J. C., Olmstead, M. P., Kaplan, A. S., McCabe, R. E., Mills, J. S., & Aimé, A. (2003). Self-help for bulimia nervosa: A randomized controlled trial. *American Journal of Psychiatry, 160*, 973–978.

Cooper, P. J., Coker, S., & Fleming, C. (1996). An evaluation of the efficacy of supervised cognitive behavioral self-help for bulimia nervosa. *Journal of Psychosomatic Research, 40*, 281–287.

Craighead, L., McNamara, K., and Horan, J. (1984). Perspectives on self-help and bibliotherapy: You are what you read. In S. Brown and R. Lent (Eds.), *Handbook of Counseling Psychotherapy* (pp. 878–929). New York: John Wiley & Sons.

Cuijpers, P. (1997). Bibliotherapy in unipolar depression: A meta-analysis. *Journal of Behavior Therapy & Experimental Psychiatry, 28*, 139–147.

Den Boer, P. C. A. M., Wiersma, D., & Van Den Bosch, R. J. (2004). Why is self-help neglected in the treatment of emotional disorders? A meta-analysis. *Psychological Medicine, 34*, 959–971.

Febbraro, G. (2005). An investigation into the effectiveness of bibliotherapy and minimal contact interventions in the treatment of panic attacks. *Journal of Clinical Psychology, 61*, 763–779.

Floyd, M., Rohen, N., Shackelford, J. A. M., Hubbard, K. L., Parnell, M. B., Scogin, F., & Coates, A. (2006). Two-year follow-up of bibliotherapy and individual cognitive therapy for depressed older adults. *Behavior Modification, 30*, 281–294.

Floyd, M., Scogin, F., McKendree-Smith, N., Floyd, D. L., & Rokke, P. D. (2004). Cognitive therapy for depression: A comparison of individual psychotherapy and bibliotherapy for depressed older adults. *Behavior Modification, 28*, 297–318.

Ghaderi, A. (2006). Attrition and outcome in self-help treatment for bulimia nervosa and binge eating disorder: A constructive replication. *Eating Behaviors, 7*, 300–308.

Glasgow, R. E., & Rosen, G.M. (1978). Behavioral bibliotherapy: A review of self-help behavior therapy manuals. *Psychological Bulletin, 85*, 1–23.

Gould, R. A., & Clum, G. A. (1993). A meta-analysis of self-help treatment approaches. *Clinical Psychology Review, 13*, 169–186.

Gregory, R. J., Canning, S. S., Lee, T. W., & Wise, J. C. (2004). Cognitive bibliotherapy for depression: A meta-analysis. *Professional Psychology, 35*, 275–280.

Hirai, M., & Clum, G. A. (2006). A meta-analytic study of self-help interventions for anxiety problems. *Behavior Therapy, 37*, 99–111.

Hynes, A. M., & Hynes-Berry, M. (1986). *Bibliotherapy—The interactive process: A handbook.* Boulder, CO: Westview Press.

Jacobs, N. N., & Mosco, E. (in press). Bibliotherapy as an adjunctive treatment. In W. T. O'Donohue and N. Cummings (Eds.), *Evidence-based adjunctive treatments.* New York: Academic Press.

Landreville, P., & Bissonnette, L. (1997). Effects of cognitive bibliotherapy for depressed older adults with a disability. *Clinical Gerontologist, 17*, 35–55.

Mains, J. A., & Scogin, F. R. (2003). The effectiveness of self-administered treatments: A practice-friendly review of the research. *Journal of Clinical Psychology/In Session, 59*(2), 237–246.

Marrs, R. W. (1995). A meta-analysis of bibliotherapy studies. *American Journal of Community Psychology, 23*, 843–870.

McKendree-Smith, N. L., Floyd, M., & Scogin, F. R. (2003). Self-administered treatments for depression: A review. *Journal of Clinical Psychology, 59*, 275–288.

Newman, M. G. (2000). Recommendations for a cost-offset model of psychotherapy allocation using generalized anxiety disorder as an example. *Journal of Consulting and Clinical Psychology, 68*, 549–555.

Newman, M. G., Erickson, T., Przeworski, A., Dzus, E. (2003). Self-help and minimal contact therapies for anxiety disorders: Is human contact necessary for therapeutic efficacy? *Journal of Clinical Psychology, 59*, 251–274.

Papworth, M. (2006). Issues and outcomes associated with adult mental health self-help materials: A "second order" review or "qualitative meta-review." *Journal of Mental Health, 15*(4), 387–409.

Pardeck, J. A. & Pardeck, J. T. (1984). An overview of bibliotherapeutic treatment approach: Implications for clinical social work practice. *Family Therapy, 11*, 241–252.

Reeves, T., & Stace, J. M. (2005). Improving patient access and choice: Assisted bibliotherapy for mild to moderate stress/anxiety in primary care. *Journal of Psychiatric and Mental Health Nursing, 12*, 341–346.

Riordan, R. J., & Wilson, L. S. (1989). Bibliotherapy: Does it work? *Journal of Counseling and Development, 67*, 506–508.

Rosen, G. M. (1981). Guidelines for the review of do-it-yourself treatment books. *Contemporary Psychology, 26*, 189–191.

Rosen, G. M. (1987). Self-help treatment books and the commercialization of psychotherapy. *American Psychologist, 42*, 46–51.

Rosen, G. M. (1993). Self-help or hype? Comments on psychology's failure to advance self-care. *Professional Psychology: Research and Practice, 24*(3), 340–345.

Rosen, G. M. (2004). Remembering the 1978 and 1990 Task Forces on Self-Help Therapies. *Journal of Clinical Psychology, 60*(1), 111–113.

Rosen, G. M., Glasgow, R. E., & Barrera, M. (2007). Good intentions are not enough: Reflections on past and future efforts to advance self-help. In P. L. Watkins & G. A. Clum (Eds.), *Handbook of Self-Help Therapies* (pp. 25–39). Mahwah, NJ: Lawrence Erlbaum.

Rosen, G. M., Glasgow, R. E., & Moore, T. E. (2003). Self-help therapy: The science and business of giving psychology away. In S. O. Lilienfeld, S. J. Lynn, & J. M. Lohr (Eds.). *Science and Pseudoscience in Clinical Psychology* (pp. 399–424). New York: Guilford.

Schrank, F. A., & Engels, D. W. (1981). Bibliotherapy as a counseling adjunct: Research Findings. *Personnel and Guidance Journal, 60*, 143–147.

Scogin, F., Bynum, J., & Stephens, G., & Calhoon, S. (1990). Efficacy of self-administered treatment programs: Meta-analytic review. *Professional Psychology: Research and Practice, 21*, 42–47.

Scogin, F., Hamblin, D., & Beutler, L. (1987). Bibliotherapy for depressed older adults: A self-help alternative. *The Gerontologist, 27*, 383–387.

Scogin, F., Jamison, C., & Gochneaur, K. (1989). Comparative efficacy of cognitive and behavioral bibliotherapy for mildly and moderately depressed older adults. *Journal of Consulting and Clinical Psychology, 57*, 403–407.

Scogin, F., Welsh, D., Hanson, A., Stump, J., & Coates, A. (2005). Evidence-based psychotherapies for depression in older adults. *Clinical Psychology: Science and Practice, 12*, 222–237.

Sharp, D. M., Power, K. G., & Swanson, V. (2000). Reducing therapist contact in cognitive behaviour therapy for panic disorder and agoraphobia in primary care: Global measures of outcome in a randomized controlled trial. *British Journal of General Practice, 50*, 963–968.

Smith, N. M., Floyd, M. R., Scogin, F., & Jamison, C. (1997). Three-year follow-up of bibliotherapy for depression. *Journal of Consulting and Clinical Psychology, 65*, 324–327.

Starker, S. (1988). Psychologists and self-help books: Attitudes and prescriptive practices of clinicians. *American Journal of Psychotherapy, 42*(3), 448–455.

Stevens, A. J., & Pfost, K. S. (1982). Bibliotherapy: Medicine for the soul? *Psychology: A Quarterly Journal of Human Behavior, 19*, 21–25.

van Lankveld, J. J. D. M. (1998). Bibliotherapy in the treatment of sexual dysfunctions: A meta-analysis. *Journal of Consulting and Clinical Psychology, 66*, 702–708.

14 BREATHING RETRAINING AND DIAPHRAGMATIC BREATHING TECHNIQUES

Holly Hazlett-Stevens and Michelle G. Craske

Breathing retraining is a widely used technique in a number of anxiety and stress reduction therapies. Slow and deep breathing from the diaphragm (i.e., the abdominal muscle located underneath the lungs near the base of the ribs) promotes a subjective state of relaxation as well as physiological effects that are contrary to hyperventilation and autonomic nervous system arousal. As a result, breathing retraining often is used to counteract the chronic anxiety seen in generalized anxiety disorder (GAD) and the hyperventilation associated with sudden, unexpected fight-or-flight activation in panic disorder. In addition to these specific anxiety reduction applications, breathing retraining is useful as a general relaxation strategy for individuals interested in learning stress management techniques (Fried, 1993).

Breathing retraining techniques typically begin with a demonstration of hyperventilation, which is followed by education about the physiology of overbreathing. The physiological effects experienced during initial hyperventilation induction are then contrasted with the slower heart rate, physical muscle relaxation, and other sensations that result from slow-paced abdominal breathing. Sometimes a cognitive meditation component is added to promote attentional focus on the deep breathing exercise. As individuals learn to engage in diaphragmatic breathing with repeated practice, they are encouraged to apply this skill whenever they detect signs of anxiety or worry or when they encounter stressful situations.

Breathing retraining has been investigated empirically as part of the larger cognitive behavioral treatment packages for panic disorder (with or without agoraphobia) and for GAD. In the treatment of panic disorder, breathing retraining is combined with psychoeducation, cognitive restructuring, and interoceptive exposure (as well as in vivo exposure in the case of agoraphobia) treatment components (Craske & Barlow, 2007). In these cases, breathing retraining is presented early in treatment as an alternative coping response to behavioral avoidance. Its utility is attributed to the reduction of hyperventilation sensations and symptoms that contribute to a vicious cycle of fear responding found during panic attacks. In the treatment of GAD, breathing retraining is taught as a useful coping response whenever anxiety symptoms or worries are detected in the course of regular and frequent anxiety level monitoring. Thus, breathing retraining is presented in the context of psychoeducation and frequent monitoring of general anxiety symptoms, and it is combined with progressive and applied relaxation training, cognitive restructuring, and imaginal exposure techniques (Newman, 2000; Borkovec & Ruscio, 2001).

WHO MIGHT BENEFIT FROM THIS TECHNIQUE

Individuals with chronic anxiety symptoms, such as panic disorder and GAD, are most likely to benefit from breathing retraining. Individuals with these particular anxiety disorder diagnoses may chronically hyperventilate, thereby contributing to somatic anxiety symptoms. Thus, breathing retraining is used in panic disorder treatment to counteract hyperventilation, which can trigger a panic attack, and therefore is used to help control and prevent panic attacks in this population. In GAD cases, diaphragmatic breathing is taught in order to promote a general state of relaxation as well as a coping response to deploy when increased anxiety or worry is detected.

However, individuals suffering from other anxiety disorders or from subclinical anxiety symptoms may also benefit from the generalized relaxation and decreased arousal this technique provides. Some research has suggested that breathing retraining can be effective when it does not target physiology by providing a subjective sense of relaxation and feelings of control (Garssen, de Ruiter, & Van Dyck, 1992). Furthermore, Fried (1993) suggested that a variety of stress-related behavioral medicine conditions, such as insomnia, hypertension, noncardiac chest pain, headache, and gastrointestinal distress, may also benefit from breathing retraining intervention. Novel clinical applications continue to appear in the treatment literature. For example, diaphragmatic breathing combined with minimized swallowing effectively treated complaints of chronic belching in a case of aerophagia, or excessive air swallowing (Cigrang, Hunter, & Peterson, 2006). Finally, breathing retraining may be a useful stress management tool for severely mentally ill psychiatric populations seeking ways to reduce general tension and anxiety (Key, Craske, & Reno, 2003).

EVIDENCE-BASED APPLICATIONS

Breathing retraining is indicated for the following conditions:

- Panic disorder (with or without agoraphobia)
- Generalized anxiety disorder
- Stress-related health conditions

CONTRAINDICATIONS OF THE TECHNIQUE

Individuals with medical conditions affecting the respiratory system, such as chronic obstructive pulmonary disease (COPD) or asthma, should first consult with their physician before breathing retraining is attempted. This caveat is particularly relevant because induced hyperventilation is conducted to demonstrate the physiological effects of overbreathing. However, the technique described presently is the same breathing technique used by physicians to teach respiratory patients how to breathe more effectively and therefore is not always contraindicated for respiratory patients.

OTHER DECISION FACTORS WHEN DECIDING TO USE THE TECHNIQUE

Certain individuals with panic disorder who enter treatment with strong convictions that panic attack symptoms represent physical harm may use breathing retraining to avoid feared panic sensations. This practice can undermine exposure-related treatment efforts by maintaining irrational fears that such hyperventilation sensations are harmful. Therefore, such clients are discouraged from using their breathing retraining skills in this way and are instructed to use diaphragmatic breathing only as a general relaxation strategy rather than as a response to panic attack episodes. Experienced therapists working with clients reporting high anxiety sensitivity (i.e., fear of anxiety-related sensations) sometimes refrain from teaching such clients breathing retraining for this reason.

In his review of this empirical literature, Taylor (2001) concluded that while hyperventilation often may not play a strong role in panic attacks, the subjective relaxation and control effects of breathing retraining identified by Garssen et al. (1992) still may hold value for some panic patients. In these cases, Taylor encouraged clinicians to teach breathing retraining only when patients understand that breathing techniques assist with unpleasant but harmless sensations. Other cognitive behavioral techniques of interoceptive exposure and cognitive restructuring are needed to teach patients that feared sensations are indeed harmless.

HOW DOES BREATHING RETRAINING WORK?

Breathing retraining teaches individuals how to reduce the shallow chest breathing associated with chronic hyperventilation by engaging in deep diaphragmatic breathing. This intentional shift to slower and deeper breaths produces a host of physiological effects consistent with a state of relaxation. Learning to breathe properly allows for optimal levels of oxygen intake, thereby preventing an imbalance of oxygen and carbon dioxide in the blood and the myriad of resulting physical sensations resulting from the body's attempt to compensate for such an imbalance. As discussed earlier, an alternative view offered by Garssen et al. (1992) posits that breathing retraining induces a subjective relaxation response by presenting a credible explanation for threatening anxiety symptoms and promoting feelings of self-control.

STEP-BY-STEP PROCEDURES[1]

See Tables 14.1 and 14.2 for an overview of key elements. Breathing retraining typically begins with a demonstration of how hyperventilation affects physiology. The client is asked to stand and to voluntarily hyperventilate by breathing very quickly and deeply as if blowing up a balloon. Exhalations should be very hard and forced so that the air is taken all the way down to the lungs. The therapist first demonstrates this for the client by taking three to four deep breaths while exhaling as forcefully as possible

at approximately three times the normal rate. The client then begins to overbreathe with the therapist. Oftentimes, the therapist will need to encourage the client to maintain speed and to exhale hard because the client may reduce the level of effort after a few breaths. The client should try to continue for 60 to 90 seconds, but should be allowed to stop in the case of excessive distress.

After this demonstration, the client is asked to sit down, close his or her eyes, and to breathe very slowly, pausing at the end of each breath. After the client begins to relax, this exercise is discussed in detail, beginning by asking the client to identify each physical sensation brought on by the voluntary hyperventilation. When treating clients with anxiety, such symptoms are discussed regarding their similarity with familiar anxiety-related sensations. In the case of panic disorder or recurrent panic attacks, similarity to the physical symptoms of a panic attack is highlighted even if the emotional aspects of the exercise differ because the client can identify the cause of the sensations. When working with panic disorder individuals, it is important to

---

1. These procedures are based on the manual entitled Mastery of *your anxiety and panic*, 4th ed. (Craske & Barlow, 2006).

TABLE 14.1   Key Elements of Breathing Retraining

- Conduct the voluntary hyperventilation exercise to demonstrate the effects of overbreathing.
- Describe the physiology of hyperventilation and explain the rationale for deep, diaphragmatic breathing.
- Teach the client how to engage in deep breathing and give corrective feedback.
- Assign homework practice exercises.
- Review client's progress with the home practice, giving feedback to help overcome any difficulties.

TABLE 14.2   Key Elements Specific to Panic Disorder

- After the voluntary hyperventilation exercise, these effects are systematically compared to feared panic attack sensations.
- Discussion of hyperventilation physiology includes identification of which effects might be misinterpreted as dangerous during a panic attack.
- Initial breathing practices are only conducted at scheduled times in a relaxed setting.
- After breathing retraining skills have been developed in the relaxed practice setting, brief practice sessions are conducted in stressful settings.
- After breathing retraining skills are mastered in stressful settings, brief practice sessions are conducted in response to physical anxiety cues.
- Clients are reminded not to use breathing retraining skills when purposefully confronting feared sensations or situations during exposure-based treatment exercises.

compare each physical effect of the hyperventilation to the client's panic symptoms and note any similarities. This exercise can then be used to launch a discussion of the role of hyperventilation in panic attacks.

The therapist then provides the rationale for breathing retraining and a brief explanation of the physiology resulting from hyperventilation. This information is crucial when treating panic disorder because it will help correct mistaken beliefs that such symptoms are harmful. This presentation of information should be explained in terms that the client can understand, and the amount of detail should be tailored to each client's individual needs. Typically, the therapist begins by explaining that the body needs oxygen in order to survive. Whenever a person inhales, oxygen is taken into the lungs and then carried around the body, where it is released for use by the body's cells. The cells use the oxygen in their energy reactions and then release carbon dioxide (CO_2) back to the blood, where it is transported to the lungs and eventually exhaled. The balance between oxygen and carbon dioxide is very important and is maintained chiefly through an appropriate rate and depth of breathing. The appropriate rate of breathing, at rest, is usually around 10–14 breaths per minute. Hyperventilation is defined as a rate and depth of breathing that is too much for the body's needs at a particular point in time. Although breathing is controlled automatically, breathing can also be put under voluntary control. Consequently, the non-automatic factors of fear and stress cause increased breathing because the muscles need more oxygen in order to fight or flee from danger. If the extra amount of oxygen is not used up at the rate at which it is brought in (as when there is no actual running or fighting going on), then the state of hyperventilation results.

The most important effect of hyperventilation is to produce a drop in carbon dioxide such that the amount of carbon dioxide is low in proportion to the amount of oxygen. This imbalance leads to constriction of certain blood vessels around the body, and the blood going to the brain is slightly decreased. Not only does less blood reach certain areas of the body, but the oxygen carried by this blood is less likely to be released to the tissues. Hence, although overbreathing

means we are taking in more oxygen than necessary, less oxygen actually gets to certain areas of our brain and body. This causes two groups of symptoms. First are symptoms produced by the slight reduction in oxygen to certain parts of the brain, including dizziness, light-headedness, confusion, breathlessness, blurred vision, and feelings of unreality. Second are symptoms produced by the slight reduction in oxygen to certain parts of the body, including increase in heartbeat to pump more blood around, numbness and tingling in the extremities, cold and clammy hands, and sometimes stiff muscles. Also, hyperventilating can produce a feeling of breathlessness, sometimes extending to feelings of choking or smothering, so that it actually feels as if there is not enough air.

Hyperventilation also causes other effects. First, the act of overbreathing is hard physical work. Hence, the person may feel hot, flushed, and sweaty. Because it is hard work, prolonged periods of hyperventilating will often cause tiredness and exhaustion. In addition, people who overbreathe often breathe from their chest rather than their abdomen; it is the latter that is really intended for breathing, as the diaphragm muscle serves this purpose and is located underneath the lungs. When chest muscles are primarily used for breathing, they become tired and tense because they are not well equipped for breathing, resulting in chest tightness or even severe chest pains. However, hyperventilation is not always obvious, especially with mild overbreathing for a long period of time. Therefore, many people are chronic hyperventilators but are unaware that such sensations may be the result of their breathing. Learning to breathe at an appropriate rate and depth can therefore reduce these sensations and promote feelings of relaxation. When treating clients with panic disorder, it is important to emphasize that hyperventilation is not dangerous. Increased respiration is central to the fight-or-flight fear response, and thus its purpose is to protect the body from danger. Hyperventilation is merely the body's natural way of compensating for such increased respiration in the absence of the physical exertion normally involved with behavioral fight or flight. Therefore, it is important for the panic disorder client to identify panic-related feared sensations that might be the consequence of overbreathing.

The next step is to teach a specific exercise to learn control over breathing. Typically, the therapist will model diaphragmatic breathing by placing one hand on his or her chest and the other hand on his or her abdomen and monitoring the movement of each. The client also attempts this while attending to the movement of each hand. The client should try to isolate breathing from the abdomen such that only that hand moves. During this process, the therapist encourages the client and gives corrective feedback until the client learns to breathe slowly (8–10 breaths per minute) yet smoothly and easily from the abdomen.

In the case of panic disorder or other chronic hyperventilators, the therapist may first instruct the client to breathe at his or her normal pace. The client would then attempt to reduce the rate of his or her breathing after one to two weeks of regular practice. This can be accomplished by matching the pace or breathing to counting and gradually slowing the counting to a rate near 10 breaths per minute. Sometimes it is helpful to pause between each step, before exhaling, and before inhaling.

The therapist then explains that regular home practice is crucial to learning breathing retraining skills, and this exercise should be practiced at least twice a day for at least 10 minutes each time. The following instructions are given:

1. Find a quiet, comfortable spot where you will not be disturbed, and allow yourself a few seconds to calm down.

2. Concentrate on taking breaths right down to your stomach. There should be an expansion of the abdomen with every breath in (inhalation). The abdomen is sucked back in with every breath out (exhalation). If you are having trouble taking the air down to your stomach, try to push your stomach out just before you inhale so that there is a space for the air to fill. Be sure to place one hand on your chest and the other hand on your stomach, as the movement should come almost entirely from the lower (abdominal) hand. Try to limit the amount of movement from the upper (chest) hand. If you are normally a chest breather, this may feel artificial and cause feelings of breathlessness. That is a natural response; just remember that you are getting enough oxygen and the feelings of breathlessness will decrease the more you practice. If you find it very hard to keep your chest still, lie on the floor, flat on your stomach (i.e., facing the floor) with your hands clasped under your head. This will make it easier to breathe from the abdomen. Once you have done that several times and feel comfortable breathing from the abdomen, practice the exercise again while in a seated position.

3. Keep your breathing smooth and fluid. Don't gulp in a big breath and then let it out all at once. When you breathe out, let the air escape equally over the whole time you are breathing out. Think of the air as oozing and escaping from your nose or mouth rather than being suddenly released. It does not matter whether you breathe through your nose or your mouth as long as you breathe slowly and smoothly. The nose is easier for this because it is a smaller opening.

4. Start to count on your inhalations. That is, when you breathe in, think the word "one" to yourself, and as you breathe out, think the word *relax*. Think *two* on your next breath in and *relax* on the breath out. Think *three* on your next breath in and *relax* on the breath out. Continue this up to around *ten* and then go backwards to *one*.

5. Focus only on your breathing and the words. This can be very difficult, and you may never be able to do it perfectly. You may not get past the first number without other thoughts coming into your mind. When this happens, do not get angry or give up. Simply allow the thoughts to pass through your mind and bring your attention back to the numbers.

6. When you first begin to count your breaths, you may become breathless or a little dizzy and begin to speed up your breathing. This should subside once you get used to the exercise. If it becomes too uncomfortable, stop for a short while and calm down, then begin again.

Individuals with panic disorder are reminded that they are learning to decrease physical feelings that may trigger panic attacks and that occur during panic attacks. These clients are warned against using this technique to cope with anxiety early on to avoid frustration. However, despite this therapist instruction not to attempt breathing retraining to combat panic sensations, panic disorder clients often will try to apply this technique during a panic attack before developing adequate skill. When such attempts are reported, the therapist can respond to client disappointment and discouragement by reminding the client that breathing control involves a skill that develops only with practice, instructing the client only to practice slow breathing in relaxed settings until this skill has developed, and addressing fears of panic sensations with cognitive restructuring techniques. These clients may also benefit from tracking levels of concentration on the breathing and counting and the ease of breathing using a practice journal.

In subsequent therapy sessions, the therapist reviews the home practices with the client. Potential problems are identified and corrected. For example, was the client getting enough air into the abdomen? If not, the stomach can be pushed out slightly before inhaling. Were symptoms of anxiety experienced during practice? This is probably due to breathing a little fast or becoming anxious about breathing while attending to it. This reaction usually diminishes with practice. If the client expresses difficulty concentrating on the counting after frequent practice, then it may help to make an audiotape on which the client records his or her voice counting at the appropriate rate. Some clients will say that they have no trouble breathing at 8–10 breaths per minute and this is how fast they usually breathe. In this case, they may not be chronic hyperventilators but may still overbreathe during times of stress or panic. This technique may still be of benefit as a method of somatic control. Clients with panic disorder may use breathing retraining out of desperation as a method of avoiding the experience of panic. This fear of panicking should be subjected to cognitive restructuring or reminders that panic is not harmful. After clients with panic disorder master slow diaphragmatic

breathing at the appropriate rate, they are encouraged to do brief practice sessions in more demanding environments. Stressful settings, such as at work or while stuck in traffic, are identified as good opportunities to practice their breathing retraining skills. Once slow diaphragmatic breathing has been effectively applied in these situations, even more challenging situations involving feared anxiety cues are attempted. However, panic disorder clients should be strongly discouraged from using breathing retraining skills to avoid panic sensations during the course of interoceptive or in vivo exposure treatment. Any thoughts about catastrophic consequences that could result from failure to control breathing in anxiety situations are subjected to cognitive restructuring.

Further Reading

Craske, M. G., & Barlow, D. H. (2006). *Mastery of your anxiety and panic: Therapist guide* (4th ed.). New York: Oxford University Press.

Fried, R. (1993). The role of respiration in stress and stress control: Toward a theory of stress as a hypoxic phenomenon. In P. M. Lehrer & R. L. Woolfolk (Eds.), *Principles and practices of stress management* (pp. 301–331). New York: Guilford Press.

Fried, R. (1987). *The hyperventilation syndrome: Research and clinical treatment.* Baltimore, MD: Johns Hopkins University Press.

References

Borkovec, T. D., & Ruscio, A. M. (2001). Psychotherapy for generalized anxiety disorder. *The Journal of Clinical Psychiatry, 62,* 37–45.

Cigrang, J. A., Hunter, C. M., & Peterson, A. L. (2006). Behavioral treatment of chronic belching due to aerophagia in a normal adult. *Behavior Modification, 30,* 341–351.

Craske, M. G., & Barlow, D. H. (2006). *Mastery of your anxiety and panic: Therapist guide* (4th ed.). New York: Oxford University Press.

Craske, M. G., & Barlow, D. H. (2007). Panic disorder and agoraphobia. In D. H. Barlow (Ed.), *Clinical handbook of psychological disorders: A step-by-step treatment manual* (4th ed.) (pp. 1–64). New York: Guilford Press.

Fried, R. (1993). The role of respiration in stress and stress control: Toward a theory of stress as a hypoxic phenomenon. In P. M. Lehrer &

R. L. Woolfolk (Eds.), *Principles and practices of stress management* (pp. 301–331). New York: Guilford Press.

Garssen, B., de Ruiter, C., & Van Dyck, R. (1992). Breathing retraining: A rational placebo? *Clinical Psychology Review, 12,* 141–153.

Key, F. A., Craske, M. G., & Reno, R. M. (2003). Anxiety-based cognitive-behavioral therapy for paranoid beliefs. *Behavior Therapy, 34,* 97–115.

Newman, M. G. (2000). Generalized anxiety disorder. In M. Hersen & M. Biaggio (Eds.), *Effective brief therapies: A clinician's guide* (pp. 157–178). San Diego, CA: Academic Press.

Taylor, S. (2001). Breathing retraining in the treatment of panic disorder: Efficacy, caveats and indications. *Scandinavian Journal of Behaviour Therapy, 30,* 49–56.

15 CLASSROOM MANAGEMENT

Steven G. Little and Angeleque Akin-Little

Managing behavior in the classroom in order to increase student learning has always been of concern to teachers and education personnel (Lewis, Romi, Qui, & Katz, 2005). Additionally, recent years have witnessed an increased focus on children's behavior in school as a result of the tragic events in locations such as Red Lake, Minnesota, and Littleton, Colorado. In spite of the fact that little reported violence involving children and youth are reported in schools (Heaviside, Rowand, Williams, & Farris, 1998; Henry, 2000) and criminal activity in schools has decreased yearly for more than a decade (Dinkes, Cataldi, Kena, & Baum, 2006), student classroom behavior is still of great concern to teachers, parents, and the general public (Brown & Beckett, 2006). Behaviors that are disruptive to the classroom such as inattention, overactivity, and noncompliance are the most common complaint of teachers (Goldstein, 1995). With prevalence rates of attention-deficit hyperactivity disorder (ADHD) estimated to be as high as 20% of the population (Coleman & Webber, 2002), rates of conduct disorder and oppositional defiant disorder both as high as 16% (American Psychiatric Association, 2000), and the growing trend toward educating all children in the regular classroom (Little & Akin-Little, 1999), the need for empirically validated approaches to classroom management is evident.

There is no one specific technique that can be called classroom management. Rather, there are a number of techniques and procedures that can be followed to help teachers better manage the classroom. The exact techniques that are implemented depend on the ecology of the classroom, the level of involvement of the psychologist in the school and classroom, the type of disruptive behavior, and the severity of the problem behaviors. For the purpose of this chapter, classroom management is defined as a set of procedures that,

if followed, should help the teacher maintain order in the classroom. The chapter is written for teachers, classroom consultants such as school psychologists, child clinical psychologists, social workers, behavioral specialists, etc. and assumes a basic understanding of the principles of applied behavior analysis and behavior modification. The chapter will present both proactive and reactive procedures that can be combined to provide a comprehensive approach to classroom management.

CLASSROOM RULES

An essential element of any classroom management program is a set of firm, but fair, classroom rules (Malone & Tietjens, 2000; McGinnis, Frederick, & Edwards, 1995; Rademacher, Callahan, & Pederson-Seelye, 1998; Wilke, 2003). While rules are necessary for effective classroom management, they alone are not sufficient to reduce rates of problem behavior in the classroom (Gettinger, 1988). Classroom rules must be integrated with a comprehensive behavior management plan. However, rules are the first place to start in effective classroom management.

In helping a teacher develop a set of classroom rules there are certain assumptions that need to be conveyed to the teacher. First and foremost is the idea that good classroom rules are the backbone of classroom management. With rules in place, other classroom management techniques will be much easier to implement. There should also be a minimum expectation for behavior for every student in the classroom. All students should be expected to follow the rules, even special education students. Once rule exceptions are made, a double standard exists and rules become worthless. Next, it is essential that students understand the resulting consequences (both positive and privilege loss) of the rules. To accomplish this it is advisable to have the teacher, during the first 2 weeks of school, randomly selecting students to read a rule, discuss why the rule is important, and explain what will happen if the rule is followed or not followed. To demonstrate that the teacher is fair, students should be allowed to question the utility or fairness of a rule during these discussion periods. It is also important that students know that rules cannot be questioned at other times, especially when a rule is broken. Further, the teacher makes the final decision and that should be clearly stated at the onset. Finally, the teacher should post the classroom rules in a visible spot in the classroom before the first day of school.

There are a number of characteristics that have been found associated with good rules (McGinnis et al., 1995; Rhode, Jenson, & Reavis, 1993; Wilke, 2003). These include:

- *Number*. The number of rules should be kept to a minimum, with five rules considered the maximum. Compliance is greatest when students can readily recall all of the rules.
- *Simplicity*. The wording of rules should be kept as simple as possible and should convey exactly what behavior is expected. Pictures or icons depicting the rules may help younger students understand the rules.
- *Positive*. Keep the wording of the rules positive if at all possible. Most rules can be stated in a positive manner; some rules cannot. However, the majority of classroom rules should be positive. It is much better to have rules that convey the behavior that is expected of the students rather than a list of don'ts.
- *Specific*. The rules should be very specific. The more ambiguous the rules are, the more difficult they are to understand. If there are loopholes in the rules, students will find them. Operational definitions of expected behavior are the best.
- *Observable*. The rules should describe behavior that is observable. The behavior must be observable so that the teacher can make an unequivocal decision as to whether or not the rule has been followed.

- *Measurable*. Rules describe behavior that is measurable. That is, behavior must be able to be counted and quantified in some way for monitoring purposes.
- *Posted*. The rules should be publicly posted in a prominent place in the classroom (e.g., in front of the classroom, near the door). The lettering should be large and block printed.
- *Consequences*. Following the rules should be connected to consequences. Spell out what happens positively if students follow the rules, and what they lose if they do not follow the rules.
- *Compliance*. A compliance rule should always be included. Classroom behavior will correspond to the posted rules. If you want to improve compliance in the classroom, a rule such as "Do what your teacher asks immediately" should be included.

ENHANCING CLASSROOM ENVIRONMENT

Keeping with the initial focus of this chapter on proactive classroom management techniques, a number of factors dealing with the classroom environment need to be considered. While consequent stimuli are frequently the focus of classroom management techniques, antecedent stimuli are equally important and need to be considered. Recognize that unstructured time in the classroom makes disruptive behavior more likely. If possible, 70% of classroom time should be devoted to academic activities (Wehby, Symons, Canale, & Go, 1998). If students are engaged in interesting academic activities, disruptive behavior will be less likely. This does not mean, however, that the teacher needs to be actively teaching 70% of the day. The utilization of strategies such as peer tutoring and cooperative learning help make this a more realistic goal. In order for sufficient time to be devoted to academic activities, an antecedent-based approach to classroom management is recommended. Strategies to consider include: (1) proximity, (2) high rates of opportunities to respond, (3) high-probability requests (behavioral momentum), and (4) choice making. Physical proximity of the teacher to students helps curtail disruptive behavior and refocus a student to instructional tasks. Shores, Gunter, and Jack (1993) reported that movement of a teacher in a classroom may be one of the most effective means of managing student behavior. Teacher movement around the classroom allows the teacher to respond quickly, improves the quality of teacher–student interactions, allows better maintenance of disruptive students, and increases the opportunity for the teacher to provide positive feedback to students.

Research has indicated that classrooms with higher rates of academic instruction tend to be those with the lowest level of problem behavior (Gunter & Denny, 1998). To accomplish this it is best to focus on improving the rate at which students are given opportunities to actively respond to instruction. This can be accomplished by the teacher's increasing the amount of instructional talk, providing prompts for correct responding, giving students adequate time to respond, and providing positive feedback for correct responding. Sutherland and Wehby, (2001) report that incorporating higher levels of active responding by students leads to fewer opportunities for inappropriate behavior and increases appropriate behavior in the classroom.

Another proactive technique is to increase the frequency of high-probability request sequencing prior to the delivery of a low-probability request. Teacher requests can be placed into two categories: high-probability requests (i.e., those that students are likely to comply with) and low-probability requests (i.e., those for which students have a history of noncompliance). High-probability request sequencing involves providing a series of high-probability requests prior to the delivery of a low-probability request. To work, the low-probability request needs to be delivered within 5 seconds of the last high-probability request, the high-probability requests need to be varied and randomized, and the high-probability requests must have an established history and be easily embedded within the context of an activity. Known as behavioral momentum, these techniques have been found to be effective at increasing the frequency of low probability behavior (Mace & Belfiore, 1990; Nevin, Mandell, & Atak, 1983).

Providing students with choice in activities has also been found to increase the frequency of appropriate behavior. Incorporating student-identified preferred activities or stimuli into the existing instructional tasks can result in decreasing the aversive nature of the task and allows students to exert more control in their daily lives (Dunlap et al., 1994). Shogren, Faggella-Luby, Bae, and Wehmeyer (2004) conducted a meta-analysis of choice making interventions and found they were effective in reducing undesirable behaviors and sustaining treatment effects.

In addition, consider the following suggestions regarding structuring the classroom space:

- Place disruptive students in the front of the classroom near the teacher, but not separated from rest of class. Do *not* place a disruptive student next to the teacher's desk facing the classroom. That is placing a major source of positive reinforcement (peer attention) directly in front of the disruptive student.
- Do not let two disruptive students sit next to each other.
- Disruptive students need more frequent reinforcement for appropriate behavior than other students. Having them close to the teacher makes this easier to accomplish.
- If there are a group of difficult students in the classroom, have the most difficult ones sit close to the teacher and spread the others out. It is best to place students who tend to behave appropriately next to disruptive students.
- Students should have only relevant materials on their desk. Relevant material includes only the material necessary for completion of the current assignment.
- Do *not* place easily distracted students near the window or other location where distraction is likely.
- Having the teacher move around the classroom frequently is one of the best proactive strategies. Walking around lets the teacher more easily detect problems before they escalate. It also allows the teacher to subtly reinforce students (e.g., a touch on the shoulder, leaning down to look at their work, saying "good job") and check on academic progress.

REINFORCEMENT STRATEGIES

Appropriate classroom behavior is maintained for many students in the classroom by naturally occurring reinforcers such as positive attention from the teacher, grades, or self-reinforcement that results from task completion. These naturally occurring reinforcers may not be sufficient to maintain all desirable behaviors in all students however. It is frequently necessary to look for more powerful reinforcers. Teachers should use caution in selecting and using positive reinforcers, however. Reinforcers should be age appropriate and the use of "natural" reinforcers is encouraged whenever it is possible (see Table 15.1). The student's level of functioning should also be considered when selecting reinforcers (e.g., Don't send a student for unsupervised free time in the library when he/she usually gets into trouble when unsupervised.). It is very important that the teacher does not use partial praise statements such as, "I'm glad you finished your work—finally!" as statements such as these may not be viewed as reinforcing to the student, but, rather, punishing.

The use of touch (e.g., pat on the back or shoulder) as an adjunct to verbal praise may increase the potency of the reinforcement. In spite of possible hesitancy to use touch, it is potentially powerful in its ability to comfort and quiet but may need to be used cautiously because of cultural considerations (Halbrook & Duplechin, 1994). Token reinforcers are generalized conditioned reinforcers that are exchangeable for a reinforcer of value to a student (Alberto & Troutman, 2006). They have been used effectively in both regular and special education classes. Finally, school–home notes consist of teachers evaluating student behavior daily and providing parents with feedback. Parents can then implement consequences based on the evaluation (Jurbergs, Palcic, & Kelley, 2007; Kelley, 1990). Parents have an important role in their children's education, and home–school communication has been shown to lead to better educational outcomes (Christenson & Conoley, 1992). One way to facilitate such a relationship is to involve both parent and teacher in home-based interventions for classroom problems (Kelley, 1990).

TABLE 15.1 Suggestions for Natural Positive Reinforcement

- Access to lunchroom snack machines (students supplies money)
- Omit certain assignments
- Be first in line (to anything)
- Run film projector or video player for class
- Be team captain
- Serve as class or office messenger or aide
- Care for class pets
- Sharpen class pencils
- Choose activity or game for class
- Sit by a friend
- Pass out paper
- Time with favorite adult or peer
- Decorate the classroom
- Tutor in class, or with younger students
- Extra portion at lunch
- Use of class walkman or tape recorder
- Extra recess or break time
- Use of magic markers and/or art supplies
- Free time to use specific equipment/supplies
- Visit the school library (individual or group)
- Give the student a place to display work
- Water class plants
- Help custodian

Key Element of Classroom Management

1. Rules
2. Classroom Environment
   a. Proximity
   b. High Rates of Opportunities to Respond
   c. High-Probability Requests (Behavioral Momentum),
   d. Choice Making
3. Positive Reinforcement
4. Effective Command Giving
5. Response Cost Procedures
6. Group Contingencies

Giving Effective Commands

Barkley (1997) provides guideline to parents in the area of effective command giving. Changing the manner in which commands are given may effectively reduce the frequency of problem behaviors and increase student compliant behavior. While Barkley's list was designed for parents, it can easily be adapted for use with teachers in the classroom. The following list summarizes effective command giving strategies for teachers and is adapted from those given by Barkley (1997) and Forehand and McMahon (1981):

- *Mean it.*—Never issue a command you do not intend to follow through to its completion.

- *Never issue a command as a question or favor.* —The command should be stated simply, directly, and in an unemotional manner.
- *Do not yell.* Getting you upset may be reinforcing to the student. Try to maintain your composure.
- *Give the student time.* When giving a command allow 5 to 10 seconds for the student to respond before (1) giving the command again, or (2) giving a new command.
- *Avoid nagging.* Issue a command only twice, then follow through on the preplanned consequence. The more you ask, the less likely they are to comply.
- *Give only one or two commands at a time.* Too many commands can confuse the student.
- *Deliver the command while maintaining eye contact.* This helps ensure that the student is paying attention to the teacher.
- *Be descriptive.* Telling the student specifically to "pick up the paper around your desk and stack your books" is much better than giving a vague instruction such as "clean up your desk."
- *Make more start requests than stop requests.* "Do" requests are better than "Don't" requests.
- *Verbally reinforce compliance.*—It is easy to forget to socially reward a student when he/she complies with your request.

Reductive Procedures

There are times when even the most proactive teacher must follow through with a negative consequence for an inappropriate behavior. Remember, however, that the worst time to select a punishment is during an episode with a student. In instances such as these the teacher may be tempted to use a punishment that is too severe for the behavior. Maag (2001) believes that educators may adopt the use of punishment because it is easy to administer, it works quickly to suppress behavior, and encouragement of punishment (i.e., discipline) is part of our cultural ethos. It is important that psychologists working in the schools recognize these issues when suggesting behavioral interventions to teachers. It is also important to recognize that some educators may evidence disdain for reinforcement-based techniques (Axelrod, 1996).

Therefore, if punishment is the initial recommendation, it may strengthen the teacher's existing bias in favor of punishment and lower the acceptability of reinforcement-based procedure. Also, it is important to understand each student for whom punishment will be used, because in some cases the intention to punish a behavior results in the behavior being inadvertently reinforced (e.g., removal of student from class for disruptive behaviors when the function of the problem behavior was to avoid doing academic work). Additionally, even in those localities where corporal punishment is legal, it is not recommended as an effective behavior management technique. For a detailed discussion of this and other important issues see Hyman and Snook (1999). Alberto and Troutman (2006) offer the following hierarchy of procedures for behavior reduction from least intrusive to most intrusive.

Level I Strategies of differential reinforcement

  a. Differential reinforcement of low-rate behavior (DRL)
  b. Differential reinforcement of other behavior(s) (DRO)
  c. Differential reinforcement of incompatible behavior (DRI)
  d. Differential reinforcement of alternative behavior(s) (DRA)

Level II Extinction (terminating reinforcement)
Level III Removal of desirable stimuli

  a. Response-cost procedures
  b. Time-out procedures

Level IV Presentation of aversive stimuli

  a. Unconditioned aversive stimuli
  b. Conditioned aversive stimuli
  c. Overcorrection procedures

The most logical reductive techniques from this list for classroom use include response-cost and overcorrection. Response cost, defined as a procedure for "reducing inappropriate behavior through withdrawal of specific amounts of reinforcer contingent upon the behavior's occurrence" (Alberto & Troutman, 2006, p. 422), is a versatile procedure with few negative side effects. It is particularly adaptable to a token reinforcement system in which students can earn token reinforcers for appropriate behaviors and lose tokens for misbehavior. Response cost procedures can also be implemented without a token economy system being in place in the classroom. A teacher who "fines" a child with the loss of free time or recess would be an example of a response cost procedure.

Overcorrection involves penalizing an undesirable behavior by having the student perform some other behavior (Kazdin, 2001). Alberto and Troutman (2006) describe two types of overcorrection. Restitutional overcorrection consists of correcting the environmental effect of the student's misbehavior, not only to its original condition but to a better condition. For example, if a student is caught writing on his/her desk, the teacher may require the child to not only erase/clean their writing, but all writing on the desk. This can be a particularly effective form of punishment for vandalism, littering, or other behavior that has a clear environmental outcome. Positive-practice overcorrection is cited much more frequently in the psychological literature and consists of repeatedly practicing the appropriate behavior, sometimes in an exaggerated or overly correct form. It has been found to be effective in reducing the incidence of a variety of behaviors including pica (Myles, Simpson, & Hirsch, 1997) and bruxism (Watson, 1993). While not technically reductive in nature, it has also been used successfully with a variety of academic behaviors such as mathematics fluency (Rhymer, Dittmer, Skinner, & Jackson, 2000) and oral reading (Singh & Singh, 1986).

Group Contingencies

A final consideration in developing classroom behavior management programs are interdependent group contingencies. When interdependent group contingencies are used, reinforcers are distributed to every member of the group contingent upon the group meeting some criteria (Litow & Pumroy, 1975). They have several advantages. Teachers can implement one program for the entire class rather than an individual program for each member of the class. The entire group either earns or doesn't earn the reinforcement; therefore teachers do not have to monitor each student's performance and give reinforcers

to some students and not to others. This not only makes the program easier to manage but also should reduce backlash because classmates are not separated into reinforcer "haves" and "have-nots" (Cashwell, Skinner, Dunn, & Lewis, 1998). Because students are attempting to earn reinforcers as opposed to avoid punishment, these programs can also be fun (Skinner & Watson, 2000). Finally, when everyone or no one receives access to positive consequences, students are not provided with information regarding their peers' performance and all students, as opposed to only a portion, get to celebrate successes (Skinner, Pappas, & Davis, 2005).

Further Reading

Alberto, P. A., & Troutman, A. C. (2006). *Applied behavior analysis for teachers* (7th ed.). Upper Saddle River, NJ: Pearson Prentice Hall.
Rhode, G., Jenson, W. R., & Reavis, H. K. (1993). *The tough kid book: Practical classroom management strategies*. Longmont, CO: Sopris West.

References

Alberto, P. A., & Troutman, A. C. (2006). *Applied behavior analysis for teachers* (7th ed.). Upper Saddle River, NJ: Pearson Prentice Hall.
American Psychiatric Association (2000). *Diagnostic and statistical manual of mental disorders*, 4th ed., (Text Revision). Washington, DC: Author.
Axelrod, S. (1996). What's wrong with behavior analysis? *Journal of Behavioral Education, 6,* 247–256.
Barkley, R. A. (1997). *Defiant children: A clinician's manual for assessment and parent training*, 2nd ed. New York: Guilford.
Brown, L. H., & Beckett, K. S. (2006). The role of the school district in student discipline: Building consensus in Cincinnati. *Urban Review, 38,* 235–256.
Cashwell, C. S., Skinner, C. H., Dunn, M. S., & Lewis, J. (1998). Group reward programs: A humanistic approach. *Humanistic Education and Development, 37,* 47–53.
Christenson, S. L., & Conoley, J. C. (1992). *Home-school collaboration: Enhancing children's academic and social competence*. Silver Springs, MD: National Association of School Psychologists.
Coleman, M. C., & Webber, J. (2002). *Emotional and behavioral disorders: Theory and practice* (4th ed.). Boston: Allyn and Bacon.
Dinkes, R., Cataldi, E. F., Kena, G., & Baum, K. (2006). *Indicators of school crime and safety: 2006* (NCES

2007-003/NCJ 214262). U.S. Departments of Education and Justice. Washington, DC: U.S. Government Printing Office.

Dunlap, G., dePerczel, M., Clarke, S., Wilson, D., Wright, S., White, R., & Gomez, A. (1994). Choice making to promote adaptive behavior for students with emotional and behavioral challenges. *Journal of Applied Behavior Analysis, 27,* 505–518.

Forehand, R. L., & McMahon, R. J. (1981). Helping the noncompliant child: A clinician's guide to parent training. New York: Guilford.

Gettinger, M. (1988). Methods of proactive classroom management. *School Psychology Review, 17,* 227–242.

Goldstein, S. (1995). Understanding and managing children's classroom behavior. New York: John Wiley & Sons.

Gunter, P. L., & Denny, R. K., (1998). Trends and issues in research regarding academic instruction of students with emotional and behavioral disorders. *Behavioral Disorders, 24,* 44–50.

Halbrook, B., & Duplechin, R. (1994). Rethinking touch in psychotherapy: Guidelines for practitioners. *Psychotherapy in Private Practice, 13,* 43–53.

Heaviside, S., Rowand, C., Williams, C., & Farris, E. (1998). *Violence and discipline problems in U. S. public schools: 1996–1997.* (NCES 98-030). Washington D.C.: U.S. Department of Education, National Center for Education Statistics.

Henry, S. (2000). What is school violence? An integrated definition. *Annals of the American Academy of Political and Social Science, 567,* 16–29.

Hyman, I. A., & Snook, P. A. (1999). Dangerous schools: What we can do about the physical and emotional abuse of our children. San Francisco: Jossey-Bass.

Jurbergs, N., Palcic, J., & Kelley, M. L. (2007). School-home notes with and without response cost: increasing attention and academic performance in low-income, ADHD children. *School Psychology Quarterly, 22,* 358–379.

Kazdin, A. E. (2001). *Behavior modification in applied settings* (6th ed.). Belmont, CA: Wadsworth/Thomson Learning.

Kelley, M. L. (1990). School-home notes: Promoting children's classroom success. New York: Guilford.

Lewis, R., Romi, S., Qui, X., & Katz, Y. J. (2005). Teachers' classroom discipline and student misbehavior in Australia, China, and Israel. *Teaching and Teacher Education, 21,* 729–741.

Litow, L., & Pumroy, D. K. (1975). A brief review of classroom group oriented contingencies. *Journal of Applied Behavior Analysis, 8,* 431–447.

Little, S. G., & Akin-Little, K. A. (1999). Legal and ethical issues of inclusion. *Special Services in the Schools, 15,* 125–143.

Maag, J. W. (2001). Rewarded by punishment: Reflections on the disuse of positive reinforcement in schools. *Exceptional Children, 67,* 173–186.

Mace, F. C., & Belfiore, P. (1990). Behavioral momentum in the treatment of escape-motivated stereotypy. *Journal of Applied Behavior Analysis, 23,* 507–514.

Malone, B. G., & Tietjens, C. L. (2000). Re-examination of classroom rules: The need for clarity and specified behavior. *Special Services in the Schools, 16,* 159–170.

McGinnis, J. C., Frederick, B. P., & Edwards, R. (1995). Enhancing classroom management through proactive rules and procedures. *Psychology in the Schools, 32,* 220–224.

Myles, B. S., Simpson, R. L. & Hirsch, N. C. (1997). A review of literature on interventions to reduce pica in individuals with developmental disabilities. *Autism, 1,* 77–95.

Nevin, J. A., Mandell, C., & Atak, J. R. (1983). The analysis of behavioral momentum. *Journal of the Experimental Analysis of Behavior, 39,* 49–59.

Rademacher, J. A., Callahan, K., & Pederson-Seelye, V. A. (1998). How do your classroom rules measure up? Guidelines for developing an effective rule management routine. *Interventions in School and Clinic, 33,* 284–289.

Rhode, G., Jenson, W. R., & Reavis, H. K. (1993). *The tough kid book: Practical classroom management strategies.* Longmont, CO: Sopris West.

Rhymer, K. N., Dittmer, K. I., Skinner, C. H., & Jackson, B. (2000). Effectiveness of a multicomponent treatment for improving mathematics fluency. *School Psychology Quarterly, 15,* 40–51.

Shogren, K. A., Faggella-Luby, M. N., Bae, S. J., & Wehmeyer, M. L. (2004). The effect of choice-making as an intervention for problem behavior: A meta-analysis. *Journal of Positive Behavior Interventions, 6,* 228–237.

Shores, R. E., Gunter, P. L., & Jack, S. L. (1993). Classroom management strategies: Are they setting events for coercion? *Behavioral Disorders, 18,* 92–102.

Singh, N. N., & Singh, J. (1986). A behavioral remediation program for oral reading: Effects on errors and comprehension. *Educational Psychology, 6,* 105–114.

Skinner, C. H., & Watson, T. S. (2000). Randomized group contingencies: Lotteries in the classroom. *The School Psychologist, 54,* 21, 24, 32, 36–38.

Skinner, C. H., Pappas, D. N., & Davis, K. A. (2005). Enhancing academic engagement: Providing opportunities for responding and influencing students to choose to respond. *Psychology in the Schools, 42,* 389–403.

Sutherland, K. S., & Wehby, J. H., (2001). Exploring the relation between increased opportunities to respond to academic requests and the academic and behavioral outcomes of students with emotional and behavioral disorders: A review. *Remedial and Special Education, 35,* 161–171.

Watson, T. S. (1993). Effectiveness of arousal and arousal plus overcorrection to reduce nocturnal bruxism. *Journal of Behavior Therapy and Experimental Psychiatry, 24,* 181–185.

Wehby, J. H., Symons, F. J., Canale, J. A., & Go, F. J. (1998). Teaching practices in classrooms for students with emotional and behavioral disorders: Discrepancies between recommendations and observations. *Behavioral Disorders, 24,* 51–56.

Wilke, R. L. (2003). *The first days of class: A practical guide for the beginning teacher.* Thousand Oaks, CA: Corwin Press.

16   COGNITIVE DEFUSION

Jason B. Luoma and Steven C. Hayes

Cognitive defusion involves a change in the normal use of language and cognition such that the ongoing *process* is more apparent and the normal functions of the *products* of thinking are broadened. The normal state of living is such that we see the world as structured by our thoughts—we do not notice that we our thinking influences how it appears to be. One purpose of cognitive defusion is to help people become more aware, in an ongoing manner, of this ubiquitous process of structuring the world through thought, so that they might relate to thinking and the world in a more flexible responsive manner even without changing the form or frequency of specific thoughts.

Cognitive defusion is a descendant of *cognitive distancing*, a technique that dates back to the origins of cognitive therapy. Cognitive distancing encourages clients to detect their thoughts, and to see them as hypotheses rather than objective facts about the world. Distancing was described as a "first, critical step in cognitive therapy" (Hollon & Beck, 1979, p. 189) because it enables clinicians to teach clients to analyze, test, dispute, and alter negative thoughts through traditional cognitive techniques. Thus, cognitive distancing is conceptualized as a preparatory step: necessary but not sufficient to produce profound change.

A contextual psychotherapy originally termed *Comprehensive Distancing* (Hayes, 1987), was one of the first to attempt to alter the functions of negative thoughts by the use of extended and elaborated forms of cognitive distancing. Later, this therapy was renamed Acceptance and Commitment Therapy (ACT; Hayes, Strosahl, & Wilson, 1999) when it expanded beyond a more narrow focus on defusion to include other elements such as acceptance, mindfulness, values, and committed action. While Cognitive Therapy attempts to reduce the believability and behavioral impact of negative thoughts disputation and test, defusion attempts to accomplish similar aims through relentless emphasis on seeing thoughts as thoughts. As such, thoughts are not so much hypotheses to be tested (as in cognitive therapy) as they are habitual constructions to be noticed and integrated into a pattern of living well. This expanded technique was named *cognitive defusion* both in order to avoid the dissociative connotations of the term *distancing*, and to emphasize the more comprehensive character of the process involved.

The purpose of cognitive defusion is to help clients who are caught up in the content of their own thinking to "defuse" from the literal meaning of thoughts and instead become more aware of thinking as an active, ongoing, process. Cognitive defusion is based on a functional contextual theory of language and cognition called relational frame theory (Hayes, Barnes-Holmes, & Roche, 2001). According to this view, thoughts work the way they do because of the context, both current and historical, in which they are experienced. The theory suggests that normal, common contexts of cognitive control and rational analysis that are directly aimed at changing the form or occurrence of particular patterns of thinking may exacerbate the behavior regulatory functions of problematic thinking, rather than weaken them. Thus, defusion attempts to alter this social/verbal context so that people are less pushed and pulled by their own idiosyncratic ways of thinking and are free to make choices in accordance with their values. While this chapter is written in a less technical style, more technical accounts of defusion that are closely linked to terms from behavior analysis and relation frame theory are available (Blackledge, 2007).

In recent years a number of related concepts and procedures have emerged within empirical clinical traditions that have similar goals, such as mindfulness procedures (e.g., Linehan, 1993; Segal, Williams, & Teasdale, 2001) and the use of metacognitive strategies (Wells, 2000). While it is clear that these concepts are related, the exact dividing lines are unclear. In this chapter the use of cognitive defusion in ACT will be emphasized.

EVIDENCE FOR THE EFFECTIVENESS OF COGNITIVE DEFUSION

Data for the impact of cognitive defusion comes from several sources. Indirect evidence comes from the body of research supporting the effectiveness of ACT, a therapy which typically includes a strong focus on the process of defusion. Outcome evidence is now available across a range of behavioral problems, including psychosis, chronic pain, workplace stress, obsessive compulsive disorder, social anxiety, drug abuse, nicotine addiction, depression, coping with physical illness, and others (Hayes, Luoma, Bond, Masuda, & Lillis, 2006). Changes in defusion related measures have also been shown to mediate outcomes in ACT interventions in studies on depression (Zettle & Hayes, 1987), counselor burnout and stigma (Hayes, Bissett et al., 2004), and two studies on psychotic behavior (Bach & Hayes, 2002; Gaudiano & Herbert, 2006). Successful mediation in these studies means that the changes seen in outcome variables occurred because of changes seen in defusion.

Studies examining the impact of a particular psychotherapy technique in isolation are quite rare, but there are experimental analogue studies of defusion. One recent study examined the impact of a common defusion technique, rapidly repeating a word until it loses its meaning, as compared to control-focused techniques such as distraction (Masuda, Hayes, Sackett, & Twohig, 2004). Results showed that the defusion technique reduced both discomfort and believability of targeted thoughts more rapidly than control conditions. Other studies of defusion techniques have reached similar conclusions,

such as Muto, Tada, and Sugiyama (2002), who tested the impact of physicalizing and "leaves on the stream" (see Table 16.1).

WHO MIGHT BENEFIT FROM THIS TECHNIQUE

Cognitive defusion can be applied to any client problems that are exacerbated by entanglement with cognitive events. The preliminary data show that these procedures can rapidly alter the functions of these events. For treatment-resistant clients who have failed in previous courses of cognitive behavior therapy, cognitive defusion holds out the promise of reducing the negative behavioral impact of harmful thoughts without having first to alter the form, frequency, or situational sensitivity of those thoughts.

CONTRAINDICATIONS OF THE TECHNIQUE

The primary contraindication is treatment inconsistency. Cognitive defusion is aimed at undermining the excessive literality of thinking itself. Cognitive defusion thus does not combine well with approaches specifically aimed at testing, disputing, arguing, suppressing, or controlling cognitive events, since all of these are heavily focused on the literal meaning of thoughts (e.g., the adequacy of evidence for truth claims). Clients with "brittle" cognitive systems can be agitated by the very idea of simply noticing thoughts without agreement or disagreement. Such clients (e.g., those with some obsessive disorders) tend to present difficulties for most forms of therapy, however, including traditional forms of cognitive therapy, and furthermore can sometimes improve through the use of defusion procedures.

OTHER DECISIONS IN DECIDING WHETHER TO USE COGNITIVE DEFUSION

Cognitive defusion can be an important supplement to a number of other therapy approaches and techniques. It may be particularly well combined with other techniques that attempt to

TABLE 16.1   Some Examples of Cognitive Defusion Techniques

"The Mind"	Treat "the mind" as an external event; almost as a separate person
Mental appreciation	Thank your mind; show aesthetic appreciation for its products
Cubbyholing	Label private events as to kind or function in a back channel communication
"I'm having the thought that"	Include category labels in descriptions of private events
Commitment to openness	Ask if the content is acceptable when negative content shows up
Just noticing	Use the language of observation (e.g., noticing) when talking about thoughts
Word repetition	Repeat a difficult thought until you can hear it as a sound
Physicalizing	Label the physical dimensions of thoughts
Put them out there	Sit next to the client and put each thought and experience out in front of you both as an object
Open mindfulness	Watching thoughts as external objects without use or involvement
Focused mindfulness	Direct attention to nonliteral dimensions of experience
Sound it out	Say difficult thoughts very, very slowly
Arrogance of word	Try to instruct nonverbal behavior and respond to each attempt "how do I do that?"
Thoughts are not causes	"Is it possible to think that thought, as a thought, *and* do x?"
Choose being right or choose being alive	If you have to pay with one to play for the other, which do you choose?
There are four people in here	Open strategize how to connect when minds are listening
Monsters on the bus	Treating scary private events as monsters on a bus you are driving
Who is in charge here?	Treat thoughts as bullies; use colorful language
Take your mind for a walk	Walk behind the client chattering like minds do, while client choose where to walk
And what is that in the service of?	Step out of content and ask this question
OK, you are right. Now what?	Take "right" as a given and focus on action
Leaves on a stream	Watch thoughts like leaves floating by on a stream
Why, why, why?	Show the shallowness of causal explanations by repeatedly asking "why"
Create a new story	Write down the normal life story, then repeatedly integrate those same facts into other stories
Carry cards	Write difficult thoughts on 3 × 5 cards and carry them with you
Carry your keys	Assign difficult thoughts and experiences to the clients keys. Ask the client to think the thought as a thought each time the keys are handled, and then carry them from there

change one's relationship to or functions of thoughts and feelings (i.e., second-order change) such as acceptance and mindfulness meditation (see Chapters 6 and 44 in this volume). It is also easily integrated with techniques that target direct change (i.e., first-order change) of overt behavior, such as behavioral activation, behavioral rehearsal and modeling, social skills training, and stimulus control strategies (see Chapters 67 and 69 in this volume). It should be used when the clinician has determined that intervention is needed to reduce the impact of a client's thoughts, but the more lengthy and perhaps difficult process of cognitive disputation and correction is not desirable due to time constraints, past treatment failures with these approaches, or comparative data.

HOW DOES THE TECHNIQUE WORK?

Thoughts have much of their impact through altering the way in which we perceive the world, without our noticing the process of thinking itself. The world simply occurs as it does, structured behind the scenes by thought. Experientially, it is as if the world as directly perceived and the world as thought about become fused into one world. Defusion is in part based on the premise that if we can catch, in flight, this act of structuring our world through thought, then perhaps we can relate to thinking in a more flexible, practical, and workable manner.

More technically, thoughts alter the functions of current situations because thoughts are mutually related to other events. For example, when you think of a lemon, some of the reactions produced by an actual lemon occur, at least in weakened form. For example, you may "see" a lemon and your mouth may water. This process is helpful in most contexts. For example, a person thinking about how to fix a car can usefully go through the steps cognitively, seeing each step in his or her mind, before actually dismantling the car. Because many contexts are of this kind, people can come to interact with the world as cognitively organized without noticing that they are constantly organizing it. Verbal/cognitive constructions come to substitute for direct contact with events.

In clinical situations, however, this kind of cognitive fusion is often unhelpful and confining. When a panic disordered client imagines how they might be trapped and socially humiliated in a particular situation they are seemingly dealing with the problem of being trapped, just as the mechanic is seemingly dealing with a car. If the literal functions of that thought dominate over all other possible functions, the issue may become how to avoid public situations so as to avoid being trapped, and not any of a thousand other possible responses. Commonly, considerable clinical attention is given to such negative thoughts and experiences with the intent of getting rid of them. However, a number of studies demonstrate that attempts to suppress, eliminate, or alter negative thoughts and feelings may result in paradoxical effects, at times actually increasing the frequency, intensity, and behavioral regulatory powers of these experiences. Furthermore, because these thoughts can be automatic and well established, altering them can be painstaking even when successful. Finally, this process can narrow the behavioral focus even more to the undesirable thought, when that very narrowness is part of the problem.

Emotions and thoughts achieve their power not only by their form or frequency, but also by the context in which they occur. In cognitive defusion, rather than trying to directly change the content or frequency of these private events, the therapist targets the context that relates them to undesirable overt behavior so as to induce greater response flexibility. The classic defusion technique of repeating a word rapidly can help clarify this point. When a person rapidly says a word or phrase over and over again for a minute or two, two things typically happen: The word temporarily loses most of its meaning and the sound of the word itself will emerge more dominantly (it is common for clients to say that they never realized the word sounded like that). The technique works best with one-syllable words (e.g., "milk"), but also works with two- or three-syllable phrases (e.g., "I'm bad") if more time is spent repeating them. In this example as in all examples of defusion techniques, the word or phrase is still present but a non-literal context is created that diminishes its normal symbolic functions and increases its more direct functions (in this example, its auditory functions). Stated another way, defusion techniques teach clients to think thoughts as thoughts, not so much through logical argument or direct instruction as through changes in the context of language and cognition itself, so as to make responding more fluid and functional.

As a result, the literal functions of problematic thoughts are less likely to dominate as a source of influence over behavior and more helpful, direct, and varied sources of control over action can gain ground. A large body of literature shows that when individuals respond to stimuli in the environment based on verbal rules, insensitivity to the direct contingencies in the environment may result and the range of behaviors available may be excessively narrowed. Individuals may continue to apply the same "logical" solution even when that solution is not working in a particular context.

The contexts that are targeted by defusion techniques include those that establish literal meaning itself, such as in the repeated word example, but also contexts that encourage people to generate verbal reasons to justify their behavior, to control private events, or to be right about their explanations for actions. Cognitive defusion acts in part through establishing contexts in which sense-making is not supported, such as paradox, confusion, meditative exercises, experiential exercises, metaphor, and undermining sense-making language conventions. Instead, clients are encouraged to focus on opportunities that the current environment affords and the workability of specific cognitive events in fostering effective action in that environment.

STEP-BY-STEP PROCEDURES

Cognitive defusion techniques can be broken down into three major groups. First, clients are introduced to the concept that language may not hold all the answers: that there may be other more flexible ways of knowing that are beyond verbal knowing. Second, thoughts and emotions are objectified through various metaphors, leading to greater distinction between thought and thinker, emotion and feeler. Third, various language conventions and experiential exercises are introduced to differentiate "buying a thought" from "having a thought," with the goal of teaching clients to evaluate thoughts based on their functional utility, rather than their literal "truth."

THINKING VERSUS EXPERIENCE

"Verbal knowing rests atop non-verbal knowing so completely that an illusion is created that all knowledge is verbal" (Hayes et al., 1999, pp. 153–154). Cognitive defusion begins the attack on clients' confidence in conscious thought by demonstrating its limits. The repeated word exercise (usual at first done with an arbitrary word such as *milk*) is often one of the earliest. Clients are first encouraged to notice all of the perceptual functions of the word (e.g., what milk tastes like) and then after a minute or two of saying the word rapidly out, to notice how these functions have changed. This exercise quickly pulls back the curtain of literality and reveals the illusion language and cognition create.

The limits of language can also be illustrated by examining how one learns any new skilled activity, such as a sport or hobby. For example, one could listen to a description of all the mechanics of how to swim down the minutest detail of how exactly to hold one's hand, how to kick one's feet, and so on. However, in order to actually learn how to swim, one needs to get in the water and practice. This can be shown by asking the client to instruct the therapist in a motor behavior, as in the following vignette:

Therapist: I'd like you to tell me how to stand up. Can you do that?

Client: Sure. You just lean forward, put your hands on the side of the chair and push up.

Therapist: Okay, how do I do that?

Client: Just shift your weight forward and flex your arm muscles to move them over to the sides of the chair.

Therapist: How do I do that?

Client: You just tell your legs to move.

Therapist (speaking to his legs): Move legs … they're not moving. [brief pause] You see what's happening here? Minds don't know how to do this. They don't know how to stand up. Lots of things we know how to do don't happen through conscious thought. Like this example, when did you learn how to walk?

Client: Oh, I don't know. I guess I was about a year old.

Therapist: Yeah, you learned how to walk even before you could talk. And then only later did your mind come in and try to claim it for itself. What if there are things that we need to do in this therapy that you can't learn through your mind, but only through practice or experience?

OBJECTIFYING THOUGHT

The natural sense of distance between self and object often disappears when those objects are thoughts because the literal functions of thought become so dominant. People tend to act as if a thought is an adequate substitute for experience. Objectifying thoughts can help people handle their thoughts in more flexible and practical ways, in much the same way that external objects can be handled in multiple ways, depending on the purpose present in the moment.

Certain language conventions are helpful in that regard. ACT therapists often react to thoughts in playful ways, such as saying

"Well, thank your mind for that thought" or congratulating clients for making dismal cognitive connections (e.g., *Client:* "So then I thought I'd completely blown it." *Therapist:* "Ah, very nice. Beautiful.") as if in appreciation for how creative minds can be. Another verbal convention has to do with labeling the type of talk clients are engaged in, rather than responding to the content of what the thought is literally about. The therapist can, as an unelaborated aside, simply label client talk by type (e.g., "Evaluation. Very good," or "Okay. Feeling."), rather than engaging in the content of the conversation. Eventually, clients can be taught to do this with their own talk, labeling evaluations as evaluations and feelings as feelings. For example, a client might verbalize the thought "I'm worthless." The client may be taught to say, "I'm having the evaluation that I'm worthless."

More extended metaphors can objectify thoughts as well. An ACT metaphor is the *passengers on the bus metaphor*, which compares the relationship between a person and his or her thoughts to that of a person and with bullies trying to take control of his or her life (Hayes et al., 1999):

> Suppose there is a bus and you're the driver. On this bus we've got a bunch of passengers. The passengers are thoughts, feelings, bodily states, memories, and other aspects of experience. Some of them are scary, and they're dressed up in black leather jackets and they have switchblade knives. What happens is that you're driving along and the passengers start threatening you, telling you what you have to do, where you have to go. . . . The threat they have over you is that if you don't do what they say, they're going to come up from the back of the bus.
>
> It's as if you've made deals with these passengers, and the deal is, "You sit in the back of the bus and scrunch down so that I can't see you very often, and I'll do what you say pretty much." Now, what if one day you get tired of that. . . . You stop the bus, and you go back to deal with the mean-looking passengers. But you notice that the very first thing you had to do was stop. Notice now, you're not driving anywhere, you're just dealing with these passengers. And they're very strong. They don't intend to leave, and you wrestle with them, but it just doesn't turn out very successfully.

> Eventually, you go back to placating the passengers, trying to get them to sit way in the back again where you can't see them. . . . Pretty soon, they don't have to tell you, "turn left"—you know as soon as you get near a left turn that the passengers are going to crawl all over you. In time you may get good enough that you can almost pretend that they're not on the bus at all. . . . However, when they eventually do show up, it's with the added power of the deals that you've made with them in the past.
>
> Now the trick about the whole thing is that the power the passengers have over you is 100% based on this: "If you don't do what we say, we're coming up and we're making you look at us." That's it. It's true that when they come up from the back they look as if they could do a whole lot more. . . . The deal you make is you do what they say so they won't come up and stand next to you and make you look at them. The driver (you) has control of the bus, but you trade off the control in these secret deals with the passengers. In other words, by trying to get control, you've actually given up control! Now notice that even though your passengers claim they can destroy you if you don't turn left, it has never actually happened. These passengers can't make you do something . . . you are just making deals with them (pp. 157–158).

Later in therapy, this metaphor can be reintroduced when clients bring up troubling thoughts, feelings, or behaviors that they feel are getting in the way of moving toward their valued goals. A therapist might say, "so what passenger is bothering you now?"

Another defusion exercise that can help clients distinguish between themselves and the content of their minds is to have clients write personally troubling thoughts cards. These cards can then be carried around by clients as homework, literally allowing them to carry their troubling thoughts as objects and still perform their daily activities.

A THOUGHT IS A THOUGHT IS A THOUGHT

Cognitive defusion presents clients experientially with the distinction between looking *at* the world as thought presents it (i.e., buying a thought) and looking at the world while simultaneously being aware of the process of thinking and being aware of the response alternatives present and choosing one of many alternatives (i.e., having a thought). This is often done through a variety of meditative and mindfulness exercises, such as by having clients, eyes closed, imagine a stream with leaves floating by on it and placing each new thought that comes up on one of the leaves. Inevitably the stream stops, or people lose the exercise when a thought comes along (e.g., "Am I doing this right?") that is not being looked *at* but is being looked *from*.

FOCUS ON THE FUNCTIONAL UTILITY
OF THOUGHTS

All of the techniques in cognitive defusion are tied together by a common focus on the functional utility of thinking. Thoughts are not to be evaluated according to their literal truth or coherence with a network of understanding, but rather by their workability. In any given situation, the primary question the therapist and client should ask is whether buying a thought would move the client towards a life in line with his or her chosen values, or whether it moves the client in some other direction.

Various language practices and verbal conventions can serve to keep the client focused on the workability of thoughts. For example, when a client begins to describe reasons to justify behavior, the therapist can ask questions like (Hayes et al., 1999, p. 164):

- "And what is that story in the service of?"
- "Is this helpful, or is this what your mind does to you?"
- "Have you told these kinds of things to yourself or to others before? Is this old?"
- "If God told you that your explanation is 100% correct, how would this help you?"
- "Okay, let's all have a vote and vote that you are correct. Now what?"

CONCLUSION

Verbal understanding is very adaptive in many situations. However, the tendency for people to become fused with thoughts, to see them as being literally true, as well as the tendency for people to cling to and defend their own verbal constructions, can serve to restrict and narrow behavior and inhibit movement towards valued life goals. Cognitive defusion loosens the grip that excessive literality can hold on behavior so that more flexible and functional behaviors can emerge. Cognitive defusion can open up a world of possible behaviors that may allow an individual to move in a direction that is more in line with his or her chosen values.

Further Reading

Hayes, S. C., Strosahl, K. D., & Wilson, K. G. (1999). *Acceptance and Commitment Therapy: An experiential approach to behavior change*. New York: Guilford.
Luoma, J. B., Hayes, S. C., & Walser, R. (2007). *Learning Acceptance and Commitment Therapy: A skills training manual for therapists*. Oakland, CA: New Harbinger (includes DVD).

References

Bach, P., & Hayes, S. C. (2002). The use of Acceptance and Commitment Therapy to prevent the rehospitalization of psychotic patients: A randomized controlled trial. *Journal of Consulting and Clinical Psychology, 70*(5), 1129–1139.
Blackledge, J. T. (2007). Disrupting verbal processes: Cognitive defusion in Acceptance and Commitment Therapy and other mindfulness-based therapies. *The Psychological Record, 57*, 555–576.
Gaudiano, B. A., & Herbert, J. D. (2006). Acute treatment of inpatients with psychotic symptoms using Acceptance and Commitment Therapy: Pilot results. *Behaviour Research and Therapy, 44*(3), 415–437.
Hayes, S. C. (1987). A contextual approach to therapeutic change. In N. Jacobson (Ed.), *Psychotherapists in clinical practice: Cognitive and behavioral perspectives* (pp. 327–387). New York: Guilford.
Hayes, S. C., Barnes-Holmes, D., & Roche, B. (2001). *Relational Frame Theory: A post-Skinnerian account of human language and cognition*. New York: Springer-Verlag.
Hayes, S. C., Bissett, R., Roget, N., Padilla, M., Kohlenberg, B. S., Fisher, G., et al. (2004). The impact of Acceptance and Commitment Training and multicultural training on the stigmatizing attitudes and professional burnout of substance abuse counselors. *Behavior Therapy, 35*(4), 821–835.

Hayes, S. C., Luoma, J. B., Bond, F. W., Masuda, A., & Lillis, J. (2006). Acceptance and Commitment Therapy: Model, processes and outcomes. *Behaviour Research and Therapy, 44*(1), 1–25.

Hayes, S. C., Strosahl, K. D., & Wilson, K. G. (1999). *Acceptance and Commitment Therapy: An experiential approach to behavior change.* New York: Guilford.

Hollon, S. D., & Beck, A. T. (1979). Cognitive therapy of depression. In P. C. Kendall & S. D. Barlow (Eds.), *Cognitive-behavioral intervention: Theory, research, and procedures* (pp. 153–203). New York: Academic Press.

Linehan, M. M. (1993). Cognitive-behavioral treatment of borderline personality disorder. New York: Guilford.

Masuda, A., Hayes, S. C., Sackett, C. F., & Twohig, M. P. (2004). Cognitive defusion and self-relevant negative thoughts: examining the impact of a ninety year old technique. *Behaviour Research and Therapy, 42*(4), 477–485.

Muto, T., Tada, M., & Sugiyama, M. (2002). Acceptance rationale and increasing pain tolerance: Acceptance-based and FEAR-based practice. *Japanese Journal of Behavior Therapy, 28,* 35–46.

Segal, Z. V., Williams, J. M. G., & Teasdale, J. D. (2001). *Mindfulness-based cognitive therapy for depression: A new approach to preventing relapse.* New York: Guilford.

Wells, A. (2000). *Emotional disorders and metacognition: Innovative cognitive therapy.* New York: John Wiley & Sons.

Zettle, R. D., & Hayes, S. C. (1987). Component and process analysis of cognitive therapy. *Psychological Reports, 64,* 939–953.

17 COGNITIVE RESTRUCTURING OF THE DISPUTING OF IRRATIONAL BELIEFS

Albert Ellis

Cognitive restructuring and the disputing of dysfunctional or irrational beliefs of people who have emotional and behavioral disturbances date back to ancient times, particularly to early Asian, Greek, and Roman philosophers, who took a constructivist view of humans. Several of these thinkers held that people have a considerable degree of agency or free will and that therefore, when their main goals and desires are thwarted by adverse conditions, they have some *choice* of reacting in a rational (self-helping) or irrational (self-defeating) manner. The idea that people's emotions are significantly connected with their modes of thinking was nicely summed up by Epictetus, a stoic philosopher, in the first century A.D. He succinctly stated that people are disturbed not by the events that happen to them but by their *view* of these events.

Nineteenth- and early twentieth-century psychologists largely based their treatment methods on this constructivist theory, as shown in the writings of Janet (1898), Dubois (1907), Coué (1923), and Adler (1927). Even Freud (1922/1960) pointed out that the small voice of reason can ultimately overcome the powerful voice of irrationality. His emphasis, however, on the overpowering influence on unconscious, often repressed, thinking and feeling led therapists to largely abandon dealing with their clients' irrational thinking; by the time the 1950s arrived they were replacing cognitive restructuring with emotional and behavioral techniques of therapy.

In 1955, however, I started to do rational emotive behavior therapy (REBT) and to forcefully favor cognitive restructuring and the disputing of irrational client beliefs. At the

same time, I pointed out that thinking, feeling, and behaving are holistically integrated and interactionally influence each other. Therefore, I hypothesized that effective therapy includes many techniques and had better be—as Arnold Lazarus indicated 15 years later—multimodal (Ellis, 1957, 1958, 1962; Lazarus, 1971). I was not the first therapist to use what became known as cognitive behavior therapy (CBT), since a few practitioners—such as Herzberg (1945) and Salter (1949)—had employed aspects of it previously. But I seem to have been the main therapist to create systematic cognitive restructuring, which I called disputing irrational beliefs, and which I will describe in this chapter. After I had promoted its use in several articles and books, it also began to be employed by several other therapists who presented their own versions of it—such as Beck (1967) and Meichenbaum (1977)—so that now it has become one of the most popular techniques of CBT.

Today, important aspects of cognitive assessment and cognitive restructuring are used, overtly or tacitly, by a great many different kinds of therapists. Thus, psychoanalysis delves into clients' unrealistic and illogical beliefs and somehow induces them to change these for healthier ideas and feelings. A few analysts, especially Karen Horney (1950), have clearly demonstrated the "tyranny of the shoulds," and some philosophers—especially Alfred Korzybski (1933/1991) described the self-defeating overgeneralizing and other thinking difficulties that people use to make themselves, as Korzybski said, "unsane." REBT and CBT pioneered in specifically showing clients their dysfunctional beliefs and how to dispute them and replace them with healthier philosophies.

REBT and CBT present an A-B-C theory of neurotic disturbance. When people are confronted with *adversities* (As) that interfere with their goals and purposes they can choose to have functional or *rational beliefs* (RBs) that will encourage them to create healthy emotional and behavioral *consequences* (Cs). But they can also choose to have irrational beliefs (IBs) that help produce unhealthy feelings and behaviors (Cs). Being constructivists (both innately and by social learning), and having language to help them, they are also able to think about their thinking, and even think about thinking about their thinking. Therefore, they can therapeutically choose to change their IBs to more rational (self-helping) beliefs.

Since people's thoughts, feelings, and actions reciprocally and sometimes powerfully affect each other, people can also simultaneously use—by themselves and with therapists' direction—a number of emotional and behavioral methods to improve their disturbed functioning. Therefore, REBT and CBT practitioners emphasize techniques of helping clients to change their dysfunctional cognitions, but at the same time they encourage clients to modify their handicapping feelings and desires. Only the main aspects of cognitive restructuring and the disputing of IBs that I largely use in my own practice of individual and group therapy will be described in this chapter (see Table 17.1 for the key elements of cognitive restructuring). I have described many of the emotional and behavioral techniques elsewhere and have emphasized

how they are to be integrated with REBT's cognitive methods (Ellis, 2001a, 2001b, 2002).

WHO MIGHT BENEFIT FROM THIS TECHNIQUE

Cognitive restructuring or the disputing of IBs may help psychotherapy clients who are convinced by their therapist or by themselves that (1) their emotional–behavioral dysfuctioning is partly the result of their irrational, unrealistic, and illogical thinking; (2) they can constructively change their IBs to RBs and will then function significantly better; (3) their irrational and dysfunctional thinking includes strong emotional and behavioral components; (4) if they persist in emotionally (strongly) feeling against and behaviorally (actively) acting against their dysfunctional beliefs, they will automatically and unconsciously create an effective new philosophy that will tend to make them less disturbed and keep them from seriously disturbing themselves in the future. Most Axis I individuals can considerably benefit from this technique, and many Axis II individuals can obtain less, but still considerable, benefit from persistently and forcefully using it.

CONTRAINDICATIONS

Some individuals with obsessive–compulsive disorder (OCD) and other severe thought disorders may take cognitive restructuring and the disputing of IBs to extremes and may become so absorbed in analyzing and changing their beliefs that they sidetrack themselves from other useful techniques of therapy. Individuals

TABLE 17.1 Key Elements of Cognitive Restructuring

- Show clients the ABCs of REBT and CBT. Show them how As alone do not lead to their disturbed Cs, but that they personally contribute to their Cs by engaging in strong and persistent beliefs (Bs) about their As. Thus, $A \rightarrow B = C$.
- Particularly show clients that when they disturb themselves (at point C) they have powerful RBs that largely consist of flexible preferences as well as strong IBs that largely consist of absolutistic, rigid musts, shoulds, and other demands.
- Show clients how to think, feel, and act against their rigid IBs with a number of cognitive, emotive, and behavioral techniques, which interrelate to each other.
- Show clients how to specifically dispute their IBs (1) realistically and empirically, (2) logically, and (3) juristically or pragmatically. Particularly show them how to change their rigid, absolutistic demands on themselves, other people, and world conditions to flexible, workable preferences.
- Show clients that when they actively and persistently dispute (D) their IBs they can create an effective new philosophy (E) that includes strong rational coping statements that can help them to feel better, get better, and stay better.

who are rigidly convinced that changing their IBs cannot have any effect on their feelings may refuse to try to do so or may waste their time and energy by trying only halfheartedly. People with abysmal self-deprecation may severely blame themselves for trying to use this technique and failing. Clients with abysmal low frustration tolerance may find it too hard to try and may give up on it.

OTHER FACTORS IN DECIDING WHETHER TO USE THIS TECHNIQUE

Even when it appears that clients are unlikely to benefit from cognitive restructuring, it can be used if the therapist thinks that they will not be harmed or too sidetracked when they try it. When the disputing of IBs is not very effective, therapists may still find that it provides useful information on how else their resistant clients may benefit. Clients may be able to distract themselves from their problems and obtain palliative relief, even when cognitive restructuring itself is not very effective.

HOW DOES THIS TREATMENT WORK?

First, clients are educated by their therapist to acknowledge the four requisites mentioned above: that dysfunctional thinking significantly contributes to emotional disturbance; that they can constructively change this thinking and function better; that their IBs include strong emotional and behavioral elements; and that they can, by cognitive restructuring, distinctly improve themselves and make themselves less disturbable.

Second, clients are specifically shown the differences between rational (self-helping) and irrational (self-defeating) beliefs. According to the theory of REBT, IBs that accompany disturbances are:

1. Rigid and extreme, instead of flexible.
2. Inconsistent instead of consistent with social reality.
3. Illogical or nonsensical instead of logical.

4. Prone to produce dysfunctional feelings (e.g., depression, panic, and rage) rather than functional feelings (e.g., disappointment, concern, and frustration) when the client's goals and purposes are thwarted.
5. Prone to lead to dysfunctional behavioral consequences (e.g., serious avoidances and compulsions) instead of functional consequences (e.g., not avoiding or compulsively dealing with adversities).
6. Demanding and musturbatory philosophies, especially (a) "I absolutely must do well at all times!" (b) "You absolutely must treat me considerately and fairly at all times!" and (c) "Life conditions absolutely must be fair and favorable!"
7. Awfulizing and terribilizing beliefs, such as "I must do well at important tasks, and it's *terrible*—almost 100% bad—if I don't!" and "Living conditions must be satisfactory, and it's *awful* if they aren't!"
8. Beliefs that depreciate human worth, such as "If I don't perform well and please significant others, as I absolutely must, I am a total failure and am thoroughly unlovable!"

Clients are taught the A-B-Cs of REBT theory and practice, which follow in the next section.

The A-B-Cs of REBT

Clients are taught how to distinguish their RBs from their IBs, to find the specific IBs of their unhealthy feelings and behaviors (C's), and then to actively and forcefully dispute (D) their IBs. Thus, their goal (G) is to lead a functional and reasonably happy life, in spite of the adversities (As) that occur, but their IBs about A's help create their dysfunctional feelings (such as panic and depression) at C (consequences). They are also shown that they often have secondary symptoms of disturbance. Thus, when they feel depressed (C) about failing a test (A), they tend to have the IB that "I must not fail, and it shows that I am an inadequate person when I do!" But they secondarily take their depressed feeling (C) and make it into a new adversity (A): "Oh, I see that I am severely depressed." Then they have an RB about this secondary A ("I don't like being depressed; I wish I weren't"), which leads them to have the healthy C of feeling sorry and disappointed about A. But they also have an IB about A ("I must not be depressed!"), which produces a secondary disturbance, self-deprecation about their depression, at C.

The REBT of cognitive restructuring or disputing of clients' IBs shows them how to strongly (emotionally) and persistently (behaviorally) argue with their IBs in an empirical, logical, and pragmatic manner. Each of these argument types is illustrated in the following sections.

Empirical or Realistic Disputing of Irrational Beliefs

This technique proposes an answer or effective new philosophy (E) for each empirical question. For example, for the empirical question, "Where is the evidence that I absolutely *must* perform well at all times and *must not* fail this test?," the answer or E might be "There is no evidence that I *must* not fail, although it would be *preferable* if I succeeded." Likewise, for the empirical question, "Why must people like me for doing well at tests?," the answer might be "Obviously, they don't have to. I would like them to like me, but they can choose not to do so."

Logical Disputing of Irrational Beliefs

This technique calls IBs into dispute through logical questioning. For example, the logical query "Does it logically follow that, because I very much want to take tests well and win the approval of others, I absolutely have to do so?" might evoke this answer: "No, it doesn't follow that no matter how much I *want* to do well, I absolutely *have* to do so." Likewise, the logical question, "Although it is highly preferable for people to like me and for me to like myself for being a good test taker, does it follow that this is *necessary*?," might lead to this answer: "No, it is great if they like me for that reason, but I can be happy and can always accept myself as a person *whether or not* I do well and *whether or not* people like me."

Pragmatic or Heuristic Disputing of Irrational Beliefs

Pragmatic questioning is another technique with which to dispute IBs. An example of a pragmatic question is "Where will it get me if I keep demanding, instead of preferring, that I absolutely must do well at test-taking and at winning people's approval for doing well?" The answer to this question might be "It will most probably get me anxious and depressed. Then I will hardly do well at test taking or almost anything else!" Another pragmatic question could follow: "Also, where will it get me if I keep demanding that I not be depressed about test-taking? The answer might be, "It will help make me depressed about my depression, and again less likely to do well at other tests."

Changing Musturbatory Demands to Preferences

REBT holds that when clients have goals, values, and preferences, they usually react to adversities by feeling healthily sorry and disappointed, but that when they have absolutistic, rigid insistences that they absolutely must do well, must be treated properly by others, and must live with conditions that are satisfactory, they then make themselves anxious, depressed, raging, compulsive, and avoiding. Thus, REBT shows clients how to keep their goals and desires but not raise them to unrealistic and illogical demands. In addition to empirically, logically, and pragmatically disputing clients' demands and helping them change them to preferences, it uses many other cognitive, emotional, and behavioral techniques. Some other forms of cognitive restructuring that clients learn through REBT include the following:

1. Working out rational coping statements— new RBs—and learning how to strongly (emotively) repeat them many times until they act on them.
2. Using positive visualization to hopefully envision their acting on efficacious and functional behaviors.
3. Working on cost–benefit analyses of their disturbed thoughts, feelings, and actions, to motivate them to see how harmful they are and how useful it will be to change them.
4. Doing cognitive homework, especially filling out regularly REBT self-help forms.
5. Modeling themselves after the therapist, after people they know, and after other people

they learn about who have successfully changed their dysfunctional beliefs, feelings, and behaviors when assailed by grim A's.

6. Reading and listening to REBT and CBT books, pamphlets, tapes, lectures, courses, and workshops.

7. Recording their own therapy sessions and playing them back several times.

8. Learning and using REBT's philosophy of unconditional self-acceptance, unconditional other-acceptance, and unconditional life-acceptance (Ellis, 2001a, 2001b, 2002, 2003).

9. Using practical problem-solving and self-management techniques when afflicted with A's in their lives.

CONCLUSION

Rational emotive behavior therapy and (to some extent) many forms of CBT hypothesize that if clients are made fully aware of their specific IBs and are strongly (emotively) and actively (behaviorally) helped to change their unrealistic, illogical, and disturbance-creating absolutistic demands into healthy preferences, they will often considerably reduce their disturbed feelings and behaviors. They can do this by empirically, logically, and heuristically doing cognitive restructuring, along with using various other emotive-evocative and active-behavioral methods.

Further Reading

Ellis, A. (2001a). *Feeling better, getting better, staying better*. Atascadero, CA: Impact Publishers.

Ellis, A. (2001b). *Overcoming destructive thinking, feeling and behaving*. Amherst, NY: Prometheus Books.

Ellis, A. (2002). *Overcoming resistance: A rational emotive behavior therapy integrative approach*. New York: Springer.

References

Adler, A. (1927). *Understanding human nature*. New York: Greenberg.

Beck, A. T. (1967). *Depression*. New York: Hoeber-Harper.

Coué, E. (1923). *My method*. New York: Doubleday-Page.

Dubois, P. (1907). *The psychic treatment of nervous disorders*. New York: Funk and Wagnalls.

Ellis, A. (1957). Outcome of employing three techniques of psychotherapy. *Journal of Clinical Psychology, 13*, 334–350.

Ellis, A. (1958). Rational psychotherapy. *Journal of General Psychology, 59*, 35–49.

Ellis, A. (1962). *Reason and emotion in psychotherapy*. New York: Lyle Stuart.

Ellis, A. (2001a). *Feeling better, getting better, staying better*. Atascadero, CA: Impact Publishers.

Ellis, A. (2001b). *Overcoming destructive thinking, feeling and behaving*. Amherst, NY: Prometheus Books.

Ellis, A. (2002). *Overcoming resistance: A rational emotive behavior therapy integrative approach*. New York: Springer.

Ellis, A. (2003). *Anger: How to live with it and without it*. New York: Citadel Press.

Freud, S. (1960). *Jokes and their relation to the unconscious* (James Strachey, Ed. & Trans.). London: Routledge & Kegan Paul. (Original work published 1922).

Herzberg, A. (1945). *Active psychotherapy*. New York: Grune & Stratton.

Horney, K. (1950). *Neurosis and human growth*. New York: Norton.

Janet, P. (1898). *Neuroses et idee fixes* [Neuroses and fixed ideas]. Paris: Alcan.

Korzybski, A. (1991). *Science and sanity*. Concord, CA: International Society for General Semantics. (Original work published 1933).

Lazarus, A. A. (1971). *Behavior therapy and beyond*. New York: McGraw-Hill.

Meichenbaum, D. (1977). *Cognitive-behavior modification*. New York: Plenum.

Salter, A. (1949). *Conditioned reflex therapy*. New York: Creative Age.

18 COGNITIVE RESTRUCTURING: BEHAVIORAL TESTS OF NEGATIVE COGNITIONS

Keith S. Dobson and Kate E. Hamilton

The power of self-observation of behavior has been recognized for a long time, and even has been the basis of developmental models of personality (Bem, 1970). Some have argued that the ability to behave, and to accurately perceive one's actions and consequences, are hallmark features of good mental health (Beck, Rush, Shaw, & Emery, 1979). Conversely, negative cognitions have been recognized as features of many different forms of psychopathology, and cognitive behavioral therapy has developed a large number of models and techniques to change these negative cognitions (Dobson, 2001).

Behavioral tests are one of the most potent techniques to challenge negative thoughts in clinical practice, and they can be applied to most problems that involve negative thinking. For example, negative cognitions that involve predictions about the future, or statements about the self, can be operationalized as hypotheses subject to empirical investigation. It is then possible to generate behavioral tests of these negative cognitions. We describe the process of conducting behavioral tests of negative cognitions, and then provide four clinical examples from the domains of anxiety, depression, marital dysfunction, and negative self-schemas (see Table 18.1 for the key techniques).

There are few cognitions that cannot be used to address this technique, although cognitions that are ideally suited to behavioral testing include negative predictions, negative attributions, negative conclusions and generalizations, and global self-assessments. In contrast, some of the more difficult types of cognitions put to a behavioral test are memories and delusions. Even in the instance of negative memories, however, it may be possible to devise strategies

to review historical phenomena or to conduct interviews with significant figures from the past, to determine whether or not the client's memory accurately portrays what the other person believes occurred. Also, in the case of delusions, there is some evidence that even the process of developing behavioral tests of delusional thinking can significantly undermine the potency of those delusions (see Kingdon & Turkington, 2005). Our perspective is that the flexibility of behavioral tests of negative cognitions is limited largely by the clinician and the client's imagination.

The specific efficacy of behavioral tests of negative cognitions has not been evaluated. However, a dismantling study has examined the comparative efficacy of cognitive behavioral therapy for depression and its two major components: (1) behavioral activation and (2) behavioral activation with automatic thought modification. The results of this study suggest that cognitive behavioral therapy was no more effective than its components either at termination or during a 2-year follow-up period (Gortner, Gollan, Dobson, & Jacobson, 1998; Jacobson et al., 1996). A more recent trial that examined the efficacy of a more purely behavioral activation therapy of depression has revealed similar results (Dimidjian, et al., 2006; Dobson, et al, in press).

HOW TO USE BEHAVIORAL TESTS TO COUNTER NEGATIVE THINKING

There are three main phases to the use of behavioral tests of negative thoughts. First, the client and therapist must agree that the negative

TABLE 18.1 Key Elements of Behavioral Tests of Negative Cognitions

1. Identify the negative cognition and its role in maintaining the problem behavior.
2. Operationalize the problem behavior and generate a behavioral test.
3. Review the outcome of the behavioral test with respect to the original negative cognition.

thought in question is important and that it plays a contributing or maintaining role in the client's overall problem. For example, the tendency to perceive threat in many situations is a negative cognition that perpetuates anxiety. A distressed wife who perceives that her husband does those things that she wants only because she nags him has a negative cognition that perpetuates marital distress. Thus, the first part of developing a behavioral test is working with the client sufficiently to ensure that he/she recognizes the critical role of the negative cognition in the current problem, and that he or she concurs that an evaluation of, or change to, this cognition may be therapeutically important. In many instances, clients only get to this perspective once they have begun to examine their negative thoughts over a period of time, or when other related techniques, such as the dysfunctional thought record, are used (J. Beck, 1995), so the critical issue at this early stage is to have them agree in principle to the examination of the thought, rather than agree that it is erroneous or faulty at the outset.

Once a client has come to the perspective that his or her thought is worthy of evaluation, the therapist can suggest the possibility of a behavioral test of that thought. Often, such suggestions are put in the form of "experiments," "assignments," or "tasks," with which the client and therapist can work collaboratively, in the spirit of truly understanding the role of these thoughts. A critical factor in this process is to ensure that the client agrees that this thought, at least in principle, can be modified through a behavioral test. If the client maintains that his/her particular cognition is absolute or, incontestable, or perhaps that the therapist doesn't understand if he or she suggests that it can be changed, then clinical wisdom suggests that more preparatory work and

data gathering about the role of the thought, is needed before the behavioral test is attempted.

A second critical element of behavior tests of negative cognitions is the behavioral test itself. The behavior in question must be clearly specified in order for a behavior test to work well, and the cognition that is being targeted by the behavioral test must also be well identified. This specification is important to reduce the possibility that the client will engage in a half-hearted attempt with the behavior and then draw the negative conclusion that this type of behavior test does not work. Behavioral recordings such as audiotapes, written descriptions of the test, dysfunctional thought records, or other methods might be employed by the therapist and client as aids to ensure that the behavior test is conducted in the way it was intended.

The third, and critical, aspect of the behavior test of cognitions is the review process. Having engaged in a behavioral assignment or experiment, the therapist and client must evaluate the conclusions that the client now draws about himself/herself, in contrast to the previous cognitions. For example, if the client had made a negative prediction, such as in the case of anxiety disorders, his/her actual experiences need to be contrasted with those expectations in order to ensure that the next time these expectations are present the client can remember that these have been invalidated in the past. Likewise, the depressed client who can more realistically evaluate negative cognitions through behavioral assignments needs to see the role of his or her negative thinking in his or her depression, in order to understand that behavioral tests can meaningfully undermine negative cognitions and depression more generally. Thus, while simple "behavioral activation" in depression may have a salutary effect on depression (Dimidjian et al., 2006), our perspective is that the client's perception of that behavior may be the critical ingredient for lasting change.

EXAMPLES OF BEHAVIORAL TESTS TO COUNTER NEGATIVE THINKING

After the client and therapist are convinced that the cognition is clinically important, and the client has accepted that the test of the thought may yield important clinical information, the therapist is in a position to develop a behavior test. The nature of the actual test will vary, depending on the clinical problem, and for this reason we provide four illustrative examples for the reader.

Panic Disorder

It is now fairly well accepted that panic-disordered clients generally have a critical cognition that involves the idea that if they experience the symptoms they associate with panic they may either be severely injured or even die (Antony & Swinson, 2000). For example, a client who monitors his heart rate may believe that if his heart rate and/or blood pressure exceed a certain value, he is likely to have a cardiac arrest or stroke and be critically injured or die. Therefore, the cognitive behavioral treatment of panic disorder typically involves a direct behavioral test of this critical negative cognition. The manner in which the test is conducted is to first have the client accept in principle that this may only be a negative catastrophic prediction, and to accept that evaluation of this cognition's role in panic is warranted. Once the client accepts these premises, the behavioral test is to have the client engage in an activity that produces panic-like symptoms, but in a way that is structured so that the panic does not actually occur. For example, the client may be instructed to walk up and down a flight of stairs in order to accelerate his or her heart rate; however, when he or she stops the exercise, the heart rate will

quickly returns to normal without a catastrophic outcome. Over time, the behavioral test can be exaggerated to the point that the client may be willing to undertake activities that he or she previously would have found too risky.

Behavioral tests of negative, anxiety-related cognitions are extremely powerful in modifying those predictions (Deacon & Abramowitz, 2004). It can be argued that without behavioral tests of these negative cognitions, successful treatment of most anxiety-related disorders is not possible. Contemporary behavior therapy of all the anxiety disorders involves exposure to the fear-provoking stimulus or situation, with cognitive restructuring attendant to behavioral tests (see Table 18.2 for the key elements of cognitive restructuring). Thus, this area probably represents the most widely accepted behavioral tests of negative cognitions.

Depressive Cognitions

Depressed clients characteristically make negative assessments of themselves, others, and the world in general (Beck et al., 1979). These "cognitive distortions" can take many and varied forms, but their characteristic feature is that they typically reflect diminution of the client's self-worth or his or her status in the world. For example, a depressed executive may believe that she can "never" get her work completed, and she may berate herself for her lack of accomplishment, even while maintaining that even if she were successful in the completion of her work assignments, it would be of little consequence anyway. Behavioral tests are a potentially

---

TABLE 18.2   Elements of Cognitive Restructuring

- Show clients the logic of Cognitive Behavior Therapy (CBT). Show them that events alone do not lead to their disturbed reactions, but that they contribute to these consequences through negative thoughts, beliefs and predictions.
- Show clients that when they disturb themselves they have strong negative thoughts that largely consist of absolutistic, rigid musts, shoulds, predictions, and other ideas.
- Show clients how to think, feel, and act against their negative thoughts with cognitive and behavioral techniques, which interrelate to each other.
- Show clients how to specifically dispute their negative thoughts: (1) realistically and empirically, (2) logically, and (3) juristically or pragmatically. Particularly show them how to change their rigid, absolutistic demands on themselves, other people, and world conditions to flexible, workable preferences.
- Show clients that when they actively and persistently dispute negative thoughts with behavioral evidence they can create a new thought that is based on experiential evidence, and that will include strong rational coping statements that can help them to get and stay better.

effective method to counter depressive cognitions, however. If this client can evaluate her negative thoughts systematically, and in particular her idea that completing her housework is of minimal benefit, the therapist and the client can work together to develop a behavioral examination of these thoughts. Thus, the therapist and client could systematically consider the various tasks that are part of her work assignments, and they could develop a behavioral plan for the successful completion of these various tasks. As the client gradually completes these tasks, her sense of accomplishment and mood can be evaluated. Depending on the client's current level of depression, these activities can be planned in a graduated fashion, so that the chances of the client's experiencing success in a gradual fashion are maximized.

Marital Distress

One of the characteristic negative thoughts in many distressed couples is that the partner is not truly committed to the success of the relationship and engages in positive activities only because of the threat of negative consequences if that activity is not done. Thus, a wife may believe that her husband engages in social activities only because she insists, and that if she did not mention these activities and did not "remind him" of the need to do these activities, they may never happen at all. The paradox of such negative expectations for the partner may lead the wife to nag or to constantly remind her husband of social obligations, and then to make negative attributions like "He only did this because I nagged him," even if the husband might have in any event engaged in the desired behavior. Thus, even if the husband were to honestly desire social relations, and if he might even engage in these without prompting, her behavior does not allow for this pattern to be recognized. If this pattern can be indentified in a distressed relationship, it lends itself nicely to a behavioral test of the negative cognition. In order to do a behavior test of this type of thought, it is first necessary for both the wife and the husband to see the pattern of negative thoughts that lead to nagging behavior and that, in effect, are reinforced by either compliance or noncompliance with the social activity.

The wife could be encouraged to elaborate her prediction of how her husband will not do these things unless he is nagged. The husband could discuss the effect nagging has on him, which is most likely that he resents it and feels that he does not get the credit he deserves when he actually engages in the things his wife wants. Both partners then need to agree that the wife will experiment with not nagging, on the understanding that if the husband cares for her and is honestly motivated to do these things, they will occur "spontaneously." Hopefully, the husband will recognize his opportunity to reduce his partner's negative behavior and will choose to engage in the desired activity without such prompting. In such a case, this behavioral test of the effect of lack of complaining can provide powerful information that the husband is more motivated in contributing to the relationship than the wife first believed. It could also enhance the husband's sense of efficacy in the relationship, and thus overall contribute to marital harmony.

Schema Change Therapy

A final example of behavior tests of negative cognitions can be seen in the recent emphasis in cognitive behavior therapy on *schema change therapy* (Young, Klosko & Weishaar, 2003). Increasingly, therapists are interested in the identification of general beliefs that clients have about themselves or how the world generally operates, and to test these beliefs behaviorally. For example, if a client comes to believe that he is a "social loser," this general belief can be put to a behavioral test. In order to perform such a test, the therapist and client first need to agree that holding this belief is important to the client, and might, for example, limit his social attainment.

The therapist and client need to agree that this thought is refutable, if sufficient contrary evidence can be gathered, and then they need to develop a behavioral test. To do so, it is important to first operationalize the belief—"What is a social loser?"—and to work with the client to develop a method to potentially invalidate this self-construction. Often, the therapist will ask the client a questions such as "What would it take for you not to believe you are a social loser?"

or "How would you know you are no longer a social loser?" This question will help the client be concrete about the activities he or she associates with being a social loser, and will help to generate behavioral tests of this construct. For example, if one of the criteria that the client enunciates is that he rarely has a date on the weekend evenings, the therapist and client could generate the assignment of getting the client a date, so that he can evaluate his social identity.

Another useful behavior test of a general belief is the "as-if" technique (J. Beck, 1995). In the as-if technique, a general self-schema that the client has adopted is first identified, and some other more positive alternative is then developed. For example, if the client's self-schema is that he or she is "unlovable," an alternative of "being loved" could be generated. The implications of holding the alternative belief would be discussed at length with the client, and then, if appropriate, the client could be encouraged to behave "as if" he or she is capable of being loved. Having done so, the client then evaluates how the adoption of this alternative way of being (both cognitively and behaviorally) affects his or her sense of self and emotional valuing. For many clients, such behavioral tests are powerful methods to demonstrate to them that they have the potential to be different than they have otherwise been. Even if they are not fully successful in the development of an alternative sense of self, these tests can be important milestones in the path to the evaluation of a range of possibilities that exist for the client.

SUMMARY AND CONCLUSIONS

We have described how behavioral tests can be used to undermine a variety of negative cognitions seen in clinical practice, ranging from specific predictions through to global negative self-assessments. We have emphasized three main phases of behavior test implementation. The first phase involves the identification of the key negative cognition and its importance in the maintenance of problem behavior. Having achieved this objective, the therapist and client collaboratively operationalize the problem behavior and generate an appropriate behavior test. Finally, the therapist and client engage in

a review process to evaluate the conclusions that the client draws regarding the negative cognition, in the face of the new behavioral evidence they have gathered. Self-observation through behavioral tests offers a potent means to challenge and modify the maladaptive cognitions associated with a broad range of clinical problems.

References

Antony, M. M., & Swinson, R. P. (2000). *Phobic disorders and panic in adults: A guide to assessment and treatment*. Washington, DC: American Psychological Association Press.

Beck, A. T., Rush, A. G., Shaw, B. F., & Emery, G. (1979). *Cognitive therapy of depression*. New York: Guilford.

Beck, J. (1995). *Cognitive therapy: Basics and beyond*. New York: Guilford Press.

Bem, D. (1970). *Beliefs, attitudes, and human affairs*. Oxford, England: Brooks/ Cole.

Deacon, B. J., & Abramowitz, J. S. (2004). Cognitive and behavioral treatments for anxiety disorders: A review of meta-analytic findings. *Journal of Clinical Psychology, 60,* 429–441.

Dimidjian, D., Hollon, S. D., Dobson, K. S., Schmaling, K. B., Kohlenberg, R. J., Addis, M. E., et al. (2006). Randomized trial of behavioral activation, cognitive therapy, and antidepressant medication in the acute treatment of adults with major depression. *Journal of Consulting and Clinical Psychology, 74,* 658–670.

Dobson, K. S. (2001). *Handbook of cognitive-behavioral therapies* (2nd ed.). New York: Guilford.

Dobson, K. S., Hollon, S. D., Dimidjian, S., Schmaling, K. B., Kohlenberg, R. J., Gallop, R., et al. (2008). Randomized trial of behavioral activation, cognitive therapy, and antidepressant medication in the prevention of relapse and recurrence in Major Depression. *Journal of Consulting and Clinical Psychology, 76,* 468–477.

Gortner, E. T., Gollan, J. K., Dobson, K. S., & Jacobson, N. S. (1998). Cognitive-behavioral treatment for depression: Relapse prevention. *Journal of Consulting and Clinical Psychology, 66,* 377–384.

Jacobson, N. S., Dobson, K. S., Truax, P. A., Addis, M. E., Koerner, K., Gollan, J. K., et al. (1996). A component analysis of cognitive-behavioral treatment for depression. *Journal of Consulting and Clinical Psychology, 64,* 295–304.

Kingdon, D. G., & Turkington, D. (2005). *Cognitive Therapy of Schizophrenia*. New York: Guilford.

Young, J. E., Klosko, K. S., & Weishaar, M. E. (2003). *Schema therapy: A practitioner's guide*. New York: Guilford Press.

19 COMMUNICATION/PROBLEM-SOLVING SKILLS TRAINING

Pamella H. Oliver and Gayla Margolin

Communication training historically has been an integral component of behavioral marital therapy and continues to be a fundamental procedure utilized in contemporary forms of therapy for marital or couple distress (Jacobson & Christensen, 1996), prevention programs for couples (Braukhaus, Hahlweg, Kroeger, Groth, & Fehm-Wolfsdorf, 2003; Floyd, Markman, Kelly, Blumberg, & Stanley, 1995; Hahlweg & Markman, 1988), and parent training programs or interventions (Dishion & Kavanaugh, 2003; Forgatch, & DeGarmo, 1999; Kazdin, 2005). Communication training involves the practice and enactment of two sets of skills—speaker/listener skills and problem-solving skills. These skills are components of many efficacious treatments, interventions or programs. For this chapter we focus on the specifics of using communication training in marital or couples therapy with the recommendation that these same techniques can be adapted for use with children and families in a variety of interventions. Based on social learning theory, behavior marital therapy focuses on improving couples' interaction through skills training and through changing conditions in the environment that establish and maintain behavioral patterns. Jacobson and Margolin (1979), the traditional treatment manual for behavior marital therapy, provides a detailed description of communication training as well as a description of other elements of therapy such as behavior exchange. The steps of communication training are also provided in other, generally more recent, manuals for therapists (Epstein & Baucom, 2002; Jacobson & Christensen, 1996) and for clients (Christensen & Jacobson, 2000; Forgatch & Patterson, 2005; Gottman, Notarius, Gonso, & Markman, 1976; Notarius & Markman, 1993).

PROPOSED MECHANISMS OF EFFECT

Many therapeutic treatments for distressed family members include communication training. Often families do not apply the basic listening and problem-solving skills presented here to the difficult, conflictual issues of their relationships. Many have never used such skills. Others, who may be skilled communicators in some situations, dispense with good listening and problem solving when such skills are most needed, that is, in moments of frustration and anger. Instead, these family members either withdraw from the interaction or resort to bombarding others with the same ill-stated point. Thus, the rationale for this procedure is derived from two models. One is a skills deficit model, the other a stimulus–response model. Communication skills training is basically a skills oriented approach. The training is sometimes prescribed to counteract family members' lack of basic interpersonal skills with which to negotiate conflict. In contrast, the stimulus–response model assumes that although family members possess communication skills in general, they do not use effective communication behavior in the particular context of relationship tension. From this perspective, communication training is used as a means of stimulus control. That is, communication training provides a structure to circumvent the family's well-developed patterns that preclude using effective communication and problem-solving skills. Whether the destructive behavioral patterns are seen as etiologic or as maintaining the problems, the therapeutic objective is twofold: to learn and practice any necessary skills, and to utilize the structured procedures in such a way that the context of conflict is fundamentally changed.

A third model describing a proposed mechanism of effect is through a constructive, positive environment. Because parents frequently are the ones facilitating change toward the goal of reducing child or adolescent problem behavior, parents' abilities to relate to their children are important, particularly their supportive communications and limit-setting communications. The general goal of increasing parents' positive emotional connection to the child can be enhanced through communication skills of initiating contact and showing interest (Liddle, Rodriguez, Dakof, Kanzki, & Marvel, 2005). Beyond developing a more positive affective interaction between parents and children, communication interventions also are used to foster a constructive environment for structured problem-solving (Forgatch & Patterson, 2005).

COMMUNICATION SKILLS TRAINING PROCEDURES

Communication training falls into two general skill sets: speaker/listener skills to generate understanding and problem-solving skills. As Weiss (1978) noted, communications often fall apart when one person simply wants to be understood and the other person starts to problem solve. Speaker/listener skills result in understanding and validation of a partner's perspective. These skills are an important goal in themselves as well as a preliminary step to problem solving. Productive problem solving occurs only when partners fully understand one another's viewpoint. Problem-solving skills lead to changes in the way partners handle a given situation. However, issues that do not require an action-oriented response need not progress to the problem-solving phase.

FUNCTION OF SPEAKER/LISTENER SKILLS

The goal of practicing speaker/listener skills is to facilitate the accurate sending and receiving of messages. A common pattern in distressed couples and families is that communication falls into highly ritualized patterns, characterized by rapidly escalating conflict or frustrated withdrawal. Such patterns generally are fueled when one person, feeling misunderstood, repeats and reiterates the same information. The other person, feeling attacked, defends or counterattacks by responding to one small segment of information. The goal of practicing speaker/listener skills is to interrupt such ritualized patterns by building in steps that guarantee family members accurately receive each other's messages. Instructions that insert additional steps in family communication dramatically slow down the communication process and thereby interrupt well-rehearsed patterns. The additional steps change the fundamental nature of the communication and promote different expectations about the purpose of the interaction. When successfully enacted, these changes allow participants to figure out and articulate what they truly want to say and to ensure that the partner has accurately received the message.

In addition to imparting new skills, speaker/listener skills training also creates a stimulus situation that triggers the enactment of constructive speaker and listener behaviors rather than angry or divisive behaviors (Margolin, 1987). The enactment of these behaviors results in a greater closeness and intimacy despite the fact that the partners do not necessarily resolve the problem. This process of using problem discussions to enhance closeness is similar to the processes of "empathic joining" (Jacobson & Christensen, 1996) or "building a joint platform" (Wile, 1993).

STEP-BY-STEP PROCEDURES FOR SPEAKER/LISTENER SKILLS

For the purposes of training and practice, the speaker and listener roles are clearly defined. One partner, the speaker, introduces a topic that she or he wants to discuss, and the other partner, the listener, is to demonstrate that she or he understands what is being said.

The Listener's Role

The therapist defines and demonstrates four separate skills of increasing complexity that demonstrate accurate listening (Jacobson & Christensen,

1996; Jacobson & Margolin, 1979). Parroting, the most straightforward skill, requires the listener simply to repeat back verbatim what the partner has said. Paraphrasing requires the listener to rephrase, in her or his own words, the content of the communication. Reflection requires the listener to discern the emotion behind the speaker's message and to verbally check out that emotional interpretation with the speaker. Validation conveys to the speaker that her/his perspective is understandable. Thus, the speaker's statement, "I can't believe you didn't call your mother to let her know we'd be late for dinner," could be repeated back in those exact words, paraphrased as "You wanted me to call my mother letting her know we'd be late," reflected as "You're angry at me for not calling my mother and maybe also embarrassed that we delayed her dinner party," or validated as "It makes sense that you'd be angry at me if you thought I had made the call." It is important to note that none of these responses require the listener to agree with the speaker.

These four listener skills are introduced sequentially. A new skill is introduced only when the previous skill has been mastered. The therapist actively directs the back-and-forth communication, prompting the listener's restatement, and asking the speaker if the listener's statement was correct. If the listener was not correct, the entire process is repeated. The communication is thus slowed down considerably by building in checks for clarity and accuracy before a reply can be given.

The Speaker's Role

At the same time that one partner is practicing listening skills, the other is practicing expressive skills. Expressive skills are as important as listening skills in fostering productive communication. Frequently, a speaker begins to present a concern without fully knowing or acknowledging what makes that situation upsetting. Accurate expressiveness, or being able to state what is truly on one's mind, often evolves through the communication process. Through clarification and feedback from the listener, be it the partner or the therapist, the speaker gains further understanding about why a given situation

is particularly distressing. According to Wile (1993), spouses' seemingly out-of-proportion anger often stems from feeling unentitled to very reasonable and normal reactions. Different dimensions of the process of expressing the core, underlying feelings associated with a problem have been described as leveling (e.g., Gottman, et. al, 1976) or as disclosing "soft" as opposed to "hard" emotions (Jacobson & Christensen, 1996).

For the listener to accurately restate the speaker's message, that message needs to be stated succinctly. Thus, an important role for the therapist is to interrupt statements that are too long and to cue the listener to restate what has been said thus far. This process of chunking speaker statements into manageable units provides the speaker with essential feedback about what portions of her/his statement have been received, thereby reducing the tendency for speakers to repeat the same message. Moreover, listeners can be encouraged to restate part of the speaker's statement but to raise questions if another part is still confusing. Only when the speaker has finished stating her or his complete point and the listener has demonstrated understanding of the entire message does the listener present her/his perspective. At that point, speaker and listener roles reverse. There is no guarantee in this process that the new speaker will not come across as angry and defensive but at least she or he has accurately heard the original speaker's point of view.

As contrasted with the equal status between two adult partners, the differential status between parents and children is reflected in somewhat different practices of speaker/listener roles. Some basic "do's" and "don'ts" still apply (e.g., see Forgatch & Patterson, 2005). Behaviors to be encouraged include: staying focused on the speaker, attempting to understand the other's perspective, and using active listening skills. Behaviors to be discouraged include: being defensive, criticizing the speaker, and lecturing or giving advice.

The Therapist's Role

As described earlier, the therapist plays an active role to maximize the likelihood of success in speaker/listener skills training. The therapist models both speaker and listener behaviors, and encourages, prompts, and reinforces the partners' efforts in this process. Most importantly, the therapist monitors and interrupts the process when it is not working to bring it back to a more productive course. Some instructions for communication training include extensive lists of rules. Certainly, it is important for the therapist to demonstrate and prompt ways for partners to express strong feelings without provoking an immediate counterattack. However, the primary objective of speaker/listener skills training should not be overshadowed by undue attention directed to a list of communication rules. The overriding goal is to create an atmosphere of mutual respect and openness so that spouses can get their most difficult and controversial points across to one another.

FUNCTION OF PROBLEM-SOLVING SKILLS

Problem-solving skills training is designed to provide spouses and family members with a strategy for examining and responding to situations that they want to change but are in disagreement about how to change. Thus, problem-solving skills are used when the family members feel "stuck" because each is entrenched in her or his own position that is different from, if not diametrically opposed to, the other's position. The steps involved in problem-solving skills are threefold. The first is to define the problem in a manner that is noninflammatory and incorporates the role of both people, thereby increasing the motivation of both to want to solve the problem. The second is to generate a broad array of solutions to the problem, thereby increasing the likelihood that the partners will find some set of solutions upon which they can agree. The third is to craft a carefully considered plan of action that can be put into effect quickly and, in subsequent sessions, can be monitored and modified. Proposed solutions are construed as 'works in progress'. Even if successful, they generally need to be updated and revised as the problem starts to resolve and/or as circumstances change. The content of each phase of the problem-solving session

should be documented in writing to help keep the process on track and to avoid disagreements about the specifics of the agreed-upon plan.

STEP-BY-STEP PROCEDURES FOR PROBLEM-SOLVING SKILLS FOR COUPLES

Defining the Problem

Problem definition is the most important and most difficult step in problem solving. It is the most important because it sets up a framework for thinking about and approaching the problem. It is the most difficult because it requires translating one person's complaint into a nonblaming relationship issue. It also requires balancing the specificity and generality of the problem definition—specificity so that participants know what problem is being addressed, and generality so that they do not solve a small manifestation of a larger issue.

Ideally, problem definition acknowledges the role of both people and the consequences of the problem for both spouses. When those components are included, spouses find it easier to collaborate with brainstorming solutions. However, in generating the problem definition, it is common for spouses to revert to a pattern in which one partner complains or criticizes and the other partner defends her or his behavior. This situation is best managed by: (1) not defining problems when either spouse is angry; (2) reminding spouses to state the problem in a way that is easiest for the partner to hear; (3) employing listener/speaker skills as needed; and (4) making sure that spouses do not sidetrack from one problem to another (Jacobson & Margolin, 1979).

Particularly when couples are first learning problem-solving skills, the therapist needs to play an active role to ensure that spouses define the problem in a way that opens up creative and constructive possibilities for addressing the problematic issue. For example, the initial complaint of a wife who comanaged a business with her husband was that the husband was obsessed with the business. This complaint directed toward the spouse was translated into the mutual issue that the couple had no relationship time apart from their business dealings. The redefinition of this problem opened up possibilities for new solutions toward reserving special relationship time as well as making sure that mutual business issues were adequately dealt with in a timely fashion.

Brainstorming Solutions

Once the partners and the therapist have agreed on a problem definition, the brainstorming process begins. The primary rules of brainstorming are that: (1) any idea, no matter how outrageous, is worthy of mention, and (2) no evaluation of ideas takes place until the entire list is generated and rated. As a result of these rules, partners are less inhibited in presenting their ideas and they stay focused on the one problem under discussion (Jacobson & Margolin, 1979). Each solution is written down until a list of 10–20 solutions is generated.

Rating Brainstormed Solutions

Still without discussion, spouses independently rate each suggestion (1 = suggestion is good; 2 = suggestion may be worthy of consideration; 3 = suggestion is bad). Each item rated as a 3 by both spouses is immediately removed from the list. Each item with a 1–1 or a 1–2 combination is discussed to develop a plan based on one or more of these ideas.

Developing and Revising the Plan

The initial plan should incorporate suggestions that can be put into effect within the next week, with the possibility of revision or incorporating other steps in future weeks. A problem solution thus is reevaluated and revised until the problem is solved or a long-range solution is in place. What makes this process of problem solving very rewarding to spouses is that they discover multiple mutually acceptable solutions to a problem that previously seemed unsolvable.

GENERALIZABILITY

Following each session of communication skills training, family members are given a homework assignment to practice and consolidate the behaviors practiced in session and extend the behaviors to a new topic. When learning speaker/listening behaviors, family members typically are asked to set aside a half-hour once or twice during the week with each person alternately taking the role as speaker and as listener. Similarly, once the family members have practiced problem solving with the therapist on several different issues, they can be asked to try the same procedures at home. For the first such assignment, the therapist may want the complete problem definition in the session and then have the clients do the brainstorming and problem solution at home.

It is generally advised that the topics selected for homework practice of speaker/listener skills or of problem-solving skills should be less conflictual than those addressed in the session. Having family members tape-record their communication skills homework is a good way for the therapist and clients to review homework practices. As with all between-session assignments, the therapist must fully debrief the homework during the next session. Ultimately, the goal is for the family to recognize when they need to use communication skills and to then employ the skills on their own.

EVIDENCE-BASED APPLICATIONS

Research on the efficacy and effectiveness of communication skills training is embedded in empirical research on behavioral marital therapy, prevention training, and parenting interventions. Baucom and colleagues (Baucom, Shoham, Mueser, Daiuto, & Stickle, 1998) have determined, based on more than 20 published, controlled treatment outcome investigations, that behavioral marital therapy is an "efficacious and specific intervention" (Chambless & Hollon, 1998) for maritally distressed couples. Similarly, a recent meta-analysis indicates behavioral marital therapy is significantly more effective than no treatment for distressed couples (Shadish & Baldwin, 2005). Research on the efficacy of communication and problem-solving skills training for committed couples has been established (Braukhaus et al., 2003; Kaiser,

Communication Training

Listener/Speaker Skills

Listener behaviors: Repeat verbatim
Paraphrase
Reflect
Validate

Speaker behaviors: Make succinct statements
Clarify and express accurate feeling statements

Problem-Solving Skills

Define problem in mutual non-blaming language
Brainstorm and then rate problem solutions
Develop plan to be enacted in stated time period
Implement plan
Review implementation and revise plan

Hahlweg, Fehm-Wolfsdorf, & Groth, 1998) with intervention couples having significantly more positive communication and less negative communication than the control couples. With respect to the long-term effects of communication skills training in particular, a component analysis of behavioral marital therapy indicated that after 6 months the communication skills training component showed superior maintenance of treatment gains over the behavioral exchange component (Jacobson, 1984). However, a subsequent 2-year follow-up indicated no differential benefit of either component, and approximately 30% of couples who had improved in therapy later relapsed (Jacobson, Schmaling, & Holtzworth-Munroe, 1987). Although research overall indicates that couples appear to benefit from communication training, there is a small set of women who demonstrate a decrease in marital satisfaction across time if, as a result of an intervention, they have been extremely positive and rarely negative in communication (Baucom, Hahlweg, Atkins, Engl, & Thurmaier, 2006). These findings indicate the importance of the expression of both negative and positive communication.

In addition to questions of efficacy, a limited number of studies also have investigated the effectiveness, or real-life generalizability of

behavioral marital therapy. These studies have reported positive consumer ratings (Baucom et al., 1998). Dropout rates are estimated to be low, as suggested by a 6% attrition rate found by Hahlweg and Markman in their meta-analysis of behavioral marital therapy studies (1988).

Improved parent–child communication generally has been examined in the context of comprehensive programs to change children's behavior or to improve family functioning around difficult issues. Parenting programs, such as Adolescent Transitions Program (Dishion & Kavanagh, 2003), based on the Patterson (1982) ecological model of antisocial behavior and coercive family interaction patterns, have empirical evidence that intervention groups of at-risk adolescents in treatment had less negative engagement and a significant reduction in home problem behavior after a program focused on parent–teen relationship skills. These relationship skills included communication skills, problem-solving skills, and negotiating. Based on similar models, there is extensive empirical evidence of the efficacy of programs that utilize components of communication skills and problem solving. A sample of these are a program for divorcing mothers and their young sons (Forgatch & DeGarmo, 1999), Incredible Years parent intervention program for young children with conduct problems (Webster-Stratton & Reid, 2003) and Parent Management Training (Kazdin, 2005) for children and adolescents with aggressive and antisocial behavior.

SUMMARY

Communication skills training sets up the structure and expectation that family members will listen to each other and approach problem solving in new ways. Interaction behaviors to be enacted are shaped with the therapist initially doing much modeling and reinforcing and family members gradually doing the steps more independently. Although the steps of communication skills training are spelled out in several manuals, the timing and sequencing are left to the therapist's judgment. Toward the goal of optimizing each person's likelihood of success at each therapeutic stage, the therapist uses her or his judgment with respect to when to introduce communication skills training, how to pace the training, whether to begin the training on more or less serious problems, whether to combine communication training with other intervention procedures, and whether to introduce communication skills in a formal, educational manner or to work them in seamlessly as needed in ongoing discussions of the couple's or family's problems.

References

Baucom, D. H., Hahlweg, K., Atkins, D. C., Engl, J., & Thurmaier, F. (2006). Long-term prediction of marital quality following a relationship education program: Being positive in a constructive way. *Journal of Family Psychology, 20,* 448–455.

Baucom, D. H., Shoham, V., Mueser, K. T., Daiuto, A. D., & Stickle, T. R. (1998). Empirically supported couple and family interventions for marital distress and adult mental health problems. *Journal of Consulting and Clinical Psychology, 66,* 53–88.

Braukhaus, C., Hahlweg, K., Kroeger, C., Groth, T., & Fehm-Wolfsdorf, G. (2003). The effects of adding booster sessions to a prevention training program for committed couples. *Behavioural and Cognitive Psychotherapy, 31,* 325–336.

Chambless, D. L., & Hollon, S. D. (1998). Defining empirically supported therapies. *Journal of Consulting and Clinical Psychology, 66,* 7–18.

Christensen, A., & Jacobson, N. S. (2000). *Reconcilable differences.* New York: Guilford.

Dishion, T. J., & Kavanagh, K. (2003). The Adolescent Transitions Program: A family-centered prevention strategy for schools. In J. B. Reid, J. J. Snyder, & G. R. Patterson (Eds.), *Antisocial behavior in children and adolescents: A developmental analysis and model for intervention* (pp. 257–272). Washington, DC: American Psychological Association.

Epstein, N. B., & Baucom, D. H. (2002). *Enhanced cognitive-behavioral therapy for couples: A contextual approach.* Washington, DC: American Psychological Association.

Floyd, F. J., Markman, H. J., Kelly, S., Blumberg, S. L., & Stanley, S. M. (1995). Preventive intervention and relationship enhancement. In N. S. Jacobson & A. S. Gurman (Eds.), *Clinical handbook of couple therapy* (pp. 212–226). New York: Guilford.

Forgatch, M. S., & DeGarmo, D. S. (1999). Parenting through change: An effective prevention program for single mothers. *Journal of Consulting and Clinical Psychology, 67,* 711–724.

Forgatch, M. S., & Patterson, G. R. (2005). Parents and adolescents living together. Part 2: Family problem solving (2nd ed.). Champaign, IL: Research Press.

Gottman, J., Notarius, C., Gonso, J., & Markman, H. (1976). *A couple's guide to communication.* Champaign, IL: Research Press.

Hahlweg, K., & Markman, H. J. (1988). Effectiveness of behavioral marital therapy: Empirical status of behavioral techniques in preventing and alleviating marital distress. *Journal of Consulting and Clinical Psychology, 56,* 440–447.

Jacobson, N. S., & Christensen, A. (1996). *Integrative couple therapy: Promoting acceptance and change.* New York: W. W. Norton.

Jacobson, N. S., & Margolin, G. (1979). Marital therapy: Strategies based on social learning and behavior exchange principles. New York: Brunner/Mazel.

Jacobson, N. S. (1984). A component analysis of behavioral marital therapy: The relative effectiveness of behavioral exchange and communication/problem-solving training. *Journal of Consulting and Clinical Psychology, 52,* 295–305.

Jacobson, N. S., Schmaling, K. B., & Holtzworth-Munroe, A. (1987). Component analysis of behavioral marital therapy: 2-year follow-up and prediction of relapse. *Journal of Marital and Family Therapy, 13,* 187–195.

Kaiser, A., Hahlweg, K., Fehm-Wolfsdorf, G., & Groth, T. (1998). The efficacy of a compact psychoeducational group training program for married couples. *Journal of Consulting and Clinical Psychology, 66,* 753–760.

Kazdin, A. E. (2005). Parent management training: Treatment for oppositional, aggressive, and antisocial behavior in children and adolescents. New York: Oxford University Press.

Liddle, H. A., Rodriguez, R. A., Dakof, G. A., Kanzki, E., & Marvel, F. A. (2005). In J. L. Lebow (Ed.), *Handbook of clinical family therapy* (pp. 128–163). Hoboken, NJ: John Wiley & Sons.

Margolin, G. (1987). Marital therapy: A cognitive–behavioral–affective approach. In N. S. Jacobson, (Ed.). *Psychotherapists in clinical practice: Cognitive and behavioral perspectives* (pp. 232–285). New York: Guilford.

Notarius, C., & Markman, H. (1993). *We can work it out: Making sense of marital conflict.* New York: G. P. Putnam's Sons.

Patterson, G. R. (1982). *Coercive family process.* Eugene, OR: Castalia.

Shadish, W. R., & Baldwin, S. A. (2005). Effects of behavioral marital therapy: A meta-analysis of randomized controlled trials. *Journal of Consulting and Clinical Psychology, 73,* 6–14.

Webster-Stratton, C., & Reid, M. J. (2003). The Incredible Years Parents, Teachers, and Children Training Series: A multifaceted treatment approach for young children with conduct problems. In A. E. Kazdin & J. R. Weisz (Eds.), *Evidence-based psycho-therapies for children and adolescents* (pp. 224–240). New York: Guilford.

Weiss, R. L. (1978). The conceptualization of marriage from a behavioral perspective. In T. J. Paolino & B. S. McCrady (Eds.). *Marriage and marital therapy: Psychoanalytic behavioral and systems theory perspectives.* New York: Brunner/Mazel.

Wile, D. (1993). After the fight: A night in the life of a couple. New York: Guilford.

20 COMPLIANCE WITH MEDICAL REGIMENS

Elaine M. Heiby and Maxwell R. Frank

In past decades, many medical regimens and public health advisories have involved prescribing individuals to modify their daily habits (O'Donohue, Naylor, & Cummings, 2005). Research has suggested that more than one-half of all deaths in the United States have behavioral determinants (Levant, 2005; McGinnis & Foege, 1993). Important health areas that have been emphasized within the context of prior intervention and research efforts have included diet, exercise, and plaque control regimens; use of safety helmets, seat belts, and safer sexual practices; as well as adoption of routine cancer screening habits (e.g., for testicular, cervical, and breast cancers). Additional important components of preventive health medicine include smoking cessation, medication compliance, and the various self-monitoring activities associated with diabetes management.

Less than half of the population is initially compliant with instructions to make a behavioral change—and this figure diminishes rapidly over time, particularly for preventive regimens (Christensen, 2004; Myers & Midence, 1998). Numerous theories have proposed situational and behavioral targets for enhancement of compliance, stimulating a large body of research identifying correlates of compliance. At this time, however, most of the theoretical literature is disunified and has failed to successfully integrate empirically supported aspects of prior theories. Subsequently, no standardized assessment device for risk of noncompliance and no empirically supported treatment or prevention package have been developed (e.g., as argued by Cramer, 1991). Therefore, this chapter will provide guidelines for enhancement of compliance that are based on consideration of what situational factors and behavioral competencies have been related to compliance and are subject to established environmental engineering and behavior

modification techniques that are described in other chapters of this volume. Variables correlated with compliance that are not subject to modification, such as demographics and personality considerations, are not addressed.

The prescription to modify health-related behavior commonly involves little more than a health care provider's verbal recommendation (Dyer, Levy, & Dyer, 2005). It is self-evident that if such prescriptions are made without prior consideration of the individual's *capacity* to comply with the prescription, nonadherence is more likely to occur. For example, has the physician assessed the patient's practical understanding of the prescription being made? Do environmental conditions exist in the patient's life such as may be necessary to succeed with the recommended behavior change? It is variables such as these that may play a role in whether the patient leaves the doctor's office and is successful in following through with the behavior change. Some prescribed changes seem fairly simple—such as taking a once-daily medication for hypertension that is inexpensive and free of troublesome side effects. Other health regimens, however, will involve the adoption of far more complex skills—for example, instructing the newly diagnosed patient with diabetes how to make sweeping changes in his or her diet, engage in a wide variety of routine monitoring behaviors (such as blood glucose testing), get regular physical exercise, and start taking self-administered injections that are not only frequent, but are commonly painful as well.

MAJOR THEORIES OF COMPLIANCE

Two prominent theories of compliance are primarily descriptive, process-oriented approaches: the transtheoretical model of behavior change (e.g., DiClemente, 1993) and the relapse prevention model (Marlatt, 1985). The former has encouraged the view that long-term strategies are needed to maintain healthy habits and examines the paths individuals may take in the behavior change process. The latter model recognizes that a range of coping skills are needed to maintain healthy habits and that these skills include unspecified cognitive, emotional, and instrumental behaviors. In addition, we have assessed four theories of compliance that are primarily explanatory models that have helped identify concrete targets for behavioral change: (1) the theories of reasoned action and planned behavior (Fishbein & Ajzen, 1975; Ajzen, 1985); (2) social cognitive theory (Bandura, 1991); (3) modified social learning theory (Wallston, 1992); and (4) the health belief model (Rosenstock, 1991). While each major compliance theory enjoys some empirical support, none provides a comprehensive framework to guide the clinician about what to assess in order to identify targets for enhancement of compliance.

The health compliance model (HCM; Heiby & Carlson, 1986; Heiby, 1986) is a cognitive behavioral approach to compliance prediction built on the principles of psychological behaviorism (Staats, 1975; 1996). Rather than simply cataloging empirically supported correlates, the HCM integrated and classified important variables according to the functional relationships they hold with behavioral outcomes (e.g., compliance behavior). Our more recent review of the compliance literature led to the formulation of a revised health compliance model (HCM-II; Frank, Cho, Heiby, Li, & Lahtela, 2006; Frank, Heiby, & Lee, 2007; Heiby & Lukens, 2006; Heiby, Lukens, & Frank, 2005) by calling upon a principle heuristic of the model as an exhaustive and systematic classifier of functional compliance-related factors. Variables were assessed according to whether they represent *facilitating conditions, discriminative stimuli, consequences,* or one of four somewhat overlapping basic behavioral personality repertoires—*language–cognitive, verbal–emotional, emotional–motivational,* or *sensorimotor.* Each of these theory components has the heuristic value of indicating the type of prevention and intervention technique that is expected to enhance compliance.

Facilitating conditions, discriminative stimuli, and consequences have implications for techniques involving environmental engineering, such as contingency contracting and stimulus control. Language–cognitive variables are conducive to techniques involving changes in knowledge and information processing, such as bibliotherapy and cognitive restructuring. Verbal–emotional variables may respond best to techniques involving manipulation of cognitions that elicit affect, such as self-management and attribution change. Emotional–motivational variables are conducive to techniques that change affective conditioning, such as exposure and systematic desensitization. And finally, sensorimotor variables may respond best to operant techniques, such as shaping and social skills training. In total, assessment of a wide range of situational factors and the behavioral repertoires related to compliance would provide the clinician with additional direction regarding what intervention may be effective given the current environmental circumstances and prior learning history of a particular individual.

GUIDELINES FOR COMPLIANCE ENHANCEMENT

Noncompliance to a medical regimen can be identified based on the following information: (1) self-report (e.g., from rating scales, or self-monitoring logs); (2) health care provider clinical assessments, such as from interviews, objective medical tests (e.g., weight, blood glucose level, and blood pressure), and previous history of adherence to scheduled appointments and prescription refill data; and (3) reports from significant others. Because each of these sources of information is subject to unique measurement error, reliability of identifying noncompliance may be enhanced by use of multimodal assessment. Similarly, because compliance may vary across situations, a time-series approach to assessment may help identify a dynamic relation to causal and maintenance factors.

We have developed a Health Behavior Schedule-II (Frank et al., 2007) which is a 209-item English-language questionnaire designed to assess 45 correlates of compliance to 12 commonly prescribed healthy practices that are conducive to a self-report. The schedule has been translated into German (Lukens, Heiby, Barkhoff, Schlicht, & Rojas, 2006) and Korean (Cho, Hahm, Lee, & Heiby, in press), and there is a form for self-monitoring of blood glucose (Frank, et al., 2006). Each version is available from the first author. Table 20.1 presents 37 correlates of compliance to healthy behaviors derived from the HCM-II and for which interventions have been established for a range of behavioral problems. While only some interventions have been evaluated with compliance to healthy habits, the table provides a guideline for the clinician while we await the development of a taxonomy of problem-specific interventions for medical regimens.

In addition to identifying noncompliance, it is important to also ascertain causal and maintenance factors, which vary not only across individuals but also by the type of medical regimen prescribed. Some medical regimens involve sensorimotor skills most people have already learned, such as swallowing a pill. In such cases, the targets for compliance enhancement would more likely include facilitating conditions and discriminative stimuli (e.g., prompts, instructions), consequences (e.g., cost of the medication, symptom relief), language–cognitive skills (e.g., accurate understanding of instructions and the verbal intention to take the medication), verbal–emotional skills (e.g., perceives self susceptible to severe disease if medication is not taken), and emotional–motivational characteristics (e.g., does not fear effects of medication). However, some medical regimens involve the acquisition of new sensorimotor skills, such as the use a blood pressure cuff or self-injecting medication with a hypodermic needle. Therefore, assessing a range of potential causal and maintenance factors is critical in identifying compliance enhancement programming for a particular client and a particular medical regimen.

The complex and multivariate nature of the HCM-II addresses the evidence that health behavior compliance is a heterogeneous construct (e.g., as argued by Norman & Conner, 1996; Marteau, 1993; Meichenbaum & Turk,

1987; Sobal, Ravicki, & DeForge, 1992). Studies using the Health Behavior Schedule-II (Cho et al., in press; Frank et al., 2006; Frank et al., 2007; Lukens, et al., 2006) found only moderate interrelatedness of compliance to various health habits and a different configuration of predictors for each habit. Overall, findings suggest that individuals do not exhibit uniform healthy lifestyles, but rather may be seen as incorporating a high degree of idiosyncrasy when assessing their unique reasons given for choosing to adhere to particular health behavior prescriptions. The task of promoting patients' successful behavior change must include components of assessment that are often overlooked in today's fast-paced, managed-care-driven health care environment. A renewed emphasis must be placed on compliance promotional efforts that pay close attention to unique differences among the determinants of behavior for an array of health practices, populations, and environments.

AN EXAMPLE OF COMPLIANCE ENHANCEMENT

We provide an example of how the clinician can consider the correlates of compliance to health behaviors and select the techniques of behavior change listed in Table 20.1. For each health behavior, it is important to assess situational factors and behavioral competencies. Please refer to other chapters in this volume for particular guidelines for implementation of the treatment and prevention techniques mentioned in the example.

Let's consider the example of an individual with arthritis who does not comply to a prescription by a rheumatologist to swim at least 30 to 45 minutes at least three times per week in order to prevent heart disease from being sedentary due to joint pain, increase muscle strength around the joints to facilitate maintaining posture, enhance joint flexibility, and reduce joint pain.

First, it is important for the clinician to assess *facilitating conditions* and *discriminative stimuli*, including flexibility in one's schedule; clear information about the reasons to swim; reminders and prompts to go swimming; access to a pool, lake, or ocean; whether there is a contract with another

TABLE 20.1   Compliance Correlates and Related Interventions

Correlates	Interventions
Facilitating conditions and discriminative stimuli	
Schedule permits time for regimen	Functional analysis
	Stimulus control
	Behavioral contracting
Pharmacist educates client with appropriate language and print	Bibliotherapy
Provider educates client	
Provider prompts client (phone calls, e-mails, letters)	Stimulus control
Physical prompts in everyday situations	
Social prompts from family and friends	
Prompts from support groups	
Minimal waiting time for appointments and distance to appointment	Functional analysis
Friendly office staff	Communication training
Provider answers client's questions	
Provider includes client in treatment decisions	
Provider assesses clients understanding of regimen	
Provider requests questions of client	
Provider contracts with client for compliance	Contingency contracting
Provider utilizes history of successful compliance	Generalization training
Consequences–punishments	
Minimize physical discomfort of regimen	Functional analysis
Minimize social embarrassment from regimen	
Minimize financial costs of regimen	
Consequences-reinforcements	
Material rewards for compliance	Contingency contracting and token economy
Symptom relief from regimen	Functional analysis
Social praise for compliance	Positive attention
Language–cognitive behavioral repertoire	
Self-prediction of compliance	Cognitive restructuring
	Self-efficacy enhancement
Knowledge about regimen	Bibliotherapy
Understands providers instructions	
Verbal-emotional behavioral repertoire	
Perceives self as susceptible to severe disease	Attribution change
	Cognitive restructuring
	Harm reduction
	Problem solving
	Relapse prevention
Perceives benefits of compliance	Problem solving
	Cognitive restructuring
Does not avoid knowledge that health is in danger	Acceptance Systematic desensitization
	Cognitive defusion
Focuses on positive sensations	Mindfulness skills
	Self-monitoring
	Self-management
Does not focus on negative sensations	Thought stopping

TABLE 20.1   *(Continued)*

Correlates	Interventions
Emotional–motivational behavioral repertoire	
Compliance elicits positive affect	Self-management
	Emotional regulation skills
Compliance elicits minimum fear and discomfort	Exposure
	Stress management
	Stress inoculation
	Systematic desensitization
Minimum anger over regimen	Anger management
Minimum depression	Self-management
	Cognitive restructuring
	Attribution change
	Assertiveness training
Sensorimotor behavioral repertoire	
Has instrumental skills for regimen	Modeling
	Behavior rehearsal
	Shaping
Uses reminders to comply	Self-management
Is assertive with others who interfere with compliance	Assertiveness training
Schedules time for regimen	Problem-solving
	Self-monitoring
	Self-management

person to swim regularly; and availability of swimming partner. Second, it would be important to assess *consequences*. These might include *punishments* such as discomfort during and after swimming due to lack of endurance and poor form; embarrassment over one's appearance in a swimsuit; and affordability (e.g., club membership and cost of a swimsuit and goggles). They might also include *negative and positive reinforcements*, such as joint pain reduction, relaxation, more energy, and social praise. Third, it would be important to assess *behavioral repertoires*. Assessment of behavioral competencies would include *language–cognitive characteristics* (self-prediction of compliance to regular swimming, knowledge of swimming techniques, and principles of successive approximation to goals), *verbal–emotional characteristics* (perceives swimming will lead to avoidance of muscle atrophy and heart disease, increase in joint flexibility, and reduction of joint pain), *emotional–motivational characteristics* (feels euphoric during and after swimming, feels reduction in joint pain and greater joint flexibility during and after swimming, and has no

fear of drowning or getting chlorinated or salt water in the eyes, ears, and nose during swimming), and *sensorimotor abilities* needed to swim comfortably (ability to stroke, kick, and breathe in the water; selection of goggles that fit; use of reminders to go swimming; assertiveness when one has scheduled a swim but faces pressure to do something else; and managing one's schedule so that there is time for a swim).

These factors can be assessed through a semi-structured interview, questionnaires, self-monitoring, and direct observation. The Health Behavior Schedule-II (Frank et al., 2007) and self-monitoring could be used to assess behavioral competencies. An interview, self-monitoring, and direct observation could be used to assess situational factors. If any of these conditions are lacking, the clinician could enhance compliance by interventions listed in Table 20.1.

For improving facilitating conditions and discriminative stimuli, decreasing punishments, and increasing reinforcement, a functional analysis, stimulus control, behavioral contracting, bibliotherapy, generalization training, and a token economy are expected to be effective. The clinician could help identify what time is available for swimming given the client's other responsibilities and engineer stimuli that prompt swimming at a scheduled time. The clinician could contract with the client to swim as scheduled, provide written information on the reasons and benefits for a person with arthritis to swim, identify past exercise skills that could facilitate the acquisition and successive approximation of a regular swimming schedule, and arrange for material reinforcement when successive goals are met (such as contingent gifts from a friend or spouse). If a swim coach is needed, the clinician could consult with the coach in effective communication with the client (e.g., is friendly, answers questions, and assesses the client's understanding of information conveyed). The clinician could also consult with the rheumatologist to ensure that he or she is communicating the prescription to swim regularly and hydrodynamically. If the client reports an increase in physical discomfort from swimming or a lack of symptom relief, the goals in successive approximation could be adjusted and immediate material and social rewards enhanced by involvement of friends, family, the coach, and physician. If the financial costs of the swimming regimen are burdensome for the client, the clinician could problem-solve how to budget these expenses or find an organization, such as the local chapter of the Arthritis Foundation, to fund them.

To improve behavioral competencies, the clinician could provide techniques that are effective for the deficient repertoire. For language–cognitive deficiencies, cognitive restructuring, self-efficacy training, and bibliotherapy could enhance self-prediction of one's ability to swim regularly and knowledge about how swimming can improve arthritic symptoms if approached in successive steps. For verbal–emotional deficiencies, attributional change, cognitive restructuring, and problem solving can enhance perception that being sedentary increases the severity of the arthritic symptoms and that swimming reduces joint pain and enhances physical and mental energy and joint flexibility. For emotional–motivational *deficiencies*,

self-management training can enhance the use of self-monitoring of the positive effects of swimming and self-reinforcement for attaining one's goals toward compliance. Exposure to swimming and systematic desensitization could reduce fears related to being in the water and the punishing consequences of being embarrassed of one's appearance in a swimsuit. Sensorimotor deficiencies can be addressed by involving a swim coach to provide praise, modeling, shaping, and behavioral rehearsal of swimming skills. Self-management skills could help the client use reminders to swim and engage in self-reinforcement for improvement of swimming skills and adherence to the regimen. Assertiveness training could help the client respond to requests to do something other than go swimming as scheduled. And problem-solving skills could help the client find the time to fit regular swimming into his or her schedule.

As with all interventions, it would be important to monitor the rate of compliance over time and evaluate the effect of treatment upon targeted situational and behavioral factors. Given that compliance tends to decrease over time for most individuals, periodic assessment of the need for further interventions is critical until the behavioral change has stabilized.

References

Ajzen, I. (1985). From intentions to actions: A theory of planned behavior. In J. Kuhl & J. Backmann (Eds.), *Action control: From cognition to behavior* (pp. 11–39). Berlin, Germany: Springer-Verlag.

Bandura, A. (1991). Self-efficacy mechanism in psychological activation and health-promoting behavior. In J. Madden (Ed.), *Neurobiology of learning, emotion and affect* (pp. 229–269). New York: Raven Press.

Christensen, A. J. (2004). Patient adherence to medical treatment regimens:Bridging the gap between behavioral science and biomedicine. New Haven, CT: Yale University Press.

Cho, S., Hahm, J., Lee, J., & Heiby, E.M. (in press). The Korean language version of the Health Behavior Schedule-II as a predictor of compliance. *International Journal of Intercultural Relations*.

Cramer, J. A. (1991). Identifying and improving compliance patterns: A composite plan for health care providers. In J. A. Cramer & B. Spilker (Eds.), *Patient compliance in medical practice and clinical trials* (pp. 387–392). New York: Raven Press.

DiClemente, C. C. (1993). Changing addictive behaviors: A process perspective. *Current Directions in Psychological Science, 2,* 101–106.

Dyer, J. R., Levy, R. M., & Dyer, R. L. (2005). An integrated model for changing patient behavior in primary care. In N. A. Cummings, W. T. O'Donohue, & E. V. Naylor (Eds.), *Psychological approaches to chronic disease management* (pp. 71–86). Reno, NV: Context Press. Fishbein, M., & Ajzen, I. (1975). Belief, attitude, intention, and behavior: An introduction to theory and research. Reading, MA: Addison-Wesley.

Frank, M. T., Cho, S., Heiby, E. M. Li, C. I., & Lahtela, A. L. (2006). The Health Behavior Schedule-II for Diabetes predicts self-monitoring of blood glucose. *International Journal of Behavioral and Consultation Therapy, 2,* 509–517.

Frank, M. R., Heiby, E. M., & Lee, J. H. (2007). Assessment of determinants of compliance to twelve health behaviors: Psychometric evaluation of the Health Behavior Schedule-II. *Psychological Reports, 100,* 1281–1297.

Heiby, E. M. (1986). A paradigmatic behavioral perspective of noncompliance to health regimens. Paper presented at the 94th Convention of the American Psychological Association, Washington, D.C: August 1986.

Heiby, E. M. & Carlson, J. (1986). The Health Compliance Model. *Journal of Compliance in Health Care, l,* 135–156.

Heiby, E. M. & Lukens, C. L. (2006). Identifying and addressing barriers to treatment adherence using behavioral analysis and modification techniques. In W. O'Donohue & E. R. Levensky (Eds.), *Promoting treatment adherence: A practical handbook for health care providers* (pp. 47–68). New York: Sage.

Heiby, E. M., Lukens, C. L., & Frank, M. R. (2005). The Health Compliance Model-II. *The Behavior Analyst Today, 6,* 27–42.

Levant, R. F. (2005). Psychological approaches to the management of health and disease: Health Care for the whole person. In N. A. Cummings, W. T. O'Donohue, & E. V. Naylor (Eds.), *Psychological approaches to chronic disease management* (pp. 37–48). Reno, NV: Context Press.

Marlatt, G. A. (1985). Relapse prevention: Theoretical rational and overview of the model. In

G. A. Marlatt & J. R. Gordon (Eds.), *Relapse prevention: Maintenance strategies in the treatment of addictive behaviors* (pp. 3–70). New York: Guilford.

Marteau, T. M. (1993). Health-related screening: The psychological predictors of uptake and impact. *International Review of Health Psychology, 2,* 149–174.

McGinnis, J. & Foege, W. (1993). Actual causes of deaths in the United States. *Journal of the American Medical Association, 270,* 2207–2212.

Meichenbaum, D., & Turk, D. C. (1987). *Facilitating treatment adherence: A practitioners' guidebook.* New York: Plenum Press.

Myers, L. G., & Midence, K. (1998). Concepts and issues in adherence. In L. B. Myers & K. Midence (Eds.), *Adherence to treatment in medical conditions* (pp. 1–24). Amsterdam: Harwood Academic Publishers.

Norman, P., & Conner, M. (1996). The role of social cognition models in predicting health behaviors: Future directions. In M. Conner & P. Norman (Eds.), *Predicting health behavior: Research and practice with social cognition models* (pp. 197–225). Buckingham, UK: Open University Press.

O'Donohue, W., Naylor, E. V., & Cummings, N. A. (2005). Disease management: Current issues. In N. A. Cummings, W. T. O'Donohue, & E. V. Naylor (Eds.), *Psychological approaches to chronic disease management* (pp. 19–36). Reno, NV: Context Press.

Rosenstock, I. M. (1991). The health belief model: Explaining health behavior through expectancies. In K. Glanz, F. M., Lewis, & B. K. Rimer (Eds.), *Health behavior and health education* (pp. 39–62). San Francisco, CA: Jossey-Bass Publishers.

Sobal, J., Ravicki, D., & DeForge, B. R. (1992). Patterns of interrelationships among health-promotion behaviors. *American Journal of Preventive Medicine, 8,* 351–359.

Staats, A. W. (1975). *Social behaviorism.* Homewood, IL: Dorsey Press.

Staats, A. W. (1996). Behavior and personality: Psychological behaviorism. New York: Springer.

Wallston, K. A. (1992). Hocus-pocus, the focus isn't strictly on locus: Rotter's social learning theory modified for health. *Cognitive Therapy and Research, 16,* 183–199.

21 CONTINGENCY MANAGEMENT INTERVENTIONS

Claudia Drossel, Christina G. Garrison-Diehn, and Jane E. Fisher

Contingency management is a general approach to behavior change that is applicable to clinical problems involving impulsivity or a lack of self-control. Its widest clinical application to date has been in the field of substance use (Sigmon, Dunn, & Higgins, 2007). The purpose of the current chapter is twofold. First, it will elaborate the principles upon which contingency management is based and describe broad guidelines for its use across problem behaviors. At the same time, this chapter will detail contingency management as an intervention for substance use, children's disruptive behavior, and childhood obesity as those are the fields for which most empirical data are available (for reviews, see DuPaul & Eckert, 1997, on attention deficit hyperactivity disorder; see Brownell, 2000, and Epstein, & Wing, 1987, on weight loss; and Lussier, Heil, Mongeon, Badger, & Higgins, 2006, on behavioral medicine).

GENERAL PRINCIPLES OF CONTINGENCY MANAGEMENT

Definitions

People's thoughts, feelings, and behavior are affected by the context within which they occur. For stylistic purposes only, we will omit references to thoughts and feelings from the following descriptions. Note, however, that contexts influence behaviors *and* thoughts and feelings.

Features of the context of behavior can be categorized as:

- *Antecedents:* Those situations in which particular thoughts, feelings, or behaviors have most frequently occurred.

- *Consequences:* The impact that these thoughts, feelings, or behaviors have had on social relationships or other outcomes.

Contingency is the term used for the description of probabilistic relations among behaviors of interest, their antecedents, and their consequences. Contingency management does not assume a "push–pull" or trigger-like cause–effect relationship among antecedents, behavior, and consequences. Rather, it assumes that the probability of behavior is higher in some situations than others and that the context plays either a facilitative or a stifling role.

By definition, facilitative contexts are called *reinforcing*, while contexts that correlate with a reduced frequency of specific behaviors are termed *punishing*. In other words, a person's behavior has a social impact or produces an outcome that, with time, either serves to maintain the behavior and increase its frequency (reinforcement) or to decrease its rate of recurrence (punishment). Note that reinforcement and punishment are strictly defined by their effects on the behavior of interest (thoughts, feelings).

Nested contingencies. Complex human behavior is affected by a multitude of contextual features at any one time. A cigarette smoker's behavior, for example, may be affected by the stimulant effects of nicotine (i.e., reinforcement = increases); avoidance of awkward social situations by joining the smokers' group at social gatherings (i.e., reinforcement = increases); and a spouse's disapproval (i.e., punishment = decreases). For this reason, contingencies can be thought of as "nested." Rather than fitting neatly with each other, such as the progressively smaller wooden Matryoshka dolls, these nested contingencies operate at the same time, overlap, and compete.

Immediate and certain versus delayed and less certain contingencies. In addition to the short-term contingencies that operate on behavior within a relatively small temporal window, there are also temporally remote and probabilistically less certain contingencies. For example, all individuals prefer long-term health to the immediate stimulant effects of smoking. Moreover, the loss of health usually punishes (i.e., decreases the rate of) smoking. However, the consequence of loss of health is remote and uncertain and thereby unable to compete with the immediate and certain reinforcing effects of smoking. When uncertain or remote consequences conflict with local, immediately available consequences, we label human behavior "impulsive" or "lacking self-control" (for a review of the basic research literature and its extension to substance use, see Rachlin, 2000a). Thus, remote and relatively uncertain contingencies—if contacted—would function to *decrease* the rate of the same behavior that locally available contingencies strongly *support*. In another example, remote and relatively less certain consequences—if contacted—could *increase* the rate of the same behavior that is strongly *reduced* by the locally available consequences: For example, overall physical fitness, the long-term relatively less certain outcome, is not able to compete with discomfort and fatigue, the short-term, immediate and certain outcome of initial workouts (for a discussion, see Rachlin, 2003, pp. 193–194). The quandary of discounting remote and uncertain contingencies is ubiquitous in human behavior.

Nonarbitrary versus arbitrary ("prosthetic") contingencies. Given the effects of competing contingencies on human behavior, Contingency management involves arranging arbitrary (prosthetic) contingencies that function as a crutch to assist individuals until their behavior contacts the long-term, delayed, or relatively less certain outcome. A child who is learning to play the piano will not be in touch with the long-term outcome of regular practice. Until the generated music itself reinforces the child's behavior, other ways must be found to maintain the piano practice. Importantly, if the child already has a long history of complying with rules and instructions and contacting delayed and less certain contingencies as a result, additional prosthetic contingencies may be unnecessary. The child does as she is told and reaps the benefits later. However, plenty of individuals do not have a sufficient history of contacting delayed and uncertain reinforcers after complying with instructions. Consequently, prosthetic contingencies are arranged for most learning situations, until skillful behavior itself produces outcomes that in turn reinforce engagement in the behavior. Once the nonarbitrary, remote, and less certain contingencies are affecting behavior, prosthetic contingencies are faded.

Caveats

While reinforcing contingencies maintain and increase the frequency of behavior, punishing contingencies decrease it. Novel behavior (whether learning to play the piano, abstaining from drug use, exercising, eating vegetables or anything else) by definition, *cannot* be shaped with punishment. Yet, many caregivers resort to punishing all behavior except the behavior of interest: To keep a child on homework tasks, for example, a parent may punish any behavior but doing homework. Given the social side effects of punishment (e.g., emotional behavior; deteriorating relationship with the person who implements the contingency; counter-control, including avoidance of the situation, such astermination of services; for a review see Van Houten, 1983), punishment contingencies alone do not serve well as prosthetic contingencies. Accordingly, many classroom-based interventions that penalize students for disruptive behavior do not produce a concurrent increase in academic or social skills (DuPaul & Eckert, 1997). Care must be taken to *reinforce* the behavior of interest (see also Sidman, 1989; and Chapter 55 on punishment).

APPLICATIONS OF CONTINGENCY MANAGEMENT

See Table 21.1 for an overview of Contingency Management.

TABLE 21.1   Applications of Contingency Management

Targets	Examples of Reinforced Behavior	Examples of Reinforcers	References
A. Behavioral Medicine			
1. Adherence to medication regimens: (1) children; (2) adults	(1) Puffs of asthma medication; (2) bottle opening recorded electronically	(1) Token economy (also with punishment procedure (penalty) for failure to adhere); (2) lottery	(1) da Costa, Rapoff, Lemanek, & Goldstein (1997); (2) Rosen et al. (2007)
2. Adherence to protocol implementation	Point-by-point protocol implementation by counselors	Participation in lottery for prizes	Andrzjeweski, Kirby, & Iguchi (2001)
3. Attendance	(1) Attending dental cleanings, testing plaque levels; (2) attending counseling sessions	(1) Fee refunds if dental plaque scores improved; (2) vouchers and prizes	(1) Iwata & Becksfort (1981); (2) Sigmon & Stitzer (2005)
4. Adherence to weight loss program	Physical activity; intake of fruits and vegetables	Social attention and gift certificates	Epstein, Gordy, Raynor, Beddome, Kilanowski, & Paluch (2001)
B. Substance use			
1. Alcohol 2. Cocaine 3. Cocaine and opiates 4. Marijuana 5. Methamphetamine 6. Nicotine 7. Opiates 8. Polydrug use and dual diagnoses	Presenting drug-negative tests (breath carbon monoxide; urinalyses; oral swabs); reducing use as evidenced by tests; participating in goal-related activities (e.g., concerning vocational rehabilitation or skills building); establishing non-using social contacts	Money; participation in lotteries or fishbowl drawings; vouchers, exchangeable for an array of goods and services; prizes; abstinent-contingent housing; abstinent-contingent vocational training	Litt, Kadden, Kabela-Cormier, & Petry (2007) Petry, Alessi, & Hanson (2007) Ghitza et al. (2007) Kadden, Litt, Kabela-Cormier, & Petry (2007) Roll et al. (2006) Lamb et al. (2007) Silverman et al. (1996) Lester et al. (2007); Silverman et al. (2007)
C. Education			
1. Classroom management	(1) Overall noise level lower than specified measure; (2) On-task academic behavior	(1) Token economy, access to or prolonged recess; (2) individualized reinforcers or vouchers	(1) Schmidt & Ulrich (1971); (2) Heering & Wilder (2006)
2. Individual disruptive behavior	Matching performance self-report with teacher's report	Token economy, access to privileges (e.g., leading class to lunch)	Shapiro, DuPaul, & Bradley-Klug (1998)

DESIGNING AN EFFECTIVE CONTINGENCY MANAGEMENT INTERVENTION

Designer Qualifications

Designers must have an understanding of principles of reinforcement, including schedule effects and concurrent contingencies (for a general introduction, see Rachlin, 2000a). They also must be able to conceptualize client behavior within a functional analytic framework (for education-related behavioral patterns, see Greer, 2002; for health-related behavioral patterns, see Bickel & Vuchinich, 2000). Therapists should have an understanding of basic behavioral principles and concepts while following a manualized approach (see Budney & Higgins, 1998, for an exemplary manual). Ideally, the contingency management intervention is based on data from a functional assessment and includes consideration of remote contingencies as well as immediate contingencies (see Drossel, Rummel, & Fisher, in press).

Therapeutic Stance

The therapist's role is analogous to that of a coach who helps define and then supports and facilitates the client's short-term and long-term goals (compare the stance advocated by Miller & Rollnick, 2002). Contingency management requires that the therapist has access to the contingencies and implements them in collaboration with the client. Behavioral contracting (see Chapter 12) is an integral part. It specifies the contingencies and ascertains that the risk of coercion and subsequent avoidance by the client is minimized.

Selecting a Behavioral Target

Programming for success is a hallmark of behavioral interventions. A behavior is chosen if it (1) can be concisely defined and (2) monitored easily. Ambiguity over whether a behavioral target has been accomplished must be minimized to maintain fairness. Moreover, the client must (3) agree to engage in that specific behavior; (4) find it relevant to his or her long-term goals; and (5) be able to accomplish the task in a specified period of time.

Special considerations include:

- *Substance use interventions.* While many of the contingency management interventions rely on the presentation of substance-negative tests for reinforcement, this behavioral target may be unattainable for severe users and result in dropout from treatment (Petry, 2000). Shaping brief initial abstinence periods may be necessary (Lamb, Kirby, Morral, Galbicka, & Iguchi, 2003; see Chapter 66). To facilitate meeting abstinence goals, most contingency management programs implement a concurrent risk analysis involving defining the antecedent situations in which drug use is most likely so the individual may alter or avoid them. Additional interventions often comprise skills building programs that shape alternative repertoires. Indeed, participation in these programs may be one of the target behaviors producing the prosthetic reinforcement (e.g., Iguchi, Belding, Morrel, & Lamb, 1997).
- *Education-based interventions.* Teachers or behavioral consultants usually choose the behaviors targeted for change. Contingency management programs can be designed to affect group or individual behavior in the classroom. If the target is the reduction of disruptive behavior, it is important to find out whether a child's engagement in disruptive behavior is related to academic deficits (see Chapter 32). Any classroom-based intervention to reduce disruptive behavior (e.g., the provision of prizes if noise levels remain low; Schmidt & Ulrich, 1971) should also provide alternative means to obtain the nonarbitrary reinforcers previously contingent on disruption. The goal is to maintain access to teacher attention, yet to make disruptive behavior unnecessary. If the teacher/consultant detects academic skill deficits, the skills themselves must be shaped and reinforced. When skills are present but need "fine-tuning" to meet class standards, alternative target behaviors may be available: Instead of academic target behaviors, Shapiro, DuPaul, & Bradley-Lug (1998) reinforced a match between students' self-reported performance and the teacher's evaluation. They found that academic deficits improved after students with attention-deficit hyperactivity disorder had learned to more accurately assess their performance, a skill that persists across specific tasks. That is, target behaviors may be chosen to facilitate future self-management and decrease reliance on external monitoring.
- *Weight loss interventions.* Access to nutritious food rather than prohibiting food may promote adherence within caloric restriction treatments (Epstein et al., 2001).

Selecting Effective Prosthetic Reinforcers

Martin and Pear (1996) describe reinforcers as "different strokes for different folks" (p. 30). As a general rule, any activity that would occur with a high frequency if the person could access it can be used to reinforce behaviors that occur with a relatively lower frequency ("Premack Principle," p. 32). Once the target behavior has occurred, reinforcer presentations must be *contingent* on the target behavior (ensuring task completion and quality to criterion), *immediate*, and *of appropriate magnitude relative to effort.* The individualized nature of what maintains or increases behavior makes the reinforcer selection a difficult process. To generate flexibility and individualization, token and voucher-based systems are usually implemented. Alternatively, individualized preference assessments may provide information on effective prosthetic reinforcers.

Special considerations include:

- *Substance-use interventions.* Substance use limits the degree to which other events are able to maintain or reinforce behavior (Rachlin, 2000b). Access to money, housing, and work programs has successfully been used to reinforce abstinence (see Table 21.1). While vouchers may be exchanged for social services, transportation, or an array of prizes, leisure-directed reinforcers may have to be reintroduced. Functionally, the narrow range of reinforcers available to substance users may resemble that of individuals with severely depressed behavior (see also the "Pleasant Event Schedule" for suggestions of potentially reinforcing activities; (Lewinsohn, Munoz, Youngren, & Zeiss, 1986). Higgins and colleagues (1991) developed a titrating schedule that systematically increases the magnitude of reinforcement with the time that a substance user has been abstinent (i.e., greater payment for longer durations). However, long durations of abstinence may not be sustainable without skill building and access to alternative, nonarbitrary reinforcers.
- *Education-based interventions.* Guidelines for the selection of reinforcers and their relation to intrinsic motivation are provided by Eisenberger & Cameron (1996). Contingencies that are designed to incorporate the previously listed principles of contingency, immediacy, and sufficient/appropriate magnitude, build (rather than reduce) intrinsic motivation.
- *Weight-loss interventions.* Guidelines for targeting increases in consumption of nutritionally dense healthy foods to promote satiation while simultaneously decreasing intake of low nutrient food are provided by Brownell (2000), Epstein et al. (2001), and Epstein, Myers, Raynor, and Saelens (1998). Contingency management programs that target simultaneous promotion of increases in activity and decreases in sedentary behaviors are associated with greater maintenance of weight loss than caloric restriction interventions alone.

Fading Out Prosthetic Reinforcers

The earlier sections emphasized the building of skills and alternative repertoires. As nonarbitrary remote and less certain contingencies are contacted (e.g., the child enjoys reading his or her first full story; the substance user may reestablish and maintain stable family relationships; an obese person may contact benefits of physical fitness), the prosthetic reinforcers matter less and thus can be faded. Nonarbitrary contingencies need time to gain influence over the person's behavior. There are currently no evidence-based strategies for fading out prosthetic reinforcers.

BARRIERS TO IMPLEMENTATION

A recent cost-effectiveness analysis suggests that high-magnitude reinforcement systems may produce outcomes at a lower per unit cost than low-magnitude systems when duration of abstinence, percentage of treatment completers, and percentage of drug-negative tests are taken into account (Sindelar, Elbel, & Petry, 2007). According to the authors, "society's willingness to pay for incremental gains in effectiveness" (p. 309) may be a major factor determining implementation.

Contingency management is a technique that provides contact with delayed and less certain reinforcement (e.g., long-term health, education, etc.) by building the requisite behavioral patterns through the use of prosthetic reinforcers, counter to the sociocultural expectation that any individual *should* be able to engage in long-term, valued patterns without help. Consequently, many clinicians are reluctant to reinforce the presentation of negative drug tests (Petry, 2007). Stereotypes of impulsive behavior as an index of lack of "willpower" and socially unacceptable "personality" characteristics may generate opposition to the provision of goods and services to reinforce target behaviors. Again, a conflict of long-term and short-term contingencies constitutes the barrier: Clinicians' behavior is not in contact with the delayed and less certain outcome of successful treatment and rather governed by the sociocultural immediate discomfort. To facilitate adherence with a contingency management protocol, Andrzejweski and colleagues (2001) arranged a prize-based contingency management intervention for substance use counselors and, indeed, found that protocol implementation improved when it was supported by immediate and relatively certain contingencies. Similarly supportive strategies might be necessary at least initially, until the effectiveness of the treatment itself convinces counselors, parents, or teachers to continue its application (Petry, 2007).

Suggested Readings

Bickel, W. K., & Vuchinich, R. E. (2000). *Reframing health behavior change with behavioral economics.* Mahwah, NJ: Lawrence Erlbaum Associates.

Budney, A. J., & Higgins, S. T. (1998). *A community reinforcement plus vouchers approach: Treating cocaine addiction.* Rockville, MD: NIDA Publication No. 98-4309, available online at www.nida.nih.gov/TXMANUALS/CRA/CRA1.HTML (accessed January 15, 2008).

Greer, D. R. (2002). *Designing teaching strategies: An applied behavior analysis systems approach.* San Diego, CA: Academic Press.

Higgins, S. T., & Silverman, K. (Eds.) (1999). *Motivating behavior change among illicit drug abusers: Research on contingency management interventions.* Washington, DC: American Psychological Association.

Martin, G., & Pear, J. (1996). *Behavior modification: What it is and how to do it* (5th ed.), Upper Saddle River, NJ: Prentice Hall.

Rachlin, H. (2000a). *The science of self-control.* Cambridge, MA: Harvard University Press.

References

Andrzejewksi, M. E., Kirby, K. C., Morral, A. R., & Iguchi, M. Y. (2001). Technology transfer through performance management: The effects of graphical feedback and positive reinforcement on drug treatment clinicians' behavior. *Drug and Alcohol Dependence, 63,* 179–186.

Brownell, K. (2000). *The LEARN program for weight management 2000.* Dallas, TX: American Health.

Da Costa, I. G., Rapoff, M. A., Lemanek, K., & Goldstein, G. L. (1997). Improving adherence to medication regimens for children with asthma and its effect on clinical outcome. *Journal of Applied Behavior Analysis, 30,* 687–691.

Drossel, C., Rummel, C., & Fisher, J. E. (In press). Functional analysis. In W. O'Donohue & J. Fisher (Eds.), *Principles and techniques of cognitive behavior therapy: An introduction.* Hoboken, NJ: John Wiley.

DuPaul, G. E., & Eckert, T. L. (1997). The effects of school-based interventions for attention deficit hyperactivity disorder. *School Psychology Review, 26*(1), 5–27.

Eisenberger, R., & Cameron, J. (1996). Detrimental effects of reward: Reality or myth? *American Psychologist, 11*(51), 1155–1166.

Epstein, L.H., Gordy, C., Raynor, H., Beddome, M., Kilanowski, C., & Paluch, R. (2001). Increasing fruit and vegetable intake and decreasing fat and sugar intake in families at risk for childhood obesity. *Obesity Research, 9*(3), 171–178.

Epstein, L. H., Myers, M. D., Raynor, H. A., & Saelens, B. E. (1998). Treatment of peditric obesity. *Pediatrics, 101*(3), 554–570.

Epstein, L., & Wing, R. (1987). Behavioral treatment of childhood obesity. *Psychological Bulletin, 101*(3), 331–342.

Ghitza, U. E., Epstein, D. H., Schmittner, J., Vahabzadeh, M., Lin, J.-L., & Preston, K. (2007). Randomized trial of prize-based reinforcement density for simultaneous abstinence from cocaine and heroin. *Journal of Consulting and Clinical Psychology, 75*(5), 765–774.

Heering, P. W., & Wilder, D. A. (2006). The use of dependent group contingencies to increase on-task behavior in two general education classrooms. *Education and Treatment of Children, 29*(3), 459–468.

Higgins, S. T., Delaney, D. D., Budney, A. J., Bickel, W. K., Hughes, J. R., Foerg, F., et al. (1991). A behavioral approach to achieving initial cocaine abstinence. *American Journal of Psychiatry, 148,* 1218–1224.

Iguchi, M. Y., Belding, M. A., Morrel, A. R., & Lamb, R. J. (1997). Reinforcing operants other than abstinence in drug abuse treatment: An effective alternative for reducing drug use. *Journal of Consulting and Clinical Psychology, 65,* 421–428.

Iwata, B. A., & Becksfort, C. M. (1981). Behavioral research in preventive dentistry: Educational and contingency management approaches to the problem of patient compliance. *Journal of Applied Behavior Analysis, 14,* 111–120.

Kadden, R. K., Litt, M. D., Kabela-Cormier, E., & Petry, N. M. (2007). Abstinence rates following behavioral treatments for marijuana dependence. *Addictive Behaviors, 32,* 1220–1236.

Lamb, R. J., Kirby, K. C., Morral, A. R., Galbicka, G., & Iguchi, M. Y. (2004). Improving contingency management programs for addiction. *Addictive Behaviors, 29*(3), 507–523.

Lamb, R. J., Morral, A. R., Kirby, K. C., Javors, M. A., Galbicka, G., & Iguchi, M. (2007). Contingencies for change in complacent smokers. *Experimental and Clinical Psychopharmacology, 15*(3), 245–255.

Lester, K. M., Milby, J. B., Schumacher, J. E., Vuchinich, R., Person, R., & Clay, O. J. (2007). Impact of behavioral contingency management on coping behaviors and PTSD symptom reduction in cocaine-addicted homeless. *Journal of Traumatic Stress, 20*(4), 565–575.

Lewinsohn, P. M., Muñoz, R. F., Youngren, M. A., & Zeiss, A. M. (1992/1986). Control your depression: Reducing depression through learning self-control techniques, relaxation training, pleasant activities, social skills, constructed thinking, planning ahead, and more. New York: Simon & Schuster.

Litt, M. D., Kadden, R. M., Kabela-Cormier, E., & Petry, N. (2007). Changing network support for drinking: Initial findings from the Network Support Project. *Journal of Consulting and Clinical Psychology, 75*(4), 542–555.

Lussier, J. P., Heil, S. H., Mongeon, J. A., Badger, G. J., & Higgins, S. T. (2006). A meta-analysis of voucher-based reinforcement therapy for substance use disorders. *Addiction, 101*, 192–203.

Miller, W. R., & Rollnick, S. (2002). *Motivational interviewing: Preparing people for change* (2nd ed.). New York: Guilford.

Petry, N. M. (2000). A comprehensive guide to the application of contingency management procedures in clinical settings. *Drug and Alcohol Dependence, 58*, 9–25.

Petry, N. M. (2007). Author's reply. *The British Journal of Psychiatry, 190*, 272.

Petry, N. M., Alessi, S. M., & Hanson, T. (2007). Contingency management improves abstinence and quality of life in cocaine abusers. *Journal of Consulting and Clinical Psychology, 75*(2), 307–315.

Rachlin, H. (2000b). The lonely addict. In W. K. Bickel, & R. E. Vuchinich (Eds.), *Reframing health behavior change with behavioral economics* (pp. 145–164). Mahwah, NJ: Lawrence Erlbaum Associates.

Rachlin, H. (2003). Privacy. In K. A. Lattal & P. N. Chase (Eds.), *Behavior Theory and Philosophy* (pp. 187–201). New York: Kluwer Academic/Plenum Publishers.

Roll, J., Petry, N. M., Stitzer, M. L., Brecht, M. L., Peirce, J. M., McCann, M. J., Blaine, J., et al. (2006).

Contingency management for the treatment of methamphetamine use disorders. *American Journal of Psychiatry, 163*, 1993–1999.

Rosen, M. J., Dieckhaus, K., McMahon, T. J., Valdes, B., Petry, N. M., Cramer, J., et al. (2007). Improved adherence with contingency management. *AIDS Patient Care and STDs, 21*(1), 30–40.

Schmidt, G. W., & Ulrich, R. E. (1971). Effects of group contingent events upon classroom noise. In C. E. Pitts (Ed.), *Operant condition in the classroom: Introductory readings in educational psychology*. New York: Thomas Y. Crowell Co.

Shapiro, E. S., DuPaul, G. J., & Bradley-Klug, K. L. (1998). Self-management as a strategy to improve the classroom behavior of adolescents with ADHD. *Journal of Learning Disabilities, 31*, 545–555.

Sidman, M. (1989). *Coercion and its fallout*. Boston, MA: Authors Cooperative, Inc.

Sigmon, S. C., Dunn, K., & Higgins, S. T. (2007). Brief history of the Contingency Management Working Group. *Drug and Alcohol Dependence, 89*, 314–316.

Sigmon, S. C., & Stitzer, M. L. (2005). Use of low-cost incentive intervention to improve counseling attendance among methadone maintained patients. *Journal of Substance Abuse Treatment, 29*(4), 253–258.

Silverman, K., Wong, C. J., Higgins, S. T., Brooner, R. K., Montoya, I. D., Contoreggi, C., et al. (1996). Increasing opiate abstinence through voucher-based reinforcement therapy. *Drug and Alcohol Dependence, 41*(2), 157–165.

Silverman, K., Wong, C. J., Needham, M., Diemer, K. N., Knealing, T., Crone-Todd, D., et al. (2007). A randomized trial of employment-based reinforcement of cocaine abstinence in injection drug users. *Journal of Applied Behavior Analysis, 40*, 387–410.

Sindelar, J., Elbel, B., & Petry, N. M. (2007). What do we get for our money? Cost-effectiveness of adding contingency management. *Addiction, 102*, 309–316.

Van Houten, R. (1983). Punishment: From the animal laboratory to the applied setting. In S. Axelrod & J. Apsche (Eds.), *The effects of punishment on human behavior*. New York: Academic Press.

22 DAILY BEHAVIOR REPORT CARDS: HOME–SCHOOL CONTINGENCY MANAGEMENT PROCEDURES

Mary Lou Kelley and Jennette L. Palcic

Behavior therapists have long relied on parents and teachers to employ interventions with children. Parents and teachers have used a variety of contingency management procedures to improve compliance, task engagement, and rule following, and for decreasing aggressive, disruptive, and disrespectful behavior. With regard to improving classroom behavior, the vast majority of studies have relied on teachers as the sole agent of change (Cohen & Fish, 1993). In the 1990s, however, collaboration between parents and teachers to improve children's classroom behavior gained increasing support in the literature (Kelley & McCain, 1995; Rhodes & Kratochwill, 1998; Rosen, Gabardi, Miller, & Miller, 1990). In part, increased parental involvement in promoting children's success in school is due to changing legal requirements and philosophical perspectives (Christenson, Hurley, Sheridan, & Fenstermacher, 1997). For example, P.L. 94–142 emphasizes teachers' legal and professional obligation to include parents in the educational process.

Although home–school collaboration is heralded in the literature, the natural environment presents many obstacles to establishing effective programs for improving academic behavior and classroom performance (Kelley, 1990). For example, a common practice is for parents to receive intermittent, negative feedback about their children. This may lead parents to avoid involvement or to become discouraged about their ability to impact the child's school behavior. Teachers and parents often disagree on the causes and solutions to problems. They may see one another as indifferent, unresponsive, or irresponsible. Finally, teachers may feel that they do not have the time for regular communication with parents given the demands of classroom instruction and management. Evans and colleagues (1993) demonstrated that just by increasing communication between teachers and parents, teachers reported an improvement in the targeted behaviors.

Daily report cards (or school–home notes) require teachers to evaluate children daily and parents to provide consequences based on the resulting data. An example of a daily report card note is seen in Table 22.1. The intervention often serves to improve parent–teacher communication and problem solving. Intervention effects are often quite substantial in spite of a great deal of variability in the specificity of target behaviors, evaluation methods, and reinforcement procedures. The procedure has been successfully used with individual students (Jurbergs, Palcic, & Kelley, 2007b) as well as entire classrooms of students (Lahey et al., 1977).

Daily report cards have proven effective in reducing a variety of children's problematic behavior, including inattention, disruptive classroom behavior, lack of classwork or homework completion, talking without permission, aggression, and poor social skills (Blechman, Kotanchik, & Taylor, 1981; Kelley, 1990; Seay, Fee, Holloway, & Giesen, 2003). The procedure has also been used successfully with children in special education classrooms to improve classroom behavior and academic performance (Dolliver, Lewis, & McLaughlin, 1985). Although the majority of studies target externalizing behavior problems or task engagement, they can be used as a treatment component for strengthening desired behaviors that are inhibited by anxiety; examples include

TABLE 22.1   Example of a School–Home Note

School–Home Note			
Name:_____ Date:_____			

Reading

Prepared for Class	Yes	So-So	No
Used Time Wisely	Yes	So-So	No
Handed in Homework	Yes	So-So	No

Comments:

Math

Prepared for Class	Yes	So-So	No
Used Time Wisely	Yes	So-So	No
Handed in Homework	Yes	So-So	No

Comments:

Recess

Played without hitting	Yes	No

Comments:

Language Arts

Prepared for Class	Yes	So-So	No
Used Time Wisely	Yes	So-So	No
Handed in Homework	Yes	So-So	No

Comments:

Consequences provided by parents at home:

Parent questions/concerns:

completing schoolwork without crying for a school-phobic child and talking in a loud voice for a shy or selectively mute child.

Home-based reinforcement of classroom behavior has been employed with children of varied ages. For example, the procedure has been shown to be effective in increasing task engagement and decreasing disruptive behavior in a preschooler with Aattention-Ddeficit Hhyperactivity Ddisorder (ADHD; McCain & Kelley, 1993); increasing attention and classroom accuracy and productivity in elementary school-aged children (Kelley & McCain, 1995); increasing academic performance and reducing disruptiveness in elementary school-aged children (Witt, Hannafin, & Martens, 1983); and reducing disruptive behavior in junior high school-aged students (Rosen et al., 1990). Some studies have shown that the behavior of high school students was improved through the use of daily report cards.

In a typical daily report card intervention, students are evaluated at intervals throughout the day on a number of behavioral dimensions. Parents provide consequences on a daily basis based on the student's evaluation. For example, McCain and Kelley (1994) required teachers to evaluate whether the student's classwork was completed correctly and whether they used class time well by circling "yes," "so-so," or "no" on the daily report card. The operational definition of each evaluative category was determined by the teacher's subjective perception, although examples and nonexamples were discussed (Kelley, 1990).

Most studies provide rewards based on positive behavior. However, two studies evaluated the additive effects of including response cost procedures to the effectiveness of a daily report card (Kelley & McCain, 1995; McCain & Kelley, 1994). On "No Response Cost" days, students were evaluated in the manner described above (McCain & Kelley, 1994). Report cards on "Response Cost" days had the addition of a series of happy faces. A face was crossed out by the teacher each time the child was corrected or redirected. Using a reversal design with alternating treatments, the effect of adding response cost was equal to or greater than the impact of the traditional note alone. Jurbergs, Palcic, and Kelley (2007b) compared the effectiveness of similar school-home notes with and without response cost in improving the classroom performance of six African-American first and second graders from low-income households, who also were diagnosed with ADHD. Both on-task classroom behavior and academic productivity improved for all participants during treatment phases. In addition, accurate classwork completion increased significantly. However, the response cost component did not demonstrate added benefit over the traditional daily report card. The response cost component was more effective in improving behavior for two participants, while the no response cost note was more effective for one participant. The other three, however, showed no differential effectiveness of the two treatments.

More recently, Jurbergs, Palcic, and Kelley (2007a) evaluated whether parent-delivered consequences are essential to the effectiveness of a daily report card or whether teacher evaluation and feedback only lead to improved behavior.

The effectiveness of a note with parent-delivered consequences was compared to a note with teacher feedback and no parent-delivered consequences. The study evaluated the on-task behavior of 43 African-American, low-income first through third graders with ADHD. The results indicated that the school–home note with home-based consequences was superior to teacher feedback, although both were significantly more effective than no treatment.

Palcic, Jurbergs, and Kelley (2007) compared the efficacy of a daily report card with parent-provided consequences to a daily report card with classroom based consequences. The notes and evaluation criteria were the same in both groups. The subjects were low-income African-American children with ADHD. Results indicated that the two interventions were equally effective in improving children's classroom attentiveness and classwork productivity, suggesting that classroom-based rewards may be substituted for home-based rewards when parents are unable to provide consistent consequences.

The comprehensiveness of school–home notes has ranged considerably. Some studies evaluated student behavior during a specific time of day (e.g., nap time, lunchtime, math class). Other studies broke the day down into a number of intervals and evaluated student behavior throughout the day (Schumaker, Hovell, & Sherman, 1977).

Consequences earned by children for improved or satisfactory behavior are varied. Consequences generally are positive and include tangible rewards and activities that children can enjoy that day after school. Praise alone is generally not an adequate consequence for increasing appropriate classroom behavior (Rosen, O'Leary, Joyce, Conway, & Pfiffner, 1984). Often the child's school day is broken down into specific classes or activities such as recess or reading. Rewards provided by parents typically include activities readily available to the family and may include access to electronics such as computer, video games, or television.

Although school–home notes typically are the source of data in determining rewards for desired classroom behavior, the information provided to parents on a daily basis can serve other valuable functions. School–home notes can also be used to inform parents about a child's progress in alternative therapies and programs. For example, the data from a school–home note are helpful in evaluating the effects and side effects of medication in children with ADHD (Pelham, 2001). The communication of brief, specific information from teacher to parent can help parents and children plan for the next school day. For instance, a few comments on a note can facilitate test preparation or problem solving regarding an issue that occurred during the day. Thus, school–home notes often convey very useful information to parents and professionals involved with the child regarding behavior trends, ancillary intervention effects, and specific problem incidents.

TREATMENT ACCEPTABILITY

The treatment acceptability of daily report cards has been examined by several studies. Daily report cards consistently are rated by teachers as being a highly acceptable intervention for managing students' classroom behavior (Chafouleas, Riley-Tillman, & Sassu, 2006; Jurbergs et al., 2007b; Pisecco, Huzinec, & Curtis, 2001). When compared to medication, teachers report that school–home notes work just as quickly as medication, but are a more acceptable form of intervention (Pisecco et al., 2001). Researchers have also found daily report cards may be preferable to response cost interventions (Pisecco et al., 2001), however, when combined with the school—home note intervention, teachers prefer school–home notes with response cost over notes without (Jurbergs et al., 2007b). Additionally, daily report cards with parent-delivered consequences were preferred over those without (Jurbergs et al., 2007a).

FOR WHOM IS THE INTERVENTION APPROPRIATE?

Daily report cards can be a useful and effective treatment whenever children will benefit from home-based rewards for appropriate classroom behavior and increased parent involvement and parent-teacher collaboration. In order for the use of notes to be effective and appropriate, parents must be willing and able to provide positive consequences for appropriate behavior on a daily basis and in a consistent manner. Though most research regarding the use of daily report cards has been conducted with middle-class families (Ayllon, Garber, & Pisor, 1975; Kelley & McCain, 1995; McCain & Kelley, 1994), recent studies have shown that school–home notes can be also an effective intervention with low-income families (Jurbergs et al., 2007a, 2007b; Palcic et al., 2007). The procedure works best with cooperative teachers who have a positive attitude, structured routines, and effective classroom management skills. Children must be able to respond to delayed reinforcement and home-based consequences.

Contraindications of the Intervention

The procedure generally is not recommended with parents who have significant functional impairment or with parents who are likely to use the procedure in a negative, erratic, or abusive manner. For example, the procedure is unlikely to succeed with disorganized, unstructured, or lax parents. Likewise, school–home notes should not be used if the child's teacher is resistant or is likely to use the intervention negatively rather than in a supportive and positive manner. With regard to child characteristics, school-home notes will be ineffective if children do not have the skills to perform the desired behaviors or if the target behavior cannot be influenced by parental consequence. However, the note may be used along with school-based consequences when delay of reinforcement appears to impede effectiveness (Palcic et al., 2007). The intervention also may be ineffective with children who are depressed or who have serious emotional or behavior problems. However, information from a daily report card may be a useful component in a comprehensive treatment program when parental involvement helps children perform better in the classroom. Sometimes implementation of a daily report card may serve to accentuate the need for alternative placement, treatments, or services.

Assessment Considerations

As with any other behavioral procedure, an appropriate assessment of the child and his or her family and classroom setting must be conducted prior to using a school-home note. Assessment commonly begins with and initial interview with the parent or teacher who initiated the referral. Assessment procedures are detailed elsewhere (Kelley, 1990), and I will only briefly review them here. It is recommended that parents, teachers, and the child be interviewed where possible to develop a list of academic and behavioral strengths and weaknesses and to identify specific target behaviors. In addition, a thorough developmental history should be obtained from a parent or guardian that includes a history of physical, social, and academic skill development. Interviewees should be asked about any emotional or behavioral problems the child might be experiencing. Parents should be screened for psychopathology and family stressors during the interviews and indications of such need to be considered.

Psychometrically sound, norm-referenced questionnaires should be obtained from the parents and the teacher(s) and the child when age appropriate. Questionnaires should be used to screen for internalizing and externalizing behavior and emotional problems for assessing the severity of symptoms. It is recommended that the clinician use a broadband, multi-informant measure such as the Child Behavior Checklist (Achenbach & Rescorla, 2001) or the Behavior Assessment System for Children (Reynolds & Kamphaus, 2004). Supplementary measures for assessing specific areas such as depression, anxiety, or ADHD may be administered where indicted. Finally, a review of the child's grades and achievement test scores should be conducted and any concerns about academic abilities addressed through norm-referenced or curriculum-based assessment.

It is very helpful to conduct a school observation in order to evaluate the child's placement in the classroom, his or her behavior, and the responses of others to the child's behavior. This information is very helpful in developing appropriate target behaviors to be included in the school–home note. The ultimate assessment question to be answered is whether a school–home note is likely to be effective and appropriate treatment. This question can be answered by defining the specific behaviors to increase or decrease and by determining whether the child is able to perform the desired behaviors and respond to parent-based rewards, whether the teacher will provide feedback fairly and consistently, and whether the parents can reliably provide consequences that alter the frequency of target behaviors in desired ways.

HOW DOES THE INTERVENTION WORK?

Parents, teachers, and usually a consultant, such as a psychologist, collaboratively select target behaviors reflective of desired change in specific situations. The daily report card is constructed with the day divided into intervals of time or specific settings, such as recess, math class, English class, or center time. Teachers evaluate student behavior throughout the day on the note. Children are provided feedback from their teacher regarding their daily performance and bring the note home to review with their parents. Parents discuss the data on the note with their children, with the emphasis on positive changes in behavior. Negative evaluations are discussed within a problem-solving context. For example, when a child brings home a "no" rating in an area such as "prepared for class," parents are encouraged to discuss with their child possible solutions for preventing the problem in the future. Finally, predetermined consequences are provided by parents daily. Consequences are generated by parents with input from their child, usually with professional guidance.

STEPS TO DEVELOPING AND USING A SCHOOL–HOME NOTE

The following sections describe in detail the steps to developing and using a daily report card and are shown in Table 22.2.

TABLE 22.2   Key Points: Steps to Using a Daily Report Card

1. Discuss the possible use of the intervention with parents and teachers.
2. Determine target behaviors to increase or decrease that are specific to the setting.
3. Divide the day into small units of time.
4. Determine anchors for evaluating behavior during the day.
5. Design an attractive, uncluttered, and developmentally appropriate note.
6. Discuss the intervention with the child prior to beginning.
7. Determine contingencies of reinforcement.
8. Begin using the note to establish baseline levels of behavior.
9. Review the completed note daily with the child.
10. Provide promised consequences.
11. Provide follow-up session to monitor effectiveness.

Step One: Discuss the Intervention with Parents and Teachers

When it is determined that a daily report card may be an effective intervention for improving a child's classroom behavior, the idea should be presented to the parents and teachers. During this meeting the overall procedure is presented along with the rationale for its use, and the likely outcomes are discussed. Concerns are addressed and the responsibilities of each involved person delineated. Children are usually responsible for remembering to get the note completed each day. However, I ask teachers to prompt children, especially in the beginning. Although it is often best to meet jointly with parents and teachers, separate meetings can be conducted, and sometimes telephone consultation with the teacher is adequate for developing the target behaviors. When parents and teachers have already established good, effective communication, parents can sometimes present the idea to the teacher along with sample school–home notes and handouts on the use of the procedure.

Step Two: Determine Target Behaviors

Selecting relevant, socially valid target behaviors is critical to the success of the daily report cards. Behaviors important to the child's academic and social success should be chosen. In general, academic products such as "completed classwork" or component behaviors such as "followed directions" or "prepared for class" should be chosen over process behaviors such as "paid attention." Although classroom conduct behaviors such as "talked only with permission" or "kept hands to self" are often included as target behaviors, it is recommended that academic–related behaviors always be included because these behaviors often lead to improved conduct. Whenever possible, target behaviors should be defined in terms of behaviors to increase rather than decrease. The written definition should be as specific as possible. Examples of common target behaviors in addition to those mentioned above include "used time wisely," "handed in homework," "participated in class discussion," "played nicely with peers," and "followed class rules." After target behaviors are determined, the behaviors should be defined and examples and non-examples of the behaviors should be discussed with the teacher, parent, and eventually the child. Target behaviors may vary as a function of the specific setting. For example, young children may have group activities or independent seatwork at different times of the day, and appropriate targets vary across those settings.

Step Three: Determine Settings and Evaluative Criteria

Generally, school–home notes are used to evaluate children's behavior throughout the day. Like other behavioral interventions, daily report cards should provide information about specific behavior in specific settings. Thus, it is recommended that the child's school day be divided into relatively small, naturally occurring units of time. For example, the day may be divided into class periods such as math, reading, language arts, science, and social studies. For some children, the periods may include those in which it is important to improve behavior.

As seen in Table 22.1, each behavior is evaluated according to certain criteria. Although only a single word anchor is provided for different criteria on the school–home note, each possible rating (yes, so-so, no) is defined in more detail and later explained to the child.

Step Four: Design the Card

As seen in the example, the card should have a place for the child's name, the date, and each setting with the target behaviors and evaluation criteria listed. A place for the teacher's and parent's comments should be included. The note can be designed by a professional, the parents, or the teacher. It is recommended that numerous examples be provided, including definitions of target behaviors, to serve as a guide. In order to reduce the number of papers the child must handle daily, the child can be provided with a daily assignment book containing large squares for recording homework assignments. A teacher planner is ideal for this purpose. Target behaviors such as "handed in homework" are stamped in the square for the teacher to complete. Stamps can be made at most office supply stores. Many examples of school–home notes are available in Kelley (1990) and Barkley (1996). Handouts detailing the use of a daily report card are provided in Kelley (1990).

Step Five: Prepare the Child

Prior to beginning, the intervention should be thoroughly explained to the child. With some children it is helpful to include them in the selection of the target behaviors and the design of the note. The child, parent, and teacher responsibilities should be determined and consequences discussed. The child should be told that the school–home note is to help the parent be more effective and that the increased feedback will help the child learn about his teacher's perceptions of his behavior. By the time a daily report card system is initiated, the parent–child relationship often is strained and quite negative with regard to discussions about school performance. It is recommended that professionals emphasize to parents that the school-home note will provide them with more complete and positive information on their child's daily behavior. This can also help reduce parents' excessive questioning about school performance. Some children are embarrassed about being singled out. These concerns should be addressed and discussed. Methods of using the procedure discreetly can be arranged and the child's self-consciousness discussed with the teacher.

Step Six: Determine Rewards

The parent and child should discuss possible daily and weekly rewards. Often, rewards include the activities that the child now enjoys in the evening, such as use of the computer, PlayStation, telephone, or television. In addition, it is recommended that an additional reward such as money, extra time watching TV, special time with Mom or Dad, or other desired consequences be included as well so children do not simply feel punished when they do not earn rewards. In many cases, use of a school–home note is well received by a child because activities that had been taken away for extended periods of time due to poor school performance are reinstated. Sometimes predetermined sanctions, such as writing an age-appropriate essay discussing how the child can avoid misbehaving the next day or performing an extra chore, are helpful when children appear to be poorly motivated to put forth effort to improve their school performance (Longanecker & O'Neill, 1990). Specific criteria for earning consequences should be written in a contract and signed by the parent and child.

Step Seven: Begin Using the Note

When first beginning the daily report card program, thoroughly review the procedures with the child. The note can be provided by either the parent or the teacher. However, it is recommended that the professional working with the family and school or the parent make copies for 2 weeks and place the copies in a notebook. In this way parents, teachers, and assisting professionals can review previous notes and make comments on the note to be used the next day. Use of a colorful notebook makes it easy for all to find. In the beginning, children are rewarded simply for bringing the note home after it is completed by the teacher. In this way, baseline rates can be used to establish appropriate levels of behavior for earning rewards.

Step Eight: Review the Note with the Child

Parents should be encouraged to be review the note with the child each day. Encourage the parent to start at the beginning of the note and proceed through the sequence of the day. In this way all aspects of the child's day are reviewed, and parents will be discouraged from overly focusing on negative behavior. Recommend to parents that they spend equal amounts of time discussing positive and negative behavior. Children can learn as much from discussing what they did well and how to repeat the performance the next day as they can from discussing ways to improve their behavior in a specific situation. Because consequences for behavior are already determined, this does not need to be discussed on a nightly basis.

Step Nine: Provide Promised Consequences

Parents should be encouraged to provide consequences as promised. It is helpful to have the parents record the consequences provided on the daily report card so that teachers are reassured about parent follow-through and the therapist can review the notes and parent-delivered consequences with the family.

Step Ten: Provide Follow-up to Assess Effectiveness

It is critical to review the completed notes with the parent and child to assess effectiveness. It is recommended that a follow-up session with the parent and child to assess effectiveness be conducted within 2 weeks, and preferably within 1 week, of beginning the intervention. Trends in behavior should be discussed, and the methods that were used to improve behavior should be outlined. For example, the therapist should discuss with the child positive days or parts of days as well as days that were not so positive and any obstacles in the classroom that impeded behavior change. The therapist should also review whether the intervention has been implemented with integrity. The follow-up session is a good opportunity to determine criteria for earning rewards. Many times, the earning of no more than a specific number of "no" ratings on the school–home note is an easy-to-understand criterion.

Use of a school–home note frequently leads to improved behavior, more effective parent involvement, and reduced conflict. When ineffective, the therapist should reassess the appropriateness of the target behaviors and other factors, such as academic skill level, that may be impeding success. It may be that alternative or additional interventions are needed. For example, for children with ADHD, the school–home note may improve behavior but not to desired levels. Parents who had hoped to avoid medication may feel differently when they see the limitation of a behavioral intervention.

Step Eleven: Fade the Note as Behavior Improves

Notes can be faded as the child consistently demonstrates acceptable behavior. I recommend fading the amount of feedback per interval or the number of intervals before fading to a weekly note without deterioration in the behavior. Children with ADHD may require the added parent involvement, structure, and external consequences provided by school–home notes in order to maintain appropriate behavior.

References

Achenbach, T. M., & Rescorla, L. A. (2001). *Manual for ASEBA School-Age Forms & Profiles*. Burlington, VT: University of Vermont, Research for Children, Youth, & Families.

Ayllon, T., Garber, S., & Pisor, K. (1975). The elimination of discipline problems through a combined school–home motivational system.. *Behavior Therapy, 6*, 616–626.

Barkley, R. (1996). Using a daily school-behavior report card. *ADHD Report, 4*(6), 1–2, 13–15.

Blechman, E. A., Kotanchik, N. L., & Taylor, C. J. (1981). Families and schools together: Early behavioral intervention with high risk children. *Behavior Therapy, 12*, 308–319.

Chafouleas, S. M., Riley-Tillman, T. C., & Sassu, K. A. (2006). Acceptability and reported use of daily behavior report cards among teachers. *Journal of Positive Behavior Interventions, 8*(3), 174–182.

Christenson, S. L., Hurley, C. M., Sheridan, S. M., & Fenstermacher, K. (1997). Parents' and school psychologists' perspective on parent involvement activities. *School Psychology Review, 26*(1), 111–130.

Cohen, J. J., & Fish, M. C. (1993). Handbook of school-based interventions: Resolving student problems and promoting healthy educational environments. California: Josey-Bass.

Dolliver, P., Lewis, A. F., & McLaughlin, T. F. (1985). Effects of a daily behvior report card on academic performance and classroom behavior. *Remedial & Special Education, 6*(1), 51–52.

Evans, I. M., Okifuji, A., Engler, L., Bromley, K., & Tishelman, A. (1993). Home–school communication in the treatment of childhood behavior problems. *Child & Family Behavior Therapy, 15*(2), 37–60.

Jurbergs, N., Palcic, J. L., & Kelley, M. L. (2007a). Daily behavior report cards with and without home-based consequences: Improving classroom behavior in low-income, African American children with ADHD. Manuscript submitted for publication.

Jurbergs, N., Palcic, J. L., & Kelley, M. L. (2007b). School-home notes with and without response cost: Increasing attention and academic performance in low-income children with attention-deficit/hyperactivity disorder. *School Psychology Quarterly, 22*(3), 358–379.

Kelley, M. L. (1990). School-home notes: Promoting children's classroom success. New York: Guilford.

Kelley, M. L., & McCain, A. P. (1995). Promoting academic performance in inattentive children: The relative efficacy of school–home notes with and without response cost. *Behavior Modification, 19*(3), 357–375.

Lahey, B. B., Gendrich, J. G., Gendrich, S. I., Schnelle, J. F., Grant, D. S., & McNees, M. P. (1977). An evaluation of daily report cards with minimal teacher and parent contacts as an efficient method of classroom intervention. *Behavior Modification, 1*(3), 381–394.

Longanecker, E. F., & O'Neill, W. J. (1990). Mediation essay: A cognitive–behavioral discipline strategy. *National Forum of Applied Educational Research Journal, 2*(2), 53–58.

McCain, A. P., & Kelley, M. L. (1993). Managing the classroom behavior of an ADHD preschooler: The efficacy of a school–home note intervention. *Child & Family Behavior Therapy, 15*(3), 33–44.

McCain, A. P., & Kelley, M. L. (1994). Improving classroom performance in underachieving preadolescents: The additive effects of response cost to a school–home note system. *Child & Family Behavior Therapy, 16*(2), 27–41.

Palcic, J. L., Jurbergs, N., & Kelley, M. L. (2007). A comparison of teacher and parent delivered consequences: Improving classroom behavior in African American children with ADHD. Manuscript submitted for publication.

Pelham, W. E. (2001). ADHD and behavioral modification. *Drug Benefit Trends, 13*(suppl. C), 11–14.

Pisecco, S., Huzinec, C., & Curtis, D. (2001). The effect of child characteristics on teachers' acceptability of classroom-based behavioral strategies and psychostimulant mediction for the treatment of ADHD. *Journal of Clinical Child Psychology, 30*(3), 413–421.

Reynolds, C., & Kamphaus, R. (2004). *Behavior Assessment System for Children*, 2nd ed. (BASC-2). Circle Pines, MN: American Guidance Service.

Rhodes, M. M., & Kratochwill, T. R. (1998). Parent training and consultation: An analysis of a homework intervention program. *School Psychology Quarterly, 13*(3), 241–264.

Rosen, L. A., Gabardi, C., Miller, D., & Miller, L. (1990). Home-based treatment of disruptive junior high school students: An analysis of the differential effects of positive and negative consequences. *Behavioral Disorders, 15*(4), 227–232.

Rosen, L. A., O'Leary, S. G., Joyce, S. A., Conway, G., & Pfiffner, L. J. (1984). The importance of prudent negative consequences for maintaining the appropriate behavior of hyperactive students. *Journal of Abnormal Child Psychology, 12,* 581–604.

Schumaker, J. B., Hovell, M. F., & Sherman, J. A. (1977). Analysis of daily report cards and parent managed privileges in the improvement of adolescents' classroom performance. *Journal of Applied Behavior Analysis, 10,* 449–464.

Seay, H. A., Fee, V. E., Holloway, K. S., & Giesen, J. M. (2003). A multicomponent treatment package to increase anger control in teacher-referred boys. *Child & Family Behavior Therapy, 25*(1), 1–18.

Witt, J. C., Hannafin, M. J., & Martens, B. K. (1983). Home-based reinforcement: Behavioral covariation between academic performance and inappropriate behavior. *Journal of School Psychology, 21,* 337–348.

DIALECTICS IN COGNITIVE AND BEHAVIOR THERAPY

Armida Rubio Fruzzetti and Alan E. Fruzzetti

"All true thoughts come from the heart."
—Chinese fortune cookie

"The opposite of a correct statement is a false statement. But the opposite of a profound truth may well be another profound truth."
—Physicist Niels Bohr

The term *dialectics* has many meanings in philosophy, history, politics, literature, and in psychotherapy. For purposes of this chapter, *dialectics* refers primarily to a set of interventions that instantiate modern cognitive and behavior therapy's embrace of both acceptance and change as important treatment strategies. Dialectical behavior therapy (DBT; Linehan, 1993), in particular, is predicated on a dialectical worldview and embraces a dialectical approach to intervention. However, an increasing number of other cognitive and behavioral therapies now utilize interventions and conceptual frameworks that may be considered dialectical. For example, many empirically supported modern cognitive behavior therapy (CBT) approaches overtly emphasize a dialectical synthesis of both acceptance and change, including acceptance and commitment therapy (ACT; Hayes, Stoshahl, & Wilson, 1999); integrative behavioral couple therapy (Jacobson & Christensen, 1996); relapse prevention for substance abuse (Marlatt & Donovan, 2005); mindfulness-based cognitive therapy (Segal, Williams, & Teasdale, 2002); CBT for anxiety disorders (Borkovec & Sharpless, 2004; Roemer & Orsillo, 2002); CBT for eating disorders (Wilson, 1996), and functional analytic psychotherapy (Kohlenberg and Tsai, 1991). This chapter will focus both on the application of the broad acceptance and change dialectic in general as well as on a variety of specific dialectical strategies and interventions found in modern cognitive and behavior therapy.

DIALECTICS IN COGNITIVE AND BEHAVIOR THERAPY

The primary dialectic in psychotherapy is that of acceptance and change. Tension often occurs in psychotherapy between acceptance-oriented strategies and targets and change-oriented strategies and targets: Patients and therapists want to promote change (e.g., enhance potential, reduce suffering) *and* at the same time the therapist needs to understand and accept the suffering, difficulties and potential limitations of the client, and the client similarly needs to accept his or her own experiences and worth. Therapies often align themselves along these apparent polarities, focusing more on acceptance (caring, warmth, support, being nondirective) or on change (identifying targets for improvement, changing thoughts, emotions, or actions, being directive). However, focusing only on change or only on acceptance may not be as helpful as integrating or synthesizing both. For example, a humanistic approach can represent the acceptance polarity and traditional behavior therapy can represent the change polarity. A dialectical approach is not neutral or in the middle between these poles, but rather offers a synthesis of these polarities: Both strong acceptance and strong change interventions are employed simultaneously, both as treatment strategies and as targets for client behavior.

Historically, dialectics provided a rationale for adding together and then synthesizing acceptance strategies (such as validating emotions, suffering, thoughts, etc.) with procedures to change behaviors and reduce problem behaviors (e.g., decreasing suicidal or crisis behaviors, reducing aversive emotional arousal such as panic or depression, etc., via skill training, stimulus control, exposure, cognitive restructuring, or contingency management). The prototype for this kind of synthesis is dialectical behavior therapy (DBT; Linehan, 1993). Dialectical principles in DBT were derived and adapted from both Western contemplative and Eastern meditative practices as well as from dialectical philosophy (Gollobin, 1986; Linehan, 1993; Pinkard, 1988), and are generally consistent with Western existential thinking applied to psychology (e.g., Binswanger, 1963). Theoretically, dialectics in CBT or DBT refers to an understanding of the nature of reality, the process of behavior change, the way that reality changes depending on the perspective employed, and to a method of engaging in persuasion (e.g., between therapist and client, therapist and treatment team), providing both an ontological and an epistemological framework for the theory and the treatment. The dialectical position informs specific applications or intervention strategies, as well as treatment targets. Consequently, dialectical interventions may be beneficial to any cognitive behavioral therapist who seeks to utilize the full acceptance–change continuum.

WHO MIGHT BENEFIT FROM DIALECTICAL STRATEGIES

Utilizing a dialectical approach provides a framework for treatment, not just a specific set of techniques. Although techniques from other therapies often illustrate only one side of the dialectic, many therapeutic approaches employ some techniques from both acceptance- and change-oriented perspectives. Of course, utilizing a dialectical approach requires the inclusion of both sides, and may be useful throughout CBT.

Evidence-Based Applications

Dialectics have been utilized, in particular in DBT, with clients meeting criteria for borderline personality disorder (who also have multiple co-occurring problems) and for other multiproblem "difficult to treat" populations (see Robbins & Chapman, 2004, or Feigenbaum, 2007 for reviews of DBT research). However, throughout CBT, a more dialectical approach (acceptance and change) has been employed in recent years to augment cognitive and behavior therapy's traditional emphasis on change. This "third wave" of behavior therapy has, in fact, had an important impact on how CBT is practiced across most modes of CBT and for most presenting problems, and there is growing evidence to support the utility of adding acceptance interventions to traditional change-oriented treatments (Fruzzetti & Erikson, in press). For example, acceptance strategies (mindfulness) have been added, with improved outcomes, to more traditional CBT change-oriented approaches to depression (e.g., Segal, Teasdale, Williams, et al., 2000), eating disorders (Wilson, 1996), and chronic pain management (Kabat-Zinn, Lipworth, & Burney, 1985), and DBT has been shown to be more effective than alternatives relying more exclusively on acceptance interventions (Linehan, et al., 2002; Turner, 2000).

Cognitive and behavior therapies have long histories of empirical support. However, change-oriented treatment strategies are not perfect, and we know relatively little about why treatments fail when they do. Making the treatments more dialectical, by integrating acceptance-oriented with change-oriented strategies often has resulted in significant improvements. Thus, a dialectical approach may be useful, especially when (1) change-oriented or acceptance-oriented approaches are not successful on their own, (2) when the treatment reaches a plateau short of its targets for improvement, (3) when clients and therapists get stuck in power struggles, or (4) for multiproblem clients in general.

Contraindications of the Treatment

At this time there are no known contraindications of utilizing dialectical strategies. More research is needed to understand if and when dialectical assessment and interventions may not be viable treatment options or may fail to add value.

THEORY OR MECHANISM BY WHICH
DIALECTICS IS HYPOTHESIZED TO WORK

Dialectical principles and strategies arise from a dialectical worldview, one in which wholeness and interrelatedness are emphasized over logical positivism and separateness. This is also consistent with a transactional model, systems theory, or contextual behavioral theory, all of which stress the interrelated nature of the individual and the social environment (Fruzzetti, Shenk, & Hoffman, 2005). Dialectics involves the synthesis of opposites (thesis and antithesis, proposition and counterproposition) in a variety of ways. The synthesis contains elements of both the thesis and antithesis. A synthesis is not a compromise, but rather a new position, proposition, perspective, idea or explanation that recognizes and includes the essence or core value of each (previously apparently contradictory) side. For example, asking for less will get more, or creating more intimacy with another can foster one's independence. Examples of dialectical syntheses will be expanded upon throughout this chapter.

A dialectical therapeutic framework accepts change as an ongoing process and as a fundamental characteristic of reality. Therefore, as treatment progresses, delivering the therapy not only changes the client, but also results in a change in the therapy itself, along with changing the therapist. In addition, dialectics helps us recognize that it may be more effective to balance attempts to help a client change with acceptance of the client and/or the client's behavior and experience (actions, thoughts, emotions, desires, etc.).

Dialectics is a concept, so of course is imbedded in language, cognition, and concepts, so these domains are core targets for the application of dialectical principles: Nondialectical language and thinking contributes to polarization and clients (and therapists) being stuck. For example, a client might encounter an undesirable event, such as argument with a partner in which the partner accuses the client of having done or said something problematic. The client may get stuck in the "fact" that the accusation is "unfair" and continue to think and say things such as, "You should not blame me, it is unfair; I did not do or say what you think." The client

and partner argue, escalate their anger, and end up very unhappy with each other. This is a situation of "nonacceptance, nonchange": The client is not able to change the partner's memory of the event, emotions, or blame of the client, and the client is not able to accept these same things. In fact, the client's nonacceptance (arguing ever more forcefully) further entrenches the partner and makes things worse. An alternative, dialectical solution might be to accept (become aware of, notice, describe, embrace, acknowledge, etc.) the partner's experiences. Acceptance would prevent the argument from escalating, thereby leading to getting along better, likely an extremely important goal of the client. In addition, by embracing the partner's experience the partner might then be soothed and thus more able, and willing, to consider the possibility that he or she is not 100% correct in his or her memory, and/or to realize that blaming is not constructive. Acceptance can, therefore, be a solution to nonacceptance/nonchange situations that result in a lot of misery. Of course, acceptance (tolerating the situation, letting go of being "right") *is* a change in this situation (Fruzzetti, 2006; Fruzzetti & Erikson, in press).

It is essential to recognize that, in a dialectical worldview, there is no "right" answer, strategy, or explanation of the causes of or solutions to behavior problems, but rather many possible reasonable and effective ones. Furthermore, the most successful explanations are those that lead to successful interventions. Deemphasizing "right" and "wrong" may have salutary effects for the relationship between the therapist and client, the client's relationships with others, and for the relationship between the therapist and other members of a treatment team. Because there is no "truth" to be found it may be easier to work together toward specified goals, with many different approaches having merit, rather than arguing over "the" correct answer or way to proceed. All parties to a discussion embrace the questions, "what is missing, what is being left out from our consideration," and/or "what do we not understand, or what have we not considered." These questions help collaborate toward a fuller meaning or explanation, one with a new synthesis and new implications for intervention.

However, a dialectical worldview is not one of nihilism. There are "truths" from given perspectives, and in cognitive behavior therapy one essential truth is outcomes: Does the perspective lead to an intervention that benefits the client in the ways for which she or he sought treatment? Similarly, dialectics in CBT is not analogous to a postmodern or constructivist perspective, because in CBT there is a meaningful, more or less objective (at least measurable) context that allows us to evaluate whether any given perspective is valid or useful: Does it facilitate improved client outcome? Thus, although it may be possible to construct an infinite number of "perspectives" on a problem, in CBT only a subset of those will lead to useful strategies, which in turn lead to meaningful client outcomes. Some other perspectives may build good stories (for other possible purposes), but lead to ineffective interventions. In a dialectical worldview those are invalid (or, at best irrelevant) perspectives vis-à-vis outcomes.

Finally, as suggested above, a dialectical approach informs the structure and the strategies of treatment when treatment becomes "stuck" and progress halted. From a dialectical point of view, failure to change suggests that something is missing from our understanding of the phenomenon (something is "missing" in the analysis), and/or that there is an imbalance between acceptance and change. The therapist may be placing too much emphasis on acceptance (feeling empathy for the client, providing a lot of soothing) or too much on change (wanting client to "just do" the plan you and he/she have come up with, etc.). A therapist who is only pushing for change can become overly critical when progress stalls. This is likely to leave a client feeling shameful or angry and is likely to damage the therapeutic relationship. On the other hand, if a therapist is "too" accepting, he/she may contribute to the client staying stuck in a painful situation rather than helping the client move on. Thus, clients may feel "cared about" but only make limited treatment gains. Similarly, therapists and clients may focus on client change to the exclusion of client self-acceptance, with less positive results.

SPECIFIC DIALECTICAL TREATMENT STRATEGIES

Dialectical strategies allow a therapist to help a client change by responding to the dialectical tensions that arise when trying to alter significant behavior patterns, sometimes just by highlighting both sides of these apparent polarities and at other times by synthesizing them. Becoming stuck at one pole or the other can often lead to a power struggle in which each tries to convince the other, leading to impediments in the relationship and treatment, decreasing the likelihood that synthesis or progress will be achieved. See Table 23.1 for a list of these strategies, which are detailed below.

Dialectical Assessment

This is a conceptualization strategy that the therapist or treatment team employs. Dialectics informs our clinical understanding about the causes of a given behavior. For example, for every proposition (or thesis) about the cause of a target behavior (e.g., excessive drinking, sad mood, emotional arousal), it is possible to generate one or more alternatives (antitheses) that expose the limitations of the original explanation and add potential explanatory power. This ongoing transaction of ideas (thesis and antithesis) forges new syntheses, which are in turn the next theses. Virtually any attribution about the cause of problem behavior has limitations, and recognizing these limitations allows for fuller understanding of the target problems and affords alternative avenues of intervention. We may regularly ask ourselves, "What is missing? What am I failing to understand or appreciate?" For example, causality that focuses on learning histories neglects present factors; biological explanations neglect environmental factors; models that see the individuals as the host of the problem behavior miss the influence of family environment factors; approaches that see the problematic consequences miss the benefits, and so on. Of course, the reverse would also be true. In a dialectical analysis of causality, the process of exploring different factors continues until an effective (not right or wrong) understanding is achieved, one

TABLE 23.1 Summary of Dialectical Strategies

Dialectical Assessment	Assess behavioral patterns, seeking "What is left out of my understanding of this behavior?"
Balanced Treatment Strategies	Use both acceptance and change strategies as solutions, and highlight the utility of both in session.
Balanced Treatment Targets	Balance acceptance of some targets while targeting change for others.
Stylistic Strategies	Balance acceptance-oriented (warmth, genuineness) and change-oriented (directive, confrontive) styles.
Dialectical Thinking and Behavior	Encourage patient to move from "either/or" thinking to "both and" thinking.
Balancing Primary and Secondary Emotions	Notice and validate primary emotions more than secondary emotions
Metaphors	Use metaphors to help patients see legitimate and useful alternative ways of thinking and responding.
Lemonade out of Lemons	Encourage patient to see that most problems also afford opportunities as well. Great care must be utilized when implementing this strategy.
Reframing	Engage the client in seeing the "problem" behavior from a different, less toxic, perspective.

from which an effective intervention is developed. Thus, dialectical assessment is conducted throughout treatment.

In order to conduct a dialectical assessment a therapist must evaluate multiple factors that are influencing a patient's behavior in the current environment. This may include past learning and larger systemic (e.g., social, familial, financial) factors, as well as current emotion, thinking and overt behavior patterns. In developing this understanding, therapist and patient are constantly asking themselves, "What are we leaving out of our understanding," until a workable intervention strategy is developed.

For example, in developing a treatment plan for a client diagnosed with alcohol abuse the therapist may utilize a dialectical assessment strategy in the following manner. Because the client's mother frequently drank a lot of alcohol as a means of emotional self-management, and the client was regularly exposed to this, it is reasonable to see the roots of her drinking historically, as learned through modeling. Whatever face validity this explanation may hold, this thesis naturally generates a critical idiographic question: "But why did she drink on Thursday morning, not Wednesday evening or Thursday afternoon?" This question about current factors exposes the limitations of the first explanation or proposition. Arriving at some synthesis, one might conclude that both early learning and current emotional factors (e.g., she

had just been criticized in a phone call with a family member) were relevant in the present drinking behavior. This proposition might naturally generate another alternative proposition (antithesis) that exposes the limitations of the synthesis (new proposition): "When criticized, she gets deeply ashamed and cannot tolerate this aversive arousal," which leads the therapist and team to consider internal, not just external, factors. The team may then propose that the therapist teaches the client ways to manage this sense of shame, perhaps via acceptance strategies (e.g., tolerating or allowing the emotion) or change (e.g., downregulation of shame, exposure, or by focusing on another primary emotion). If this conceptualization and the accompanying strategies work (i.e., she drinks a lot less), the synthesis will be considered sufficient. However, if this assessment does not identify effective targets for intervention, the assessment would continue dialectically until such targets and intervention strategies were identified and implemented successfully.

Balanced Treatment Strategies

In order to maintain collaboration in session, the therapist may alternate and balance acceptance and change strategies. This requires integrating traditional, change oriented strategies (cognitive and behavior therapy interventions such as skill training, contingency management, problem solving, cognitive restructuring, exposure and response prevention, etc.) with mindfulness-, acceptance-, or validation-based treatment strategies. The therapist maintains a stance of flexibility and stability, is nurturant and challenging, recognizing a client's limitations (acceptance) while simultaneously pushing for increasing capabilities (change). For example, a therapist and patient may have been practicing how the client will be assertive with her ex-husband who has become increasingly hostile and demanding toward her. The patient is going to meet the ex-husband the next day and the therapist is pushing the client to carry out her plan for asserting herself, highlighting for her all the pros of being able to do so. While pushing the patient to engage in this behavior, the therapist will need to ensure that he/she verbally validates of the legitimate fears the patient has of doing this behavior. Further acceptance and validation could take the form of helping her develop a safety plan (e.g., bringing along a mutual friend) or some alternative to achieve her goals.

Balanced Treatment Targets

Clients typically have problem behaviors (e.g., panic, social withdrawal, aggression, disordered eating, substance abuse, suicidality) that are the target of change in cognitive and behavior therapy. However, these problem behaviors occur in a complex cognitive–emotive–physiological–social context, and it is common for some of these contextual variables to become targeted for change along with the specific problem behavior. Disaggregating behaviors and focusing on acceptance of some while targeting change for others may be an effective alternative approach. For example, a client may binge and purge following awkward social interactions in which she feels a lot of shame about her body. It might be desirable simply to reduce her shame, her binging and her purging all together. But because of the high levels of implicit criticism of her body from various media, and explicit criticisms from her family and peers, it may be extremely difficult to reduce her shame significantly. Thus, it may be useful instead to help her learn to accept some shame as a normal emotional response to social

criticism, then help her disaggregate her binging and purging from shame, and thus reduce or eliminate her disordered eating.

Stylistic Strategies: Acceptance-Oriented versus Change-Oriented Communication

Therapists can also use communication strategies to maintain balance in session by varying the intensity of emotion, communication, and speed in the session (Linehan, 1993). Varying intensity conveys certainty and strength and responsiveness to a client's movement such that the therapist is able to match the client, push the client to move faster, or slow the client down. Varying speed keeps the client and therapist moving so that neither get "stuck" maintaining a position. This can be akin to driving a car with a manual transmission. Varying intensity is similar to paying attention to when you must shift up or down to maintain a smooth ride and not stall the car or other traffic, and not to crash. Also, sufficient speed allows for smooth changing of gears so that you do not grind the gears when shifting.

Acceptance-oriented communication is responsive, warm and genuine. This type of communication is common in most therapies at some times. It generally communicates acceptance of the client and facilitates trust and respect in the therapeutic relationship. Alternatively, change-oriented communication is often quite directive, but also can include an off beat style or a stimulus that is novel to that situation. This unorthodox communication, or any strong push for change, must come from a place of caring and genuineness, lest it simply be seen as uncaring, or not taking the patient's difficulties seriously. When using irreverent, change-oriented communication, a therapist may present a more extreme or opposite style, to that of the patient, either being "deadpan" or highly emotional, responding to what a patient says but not in the manner he or she expects. Imagine a patient who has recently attempted suicide while on the inpatient ward. She expresses anger over her treatment by the staff (who watch her, tell her when to shower, etc.). A therapist may respond by saying, "Well, what do you expect, if you act like a mental patient the staff are likely to treat you as one." Or the therapist may vary her or his tone intentionally to communicate to a client the dysfunctional nature of her behavior, "You aren't *really* thinking that's a good idea are you?!" Acceptance-oriented and change-oriented communication must be used together to provide balance. Balance does not necessarily mean 50–50; the balance is achieved in relation to what is occurring in the session in terms of what is needed to ensure movement and progress.

Increasing Dialectical Thinking and Behavior as a Target for Clients

Encouraging dialectical thinking emphasizes patient's becoming aware of "all-or-none" thinking and challenging this type of thinking. However, as should be clear, dialectical thinking does not encourage finding absolute "truths" based on logic. Thus, therapist and patient are encouraged to move from "either/or" thinking to "both/and" thinking. For example, a patient may be angry with a therapist for "pushing me too much" and instead wants the therapist to "just be caring." One synthesis may be to help the client gain the perspective that in fact the therapist is doing the most caring thing possible by pushing him to make difficult changes needed to achieve his goals. Or the therapist could focus on finding more caring ways to push for change. Another example is when a client proclaims, "If my girlfriend loved me, she'd be willing to do X." One synthesis is to recognize that his girlfriend can love him and still not be willing to do what he wants.

Clients often become stuck making negative, critical, or judgmental self-statements or having negative or judgmental thoughts about themselves. It is common in cognitive therapy to attempt to refute or disprove these thoughts. However, research by Swan (1997) suggests that when these kinds of thoughts are consistent with a person's self-view, such attempts may actually increase distress. Similarly, work on thought suppression (e.g., Wegner, Schneider, Carter, & White, 1987) suggests that attempts to push out these kinds of thoughts may backfire and result in a "rebound" in which the negative thoughts or self-statements become even more distressing.

Dialectical thinking is an alternative to refutation. In a dialectical approach to critical or judgmental thoughts about themselves, clients are encouraged first to notice or observe the fact that they are having the thought (e.g., "She doesn't love me because I'm so awful"), thereby helping the client to see thinking as another behavior and to decrease its literality and power. A therapist might say, "I know you *think* you're a bad person and are undeserving of caring from your fiancé." The therapist might emphasize the legitimacy of this thought by noting, "You really did say some pretty awful things to her." And then, instead of trying to refute the self-judgment or directly blocking any "catastrophizing," the therapist might attempt to provide another valid, albeit quite different, point of view: "Of course, at other times you have done many, nicer things. Let's see if there is some repair you can do for when you were nasty. Repairing the damage would also be a nice thing." In dialectical thinking it is possible, even desirable, to notice both valued and problematic behaviors, along with their accompanying thoughts.

Encouraging dialectical behavior patterns involves having the patient learn to respond in a "balanced" way to situations. An unbalanced situation that patients often present occurs when they have had a major disagreement with someone. Their position is "right" and the person with whom they are having a disagreement with is "wrong," therefore justifying their displays of bitter anger. A dialectical stance is not simply to try to be a "good" therapist by supporting our clients against the world. Instead, it is to help patients recognize that they may disagree with someone and that this does not make the other evil, a maltreater, or worthless, just as they are not evil, bad, or worthless; both sides have their validity and their value. This stance facilitates a client's responding in a more balanced way to the individual. The idea that neither is right or wrong at the level of absolute "truth" is very difficult to grasp for many patients and therapists. Most psychotherapy, and indeed Western culture more generally, places values on behaviors as being either "good behaviors" or "bad behaviors." A dialectical point of view is that behaviors simply are what they are: Things we do that are effective or ineffective in achieving goals, and that bring certain consequences. Describing literal or objective reality, including events, emotional reactions, and the consequences of those events vis-à-vis desired goals (e.g., "he came home 45 minutes late and then it was too late to go, and I was disappointed" rather than "he is such a selfish jerk"), can help turn attention away from good/bad thinking toward more dialectical thinking.

Balancing Primary and Secondary Emotions

Emotional distress is a core part of most problems for which people seek psychotherapy. Emotional reactions to events big and small are often adaptive, predictable, and generally universal—what we typically call primary emotions. However, sometimes people have emotional reactions to their emotional reactions (or in anticipation of them) or change the quantity or quality of their emotional responses via judgments (right/wrong thinking) or other interpretations. These are typically less adaptive and may be considered secondary emotions (Greenberg & Safron, 1989). How therapists attend to primary versus secondary emotions can be very important (see Chapter 28).

For example, a client may describe a situation at home or at work in which he or she did not get what he or she wanted (e.g., someone to listen and support, or someone to provide instrumental help with a task). A primary emotional response is likely to include disappointment when we do not get what we desire. Yet, the client may express a lot of anger or shame, around the incident, maybe as a result of becoming judgmental toward another (creating anger) or toward him- or herself (creating shame). By calling attention both to what the client is experiencing (anger or shame, more secondary emotions in this situation) as well as what the client may be missing (disappointment, a likely primary emotion in this situation), the therapist highlights the existence of both kinds of emotions, but may direct attention to the "missing" primary emotion. Recognizing the disappointment may lead the client to do something much more constructive than suggested by the more destructive urges that often originate with secondary emotions.

Metaphors

Metaphors or stories encourage dialectical thinking and balanced responding. The use of metaphors generates alternatives because the content of the metaphor does not elicit as big of an emotional reaction as the actual situation, and the client may more easily take the "observer" role (a different perspective). Thus, metaphors are generally easier to "hear" because they often convey a profound understanding of the client's experience, and then clients are less likely to feel that they are being "nagged at" or "lectured to" by their therapist.

Using metaphors or stories as a strategy takes practice. There are many examples of metaphors that can be used routinely in therapy. Their use could be planned (e.g., to help someone find a new perspective on a situation that recurs) or could be spontaneous. For example, when a client is refusing to try to participate in a particular behavior that would likely be effective (e.g., unwilling to report important activities to the therapist, or refusing to engage in a role-playing a situation with the therapist), his or her unwillingness could be compared to going to the dentist's office and not opening one's mouth. Or when describing the need for the patient to practice at home something he or she has been working on in the session, the therapist could employ a swimming metaphor: The therapist, who is the coach, can teach the swimmer (patient) to swim in a calm pool (therapist's office). But because the swimmer lives in the ocean, the swimmer needs to practice swimming there as well.

It may also be useful to ask a client to describe images, stories, or metaphors that he or she notices. The metaphor may help increase dialectical assessment and understanding of both the therapist and the client.

Make Lemonade Out of Lemons

This strategy, when executed well, can be very helpful. However, when done poorly or misused, it can lead to serious damage to the therapeutic relationship. Therefore, this strategy must be performed delicately. The therapist takes a problem and balances the problem with the "opportunity" the problem presents for something desirable. The therapist must be careful to not invalidate the difficulties the patient is having and that making lemonade itself can be difficult. This must be done in the context of a caring relationship, lest it seem the therapist is being callous. For example, imagine a client who presented with difficulties with relationships and has been working on social skills with the therapist. All has been smooth for sometime. Then one day he comes to session complaining that his new supervisor and he just "don't get along" and that he is thinking of "just quitting," given all the problems he has had at work in the past. A response of "It makes sense that you might want to quit given all the past problems you've had and how hard it will be to manage this situation. But I need to point out to you that this is fantastic in another way. This is exactly the kind of opportunity we've needed so that now you can really practice!" Again, this is not to take lightly the problem encountered, but to highlight that the problem may be balanced with the "opportunity" it brings. Again, this is a strategy to be used with great care.

Reframing

One of the core ideas in dialectics is that multiple perspectives about reality may be valid. In CBT, this principle can be used to help clients who are suffering in part because they are "stuck" in one, limited, painful perspective. Helping them understand or experience at least one alternative, legitimate perspective is called reframing, and this can help them get "unstuck."

For example, the client may be stuck in judgments and anger because his or her partner regularly works late or brings work home. The client may take the perspective that his or her partner doesn't care about the relationship, is not committed to the relationship, and so on. However, the "hard working" partner may have the experience that it is because of his or her commitment to their relationship and to their family that he or she works so hard (to provide for them). He or she feels unappreciated and unjustly criticized. If the therapist can help reframe the "problem" so that it includes the partner's heretofore missing perspective, a shift might occur that helps the client express his or her feelings more gently and accurately (primary emotions, such as missing the partner, rather than secondary emotions such as anger), which reduces their conflict and helps them meet each other's needs better. Unlike cognitive restructuring per se, the idea with reframing is to see the validity in another perspective *in addition to* the one the client already has, not to invalidate or drop that initial perspective, which is also valid.

CONCLUSIONS

From a CBT perspective, all behaviors (thoughts, emotions, actions, etc.) are multidetermined, so in this way dialectical approaches are quite compatible with the foundations of CBT in general. Thus, dialectical strategies may, in principle, enhance virtually any traditional interventions in CBT, and emerging evidence suggests that employing dialectical interventions can improve outcomes. Dialectical strategies should be employed in a context of caring, honesty, and commitment to the client. The therapist must maintain a stance in which she/he appreciates both sides of any apparent polarity or disagreement. The therapist also must recognize that she/he does not have the corner on "truth" or "the answers" but, rather, genuinely search for what is left out, for alternate perspectives, so that balance may be achieved and outcomes enhanced.

Further Reading

Hayes, S. C., Follette, V. M., & Linehan, M. M. (Eds.) (2004). *Mindfulness and acceptance: Expanding the cognitive-behavioral tradition.* New York: Guilford.
Linehan, M. M. (1993). *Cognitive behavioral treatment of borderline personality disorder* New York: Guilford.

References

Binswanger, L. (1963). *Being-in-the-world: Selected papers of Ludwig Binswanger* (trans. J. Needleman). New York: Basic Books.
Borkovec, T. D., & Sharpless, B. (2004). Generalized anxiety disorder: Bringing cognitive–behavioral therapy into the valued present. In S. C. Hayes, V. M. Follette, & M. M. Linehan (Eds.), *Mindfulness and acceptance: Expanding the cognitive-behavioral tradition* (pp. 209–242). New York: Guilford Press.

Feigenbaum, J. (2007). Dialectical behaviour therapy: An increasing evidence base. *Journal of Mental Health, 16,* 51–68.

Fruzzetti, A. E. (2002). Dialectical behavior therapy for borderline personality and related disorders. In T. Patterson (Ed.), *Comprehensive handbook of psychotherapy.* New York: John Wiley & Sons.

Fruzzetti, A. E. (2006). The high conflict couple: A dialectical behavior therapy guide to finding peace, intimacy, and validation. Oakland, CA: New Harbinger Press.

Fruzzetti, A. E., & Erikson, K. M. (in press). Acceptance based interventions in cognitive–behavioral therapies. In K. Dobson (Ed.), *Handbook of Cognitive-Behavioral Therapies* (3rd ed.). New York: Guilford.

Fruzzetti, A. E., Shenk, C., & Hoffman, P. D. (2005). Family interaction and the development of borderline personality disorder: A transactional model. *Development and Psychopathology, 17,* 1007–1030.

Gollobin, I. (1986). Dialectical materialism: Its laws, categories, and practice. New York: Petras Press.

Greenberg, L. S., & Safran, J. D. (1989). Emotion in psychotherapy. *American Psychologist, 44,* 19–29.

Hayes, S. C., Follette, V. M., & Linehan, M. M. (Eds.) (2004). *Mindfulness and acceptance: Expanding the cognitive–behavioral tradition.* New York: Guilford.

Hayes, S. C., Stroshahl, K. D., & Wilson, K. E. (1999). Acceptance and commitment therapy: An experiential approach to behavior change. New York: Guilford.

Jacobson, N., & Christensen, A. (1996). Acceptance and change in couple therapy: A therapist's guide to transforming relationships. New York: Norton.

Kabat-Zinn, J., Lipworth, L., Burney, R. (1985). The clinical use of mindfulness meditation for the self-regulation of chronic pain. *Journal of Behavioral Medicine, 8,* 163–190.

Kohlenberg, R. J., & Tsai, M. (1991). Functional analytic psychotherapy. New York: Plenum Press.

Linehan, M. M. (1993). Cognitive behavioral treatment of borderline personality disorder. New York: Guilford.

Linehan, M. M., et al. (2002). DBT versus comprehensive validation plus 12-step for the treatment of opioid dependent women meeting criteria for borderline personality disorder. *Drug and Alcohol Dependence, 67,* 13–26.

Marlatt, G. A., & Donnovan, D. M. (2005). *Relapse prevention: Maintenance strategies in the treatment of addictive behaviors* (2nd ed.). New York: Guilford.

Pinkard, T. (1998). *Hegel's dialectic: The explanation of possibility.* Philadelphia: Temple University.

Robins, C. J., & Chapman, A. L. (2004). Dialectical behavior therapy: Current status, recent developments, and future directions. *Journal of Personality Disorders, 18,* 73–89.

Roemer, L., & Orsillo, S. (2002). Expanding our conceptualization of and treatment for generalized anxiety disorder: Integrating mindfulness/acceptance-based approaches with existing cognitive-behavioral models. *Clinical Psychology: Science and Practice, 9,* 54–68.

Segal, Z. V., Williams, J. M. G., Teasdale, J. D. (2002). Mindfulness-based cognitive therapy for depression: A new approach to preventing relapse. New York: Guilford.

Swan, W. B. (1997). The trouble with change: Self-verification and allegiance to the self. *Psychological Science, 8,* 177–180.

Teasdale, J. D., Segal, Z. V., Williams, J. M. G., Ridgeway, V. A., Souslby, J. M., & Lau, M. A. (2000). Prevention of relapse/recurrence in major depression by mindfulness-based cognitive therapy. *Journal of Consulting and Clinical Psychology, 68,* 615–623.

Turner, R. M. (2000). Naturalistic evaluation of dialectical behavior therapy–oriented treatment for borderline personality disorder. *Cognitive and Behavioral Practice, 7,* 413–419.

Wegner, D. M., Schneider, D. J., Carter, S. R., & White, T. L. (1987). Paradoxical effects of thought suppression. *Journal of Personality and Social Psychology, 53,* 5–13.

Wilson, T. G. (1996). Acceptance and change in the treatment of eating disorders and obesity. *Behavior Therapy, 27,* 417–439.

24 DIFFERENTIAL REINFORCEMENT OF LOW-RATE BEHAVIOR

Mark Alavosius, Joseph Dagen,
and William D. Newsome

OVERVIEW

Sometimes behaviors are acceptable or desired when performed at low rates but problematic when performed frequently. Procedures that use reinforcement to establish acceptably low rates of frequent behavior are termed *differential reinforcement of low-rate behavior* (DRL). Definitions of DRL can be found in many various sources including basic research procedures (Ferster & Skinner, 1975; Holz & Azrin, 1963) and applied interventions (Repp & Deitz, 1973, 1974; Deitz, 1977). Although DRL relies on many complex behavioral concepts (e.g., reinforcement, operant conditioning, extinction, interresponse time, etc.), it is not itself a novel construct, but rather an arrangement of them. Thus, the definitions provided for DRL are not generally explanatory. Rather, they are descriptive, detailing the procedural characteristics of implementation. Essentially, DRL procedures are designed to lower the rate of some target behavior but not eliminate it. The actual DRL procedure chosen can vary in how it is managed but will have the essential property of managing reinforcement in such a way as to maintain some behavior at some acceptable rate below the levels deemed too high for the circumstances.

DRL schedules are reductive procedures that manipulate the schedule of reinforcement to moderate behavior. This is in contrast to punishment procedures that apply an aversive consequence to reduce or eliminate behavior. Thus DRL would be preferred to punishment when the goal is behavioral reduction as it reduces the negative side effects (e.g., escape, avoidance) usually associated with punishment. DRL is likely to not have a quick effect, however, and should be used when gradual behavior change is acceptable and elimination of the behavior is not desired.

EXAMPLES OF DRL

There are many situations where a low rate of a behavior is acceptable or desirable but high rates raise problems. For example, in work situations where workers' high sustained rates of behavior may cause disabilities such as repetitive motion injuries (e.g., carpal tunnel disorders due to repetitious wrist rotations), a DRL procedure might be used to pace work or lower rates of awkward twisting motions but still maintain productive behavior. In educational settings, DRL procedures might be used to manage students' rate of misbehavior such as seeking help excessively from the teacher. A low level of such requests is desirable but when the demands become frequent, the behavior interferes with other classroom activities and DRL contingencies might be designed to moderate the requests. In sport settings, high rates of vigorous exercise might be excessive and weaken an athlete before competition. A DRL schedule might be designed to moderate exertion in the days before competition and insure the athlete is fit and rested at the starting line. In clinical settings, DRL can be used to moderate behaviors that are acceptable or tolerable at low rates but disruptive or disturbing when performed frequently. The pace of eating might be problematic for individuals with health complications exacerbated by rapid eating (Lennox, Miltenberger, & Donnelly, 1987; Wright & Vollmer, 2002) and DRL schedules can be programmed to slow the behavior. As another example where DRL might be useful, ingestion of small amounts of sugar might be acceptable for persons with diabetes, but too much poses risks. Special-needs populations such as persons with autism and developmental disabilities engage in stereotypic behaviors that have been moderated with DRL procedures (Singh, Dawson, & Manning, 1981). Thus, DRL procedures have a solid foundation in basic research yielding predictable behavioral patterns, and successful applications have been replicated with numerous populations and target behaviors.

DRL procedures manage the schedule and delivery of reinforcement. They may be part of a treatment package that includes antecedent controls to bolster treatment effects. For example, goals for behavioral reduction and rules specifying when and how often behavior may occur may combine with reinforcement procedures to establish and maintain low-rate behavior. The effects of rules on responding to operant contingencies are complex and research is investigating the complexity of learning histories and rule-governance. For example, Wulfert, Greenway, Farkas, Hayes, & Dougher (1994) investigated the effects of sensitivity to changing reinforcement contingencies under types of rules (minimal and accurate) and subject's self-reports of rigidity. Results indicated the accuracy of rules affects control by reinforcement contingencies when the schedule changes. In particular subjects given inaccurate rules may not acquire control by DRL schedules put in place after a history of FR reinforcement. The point being that the instructions provided to individuals about the contingency arrangements they encounter may enhance or impair control by newly established contingencies. Accurate and detailed rules are most likely to occasion control by the newly established contingencies and inaccurate or absent rules may result in the persistence of behavior established under previous conditions and insensitivity to new treatment contingencies (e.g., a DRL procedure).

USING DRL SCHEDULES

The goal of DRL procedures is to lower the rate of behavior and it is chosen when simpler procedures such as requests for reduced behavior rates alone are not effective. DRL procedures require that the rate of behavior be measured and schedules of reinforcement managed to support rate reductions. This entails some measurement of responding over time with the necessity of measuring occurrences of the behavior and tracking the passage of time. It also requires identification of effective reinforcers whose delivery can be managed. Once baseline measures of behavior are established that indicate rates are unacceptably high, a desired lower rate of behavior can be prescribed. This is probably done in consultation with the client and those affected by the high rates. For example, an assembly-line employee suffering from carpal tunnel syndrome might benefit from a DRL procedure to lower the rate of repetitive motion. The optimal rate is probably set by experts such as an occupational therapist or rehabilitation nurse who can judge rates of behavior likely not to worsen existent symptoms. With a terminal rate of behavior established, various DRL methods can be used to pace the rate of behavior by scheduling delivery of reinforcement contingent on lower rates of behavior. In some cases, a shaping procedure might be employed to thin the schedule of reinforcement and in a stepwise fashion lower the rate of behavior to some acceptable level. How the behavioral occurrences are measured, how time is partitioned, and what reinforcements are managed dictate the types of DRL variations that might be used. As noted above, explaining accurately to the worker the DRL contingencies is likely to be a useful component of the procedure and enhance treatment effectiveness.

Full-Session DRL

Say a math teacher is concerned that a student's requests for assistance are excessive and disruptive to instruction provided to the rest of the class. The teacher measures the occurrences of that student's help requests during the entire class time and determines an unacceptably high rate (e.g., eight per hour). The teacher then sets a criterion for acceptable requests (e.g., four per hour). This determination rests on judgment of what levels of interruptions are tolerable. The teacher provides reinforcement of the student's low-rate behavior at the end of class time if the count of help requests is measured at four or fewer occurrences. This method is straightforward and simply requires a count of occurrences during the entire class session. Reinforcement of low-rate behavior is provided at the end of class only if the target goal is met. The teacher might instruct the child about the exact contingencies and provide clear rules about what amount of help seeking will earn reinforcement and what amount results in forfeiture.

Interval DRL

In the preceding example, the student may not meet the response rate criterion and help seeking persists at unacceptably high rates. The class period can be divided into intervals (say four 15-minute blocks) to make achievement of reinforcement more probable. Now the rate would be one occurrence per 15 minutes. With this variation, the teacher provides reinforcement at the end of 15-minute blocks if the child asks for help once or less per interval. Note that in this example there are more opportunities to earn reinforcement, and hence learning is likely to occur more rapidly. It does require more effort by the teacher to track occurrences through time and deliver reinforcement. Note that the procedure can be adjusted by changing the response criterion and/or changing the duration of the intervals. Such decisions are based made in light of the baseline data. Challenging but attainable goals can be used to gradually reduce the rate of undesired high-rate behavior while desired alternative behaviors (e.g., working independently) are strengthened and maintained by other contingencies. These other contingencies are important, as they establish desired alternative behaviors (e.g., working independently) in the child's repertoire. Thus, DRL procedures operate in the context of other reinforcement systems and work to alter the allocation of behavior to the availability of reinforcement.

The intervals between behaviors might be measured during baseline to establish an average IRT (inter-response time). The baseline would provide information about the client's pattern of responding and inform judgments about goals for increasing the interval between behaviors. Reinforcement would be provided if the client meets the desired interval between behaviors. Goals for increasing the interval between behaviors would likely begin near or just longer than the average interval established during baseline then gradually increase as the client's rate of the target behavior decreases. Note that this is more effortful for the contingency manager than the two previous options as it requires more fine-grained monitoring of behavior and more frequent delivery of reinforcement.

DRL using the whole session and interval blocks specify a ceiling number of behaviors during a certain time interval (full session or block of time) in order for reinforcement to be delivered. If no behavior occurs during the interval, reinforcement would still be delivered. Thus the behavior may cease to occur. It is a relatively easy procedure to implement. The IRT method requires that a specified behavior does not occur during a specified interval and, after the interval has passed, that an instance of that behavior must occur for reinforcement. In other words, occurrences of a specific behavior are spaced out over time. The IRT DRL is useful when the behavior you want to reduce is desirable, provided that is does not occur at too high a rate.

LIMITATIONS OF DRL

DRL procedures produce behavior change gradually. If you need to reduce an inappropriate behavior quickly, DRL would not be the method of first choice. DRL would not be advisable for use with self-injurious, violent or potentially dangerous behaviors that must be reduced quickly. Note that the DRL procedure focuses measurement and reinforcement on the inappropriate behavior targeted for reduction. When resources are limited, efforts to increase desired, effective behaviors may be short-changed. When designing a treatment program, a combination of procedures that increase desired behavior and reduce problem behavior is optimal and DRL is therefore likely part of a package of interventions. The ease of use becomes important and the choice of procedure should consider the demands placed on the practitioner so that consistent and effective implementation is maintained.

FUTURE WORK

Applied DRL research has almost exclusively occurred in the context of schoolchildren, autism, or developmental disabilities. While DRL procedures have produced pragmatic outcomes with these populations, multiple domains beyond developmental disabilities remain relatively unexplored. It is provocative to consider some of these alterative application domains.

Diet

An obesity epidemic is spreading across America. Obese individuals face severe health complications, and the country faces increasing health care costs as a result. In the war against obesity, diet and portion control have been identified as important components of a healthy lifestyle. Altering one's diet, however, remains a difficult challenge as low-nutrient, high-calorie foods typically function as extremely powerful reinforcers. The omission of these unhealthy foods is an incredible challenge for individuals with a long history of consuming them. DRL procedures offer an unexplored tool for decreasing the rate of unhealthy eating behaviors. Within a DRL schedule, individuals may still contact the potent reinforcers inherent in nonnutritious foods, but will necessarily contact the natural consequences of a healthier diet: increased energy, attention, improved sleep, and so on. Additionally, by still contacting unhealthy foods at low, regular intervals, powerful establishing operations that increase the reinforcing properties of healthy foods may be created. Thus, established operations created during dieting that function to decrease the reinforcing properties of healthy foods may be combated by contacting unhealthy alternatives during dieting, thus reestablishing reinforcing properties for healthy foods. Research is needed to determine the necessary conditions under which these schedules are most effective.

Sports

DRL procedures could find multiple uses with athletes. For example, some elite endurance athletes consistently train at too high an intensity at the expense of their fitness. In the absence of programmed recovery periods, fitness rapidly deteriorates and performance gains are never fully realized. Data provided by heart-rate monitors and power-output monitors could serve as an intensity measurement with sponsors, coaches, and fellow athletes, providing monetary or social reinforcement contingent upon low rates of high-intensity training. Thus, the athlete's low rate of high-intensity training provides reinforcement based on the programmed consequences within the contingency, but also will likely produce significant fitness gains. These procedures can therefore bring athletes into contact with the natural consequences of refined training regimens: higher performance. Combined with other interventions in a package treatment (e.g., goal setting and public posting), DRL procedures could produce pragmatic effects.

Child Rearing

These procedures may be particularly effective in decreasing the rate of certain sedentary behaviors in children. As current childhood obesity prevalence increases, parents and educators are looking for ways to promote healthy behaviors. Restricting access to potent reinforcers such as television and videogames may help parents promote healthier alternatives for their children. Current televisions and videogame systems could readily be programmed such that the devices would operate only after a programmed duration of inactivity. Thus, a child may attempt to turn on the television, but find that it will not operate if the child has attempted to turn the device on too often during the previous period of time. Only after a particular duration might the child's attempt to operate the device result in the device's turning on. Thus, the child's behavior is reduced, but not completely extinguished. Further duration contingencies during the operation of these devices could reduce their reinforcing properties while still allowing the child to contact reinforcement. DRL schedules applied to technology may be particularly effective because reinforcement delivery can be programmed into the devices themselves rather than be delivered by an individual who must necessarily be vigilant about observation, data collection, and the reinforcement schedule.

Worker Safety

High rates of behavior are a contributing factor to repetitive-motion injuries and cumulative trauma disorders. Jobs that entail routines of high-rate physical motions, such as assembly-line workers, cashiers, phone operators, musicians, and others, are at heightened risk for disorders such as carpal tunnel syndrome and tendinitis. One strategy to lower risks for injury would be to arrange schedules of reinforcement and feedback to moderate activity rates and reduce physical stressors created by high-rate behavior. In addition to prevention of onset of these disorders, DRL schedules might be particularly useful in return-to-work programs for injured workers. Schedules that pace work and progressively reintroduce workers to jobs that produced injury might be very effective ingredients in work hardening programs. Keyboard operators (e.g., data entry clerks) might have their keystrokes measured by their equipment and software could program the delivery of DRL reinforcement to moderate the pace of repetitive motion exposures. More work is needed to explore this and examine how schedule manipulations can be integrated into work safety technologies.

CONCLUSION

DRL procedures are used often in basic research to establish predictable patterns of behavior. Clinical interventions using DRL procedures have been effective in lowering the rate of undesired, maladaptive behaviors. As a treatment procedure it is useful as a reductive technique when the goal is reduction of behavior rates to some tolerable level. The procedure is a relatively straightforward contingency management technique. Applied research is needed to further understand the variables influencing its effectiveness. Understanding how individuals' learning histories and provision of rules interact with DRL contingencies will help understand optimal administration of this procedure. Looking ahead, DRL applications may expand toward treatment of everyday behavioral excesses that diminish health and well-being.

References

Dietz, S. M. (1977). An analysis of programming DRL schedules in educational settings. *Behavior Research and Therapy. 15*, 103–111.

Dietz, S. M., & Repp, A. C. (1973). Decreasing classroom misbehavior through the use of DRL schedules of reinforcement. *Journal of Applied Behavior Analysis. 6*, 457–463.

Deitz, S. M., & Repp, A. C. (1974). Differentially reinforcing low rates of misbehavior with normal elementary school children. *Journal of Applied Behavior Analysis. 7*, 622.

Ferster, C. B., & Skinner, B. F. (1957). *Schedules of reinforcement.* New York: Appleton-Century-Crofts.

Holz, W. C., & Azrin, N. H. (1963). A comparison of several procedures for eliminating behavior. *Journal of the Experimental Analysis of Behavior, 6*, 399–406.

Lennox, D. B., Miltenberger, R. G., & Donnelly, D. R. (1987). Response interruption and DRL for the reduction of rapid eating. *Journal of Applied Behavior Analysis. 20*, 279–284.

Singh, N. N., Dawson, M. J., & Manning, P. (1981). Effects of spaced responding DRL on the stereotyped behavior of profoundly retarded persons. *Journal of Applied Behavior Analysis. 14*, 521–526.

Wright, C. S., & Vollmer, T. R. (2002). Evaluation of a treatment package to reduce rapid eating. *Journal of Applied Behavior Analysis. 35*, 89–93.

Wulfert, E., Greenway, D. E., Farkas, P., Hayes, S. C., & Dougher, M. J. (1994). Correlation between self-reported rigidity and rule-governed insensitivity to operant contingencies. *Journal of Applied Behavior Analysis. 27*, 659–671.

25 DIFFERENTIAL REINFORCEMENT OF OTHER BEHAVIOR AND DIFFERENTIAL REINFORCEMENT OF ALTERNATIVE BEHAVIOR

Michele D. Wallace and Adel C. Najdowski

Differential reinforcement procedures, namely differential reinforcement of other behavior (DRO), which involves providing reinforcement contingent upon the absence of the problem behavior for a specified time interval and differential reinforcement of alternative behavior (DRA), which involves providing reinforcement contingent on a desirable replacement behavior (Cooper, Heron, & Heward, 2007), have been repeatedly demonstrated to be relatively effective treatments for eliminating problem behavior (Poling & Ryan, 1982; Vollmer & Iwata, 1992). In fact, there is an extensive body of literature demonstrating that both procedures are effective alternatives in decreasing undesirable behavior presented by a client (see Table 25.1). Thus, what follows is a review of various issues that should be considered prior to implementation as well as a step-by-step guideline for how to properly implement both DRO and DRA procedures (see Table 25.2).

CONSIDERATIONS PRIOR TO IMPLEMENTING A DRO/DRA PROCEDURE

Conducting a Functional Behavioral Assessment

The most effective differential reinforcement procedures have been those conducted in combination with the use of extinction for problem behavior (Mazaleski, Iwata, Vollmer, Zarcone, & Smith, 1993). However, in order to use extinction for problem behavior, it is necessary to first determine the reinforcer maintaining such behavior. Therefore, a functional behavioral assessment of problem behavior (Iwata, Kahng, Wallace,

& Lindberg, 2000; Iwata, Vommer, & Zarcone, 1990) should be conducted to identify possible maintaining sources of reinforcement prior to implementing a differential reinforcement procedure (see Chapter 32).

Selecting Reinforcers to Deliver during Differential Reinforcement

Reinforcers scheduled to be delivered during differential reinforcement procedures should be chosen prior to implementation. They can be either the reinforcer maintaining problem behavior or an arbitrarily chosen reinforcer. As previously mentioned, the most efficient treatments involve delivery of maintaining reinforcers. Thus, it should be noted that in order for arbitrarily chosen reinforcers to effectively reduce problem behavior, they must be more potent than the reinforcer maintaining problem behavior (Vollmer & Iwata, 1992).

If the item to be delivered during the differential reinforcement procedure is arbitrary, a stimulus preference assessment (SPA) should always be conducted to increase the likelihood that the item will function as a reinforcer (see Pace, Ivancic, Edwards, Iwata, & Page, 1985). Items approached most often during the SPA should subsequently be used during the differential reinforcement procedure.

DIFFERENTIAL REINFORCEMENT OF OTHER BEHAVIOR (DRO)

In DRO procedures, problem behavior is reduced by scheduling a reinforcer contingent upon the

TABLE 25.1   Evidence-Based Applications

Behavior	DRO	DRA
Aggression	Figueroa, Thyer, & Thyer (1992); Repp & Deitz (1974)	Hagopian, Fisher, Sullivan, Acquisto, & LeBlanc (1998); Lalli, Casey, & Kates (1995)
Bedtime Problem Behavior	Freman (2006)	
Cigarette Smoking	Glenn & Dallery, (2007); Peine, Darvish, Blakelock, Osborne, & Jenson (1998)	_____
Disruption	Allen, Gottselig, & Boylan (1982); Conyers, Miltenberger, Maki, Barenz, Jurgens, Sailer, Haugen, & Kopp (2004); Deitz, Repp, & Deitz (1976); Repp, Barton, & Brulle (1983)	Hagopian, Fisher, Sullivan, Acquisto, & LeBlanc (1998); Marcus & Vollmer (1995)
Elopement	Piazza, Hanley, Bowman, Ruyter, Lindauer, & Saiontz (1997)	Tarbox, Wallace, & Williams (2003)
Food Refusal	_____	Riordan, Iwata, Finney, Wohl, & Stanley (1984); Riordan, Iwata, Wohl, & Finney (1980);
Food Stealing	Page, Finney, Parrish, & Iwata (1983)	_____
Hyperactivity	Doubros & Daniels (1986); Patterson, Jones, Whittier, & Wright (1965)	Twardosz & Sajwaj (1972)
Inappropriate Sexual Behavior	Foxx, McMorrow, Fenlon, & Bittle (1986)	Fyffe, Kahng, Fittro, & Russell (2004)
Inappropriate Verbal Behavior	_____	Dixon, Benedict, & Larson (2001); Durand, & Crimmins (1987); Rehfeldt & Chambers (2003); Wilder, Masuda, O'Connor, & Baham (2001)
Noncompliance	Kodak, Miltenberger & Romaniuk, C. (2003)	Marcus & Vollmer (1995); Wilder, Harris, Reagan, & Rasey (2007)
Pica	_____	Hagopian, Fisher, Sullivan, Acquisto, & LeBlanc (1998)
Precursors to Challenging Behavior	_____	Najdowski, Wallace, Ellsworth, MacAleese, & Cleveland (in press)
Psychogenic Cough	Watson & Heindl (1996)	_____
Self-Injury	Cowdery, Iwata, & Pace (1990); Frankel, Moss, Schofield, & Simmons (1976); Vollmer, Iwata, Zarcone, Smith, & Mazeleski (1993)	Hagopian, Fisher, Sullivan, Acquisto, & LeBlanc (1998); Lalli, Casey, & Kates (1995); Steege, Wacker, Berg, Cigrand, & Cooper (1989); Vollmer, Iwata, Smith, & Rodgers (1992)
Self-Scratching	Allen & Harris (1966)	_____
Sibling Fighting	Leitenberg, Burchard, Burchard, Fuller, & Lysaght (1977)	Leitenberg, Burchard, Burchard, Fuller, & Lysaght (1977)
Stereotypy	Patel, Carr, Kim, Robles, & Eastridge (2000); Repp, Dietz, & Spier (1974)	Steege, Wacker, Berg, Cigrand, & Cooper (1989)
Tantrums	Wilder, Chen, Atwell, Pritchard, & Weinstein (2006)	Carr & Durand (1985)
Thumb Sucking	Lowitz & Suib (1978)	Knight & McKenzie (1974)
Tics	Himle, Woods, Conelea, Bauer, & Rice (2007); Wagaman, Miltenberger, & Williams (1995); Woods & Himle (2004)	_____
Rumination	McKeegan, Estill, & Campbell (1987); Conrin, Pennypacker, Johnston, & Rast (1982)	_____
Wandering	Heard & Watson (1999)	_____

TABLE 25.2   Steps in the Use of DRO and DRA to Reduce Problem Behavior

---

I. Preparation

    Step 1. Conduct a functional assessment.

    Step 2. Select reinforcers to deliver during differential reinforcement that fit the functional assessment.

II. DRO procedures

    Step 1. Select the reinforcement interval length (e.g., use an interval slightly shorter than the mean interresponse time), focus (e.g., absence of the response during the whole interval or only at the end of an interval), and resetting feature (e.g., decide whether the time interval resets if problem behavior occurs at any point during the interval).

    Step 2. Implement the DRO in a setting that is associated with the problem behavior.

    Step 3. Thin the reinforcement schedule as problem behavior is reduced.

III. DRA procedures

    Step 1. Select an alternative response (e.g., one that is functionally or literally incompatible with the behavior that needs to decrease).

    Step 2. Select a reinforcement schedule (usually initially continuous reinforcement).

    Step 3. Implement the DRA in a setting in which reinforcement can be immediate.

    Step 4. Thin reinforcement schedule as behavior is acquired.

---

absence of problem behavior for a specific time interval. There are a number of mechanisms suggested to be responsible for the effectiveness of DRO procedures. First, because preferred consequences are delivered only when problem behavior is absent, these behaviors are no longer reinforced. In this manner, problem behavior may be suppressed through the process of extinction. Second, because DRO procedures require scheduled reinforcement, individuals are less likely to experience deprivation from reinforcement. Third, scheduled reinforcement increases the probability of whatever response it follows. Thus, behavior other than problem behavior is likely to be strengthened (Miltenberger, 2007).

Advantages and Disadvantages of DRO

The advantages and disadvantages of DRO procedures should be considered prior to determining if DRO would be a suitable treatment. There are many advantages of using DRO to reduce problem behavior. First, the procedure is relatively easy to implement and capable of rapidly (Reynolds, 1961) and successfully (Poling & Ryan, 1982; Vollmer & Iwata, 1992) treating a multitude of behavior problems. Second, the procedure involves frequently scheduled reinforcement of many other behaviors. Third, the technique itself is nonaversive in that in does not rely on punishment.

Regardless of the benefits of DRO, there are a number of disadvantages that should be considered prior to implementation:

1. The function of reinforcement delivery during DRO is to ensure relatively low levels of deprivation; however, if an individual engages in high rates of problem behavior, he or she will likely fail to meet the schedule requirements for reinforcement and will become more and more deprived of the reinforcer. In this case, an individual may continue to engage in problem behavior or start engaging in other inappropriate behavior to ensure reinforcement.

2. Because the procedure does not reinforce any replacement behavior in particular, it may unintentionally reinforce other inappropriate behavior. That is, DRO reinforces any behavior going on other than a specified problem behavior, and sometimes these behaviors may be inappropriate. For example, if one is using DRO to decrease aggression maintained by attention and one delivers reinforcement for not engaging in aggression just after the child swears, swearing might be in advertently strengthened because you would be delivering reinforcement following inappropriate vocalizations. Additonally, DRO is not considered to be a constructive approach to behavior management in that it does not

teach a specific alternative response to obtain reinforcement.

3. Behavioral contrast may be another adverse side effect of a DRO procedure. Problem behavior may increase in other situations (in which DRO is not implemented) if reinforcement for problem behavior is still being provided in those situations, in part due to the contrast with the situation in which DRO contingencies apply.

4. DRO has been suggested to be less adequate in treating problem behavior maintained by automatic reinforcement (e.g., sensory reinforcement), because the reinforcer delivered during the procedure must compete with reinforcers produced by problem behavior (Harris & Wolchik, 1979). Therefore, when choosing to use DRO with an individual who engages in problem behavior maintained by automatic reinforcement, it is advised that the reinforcer used in the DRO procedure compete with problem behavior as demonstrated in a competing item assessment (see Piazza, Adelinis, Hanley, Goh, & Delia, 2000).

Steps for Effective Usage of DRO

As previously mentioned, a functional behavioral assessment as well as careful reinforcer selection is advised prior to implementing any differential reinforcement procedure. Once these requirements for effective implementation of DRO have been met, there are a number of other important factors to consider, such as selecting reinforcement intervals, implementing the procedures, and thinning the DRO interval.

Selecting Reinforcement Intervals

In DRO, reinforcers are delivered following a period of time whereby problem behavior is absent. Thus, time requirements for the absence of problem behavior are based on either fixed intervals (FIs) or variable intervals (VIs). While FI are most commonly used during DRO procedures, there are no hard rules for choosing reinforcement intervals (Poling & Ryan, 1982).

One effective method for determining reinforcement intervals begins by measuring baseline rates of problem behavior, calculating the mean interresponse time (IRT), and subsequently using an interval slightly shorter than the mean IRT (Deitz & Repp, 1983). For example, if baseline responding occurs at a rate of 6 responses per minute (rpm), the mean IRT would be 10 s. Thus, the initial DRO schedule should be under 10 s. Moreover, it may be necessary to use even shorter time intervals if an extinction burst of problem behavior occurs during initial treatment sessions to ensure the delivery of reinforcement.

Once the necessary time interval is chosen, within interval requirements for reinforcer deliverance must also be considered. Whole-interval and momentary-interval requirements are two such possibilities. A whole-interval requirement involves the absence of problem behavior during an entire interval, while a momentary requirement involves the absence of problem behavior only at the end of an interval. Both procedures have been shown to be effective in reducing problem behavior (Lindberg, Iwata, Kahng, & DeLeon, 1999; Repp, Barton, Brulle, 1983).

Whether the interval will involve a resetting or nonresetting feature should also be considered. A resetting feature is most common for DRO procedures (Vollmer & Iwata, 1992), whereby a time interval resets if problem behavior occurs at any point during the interval (Repp et al., 1974). Contrarily, a nonresetting feature involves a time interval, which is not reset if problem behavior occurs during the interval (Repp, Deitz, & Deitz, 1976). In the latter case, the reinforcer would either be delivered at the end of the interval (nonresetting in conjunction with momentary DRO) or the remainder of the interval would be added to the subsequent interval (nonresetting in conjunction with whole-interval DRO). As such, the intervals may seemingly grow lengthier, and it is noteworthy that this could potentially lead to increased levels of deprivation when an individual continuously fails to meet the reinforcement requirement. A nonresetting DRO schedule might be useful, however, in a classroom or institutional setting, where staff-to-client ratios are low and several clients are observed simultaneously.

Implementing DRO

DRO implementation should begin with choosing a reasonable portion of the day in which it can consistently be implemented (Poling & Ryan, 1982). This may mean choosing an activity in which the problem behavior is most interfering. As problem behavior decreases one setting at a time, subsequent settings should be systematically targeted.

Using a stopwatch, DRO intervals should be timed, and reinforcers should be delivered contingent upon the absence of problem behavior for a specified period of time (Miltenberger, 2007). If problem behavior occurs during a point at which reinforcement is scheduled to be delivered, the reinforcer should be withheld. Following reinforcement, the timer should be reset, and the steps outlined above should be repeated. Once problem behavior begins to decrease to a specified criterion, it will be necessary to increase the interval requirement, thereby reducing the intensity of reinforcement. The criterion for increasing the interval length should be one in which an individual is successfully receiving reinforcement for the absence of problem behavior during most intervals (Miltenberger, 2007). An effective criterion for accomplishing this is to increase interval requirements following two consecutive sessions where little or no problem behavior occurs. This may also be operationally defined as problem behavior occurring at or less than 85%–90% of baseline rates (Hanley, Iwata, & Thompson, 2001).

Thinning the DRO Interval

Lengthening the DRO interval can be achieved across sessions or within sessions (Repp & Slack, 1977). Either way, it involves increasing intervals by fixed increments, proportional increments, or utilizing an IRT-adjusting method. Lengthening intervals by fixed increments simply involves consistently increasing interval requirements by a fixed length of time (Poling & Ryan, 1982). For example, a fixed 1-min increment would involve increasing a 2-min DRO interval to 3 min, 4 min, and 5 min, respectively.

Increasing the interval by proportional increments involves consistently lengthening interval requirements by a fixed or adjusted percentage of time. For example, a fixed 50% increment would involve increasing a 2-min interval to 3 min, 4.5 min, and 6.75 min, respectively. Conversely, an adjusted proportional increase would

often involve increasing the DRO interval by 33%–100%, depending on the current interval. For example, when beginning with a short interval such as 15 s, an initial increase of 100% to 30 s might be used. This might then increase across sessions to 45 s (50%), 60 s (33%), 90 s (50%), 120 s (33%), 160 s (33%), 230 s (44%), 330 s (43%), 450 s (37%), and 600 s (33%). This process could also be accompanied by periodic probes to determine if steps can be skipped. For example, after three consecutive sessions with no or little problem behavior, three steps ahead could be probed. If unsuccessful, then it would be appropriate to return to the previously successful step and proceed through the three intermediate steps before probing three steps ahead again (LeBlanc, Hagopian, Maglieri, & Poling, 2002).

Lengthening intervals by using an IRT-adjusting method involves continually adjusting the interval by setting the current interval slightly lower than the mean IRT measured in the previous 3–5 sessions (Deitz & Repp, 1983; Vollmer, Iwata, Zarcone, Smith, & Mazaleski, 1993). For example, if the initial DRO schedule was 10 s and the rate of responding from the last five sessions was 3 rpm, the new mean IRT would be 20 s. Thus, one would increase the interval from 10 s to 15 s for the next DRO session/requirement.

Once again, the criterion adopted for increasing the interval (based on a percentage decrease from baseline rates or visual inspection concluding the occurrence of little or no problem behavior) should be met within each phase of this process. In the event that an individual fails to meet the new criterion for a number of sessions (e.g., two to three), the previously successful interval requirement should be reinstated, to ensure that the individual successfully contacts reinforcement, until little or no problem behavior is occurring before again beginning to further increase the DRO interval (LeBlanc, Hagopian, & Maglieri, 2000).

DIFFERENTIAL REINFORCEMENT OF ALTERNATIVE BEHAVIOR (DRA)

In DRA procedures, problem behavior is reduced by increasing an alternative behavior that has been identified as a replacement for problem behavior. Thus, reinforcement is provided for alternative behavior while problem behavior is often (but not always) extinguished (Miltenberger, 2007). There are a number of mechanisms suggested to be responsible for the effectiveness of DRA procedures:

1. When reinforcement is no longer delivered contingent upon problem behavior, suppression of problem behavior may occur through the process of extinction (Fisher et al., 1993).
2. Alternative behavior is increased by deliverance of the reinforcer maintaining problem behavior. Thus, it is no longer necessary for an individual to engage in problem behavior to gain access to a specific reinforcer (Carr, 1988).
3. DRA procedures allow individuals to access reinforcement at whatever rate they choose to engage in the alternative behavior. Thus, it has been suggested that DRA allows individuals to exert control over reinforcement (Carr & Durand, 1985).

Variations of DRA

Differential Reinforcement of Incompatible Behavior (DRI)

In DRI, the topography of alternative behavior is incompatible with problem behavior. That is, problem behavior cannot occur while the individual is engaging in the alternative behavior. In this sense, incompatible behavior competes with problem behavior (Tarpley & Schroeder, 1979). For example, a child engaging in hand mouthing during a first grade "circle time" activity may be provided reinforcement for sitting with folded hands during the course of the activity. In this example, the child cannot physically fold his/her hands and hand mouth simultaneously.

Functional Communication Training (FCT)

In another variation of DRA, FCT, the alternative behavior is a communicative response. Thus, the replacement behavior allows an individual to communicate or request access to the reinforcer maintaining problem behavior. For example, in the case that problem behavior is maintained by escape from demands, an individual would be taught to request a break. The FCT response

(requesting a break) would be reinforced, while problem behavior (e.g., aggression, disruption, etc.) would be extinguished.

Advantages and Disadvantages of DRA

Consideration of the advantages and disadvantages associated with DRA procedures should be considered prior to implementation. There are many advantages to using DRA to treat problem behavior. As in the case of DRO, the first two involve the fact that: (1) DRA has been demonstrated to successfully treat a multitude of behavior problems (Vollmer & Iwata, 1992) and (2) the procedure is a nonpunishing and non-aversive treatment because it occasions reinforcement regularly (Deitz & Repp, 1983). A third advantage is that DRA replaces problem behavior with more appropriate behavior (LaVigna & Donnellan, 1986), and as long as alternative behavior is reinforced and maintained, problem behavior is less likely to occur (Deitz & Repp, 1983). Thus, DRA is considered to be a constructive approach to behavioral management.

Regardless of the benefits, there are at least two important disadvantages of DRA that should be addressed before implementation. First, results of the procedure are not necessarily achieved rapidly. Because DRA requires the acquisition of an alternative response, the target behavior may continue to occur until the alternative response has been strengthened. This means that decreases in the problem behavior and increases in the alternative behavior may occur slowly in some individuals. Second, individuals who have been taught an alternative response may use it at unmanageably high rates. For example, if you teach a child to request attention from Mom by saying "excuse me," the child might say "excuse me" 100-plus times throughout dinner preparation. Consequently, until the reinforcement schedule is thinned, DRA may be a tedious and labor-intensive intervention unless the new behavior is extinguished by no longer reinforcing it. However, it should be pointed out that extinguishing the new replacement behavior, even if it is now occurring at unmanageably high rates, would actually be considered a step backwards in that recovery of the initial problem behavior or development of new problem behavior) may be promoted.

Steps for Effective Usage of DRA

Subsequent to conducting a functional assessment and carefully selecting reinforcers, there are a number of other important factors to consider prior to implementation such as selecting an alternative response, selecting reinforcement intervals, implementing DRA, and thinning reinforcement.

Selecting an Alternative Response

Responses chosen to replace problem behavior should be responses that already occasionally occur in an individual's repertoire when possible. Additionally, responses should be ones that natural contingencies are likely to reinforce, that is, ones that the social environment would naturally support. Moreover, the alternative response should require little response effort, such that an individual would be more likely to engage in the alternative behavior than problem behavior (Miltenberger, 2007). Finally, it may also be beneficial to choose a number of alternative responses to reinforce (Kazdin, 1994). This might involve teaching an individual engaging in problem behavior maintained by attention to not only approach others but to also initiate conversation by saying "hello" or "let's talk." If it is not possible to choose an alternative response within the individual's repertoire, it will be necessary to devote time to training the desired responses via either shaping or transfer of stimulus control. For example, providing differential reinforcement for successive approximations of a specified alternative behavior or using a prompting procedure.

Selecting Reinforcement Intervals

Any reinforcement schedule, including fixed ratio (FR) and variable ratio (VR), may be used to reinforce an alternative response. However, an initial continuous reinforcement schedule (CRF) in which an alternative response is reinforced for every occurrence is recommended. A CRF schedule will allow the alternative response to increase more rapidly (Miltenberger, 2007).

Implementing DRA

During DRA implementation, reinforcement for alternative behavior should not only be delivered continuously, but also contingently and immediately. This means that contingent upon each occurrence of alternative behavior; reinforcement should be delivered without delay. Once problem behavior begins to decrease and alternative behavior has become efficient, it will be necessary to thin the reinforcement schedule (Miltenberger, 2007). The thinning criterion already outlined in the DRO section of this chapter is also recommended for DRA.

Thinning Reinforcement

Thinning the reinforcement schedule within a DRA procedure involves either gradually increasing the reinforcement schedule by fixed or proportional ratios, inserting delays to reinforcement, altering the magnitude or quality of reinforcement, arranging a multiple schedule requirement, or restricting access to the materials needed to engage in the alternative response. Thinning ratio schedules by fixed increments involves consistently increasing response requirements by specific number of responses. Thinning ratio schedules by proportional increments involves consistently increasing ratio requirements by a fixed or adjusted percentage of responses (see the DRO section for details on fixed and proportional methods).

Since intermittent FR schedules and VR schedules result in moderate to high increases in response rates, the thinning method of increasing ratio requirements should only be used for alternative responses that are desired to occur at high rates (LeBlanc et al., 2002). For example, a desirable high-rate alternative response would be completion of math problems, whereas an undesirable high-rate alternative response would be asking for help. The latter is undesirable because asking for help may begin to occur at unmanageably high rates.

Another method for reducing the intensity of reinforcement for alternative responses that are undesirable when they occur at high rates is to insert a delay between when the alternative response occurs and when the reinforcer is delivered. This delay to reinforcement would begin with just a few seconds and increase after two to three sessions, with problem behavior remaining low until the terminal delay is reached (Hagopian, Fisher, Sullivan, Acquisto, & LeBlanc, 1998). Additionally, since the individual is required to wait for the reinforcer, it might be useful to increase the magnitude of the reinforcer when possible (Logue, 1988).

One practical way of thinning reinforcement involves using a response chaining method. In response chaining, individuals are taught to complete a series of steps in a task before obtaining reinforcement. For example, individuals engaging in problem behavior to access escape may initially be taught to request a break. However, as individuals become efficient in requesting a break, they should be taught to complete one homework problem prior to requesting a break. In this manner, response chaining would ultimately lead to the completion of an entire worksheet of homework problems before a break is obtained (Lalli, Casey, & Kates, 1995).

The reinforcement schedule for the alternative response can also be reduced by arranging a multiple schedule wherein periods of reinforcement and extinction for the alternative response are signaled by correlating each of these periods with a different stimulus. For example, a green card could be correlated with a period of reinforcement, while a red card could be correlated with a period of extinction for alternative behavior. These periods would initially alternate in a fashion that would allow the reinforcement period to be greater than the extinction period. For example, it might be feasible to start by delivering continuous reinforcement for an alternative response for a period of 45 s followed by a period of 15 s in which no reinforcement is provided. Then, the multiple schedule could be further thinned (e.g., from 45/15 to 60/30, 60/45, 60/60, 60/90, 60/120 . . .) upon achieving no or little problem behavior for two consecutive sessions (Hanley et al., 2001; Najdowski, Wallace, Ellsworth, MacAleese, & Cleveland, in press).

A final alternative method for reducing the intensity of reinforcement is to restrict the individual's access to the materials needed to engage in the alternative response. For example, when the alternative response involves handing over a communication card to request attention, a break, or access to a tangible item, the card is initially present continuously and the alternative response of handing in the card is reinforced on a continuous schedule. Following this phase, a short restriction interval can be put into place (e.g., 3 s), where in the card in not available for 3s. Subsequently, the restriction interval is slowly increased as long as problem behavior remains low (Roane, Fisher, Sgro, Falcomata, & Pabico, 2004).

SUMMARY

DRO and DRA, two of the most commonly used contingency-based procedures for the reduction of problem behavior, have been demonstrated to be easily implemented and an effective treatment strategy. When choosing to use DRO or DRA procedures, it is advised that one first identify the maintaining variables associated with the undesirable behavior. Moreover, when determining the suitability of differential reinforcement treatments, one should take into account possible advantages and disadvantages (outlined above) prior to implementation. Finally, if implemented in accordance to the above mentioned guidelines, one should be able to make lasting behavioral change with either DRO or DRA procedures.

References

Allen, L. C., Gottselig, M., & Boylan, S. (1982). A practical mechanism for using free time as a reinforcer in classrooms. *Education and Treatment of Children, 5*, 347–353.

Allen, E. K., & Harris, F. R. (1966). Elimination of a child's excessive scratching by training the mother in reinforcement procedures. *Behavior Research and Therapy, 4*(2), 79–84.

Carr, E. G. (1988). Functional equivalence as a means of response generalization. In R. H. Horner & G. Dunlap & R. L. Koegel (Eds.), *Generalization and maintenance: Life-style changes in applied settings* (pp. 221–241). Baltimore: Paul H. Brooks.

Carr, E. G., & Durand, V. M. (1985). Reducing behavior problems through functional communication training. *Journal of Applied Behavior Analysis, 18*, 111–126.

Conrin, J. H., Pennypacker, H. S., Johnston, J., & Rast, J. (1982). Differential reinforcement of other behaviors to treat chronic rumination of mental retardates. *Journal of Behavior Therapy and Experimental Psychiatry, 13*(4), 325–329.

Conyers, C., Miltenberger, R., Maki, A., Barenz, R., Jurgens, M., Sailer, et al. (2004). A comparison of response cost and differential reinforcement of other behavior to reduce disruptive behavior in a preschool classroom. *Journal of Applied Behavior Analysis, 37,* 411–415.

Cooper, J. O., Heron, T. E., & Heward, W. L. (2007). *Applied behavior analysis.* Upper Saddle River, NJ: Pearson Education, Inc.

Cowdery, G. E., Iwata, B. A., & Pace, G. M. (1990). Effects and side effects of DRO as treatment for self-injurious behavior. *Journal of Applied Behavior Analysis, 23,* 497–506.

Deitz, D. E., & Repp, A. C. (1983). Reducing behavior through reinforcement. *Exceptional Education Quarterly, 3,* 34–46.

Deitz, S. M., Repp, A. C., & Deitz, D. E. D. (1976). Reducing inappropriate classroom behaviour of retarded students through three procedures of differential reinforcement. *Journal of Mental Deficiency Research, 20,* 155–226.

Dixon, M. R., Benedict, H., & Larson, T. (2001). Functional analysis and treatment of inappropriate verbal behavior. *Journal of Applied Behavior Analysis, 34,* 361–363.

Donnelly, D. R., & Olczak, P. V. (1990). The effect of differential reinforcement of incompatible behaviors (DRI) on pica for cigarettes in persons with intellectual disability. *Behavior Modification, 14,* 81–96.

Doubros, S. G., & Daniels, G. J. (1986). An experimental approach to the reduction of overactive behavior. *Behaviour Research and Therapy, 4,* 251–258.

Durand, V. M., & Crimmins, D. B. (1987). Assessment and treatment of psychotic speech in an autistic child. *Journal of Autism and Developmental Disorders, 17,* 17–28.

Figueroa, R. G., Thyer, B. A., & Thyer, K. B. (1992). Extinction and DRO in the treatment of aggression in a boy with severe mental retardation. *Journal of Behavior Therapy and Experimental Psychiatry, 23*(2), 133–140.

Fisher, W., Piazza, C., Cataldo, M., Harrell, R., Jefferson, G., & Conner, R. (1993). Functional communication training with and without extinction and punishment. *Journal of Applied Behavior Analysis, 26,* 23–36.

Frankel, F., Moss, D., Schofield, S., & Simmons (1976). Case study: Use of differential reinforcement to suppress self injurious and aggressive behavior. *Psychological Reports, 39*(3), 843–849.

Freeman, K. A. (2006). Treating bedtime resistance with the bedtime pass: A systematic replication and component analysis with 3-year-olds. *Journal of Applied Behavior Analysis, 39,* 423–428.

Foxx, R.M., McMorrow, M.J., Fenlon, S., & Bittle, R.G. (1986). The reductive effects of reinforcement procedures on the genital stimulation and stereotypy of a mentally retarded adolescent male. *Analysis and Intervention in Developmental Disabilities, 6*(3), 239–248.

Fyffe, C. E., Kahng, S., Fittro, E., & Russell, D. (2004). Functional analysis and treatment of inappropriate sexual behavior. *Journal of Applied Behavior Analysis, 37,* 401–404.

Glenn, I. M., & Dallery, J. (2007). Effects of Internet-based voucher reinforcement and a transdermal nicotine patch on cigarette smoking. *Journal of Applied Behavior Analysis, 40,* 1–13.

Hagopian, L. P., Fisher, W. W., Sullivan, M. T., Acquisto, J., & LeBlanc, L. A. (1998). Effectiveness of functional communication training with and without extinction and punishment: A summary of 21 inpatient cases. *Journal of Applied Behavior Analysis, 31,* 211–235.

Hanley, G. P., Iwata, B. A., & Thompson, R. H. (2001). Reinforcement schedule thinning following treatment with functional communication training. *Journal of Applied Behavior Analysis, 34,* 17–38.

Harris, S. L., & Wolchik, S. A. (1979). Suppression of self-stimulation: Three alternative strategies. *Journal of Applied Behavior Analysis, 12,* 199–210.

Heard, K., & Watson, T. S. (1999). Reducing wandering by persons with dementia using differential reinforcement. *Journal of Applied Behavior Analysis, 32,* 381–384.

Himle, M. B., Woods, D. W., Conelea, C. A., Bauer, C. C., & Rice, K. A. (2007). Investigating the effects of tic suppression on premonitory urge ratings in children and adolescents with Tourette's syndrome. *Behavior Research and Therapy, 45*(12), 2964–2976.

Iguchi, M. Y., Belding, M. A., Morral, A. R., Lamb, R., & Husband, S. D. (1997). Reinforcing operants other than abstinence in drug abuse treatment: An effective alternative for reducing drug use. *Journal of Consulting and Clinical Psychology, 65*(3), 421–428.

Iwata, B. A., Kahng, S., Wallace, M. D., & Lindberg, J. S. (2000). The functional analysis model of behavioral assessment. In J. Austin & J. E. Carr (Eds.), *Handbook of applied behavior analysis.* Reno, NV: Context Press.

Iwata, B. A., Vollmer, T. R., & Zarcone, J. R. (1990). The experimental (functional) analysis of behavior disorders: Methodology, applications, and limitations. In A. C. Repp & N. N. Singh (Eds.), *Perspectives on the use of nonaversive and aversive interventions for persons with developmental disabilities* (pp. 301–330). Sycamore, IL: Sycamore Publishing Co.

Kazdin, A. E. (1994). *Behavior modification in applied settings* (5th ed.). Pacific Grove: Brooks/Cole Publishing Company.

Knight, M. F., & McKenzie, H. S. (1974). Elimination of bedtime thumbsucking in home settings through contingent reading. *Journal of Applied Behavior Analysis, 7*(1), 33–38.

Kodak, T., Miltenberger, R. G., & Romaniuk, C. (2003). The effects of differential negative reinforcement of other behavior and noncontingent escape on compliance. *Journal of Applied Behavior Analysis, 36*, 379–382.

Lalli, J. S., Casey, S., & Kates, K. (1995). Reducing escape behavior and increasing task completion with functional communication training, extinction, and response chaining. *Journal of Applied Behavior Analysis, 28*, 261–268.

LaVigna, G. W., & Donnellan, A. M. (1986). Alternatives to punishment: Solving behavior problems with non-aversive strategies. New York: Irvington Publishers Inc.

LeBlanc, L. A., Hagopian, L. P., & Maglieri, K. A. (2000). Use of a token economy to eliminate excessive inappropriate social behavior in an adult with developmental disabilities. *Behavioral Interventions, 15*(2), 135–143.

LeBlanc, L. A., Hagopian, L. P., Maglieri, K. A., & Poling, A. (2002). Decreasing the intensity of reinforcement-based interventions for reducing behavior: Conceptual issues and a proposed model for clinical practice. *The Behavior Analyst Today, 3*(3), 289–300.

Leitenberg, H., Burchard, J. D., Burchard, S. N., Fuller, E. J., & Lysaght, T. V. (1977). Using positive reinforcement to suppress behaviors: Some experimental comparisons with sibling conflict. *Behavior Therapy, 8*, 168–182.

Lindberg, J. S., Iwata, B. A., Kahng, S., & DeLeon, I. G. (1999). DRO contingencies: An analysis of variable-momentary schedules. *Journal of Applied Behavior Analysis, 32*, 123–136.

Lockwood, K., Maenpaa, M., & Williams, D. E. (1997). Long-term maintenance of a behavioral alternative to surgery for severe vomiting and weight loss. *Journal of Behavior Therapy and Experimental Psychiatry, 28*, 105–112.

Logue, A. W. (1988). Research on self-control: An integrating framework. *Behavioral and Brain Sciences, 11*(4), 665–709.

Lowitz, G. H., & Suib, M. R. (1978). Generalized control of persistent thumbsucking by differential reinforcement of other behaviors. *Journal of Behavior Therapy and Experimental Psychiatry, 9*(4), 343–346.

Marcus, B. A., & Vollmer, T. R. (1995). Effects of differential negative reinforcement on disruption and compliance. *Journal of Applied Behavior Analysis, 28*, 229–230.

Mazaleski, J. L., Iwata, B. A., Vollmer, T. R., Zarcone, J. R., & Smith, R. G. (1993). Analysis of the reinforcement and extinction components in DRO contingencies with self-injury. *Journal of Applied Behavior Analysis, 26*, 143–156.

McKeegan, G. F., Estill, K., & Campbell, B. (1987). Elimination of rumination by controlled eating and differential reinforcement. *Journal of Behavior Therapy and Experimental Psychiatry, 18*(2), 143–148.

Miltenberger, R. G. (2007). *Behavior modification: Principles and procedures* (4th ed.). Belmont, CA: Wadsworth Thomson Learning.

Najdowski, A. C., Wallace, M. D., Ellsworth, C. L., MacAleese, A. N., & Cleveland, J. M. (in press). Addressing severe problem behavior through functional analyses and treatment of precursor behavior. *Journal of Applied Behavior Analysis.*

Pace, G. M., Ivancic, M. T., Edwards, G. L., Iwata, B. A., & Page, T. J. (1985). Assessment of stimulus preference and reinforcer value with profoundly retarded individuals. *Journal of Applied Behavior Analysis, 18*, 249–255.

Page, T. J., Finney, J. W., Parrish, J. M., & Iwata, B. A. (1983). Assessment and reduction of food stealing in Prader–Willi children. *Applied Research in Mental Retardation, 4*(3), 219–228.

Patel, M. R., Carr, J. E., Kim, C., Robles, A., & Eastridge, D. (2000). Functional analysis of aberrant behavior maintained by automatic reinforcement: Assessments of specific sensory reinforcers. *Research and Developmental Disabilities, 21*(5), 393–407.

Peine, H. A., Darvish, R., Blakelock, H., Osborne, J. G., & Jenson, W. R. (1998). Non-aversive reduction of cigarette smoking in two adult men in a residential setting. *Journal of Behavior Therapy and Experimental Psychiatry, 29*(1), 55–65.

Piazza, C. C., Adelinis, J. D., Hanley, G. P., Goh, H., & Delia, M. D. (2000). An evaluation of the effects of matched stimuli on behaviors maintained by automatic reinforcement. *Journal of Applied Behavior Analysis, 33*, 13–27.

Piazza, C. C., Hanley, G. P., Bowman, L. G., Ruyter, J. M., Lindauer, S. E., & Saiontz, D. M. (1997). Functional analysis and treatment of elopement. *Journal of Applied Behavior Analysis, 30*, 653–672.

Poling, A., & Ryan, C. (1982). Differential reinforcement of other behavior schedules: Therapeutic applications. *Behavior Modification, 6*, 3–21.

Rehfeldt, R. A., & Chambers, M. R. (2003). Functional analysis and treatment of verbal perseverations displayed by an adult with autism. *Journal of Applied Behavior Analysis, 36*, 259–261.

Repp, A. C., Barton, L. E., & Brulle, A. R. (1983). A comparison of two procedures for programming the differential reinforcement of other behavior. *Journal of Applied Behavior Analysis, 16*, 435–445.

Repp, A. C., & Deitz, S. M. (1974). Reducing aggressive and self-injurious behavior of institutionalized children through reinforcement of other behaviors. *Journal of Applied Behavior Analysis, 7,* 313–325.

Repp, A. C., Deitz, S. M., & Deitz, D. E. (1976). Reducing inappropriate behaviors in a classroom and in individual sessions through DRO schedules of reinforcement. *Mental Retardation, 14,* 11–15.

Repp, A. C., Deitz, S. M., & Speir, N. C. (1974). Reducing stereotypic responding of retarded persons by the differential reinforcement of other behavior. *American Journal of Mental Deficiency, 79,* 279–284.

Repp, A. C., & Slack, D. J. (1977). Reducing responding of retarded persons by DRO schedules following a history of low-rate responding: A comparison of ascending interval sizes. *Psychological Record, 3,* 581–588.

Reynolds, G. S. (1961). Behavioral contrast. *Journal of the Experimental Analysis of Behavior, 4,* 57–71.

Riordan, M. M., Iwata, B. A., Finney, J. W., Wohl, M. K., & Stanley, A. E. (1984). Behavioral assessment and treatment of chronic food refusal in handicapped children. *Journal of Applied Behavior Analysis, 17,* 324–341.

Riordan, M. M., Iwata, B. A., Wohl, M. K., & Finney, J. W. (1980). Behavioral treatment of food refusal and selectivity in developmentally disabled children. *Applied Research in Mental Retardation, 1,* 95–112.

Roane, H. S., Fisher, W. W., Sgro, G. M., Falcomata, T. S., & Pabico, R. R. (2004). An alternative method of thinning reinforcer delivery during differential reinforcement. *Journal of Applied Behavior Analysis, 37,* 213–218.

Steege, M. W., Wacker, D. D., Berg, W. K., Cigrand, K. K., & Cooper, L. J., (1989). The use of behavioral assessment to prescribe and evaluate treatments for severely handicapped children. *Journal of Applied Behavior Analysis, 22,* 23–33.

Tarbox, R. S. F., Wallace, M. D., & Williams, L. (2003). Assessment and treatment of elopement: A replication and extension. *Journal of Applied Behavior Analysis, 36*(2), 239–244.

Tarpley, H. D., & Schroeder, S. R. (1979). Comparison of DRO and DRI on rate suppression of self-injurious behavior. *American Journal of Mental Deficiency, 84,* 188–194.

Twardosz, S., & Sajwaj, T. (1972). Multiple effects of a procedure to increase sitting in a hyperactive, retarded boy. *Journal of Applied Behavior Analysis, 5,* 73–78.

Vollmer, T. R., & Iwata, B. A. (1992). Differential reinforcement as treatment for behavior disorders: Procedural and functional variations. *Research in Developmental Disabilities, 13,* 393–417.

Vollmer, T. R., Iwata, B. A., Zarcone, J. R., Smith, R. G., & Mazaleski, J. L. (1993). Within-session patterns of self-injury as indicators of behavioral function. *Research in Developmental Disabilities, 14,* 479–492.

Wagaman, J. R., Miltenberger, R. G., & Williams, D. E. (1995). Treatment of a vocal tic by differential reinforcement. *Journal of Behavior Therapy and Experimental Psychiatry, 26*(1), 35–39.

Watson, T. S., & Heindl, B. (1996). Behavioral case consultation with parents and teachers: An example using differential reinforcement to treat psychogenic cough. *Journal of School Psychology, 34*(4), 365–378.

Wilder, D. A., Chen, L., Atwell, J., Pritchard, J., & Weinstein, P. (2006). Brief functional analysis and treatment of tantrums associated with transitions in preschool children. *Journal of Applied Behavior Analysis, 39,* 103–107.

Wilder, D. A., Harris, C., Reagan, R., & Rasey, A. (2007). Functional analysis and treatment of noncompliance by preschool children. *Journal of Applied Behavior Analysis, 40,* 173–177.

Wilder, D. A., Masuda, A., O'Connor, C., & Baham, M. (2001). Brief functional analysis and treatment of bizarre vocalizations in an adult with schizophrenia. *Journal of Applied Behavior Analysis, 34,* 65–68.

Woods, D. W., & Himle, M. B. (2004). Creating tic suppression: Comparing the effects of verbal instruction to differential reinforcement. *Journal of Applied Behavior Analysis, 37,* 417–420.

26 DIRECTED MASTURBATION: A TREATMENT OF FEMALE ORGASMIC DISORDER

Stephanie Both and Ellen Laan

INTRODUCTION

Directed masturbation, a behavioral treatment for female orgasmic disorder, was developed in the early 1970s. Like most sex therapy methods, directed masturbation is based on the sex therapy format introduced by Masters and Johnson. The pioneer laboratory work of Masters and Johnson (1966) showed that men and women are equally capable of responding sexually. In addition, their work in the field of treatment of sexual dysfunctions, described in the book *Human Sexual Inadequacy* (1970), showed that people with sexual dysfunctions could benefit substantially from a brief and directive treatment. The more liberal sexual climate in the 1960s and the increased liberation of women, together with the work of Masters and Johnson, initiated the assertion that for women it should be equally possible to experience sexual pleasure and orgasm as for men.

Masters and Johnson already included specific interventions in their treatment method for making possible orgasms for women who never or seldom experienced them. LoPicollo and Lobitz (1972) elaborated on the work of Masters and Johnson, and designed a nine-step masturbation program for anorgasmic women. This program consisted of a number of basic elements: education, self-exploration and body awareness, directed masturbation, and sensate focus. Initially, the program involved both partners of a couple, similar to Masters and Johnson's approach. Later, Barbach (1974) transformed the masturbation program of LoPicollo and Lobitz to a format for group treatment for women without their partners, the so-called preorgasmic women's groups. The use of the word *preorgasmic* stressed the view that anorgasmia in women

was thought to be mainly the result of an inadequate learning process. In this view, women who never experienced orgasm missed a history of discovery of their own sexuality. This omission was supposed to be repaired through learning of adequate "masturbation skills" that result in sexual arousal and orgasm. Eventually, these skills could be applied in interaction with a partner. In Barbach's approach there was an emphasis on facilitating women's autonomy and assertiveness in their sexual relationships. Later on, the masturbation program became available for a larger audience through the self-help books *For Yourself: The Fulfillment of Female Sexuality* (Barbach, 1975) and *Becoming Orgasmic* (Heiman, LoPicollo, & LoPicollo, 1976).

The assumption that sexual behavior is learned is common across theories of sexual behavior. Many theories state that sexual behavior is learned through associative learning processes like classical and operant conditioning. Through conditioning, sexual behaviors and positive feelings become associated, which facilitates behavior that may result in sexual arousal and orgasm. In anorgasmic women such positive associations may be missing, or sexual behavior may be associated with negative feelings. It is assumed that through directed masturbation positive associations can be learned. The goal of the treatment is to stimulate behavior that facilitates sexual arousal and orgasm, and to replace inadequate behavior that prevents sexual arousal and orgasm to come about for more appropriate behavior. Feelings of anxiety, shame, or guilt, which may restrain the woman to try various kinds of sexual stimulation, are reduced by systematic desensitization.

Other cognitive theories on sexual functioning stress the importance of anxiety and attention and fear of losing control. Anxiety associated with sexual experiences can interfere with the ability to relax and can lead to attention to a number of (nonsexual) concerns resulting in inhibition of sexual arousal and orgasm (Barlow, 1986). Women who feel that they must remain in control, and who may have learned to fear the loss of control, are more likely to have problems in "letting go," which is a necessary condition for orgasm to occur (Heiman, 2000). The present method of directed masturbation is based on both learning and cognitive principles.

Directed masturbation is characterized by the prescription of behavioral exercises that are performed privately at home. The exercises focus initially on body awareness and body acceptance, and on visual and tactile exploration of the body. Second, women are encouraged to discover the areas of the body that produce pleasure when touched. After that, women are instructed in techniques of masturbation, and to use fantasy and imaging to increase sexual excitement. The use of topical lubricants, vibrators, and erotic literature or videotapes is often recommended. Frequently, Kegel exercises (contraction and relaxation of the pelvic floor muscles) (Kegel, 1952) are prescribed, since they may increase women's awareness of sensations in the genitals and because that may enhance sexual arousal (Messen & Geer, 1985). For women who are inhibited in achieving orgasm due to fear of losing control, the use of "role-play" orgasm is recommended (Heiman & LoPicollo, 1986). In such role-play, a woman pretends she is losing control and is experiencing high sexual arousal and orgasm. This may help to overcome the fear of showing the uncontrolled behavior that may accompany orgasm.

EVIDENCE-BASED APPLICATIONS

The treatment has been applied in different settings, including group, individual, couple, and bibliotherapy. Generally, the treatment is brief, between 12 and 20 sessions. It is proven to be equally successful in different settings. Most outcome studies report high success rates in women with lifelong anorgasmia, with greater than 80% of women being able to experience orgasm by masturbation, and a lower percentage, 20%–60%, being able to experience orgasm with their partner (Heiman, 2000). Reviews of treatments for sexual dysfunctions in women that follow the criteria for validated or evidence-based practice (APA, 1995) conclude that directed masturbation treatments for primary anorgasmia fulfill the criteria of "well established" (Heiman & Meston, 1997), or at least "probably efficacious" (O'Donohue, Dopke & Swingen, 1997). Learning how to become orgasmic during masturbation does not necessarily generalize to being orgasmic during sexual activity with a partner (de Bruijn, 1982; Hurlbert & Apt, 1995; Leff & Israel, 1983). If a woman is able to attain orgasm through masturbation but not with her partner, couple treatment with a focus on communication, anxiety reduction, adequate clitoral stimulation, and engaging in intercourse using positions that maximize clitoral stimulation, may be more effective (Meston & Levin, 2005).

WHO MIGHT BENEFIT FROM THIS TREATMENT

In the *Diagnostic and Statistical Manual of Mental Disorders*, 4th edition, text revision *(DSM-IV-TR)* female orgasmic disorder is described as a persistent or recurrent delay in, or absence of, orgasm following a normal sexual excitement phase (APA, 1994). To meet criteria for orgasmic disorder, the disturbance must cause marked distress or interpersonal difficulty. The *DSM-IV-TR* describes subtypes of female orgasmic disorder as lifelong versus acquired and generalized (never experiencing orgasm) versus situational (reaching orgasm only with specific stimulation). Acknowledging the variability within and between women in the type or intensity of stimulation required to trigger orgasm, even in standardized conditions (Laan & van Lunsen, 2002; Levin & Wagner, 1985), the diagnosis of the disorder is based on "the clinician's judgment that the woman's capacity to orgasm is less than would be reasonable for her age, sexual experience, and the adequacy of sexual stimulation she receives." However, indications of what is reasonable, and a definition of orgasm are not provided by the *DSM-IV-TR*. *The Hite Report* (1976) showed that 72% of women did not regularly have orgasm during coitus, yet 93% could reach orgasm pleasurably with self-stimulation that was dissimilar to the stimulation received during coitus. The clinical consensus is that a woman who can obtain orgasm through intercourse with manual stimulation but not through intercourse alone would not meet criteria for clinical diagnosis, unless she is distressed by the frequency of her sexual response (Meston & Bradford, 2007).

Orgasm is usually defined as a combination of subjective experience and physiological changes. Meston and Bradford (2007) offer the following definition: "An orgasm in the human female is a variable, transient peak sensation of intense pleasure, creating an altered state of consciousness, usually accompanied by involuntary, rhythmic contractions of the pelvic striated circumvaginal musculature, often with concomitant uterine and anal contractions and myotonia that resolves the sexually-induced vasocongestion, usually with an induction of well-being and contentment" (p. 244).

Given the variance in type and intensity of stimulation needed to reach orgasm, and the two components of orgasm (subjective experience and physiological changes), it is not surprising that there exists a substantial variety in the orgasmic problems women report. Women may seek help because they never have experienced orgasm; because they are capable of reaching orgasm by masturbation but not during sexual contact with a partner; because they can reach orgasm with a partner but not or seldom through intercourse; because they cannot reach orgasm except with a vibrator or through other specific types of sexual stimulation (e.g., by lying face down on the bed with legs pressed together while moving the pelvis); or because they orgasm physically but do not, or only weakly, experience feelings of pleasure or release of tension.

Directed masturbation is most effective in treating women with lifelong, generalized orgasmic disorder (Heiman & Meston, 1997; O'Donohue et al. 1997). However, the treatment may also be effective in women with situational orgasmic disorder who can reach orgasm only through very specific masturbation manners.

The focus in directed masturbation on discovery of various areas of the body that may produce pleasure when touched, and the encouragement to experiment with various techniques of masturbation, can expand a woman's skills to reach orgasm.

Following the definition of *DSM-IV-TR*, orgasmic disorder is diagnosed only when there is a normal sexual excitement phase that is not followed by orgasm. But many women with lifelong, generalized anorgasmia experience only little sexual excitement or report problems in keeping a certain level of sexual excitement (Morokoff, 1989). Thus, in clinical practice, the diagnosis orgasmic disorder may be made when, according to *DSM-IV-TR* criteria, the diagnosis "female sexual arousal disorder" may be more accurate. In fact, directed masturbation is, given the emphasis on learning of behavior that makes sexual excitement and orgasm to come about, especially aimed at women who experience little sexual excitement. Some women with hypoactive sexual desire disorder have a history of sexual excitement problems and anorgasmia, resulting in a lack of sexually rewarding experiences. Thus, orgasmic problems often involve sexual arousal problems, and desire problems can be caused by arousal and orgasmic problems. Not surprisingly, there is often comorbidity of anorgasmia, sexual arousal disorder, and sexual desire disorder (Segraves & Segraves, 1991). Several theorists have suggested that the majority of female sexual difficulties reflect disruptions in sexual arousal (Laan, Everaerd, & Both, 2005; Meston & Bradford, 2007). To summarize, given the overlap of sexual arousal, orgasmic, and desire problems, directed masturbation can be suitable for women with lifelong generalized orgasmic problems, women with generalized sexual arousal problems, and for women with sexual desire problems combined with generalized low sexual arousal.

As noticed before, orgasmic problems can be related to a lack of "skills" to achieve arousal and orgasm, or to inhibition of the orgasmic response due to, for example, fear of losing control, or both. Unfortunately, no studies have examined the prevalence of, or the effect of, directed masturbation in these distinct forms of orgasmic disorder.

CONTRAINDICATIONS FOR TREATMENT

Various conditions, like medical illness, anxiety and depression disorders, posttraumatic stress disorder (PTSD) after sexual assault, drug addiction, or serious relationship problems can have a profound impact on sexual functioning. In case of such conditions, specific treatment for these conditions is indicated rather than sex therapy.

Little can be said about physical causes of inhibited female orgasm due to a lack of knowledge of the neurophysiological basis of orgasm. Damage to the central nervous system, the spinal cord, or the peripheral nerves caused by trauma or multiple sclerosis may lead to orgasmic difficulties (Sipski, 1998). The role of estrogen or testosterone in orgasmic function is a topic of debate; positive associations between testosterone and orgasm have been observed, but may be mediated by increased sexual desire and sexual activity (Bianchi-Demichelli & Ortigue, 2007). Drugs that increase serotonergic activity (e.g., antidepressants; paroxetine, fluoxetine, sertraline) or decrease dopaminergic activity (e.g., antipsychotics) are reported to delay or inhibit orgasm in women (Meston & Bradford, 2007). For women taking selective serotonin reuptake inhibitors (SSRIs), in which the orgasmic difficulties coincide with the onset of drug treatment, a change in prescription to an antidepressant with fewer sexual side effects may be recommended (e.g., bupropion, nefazodone, mirtazapine) (Gregorian, Golden, Bahce et al., 2002). For women with orgasmic disorder using psychotropic medication that is known to impair orgasm, it is recommended to start directed masturbation only after medication is reduced or changed. However, if a change or reduction of medication is not possible, treatment may be started to see what improvements can be made.

A relationship between sexual abuse and various sexual difficulties has been reported (e.g., van Berlo & Ensink, 2000), and there is evidence for an association between childhood sexual abuse and sexual aversion (Noll, Trickett, Putnam et al., 2003). There is, however, no consistent evidence for an association between sexual abuse and anorgasmia (Meston & Levin, 2005; Lutfey, Link, Litman et al., 2007). A history of sexual abuse is no contraindication for directed masturbation, but it is important to determine carefully whether there is a strong fear or aversion for sex. When extreme fear or sexual aversion is present, gradual exposure or counterconditioning is indicated rather than directed masturbation. Also, in women with a history of sexual abuse, it is recommended to check carefully if the woman is capable to cope with memories of sexual abuse or whether such memories are likely to occur before treatment is started. When the woman becomes substantially disordered by talking about the sexual abuse, and reports posttraumatic stress symptoms, treatment for PTSD is indicated. After treatment for PTSD, a directed masturbation program can be considered.

In case of evident problems in the sexual relationship with the partner, we recommend clinicians to start couple therapy prior to an individual directed masturbation program or to incorporate directed masturbation in couple therapy.

THE INITIAL INTERVIEW

The behavioral exercises that are used in directed masturbation have to be tailored to the individual needs of the client. Therefore, a thorough clinical interview is needed to get a full picture of the client and the nature of her orgasmic problem. The aim of the initial interview is to gather information concerning current sexual functioning, onset of the complaints, and the context in which the problem occurs. Specific attention should be given to the amount of subjective and physiological sexual excitement the woman experiences. In women who report to be capable of reaching high levels of sexual excitement and who feel that they are almost reaching orgasm, fear for losing control may be an important factor.

An extensive sexual history should be taken, and the clinician should ask if the woman ever experienced sexual abuse or trauma. To indicate to what extent the woman has discovered her own sexuality it is necessary to ask about her feelings toward her body; masturbation experience; and familiarity with, and response to, different forms of sexual stimulation (e.g., erotic fantasy, vibrators, sexual activity with partners). An impression should be obtained of the woman's cognitions and feelings about sexuality, and about masturbation specifically. Besides sexual history, the psychiatric and medical history should be addressed. If a stable relationship exists, the nature of the general relationship should be examined. A conjoint partner interview is desirable to provide information concerning possible sexual problems of the partner. For a detailed general psychosocial and sexual assessment, we refer to Meston and Bradford (2007).

STEP-BY-STEP PROCEDURES

The directed masturbation procedure described here is a fixed program of 10 sessions largely based on the programs described by LoPicollo and Lobitz (1972) and Barbach (1974), extended with more cognitive behavioral interventions (Both, de Groot, & Rossmark, 2001). Throughout the whole program, there is a strong emphasis on increasing autonomy and assertiveness. The program can be applied in a group therapy setting, in individual therapy, and within couple therapy. Women differ in the speed with which they go through the program. To tailor the program to the individual needs of the client, the individual focus of the woman is explicitly discussed during the therapy.

The behavioral exercises that are assigned each session have to be practiced at home for an hour each day. During each session the woman's experiences with the assigned homework is extensively discussed. The woman is asked to keep a diary to record her behavior and feelings in response to the exercises.

We will now describe each session in more detail, including the exercises (homework) that are assigned.

Session 1

The rationale of the program is explained. After that, the woman is asked to formulate her personal goals: What does she want to achieve through the therapy? The woman is encouraged to formulate intermediate goals, and the therapist helps to phrase concrete goals and to express them in positive terms. Expressions such as "I do not want to have so many negative feelings toward my body" are rephrased in positive terms such as "I want to accept my body as it is" or "I want to have more positive feelings toward my body."

Homework: Taking a shower and concentrating on the water touching the body, followed by examination of the nude body in a full-length mirror in minute detail.

Session 2

The discussion of the homework is tailored toward creating time for yourself and concentration on bodily sensations. Negative and positive reactions to the body are discussed. Women who express mainly negative feelings toward their body are encouraged to name three parts they value positively the next time they examine their body.

Homework: Taking a shower and examining the body in the mirror, followed by touching the whole body, with an emphasis on experimenting and discovery of parts of the body that are nice to be touched.

Session 3

The discussion of the exercise concentrates on "spectatoring" (watching yourself touching your body rather than experiencing the sensations generated by touching), and on the discovery of sensitive areas of the body and pleasurable ways of touching. The subject of sexual upbringing is introduced. The impact of subtle messages regarding sexuality that may have been given by the client's family is discussed. Terminology for male and female genitals and sexual contact is discussed. The woman is asked to choose terms she wants to use for her genitals.

Homework: Repetition of exercise 2, extended by visual exploration of the genitals with the aid of a hand mirror. She is also asked to write down the messages regarding sexuality given by her family (or other significant persons).

Session 4

Reactions to the visual exploration of the genitals are discussed. The therapist shows photographs of female genitals and explains the anatomy. Common concerns regarding genital anatomy (e.g., the size of the labia minora) are addressed. The impact of the messages regarding sexuality given by significant others is discussed, and the woman is invited to formulate a new message for herself that will serve the achievement of her personal goals. Kegel exercises (contraction and relaxation of the pelvic floor muscles) are introduced (Kegel, 1952).

Homework: Repetition of exercise 3, extended with exploring the genitals by touching, and Kegel exercises.

Session 5

The thoughts and feelings elicited by touching of the genitals are discussed, as well as the importance of relaxation during touching, followed by a progressive relaxation exercise (see Chapter 58). It is explained that the Kegel exercises can be used to enhance sexual arousal.

Homework: The formerly assigned exploration and touching exercises with a focus on pleasurable erotic feelings. Visit to a female-oriented sex shop or Internet site to look for erotic books or movies.

Session 6

The exploration and touching exercises are discussed, with emphasis on attention for pleasurable and sexual feelings. Education is given about the inhibiting or facilitating effect of cognitions; for example, "I should experience more arousal now; it doesn't work" (inhibiting) or "I focus on what I feel; this feels nice, let's go on" (facilitating). With reference to the visit to the sex shop or Internet site, materials that may be sexually arousing—and how to use them—is discussed.

A female masturbation movie is shown (Liekens & Drenth, 1991). This movie is especially produced for use in sex therapy. Attitudes toward masturbation are explored, and myths around female sexual arousal and orgasm are discussed and refuted. Physical and subjective changes during sexual arousal and orgasm are explained. Different stimulation techniques are described. The importance of the "solo phase" (secluding oneself from the environment

and concentrating completely on one's sexual sensations) to intensify arousal and to reach orgasm is explained.

Homework: Touching exercises combined with intensifying arousal through experimenting with different stimulation techniques with or without a lubricant.

Session 7

Exercises are discussed with a focus on techniques that the woman can use to facilitate her arousal, for example "teasing" (suspending stimulation at the point that sexual excitement is high, waiting for a moment, and then continuing stimulation). The use of erotic fantasy and imagery to enhance sexual arousal is discussed, including fantasy not necessarily being about things a woman wants to experience in real life. In addition, the woman is asked to remember as vividly as possible a situation in which she enjoyed sexual arousal. She is encouraged to use this memory as an arousal-enhancing fantasy and to expand upon it.

Homework: Touching exercise and trying to enhance arousal by use of fantasy, erotic books or film, and/or teasing.

Session 8

The discussion of the exercises is tailored to the specific difficulties of the woman. The use of a vibrator is brought in. The subject "fear of losing control" is introduced. Different possible fears are discussed, for example, "fear of behaving in an uncontrolled, unladylike fashion" or "fear of losing urine during orgasm." Women may be afraid that during orgasm they will behave in a wild and uncontrolled manner, or that they will be completely unconscious for a period of time. To modify such irrational beliefs, physiological and psychological changes during orgasm are explained, with reference to what was shown in the female masturbation film that was introduced in session 6. Some women are inhibited sexually after experiencing an embarrassing situation in which they lost much fluid, probably during orgasm. The existence of female ejaculation is discussed to reassure that losing fluid is an uncommon but recognized part of female sexual responses.

Sexual contact with a partner is discussed, with an emphasis on the wishes and expectancies of the woman. Explicit attention is given to the impossibility, for many women, to reach orgasm with intercourse alone.

Homework: The same as session 7 plus experimenting with a vibrator and "role-play orgasm."

Session 9

Discussion of the exercises is tailored to the woman's specific difficulties. Partner sex is discussed more extensively with a focus on assertiveness and communication.

Homework: Identical to session 8.

Session 10: Evaluation

The woman is asked to indicate to what extent she reached the goals she formulated in the first session. The therapist helps to describe the changes in behavior or subjective experience that appeared during the program. The woman formulates what is needed in the future to maintain the reached goals and to make further progress.

Session 11: Follow-Up Session After 3 Months

The woman's specific experiences and difficulties during the follow-up period are discussed.

KEY ELEMENTS OF THE DIRECTED MASTURBATION PROGRAM

a. Visual and tactile exploration of the body with a focus on body awareness and body acceptance
b. Masturbation instructions and exercises
c. Education about female sexual response
d. Education about "spectatoring"
e. Instructions to explore the use of sexual fantasy, lubricants, and a vibrator to increase sexual arousal
f. Discussion of the impact of sexual upbringing
g. Emphasis on assertiveness and autonomy in sexual relationships

h. Education about inhibiting and facilitating effects of cognitions on sexual arousal
i. Disinhibition strategies (e.g. "role play orgasm")

PROBLEMS TO DEAL WITH DURING THE TREATMENT PROGRAM

One of the problems that may occur during directed masturbation is resistance to perform the assigned exercises. Resistance to the assignments involving genital touching may be related to strong prohibitions to masturbation. Besides discussion of such prohibitions, the woman should be confronted with the question of how the avoidance behavior serves her. She has to choose whether to engage in the exercises that could help her or to continue the avoidance behavior. Limiting the number of sessions beforehand may prevent avoidance to prolong.

A well-known pitfall in directed masturbation is becoming too goal oriented. A strong focus on reaching orgasm may have a counterproductive effect. The therapist should help the woman, all along the treatment program, to focus during the exercises on the pleasurable feelings she is experiencing, instead of on feelings she thinks she is expected to experience.

Directed masturbation is a highly directive therapeutic approach, and there is a risk that clients place the responsibility for the achievement of orgasm on the therapist. The therapist has to be clear that it is the client who is responsible for the discovery of her own sexual capacities. A coaching attitude, providing information, support, and permission, but confronting in case of avoidance behavior, is the most fruitful therapeutic approach.

DISCUSSION

During the evaluation and follow-up sessions of the directed masturbation program described in this chapter, a majority of the clients report improvements in body awareness, body acceptance, sexual arousal, enjoyment in sex, and decreased feelings of shame or fear of being "abnormal." Our clinical experience is, however, that far less than the 80% in the effects studies reported in the 1970s and 1980s (Heiman, 2000) is able to experience orgasm by masturbation at the end of the program. Thus, nowadays, the results seem not as good as those reported previously. The difference in success can perhaps be explained by selection. The increased availability of information about female sexuality may help many anorgasmic women to find out, by themselves, how to reach orgasm. The women who seek help today may be a group with more complicated problems. Clearly, more recent treatment efficacy data are needed. Given the high comorbidity of orgasmic and arousal problems, it would be meaningful in outcome studies to distinguish women with both orgasmic and arousal disorder from women with orgasmic disorder only.

It can be expected that during the upcoming years there will be more information on medications for treating sexual arousal and orgasm disorders in women. There is some preliminary evidence for a positive effect of apomorphine in anorgasmia (Bechara, Bertolino, Casabé, & Fredotovich, 2004). Placebo controlled research is needed to examine the effectiveness of pharmacological agents such as dopaminergic drugs, granisetron, sildenafil, or testosterone, that may facilitate orgasmic function in women (Uckert, Mayer, Jonas, & Stief, 2006). Possibly, a combination of directed masturbation and pharmacological treatments may lead to an even more efficacious treatment method for female orgasmic disorder in the future.

Further Reading

Everaerd, W., Laan, E., Both, S., & van der Velde, J. (2000). Female Sexuality. In L.T. Szuchman & F. Muscarella (Eds.), *Psychological perspectives on human sexuality.* New York: John Wiley & Sons.

Meston, C. M., & Levin, R. J. (2005). Female orgasm dysfunction. In R. Balon & R. T. Segraves (Eds.), *Handbook of sexual dysfunction.* London/New York: Taylor & Francis.

References

American Psychiatric Association (1994). *Diagnostic and statistical manual of mental disorders* (4th ed.). Washington, DC: Author.

Barbach, L. G. (1974). Group treatment of preorgasmic women. *Journal of Sex and Marital Therapy, 1,* 139–145.

Barbach L. G. (1975). *For yourself.* New York: Doubleday.

Barlow, D. H. (1986). Causes of sexual dysfunction. *Journal of Consulting and Clinical Psychology, 54,* 140–148.

Bechara, A., Bertolino, M. V., Casabé, A., & Fredotovich, N. (2004). A double-blind randomized placebo control study comparing the objective and subjective changes in female sexual response using sublingual apomorphine. *Journal of Sexual Medicine, 1,* 209–214.

Bianchi-Demicheli F., & Ortigue, S. (2007) Toward an understanding of the cerebral substrates of woman's orgasm. *Neuropsychologia, 45,* 2645–2659.

Both, S., de Groot, H. E., & Rossmark, M. (2001). Orgasmestoornissen bij de vrouw. Een cognitief-gedragstherapeutische groepsbehandeling [Orgasmic disorders in women: A cognitive-behavioural group treatment program]. In M. W. Hengeveld & A. Brewaeys (Eds.). *Behandelingsstrategieën bij seksuele dysfuncties [Treatment strategies for sexual dysfunctions].* Houten: Bohn Stafleu van Loghum.

de Bruijn, G. (1982). From masturbation to orgasm with a partner: How some women bridge the gap—and why others don't. *Journal of Sex & Marital Therapy, 8,* 151–167.

Gregorian, R. S., Golden, K. A., Bahce, A., Goodman, C., Kwong, W. J., & Khan, Z. M. (2002). Antidepressant-induced sexual dysfunction. Annals of Pharmacotherapy, *36,* 1577–1589.

Heiman, J. R. (2000). Orgasmic disorders in women. In R. E. Leiblum & R. C. Rosen (Eds.), *Principles and practices of sex therapy* (3rd ed.). New York: Guilford.

Heiman, J., & LoPicollo, J. (1986). *Becoming orgasmic: A sexual growth program for women.* Englewood Cliffs, NJ: Prentice Hall.

Heiman, J. R., LoPicollo, L., & LoPicollo, J. (1976). *Becoming orgasmic: A sexual growth program for women.* Englewood Cliffs, NJ: Prentice Hall.

Heiman, J. R., & Meston, C. M. (1997). Evaluating sexual dysfunction in women. *Clinical Obstetrics and Gynecology, 40,* 616–629.

Hite, S. (1976). *The Hite report.* New York: Dell.

Hurlbert, D. F., & Apt, C. (1995). Coital alignment technique and directed masturbation: A comparative study on female orgasm. *Journal of Sex and Marital Therapy, 21,* 21–29.

Kegel, A. H. (1952). Sexual function of the pubococcygeus muscle. *Western Journal of Surgery, Obstetrics, and Gynecology, 60,* 521–524.

Laan, E., Everaerd, W., & Both, S. (2005). Female sexual arousal disorders. In R. Balon & R. T. Segraves (Eds.), *Handbook of Sexual Dysfunctions* (pp. 123–154). New York: Marcel Dekker Inc.

Laan, E., & van Lunsen, R. H. W. (2002, June). Orgasm latency, duration and quality in women: Validation of a laboratory sexual stimulation technique. Poster presented at 28th Conference of the International Academy of Sex Research, Hamburg, Germany.

Leff, J. J., & Israel, M. (1983). The relation between mode of female masturbation and achievement of orgasm in coitus. *Archives of Sexual Behavior, 12,* 227–236.

Levin, R. J., & Wagner, G. (1985). Orgasm in women in the laboratory: Quantitative studies on duration, intensity, latency, and vaginal blood flow. *Archives of Sexual Behavior, 14,* 439–449.

Liekens, G., & Drenth, J. (1991). Het vrouwelijk orgasme [Female orgasm]. Amsterdam: Select Movies Video.

LoPicollo, J., & Lobitz, W. C. (1972). The role of masturbation in the treatment of orgasmic dysfunction. *Archives of Sexual Behavior, 2.* 163–171.

Lutfey, K. E., Link, C. L., Litman, H. J., Rosen, R. C., & McKinlay, J. B. (2007). An examination of the association of abuse (physical, sexual, or emotional) and female sexual dysfunction: Results from the Boston Area Community Health Survey. *Fertility and Sterility.* doi:10.1016/j.fertnstert.2007.07.1352

Masters, W., & Johnson, V. (1966). *Human sexual response.* Boston: Little, Brown.

Masters, W., & Johnson, V. (1970). *Human sexual inadequacy.* Boston: Little, Brown.

Messe, M. R., & Geer, J. H. (1985). Voluntary vaginal musculature contractions as an enhancer of sexual arousal. *Archives of Sexual Behavior, 14,* 13–28.

Meston, C. M., & Bradford, A. (2007). Sexual dysfunctions in women. *Annual Review of Clinical Psychology, 3,* 233–256.

Meston, C. M., & Levin, R. J. (2005). Female orgasm dysfunction. In: R. Balon & R. T. Segraves (Eds.), *Handbook of Sexual Dysfunction.* London/New York: Taylor & Francis.

Morokoff, P. (1989). Sex bias and POD. *American Psychologist, 44,* 73–75.

Noll, J. G., Trickett, P. K., Putnam, F. W. (2003). A prospective investigation of the impact of childhood sexual abuse on the development of sexuality. *Journal of Consulting and Clinical Psychology, 71,* 575–586.

O'Donohue, W. T., Dopke, C. A., & Swingen, D. N. (1997). Psychotherapy for female sexual dysfunction: A review. *Clinical Psychology Review, 17,* 537–566.

Sipski, M. L. (1998). Sexual functioning in the spinal cord injured. *International Journal of Impotence Research, 10,* S128–S130.

Uckert, S., Mayer, M. E., Jonas, U., & Stief, C. G. (2006). Potential future options in the pharmacotherapy of female sexual dysfunction. *World Journal of Urology, 24,* 630–638.

van Berlo, W., & Ensink, B. (2000). Problems with sexuality after sexual assault. *Annual Review of Sex Research, 11,* 235–285.

27 DISTRESS TOLERANCE

Michael P. Twohig and Katherine A. Peterson

Aversive private experiences are ubiquitous. In many cases, private events cannot be wholly managed (e.g., urges to smoke, chronic pain), and sometimes attempts at changing the thought, feeling, or bodily sensation result in their increased importance and greater limitations on quality of life than simply tolerating the private event (Hayes, Wilson, Gifford, Follette, & Strosahl, 1996; Linehan, 1993a; 1993b). Distress tolerance training provides skills to overcome impulsive and maladaptive action tendencies, thus allowing more functional and goal oriented behavior.

Distress tolerance is generally defined as the ability to experience negative private events and not allowing them to interfere with engaging in goal oriented actions. Cognitively oriented descriptions of distress tolerance focus on perceptions and appraisals of negative private events and one's perceived ability to tolerate distress as the mediating factors in tolerating distress (Simons & Gaher, 2005). Whereas, more behaviorally oriented descriptions of distress tolerance have less focus on the exact cognitive processes underling the ability to tolerate distress, and instead focus on the skill of experiencing aversive private events while continuing to engage in goal oriented actions (e.g., Brown, Lejuez, Kahler, Strong, & Zvolensky, 2005). In general, low distress tolerance is exhibited if psychological discomfort is experienced as "unendurable," and distress is decreased by engaging compensatory behaviors that function to alleviate the distress, resulting in negative overall functioning. Whereas high distress tolerance is evidenced when aversive private events are experienced and either effectively regulated or "accepted" by not regulating them and not letting them interfere with goal-oriented actions.

The ability to tolerate distress is not a distinct concept; there are several other constructs that have a similar focus. Experiential avoidance generally focuses on the possible adverse effects of attempting to control or manage private events (Hayes et al., 1996), anxiety sensitivity is the fear of anxiety related sensations (Reiss & McNally, 1985), emotional regulation refers to the ability to effectively manage and express emotions (Linehan, 1993a), and discomfort intolerance focuses on tolerance of physical sensations (Simons & Gaher, 2005). All of these concepts share similarities with distress tolerance.

EMPIRICAL EVIDENCE SUPPORTING THE USE OF DISTRESS TOLERANCE

The use of distress tolerance skills in clinical situations are well supported as components of several empirically supported treatments, most notably dialectical behavioral therapy (DBT), where distress tolerance skills are used to target emotion dysregulation (Linehan, 1993a). Similar skills are taught in acceptance and commitment therapy (ACT) to address experiential avoidance (Hayes, Strosahl, & Wilson, 1999). Debatably, exposure-based therapies directly increase distress tolerance skills by teaching clients to stay in contact with feelings of anxiety and anxiety related cognitions while engaging in goal-oriented actions. The ability to tolerate distress has also been found to be useful in many other clinical situations regardless of the type of therapy utilized.

Increased distress tolerance skills are positively related to longer abstinence from cigarette smoking after smoking cessation trails (Brown, Lejuez, Kahler, & Strong, 2002; Brown, et al., 2005; Daughters, Lejuez, Kahler, Strong & Brown, 2005). Training in acceptance of private events (a type of distress tolerance) is useful in the treatment of anxiety disorders. Acceptance has been shown to increase willingness to experience panic sensations and regulate anxiety related cognitions in carbon dioxide challenges (Eifert & Heffner, 2003; Levitt, Brown, Orsillo, & Barlow, 2004), effectively regulate affect and heart rate when exposed to an emotionally provoking film (Campbell-Sills, Barlow, Brown, & Hofmann, 2006), and experience unwanted thoughts (Marcks & Woods, 2004).

Training in acceptance skills has also been shown to increase pain tolerance (Vowles et al., 2007; Masedo & Esteve, 2006), and increase tolerance of food cravings (Forman, Hoffman, McGrath, Herbert, Brandsma, & Lowe, 2007). Finally, greater distress tolerance is associated with better overall functioning and medication adherence with HIV-positive individuals (O'Cleirigh, Ironson, & Smits, 2007), and training in acceptance procedures results in decreased anxiety and depression and greater quality of life after diagnosis of breast cancer compared to a control condition (Páez, Luciano, & Gutiérrez, 2007).

WHO MIGHT BENEFIT FROM THIS TECHNIQUE

It has been suggested that many behaviors serve avoidance and escape functions (e.g., Hayes et al., 1996). As noted by Linehan (1993a), aversive private events are part of life; attempts to avoid them work in the short term but reinforce the process in the long term, thus tolerating distress seems to be a necessary part of life. Therefore, training in distress tolerance is suitable for clients who engage in maladaptive avoidance behaviors in response to negatively evaluated private events.

Distress tolerance training has been found useful with individuals diagnosed with borderline personality disorder who engage in risky or self-harming behaviors (e.g., cutting, substance abuse, suicide attempts). It enables clients to cope with physical discomforts or symptoms of withdrawal associated with substance abuse or dependence. Distress tolerance helps clients diagnosed with eating disorders experience urges to overeat or engage in compensatory behaviors while engaging in goal-directed behavior. Finally, it helps individuals with chronic pain endure the pain, and it can increase enagement in exposure therapy for anxiety disorders. This is a list of known clinical applications of distress tolerance training, but distress tolerance skills would likely be useful for decreasing problematic avoidance or escape in many additional situations.

CONTRADICTIONS

Distress tolerance can generally be taught in two fashions: acceptance or change strategies. Acceptance procedures are favored by certain therapeutic approaches such as ACT, whereas DBT teaches several skills that utilize both acceptance and change strategies (Linehan, 1993a; 1993b). As indicated in the distress tolerance module of DBT, skills learned such as distraction and relaxation utilize methods of change to alleviate distress but also teach several acceptance skills such as making the best of the moment or evaluating the pros and cons of enduring distress. Thus, several theoretical approaches utilize distress tolerance skills, but the focus on change or acceptance varies in these treatments.

DECIDING TO USE DISTRESS TOLERANCE

Distress tolerance is a suitable therapeutic technique for clients who have target behaviors in their repertoires, but lack the skills to manage or accept the aversive private events that are involved in engaging in these actions. For example, most smokers know how to stop smoking, but the urges involved in stopping are experienced as too strong to maintain abstinence. Once distress tolerance skills are learned, clients undergo other treatment strategies to attain greater goals. Distress tolerance may be thought of as a stepping-stone in therapeutic change because it is frequently implemented as a means to achieve larger therapeutic goals, but distress tolerance alone is generally not the focus of treatment. Additional therapeutic procedures that strengthen or increase goal-oriented actions should compliment distress tolerance training.

DISTRESS TOLERANCE TECHNOLOGY

Several therapies focus on the inability to tolerate distress, and this process is generally supported in clinical research. Nevertheless, this construct varies slightly between therapies and the mechanism through which these therapies increase distress tolerance is being studied but remains somewhat unclear. Generally, distress tolerance is taught in DBT through acceptance or change procedures, or both. Acceptance techniques assist clients in enduring difficult situations and emotional states without altering the associated aversive private event. Change procedures generally involve regulating private events to a level where chances of engaging in goal-oriented activities while the private event is present are increased. For example, instead of experiencing all the anger from an insult, the client might be taught to regulate anger through distraction or mindfulness training. In ACT, "distress tolerance" is trained through acceptance and defusion (treating private events nonliterally), and is done in the service on one's values (meaningful areas of life). In exposure-based therapies, distress tolerance is generally utilized to assist in more fully participating in exposures, and ultimately as part of a new way of living.

PROCEDURES

DBT is the only treatment that specifically targets "distress tolerance" as an identified skill set. Although, distress tolerance is part of many therapies, it is functionally defined as *the ability to experience aversive private events while continuing in one's chosen direction*. There are many ways to train distress tolerance skills. The following four areas—acceptance, exposure, change strategies, and evaluation of pros and cons or values—have been identified as overarching representations of the strategies utilized in distress tolerance (for additional exercises and examples see Table 27.1).

Acceptance

In general, acceptance of private experiences is necessary in any distress tolerance skill set. Acceptance can be defined as experiencing one's private experiences in their entirety, without public or private regulation. In DBT, Linehan (1993b) refers to three types of acceptance strategies: (1) radical acceptance, or a complete acceptance of reality; (2) turning the mind, or actively choosing to accept one's situations; and (3) willfulness versus willingness. Radical acceptance can involve the process of recognizing the importance of human pain and suffering as part of life, and behaving in accepting ways in response to it when it is useful. For example, pain can be adaptive by signaling when something is wrong (e.g., burning one's hand on the stove), and in those situations avoidance is suggested, but anxiety in social situations may be part of life. Acceptance is something that must be consciously chosen, repeatedly, possibly every day. This continual choice in accepting reality is what is meant when referring to turning the mind.

Individuals who are being *willful* are trying to impose their own will on reality rather than being *willing*, which implies engaging in what works or what is beneficial and needed in the current moment despite unwanted stimuli or situations. While utilizing acceptance as described in DBT, therapists are encouraged to foster willingness versus willfulness by teaching clients to identify situations as they arise and labeling them as willing or willful. For example, if the client is upset about a situation at work, the therapist might say something such as, "Are you being *willful* in trying to change your boss, or *willing* and doing what would help you most at this time?" The therapist might create examples in therapy sessions such as saying, "Every time I go shopping, the traffic drives me crazy. People need to learn how to drive or have their licenses revoked!" Then ask the client, "Am I being *willful* or *willing* right now?"

ACT uses similar methods of acceptance as DBT. ACT postulates that experiential avoidance is central to many forms of psychopathology, and attempting to control or regulate private events often leads to a lower quality of life rather than an improved one. ACT therapists often illustrate this concept by asking clients to report or test attempts at controlling private events versus accepting them. Often, clients

TABLE 27.1   Distress Tolerance Skills

I. Acceptance
- *Two games exercise*—Client is taught to shift focus from winning first game (involving regulating distress) to a second game (working toward increased quality of life).
- *Mindfulness training*—Client is taught to "just notice" private events as they occur and to not attempt to control or change them.
- *Radical Acceptance*—Client learns how to authentically accept reality for what it is, and accept that pain can be tolerated and may in some cases be beneficial (e.g., when placing a hand on a hot stove, the elicited pain sensation causes the hand to move).

II. Exposure
- *In vivo*—Exposing the client to "live" stimuli that evoke the target private event.
- *Imaginal*—Guiding the client through thoughts of feared stimuli in order to evoke the target private event.
- *Exposure script*—Client creates a written or recorded scrip of the feared situation or stimuli that he or she reads or listens to as a form of exposure.

III. Change Strategies
- *Distraction*—Client is taught to shift focus from distressing event to less distressing one.
- *Imagery*—Client is taught to create situations mentally different from the present one.
- *Relaxation*—Client learns how to change the body's response to aversive interoceptive stimuli (e.g., diaphragmatic breathing, progressive relaxation techniques).

IV. Evaluation of Pros and Cons
- *Pros and cons practice exercise*—Client is instructed to make a list of "pros" and "cons column," of tolerating psychological discomfort without engaging in impulsive action tendencies.
- *What do you want your life to stand for exercise*—Client envisions she has died and is listening to what her loved ones say about her in her absence. Client is encouraged to think about what she would most like to have said about her and works towards being that person.
- *Competency exercise*—Client evaluates values and the rationalization behind them. The therapist may implement this exercise by asking something like, "What do you want in your life that you feel is currently missing, and why?"

---

report that attempting to control or regulate private events results in an increased frequency in those thoughts, feelings, and bodily sensations and a co-occurring decrease in quality of life. Based on the client's reported experience, the therapist offers acceptance of private events as an alternative to control or regulation in order to foster behavior change. Acceptance is then solidified by the use of metaphors and exercises such as the *two-scales exercise* (Hayes et al., 1999). In this exercise, the therapist discusses two scales, the first representing the private event the client is struggling with, and the second representing willingness to experience (or accept) what is on the first scale. The therapist might explain the *two-scales exercise* as follows:

Pretend that there are two scales over your shoulders and that each scale has a corresponding dial that should regulate it. The first scale represents the private event you are struggling with, and the dial associated with it is like a like a socket wrench and only spins the bolt one way. In this situation

you can only increase these private events—the dial does not turn the other way allowing you to decrease it. The dial to the second scale represents willingness to experience the private event, and it actually works—you can increase or decrease your willingness. By increasing the willingness scale, you are allowing the private event to be there without fighting with it. Increasing the willingness scale will not decrease the private event, but it will allow it to change depending on the situation. It will be there when appropriate and probably will not be there when it is not. Can we try shifting the focus from the first scale to the second?

Exposure

Exposure, as a technique, can have many functions, one of which is increasing distress tolerance. When using exposure in training distress tolerance, individuals are primarily engaging in interoceptive work. Rather than being exposed to particular stimuli, clients are undergoing exposure to private events in order to practice tolerance of them. Exposure is conducted in one of two formats: graduated or massed. In graduated exposure, clients are exposed to increasingly strong private experiences in a steplike fashion, whereas in massed exposure, clients are exposed to intense levels of distress and must quickly adapt. Graduated exposure is generally found to be more acceptable and time consuming, but both procedures are useful in training distress tolerance.

Using graduated exposure for distress tolerance in smoking cessation involves repeated exposure to increasingly strong urges to smoke through longer periods of abstinence or reductions in numbers of cigarettes. For example, the client might not smoke for one hour, then two hours, and so on, or the client might smoke one pack in a day, then 15 cigarettes the next, then 10, and so on. Massed exposure for smoking might involve stopping smoking completely and exposing the client to stimuli that evoke strong urges to smoke such as cigarettes or situations where smoking commonly occurs while refraining from smoking. Interoceptive reactions occurring from nicotine withdrawal are generally what are being avoided through smoking. Exposure to these aversive sensations increases tolerance of these "cravings" and increases likelihood of abstinence (Brown et al., 2005). These same procedures can be utilized with other private events.

Change Strategies

Change strategies offer an alternate method for coping with aversive private events compared to acceptance. Change strategies often include skills that foster a sense of control or the ability to change situations in order to foster greater goal-oriented actions. Techniques such as distraction, imagery, or taking a "vacation" are all skills learned in DBT to aid clients in increasing distress tolerance. Distraction, for example, uses several skills to help achieve cognitive and emotional distance from the aversive experience. Replacing negative emotions with opposite emotions, or leaving aversive situations, either mentally or physically, are skills taught as part of distraction strategies. Imagery is a distraction

method that uses mentally created situations to increase coping or manage current crisis situations.

As indicated by Linehan (1993b) clients may benefit from a "vacation," which is discussed as either a mental vacation for a few moments (client may think about a favorable place or event rather than ruminating or maintaining an anxiety-provoking thought) or a physical vacation for no longer than a day to provide time to regroup. Removal from distressing situations, if only briefly, allows clients the freedom to change situations and provides a sense of control (Linehan, 1993b). Other change strategies include relaxation techniques such as progressive relaxation or diaphragmatic breathing. Another relaxation technique taught in DBT includes the *half-smile* technique, which may be described to the client as follows:

> Begin by sitting still and focusing on making a nonexpressive face. I want you to notice how this particular expression feels. Try relaxing all the muscles in your face, and while you do that, notice those sensations as well. Now, give me a half-smile. Half-smiling includes relaxing the face, neck, and shoulders, and then half-smiling with only your lips. Once you have your half-smile going, shift your attention to what this expression feels like—really pay attention to what your lips, cheeks, and jaw muscles feel like. [Continue practicing this until the client is familiar with this expression.]

After the client is familiar with this feeling, ask her to practice half-smiling throughout the day such as when irritated, contemplating a person she dislikes, first waking, or when listening to music. The function of this exercise is to create a sense of controlled relaxation.

Evaluation of Pros and Cons, and Values Training

Elucidating the importance and benefit of enduring aversive emotional states rather than exerting unnecessary and often maladaptive energy avoiding them is a useful skill employed in several empirically supported treatments. DBT teaches this distress tolerance skill through "thinking of pros and cons." This exercise involves, first, helping the client create a list of costs versus benefits of enduring psychological discomfort. Second, a second list is created that examines the pros and cons of not enduring the discomfort. Finally, the client is encouraged to think of long-term goals and evaluate the benefits of each strategy in achieving those goals.

Evaluation of "pros and cons" of distress tolerance assists clients in finding meaning in engaging in, or at least enduring, higher levels of discomfort while working toward greater treatment goals.

Values training in ACT assists clients in identifying life goals and pursuing them despite psychological challenges or crisis that arise. In values training, clients are often asked to think about what they want their lives to be about and the benefits of engaging in actions that are consistent with those values versus not pursuing them and attempting to control aversive private events. Accepting aversive private events are linked to areas of life such that "tolerating distress" ends up being in the service of following one's values. For example, a client diagnosed with social phobia, might be told that gradually exposing herself to anxiety provoking stimuli will ultimately help her go to public places with her family or participate more in her occupation. Values training can give meaning to tolerating distress and ultimately increase distress tolerance skills. Values can be clarified by simply asking the client, "What would you do if the urge to smoke [use target private event] were not present?" If the client responds that he would change his behavior, the therapist can say, "It seems that the largest variable in your way is your own thoughts, feelings, and bodily sensation and not a lack of skill." Next, the therapist can link tolerating distress to the client's values by saying something such as, "Let's try not smoking for two consecutive hours per day this week so that you can get used your urges to smoke, which will help you ultimately stop."

CONCLUSION

The construct of distress tolerance shares similarities to techniques and constructs such as experiential avoidance, anxiety sensitivity, emotional regulation, and discomfort tolerance.

It teaches the ability to withstand aversive private events while pursuing personal goals and discourages impulsive escape or avoidance strategies. Even though the concept of distress tolerance is relatively new, research supporting similar processes and functions is rapidly growing, especially with regard to substance abuse, anxiety, physical pain, eating disorders, and other disorders, including borderline personality disorder. Albeit most of the current research focuses on specific pathologies, distress tolerance skills may be effective in treating any client who is regularly engaging in maladaptive avoidance behaviors.

Further Reading

Hayes, S. C., Strosahl, K. D., & Wilson, K. G. (1999). *Acceptance and commitment therapy: An experiential approach to behavior change.* New York: Guilford.
Linehan, M. M. (1993a). *Cognitive behavioral treatment of borderline personality disorder.* New York: Guilford.
Linehan, M. M. (1993b). *Skills training manual for treating borderline personality disorder.* New York: Guilford.
Louma, J. B., Hayes, S. C., & Walser, R. D. (2007). *Learning ACT: An acceptance and commitment therapy skills-training manual for therapists.* Oakland: New Harbinger Publications.

References

Brown, R. A., Lejuez, C. W., Kahler, C. W., & Strong, D. R. (2002). Distress tolerance and duration of past smoking cessation attempts. *Journal of Abnormal Psychology, 111,* 180–185.
Brown, R. A., Lejuez, C. W., Kahler, C. W., Strong, D. R., & Zvolensky, M. J. (2005). Distress tolerance and early smoking lapse. *Clinical Psychology Review, 25,* 713–733.
Campbell-Sills, L., Barlow, D. H., Brown, T. A., & Hofmann, S. G. (2006). Effects of suppression and acceptance on emotional responses of individuals with anxiety and mood disorders. *Behaviour Research and Therapy, 44,* 1251–1263.
Daughters, S. B., Lejuez, C. W., Kahler, C. W., Strong, D. R., & Brown, R. A. (2005). Psychological distress tolerance and duration of most recent abstinence attempt among residential treatment-seeking substance abusers. *Psychology of Addictive Behaviors, 19,* 208–211.
Eifert, G. H., & Heffner, M. (2003). The effects of acceptance versus control contexts on avoidance of panic-related symptoms. Journal of Behavior

Therapy and Experimental Psychiatry *34*, 293–312.

Forman, E. M., Hoffman, K. L., McGrath, K. B., Herbert, J. D., Brandsma, L. L., & Lowe, M. R. (2007). A comparison of acceptance- and control-based strategies for coping with food cravings: An analog study. *Behaviour Research and Therapy*, *45*, 2372–2386.

Hayes, S. C., Strosahl, K. D., & Wilson, K. G. (1999). *Acceptance and commitment therapy: An experiential approach to behavior change.* New York: Guilford.

Hayes, S. C., Wilson, K. G., Gifford, E. V., Follette, V. M., & Strosahl, K. (1996). Emotional avoidance and behavioral disorders: A functional dimensional approach to diagnosis and treatment. *Journal of Consulting and Clinical Psychology*, *64*, 1152–1168.

Levitt, J. T., Brown, T. A., Orsillo, S. M., & Barlow, D. H. (2004). The effects of acceptance versus suppression of emotion on subjective and psychophysiological response to carbon dioxide challenge in patients with panic disorder. *Behavior Therapy*, *35*, 747–766.

Linehan, M. M. (1993a). *Cognitive behavioral treatment of borderline personality disorder.* New York: Guilford.

Linehan, M. M. (1993b). *Skills training manual for treating borderline personality disorder.* New York: Guilford.

Marcks, B. A., & Woods, D. W. (2005). A comparison of thought suppression to an acceptance-based technique in the management of personal intrusive thoughts: A controlled evaluation. *Behaviour Research and Therapy*, *43*, 433–445.

Masedo, A. I., & Esteve, M. R. (2007). Effects of suppression, acceptance and spontaneous coping on pain tolerance, pain intensity and distress. *Behaviour Research and Therapy*, *45*, 199–209.

Páez, M., Luciano, M. C., & Gutiérrez, O. (2007). Psychological treatment for breast cancer. Comparison between acceptance based and cognitive control based strategies. *Psicooncología*, *4*, 75–95.

O'Cleirigh, C., Ironson, G., & Smits, J. A. (2007). Does distress tolerance moderate the impact of major life events on psychosocial variables and behaviors important in the management of HIV? *Behavior Therapy*, *38*, 314–323.

Reiss, S., & McNally, R. J. (1985). Expectancy model of fear. In S. Reiss, & R. R. Bootzin (Eds.), *Theoretical issues in behavior therapy* (pp. 107–121). San Diego: Academic Press.

Simons, J. S., & Gaher, R. M. (2005). The distress tolerance scale: Development and validation of a self-report measure. *Motivation and Emotion*, *29*, 83–102.

Vowles, K. E., McNeil, D. W., Gross, R. T., McDaniel, M. T., Mouse, A., Bates, M., et al. (2007). Effects of pain acceptance and pain control strategies on physical impairment in individuals with chronic low back pain. *Behavior Therapy*, *38*, 412–425.

28 EMOTION REGULATION

Alan E. Fruzzetti, Wendy Crook,
Karen M. Erikson, Jung Eun Lee,
and John M. Worrall

The central role of regulating emotions is now widely accepted across many cognitive and behavioral conceptualizations of psychopathology (e.g., Ehring, Fischer, Schnülle, Bösterling, & Tuschen-Caffier, 2008; Fox, Hong, & Sinha, 2008; Fruzzetti, Shenk, & Hoffman, 2005; Keltner & Kring, 1998; Southam-Gerow & Kendall, 2002). Consequently, the incorporation of emotion regulation concepts and strategies into cognitive behavioral therapies (CBT) has increased rapidly to include applications for a wide range of problems and disorders, including borderline personality disorder, anxiety disorders, substance abuse, depression, couple and family distress, severe medical problems, and a variety of other problems (e.g., Burum & Goldfried, 2007; Ehrenreich, Buzzella, & Barlow, 2007; Cameron et al., 2007; Fruzzetti, 2006; Hayes & Feldman, 2004; Linehan, Bohus, & Lynch, 2007; Menin, 2006).

In this chapter we will first establish some common ground by defining emotion regulation and dysregulation, and describing a basic model for the development of emotion dysregulation problems. We will then explicate many of the core components of CBT-compatible interventions, or emotion regulation treatment strategies, designed to help clients regulate their emotion.

UNDERSTANDING EMOTION REGULATION AND DYSREGULATION

Prior to identifying a suitable definition of emotion regulation and dysregulation, it is important to note that understanding these processes fully is tantamount to resolving longstanding problems in defining emotions. Although psychologists have studied emotions, and disagreed about

emotion, at least since William James (1884), we continue to employ a lexicon that implies that an emotion is a thing inside a person. A more accurate and helpful way to conceptualize emotion may be to consider emotion as a process and a multisystemic response involving neurobiology, cognition, and behavior, most often occurring in a largely social context. For example, Linehan, Bohus, and Lynch (2007) view the process of emotion not only as a response to internal and external events, but also as encompassing emotional cues and the biological and psychological state of the individual. Therefore, the process of emotion includes several interacting subsystems, including "(1) emotional vulnerability to cues; (2) internal and/or external events that serve as emotional cues, including attention to and appraisals of the cues; (3) emotional responses, including physiological responses, cognitive processing, experiential responses, and action urges; (4) nonverbal and verbal expressive responses and actions; and (5) aftereffects of the initial emotional firing" (Linehan et al., 2007, p. 582). In addition, the social context (cues themselves, or moderating factors, both antecedent and consequent to emotional reactions) are core factors in determining emotional responding (Fruzzetti & Iverson, 2006).

Defining Emotion Regulation and Dysregulation

Emotion regulation was defined by Gross (1998) as "the process by which individuals influence which emotions they have, when they have them, and how they experience and express these emotions" (p. 275). Thompson (1994) described emotion regulation as both the "extrinsic and intrinsic processes responsible for monitoring, evaluating and modifying emotional reactions ... to accomplish one's goals" (p. 27–28). Individuals modulate their emotions by modifying any part of the emotion process described above, either by accepting or changing aspects of the ongoing emotional response or its context. For example, emotion regulation strategies that target emotional cues may include actions such as choosing between different situations or changing a topic of conversation in order to turn one's attention away from an upsetting subject (Gross, 2002), but may also include habituating to that same upsetting subject, up- or downregulating the emotional reaction to the subject or event, changing appraisals of the subject or event, or a variety of other strategies. Regardless, once an emotion has been triggered, an individual may regulate emotion by engaging in a variety of responses that have in common only the fact that they keep emotional arousal moderated, prevent escape responses, and allow the individual to maintain self-control.

Emotion dysregulation occurs when an individual is unable to accept or change different components of the emotion process and experiences such a high level of emotional arousal that it disrupts effective self-management. However, a person should not be considered to be emotionally dysregulated when he or she is simply upset or experiencing an intense emotion. Rather, the hallmark of dysregulation is negative emotional arousal of sufficient intensity or duration to interfere with the person's goals and self-control. Markers of emotion dysregulation typically include an excess of negative emotional arousal (although "dysregulated" actions may truncate escalating emotional arousal), difficulty averting attention away from negative emotional stimuli, cognitive distortions, inability to control impulsive or other "escape" behaviors, and difficulty organizing behavior in a manner consistent with the individual's long-term goals (identified more or less consistently when the person is not highly emotionally aroused).

Thus, regulating emotion involves managing emotional reactions, or any aspect thereof (physiological arousal, cognition, attention, awareness, musculature and facial expression, etc.), and/or managing the antecedents (or cues) for rapidly escalating negative affect, or the consequences of high negative affect that

maintain the emotion regulation system on "hair-trigger" alert for dysregulation (such as dysfunctional, escape-oriented coping responses including self-harm, drug use, etc.). Emotions are, therefore, dialectical in nature: They are understood to regulate other behaviors of the individual (e.g., cognition, action, physiology), while they are themselves the phenomenon to be regulated (Baumeister, Zell, & Tice, 2007; Southam-Gerow & Kendall, 2002).

Everyone presumably becomes emotionally dysregulated at times. However, chronically emotionally dysregulated individuals experience certain emotions frequently as overwhelming and extremely distressing. As a result, chronically dysregulated individuals experience difficulties in most areas of life. Self-injury, substance use, eating disordered behavior, agoraphobia, and the like, are examples of the dysfunctional and clinically relevant impulsive behaviors in which a dysregulated individual may engage in an effort to alleviate (or prevent) distressing emotions and decrease negative emotional arousal. Extreme mood lability and intense emotional reactions, such as intense anger, shame, anhedonia, anxiety, and even numbing, form the core experience of people who are chronically dysregulated. Close relationships, of course, are inescapably affected by the behaviors and emotional reactions resulting from a person's dysregulation. Therefore, chronically emotionally dysregulated individuals can have chaotic and dysfunctional relationships that, in turn, perpetuate the emotion dysregulation process.

Development of Chronic Emotion Dysregulation: Transactions between the Person and the Social Environment

Socialization of Emotion

An understanding of the development of emotion regulation skills and emotion dysregulation can facilitate treatment of disorders associated with emotion regulation deficits. Although different language is employed in various subfields, most theories of emotion regulation and dysregulation employ a variation of a biosocial or transactional model (Fruzzetti, et al., 2005).

Developmental psychology has perhaps been most influential in explicating the socialization of emotion. For example, Eisenberg, Spinrad, and Smith (2004) note that parental discussion of emotions with children is associated with the development of emotion regulation skills. Overall, parents who are active in labeling the child's feelings and responses, identifying causes and effects of emotion, and proposing methods to regulate emotion have children who are more emotionally regulated (Rimé, 2007). Thus, it is likely that if parents do not provide accurate labels or teach effective regulation techniques, their children will have difficultly with one or more aspects of emotion regulation later in life.

Of course, the socialization of emotion does not necessarily end in childhood. Evidence suggests that we continue to seek social input to facilitate emotion regulation as adults. Rimé (2007) describes this as the "social sharing of emotion," which entails "a description, in a socially shared language, of an emotional episode to some addressee by the person who experienced it." (p. 467; see "Accurate Expression" later in this chapter), suggesting that when a person *effectively* shares an emotional experience, the emotional story elicits emotion in the listener, which in turn leads to enhanced empathy and improved emotional communication. Specifically, listeners provide help and support, comfort and soothing, legitimization, validation, clarification and meaning, and advice and solutions, all of which facilitate regulation (Fruzzetti & Iverson, 2006; Rimé, 2007).

Transactional Model

Linehan and colleagues (e.g., Fruzzetti, et al., 2005; Linehan, 1993a) perhaps have been most explicit in detailing the components of emotion regulation and dysregulation and the development of problems with emotion regulation, using borderline personality disorder (BPD) as a model. Because BPD may be considered the prototype for emotion dysregulation problems and disorders (Fruzzetti, 2002), BPD serves as a useful model for understanding dysregulation in psychopathology more broadly. Indeed, there are many similarities between models of the socialization of emotion and the transactional model for the development of BPD. For example, "healthy" transactions (Fruzzetti et al., 2005) parallel those outlined by Rimé (2007): An emotional event (either positive or negative) leads to moderate emotional arousal, which in turn leads to accurate (or effective) expression of the emotion and a validating response from the listener. A validating response is one that communicates understanding and implicitly or explicitly acknowledges the legitimacy (even the existence) of an experience or behavior and helps reduce emotional arousal (Fruzzetti & Iverson, 2004, 2006).

At least two different kinds of factors affect an individual's vulnerability to negative emotional arousal and dysregulation. One kind of emotional vulnerability is more temperamental and includes: (1) increased sensitivity to emotional stimuli, (2) higher reactivity to emotional stimuli, and (3) slow or delayed return to an emotional baseline following an emotional event. This kind of vulnerability varies from person to person. A second kind of vulnerability is simply the level of affectivity the person has as a "baseline" prior to the current emotional event, and varies within the individual. Obviously, if a person's arousal is relatively high, a smaller event will be sufficient to lead to aversive arousal and/or dysregulation. A number of specific factors influence current arousal, such as how tired a person is, whether he or she has had enough to eat, whether the person is under the influence of drugs or alcohol, and so on. Vulnerabilities of all kinds contribute to heightened emotional arousal following an emotional event (usually of negative valence). If the arousal is high enough, *inaccurate* expression (or ineffective communication) of the emotion (or beliefs, desires, etc.) follows. Inaccurate expression can include expressing a secondary emotion (such as anger or shame) as opposed to the primary emotion (such as sadness, disappointment, or worry). Inaccurate expression, in turn, makes it much more likely the individual will receive an invalidating response from the listener. An invalidating response can be described as one in which the phenomenologically valid experiences and behaviors of the individual are not understood and instead are invalidated by criticism, inattention, punishment, dismissal, blaming, or unresponsiveness, or by erratic, extreme, or otherwise socially and developmentally inappropriate responses.

The transactional nature of this model is important both to the development and treatment of emotion dysregulation. As a transaction, both components (individual emotional vulnerabilities and invalidating social responses) reciprocally influence one another as a person goes through daily life. Thus, an individual with high emotional vulnerability and a lot of dysregulation may perpetuate or exacerbate invalidating responses just as invalidating responses may heighten emotional vulnerabilities and increase dysregulation.

The consequences of the transaction between emotionally vulnerable individuals and invalidating responses include the following (cf. Linehan, 1993a):

• The individual may not learn to discriminate emotions and label them in a manner that is consistent with the social community.
• The person has limited emotional understanding, which results in little proactive emotion management activities, such as reducing vulnerability to negative emotion or increasing positive emotional experiences to buffer against negative experiences.
• Because the individual is usually instructed to control her or his emotions and suppress emotional displays but is not taught *how* to do so, the person does not learn to regulate emotional arousal (and in fact may rely on others for this function) and may express emotions and other negative experiences very inaccurately.
• Because of unresponsiveness to the communication of pain or misery, the person may develop very extreme responses (high reactivity) to negative situations and emotion (all-or-nothing emotional reactions).
• Because of inattention or punishing responses, the person is likely to have very high emotional sensitivity, along with difficulty differentiating among some emotions, in particular differentiating between *primary* and *secondary* emotions (primary emotions are typically universal responses to the situation, whereas secondary emotions are those in response to the primary emotion

or mediated by judgments and appraisals; Greenberg & Safran, 1989).
• Individuals may learn not to trust their own experience and may instead invalidate their own emotions, experiences, beliefs, reactions, desires, and so on.

Redressing these negative consequences are the primary goals of emotion regulation skills.

EMOTION REGULATION STRATEGIES AND INTERVENTIONS

Because emotional responses may be understood as occurring within a transaction, intervening on any component of the transaction can change the functioning of the entire system. In addition, there are at least two distinct approaches to intervening on each step in the transaction (emotion dysregulation process): acceptance strategies and change strategies. Skills designed to help clients accept their emotions include skills focusing on emotion discrimination, accurate labeling of emotions, and accurate emotional expression. Skills designed to help clients change their emotions include skills focusing on changing the type of emotion, or the intensity or duration of the emotion. In addition, some skills or strategies may incorporate elements of both acceptance and change dialectically (Fruzzetti & Fruzzetti, this volume), which may be beneficial at times.

Empirical Support

There is considerable evidence supporting the use of acceptance strategies, change strategies, or their combination, in regulating emotion, in particular in dialectical behavior therapy (DBT), the central focus of which is emotion regulation. Although a comprehensive review of DBT is beyond the scope of this chapter, dozens of studies have demonstrated the effectiveness of DBT with a variety of problems related to emotion dysregulation (see Feigenbaum, 2007, or Robbins & Chapman, 2006 for recent reviews). Studies typically have examined DBT as applied to individuals with borderline personality disorder or other severely dysfunctional behaviors such as self-injury and suicidality, but also employ DBT for substance use, depression, bulimia nervosa, anxiety disorders, binge-eating disorder, aggression and violence, couple and family problems, and other problems associated with intense negative emotional arousal and dysregulation. Increasingly, a variety of CBT approaches have incorporated an emphasis on emotion regulation, with successful outcomes as noted earlier. However, few CBT studies have evaluated the specific components of treatment related to emotion regulation per se. Thus, DBT studies, which inherently target emotion regulation and utilize emotion regulation strategies, provide the best evidence for the use of these interventions for a wide range of problems.

Acceptance Strategies

Acceptance strategies include understanding emotions, mindfulness, identification and discrimination of emotion, accurate labeling, tolerating painful emotional experience, allowing (and participating in) emotions, letting go of secondary emotions, accurate expression of emotions, self-validation, and validation from others. In a sense, acceptance of an emotion leads to effective management of the consequences of the emotion, thereby regulating cognition and overt behavior. Moreover, by "accepting" current emotional experiences the client does not engage in escape behaviors (e.g., drug use, aggression, or social withdrawal) or secondary emotional responses that might trigger arousal further (Fruzzetti & Erikson, in press).

Understanding Emotions

Although complex, it can be useful to provide psychoeducation in the functions of emotion and in the various factors that influence emotion (e.g., events, appraisals, biological functioning, learning history or emotional disposition, facial expression, body posture, labels for events and emotional responses, availability of supportive/validating versus unsupportive/invalidating others). Although it is obvious to some, many clients may not understand the multiple determinants of ordinary emotion, and this lack of understanding can increase fear and the development of secondary emotional reactions. Client understanding about

emotion can provide a quick avenue toward self-assessment of the factors that are leading to dysregulated emotion, and may be useful alone or in combination with other skills.

Mindfulness: Discriminating and Accurately Labeling Emotions

The incorporation of mindfulness into CBT has occurred rapidly in recent years (Fruzzetti & Erikson, in press). Mindfulness includes a variety of different strategies, ranging from intensive, long-term meditation practice (e.g., mindfulness-based cognitive therapy; Segal et al., 2001) to a careful breakdown of the psychological components of mindfulness and applying them as skills in daily living (e.g., Linehan, 1993b). Perhaps most importantly, the role of mindfulness skills as an intervention, in particular in regulating emotion, has begun to receive empirical support (Baer, 2003). For example, Wupperman, Neumann & Axelrod (in press) have demonstrated that mindfulness skills are inversely related to emotion regulation problems and other features of borderline personality disorder, even after covarying out other related factors.

Although there are many definitions of mindfulness, at their core they include the ability to focus attention and awareness in a non-judgmental manner (Bishop et al., 2004; Brown & Ryan, 2003). In her pioneering work, Linehan (1993b) separates the components of mindfulness into "what" a person does when mindful (either observe, describe, or participate), and "how" to do these things (nonjudgmentally, one at a time, and with a focus on doing what is effective, in particular what is effective in terms of long-term goals), and frames each as a skill to be learned. Learning mindfulness skills in general may be very helpful for clients. In addition, even applying elements of mindfulness to emotions may be useful.

Before any specific treatment of problematic emotion can be attempted, the client's actual primary emotion must be identified and labeled accurately. This process can be achieved by using mindfulness to discriminate sensations, urges, and situations (discrimination training) in order to identify emotions accurately, and in this context includes several steps. First, it may be useful to notice and become aware of the prompting events or stimuli. Emotions could be elicited not only by the event itself, but also by a person's interpretation of an event, thoughts, and memories (or a combination). Then, noticing bodily responses such as sweating, body gestures, facial expression, muscle tension, and other sensations helps clients to become aware that they are experiencing emotional arousal. Simply being aware may help the client to habituate both to the situation and to the emotion itself, reducing secondary emotional reactions (below). In addition, certain action urges are associated specifically with certain emotions (e.g., urge to hide: shame; to attack: anger; to withdraw: sadness; to run away or avoid: fear). Noticing these action urges can help identify the specific emotion being experienced. The next step is to describe what has been observed in a nonjudgmental way, connecting sensations, cognitions and action tendencies to the situation. Nonjudgmental description means describing a more or less objective reality, without interpretation or any value valence: without right/wrong, should/ shouldn't, or good/bad evaluations. Description itself may slow or lower emotional arousal (and secondary emotional responses), thereby soothing painful emotions and making aware- ness, accurate labeling, and acceptance, more likely.

However, for some clients, awareness and description may be too difficult for a first step, especially in high-arousal situations. For them, it may be helpful to imagine other people in their situation and describe how they might feel. This may be useful if the client is overwhelmed with judgments and interpretations, or simply does not have much skill at observing and describing his or her own private experiences. Observing his or her own experience also creates an immediate step away from the emotional intensity of the situation, further enabling the client to practice emotion awareness and accurate labeling. If emotions are labeled inaccurately, the individual loses the effective path of accurate expression and other emotion strategies, and is more likely to receive inval- idating responses that further fuel arousal and dysregulation.

Discriminate between Primary and Secondary Emotions

Primary emotions are normative, adaptive, and universal responses in a given context. In contrast, secondary emotions are reactions to the primary emotion (Greenberg & Safran, 1989), and may be learned responses to primary emotions, or may be mediated by judgments or other negative appraisals of factors related to the emotional event (such as judgments about another person, self, the situation, etc.). Regardless, secondary emotions typically bring with them a variety of maladaptive responses. In fact, emotion regulation skills are often most relevant for use on dysregulated secondary emotions. Thus, emotion regulation skills often help the client either avoid secondary emotional reactions (by staying in the experience of the primary emotion) or focus on regulating the intensity of secondary emotional reactions. For example, although how to manage anger in psychotherapy is somewhat controversial (cf. Greenberg, 2007), anger often may be conceptualized as a secondary emotional re- sponse to fear, sadness or shame, especially in a relational context (Fruzzetti, 2006). The person may have learned to escape from the primary emotion to anger, which may now be a conditioned emotional reaction in the situation (Fruzzetti & Levensky, 2000). Of course, other emotions may also be secondary emotions.

Thus, the "regulation" of primary and sec- ondary emotions is different. If the client has a tendency to react with secondary emotions, it is essential to use emotion identification skills (mindfulness) to turn awareness and attention toward the missed primary emotion. Otherwise, the client is likely to react and express in ways that are nonnormative to the situation; consequently he or she will be less likely to regulate and achieve his or her goals, and will be more likely to be invalidated by others, making further dysregulation likely. Because secondary emotions are often accompanied by judgments, letting go of judgments (using mindfulness skills such as description) can be a very useful step. Then, attention can be focused back on primary emotions slowly, or focused back on the situation (which will retrigger the primary emotion). Refocusing attention back to primary emotions may be sufficient to regulate the person's emotion. If not, additional emotion regulation strategies may be employed.

Tolerating Painful Emotion

Regulating emotion requires that the person be able to tolerate the emotion (primary or secondary), at least briefly, either until it subsides naturally or until the person can employ other strategies. Tolerating intense negative emotional arousal clearly is an acceptance strategy in many ways. Because our emotion systems are constantly reacting to new stimuli, the act of tolerating the emotion may, in fact, lead to arousal reduction. The most common and effective strategies include distracting away from the stimulus for the negative emotion and/or distracting away from the experience of the emotion itself by engaging fully in some other activity; soothing oneself (or soliciting soothing by others); engaging in relaxation; or engaging in some sort of cognitive activity such as imagery or prayer.

Allowing or Participating in the Emotion

Emotionally dysregulated clients often expend a great deal of effort trying to escape from, cut off, and/or preempt negative emotions. However, it is necessary in living life to have regular negative emotional experiences (many times every day). Rather than trying to suppress or avoid them, which is counterproductive, an alternative is to allow or embrace them, without becoming consumed or dysregulated by them. This involves the ability to simultaneously be aware of one's emotion and aware of the context (whole person, situation, events) of the emotion. The skill involves titrating one's level of awareness between noticing the emotion itself and observing oneself as the person experiencing the emotion, while neither suppressing nor avoiding the emotion. The idea is that a person can have an emotion without acting on it and can actually feel alive and content while experiencing even "negative" emotions. For example, following the death of a loved one, it is healthy to feel sadness and grief. People mourn loved ones by going back and forth between noticing the sadness, communicating about it (titrating away from the emotional intensity), soothing themselves, and

engaging in other activities (ordinary ones like eating, driving, reading, working, or recreation). Allowing or participating in the emotional experience does not change the emotion per se, but does change the person's relationship with his or her emotion.

Accurate Expression

As noted earlier, when a person *accurately* expresses his or her emotional experience, this has an effect on the listener, who is much more likely to be able to validate the person's experience and soothe his or her emotion. In general, all of the strategies noted above to help observe and describe emotions, and to discriminate between primary and secondary emotions, are relevant here as well. In addition, there are social or interpersonal skills that allow the person to connect verbally his or her experience both to the event that precipitated it and to his or her vulnerabilities. This kind of description is the most complete and accurate, and therefore the most likely to be understood by the listener, and in turn the most likely to elicit a response that helps the individual regulate further (soothing, validation). Accurate expression is an acceptance-oriented skill in part because it also allows the individual to take the observer role, which facilitates allowing or participating in his or her own experience.

Self-Validating Emotions

Clients who are emotionally dysregulated often invalidate their own experience, which further dysregulates them. For example, dysregulated individuals often become judgmental about their experience, delegitimize or pathologize their own suffering (e.g., "I deserve this pain" or "I should be able to do this without feeling so bad"), identify their emotions inaccurately, or do not even notice (for some time, anyway) that they have a particular emotion. Self-validation is the opposite of these behaviors, and is about accepting one's own experience. Self-validation often starts with interrupting self-judgments simply by noticing and describing (without interpretation) the "facts" of the situation (what happened, how it feels, what the emotion is). Next, clients can notice the legitimacy of their own emotional reaction, either because of their own history or disposition, or because their responses are quite normative (Fruzzetti & Iverson, 2006; Linehan, 1997). For example, a person whose friend didn't show up for lunch might say, "I shouldn't have counted on this person anyway. I feel stupid and ashamed." Coaching in self-validation would help the client notice her or his actual emotion (e.g., disappointment) and notice that this feeling makes sense (is normative) in this particular situation. So the person might end up saying, "I'm disappointed. Of course, I am; I was looking forward to lunch with my friend. I'll find out what happened to her/him." Thus, self-validation is predicated on accurate labeling and the ability to tolerate negative emotion, at least for a while. And not only does self-validation interrupt escalating emotional arousal, it also promotes effective interpersonal behaviors and more regulated relationships, which in turn facilitate more effective emotion regulation.

Validation from Others

Being understood and validated by other people soothes frayed emotions and helps reduce negative emotional arousal even under stressful circumstances (Fruzzetti, 2006; Shenk & Fruzzetti, 2008). A validating response communicates understanding and acceptance of the person's experience. Consequently, validating can be both an essential therapeutic tool (Linehan, 1997) and a key client skill (Fruzzetti & Iverson, 2006). In the context of regulating one's own emotion, being able to seek validation (acceptance) is important.

The idea here is for the client to seek validation from another person who is able and willing to validate the *valid* parts of the person's experience in the ways that they are valid, and not to validate (at least not in the same ways) the less valid parts (e.g., secondary emotions, judgments). It is important to understand that validation is not agreement per se, although it often involves finding the areas of agreement. For example, an emotionally dysregulated client might also be cognitively dysregulated, and approach another person seeking validation by saying something like, "You won't believe what an asshole my spouse is . . . " and spend several minutes criticizing his or her partner. A truly validating response *will not agree* with this characterization of the partner. Instead, the person would respond by validating the person's *experience*, and especially, the primary emotion: "Wow, you really are upset. It makes sense that after she/he did that you would feel disappointed and let down" (see Chapter 78 for further discussion).

Change-Oriented Strategies

There are a number of different skills and strategies that may be instrumental in changing the experience of an emotion (its intensity or duration), changing the emotion itself in a given situation, or changing or avoiding situations that lead to dysregulated emotion. However, given that individuals with emotion regulation problems likely learn emotional avoidance as a key coping strategy (e.g., Linehan et al., 2007), it is important to help clients discriminate the appropriate contexts in which to apply change-oriented skills and strategies to regulate their emotion (rather than acceptance-oriented ones). For example, when clients are emotionally dysregulated, they may have trouble applying even the most rudimentary problem-solving skills to their situation, and in this case removing themselves from the situation may be the most effective first step. Simply avoiding difficult situations, however, will create enormous problems, and that is why avoidance per se is not considered an emotion regulation skill. Temporarily avoiding by distracting or self-soothing (cf. distress tolerance skills; Linehan, 1993b) may be useful in combination with emotion regulation, but is not likely to lead to long-term solutions on its own.

Effective change strategies may include exposure and response prevention, or other stimulus control strategies, either in the therapy session or in vivo. Additional change strategies include reducing vulnerability to negative emotion, increasing positive events (activation), modulation of physiological and other transitory responses, problem solving, and improving interpersonal transactions and close relationships. These are all discussed in this chapter.

Exposure and Response Prevention

At times, emotion dysregulation (hyperarousal or numbing) occurs in response to discrete stimuli (e.g., stimuli associated with trauma), and can be treated using formal exposure and response prevention strategies (see Chapters 39 and 59 for a full description of these procedures). However, at other times, the stimuli associated with dysregulated emotion are many and diffuse, or the stimulus for dysregulation is itself another emotion (a secondary emotion in response to a primary one). In these situations, the same principles of exposure and response prevention can be applied, but may be augmented by mindfulness and acceptance-oriented regulation strategies Fruzzetti & Erikson, in press). For example, a client might have such a long history of being criticized and invalidated, in combination with a lot of emotion sensitivity, that countless stimuli elicit shame and sadness. However, she may have experienced shame and sadness as more painful than anger, and anger as more effective in pushing away invalidating others. Consequently, she may experience and express anger quite consistently, neither noticing nor expressing sadness or shame. Here, of course, anger is her secondary emotion. Thus, her therapist may try to help her to ignore her feelings of anger (thoughts, labels, etc.) and block the action urges associated with anger (facially, verbally, etc.) and instead try to discriminate sadness or shame, which are the primary emotions among her sensations, notice or increase awareness of her judgments (and let them go), notice appraisals, experiences, recent events or triggers, and so on. If she also has fewer invalidating social encounters she may be able to learn to: (1) ignore her anger; (2) block her angry behaviors; (3) notice her sadness or shame; (4) attenuate her sadness and shame with repeated exposure to life situations that do not naturally elicit sadness or shame; and (5) build more effective relationships.

Other Stimulus Control Strategies

When high negative emotional arousal is predictably elicited by certain cues, clients can regulate emotion by titrating exposure to those cues or by changing the eliciting properties of the stimuli. Again, because of the problems associated with overreliance on avoidance, the idea is not to avoid per se. Rather, one strategy might be to control exposure to the cues in combination with other emotion regulation strategies. For example, the client might delay entering into a situation (stimulus control) in order first to engage in arousal reduction, knowing that just being in that situation will elicit a large emotional response. Alternatively, the stimulus itself may be reconditioned not to elicit a high negative emotional response. For example, some clients who have lived in extreme but inconsistent and unpredictable families have an aversive response to being praised. However, praise typically is expected to elicit more positive emotion (e.g., satisfaction, pride). If praise elicits fear or shame, presumably maladaptive learning has occurred, and praise can be reconditioned by directing the client to be aware of the current circumstances (e.g., in-session), and try to notice what gets in the way of a positive response. With repeated pairings (praise that is genuine, awareness of safety, predictability, and being appreciated), the stimulus properties of praise will change and it will no longer elicit an aversive reaction.

Reducing Vulnerability to Dysregulation

As noted earlier, both temperament and the individual's emotional baseline can make a person more (or less) vulnerable to being dysregulated in a given situation. Consequently, reducing those vulnerabilities reduces dysregulation, even if the same events occur. Individuals can minimize vulnerability by influencing their biological processes, for example by treating physical illnesses effectively (e.g., taking medication for disease, stretching or exercising for backache), balancing eating (e.g., consuming healthy amounts of nutritional foods), not ingesting mood-altering drugs (e.g., alcohol, illicit drugs), practicing good sleep hygiene (e.g., getting enough sleep on a regular schedule; see Chapter 40 on the treatment of insomnia), and exercising regularly.

In addition, the client can create an environment more conducive to emotional resiliency (less vulnerability). This may involve working to increase the number of pleasant events in an individual's day (see activation, below), and/or reducing the number of stressors. It may involve taking effective action consistent with the pursuit of important goals, which builds up resistance to negative emotional cues by helping to engender more feelings of optimism and hope, as well as generating competencies. It may also include making structural changes such as taking a new job that has more flexible hours, or an individual may be able to mange time in other ways so that it is easier to get regular sleep or exercise (and thus decrease biological vulnerability), or spend more time engaging in valued activities (rather than mindless ones).

Behavioral Activation

Behavioral activation utilizes the relationship between a person's mood, environment and activities to reduce negative emotion (and build positive experiences). This skill teaches a client that mood can be improved by engaging in activities that are pleasurable (or at least were at one time). These activities need to be tailored to the individual and in service to the individual's long-term goals (see Chapter 10). Clients ideally should schedule activities daily and then use self-monitoring to determine how they felt during and after engaging in the activities. Activation should be augmented with the mindfulness skills of observing and participating because full engagement in activities is essential. Therefore, participating mindfully helps the individual engage in activities one mindfully and absent of distractions (rather than being aware primarily of his or her negative mood). Similarly, mindfulness skills such as noticing or observing (awareness) help the client to be aware of any incipient positive emotional changes that result from new or renewed activities and prevent reorientation of attention back to preexisting negative emotions.

Modulating Physiology and Attention

Emotions may be either up- or downregulated physiologically. In situations of high emotional arousal, intense physical exercise may paradoxically help reduce arousal. Exercise raises physiological arousal to match emotional arousal; as the physiological arousal decreases after cessation of exercise, emotional arousal may follow. Splashing cold water on the face can also decrease

arousal quickly. Progressive muscle relaxation, which involves tensing a part of the body, holding the tension and then relaxing the muscles, reduces tension and decreases intense emotional arousal, as does relaxing facial musculature and body posture. Breathing retraining (also mindful breathing) can help the client condition a relaxation response to a single deep breath. Engaging in activities that are soothing to one of the senses, such as massaging the palm of the hand or taking a hot (or cool) bath are also helpful in decreasing arousal. Physiological techniques have the advantage of affecting emotional arousal rapidly and do not require a high level of cognitive processing. These techniques appear to work by focusing attention away from the original arousing stimuli and also by interfering with the sensations evoked by the negative emotion (Linehan, 1993).

Using mindfulness skills, an individual may shift the focus of attention away from an unpleasant stimulus. Additionally, the client can turn the focus of his or her attention to long-term goals versus shorter-term goals, which help the client ride out the urge to use "escape" behaviors. Mindfulness may also be employed to focus attention to the client's values, which can helpful in lowering negative arousal enough to re-regulate and engage in effective problem solving. Mindfulness is also helpful in inhibiting, or letting go, of judgments, negative thinking, or perseveration on negative stimuli, all of which are contributory factors to negative emotional arousal and dysregulation. Cognitive restructuring techniques may be used to modify negative interpretations and attributions of events, especially prior to peak arousal states.

Opposite Action

Because every emotion has associated action urges, and the relationship between the emotions and urges are reciprocal, a client can act in a way that is inconsistent with, and in opposition to, the current action urge as a way to reduce the emotion itself. Although this strategy is similar to exposure and response prevention in principle, in practice it does not require formal exposure or therapist assistance, and has been shown to be an effective intervention strategy (e.g., Rizvi & Linehan, 2005). Acting opposite begins with accurate identification and labeling of a current negative emotion that the person wants to change (i.e., either reduce the intensity or duration of the emotion, or change the quality of the emotion) and its associated action urge. Then the client can identify actions that are opposite to the present action urge tendency and try to engage in this opposite action (assuming it is safe to do so). For example, a person with a lot of social fears is likely to have a tendency (urge) to avoid social situations. The opposite action would be to engage mindfully in some social activity and to notice other aspects of the experience (in particular that nothing dangerous occurs, and also any incipient positive emotional experience). Similar opposite actions could be practiced for shame or guilt (talking to someone instead of avoiding or hiding), sadness (becoming active instead of withdrawing), or anger (gently avoiding instead of attacking). Again, opposite action is likely to be most successful when the client already has many of the other skills described (identifying and labeling emotions accurately, tolerating painful emotion, being mindful of less painful aspects of emotional experience, etc.).

Problem Solving

Problem-solving skills can be used to regulate emotions by reducing the number of negative events in daily living (or at least changing the ratio of positive to negative events), effectively reducing the triggers for negative emotional arousal and dysregulation. Or, problem-solving can be used to change current situations or stimuli that are triggers for emotional distress and dysregulation. The first step is the identification of situations that cue distressing emotions. Mindfulness can be used to appraise accurately the situation and differentiate the facts of the situation from interpretations, assumptions, and worries. Interpersonal problem-solving can then be employed to help attain desired goals in a way that preserves self-respect and long-term goals (Linehan, 1993b). Problem solving is effective in regulating emotions in part because it prevents perseveration on a distressing situation, reduces negative events, and involves activation.

Improving Relationship Skills and Interactions with Others

A longer-term change strategy involves helping the client improve interactions with others. A variety of social, relationship, or interpersonal skills may be employed to help clients improve the quality of their close relationships. Helping clients to pay attention to and validate others more often is likely to result in them being understood and validated in return. These kinds of changes would serve to alter some of the situational factors that contribute to emotion dysregulation and prevent the escalation of negative emotional arousal. Another application of this strategy would be to assist the client in repairing relationships that are important to them and in building new healthy relationships (Fruzzetti, 2006).

Changing the Social and Family Environment

Although the focus of this chapter is on how individuals can learn to regulate their emotions, it would be incomplete without mentioning the importance of having a supportive or validating social or family environment (or at least the absence of a critical or invalidating one). Delineating the many interventions that can be employed to help family members and friends become less invalidating and more validating is beyond the scope of this chapter. However, it is important to realize that when nascent emotion regulation skills learned in treatment are punished by the client's family or friends they are unlikely to develop successfully. Thus, assessing for the consequences when clients try out their newly learned skills in their family and social environment is an essential part of any skill training. Intervening to make family members and friends more receptive to and reinforcing of client emotion regulation skills may make the difference between success and failure.

Further Reading

J. J. Gross (2007). *Handbook of emotion regulation*. New York: Guilford.

Philippot, P., & Feldman, R. (2004). *The regulation of emotion*. Mahwah: NJ: Lawrence Erlbaum.

D. K. Snyder, J. Simpson, & J. Hughes (2006). *Emotion regulation in couples and families: Pathways to dysfunction and health*. Washington, DC: American Psychological Association.

References

Baer, Ruth A. (2003). Mindfulness training as a clinical intervention: A conceptual and empirical review. *Clinical Psychology: Science and Practice, 10,* 125–143.

Baumesiter, R. F., Zell, A. L., & Tice, D. M. (2007). How emotions facilitate and impair self-regulation. In J. J. Gross (Ed.), *Handbook of emotion regulation* (pp. 408–426). New York: Guilford Press.

Bishop, S. R., Lau, M., Shapiro, S., Carlson, L., Anderson, N. D., Carmody, J., et al. (2004). Mindfulness: A proposed operational definition. *Clinical Psychology: Science & Practice, 11,* 230–241.

Brown, K. W., & Ryan, R. M. (2003). The benefits of being present: Mindfulness and its role in psychological well-being. *Journal of Personality and Social Psychology, 84,* 822–848.

Burum, B. S., & Goldfried, M. R. (2007). The centrality of emotion to psychological change. *Clinical Psychology: Science and Practice, 14,* 407–413.

Cameron, L. D., Booth, R. J., Schlatter, M., Ziginskas, D., & Harman, J. E. (2008). Changes in emotion regulation and psychological adjustment following use of a group psychosocial support program for women recently diagnosed with breast cancer. *Psycho-Oncology, 16,* 171–180.

Ehrenreich, J. T., Fairholm, C. P., Buzzella, B. A., Ellard, K., & Barlow, D. H. (2007). The role of emotion in psychological therapy. *Clinical Psychology: Science and Practice, 14,* 422–428.

Ehring, T., Fischer, S., Schnülle, J., Bösterling, A., & Tuschen-Caffier, B. (2007). Characteristics of emotion regulation in recovered depressed versus never depressed individuals. *Personality and Individual Differences, 44,* 1574–1584.

Eisenberg, N., Spinrad, T., & Smith, C. (2004). Emotion-related regulation: Its conceptualization, relations to social functioning, and socialization. In P. Philippot & R. Feldman (Eds.), *The regulation of emotion* (pp. 277–306). Mahwah: NJ: Lawrence Erlbaum.

Feigenbaum, J. (2007). Dialectical behaviour therapy: An increasing evidence base. *Journal of Mental Health, 16,* 51–68.

Fox, H. C., Hong, K. A., & Sinha, R. (2008). Difficulties in emotion regulation and impulse control in recently abstinent alcoholics compared with social drinkers. *Addictive Behaviors, 33,* 388–394.

Fruzzetti, A. E. (2002). Dialectical behavior therapy for borderline personality and related disorders. In T. Patterson (Ed.), *Comprehensive Handbook of Psychotherapy* (Vol. 2, pp. 215–240). New York: John Wiley & Sons.

Fruzzetti, A. E. (2006). The high conflict couple: A dialectical behavior therapy guide to finding peace, intimacy, and validation. Oakland, CA: New Harbinger Press.

Fruzzetti, A., & Iverson, K. (2004). Mindfulness, acceptance, validation, and "individual" psychopathology in couples. In S. C. Hayes, V. M. Follette, & M. M. Linehan (Eds.), *Mindfulness and acceptance: Expanding the cognitive-behavioral tradition* (pp. 192–208). New York: Guilford.

Fruzzetti, A. E., & Iverson, K. M. (2006). Intervening with couples and families to treat emotion dysregulation and psychopathology. In D. K. Snyder, J. Simpson, & J. Hughes (Eds.), *Emotion regulation in couples and families: Pathways to dysfunction and health* (pp. 249–267). Washington, DC: American Psychological Association.

Fruzzetti, A. E., & Levensky, E. R. (2000). Dialectical behavior therapy for domestic violence: Rationale and procedures. *Cognitive and behavioral practice, 7,* 435–447.

Fruzzetti, A. E., Shenk, C., & Hoffman, P. D. (2005). Family interaction and the development of borderline personality disorder: A transactional model. *Development and Psychopathology, 17,* 1007–1030.

Greenberg, L., & Bischkopf, J. (2007). Anger in psychotherapy: To express or not to express? That is the question. In T. A. Cavell & K. T. Malcolm (Eds.), *Anger, aggression and interventions for interpersonal violence.* Mahwah, MJ: Lawrence Erlbaum.

Greenberg, L. S., & Safran, J. D. (1989). Emotion in psychotherapy. *American Psychologist, 44,* 19–29.

Gross, J. J. (1998). The emerging field of emotion regulation: An integrative review. *Review of General Psychology, 2,* 271–299.

Hayes, A. M., & Feldman, G. (2004). Clarifying the construct of mindfulness in the context of emotion regulation and the process of change in therapy. *Clinical Psychology: Science and Practice, 11,* 255–262.

James, W. (1884). What is an emotion? *Mind, 9,* 188–205.

Keltner, D., & Kring, A. M. (1998). Emotion, social function, and psychopathology. *Review of General Psychology, 2,* 320–342.

Linehan, M. (1993a). Cognitive–behavioral treatment of borderline personality disorder. New York: Guilford.

Linehan, M. (1993b). Skills training manual for treating borderline personality disorder. New York: Guilford.

Linehan, M. M. (1997). Validation and psychotherapy. In A. Bohart & L. S. Greenberg (Eds.), *Empathy and psychotherapy: New directions to theory, research, and practice* (pp. 353–392). Washington, DC: American Psychological Association.

Linehan, M., Bohus, M., & Lynch, T. (2007). Dialectical behavior therapy for pervasive emotion dysregulation: Theoretical and practical underpinnings. In J. J. Gross (Ed.), *Handbook of emotion regulation* (pp. 581–605). New York: Guilford.

Menin, D. S. (2006). Emotion regulation therapy: An integrative approach to treatment-resistant anxiety disorders. *Journal of Contemporary Psychotherapy, 36,* 95–105.

Rimé, B. (2007). Interpersonal emotion regulation. In J. J. Gross (Ed.), *Handbook of emotion regulation* (pp. 466–485). New York: Guilford.

Rizvi, S. L., & Linehan, M. M. (2005). The treatment of maladaptive shame in borderline personality disorder: A pilot study of "opposite action." *Cognitive and Behavioral Practice, 12,* 437–447.

Robins, C. J., & Chapman, A. L. (2004). Dialectical Behavior Therapy: Current status, recent developments, and future directions. *Journal of Personality Disorders, 18,* 73–89.

Robins, C., Schimidt, H., & Linehan, M. (2004). Dialectical behavior therapy: Synthesizing radical acceptance with skillful means. In S. C. Hayes, V. M. Follette, & M. M. Linehan (Eds.), *Mindfulness and acceptance: Expanding the cognitive-behavioral tradition* (pp. 30–44). New York: Guilford.

Southam-Gerow, M. A., & Kendall, P. C. (2002). Emotion regulation and understanding: Implications for child psychopathology and therapy. *Clinical Psychology Review, 22,* 189–222.

Wupperman, P., Neumann, C. S., & Axelrod, S. R. (in press). Do deficits in mindfulness underlie borderline personality features and core difficulties? *Journal of Personality Disorders.*

29 ENCOPRESIS: BIOBEHAVIORAL TREATMENT

Patrick C. Friman, Jennifer Resetar,
and Kim DeRuyk

INTRODUCTION

Since the publication of the first edition of this book, the literature on functional encopresis (FE) has not changed significantly. There have been no substantive changes in the literature on its definition, underlying processes, or methods for its evaluation. There have been some modest additions to literature on treatment, but these additions fundamentally involve replication, minor variations on previously reported treatments, or alterations in methods of treatment delivery (e.g., via Internet: Ritterband et al., 2003, 2006). The additions do not change the overall clinical picture, nor do they require exhaustive coverage in this chapter. Thus, the body of this chapter will closely mirror the previous one, with a few modest exceptions. The most substantive of these is a table listing major empirical investigations of biobehavioral treatment for FE and it is divided between single subject and group studies (see Table 29.1). New references to recent reviews of incontinence are included in the Further Reading section. New information has been added to the sections on Facilitating Medication and Nonretentive FE, and some phrasing changes were made throughout. Finally, arguments against assumptions about the psychopathological basis of FE have been added.

FE involves fecal incontinence not attributable to pathophysiological or substance-based processes (more on this later). Although all forms of incontinence require evaluation and treatment, when left untreated, FE is more likely than other forms such as enuresis to lead to serious and potentially life-threatening medical sequelae and seriously impaired social acceptance, relations, and development. The reasons for the

medical sequelae are described in the Evaluation section. The primary reason for the social impairment is that soiling evokes more revulsion from peers, parents, and important others than other forms of incontinence (and most other behavior problems). As an example, severe corporal punishment for fecal accidents was still recommended by professionals in the late nineteenth century (Henoch, 1889). The professional approach to FE has evolved substantially since then but the approaches by laypersons (and still some professionals) are not keeping pace. Children with FE are still frequently shamed, blamed, and punished for a condition that is almost totally beyond their control (Friman, Hofstader, & Jones, 2006; Levine, 1982).

The definition of FE has remained relatively consistent across versions of the *Diagnostic and Statistical Manual of Mental Disorders (DSM)*; the *DSM-IV* (American Psychiatric Association, 1994) lists four criteria for FE: (1) repeated passage of feces into inappropriate places whether involuntary or intentional; (2) at least one such event a month for at least 3 months; (3) chronological age is at least 4 years (or equivalent developmental level); and (4) the behavior is not due exclusively to the direct physiological effects of a substance or a general medical condition except through a mechanism involving constipation. In terms of presentation, the *DSM-IV* describes two subtypes, one with and without constipation and overflow incontinence. The subtype without constipation and overflow incontinence is much less common and understood than the other subtype (more on this in the section on FE without constipation). In terms of course, the *DSM-IV* also describes two subtypes: primary, in which the child has never

TABLE 29.1   Sample Empirical Evaluations of Biobehavioral Treatment for Encopresis

Authors	Age	n
Group Design		
Cox, Sutphen, Ling, Quillian, & Borowitz (1996)	6–15	44
Dawson, Griffith, & Boeke (1990)	6–14	16
Fireman & Koplewicz (1992)	52	3–17
Levine & Bakow (1976)	_[a]	127
Lowery, Srour, Whitehead, & Schuster (1985)	4–16	58
Ritterbrand, Cox, Gordon, Borowitz, Kovatchev, Walker, & Sutphen (2006)	5–12	49
Ritterband, Cox, Walker, Kovatchev, McKnight, Patel, Borowitz, & Sutphen (2003)	6–12[b]	24
Stark, Owens-Stively, Spirito, Lewis, & Guevremont (1990)	4–11	18
Stark, Opipari, Donaldson, Danovsky, Rasile, & DelSanto (1997)	2–12	59
Young, Brennen, Baker, & Baker (1995)	6–12	76
Single Subject Design		
Bornstein, Sturm, Retzlaff, Kirby, & Chong (1981)	9	1
Houts, Mellon, & Whelan (1988)	6–8	3
O'Brien, Ross, & Christopherson (1986)	4–5	4
Rolider & Van Houten (1985)	12	1

[a]Participants ages were not specified.
[b]Participants ages were not specified, criteria for participant age ranged from 6 to 12.

had fecal continence; and secondary, in which incontinence returns after at least 6 months of continence. Approximately 3% of the general pediatric population meets these criteria.

UNDERLYING PROCESSES

Successful treatment for FE targets the processes that cause the condition and 90% to 95% of cases occur as a function of, or in conjunction with, reduced colonic motility, constipation, and fecal retention, and the various behavioral/dietary factors contributing to these conditions, including: (1) insufficient roughage or bulk in the diet; (2) irregular diet; (3) insufficient oral intake of fluids; (4) medications that may have a side effect of constipation; (5) unstructured, inconsistent, and/or punitive approaches to toilet training; and (6) toileting avoidance by the child. Any of these factors, singly or in combination, puts the child at risk for reduced colonic motility, actual constipation, and corresponding uncomfortable or painful bowel movements. Uncomfortable or painful bowel movements, in turn, negatively reinforce fecal retention, and retention leads to

a regressive reciprocal cycle, often resulting in regular fecal accidents. When the constipation is severe or the cycle is chronic, the child may develop fecal impaction, a large blockage caused by the collection of hard, dry stool. Not infrequently, liquid fecal matter will seep around the fecal mass, producing "paradoxical diarrhea." Although the child is actually constipated, he or she appears as to have diarrhea. Some parents will attempt to treat this type of "diarrhea" with the over-the-counter antidiarrheal agents, which only worsen the problem.

EVALUATION

The therapist faced with an encopretic child should essentially go no further with treatment until the child has received a medical evaluation. Two primary reasons for this cautionary dictate are the possibility of organic disease (see Contraindications) and the medical risk posed by fecal matter inexorably accumulating in an organ with a limited amount of space. An unfortunately all-too-frequent presenting problem in medical clinics is an encopretic child who has been in extended therapy with a nonmedical professional whose initial evaluation did not include referral for a medical evaluation and whose treatment did not address the etiology of FE (see Underlying Process). As a result, the children's colonic systems can become painfully and dangerously distended, sometimes to the point of being life threatening (e.g., McGuire, Rothenberg, & Tyler, 1984).

The medical evaluation will typically involve a thorough medical, dietary, and bowel history. In addition, abdominal palpation and rectal examination are used to check for large amounts of fecal matter, very dry fecal matter in the rectal vault and poor sphincter tone. Approximately 70% of constipation can be determined on physical exam, and detection can be increased to above 90% with a KUB (x-ray of kidneys, ureter, and bladder) (Barr, Levine, & Watkins, 1979).

Despite the emphasis on diet and behavior here, gleaned from the most empirical parts of literature, some psychologists and psychiatrists persist in viewing FE as a psychological problem. Yet over the past 15 years, several studies have concluded that, although some children with FE also have psychological problems, the incidence is simply not high enough to suggest a causal relationship between the two conditions (Friman et al., 2006). Thus, targeting psychological problems in order to obtain fecal continence would seem imprudent from the perspective of the scientific literature. Rather, when FE and behavioral/psychological problems co-occur, they often have to be treated separately. For example, children who have poorly developed instructional control skills are at risk for being noncompliant with treatment and thus instructional control training may need to precede or accompany treatment for FE.

CONTRAINDICATIONS

Some medical conditions (e.g., Hirschsprung's disease, hypothyroidism), if identified, may preclude referral to a therapist. The most common organic cause of bowel dysfunction is Hirschsprung's disease, a condition involving segments of nonenervated tissue in the colon. To become familiar with the differential presentation of

Hirschsprung's and FE, therapists may wish to consult publications that compare and contrast the symptoms of the two disorders (e.g., Levine, 1981). Additionally, slow or absent weight gain in children who are below age-expected weight levels may indicate a malabsorption syndrome and thus require specialized medical treatment (cf. Barr et al., 1979). Finally, in a small percentage of cases, FE is secondary to extraordinary emotional disturbance and thus resistant to behavioral/medical treatment focused primarily on FE (e.g., Landman & Rappaport, 1985). In such cases, the emotional condition may be a treatment priority especially when there is no evidence of constipation or fecal retention.

TREATMENT OF FE

Retentive FE

Although the child is the target of treatment, the parent (or primary caregiver) is the delivery agent and thus the primary recipient of the information about treatment. Discussing treatment in general terms with the child while expressing optimism about outcome is good practice. Additionally, any punitive parental responses toward fecal accidents, intentional and unintentional, are to be terminated immediately. Requesting a related promise from the parent in the presence of the child can increase the child's interest in participation. Treatment is then laid out in a series of steps. (See Table 29.2 for a sample treatment plan.)

Demystification

During or immediately following the evaluation, the entire elimination process including its disordered manifestations should be "demystified" (Levine, 1982). The belief, born of longstanding characterological and psychopathological perspectives on FE, that bowel retention and bowel accidents are generally associated with personality development, and specifically with such characteristics as stubbornness, immaturity, or laziness, can result in parents shaming and blaming their children into the bathroom. But a disordered process of elimination such as FE should no more be a target for censure and blame than

TABLE 29.2   Sample Biobehavioral Treatment Plan

1. Refer to appropriately trained physician for evaluation.
2. Demystify bowel movements and problems and eliminate all punishment.
3. Completely evacuate bowel. Procedures are prescribed and overseen by physician.
4. Establish stool-softening regimen with facilitating medication. Procedures are prescribed and overseen by physician.
5. Establish regular toileting schedule. Ensure that child's feet are on a flat surface during toileting.
6. Establish monitoring and motivational system.
7. Require child participation in clean up.
8. Teach appropriate wiping and flushing.
9. Implement dietary changes that include regularity of meals and increases in fluid and fiber intake.
10. Utilize facilitative medication. What, when, and how much to be established by physician.
11. Establish method for fading facilitative medication.

should a disordered process of respiration, digestion, or motor movement. As indicated above, the literature does not reflect a significant association between psychological profiles and child bowel problems.

Bowel Evacuation

The primary goal of FE treatment is the establishment of regular bowel movements in the toilet and the first step is to cleanse the bowel completely of resident fecal matter. A variety of methods are used, the most common of which involve enemas and/or laxatives. Although the therapist can assist with the prescription of these (e.g., with suggestions about timing, interactional style, behavioral management, etc.) the evacuation procedure must be prescribed and overseen by the child's physician. Typically, evacuation procedures are conducted in the child's home, but severe resistance can necessitate medical assistance in which case they must be completed in a medical setting. The ultimate goal, however, is complete parent management of evacuation procedures because they are to be used whenever the child's eliminational pattern suggests excessive fecal retention.

Toileting Schedule

The parent and therapist should choose a regular time for the child to attempt bowel movements. The time should not be during school hours because unpleasant social responses to bowel movements in the school setting can cause regressive responses to treatment (e.g., retention). Choosing among the times that remain (morning, afternoon, or evening) should

be guided by the child's typical habits and child–parent time constraints. Establishing a time shortly after food intake can increase chances of success through the influence of the gastrocolonic reflex. In the early stages of treatment or in difficult cases, two scheduled attempts a day (e.g., after breakfast and dinner) may be necessary. The time the child is required to sit on the toilet should be limited 10 or fewer minutes in order to avoid unnecessarily increasing the aversive properties of the toileting experience. The child's feet should be supported by a flat surface (e.g., floor or a small stool) to increase comfort, maintain circulation in the extremities, and facilitate the abdominal push necessary to expel fecal matter from the body. The time should also be unhurried and free from distraction or observation by anyone other than the managing parent. Allowing children to listen to music, read, or talk with the parent can improve the child's attitude toward toileting requirements. Generally, toileting should be a relaxed, pleasant, and ultimately private affair.

Response to Toileting Efforts

If the child has a bowel movement in the toilet, he or she should be praised. In the early stages of treatment it is also helpful to have a reward system in place. An easy system involves a dot-to-dot drawing and a grab bag. The child identifies an affordable and desirable prize and the parent draws (or traces) a picture of it using a dot-to-dot format with every third or fourth dot bigger than the rest. The child connects two dots for each bowel movement in the toilet and when the line reaches a larger dot, they earn access to a grab bag with small rewards (e.g., small toys, edibles, money, privileges). When all the dots are connected, the child earns the prize (Friman et al., 2006). A less elaborate, more naturalistic, but also more time intensive procedure involves the provision of special time. For example, following successful toileting a child might be allowed 10–15 minutes of special time with a parent during which the child is allowed to choose the activity. If the child does not have a bowel movement their effort should be praised and another session should be scheduled for later in the day.

Response to Accidents

Accidents should not be the object of punishment or criticism. However, the child should participate in cleaning up the mess that has been made. With younger children this may merely mean bringing soiled clothing to the laundry area and allowing themselves to be cleaned by the parent. With older children it may mean managing the entire mess themselves, including doing the laundry and cleaning their person. Children should earn praise and rewards for any bowel movements in the toilet, even if they had a prior accident.

In treatment-resistant cases, however, mild aversive consequences are sometimes used. Although there is little documentation of their effects, there is ample evidence of their use. One example, a procedure called positive practice, involves intensive practice of appropriate toileting behaviors following detection of an accident (e.g., a series of "dry run" trips to the bathroom from locations near detection of the accident). Another example for which a small amount of data has been published involves a response cost procedure—using small tokens to reward toileting success and withdrawal of tokens (i.e., small "fines") for accidents (Reimers, 1996).

Cleanliness Training

Successful toileting is a complex arrangement of small tasks and two that are critical to overall success but often overlooked in fecal incontinence programs are wiping and flushing. The therapist should provide the parents instructions on how to motivate and teach children to complete these tasks.

Monitoring

Frequent monitoring accomplishes at least three goals, early detection of accidents, assessment of progress, and multiple opportunities for praise. Two levels of monitoring are usually employed. The first, involves regular "pants checks" that result in praise when pants are accident free and the procedure for accidents described above when they are not. The second involves a record completed by the parent that documents toileting successes and accidents and the size and consistency of both. The latter record is made easier by providing the parent with a user-friendly data sheet.

Dietary Changes

As discussed in the section on underlying processes, diet often plays a causal role in FE and dietary changes are almost always part of treatment. One of the keys to establishing full fecal continence is a regular diet with a high level of dietary fiber. Fiber increases colonic motility and the moisture in colonic contents and thus facilitates easier and more regular bowel movements. To aid the parents in increasing the fiber content in their child's diet, an educational handout can be helpful. Dietary changes can also be enhanced with over the counter preparations with dense fiber content (e.g., Metamucil, Perdiem).

Facilitating Medication

Successful treatment for FE will almost always require inclusion of medications that soften fecal matter, ease its migration through the colon, and/or aid its expulsion from the rectum. The decision to use medication and the type is the consulting physician's to make, however, the therapist can inform the decision and educate the parent about its use. Generally, it is best to avoid interfering with the sensitive biochemistry of the alimentary system, the colonic portion of it in particular, and thus inert substances are usually used. Formerly, the most frequently used substance was mineral oil, either alone or in combination with other ingredients such as magnesium. As indicated, prescription of the substance is the physician's prerogative, but ensuring compliance with the prescription is typically the therapist's task. Children will often resist ingesting substances with odd tastes and textures, and thus to gain their cooperation it is often necessary to mix the substances with a preferred liquid (e.g., orange juice) and follow ingestion with praise and appreciation. A recent development, however, makes this task even easier while also improving outcomes for children with FE. Polyethylene glycol 3350 (trade name, Miralax) is an odorless, tasteless powdered laxative that can be mixed with food or liquid with limited possibility of child detection, and it has produced excellent results in treatment of childhood constipation and FE and is increasingly becoming the preferred medical treatment option (Bishop, 2001; Pashankar & Bishop, 2001).

A more invasive substance involves glycerin suppositories. Some physicians prescribe these because their use increases the predictability of bowel movements and reduces the likelihood of an out-of-home accident. When prescribed, suppositories should be used in the following sequence. Prior to the meal closest in time to the regularly scheduled toileting, the child should attempt a bowel movement. If successful, regular procedures are followed and no suppository is given. If unsuccessful, a suppository should be inserted by the parent, the meal eaten by the child, and another attempt made after the meal. The combination of the gastrocolonic reflex initiated by the meal and the lubrication and mechanical stimulation provided by the suppository is usually sufficient to inaugurate a bowel movement. These advantages notwithstanding, inserting suppositories into a child's body can engender resistance and in such cases the therapist can assist the process by teaching the child how to relax under stressful circumstances and the parent how to use instructional and motivational procedures to enhance compliance.

Fading Facilitative Medication

Although medication is the province of the physician, therapists can assist with its use by establishing methods to ensure it is taken (as above) and to design systematic steps for its ultimate withdrawal. Obviously, partnership with the consulting physician is necessary in both cases. A frequently used withdrawal method is to eliminate the medication on one day a week contingent upon a series of consecutive accident-free, toileting success days (e.g., 14). The child is allowed to choose the day. If another similar series occurs, another day is chosen. If the child has an accident, the medication is replaced on one day. The parent and child go back and forth inside this system until the medication is completed faded out.

Treatment Resistance

As indicated earlier, in some cases direct FE treatment may be forestalled by, or conducted in conjunction with, treatment for the resistance (e.g., with instructional control training, and/or psychotherapy). Some treatment-resistant cases, however, involve abnormal defecation dynamics (e.g., rectal distention, decreased sensitivity) much more than abnormal externalizing or internalizing behavior problems. For these cases, various forms of biofeedback have been used to increase awareness and establish bowel habits (e.g., Loening-Baucke, 1990).

Evidence of Effectiveness

The first treatment-based break with characterological (punishment) and psychopathological (psychotherapy) perspectives on FE was provided by Murray Davidson, who described what has come to be called the pediatric approach (Davidson, 1958). The regimen involved starting a child on a daily dose of mineral oil and increasing the dosage until regular bowel functioning was established. The mineral oil regimen was often accompanied by reductions in dairy products and increases in fruits and vegetables and its initial evaluation yield a high rate of success (90%) (Davidson et al., 1963).

Over the past 20 years, several descriptive and controlled experimental studies have supported incorporating Davidson's pediatric regimen into the multicomponent biobehavioral approach recommended here (see Table 29.1 for published research; see Christophersen & Friman, 2004; Field & Friman, 2006; Friman, 2007; 2008; Friman et al., 2006 for published reviews) and numerous documentations of success have led to the listing of this approach as an empirically supported treatment by the *Journal of Pediatric Psychology* (McGrath, Mellon, & Murphy, 2000). In fact, the literature on this comprehensive approach has progressed sufficiently to lead to group implementation. In the initial evaluation of group treatment, 18 encopretic children between the ages of 4 and 11 years and their parents were seen in groups of three to five families for six sessions. Noteworthy is that all of these children had previously failed a solely medical regimen. Soiling accidents decreased by 84% across the groups and these results were maintained or improved at 6-month follow-up (Stark, Owens-Stively, Spirito, Lewis, & Guevremont, 1990). As additional evidence of the effectiveness of the biobehavioral approach to treatment, there is mounting evidence, including a randomized clinical trial, showing that Internet delivery of the biobehavioral treatment for FE produces statistically and clinically significant benefits for afflicted children (e.g., Ritterband et al., 2003; 2006). Finally, for even more evidence, please refer again to Table 29.1, which lists samples of single subject and group studies that have evaluated the biobehavioral treatment approach to FE.

Targeting Only the Symptom?

A small but persistent concern with the direct biobehavioral treatment approach is that targeting only the symptoms of FE may produce behavioral or psychological side effects (e.g., "symptom substitution"). At least two large studies have undermined this concern. The first used a behavioral inventory to compare (before and after treatment and at 3-year follow-up) a group of encopretic children who were cured with a group who were not cured to determine whether any significant symptom substitution occurred in children cured of FE (Levine, Mazonson, and Bakow, 1980). The conclusion of the first study—that successful treatment was not accompanied by any problematic behavioral side effects—was replicated in the second, which used even more measures and analytic methods (e.g., Young, Brennen, Baker, & Baker, 1995).

Another persistent concern is that FE is thought to be part of a constellation of problems such as oppositional defiant disorder (ODD) or conduct disorder (CD). Although the evidence indicates a slight increase in behavior problems in children with FE, for the majority of these children the increase does not rise to the level of clinical significance and is more plausibly attributed to the FE than as a cause or a correlate of it (e.g., Friman, 2002; Friman, Mathews,

Finney, Christophersen, & Leibowitz, 1988). The small data-based literature making a case to the contrary (e.g., Fatih, & Pehlivanturk, 2004) is rife with selection and Berkson's biases (cf. Berkson, 1946; Du Fort, Newman, & Bland, 1993; Friman, 2002). These points are made here so that clinicians are not daunted or distracted by the readily available but empirically unsupported assertions about the psychopathological basis of FE. Furthermore, even in the very small number of cases where psychopathology is a factor, the biobehavioral approach to treatment of FE is the optimal approach to soiling. An optimal approach to the psychopathology, however, has not been established.

Nonretentive FE

Treatment of nonretentive FE has been the focus of very little research, none of which appears to have involved experimental controls. Thus, recommending an optimal course of treatment, based on empirical evidence, is premature. Attributions about psychopathology are more frequently made about nonretentive than retentive FE. As one particularly sensational example, the DSM-IV states that nonretentive FE is "usually associated with the presence of Oppositional Defiant Disorder or Conduct Disorder or may be the consequence of anal masturbation" (American Psychiatric Association, 1994, p. 106). Note that a thorough literature search revealed no published research to support either claim. Some clinical case studies have linked nonretentive FE with ODD and/or CD, but the claim about anal masturbation is pure speculation. The basic fact is that the etiological mechanisms for nonretentive FE have not been established. Logic and clinical lore do suggest that when bowel movements are not difficult or painful to pass, as they are in retentive FE, other more psychological factors may be contributing to fecal accidents. But logic and clinical lore are no substitute for scientific evaluation.

Nonetheless, nonretentive FE has to be treated, the gap in the literature notwithstanding. Perhaps the best approach would begin with a comprehensive psychological evaluation that includes behavioral assessment techniques. Most all investigators who have described this subsample of children report emotional and behavioral problems and treatment resistance (e.g., Landman & Rappaport, 1985), and it is possible that some of these children's soiling is related to modifiable aspects of their social ecology. Some investigators have employed versions of the biobehavioral approach to retentive FE coupled with supportive verbal therapy (Landman & Rappaport, 1985). A relatively recent multicomponent approach recommends an initial full developmental and behavioral assessment to determine whether the incontinent child is even ready for treatment (Kuhn, Marcus, & Pitner, 1999). If the child is deemed to be ready, subsequent assessments should focus on any potential barriers to success, particularly disruptive behavior problems, and address those (cf. Stark et al., 1990). According to this approach, success is likely to depend on the presence of soft, comfortable bowel movements and a direct focus on toilet refusal behavior. The treatment includes daily scheduled positive toilet sits are recommended with incentives for successful bowel movements (similar to treatment for retentive FE). If this approach to treatment results in stool withholding, the therapist could proceed with the treatment for retentive FE prescribed above. The general theme of the scant literature on nonretentive FE is that various problems, other than soiling exhibited by this subsample require some form of treatment, but the soiling itself needs direct treatment, too.

PREVENTION

FE can be a preventable condition. There are known risk factors and often a predictable developmental course. In his discussion of the causes of FE, Levine (1982) described three stages of its development. Such descriptions would aid the identification of children who would be most likely to benefit from preventive interventions.

According to Levine, in stage I (infants and toddlers) the primary causal variables are simple constipation and parental overreaction. In this stage a provider (probably a pediatrician but possibly a psychologist) should use demystification (described earlier) to initiate a preventive

intervention. The general demystified instructions for parents should emphasize consistent, nonaggressive, well-informed management of any or all bowel problems, especially constipation. Parents should also be provided information on toileting readiness (e.g., Friman et al., 2006) before setting up a bowel-training program. In general, no reaction at all to a bowel problem is better than an overreaction (Levine, 1982).

During stage II (3–5 years) the various stresses associated with toilet training are of paramount concern. Preventive efforts should include continued demystification, which at this stage involves gentle assistance with all toileting tasks, and encouragement to work on, and to talk about, toileting tasks. During stage II such aids as toilet seats and small stools for foot leverage may be helpful. Also, increased dietary fiber will loosen and moisten stools and help to prevent painful passage of hard stools. Most important is the avoidance of coercion, negative feedback, and inducements to rush the toileting process. The child should be encouraged to sit on the toilet at least once a day but for not longer than 5 minutes. The time for this toileting episode should be consistent across days. And the child should be praised for adherence to the schedule (2001; Friman et al., 2006; Levine, 1982).

During stage III (early school years) scheduling toileting episodes becomes the primary concern. Toileting schedules at this stage are particularly critical for children whose risk of FE has increased because of problems during stages I and II. The psychosocial reactions to bowel movements at school, especially schools without doors on toilets stalls, can be a problem for the child at risk (Levine, 1982). For such children a preventive effort should involve the regulation of bowel movements so that they occur in the children's home either before or after school. Perhaps the best method of increasing adherence to a home schedule is the use of suppositories (although potential problems with their use were noted earlier). In addition to regulation of bowel movements, the preventive intervention for the school-aged child at risk should include increased dietary fiber, elevated activity levels, increased fluid intake, continued demystification, and praise for the absence of accidents (Levine, 1982).

The preventive intervention recommended here, however, is at its most burdensome point a mild treatment procedure and at its least burdensome point a mild toilet-training procedure. Thus, implementation of the intervention may not require a great deal of extra effort from the parents or the therapist. In fact, with the exception of those cases where suppositories are needed, prevention is equivalent to ordinary toilet training conducted at an appropriate age level. Therefore, the best preventive maneuver would be to provide the intervention recommended for children at risk for all children. Bowel training is, after all, a human experience that is often fraught with complications (Levine, 1982). It is difficult to ascertain how the interventions used to ease those complications in children at risk for FE would cause problems when used with children whose risk is lower. Conversely, the procedure might simplify the entire bowel-training process for everyone concerned.

CONCLUSION

FE has been misunderstood, misinterpreted, and mistreated for centuries. During the last half of the twentieth century, however, and particularly toward its end, a fuller, biobehavioral understanding of FE's causal conditions was obtained and an empirically supported approach to its treatment established. The biobehavioral understanding and approach to FE is dramatically different than the psychogenic understanding and approach of history. The biobehavioral approach addresses the physiology of defecation primarily and addresses the psychology of the child as a set of variables that are not causal but can be critical to active participation in treatment. The psychogenic approach, however, addressed the psychology of child primarily, especially insofar as causal variables were of interest, and gave minimal attention to the physiology of defecation. Although evaluation and treatment of FE absolutely requires the direct involvement of a physician, ideal management involves a partnership between the physician, therapist,

and family. In simple terms, the physician prescribes the treatment for FE, especially the parts pertaining to defection dynamics in general and evacuating the colon, changing the texture of fecal matter, and increasing colonic motility in particular. In an alliance with the physician (and family), the therapist addresses the educational, behavioral, and motivational variables that are critical to the implementation of treatment and a successful outcome. This united, biobehavioral approach can eliminate or at least minimize the possibility of the damaging overinterpretation and dangerous forms of treatment that blemished the approach to FE from antiquity through most of the twentieth century.

Further Reading

Christophersen, E. R., & Friman, P. C. (2004). Elimination disorders. In R. Brown (Ed.), *Handbook of pediatric psychology in school settings* (pp. 467–488). Mahwah, NJ: Lawrence Erlbaum.

Field, C., & Friman, P. C. (2006). Encopresis. In J. Fisher & W. O'Donohue (Eds.), *Practitioners guide to empirically to evidence based psychotherapy* (pp. 277–283). New York: Springer.

Friman, P. C. (2007). Encopresis and enuresis. In M. Hersen (Ed. In Chief) & D. Reitman (Vol. Ed.), *Handbook of assessment, case conceptualization, and treatment: Vol 2: Children and adolescents* (pp. 589–621). Hoboken, NJ: John Wiley & Sons.

Friman, P. C. (2008). Evidence based therapies for enuresis and encopresis. In R. G. Steele, T. D. Elkin, & M. C. Roberts (Eds.), *Handbook of evidence-based therapies for children and adolescents* (pp. 301–323). New York: Springer.

Friman, P. C., Hofstadter, K. L., & Jones, K. M. (2006). A biobehavioral approach to the treatment of functional encopresis in children. *Journal of Early and Intensive Behavioral Interventions, 3,* 263–272.

Reimers, T. M. (1996). A biobehavioral approach toward managing encopresis. *Behavior Modification, 20,* 469–479.

References

American Psychiatric Association (1994). *Diagnostic and statistical manual of mental disorders* (4th ed.). Washington, DC: Author.

Barr, R. G., Levine, M. D., Wilkinson, R. H., & Mulvihill, D. (1979). Chronic and occult stool retention: A clinical tool for its evaluation in school aged children. *Clinical Pediatrics, 18,* 674–686.

Berkson, J. (1946). Limitations of the application of the fourfold table analysis to hospital data. *Biometric Bulletin, 2,* 47–53.

Bishop, W. (2001). Miracle laxative? *Journal of Pediatric Gastroenterology and Nutrition, 32,* 514–515.

Bornstein, P. H., Sturm, C., Retzlaff, P. D., Kirby, K., & Chong, H. (1981). *Journal of Behavior Therapy and Experimental Psychiatry, 12,* 167–170.

Davidson, M. (1958). Constipation and fecal incontinence. *Pediatric Clinics of North America, 5,* 749–757.

Dawson, P. M., Griffith, K., & Boeke, K. M. (1990). Combined medical and psychological treatment of hospitalized children with encopresis. *Child Psychiatry and Human Development, 20,* 181–190.

Cox, D. J., Sutphen, J., Ling, W., Quillan, W., & Borowitz, S. (1996). Additive benefits of laxative, toilet training, and biofeedback therapies in the treatment of pediatric encopresis. *Journal of Pediatric Psychology, 21,* 659–670.

Du Fort, G. G., Newman, S. C., & Bland, R. C. (1993). Psychiatric comorbidity and treatment seeking: Sources of selection bias in the study of clinical problems. *Journal of Nervous and Mental Disease, 181,* 467–474.

Fatih, U., & Pehlivanturk, B. (2004). Comorbid psychiatric disorders in 201 cases of encopresis. *Turkish Journal of Pediatrics, 46,* 350–353.

Fireman, G., & Koplewicz, H. S. (1992). Short term treatment of children with encopresis. *Journal of Psychotherapy Practice and Research, 1,* 64–71.

Friman, P. C. (2002). The psychopathological interpretation of common child behavior problems: A critique and related opportunity for behavior analysis. Invited address at the 28th annual convention of the Association for Behavior Analysis, Toronto, Canada. (Video available from ABA International).

Friman, P. C., Mathews, J., Finney, J. W., Christophersen, E. R., Leibowitz, J. M. (1988). Do encopretic children have clinically significant behavior problems? *Pediatrics, 82,* 407–409.

Henoch, E. H. (1889). Lectures on children's diseases (Vol. 2, J. Thompson translator). London: New Syndenham Society.

Houts, A. C., Mellon, M. W., & Whelan, J. P. (1988). Use of dietary fiber and stimulus control to treat retentive encopresis: A multiple baseline investigation. *Journal of Pediatric Psychology, 13,* 435–445.

Kuhn, B. R., Marcus, B. A., & Pitner, S. L. (1999). Treatment guidelines for primary nonretentive encopresis and stool toileting refusal. *American Family Physician, 59,* 2171–2178.

Landman, G. B., & Rappaport, L. (1985). Pediatric management of severe treatment resistant encopresis.

Journal of Developmental and Behavioral Pediatrics, 6, 349–351.

Levine, M. D. (1982). Encopresis: Its potentiation, evaluation, and alleviation. *Pediatric Clinics of North America, 29,* 315–330.

Levine, M. D., & Bakow, H. (1976). Children with encopresis: A study of treatment outcome. *Pediatrics, 58,* 845–852.

Loening-Baucke, V. A. (1990). Modulation of abnormal defecation dynamics by biofeedback treatment in chronically constipated children with encopresis. *Journal of Pediatrics, 116,* 214–221.

Lowery, S., Srour, J., Whitehead, W. E., & Schuster, M. M. (1985). Habit training as treatment of encopresis secondary to chronic constipation. *Journal of Pediatric Gastroenterology and Nutrition, 4,* 397–401.

McGuire, T., Rothenberg, M., & Tyler, D. (1984). Profound shock following interventions for chronic untreated stool retention. *Clinical Pediatrics, 23,* 459–461.

Pashankar, D. S. & Bishop, W. P. (2001). Efficacy and optimal dose of daily polyethylene glycol 3350 for treatment of constipation and encopresis in children. *Journal of Pediatrics, 139,* 428–432.

O'Brien, S., Ross, L., & Christophersen, E. R. (1986). Primary encopresis: Evaluation and treatment. *Journal of Applied Behavior Analysis, 19,* 137–145.

Ritterband, L. M., Cox, D. J., Gordon, T. L., Borowitz, S. M., Kovatchev, B. P., Walker, L. S., et al. (2006). Examining the added value of audio, graphics, and interactivity in an internet intervention for pediatric encopresis. *Children's Health Care, 35,* 47–59.

Ritterband, L. M., Cox, D. J., Walker, L. S., Kovatchev, B., McKnight, L., Patel, K., et al. (2003). An Internet intervention as adjunctive therapy for pediatric encopresis. *Journal of Consulting and Clinical Psychology, 71,* 910–917.

Rolider, A., & Van Houten, R. V. (1985). Treatment of constipation caused encopresis by a negative reinforcement procedure. *Journal of Behavior Therapy and Experimental Psychiatry, 16,* 67–70.

Stark, L. J., Opipari, L. C., Donaldson, D. L., Danovsky, M. R., Rasile, D. A., & DelSanto, A. F. (1997). Evaluation of a standard protocol for retentive encopresis: A replication. *Journal of Pediatric Psychology, 22,* 619–633.

Stark, L. J., Owens-Stively, J., Spirito, A., Lewis, A., & Guevremont, D. (1990). Group behavioral treatment of retentive encopresis. *Journal of Pediatric Psychology, 15,* 659–671.

Young, M. H., Brennen, L. C., Baker, R. D., & Baker, S. S. (1995). Functional encopresis symptom reduction and behavioral improvement. *Developmental and Behavioral Pediatrics, 16,* 226–232.

30 EXPRESSIVE WRITING

Jenna L. Baddeley and James W. Pennebaker

Writing about upsetting experiences has been shown to be beneficial for people's physical and psychological health. The disclosure of personal thoughts and feelings is, of course, a component of all psychotherapies. Psychotherapists have long assumed that the effectiveness of psychotherapy hinges on how the therapist responds to the patient's disclosures. Freud thought that psychological dysfunction was caused by past traumatic events which the patient had repressed but which continued to shape the patient's behavior. A therapist could alleviate a person's symptoms by interpreting the origins (in past events and relationships) of the patient's transference reactions toward the therapist. Rogers believed that for therapy to be effective, client disclosures must be met with therapist responses that reflect unconditional positive regard for the client. For Beck, the therapist helps the patient learn how to identify and empirically challenge the dysfunctional patterns of thinking that are revealed in the patient's disclosures. In short, different schools of therapy have different conceptions of the kinds of responses that therapists should provide to their clients. Despite these differences, almost all therapies are effective. The expressive writing intervention is effective in the absence of a therapist or any other audience, which suggests that disclosure itself is therapeutic.

The expressive writing technique is straightforward. People write about emotional upheavals in their lives three or four times over the space of about a week. The expressive writing method was first developed in the 1980s (Pennebaker & Beall, 1986) and since that time almost 200 published empirical articles have documented the method's success in improving mental and physical health.

The evidence supporting this intervention comes both from self-reports and from biological and behavioral measures. People who have done expressive writing are less vulnerable to illness, as suggested by both biological measures (i.e., improved immune functioning) and behavioral ones (i.e., fewer visits to a health care provider for illness reasons in the months after writing). Expressive writing also appears to improve people's cognitive functioning, suggested by improved performance on tests of working memory and improved grades among college students. A recent and comprehensive meta-analysis of the studies has computed an average r effect size of .075 (Cohen's $d = .151$) for the expressive writing intervention. This effect size represents the average across 146 studies and three outcome domains (reported physical health, psychological health, and subjective impact). An effect size of .075 suggests that this intervention can be expected to produce small but important changes in people's psychological and physical health.

HOW TO DO EXPRESSIVE WRITING

Writing Topics and Instructions

Originally, the expressive writing instructions focused on trauma, but a number of studies have since demonstrated that writing about positive experiences is just as beneficial as writing about negative ones. Instructions that include a more detailed description of the kinds of topics and questions that participants might write about produce more improvement in physical health. Yet instructions should also allow for topic switching. We have found that the less the writing instructions constrain the writer to a particular topic or event, the more successful the intervention is. Expressive writing instructions are typically a variation on the following:

> Over the next four days, I want you to write about your deepest emotions and thoughts about the most

upsetting experience in your life. Really let go and explore your feelings and thoughts about it. In your writing, you might tie this experience to your childhood, your relationship with your parents, people you have loved or love now, or even your career. How is this experience related to who you would like to become, who you have been in the past, or who you are now?

Many people have not had a single traumatic experience but all of us have had major conflicts or stressors in our lives and you can write about them as well. You can write about the same issue every day or a series of different issues. Whatever you choose to write about, however, it is critical that you really let go and explore your very deepest emotions and thoughts.

No Feedback

Participants in expressive writing studies receive no feedback on their writing. It appears that when people in controlled studies write in private and can keep their writing to themselves, the intervention is more effective. Studies that have participants write at home rather than in a public place such as a lab, and studies that have participants keep their writing rather than giving it to the experimenter tend to result in larger improvements in psychological health.

Timing and Sequencing

In the typical expressive writing intervention, three or four sessions of 15–20 minutes each are spaced a few days apart over the course of a week. Although writing at least three times and for at least 15 minutes tends to provide the best physical health outcomes, evidence suggests that a single writing session can provide benefits (Greenberg, Stone, & Wortman, 1996), as can a series of short writing sessions (Burton & King, 2008). It is our observation, too, that the best outcomes result if people write for a fixed rather than open-ended number of times. The spacing of the writing sessions does not appear to affect the outcome; writing sessions may be conducted weekly or daily with similar results. When writing sessions are massed into a single hour, benefits in psychological and physical health are comparable to those in studies in which the writing

sessions are spaced farther apart, although participants perceive the intervention as less helpful (Chung & Pennebaker, 2008).

Timing after an Emotional Upheaval

In studies reviewed in Frattaroli's (2006) meta-analysis, participants wrote about events that had taken place an average of 15 months ago. People who wrote about more recent events experienced greater improvements in psychological and physical health than those who wrote about more distant events. However, instructing people to write about recent events does not seem to result in bigger improvements than instructing them to write about less recent events or giving them a choice whether to write about recent or less recent events. It may be that people who choose to write about more recent events are simply better able to cope than people who choose to write about less recent events.

For therapists, the question still remains regarding when to assign an expressive writing intervention to a patient. We caution against beginning an expressive writing intervention with patients who have very recently undergone a traumatic experience and who may not yet be ready to examine or confront it. Our caution is based on the fact that no evidence supports any psychological intervention in the immediate aftermath of a potentially traumatic event. Research on critical incident stress debriefing, a popular intervention that encourages people to disclose their thoughts and feelings about a traumatic experience within 72 hours after the trauma, shows that the method is at best ineffective and at worst downright harmful (NcNally, Bryant & Ehlers, 2003).

We urge clinicians to wait at least 2 weeks after a trauma has occurred before recommending expressive writing. Research on natural disclosure patterns following socially shared upheavals such as the Loma Prieta earthquake and the first Persian Gulf war (Pennebaker & Harber, 1993) as well as September 11, 2001 (Cohn, Mehl, & Pennebaker, 2004) suggest that people talk about the event a great deal for about 2 to 3 weeks. In the weeks afterwards, however, individuals often find it more difficult or socially awkward to talk. Expressive writing may be a useful outlet for people during the time when social sharing is constrained, but the event is still on their mind.

Mode of Disclosure

In expressive writing studies to date, participants have typically disclosed in longhand writing, typing, or speaking into a voice recorder. Although similar in terms of effectiveness, there may be a slight advantage to writing in longhand because it slows down the writing and thinking process.

WHO BENEFITS FROM EXPRESSIVE WRITING?

Our studies have shown that expressive writing benefits a broad range of groups, from college students of all racial and ethnic backgrounds to highly educated professionals to maximum security prisoners with a sixth-grade education.

The positive impact of expressive writing on physical health makes it an especially useful intervention for clients who suffer from co-morbid physical illness. As mentioned previously, a number of studies now show that expressive writing leads to enhanced immune functioning. Evidence is promising but more preliminary that it may lead to improvements in HIV viral load and liver function. Expressive writing tends to improve the physical health of already healthy people, but it is even more effective in improving the physical health of people with physical illnesses and/or high levels of life stress.

Expressive writing is not effective for individuals experiencing normal grief reactions to an expected death of a friend or family member. People who grieve normally will recover over time, and expressive writing does not speed this process. People who are experiencing complicated grief, however, can benefit from expressive writing.

CONTRAINDICATIONS

The only situation in which we have seen clear negative outcomes following an expressive writing intervention was a study involving patients with posttraumatic stress disorder (PTSD), who were asked to share their writings with a group (Gidron, Peri, Connolly & Shaler, 1996). The expressive writing participants who shared their writings with others in a group had worse emotional and physical health outcomes 5 weeks later compared to controls who wrote and shared superficial writing samples. Because other studies testing the use of expressive writing on patients with PTSD have not shown negative effects, we believe that the sharing of the writing with the group may have been the cause of the negative effects. Thus, we caution against group discussion of expressive writing.

WHY DOES EXPRESSIVE WRITING WORK?

No one knows exactly why expressive writing works. Our initial theory was that expressive writing circumvents the inhibition of thoughts and feelings, thus freeing the writer from the deleterious health consequences of inhibition. However, the inhibition theory cannot explain why writing about previously disclosed memories produces comparable benefits to writing about previously undisclosed (presumably inhibited) memories. It also cannot explain why people who are higher in trait inhibition are no more likely to benefit from expressive writing than people lower in trait inhibition.

Another explanation for the benefits of expressive writing is that focusing on and repeatedly reexperiencing the negative emotions associated with a remembered event causes people to habituate to these emotions and memories. This theory is supported by evidence that when people with PTSD write about the same topic on successive writing sessions, they will benefit more than if they switch topics (Sloan, Marx, & Epstein, 2005). However, Frattaroli's (2006) meta-analysis shows no difference in outcome between studies with instructions against topic switching and studies with instructions that suggested topic switching.

At the core of expressive writing is the verbal labeling of emotions. This may be a key mechanism underlying the effects of expressive writing. Labeling, or verbally representing, emotions fundamentally changes those emotions as the verbal representation takes the place of the original emotion in the person's memory. Making linkages between emotions and events may provide a sense of meaning and closure to past experiences, which may make them less cognitively disruptive.

There is also compelling evidence that expressive writing works by enabling writers to generate affirming statements about themselves (Creswell, Lam, Stanton, Taylor, Bower, & Sherman, 2007). Similarly, people who use more positive emotion words in their writing tend to have better health outcomes (Pennebaker & Chung, 2007). However, instructing people to write about positive experiences or positive aspects of a trauma does not typically produce better outcomes than the standard trauma writing instructions.

SUGGESTED USES

Expressive writing is a remarkably easy, cost-effective intervention, requiring little oversight from therapists. This makes the expressive writing intervention a promising adjunct to traditional psychotherapy as well as means of providing psychotherapeutic benefit to people who lack access to traditional psychotherapeutic treatment.

Therapists could assign expressive writing to new patients (perhaps they could write for 15 minutes in the therapist's waiting room) to clarify what their most important difficulties are. Anecdotal evidence from participants in our studies suggests that they may start writing about their "presenting" problem but turn their attention to another problem or problems that are in fact more significant. Once therapy has begun, therapists could augment the effectiveness of their treatments by assigning expressive writing exercises as homework. Because expressive writing is portable and requires no therapist feedback, the patient could substitute an expressive writing exercise for a therapy session in the event that patient and therapist have to miss one or more of their scheduled meetings. For clients who have successfully completed a course of therapy, expressive writing exercises may provide easy and effective booster sessions.

The expressive writing technique has traditionally been used outside of traditional therapy settings with good effect. Support group leaders, many of whom are not professionally trained as psychotherapists, can make the expressive writing intervention available to their group members. For people who are reluctant to disclose to anyone—including potential therapists—the technique may help them to gain the benefits of disclosure by removing the social constraints that may be imposed by an audience.

Further Reading

Pennebaker, J. W. (1997). *Opening up: The healing power of expressing emotion.* New York: Guilford.

Pennebaker, J. W. (2004). Writing to heal: A guided journal for recovering from trauma and emotional upheaval. Oakland, CA: New Harbinger Press.

References

Burton, C. M., & King, L. A. (2008, in press). The effects of (very) brief writing on health: The ten minute miracle. *British Journal of Health Psychology.*

Chung, C. K., & Pennebaker, J. W. (2008). Variations in the spacing of expressive writing sessions. *British Journal of Health Psychology, 13,* 15–21.

Cohn, M. A., Mehl, M. R., & Pennebaker, J. W. (2004). Linguistic markers of psychological change surrounding September 11, 2001. *Psychological Science, 15,* 687–693.

Creswell, J. D., Lam, S., Stanton, A. L., Taylor, S. E., Bower, J. E., & Sherman, D. K. (2007). *Personality and Social Psychology Bulletin, 33,* 238–250.

Frattaroli, J. (2006). Experimental disclosure and its moderators: A meta-analysis. *Psychological Bulletin, 132,* 823–865.

Gidron, Y., Peri, T., Connolly, J. F., & Shaler, A. Y. (1996). Written disclosure in posttraumatic stress disorder: Is it beneficial for the patient? *Journal of Nervous & Mental Disease, 184,* 505–507.

Greenberg, M. A., Stone, A. A., & Wortman, C. B. (1996). Health and psychological effects of emotional disclosure: A test of the inhibition-confrontation approach. *Journal of Personality and Social Psychology, 71,* 588–602.

McNally, R. J., Bryant, R. A., & Ehlers, A. (2003). Does early psychological intervention promote recovery from posttraumatic stress? *Psychological Science in the Public Interest, 4,* 45–79.

Pennebaker, J. W. & Beall, S. K. (1986). Confronting a traumatic event: Toward an understanding of inhibition and disease. *Journal of Abnormal Psychology, 95,* 274–281.

Pennebaker, J. W. & Chung, C.K. (2007). Expressive writing, emotional upheavals, and health. In H. Friedman and R. Silver (Eds.), *Handbook of health psychology* (pp. 263–284). New York: Oxford University Press.

Pennebaker, J. W., & Harber, K. D. (1993). A social stage model of collective coping: The Loma Prieta Earthquake and the Persian Gulf War. *Journal of Social Issues, 49,* 125–145.

Sloan, D. M., Marx, B. P., & Epstein, E. M. (2005). Further examination of the exposure model underlying the efficacy of written emotional disclosure. *Journal of Consulting and Clinical Psychology, 73,* 549–554.

31 FLOODING

Lori A. Zoellner, Jonathan S. Abramowitz, Sally A. Moore, and David M. Slagle

Flooding involves prolonged exposure to stimuli that evoke relatively high levels of inappropriate or excessive anxiety or fear. This procedure differs from other exposure-based procedures in that flooding begins with exposure to highly fear-evoking stimuli whereas other techniques employ graduated exposure, progressing from less anxiety provoking stimuli. Flooding may be conducted in real life, termed *in vivo* exposure, or in fantasy, termed *imaginal* exposure. The basics of exposure-based procedures include engagement with the fear-arousing stimuli, systematic prolonged and repeated exposure to this stimuli, and learning of corrective information regarding its lack of dangerousness until the anxiety and fear associated have been greatly reduced.

WHEN ARE FLOODING PROCEDURES USED?

Clinicians are often reluctant to use flooding procedures since the client invariably experiences high levels of discomfort. However, flooding is a useful method for reducing fear and should be considered in several circumstances. *In vivo* flooding is often employed when a time-limited intervention is desired; for example, in the treatment of a hospital phobic whose spouse needs to spend time in the hospital, or an airplane phobic who has an important business trip. *Imaginal* flooding is often useful in instances where it is not possible to conduct *in vivo* exposure. For example, imaginal exposure may be used for intrusive fear-evoking memories of a traumatic event in individuals with posttraumatic stress disorder (PTSD) or feared consequences in individuals with obsessive–compulsive disorder (OCD).

Although there is limited research examining who does or does not make a good candidate for flooding procedures, clinical experience provides some guidelines about when to pursue other treatment options. The therapist should consider factors that could interfere with motivation to complete the intense therapy (e.g., severe depression) or contribute to a client being unable to successfully tolerate extreme distress before, during, or after exposure (e.g., psychosis, severe dissociative symptoms, and suicidality). Further, imaginal flooding procedures are typically not recommended for PTSD symptoms related to realistic guilt or shame (e.g., murdering or raping), though recent work has suggested that this caution may be unwarranted (Rogers, Gray, Williams, & Kitchner, 2000; Rothbaum, Ruef, Litz, Han, & Hodges, 2003).

ARE FLOODING PROCEDURES EFFECTIVE IN REDUCING FEAR?

We will consider both *in vivo* and *imaginal* types of flooding separately as we discuss the efficacy of flooding in reducing fear.

Flooding *In Vivo*

The efficacy of *in vivo* flooding is well documented across the anxiety disorders, including: specific phobias (Mannion & Levine, 1984), social phobia (Turner, Beidel, & Jacob, 1994), panic disorder and agoraphobia (e.g., Deacon & Abramowitz, 2006; Lang & Hoyer, 2007), and posttraumatic stress disorder (e.g., Başoğlu, Şalcioğlu, & Livanou, 2006; Boudewyns, & Hyer, 1990). Perhaps its greatest use is in the treatment of specific phobias. Öst and colleagues (e.g., Öst, Svensson, Hellstrom, & Lindwall, 2001) have shown that a single two- to three-hour session of therapist-supervised *in vivo* flooding can lead to significant and lasting improvement for many phobias, including claustrophobia and fears of animals, blood, injections, and flying for both adults and children.

Flooding in Imagination

Imaginal flooding, often in conjunction with other procedures, is also used in the treatment of many anxiety disorders including obsessional problems (e.g., Freeston et al., 1997), PTSD (e.g., Foa et al., 1999; 2005), generalized anxiety disorder (e.g., Borkovec & Costello, 1993), and social phobia (e.g., Heimberg, Becker, Goldfinger, & Vermilyea, 1985). Although imaginal exposure has been shown to be an effective procedure for targeting specific feared situations and thoughts (e.g., fears of disastrous consequences in OCD; Foa, Steketee & Grayson, 1995), research does not indicate that it is clearly more effective by itself than *in vivo* exposure as a monotherapy or in combination with other techniques (e.g., Bryant, Moulds, Guthrie, Dang, & Nixon, 2003; Abramowitz, 1996). Thus, imaginal exposure is frequently used as a treatment component (paired with *in vivo* exposure or cognitive therapy) rather than as a stand-alone treatment. Perhaps the most common usages of flooding in imagination as a treatment component are in the areas of PTSD and OCD.

WHY DOES FLOODING WORK?

Many theories have been proposed to explain the general process of anxiety reduction during exposure-based therapy but none yet account for all of the data. Three theories that we use most often to discuss the fear reduction process with our clients are described below. First, emotional processing theory (Rachman, 1980) proposes that exposure involves the modification of a pathological *fear structure*, defined by Lang (1977) as an underlying memory structure that contains excessive and distorted stimulus (e.g., quick movement in the grass), response (e.g., standing still, heart racing), and meaning (e.g., a snake is going to bite me) propositions. Foa and Kozak (1986) elaborated on this idea, suggesting that a fear structure can be modified

by accessing it through fear evocation and then providing corrective information.

Second, Bouton (1988) proposed a context specificity hypothesis for anxiety reduction. In this theory, exposure can be viewed as an example of retroactive interference, where new learning is introduced to interfere with information that was learned at an earlier point. Specifically, new learning during exposure helps make the meaning of a feared stimulus become ambiguous because memories of both the fear and fear reduction are retained. Bouton argued that context (e.g., internal or environmental backgrounds) serves to resolve this ambiguity by determining the meaning of the stimuli and the response. By repeated experience with fear reduction and its association with multiple contexts, the memory for reduction is strengthened and the memory for the fear itself becomes more inhibited.

Third, Bandura (1983) proposed a self-efficacy theory of anxiety reduction. He suggested that an *efficacy expectation* is the conviction that one can successfully execute the behavior required to produce an outcome. Therefore, a treatment reduces fear to the extent that a person's sense of self-efficacy has been elevated and strengthened (Bandura, 1983). Bandura further suggested that one of the best means for raising and strengthening self-efficacy is direct behavioral experience and accomplishment.

HOW TO CONDUCT FLOODING IN VIVO

Although the exact flooding procedures depend upon the client's idiosyncratic fears, there are important common principles across all anxiety disorders. See Table 31.1. The procedures for *in vivo* flooding are largely similar to those used in graduated *in vivo* exposure (see Chapter 42). The first step is to provide a foundation for the treatment by presenting a clear therapeutic rationale, forming a strong therapeutic alliance, and a thoroughly assessing the client's fears and related avoidance. This foundation helps the client make better choices regarding treatment options (i.e., the choice of confronting their fear), increases commitment to the choice made, and

TABLE 31.1   Steps in Using Flooding

1. Form a strong therapeutic alliance.
2. Thoroughly assess the client's fears and related avoidance.
3. Provide an effective rationale.
4. Provide prolonged therapist-directed exposure to the most anxiety arousing situations.
    a. Therapist describes the situation.
    b. Therapist demonstrates how to perform the task.
    c. Therapist instructs the client to do the same.
5. During imaginal exposure, particularly, titrate the client's level of engagement and distress.
6. Stay in the fear-producing situation until there is at least a 50% reduction in fear.
7. Debrief client's reactions to exposure as therapy proceeds.
8. Repeat until fear has been significantly reduced and all relevant areas of avoidance have been addressed.

provides a preview of what is to be expected during treatment.

Client understanding and acceptance of treatment rationales has been linked to positive therapeutic outcome (e.g., Addis & Jacobson, 1996). Initially, we clarify that therapy will be time limited and specific to the client's fears and related symptoms. A cognitive behavioral model of the maintenance of fear is presented in which avoidance of fear-related thoughts, feelings, situations, and memories prolongs excessive, irrational fear responses by preventing the client from learning that their anticipated outcomes are not likely to occur. Thus, the goal of flooding is to help the client approach fear-eliciting stimuli, prevent avoidance behaviors, and disconfirm their overestimates of danger. Although this discussion is largely didactic, often the client can provide good examples of the role of avoidance in his or her life.

It is useful to explain that while an initial increase in fear can be expected, this is temporary, and that fear will eventually decline. Moreover, with repeated exposure the amount of fear evoked will continue to lessen. Often, we diagram the relationship between time and level of fear to illustrate how fear initially increases, but then gradually decreases if exposure continues; and how the level of fear is less at each successive repetition (see Figure 31.1). It may also be helpful to elicit an example from the client's life when they overcame a fear (i.e., riding a roller coaster) by facing the situation despite an initially high level of anxiety. Analogies can also be helpful in describing the process to clients. A good example to use is that of helping a child

get comfortable diving off a high diving board. One approach, a graduated method, would start with the child getting comfortable diving into the water at the side of the pool, gradually diving off a low diving board, and then eventually up to the high dive. Another approach, a flooding method, would be to simply have the child, despite his or her fear, repeatedly dive off the high dive. The point can be made that the results are similar; however, the process is different. Once described, the client can help by generating the advantages and disadvantages of each method (e.g., distress, time, etc.).

An integral part of the initial sessions is forming a therapeutic relationship by discussing the collaborative nature of therapy. The client is informed that the treatment is conducted as "teamwork," with both the therapist and the client taking responsibility for achieving good results. The therapist plays the role of "coach" and "cheerleader" and *never forces* the client into any situation. Moreover, all situations are discussed and demonstrated before the flooding session begins. Other elements of forming a good alliance include praising the client for coming into treatment and acknowledging his or her courage, communicating an understanding of the client's symptoms, validating the client's experience, and being nonjudgmental.

Next, a thorough assessment of activities, situations, or places that are avoided, and fear-related cognitions is conducted. Attention must be paid not only to areas of actual avoidance but also underlying reasons for avoidance. For example, there may be many reasons why someone is afraid of flying on an airplane: "I'm afraid

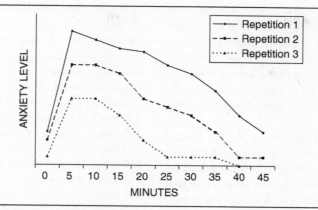

FIGURE 31.1 Chart illustrating the relationship between time and the degree of anxiety/fear during flooding sessions.

that turbulence will cause the plane to crash"; "I'm afraid of being in such a small, confined space"; or "I'm afraid the plane will be high-jacked." In this example, only in one case would flying alone on a bumpy flight be a target for treatment. Attention should also be paid to subtle forms of avoidance (e.g., distraction) and possible safety cues (e.g., carrying antianxiety medication, a cell phone). A list of activities/situations is generated, and a subjective unit of discomfort scale (SUDs, where 0 indicates "no discomfort at all" and 100 indicates "severe discomfort") is used to rank these activities or situations. With flooding *in vivo*, the top areas of avoidance are targeted for treatment at the onset of exposure.

Flooding *in vivo* consists of prolonged therapist-directed exposure to the most anxiety arousing situations, selecting from key domains at the top of the list. For example, in the treatment of claustrophobia, situations or activities might include being in a small, windowless room with the door locked, riding in elevators, and so on. As described above, the therapist describes the situation, demonstrates how to perform the task, and then instructs the client to do the same. SUDs levels are monitored throughout exposure and the client is encouraged to stay in the fear-producing situation until there is at least a 50% reduction in fear or SUDs levels decline to around 20 or 30. Exposure is repeated until fear has significantly

reduced and until all relevant areas of avoidance have been addressed.

HOW TO CONDUCT FLOODING
IN IMAGINATION

How flooding in imagination, or imaginal exposure, is conducted also varies greatly across the anxiety disorders. For example, in OCD, imaginal exposure often focuses on a client's feared consequences; in PTSD, imaginal exposure often focuses on the memory of the traumatic event. Below, we present examples of how imaginal flooding is implemented in the treatment of OCD and PTSD. In both examples, imaginal exposure is only one component of a treatment package that usually includes *in vivo* exposure and/or cognitive therapy.

Procedures for Imaginal Exposure in the Treatment of OCD

Assessment of distressing obsessional thoughts, ideas, or images is necessary for effective imaginal exposure. Therefore, the clinician should inquire about clients' feared consequences associated with obsessional situations or stimuli. For example, a client fearing the number "666" may be scared that as a result of confrontation with this number she will be possessed by the devil. "Unacceptable" anxiety-evoking intrusive thoughts, ideas, or urges should also be identified. Common examples include unacceptable sexual thoughts (e.g., incest) or ideas of accidents or illnesses occurring to loved ones. Clinicians should assess the degree of distress evoked by the obsessional thoughts and any behavioral or mental strategies used to control/neutralize the thoughts.

Appraisals of obsessional thoughts should also be assessed. In OCD, it is common for clients to ascribe undue significance to unwanted upsetting thoughts. For example, the assumption that having an immoral thought is tantamount to performing an immoral action is common. Clients may also mistakenly believe their unwanted thoughts about disasters are equivalent to wishes for such disasters. Another misperception frequently observed in OCD is the belief that obsessional thoughts imply responsibility for harm or its prevention (e.g., "The plane may crash if I think about it"). It is beneficial to determine specific distorted beliefs about thoughts since imaginal exposure will be used as a tool to demonstrate that such upsetting thoughts or ideas do not, themselves, indicate/produce harmful consequences.

The next step is to present a rationale for imaginal exposure as a therapeutic tool. This may be accomplished by helping the client to understand that most people normally experience upsetting thoughts (see Rachman & DeSilva, 1978); thus, such thoughts are quite normal. The problem, therefore, is not the thoughts per se, but the *misinterpretation* of such thoughts as highly significant. Specific information obtained in assessment should be used to illustrate how such misinterpretations evoke anxiety, preoccupation with the thought, and urges to control or dismiss the thought (i.e., compulsive rituals). Thus, one focus of treatment for OCD must be to modify the connection between essentially normal (harmless) thoughts and excessive anxiety. Repeated practice confronting (rather than avoiding or neutralizing) such thoughts will help clients to learn that these thoughts themselves do not pose any significant threat.

Imaginal exposure is often used as an adjunct to *in vivo* exposure and response prevention for OCD. For example, if *in vivo* exposure for a client with contamination obsessions involves touching a bathroom door handle and then holding a baby (without washing), imaginal exposure will include imagining the feared consequences of this exposure exercise. The client and therapist together generate a script that incorporates all elements of the client's obsessional fear. As a general rule, it is helpful to include *uncertainty* as a theme in imaginal exposure since obsessional fears often involve uncertainty about possible harm. The client or therapist next reads the imaginal script into a tape recorder (it is useful to use loop-tapes, which repeat without having to manually rewind) or digital voice recorder. An example of such a script appears below:

> ... You usually go out of your way to avoid touching bathroom doors, and always wash your hands if you do touch them. But this time you didn't wash, and instead held [baby] and touched her face and hands for a long time. Now, you're thinking that she's contaminated, and may become very sick. You desperately want to wash both [baby] and yourself to be sure that there will be no illness. But you know that you must not ritualize if you are to beat your OCD. So, you decide to risk it, remaining unsure of whether both of you will become sick from touching the door. You picture little [baby] in the infectious disease unit of the hospital and the doctors telling you that she may have become sick because someone forgot to wash their hands after using the bathroom. You should have known that little babies don't have fully developed immune systems. Perhaps you have caused your child to become deathly ill. The uncertainty is excruciating. ...

Clients are instructed to repeatedly listen to the tape and fully engage in the upsetting imagery. Urges to suppress the thought, engage in compulsive rituals, or obtain reassurances should be resisted, although reminding oneself that obsessional thoughts are normal and harmless is acceptable.

Procedures for Imaginal Exposure in the Treatment of PTSD

Imaginal exposure is introduced after the therapist and the client have discussed the common nature of posttrauma reactions and the rationale for exposure, working to provide a firm therapeutic alliance as a background for exposure. See Foa and colleagues (1998, 2007) for a detailed discussion. In imaginal exposure for PTSD, the focus is on the trauma memory. Trauma survivors often try hard to push intrusive memories of the event out of their minds. However, by engaging in the memory rather than avoiding it, they learn that the memories of the trauma are not intrinsically dangerous. Consequently, the trauma can be remembered without intense or disruptive anxiety. During imaginal exposure, the client recalls the memory as vividly as possible, imagining the trauma as if it is happening at that moment. The client is encouraged to describe the trauma in the present tense and recount as many details as possible, including specific thoughts and feelings. The therapist monitors SUDs levels every 5 minutes during flooding and checks to ensure that the client maintains a vivid image of the events being recalled. The goal of imaginal exposure is to help the client to access important, fear-related elements of the trauma memory but also to remain firmly grounded in the present. Thus, the client relives the trauma knowing that he or she is safe, and that the memory, although upsetting, cannot hurt him or her.

Imaginal exposure, during a therapy session, typically continues for approximately 45–60 minutes, repeating the memory several times. Although details are helpful in enhancing vividness, the goal is not to recall as many details as possible or recover "lost" memories. As therapy proceeds, the imaginal exposure shifts focus to the most difficult parts of the trauma ("hot spots") to promote fear reduction. The therapist's key role is to help titrate the client's level of engagement and distress, either by encouraging more detail and affect (for underengagement) or by diminishing detail and affect (for overengagement). Clients who underengage may be able to describe the trauma in detail but may be unable to connect with the emotional content of the memory. Conversely, those who overengage may show visual signs of distress (e.g., making physical movements reminiscent of the trauma happening again) and have difficulty maintaining their sense of grounding and safety. Several procedural modifications help to increase or decrease engagement with the memory. For underengagement, the client is encouraged to keep his or her eyes closed and to use present tense. Often, it is helpful for the therapist to probe for details, sensory information (e.g., see, hear, smell, touch), thoughts, and feelings. For overengagement, the client is encouraged to keep his or her eyes open, or if closed, to periodically open them to promote grounding. Often, with overengagement, the therapist will increase verbal communication, helping to focus the client and communicating empathy (e.g., "You're doing a great job staying with the memory even though it's hard.")

Following imaginal exposure, time is always allotted to discuss the client's reaction to the reliving experiences. This part of the session is typically termed *processing* and involves discussion of salient themes and reactions. The client is instructed to listen to the audiotape of the imaginal exposure daily and to record pre-, post-, and peak SUD levels. The therapist monitors the imaginal exposure homework to make sure that the client is listening to the tape in a manner that will encourage full engagement with the trauma memory (e.g., the client is not listening to the tape in the car on the way to work). Imaginal exposure to the trauma memory and homework is repeated until fear regarding the trauma memory has been greatly reduced.

CONCLUSION: HELPING THE CLIENT HANDLE DISTRESS

Possibly more so than with other exposure-based therapies, flooding demands that both the therapist and client are able to tolerate distress. When a client is having problems tolerating exposures, we often fall back on the basics of the therapy to help the client (and ourselves) through the distress. A therapist should convey a calm and relaxed manner when a client is distressed. One of the first things we do is reiterate the rationale for the therapy: reminding the client of the process of fear reduction, the efficacy of the therapy, and, if possible, their previous successes with the process. We also fall back on the therapeutic alliance. Here, we remind the client that the exposures are the client's choice and that we will support and work with them through the process. Finally, even if the exposure itself (e.g., a very difficult traumatic event) or the client's distress is distressing to you as a therapist, its helpful to remember that you, too, will grow more comfortable with time and repetition.

FUTURE DIRECTIONS

Future research in several areas can improve the effectiveness of flooding. Specifically, little is known about what constitutes optimal levels of exposure intensity, duration, and repetitions of the fear stimulus during *in vivo* and imaginal exposure. There also exists a dearth of knowledge about how individual differences (e.g., distress tolerance, coping skills, dissociation proneness, comorbid conditions) affect an individual's response to these procedures. Lastly, preliminary evidence suggests the efficiency of exposure may be maximized with the introduction of pharmacological agents shown to enhance learning and expedite the extinction of fear. D-cycloserine (DCS), for instance, has been used as an adjunct with intensive exposure therapy in the treatment of acrophobia, social anxiety, obsessive–compulsive disorder, and posttraumatic stress disorder (Guastella, Dadds, Lovibond, Mitchell, & Richardson, 2007; Heresco-Levy, Kremer, & Javitt, 2002; Hofmann, 2007; Hofmann, Meuret, & Smits, 2007; Kushner et al., 2007; Ressler, Rothbaum, & Tannenbaum, 2004; Storch et al., 2007). The results of these studies, although mixed, are somewhat encouraging. Further controlled clinical trials are needed to determine whether pharmacological agents such as DCS effectively augment exposure procedures.

EVIDENCE-BASED APPLICATIONS

Flooding procedures have been successfully applied as a stand-alone intervention and as a component to multicomponent treatment packages for a number of anxiety disorders. The following is a list of anxiety disorders with accompanying references describing how the procedure has been used effectively for the disorder:

Specific phobia: Öst, Alm, Brandberg, and Breitholtz (2001), Öst, Ferebee, and Furman, (1997), Öst, Hellstrom, & Kerstin, 1992).

Obsessive–compulsive disorder: Freeston et al. (1997); Abramowitz (2006).

Posttraumatic stress disorder: Başoğlu, Şalcioğlu, and Livanou (2006); Boudewyns and Hyer (1990); Foa et al. (1999, 2005).

Panic disorder: Deacon (2007); Lang and Hoyer (2007); Morissette, Spiegel, and Heinrichs (2005).

Generalized anxiety disorder: Borkovec and Costello (1993); Dugas and Koerner (2005).

Social phobia: Heimberg, Becker, Goldfinger, and Vermilyea (1985); Lincoln et al. (2005); Scholing and Emmelkamp (1996); Turner, Beidel, Long, and Greenhouse (1993); Turner, Beidel, and Jacob (1994).

References

Abramowitz, J. S. (1996). Variants of exposure and response prevention in the treatment of obsessive-compulsive disorder: A meta-analysis. *Behavior Therapy, 27,* 583–600.

Abramowitz, J. S. (2006). Understanding and treating obsessive–compulsive disorder: A cognitive–behavioral approach. Mahwah, NJ: Lawrence Erlbaum.

Addis, M. E., & Jacobson, N. S. (1996). Reasons for depression and the process and outcome of cognitive-behavioral psychotherapies. *Journal of Consulting and Clinical Psychology, 64,* 1417–1424.

Bandura, A. (1983). Self-efficacy determinants of anticipated fears and calamities. *Journal of Personality and Social Psychology, 45,* 464–469.

Başoğlu, M., Şalcioğlu, E., & Livanou, M. (2006). A randomized control study of single-session behavioural treatment of earthquake-related post-traumatic stress disorder using an earthquake simulator. *Psychological Medicine, 37,* 203–213.

Borkovec, T. D., & Costello, E. (1993). Efficacy of applied relaxation and cognitive–behavioral therapy in the treatment of generalized anxiety disorder. *Journal of Consulting & Clinical Psychology, 61*(4), 611–619.

Bouton, M. E. (1988). Context and ambiguity in the extinction of emotional learning. Implications for exposure therapy. *Behavior Research and Therapy, 26*, 137–149.

Boudewyns, P. E., & Hyer, L. (1990). Physiological response to combat memories and preliminary treatment outcome in Vietnam veteran PTSD clients treated with direct exposure therapy. *Behavior Therapy, 21*(1), 63–87.

Bryant, R. A., Moulds, M. L., Guthrie, R. M., Dang, S. T., & Nixon, R. (2003). Imaginal exposure alone and imaginal exposure with cognitive restructuring in treatment of posttraumatic stress disorder. *Journal of Consulting & Clinical Psychology, 71*, 706–712.

Deacon, B. J., & Abramowitz, J. S. (2006). A pilot study of two-day cognitive–behavioral treatment for panic disorder. *Behaviour Research and Therapy, 44*, 807–817.

Dugas, M. J., & Koerner, N. (2005). Cognitive–behavioral treatment for generalized anxiety disorder: Current status and future directions. *Journal of Cognitive Psychotherapy: An international quarterly, 19*(1), 61–81.

Foa, E. B., Dancu, C. V., Hembree, E. A., Jaycox, L. H., Meadows, E. A., & Street, G. P. (1999). A comparison of exposure therapy, stress inoculation training, and their combination for reducing posttraumatic stress disorder in female assault victims. *Journal of Consulting and Clinical Psychology, 67*, 194–200.

Foa, E. B., Hembree, E. A., Cahill, S. P., Rauch, S. L., Riggs, D. S., Feeny, N. C., et al. (2005). Randomized trial of prolonged exposure for posttraumatic stress disorder with and without cognitive restructuring: Outcome at academic and community clinics. *Journal of Consulting and Clinical Psychology, 73*(5), 953–964.

Foa, E. B., Hembree, E. A., & Rothbaum, B. O. (2007). *Prolonged exposure therapy for PTSD: Emotional processing of traumatic experiences.* New York: Oxford University Press.

Foa, E. B., & Kozak, M. S. (1986). Emotional processing of fear: Exposure to corrective information. *Psychology Bulletin, 99*, 20–35.

Foa, E. B., & Rothbaum, B. O. (1998). *Treating the trauma of rape.* New York: Guilford.

Foa, E. B., Sketee, G., & Grayson, J. B. (1985). Imaginal and in vivo exposure: A comparison with obsessive-compulsive checkers. *Behavior Therapy, 16*, 292–302.

Freeston, M. H., Ladouceur, R., Gagnon, F., Thibodeau, N., Rheaume, J., Letarte, H., et al. (1997). Cognitive-behavioral treatment of obsessive thoughts: A controlled study. *Journal of Consulting & Clinical Psychology, 65*(3), 405–413.

Guastella, A. J., Dadds, M. R., Lovibond, P. F., Mitchell, P., & Richardson, R. (2007). A randomized control trial of the effect of D-cycloserine

on exposure therapy for spider phobia. *Journal of Psychiatric Rsearch, 41*(6), 466–471.

Heimberg, R. G., Becker, R. E., Goldfinger, K., & Vermilyea, J. A. (1985). Treatment of social phobia by exposure, cognitive restructuring, and homework assignments. *Journal of Nervous and Mental Disease, 173*(4), 236–245.

Heresco-Levy, U., Kremer, I., & Javitt, D. C. (2002). Pilot-control trial of D-cycloserine for the treatment of posttraumatic stress disorder. *International Journal of Neuropsychopharmacology, 5*(4), 310–307.

Hofmann, S. G. (2007). Enhancing exposure-based therapy from a translational research perspective. *Behaviour Research and Therapy, 45*(9), 1987–2001.

Hofmann, S. G., Meuret, A. E., & Smits, J. A. J. (2007). Augmentation of exposure therapy with D-cycloserine for social anxiety disorder. *Archives of General Psychiatry, 63*(3), 298–304.

Kushner, M. G., Kim, S. W., Donohue, C., Thuras, P., Adson, D., Kotlyar M., et al. (2007). D-cycloserine augment exposure therapy for obsessive-compulsive disorder. *Biological Psychiatry, 62*(8), 835–838.

Lang, P. J. (1977). Imagery in therapy: An information processing analysis of fear. *Behavior Therapy, 8*, 862–886.

Lang, P. J. (1977). Physiological assessment of anxiety and fear. In J. D. Cone & R. A. Hawkins (Eds.), *Behavioral assessment: New directions in clinical psychology.* New York: Brunner/Mazel.

Lang, T., & Hoyer, J. (2007). Massed exposure and fast remission of panic disorder with agoraphobia: A case example. *Behavioural and Cognitive Psychotherapy, 35*(3), 371–375.

Lincoln, T. M., Reif, W., Hahlweg, K., Frank, M., Von Witzleben, I., Schoeder, B., et al. (2005). Who comes, who stays, who profits? Predicting refusal, dropout, success, and relapse in a short intervention for social phobia. *Psychotherapy Research, 15*(3), 210–225.

Mannion, N. E., & Levine, B. A. (1984). Effects of stimulus representation and cue category level on exposure (flooding) therapy. *British Journal of Clinical Psychology, 23*, 1–7.

Morissette, S. B., Spiegel, D. A., & Heinrichs, N. (2005). Sensation-focused intensive treatment for panic disorder with moderate to severe agoraphobia. *Cognitive and Behavioral Practice, 12*(1), 17–29.

Öst, L. G., Alm, T., Brandberg, M., Breitholtz, E. (2001). One vs five sessions of exposure and five sessions of cognitive therapy in the treatment of claustrophobia. *Behaviour Research and Therapy, 39*(2), 167–183.

Öst, L. G., Ferebee, I., & Furman, T. (1997). One-session group therapy of spider phobia: Direct versus indirect treatments. *Behaviour Research and Therapy, 35*(8), 721–732.

Öst, L. G., Svensson, L., Hellstrom, K., & Lindwall, R. (2001). One-session treatment of specific phobias in youths: A randomized clinical trial. *Journal of Consulting and Clinical Psychology, 69,* 814–824.

Rachman, S. (1980). Emotional processing. *Behaviour Research and Therapy, 18,* 51–60.

Rachman, S., & de Silva, P. (1978). Abnormal and normal obsessions. *Behaviour Research and Therapy, 16,* 233–238.

Ressler, K. J., Rothbaum, B. O., & Tannenbaum, L. (2004). Cognitive enhancers as adjuncts to psychotherapy: Use of D-cycloserine in phobic individuals to facilitate extinction of fear. *Archives of General Psychiatry, 61*(11), 1136–1144.

Rogers, P., Gray, N. S., Williams, T., & Kitchner, N. (2000). Behavioral treatment of PTSD in a perpetrator of manslaughter: A single case study. *Journal of Traumatic Stress, 13,* 511–519.

Rothbaum, B. O., Ruef, A. M., Litz, B. T., Han, H., & Hodges, L. (2003). Virtual reality exposure therapy of combat-related PTSD: A case study using psychophysiological indicators of outcome. *Journal of Cognitive Psychotherapy, 17,* 163–177.

Scholing, A., & Emmelkamp, P. M. G. (1996). Treatment of generalized social phobia: Results at long-term follow-up. *Behaviour Research and Therapy, 34*(5-6), 447-452.

Storch, E. A., Merlo, L. J., Bengston, M., Murphy, T. K., Lewis, M. K., Yang M. C., et al. (2007). D-cycloserine does not enhance exposure-response prevention in obsessive compulsive disorder. *International Clinical Psychopharmacology, 22*(4), 230–237.

Turner, S. M., Beidel, D. C., Long, P. J., & Greenhouse, J. (1993). Reductions of fear in social phobics: An examination of extinction patterns. *Behavior Therapy, 23*(3), 389–403.

Turner, S. M., Beidel, D. C., & Jacob, R. G. (1994). Social phobia: A comparison of behavior therapy and atenolol. *Journal of Consulting & Clinical Psychology, 62*(2), 350–358.

32 EXPERIMENTAL FUNCTIONAL ANALYSIS OF PROBLEM BEHAVIOR

James E. Carr, Linda A. LeBlanc, and Jessa R. Love

BACKGROUND

In 1977, E. G. Carr proposed five hypotheses regarding the motivation of self-injury of individuals with developmental disabilities. Three of the hypotheses, and perhaps the most provocative at the time, suggested that self-injury could be acquired and maintained through contingencies of reinforcement (i.e., self-injury could be operant behavior). These three sources of reinforcement were: (1) attention from others, (2) escape from aversive situations, and (3) sensory stimulation. The practical implication of E. G. Carr's operant hypotheses was that, once identified, the reinforcer responsible for maintaining self-injury could be modified as a form of treatment.

Several years later, Iwata and colleagues (Iwata, Dorsey, Slifer, Bauman, & Richman, 1994/1982) developed the *functional analysis*, an experimental procedure used to determine whether self-injury was indeed maintained by the operant variables proposed by E. G. Carr (1977). The convergence of an operant framework for considering the motivation of problem behavior with a procedure to identify such functions resulted in a pervasive change in the way clinicians and researchers assess and treat problem behavior. Since the publication of these two seminal articles, the field has moved toward a function-based model of treatment selection and away from the previously endemic topography-based model. In other words, instead of selecting a treatment for a problem behavior based on its topographical classification (e.g., aggression, pica), treatments are now generally selected based on the behavior's function (e.g., attention from others). This more contemporary function-based approach to treatment selection is considered beneficial

because it: (1) directly addresses the individual's "motivation" for engaging in the behavior instead of ignoring or overpowering it, (2) facilitates the teaching of replacement behaviors, and (3) diminishes reliance on aversive procedures (J. E. Carr, Coriaty, & Dozier, 2000).

The functional analysis is but one method within the broader *functional assessment*[1] process of which the ultimate purpose is the identification of variables that maintain problem behavior. Functional assessment is often characterized as three distinct, but compatible, methods (Lennox & Miltenberger, 1989). Informant assessments, often the first step in functional assessment, involve the use of rating scales and interviews to generate hypotheses about behavioral function (e.g., what consequences the behavior produces). Descriptive assessments entail direct observation of the problem behavior in the natural environment to determine when the behavior occurs (e.g., with a scatter plot; Kahng et al., 1998; Touchette, MacDonald, & Langer, 1985) and its immediate environmental antecedents and consequences (e.g., with an A-B-C assessment; Lerman & Iwata, 1993). The third method, the experimental functional analysis, involves brief experimentation to confirm hypotheses often generated by prior informant and descriptive

---

1. In applied behavior analysis, especially as it pertains to developmental disabilities, the term *functional analysis* refers specifically to experimental methods for identifying behavioral function (Mace, 1994) because of the longstanding meaning of the term *analysis* within the field (Baer, Wolf, & Risley, 1968). The term *functional assessment* refers more broadly to all methods used to infer or identify behavioral function. However, in other areas, the term *functional analysis* has been used synonymously with functional assessment (e.g., Martell, 2003).

assessments. In a functional analysis, the variables hypothesized to maintain problem behavior are delivered contingent on that behavior within brief sessions. When the problem behavior increases in rate (i.e., is reinforced) compared to a control condition, this is considered indicative of a demonstrated behavioral function.

Numerous studies have been conducted in an effort to improve the functional analysis (e.g., Neef & Iwata, 1994). Iwata and colleagues (e.g., Iwata, Duncan, Zarcone, Lerman, & Shore, 1994; Vollmer, Iwata, Duncan, & Lerman, 1993; Vollmer, Iwata, Zarcone, Smith, & Mazaleski, 1993) have developed several variations of and extensions to their original functional analysis, which employed a multielement experimental design (i.e., rapidly alternating sessions of different conditions). These methodological variations have improved our ability to identify behavioral function in cases in which the original multielement functional analysis (described later in "Step-by-Step Instructions") has proved inconclusive. Similarly, Derby et al. (1992) made a significant contribution with the development of their brief functional analysis, which can be conducted in a few hours. Such brevity was a significant achievement for managed behavioral healthcare because a standard functional analysis sometimes requires several weeks to complete. Vollmer, Marcus, Ringdahl, and Roane (1995) further extended this line of research by providing a progressive model for conducting a functional analysis. The model began with a brief functional analysis, and, if necessary, was followed by the more traditional multielement analysis along with additional analyses for clarifying ambiguous functional analysis outcomes. As a result of over 20 years of research and development, clinicians and researchers today have access to a number of functional analysis methods with which to identify the function of problem behavior (Hanley, Iwata, & McCord, 2003).

WHO MIGHT BENEFIT FROM THE FUNCTIONAL ANALYSIS

The functional analysis has proved remarkably general. In the years since its introduction, the functional analysis has been effectively applied to a number of populations including children and adults with developmental disabilities (e.g., autism, mental retardation), children and adults with brain injuries, children with and without clinical diagnoses (e.g., attention-deficit hyperactivity disorder), and elders with dementia. The common feature of these groups of individuals is that they often have somewhat impaired verbal repertoires. The functional analysis achieves its effects via contingency-shaped behavior. Therefore, any rules a verbally competent client might generate could interfere with the analysis. For example, if a client followed a rule such as "Each time I hit the therapist, she lets me stop working," the functional analysis outcome would be indicative of rule-governed behavior instead of reinforcement contingencies. A client might also follow an incorrect rule during a session, which might produce data that would result in an erroneous interpretation of the behavioral function. In addition, verbally competent clients might experience the functional analysis as artificial, possibly resulting in further interference.

The functional analysis has also been successfully applied to a wide variety of problem behaviors, including self-injury (Iwata, Pace, Dorsey et al., 1994), aggression (Marcus, Vollmer, Swanson, Roane, & Ringdahl, 2001), tantrums (Vollmer, Northup, Ringdahl, LeBlanc, & Chauvin, 1996), stereotypy (Kennedy, Meyer, Knowles, & Shukla, 2000), pica (Piazza et al., 1998), psychotic speech (Wilder, Masuda, O'Connor, & Baham, 2001), noncompliance (Wilder, Harris, Reagan, & Rasey, 2007), food refusal (Piazza et al., 2003), and vocal tics (J. E. Carr, Taylor, Wallander, & Reiss, 1996). Finally, and perhaps most importantly, the functional analysis has been used successfully with a wide variety of behavioral functions, including attention from others, access to tangible items, access to a previously interrupted preferred activity, escape from instructional demands, escape from social interaction, escape from unpleasant noise, and automatic/sensory stimulation, among others.

POSSIBLE CONTRAINDICATIONS

Although the functional analysis has been successfully applied to a number of problem behaviors, there are at least three classes of behavior for which the functional analysis might not be appropriate.

Low-Rate Behavior

Since one of the requirements of the functional analysis is a moderate- to high-rate behavior—that is, a behavior that is likely to occur at least once during a 10- to 15-min session—the functional analysis is generally inappropriate for problem behavior that occurs less often. When a functional analysis is attempted with a low-rate behavior, the behavior is unlikely to occur during sessions and, therefore, will not come into contact with the arranged contingencies. Instead, informant and descriptive assessments are typically used to assess the function of low-rate problem behavior (Radford & Ervin, 2002; Sprague & Horner, 1999).

Life-Threatening Behavior

An additional concern is the use of a functional analysis with life-threatening behaviors. Because the functional analysis achieves its outcome via the planned reinforcement of problem behavior during brief sessions, it may be unethical in some cases to use this procedure with behavior that is potentially life threatening. Examples of such behavior include pica with dangerous objects (e.g., pushpins), suicidal behavior, and self-injury that occurs at a high intensity and/or involves a vulnerable area of the body (e.g., eye poking). However, it may be possible to conduct a functional analysis with such behaviors by using protective equipment (e.g., helmets, eye patches) for some forms of self-injury and using simulated, but safe pica objects (Piazza et al., 1998).

Covert Behavior

Functional analyses cannot be conducted with problem behaviors that only occur in private. For example, although operant variables may maintain trichotillomania (clinically problematic hair pulling), some individuals will not engage in this behavior in the presence of others (Elliott & Fuqua, 2000).

ADDITIONAL CONSIDERATIONS

Because functional analysis involves the deliberate, controlled reinforcement of problem behavior, the procedure should be conducted only by trained professionals who are properly supervised. In addition, it can be politically advantageous to have the agency in which the analysis is conducted to support its use. It is also important to consider safety precautions for the client and staff when conducting a functional analysis for behavior such as self-injury or aggression. For some behaviors that might result in significant injury to the client or staff, it may be necessary to have medical staff available on site. In addition, safety guidelines that specify criteria for terminating a session should be established prior to beginning the analysis.

HOW DOES THE FUNCTIONAL ANALYSIS WORK?

A functional analysis typically includes multiple conditions that test the reinforcing properties of various programmed consequences. The necessary features of these test conditions are as follows: (1) the relevant *establishing operation*[2] must be present (e.g., deprivation of attention within the session), (2) discriminative stimuli must be present (e.g., the presence of a therapist), and (3) the putative reinforcer (e.g., attention) is delivered only contingent on problem behavior. These three components work together to simulate the complete reinforcement contingency for a problem behavior. In other words, the functional analysis is effective because, within the

---

2. An establishing operation (EO) is an event that increases or decreases the reinforcing (or punishing) effect of a consequence (for further information, see McGill, 1999). In other words, it alters the client's "motivation" for a specific consequence. In a functional analysis test condition, the EO must be present in order for the programmed consequence to function as a reinforcer. For example, in a demand condition in which brief escape from a task is being evaluated, the task itself must be at least somewhat unpleasant. The unpleasantness of the task is classified as an EO that increases the value of escape from the task as a reinforcer.

session, problem behavior is evoked and is subsequently exposed to differential consequences that should result in increased levels of problem behavior when the maintaining reinforcer is delivered.

EMPIRICAL SUPPORT FOR THE FUNCTIONAL ANALYSIS

A number of studies (e.g., Iwata, Pace, Cowdery, & Miltenberger, 1994; Repp, Felce, & Barton, 1988) have demonstrated superior treatment effects with procedures prescribed by the outcome of a functional assessment compared to a default, non-function-based alternative (see also Campbell, 2003). For example, Iwata, Pace, Cowdery et al. demonstrated that only variations of extinction that were matched to behavioral function were effective in treating self-injury. For example, the attention-maintained head hitting of one individual was successfully treated using planned ignoring (i.e., attention extinction). However, having the individual wear a helmet to attenuate sensory stimulation (i.e., sensory extinction) for the same behavior was ineffective. Although the ultimate validity of a functional analysis is a successful treatment based on its results, additional empirical support can be found by examining the percentage of functional analysis cases that resulted in interpretable data from experimental–epidemiological analyses. For example, Iwata, Pace, Dorsey et al. (1994) reported that, out of 152 functional analyses, 138 (91%) resulted in data clearly indicating a behavioral function. Similarly, Asmus et al. (2004) reported the successful identification of behavioral function in 96% of 138 functional analyses of the problem behavior of individuals with and without developmental disabilities.

STEP-BY-STEP INSTRUCTIONS

Preliminary Assessment

As mentioned previously, there are three types or levels of functional assessment: informant, descriptive, and experimental functional analysis. These three methods progress from less time-and-labor intensive to more time-and-labor intensive with an increasing degree of certainty about likely maintaining variables. Many clinicians begin the functional assessment process at the informant level during which caregivers complete rating scales or are interviewed to provide preliminary information on the problem behavior. Some examples of structured informant assessments that researchers have developed include the Questions about Behavioral Functional checklist (Paclawskyj, Matson, Rush, Smalls, & Vollmer, 2000) and the Functional Analysis Interview (O'Neill et al., 1997). Sturmey (1994) reviewed the psychometric properties of several informant rating scales and suggested that additional demonstration of their reliability and validity is needed.

Next, the client is typically observed in the natural environment to further assess the problem. This practice is referred to as "descriptive assessment." Typically, when the problem behavior occurs the therapist should record its occurrence, as well as its immediate, observable antecedent and consequence. The therapist may also note the date, time, and location of the behavior as well as what activity was occurring and which persons were present. Data obtained using this method are summarized to examine potential patterns associated with the occurrence of behavior (Lalli & Goh, 1993). A benefit of the descriptive assessment is that the therapist is actually observing the problem behavior in the natural setting (as opposed to an artificial one) and is not relying on the verbal information from others. Another potential benefit of the descriptive assessment is its ability to assess the function of behavior that does not occur frequently but is, nonetheless, problematic. Unfortunately, all data collected using this method are correlational and cannot be considered definitive. However, information from descriptive and informant assessments can be useful in designing a subsequent functional analysis (Hanley et al., 2003).

Finally, a functional analysis can be conducted to confirm hypotheses generated by the informant and descriptive assessments. The purpose of the functional analysis is to conduct a brief experiment to test the effects of different antecedent conditions and reinforcers on problem behavior.

Setting and Session Features

Most functional analyses are conducting in analogue rather than naturalistic settings because the analogue setting is more likely to produce interpretable results because extraneous variables are eliminated. However, a naturalistic setting may be more likely to evoke the problem behavior due to the presence of relevant idiosyncratic stimuli. A compromise between these styles is to have an individual from the client's natural environment deliver consequences during an analogue functional analysis.

Wallace and Iwata (1999) determined that sessions 10 or 15 min in duration resulted in clearer outcomes than 5-min sessions; however, 5-min sessions are still adequate for many functional analyses. Sessions should be conducted using a rapidly alternating multielement design (Barlow & Hersen, 1984) with randomized presentation of experimental conditions. For example, a therapist might conduct a block of five 10-min sessions in approximately 1 hour (e.g., attention → escape → alone → control → escape). Sessions should be separated from each other by at least a few minutes to (1) allow the therapist to prepare for the next session, and (2) help produce response differentiation between conditions. Each condition should generally be conducted a minimum of three times, although additional sessions might produce clearer data (Kahng & Iwata, 1999). Although it is possible to conduct the entire functional analysis in one time period (e.g., 4 hours), sessions are generally conducted over at least several days due to therapist availability and to prevent client fatigue.

As stated earlier, in each condition, the therapist creates specific antecedent situations, provides specific consequences for the problem behavior, and ultimately looks for an increase in response rate (i.e., a reinforcement effect). Each condition should contain some physical element to serve as a discriminative stimulus to facilitate the development of stimulus control over the problem behavior in each condition (Conners et al., 2000). Examples of these elements include therapists, rooms, T-shirts, and colored posters assigned to each condition (e.g., the therapist wears a yellow T-shirt during the attention condition and a blue T-shirt during the escape condition).

Common Test Conditions

The following are descriptions of the most commonly used functional analysis conditions:

Attention from others. The purpose of this condition is to determine whether the behavior is maintained by attention from others (i.e., social positive reinforcement). The client should be seated and may be given a medium-preference leisure item with which to interact. We refer the reader to McCord and Neef (2005) in which a flowchart is presented for determining whether to include leisure items in an attention condition. Each time the behavior occurs, the client should receive 3–5 s of attention for the behavior. The content of these attention deliveries typically involves social disapproval (e.g., "Please don't do that."). However, the type and specific content of attention (positive or negative) used should match what the therapist believes occurs in the client's environment (perhaps from a prior descriptive assessment), as different forms of contingent attention—both verbal and physical—have been found to differentially affect problem behavior (Kodak, Northup, & Kelley, 2007).

Escape from instructional demands. The purpose of this condition is to determine whether the behavior is maintained by escape from or avoidance of instructional demands (i.e., social negative reinforcement). The therapist should provide a task (e.g., academic, habilitative) that has been demonstrated as at least moderately difficult for the client. When the problem behavior occurs, give the client a 20- to 30-s break before resuming instruction. Always praise task compliance. Consider carefully the nature of the demands presented in this condition. The task demands should be similar to those delivered in the natural environment in terms of the type of task, rate of presentation of tasks, and level of task difficulty. This information is often obtained during informant and descriptive assessment.

Access to tangible items. The purpose of this condition is to determine whether the behavior is maintained by access to preferred tangible items (e.g., toys, leisure materials). Before the session begins, give the client brief, free access to the preferred item. At the beginning of the session, remove the item and give it back for 20-30 s if the problem behavior occurs. We recommend against providing the client with any additional attention (e.g., saying "You can have your toy back," providing eye contact) when delivering the item, as this may confound the outcomes of the functional analysis when problem behavior is attention maintained (Moore, Mueller, Dubard, Roberts, & Sterling-Turner, 2002). This condition should only be conducted when there is strong evidence from prior functional assessment to indicate that access to preferred items may serve a likely maintaining function (Hanley et al., 2003).

Alone/No interaction. This condition is designed to determine whether the behavior is maintained by automatic reinforcement (i.e., sensory reinforcement or self-stimulation). Hanley et al. (2003) recommend that this condition be included in a functional analysis whenever feasible, as its omission may lead to erroneous conclusions about the social nature of the behavioral function. In an alone-condition session, the client is typically left alone for the duration of the session. However, if this is not practically feasible, the therapist can be present, but should not interact with the client during the session. In addition, there should be little stimulation in the environment (e.g., no radio, television, or other tangible items). High rates of behavior in this condition might be indicative of an automatic reinforcement function.

Control. The purpose of the control condition is to provide an "ideal" environment for the client so that problem behavior should not occur. Therefore, the environment should be enriched with preferred items. The client should also be given frequent attention on a reasonable schedule (usually 3–5 s of attention every 30 s and in response to appropriate initiations) and no demands should be presented. The purpose of this condition is to reduce the "motivation" to engage in problem behavior by making freely available all of the potential reinforcers provided contingently in the test conditions. The control condition should generally produce few problem behaviors; therefore, data from each test condition should be compared with data from this condition to determine whether reinforcement has occurred.

Customized test conditions. Although the common conditions described above cover the majority of maintaining environmental variables for problem behavior, it may sometimes be necessary to customize test conditions to assess for an idiosyncratic function. For example, McCord, Iwata, Galensky, Ellingson, and Thomson (2001) used functional analyses with problem behaviors whose function was escape from unpleasant noise (i.e., problem behavior terminated the noise). When developing a customized test condition, ensure that the relevant antecedent conditions are present (e.g., unpleasant noise, an adult who can terminate the noise) and that the hypothesized reinforcer (e.g., termination of noise) is delivered contingent on each problem behavior.

We recommend always including at least the control and alone/no-interaction conditions in the analysis, plus any additional test conditions that are deemed relevant from the preliminary assessment. Although the control condition should always be included, the alone condition could be eliminated in instances in which another person's presence is necessary for the problem behavior (e.g., aggression) to occur. The ability to customize the functional analysis by including only relevant conditions and by developing new conditions makes it particularly suitable for clinical practice. We refer the reader to a literature review by Hanley et al. for additional recommendations on functional analysis design (Hanley et al., 2003).

Data Collection and Analysis

During each session, observational data should be collected on some aspect of problem behavior such as its frequency or duration (Cooper, Heron,

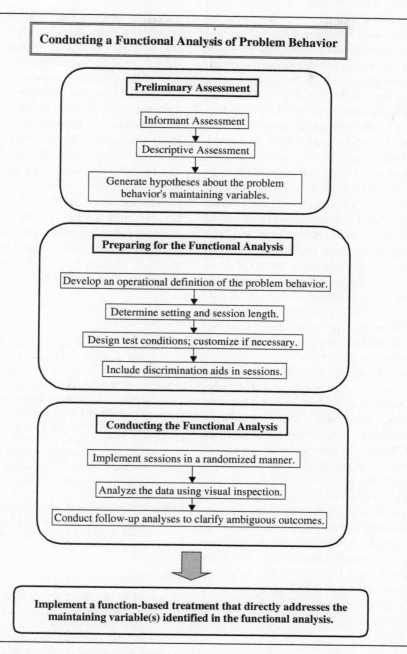

FIGURE 32.1   Key steps in conducting a functional analysis of problem behavior.

& Heward, 2007). The nature of the behavior (e.g., whether each instance of the behavior is discrete, whether instances of the behavior occur for variable durations) will determine the appropriate recording system (e.g., frequency counts, momentary time sampling). For settings with ample resources, computerized data collection might be a viable option (Jackson & Dixon, 2007). Data should be plotted on a line graph one session at a time. Using visual inspection, the data from each test condition should then be compared with data from the control condition. Test conditions with consistently higher rates of problem behavior are indicative of identified reinforcement functions. Hagopian et al. (1997) developed specific criteria that can be used during the visual inspection of functional analysis data. In general, the procedure requires one to compare each test condition to the control condition to determine if a substantial percentage of those sessions had behavior rates at least two standard deviations above the average of the control condition sessions.

Although the standard, multielement-design functional analysis often results in interpretable data, additional analyses are needed when they do not. We refer the reader to the protocol developed by Vollmer et al. (1995) for conducting a series of follow-up analyses when functional analysis outcomes are ambiguous. One of the final phases of this protocol is a series of consecutive alone/no-interaction sessions. If problem behavior persists during these sessions, the common conclusion is that the behavior is maintained by automatic (i.e., sensory, self-stimulatory) reinforcement. We refer the reader to an article by LeBlanc, Patel, and J. E. Carr (2000) for a description of assessments that are designed to clarify the specific sensory consequences that may maintain problem behavior.

LINKING THE FUNCTIONAL ANALYSIS TO TREATMENT

At the conclusion of the functional assessment process (see Figure 32.1), the therapist should have a clearer understanding of the variables that maintain the client's problem behavior. It is then necessary to develop a treatment plan that incorporates this information. For example, if a functional analysis identified an attention function, this maintaining variable should be directly addressed in subsequent treatment. Common approaches for treating attention-maintained behavior include planned ignoring of the problem behavior (Ducharme & Van Houten, 1994), providing noncontingent (free) attention to the client throughout the day (Carr & LeBlanc, 2006; Wilder & Carr, 1998), and teaching the client more appropriate ways to obtain attention (Durand, 1990). Regardless of the specific treatment that is selected, however, the therapist should ensure that it directly addresses the behavior's function so that the client ultimately receives the most effective and relevant treatment possible (Iwata, Vollmer, Zarcone, & Rodgers, 1993).

Further Reading

Hanley, G. P., Iwata, B. A., & McCord, B. E. (2003). Functional analysis of problem behavior: A review. *Journal of Applied Behavior Analysis, 36*, 147–185.

Neef, N. A., & Iwata, B. A. (Eds.) (1994). Special issue on functional analysis approaches to behavioral assessment and treatment [Special Issue]. *Journal of Applied Behavior Analysis, 27*(2).

O'Neill, R. E., Horner, R. H., Albin, R. W., Sprague, J. R., Storey, K., & Newton, J. S. (1997). *Functional assessment and program development for problem behavior: A practical handbook* (2nd ed.). Pacific Grove, CA: Brooks/Cole.

Repp, A. C., & Horner, R. H. (1999). *Functional analysis of problem behavior: From effective assessment to effective support.* Belmont, CA: Wadsworth.

References

Asmus, J. M., Ringdahl, J. E., Sellers, J. A., Call, N. A., Andelman, M. S., & Wacker, D. P. (2004). Use of a short-term inpatient model to evaluate aberrant behavior: Outcome data summaries from 1996 to 2001. *Journal of Applied Behavior Analysis, 37*, 283–304.

Baer, D. M., Wolf, M. M., & Risley, T. R. (1968). Some current dimensions of applied behavior analysis. *Journal of Applied Behavior Analysis, 1*, 91–97.

Barlow, D. H., & Hersen, M. (1984). *Single case experimental designs: Strategies for studying behavior change* (2nd ed.). Boston: Allyn and Bacon.

Campbell, J. M. (2003). Efficacy of behavioral interventions for reducing problem behavior in persons with autism: A quantitative synthesis of single-subject research. *Research in Developmental Disabilities, 24*, 120–138.

Carr, E. G. (1977). The origins of self-injurious behavior: A review of some hypotheses. *Psychological Bulletin, 84*, 800–816.

Carr, J. E., Coriaty, S., & Dozier, C. L. (2000). Current issues in the function-based treatment of aberrant behavior in individuals with developmental disabilities. In J. Austin & J. E. Carr (Eds.), *Handbook of applied behavior analysis* (pp. 91–112). Reno, NV: Context Press.

Carr, J. E., & LeBlanc, L. A. (2006). Noncontingent reinforcement as antecedent behavior support. In J. K. Luiselli (Ed.), *Antecedent assessment & intervention: Supporting children & adults with developmental disabilities in community settings* (pp. 147–164). Baltimore, MD: Brookes.

Carr, J. E., Taylor, C. C., Wallander, R. J., & Reiss, M. L. (1996). A functional–analytic approach to the diagnosis of a transient tic disorder. *Journal of Behavior Therapy and Experimental Psychiatry, 27*, 291–297.

Conners, J., Iwata, B. A., Kahng, S., Hanley, G. P., Worsdell, A. S., & Thompson, R. H. (2000). Differential responding in the presence and absence of discriminative stimuli during multielement functional analyses. *Journal of Applied Behavior Analysis, 33*, 299–308.

Cooper, J. O., Heron, T. E., & Heward, W. L. (2007). *Applied behavior analysis* (2nd ed.). Upper Saddle River, NJ: Prentice Hall.

Derby, K. M., Wacker, D. P., Sasso, G., Steege, M., Northup, J., Cigrand, K., & Asmus, J. (1992). Brief functional assessment techniques to evaluate aberrant behavior in an outpatient setting: A summary of 79 cases. *Journal of Applied Behavior Analysis, 25*, 713–721.

Ducharme, J. M., & Van Houten, R. (1994). Operant extinction in the treatment of severe maladaptive behavior: Adapting research to practice. *Behavior Modification, 18*, 139–170.

Durand, V. M. (1990). *Severe behavior problems: A functional communication training approach.* New York: Guilford.

Elliott, A. J., & Fuqua, R. W. (2000). Trichotillomania: Conceptualization, measurement, and treatment. *Behavior Therapy, 31*, 529–545.

Hanley, G. P., Iwata, B. A., & McCord, B. E. (2003). Functional analysis of problem behavior: A review. *Journal of Applied Behavior Analysis, 36*, 147–185.

Hagopian, L. P., Fisher, W. W., Thompson, R. H., Owen-DeSchryver, J., Iwata, B. A., & Wacker, D. P. (1997). Toward the development of structured criteria for interpretation of functional analysis data. *Journal of Applied Behavior Analysis, 30*, 313–326.

Iwata, B. A., Dorsey, M. F, Slifer, K. J., Bauman, K. E., & Richman, G. S. (1994). Toward a functional analysis of self-injury. *Journal of Applied Behavior Analysis, 27*, 197–209. (Reprinted from *Analysis and Intervention in Developmental Disabilities, 2*, 3–20, 1982).

Iwata, B. A., Duncan, B. A., Zarcone, J. R., Lerman, D. C., & Shore, B. A. (1994). A sequential, test-control methodology for conducting functional analyses of self-injurious behavior. *Behavior Modification, 18*, 289–306.

Iwata, B. A., Pace, G. M., Cowdery, G. E., & Miltenberger, R. G. (1994). What makes extinction work: An analysis of procedural form and function. *Journal of Applied Behavior Analysis, 27*, 131–144.

Iwata, B. A., Pace, G. M., Dorsey, M. F., Zarcone, J. R., Vollmer, T. R., Smith, R. G., et al. (1994). The functions of self-injurious behavior: An experimental–epidemiological analysis. *Journal of Applied Behavior Analysis, 27*, 215-240.

Iwata, B. A., Vollmer, T. R., Zarcone, J. R., & Rodgers, T. A. (1993). Treatment classification and selection based on behavioral function. In R. Van Houten & S. Axelrod (Eds.), *Behavior analysis and treatment* (pp. 101–125). New York: Plenum.

Jackson, J., & Dixon, M. R. (2007). A mobile computing solution for collection functional analysis data on a pocket PC. *Journal of Applied Behavior Analysis, 40*, 359–384.

Kahng, S., & Iwata, B. A. (1999). Correspondence between outcomes of brief and extended functional analyses. *Journal of Applied Behavior Analysis, 32*, 149–159.

Kahng, S., Iwata, B. A., Fischer, S. M., Page, T. J., Treadwell, K. R. H., Williams, D. E., et al. (1998). Temporal distributions of problem behavior based on scatter plot analysis. *Journal of Applied Behavior Analysis, 31*, 593–604.

Kennedy, C. H., Meyer, K. A., Knowles, T., & Shukla, S. (2000). Analyzing the multiple functions of stereotypical behavior for students with autism: Implications for assessment and treatment. *Journal of Applied Behavior Analysis, 33*, 559–571.

Kodak, T., Northup, J., & Kelley, M. E. (2007). An evaluation of the types of attention that maintain problem behavior. *Journal of Applied Behavior Analysis, 40*, 167–171.

Lalli, J. S., & Goh, H. (1993). Naturalistic observations in community settings. In J. Reichle & D. P. Wacker (Eds.), *Communicative alternatives to challenging behavior: Integrating functional assessment and intervention strategies* (pp. 11–40). Baltimore, MD: Paul H. Brookes.

LeBlanc, L. A., Patel, M. R., & Carr, J. E. (2000). Recent advances in the assessment of aberrant behavior maintained by automatic reinforcement in individuals with developmental disabilities. *Journal of Behavior Therapy and Experimental Psychiatry, 31,* 137–154.

Lennox, D. B., & Miltenberger, R. G. (1989). Conducting a functional assessment of problem behavior in applied settings. *Journal of the Association for Persons with Severe Handicaps, 14,* 304–311.

Lerman, D. C., & Iwata, B. A. (1993). Descriptive and experimental analyses of variables maintaining self-injurious behavior. *Journal of Applied Behavior Analysis, 26,* 293–319.

Mace, F. C. (1994). The significance and future of functional analysis methodologies. *Journal of Applied Behavior Analysis, 27,* 385–392.

Marcus, B. A., Vollmer, T. R., Swanson, V., Roane, H. R., & Ringdahl, J. E. (2001). An experimental analysis of aggression. *Behavior Modification, 25,* 189–213.

Martell, C. R. (2003). Behavioral activation treatment for depression. In W. O'Donohue, J. E. Fisher, & S. C. Hayes (Eds.), *Cognitive behavior therapy: Applying empirically supported techniques in your practice* (pp. 28–32). New York: John Wiley & Sons.

McCord, B. E., Iwata, B. A., Galensky, T. L., Ellingson, S. A., & Thomson, R. J. (2001). Functional analysis and treatment of problem behavior evoked by noise. *Journal of Applied Behavior Analysis, 34,* 447–462.

McCord, B. E., & Neef, N. A., (2005). Leisure items as controls in the attention condition of functional analyses. *Journal of Applied Behavior Analysis, 38,* 417–426.

McGill, P. (1999). Establishing operations: Implications for the assessment, treatment, and prevention of problem behavior. *Journal of Applied Behavior Analysis, 32,* 393–418.

Moore, J. W., Mueller, M. M., Dubard, M., Roberts, D. S., & Sterling-Turner, H. E. (2002). The influence of therapist attention on self-injury during a tangible condition. *Journal of Applied Behavior Analysis, 35,* 283–286.

Neef, N. A., & Iwata, B. A. (Eds.) (1994). Special issue on functional analysis approaches to behavioral assessment and treatment [Special Issue]. *Journal of Applied Behavior Analysis, 27*(2).

O'Neill, R. E., Horner, R. H., Albin, R. W., Sprague, J. R., Storey, K., & Newton, J. S. (1997). *Functional assessment and program development for problem behavior: A practical handbook* (2nd ed.). Pacific Grove, CA: Brooks/Cole.

Paclawskyj, T. R., Matson, J. L., Rush, K. S., Smalls, Y., & Vollmer, T. R. (2000). Questions About Behavioral Function (QABF): A behavioral checklist for functional assessment of aberrant behavior. *Research in Developmental Disabilities, 21,* 223–229.

Piazza, C. C., Fisher, W. W., Brown, K. A., Shore, B. A., Patel, M. R., Katz, R. M., et al. (2003). Functional analysis of inappropriate mealtime behaviors. *Journal of Applied Behavior Analysis, 36,* 187–204.

Piazza, C. C., Fisher, W. W., Hanley, G. P., LeBlanc, L. A., Worsdell, A. S., Lindauer, S. E., & Keeney, K. M. (1998). Treatment of pica through multiple analyses of its reinforcing functions. *Journal of Applied Behavior Analysis, 31,* 165–189.

Radford, P. M., & Ervin, R. A. (2002). Employing descriptive functional assessment methods to assess low-rate, high-intensity behaviors: A case example. *Journal of Positive Behavior Interventions, 4,* 146–155.

Repp, A. C., Felce, D., & Barton, L. E. (1988). Basing the treatment of stereotypic and self-injurious behaviors on hypotheses of their causes. *Journal of Applied Behavior Analysis, 21,* 281–289.

Sprague, J. R., & Horner, R. H. (1999). Low-frequency high-intensity problem behavior: Toward an applied technology of functional assessment and intervention. In A. C. Repp & R. H. Horner (Eds.), *Functional analysis of problem behavior: From effective assessment to effective support* (pp. 98–116). Belmont, CA: Wadsworth.

Sturmey, P. (1994). Assessing the functions of aberrant behaviors: A review of psychometric instruments. *Journal of Autism and Developmental Disorders, 24,* 293–304.

Touchette, P. E., MacDonald, R. F., & Langer, S. N. (1985). A scatter plot for identifying stimulus control of problem behavior. *Journal of Applied Behavior Analysis, 18,* 343–351.

Vollmer, T. R., Iwata, B. A., Duncan, B. A., & Lerman, D. C. (1993). Extensions of multielement functional analysis using reversal-type designs. *Journal of Developmental and Physical Disabilities, 5,* 311–325.

Vollmer, T. R., Iwata, B. A., Zarcone, J. R., Smith, R. G., & Mazaleski, J. L. (1993). Within-session patterns of self-injury as indicators of behavioral function. *Research in Developmental Disabilities, 14,* 479–492.

Vollmer, T. R., Marcus, B. A., Ringdahl, J. E., & Roane, H. S. (1995). Progressing from brief assessments to extended experimental analyses in the evaluation of aberrant behavior. *Journal of Applied Behavior Analysis, 28,* 561–576.

Vollmer, T. R., Northup, J., Ringdahl, J. E., LeBlanc, L. A., & Chauvin, T. M. (1996). Functional analysis of severe tantrums displayed by children with language delays: An outclinic assessment. *Behavior Modification, 20,* 97–115.

Wallace, M. D., & Iwata, B. A. (1999). Effects of session duration on functional analysis outcomes. *Journal of Applied Behavior Analysis, 32,* 175–183.

Wilder, D. A., & Carr, J. E. (1998). Recent advances in the modification of establishing operations to reduce aberrant behavior. *Behavioral Interventions,* *13,* 43–59.

Wilder, D. A., Harris, C., Reagan, R., & Rasey, A. (2007). Functional analysis and treatment of noncompliance by preschool children. *Journal of Applied Behavior Analysis, 40,* 173–177.

Wilder, D. A., Masuda, A., O'Connor, C., & Baham, M. (2001). Brief functional analysis and treatment of bizarre vocalizations in an adult with schizophrenia. *Journal of Applied Behavior Analysis, 34,* 65–68.

33 FUNCTIONAL COMMUNICATION TRAINING TO TREAT CHALLENGING BEHAVIOR

V. Mark Durand and Eileen Merges

Children and adults with developmental disorders often engage in behaviors that are disturbing and, at times, dangerous to themselves and others. Aggression, self-injurious behavior, and other disruptive behaviors pose such a serious threat to efforts to help these individuals lead more independent lives that a great deal of research has focused on the treatment of these behaviors (Durand & Merges, 2001). A wide range of consequences have been tried in efforts to reduce the behavior problems exhibited by persons with disabilities, including time-out from positive reinforcement (Wolf, Risley & Mees, 1964), contingent restraint (Azrin, Besalel, & Wisotzek, 1982), overcorrection (Johnson, Baumeister, Penland, & Inwald, 1982), and contingent electric shock (Corte, Wolf, & Locke, 1971; Tate & Baroff, 1966; Luiselli, 1992). Although many of these interventions demonstrate effectiveness in the initial reduction of challenging behaviors, sustained and clinically relevant improvements are elusive (Durand & Carr, 1989; Luiselli, 1992). An alternative behavioral approach to the traditional treatments for challenging behaviors was developed in the mid-1980s and has been referred to as functional communication training (FCT) (Durand, 1990). FCT specifically uses communication to reduce challenging behavior (Carr & Durand, 1985; Halle, Ostrosky, & Hemmeter, 2006; Mancil, 2006). This strategy includes assessing the variables maintaining the behavior to be reduced and providing the same consequences for a different behavior. It is assumed that if individuals can gain access to desired consequences more effectively with the new response, they will use this new response and will reduce their use of the undesirable response. Applying this logic to challenging behavior, one is able to teach individuals more acceptable behaviors that serve the same function as their problem behavior. So, for example, we could teach people to ask for attention by saying, "Am I doing good work?" This would allow them to gain teacher attention in this appropriate way rather than in an inappropriate way such as through slapping their face.

WHO MIGHT BENEFIT FROM THIS TREATMENT

Although the majority of research on FCT involves individuals with autism and related disorders, this research has expanded to include other populations (e.g., children with ADHD, traumatic brain injury). Research on FCT has focused on severe challenging behaviors such as aggression and self-injurious behavior (e.g., Casey & Merical, 2006; Kurtz et al., 2003), stereotyped behavior (e.g., Durand & Carr, 1987; Wacker et al., 1990), and a variety of communication disorders (e.g., Carr & Kemp, 1989; Durand & Crimmins, 1987). Intervention has been conducted in group homes (e.g., Durand & Kishi, 1987), schools (e.g., Reeve & Carr, 2000), and vocational settings (e.g., Bird et al., 1989) (see Table 33.1).

CONTRAINDICATIONS OF THE TREATMENT

Because of its reliance on communication, those individuals who are in environments that are relatively unresponsive to their needs and requests will often be frustrated in their attempts to gain access to preferred reinforcers. Therefore, major

TABLE 33.1 Evidence-Based Applications

Parameter	Examples
Target behaviors	
Self-injurious behavior	Casey & Merical (2006)
Aggression	Mildon et al. (2004)
Tantrums	Mancil et al. (2006)
Stereotyped behavior	Durand & Carr (1987)
Off-task	Flood & Wilder (2002)
Enhance prelinguistic behavior	Tait et al. (2004)
Echolalia and perseverative speech	Ross (2002)
Inappropriate sexual behavior	Fyffe et al. (2004)
Populations	
Attention-deficit hyperactivity disorder (ADHD)	Flood & Wilder (2002)
Autism spectrum disorders	Brown et al. (2000)
Developmental delay	Dunlap, et al. (2006); Wacker, et al. (2005) ; Winborn et al. (2002)
Severe cognitive impairment	Bailey et al. (2002)
Traumatic brain injury	Fyffe et al. (2004)
Settings	
Home	Tait et al. (2004)
School	Hagopian et al. (2001); Peck Peterson et al. (2005)
Residential	Lindauer et al. (2002)
Clinic	Kurtz et al. (2003)

environmental modifications are required prior to any attempt to implement FCT.

HOW DOES THE TREATMENT WORK?

The mechanism behind the success of FCT is assumed to rely on *functional equivalence* (Durand, 1990). In other words, behaviors maintained by a particular reinforcer (e.g., escape from work) are replaced by other behaviors if these new behaviors serve the same function and are more efficient at gaining the desired reinforcers. Using communication as the replacement behavior provides an added benefit because of its ability to recruit natural communities of the desired reinforcers (Durand, 1999). One effect of this view of behavior problems is the suggestion that these behaviors are not just responses that need to be reduced or eliminated. This perspective reminds us that attempting to eliminate these behaviors through some reductive technique would leave these individuals with no way of accessing their desired reinforcers and therefore you could anticipate that other maladaptive behaviors would take their place (also called *symptom substitution* or *response covariation*).

EVIDENCE FOR THE EFFECTIVENESS OF FCT

Empirical support for the success of FCT is growing (Halle, Ostrosky, & Hemmeter, 2006; Mancil, 2006), and this approach is one of the few skills-focused interventions for autism described as having "extensive support from initial efficacy studies" (Smith, Scahill, Dawson, Guthrie, Lord, Odom, Rogers, & Wagner, 2007, p. 363). Researchers are exploring the boundaries of this intervention approach through the study of maintenance (e.g., Bird et al., 1989; Durand, 1999; Durand & Carr, 1991; Durand & Carr, 1992), the role of response efficiency (Horner, Sprague, O'Brien, & Heathfield, 1990) as well as a variety of other important parameters (Brown, Wacker, Derby, Peck, Richman, Sasso, Knutson, & Harding, 2000; Hagopian, Kuhn, Long, &

Rush, 2005; Kelley, Lerman, & Van Camp, 2002; Lerman, Kelley, Vorndran, & LaRue, 2002).

With growing evidence of the value of this intervention approach in reducing a variety of problem behaviors, it is important to evaluate how FCT compares with other interventions. Hanley and colleagues, for example, compared the effectiveness of FCT with noncontingent reinforcement (NCR) on the multiple behavior problems of two children (Hanley, Piazza, Fisher, Contrucci, & Maglieri, 1997). They found that both interventions initially reduced problem behaviors, but that the participants demonstrated a preference for FCT.

An important aspect of FCT—its usefulness outside of specially designed settings—has also been investigated. Durand and Carr (1992) and Durand (1999) found that not only could individuals be taught to communicate to reduce their behavior problems, their requests could be adapted (at times using alternative communication systems) so that they were effective outside of school and with untrained community members. The research to date suggests that we can teach people with behavior problems ways of communicating that will be understood even by people who do not have training in the area of communication difficulties or intellectual disabilities.

STEP-BY-STEP PROCEDURES

Table 33.2 illustrates the basic steps used to assess behavior and conduct FCT. These steps can often be complicated, and readers are referred to the Further Reading section for more detailed instructions.

Step 1: Assess the Function of Behavior

In order to assess the function of a problem behavior, the antecedents and consequences of that behavior need to be identified. Challenging behaviors are often found to serve one or more of the following functions: (1) to avoid or escape nonpreferred stimuli (e.g., difficult demands; nonpreferred staff); (2) to access preferred stimuli (e.g., toys, attention); or (3) to increase sensory stimulation. Once the purpose of a targeted behavior is understood, individuals can be taught to request the variables previously obtained by the challenging behavior.

There are a number of functional assessment strategies that are useful for determining the function of behavior, including A-B-C charts, functional analyses, and a variety of rating scales. We always begin with informal observations and interviews of significant others, but we continue the process using *multiple forms of assessment*, including the Motivation Assessment Scale (MAS) and structured observations in the individuals' environment. The MAS is a questionnaire that we can give to teachers, paraprofessionals, family members, or anyone else who has a great deal of contact with the individual (Durand & Crimmins, 1988, 1992). The MAS asks questions that determine where, when, and under what conditions problem behaviors occur and determines their functions. Information from the MAS, along with other forms of functional behavioral assessments, is used to design plans for reducing the behavior problems.

A functional analysis—manipulating aspects of the environment to assess behavior change—is frequently cited as the best method of determining the function of a behavior problem (Mace, 1994). However, there are also a number of issues to consider prior to conducting this type of assessment (Durand, 1997). One issue is *accessibility to manipulation*. There are certain influences that you cannot or would not manipulate or change in order to perform a functional analysis. Factors such as some illnesses, disrupted family life, and chromosomal aberrations can certainly affect behavior problems, but they cannot or should not be turned on and off in order to assess their influence.

Another concern involves the *ethics* of conducting a functional analysis. There are other influences that you could manipulate, but you may not want to change if they will result in an increase in challenging behavior. In many instances, deliberately increasing a severe behavior problem in order to assess it (e.g., by reinforcing challenging behavior) can be questioned on ethical grounds. In these cases, assessment that does not involve manipulation (and subsequent increases in challenging behavior) would

TABLE 33.2 Step-by-Step Instructions for Functional Communication Training

Steps	Description
1. Assess the function of behavior	Use two or more functional assessment techniques to determine what variables are maintaining the problem behavior.
2. Select the communication modality	Identify how you want the individual to communicate with others (e.g., verbally, through alternative communication strategies).
3. Create teaching situations	Identify situations in the environment that are triggers for problem behavior (e.g., difficult tasks) and use these as the settings for teaching the alternative responses.
4. Prompt communication	Prompt the alternative communication in the setting where you want it to occur. Use the least intrusive prompt necessary.
5. Fade prompts	Quickly fade the prompts, insuring that no problem behaviors occur during training.
6. Teach new communicative responses	When possible, teach a variety of alternative communicative responses that can serve the same function (e.g., saying "Help me" or "I don't understand").
7. Environmental modification	When appropriate, changes in the environment—such as improving student-task match in school—should be implemented.

be recommended (for a more detailed discussion of these issues, see Durand, 1993).

Step 2: Select the Communication Modality

The type of response to encourage from the individual needs to be determined. If the individual already has some facility in one mode of communication (e.g., verbal, signing), then that mode should be considered for functional communication training. Usually, if an individual has been unsuccessful in learning to communicate effectively after extensive verbal language training, then the communication modality to be used should either be signing or symbolic. If the person has also been unsuccessful with sign language training (e.g., has not learned to sign or uses "sloppy" and incomprehensible signs), we recommend symbolic communication training, at least initially. Symbolic communication training can involve the use of picture books, tokens with messages written on them, or other assistive devices (e.g., vocal output devices). This form of communication training has the advantage of being relatively easy to teach, and is universally recognizable.

Step 3: Create Teaching Situations

The environment is arranged to create opportunities for communication (e.g., putting an obstacle in the way of a person trying to open a door and prompting him or her to ask for assistance). This use of *incidental teaching* (McGee, Morrier, & Daly, 1999)—arranging the environment to establish situations that elicit interest and that are used as teaching opportunities—is an important part of successful communication training. Using the person's interest in some interaction, whether it be a desire to stop working on a difficult task or to elicit the attention of an adult, is a very powerful tool in teaching generalized communication. As soon as possible, training trials are interspersed throughout the individual's day where appropriate. Generalization and maintenance of intervention effects may be facilitated by using the criterion environment (i.e., where you want the person to communicate) as the training environment. With the typical model of teaching skills in a separate setting (e.g., in the speech therapist's office), once the response is learned you need to encourage the performance of that behavior in settings where you want it to occur (e.g., in the cafeteria). By beginning training in the natural or criterion setting, extensive programming for generalization is not necessary because it will be occurring where you want it to occur. In addition, obstacles to maintenance can be immediately identified when teaching in the criterion environment (e.g., are the consequences being provided in that setting going to maintain the new response).

Step 4: Prompt Communication

Teaching individuals to communicate as a replacement for their challenging behavior requires a range of sophisticated language training techniques (Durand, Mapstone, & Youngblade, 1999). A multiphase prompting and prompt fading procedure is used to teach the new communicative response. Prompts are introduced as necessary, then faded as quickly as possible. Some learners "negatively resist" attempts to teach important skills (e.g., individual screams and kicks), others "positively resist" (e.g., individual laughs and giggles instead of working), and still others "passively resist" (e.g., individual does not look at materials, makes no response). When an individual kicks, screams, and rips up work materials whenever they are presented, or passively ignores efforts to get them to attend to a task, teaching becomes a major challenge and learning becomes highly unlikely.

One procedure we have used for these types of problems is to teach the individual to request assistance (e.g., "Help me") or a brief break from work. Often, the problem behaviors appear to be attempts to avoid or escape from unpleasant situations. It makes sense, then, that if the individual is taught to appropriately request assistance *and receives it*, then the task will seem easier and problem behaviors should be reduced. Similarly, if an individual has been working for some time on a task and is allowed to ask for a break *and receives it*, then this individual's problem behavior should also be reduced

Step 5: Fade Prompts

We begin reducing the individual's reliance on prompts by fading back on the most intrusive assistance being used. In the case of teaching a student to point to a picture book to make a request, we do this by going from a full physical prompt to partial prompts (e.g., just touching his hand), to gestural prompts (e.g., motioning to prompt his hands), to, finally, only the verbal prompt, "What do you want?" Throughout his

training we rely heavily on delayed prompting. After several trials, we would intersperse a trial with a delayed prompt (i.e., we waited approximately 5 seconds), to see if the individual would respond without the next level of prompt. For example, if a student had been responding to just a touch of his hand to point to a picture, we would make a gesture as if we were going to prompt him, and then wait 5 seconds.

We do not wait until responding is extremely stable to move on to the next level of prompting. In other words, the person does not have to be correctly responding to say, 9 out of 10 prompts for 2 weeks for us to move to the next step. We would attempt to move to the next step if the individual was successful at a step for three to five consecutive responses. We do this in order to prevent the person from becoming prompt dependent (i.e., too reliant on prompts to respond).

Training progresses quickly over several weeks to the point where the individual can communicate with no external prompting. As is typical in our training, behavior improves most dramatically as soon as the individual begins to make requests without prompts.

Step 6: Teach New Communicative Responses

Once successful, intervention continues by introducing new communicative forms (e.g., requests for food, music, work), reintroducing work demands, expanding the settings in which communication is encouraged to include the whole day, and introducing new staff into the training program.

Step 7: Environmental Modification

Recommendations are often made concerning environmental and curricula changes. For example, it can be useful to consider curricular changes for a student who is attempting to escape from academic tasks. However, we typically approach these types of changes with considerable caution. The fear is that we will create such an artificial environment that the student may not be able to adapt to new challenges or new environments. The goal of FCT is to teach the student a form of coping skill to be able to appropriately respond to new and unexpected situations (e.g., a new teacher, more difficult work). Therefore, we view environmental modifications as a form of short-term prevention strategy rather than the main programmatic intervention.

PREDICTING SUCCESSFUL OUTCOMES

We have identified a number of factors that seem to influence the success or failure of functional communication training. These elements of training appear to be necessary conditions for initial reductions in behavior, generalization across people and stimulus conditions, and/or maintenance across time.

Response match—matching the communicative behavior to the function of the challenging behavior. In other words, the new trained response should evoke the same consequences as the targeted challenging behavior.

Response success—whether or not significant others respond to the trained communicative responses. Simply engaging in these communicative acts (i.e., making responses that match the function of challenging behavior) without a subsequent response by others will not result in reductions in challenging behavior.

Response efficiency—whether or not the response is more effective and efficient in getting the student the reinforcers he or she obtained with his or her problem behavior. In a series of studies, Horner and his colleagues examined this aspect of functional communication training (Horner & Day, 1991; Horner, Sprague, O'Brien, & Heathfield, 1990).

Response acceptability—whether or not the response is acceptable to significant others. If the new communicative response is seen as unacceptable in community settings, then others will not respond appropriately and the desired consequences will not be obtained.

Response recognizability—whether or not the response can be recognized, especially by others who may not be highly trained. If the

trained response is not easily recognizable by significant others in the environment, then these other people will not respond, and challenging behavior will not be reduced.

Further Reading

Carr, E. G., Levin, L, McConnachie, G., Carlson, J. I., Kemp, D. C., & Smith, C. E. (1994). *Communication-based intervention for problem behavior: A user's guide for producing positive change.* Baltimore, MD: Paul H. Brookes.

Durand, V. M. (1990). *Severe behavior problems: A functional communication training approach.* New York: Guilford.

Durand, V. M., & Hieneman, M. (2008). *Helping parents with challenging children: Positive family intervention—facilitator's guide.* New York: Oxford University Press.

Durand, V. M., & Hieneman, M. (2008). *Helping parents with challenging children: Positive family intervention—workbook.* New York: Oxford University Press.

References

Azrin, N. H., Besalel, V. A., & Wisotzek, I. E. (1982). Treatment of self-injury by a reinforcement plus interruption procedure. *Analysis and Intervention in Developmental Disabilities, 2,* 105–113.

Bailey, J., McComas, J., Benavides, C., Lovascz, C. (2002). Functional assessment in a residential setting: Identifying an effective communicative replacement response for aggressive behavior. *Journal of Developmental and Physical Disabilities, 14*(4) 353–369.

Bird, F., Dores, P. A., Moniz, D., & Robinson, J. (1989). Reducing severe aggressive and self-injurious behaviors with functional communication training: Direct, collateral and generalized results. *American Journal on Mental Retardation, 94,* 37–48.

Brown, K. A., Wacker, D. P., Derby, K. M., Peck, S. M., Richman, D. M., Sasso, G. M., et al. (2000). Evaluating the effects of functional communication training in the presence and absence of establishing operations. *Journal of Applied Behavior Analysis, 33,* 53–71.

Carr, E. G., & Durand, V. M. (1985). Reducing behavior problems through functional communication training. *Journal of Applied Behavior Analysis, 18,* 111–126.

Carr, E. G., & Kemp, D. C. (1989). Functional equivalence of autistic leading and communicative pointing: Analysis and treatment. *Journal of Autism and Developmental Disorders, 19,* 561–578.

Casey, S. D., & Merical, C. L. (2006). The use of functional communication training without additional treatment procedures in an inclusive school setting. *Behavioral Disorders, 32*(1), 46–54.

Corte, H. E., Wolfe, M. M., & Locke, B. J. (1971). A comparison of procedures for eliminating self-injurious behavior of retarded adolescents. *Journal of Applied Behavior Analysis, 4,* 201–213.

Dunlap, G., Ester, T., Langhans, S., & Fox, L. (2006). Functional communication training with toddlers in home environments. *Journal of Early Intervention, 28*(2), 81–96.

Durand, V.M. (1990). Severe behavior problems: A functional communication training approach. New York: Guilford.

Durand, V. M. (1993). Functional assessment and functional analysis. In M. D. Smith (Ed.), *Behavior modification for exceptional children and youth* (pp. 38–60). Baltimore, MD: Andover Medical Press.

Durand, V. M. (1997). Functional analysis: Should we? *Journal of Special Education, 31,* 105–106.

Durand, V.M. (1999). Functional communication training using assistive devices: Recruiting natural communities of reinforcement. *Journal of Applied Behavior Analysis, 32,* 247–267.

Durand, V. M., & Carr, E. G. (1987). Social influences on "self-stimulatory" behavior: Analysis and treatment application. *Journal of Applied Behavior Analysis, 20,* 119–132.

Durand, V. M., & Carr, E. G. (1989). Operant learning methods with chronic schizophrenia and autism: Aberrant behavior. In J. L. Matson (Ed.), *Chronic schizophrenia and autism: Issues in diagnosis, assessment, and treatment* (pp. 231–273). New York: Springer.

Durand, V. M., & Carr, E. G. (1991). Functional communication training to reduce challenging behavior: Maintenance and application in new settings. *Journal of Applied Behavior Analysis, 24,* 251–264.

Durand, V. M., & Carr, E. G. (1992). An analysis of maintenance following functional communication training. *Journal of Applied Behavior Analysis, 25,* 777–794.

Durand, V. M., & Crimmins, D. B. (1987). Assessment and treatment of psychotic speech in an autistic child. *Journal of Autism and Developmental Disorders, 17,* 17–28.

Durand, V. M., & Crimmins, D. B. (1988). Identifying the variables maintaining self-injurious behavior. *Journal of Autism and Developmental Disorders, 18,* 99–117.

Durand, V. M., & Crimmins, D. B. (1992). *The Motivation Assessment Scale (MAS) Administration Guide.* Topeka, KS: Monaco & Associates.

Durand, V. M., & Kishi, G. (1987). Reducing severe behavior problems among persons with dual sensory impairments: An evaluation of a technical assistance model. *Journal of the Association for Persons with Severe Handicaps, 12,* 2–10.

Durand, V. M., Mapstone, E., & Youngblade, L. (1999). The role of communicative partners. In J. Downing (Ed.), *Teaching communication skills to students with severe disabilities within general education classrooms* (pp. 139–155). Baltimore, MD: Paul H. Brookes.

Durand, V. M., & Merges, E. (2001). Functional communication training: A contemporary behavior analytic intervention for problem behaviors. *Focus on Autism and Other Developmental Disabilities, 16,* 110–119.

Flood, W. A., & Wilder, D. A. (2002). Antecedent assessment and assessment-based treatment of off-task behavior in a child diagnosed with attention deficit-hyperactivity disorder (ADHD). *Education and Treatment of Children, 25*(3), 331–338.

Fyffe, C. E., Kahng, S. W., Fittro, E., & Russell, D. (2004). Functional analysis and treatment of inappropriate sexual behavior. *Journal of Applied Behavior Analysis, 37*(3), 401–404.

Halle, J. W., Ostrosky, M. M., & Hemmeter, M. L. (2006). Functional communication training: A strategy for ameliorating challenging behavior. In R. J. McCauley & M. E. Fey (Eds.), *Treatment of Language Disorders in Children* (pp. 509–548). Baltimore, MD: Paul H. Brookes.

Hagopian, L. P., Wilson, D. M., & Wilder, D. A. (2001). Assessment and treatment of problem behavior maintained by escape from attention and access to tangible items. *Journal of Applied Behavior Analysis, 34*(2), 229–232.

Hagopian, L. P., Kuhn, S. A. C., Long, E. S., & Rush, K. S. (2005). Schedule thinning following communication training using competing stimuli to enhance tolerance to decrements in reinforcer density. *Journal of Applied Behavior Analysis, 38*(2), 177–193.

Hanley, G. P., Piazza, C. C., Fisher, W. W., Contrucci, S. A., & Maglieri, K. A. (1997). Evaluation of client preference for function-based treatment packages. *Journal of Applied Behavior Analysis, 30,* 459–473.

Horner, R. H., & Day, H. M. (1991). The effects of response efficiency on functionally equivalent competing behaviors. *Journal of Applied Behavior Analysis, 24,* 719–732.

Horner, R. H., Sprague, J. R., O'Brien, M., & Heathfield, L. T. (1990). The role of response efficiency in the reduction of problem behaviors through functional equivalence training: A case study. *Journal of the Association for Persons with Severe Handicaps, 15,* 91–97.

Johnson, W. L., Baumeister, A. A., Penland, M. J., & Inwald, C. (1982). Experimental analysis of self-injurious, stereotypic, and collateral behavior of retarded persons: Effects of overcorrection and reinforcement of alternative responding. *Analysis and Intervention in Developmental Disabilities, 2,* 41–66.

Kelley, M. E., Lerman, D. C., & Van Camp, C. M. (2002). The effects of competing reinforcement schedules on the acquisition of functional communication. *Journal of Applied Behavior Analysis, 35,* 59–63.

Kurtz, P. F., Chin, M. D., Huete, J. M., Tarbox, R. S. F., O'Connor, J. T., Paclawskyj, T.R., et al. (2003). Functional analysis and treatment of self-injurious behavior in young children: A summary of 30 cases. *Journal of Applied Behavior Analysis, 36*(2), 205–219.

Lerman, D. C., Kelley, M. E., Vorndran, C. M., Kuhn, S. A. C., & LaRue, R. H. Jr. (2002). Reinforcement magnitude and responding during treatment with differential reinforcement. *Journal of Applied Behavior Analysis, 35,* 29–48.

Lindauer, S. E., Zarcone, J. R., Richman, D. M., & Schroeder, S. R. (2002). A comparison of multiple reinforcer assessments to identify the function of maladaptive behavior. *Journal of Applied Behavior Analysis, 35* (3), 299–303.

Luiselli, J. K. (1992). Assessment and treatment of self-injury in a deaf-blind child. *Journal of Developmental and Physical Disabilities, 4,* 219–226.

Mace, F. C. (1994). The significance and future of functional analysis methodologies. *Journal of Applied Behavior Analysis, 27,* 385–392.

Mancil, G. R. (2006). Functional communication training: A review of the literature related to children with autism. *Education and Training in Developmental Disabilities, 41*(3), 213–224.

Mancil, G. R., Conroy, M. A., Nakao, T., & Alter, P. J. (2006). Functional communication training in the natural environment: A pilot investigation with a young child with autism spectrum disorder. *Education and Treatment of Children, 29*(4), 615–633.

McGee, G. G., Morrier, M. J., & Daly, T. (1999). An incidental teaching approach to early intervention for toddlers with autism. *Journal of the Association for Persons with Severe Handicaps, 24,* 133–146.

Mildon, R. L., Moore, D. W., & Dixon, R. S. (2004). Combining noncontingent escape and functional communication training as treatment for negatively reinforced disruptive behavior. *Journal of Positive Behavior Interventions, 6*(2), 92–102.

Peck Peterson, S. M., Caniglia, C., Royster, A. J., Macfarlane, E., Plowman, K., Baird, S. J., & Wu, N. (2005). Blending functional communication training and choice making to improve task engagement and decrease problem behaviour. *Educational Psychology, 25*(2–3), 257–274.

Reeve, C. E., & Carr, E. G. (2000). Prevention of severe behavior problems in children with developmental disorders. *Journal of Positive Behavior Interventions, 2*(3), 144–160.

Ross, D. E. (2002). Replacing faulty conversational exchanges for children with autism by establishing a functionally equivalent alternative response. *Education and Training in Mental Retardation and Developmental Disabilities, 37*(4), 343–362.

Smith, T., Scahill, L., Dawson, G., Guthrie, D., Lord, C., Odom, S., Rogers, S., & Wagner, A. (2007). Designing research studies on psychosocial interventions in autism. *Journal of Autism and Developmental Disorders, 37*(2), 354–366.

Tait, K., Sigafoos, J., Woodyatt, G., O'Reilly, M. F., & Lancioni, G. E. (2004). Evaluating parent use of functional communication training to replace and enhance prelinquistic behaviours in six children with developmental and physical disabilities. *Disability and Rehabilitation: An International, Multidisciplinary Journal, 26*(21–22), 1241–1254.

Tate, B. G., & Baroff, G. S. (1966). Aversive control of self-injurious behavior in a psychotic boy. *Behavior Research and Therapy, 4,* 281–287.

Wacker, D. P., Berg, W. K., Harding, J. W., Barretto, A., Rankin, B., & Ganzer, J. (2005). Treatment effectiveness, stimulus generalization, and acceptability to parents of functional communication training. *Educational Psychology, 25*(203), 233–256.

Wacker, D. P., Steege, M. W., Northup, J., Sasso, G., Berg, W., Reimers, T., et al. (1990). A component analysis of functional communication training across three topographies of severe behavior problems. *Journal of Applied Behavior Analysis, 23,* 417–429.

Winborn, L., Wacker, D. P., Richman, D. M., Asmus, J., & Geier, D. (2002). Assessment of mand selection for functional communication training packages. *Journal of Applied Behavior Analysis, 35*(3), 295–298.

Wolf, M. M., Risley, T. R., & Mees, H. (1964). Application of operant conditioning procedures to the behavior problems of an autistic child. *Behavior Research and Therapy, 1,* 305–312.

34 FUNCTIONAL SELF-INSTRUCTION TRAINING TO PROMOTE GENERALIZED LEARNING

Frank R. Rusch and Douglas Kostewicz

Over the past 15 years, educators and researchers have made great strides in their ability to provide individuals with diverse levels of disabilities the use of functional self-instructional strategies. Without the constant direction of others, individuals using these strategies rely upon their own abilities to perform a variety of skills independently, under new circumstances, and at different points in time. Maybe most importantly, these strategies allow individuals to become causal agents in their lives instead of the targets of others employed to direct and manage their behaviors and routines.

Research suggests a number of traditional self-management strategy features that, when combined with multiple examples during training, promote a level of learning far exceeding results found in previous literature that use these strategies and single examples. Educators typically use single examples when teaching the strategy to individuals with disabilities. For example, when teaching young children to put on their shoes, parents or teachers typically use one example—the shoes that the child is wearing. New evidence suggests that teaching the child to put on another pair of shoes, combined with self-instructions, will result in the child putting on shoes used during training as well as shoes not used during training. Typically, an individual's generalized learning results from training that includes more than one example of the type of problem situation that the strategy is directed toward. Rarely, however, has training been reported whereby multiple tasks (e.g., more than one pair of shoes) or behaviors are employed while teaching the individual traditional self-management strategies.

A few investigations have reported generalization across untrained tasks. These investigations have used traditional self-management (self-instructional) strategies with multiple examples of the problem or tasks to be performed. One of the first examples of promoting generalization across untrained tasks was reported by Martin et al. (1982). In this investigation, Martin et al. utilized self-instructional strategies to teach three adults with moderate mental retardation to prepare and cook five complex meals. One of the unintended effects of using multiple meals to study the effects of self-instruction was the spillover effect produced by using more than one meal during training. Participants learned to prepare untrained meals faster and with fewer errors. Data collected during one of the baselines, for example, indicated that one of the participants learned to prepare meals independent of learning self-instruction. Adding self-instruction appeared to promote additional task acquisition; the use of more than one example appeared to promote generalization across untrained meals.

Hughes and Rusch (1989) studied the effects of self-instruction and the use of multiple examples during training. In this investigation, employees with severe mental retardation were required to solve problems related to those typically encountered in work settings (e.g., determining what to do when work-related materials are depleted). Hughes and Rusch identified an analytic model for identifying "typical" problems and classifying these problems based on similarities (i.e., shared stimulus properties), which allowed the employees to identify similar solutions (i.e., responses to problems). These researchers also identified a model for evaluating acquisition of self-instruction when using one versus multiple problems during the functional self-instruction training as well as to similar and untrained (generalization) problems. Hughes and Rusch found that the combined effects of using multiple examples when teaching self-instruction produced generalized responding to similar as well as topographically dissimilar problems. Hughes (1992) subsequently went on to determine if four residents with severe mental retardation could be taught to solve typical problems that arose while completing daily, residential chores in their respective residences. Again, the training approach combined using a self-instructional strategy with multiple examples that defined typical, but not all, problems. The results of this study complemented those reported by Hughes and Rusch (1992).

Utilizing multiple examples (also referred to as "multiple exemplars") alone has been reported to be an effective approach to producing task acquisition as well as generalized responding in the applied behavioral literature. Horner, Jones, and Williams (1985), for example, taught three individuals to cross streets using multiple exemplars. The primary strategy focused on teaching students to cross more than one intersection while also measuring their ability to cross untrained intersections after introducing additional intersections. All three students demonstrated the ability to cross untrained and more difficult intersections (intersections with lights and traffic) after instruction on less difficult intersections (intersections with stop signs and little or no traffic).

A primary difference exists between the multiple exemplar approach introduced by Horner and his colleagues versus the self-instructional approach reported by Rusch and his colleagues. While the multiple exemplar approach relies primarily upon external mediation strategies that orient the student to the stimulus properties of the problem to be solved, a self-instructional approach directs the person to identify that a problem exists and that the problem demands a solution that can be guided by the individual. The importance of the self-instruction approach to learning is that the individual learns to guide current and future behavior to similar and dissimilar problem situations. Clearly, teaching someone to rely upon and in effect develop their own ability to independently perform has potential advantages that far outweigh an approach that relies upon others to direct behavior, even given the positive outcomes historically associated with external mediation.

In response to an exhaustive review of the literature related to employment outcomes and cognitive strategies, Rusch, Hughes, and Wilson (1995) introduced a problem-solving model that proposed six steps that include self-instruction combined with incorporating the multiple exemplar strategies introduced by Horner and his colleagues. Although more recent reviews of the literature exist (e.g., Mechling, 2007; Storey, 2007), these reviews do not report attempts to promote generalization across tasks, such as problems that typically confront individuals on a day-by-day basis or problems that confront students in typical classrooms, apart from those problems that define the training paradigm.

The major components of the functional self-instruction model comprise the following steps:

1. Selecting an array of examples (responses) a student may be required to execute in an environment
2. Classifying these responses into teaching sets based on a functional analysis
3. Dividing members of the teaching set into responses that serve as training examples (typically two) and responses that serve as generalization probes (typically more than two)
4. Teaching self-instruction using the training examples
5. Evaluating (a) the effects of training on the trained and untrained examples (i.e., generalization probes) as well as (b) the student's ability to use self-instructional statements
6. Withdrawing training based on performance (Rusch et al.,1995)

In this chapter, the functional self-instruction training model we introduce primarily draws upon work that has been reported in employment settings. The competitive employment environment is a dynamic, fluid setting. An employee may have to respond to a variety of stimulus conditions, including personnel, materials, coworkers, supervisors and consumer demands. For employees to maintain their employment, they must be able to perform tasks that have been taught as well as new tasks that may be assigned after the initial training period (cf. Rusch, 2008). It is impractical and impossible to teach each and every response required to each and every stimulus situation that may arise in a work environment. Consequently, exploring new instructional strategies that promote generalized learning is tantamount to the long-term success of individuals remaining employed.

Functional self-instruction training is a new approach to facilitating competent performance. This self-instructional training approach is referred to as "functional" because the approach relies on our ability to identify an array of representative stimulus conditions that can be selected to serve as training examples (Hughes & Rusch, 1989). This array of stimulus conditions defines functional responses that result in correct responses that serve as solutions. For example, a maid who is attempting to vacuum a rug and an obstacle is in the way (the stimulus condition) would need to move the obstacle which serves as the solution. The model is based upon empirical research that has shown that combining multiple exemplars (moving a different obstacle) with self-instructions promote one's ability to respond more reliably to known and unknown situations that may and typically do arise in diverse settings (a maid moving new and different obstacles). Table 34.1 provides a list of studies that contain empirical evidence for the functional self-instruction training model outlined below.

Table 34.2 provides an overview of the functional self-instruction training model. Additionally, a social behavior example is presented that illustrates the model in an educational context.

STEP 1: SELECT AN ARRAY OF EXAMPLES

Identifying typical social situations that may occur in schools requires the teacher to identify the range of situations that the student is likely to encounter. Because it is not practical to teach responses to all possible social initiations, for example, representative examples of the "array of examples" and typical responses are selected as teaching examples. These examples are selected based upon a survey of typical responses. For example, when students enter classrooms they are likely to encounter greetings from other students, teachers, as well as others who may be present (e.g., a teaching aide). These can encompass a wide variety depending on the greeter, time of day, and individual receiving the greeting. Additionally, when the same students enter the hallway in transition to another class they also encounter a range of possible greetings, some similar and some varied. For example, the student may encounter greetings in multiple settings across the school day that include "hi," "hello," "whatup," "how's it going?," "dude," and so on. Once the list of possible examples is known (the stimulus situations), then the correct response(s) to each of the stimulus situations is identified. These representative examples (multiple exemplars) serve as teaching examples as well as measures of generalized learning.

STEP 2: CLASSIFY RESPONSES INTO TEACHING SETS

Identifying responses (social greetings) to specific stimulus situations ("hi," "whatup") requires a traditional functional analysis to determine the response operations required to satisfy the social act. For example, after teaching a student to respond to "hi" and "whatup" by replying "hey," you would expect the student to respond "hey" to someone who says, "dude"—a variation of the greeting discriminative stimulus. We expect the student to "generalize" the use of a learned greeting to different, but similar stimulus conditions. As many as 10 situations should be selected from the full range (array) to serve as the teaching set.

STEP 3: DIVIDE MEMBERS OF THE TEACHING SET INTO TRAINING EXAMPLES THAT WILL SERVE AS GENERALIZATION EXAMPLES

Because the goal is to produce generalized responding, we must determine if similar responses

TABLE 34.1   Evidence-Based Practices

- Wilson, P. G., Rusch, F. R., & Lee, S. (1992). Strategies to increase exercise-report correspondence by boys with moderate mental retardation: Collateral changes in intention-exercise correspondence. *Journal of Applied Behavior Analysis, 25,* 681–690.

- Rusch, F. R., Hughes, C., & Wilson, P. G. (1995). Utilizing cognitive strategies in the acquisition of employment skills. In W. O'Donohue & L. Krasner (Eds.). *Handbook of psychological skills training clinical techniques and applications.* (pp. 363–382). New York: Pergamon Press.

- Rusch, F. R., Morgan, T. K., Martin, J. E., Riva, M., & Agran, M. (1985). Competitive employment: Teaching mentally retarded adults self-instructional strategies. *Applied Research in Mental Retardation, 6,* 389–407.

- Rusch, F. R., Martin, J. E., & White, D. M. (1985). Competitive employment: Teaching mentally retarded employees to maintain their work behavior. *Education and Training of the Mentally Retarded, 20,* 182–189.

TABLE 34.2   Model for Teaching Functional Self-Instruction Utilizing Multiple Exemplars

Step 1: Select an array of examples (responses)

1. Survey setting.
2. Determine range of situations (stimulus) that one is likely to encounter.
3. Determine the correct responses to stimuli.
4. Select representative examples from among available stimulus situations.

Step 2: Classify examples into teaching sets.

1. Conduct traditional functional analysis of response requirements.
2. Determine similarity among responses based on functional analysis.
3. Classify related responses into teaching sets based on common operations.

Step 3: Divide members of the teaching set into training examples that will serve as generalization examples.

1. Divide members of each teaching set equally.
2. Assign members to groups of responses to be trained or to serve as generalization probes (assignment should be random).

Step 4: Teach self-instruction.

1. Use teaching sequence
   a. Teacher provides rationale for teaching and tells student to respond as if in response to instructional demands.
   b. Teacher models correct responses while self-instructing aloud, using multiple exemplars.
   c. Student performs same responses while teacher instructs aloud, then whispering, and then mouthing.
   d. Student performs response while self-instructing aloud, then whispering, and then mouthing.
   e. Teacher provides corrective feedback and/or prompting if student does not perform correct responses.
2. Teach self-instruction statements
   a. Statement of situation (e.g., "he said 'hi' to me"),
   b. Statement of generic response (e.g., "say something back"),
   c. Statement of specific response (e.g., "hey"),
   d. Self-report (e.g., "I said hi"),
   e. Self-reinforce (e.g., "I did a good job").
3. Adjust training time.
   a. Determine student's ability level.
   b. Adjust number and length of instructional sessions to student ability level.

Step 5: Evaluate the effects of training.

1. Take repeated measures of self-instruction steps verbalized and responses to multiple exemplars made during training.
2. Take repeated measures of responses to untrained problems (generalization probes).

Step 6: Withdraw training based on student performance.

1. Establish range of acceptable behavior within setting.
2. Determine performance criteria.
3. Systematically withdraw training.

that are acquired under similar stimulus conditions will also occur under dissimilar stimulus conditions. In order to provide an assessment of a student's generalized responding across related but novel (social) situations not encountered during training, members of the teaching set should be randomly assigned to a group of stimulus situations to be presented and used for training and a group of stimulus situations to be used as generalization probes. The skills to be taught are selected based on situations that students are likely to experience throughout their school day. For example, situations involving "hey" and "hello" may make up part of the teaching set, while other greetings such as "dude" and "whatup" would be reserved for generalization examples.

STEP 4: TEACH SELF-INSTRUCTION

The fourth step is to teach self-instruction. The success of self-instruction appears to be related to three factors: (1) training sequence used, (2) self-instruction statements taught, and (3) length of training time (Rusch et al., 1995). The training sequence starts with the teacher providing a rationale for instruction and is followed with the teacher modeling the correct response using self-instruction. The student is then asked to execute the same response (responding to a greeting) while the teacher instructs aloud. Several opportunities are provided for practice with the student performing the same responses while self-instructing aloud. Next, the teacher provides corrective feedback and/or additional prompting if the student does not execute the correct response (i.e., saying "hi" in response to "hi, Bob").

Self-instruction includes actual verbal statements made by the student that guide the student's response. Five different statements need to be taught, including:

1. A statement of the situation ("he said 'hi' to me")
2. A statement of generic response ("say something back")
3. A statement of specific response (say "hey")
4. A self-report statement ("I said hey")

5. A self-reinforcement statement (e.g., "I did a good job")

A major limitation of self-instructional training is that the teaching strategy starts by asking the student to talk out loud followed by talking quietly and eventually talking to oneself silently. If a student is to perform a socially valued response in an integrated school, community or employment setting, that response should be performed with minimal impact on the student's social status in the integrated setting. When the student reliably produces the sequence of verbal statements out loud, the student should then whisper the sequence of self-instructions and eventually "mouth" the sequence. This instructional transition should take place in a private place. The final step would include the individual performing the target task and not mouthing the self-instructions. The final step requires that the individual "think" about what is to be done.

Finally, the number and length of instructional sessions is based on data collected on learning to independently produce the verbal sequence that will lead to the student eventually "thinking" of the self-instructions.

STEP 5: EVALUATE THE EFFECTS OF TRAINING

In order to isolate the point at which a student learns to self-instruct, the teacher needs to take repeated measures of self-instruction verbalizations and responses to multiple exemplars made during training. Additionally, in order to assess generalization, repeated measures of the responses to untrained problems (generalization probes) must also be taken (Rusch et al., 1995).

STEP 6: WITHDRAW TRAINING BASED ON STUDENT PERFORMANCE

The final step in the model is to withdraw training and evaluate the effect of training withdrawal. Withdrawal of training should be based on the frequency of correct responses that is within the range of acceptable behavior. The student must execute the correct responses to stimuli in settings where training did not occur, for example, and under novel conditions. For example, after teaching a student to respond to different greetings during training (saying "hey" and "hi" to two different social greetings "what's up" and "dude" by a male peer, then assessing social responses to a different peer and in a different setting is assessed (saying "hi" and "good morning" to a female peer who say's "hi Bob" or "good morning, Bob").

CONCLUSION

Generalized learning has been a fairly elusive, yet desired, outcome in education, especially for children and youth with disabilities. That we have demonstrated this population's ability to learn cannot be disputed—countless books and articles attest to our ability to teach complex responses. Teaching students to respond correctly apart from instructional settings has not been as successful. In part, our failure to teach generalized responding may be due, in part, to our teaching approach, which typically includes teaching single instances of a solution to single examples of the problem.

This chapter introduced a departure from traditional single instance training using teacher-directed cues to perform. This departure in the form of self-instructional strategies identifies multiple examples of typical situations that demand an equally broad array of solutions. After instruction, students then have the responsibility to identify salient responses based on the situation that allow them to independently generate the solution (i.e., by using self-instruction strategies learned when deriving solutions to multiple examples, not single examples, of the problem).

References

Horner, R. H., Jones, D. N., & Williams, J. A. (1985). General case programming for community activities. In B. Wilcox & G. T. Bellamy (Eds.), *Design of high school programs for severely handicapped students.* (pp. 61–98). Baltimore: Paul H. Brookes.

Hughes, C. (1992). Teaching self-instruction utilizing multiple exemplars to produce generalized problem solving among individuals with severe mental retardation. *American Journal on Mental Retardation, 97,* 302–314.

Hughes, C., & Rusch, F. R. (1989). Teaching supported employees with severe mental retardation to solve problems. *Journal of Applied Behavior Analysis, 22,* 365–372.

Martin, J. E., Rusch, F. R., James, V. L., Decker, P. L., & Trtol, K. A. (1982). The use of picture cues to establish self-control in the preparation of complex meals by mentally retarded adults. *Applied Research in Mental Retardation, 3,* 105–119.

Mechling, L. C. (2007). Assistive technology as a self-management tool for promoting students with intellectual disabilities to initiate and complete daily tasks: A literature review. *Education and Training in Developmental Disabilities, 42,* 252–269.

Rusch, F. R., Hughes, C., & Wilson, P. G. (1995). Utilizing cognitive strategies in the acquisition of employment skills. In W. O'Donohue & L. Krasner (Eds.). *Handbook of psychological skills training clinical techniques and applications* (pp. 363–382). New York: Pergamon Press.

Storey, K. (2007) Review of research on self-management interventions in supported employment settings with employees with disabilities. *Career Development for Exceptional Individuals, 30,* 27–34.

35 GROUP INTERVENTIONS

Claudia Drossel

INTRODUCTION

Group Interventions

Joseph Pratt's (1907) "class method" for providing education to socioeconomically disadvantaged tuberculosis patients represents the formal beginning of professional interest in group interventions. Pratt's "class method" seemed to adventitiously decrease depressed behavior and increase treatment adherence (Spitz & Spitz, 1999). Subsequently, group interventions were the preferred mode of treatment delivery both when demand for treatment outweighed the system's supply (e.g., World War II, Vietnam War) and the burgeoning era of managed care called for cost-effective treatments (Spitz & Spitz, 1999). Since Pratt's initiation more than a century ago, research on group interventions incorporating a range of therapeutic approaches has generated a multifaceted and extensive body of literature. Many of the empirically supported techniques described in the current text have been applied in a group format for 30 to 40 years (e.g., Lazarus, 1961: systematic desensitization; Lewinsohn, Weinstein, & Alper, 1970: social skills training; Shaw, 1977: cognitive restructuring). This initial group application rested on the assumptions that empirically supported techniques, derived from behavioral principles based on basic research, could be transferred seamlessly into the group context and, furthermore, that the effects of nonspecific factors inherent to group processes were negligible (for a critique, see Rose, Tolman, & Tallant, 1985). However, the latter assumption proved untenable; later studies suggested that group processes might contribute to the results of cognitive-behavioral therapy outcome studies (e.g., Hope, Heimberg, & Bruch, 1995). Current research focuses on the delivery of cognitive-behavioral techniques through, rather than simply within, the group context, but vaguely defined group process constructs adopted from psychodynamic theory have contributed to controversy and inconclusive results. To facilitate practitioners' use of empirically supported cognitive-behavioral strategies in a group context, the present chapter will contrast group cognitive-behavioral interventions with other group interventions; summarize their efficacy; introduce nonspecific, group-inherent factors that might affect therapy outcome; and provide general considerations for the implementation of empirically supported techniques within a group context.

Overview of Group Formats

As pointed out by White (2000), *group cognitive behavioral interventions* distinguish themselves from other group interventions by their *task focus*. Regardless of the components that make up the group cognitive-behavioral intervention package (skills training, cognitive restructuring, relaxation, acceptance, mindfulness, etc.), groups led by professionals and paraprofessionals follow an explicit, formal structure that integrates didactic instruction, a flexible discussion agenda, and attainable goal-setting with performance feedback (e.g., Daniels, 1989). Step-by-step treatment manuals are available for a range of presentations.

In contrast, *mutual aid groups*, such as peer support and self-help groups, employ a wide range of styles and structures and cannot be easily categorized along dichotomous dimensions. Shepherd and colleagues (1999) investigated a sample of 246 mutual aid groups and found that professional facilitation of these groups occurred on a continuum. Generally, mutual aid groups are based upon social learning theory (Bandura,

1976) and assume that nonspecific factors, such as social standard setting by members, shared experience, and commonality of suffering, lead to positive outcomes for group members. Correspondingly, Davison, Pennebaker, and Dickerson (2000) reported that individuals with highly stigmatizing diseases (e.g., HIV-infection, alcoholism) and thus at risk of loss of social support were most likely to seek alternative support from mutual aid groups.

Psychoeducational groups can be viewed on a continuum with mutual aid groups. While groups implementing empirically supported cognitive behavioral strategies also incorporate psychoeducation into their curriculum, their focus is on structured participant activities and application of skills (e.g., through homework) rather than the exclusive accumulation of knowledge. Psychoeducational groups, often led by professionals, paraprofessionals, or trained volunteers, assume that knowing *what* is affecting group members is sufficient for knowing *how* to master individual difficulties.

Psycho-education groups typically implement a *combination* of empirically supported techniques, social support and psychoeducation. For example, supportive-expressive group therapy for cancer patients (Spiegel & Classen, 2000) places a high value on building relationships and expressing emotions. The group is viewed as a "social microcosm" (Yalom, 1995), which provides therapists with the opportunity to shape members' social behavior in the "here and now" of group interactions, rather than using a didactic approach. In addition to social shaping and psychoeducation, supportive-expressive group therapy also emphasizes concurrent skills training, particularly problem-focused coping. Most group interventions are combination treatments consisting of a range of often unspecified treatment components. This lack of specificity has impeded comparisons and evaluative summaries of outcome studies.

Evidence of Efficacy

Rather than constituting a secondary or inferior alternative to individual therapy, forced upon professionals and consumers for convenience or cost-savings, *group cognitive behavioral interventions* are treatments of choice and deemed as efficacious as individualized treatment (Morrison, 2001; Shaffer, Shapiro, Sank, & Coghlan, 1981). Petrocelli (2002) reviewed the literature on group cognitive-behavioral therapy packages that include cognitive restructuring and reported an overall pre- to post-treatment weighted mean effect size of 0.77 for a wide range of presenting problems, or "four-fifths of a standard deviation better on post-treatment than on pre-treatment measures" (p. 97). Compared to no-treatment controls, individuals who completed group cognitive-behavioral interventions scored on average three-fifths of a standard deviation better on posttreatment measures.

Acceptance-based approaches (e.g., acceptance and commitment therapy (ACT), Hayes, Strosahl, & Wilson, 1999; mindfulness-based cognitive therapy (MBCT), Segal, Williams, & Teasdale 2002) incorporate the finding that changing the literal content of thought may not be necessary for behavior change. Rather, training to observe thinking and feeling as a process ("distancing;" e.g., Beck, Rush, Shaw, & Emery, 1979) suffices in and of itself to promote effective behavior by decoupling it from negative or distorted cognitions and feelings (e.g., Segal, Teasdale, & Williams, 2004). Acceptance or mindfulness-based cognitive behavioral approaches, which omit the cognitive restructuring component and instead focus on removing cognitive barriers to behavior change by teaching how to act effectively in the presence of distorted or dysfunctional cognitions through acceptance (see Chapter 6), mindfulness (see Chapter 44), cognitive defusion (see Chapter 16), and values clarification (global statements that lead to specific goal-setting; see Chapter 79), have also demonstrated improved pre-/post-scores in group contexts (see Walser & Pistorello, 2004, for a description of studies involving a wide range of presenting problems and for a description of ACT in a group context). The U.K. National Institute for Health and Clinical Excellence (NICE) recommends MBCT as an effective treatment for recurrent depression (National Institute for Health and Clinical Excellence, 2007).

Mutual aid groups, as defined earlier, with their focus on shared experience, have been found to affect measures of social support and have produced self-reports of increased personal relationships and sense of community among group members (see Hogan, Linden, & Najarian, 2002, for a review). As Yalom (1995) noted, however, "emotional expression, though necessary, is not a *sufficient* condition for change" (p. 27). Accordingly, participation in mutual aid groups does not affect other outcome measures, for example, quality of life for women with early-stage breast cancer (Helgeson, Cohen, Schulz, and Yasko, 2001; Macvean, White, & Sanson-Fisher, 2008); depression related to bereavement (Huss & Ritchie, 1999; Tudiver, Hilditch, Permaul, & McKendree, 1992); eating attitudes and behaviors (McVey, et al., 2003); or medication adherence (Simoni, Pantalone, Plummer, & Huang, 2007).

Psychoeducational groups have been found to be efficacious in prevention and risk-reduction studies (e.g., Malow, West, Corrigan, Pena, & Cunningham, 1994). In addition to increasing knowledge, psychoeducational groups also may reduce relapse and rehospitalization rates when implemented as add-on interventions for both individuals with chronic behavioral health issues and their families, but do not affect symptoms, functioning, or medication adherence (Lincoln, Wilhelm, & Nestoriuc, 2007; Dolder, Lacro, Leckband, & Jeste, 2003).

WHO MIGHT BENEFIT FROM GROUP INTERVENTIONS?

Generally, group interventions (i.e., empirically supported cognitive behavioral components or packages, mutual aid, psychoeducation) have domain or target-specific outcomes (Mueser et al., 2002). A functional assessment of client repertoires and needs determines whether a particular client will benefit from unstructured social support (i.e., mutual aid groups), increased knowledge (i.e., psychoeducation in isolation), or specifically targeted therapeutic interventions to reduce behaviors that interfere with daily psychosocial functioning and to build repertoires that increase quality of life.

The decision whether to offer group versus individualized cognitive-behavioral interventions

depends on the functional assessment as well: To successfully complete structured group interventions, clients must be (1) able to understand and agree to the function and rationale of treatment and (2) have the repertoires necessary for participation and task as well as group completion (e.g., arranging for transportation or respite; following through on homework assignments; prioritizing group attendance over other, possibly interfering events; being on time; temporarily foregoing alcohol or illicit drug use to be alert and attentive during group). Cognitive impairment (e.g., related to organic brain syndromes, acute psychosis, or mania) should be ruled out and sufficient skill in reading and writing ascertained. As multiple clients inevitably will give and receive feedback on behaviors, thoughts, or feelings from other group members, all members must be willing to engage with others and be able to follow the social guidelines of the particular group (e.g., being responsive to requests for respectful behavior, for yielding the floor, or for managing crises in individually scheduled meetings only).

CONTRAINDICATIONS

Group psychoeducational or cognitive behavioral interventions may be contraindicated for groups of individuals who have counterpliant repertoires (i.e., usually behave in opposition to any stated rule or request for compliance) that are maintained by peer approval or attention. Dishion and Andrews (1995), for example, reported that groups for high-risk adolescents consisting of psychoeducation and cognitive behavioral skills components resulted in more favorable attitudes toward substance use, higher tobacco use, and more behavioral problems at school than other, parent-directed interventions. Thus, if the peer group is likely to reinforce problem behavior, group interventions must be structured to prevent, override, or counteract these adventitious group dynamics (see also Poulin, Dishion, & Burraston, 2001).

Mutual aid groups may carry the inherent risk that group members engage in corumination, that is, non-problem-focused excessive discussion of problems, without a facilitator who sets an agenda for the meeting and offers expert information. Consequently, some studies have reported potentially harmful effects of mutual aid groups on the functioning of members who initially entered the group with a high-level of perceived social support in their natural, nongroup environment (e.g., Helgeson, Cohen, Schulz, & Yasko, 2000). Given the suggested role of rumination and avoidance in recent models of psychopathology (Hayes, Strosahl, & Wilson, 1999; Segal, Williams, & Teasdale, 2002), mutual aid groups may have iatrogenic effects when individuals interpret thoughts and feelings as strict determinants of behavior and already have access to a social support system. The sharing of negative experiences in the absence of structured components to promote coping and social skills may increase the frequency of negative thoughts and feelings and thereby prompt a (negative) re-evaluation of existing support networks and decreased individual functioning (Helgeson, Cohen, Schulz, & Yasko, 2000).

PRACTICAL CONSIDERATIONS

Group Selection

The current categorization of client presenting problems according to the *Diagnostic and Statistical Manual of Mental Disorders* (*DSM-IV*, American Psychiatric Association, 1994) has led to the definition of group homogeneity based on diagnostic criteria. While standard group cognitive-behavioral intervention protocols have been developed based on these categorizations (e.g., White & Freeman, 2000), a functional assessment of client repertoires may reveal differences in the function of problematic behaviors that are important for predicting the effectiveness of specific group interventions. Depressed behavior, for example, may function to avert family conflict (e.g., Hops, Biglan, Sherman, & Arthur, 1987), may represent a general lack of access to positive reinforcement (behavioral activation; Jacobson, Martell, & Dimidijan, 2001), or may be indicative of cognitive barriers, such as dysfunctional schemata of how the world works

(cognitive restructuring; White, 2000), excessive rumination (MBCT; Segal, Teasdale, & Williams, 2002), or excessive sensitivity to evaluation and concurrent avoidance of all events that correlate with depressive self-talk or feelings (ACT; Zettle, 2007). Moreover, clients with the same *DSM-IV* diagnosis may have different knowledge, instrumental problem solving, or interpersonal skill levels. Consequently, when inclusion in a group is based on *DSM-IV* criteria, the degree to which individuals benefit from the chosen group cognitive-behavioral treatment protocol may reflect the degree to which the function of the presenting problem matches the intervention, regardless of perceived group homogeneity. Therapist referral based on diagnosis with subsequent telephone screening does not replace a thorough functional assessment of the client's presenting problem. As Rapin (2004) underscores, "knowledge of who might most benefit from a particular type of group and group format is central to ethical practice" (p. 161).

Other Group Characteristics

Cognitive behavioral strategies are commonly implemented in groups of six to 12 people who meet for one-and-a-half to two hours eight to 20 times (Morrison, 2001). Smaller groups might be indicated for individuals with high levels of social fear and avoidance. A cotherapist might be needed to manage homework reviews for groups with more than six members (Hollon & Shaw, 1979).

In addition, brief four- to six-session interventions with a more didactic psychoeducational format, incorporating exercises but not discussion of individual problems, have been conducted with 20 to 40 participants (Hayes & Bach, 2002; White & Keenan, 1990). More cost-effective modes of delivery are also available in the form of workshops that consist of a combination of psychoeducation, skills training, or *in vivo* exercises (e.g., Evans, Holt, & Oei, 1991).

Nonspecific Group Processes

White (2000) emphasizes task focus and group cohesiveness as the principles governing the successful implementation of cognitive-behavioral techniques in groups. *Group cohesiveness* is a construct that parallels the client–therapist working alliance in individual therapy and refers to the degree to which members perceive the group as a meaningful, collaborative entity and feel a sense of belonging to it (Yalom, 1995). As vagueness in the construct and a wide range of measures have hindered a comparison of divergent outcome studies (e.g., Taube-Schiff, et al., 2007; Woody & Adessky, 2002), some researchers (e.g., Hornsey, Dwyer, & Oei, 2007) have suggested to abandon "cohesiveness" as a global construct and to focus on specific group processes instead. Specific therapist behaviors and strategies that may enhance client participation and collaboration include the following:

Group preparation:

1. *Limits of confidentiality:* Roback, Moore, Bloch, and Shelton (1996) have drawn attention to the fact that most discussions of confidentiality refer to the therapist's professional obligations but do not inform group members about the risk that other members might break confidentiality. To fully inform and protect group therapy clients, the authors suggested the following consent statement:

   If you reveal secrets in the group, those secrets might be told outside the group by other members of the group. If your secrets are told outside the group, then people you know might learn these secrets. You could be hurt emotionally and economically if your secrets are told outside the group. Other group members might tell their secrets to you. If you tell those secrets outside the group, then the members whose secrets you tell might have legal grounds to sue you for money for telling those secrets. If you violate the confidentiality rules of the group, then the group leader might expel you from the group. (p. 135)

2. *Treatment rationale:* There is some evidence that the degree to which clients accept the treatment rationale affects attrition and outcome (Addis & Carpenter, 2000; Hoffman & Suvak, 2006). As cognitive

behavioral strategies require active participation in the form of in-session exercises, *in vivo* exposure (e.g., for social anxiety), and homework, therapists must link the amount of effort expended by the client to the treatment rationale and outcome expectations. Any client concerns or foreseeable barriers to client engagement should be addressed prior to entering the group. Group pretraining allows the therapist to challenge any myths or misconceptions about how the group will function and the client to make a fully informed choice and commitment to group attendance. Client responses during this pregroup preparation phase will provide additional information about group fit.

Group leadership. Morran, Stockton, and Whittingham (2004) outline two general skill sets for managing the behavior of group members:

1. *Protecting:* Clarifying and establishing group norms; preventing excessive risk-taking in the form of disclosure by any particular member; skillfully and gently blocking member responding that disrupts group functioning (e.g., story-telling, unwarranted confrontation, criticism, or pressure to self-disclose); and reinforcing appropriate participation.

2. *Involving:* Inviting individual or groups of members to participate; modeling effective interpersonal behavior (including feedback delivery and acceptance); linking statements to the group's goals or other members' statements; exploring with group members the meaning of their current experience and interpreting events within the cognitive behavioral framework; self-disclosing information or reactions to model effective interpersonal behavior for the group; providing and accepting contingent feedback; facilitating and guiding member-to-member feedback. The provision of contingent feedback within the group setting may be especially important when members engage in interpersonal behaviors that disrupt group functioning, such as monopolizing group time, refusing to participate, rejecting suggestions, or displaying hostility toward

the therapist or other group members. Yalom (1995) describes the group feedback process as clients

- Learning to describe their interpersonal patterns
- Coming to know how these patterns impact others
- Choosing whether to ask for the group's assistance in changing any of these patterns
- Working within the group on behavior change

Note that the client's behavior is addressed in group, rather than separately outside of the group context. Kohlenberg and Tsai (1991) provide a cognitive behavioral interpretation and guidelines to contingent feedback within dyadic interactions (see also Kohlenberg, Kanter, Bolling, Parker, & Tsai, 2002).

Attrition. As White (2000) points out, any group member who discontinues attendance may do so because of negative experiences in the group setting. To prevent ruptures in cohesiveness, White (2000) recommends that therapists encourage group members to voice any dissatisfaction with the group or thoughts of dropping out. If members decide to leave the group, they are asked to consent to the therapist's sharing of their rationale with other group members and reassuring the remaining group members of the departed's well-being as well as continuity of care. Given that many group attendees do not have access to social support networks, their concern about the departure of fellow group members may be clinically relevant and, if ignored, may negatively affect outcome (e.g., Hope, Heimberg, & Bruch, 1995).

Nonspecific factors related to group preparation, group leadership, and the management of attrition may be necessary, albeit not sufficient, to generate positive outcomes for group members (Beck, Rush, Shaw, & Emery, 1979). Studies that have found that professionally led, manual-based cognitive behavioral groups are more effective than those led by paraprofessionals have suggested that paraprofessionals'

"ability to convey sophisticated therapeutic techniques in highly structured CBT groups is relatively weaker" (Bright, Baker, & Neimeyer, 1999, p. 499). Thus, when training paraprofessionals to deliver cognitive-behavioral strategies in groups, it may be worthwhile to include nonspecific factors, even if the research literature is still inconclusive with respect to the magnitude and nature of impact (Atkins & Christensen, 2001). It may not be the presence of nonspecific factors but their absence that is mostly felt.

STEP-BY-STEP PROCEDURES

Assessment and group pretraining has occurred before clients enter their first cognitive behavioral group session. The first session functions as an introductory session: Clients meet each other; review the treatment rationale, group goals and rules; and may be introduced to the first record-keeping instruments. All following sessions resemble the following structure:

1. Weekly progress assessment (standardized measures)
2. Review of principles/teaching points of the last session, including clarification if needed
3. Review of homework (e.g., record-keeping instruments; tasks)
4. Review of client's status in the context of the homework
5. Introduction of new agenda items
6. New homework
7. Recapitulation of the session from the client's perspective; clarification if needed

The reader may refer to each of the chapters of this text to examine specific cognitive behavioral techniques for inclusion in a group program. Descriptions of existing group protocols for specific *DSM-IV* diagnoses as well as specific populations have been aggregated by White and Freeman (2000).

Further Reading

Daniels, A. C. (1989). *Performance management: Improving quality productivity through positive reinforcement.* Tucker, GA: Performance Management Publications.

Kohlenberg, R. J., & Tsai, M. (1991). *Functional analytic psychotherapy: Creating intense and curative therapeutic relationships.* New York: Plenum Press.

Morran, K. D., Stockton, R., & Whittingham, M. H. (2004). Effective leader interventions for counseling and psychotherapy groups. In J. L. DeLucia-Waack, D. A. Gerrity, C. R. Kalodner, & M. T. Riva (Eds.), *Handbook of group counseling and psychotherapy* (pp. 91–103). Thousand Oaks, CA: Sage Publications.

Rapin, L. S. (2004). Guidelines for ethical and legal practice in counseling and psychotherapy groups. In J. L. DeLucia-Waack, D. A. Gerrity, C. R. Kalodner, & M. T. Riva (Eds.), *Handbook of group counseling and psychotherapy* (pp. 151–165). Thousand Oaks, CA: Sage Publications.

Roback, H. B., Moore, R. F., Bloch, F. S., & Shelton, M. (1996). Confidentiality in group psychotherapy: Empirical findings and the law. *International Journal of Group Psychotherapy, 46*(1), 117–135.

White, J. R., & Freeman, A. S. (Eds.). (2000). *Cognitive-behavioral group therapy for specific outcomes and populations.* Washington, DC: American Psychological Association.

Yalom, I. D. (1995). *The theory and practice of group psychotherapy* (4th ed.). New York: Basic Books.

References

Addis, M. E., & Carpenter, K. M. (2000). The treatment rationale in cognitive behavioral therapy: Psychological mechanisms and clinical guidelines. *Cognitive and Behavioral Practice, 7*(2), 147–156.

American Psychiatric Association (1994). *Diagnostic and statistical manual of mental disorders* (4th ed.). Washington, DC: Author.

Atkins, D. C., & Christensen, A. (2001). Is professional training worth the bother? A review of the impact of psychotherapy training on client outcome. *Australian Psychologist, 36*(2), 122–130.

Bach, P., & Hayes, S. C. (2002). The use of acceptance and commitment therapy to prevent the rehospitalization of psychotic patients: A randomized controlled trial. *Journal of Consulting and Clinical Psychology, 70*(5), 1129–1139.

Bandura, A. (1977). *Social learning theory.* Englewood Cliffs, NJ: Prentice Hall.

Beck, A. T., Rush, A. J., Shaw, B. F., & Emery, G. (1979). *Cognitive therapy of depression.* New York: Guilford.

Bright, J. I., Baker, K. D., & Neimeyer, R. A. (1999). Professional and paraprofessional group treatments for depression: A comparison of cognitive-behavioral and mutual support interventions. *Journal of Consulting and Clinical Psychology, 67*(4), 491–501.

Davison, K. P., Pennebaker, J. W., & Dickerson, S. S. (2000). Who talks? The social psychology of illness support groups. *The American Psychologist, 55*(2), 205–217.

Dishion, T. J., & Andrews, D. W. (1995). Preventing escalation in problem behaviors with high-risk young adolescents: Immediate and 1-year outcomes. *Journal of Consulting and Clinical Psychology, 63*(4), 538–548.

Dolder, C. R., Lacro, J. P., Leckband, S., & Jeste, D. V. (2003). Interventions to improve antipsychotic medication adherence: A review of recent literature. *Journal of Clinical Psychopharmacology, 23*(4), 389–399.

Evans, L., Holt, C., & Oei, T. P. S. (1991). Long-term follow-up of agoraphobics treated by brief intensive group cognitive behavioural therapy. *Australia and New Zealand Journal of Psychiatry, 25,* 343–349.

Hayes, S. C., Strosahl, K. D., & Wilson, K. G. (1999). *Acceptance and commitment therapy: An experiential approach to behavior change.* New York: Guilford.

Helgeson, V. S., Cohen, S., Schulz, R., & Yasko, J. (2000). Group support interventions for women with breast cancer: Who benefits from what? *Health Psychology, 19*(2), 107–114.

Hofmann, S. G., & Suvak, M. (2006). Treatment attrition during group therapy for social phobia. *Journal of Anxiety Disorders, 20*(7), 961–972.

Hogan, B. E., Linden, W., & Najarian, B. (2002). Social support interventions: Do they work? *Clinical Psychology Review, 22*(3), 381–440.

Hollon, S. D., & Shaw, B. F. (1979). Group cognitive therapy for depressed patients. In A. T. Beck, A. J. Rush, B. F. Shaw, & G. Emery, *Cognitive therapy of depression* (pp. 328–353). New York: Guilford.

Hope, D. A., Heimberg, R. G., & Bruch, M. A. (1995). Dismantling cognitive–behavioral group therapy for social phobia. *Behavior Research and Therapy, 33*(6), 637–650.

Hops, H., Biglan, A., Sherman, L., & Arthur, J. (1987). Home observations of family interactions of depressed women. *Journal of Consulting & Community Psychology, 55*(3), 341–346.

Hornsey, M. J., Dwyer, L., & Oei, T. P. S. (2007). Beyond cohesiveness: Reconceptualizing the link between group processes and outcomes in group psychotherapy. *Small Group Research, 38*(5), 567–592.

Huss, S. N., & Ritchie, M. (1999). Effectiveness for a group for parentally bereaved children. *Journal for Specialists in Group Work, 24*(2), 186–196.

Jacobson, N. S., Martell, C. R., & Dimidijan, S. (2001). Behavioral activation treatment for depression: Returning to contextual roots. *Clinical Psychology: Science and Practice, 8*(3), 255–270.

Kohlenberg, R. J., Kanter, J. W., Bolling, M. Y., Parker, C. R., & Tsai, M. (2002). Enhancing cognitive therapy for depression with functional analytic psychotherapy: Treatment guidelines and empirical findings. *Cognitive and Behavioral Practice, 9*(3), 213–229.

Lazarus, A. A. (1961). Group therapy of phobic disorders by systematic desensitization. *Journal of Abnormal and Social Psychology, 63*, 504–510.

Lewinsohn, P. M., Weinstein, M. S., & Alper, T. (1970). A behavioral approach to the group treatment of depressed persons: A methodological contribution. *Journal of Clinical Psychology, 26*(4), 525–532.

Lincoln, T., Wilhelm, K., & Nestoriuc, Y. (2007). Effectiveness of psychoeducation for relapse, symptoms, knowledge, adherence and functioning in psychotic disorders: A meta-analysis. *Schizophrenia Research, 96*(1–3), 232–245.

Macvean, M. L., White, V. M., & Sanson-Fisher, R. (2008). One-to-one volunteer support programs for people with cancer: A review of the literature. *Patient Education and Counseling, 70*(1), 10–24.

Malow, R. M., West, J. A., Corrigan, S. A., Pena, J. M., & Cunningham, S. C. (1994). Outcome of psychoeducation for HIV risk reduction. *AIDS Education and Prevention, 6*(2), 113–125.

McVey, G., Lieberman, M., Voorberg, N., Wardrope, D., Blackmore, E., & Tweed, S. (2003). Replication of a peer support program designed to prevent disordered eating: Is a life skills approach sufficient for all middle school students? *Eating Disorders, 11*(3), 187–195.

Morrison, N. (2001). Group cognitive therapy: Treatment of choice or sub-optimal option? *Behavioural and Cognitive Psychotherapy, 29*(3), 311–332.

Mueser, K. T., Corrigan, P. W., Hilton, D. W., Tanzman, B., Schaub, A., Gingerich, S., et al. (2002). Illness management and recovery: A review of the research. *Psychiatric Services, 53*(10), 1272–1284.

National Institute for Health and Clinical Excellence. (2007). Quick reference guide (amended). www.nice.org.uk/nicemedia/pdf/CG23quick refguideamended.pdf, accessed March 26, 2008.

Petrocelli, J. V. (2002). Effectiveness of group cognitive-behavioral therapy for general symptomatology: A meta-analysis. *Journal for Specialists in Group Work, 27*(1), 92–115.

Poulin, F., Dishion, T. J., & Burraston, B. (2001). 3-year iatrogenic effects associated with aggregating high-risk adolescents in cognitive–behavioral preventive interventions. *Applied Developmental Science, 5*(4), 214–224.

Pratt, J. H. (1907). The class method of treating consumption in the homes of the poor. *Journal of the American Medical Association, 49*, 755–759.

Rose, S. D., Tolman, R., & Tallant, S. (1985). Group process in cognitive–behavioral therapy. *The Behavior Therapist, 8*(4), 71–75.

Segal, Z. V., Teasdale, J. D., & Williams, J. M. G. (2004). Mindfulness-based cognitive therapy: Theoretical rationale and empirical status. In S. C. Hayes, V. M. Follette, & M. M. Linehan (Eds.), *Mindfulness and acceptance: Expanding the cognitive–behavioral tradition.* New York: Guilford.

Segal, Z. V., Williams, J. M. G., & Teasdale, J. D. (2002). *Mindfulness-based cognitive therapy for depression: A new approach to preventing relapse.* New York: Guilford.

Shaffer, C. S., Shapiro, J., Sank, L. I., & Coghlan, D. J. (1981). Positive changes in depression, anxiety, and assertion following individual and group cognitive behavior therapy intervention. *Cognitive Therapy and Research, 5*(2), 149–157.

Shaw, B. F. (1977). Comparison of cognitive therapy and behavior therapy in the treatment of depression. *Journal of Consulting and Clinical Psychology, 45*(4), 543–551.

Shepherd, M. D., Schoenberg, M., Slavich, S., Wituk, S., Warren, M., & Meissen, G. (1999). Continuum of professional involvement in self-help groups. *Journal of Community Psychology, 27*(1), 39–53.

Simoni, J. M., Pantalone, D. W., Plummer, M. D., & Huang, B. (2007). A randomized controlled trial of a peer support intervention targeting antiretroviral medication adherence and depressive symptomatology in HIV-positive men and women. *Health Psychology, 26*(4), 488–495.

Spiegel, D., & Classen, C. (2000). *Group therapy for cancer patients: A research-based handbook of psychosocial care.* New York: Basic Books.

Spitz, I., & Spitz, T. (1999). *A pragmatic approach to group psychotherapy.* Philadelphia, PA: Brunner/Mazel, Taylor & Francis Group.

Taube-Schiff, M., Suvak, M. K., Antony, M. M., Bieling, P. J., & McCabe, R. E. (2007). Group cohesion in cognitive-behavioral group therapy for social phobia. *Behaviour Research and Therapy, 45*(4), 687–698.

Tudiver, F., Hilditch, J., Permaul, J. A., & McKendree, D. J. (1992). Does mutual help facilitate newly bereaved widowers? *Evaluation and the Health Professions, 15*(2), 147–162.

Walser, R., & Pistorello, J. (2004). ACT in group format. In S. C. Hayes & K. D. Strosahl (Eds.), *A practical guide to acceptance and commitment therapy* (pp. 347–389). New York: Springer.

White, J. R. (2000). Depression. In J. R. White & A. S. Freeman (Eds.), *Cognitive–behavioral group therapy for specific problems and populations.* Washington, DC: American Psychological Association.

White, J., & Keenan, M. (1990). Stress control: A pilot study of large group therapy for generalized anxiety disorder. *Behavioural Psychotherapy, 19*, 143–146.

Woody, S. R., & Adessky, R. S. (2002). Therapeutic alliance, group cohesion, and homework compliance during cognitive-behavioral group treatment of social phobia. *Behavior Therapy*, 33(1), 5–27.

Zettle, R. (2007). *ACT for depression: A clinician's guide to using acceptance and commitment therapy in treating depression.* Oakland, CA: New Harbinger Publications, Inc.

36 HABIT REVERSAL TRAINING

Amanda Nicolson Adams, Mark A. Adams, and Raymond G. Miltenberger

Habit reversal was developed by Nathan Azrin and his colleagues in the early 1970s as a treatment for nervous habits and tics. An article appearing in *Behaviour Research and Therapy* (1973) and reprinted in Rachman (1997) theorized that nervous habits persist because of response chaining, limited awareness, excessive practice, and social tolerance. Habit Reversal was designed to counteract these influences. Prior to the development of habit reversal, negative practice (i.e., numerous forced repetitions; developed by Knight Dunlap in the 1930s) was a popular and validated method of treating tic disorders. Although ahead of its time in 1930, inconsistent results following from the application of negative practice led to a decrease in both research and application of negative practice for habit treatment. Habit reversal, now called habit reversal training (HRT; Piacentini & Chong, 2005) is not only a more effective treatment for tic disorders, but has efficacy for the treatment of many other "nervous habits" or habit disorders as well.

WHO MIGHT BENEFIT FROM THIS TECHNIQUE

The treatment of Tourette's disorder (Himle, Woods, Conelea, Bauer, & Rice, 2007; Himle, Woods, Piacentini, & Walkup, 2006; Meidinger et al., 2005; Woods, Twohig, Flessner, & Roloff, 2003; Woods, Watson, Wolfe, Twohig, & Friman, 2001), other tic disorders (Clarke, Bray, Kehle, & Truscott, 2001; Himle et al., 2006; Himle & Woods, 2005; Woods & Himle, 2004; Woods & Miltenberger, 1995), and trichotillomania or chronic hair pulling (Diefenbach, Reitman, & Williamson, 2000; Elliot & Fuqua, 2000; Kraemer, 1999; Rapp, Miltenberger, Long, Elliott, & Lumley, 1998;

Romaniuk, Miltenberger, & Deaver, 2003; Rothbaum & Ninan, 1999; Woods, Flessner, et al., 2006; Woods, Wetterneck, & Flessner, 2006;) have emerged as primary application areas for HRT procedures. In addition to these prominent disorders, other repetitive behavior disorders have been successfully treated using HRT (Woods & Miltenberger, 2001), including stuttering (Azrin & Nunn, 1974; de Kinkelder & Boelens, 1998; Wagaman, Miltenberger, & Arndorfer, 1993; Woods, Fuqua, & Waltz, 1997), nail biting (Woods, Fuqua, et al., 2001), oral habits such as lip or mouth biting and teeth grinding (Azrin, Nunn, & Frantz-Renshaw, 1982), oral–digital habits or thumbsucking (Woods et al., 1999; Long, Miltenberger, Ellingson, & Ott, 1999), pica (Woods, Miltenberger, & Lumley, 1996), scratching (Rosenbaum & Ayllon, 1981), chronic skin picking (Teng, Woods, & Twohig, 2006; Twohig & Woods, 2001a), self-choking (Higa, Chorpita, & Yim, 2001), social competence (Anderson & Allen, 2000), chronic facial pain including chronic headaches (Townsend, 2000), self-biting (Jones, Swearer, Friman, 1997), and the reduction of disruptive outbursts (Allen, 1998). In sum, there are data-based evaluations of HRT for tic disorders, and a wide variety of habit behaviors or repetitive behavior disorders, as indicated above. Although not intended as an exhaustive list of behaviors treated using HRT, this list speaks to the vast scope of applications for this technique.

CONTRAINDICATIONS OF THE TREATMENT

HRT does not seem contraindicated for most people. There are some situations, however, that may present limitations. Applications of HRT that include a pretreatment functional analysis component have recently appeared in the literature. It is interesting, but not surprising to find that behaviors shown to be controlled by automatic reinforcement (i.e., self-stimulatory behaviors) tend to respond best to HRT, whereas behaviors that function for escape, attention, or other social consequences respond less consistently to HRT as treatment (Higa et al., 2001; Woods, Fuqua, et al., 2001). Although this line of research is extremely limited in scope at this time, and the vast majority of studies show the effectiveness of HRT independent of knowledge of behavioral function, this research does suggest that the function of the habit may be an important consideration when selecting a treatment for tics, habits, or repetitive behavior disorders.

Wright and Miltenberger (1987) and Woods, Miltenberger, et al. (1996) found awareness training by itself to be an effective treatment for some individuals' tics. In what could be considered a contrary finding, Long, Miltenberger, Ellingson, et al. (1999) found that limitations exist in the success of HRT for individuals with mental retardation. Although the authors do not state that the inability to successfully train awareness was responsible for poor results with a developmentally delayed population, they found that more immediate and clear contingency procedures were needed. Other studies also have found that HRT was not effective and contingency management was needed for hair pulling and thumb sucking exhibited by young children and individuals with mental retardation (Long, Miltenberger, & Rapp, 1999; Rapp, Miltenberger, Galensky, Roberts, & Ellingson, 1999; Rapp, Miltenberger, & Long, 1998). The limited results to date suggest that different HRT components or other treatment procedures may be called for depending on the client population, the particular habit being treated, and the function of the habit being treated. Acceptance and commitment therapy (ACT) and adjunct therapies have recently been cited in habit reversal literature, indicating a possibility to combine traditional HRT and simplified HRT procedures with other behaviorally based therapy (e.g., Woods, Wetterneck, et al., 2006; Twohig & Woods, 2004: Romaniuk et al., 2003).

HOW DOES THE TECHNIQUE WORK?

Azrin and Nunn (1973) developed HRT with 10 procedures grouped into four components: (1) motivation procedures, (2) awareness training, (3) competing response training, and (4) generalization procedures. Relaxation training has been added as a component in a number of studies (Azrin & Nunn, 1974; Finney, Rapoff, Hall, & Christopherson, 1983). Given the multicomponent nature of HRT, some research has focused on component analyses of HRT (Miltenberger, Fuqua, & Woods, 1998; Twohig & Woods 2001b) and has implemented simplified procedures consisting of three steps: (1) awareness training, (2) competing response training, and (3) social support (Elliot, Miltenberger, Rapp, Long, & McDonald, 1998; Long, Miltenberger, Rapp & 1999; Rapp et al., 1998).

Awareness Training

Awareness training involves extensive self-assessment to ensure that the client is aware of the individual responses that make up the habit and their environmental antecedents. Clients are asked to practice detecting the first signs of the particular behavior excess so that they will be able to stop the response before it is emitted or early in the sequence.

Competing Response Training

Clients practice performing a response that competes with the behavior excess. For example, a person who bites nails may practice putting on hand lotion or squeezing a ball so that their hands are not available for nail biting. This response must be one that the client can sustain for several minutes, one that is compatible with everyday activities, and one that is inconspicuous to others.

Research on HRT components has asserted that awareness training and competing response training (i.e., a planned, practiced alternate response) seem to be the critical components (Miltenberger & Fuqua, 1985; Miltenberger, Fuqua, & McKinley, 1985; Woods, Miltenberger, & Lumley, 1996). Sharenow, Fuqua, and Miltenberger (1989) and Woods and colleagues (1999) have examined the competing response component by comparing a topographically similar versus a dissimilar competing response. Results were roughly comparable for the similar and dissimilar competing responses, leading to the possible conclusion that the competing response does not necessarily have to be a physically incompatible behavior.

Motivation Procedures

In an attempt to motivate the client to work at eliminating the habit, Azrin and Nunn (1973) used three procedures. First, they had clients review the inconveniences caused by the habit. Second, they enlisted significant others to provide social support, including prompts to use the competing response when needed and praise for using the competing response and refraining from engaging in the habit behavior. Flessner and colleagues (Flessner et al., 2005) evaluated simplified habit reversal with and without the social support component for nail biting in adults and found no difference between the two groups. As a third motivation strategy, Azrin and Nunn had the client publicly display his or her control of the habit and solicit reinforcement from significant others.

Generalization Procedures

The primary procedure used to enhance generalization was for the client to engage in symbolic rehearsal by imagining successful control of the habit in situations where the habit previously occurred. For example, one might imagine having to wait in line (an occasion that had previously prompted nail biting), and mentally rehearse engaging in alternative behaviors to nail biting.

STEP-BY-STEP PROCEDURES

Typically, HRT is implemented in a small number of treatment sessions followed by booster sessions as needed. The first session is devoted to assessment and the establishment of data collection. In the following sessions the therapist describes HRT procedures and provides instructions for the client to use the procedures in the natural environment.

Assessment and Data Collection

The therapist asks the client to describe the sequence of behaviors involved in each occurrence of the habit. For example, a client who engages in hair pulling might describe a sequence in which she strokes her hair, finds a strand, twirls it between her finger and thumb, reaches down to the root, pulls out the hair, looks at it, rubs it on her lips, and then drops it to the floor. The therapist also asks about antecedents and consequences related to the habit behavior to identify antecedents that may have stimulus control over the behavior and to determine whether any form of social reinforcement may be involved in the maintenance of the behavior. If the habit behavior serves a social function (e.g., the client receives attention for engaging in the habit), operant procedures may be used in place of, or in addition to, HRT procedures. Information on antecedents is also valuable for proper use of HRT procedures.

The therapist works with the client in the first session to develop a data collection plan. The client (or the parents in the case of a child) may record the occurrence of the habit behavior using frequency, duration, or time sample recording. For example, an adult may keep a simple tally of the number of times he bites his nail each day (frequency recording). Alternately, a parent may observe a child periodically while the child is studying or watching television and record whether hair pulling was observed during each observation (time sample recording). In addition to direct observation of the habit behavior, the client may record a permanent product of the habit behavior, such as nail length for a nail biter or number of hairs collected or the size of the depilated area for a hair puller.

Implementing HRT Components

HRT procedures are implemented after the assessment and data collection plan are completed. Before implementing HRT procedures, the therapist provides an overview of the procedures and a rationale for the treatment components A description of the procedures in implementing HRT are now discussed in some detail. For a summary of the key elements of HRT, please see Table 36.1.

TABLE 36.1   Key Elements of Habit Reversal

1. Inconvenience review: Help client see how habit interferes with life.
2. Awareness training: Teach client to become aware of each instance of the habit.
3. Competing response training: Teach client to engage in one or more incompatible behaviors to replace the habit.
4. Social support: Involve the assistance of others to help the client use the competing response successfully.
5. Generalization procedure: Practice symbolic rehearsal and other steps to promote success in the client's everyday life.

Inconvenience Review

The purpose of this procedure is to have the client consider all of the ways in which the habit has caused inconvenience, embarrassment, or disruption of the client's life. After reviewing the various ways that the habit has had a negative impact on the client's life, the client may become more motivated to work at implementing the HRT procedures. The therapist can conduct the inconvenience review by asking the client open-ended questions such as, "How has your hair pulling caused difficulty in your life?" or "How has your hair pulling inconvenienced or embarrassed you?" The therapist may also use a checklist of possible negative consequences resulting from the habit. Keuthen, Stein, and Christenson (2001) developed a checklist for hair pullers that listed physical consequences (e.g., bald spots), emotional consequences (e.g., shame/embarrassment), economic consequences (e.g., cost of wigs), and interpersonal consequences (e.g., avoidance of intimate relationships). Whether the therapist uses open-ended questions or a checklist, the use of this procedure should help the client see the negative impact the habit has had and motivate the client to direct more substantial effort toward therapy.

Awareness Training

The goal of awareness training is for the client to become aware of each instance of the habit as it occurs and to become aware of antecedents to the habit. The client is told that she must be aware of each occurrence of the habit in order to be able to control the habit. Increased awareness is critical for the use of the competing response. The first

step in awareness training is to have the client describe all of the behaviors involved in the occurrence of the habit (response description). If clearly described in the initial interview, the therapist will review the information with the client at this time. The next step is response detection. For some target behaviors, such as motor and vocal tics or stuttering, the client is instructed to identify each occurrence of the habit in session. The therapist praises the client for detecting each instance of the habit and prompts the client when the client fails to identify an instance of the habit. With practice in session, the client should identify each occurrence of the habit behavior at close to 100% accuracy.

Some habit behaviors may not occur in session, such as nail biting, thumb sucking, hair pulling, and other "nervous habits." For target behaviors such as these, the therapist asks the client to simulate the occurrence of the habit in session in order to facilitate awareness of the habit. The client attempts to simulate the sequence of behaviors involved in the habit exactly as the behaviors would occur in the natural environment. While simulating the habit behavior, the therapist will tell the client to stop at various points in the sequence of behaviors and to notice how the behavior looks or feels in an attempt to enhance awareness. As the client is simulating the habit behavior, the client should also simulate the activities or situations during which the behavior occurs. For example, the client simulates sitting at his desk at school as he reaches up to pull his hair.

In addition to response description and detection procedures, the therapist will also help the client become more aware of antecedents to the habit, including overt environmental antecedents and covert antecedents. Questions about antecedents are asked in the first session and revisited during awareness training. Examples of overt antecedents may include specific activities, times of day, locations, or the client's own behavior. For example, hair stroking or twirling may be an antecedent to hair pulling. A child may be more likely to bite her nails when she is resting her face on her hands while at her desk at school or while watching television. Covert antecedents may be relevant to a number of habit behaviors. For example, hair pulling may be more likely to occur when the client experiences tension or anxiety and motor tics may be more likely to occur when the client experiences specific sensations in the area affected by the tic (e.g., itching, burning, tickling, etc.). Discussion of overt and covert antecedents should increase the client's awareness of the incipient occurrence of the habit in the natural environment. Such awareness should facilitate the proper use of the competing response.

Competing Response Training

The goal of competing response training is to teach the client to engage in one or more physically incompatible behaviors to replace the habit behavior. The client is told that she will learn to engage in a different behavior to replace the habit behavior and that with practice the new behavior will become a habit itself. The competing response should be inconspicuous, require little response effort, and compete physically with the habit. For a motor tic, the competing response would involve tensing the muscles involved in the tic. For a vocal tic, the competing response would involve diaphragmatic breathing with the mouth closed. For a hand-to-head habit such as hair pulling, nail biting, or thumb sucking, the competing response would involve an alternative use of the hand(s) such as clenching a fist, holding an object, folding the hands, sitting on the hands, putting hands in pockets, and so on. The client is instructed to engage in the competing response for about one minute contingent on the occurrence of the habit behavior or the antecedents to the habit behavior. In this way, the competing response will interrupt the habit or prevent its occurrence.

After providing a rationale for the use of the competing response, the therapist works with the client to choose a number of competing responses that the client could use in each of the situations where the habit occurs. The client then practices the use of the competing response(s) in session. For habits that occur in session (e.g., tics, stuttering), the client uses the competing response immediately contingent on the occurrence of the habit or the antecedents to the habit. The therapist praises the client for proper use of the competing response and prompts the client to use the competing response if the client fails

to do so at the appropriate time. Competing response practice should continue until the client is using the competing response consistently. For habits that do not occur in session, the therapist has the client simulate the habit behavior and practice the competing response. The client will simulate different situations in which the habit occurs and engage in the competing response contingent on the simulation of the habit. The therapist instructs the client to use the competing response when antecedents are present or early in the chain of behaviors so that the competing response prevents the occurrence of the habit.

Social Support

Social support involves the assistance of a significant other to help the client use the competing response successfully. A parent, a spouse, or a good friend may serve as the social support person. The social support person attends the treatment sessions and learns to assist the client in three ways. First, the social support person is told to praise the client for the absence of the habit in situations where the habit typically occurs. Second, the support person is instructed to praise the client for using the competing response appropriately. Third, the support person is instructed to prompt the client to use the competing response when the habit occurs and the client fails to use the competing response to control the habit. The social support person practices these three activities with the client in the presence of the therapist.

Generalization Procedures

A number of procedures are used to promote the use of the HRT procedures outside of the session in the client's everyday life. First, the social support person provides prompts and reinforcement. Second, the client is instructed to engage in symbolic rehearsal in the session. The therapist has the client imagine using the competing response to successfully control the habit behavior in situations where the habit behavior has been most likely to occur. Third, the therapist has the client enter into situations where the habit has typically occurred, use the competing response, and solicit praise from the social support person. Fourth, the therapist gives specific instructions for the client and social support person to practice the use of the skills learned in session to control the habit in the natural environment. Practice in the natural environment may involve short daily practice sessions and the routine use of the procedures wherever and whenever the habit occurs.

Booster Sessions

Following the initial sessions during which the therapist describes the HRT procedures to the client and instructs the client to use the procedures in the natural environment, the therapist will conduct a number of booster sessions as needed. In these sessions, the therapist reviews the data with the client to see if the habit behavior is decreasing and reviews the client's use of the treatment procedures. The therapist praises the client's efforts and discusses any difficulties the client may be having. In some cases, the initial treatment sessions and two or three booster sessions may be sufficient for success (e.g., Rapp et al., 1998). In other cases, a number of booster sessions may be needed to achieve success (e.g., Wagaman et al., 1993). Depending on the case, adjunct treatment procedures (including operant contingencies and other cognitive behavioral strategies) may be called for if the habit behavior is not decreasing as expected (e.g., Keuthen et al., 2001; Woods & Miltenberger, 2001).

Further Reading

Azrin, N. H., & Nunn, R. G. (1973). Habit reversal: A method of eliminating nervous habits and tics. *Behaviour Research and Therapy, 11,* 619–628.

Miltenberger, R., Fuqua, R. W., & Woods, D. W. (1998). Applying behavior analysis with clinical problems: Review and analysis of habit reversal. *Journal of Applied Behavior Analysis, 31,* 447–469.

Woods, D., & Miltenberger, R. (Eds.) (2001). *Tic disorders, trichotillomania, and other repetitive behavior disorders: behavioral approaches to analysis and treatment.* Boston, MA: Kluwer.

References

Allen, K. D. (1998). The use of an enhanced simplified habit-reversal procedure to reduce disruptive outbursts during athletic performance. *Journal of Applied Behavior Analysis, 31(3),* 489–492.

Anderson, C. M., & Allen, K. D. (2000). Making social competence a habit. *Cognitive & Behavioral Practice, 7(2),* 239–241.

Azrin, N. H., & Nunn, R. G. (1973). Habit reversal: A method of eliminating nervous habits and tics. *Behaviour Research and Therapy, 11,* 619–628.

Azrin, N. H., & Nunn, R. G. (1974). A rapid method of eliminating stuttering by a regulated breathing approach. *Behaviour Research and Therapy, 12,* 279–286.

Azrin, N. H., & Nunn, R. G., & Frantz-Renshaw, S. E. (1982). Habit reversal versus negative practice treatment of self-destructive oral habits (biting, chewing, or licking of the lips, cheek, tongue, or palate). *Journal of Behavior Therapy and Experimental Psychiatry, 13,* 49–54.

Clarke, M. A., Bray, M. A., Kehle, T. J., Truscott, S. D. (2001). A school-based intervention designed to reduce the frequency of tics in children with Tourette's syndrome. *School Psychology Review, 30(1),* 11–22.

De Kinkelder, M., & Boelens, H. (1998). Habit-reversal treatment for children's stuttering: Assessment in three settings. *Journal of Behavior Therapy & Experimental Psychiatry, 29(3),* 261–265.

Diefenbach, G. J., Reitman, D., & Williamson, D. A. (2000). Trichotillomania: A challenge to research and practice. *Clinical Psychology Review, 20(3),* 289–309.

Elliott, A. J., & Fuqua, R. W. (2000). Trichotillomania: Conceptualization, measurement, and treatment. *Behavior Therapy, 31,* 529–545.

Elliott, A. J., Miltenberger, R. G., Rapp, J. T., Long, E. S., & McDonald, R. (1998). Brief application of simplified habit reversal to treat stuttering in children. *Journal of Behavior Therapy & Experimental Psychiatry, 29(4),* 289–302.

Finney, J. W., Rapoff, M. A., Hall, C. L., & Christopherson, E. R. (1983). Replication and social validation of habit reversal treatment for tics. *Behavior Therapy, 14,* 116–126.

Flessner, C. A., Miltenberger, R. G., Egemo, K., Kelso, P., Jostad, C., Johnson, B., et al. (2005). An evaluation of the social support component of simplified habit reversal. *Behavior Therapy, 36,* 35–42.

Higa, C. K., Chorpita, B. F., & Yim, L. M. (2001). Behavioral treatment of self-choking in a developmentally normal child. *Child & Family Behavior Therapy, 23(2),* 47–55.

Himle, M. B., Chang, S., Woods, D. W., Pearlman, A., Buzzella, B., Bunaciu, L., & Piacentini, J. C. (2006). Establishing the feasibility of direct observation in the assessment of tics in children with chronic tic disorders. *Journal of Applied Behavior Analysis, 39,* 429–440.

Himle, M. B., & Woods, D. W. (2005). An experimental evaluation of tic suppression and the tic rebound effect. *Behaviour Research and Therapy, 43,* 1443–1451.

Himle, M. B., Woods, D. W., Conelea, C. A., Bauer, C. C., & Rice, K. A. (2007). Investigating the effects of tic suppression on premonitory urge ratings in children and adolescents with Tourette's syndrome. *Behaviour Research and Therapy, 45,* 2964–2976.

Himle, M. B., Woods, D. W., Piacentini, J. C., & Walkup, J. T. (2006). Brief review of habit reversal training for Tourette syndrome. *Journal of Child Neurology, 21*(8), 719–725.

Jones, K. M., Swearer, S. M., Friman, P. C. (1997). Relax and try this instead: Abbreviated habit reversal for maladaptive self-biting. *Journal of Applied Behavior Analysis, 30*(4), 697–699.

Keuthen, N. J., Stein, D. J., & Christenson, G. A. (2001). *Help for hair pullers: Understanding and coping with trichotillomania.* Oakland, CA: New Harbinger.

Kraemer, P. A. (1999). The application of habit reversal in treating trichotillomania. *Psychotherapy: Theory, Research, Practice, Training, 36*(3), 289–304.

Long, E. S., Miltenberger, R. G., Ellingson, S. A., & Ott, S. M. (1999). Augmenting simplified habit reversal in the treatment of oral–digit habits exhibited by individuals with mental retardation. *Journal of Applied Behavior Analysis, 32*(3), 353–365.

Long, E. S., Miltenberger, R. G., & Rapp, J. T. (1999). Simplified habit reversal plus adjunct contingencies in the treatment of thumb sucking and hair pulling in a young child. *Child & Family Behavior Therapy, 21*(4), 45–58.

Meidinger, A. L., Miltenberger, R. G., Himle, M., Omvig, M., Trainor, C., & Crosby, R. (2005). An investigation of tic suppression and the rebound effect in Tourette's disorder. *Behavior Modification, 29,* 716–745.

Miltenberger, R., & Fuqua, W. (1985). Contingent vs. non-contingent competing response practice with nervous habits. *Journal of Behavior Therapy and Experimental Psychiatry, 16,* 195–200.

Miltenberger, R., & Fuqua, W., & McKinley, T. (1985). Habit reversal with muscle tics: Replication and component analysis. *Behavior Therapy, 16,* 39–50.

Miltenberger, R., Fuqua, R. W., & Woods, D. W. (1998). Applying behavior analysis with clinical problems: Review and analysis of habit reversal. *Journal of Applied Behavior Analysis, 31,* 447–469.

Piacentini, J., & Chong, S. (2005). Habit reversal training for tic disorders in children and adolescents. *Behavior Modification, 29,* 803–855.

Rachman, S. (Ed). (1997). *Best of Behaviour Research and Therapy.* Amsterdam, Netherlands: Pergamon/ Elsevier Science Inc.

Rapp, J., Miltenberger, R., Galensky, T., Roberts, J., & Ellingson, S. (1999). Brief functional analysis and simplified habit reversal treatment of thumb sucking in fraternal twin brothers. *Child & Family Behavior Therapy, 21*(2), 1–17.

Rapp, J., Miltenberger, R., & Long, E. (1998). Augmenting simplified habit reversal with an awareness enhancement device: Preliminary findings. *Journal of Applied Behavior Analysis, 31,* 665–668.

Rapp, J., Miltenberger, R., Long, E., Elliott, A., & Lumley, V. (1998). Simplified habit reversal for chronic hair pulling in three adolescents: A clinical replication with direct observation. *Journal of Applied Behavior Analysis, 31,* 299–302.

Romaniuk, C., Miltenberger, R. G., & Deaver, C. (2003). Long-term maintenance following habit reversal and adjunct treatment for trichotillomania. *Child and Family Behavior Therapy, 25,* 45–59.

Rosenbaum, M. S., & Ayllon, T. (1981). The behavioral treatment of neurodermatitis through habit reversal. *Behaviour Research and Therapy, 19,* 313–318.

Rothbaum, B. O., & Ninan, P. T. (1999). Trichotillomania. In Stein, D. J., & Christenson, G. A., et al., (Eds.), *Manual for the cognitive-behavioral treatment of trichotillomania.* American Psychiatric Press.

Sharenow, E., Fuqua, R. W., & Miltenberger, R. (1989). The treatment of motor tics with dissimilar competing response practice. *Journal of Applied Behavior Analysis, 22,* 35–42.

Teng, E. J., Woods, D. W., Twohig, M. P. (2006). Habit reversal as a treatment for chronic skin picking. *Behavior Modification, 30*(4), 411–422.

Townsend, D. R. (2000). The use of a habit reversal treatment for chronic facial pain in a minimal therapist contact format. *Dissertation Abstracts International, 60*(12-B), 6387.

Twohig, M. P., & Woods, D. W. (2001a). Habit reversal as a treatment for chronic skin picking in typically developing adult male siblings. *Journal of Applied Behavior Analysis. 34*(2), 217–220.

Twohig, M. P., & Woods, D. W. (2001b). Evaluating the duration of the competing response in habit reversal: a parametric analysis. *Journal of Applied Behavior Analysis, 34*(4), 517–520.

Twohig, M. P., & Woods, D. W. (2004). A preliminary investigation of acceptance and commitment therapy and habit reversal as a treatment for trichotillomania. *Behavior Therapy, 35,* 803–820.

Wagaman, J., Miltenberger, R., & Arndorfer, R. (1993). Analysis of a simplified treatment for stuttering in children. *Journal of Applied Behavior Analysis, 26,* 53–61.

Woods, D. W., Flessner, C., Franklin, M. E., Wetterneck, C. T., Walther, M. R., Anderson, E. R., & Cardona, D. (2006). Understanding and treating trichotillomania: what we know and what we don't know. *Psychiatric Clinics of North America, 29,* 487–501.

Woods, D. W., & Fuqua, R. W., Siah, A., Murray, L. K., Welch, M., Blackman, E., et al. (2001). Understanding habits: a preliminary investigation of nail biting function in children. *Education & Treatment of Children*, 24(2), 199–216.

Woods, D. W., Fuqua, R. W., & Waltz, T. J. (1997). Evaluation and elimination of an avoidance response in a child who stutters: a case study. *Journal of Fluency Disorders*, 22(4), 287–297.

Woods, D. W., & Himle, M. B. (2004). Creating tic suppression: Comparing the effects of verbal instruction to differential reinforcement. *Journal of Applied Behavior Analysis*, 37, 417–420.

Woods, D., & Miltenberger, R. (1995). Habit reversal: A review of applications and variations. *Journal of Behavior Therapy and Experimental Psychiatry*, 26, 123–131.

Woods, D., & Miltenberger, R. (Eds.) (2001). Tic disorders, trichotillomania, and repetitive behavior disorders: Behavioral approaches to analysis and treatment. Norwell, MA: Kluwer.

Woods, D., Miltenberger, R., & Lumley, V. (1996). Sequential application of major habit reversal components to treat motor tics in children. *Journal of Applied Behavior Analysis*, 29, 483–493.

Woods, D. W., Murray, L. K., Fuqua, R. W., Seif, T. A., Boyer, L. J., Siah, A. (1999). Comparing the effectiveness of similar and dissimilar competing responses in evaluating the habit reversal treatment for oral-digital habits in children. *Journal of Behavior Therapy & Experimental Psychiatry*, 30(4), 289–300.

Woods, D. W., Twohig, M. P., Flessner, C. A., & Roloff, T. J. (2003). Treatment of vocal tics in children with Tourette syndrome: Investigating the efficacy of habit reversal. *Journal of Applied Behavior Analysis*, 36, 109–112.

Woods, D. W., Watson, T. S., Wolfe, E., Twohig, M. P., & Friman P. C. (2001). Analyzing the influence of tic-related talk on vocal and motor tics in children with Tourette's syndrome. *Journal of Applied Behavior Analysis*, 34, 353–356.

Woods, D. W., Wetterneck, C. T., & Flessner, C. A. (2006). A controlled evaluation of acceptance and commitment therapy plus habit reversal for trichotillomania. *Behaviour Research and Therapy*, 44, 639–656.

Wright, K., & Miltenberger, R. (1987). Awareness training in the treatment of head and facial tics. *Journal of Behavior Therapy and Experimental Psychiatry*, 18, 269–274.

37 HARM REDUCTION

Arthur W. Blume and G. Alan Marlatt

The principal goal of harm reduction is to reduce the risk of harmful health consequences related to a targeted behavior. Unlike some behavior change strategies, harm reduction does not necessarily seek extinction of the behavior (although it can be one of the goals), but instead seeks to modify the targeted behavior in order to reduce its risk to the person (Marlatt, 1998a).

Harm reduction strategies were first developed for addictive behaviors because of a couple of reasons. First, many substance using clients felt marginalized by the strict abstinence requirements demanded by traditional substance abuse treatment programs. Second, with the rapid spread of communicable and preventable diseases that can be contracted by unsafe substance use, such as HIV and hepatitis, it became critical to develop a new therapeutic approach that targeted the possible negative sequelae of substance use among those who were not willing or able to abstain (Marlatt, 1998b).

Although harm reduction often utilizes empirically supported cognitive behavioral strategies, some well-known harm reduction strategies are pharmacological. Methadone replacement as an alternative to heroin use may be the most common. The literature suggests that methadone replacement has been helpful in reducing the risks related to heroin usage in a very cost-effective way for many people over a number of years (Barnett, Zaric, & Brandeau, 2001; Yoast, Williams, Deitchman, & Champion, 2001).

More recently, other pharmacological harm reduction techniques have been used successfully in an effort to reduce the risks of substance abuse by controlling cravings (in an effort to reduce the amount used), or by reducing aversive consequences of other conditions to make substance use less attractive. In order to reduce cravings, naltrexone and acamprosate may hold

some promise (Anton et al., 2006; Kranzier & Van Kirk, 2001). However, some pharmacological interventions may reduce the potential harm of substance use by reducing other comorbid aversive conditions. For instance, medicines to control psychiatric symptoms or using therapeutic doses to properly medicate a person for pain may reduce specific factors contributing to substance abuse via "self-medication" (Blume, Anderson, Fader, & Marlatt, 2001; Blume, Schmaling, & Marlatt, 2000).

Needle exchanges are perhaps the best-known nonpharmacological harm reduction programs and often use cognitive behavioral principles to modify injectable drug use behavior. Needle exchanges arose in order to reduce the risk of HIV and hepatitis infection among injectable drug users who often share syringes if clean syringes are not easily accessible. With needle exchanges, clean syringes are distributed on the streets in easily accessible locations in neighborhoods of high substance use. The person using the injectable drugs is asked to "trade" used syringes for new ones, with the old syringes being properly disposed to eliminate the possibility of reuse. At the exchanges, education is frequently offered on how to clean used syringes, and is accompanied by the distribution of condoms, another harm reduction technique targeting high risk sexual behavior. The use of needle exchanges has been shown to effectively reduce the spread of HIV and other communicable diseases (Gibson, 2001) and has been associated with ultimate reductions in substance use and increased treatment seeking in one study (Hagan et al., 2000); moreover, needle exchanges have been found to be very cost effective, since in terms of public money the cost of prevention is lower than the cost of treating HIV-positive patients (Kahn, 1998). Federal funding of needle exchanges was recommended by a panel of highly regarded scientists, but unfortunately the report has been ignored (Yoast et al., 2001).

EVIDENCE-BASED APPLICATIONS OF HARM REDUCTION

Harm reduction interventions have been tested empirically for a number of high-risk health and mental health behaviors. Behavioral harm reduction interventions have been shown to be effective for treating alcohol and other substance abuse and misuse among adolescents (e.g., Rivers, Greenbaum, & Goldberg, 2001), ethnic majority and minority college students (e.g., Baer, Kivlahan, Blume, McKnight, & Marlatt, 2001; Caudill et al., 2007; Fromme & Orrick, 2004; Hernandez et al., 2006), and adults (e.g., Larimer et al., 1998), prevention of HIV and other sexually transmitted diseases (e.g., Ball, 2007; Emmanuelli & Desenclos, 2005), high-risk eating behavior (e.g., Wilson, Grilo, & Vitousek, 2007), and smoking among adolescents (e.g., Hamilton, Cross, Resnicow, & Hall, 2005). Pharmacological harm reduction interventions have been empirically supported for treating substance abuse, especially for alcohol (e.g., Anton et al., 2006), opioids (e.g., van den Brink & Haasen, 2006) and nicotine (e.g., Ferguson, Shiffman, & Gwaltney, 2006).

WHO MIGHT BENEFIT FROM THIS TECHNIQUE

Harm reduction works well for people who are unable or unwilling to abstain from substances (Marlatt, 1998a) by intervening upon risky substance use patterns to minimize the experience of potentially risky consequences (e.g., Baer, Kivlahan, Blume, McKnight, & Marlatt, 2001; Hagan et al., 2000). Harm reduction is a viable option for clients who have not done well in programs that demand abstinence or cessation of the targeted behavior (Marlatt, 1998a, Marlatt, Blume, & Parks, 2001), clients with co-occurring mental health and substance use disorders (Blume et al., 2001; Little, 2001), and clients with a history of multiple relapses (Marlatt et al., 2001). Harm reduction strategies also are effective interventions for risky behaviors where complete

abstinence is impractical, such as risky binge eating or overeating patterns, and works well in the secondary prevention of particular health problems when a person has already made the decision to engage in a particular behavior that has the capacity for harm (e.g., use of safe sex practices with sexually active individuals).

CONTRAINDICATIONS OF THIS THERAPY

Harm reduction may not be the most appropriate intervention if the person is willing and able to abstain from a potentially harmful behavior, such as substance abuse. Many practitioners of harm reduction believe that extinction of the targeted behavior for some clients represents the most optimal outcome and that harm reduction is a step-wise method for reaching that goal. A stepped-up care model of therapy starting with harm reduction and moving toward an abstinence goal if harm reduction is not leading to improvement is an effective treatment approach (e.g., Denning, 2001; Marlatt, 1998a). Furthermore, if harm reduction techniques have not worked to reduce risky behavior among clients, other interventions should be considered.

Finally, the successful outcomes of self-directed harm reduction programs rely upon the capacity of clients to carry out the plan, suggesting a certain level of skills are necessary to succeed. If those skills are not present (for instance, critical cognitive skills), then self-directed harm reduction strategies should not be encouraged. However, even with these caveats, harm reduction will be appropriate for a great many people who will benefit by taking steps to reduce the potential harmful consequences of a behavior. In this context, harm reduction may provide accessible treatment options to populations that are often underserved and excluded.

HOW DOES THE TECHNIQUE WORK?

The principal goal of harm reduction is to protect the client's health while respecting the goals for behavior change she or he has developed. Harm reduction is very client centered: The client decides what the goals of behavior change may be. The therapist is available to support the client in reaching her or his goals for therapy by suggesting behavioral change strategies and encouraging behavior modification that validates client goals. Successive approximations toward reduced health risks are evidence of the success of harm reduction strategies.

STEP-BY-STEP PROCEDURES

The following sections will elaborate on the procedures for harm reduction outlined in Table 37.1.

Step 1: Determination of Client Goals for Behavior Change

The client and therapist first determine what the goals of the client are for modifying the targeted behavior. An assessment of personal motivation to change is made, often utilizing the Transtheoretical Stages of Change Model (Prochaska & DiClemente, 1982). The therapist may use motivational interviewing strategies (Miller & Rollnick, 1991) to enhance commitment to behavioral goals, or to investigate the willingness of the client to modify other behavior that the therapist perceives to be risky. Prompting the client to discuss the pros and cons of change versus no change may be utilized to enhance motivation to change. The therapist also may wish to highlight potential health risks in a disarming fashion, and then asking the client what she or he may think about those risks, and if the client has concerns about other consequences of her or his behavior.

TABLE 37.1   Harm Reduction Step by Step

1. Determine the client's goal for behavior change.
2. Assess the behavior chain of the client's targeted behavior.
3. Education about the targeted behavior and its consequences.
4. Develop a consensus about the type of intervention strategies with the client.
5. Provide continued assessment and, when necessary, reevaluation of goals and strategies.
6. Teach maintenance strategies.

Step 2: Self-Monitoring and Other Assessment of Targeted Behavior Chain

The next step is to encourage behavioral monitoring via either self-monitoring forms or diaries in order to assess current behavior patterns. Monitoring will provide data concerning risky behavioral patterns and will suggest places for intervention in the behavior chains of clients. As an example, self-monitoring is a very effective strategy to help the client understand the scope and relationship of problems with the substance use. Clients keep daily diaries of time, type, amount, cues to use substances, patterns of substance use, and consequences of substance use which can be quite helpful for clarifying what the change strategies and goals of modification should be (Blume et al., 2001; Dimeff, Baer, Kivlahan, & Marlatt, 1999).

Use of assessment with standardized social norms also may allow clients to objectively reflect upon consequences of substance use in comparison to normative data. Some researchers have suggested that assessment alone (without feedback) may contribute to reductions in substance use, presumably by increasing personal awareness of the desirability for behavior change (e.g., Carey, Carey, Maisto, & Henson, 2006; Epstein et al., 2005). Some people are genuinely unaware that their behavior deviates significantly from social norms, and providing evidence of this deviation may enhance personal motivation to consider behavior change (e.g., Miller, Zweben, DiClemente, & Rychtarik, 1999).

Step 3: Education about the Targeted Behavior and Its Consequences

Educating the client about the potential consequences of the risky behavior is the next step. Education includes providing new information about the targeted behavior and its consequences and challenges to positive outcome expectancies and personal or cultural myths associated with the targeted behavior (Dimeff et al, 1999). As an example, a therapist may wish to challenge the "that won't happen to me" myth with data related to infection rates after engaging in high-risk sex. As another example, a therapist may wish to challenge positive alcohol expectancies by walking a person through an episode of drinking, from first drink to the consequences of withdrawal.

Step 4: Agreed-upon Intervention Strategies

The client and the therapist jointly develop a behavior modification plan utilizing agreed-upon strategies developed specifically to support the client in reaching her or his goals for behavior change. After the plan is developed, the client acts upon the plan and the therapist gathers data to be used to assess the effectiveness of the plan to achieve the client's goals. The therapist reinforces successive approximations toward reduced health risks by the client in session. Behavioral and pharmacotherapy harm reduction strategies, initially developed for substance use modification, are described subsequently and the broad concepts are also very applicable for non-substance-related harm reduction.

Switching and Alternating

One effective method for reducing harm is to encourage the client to switch to a less harmful alternative behavior. For example, a therapist may suggest a switch to a less harmful substance or to alternate what they typically use with something less harmful. One example of the former would be to encourage beer drinkers to switch from high-alcohol-content to low-alcohol-content beer. Switching people from harder drugs to marijuana has been used successfully in European countries to reduce the harmful consequences of substance abuse (Marlatt, 1998b). Alternating between an alcoholic beverage and a nonalcoholic beverage, or eating while drinking alcohol (alternating drinking with eating), can effectively slow the rate of alcohol consumption.

Tapering

Tapering is a frequently used harm reduction strategy that promotes change via successive approximations toward the client's goal. Tapers often begin by switching to safer alternatives. Limiting access is one strategy related to tapering the targeted behavior. As an example, harm reduction therapists may encourage heavy-drinking clients to buy less alcohol at a time and keep less on hand, rather than stockpiling alcohol. This instills inconvenience into drinking events by limiting easily available alcohol. Furthermore, therapists may wish to emphasize to clients enhancing the quality of drinking rather than quantity by upgrading to more expensive and better tasting alcohol with the goal of promoting sipping rather than gulping. In addition, therapists will want to emphasize that tolerance actually diminishes the positive effects of substance use, a powerful motivator for clients to drink more moderately in order to enhance the positive effects of drinking alcohol.

Structuring Time

Engaging in activities that are incompatible with the targeted behavior will provide fewer opportunities to experience aversive consequences related to that behavior. It is important to help clients structure their time with activities that discourage engaging in the targeted behavior. As an example, harm reduction interventions targeting substance use include plans for exciting, interesting, and challenging alternative activities that diminish available free time in which to use substances. Furthermore, if clients choose to engage in the targeted behavior, they should be taught where and when to do so more safely. For example, many people overdose on substances when in unfamiliar surroundings or using unfamiliar substances, especially when they are alone. Harm reduction for substance abuse teaches clients to use familiar substances in familiar surroundings with familiar people who can provide help in case of emergency (e.g., drug overdose).

Distress Management

Client distress may occur as a result of reducing or extinguishing a targeted behavior, and distress may lead to treatment disengagement if unaddressed. Distress management skills are used in harm reduction to cope with distress. Strategies may include urge surfing (see Chapter 71) and other distress tolerance strategies (Linehan, 1993; Marlatt, 1985), and meditation (Marlatt & Kristeller, 1999), teaching that discomfort is transitory, and that observing dispassionately may be more useful than attempting to control the distress.

Trial Cessation

Another strategy is to ask a client to voluntarily cease the behavior for a prearranged period of time in order to regain control. As an example, harm reduction therapists may ask clients to engage upon a trial period of abstinence (called *sobriety sampling*), which can provide useful information for client and therapist about the persistent nature of the habit. Also, a period of abstinence may allow cognitive abilities to improve, increasing clients' abilities to make better choices.

Skills Training

Skills training is also an important harm reduction strategy to empower clients to reach their goals for therapy. Skills are accessed to see if they seem at an appropriate level to make it likely that the client will reach her or his goals for behavior change. If not, then the therapist will teach and rehearse skills with the client specifically related to the behavior modification goals of the client and to the context in which the skills will be used.

Environmental Interventions

Harm reduction also includes interventions that target the environment surrounding the client. Part of the intervention may be intervening in such a way that alters the reinforcement qualities of the targeted behavior, perhaps by changing the way collaterals act toward the client when engaging in the behavior. At the same, interventions in the environment may be made to reinforce behavior change. A client may be asked to change her or his routine in order to alter their environment. As an example, clients may be asked to drink at home rather than out at their favorite tavern in order to prevent drinking and driving.

Pharmacotherapy

As previously mentioned, pharmacotherapy can be a particularly helpful harm reduction intervention. For example, with substance abuse, pharmacotherapy can help people who are tapering to avoid distress and discomfort (e.g., anxiety or depression) or help reduce cravings to use. Furthermore, clients can

be taught to improve nutritional habits (for example, ingesting more thiamine), as well as avoid potentially harmful over-the-counter medication (e.g., acetaminophen with heavy drinking can harm the liver).

Step 5: Continued Behavior Monitoring and Reevaluation of Behavior Change Goals

Continued monitoring of behavior reveals progress toward achieving client goals. Therapist and client use sessions to review progress, and the therapist may suggest strategy changes as needed. Reevaluation of goals regarding the targeted behavior may lead to revised change goals by the client and a new behavioral plan developed and implemented in consultation with the therapist.

Step 6: Maintenance of Changes

The final step involves use of maintenance strategies when the client's change goals have been reached. Relapse prevention and management strategies may work well for maintaining the behavioral changes at this stage even if extinction of the behavior is not the ultimate goal of therapy (Larimer & Marlatt, 1990).

CONCLUSION

Harm reduction is useful for modifying behavior when extinction may not be a goal, and it also may serve as a first step toward extinction for some clients. A pragmatic approach to behavior change, harm reduction incorporates many different empirically validated cognitive behavioral change strategies into the treatment plan. The therapy often includes grassroots participation by key stakeholders, such as consumers of mental health care, that provide consultation on what change strategies may work best for them. Harm reduction interventions have been empirically supported for a number of targeted behaviors, and offer promise for a number of other areas yet untested. One of the strengths of this technique is its collaborative style and client-centered approach for therapy. Because of this style, harm reduction holds great promise in helping people in traditionally underserved populations who often do not access or do well in conventional treatment environments. Harm reduction is able to serve a more broad-based clientele because it attempts to serve the needs of clients along a continuum of change, rather than expecting certain preconditions from clients in order to receive services (such as abstinence for substance using clients). Harm reduction therefore avoids a moralistic approach to therapy and instead uses pragmatism and sound psychological science to improve public health.

Further Reading

Marlatt, G. A. (Ed.). (1998). *Harm reduction: Pragmatic strategies for managing high risk behaviors.* New York: Guilford.

Denning, P. (2000). *Practicing harm reduction psychotherapy: An alternative approach to addictions.* New York: Guilford.

References

Anton, R. F., O'Malley, S. S., Ciraulo, D. A., Cisler, R. A., Couper, D., Donovan, D. M., et al. (2006). Combined pharmacotherapies and behavioral interventions for alcohol dependence: The COMBINE study: A randomized controlled trial. *Journal of the American Medical Association, 295,* 2003–2017.

Baer, J. S., Kivlahan, D. R., Blume, A. W., McKnight, P., & Marlatt, G. A. (2001). Brief intervention for heavy drinking college students: Four-year follow-up and natural history. *American Journal of Public Health, 91,* 1310–1316.

Ball, A. L. (2007). HIV, injecting drug use and harm reduction: A public health response. *Addiction, 102,* 684–690.

Barnett, P. G., Zaric, G. S., & Brandeau, M. L. (2001). The cost-effectiveness of buprenorphine maintenance therapy for opiate addiction in the United States. *Addictions, 96,* 1267–1278.

Blume, A. W., Anderson, B. K., Fader, J. S., & Marlatt, G. A. (2001). Harm reduction programs: Progress rather than perfection. In R. H. Coombs (Ed.), *Addiction recovery tools: A practical handbook.* Thousand Oaks, CA: Sage Publications.

Blume, A. W., Schmaling, K. B., & Marlatt, G. A. (2000). Revisiting the self-medication hypothesis from a behavioral perspective. *Cognitive and Behavioral Practice, 7,* 379–384.

Carey, K. B., Carey, M. P., Maisto, S. A., & Henson, J. M. (2006). Brief motivational interventions for heavy college drinkers: A randomized controlled trial. *Journal of Consulting and Clinical Psychology, 74,* 943–954.

Caudill, B. D., Luckey, B., Crosse, S. B., Blane, H. T., Ginexi, E. M., & Campbell, B. (2007). Alcohol risk-reduction skills training in a national fraternity: A randomized intervention trial with longitudinal intent-to-treat analysis. *Journal of Studies on Alcohol and Drugs, 68,* 399–409.

Denning, P. (2001). Strategies for implementation of harm reduction in treatment settings. *Journal of Psychoactive Drugs, 33,* 23–26.

Dimeff, L. A., Baer, J. S., Kivlahan, D. R., & Marlatt, G. A. (1999). *Brief alcohol screening and intervention for college students (BASICS): A harm reduction approach.* New York: Guilford.

Emmanuelli, J., & Desenclos, J-C. (2005). Harm reduction interventions, behaviours and associated health outcomes in France, 1996–2003. *Addiction, 100,* 1690–1700.

Epstein, E. E., Drapkin, M. L., Yusko, D. A., Cook, S. M., McCrady, B. S., & Jensen, N. K. (2005). Is alcohol assessment therapeutic? Pretreatment change in drinking among alcohol-dependent women. *Journal of Studies on Alcohol, 66,* 369–378.

Ferguson, S. G., Shiffman, S., & Gwaltney, C. J. (2006). Does reducing withdrawal severity mediate nicotine path efficacy? A randomized controlled trial. *Journal of Consulting and Clinical Psychology, 74,* 1153–1161.

Fromme, K., & Orrick, D. (2004). The lifestyle management class: A harm reduction approach to college drinking. *Addiction Research & Theory, 12,* 335–351.

Gibson, D. R. (2001). Effectiveness of syringe exchange programs in reducing HIV risk behavior and HIV seroconversion among injecting drug users. *AIDS, 15,* 1329–1341.

Hagan, H., McGough, J. P., Thiede, H., Hopkins, S., Duchin, J., & Alexander, E. R. (2000). Reduced injection frequency and increased entry and retention in drug treatment associated with needle-exchange participants in Seattle drug injectors. *Journal of Substance Abuse Treatment, 19,* 247–252.

Hamilton, G., Cross, D., Resnicow, K., & Hall, M. (2005). A school-based harm minimization smoking intervention trial: Outcome results. *Addiction, 100,* 689–700.

Hernandez, D. V., Skewes, M. C., Resor, M. R., Villanueva, M. R., Hanson, B. S., & Blume, A. W. (2006). A pilot test of an alcohol skills training programme for Mexican-American college students. *International Journal of Drug Policy, 17,* 320–328.

Kahn, J. G. (1998). Economic evaluation of primary HIV prevention in injection drug users. In D. R. Holtgrave (Ed.), *Handbook of economic evaluation of HIV prevention program, AIDS prevention, and mental health.* New York: Plenum Press.

Kranzier, H. R., & Van Kirk, J. (2001). Efficacy of naltrexone and acamprosate for alcoholism treatment: A meta-analysis. *Alcoholism: Clinical and Experimental Research, 25,* 1335–1341.

Larimer, M. E., & Marlatt, G. A. (1990). Applications of relapse prevention with moderation goals. *Journal of Psychoactive Drugs, 22,* 189–195.

Larimer, M. E., Marlatt, G. A., Baer, J. S., Quigley, L. A., Blume, A. W., & Hawkins, E. H. (1998). Harm reduction for alcohol problems: Expanding access to and acceptability of prevention and treatment services. In G. A. Marlatt (Ed.), *Harm reduction: Strategies to manage high risk behavior* (pp. 69–121). New York: Guilford Press.

Linehan, M. M. (1993). *Skills training manual for treating borderline personality disorder.* New York: Guilford.

Little, J. (2001). Treatment of dually diagnosed clients. *Journal of Psychoactive Drugs, 33,* 27–31.

Marlatt G. A. (1985). Cognitive assessment and intervention procedures for relapse prevention. In Marlatt G. A. & Gordon J. R. (Eds.), *Relapse prevention: Maintenance strategies in the treatment of addictive behaviors,* (pp. 3–70). New York: Guilford.

Marlatt, G. A. (1998). Basic principles and strategies of Harm Reduction. In G. A. Marlatt (Ed.), *Harm reduction: Pragmatic strategies for managing high risk behaviors,* (pp. 49–66). New York: Guilford.

Marlatt, G. A. (1998). Harm reduction around the world: A brief history. In G. A. Marlatt (Ed.), *Harm reduction: Pragmatic strategies for managing high risk behaviors,* (pp. 30–48). New York: Guilford.

Marlatt, G. A., Blume, A. W., & Parks, G. A. (2001). Integrating harm reduction therapy and traditional substance abuse treatment. *Journal of Psychoactive Drugs, 33,* 13–21.

Marlatt, G. A., & Kristeller, J. (1999). Mindfulness and meditation. In W. R. Miller (Ed.), *Integrating spirituality into treatment.* Washington, DC: American Psychological Association.

Miller, W. R., Zweben, A., DiClemente, C. C., & Rychtarik, R. G. (1999). Motivational enhancement therapy manual: A clinical research guide for therapists treating individual with alcohol abuse and dependence. Project MATCH Monograph Series, Volume 2, M. E. Mattson, (Ed.). Rockville, MD: National Institute on Alcohol Abuse and Alcoholism.

Miller, W. R., & Rollnick, S. (1991). *Motivational interviewing.* New York: Guilford.

Rivers, S. M., Greenbaum, R. L., & Goldberg, E. (2001). Hospital-based adolescent substance abuse treatment: Comorbidity, outcomes, and gender. *Journal of Nervous and Mental Disease, 189,* 229–237.

Van den Brink, W., & Haasen, C. (2006). Evidenced-based treatment of opioid-dependent patients. *Canadian Journal of Psychiatry, 51,* 635–646.

Wilson, G. T., Grilo, C. M., & Vitousek, K. M. (2007). Psychological treatment of eating disorders. *American Psychologist, 62,* 199–216.

Yoast, R., Williams, M. A., Deitchman, S. D., & Champion, H. C. (2001). Report of the Council on Scientific Affairs: Methadone maintenance and needle-exchange programs to reduce the medical and public health consequences of drug abuse. *Journal of Addictive Diseases, 20,* 15–40.

38 PUTTING IT ON THE STREET: HOMEWORK IN COGNITIVE BEHAVIORAL THERAPY

Patricia Robinson

The importance of homework has long been recognized, and its use was first documented in the literature over 60 years ago (Herzberg, 1941). It has been described as "the most generic of behavioral interventions" (Goisman, 1985, p. 676), and early developers of cognitive behavioral therapy advised that it was the client's ability to apply behavioral and cognitive skills learned in therapy that determine long-term gains (Beck, Rush, Shaw, & Emery, 1979). Homework is a fundamental strategy for creating necessary opportunities for applying skills learned in client and therapist interactions. In recent years, empirical studies have demonstrated a link between client homework compliance and reduced symptoms at posttreatment (Beutler et al., 2004; Kazantzis, Deane, & Ronan, 2000), and the push is on to explore reliable measures for compliance and homework's causal effects on symptom reduction.

However, several barriers limit the potentially pervasive and positive impact that competent use of homework could have on outcomes of cognitive behavioral therapy. These include cognitive behavioral therapists' inconsistent use of homework, as well as the lack of a systematic approach to homework. The optimal process for integrating homework into therapy is a recent topic for empirical investigation (Zazantzis & Dattilio, 2007) and support for effective use of homework is growing. This chapter addresses barriers and suggests practical guidelines for using homework systematically to obtain optimal outcomes with a diverse group of clients, including challenging and complex clients.

THERAPIST USE OF HOMEWORK

Over 25 years ago, Shelton and Levy (1981) published a manual describing a systematic approach to use of homework in clinical practice. Contemporary writers continue to emphasize homework in formulations of cognitive behavioral therapy (Alford & Beck, 1994; Hollon & Beck, 1994) and to specify homework assignments in manualized, empirically supported treatments for specific disorders, such as panic disorder, generalized anxiety disorder (Barlow & Craske, 1989; Craske, Barlow, & O'Leary, 1992), psychosis (Nelson, H. E. (2005), anxious youth (Kendall & Hedtke, 2006), and with families and couples (Bevilacqua & Dattilio, 2001, Dattilo & Jongsma, 2000, O'Leary, Heyman, & Jongsma, 1998).

While the promotion of homework as an integral part of cognitive behavioral therapy has had a positive impact, its potential is greater than its current impact. Kazantzis and Deane (1999) found that 98% of a group of 221 New Zealand practicing psychologists used homework assignments. However, only one in four reported use of a systematic approach to homework, such as was recommended by Shelton and Levy (1981). Cognitive behavioral therapists responding to the survey, in comparison with therapists practicing other models of treatment, were significantly more likely to use homework activities involving explicit recording (53% vs. 36%) and to recommend homework in more sessions (66% of sessions vs. 57%).

Available evidence suggests that therapist competence is a potent factor in successful use of homework. Young and Beck's (1980) Cognitive Therapy Scale (CTS) includes use of homework as a therapist competency area. Several studies using CTS constructs as well as other sources of data suggest that therapist review (Bryant, Simons, & Thase, 1999), design, and assignment of homework are associated with desired therapy outcomes (Detweiler-Bedell & Whisman, 2005; Startup & Edmonds, 1994).

Kazantis, MacEwan, et al. (2005) offer a model for use of homework in clinical practice that emphasizes therapist beliefs, as well as specific therapist behaviors in reviewing, designing, and assigning homework. In the "Therapist's Quick Reference" (TQR; Kazantzis, Deane, Ronan, & L'Abate, 2005) specific therapist behaviors for three phases—design, assign, and review—are offered to support training and consistency in effective use of homework.

Shelton and Levy (1981) stress the importance of taking a systematic approach to homework and suggest that such include (1) specification of the location and length of the homework assignment, (2) provision of a written note for the client concerning the homework plan, and (3) completion of a written note in the treatment record indicating the extent or quality of homework completion for each session. In an effort to boost consistent and effective use of homework with a wide range of clients, this chapter offers a step-by-step guide to systematic use of homework. Prior to the practicalities of homework a brief review of the evidence for the effectiveness of homework with specific populations is in order.

EVIDENCE-BASED APPLICATIONS OF HOMEWORK

Empirical evidence supports involving clients in homework assignments, and it is likely that clients who actively engage in homework are more likely to benefit from therapy (Kazantzis, Dattilio, & MacEwan, 2005). The first evidence for the effectiveness of homework was reported over 65 years ago: "short treatment of neuroses by graduated tasks" was effective with approximately 60% of a client sample (Herzberg, 1941). Subsequently, numerous studies have suggested a positive correlation between homework adherence and treatment outcome (Burns &

Auerbach,1992; Burns & Nolen-Hoeksema, 1991; Leung & Heimberg, 1996), as well as between homework adherence and posttreatment symptom reduction (Beutler et al., 2004; Kazantis, Deane, & Ronan, 2000). While the evidence for homework's causal effects on symptom reduction needs clarification, lack of clarity in findings may be the result of low sample sizes and limited assessments of homework compliance (Kazantzis & Dattilo, 2007). In this section, evidence is presented in two parts. The first concerns general casual effects and factors associated with homework compliance; the second provides examples of evidence for use of homework with specific populations.

WHAT IS THE PROCESS BY WHICH HOMEWORK PRODUCES ITS EFFECTS IN THERAPY?

In order for homework assignments to improve therapy outcomes, clients presumably need to complete them. In other words, in order for homework to contribute to positive outcomes in therapy, clients need to implement them. Burns and Spangler (2000) used structural equation modeling to suggest a causal link between homework and outcome. They reported effect sizes in their two client samples similar in magnitude to those reported by Persons, Burns, and Perloff (1988). Persons and her colleagues found a mean reduction in Beck Depression Inventory scores of 16.6 points for clients who did home work in comparison to a 2.4-point reduction for clients who did little or no homework. An effect size of this magnitude is of a sufficient size to lead to nearly complete elimination of symptoms for clients with mild to moderate levels of depression.

Several studies indicate that completion of homework also supports the maintenance of gains after treatment completion. Edelman and Chambless (1995) evaluated the relationship of homework completion and long-term change among social phobic clients in a cognitive behavioral group treatment. At the 6-month follow-up, clients who adhered more to homework instructions reported less anxiety during a behavioral task, greater decrements in anxiety, and more change in avoidant behavior. Thompson and

Gallagher (1984) also found that homework during the later phase of treatment helped older, depressed adults maintain gains following treatment completion.

In regards to the question of why some clients complete assignments and others do not, definitive studies are lacking. Factors related to homework adherence include therapist factors, client factors, and environmental factors. As mentioned previously, therapist competence in designing homework is a potent factor. Additionally, therapeutic collaboration probably plays a significant role. Clients may be more likely to adhere, when they participate actively in the formulation of the homework plan. In a trial of two approaches to teaching parenting skills, participants in the coping modeling problem-solving group completed more homework and rated the program more highly than participants in the master modeling approach (Cunningham, Davis, Bremner, & Dunn, 1993). Additionally, client acceptance of treatment rationale, in addition to homework compliance, has been found to make an independent contribution to treatment outcome (Addis & Jacobson, 2000). It appears that collaborative development and providing an acceptable rationale for treatment and related homework may be critical components of homework assignments that lead to clinical improvements.

The *Cognitive Behavior Therapy Homework Project* at Massey University, New Zealand, is an international collaborative project whose purpose is to clarify the process by which homework produces its effects in therapy (Kazantzis, 2005). Publications from this group include theoretical and practical integration of homework in behavior therapy (Roth-Ledley & Huppert, 2007), cognitive therapy (Beck & Tompkins, 2007), personal construct therapy (Neimeyer & Winter, 2007), acceptance and commitment therapy (Twohig, Pierson, & Hayes, 2007) and dialectical behavior therapy (Lindenboim, Chapman, & Linehan, 2007). They are sure to produce more needed information about client, therapist, and environmental processes that affect homework design, implementation, and review in coming years.

USE OF HOMEWORK WITH SPECIFIC POPULATIONS

Homework is likely an important treatment component in treatment of most behavioral health problems and in delivery of cognitive behavioral as well as other types of therapy. Data suggest that homework is a critical component in marital and family therapy (Carr, 1997; Hansen & MacMillan, 1990), solution-focused therapy (Beyebach, Morejon, Palenzuela, & Rodriguez-Arias, 1996), and addiction treatment (Annis, Schober, & Kelly, 1996). However, the nature of determining the effectiveness of homework with specific populations limits understanding of the specific role homework contributes to treatment outcomes with specific populations.

Our tradition is to establish empirical validation for a therapeutic procedure by applying it in controlled circumstances to a specific problem, such as depression or anxiety. We have yet to conduct studies that define the specific contribution of homework in empirically supported cognitive behavioral treatments for specific populations. This type of study would involve randomization a group of clients, for example depressed clients, to two groups—one whose therapists follow the empirically established protocol, including use homework, and one whose therapists follow the protocol excepting an exclusion of the use of homework. The data we have concern use of homework as a part of a treatment package for which empirical effectiveness has been established.

A special series in cognitive and behavioral practice (Kazantzis & Dattilio, 2007) provides guidance on the use of homework with complex and challenging clients. Illustrative case examples range from an older adult with dementia to a treatment-resistant case of obsessive–compulsive disorder. The following two examples are selected for brief review here because they rely on an empirically supported treatment package and they illustrate important adaptations that increase the likelihood of client participation in development, enactment, and review of homework.

Anxious Youth. Child-focused cognitive behavioral therapy for anxious youth (e.g., Albano & Kendall, 2002) is a "probably efficacious" treatment (Chambless & Hollon, 1998). Kendall and Barmish (2007) use Show-That-I-Can (STIC) (Homework) tasks in the Coping Cat program, a 12–16-week program modeled after empirical studies. STIC tasks, unlike academic homework, have no right or wrong answers, do not involve evaluation of spelling or grammar, and are not graded.

Psychosis. Given numerous randomized controlled trial studies demonstrating the efficacy of cognitive behavioral therapy for psychosis (cf. Pilling et al., 2002; Tarrier & Wykes, 2004), it is now a recommended component of evidence-based care in the National Institute for Health and Clinical Excellence (NICE, 2003). Rector (2007) describes a systematic approach to use of homework in seven phases of treatment, beginning with assessment and engagement and ending with relapse prevention. Common homework options include self-monitoring, bibliotherapy/resources, cognitive tasks, and behavioral tasks.

HOW DOES HOMEWORK WORK?

The causal structure that accounts for the positive association between homework compliance and degree of improvement is not understood. In the case of depression, Burns and Spangler (2000) have suggested four possibilities:

1. Homework has positive causal effects on changes in depression.
2. Depression influences the amount of homework completed between sessions.
3. A positive feedback loop exists in which homework assignments lead to improvement in depression, and the uplift in mood increases the likelihood of homework compliance.
4. Homework compliance is only spuriously correlated with depression because of an unknown third variable with simultaneous casual effects on homework compliance and depression.

In their study (Burns & Spangler, 2000), homework compliance had a causal effect on changes in depression, and the magnitude of this effect was large. Clients who did the most homework improved much more than clients who did little or no homework. Homework compliance did not appear to be a proxy for any other, unobserved variable, such as motivation.

WHO MIGHT BENEFIT FROM HOMEWORK ASSIGNMENTS

Homework provides critical information for the therapist and client to use in formulating and evaluating change plans, as well as opportunities for the client to practice new skills introduced in treatment sessions. Therefore, treatment outcome is presumably very closely linked to consistent development of high-quality homework and client and therapist adherence. Available literature suggests that depressed clients benefit from homework assignments (Burns & Nolen-Hoeksema, 1991; Persons et al., 1988; Neimeyer & Feixas, 1990; Startup & Edmonds, 1994; Addis & Jacobson, 2000; Burns & Spangler, 2000). Additionally, homework compliance has been related to a positive treatment outcome with social phobia (Leung & Heimberg, 1996) and agoraphobic men and women (Edelman, & Chambless, 1995). The relative contribution of homework to treatment outcome has not been established for other disorders.

Survey data suggest that 80% of psychologists believe homework is of great importance in the treatment of anxiety, nonassertiveness, and social skills, and 65% see homework as being of great importance in the treatment of depression, anxiety disorders, insomnia, obsessions and compulsions, and sexual dysfunction (Kazantzis & Deane, 1999). Data from the same survey suggest that 50% see homework being as of little or moderate importance for treatment of delusions and hallucinations, learning disorders, and sexual abuse.

Since there are many reports of the success of homework, and only speculations to the contrary, it seems possible that the vast majority of clients benefit from completion of well-developed homework assignments. Critical issues for developing beneficial homework assignments include (1) accurate evaluation of the client's readiness for change, (2) the quality of the therapeutic alliance, (3) the level of collaboration in homework development, (4) the rationale given for homework, (5) the utilization of client strengths in formulation of the homework plan, and (6) the extent to which homework adherence is positively reinforced both inside and outside of the treatment session.

CONTRAINDICATIONS FOR HOMEWORK ASSIGNMENTS

Practitioners need to use homework systematically with almost all clients, but they should use it with caution with clients with cognitive and/or motivational deficits. Highly symptomatic clients with delusions and hallucinations may have difficulty with written homework tasks (Nelson, 1997). This is because many of these clients may be unwilling or unable to complete written homework assignments and because they find it difficult to work at the abstract level of thinking about thinking. However, some of these clients may benefit from homework assignments involving completion of practical tasks between sessions and reporting back to the therapist from memory (Chadwick, Birchwood, & Trower, 1996).

Obesity treatment clients who fail to comply with self-monitoring instructions at the beginning of therapy have been observed to be likely to fail to lose weight (Wadden & Letizia, 1992). Clinical experience suggests that obesity treatment clients who continue to not complete self-monitoring assignments despite the therapist's best efforts to collaborate, provide a rationale for self-monitoring, and positively reinforce any approximation toward completion of self-monitoring assignments do not do well in treatment (Wilson & Vitousek, 1999). This may be the case with clients with other complaints who do not intend to make a change within the next 6 months.

Prochaska and DiClemente (1983) have proposed a transtheoretical model that applies to intentional change and individual decision-making about health behavior, and this approach is often useful with less motivated psychotherapy clients. This model suggests specific strategies for working with clients to help them move from the precontemplation stage to the action stage of change (Prochaska, 1994). Miller and Rollnick (1991), developers of motivational interviewing, also offer ideas for working successfully with clients who are in the contemplation stage of change.

OTHER FACTORS IN DECIDING WHETHER TO USE HOMEWORK

If a client fails to adhere to a homework assignment, the therapist needs to avoid repeating assignment of the same homework and should share in responsibility for the adherence failure. The therapist is the expert on behavior change, and, hence, has ultimate responsibility for the feasibility of assigned homework. When a client fails to implement a homework plan, the therapist needs to take time to identify the specific obstacles to implementation and to address these thoughtfully in a new homework assignment. When motivation for change is lacking, the therapist will need to accommodate the willingness level of the client and plan homework consistent with that level. It is important to scale client confidence in a homework plan developed immediately after a failed homework plan. This can be accomplished by asking the client to rate his or her confidence on a scale of 1 (no confidence) to 10 (total confidence). When client confidence is lacking, the therapist may want to revise the plan and/or offer additional support to the client. The therapist's offer of a brief phone call check-in may inspire more client confidence, particularly after a failed homework assignment. For the vast majority of client contacts, the therapist will develop homework assignments that are adjusted to the client's level of organization and motivation and that are supported optimally by the client's social network, the client's own self-reinforcement plan, and/or the therapist.

TABLE 38.1   Step-by-Step Procedures for Developing Homework Assignments

Phase of Treatment Process of Care Target

Homework Target.

    Initial: The M&Ms of Monitoring Assignments

    Motivation for Change

    Monitoring Method Selection

Middle: The 6 S's of Successful Behavior Change Assignments

    Self-Efficacy/Strengths

    Soundness of Rationale

    Size and Place of Assignment

    Skills Required

    Self-Reinforcement

    Support (Social, Therapist)

Conclusion: The Four R's of Effective Maintenance Assignments

    Related to Values

    Relapse Prevention Plans

    Regular Review

    Revised to Support Lifestyle

TABLE 38.2   Questions to Use as a Quality Check for Use of Homework in Cognitive Behavioral Treatment

Homework Quality Check Questions.

Phase of Treatment Question.

Initial

    1. Does the client intend to change in the next 6 months?

    2. What is the most feasible method of self-monitoring?

Middle

    3. What client strengths relate to the homework task, and how strong is the client's belief in his or her ability to complete the task?

    4. What are the client's beliefs about the cause of and solution for the problem?

    5. How much time will homework take, and where will it occur?

    6. What skills are required to implement the homework?

    7. What are the planned potential positive reinforcers for the homework assignment (self, others, therapist)?

    8. Is the homework plan in written form for the client (as a take-home) and for the therapist (in records)?

Conclusion

    9. How are most beneficial homework tasks related to client values?

    10. What changes and/or new skills helped the client improve; how often and when will they continue to be performed, and who will support them?

    11. What is the emergency plan?

    12. How can the most beneficial homework assignments be integrated into the client's lifestyle?

STEP-BY-STEP PROCEDURES FOR USING HOMEWORK

Although homework is a potentially beneficial part of cognitive behavioral treatment with most disorders and in all phases, homework assignments are more likely to contribute to client improvement when they match the demands of the phase of treatment and are sensitive to process-of-care factors. Table 38.1 offers a conceptual structure for systematic use of homework in cognitive behavioral therapy. In Table 38.2, there are 12 questions that therapists can use as a quality check on homework. Applying these questions with one new client each week will help therapists become more systematic in developing and evaluating homework in their practice setting.

In the initial contact, the most common assignment will involve some form of self-monitoring. Self-monitoring is the act of tracking the frequency, intensity, or duration of a clinical target behavior and recording this information in some type of written record. The process-of-care factor that is most critical in determining the success of self-monitoring assignments is the client's level of motivation for change.

During the behavior change phase of treatment, self-efficacy and skills are important factors in homework design. Finally, the relationship of homework assignments to client values merits focus in tailoring homework assignments for the maintenance phase of treatment. Although all three of the suggested process-of-care variables may play a critical role at any phase of treatment, they are often more salient at the treatment phase suggested earlier and indicated in Table 38.1.

The M&M's of Monitoring Assignments: Initial Homework Assignments

The M&M's of monitoring assignments consist of (1) motivation for change and (2) monitoring method selection. Client level of motivation can change significantly even within a single session.

A homework assignment that permits assessment of the level of motivation for change on an ongoing basis according to a structured method can open the door for later action-oriented psychotherapy. Of course, self-monitoring is at the heart of cognitive behavioral therapy.

Motivation for Change

In introducing the concept of homework, the therapist may tell clients that research findings suggest that clients who commit themselves to developing and implementing homework assignments may experience significantly more benefit from treatment than clients who do little or no homework. The therapist can explain that most of the client's life happens between treatment sessions and that it's putting it on the street, so to speak, that facilitates improvement.

Given encouragement, most clients will readily state their level of intention to change. When others send clients to treatment, they may have not had the opportunity to sort out the pros and cons of behavior change. They may lack information about the options for change and the related benefits. When a client indicates ambivalence, the therapist may offer assignments that increase the client's information level and/or help the client clarify costs and benefits of treatment at the present time.

It is important to avoid strong-arming clients and to offer them a choice. This stance will help to keep the door open for treatment later. Therapists may even offer phone call check-ins on a quarterly basis, particularly to clients at risk for poor outcomes. With this approach, there is the possibility that services will become available close to the time when the client's level of motivation increases.

New models of care, such as the Primary Care Behavioral Health Model (Robinson & Reiter, 2007; Robinson, Wischman, & Del Vento, 1996; Strosahl, 1997) support strategic work with less motivated members of a population, because the mission of the model is to improve the health status of an entire population. In these therapeutic relationships, the client's homework is to participate in discussion of the pros and cons of change during quarterly telephone calls.

Monitoring Method Selection

Monitoring methods need to be feasible, meaning that the client has the necessary skills, time, and interest required to complete the monitoring. Many clients will have difficulties with monitoring assignments that require them to carry around workbooks or even large pieces of paper. A single half-sheet or a small pocket notebook (with the instructions written inside the cover) is often more feasible. Another option is to ask the client to record monitored information in his or her personal calendar, whether that is a monthly calendar in their bedroom, a daily appointment book, or a palm pilot. The nature of the monitoring assignment needs to be simple and straightforward, and the assignment should be practiced in session, followed by a self-reinforcing activity, and acknowledged by the therapist in all follow-up sessions.

The Six S's of Successful Behavior Change Assignments: Homework in the Middle Phase

The six S's of successful behavior change homework assignments include self-efficacy strengths, soundness of rationale, and size of assignment, skills required, self-reinforcement, and support. In order for behavior change homework assignments to contribute their maximum impact to client improvement, both the therapist and client must be intentional and thorough in their development, implementation, and follow-up.

Self-Efficacy/Strengths

It is important to identify client strengths and to incorporate them into the homework assignment. Although this seems simple in principle, it can be deceptively difficult in practice. An example of working with a more challenging client will illustrate this point. The client was a woman with substantial economic challenges, who reported moderate symptoms of depression, as well as marital, parent–child, occupational, and health problems. When asked, the client indicated that she had no strengths. When asked what brought her pleasure, she indicated that nothing brought her pleasure. When asked if she liked to go outside, she said that she did like to sit on the steps of her trailer, but that she often felt afraid there because neighbors of a different race had thrown rocks at her. Within a few minutes of questioning, the following homework assignment was developed: She would ask her 21-year-old daughter (the only licensed driver in the family) to drive her to a safe park twice weekly, where she would walk and enjoy the plants for 30 minutes. Her self-efficacy about this plan was high. She knew that she could ask her daughter, that she could walk, and that she would enjoy seeing the plants at the park.

Soundness of Rationale

Client beliefs about the nature of their problem may play a role in developing rationales for homework that make sense to the client. Addis and Jacobson (2000) found that depressed clients who gave existential reasons for their depression had better outcomes with cognitive therapy, while clients who espoused relationship-oriented reasons as causing their depression had consistently more negative process (including homework) and treatment outcomes with cognitive therapy. This finding may speak in part to the acceptability of the rationale for treatment, including the nature of the homework assigned. Often, an understanding of the clients' beliefs about the cause of their problem helps the therapist to construct a more meaningful rational for treatment, including homework.

Because depression is a very common reason for seeking treatment, it will be used in illustrating this point. Some clients believe the cause of depression is biochemistry or bad genes. Others insist that it is due to life circumstances. Conceivably, a similar behavioral activation plan (e.g., going to a movie with a friend and evaluating the impact on mood) could be collaboratively developed for both clients. However, the rationale would need to be tailored to each client. In the case of the client who believes in biochemical causation, the rationale might be that this assignment made sense because the activity might facilitate a biochemical change that would improve brain chemistry and mood functioning. For the other client, the rationale might be that the assignment could provide a counterbalance to difficult situations, therefore, reducing the overall impact of the life circumstance problems. When the therapist provides an acceptable rationale, the client is able to put the homework assignment into a framework that is consistent with his or her prevailing worldview.

Size of Assignment

The size of the assignment depends on the client's readiness for change, his or her self-efficacy, and his or her resources, including mastery of prerequisite skills and availability of potential positive reinforcers. Some clients come to the initial session with a great deal of motivation, self-efficacy, and resources. This type of client may participate collaboratively in developing a homework plan and require no follow-up beyond a brief phone check-in concerning implementation of the homework plan. By way of illustration, consider the case of a pregnant woman who came to therapy with the complaint that her best friend had died. She explained that she was experiencing a great deal of sadness and was worried about the impact on her unborn child. The planned homework assignment included development of a weekly schedule of health-related behaviors (e.g., exercise and relaxation activities) and social activities, along with scheduled times when she could experience her loss and her sadness. Although size of the homework was huge (i.e., 6 hours of exercise, 7 hours of grieving, 5 hours of social activities, 4 hours of pleasurable activities, etc.), the client was completely confident because it matched her readiness to change, her self-efficacy, and her resources.

Skills Required

Many good homework assignments blow up because the client simply does not have the prerequisite skills necessary to succeed at the assignment. In one such case, a young therapist developed a homework assignment for an inpatient adolescent that involved independent use of a washing machine to laundry her clothes. The therapist planned the time and location for the task and identified planned reinforcers. Unfortunately, the client came from a family that did not have an automatic washer and she had never operated a washing machine. The client made an effort, but placed a bar of soap, rather than laundry detergent, in the machine, and the result was not a positive experience. A good way to identify specific skill requirements is to ask the client to visualize doing the homework assignment in session and to report on perceived obstacles. Then, the therapist can help the client develop the skills needed to overcome the obstacles or change the homework assignment.

Self-Reinforcement

Since many homework assignments involve asking the client to engage in different, more effective behaviors, it is important to reward these behaviors immediately after they occur. Many clients who are motivated to change behavior don't succeed because there are no immediately available reinforcements in their natural environment. They are forced to rely on an intrinsic sense of gratification, which may be absent, or they may receive negative feedback when they behave in more personally effective ways (e.g., a woman who asserts herself rather than submitting to a verbally aggressive husband). The therapist can explain that most people don't have someone to cheer them on during the difficult process of self-change. Therefore, learning to make and implement self-reinforcement plans is an important life skill. Self-reinforcement plans need to have all of the qualities of good homework plans (i.e., they should be specific, simple, etc.) and to be affordable. Examples of self-reinforcement following a desired homework assignment include going to a movie, watching a favorite television show, listening to a favorite CD, taking a long warm bath, and so forth.

Support (Therapist, Social)

Early in treatment, it is important to identify whom the client can rely on to provide social support and social reinforcement for completing a homework assignment. Who cares about the changes she or he is trying to make? It is often useful to jot down the name of the identified social supporter and to suggest to the client that they give a brief report to the person (or pet) close to the time that they complete a homework assignment. The therapist also needs to understand this his\her attention is a powerful secondary reinforcer. Because of this, the therapist must be entirely committed to monitoring homework assignments and providing praise and social reinforcement when the assignment has been completed.

This support can be accomplished in a number of ways and depends on the needs of the client. All clients need to know that completion of homework is important, and the therapist demonstrates this by asking the client about homework completion in the first 5 minutes of the follow-up session. The therapist should be thorough in asking about all aspects of the homework experience and acknowledge all aspects of the homework experience, from effort to implement to interest in learning from the experiment.

At times, a client will need the therapist to provide this type of support between sessions. This can be offered when a client is planning a homework assignment that is particularly challenging and during the termination phase of treatment, when visits may be weeks or months apart. The therapist can provide support to enhance adherence by giving a 2-minute phone call: "Did you do it? Good for you!" Mail, Internet, or voice mail communications may accomplish support of homework, as well. Additionally, follow-up of homework assignments by other team members (e.g., primary care physicians, nurses, or teachers) is an option for behavioral health providers who provide consultation services as part of a team or staff in a primary care clinic or school.

The Four R's of Effective Homework Assignments during the Maintenance Phase

The maintenance phase of treatment includes development of a large homework assignment— the relapse prevention plan. A strong plan will link the client's intention to maintain new changes to important values and thoughtfully integrate the continued shaping of new behaviors into the client's lifestyle.

Related to Values

As treatment concludes, whether at the second or tenth contact, the client and therapist need to address questions related to values, such as why maintenance of the changed behavior(s) matters in the long run and what value the client will use at the moment when the choice to continue or return to past behavior patterns presents itself. Success in the maintenance phase of treatment requires the client to engage in independent committed action. Hayes, Strosahl, and Wilson (1999) suggest strategies for furthering client preparation for successful development of homework assignments in this phase of treatment.

Relapse Prevention Plans

Development of an effective relapse prevention plan involves identification of the skills that have contributed most to the client's improvement (many of which were likely discovered or fine-tuned in homework assignments) and packaging these into a feasible lifestyle plan. Because of the importance of providing positive reinforcement for newly acquired skills, the plan needs to specify self-reinforcement and social reinforcement strategies for newly learned behaviors. This may involve the client's participation in supportive group programs (e.g., attendance at Toastmasters after treatment for public speaking phobia), reports to buddies (e.g., calling a close friend to report completion of a monthly self-monitoring procedure), or follow-up with other professionals (teachers, spiritual leaders, primary care providers).

Regular Review

Clients vary in their personal organizational style, and some may prefer to plan a regular review of relapse prevention plans with a therapist or case manager. This review can be conducted in a brief phone call that targets the relapse prevention plan (Katon et al., 1996) or in a group booster session. Providing a generic, drop-in psychoeducational group on a weekly basis at an accessible location, such as a primary care clinic (cf. Robinson, 1996, for curriculum for a Quality of Life class), allows clients who need more direct support to receive it. Use of a curriculum that furthers development of self-management skills through structured, empirically supported homework assignments allows the therapist to be more efficient in meeting the needs of clients who are in the process of creating stable change in chronic dysfunctional patterns.

Revised to Support Lifestyle

Many aspects of a client's life may change during the first 6 months after a successful episode of psychotherapy. A follow-up appointment 6 months after the completion of active treatment provides an opportunity for the client and therapist to revise the relapse prevention plan with better understanding of the person's more functional lifestyle. As more effective behaviors are developed and integrated into the client's native repertoire, it is only natural to see the relapse prevention plan evolve in content and complexity. These changes should be anticipated as part of a successful psychotherapy maintenance plan.

Further Reading

N. Kazantzis, & L'Abate, L. (2007). *Handbook of homework assignments in psychotherapy: Research, practice, and prevention.* New York: Springer.

Shelton, J. L., & Levy, R. L. (1981). *Behavioral assignments and treatment compliance: A handbook of clinical strategies.* Champaign, IL: Research Press.

References

Addis, M., & Jacobson, N. S. (2000). A closer look at the treatment rationale and homework compliance in cognitive behavioral therapy for depression. *Cognitive Therapy and Research,* 24(3), 313–326.

Albano, A. M., & Kendall, P. C. (2002). Cognitive behavioral therapy for children and adolescents with anxiety disorders: Clinical research advances. *International Review of Psychiatry,* 14, 129–134.

Alford, B. A., & Beck, A. T. (1994). Cognitive therapy of delusional beliefs. *Behavioral Research and Therapy,* 32(3), 369–380.

Annis, H. M., Schober, R., & Kelly, E. (1996). Matching addiction outpatient counseling to client readiness for change: The role of structured relapse prevention counseling. *Experimental and Clinical Psychopharmacology,* 4(1), 37–45.

Barlow, D. H., & Craske, M. G. (1989). *Mastery of your anxiety and panic.* Albany, NY: Graywind Publications.

Beck, A. T., Rush, J. A., Shaw, B. F., & Emery, G. (1979). *Cognitive therapy of depression.* New York: Guilford.

Beutler, L. E., Malik, M., Alimohamed, S., Harwood, T. M., Talebi, H., Noble, S., et al. (2004) Therapist variables. In M. J. Lamber (Ed.), *Bergin and Garfield's handbook of psychotherapy and behavior change.* (5th ed., pp. 227–306). New York: Springer.

Bevilacqua, L. J., & Dattilio, F. M. (2001). *Brief family therapy homework planner.* New York: John Wiley & Sons.

Beyebach, M., Morejon, A. R., Palenzuela, D. L., & Rodriguez-Arias, J. L. (1996). Research on the process of solution-focused therapy. In S. D. Miller, M. A. Hubble, & B. L. Duncan (Eds.), *Handbook of solution-focused brief therapy* (pp. 299–334). San Francisco, CA: Jossey-Bass.

Bryant, M. J., Simons, A. D., & Thase, M. E. (1999). Therapist skill and patient variables in homework compliance: Controlling an uncontrolled variable in cognitive therapy outcome research. *Cognitive Therapy and Research, 23*, 381–399.

Burns, D. D., & Auerbach, A. H. (1992). Does homework compliance enhance recovery from depression? *Psychiatric Annals, 22*(9), 464–469.

Burns, D. D., & Nolen-Hoeksema, S. (1991). Coping styles, homework compliance, and the effectiveness of cognitive-behavioral therapy. *Journal of Consulting and Clinical Psychology, 59*(2), 305–311.

Burns, D. D., & Spangler, D. L. (2000). Does psychotherapy homework lead to improvements in depression in cognitive-behavioral therapy or does improvement lead to increased homework compliance? *Journal of Consulting and Clinical Psychology, 68*(1), 46–56.

Carr, A. (1997). Positive practice in family therapy. *Journal of Marital and Family Therapy, 23*(3), 271–293.

Chadwick, P., Birchwood, M., & Trower, P. (1996). *Cognitive therapy for delusions, voices and paranoia.* Chichester, England: Wiley.

Chambless, D., & Hollon, S. (1998). Defining empirically supported treatments. *Journal of Consulting and Clinical Psychology, 66*, 5–17.

Craske, M. G., Barlow, D. H., & O'Leary, T. (1992). *Mastery of your anxiety and worry.* Albany, NY: Graywind Publications.

Cunningham, C., Davis, J. R., Bremner, R., & Dunn, K. W. (1993). Coping modeling problem solving versus mastery modeling: Effects on adherence, in-session process, and skill acquisition in a residential parent-training program. *Journal of Consulting and Clinical Psychology, 61*(5), 871–877.

Dattilio, F. M., & Jongsma, A. E. (2000). *The family treatment planner.* New York: John Wiley & Sons.

Detweiler-Bedell, J. B., & Whisman, M. A. (2005). A lesson in assigning homework: Therapist, client, and task characteristics in cognitive therapy for depression. *Professional Psychology: Research and Practice, 36*, 223–319.

Edelman, R. E., & Chambless, D. L. (1995). Adherence during sessions and homework in cognitive-behavioral group treatment of social phobia. *Behaviour Research & Therapy, 33*(5), 573-577.

Goisman, R. M. (1985). The psychodynamics of prescribing in behavior therapy. *American Journal of Psychiatry, 142*, 675–679.

Hansen, D. J., & MacMillan, V. M. (1990). Behavioral assessment of child-abuse and neglectful families: Recent developments and current issues. *Behavior Modification, 14*(3), 255–278.

Hayes, S., Strosahl, K., & Wilson, K. (1999). *Acceptance and commitment therapy: An experiential approach to behavior change.* New York: Guilford.

Herzberg, A. (1941). Short treatment of neuroses by graduated tasks. *British Journal of Medical Psychology, 19*, 19–36.

Hollon, S. D., & Beck, A. T. (1994). Cognitive and cognitive-behavioral therapies. In A. E. Bergin & S. L. Garfield (Eds.), *Handbook of psychotherapy and behavior change* (4th ed., pp. 428–466). New York: John Wiley & Sons.

Katon, W., Robinson, P., Von Korff, M., Lin, E., Bush, T., Ludman, E., et al. (1996). A multifaceted intervention to improve treatment of depression in primary care. *Archives of General Psychiatry, 53*, 924–932.

Kazantzis, N., & Dattilio, F. M. (2007). Special series beyond basics: Using homework in cognitive behavior therapy with challenging patients. Introduction. *Cognitive and Behavioral Practice, 14*, 249–251.

Kazantzis, N., & Deane, F. P. (1999). Psychologists' use of homework assignments in clinical practice. *Professional Psychology: Research and Practice, 30*(6), 581–585.

Kazantzis, N., Deane, F. P., & Ronan, K. R. (2000). Homework assignments in cognitive and behavioral therapy: A meta-analysis. *Clinical Psychology: Science and Practice, 7*, 189–202.

Kazantzis, N., Deane, F. P., & Ronan, K. R. (2004). Assessing compliance with homework assignments: Review and recommendations for clinical practice. *Journal of Clinical Psychology, 60*, 627–641.

Kazantzis, N., Deane, F. P., & Ronan, K. R. (2005). Assessment of homework completion. In N. Kazantzis, F. P. Deane, K. R. Ronan, & L. L'Abate (eds.), *Using homework assignments in cognitive behavior therapy* (pp. 61–72). New York: Routledge.

Kazantzis, N. MacEwan, J., & Dattilio, F. M. (2005). A guiding model for practice. In N. Kazantzis, F. D. Deane, K. R. Ronan, & L. L'Abate (Eds.), *Using homework assignments in cognitive—behavioral therapy* (pp. 35–404). New York: Brunner-Routledge.

Kendall, P. C., & Barnish, A. J. Show-that-I-can (homework) in cognitive-behavioral therapy for anxious youth: Individualizing homework for Robert. *Cognitive and Behavioral Practice, 14*, 289–296.

Kendall, P. C., Chu, B., Gifford, A., Hayes, C., & Nauta, M. (1998). Breathing life into a manual: Flexibility and creativity with manual-based treatments. *Cognitive and Behavioral Practice, 5*, 177–198.

Leung, A. W., & Heimberg, R. G. (1996). Homework compliance, perceptions of control, and outcome of cognitive behavioral treatment of social phobia. *Behaviour Research & Therapy, 34*(5–6), 423–432.

Miller, W. R., & Rollnick, S. (1991). *Motivational interviewing.* New York: Guilford.

National Institute of Health and Clinical Excellence (2003). *Schizophrenia: Core interventions in the treatment and management of schizophrenia in primary and secondary care.* London: Author.

Nelson, H. E. (2005). *Cognitive-behavioral therapy with delusions and hallucinations: A practice manual,* 2nd ed. Cheltenham: Nelson Thornes Ltd.

Nelson, H. E. (1997). *Cognitive behavioural therapy with schizophrenia: A practice manual.* Cheltenham, England: Stanley Thorne.

Neimeyer, R. A., & Feixas, G. (1990). The role of homework and skill acquisition in the outcome of group cognitive therapy for depression. *Behavior Therapy, 21*(3), 281–292.

O'Leary, K. D., Heyman, R. E., & Jongsma, A. E. (1998). *The couples psychotherapy treatment planner.* New York: John Wiley & Sons.

Persons, J. B., Burns, D. D., & Perloff, J. M. (1988). Predictors of dropout and outcome in cognitive therapy for depression in a private practice setting. *Cognitive Therapy and Research, 12*(6), 557–575.

Pilling, S., Bebbington, P., Kuipers, E., Garety, P., Geddes, J., Orback, G., et al. (2002). Psychological treatments in schizophrenia: I. Meta-analysis of family interventions and cognitive behaviour therapy. *Psychological Medicine, 32,* 763–782.

Prochaska, J. O. (1994). Strong and weak principles for progressing from precontemplation to action on the basis of twelve problem behaviors. *Health Psychology, 13,* 47–51.

Prochaska, J. O., & DiClemente, C. C. (1983). Stages and processes of self-change of smoking: Toward an integrative model of change. *Journal of Consulting and Clinical Psychology, 51,* 390–395.

Rector, N. A. (2007). Homework use in cognitive therapy for psychosis: A case formulation approach. *Cognitive and Behavioral Practice, 14,* 303–316.

Robinson, P. (1996). *Living life well: New strategies for hard times.* Reno, NV: Context Press.

Robinson, P., Wischman, C., & Del Vento, A. (1996). Treating depression in primary care: A manual for primary care and mental health providers. Reno, NV: Context Press.

Robinson, P. J., & Reiter, J. T. (2007). *Behavioral consultation and primary care: A guide to integrating services.* New York: Springer.

Shelton, J. L., & Levy, R. L. (1981). *Behavioral assignments and treatment compliance: A handbook of clinical strategies.* Champaign, IL: Research Press.

Startup, M., & Edmonds, J. (1994). Compliance with homework assignments in cognitive behavioral psychotherapy for depression: Relation to outcome and methods of enhancement. *Cognitive Therapy, 18,* 567–579.

Strosahl, K. (1997). Building integrated primary care behavioral health delivery systems that work: A compass and a horizon. In N. Cummings, J. Cummings, & J. Johnson (Eds.), *Behavioral health in primary care: A guide for clinical integration* (pp. 37–58). Madison, CN: Psychosocial Press.

Tarrier, N., & Wykes, T. (2004). Cognitive-behavioral treatments of psychosis: Clinical trials and methodological issues in clinical psychology. In S. Day, S. Greene, & D. Machin (Eds.), *Textbook of clinical trials* (pp. 273–296). Chichester, UK: Wiley.

Thompson, L. W., & Gallagher, D. (1984). Efficacy of psychotherapy in the treatment of late-life depression. *Advances in Behaviour Research and Therapy, 6,* 127–139.

Wadden, T. A., & Letizia, K. A. (1992). Predictors of attrition and weight loss in patients treated by moderate and severe caloric restriction. In T. A. Wadden & T. B. VanItallie (Eds.), *Treatment of the seriously obsessed patient* (pp. 383–410). New York: Guilford Press.

Wilson, G. T., & Vitousek, K. M. (1999). Self-monitoring in the assessment of eating disorders. *Psychological Assessment, 11*(4), 480–489.

THE PROLONGED CS EXPOSURE
39 TECHNIQUES OF IMPLOSIVE
(FLOODING) THERAPY

Donald J. Levis

As one of the early contributors to the development of the behavior therapy movement, my youthful enthusiasm for the potential of this movement resulted in my (Levis, 1970) christening this new approach the "Fourth Psychotherapy Revolution" following the "revolutionary" labels historically ascribed to moral therapy, psychoanalysis, and the community mental health movement (Tourney, 1967). What made this movement revolutionary for me involved the movement's commitment to three objectives: (1) the adoption of a scientific philosophy that required operational specificity of theoretical constructs and treatment procedure; (2) its stated objective of extending established laboratory principles from the field of experimental psychology to the treatment of psychopathology; and (3) its commitment to provide objective assessment and experimental evaluation of its procedures. As a cautionary move, I wisely ended my new label for this movement with a question mark.

Over 50 years have passed since the founding fathers outlined the above stated objectives. As the years passed, deep cracks in the foundation of the movement were noted by those responsible for the movement's initial growth. Numerous and repeated warnings criticizing the changing nonbehavioral developments in the field were made (e.g., Agras, 1987; Krasner, 1985; Levis, 1999; Skinner, 1974, 1984; Stampfl, 1983; and Wolpe, 1976, 1989, 1993). Despite the compelling message addressed by these critics, the warnings were not heeded. Today, it is clear the current scientific status of both the behavior

therapy movement and the field of psychotherapy are in jeopardy. Perhaps Norcross (1986, 1989) stated it best when he concluded that the abundance of treatment approaches that exist today, coupled with the continual influx of new approaches has been accompanied by a deafening cacophony of rival claims resulting in a field characterized by confusion, fragmentation, and discontent (see Levis, 1999, for a review of this issue).

If the behavior therapy movement is ever going to be evaluated historically as a therapeutic revolution and not as a passing fashionable fad, the field must remove the current fragmentation and confusion by reassessing what key behavioral principles work by determining through a functional analysis whether their presence is a key contributing factor in other approaches and then assess which technique maximizes the effectiveness of the principles that work. Such a strategy should not only reduce the complexity of a given approach but also reduce the number of effective principles and techniques to a few.

The purpose of this chapter is to describe a theoretical treatment approach that has not only withstood the test of time, but strives to address the previous outlined recommendation by focusing on the importance of maximizing a single established therapeutic change agent, the principle of direct Pavlovian extinction. This principle states that the repeated presentation of an emotionally conditioned stimulus (CS) in the absence of a biological unconditioned stimulus (UCS) will lead to the extinction of the conditioned response (CR; the symptom). Not only can the presence of this principle be found to be operating in most psychotherapy techniques, it is my belief that it represents the key principle responsible for producing behavior and cognitive changes. My treatment experience also suggests that cognitive restructuring occurs *after* and not before the emotional stimuli maintaining maladaptive behavior are extinguished.

The approach under consideration was developed by Thomas G. Stampfl. He was the first behavior therapist to recommend and promote the maximization of this principle via repeated presentation of prolonged CS exposure and the first to apply it to the treatment of a wide variety of clinical nosologies. His technique and supporting learning theory was developed in 1959.

At the time, Stampfl recognized his technique would be considered radical and controversial eliciting fears it may prove to be harmful. He was influenced by a number of factors including his therapeutic work with emotionally disturbed children. While using nondirective play therapy, he observed that the children he treated would frequently confront their most dreaded fears in play activity. This in turn would result in the elicitation of intense emotional responding, which would weaken with repetitive play behavior and lead to positive changes. At this point, he rejected the widely held analytic notion that "insight" was the corrective therapeutic change agent. His knowledge of learning theory led him to conclude that the change agent noted in his children involved the Pavlovian principle of experimental extinction (Stampfl, 1960). He also was convinced that Maslow and Mittlemann (1951) were correct in their insistence that neurotic symptoms defense mechanisms and general maladaptive behavior resulted from a state of anticipation of some catastrophic event, unspecifiable by the patient, which in turn provided the motivational source for symptom development and maintenance. They also concluded what was feared involved an anticipation of abandonment, condemnation, disapproval, humiliation, bodily injury, loss of love, and utter deprivation. Stampfl labeled his new approach implosive therapy (IT). The term, borrowed from physics, was selected to reflect the internal "dynamic" process he

believed was inherent in the release of affective loaded stimuli encoded in the brain. Once the process of cue release begins, he hypothesized an internal chain reaction begins in which the first set of cues leads to the second set, which in turn generates another set, and so on.

Stampfl first adopted an *in vivo* method of CS presentation but he soon changed to an imagery technique to permit the presentation of hypothesized cues such as those suggested by Maslow and Mittlemann and those generated through the initial interview and during treatment. The imagery approach has the additional advantage of dealing directly with what is stored in memory, an image, thus, the IT technique can be described as a dynamic behavior cognitive therapy approach.

Despite considerable pressure from his colleagues to publish, Stampfl refused until data were available to confirm the procedure was safe and supported by two experimental studies (Hogan, 1966; Levis and Carrera, 1967). However, word of his new approach spread through the dissemination of two unpublished papers (Stampfl 1960, 1961) and through a series of lectures conducted by Stampfl and this writer. Perry London (1964) after interviewing Stampfl, published the first description of the technique. Stampfl's first publication in a major journal occurred in 1967 (Stampfl & Levis, 1967). Some later investigators chose the term *flooding* rather than *implosion*. At first, this term was restricted to the use of an *in vivo* procedure. However, today the term is also applied to the imagery use of hypothesized cues, which in effect prevent any meaningful operational distinction. Both terms imply they used a direct extinction procedure and their use appears to be determined by the preference of the writer.

To fully comprehend the diversity and power of this approach, it is essential for the practitioner to comprehend the underlying learning theory supporting this treatment technique. Since detailed reports of Stampfl's theory have been presented elsewhere, only a cursory review will be provided here (Boudwyns & Shipley, 1983; Levis, 1980, 1981, 1985, 1987, 1989, 1991, 1995; Levis & Krantweiss, 2003; Stampfl, 1970, 1983, 1987, 1991; Stampfl & Levis, 1967, 1969, 1973, 1976).

IMPLOSIVE THEORY

Stampfl viewed maladaptive behavior as a learned response that is considered to be an end product of antecedent aversive conditioning. The theoretical learning model adapted by Stampfl is primarily based on an extension to the area of psychopathology of O. H. Mowrer's two-factor theory of avoidance learning (Mowrer, 1947, 1960). In theory, the learning of maladaptive behavior can be separated into two different response categories. The first involves the conditioning of an aversive emotional state, which is based on the well-established laws of classical conditioning. Fear and other emotional aversive conditioning result from the simple contiguity of pairing of nonemotional stimulation in space and time with an inherent primary aversive event producing pain fear, frustration, or severe deprivation. Following sufficient repetition, the nonemotional stimulus acquires the capability of eliciting the aversive emotional state. Most importantly, Stampfl believes the conditioning events of patients involve multiple complex sets of stimuli, which comprise both external and internal aversive stimuli that are encoded in long-term memory. Thus, the assumption is made that central state constructs such as images, thoughts and memories function as conditioned stimuli, which represent the major controlling stimulation maintaining psychopathology (Levis, 1995; Stampfl, 1970).

Emotional conditioning is also viewed as a secondary source of drive possessing both motivational and reinforcing properties that set the stage for the learning of the second response class, avoidance or escape behavior. This second response class is governed by the laws of instrumental learning. Avoidance and escape behavior are learned by the organism in an attempt to prevent, remove, or reduce the aversive state elicited by the presence of conditioned emotional stimuli. In theory, any response that achieves this objective is, in turn, reinforced by the resulting reduction in this aversive state. The more effective the avoidance response is in achieving this objective, the greater the amount of reinforcement. The conceptualization of clinical symptoms and maladaptive behavior as avoidance behavior is a central component of IT theory.

From the foregoing analysis it would follow that because patients' symptoms occur in the absence of any primary reinforcement, their symptoms should eventually undergo an extinction effect. Clinical evidence exists that this is true for some cases, but for other cases, patients' symptoms appear to persist for years. Freud (1936) first raised this issue of sustained symptom maintenance and Mowrer (1948) labeled it as the "neurotic paradox." More specifically, the paradox is why neurotic behavior is at one and the same time self-defeating and yet self-perpetuating instead of self-eliminating. To provide a resolution of this paradox, Stampfl extended Solomon and Wynne's (1954) conservation of anxiety hypotheses, which basically states that any part of the CS complex that is not exposed will maintain its aversive properties until full exposure results in an extinction effect. Stampfl postulated that the eliciting set of cues triggering symptoms' onset are backed by a multiple network of unexposed CS cues stored in long-term memory. These cues are believed to be ordered in a sequential or serial arrangement according to their accessibility along a dimension of stimulus intensity, with the more aversive cues being least accessible. As the initial set of cues undergo an extinction effect from repeated exposure, it is replaced with another, more aversive set of cues which secondarily reconditions the first set of cues reinstating symptom occurrence. This process continues to repeat itself, resulting in the maintenance of symptomatology over long periods of time until each set of cues encoded in the serial arrangements is fully extinguished (for a more detailed presentation of this important theoretical contribution along with the supporting experimental evidence, see Levis, 1991; 1995; Levis & Brewer, 2001; Stampfl, 1987, 1991).

OVERVIEW OF THE THERAPEUTIC EXTENSION OF IMPLOSIVE THEORY

The implementation of this well-established principle of experimental extinction is straightforward in a laboratory setting where the CS cues eliciting avoidance responding are known conditions and therefore easily reproducible. However, the contingencies of the conditioning history of a patient upon first contact are unknown. Despite the fact that it is difficult, if not impossible, to specify the aversive conditioning events with exact precision, it is feasible, as Stampfl noted, for a trained clinician following a few diagnostic interviews to locate key stimuli associated with the problem areas of the patient. Once these are located it is not difficult to formulate hypothesis as to the type of traumatic events which may have contributed to the client's behavior. Of course, these initial hypotheses must be conceived as only first approximations of the original conditioning sequences, but it is quite possible that they incorporate a number of the more significant avoided components. As therapy progresses it is usually possible to obtain additional information as to the validity of these cues and to generate new hypotheses. A key advantage of the IT technique is that it is an operational treatment procedure, in that confirmation or disconfirmation of a hypothesized cue area is determined by whether or not the presentation of the material elicits a strong emotional response. The assumption is made that the stronger the overt emotional response obtained, the greater the support is for the continual presentation of the cue area until extinction is obtained. The technique is also a feedback approach in that the therapist has the added advantage of being able to alter or restructure a given hypothesis by focusing on the patient's reported associations to the stimuli being presented and incorporating them into the development of additional hypotheses. Thus, the therapist can produce a chain of associations that not only releases new unexposed fear cues but also frequently results in the decoding of an actual traumatic memory. However, knowledge of the actual historical conditioning events is not required, because the technique is based on the premise that if the anxiety-eliciting hypotheses are close to the actual event, the principle of generalization of extinction should produce an extinction effect.

In an attempt to aid the therapist in the selection, classification, and ordering of cues to be presented, Stampfl (1970) suggested the use of a four-cue category system. These cue categories can be conceptualized in terms of a progression along a continuum that ranges from extremely concrete and physical cues at one end to more hypothetical and dynamic cues at the other end. These cue categories are as follows:

1. *Symptom-contingent cues,* or those environmental cues that are correlated with the elicitation of symptom onset
2. *Patient reportable, internally elicited cues*—the thoughts, feelings, and physical sensation that the patient reports experiencing while engaging in their problematic behavior
3. *Unreportable cues,* which are hypothesized to be related to reportable internally related cues (e.g., feeling of loss of control)
4. *Hypothesized dynamic cues,* which are cues associated with death, the afterlife, sexual fear, or primary process thoughts.

CONTRAINDICATION OF THE TREATMENT

Although no experimental data exists for the contraindication of use of this technique, it is essential in order for the technique to be effective that the patient be willing to cooperate in the technique's administration. Although the vast majority of the patients willingly participate, occasionally the initial fear level of a given patient may be so strong that cooperation is not obtained, requiring the use of an alternate or modified technique. It is also critical for the technique's effectiveness that the procedure elicit emotional responding. Although the technique has been readily used with patients on psychotropic medication, it is possible that some medication especially designed for the treatment of psychotic symptoms may result in the blocking or retardation of emotional responding. Prior to the start of treatment, all patients are instructed to have a physical exam to insure the technique will not exacerbate an existing medical condition. Concerns in this area should be coordinated with the patient's medical doctor. Finally, data does not exist for the use of this technique in cases of substance abuse, psychopathic behavior, or sexual predation.

OTHER ISSUES IN DECIDING WHETHER TO USE AN EXPOSURE BEHAVIORAL APPROACH

Despite the strong experimental support for the clinical efficacy of exposure-based technique, considerable resistance to its use still exists. It may prove beneficial to review some of the concerns that have been raised in the past and that emerged during our experience when training new therapists in the technique. Historically concerns were initially expressed by behavior therapists who objected to Stampfl's inclusion of dynamic cues because of their psychoanalytic implications. Because of this false impression, Stampfl, prior to his death, lamented his use of the term *psychodynamics* in his first publication. This objection persisted despite the finding that these cues were often reported to be present in the thoughts of the patients and that such cues were readily interpreted within a behavioral learning theory framework. Interestingly, many IT therapists report that the use of dynamic cues frequently produces the greatest clinical gains. A second concern, which still emerges with new therapists, centers on the fear that the elicitation of high level of affect with a patient may produce a harmful effect or create a psychotic reaction. This hypothesis was directly tested with hospitalized patients who manifested a low degree of ego strength and was disconfirmed (Boudwyns, 1975; Boudwyns & Levis, 1972; Boudwyns & Wilson, 1972; Hogan, 1966). These data, combined with the survey study of Shipley & Boudwyns (1983) and over 40 years of successful therapeutic use, have empirically put this concern to rest. The final resistant point encountered relates to the therapist's own avoidance of presenting to patients anxiety-eliciting cues involving such content areas as rejection, anger, sex, guilt, shame, and fears of loss of control. The clinical gains achieved from the use of this technique quickly extinguish this concern.

Patients, however, report that they stay in treatment because the treatment rationale makes sense to them, they recover quickly from each session, can see the changes in their lives and they like the fact that they are trained in how to use the technique between sessions which gives them a sense of control over their fears. The overall attrition and noncompliance rate of patients exposed to IT is very low, with missing of sessions being rare.

HOW DOES THE TECHNIQUE WORK?

Implosive therapy and related exposure therapies base their treatment effectiveness on the established laws of direct experimental extinction, the repeated presentation of aversive stimuli that elicit symptom behavior in the absence of any aversive reinforcement. Laboratory and clinical evidence strongly confirms that procedures that prevent or block the occurrence of the avoidance behavior or repeatedly present the aversive complex of stimuli that elicit symptomatic behavior, to result in a rapid unlearning (extinction) of both the eliciting emotional state and the resulting avoidance behavior. These manipulations at first result in the elicitation of a strong emotional response, which is followed by an equally strong extinction effect, relegating the aversive eliciting stimuli to a neutral state devoid of its motivational properties. Clinical evidence supports the contention that therapeutic cognitive restructuring takes place following the process of emotional extinction.

Stimulus Mode of Conditioned Stimulus Presentation

The execution of the principle of experimental extinction is achieved by representing, reinstating, or symbolically reproducing in the absence of physical pain those conditioned cues responsible for motivating and maintaining the patient's symptomatology. In those cases where the CS patterns being avoided involve discrete external stimuli, *in vivo* exposure to those cues can be presented by encouraging the patient to confront the phobic object directly (e.g., a snake) or by directly blocking the patient's symptoms (e.g., hand washing in a case of obsessive–compulsive behavior). If the therapeutic decision is made to present only *in vivo* cues, the procedure outlined by Foa and Tillmanns (1980) can be adopted. However, most IT therapists adopt both an *in vivo* and imagery mode of CS presentation. The advantage of presenting *in vivo* cues in imagery is that they can be combined with the presentation of symptom-related internal cues, such as those cues and events associated with guilt, anger, fear of rejection, pain, punishment, and loss of control. Thus, the imagery mode enhances the ability of the therapist to expose the patient to a variety of stimuli (visual, auditory, and tactile) hypothesized to be links to the original conditioning history.

A STEP-BY-STEP PROCEDURAL OUTLINE OF IMPLOSION THERAPY

The following sections describe the five key steps that make up the process of Implosion Therapy (IT). They are as follows.

Step 1: Performing In-Depth Pretreatment Diagnostic Interview

The first task of the therapist is to identify as accurately as possible those conditioned aversive stimuli that are presumed to mediate the emotional responses (e.g., anxiety, anger, rejection, depression) that are determinants of the symptoms and problems of the client. To achieve this objective two or three 1-hour sessions are conducted with the patient in an ordinary office or therapy room. The key question that constantly guides the therapist is "What cue areas do the patient's symptoms prevent from full exposure?" The diagnostic workup should include not only a thorough analysis of the situational cues surrounding the onset of each symptom reported by the patient but also a thorough review of the individual's family, sexual, religious, cultural and medical history. Early memories of aversive events with family members should be solicited, as well as any reoccurring nightmares or other such material that may aid the therapist in an attempt to restructure the life-history conditioning events. Careful notes are taken listing both internal stimuli (images, thoughts, and impulses) and external stimuli (stimuli associated with public events; e.g., phobic objects, social situations, parental arguments, etc.). Experience indicates that rapport can be facilitated by skillfully discussing difficult areas of sexuality, expression of anger, or thoughts of suicide. To maximize the obtainment of

information it is important to raise these "base-rate" questions in a manner that implies that the therapist assumes such conflicts exist. The administration of global personality inventories like the Minnesota Multiphasic Personality Inventory (MMPI-2) also has been shown to be useful.

Step 2: Formulating a Treatment Plan

Following the interview phase and the classification of the obtained material into hypothesized cue areas, a treatment plan is developed by the therapist. Cue areas hypothesized by the therapist to be maintaining the patient's symptoms are then integrated by the therapist into scenes along a dimension from the least to the most anxiety eliciting. This serial cue hierarchy can then be incorporated into Stampfl's four cue categories previously outlined.

Step 3: Presenting a Treatment Rationale

It is helpful to first provide a simple explanation to the patient of the underlying avoidance model of conditioning and the role the serial CS hypothesis plays in maintaining the patient's symptomatology. Next, a treatment rationale is presented:

> Before we actually start the treatment procedure, I would like to take a little time and describe to you the rationale behind the technique we are going to use. First, let me ask you a question. If you were learning to ride a horse and you fell off, what would your instructor have you do? (The usual answer given is to get back on the horse). Exactly, and if you didn't, your fear may increase and generalize not only to the surrounding stimuli but may even back up to the entrance of the stable. By forcing you to be exposed to what you are afraid of, you can overcome your fears. Let me try another example. Have you ever been frightened by a horror movie? If you have and you stayed to see the movie over and over again, it is unlikely by the tenth showing you would have any fear of the situation. It is the same situation that confronts a young medical intern who, upon seeing his or her first operation, faints from fear of the sight of an open chest. However, with continual exposure to

such operations, the fear is overcome. The technique we are going to use follows the same basic principle of extinction. You will be asked to imagine various scenes in imagery that are designed to elicit anxiety. Repeating the scene many times will reduce or extinguish your fear level. Your fears are learned and can be unlearned by confronting them directly in imagery. Images can't hurt you in reality. Do you have any questions.

Step 4: Using First-Session Instructional Set

Approximately 20 minutes should be set aside at the end of the last diagnostic interview to assess the patient's imagery ability. The purpose of such training is to allow the therapist to establish a crude baseline for the patient's ability to imagine various sensory modalities (e.g., visual, auditory, tactile) and to establish the therapist as the director of the scenes. Such neutral imagery may include watching TV, walking down a street, eating a meal, and the like. Details of the scenes should be fully described (e.g., facial expressions), and scenes should be designed not to elicit any anxiety.

Step 5: Executing Effective Treatment Scenes

The first IT session is initiated during the third or fourth session. After a few minutes of conversation, the patient is asked to play out various scenes presented by the therapist. A typical instructional set is provided by the following excerpt:

Your task is much like that of an actor (actress). You will be asked to play the part of yourself and to portray certain feelings and emotions in imagery. Like an actor (actress) you are to "live" the scenes with genuine emotions and affect. I (the therapist) will direct the scene. You will be asked to close your eyes and follow the scenes in imagery. Please put yourself in the scene as best as you can and imagine the events I describe as clearly as possible. The scenes, like movies, do not necessarily involve real events. You only have to believe or accept the scenes as real when you are visualizing them. The greater the level of affect you can experience, the greater the benefits received. Do you have any questions before we start?

In order to circumvent resistance, it is important that the therapist make little or no attempt to secure admission from the patient that the content of the scene actually applies to the patient. It is usually convenient to begin the first session by incorporating relevant material reported by the client (e.g., symptom-contingent cues, active memory of a traumatic experience, or a frequently recurring dream). It is useful to develop a scene slowly, allowing the client sufficient time to formulate a relatively good image by having him or her to describe context cues (setting cues). The relevant material within a scene can be played over and over again even though other features of the scene are changing. A given scene is usually terminated after some diminution in anxiety is noted. Never stop a scene in the middle of a given theme; always complete the sequence. Following the last scene in the session, allow at least 10 minutes to pass to ensure that the patient's anxiety level is back to normal. When patients are asked to open their eyes, the anxiety level elicited usually returns to baseline within 5 minutes. Repetition is a critical component of IT, and each scene presented within a session should be repeated at least once. To facilitate the extinction process at the end of each session, the patient is assigned homework which involves repeating the scenes administered during the session for at least a 20-minute period daily until the next session.

The therapist's attitude and method of scene presentation play an important role. The more sensitive and empathetic the therapist is in understanding the client's problem, the better able the therapist is to present the scene material. The therapist should try to feel the role being played. By varying the vocal inflection at appropriate places, the therapist can produce a greater effect. The more involved and dramatic the therapist becomes in describing a given scene, the more realistic the scene becomes, and the easier it is for the client to participate.

DEALING WITH RESISTANCE AND DEFENSES

Cooperation on this patient's part is essential for maximum effects to be obtained. The skills of the therapist are critical in this regard. Because of the nature of the material being presented, resistance should be expected. When encountered, three strategies can be adapted. The first is to override or overpower the resistance directly. For example, it is common for a patient to say "It is not true." The therapist's response is "Whether it's true or not, just imagine it." If the patient says, "I can't see that," the therapist's response is "Yes, you can see it." If this direct approach doesn't work after several minutes of pressure, the second strategy of circumventing the patient's defenses can be used. This can be achieved by changing the content of the scene to a lesser anxiety-arousing level. After a while the therapist can return to the more anxiety-eliciting material previously awarded. The third strategy involves "imploding" the defense directly. For example, if the patient says, "I can't do this; it will make me worse or I will lose control," the therapist's response is to have the patient close his or her eyes and describe an IT scene in which the patient, as a function of coming to therapy, loses control and ends up in the back ward of a mental hospital, to remain there for the rest of his or her life. The first author's experience has been that this scene never fails to work and that after one repetition the patient readily goes back to working on the scene where the defense materialized.

SESSION SPACING AND TREATMENT DURATION

It should be clear from this discussion that a given therapy session cannot necessarily be held to the usual 50-minute session. The therapist must be flexible in this regard. If a session of 50 minutes is allotted for scenes to be presented, allow half an hour between patients. Some sessions have run 2 or 3 hours, some 20 minutes. The desired spacing between sessions is also unknown. Usually, one meeting a week is scheduled, but more frequent visits have also produced good effects. Duration of treatment clearly varies with the individual case. Symptom removal has occurred following one session, and usually reduction in symptomatology is obtained after 10–15 sessions.

However, with more difficult cases involving multiple problems or longstanding problems, more time may be needed to obtain significant gains. Longer periods of treatment are also needed when the defense structure of the patient is strong and the therapist finds it difficult to evoke much anxiety. (For a more detailed discussion of the above procedure steps, see Levis & Boyd, 1985, for further discussion of this topic).

EVIDENCE-BASED APPLICATIONS

Since Stampfl first published his technique of implosive (flooding) therapy, perhaps no other behavioral therapy approach has been suggested to such an extensive research scrutiny or has received such strong experimental support. In the Levis and Hare (1977) review article, 135 supporting experimental analogue and patient outcome studies were found as were an additional 16 studies that dealt with psychiatric hospitalized patients. Reported effectiveness for the use of this approach has been documented for the treatment of diverse phobic behavior, including agoraphobia, obsessive–compulsive behavior, panic and anxiety disorders, depression, and posttraumatic stress (see Levis & Boyd, 1985). Since that time, considerable additional research has been conducted, which also supports the use of a prolonged CS exposure treatment technique (see Richard and Lauterbach, 2007). Finally, the underlying theoretical model developed by Stampfl (see Levis, 1985) has also received strong experimental support from research conducted with animals, humans, and clinical patients (see Levis, 1985, 1989, 1991; and Levis & Brewer 2001).

ADDENDUM

This section is designed to provide a cursory review of the ongoing development and content research analysis of an ancillary technique that appears capable of greatly enhancing the memorial reactivation component of IT.

This technique is referred to as patient-directed implosive therapy or brain release therapy to distinguish it from Stampfl's therapist-directed technique (Levis, 1988). The data forthcoming from its therapist with over 20 years' use of this procedure, with a large sample of patients manifesting a history of repeated traumatic experiences, strongly suggests the technique is capable of decoding those key traumatic memories responsible for the development and maintenance of the patient's psychopathology. The release of the encoded memorial content of a given memory appears to be complete in that both the internal and external stimuli associated with the beginning, middle, and end of a given traumatic event are reproduced in great detail. This includes (1) the release of the sensory systems involved in the original conditioning event including the visual, tactual, auditory, kinesthetic, and odoriferous systems; (2) the release of the cognitive components encoded including words spoken, internal thoughts, and fears elicited; and, most importantly, (3) the release of the autonomous responses conditioned, including the reactivation of intense physical and psychological pain cues. The procedure for facilitating the start of the decoding process is surprisingly simple. All the therapist is required to do is to select any partial memory fragment previously reported that is suspected to be related to a trauma experience. The patient is then asked to close his or her eyes, go back in time, and focus on the details of what is remembered as suggested by Stampfl's instructional set. If new associations are reported, the process is repeated, which should elicit more content until the details of the memory are fully decoded. The brain will then start the release of the next memory encoded in the sequence, and so forth. If the patient's defense mechanism inhibits the elicitation of new associations, the procedure can be tried at a later point in therapy. It appears the key factor in facilitating the release of new memories involves both the shifting of the responsibility for eliciting the content of the memory to the patient and the willingness of the patient to continue the process. Once the patient is fully involved in the decoding process, the therapist participation becomes minimal, being relegated to the role of a data recorder and supporting witness of the unfolding patient's traumatic experiences. At no point should the therapist confirm or disconfirm the accuracy of the material being elicited.

Acceptance or nonacceptance is believed to be best left up to the patient.

The approach has been successful in reducing the patient's maladaptive behavior in a number of cases. The material being elicited appears to be unaffected by attempts to alter the content through suggestive manipulations. The process of decoding also appears to be lawful and identical across and within patients. Patients also appear to fully recover from the high levels of affect elicited by the procedure within a 10–15-minute period. Interestingly, patients report they are willing to expose themselves to their reliving the past trauma, because of the relief they experience following each session and because they report a strong desire to understand why the memories of the past have been blocked out from their conscious awareness. Once the content of a given memory is fully elicited and its accompanying affect is fully extinguished, it ceases to have any further behavior control over the patient, which in turn leads to significant symptom reduction.

However, it is recommended that prior to the implementation of this "free" recall procedure, the patient should be informed that the process of decoding a given memory may take months of treatment and the time required in decoding all of the patient's key traumatic experiences may take years, which is the major disadvantage of the technique. Surprisingly, few patients have chosen not to try the technique. Fortunately, throughout the treatment, positive changes are regularly reported. The second disadvantage of the approach is that the technique requires the willingness of the therapist to subject him or herself to witness the high levels of affect and horrifying content generated by the patient's release of this material.

The primary interest of this researcher is in the potential theoretical and applied benefits that may emerge from an analysis or the data produced by this approach. Since 1978, a team of trained researchers have been systematically behaviorally encoding the audio and video transcripts of over 5,000 recorded sessions of memory release. The primary objective of this ongoing longitudinal project is to map out how the brain encodes trauma memories by analyzing how it releases them. This process appears to be lawful across patients. This effort should lead to a better understanding of the principle responsible for both eliciting and inhibiting the release of memory, as well as how the process can be shortened. Some of the preliminary findings from this project can be found in Kirch & Levis (2001), and Levis (1991a, 1991b, and 1995).

References

Agras, W. S. (1987). So where do we go from here? *Behavior Therapy, 18,* 203–218.

Boudwyns, P. A. (1975). Implosive therapy and desensitization therapy with inpatients: A five-year follow-up. *Journal of Abnormal Psychology, 84,* pp. 159–160.

Boudwyns, P. A., & Levis, D. J. (1975). Autonomic reactivity of high and low ego-strength to repeated anxiety eliciting scenes. *Journal of Abnormal Psychology, 84,* pp. 682–692.

Boudwyns, P. A., & Shipley, R. H. (1983). *Flooding and implosive therapy.* New York: Plenum.

Boudwyns, P. A., & Wilson, A. E. (1972). Implosive therapy and densensitization therapy using free-association in the treatment of inpatients. *Journal of Abnormal Psychology, 79,* pp. 259–268.

Foa, E. B, & Tillmanns, A. (1980). The treatment of obsessive-compulsive neurosis. In A. Goldstein & E. B. Foa (Eds.), *Handbook of behavioral interventions: A clinical guide* (pp. 416–500). New York: John Wiley & Sons.

Freud, S. (1936). *The problems of anxiety.* (H. A. Bunker, Trans.) New York: Norton.

Hogan, R. A. (1966). Implosive therapy in the short-term treatment of psychotics. *Psychotherapy: Theory Research, and Practice, 3,* 25–31.

Kirch, M. V., & Levis, D. J. (2001). An assessment of the accuracy of two clinical imagery procedures to elicit in a non-patient population recall of a reportedly forgotten long-term memory: An exploratory study. *Journal of Mental Imagery, 25*(3–4), 63–78.

Krasner, L. (1985). Review of International handbook of behavior modification and therapy. *Behavior Therapist, 8,* 13.

Levis, D. J., & Carrera, R. N. (1967). Effects of ten hours of implosive therapy in the treatment of outpatients. *Journal of Abnormal Psychology, 72,* 504–508.

Levis, D. J. (1970). Behavioral therapy: The fourth therapeutic revolution? In D. J. Levis (Ed.), *Learning approaches to therapeutic behavior change* (pp. 1–35), Chicago: Aldine.

Levis, D. J., & Hare, N. (1977). A review of the theoretical rationale and empirical support for the extinction approach of implosive (flooding) therapy. In M. Hersen, R. M. Eisler, & P. M. Miller (Eds.), *Progress in behavior modification IV* (pp. 300–376). New York: Academic Press.

Levis, D. J. (1980). Implementing the technique of implosive therapy. In A. Goldstein & E. B. Foa (Eds.). *Handbook of behavioral interventions: A clinical guide* (pp. 92–151). New York: John Wiley & Sons.

Levis, D. J. (1981). Extrapolation of two-factor learning theory of infrahuman avoidance behavior to psychopathology. *Neuroscience and Biobehavioral Review, 5,* 355–370.

Levis, D. J. (1985). Implosive theory: A comprehensive extension of conditioning theory of fear/anxiety to psychopathology. In S. Reiss & R. R. Bootzin (Eds.), *Theoretical issues in behavior therapy* (pp. 49–82). New York: Academic Press.

Levis, D. J., & Boyd, T. L. (1985). The CS exposure approach of implosive therapy. In R. McMillan Turner & L. M Ascher (Eds.), *Evaluation of behavior therapy outcome* (pp. 56–94). New York: Springer.

Levis, D. J. (1987). Treating anxiety and panic attacks: The conflict model of implosive therapy. *Journal of Integrative and Eclectic Psychotherapy, 6*(4), pp. 450–461.

Levis, D. J. (1988). Observation and experience from clinical practice: A critical ingredient for advancing behavioral theory and therapy. *The Behavior Therapist, 11,* 95–99.

Levis, D. J. (1989). The case for a two-factor theory of avoidance: Do non-fear interpretations really offer an alternative. In S. B. Klein & R. R. Mowrer (Eds.), *Contemporary learning theories* (pp. 227–277). Hillsdale, NJ: Lawrence Erlbaum.

Levis, D. J. (1991). A clinician's plea for a return to the development of nonhuman models of psychopathology: New clinical observations in need of laboratory study. In M. R. Denny (Ed.), *Fear, avoidance, and phobias: A fundamental analysis* (pp. 395–427). Hillsdale, NJ: Lawrence Erlbaum.

Levis, D. J. (1991a). The recovery of traumatic memories: The etiological source of psychopathology. In R. G. Kunzendorf (Ed.), *Mental imagery* (pp. 233–240). New York: Plenum.

Levis, D. J. (1995). Decoding traumatic memory: Implosive theory of psychopathology. In W. O'Donohue & L. Krasner (Eds.), *Theories in behavior therapy* (pp. 173–207). Washington, DC: American Psychological Association.

Levis, D. J. (1999). The negative impact of the cognitive movement on the continued growth of the behavior therapy movement: A historical perspective. *Genetic, social and general psychology monographs, 125*(2), 157–171.

Levis, D. J. & Brewer, K. E. (2001). The neurotic paradox: Attempts by two-factor fear theory and alternative avoidance models to resolve the issues associated with sustained avoidance responding in extinction. In R. R. Mowrer & S. B. Klein (Eds.), *Handbook of Contemporary Learning Theories* (pp. 561–597). Mahwah, NJ: Lawrence Erlbaum.

Levis, D. J., & Krantweiss, A. R. (2003). Working with implosive (flooding) therapy: A dynamic cognitive–behavioral exposure psychotherapy treatment approach. In W. O'Donohue, J. E. Fisher, & S. E. Hayes (Eds.) *Cognitive behavior therapy*, pp. 463–470. Hoboken, NJ: Wiley.

London, P. (1964). *The modes and morals of psychotherapy.* New York: Holt, Rinehart & Winston, Inc.

Marlow, A. H. & Mittelmann, B. (1951). *Principles of abnormal psychology: The dynamics of psychic illness.* New York: Harper & Brothers Publishers.

Mowrer, O. H. (1947). On the dual nature of learning—A re-interpretation of conditioning and problem-solving. *Harvard Educational Review, 17,* 102–148.

Mowrer, O. H. (1948). Learning theory and the neurotic paradox. *American Journal of Orthopsychiatry, 18,* 571–610.

Mowrer, O. H. (1960). *Learning theory and behavior.* New York: John Wiley & Sons.

Norcross, J. D. (1986). *Handbook of eclectic psychotherapy.* New York: Brunner/Mazel.

Norcross, J. C. (1989). Eclecticism and integration in counseling and psychotherapy: Major themes and obstacles. *British Journal of Guidance and Counseling, 17,* 227–247.

Richard, C. S., & Lauderbach, D. L. (2007) (Eds.), *Handbook of exposure therapies.* Burlington, MA: Academic Press.

Shipley, R. H., & Boudwyns, P. A. (1983). Flooding and implosive therapy: Are they harmful? *Behavior Therapy, 11,* pp. 503–508.

Skinner, B. F. (1974). *About behaviorism.* New York: Knopf.

Skinner, B. F. (1984). The shame of American education. *American Psychologist, 34,* 947–954.

Solomon, R. L., & Wynne, L. C. (1954). Traumatic avoidance learning: The principle of anxiety conservation and partial irreversibility. *Psychological Review, 61,* 353–385.

Stampfl, T. G. (1960). Avoidance conditioning reconsidered: An extension of Mowrerism theory. Unpublished manuscript. John Carroll University, Cleveland, OH.

Stampfl, T. G. (1961). Implosive therapy: A learning theory derived psychodynamic technique. Unpublished paper presented at a colloquium of the University of Illinois.

Stampfl, T. G. (1970). Implosive therapy: An emphasis on covert stimulation. In D. J. Levis (Ed.), *Learning approaches to therapeutic behavior change* (pp. 182–204). Chicago: Aldine.

Stampfl, T. G. (1983). Exposure treatment for psychiatrists? *Contemporary Psychology, 28,* 527–529.

Stampfl, T. G. (1987). Theoretical implications of the neurotic paradox as a problem in behavior theory: An experimental resolution. *The Behavior Analyst, 10,* 161–173.

Stampfl, T. G. (1991). Analysis of aversive events in human psychopathology: Fear and avoidance. In M. R. Denny (Ed.), *Fear, avoidance and phobias* (pp. 363–393). Hillsdale, NJ: Lawrence Erlbaum Associates.

Stampfl, T. G., & Levis, D. J. (1967). The essentials of implosive therapy: A learning theory based on psychodynamic behavioral therapy. *Journal of Abnormal Psychology, 72,* 496–503.

Stampfl, T. G., & Levis, D. J. (1969). Learning theory: An aid to dynamic therapeutic practice. In L. D. Eron & R. Callahan (Eds.), *Relationship of theory to practice in psychotherapy* (pp. 85–114). Chicago: Aldine.

Stampfl, T. G., & Levis, D. J. (1973). Implosive therapy. In R. M. Jurjevich (Ed.), *Direct psychotherapy: 28 American originals* (pp. 83–105). Coral Gables, FL: University of Miami Press.

Stampfl, T. G., & Levis, D. J. (1976). Implosive therapy: A behavioral therapy. In J. T. Spence, R. C. Carson, & J. W. Thibaut (Eds.), *Behavioral approaches to therapy* (pp. 86–110). Morristown, NJ: General Learning Press.

Tourney, G. (1967). A history of therapeutic fashions in psychiatry, 1800–1966. *American Journal of Psychiatry, 124,* 784–796.

Wolpe, J. (1976). Behavior therapy and its malcontents—II. Multimodal eclecticism, cognitive exclusions, and "exposure" empiricism. *Journal of Behavior Therapy and Experimental Psychology, 7,* 109–116.

Wolpe, J. (1989). The derailment of behavior therapy. *Journal of Behavior Therapy and Experimental Psychiatry, 20,* 3–15.

Wolpe, J. (1993). The cognitivist oversell and comments on symposium contributions. *Journal of Behavior and Experimental Psychiatry, 24,* 141–147.

40 COGNITIVE BEHAVIORAL TREATMENT OF INSOMNIA

Wilfred R. Pigeon and Michael L. Perlis

INTRODUCTION AND BACKGROUND

Insomnia is a highly pervasive condition. Approximately 5%–35% of the population of the United States report sleep disturbance problems at some point in their lives (Ford & Kamerow, 1989; Gallup Organization, 1995; Mellinger, Balter, & Uhlenhuth, 1985) and approximately 10% suffer from persistent insomnia (Ancoli-Israel & Roth, 1999). The day-to-day cost of insomnia is not limited to fitful sleep. Insomnia, when chronic, tends to be unremitting, disabling, costly, and insidious.

Chronic insomnia seldom spontaneously resolves although the presenting form of insomnia (i.e., initial, middle, or late) can vary over time (Young, 2005; LeBlanc, Merette, Savard, & Morin, 2007). For instance, subjects in one study presented with an average chronicity of 10 years at their initial assessment and 88% continued to report insomnia 5 years later (Mendelson, 1995). A number of investigations suggest that individuals with chronic insomnia, as opposed to no or occasional insomnia, have impaired cognitive performance (Roth & Roehrs, 2003) (Carey, Moul, Pilkonis, Germain, & Buysse, 2005; Shochat, Umphress, Israel, & Ancoli-Israel, 1999), decreased ability to handle minor irritations, decreased ability to enjoy family/social life, and poorer interpersonal relationships with spouses (Shochat et al., 1999), less job satisfaction, lower performance scores, less productivity, and higher rates of errors and absenteeism (Kupperman, Lubeck, & Mazonson, 1995; Johnson & Spinweber, 1983), (Leger, Guilleminault, Bader, Levy, & Paillard, 2002). Interestingly, neuropsychological evaluations of patients with chronic insomnia have not yielded reliable data regarding specific cognitive deficits (Orff, Drummond, Nowakowski, & Perlis, 2007). This discrepancy between perceived and measured impairment may be reflective of patient's real appreciation of the fact that extra effort is required to maintain normal or near normal performance (Orff et al., 2007).

In the United States alone, the direct and indirect costs attributable to insomnia exceed $100 billion annually at the societal level (Fullerton, 2006). Direct costs include physician visits, prescriptions and procedures and exceed $13 billion per year (Walsh & Engelhardt, 1999; Leger et al., 2002). Indirect costs (motor vehicle and workplace accidents, reduced productivity, and absenteeism) account for the majority of the economic consequences of insomnia (Aldrich, 1989; Roth & Ancoli-Israel, 1999; Hillman, Murphy, & Pezzullo, 2006). At the individual level, recent work estimates the excess cost per annum of insomnia at $1,253 in younger adults and $1,143 in older adults for direct health care expenses above that expended by similar patients without insomnia (Ozminkowski, Wang, & Walsh, 2007).

Insomnia is also associated with increased vulnerability for a variety of medical conditions and psychiatric disorders. With respect to medical disease, the data suggesting that insomnia confers risk are preliminary and somewhat indirect. These data include that patients with insomnia (or those with poor sleep quality) are more likely to suffer from pain conditions and gastrointestinal distress (Kupperman et al., 1995), are at risk for hypertension (Phillips & Mannino, 2007; Suka, Yoshida, & Sugimori, 2003), heart disease (Phillips et al., 2007; Schwartz et al., 1999), and poor glycemic regulation (Ryden, Knutson, Mander, & Van Cauter, 2002). Insomnia and/or short sleep duration are also associated with increased mortality (Kripke, Simons, Garfinkel, & Hammond, 1979; Dew et al., 2003). With respect to psychiatric disease, there is a preponderance of data to suggest that insomnia confers increased risk for new onset and recurrent depression/major depressive disorder (MDD) (Pigeon & Perlis, 2007) and even that insomnia may be a prodromal symptom of depression (Perlis, Buysse, Giles, Tu, & Kupfer, 1997), and a barrier to remission (Pigeon et al., 2008). Fewer data are available for the anxiety disorders, although insomnia is equally or more prevalent in anxiety, as compared to mood disorders (Stewart et al., 2006; Mahendran, Subramaniam, & Chan, 2007; Mellinger et al., 1985; Taylor, Lichstein, Durrence, Reidel, & Bush, 2005). As in the depression literature, available data suggest that subjects with insomnia are more likely to have an anxiety disorder than those without insomnia (Ford et al., 1989).

Whether any of these associations to medical and psychiatric conditions are causal, remains to be determined as does what factors related to insomnia in specific confer and moderate/mediate risk. Nonetheless, given the personal and societal costs of insomnia, it follows that this is a disorder that should be aggressively treated. Fortunately, there are a variety of cognitive and behavioral interventions which are rooted in behavioral and cognitive principles, target insomnia as a clearly defined disease entity and are empirically validated. As will be shown, insomnia is a disorder in which theory, diagnosis, assessment, and treatment are intertwined.

THE COGNITIVE BEHAVIORAL MODEL OF INSOMNIA

A theoretical understanding of the etiology and pathophysiology of insomnia is a valuable starting point when considering its behavioral treatments. There is currently more than one "cognitive behavioral model of insomnia." All such models, however, recognize that insomnia is a condition that develops over time, is related to maladaptive behaviors and cognitions, and whose developmental course is typically a chronic one unless it is treated aggressively in its initial phases (American Academy of Sleep Medicine, 2005; Perlis, Smith, & Pigeon, 2005).

The behavioral components of "the model" were originally set forth by Spielman and colleagues (Spielman, Caruso, & Glovinsky, 1987). This model is used as a foundation for most models of insomnia (and for its behavioral treatment). The Spielman model (also known as the "3-P Model") posits that insomnia occurs acutely in relation to both predisposing and precipitating factors. Thus, an individual may be prone to insomnia due to predisposing characteristics, but experiences actual episodes because of precipitating factors. The acute insomnia becomes sub-chronic when it is reinforced by perpetuating factors (often in the form of maladaptive coping strategies). These strategies, in turn, result in conditioned arousal and chronic insomnia. A graphic representation of this model is presented in Figure 40.1.

Predisposing factors extend across the entire biopsychosocial spectrum. Biological factors include hyperarousal or hyperreactivity. Psychological factors include worry or the tendency to be excessively ruminative. Social factors, although rarely a focus at the theoretical level, include such things as the bed partner keeping an incompatible sleep schedule or social pressures to sleep according to a non-preferred sleep schedule. Precipitating factors, as the name implies, are acute occurrences that constitute stressful life events.

Perpetuating factors occur once an insomnia episode is initiated and individuals adopt maladaptive strategies in the attempt to get more sleep or recover from sleep loss. Research and treatment have focused on two in particular: excessive time in bed and the practice of staying in bed while awake. Excessive time in bed refers to the tendency of patients with insomnia to go to bed earlier and/or to get out of bed later. Such changes are enacted in order to increase the opportunity to get more sleep. These behaviors, however, lead to decreased sleep efficiency. That is, when the opportunity to sleep exceeds basal ability to generate sleep, the consequence is more frequent, and longer awakenings. The practice of staying in bed while awake, as with the prior strategy is enacted to increase the opportunity to get more sleep. In addition, the practice is often adopted under the rationale that staying in bed is at least "restful." While a

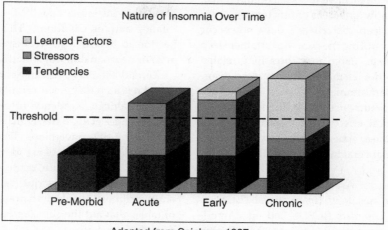

Adapted from Spielman 1987

FIGURE 40.1   The Development of Chronic Insomnia: A Conceptual Model

seemingly reasonable behavior, staying in bed while awake leads to an association of the bed and bedroom with arousal, not sleepiness and sleep. That is, when confronted with stimuli that are typically associated with sleep, they elicit arousal responses via classical conditioning. The two maladaptive behaviors are likely to occur concurrently and promote one another. Excessive time in bed increases the likelihood that the individual will be awake while in bed. Being awake while in bed increases the likelihood that the individual will attempt to get more sleep by increasing sleep opportunity. These behaviors become targets for behavioral interventions.

The Spielman model of insomnia has received a fair amount of support largely due to the empirical support available for the therapies that are derived from its principles. These therapies appear to be effective, both in comparison to placebo conditions (Murtagh & Greenwood, 1995) and compared to pharmacologic interventions (Smith et al., 2002). Other models have increased our understanding of the etiology of insomnia (for a thorough review, see Perlis et al., 2005). Such models incorporate other aspects of insomnia including cognitive and hyperarousal factors. They draw our attention to how patients may engage in safety behaviors, harbor dysfunctional beliefs about sleep, engage in excessive rumination and catastrophizing, as well as being

cortically primed for presleep arousal and overt attention to stimuli that good sleepers easily ignore (Espie, Broomfield, MacMahon, Macphee, & Taylor, 2005; Harvey, 2001; Morin, Stone, Trinkle, Mercer, & Remsberg, 1993; Perlis, Giles, Mendelson, Bootzin, & Wyatt, 1997). All of these are antithetical to initiating and maintaining sleep and can be the focus of treatment.

DIAGNOSIS AND ASSESSMENT OF INSOMNIA

Definition of Insomnia

The American Psychiatric Association's nosology (*Diagnostic and Statistical Manual of Mental Disorders*, 4th ed. [DSM-IV]; American Psychiatric Association, 2000) includes a formal diagnosis of "primary insomnia" under the category of "dyssomnias." The dyssomnias include problems of initiating or maintaining sleep or of excessive sleepiness characterized by disturbances associated with the amount, quality, timing, or perception of sleep. The DSM-IV diagnostic criteria for primary insomnia (307.42) requires:

1. The predominant complaint of difficulty in initiating or maintaining sleep, or nonrestorative sleep, for at least 1 month
2. That the sleep disturbance (or associated daytime fatigue) causes clinically significant

distress or impairment in social, occupational, or other important areas of functioning

3. That the sleep disturbance does not occur exclusively during the course of another sleep disorder (e.g., narcolepsy, breathing-related sleep disorder, circadian rhythm sleep disorder, or a parasomnia, etc)

4. That the disturbance is not due to the direct physiological effects of a substance (e.g., a drug of abuse, a medication) or another psychiatric or general medical condition

The American Academy of Sleep Medicine uses its own nosology (*International Classification of Sleep Disorders* [ICSD], 2nd ed.; American Academy of Sleep Medicine, 2005). Within this classification system, the *DSM-IV* definition of "primary" insomnia is further refined. Of the three subtypes of insomnia (psychophysiological, paradoxical, and idiopathic), two are classified based on the factors that are thought to contribute to the occurrence and/or severity of the disorder (psychophysiological and idiopathic). The remaining subtype (paradoxical) is reserved for a small subset of patients who have an extreme discrepancy between their subjective report of insomnia and traditional polysomnographic findings, which demonstrate normal sleep architecture.

Psychophysiological insomnia, as characterized by the ICSD, is a disorder of somaticized tension and learned sleep-preventing associations that leads to difficulties initiating and/or maintaining sleep, excessive daytime fatigue, and complaints of impaired daytime function (e.g., concentration and memory difficulties).

Paradoxical insomnia is a disorder in which the complaint of insomnia and/or nonrestorative sleep occurs without objective evidence of a sleep disturbance. Complaints of poor sleep in these individuals appear to be clinically genuine, yet polysomnographic (PSG) or actigraphic measures of sleep do not reveal sleep continuity or sleep architecture disturbances. This condition, unlike that of psychophysiologic insomnia, requires PSG or actigraphic measures to establish the diagnosis.

Idiopathic insomnia is a lifelong and unremitting inability to obtain adequate sleep that is presumably due to an abnormality of the

neurological control of the sleep–wake system. Idiopathic insomnia usually is present during infancy and/or childhood. This disorder may be due to heritable neurochemical imbalances and/or neuroanatomical abnormalities.

Recently, the sleep research community established research diagnostic criteria for the insomnias (American Academy of Sleep Medicine, 2005; Edinger et al., 2004), which closely approximate the ICSD conventions. The value of these criteria lies in their being derived from the evidence-based literature, made available in one easily accessible manuscript (as opposed to an entire diagnostic book), and presented in a series of tables that aid the clinician and researcher in differential diagnosis.

Despite the existence of these nosologies, the field does not have published criteria for severity and frequency of the illness. Most classification schemes (regardless of the type of insomnia) do not specify criteria for: (1) how much wakefulness (prior to desired sleep onset or during the night) is considered abnormal, (2) how little total sleep must be obtained to fall outside the normal range, or (3) how frequently these difficulties must occur to be considered pathologic.

Most clinicians and investigators consider 30 or more minutes to fall asleep and/or 30 or more minutes of wakefulness after sleep onset to represent the threshold between normal and abnormal sleep. With respect to total sleep time, many are reluctant to fix a value for this parameter. In part, establishing such a value is difficult because representing what is pathological with one number is too confounded by factors like age, prior sleep, and the individual's basal level of sleep need. In addition, such values can be misleading, as it is also possible that an individual can experience profound sleep initiation or maintenance problems in the absence of sleep loss. For research purposes, most investigators specify that the amount of sleep obtained on a regular basis be equal to or less than 6.5 or 6.0 hours per night. In terms of frequency most investigators require problems on three or more nights per week, but this may have more to do with increasing the odds of studying the occurrence of the disorder in laboratory than an inherent belief that fewer than three nights per week of sleep difficulties are normal. Regardless of the nosology used to diagnose the insomnias, assessment proceeds along the same line.

Assessment of Insomnia

The assessment of a patient with insomnia includes a thorough sleep, medical and psychiatric history. The sleep history includes a chronological review of sleep going back to childhood and working up to the present. Particular attention is given to factors that may have precipitated the insomnia, whether these factors abated or changed over time, and to what extent perpetuating factors and various life stressors are currently present. It is also useful to have the patient go through a typical 24-hour period in terms of their sleep behaviors and schedule. Simlarly, it is useful to know how often a typical night occurs, if there are any identifiable patterns and how a "really bad night" differs from a "really good night." As with any disorder, the clinician will want to explore what has been tried to correct the sleep disturbance and to what extent such strategies worked. A sleep history also includes questions to rule out other possible sleep disorders.

Similarly, the clinician must distinguish the primary insomnias from co-morbid insomnia in the clinical evaluation. It is noteworthy that of all the insomnias (the ICSD lists 10 separate chronic insomnia diagnoses), the primary insomnias account for only 10%–20% (Ohayon & Roth, 2001; Ohayon, 2002). Most insomnias, therefore, are related to medical conditions (e.g., chronic pain, cancer), psychiatric conditions (e.g., depression, posttraumatic stress disorder), substances of abuse, and medication side effects. Differential diagnosis is important for at least two other reasons.

First, clinical experience suggests that while medical and psychiatric disorders may precipitate insomnia, the sleep initiation and maintenance problems may often persist long after the parent conditions are stable or resolved. The common strategy of treating what might be considered primary (e.g., chronic pain or depression) and forgoing insomnia interventions rests in the belief that if the latter is only a symptom. While this is certainly true for some individuals, such a strategy may ill serve a sizable number of patients.

Second, a careful clinical history may indeed determine that the inability to fall asleep, stay asleep, or the tendency to awaken early in the morning may be related to a variety of factors including primary medical or psychiatric conditions, drug use or abuse, or other extrinsic or intrinsic sleep disorders. To the extent that any of these may be contributing to insomnia, the interview session may be used to acquire consents to contact the patient's primary care provider and/or other providers to assist in treatment planning and discuss possible contraindications for treatment. Some of these conditions do warrant targeted intervention prior to treating the presenting insomnia. Typical medical exclusions for initiating insomnia treatment include untreated or unstable gastrointestinal disorders (e.g., gastroesophageal reflux disease), cardiopulmonary disorders (e.g., heart disease), and neuroendocrine disorders (e.g., estrogen deficiency). Typical psychiatric exclusions include untreated or unstable affective and/or anxiety disorders. Typical drug use or abuse exclusions include the use of medications and/or "recreational" drugs that have insomnia as a direct effect or as a withdrawal effect. Typical sleep disorders exclusions include other intrinsic sleep disorders (e.g., sleep apnea), circadian rhythm disorders (e.g., shift work sleep disorder), and extrinsic sleep disorders (e.g., inadequate sleep hygiene). It is imperative to note that comorbid insomnia may nonetheless be treated in conjunction with the treatment of a "primary" disorder or even as a front line intervention as demonstrated in several patient populations (see Efficacy section later in this chapter).

Having reviewed its theoretical underpinnings, and completed a primer in diagnosis and assessment, this chapter now turns to a description of the cognitive behavioral treatment of insomnia.

THE COGNITIVE BEHAVIORAL TREATMENT OF INSOMNIA

Standard Behavioral Treatment of Insomnia

In general, there are three main types of therapy that can be employed, from a behavioral standpoint, to deal with chronic insomnia: stimulus control, sleep restriction, and sleep hygiene therapies. These therapies comprise the standard behavioral therapy of insomnia. The session-to-session clinical regimen is described below, while a description of cognitive and other therapies follows in the next section.

Stimulus Control Therapy

Stimulus control therapy is considered to be the first-line behavioral treatment for chronic primary insomnia and therefore should be prioritized accordingly (Chesson Jr. et al., 1999). Stimulus control instructions limit the amount of time patients spend awake in bed or the bedroom and are designed to decondition presleep arousal. Typical instructions include: (1) keep a fixed wake time 7 days per week, irrespective of how much sleep you get during the night; (2) avoid any behavior in the bed or bedroom other than sleep or sexual activity; (3) sleep only in the bedroom; (4) leave the bedroom when awake for approximately 15–20 minutes; (5) return only when sleepy. The combination of these instructions reestablishes the bed and bedroom as strong cues for sleep and entrains the circadian sleep–wake cycle to the desired phase.

Sleep Restriction

Sleep restriction therapy (SRT) requires patients to limit the amount of time they spend in bed to an amount equal to their average total sleep time. In order to accomplish this, the clinician works with the patient to (1) establish a fixed wake time and (2) decrease sleep opportunity by prescribing a later bedtime. This is called the sleep window. Initially, the therapy results in a reduction in total sleep time, but over the course of several days results in decreased sleep latency and decreased wake time after sleep onset. As sleep efficiency increases, patients are instructed to gradually widen their sleep window by increasing the amount of time they spend in bed. In practice, patients roll back their bedtime in 15-minute increments per week (i.e., they keep their morning wake time the same but move their bedtime to 15 minutes earlier). This is based on sleep diary data, which shows that on the prior week the patient's sleep was on average efficient (90% or more of the time spent

in bed was spent asleep [TST/TIB]). If that ratio is less than 90% and $\geq 85\%$, then the sleep window remains the same for another week. If the sleep efficiency drops below 85%, then the sleep window is shrunk by 15 minutes. This process continues on a weekly basis until therapy is completed, at which point the subject is instructed to continue the practice on his or her own.

This therapy is thought to be effective for two reasons. First, it prevents the patient from coping with their insomnia by extending sleep opportunity. This strategy, while increasing the opportunity to get more sleep, produces a form of sleep that is shallow and fragmented. Second, the initial sleep loss that occurs with SRT is thought to increase the "pressure for sleep," which in turn produces quicker sleep latencies, less waking after sleep onset, and more efficient sleep. It should be noted that the treatment has a paradoxical aspect to it. Patients who report being unable to sleep are in essence being told: "sleep less." Such a prescription needs to be delivered with care and compliance must be monitored. Sleep restriction is contraindicated in patients with histories of bipolar disorder or seizures, because it may aggravate these conditions.

Sleep Hygiene

This requires that the clinician and patient review a set of instructions that are geared toward helping the patient maintain good sleep habits (see Table 40.1). It should be noted that sleep hygiene instructions are not helpful when provided as a monotherapy (Lacks & Morin, 1992) and might be even less helpful when provided as written instructions, which are not tailored to the individual or cast in absolute terms. With respect to the former, providing patients with a "handout" (especially without an explanation of the clinical science behind the issues) is likely to lead to noncompliance, a loss of confidence in the provider, and a sense that there may be nothing other than these "sleep tips" medications to help with insomnia. With respect to the latter, sleep hygiene instructions have within them several absolute dictums, e.g., "Avoid caffeinated products" and "Do Not Nap." Both of these instructions are too simple. For example, caffeine may be used to combat some of the daytime sequaelae of insomnia and withdrawal from

TABLE 40.1   Sleep Hygiene Instructions

1. *Sleep only as much as you need to feel refreshed during the following day.* Restricting your time in bed helps to consolidate and deepen your sleep. Excessively long times in bed lead to fragmented and shallow sleep. Get up at your regular time the next day, no matter how little you slept.
2. *Get up at the same time each day, 7 days a week.* A regular wake time in the morning leads to regular times of sleep onset, and helps to set your "biological clock."
3. *Exercise regularly.* Schedule exercise times so that they do not occur within 3 hours of when you intend to go to bed. Exercise makes it easier to initiate sleep and deepen sleep.
4. *Make sure your bedroom is comfortable and free from light and noise.* A comfortable, noise-free sleep environment will reduce the likelihood that you will wake up during the night. Noise that does not awaken you may also disturb the quality of your sleep. Carpeting, insulated curtains, and closing the door may help.
5. *Make sure that your bedroom is at a comfortable temperature during the night.* Excessively warm or cold sleep environments may disturb sleep.
6. *Eat regular meals and do not go to bed hungry.* Hunger may disturb sleep. A light snack at bedtime (especially carbohydrates) may help sleep, but avoid greasy or "heavy" foods.
7. *Avoid excessive liquids in the evening.* Reducing liquid intake will minimize the need for nighttime trips to the bathroom.
8. *Cut down on all caffeine products.* Caffeinated beverages and foods (coffee, tea, cola, chocolate) can cause difficulty falling asleep, awakenings during the night, and shallow sleep. Even caffeine early in the day can disrupt nighttime sleep.
9. *Avoid alcohol, especially in the evening.* Although alcohol helps tense people fall asleep more easily, it causes awakenings later in the night.
10. *Smoking may disturb sleep.* Nicotine is a stimulant. Try not to smoke during the night when you have trouble sleeping.
11. *Don't take your problems to bed.* Plan some time earlier in the evening for working on your problems or planning the next day's activities. Worrying may interfere with initiating sleep and produce shallow sleep.
12. *Train yourself to use the bedroom only for sleeping and sexual activity.* This will help condition your brain to see bed as the place for sleeping. Do *not* read, watch TV, or eat in bed.
13. *Do not try to fall asleep.* This only makes the problem worse. Instead, turn on the light, leave the bedroom, and do something different like reading a book. Don't engage in stimulating activity. Return to bed only when you are sleepy.
14. *Put the clock under the bed or turn it so that you can't see it.* Clock watching may lead to frustration, anger, and worry, which interfere with sleep.
15. *Avoid naps.* Staying awake during the day helps you to fall asleep at night.

Author's note: The above list includes the usual practices described as "good sleep hygiene," but it also includes some principles subsumed under "Stimulus Control therapy" (#2,12,13), "Sleep Restriction Therapy" (#1,2,15), and "Relaxation" (#11,13).

the substance and, if timed appropriately, may actually enhance subjects' ability to fall asleep more quickly. Napping may be useful to sustain high levels of daytime function and performance. Such a compensatory strategy, however, should be allowed only provided that time to bed is delayed. In sum, sleep hygiene is best deployed with other strategies, in a didactive therapy session, with attention to the individual patient's experience.

Standard Eight-Session Behavioral Intervention

Behavioral interventions for insomnia are typically structured to allow for weekly sessions over 6–8 weeks. The preponderance of the efficacy data is based on structured protocols of this length as are the detailed treatment manuals available, for example (Morin & Espie, 2003; Perlis, Jungquist, Smith, & Posner, 2005). There

are several good reasons for having this many sessions (as opposed to fewer). First, it allows the clinician to deal with initial noncompliance with the behavioral interventions, which clients can find somewhat onerous. Second, sleep restriction therapy can often reduce time in bed (and thus the maximal possible nightly sleep time to 5–6 hours per night and the sleep window is only increased at 15 minutes per week. This means that a patient initially restricted to 5.5 hours in bed based on their sleep diaries, could at best achieve 7.25 hours of total sleep time per night by the end of therapy. Thus, an eight-session structure allows the patient and clinician to monitor progress, maintain compliance over this interval, and arrive at treatment end with what is usually an acceptable level of total sleep time. It is often the case that as patients continue to apply sleep restriction, their total sleep time continues to increase following treatment. Finally, an eight-session format is useful in that many patients' sleep continuity may improve, but that they do not subjectively "feel" much better until one or more weeks of better than average sleep. For some, this does not occur until later sessions, so that initial and middle treatment sessions serve to bolster the patient's confidence that subjective wellness is within sight. For these reasons, an eight-session protocol remains the standard research grade form of delivery for the behavioral treatment of insomnia.

In a clinical practice, the clinician may alter the number of sessions based on factors such as the patient's progress and their ability to self-administer the treatment regimen in a consistent and compliant manner. More recently, efforts to shorten treatment so that it may be offered outside the traditional therapy setting have been undertaken. Brief behavioral therapy for insomnia has been delivered in three to four sessions with good efficacy (Edinger & Sampson, 2003). It remains to be seen whether the treatment gains are as enduring as those evidenced in treatments with more sessions.

The following is a summary description of just such an eight-session intervention using behavioral techniques alone. The reader is encouraged to refer to the treatment manuals noted earlier for more detailed information.

Session 1 (clinical evaluation and 2-week baseline). During this session, the patient's sleep complaints are reviewed with the clinician responsible for treatment and the patient is instructed to keep a sleep diary for a baseline period of 2 weeks. All subjects are carefully instructed on how to complete this measure. Diaries can be commenced simultaneously with treatment for other existing conditions or in conjunction with sleep medication usage. Note that session 2 is scheduled 2 weeks after session 1; all other sessions are scheduled at 1-week intervals.

Session 2 (sleep restriction and stimulus control therapy). Baseline sleep diary data are reviewed. This information sets the parameters for sleep restriction therapy and guides the patient toward the treatment to be prescribed. The standard approach is interactive/didactic. The patient and the clinician

evaluate the data together. After reviewing the data and identifying basic assumptions, most patients easily deduce what might represent a good "counterstrategy." The primary assumption most patients identify is what we call "the positive correlation fallacy": the more time in bed, the more sleep one will get. When the patient has identified one or more components of therapy, the clinician explains in detail the rationale and procedures for sleep restriction and stimulus control therapy (see above).

Session 3 (sleep hygiene and sleep restriction therapy adjustments). As with all sessions, sleep diary data are reviewed and charted. The upward titration process is begun and sleep hygiene instructions are reviewed by having the patient read aloud the various imperatives and the corresponding rationales. After the patient and the clinician have identified the relevance of the issue, the clinician reviews in more detail the basic concepts and related clinical research. The amount of, and manner in which, information is presented varies according to patient interest.

Sessions 4–7 (sleep restriction therapy adjustments). Sleep diary data are reviewed and charted. Upward titration continues.

Session 8 (relapse prevention). This last session is largely psychoeducational. The clinician reviews (1) "how insomnia gets started" and the strategies that maintain poor sleep and (2) the strategies that are likely to abort an extended episode of insomnia.

Adjunctive Therapies or Multicomponent CBT

In addition to these principal behavioral techniques, there are also several adjunctive therapies that may prove helpful to the patient and can be included in the treatment plan: relaxation training, phototherapy, and cognitive therapy. Some or all of these, when added to the behavioral therapies, comprise what is called a multicomponent CBT for insomnia. These additional strategies are often inserted in the six- to eight-session structure above (i.e., there is usually no need to lengthen the number of sessions to add these components).

Relaxation Training

Different relaxation techniques target different physiological systems. Progressive muscle relaxation is used to diminish skeletal muscle tension. Diaphragmatic breathing is used to make breathing slower and shallower and resembles the form of breathing, interestingly, that naturally occurs at sleep onset. Autogenics training focuses on increasing peripheral blood flow. Biofeedback may similarly target specific systems with a common goal of achieving a relaxed state. To the list of relaxation techniques can be added hypnosis and mindfulness-based stress reduction. While the latter involves more than learning a relaxation technique, this is nonetheless its core practice. Most practitioners select the optimal relaxation method based on which technique is easiest for the patient to learn, which is most consistent with how the patient manifests arousal, and which technique is not contraindicated by medical conditions (e.g., progressive muscle relaxation might not be an ideal choice for patients with certain neuromuscular disorders).

Phototherapy

There is substantial empirical evidence that bright light has antidepressant and sleep-promoting effects. The sleep-promoting effects of bright light may occur via several mechanisms, including shifting the circadian system; enhancement of the amplitude of the circadian pacemaker, promoting wakefulness during the day and sleep at night; or indirectly via its antidepressant effects. In practice, bright light is used to shorten or lengthen the diurnal phase of the patient's day. In the case where the patient's insomnia has a phase delay component (i.e., the patient prefers to go to bed late and wake up late), waking early by alarm and being exposed to bright light in the morning for a period of time may enable them to "feel sleepy" at an earlier time in the evening. In the case where the patient's insomnia has a phase advance component (i.e., the patient prefers to go to bed early and wake up early), bright light exposure in the evening may enable them to stay awake later and wake up later. It is generally assumed that phototherapy has no significant side effects, but this is not always the case. Mania may be triggered by bright light in patients not previously diagnosed with bipolar mood disorder. Other side effects include insomnia, hypomania, agitation, visual blurring, eyestrain, and headaches. Individuals with eye-related problems or who are at risk for such conditions such as diabetes should consult an eye care specialist prior to initiating light therapy.

Cognitive Therapy

Several forms of cognitive therapy for insomnia have been developed and often overlap. Some have a more didactic focus (Morin, 1993), others use paradoxical intention (Shoham-Salomon & Rosenthal, 1987), others use a form of cognitive restructuring (Buysee D.J. & Perlis, 1996) and others focus on safety behaviors (Harvey, 2002) and attention (Espie, Broomfield, MacMahon, Macphee, & Taylor, 2006). While the approaches differ in procedure, all are based on the observation that patients with insomnia have negative thoughts and beliefs about their condition and its consequences. Helping patients to challenge the veracity and usefulness of these beliefs is thought to decrease the anxiety and arousal associated with insomnia.

Techniques for Dealing with Client Noncompliance

CBT techniques for insomnia can be challenging for both the client and the practitioner. This may be particularly true early in the therapeutic process as the client will be asked to accept a difficult regimen of behavioral change and concomitant sleep deprivation. Sleep loss alone may try the patience of a client and this makes compliance with any therapeutic modality a problematic issue. There are, however, some strategies (most based in clinical experience) that may enhance the likelihood of a successful clinical outcome. Examples of these techniques include using:

- *Good salesmanship (a motivational approach to therapy)*. There is no more important a method than the demonstration of a good knowledge base regarding (in general) sleep medicine and (in specific) the principles behind the behavioral interventions. Patients will often have challenging questions regarding the procedures. Clear and compelling explanations go a long way toward gaining patient trust and compliance. Sharing information about the clinical efficacy and effectiveness of treatment can often be a powerful aid in obtaining compliance.

- *A Socratic versus pedantic approach to patient education.* It is important to both educate and work collaboratively with the client throughout the treatment process. Whenever possible, clients should be led to answers that they discover, rather than being simply told what to do and why to do it. This process will reduce patient resistance, particularly in reactant patients or in patients who are not treatment naive.

- *Realistic goal setting.* It is of great importance for the therapist to understand the goals of the client and determine if and how they can be realistically met. Such evaluation of the client should include a discussion of life circumstances, as it would be unwise to start a client through treatment at a time where personal situations may make compliance an issue. Part of the psychoeducational process involves some discussion the notion that even good sleepers do not necessarily sleep for 8 uninterrupted hours per night and that they do not necessarily sleep well every night. It is also important to make clients aware from the very first session that CBT will be difficult and that their insomnia symptoms may get worse before they get better.

- *A scientific approach to treatment.* Finally, it is quite helpful to keep graphs of client progress throughout treatment. Rewarding a client by showing them their progress graphically from week to week makes the process more tangible and has the effect of proving to the client that the treatment is working and that they are gaining control over their problem and achieving success.

Efficacy of Cognitive Behavioral Treatment Strategies

There is clear evidence that the cognitive behavioral modalities are effective and that the clinical gains are comparable to those produced by hypnotics. A meta-analysis has shown that behavioral treatments lead to very good long-term results for chronic insomnia (Murtagh et al., 1995). In another meta-analysis (Morin, Culbert, & Schwartz, 1994), improvements in sleep of 30%–40% were observed when using behavioral strategies. Sleep latency was reduced by 39%–43%, number of awakenings was reduced by 30%–73%, duration of awakenings was reduced by 46%, and total sleep time was increased 8%–9.4%. In real numbers this amounted to patients falling asleep approximately 25 minutes sooner, having 0.5–1.2 fewer awakenings per night, and sleeping about 30 minutes longer per night. These outcomes are comparable to the gains that can be obtained with medication and in the case of sleep initiation difficulties may actually be superior to pharmacotherapy (Smith et al., 2002).

Cognitive-behavioral treatments can be employed with patients who are classified as having either primary insomnia or insomnia co-morbid with another medical or psychiatric condition (Smith & Perlis, 2006; Lichstein, Wilson, & Johnson, 2000). A number of co-morbid insomnias have responded to CBT for insomnia, these include chronic pain (Currie, Wilson, Pontefract, & deLaplante, 2000; Pigeon et al., 2007), fibromyalgia (Edinger, Wohlgemuth, Krystal, & Rice, 2005), breast cancer (Savard, Simard, Ivers, & Morin, 2005), depression (Taylor, Lichstein, Weinstock, Temple, & Sanford, 2007), and PTSD (Deviva, Zayfert, Pigeon, & Mellman, 2005; Germain, Shear, Hall, & Buysse, 2007; Krakow et al., 2001). Depending on the primary disorder in question, alterations or additions to the standard therapies may be in order. For instance, in cancer survivors, the clinician may wish to limit the amount of sleep restriction prescribed so as to not create additional fatigue and immunological stress by creating additional sleep loss in these patients. In patients whose PTSD stems from trauma that occurred during sleep and/or in the sleep environment, there may be increased amounts of safety behaviors and cognitions related to sleep that may need to be addressed in the course of treatment. Those patients who also present with frequent nightmares may also benefit from focused nightmare therapies (Krakow, Kellner, Pathak, & Lambert, 1995). For an excellent review of comorbid insomnias, see Smith, Huang, and Manber (2005).

CONCLUSION

Sleep is thought to be essential to many vital processes including, but not limited to, physiologic restoration, immune system function, memory consolidation, and mood. Without good quality and/or quantity sleep the careful balance that exits in these many complex systems is susceptible to dysregulation.

Insomnia represents one of the more ubiquitous forms of sleep disturbance. Unfortunately, despite it prevalence and associated negative sequaelae, only a small fraction of patients seek out treatment or have access to behavioral sleep medicine specialists. This is especially unfortunate given the existence of multiple forms of effective therapy. We hope the material presented in this chapter (1) highlights the need to treat insomnia, (2) provides health care professionals with information on the techniques employed by behavioral sleep medicine specialists, and (3) presents enough information so as to allow clinicians to decide whether to refer patients to a specialist or to seek specific training in this form of CBT treatment. While this chapter provides a good introduction to the CBT of insomnia, the chapter cannot provide a good substitute for mentored clinical experience. We encourage those interested in developing an expertise in the CBT for insomnia to seek out additional training in behavioral sleep medicine through a variety of mechanisms including accredited fellowships and courses offered through the American Academy of Sleep Medicine, half- and full-day workshops at national meetings (e.g., the Associated Professional Sleep Societies, the American Psychological Association, the Society for Behavioral Medicine, and the Association for Behavioral and Cognitive Therapies) and via day-long and weekend-long CME/CEU programs delivered by individual institutions.

Further Reading

Hauri, P. (1991). *Case studies in insomnia*. New York, New York: Plenum.

Morin, C. M., & Espie, C. A. (2003). *Insomnia: A clinical guide to assessment and treatment management*. New York: Kluwer Academic/Plenum.

Perlis, M., & Lichstien, K. (Eds.). (2003) *Treating sleep disorders: The principles & practice of behavioral sleep medicine*. Philadelphia: JohnWiley & Sons.

References

Aldrich, M. S. (1989). Automobile accidents in patients with sleep disorders. *Sleep, 12*, 487–494.

American Academy of Sleep Medicine. (2005). *International classification of sleep disorders. Diagnostic and coding manual* (2nd ed.). Westchester, IL: American Academy of Sleep Medicine.

American Psychological Association (2000). *Diagnostic and Statistical Manual of Mental Disorders*, 4th ed., Text Revision *(DSM-IV-TR)*. Washington DC: author.

Ancoli-Israel, S., & Roth, T. (1999). Characteristics of insomnia in the United States: Results of the 1991 National Sleep Foundation Survey I [in process citation]. *Sleep, 22*(suppl 2), S347–S353.

Buysee, D. J., & Perlis, M. L. (1996). The evaluation and treatment of insomnia. *Journal of Practical Psychchiatry and Behavioral Health, 2*, 80–93.

Carey, T. J., Moul, D. E., Pilkonis, P., Germain, A., & Buysse, D. J. (2005). Focusing on the experience of insomnia. *Behavioral Sleep Medicine, 3*, 73–86.

Chesson, A. L., Jr., Anderson, W. M., Littner, M., Davila, D., Hartse, K., Johnson, S., et al. (1999). Practice parameters for the nonpharmacologic treatment of chronic insomnia. An American Academy of Sleep Medicine report. Standards of Practice Committee of the American Academy of Sleep Medicine [in process citation]. *Sleep, 22*, 1128–1133.

Currie, S. R., Wilson, K. G., Pontefract, A. J., & de Laplante, L. (2000). Cognitive–behavioral treatment of insomnia secondary to chronic pain. *Journal of Consulting Clinical Psychology., 68*, 407–416.

Deviva, J. C., Zayfert, C., Pigeon, W. R., & Mellman, T. A. (2005). Treatment of residual insomnia after CBT for PTSD: Case studies. *Journal of Traumatic Stress, 18*, 155–159.

Dew, M. A., Hoch, C. C., Buysse, D. J., Monk, T. H., Begley, A. E., Houck, P. R., et al. (2003). Healthy older adults' sleep predicts all-cause mortality at 4 to 19 years of follow-up. *Psychosomatic Medicine, 65*, 63–73.

Edinger, J. D., Bonnet, M. H., Bootzin, R. R., Doghramji, K., Dorsey, C. M., Espie, C. A. et al. (2004). Derivation of research diagnostic criteria for insomnia: Report of an American Academy of Sleep Medicine Work Group. *Sleep, 27*, 1567–1596.

Edinger, J. D., & Sampson, W. S. (2003). A primary care "friendly" cognitive behavioral insomnia therapy. *Sleep, 26*, 177–182.

Edinger, J. D., Wohlgemuth, W. K., Krystal, A. D., & Rice, J. R. (2005). Behavioral insomnia therapy for fibromyalgia patients: A randomized clinical trial. *Archives of Internal Medicine, 165,* 2527–2535.

Espie, C. A., Broomfield, N. M., MacMahon, K. M. A., Macphee, L. M., & Taylor, L. M. (in press). The attention–intention–effort pathway in the development of psychophysiologic insomnia: An invited theoretical review. *Sleep Medecine Reviews.*

Espie, C. A., Broomfield, N. M., MacMahon, K. M. A., Macphee, L. M., & Taylor, L. M. (2006). The attention–intention–effort pathway in the development of psychophysiologic insomnia: An invited theoretical review. *Sleep Medicine Reviews, 10,* 215–245.

Ford, D. E., & Kamerow, D. B. (1989). Epidemiologic study of sleep disturbances and psychiatric disorders. An opportunity for prevention? *Journal of the American Medical Association, 262,* 1479–1484.

Fullerton, P. (2006). The economic impact of insomnia in managed care: A clearer picture emerges. *American Journal of Managed Care,* S246–S252.

Gallup Organization (1995). *Sleep in America.* Princeton, NJ: The Gallup Organization.

Germain, A., Shear, M. K., Hall, M., & Buysse, D. J. (2007). Effects of a brief behavioral treatment for PTSD-related sleep disturbances: A pilot study. *Behaviour Research and Therapy, 45,* 627–632.

Harvey, A. G. (2001). A cognitive model of insomnia. *Behavior Research and Therapy,* 1–25.

Harvey, A. G. (2002). Identifying safety behaviors in insomnia. *Journal of Nervous and Mental Disease, 190,* 16–21.

Hillman, D. R., Murphy, A. S., & Pezzullo, L. (2006). The economic cost of sleep disorders. *Sleep, 29,* 299–305.

Johnson, L. & Spinweber, C. (1983). Quality of sleep and performance in the navy: A longitudinal study of good and poor sleepers. In C. Guilleminault & E. Lugaresi (Eds.), *Sleep/wake disorders: Natural history, epidemiology, and long-term evaluation* (pp. 13–28). New York: Raven Press.

Krakow, B., Johnston, L., Melendrez, D., Hollifield, M., Warner, T. D., Chavez-Kennedy, D., et al. (2001). An open-label trial of evidence-based cognitive behavior therapy for nightmares and insomnia in crime victims with PTSD. *American Journal of Psychiatry, 158,* 2043–2047.

Krakow, B., Kellner, R., Pathak, D., & Lambert, L. (1995). Imagery rehearsal treatment for chronic nightmares. *Behaviour Research and Therapy, 33,* 837–843.

Kripke, D. F., Simons, R. N., Garfinkel, L., & Hammond, E. C. (1979). Short and long sleep and sleeping pills: Is increased mortality associated? *Archives of General Psychiatry, 36,* 103–116.

Kupperman, M., Lubeck, D. P., & Mazonson, P. D. (1995). Sleep problems and their correlates in a working population. *Journal of General Internal Medicine, 10,* 25–32.

Lacks, P., & Morin, C. M. (1992). Recent advances in the assessment and treatment of insomnia. [Review] [105 refs]. *Journal of Consulting & Clinical Psychology, 60,* 586–594.

LeBlanc, M., Merette, C., Savard, J., & Morin, C. (2007). Incidence and risk factors of insomnia in a population-based sample. *Sleep, 30* (abstract Suppl), A261–A262.

Leger, D., Guilleminault, C., Bader, G., Levy, E., & Paillard, M. (2002). Medical and socio-professional impact of insomnia. *Sleep, 25,* 625–629.

Lichstein, K. L., Wilson, N. M., & Johnson, C. T. (2000). Psychological treatment of secondary insomnia. *Psychology of Aging, 2,* 232–240.

Mahendran, R., Subramaniam M., & Chan, Y. M. (2007). Psychiatric morbidity of patients referred to an insomnia clinic. *Singapore Medical Journal, 48,* 163–165.

Mellinger, G. D., Balter, M. B., & Uhlenhuth, E. H. (1985). Insomnia and its treatment: prevalence and correlates. *Archives of General Psychiatry, 42,* 225–232.

Mendelson, W. B. (1995). Long-term follow-up of chronic insomnia. *Sleep, 18,* 698–701.

Morin, C. M., & Espie, C. A. (2003). *Insomnia: A clinical guide to assessment and treatment.* New York: Kluwer Academic/Plenum.

Morin, C. M. (1993). *Insomnia: Psychological assessment and management.* New York: Guilford.

Morin, C. M., Culbert, J. P., & Schwartz, S. M. (1994). Nonpharmacological interventions for insomnia: A meta-analysis of treatment efficacy. *American Journal of Psychiatry, 151,* 1172–1180.

Morin, C. M., Stone, J., Trinkle, D., Mercer, J., & Remsberg, S. (1993). Dysfunctional beliefs and attitudes about sleep among older adults with and without insomnia complaints. *Psychology and Aging., 8,* 463–467.

Murtagh, D. R., & Greenwood, K. M. (1995). Identifying effective psychological treatments for insomnia: a meta-analysis. *Journal of Consulting & Clinical Psychology, 63,* 79–89.

Ohayon, M. M. (2002). Epidemiology of insomnia: what we know and what we still need to learn. *Sleep Medicine Reviews, 6,* 97–111.

Ohayon, M. M., & Roth, T. (2001). What are the contributing factors for insomnia in the general population? *Journal of Psychosomatic Research, 51,* 745–755.

Orff, H. J., Drummond, S. P. A., Nowakowski, S., & Perlis, M. L. (in press). Discrepancy between subjective symtomatology and objective neuropsychological performance in insomnia. *Sleep.*

Ozminkowski, R. J., Wang, S. H., & Walsh, J. K. (2007). The direct and indirect costs of untreated insomnia in adults in the United States. *Sleep, 30,* 263–273.

Perlis, M., Jungquist, C., Smith, M. T., & Posner, D. (2005). *The cognitive behavioral treatment of insomnia: A treatment manual.* New York: Spinger Verlag.

Perlis, M. L., Buysse, D., Giles, D. E., Tu, X., & Kupfer, D. J. (1997). Sleep disturbance may be a prodromal symptom of depression. *Journal of Affective Disorders, 42,* 209–212.

Perlis, M. L., Giles, D. E., Mendelson, W. B., Bootzin, R. R., & Wyatt, J. K. (1997). Psychophysiological insomnia: The behavioural model and a neurocognitive perspective. *Journal of Sleep Research, 6,* 179–188.

Perlis, M. L., Smith, M. T., & Pigeon, W. R. (2005). Etiology and Pathophysiology of Insomnia. In M. Kryger, T. Roth, & W. C. Dement (Eds.), *Principles and Practice of Sleep Medicine* (4th ed., pp. 714–725). Philadelphia: Elsevier Saunders.

Phillips, B., & Mannino, D. (2007). Do insomnia complaints cause hypertension or cardiovascular disease? *Journal of Clinical Sleep Medicine, 3,* 489–494.

Pigeon, W., Jungquist, C., Matteson, S., Swan, J., Stoll, J., O'Brien, C. et al. (2007). Pain, sleep and mood outcomes in chronic pain patients following cognitive behavioral therapy for insomnia. *Sleep, 30,* A255–A256.

Pigeon, W., & Perlis, M. L. (2007). Insomnia and depression: Birds of a feather? *International Journal of Sleep Disorders, 1,* 82–91.

Pigeon, W. R., Hegel, M. T., Unutzer, J., Fan, M.-Y., Sateia, M., Lyness, J. M. et al. (2008). Is insomnia a perpetuating factor for late-life depression in the IMPACT cohort? *Sleep.*

Roth, T., & Ancoli-Israel, S. (1999). Daytime consequences and correlates of insomnia in the United States: Results of the 1991 National Sleep Foundation Survey. II [in process citation]. *Sleep,* 22(suppl 2), S354–S358.

Roth, T., & Roehrs, T. (2003). Insomnia: epidemiology, characteristics, and consequences. *Clinical Cornerstone, 5,* 5–15.

Ryden, A. M., Knutson, K. L., Mander, B. A., & Van Cauter, E. Y. (2002). Association between sleep quality and glycemic control in type 2 diabetic African-American women. *Diabetes, 51,* A620.

Savard, J., Simard, S., Ivers, H., & Morin, C. M. (2005). A randomized study of on the efficacy of cognitive–behavioral therapy for insomnia secondary to breast cancer: I. Sleep and psychological effects. *Journal of Clinical Oncology, 23,* 6083–6096.

Schwartz, S., McDowell, A. W., Cole, S. R., Cornoni-Huntley, J., Hays, J. C., & Blazer, D. (1999). Insomnia and heart disease: A review of epidemiologic studies. *Journal of Psychosomatic Research, 47,* 313–333.

Shochat, T., Umphress, J., Israel, A. G., & Ancoli-Israel, S. (1999). Insomnia in primary care patients. *Sleep,* 22(suppl 2), S359–S365.

Shoham-Salomon, V., & Rosenthal, R. (1987). Paradoxical interventions: A meta-analysis. *Journal of Consulting & Clinical Psychology, 55,* 22–28.

Smith, M. T., Huang, M. I., & Manber, R. (2005). Cognitive behavior therapy for chronic insomnia occurring within the context of medical and psychiatric disorders. *Clinical Psychology Review, 25,* 559–611.

Smith, M. T. & Perlis, M. L. (2006). Who is a candidate for cognitive–behavioral therapy for insomnia? *Health Psychology, 25,* 15–19.

Smith, M. T., Perlis, M. L., Park, A., Smith, M. S., Pennington, J., Giles, D. E., et al. (2002). Comparative meta-analysis of pharmacotherapy and behavior therapy for persistent insomnia. *American Journal of Psychiatry, 159,* 5–11.

Spielman, A., Caruso, L., & Glovinsky, P. (1987). A behavioral perspective on insomnia treatment. *Psychiatric Clinics of North America, 10,* 541–553.

Stewart, R., Besset, A., Bebbington, P., Brugha, T., Lindesay, J., Jenkins, R. et al. (2006). Insomnia comorbidity and impact and hypnotic use by age group in a national survey population aged 16 to 74 years. *Sleep, 29,* 1391–1397.

Suka, M., Yoshida, K., & Sugimori, H. (2003). Persistent insomnia is a predictor of hypertension in Japanese male workers. *Journal of Occupational Health, 45,* 344–350.

Taylor, D. J., Lichstein, K., Weinstock, J., Temple, J., & Sanford, S. (2007). A pilot study of cognitive–behavioral therapy of insomnia in people with mild depression. *Behavior Therapy, 38,* 49–57.

Taylor, D. J., Lichstein, K. L., Durrence, H. H., Reidel, B. W., & Bush, A. J. (2005). Epidemiology of insomnia, depression, and anxiety. *Sleep, 28,* 1457–1464.

Walsh, J. K., & Engelhardt, C. L. (1999). The direct economic costs of insomnia in the United States for 1995. *Sleep,* 22(suppl 2), S386–S393.

Young, T. B. (2005). Natural history of chronic insomnia. *Journal of Clinical Sleep Medicine, 1,* e466–e467.

41 INTEROCEPTIVE EXPOSURE FOR PANIC DISORDER

John P. Forsyth, Tiffany Fusé, and Dean T. Acheson

Interoceptive exposure is at the core of most efficacious cognitive behavioral interventions for panic disorder (PD) and is based, in large part, on the biopsychosocial model of panic (Barlow, 2001). This model affords conditioning or associative learning processes a prominent role in the development and maintenance of panic pathology. In short, otherwise benign bodily and/or environmental cues that precede or co-occur with an unexpected false alarm (i.e., panic attack) may acquire fear-evoking functions to elicit subsequent learned alarms or panic attacks (see Acheson, Forsyth, Prenoveau & Bouton, 2007; Barlow, 2001; Bouton, Mineka, & Barlow, 2001; Forsyth & Eifert, 1996a, 1996b, 1998).

This process, in turn, is thought to contribute to the development of hypervigilance and sensitivity to bodily and environmental cues that were associated with panic in the past, and thus to a positive feedback spiral. For instance, unexpected arousal (e.g., a heart flutter) evokes fear and is responded to as such (e.g., avoidance, escape, suppression; Forsyth, Eifert, & Barrios, 2006). Such behavior can further amplify unpleasant arousal, leading to stronger negative emotional learning, while strengthening associations between learned alarms and other bodily or environmental cues, including arbitrary verbal events (e.g., the thought "I am dying" may seem real and frightening to panic sufferers, despite never having direct experience with death during prior panic attacks). Anxious apprehension is a feature of this cycle and covert and overt forms of behavioral avoidance are common, if not central, to the process that transforms panic from being an unpleasant event to a life shattering clinical problem (Forsyth et al., 2006).

Cognitive behavior therapy (CBT) is designed to modify several elements that are believed to maintain PD, whereas interoceptive exposure

(IE) is used explicitly to modify learned relations between bodily cues and subsequent panic. Indeed, all effective treatments for PD have IE as a component (Barlow, 2001; Craske & Barlow, 2000; Craske, Rowe, Lewin, & Noriega-Dimitri, 1997; Penava, Otto, Maki, & Pollack, 1998; Klosko, Barlow, Tassinari, & Cerny, 1990), and IE is also effective as a treatment for PD when used alone (e.g., Beck, Shipherd, & Zebb, 1997; Griez & van den Hout, 1986; van den Hout, van der Molen, Griez, Lousberg, & Nansen, 1987). Increasingly, IE is also being used as a core intervention for persons with any anxiety disorder (Barlow, Allen, & Choate, 2004; Eifert & Forsyth, 2005).

IE can be thought of as the behavioral component of CBT for PD and, like other forms of exposure therapy (see Chapter 38 on *in vivo* exposure and Chapter 66 on systematic desensitization in this volume), is designed to provide a structured context that facilitates approaching discomfort fully and without defense as it is, and thus opportunities for new emotional learning. Interoceptive exposure differs from other forms of exposure therapy only in that it involves exercises designed to evoke feared bodily cues and sensations. IE capitalizes on extinction processes like other forms of exposure therapy, with the goal being to reduce the tendency for bodily cues to evoke strong fear and avoidance behavior.

WHO MIGHT BENEFIT FROM THIS TREATMENT?

Interoceptive exposure, whether in an individual or group therapy format, is a brief (4–15 sessions) and highly effective intervention for problems where panic attacks are a prominent feature (e.g., Clum, Clum, & Surls, 1993; Craske,

Brown, & Barlow, 1991; Craske et al., 1997; Gould, Otto, Pollack, 1995; Westen & Morrison, 2001; Zuercher-White, 1997). Approximately 85%–100% of persons suffering from PD remain free from panic at 1- and 2-year follow-ups when IE is included as part of a comprehensive treatment package (Craske, Brown, & Barlow, 1991). Moreover, CBT for PD produces more durable long-term outcomes at 6 months compared to pharmacotherapy (e.g., imipramine) and has lower attrition rates (Barlow, Gorman, Shear, & Woods, 2000; see also Gould et al., 1995).

Interoceptive exposure also appears to be effective as a treatment for nocturnal panic (Craske & Tsao, 2005). Exercises are tailored to evoke sensations that accompany sleep and sudden waking from a sleeping state (e.g., relaxation and startle). Fears of gastrointestinal symptoms that accompany irritable bowel syndrome—a stress-related condition that tends to co-occur with PD—also responds well to IE. Interoceptive exposure also may be appropriate for problems other than panic, and particularly cases in which (1) bodily signs and discomfort evoke distress or psychological suffering, and (2) responding to bodily signs and symptoms with avoidance and excessive emotion regulation gets in the way of more effective action (Forsyth et al., 2006). Examples of such problems include, but are not limited to, conditioned nausea resulting from chemotherapy, hypochondriacal symptoms, illness phobia (e.g., cardiophobia), chronic pain, abuse of controlled substances (e.g., withdrawal), and the anxiety disorders more broadly. That is, IE may be helpful for problems wherein unpleasant bodily sensations and emotional events are related with excessive distress, avoidance, and/or escape behavior.

It should be stressed that efficacy data are limited regarding the utility of IE for problems other than panic. Though IE does appear effective when included as part of routine CBT for individuals with panic and other comorbid conditions, most studies exclude persons with active substance abuse or dependence, psychosis, and suicidal or homicidal ideation or intent; additionally, data regarding the efficacy of IE in ethnic minorities, children, and young adults, are limited at best (Chosak, Baker, Thorn, Spiegel, & Barlow, 1999).

CONTRAINDICATIONS OF THE TREATMENT

Interoceptive exposure is a structured, non-pharmacologic intervention that encourages clients to confront feared bodily sensations in a supportive therapeutic environment while resisting the natural tendency to engage in covert and overt avoidance or escape strategies. In many respects it can be thought of as an *in vivo* method of directly confronting the natural tendency toward experiential avoidance of unwanted private events (see Chapter 6 on acceptance in this volume)—events that are otherwise harmless and perfectly adaptive components of human emotional responding (Forsyth et al., 2006). Yet IE is certainly not to be used for all clients, and it is even contraindicated in some cases.

For instance, IE exercises designed to elicit cardiorespiratory cues (e.g., jogging, running up a staircase, hyperventilation) are inappropriate for those suffering from certain cardiovascular conditions. Moreover, exercises such as breathing through a straw, rebreathing expired air, or inhaling enhanced concentrations of carbon dioxide–enriched air are contraindicated for clients with asthma, chronic obstructive lung disease, renal disease, seizure disorders, certain blood disorders such as anemia, and for women who are pregnant.

If the therapist is uncertain about the appropriateness of a particular IE exercise, then it is recommended that the therapist consult with the client's primary care physician or select an alternate exercise. When a particular exercise is not feasible for a client, the therapist may model the exercise so as to demonstrate both how ordinary activities may cause somatic sensations and that such sensations are not harmful.

Moreover, some medications, particularly those that attenuate physical symptoms such as benzodiazapines and other anxiolytics, can interfere with the processes that IE is designed to target and change. For instance, medications that attenuate arousal work against a client fully experiencing both conditioned and unconditioned autonomic arousal during exposure, and hence extinction processes. In fact, poorer long-term outcomes have been noted when IE is combined with benzodiazapines and other anxiolytic medications (e.g., Brown & Barlow, 1995; Klosko et al., 1990; Spiegel & Bruce, 1997). Here, there also is the risk that patients may erroneously attribute any improvement to the medication, and not to their efforts during IE.

Severe cases of depression, including suicidal or homicidal ideation or intent, contradict IE as a first-line of treatment, whereas the presence of Axis II disorders may simply result in some delayed therapeutic benefit (Tsao & Craske, 2000). Moreover, elevated cortisol and plasma catecholamine levels are associated with panic attacks and may harm a developing fetus (Nonacs, Cohen, & Altshuler, 1988). Thus, therapists should be cautious about using IE to generate intense arousal in pregnant women, particularly during the third trimester, due to the risk of inducing false labor.

Finally, noncompliance is a frequent concern with IE and can occur for several reasons (e.g., extremely fearful clients, lack of faith in the treatment, lack of social support and/or motivation). Noncompliance is not a contraindication for IE, but it should be addressed in a creative and supportive manner and may even require a slower pace of IE exercises and/or structuring of such exercises in a more graduated fashion.

OTHER CONSIDERATIONS IN DECIDING WHETHER TO USE INTEROCEPTIVE EXPOSURE

Whether IE alone is sufficient to result in changes in the way client's think about their bodily sensations and panicogenic responses is a source of continuing controversy and debate. In fact, IE is most often bundled with some form of cognitive restructuring intervention that is designed to challenge and replace the tendency of patient's with PD to catastrophically misinterpret signs and symptoms of arousal. Such cognitive conceptualizations could, and probably should, be routinely integrated with IE.

For instance, during exposure exercises, clients could be taught to approach and experience feared bodily sensations while also confronting misinterpretations or catastrophic patterns of consequential thinking (e.g., heart palpitations mean "I am having a heart attack" versus "I am having the thought that I am having

a heart attack"; see Eifert & Forsyth, 2005). Thus, IE could be conceived of as an experiential exercise to evoke both bodily cues and the associated verbal and symbolic thoughts associated with them. The context and consequences of such thinking could then be incorporated into IE without necessarily focusing on the thought content. As another example, a therapist might focus on a client's tendencies to respond to their own responses and the strategies they use to reduce, escape from, or avoid such feelings, and then focus on the ways both contribute to other problems in living (Eifert & Forsyth, 2005). The goal then would not be to eliminate or replace autonomic responses and associated thoughts, but to use IE to learn how to respond to them differently and how to behave differently when such private events occur.

HOW DOES INTEROCEPTIVE EXPOSURE WORK?

Interoceptive exposure, like other forms of exposure therapy, is predicated on two interrelated learning processes. The first of these is based on extensive laboratory research showing that stimuli can acquire fear-evoking functions via Pavlovian or respondent learning processes (see Acheson et al., 2007; Bouton et al., 2001; Forsyth & Eifert, 1996a, 1996b), and that the capacity of such stimuli to evoke fearful responding can be attenuated via the controlled and systematic presentation of fear evoking cues without the anticipated aversive consequences. Such attenuation in fearful responding over repeated nonreinforced exposure trials, in turn, is based on the principle of extinction—a principle that should not be confused with elimination or a response. Indeed, no response is eliminated via exposure-based interventions, although this has become a common way to talk about extinction. Moreover, extinction is based on a learning process, whereas habituation is generally regarded as an unlearned process involving similar attenuation of responding to stimuli upon repeated presentation. Interoceptive exposure and the underlying principles driving its operation are fairly well worked out.

The second learning process, however, is not as well understood, namely, the tendency to respond fearfully to conditioned processes associated with otherwise normal bodily cues, and specifically how IE alone changes this tendency. This issue is critical for this reason: There is nothing inherently pathogenic about conditioned fear. The responses themselves are quite adaptive. Most mammals, however, respond to the sources of threat in the external environment (i.e., freeze, avoid, escape, or fight). Nonverbal organisms do not act to regulate their own emotional responses directly. This understanding is key.

Humans will experience fear and act on that response in an attempt to regulate it. New research suggests that excessive emotion regulation may be a key process that transforms normal fear and fear learning into a significant life problem, in part, because such regulation is effortful, does not work well in the long-term to change the onset, duration, or frequency of unpleasant emotional experiences (and, in fact, tends to amplify them), and by definition demands time, energy, and resources that complete directly with the actions that are necessary for the achievement of valued ends or goals (see Chapter 6; see also Forsyth et al., 2006; Hayes, Strosahl, & Wilson, 1999). The goal of IE is to expose clients to feared bodily sensations that are tailored to their unique concerns, thereby allowing clients to resist the natural tendency to engage in avoidance or escape behaviors, or which emotion regulation is a part. As such, IE could be thought of as a process to promote greater experiential and psychological flexibility in the service of valued action (see Forsyth et al., 2006; Forsyth & Eifert, 2008).

If successful, clients learn to respond to their responses differently, and this corrective emotional experience makes the natural tendency to avoid or escape nonsensical as a solution. This process will be accelerated initially to the extent that the exposure exercises are taught and repeated in a controlled systematic fashion with minimal variability. Later, such exercises should be practiced by the client in a variety of settings to maximize generalization. Therapists and clients should be aware that generalization training will likely result in some reemergence of fearful responding based on what is known about spontaneous recovery and contextual control over

behavior (e.g., exposure to racing heart sensations will tend to evoke a different response in the safe confines of the therapist's office as opposed to driving on the interstate during rush hour traffic).

STEP-BY-STEP GUIDE ON HOW TO IMPLEMENT INTEROCEPTIVE EXPOSURE

Interoceptive exposure is predicated on the conceptual learning framework described previously, and consists of structured exposure exercises to elicit bodily sensations that are of primary concern to the client. Thus, the nature of IE exercises will vary from client to client depending on their principal complaints. That said, we recommend using broad range of IE exercises so as to foster skill development, behavioral flexibility, treatment generalization.

The treatment consists of activities designed to evoke signs and symptoms of autonomic arousal so that the client can fully experience such sensations in a voluntary and deliberate manner while resisting any tendency toward avoidance or escape. The nature and structure of IE activities should be tailored idiographically to the client and should be derived from a through assessment. See Table 41.1 for a quick reference to the steps involved in conducting IE.

CONDUCTING AN IDIOGRAPHIC ASSESSMENT AND FUNCTIONAL ANALYSIS

It is important for the therapist to determine the appropriateness of IE for the client before beginning. Prior to initiating IE, the therapist will want to conduct a thorough assessment of the client's medical history with respect to problematic experiences of autonomic arousal, and the antecedents and consequences of such experiences, including how the client normally responds to them.

In this context, the therapist should have the client begin self-monitoring in his or her natural environment. Self-monitoring data, in turn, will be used to develop a fear hierarchy and to select appropriate IE exercises in therapy. Self-monitoring of panic attacks, for instance,

TABLE 41.1 Steps Involved in the Conduct of Interoceptive Exposure

1. Perform idiographic assessment and functional analysis.
2. Begin self-monitoring of panic attacks and associated behaviors.
3. Provide client with adequate rationale for using interoceptive exposure.
4. Construct fear hierarchy from self-monitoring and behavioral experiments.
5. Arrange exercises from least feared/easiest to most feared/most difficult.
6. Begin in-session exposure with client's least feared exercise and symptoms.
7. Assign in-session exposure exercises for homework between sessions.
8. Monitor and address subtle and overt forms of avoidance and escape behavior.
9. Arrange for generalization via naturalistic interoceptive exposure exercises.
10. Continuously review and plot data and use to guide treatment decisions.

Note. Item 3 above can be framed more traditionally in terms of anxiety management and control (i.e., fear reduction) or as a way to learn to be with and move with discomfort in the service of value-guided goals and actions (Eifert & Forsyth, 2005). Item 6 can be framed in terms of willingness exercises (Forsyth & Eifert, 2007), with the term homework being replaced with "Experiential Life Enhancement Exercises" to avoid negative connotations associated with doing homework (e.g., negative evaluation, failure, having to do it, etc.).

should be made immediately following each attack and should be structured to include prompts for the following information:

1. Date and time of the attack
2. The situation in which the attack occurred
3. A self-rating of the distress and fear associated with the attack (e.g., 0 = *no distress/fear* to 9 = *extreme distress/fear*)
4. A list of signs and symptoms from the *Diagnostic and Statistical Manual of Mental Disorders*, 4th ed. (*DSM-IV*), so that the client can indicate which experiences occurred during the attack
5. A place to note what was occurring before the panic attack (i.e., antecedents that could include environmental cues, thoughts, bodily sensations, stressors, particular foods, drugs, or beverages consumed) and what the client did following the attack (i.e., consequences that may include self-mediation, and overt

and covert forms of escape and avoidance), including any accompanying self-statements
6. An estimate in minutes of how long the panic attack lasted at its peak

Self-monitoring is important for several reasons. First, it provides the therapist with information about the nature and extent of the client's problems as they occur naturally (i.e., is the problem really a problem?). Second, it provides information about potential contextual factors that may maintain or exacerbate the problem, including information about contexts (e.g., people, places, times of day, behaviors) that are not problematic for the client (e.g., being at home vs. being in a crowd of people). Third, it provides the therapist with information that can be used to better conceptualize the client's problem. For example, self-monitoring data are often useful as a means to identify overt and covert triggers for panic attacks, which are often difficult for the client to identify early in therapy. Fourth, and most important for present purposes, self-monitoring provides data that will be used to construct a hierarchy of feared bodily signs and symptoms and to select appropriate IE exercises. Therapists should take great care to explain the nature and purposes of self-monitoring, including how it should be done properly. Usually, self-monitoring begins at the outset of therapy in conjunction with basic psychoeducation about fear and panic and continues throughout therapy.

PROVIDING CLIENTS WITH AN ADEQUATE RATIONALE FOR INTEROCEPTIVE EXPOSURE

Inexperienced therapists often make the mistake of implementing IE too soon before a good working therapist–client relationship has had time to develop, and without providing their clients with an easy-to-understand explanation of the procedure, the rationale underlying it, and anticipated costs and benefits. This is a mistake.

The bodily sensations and thoughts evoked by IE are precisely those that the client wishes not to experience. After all, therapy is supposed to make clients feel better, not worse. In the case of IE, however, there is some truth to the trite phrase "no pain, no gain." Clients need to be provided with an explanation of the nature of fear and anxiety as adaptive responses, and informed of how those same responses can become life constricting and debilitating. That is, clients need a tailored conceptualization regarding the role that learning plays in the development of their difficulties with panic, and particularly how subtle and overt forms of avoidance and escape behavior serve to maintain their difficulties.

Interoceptive exposure can then be explained as a means for clients to do something different, namely, to face their fear in a gradual fashion so as to learn new ways of responding to their own responses. Therapists can guarantee their clients that as long as they respond the way they have been responding (i.e., attempting to avoid or escape from their own responses), they will continue to have the problems that they are presently having. At some level, most clients suffering from panic attacks know this already. "Every time I take a step in a direction I want to move, I get something I don't want to experience. To get a different outcome, I need to risk doing something new with my discomfort."

As such, IE could be thought of an experiential strategy that is designed to assist clients in mastering their ability to experience a full range of emotional responses, fully and without defense, for what they are and not for what clients they think they are (i.e., something dangerous and harmful; Eifert & Forsyth, 2005). Interoceptive exposure is not a means to get rid of fear—an approach that would maladaptive for humans and most non-human species as well. Providing a thorough rationale—a topic that has been discussed extensively by others in several places elsewhere—presents an opportunity for the therapist and client to develop a collaborative effort, to set expectations, and to prepare the client for exercises that will be somewhat difficult to do initially but will get easier with repeated practice (Craske & Barlow, 2000).

STRUCTURE AND SELECTION OF INTEROCEPTIVE EXPOSURE EXERCISES

Self-monitoring data should be reviewed prior to each session and noncompliance or obstacles to successful self-monitoring should be addressed and corrected. The therapist and client should then begin the process of arranging the problematic sensations gleaned from self-monitoring data in a hierarchy from least-to-most severe or distressing. The sensations placed in the hierarchy should occur with sufficient frequency or intensity and be associated with significant life disruption to warrant their inclusion. Once the list is compiled, the therapist can then solicit in-session verbal ratings of distress from the client in response to each element of the hierarchy. This may be done so as to provide additional information about how the client currently responds to each element of the hierarchy.

The next step involves selection of IE exercises. These should be selected for their ability to evoke problematic bodily sensations that the client is afraid of and struggles with in some way (Antony, Ledley, Liss, & Swinson, 2006; Forsyth & Eifert, 2008; Schmidt & Trakowski, 2004; Taylor, 2000). Initially, this process should be conducted in-session under careful therapist guidance. To the extent feasible, the therapist should opt for using mini in-session behavioral experiments that involve exercises (to be described) to evoke the problematic sensations from the hierarchy. While the client is completing the exercises, the therapist notes which exercises produce the highest level of anxiety (and struggle, avoidance) for the client, regardless of their similarity to the client's most feared sensations. The therapist should also ask the client whether the sensations evoked by a particular IE exercise are similar to sensations that accompany naturally occurring panic, including any associated catastrophic and noncatastrophic thoughts, and urges to avoid.

For example, a client who fears the sensation of dizziness may be asked to be "willingly dizzy" by spinning in an office chair for a minute, immediately after which the therapist may prompt for a rating of distress or fear, a report of any catastrophic self-statements (e.g., "I feel like I'm losing control or going crazy"), and any urges to avoid or escape. This is also a good time to assess whether the induced sensations are similar or different from experiences that accompany the client's panic outside of therapy.

Such mini behavioral experiments for each element of the hierarchy can be used to (1) confirm the ordering of the IE exercises that will follow, (2) test catastrophic beliefs and predictions, and (3) begin the process of helping the client to discover the likely noncatastrophic ways that feared somatic cues may come about. Moreover, they provide important directly observable information about how the client responds to autonomic arousal and bodily discomfort, some of which may be unexpected (Zuercher-White, 1997). This kind of information is difficult to glean from paper-and-pencil self-monitoring alone.

TYPES OF INTEROCEPTIVE EXPOSURE EXERCISES

The universe of possible IE exercises is only limited by the therapist's creativity and available resources. Antony et al. (2006) and Schmidt and Trakowski (2004) have systematically examined the effectiveness of an array of exercises in producing sensations that are both anxiety provoking as well as similar to naturally occurring panic. These manuscripts serve as good, detailed references for the therapist when choosing potential exercises (see also Forsyth & Eifert, 2008). The following is a brief list of some commonly used in-session IE exercises, including information about their implementation and typical effects.

Breath Holding

Breath holding involves asking the client to hold his or her breath for a period of time. The duration of breath holding can be increased in a graduated fashion over exposure trials. This procedure typically evokes shortness of breath, light-headedness, dizziness, and a pounding or racing heart (Antony et al., 2006; Schmidt & Trakowski, 2004; see the earlier discussion of contraindications). This exercise tends to be experienced as mildly similar to natural panic and is capable of producing at least moderate fear in 1 out of 4 panic prone individuals; see Antony et al., 2006).

Breathing through a Straw

Several inexpensive small- and large-bore straws can be used for this IE exercise. The nose should be occluded while the client breathes through a straw for 30 seconds or more. This exercise can evoke shortness of breath, choking, suffocation, pounding or racing heart, and dizziness. Further, it can be combined with other IE exercises such as climbing stairs. Studies show that this is one of the most effective exercises to induce a broad range of intense physical sensations, similar in kind to naturally occurring panic (Antony et al., 2006).

Climbing Steps

This exercise and its variants (e.g., fast walking, jogging in place) evoke cardiorespiratory sensations and more widespread sensations of autonomic arousal associated with physical exertion (see contraindications). Modifications to this procedure can range from climbing up and down one or two steps to climbing several flights of stairs. As appropriate, the pace can be graduated within different levels (e.g., 2 steps, 5 steps, 10 steps, and within each level, for varied durations).

Spinning

This IE exercise can also take several forms, and typically evokes sensations of dizziness and vertigo, and may yield light-headedness, pounding or racing heart, breathlessness, nausea, and blurred vision (Antony et al, 2006; Schmidt & Trakowski, 2004). Such exercises may include therapist- and non-therapist-assisted spinning in an office chair, spinning while standing, and placing the head between the knees and suddenly moving into an upright sitting position. Spinning yields moderate fear in about a third of panic prone individuals and a range of sensations that are similar to natural panic (Antony et al., 2006).

Hyperventilation

This procedure involves voluntary and exaggerated over breathing and is capable of inducing panic attacks, including dissociative symptoms, in susceptible individuals. This occurs, in part, because carbon dioxide is expired at a rate greater than metabolic demand. The therapist demonstrates full exhalations and inhalations through the mouth at a pace of about one breath for every 2 seconds. This procedure may be extended for up to 3–5 minutes (see contraindications), and can induce a range of sensations that mirror naturally occurring panic, including dizziness, breathlessness, pounding or racing heart, tingling in the extremities, light-headedness, derealization, dry mouth or throat, shaking or trembling, and hot flashes (Antony et al, 2006; Schmidt & Trakowski, 2004).

Rebreathing Expired Air

Rebreathing expired air into a bag is also capable of inducing wide-ranging bodily sensations similar to panic. The sensations occur, in part, because of a rise in partial pressure of carbon dioxide relative to oxygen over and above metabolic demand. For this exercise a client may be provided with a brown lunch bag and asked to inhale and exhale directly into the bag. This procedure may be extended for up to 3–5 minutes, or longer in some cases, depending on how well the procedure is producing its intended effects for a given client (see also contraindications).

Head between Legs

This exercise involves having the client, while sitting, place his or her head between the knees for 30 seconds and then lift the head quickly to the normal position. This procedure has the potential to induce sensations that are mildly similar to naturally occurring panic such as pressure in the head, dizziness, breathlessness, light-headedness, and numbness in the face and extremities (Antony et al, 2006; Schmidt & Trakowski, 2004).

Tongue Depressor

This exercise involves having the client place a tongue depressor on the back of his or her tongue for 30 seconds. The tongue depressor should be far enough to the rear of the mouth

to slightly stimulate the gag reflex. This exercise has the potential to invoke symptoms such as choking, suffocation, breathlessness, nausea, and general discomfort (Antony et al, 2006; Schmidt & Trakowski, 2004). This exercise tends to be less effective than the previous exercises in producing symptoms similar to natural panic. However, it is capable of producing moderate fear in 1 out of 3 panic-prone individuals and may be useful for clients who experience nausea or choking fears as a primary complaint (Antony et al., 2006).

IMPLEMENTATION OF INTEROCEPTIVE EXPOSURE

Interoceptive exposure is typically utilized as an integral component of a larger CBT package in the treatment of PD and is often initiated after psychoeducation, relaxation procedures, and cognitive restructuring. The sessions on cognitive restructuring focus on challenging automatic thoughts and changing core beliefs (Zuercher-White, 1997), whereas mindfulness and acceptance-based approaches tend to focus on skills to simply notice and defuse from such thoughts without challenging them directly (see Eifert & Forsyth, 2005; Hayes et al., 1999). In randomized controlled trials, the treatment is typically between 12 and 15 sessions (Otto & Dekersbach, 1998).

All IE exercises should be explained and modeled by the therapist first before the client attempts them. This does not mean, however, that all IE exercises are introduced in one session. As indicated, IE exercises are introduced and practiced in-session in a graduated fashion. Typically, this means that a client will begin with the easiest-to-tolerate IE exercise from the hierarchy. The therapist should first model the IE exercise and then carefully observe the client doing it him- or herself to ensure that it is completed correctly. Correct completion of the exercise depends largely on the approach one adopts.

For instance, some argue that clients should simply be instructed to induce the feared somatic sensations, and then focus on simply experiencing the symptoms, without trying to change them (Otto & Dekersbach, 1998). Others, however, have suggested that to obtain the maximum benefit from IE, the therapist should instruct the client to attempt to intensify the sensations after inducing the somatic cues (Taylor, 2000). We see both approaches as complementary, because both are consistent with maximizing the process of corrective emotional learning and the general aim of teaching the client new ways of responding to his or her own responses. In either case, therapists will want to be particularly watchful for subtle and overt forms of escape or avoidance (e.g., distraction, taking fewer and more shallow breaths during hyperventilation), because such avoidance can retard the process of extinction and new learning.

It is important that the client practice each exercise a sufficient number of times during the therapy session for two reasons. First, such practice provides the opportunity for the client to experience some therapeutic benefit. Second, it ensures that the exercise is rehearsed well enough that it can be performed willingly by the client outside of therapy. It is also important for the therapist to assess the client's ratings of distress, fear, and the presence and severity of physical and cognitive responses to each exercise. To the extent possible, this assessment should be quantitative, structured (e.g., using a 0 to 10 visual scale to solicit ratings of distress and fear), and ongoing throughout IE. Such data are critical for clinical decision making about the pace and structure of IE. They also provide important information to the client regarding his or her progress and can even help to facilitate compliance with therapy.

In our work, we like to see that a client can show at least a 50% pre- to post exposure reduction in reported fear and anxiety in response to the same exercise. Moreover, we like to see that this reduction is stable over at least three repetitions of the same exercise in-session before we assign the exercise for homework and, before we decide to move on to other exercises in the hierarchy. Some exercises for some clients will undoubtedly require several in-session exposure trials before any clinically meaningful reductions in anxious and fearful responding are observed. This is fine and to be expected. Interoceptive

exposure exercises that are completed successfully in-session should then be assigned as client homework outside of session.

EXPOSURE HOMEWORK

Completing homework (i.e., client practice of exposure exercises outside of therapy) is an integral component of the treatment. The simple metaphor of learning to ride a bicycle for the first time can be helpful to convey to the client the importance of practice, commitment, and skill development (Forsyth & Eifert, 2008).

No one learns to ride a bike by reading about bicycling riding or watching movies about how to do it. To learn to ride a bike, one must get on a bike and do it. Initially, this process can be painful. To make learning a bit easier, we add training wheels. Yet no one wants to ride a bicycle with training wheels for the rest of his or her life. With repeated practice and effort we expect to get to the point of being able to remove the training wheels and ride without them. At that point, there may be a few more bumps and bruises along the way. Even seasoned bicyclists fall once in a while, but they spend more time on the bike riding than they do falling on the ground. A similar process is at work with IE practice outside of therapy.

Interoceptive exposure should start in a comfortable environment (e.g., the privacy of one's home) and be structured at regular (i.e., several times a day) clustered intervals so that the client masters the skill (Craske & Barlow, 2000; Craske, Barlow, & Meadows, 2000). Home practice is analogous to using training wheels to ride a bike in that the goal is to master the basic skills first, before applying those skills in other situations that are more challenging. Initially, such homework may simply include practice with the exposure exercises covered in session (e.g., practicing breath holding at home), and later it may progress to exposures in other contexts and settings. Such homework should be completed regardless of whether the client is feeling anxious or distressed about IE or other matters. In fact, it may be particularly valuable for the client to perform IE exercises when he or she is under stress (Taylor, 2000), although not initially.

It is essential that the therapist convey to the client the importance of completing homework assignments and performing the IE exercises correctly. To facilitate compliance, the therapist should provide homework sheets with columns and spaces for the date, the setting, the start and end times of practice (i.e., duration), pre- and post-practice ratings of fear, distress (using some interval scale with anchor points), and type of sensations experienced, and a place to note associated catastrophic and non-catastrophic thoughts and avoidance. Such homework should be routinely collected and reviewed by the therapist during each session, and the therapist should reinforce the client for successfully completing or attempting the homework exercises. The therapist should also routinely plot both in-session and outside session data and periodically review these data with the client. Reviewing client progress in this manner can be a powerful motivator, and can also highlight areas that remain problematic or require more work.

The therapist will want evidence that the client has shown clinically meaningful and stable attenuation of fearful responding to a given IE exercise in-session and outside session before moving on to the next step: instructing the client to go about his or her usual activities while experiencing feared somatic sensations. The purpose here is to remove the training wheels and to start allowing the client to practice experiencing somatic symptoms while performing routine activities.

Practice with IE exercises should continue several times during the day; however, now the practice will occur in those situations where the signs and symptoms of arousal are particularly disruptive or problematic (e.g., school, work, driving, walking, waiting in line). For example, IE exercises such as applying pressure to the throat or standing up suddenly can be performed at a desk while at work (Zuercher-White, 1997). To derive the maximum benefit from the treatment, clients should perform IE exercises in as many different contexts and situations as possible (Taylor, 2000). As before, the therapist should provide rating forms for the client to complete and the resultant data should be plotted and reviewed regularly in therapy. Failure on the part of the therapist to review, discuss, and plot the homework assignments regularly, and to use such data to guide treatment decisions sends the client the wrong message—namely, that the homework is really not important, and so why should the client bother doing it.

PROMOTING GENERALIZATION USING NATURALISTIC EXPOSURE

It is important for clients to perform IE exercises in many different situations and under diverse circumstances. Doing so helps to promote generalization while also helping clients learn that feared interoceptive cues are not harmful to them (Taylor, 2000), and most importantly that unpleasant bodily sensations are not barriers to effective action (Eifert & Forsyth, 2005; Forsyth & Eifert, 2008).

Naturalistic IE is a component of this process and involves exposure to common daily activities or situations that produce feared somatic sensations. Such situations are typically those that are of great importance to the client and contribute to a good quality of life (e.g., value of work, family, recreation; Forsyth & Eifert, 2007). Prior to treatment, these situations and activities are typically avoided or else endured with great distress, hence functional impairment. With naturalistic IE, the focus shifts to structured exercises that are performed by the client in increasingly feared and less safe situations (Otto & Dekersbach, 1998).

For example, the client may begin by performing IE homework exercises at home with his or her spouse present. This may be followed by practice at home but without a safe person present, doing an IE exercise in a shopping mall with a safe person present, and ultimately going to the mall alone. Other common examples of naturalistic IE include going to an amusement park and going on scary rides, or engaging in a workout program such as running, cycling, or aerobics. Swimming may be a viable option for clients with medical conditions that contradict participation in other forms of exercise (Taylor, 2000).

Though naturalistic IE and situational exposure have common elements (i.e., both induce discomfort and counteract avoidance with approach behavior), they differ in that the goal of naturalistic IE is to induce symptoms of autonomic arousal, whereas the goal of situational exposure is to expose the client to the feared situations themselves, without regard for the somatic sensations they produce (Taylor, 2000). However, naturalistic IE and situational exposure may be combined in some exercises. For example, a client could join an aerobics class, which will certainly involve the experience of some cardiac and respiratory sensations in the presence of a group of people. Both the therapist and client should arrange for such exposures in a structured and deliberate fashion, preferably one that progresses from least-to-most difficult. Homework should be assigned and reviewed regularly in therapy as before.

STRATEGIES TO UNDERMINE AVOIDANCE AND SAFETY-SEEKING BEHAVIORS

Safety signals (i.e., stimuli that the person associates with the absence of feared outcomes; e.g., reassurance, repeated checking, being with a significant other, carrying an empty pill bottle) and safety behaviors (i.e., actions designed to ward off fear events; e.g., escape and avoidance behavior) are problematic because they prevent fearful responses to interoceptive cues from being extinguished, block the process of corrective emotional learning, and generally do not work as a long-term solution (Forsyth et al., 2006). Here, we briefly outline three strategies to undermine safety signals and behaviors (cf. Taylor, 2000). Functionally speaking, most of these are avoidance moves—they buy clients a brief honeymoon from their discomfort, but at significant cost in the long-term (cf. Forsyth & Eifert, 2008).

Identify Subtle and Obvious Safety Signals and Behaviors

First, the therapist and client work together to identify both subtle and obvious safety signals and behaviors. The therapist may also observe the client during in-session IE activities and then ask the client whether he or she did anything in

order to prevent catastrophic outcomes or make the situation less frightening. The therapist and client should arrive at a list of safety signals and behaviors and both domains should be continually assessed, particularly as IE is practiced by the client in other more naturalistic contexts. Indeed, it is common to find that clients utilize different safety signals and behaviors in different situations, or even several different safety signals and behaviors across similar situations (Taylor, 2000). You may also explore the costs associated with such behaviors, with an eye on what the client cares about in his or her life (e.g., "what am I missing out on or am unable to do in the service of feeling safe or managing my panic?"; Forsyth & Eifert, 2008).

Demonstrate that Safety Signals and Behaviors are Ineffective as a Solution

The second step involves demonstrating to the client that safety signals and behaviors are ineffective as a solution for his or her problems. At some level, most clients know that such strategies don't work, otherwise they wouldn't be in the room with you. You can make this more transparent by discussing what the client has tried and how it has worked (short and long term). You may also make this more experiential by doing mini in-session behavioral experiments in which the client first engages in an IE exercise while also engaging in a safety behavior, or in the presence of a safety signal, and then performs the IE exercise again but without the safety signals or behaviors (Taylor, 2000).

Help Clients Abandon Safety Behaviors and Develop Repertoire Expanding Solutions

Finally, it is essential that the therapist educate the client about the functional role safety signals and avoidance behavior play in maintaining the problem, including the ways they may actually constrict the client's ability to live a full and valued life. Most clients will be reluctant to simply give up their tendency to use safety signals and behaviors; however, the therapist may assist the client to discard them in a gradual fashion over repeated exposure exercises (Taylor, 2000).

Clients may be more willing to give up unworkable avoidance behavior if they are helped to see how such behavior amplifies their suffering and gets in the way of the things that they care about doing.

In this regard, exploring how avoidance gets in the way of valued action may be critical as a way to contextualize and dignify the entire treatment. In a way, it shifts the focus from feeling better in order to live better to living well with whatever one is thinking and feeling. This approach, in turn, can function to transform exposure from panic management to something bigger than that, namely, a life lived well. This framework is part of a newer third generation CBT for anxiety problems based on acceptance and commitment therapy (or ACT, said as one word: see Chapter 6; see also Eifert & Forsyth, 2005; Forsyth & Eifert, 2008).

Further Reading

Antony, M. M., Ledley, D. R., Liss, A., & Swinson, R. P. (2006). Responses to symptom induction exercises in panic disorder. *Behaviour Research and Therapy*, 44, 85–98.

Barlow, D. H. (2001). *Anxiety and its disorders: The nature and treatment of anxiety and panic*, (2nd ed.). New York: Guilford.

Bouton, M. E., Mineka, S., & Barlow, D.H. (2001). A modern learning theory perspective on the etiology of panic disorder. *Psychological Review, 108*(1), 4–32.

Carter, M. M., & Barlow, D. H. (1993). Interoceptive exposure in the treatment of panic disorder. In L. VandeCreek, S. Knapp, & T. L. Jackson (Eds.), *Innovations in clinical practice: A source book: Vol. 12.* (pp. 329–336). Sarasota, FL: Professional Resource Press/Professional Resource Exchange.

Eifert, G. H., & Forsyth, J. P. (2005). *Acceptance and commitment therapy for anxiety disorders: A practitioner's treatment guide to using mindfulness, acceptance, and value-guided behavior change strategies*. Oakland, CA: New Harbinger.

Forsyth, J. P., & Eifert, G. H. (2008). *The mindfulness and acceptance workbook for anxiety: A guide to breaking free from anxiety, phobias, and worry using acceptance and commitment therapy*. Oakland, CA: New Harbinger.

Schmidt, N. B., & Trakowski, J. (2004). Interoceptive assessment and exposure in panic disorder: A descriptive study. *Cognitive and Behavioral Practice, 11*, 81–92.

References

Acheson, D. T., Forsyth, J. P., Prenoveau, J., & Bouton, M. E. (2007). Interoceptive fear conditioning as a learning model of panic disorder: An experimental evaluation using 20% CO_2-enriched air in a non-clinical sample. *Behaviour Research and Therapy, 45*, 2280–2294.

Antony, M. M., Ledley, D. R., Liss, A., & Swinson, R. P. (2006). Responses to symptom induction exercises in panic disorder. *Behaviour Research and Therapy, 44*, 85–98.

Barlow, D. H. (2001). *Anxiety and its disorders: The nature and treatment of anxiety and panic*, (2nd ed.). New York: Guilford.

Barlow, D. H., Allen, L. B., & Choate, M. L. (2004). Toward a unified treatment for emotional disorders. *Behavior Therapy, 35*, 205–230.

Barlow, D. H., Gorman, J. M., Shear, K., & Woods, S. W. (2000). Cognitive-behavioral therapy, imipramine, or their combination for panic disorder: A randomized controlled trial. *Journal of the American Medical Association, 283*, 2529–2536.

Beck, J. G., & Shipherd, J. C. (1997). Repeated exposure to interoceptive cues: Does habituation of fear occur in panic disorder patients? A preliminary report. *Behaviour Research and Therapy, 35*(6), 551–557.

Beck, J. G., Shipherd, J. C., & Zebb, B. J. (1997). How does interoceptive exposure for panic disorder work? An uncontrolled case study. *Journal of Anxiety Disorders, 11*, 541–556.

Bouton, M. E., Mineka, S., & Barlow, D. H. (2001). A modern learning theory perspective on the etiology of panic disorder. *Psychological Review, 108*, 4–32.

Chosak, A., Baker, S. L., Thorn, G. R., Spiegel, D. A., & Barlow, D. H. (1999). In D. J. Nutt, J. C. Ballenger, & J. Lépine (Eds.), *Panic Disorder: Clinical diagnosis, management and mechanisms* (pp. 203–220). London: Martin Dunitz Ltd.

Clum, G. A., & Surls, R. (1993). A meta-analysis of treatments for panic disorder. *Journal of Consulting and Clinical Psychology, 61*, 317–326.

Craske, M. G., & Barlow, D. H. (2000). *Mastery of your anxiety and panic (MAP-3)* 3rd ed. San Antonio, TX: The Psychological Corporation.

Craske, M. G., Barlow, D. H., & Meadows, E. A. (2000). *Mastery of your anxiety and panic (MAP-3): Therapist guide for anxiety, panic, and agoraphobia*, 3rd ed. San Antonio, TX: The Psychological Corporation.

Craske, M. G., Brown, T. A., & Barlow, D. H. (1991). Behavioral treatment of panic disorder: A two-year follow-up. *Behavior Therapy, 22*, 289–304.

Craske, M. G., Rowe, M., Lewin, M., & Noriega-Dimitri, R. (1997). Interoceptive exposure versus breathing retraining within cognitive-behavioural therapy for panic disorder with agoraphobia. *British Journal of Clinical Psychology, 36,* 85–99.

Craske, M. G., & Tsao, J. C. I. (2005). Assessment and treatment of nocturnal panic attacks, *Sleep Medicine Reviews, 9,* 173–184.

Forsyth, J. P., & Eifert, G. H. (1998). Phobic anxiety and panic: An integrative behavioral account of their origin and treatment. In J. J. Plaud & G. H. Eifert (Eds.), *From behavior theory to behavior therapy* (pp. 38–67). Needham, MA: Allyn & Bacon.

Forsyth, J. P., & Eifert, G. H. (1996a). Systemic alarms in fear conditioning—I: A reappraisal of what is being conditioned. *Behavior Therapy, 27,* 441–462.

Forsyth, J. P., & Eifert, G. H. (1996b). The language of feeling and the feeling of anxiety: Contributions of the behaviorisms toward understanding the function-altering effects of language. *Psychological Record, 46,* 607–649.

Forsyth, J. P., Eifert, G. H., & Barrios, V. (2006). Fear conditioning in an emotion regulation context: A fresh perspective on the origins of anxiety disorders. In M. G. Craske, D. Hermans, & D. Vansteenwegen (Eds.), *Fear and learning: From basic processes to clinical implications* (pp. 133–153). Washington, DC: American Psychological Association.

Gould, R. A., Otto, M. W., & Pollack, M. H. (1995). A meta-analysis of treatment outcome for panic disorder. *Clinical Psychology Review, 15,* 819–844.

Griez, E., & van den Hout, M. A. (1986). CO_2 inhalation in the treatment of panic attacks. *Behaviour Research and Therapy, 24,* 145–150.

Hayes, S. C., Strosahl, K. D., & Wilson, K. G. (1999). *Acceptance and commitment therapy: An experiential approach to behavior change.* New York: Guilford.

Klosko, J. S., Barlow, D. H., Tassinari, R., & Cerny, J. A. (1990). A comparison of alprazolam and behavior therapy in treatment of panic disorder. *Journal of Consulting and Clinical Psychology, 58,* 77–84.

Nonacs, R., Cohen, L. S., & Altshuler, L. L. (1998). Course and treatment of panic disorder during pregnancy and the postpartum period. In J. F. Rosenbaum & M. H. Pollack (Eds.), *Panic Disorder and its treatment* (pp. 229–246). New York: Marcel Dekker.

Otto, M. W., & Deckersbach, T. (1998). Cognitive–behavioral therapy for panic disorder: Theory, strategies, and outcome. In J. F. Rosenbaum & M. H. Pollack (Eds.), *Panic disorder and its treatment* (pp. 181–204). New York: Marcel Dekker.

Penava, S. J., Otto, M. W., Maki, K. M., & Pollack, M. H. (1998). Rate of improvement during cognitive-behavioral group treatment for panic disorder. *Behavior Research and Therapy, 36,* 665–673.

Schmidt, N. B. & Trakowski, J. (2004). Interoceptive assessment and exposure in panic disorder: A descriptive study. *Cognitive and Behavioral Practice, 11,* 81–92.

Taylor, S. (2000). *Understanding and treating panic disorder.* Chichester, UK: John Wiley & Sons.

Tsao, J. C. I., & Craske, M. G. (2000). Panic disorder. In M. Hersen & M. Biaggio (Eds.), *Effective brief therapies: A clinician's guide* (pp. 63–78). New York: Academic Press.

van den Hout, M., van der Molen, M., Griez, E., Lousberg, H., & Nansen, A. (1987). Reduction of CO_2-induced anxiety in patients with panic attacks after repeated CO_2 exposure. *American Journal of Psychiatry, 144,* 788–791.

Westen, D, & Morrison, K. (2001). A multidimensional meta-analysis of treatments for depression, panic, and generalized anxiety disorder: An empirical examination of the status of empirically supported therapies. *Journal of Consulting and Clinical Psychology, 69,* 875–899.

Zuercher-White, E. (1997). *Treating panic disorder and agoraphobia: A step-by-step guide.* Oakland, CA: New Harbinger.

42 LIVE (*IN VIVO*) EXPOSURE

Holly Hazlett-Stevens and Michelle G. Craske

Live (*in vivo*) exposure to feared situations has been a cornerstone of behavior therapy for decades. Even psychoanalytic and Gestalt therapy techniques relied on the principle of exposure to treat neuroses (Foa & Kozak, 1986). Mary Cover Jones is credited with one of the earliest documented cases of *in vivo* exposure for treating a case of phobia in the 1920s (Barlow & Durand, 2004). After observing how fear could be classically conditioned by pairing presentations of aversive, unconditioned stimuli with neutral, innocuous objects, she successfully extinguished a young boy's fear response to furry animals by gradually and systematically exposing him to white rabbits (Jones, 1924). Thus, this therapeutic technique is historically linked to early experimental studies of classical conditioning and related principles of conditioned stimulus (CS)—unconditioned stimulus (UCS) extinction.

One of the most influential exposure techniques is the procedure of systematic desensitization developed by Salter (1949) and by Wolpe (1958). Systematic desensitization involves a series of exposure exercises presented in gradual steps of increased fear intensity. These exposures are conducted during relaxation, an emotional and physiological state considered incompatible with the conditioned anxiety or fear response. Systematic desensitization has received a wealth of empirical support for its efficacy (Leitenberg, 1976), but the role of relaxation in its effectiveness has been the subject of much debate (Borkovec & O'Brien, 1976; Levin & Gross, 1985). In general, the incorporation of contiguous relaxation (i.e., systematic desensitization) is indicated when the therapist maintains control over the exposure (Borkovec & O'Brien, 1976) and when generalization of treatment effects to untreated phobias is desired (AuBuchon & Calhoun, 1990). However, *in vivo* exposure alone without relaxation training is widely used to treat a number of anxiety disorders and phobias, and much research supports this practice (see reviews by Foa & Kozak, 1985; Öst, 1996). Furthermore, *in vivo* exposure without relaxation training is a crucial component of effective psychological treatments for panic disorder with agoraphobia (Craske & Barlow, 2007), social phobia (Heimberg, Dodge, Hope, Kennedy, Zollo, & Becker, 1990), and obsessive–compulsive disorder (Franklin & Foa, 2007).

In vivo exposure techniques are useful in the treatment of anxiety related to circumscribed objects or situations. Treatment typically begins with assessment of which objects or situations an individual fears and avoids as well as any contextual cues and features of the phobic stimuli that enhance this fear response. The therapist and client then work together to generate a hierarchy of situations or stimuli for the client to face in ascending order of difficulty. Finally, these exposures are conducted, often in a graded fashion such that the client moves up to the next hierarchical step only after mastering the previous one. The client is encouraged to experience the full fear response during exposures without engaging in subtle forms of avoidance, such as distraction or looking away from the stimulus. Depending on the nature of the fear, such exposure can produce therapeutic effects quickly, at times in only a single session (Öst, 1996).

WHO MIGHT BENEFIT FROM *IN VIVO* EXPOSURE

Most individuals with anxiety involving circumscribed, irrational fears of external objects or situations benefit from this technique.

This applies to people diagnosed with panic disorder with agoraphobia, specific phobia, or agoraphobia without panic (i.e., the situational avoidance associated with other anxiety-related bodily responses such as generalized anxiety disorder or irritable bowel syndrome). *In vivo* exposure is equally important in the treatment of social phobia (Heimberg et al., 1990), obsessive–compulsive disorder (Franklin & Foa, 2007), and situational avoidance resulting from traumatic events (Foa & Meadows, 1997).

EVIDENCE-BASED APPLICATIONS

Specific phobia
Panic disorder with agoraphobia
Agoraphobia without history of panic disorder
Social phobia/social anxiety disorder
Obsessive–compulsive disorder (combined with ritual/response prevention)
Posttraumatic stress disorder

CONTRAINDICATIONS

Individuals with cardiovascular medical conditions (e.g., arrhythmia, heart disease) may be physically unable to tolerate the fear activation associated with *in vivo* exposure and should seek medical advice before attempting this form of treatment. Individuals currently living in physically dangerous or volatile situations in which their behavioral avoidance serves a realistic self-protective function should not attempt this form of treatment until conditions of physical safety have been restored. For example, if a client who is currently involved in a domestic violence situation is afraid to shop at local stores, ride public transportation, and so on due to a realistic fear of encountering an abusive partner, this client should not attempt such exposure until this external threat has been addressed. *In vivo* exposure may also be inappropriate for individuals suffering from psychosis, other thought disorders, or dementia, especially when behavioral avoidance of certain situations is considered adaptive for that individual.

ANY OTHER DECISION FACTORS IN DECIDING WHETHER TO USE THE TECHNIQUE

Some clients may not be prepared or willing to engage in live exposure when first presenting for psychological treatment. For example, a client with severe panic disorder with agoraphobia convinced that a panic attack could result in a heart attack may not be willing to enter such situations at first. Treatment for this individual would first require psychoeducation to increase understanding of the harmless nature of the fight-or-flight panic attack response and/or cognitive restructuring to correct catastrophic misinterpretations about racing heart sensations before *in vivo* exposure to agoraphobic situations could be attempted.

Imaginal exposure can be done before *in vivo* exposure when a client's fear is so severe that the individual is unable to begin with live exposure items on the hierarchy, or if the situation cannot be recreated for live exposure. One recently developed imaginal exposure treatment, known as active imaginal exposure, teaches clients to perform adaptive coping responses physically while engaging in traditional imaginal exposure (Rentz, Powers, Smits, Cougle, & Telch, 2003). Inspection of effect sizes suggested that active imaginal exposure outperformed traditional imaginal exposure alone, although this between-group difference was not statistically significant (Rentz et al.). Another interesting alternative is the use of virtual reality equipment. This medium provides sensory exposure to stimuli resembling the actual feared situation, and may be particularly helpful when treating fear of heights (Rothbaum, Hodges, Kooper, Opdyke, Williford, & North, 1995), spiders (Carlin, Hoffman, & Weghorst, 1997), or flying (Mühlberger, Herrmann, Wiedemann, Ellgring, & Pauli, 2001), or cases of claustrophobia (Botella, Banos, Perpina, Villa, Alcaniz, & Rey, 1998).

In the special case of blood–injection–injury type-specific phobias, the fear reaction usually involves a vasovagal physiological response, leading to a drop in blood pressure and the possibility of fainting (Öst, 1992). When treating this disorder, exposure exercises should be accompanied by applied muscle tension so that the client purposefully increases blood pressure to prevent the fainting response when confronting feared blood-, injection-, or injury-related stimuli (Öst, 1996).

HOW DOES *IN VIVO* EXPOSURE WORK?

In vivo exposure techniques originally were based on the behavioral principle of extinction. Thus, live exposure is believed to reduce anxiety because the CS is repeatedly presented in the absence of any accompanying aversive UCS. However, more recent accounts suggest that exposure also promotes cognitive restructuring because clients learn during exposure trials that the feared stimuli are in fact harmless (e.g., Craske & Barlow, 2007). In 1986, Foa and Kozak presented a neobehavioristic theory of emotional processing to explain how repeated exposure leads to fear reduction. Based on the work of Peter Lang, they conceptualized fear as a program for escape or avoidance and suggested two conditions needed for successful fear reduction. First, the full fear structure must be activated, in which fear-relevant information become available in a form sufficient to activate the fear memory. Second, new information that is incompatible with elements of the original fear structure must then be presented and processed in order to change the threat-related meanings contained within the fear structure. As a result, new cognitive, affective, physiological, and environmental information become integrated into memory, and this hypothetically leads to emotional change. In a recent review, Foa and Kozak (1998) examined the contributions of Peter Lang's work to fear reduction theory and suggested new applications of this theory to specific anxiety disorder groups.

However, some aspects of this emotional processing theory have not always been empirically supported. For example, within-session habituation during exposure was not associated with long-term fear reduction or improved outcome in investigations of obsessive–compulsive disorder (Kozak, Foa, & Steketee, 1988), posttraumatic stress disorder (Pitman, Orr, Altman, & Longpre, 1996; van Minnen & Hagenaars, 2002), panic disorder with agoraphobia (Riley, McCormick,

Simon, Stack et al., 1995), public speaking anxiety (Tsao & Craske, 2000), acrophobia (A.J. Lang & Craske, 2000), and claustrophobia (Kamphuis & Telch, 2000; Sloan & Telch, 2002). Furthermore, effective exposure therapy has been demonstrated in several studies when exposure trials were terminated at high anxiety levels (see Craske, Kircanski, Zelikowsky, Mystowski et al., 2008 for a review of this literature). Craske and colleagues also found evidence that significant declines in physiology across exposure trials are not always necessary for clinical improvement.

Given the weak empirical support for the earlier emotional processing theory, Craske et al. (2008) proposed that extinction during exposure is better characterized by an inhibitory learning process. That is, the original CS–UCS fear conditioning association remains intact while new secondary learning that inhibits this previous meaning develops (e.g., Bouton & King, 1983; Bouton, 1993). From this perspective, toleration of fear during exposure is considered more crucial to successful long-term fear reduction than any short-term fear reduction experienced during the exposure treatment.

STEP-BY-STEP PROCEDURES[1]

The first therapeutic step (see Table 42.1) involves a functional analysis of the avoidance behavior to determine exactly what the client fears. The therapist asks pointed questions to determine which aspects of the situation or object are responsible for the fear response. This ensures that a fear hierarchy relevant for that individual is generated, because certain context features that make the situation more or less fearful will be used to design subsequent exposure exercises. Assessment also is conducted for any safety signals or for other subtle avoidance behaviors (such as distraction or averting eyes) the client relies upon when overt behavioral avoidance is not an

---

1. These procedures are based on the manuals of Craske, Antony, and Barlow (2006) and of Craske and Barlow (2006).

TABLE 42.1   Key Elements of *In Vivo* Exposure

- Conduct a functional analysis of avoidance behavior.
- Describe the purpose and value of exposure to feared situations or objects.
- Generate a hierarchy of fear items.
- Begin repeated, systematic exposure to fear items, beginning at the bottom of the hierarchy.
- Continue with repeated exposure to the next fear hierarchy item when exposure to the previous item generates only mild fear.
- Assign self-directed exposure exercises for home practice.
- Review client's progress with the home practice, giving feedback to overcome any difficulties.

option; these behaviors can undermine the functional exposure experienced during the exposure exercises.

Next, the therapist provides a brief rationale so that the client understands the value and purpose of the exposure. This typically begins with a description of the nature of fear and avoidance and the principle of classical conditioning. The client's anxiety is conceptualized as a conditioned reaction of increased physiological arousal and subjective fear to certain external cues that were somehow associated with danger in the past. Exposure exercises are therefore considered necessary to break the CS–UCS association previously learned, and they allow the client's mind and body to learn that no danger actually exists. Oftentimes this will lead to a discussion of how the client acquired the fear originally, making the notion of classical fear conditioning more salient. In the case of panic disorder with agoraphobia, fears of interoceptive bodily sensations are also discussed, and ideally, *in vivo* exposure is conducted in combination with interoceptive exposure (Craske & Barlow, 2007).

Once the client clearly understands the rationale, the therapist and client work together to generate a hierarchy of feared items. At this time, the value of gradual exposure is presented as a means for the client to develop a sense of mastery over manageable situations, preventing feelings of overwhelming fear and the risk of inadvertently strengthening the fear. Although *in vivo* exposure is typically done in this gradual fashion, some cases may warrant more the more intensive exposure procedure known as *flooding* (see Chapter 31). The exposure hierarchy is often generated by asking the client to list situations that would be anxiety provoking while ranking each for its anxiety level (this can be done using a 0–8-point Likert scale). The variety of situations generated will depend on how circumscribed the fear is. For example, if the client presents with a specific fear of heights, all hierarchy items will involve situations involving height. Conversely, if an individual experiences agoraphobia encompassing a number of situations, then these different places should be identified and ranked. Each item should include as specific detail as possible, and the same type of situation may be repeated in another step with the alteration of important stimulus features. For example, the first hierarchy step for an individual fearful of driving might involve simply sitting in a parked car while resting the hands on the steering wheel. Higher steps on the hierarchy may include pulling the car out of the driveway, followed by driving one loop around a block in the neighborhood, followed by driving the distance of one exit on the freeway, and so on. The anxiety levels assigned to each step can then be used to rank order the hierarchy items according to difficulty.

This step is followed by selection of exposure exercises to be done on a scheduled basis. The therapist can model the exposure exercise and then coach the client during in-session exposure to the first hierarchy item. This coaching includes encouraging the client to fully experience all aspects of the external situation as well as any internal anxiety response. The client is discouraged from simply stopping the exposure as soon as anxiety is detected. Rather, the client is instructed to monitor the anxiety level during the exposure and experience the extinction of anxiety before discontinuing the exercise. When an exposure trial has ended, the therapist asks the client to rate his or her current anxiety level and to describe the experience. If the client noticed anxiety-provoking thoughts during the exposure, these thoughts can be discussed and put into perspective with psychoeducation or with cognitive restructuring. If the client reports low anxiety during the exposure, the therapist queries for any reasons the client did not experience greater anxiety (e.g., if the client was using distraction and not attending to the stimulus) and try again. As a general rule, the client continues repeated exposure to that hierarchy item until exposure results in an anxiety level of only around 2 (on the 0–8-point scale). At that time, the next hierarchy item is selected for subsequent exposure.

If it is most important for the client also to engage in self-directed exposure exercises in between therapy sessions. If therapist-directed, in-session exposure is not feasible, clients can be instructed to ascend the hierarchy on their own. The following instructions should be given to guide clients in this homework:

1. Clients begin with the least feared items from the hierarchy list. In the case of agoraphobia in which the individual fears more than one situation, different types of exposures can be conducted over the same homework period.
2. Some items may require practice only a couple of times before mild levels of anxiety are reached. Other more difficult items may require practice 5, 10, or 20 times. Practice is recommended at least 3 times per week, although the more the better.
3. A long, continuous practice is usually more helpful than shorter, interrupted practices. In other words, it is more helpful to do a solid hour of practice rather than four separate 15-minute practices. Practices that are too short will only resemble current avoidance behavior (i.e., escaping from the phobic situation as soon as possible or remaining for a short while but with a sense of "holding on for dear life" until the practice is over). These attitudes only strengthen the mistaken belief that the exposure involves actual risk.
4. Exposure is most effective when all aspects of the task are attempted in the same manner as if there were no fear. For example, if the hierarchy item was to walk across a certain bridge, then walking very quickly across the bridge without ever looking over the edge would be much less effective than walking at a slower pace, stopping every now and then to look over the rail.

5. In the case of panic disorder with agoraphobia, the client might also be encouraged to identify and challenge anxiety-provoking thoughts associated with the feared situation before engaging in the exposure exercise.
6. If the client feels it is absolutely necessary to prematurely terminate an exposure exercise due to intense fear, the best strategy is to stop and allow the anxiety to reduce but then to resume the exposure, even if only for a few minutes longer. If not, another practice is scheduled soon afterward involving an item expected to generate significant anxiety levels that are less than that experienced during the previous exposure trial.
7. After each exposure trial, the client records his or her anxiety level. The previous exposure item is repeated until the fear response reduces to a mild level. Clients are encouraged to appreciate a sense of accomplishment after each exposure, rather than minimizing its significance.

In subsequent treatment sessions, the therapist reviews these exposure attempts with the client by reinforcing attempts, reassuring clients that progress is not always linear and more often fluctuates up and down, and giving corrective feedback. The therapist and client can collectively problem-solve any practical difficulties in conducting the exercises. If the client does not learn something new following repeated exposure, then further assessment of factors that could be maintaining the fear response should be conducted. For example, the client may be engaging in maladaptive coping styles during the exposure, such as holding onto a good luck charm or other safety signal believed to protect the client from danger. Merely perceiving that such safety signals are available also could undermine exposure treatment efforts. In a recent experiment (Powers, Smits, & Telch, 2004), one group of participants suffering from claustrophobia were told they could access safety aids if needed during exposure. These participants experienced the same degree of disruption on fear reduction as another group of participants required to use such safety aids. Safety behavior utilization also appears disruptive during imaginal exposure treatment (Rentz et al., 2003). Other factors that might maintain fear despite repeated exposure include attempting the exposure with great caution (thereby reinforcing beliefs that the situation is harmful), and avoiding aspects of the stimulus through mental distraction or by looking away from fearful stimuli. Indeed, participants with claustrophobia who performed a distracting cognitive load task during exposure treatment experienced less fear reduction than other exposure participant groups (Telch, Valentiner, Ilai, Young et al., 2004). The therapist also assesses the number of trials and the length of exposures attempted, because exceedingly brief exposures may not allow for corrective learning.

Finally, unsuccessful fear reduction can result from resisting the fear response during exposure. If clients try to "fight" the anxiety and suppress their fear response, this may paradoxically increase the anxious meaning of the situation. Such clients are reminded that the goal of exposure is to learn that they can tolerate anxiety, fear, and discomfort, and clients are encouraged to embrace and to closely monitor their anxiety responses so that they can experience eventual decreases over time. The therapist continues to track the client's progress in this manner as the client ascends up his or her exposure hierarchy. Depending on the nature and severity of the fear, some clients (especially specific phobia cases) may show dramatic fear reduction over only a few sessions. However, more generalized fears associated with social phobia and agoraphobia may involve much more complex hierarchies, including many steps spanning over several weeks. Once fear reduction has been achieved, some clients may experience a return of fear in new contexts that differ significantly from the original exposure treatment context (Mystkowski, Craske, & Echiverri, 2002). In these cases, mental reinstatement of the treatment context before encountering the phobic stimulus or situation in the new context might address this clinical problem (Mystkowski, Craske, Echiverri, & Labus, 2006).

Further Reading

Antony, M. M., Craske, M. G., & Barlow, D. H. (2006). *Mastering your fears and phobias: Workbook* (2nd ed.). New York: Oxford University Press.

Craske, M. G., Antony, M. M., & Barlow, D. H. (2006). *Mastering your fears and phobias: Therapist guide* (2nd ed.). New York: Oxford University Press.

Barlow, D. H., & Craske, M. G. (2006). *Mastery of your anxiety and panic: Workbook* (4th ed.). New York: Oxford University Press.

Craske, M. G., & Barlow, D. H. (2006). *Mastery of your anxiety and panic: Therapist guide* (4th ed.). New York: Oxford University Press.

Barlow, D. H. (Ed.) (2007). *Clinical handbook of psychological disorders: A step-by-step treatment manual* (4th ed.). New York: Guilford.

References

AuBuchon, P. G., & Calhoun, K. S. (1990). The effects of therapist presence and relaxation training on the efficacy and generalizability of in vivo exposure. *Behavioural Psychotherapy, 18*, 169–185.

Barlow, D. H., & Durand, V. M. (2004). *Abnormal psychology* (4th ed.). Belmont, CA: Thomson Wadsworth.

Borkovec, T. D., & O'Brien, G. T. (1976). Methodological and target behavior issues in analogue therapy outcome research. *Progress in Behavior Modification, 3*, 133–172.

Botella, C., Banos, R. M., Perpina, C., Villa, H., Alcaniz, M., & Rey, A. (1998). Virtual reality treatment of claustrophobia: A case report. *Behaviour Research and Therapy, 36*, 239–246.

Bouton, M. E. (1993). Context, time and memory retrieval in the interference paradigms of Pavlovian learning. *Psychological Bulletin, 114*, 90–99.

Bouton, M. E., & King, D. A. (1983). Contextual control of the extinction of conditioned fear: Tests for the associative value of the context. *Journal of Experimental Psychology: Animal Behavior Processes, 9*, 248–265.

Carlin, A. S., Hoffman, H. G., & Weghorst, S. (1997). Virtual reality and tactile augmentation in the treatment of spider phobia: A case report. *Behaviour Research and Therapy, 35*, 153–158.

Craske, M. G., Antony, M. M., & Barlow, D. H. (2006). *Mastering your fears and phobias: Therapist guide* (2nd ed.). New York: Oxford University Press.

Craske, M. G., & Barlow, D. H. (2006). *Mastery of your anxiety and panic: Therapist guide* (4th ed.). New York: Oxford University Press.

Craske, M. G., & Barlow, D. H. (2007). Panic disorder and agoraphobia. In D. H. Barlow (Ed.), *Clinical handbook of psychological disorders: A step-by-step treatment manual* 4th ed.) (pp. 1–64). New York: Guilford.

Craske, M. G., Kircanski, K., Zelikowsky, M., Mystowski, J., Chowdhury, N., & Baker, A.

(2008). Optimizing inhibitory leaning during exposure therapy. *Behaviour Research and Therapy, 46*, 5–27.

Foa, E. B., & Kozak, M. J. (1985). Treatment of anxiety disorders: Implications for psychopathology. In A. H. Tuma & J. D. Maser (Eds.), *Anxiety and the anxiety disorders* (pp. 421–452). Hillsdale, NJ: Erlbaum.

Foa, E. B., & Kozak, M. J. (1986). Emotional processing of fear: Exposure to corrective information. *Psychological Bulletin, 99*, 20–35.

Foa, E. B., & Kozak, M. J. (1998). Clinical applications of bioinformational theory: Understanding anxiety and its treatment. *Behavior Therapy, 29*, 675–690.

Foa, E. B., & Meadows, E. A. (1997). Psychosocial treatments for posttraumatic stress disorder: A critical review. *Annual Review of Psychology, 48*, 449–480.

Franklin, M. E., & Foa, E. B. (2007). Obsessive-compulsive disorder. In D. H. Barlow (Ed.), *Clinical handbook of psychological disorders: A step-by-step treatment manual* 4th ed.) (pp. 164–215). New York: Guilford.

Heimberg, R. G., Dodge, C. S., Hope, D. A., Kennedy, C. R., Zollo, L. J., & Becker, R. E. (1990). Cognitive behavioural group treatment for social phobia: Comparison with a credible placebo control. *Cognitive Therapy and Research, 14*, 1–23.

Jones, M. C. (1924). A laboratory study of fear. The case of Peter. *Pedagogical Seminary, 31*, 308–315.

Kamphuis, J. H., & Telch, M. J. (2000). Effects of distraction and guided threat reappraisal on fear reduction during exposure-based treatments for specific fears. *Behaviour Research and Therapy, 38*, 1163–1181.

Kozak, M. J., Foa, E. B., & Steketee, G. (1988). Process and outcome of exposure treatment with obsessive-compulsives: Psychophysiological indicators of emotional processing. *Behavior Therapy, 19*, 157–169.

Lang, A. J., & Craske, M. G. (2000). Manipulations of exposure-based therapy to reduce return of fear: A replication. *Behaviour Research and Therapy, 38*, 1–12.

Leitenberg, H. (Ed.) (1976). Behavioral approaches to treatment of neuroses. In *Handbook of behavior modification and behavior therapy.* Englewood Cliffs, NJ: Prentice Hall.

Levin, R. B., & Gross, A. M. (1985). The role of relaxation in systematic desensitization. *Behaviour Research and Therapy, 23*, 187–196.

Mühlberger, A., Herrmann, M.J., Wiedemann, G., Ellgring, H., & Pauli, P. (2001). Repeated exposure of flight phobics to flights in virtual reality. *Behaviour Research and Therapy, 39*, 1033–1050.

Mystkowski, J. L., Craske, M. G., & Echiverri, A. M. (2002). Treatment context and return of fear in spider phobia. *Behavior Therapy, 33*, 399–416.

Mystkowski, J. L., Craske, M. G., Echiverri, A. M., & Labus, J. S. (2006). Mental reinstatement of context and return of fear in spider phobia. *Behavior Therapy, 37*, 49–60.

Öst, L.-G. (1992). Blood and injection phobia: Background and cognitive, physiological, and behavioral variables. *Journal of Abnormal Psychology, 101*, 68–74.

Öst, L.-G. (1996). Long-term effects of behavior therapy for specific phobia. In M. R. Mavissakalian, & R. F. Prien (Eds.), *Long-term treatments of anxiety disorders* (pp. 171–199). Washington, D.C.: American Psychiatric Press.

Pitman, R. K., Orr, S. P., Altman, B., & Longpre, R. E. (1996). Emotional processing and outcome of imaginal flooding therapy in Vietnam Veterans with chronic posttraumatic stress disorder. *Comprehensive Psychiatry, 37*, 409–418.

Powers, M. B., Smits, J. A. J., & Telch, M. J. (2004). Disentangling the effects of safety-behavior utilization and safety-behavior availability during exposure-based treatment: A placebo-controlled trial. *Journal of Consulting and Clinical Psychology, 72*, 448–454.

Rentz, T. O., Powers, M. B., Smits, J. A. J., Cougle, J. R., & Telch, M. J. (2003). Active-imaginal exposure: Examination of a new behavioral treatment for cynophobia (dog phobia). *Behaviour Research and Therapy, 41*, 1337–1353.

Riley, W. T., McCormick, M. G. F., Simon, E. M., Stack, K., Pushkin, Y., Overstreet, M. M., et al. (1995). Effects of alprazolam dose on the induction and habituation processes during behavioral panic induction treatment. *Journal of Anxiety Disorders, 9*, 217–227.

Rothbaum, B. O., Hodges, L., Kooper, R., Opdyke, D., Williford, J. S., & North, M. (1995). Effectiveness of computer-generated (virtual reality) graded exposure in the treatment of acrophobia. *American Journal of Psychiatry, 152*, 626–628.

Salter, A. (1949). *Conditioned reflex therapy.* New York: Creative Age.

Sloan, T., & Telch, M. J. (2002). The effects of safety-seeking behavior and guided threat reappraisal on fear reduction during exposure: An experimental investigation. *Behaviour Research and Therapy, 40*, 235–251.

Telch, M. J., Valentiner, D. P. Ilai, D., Young, P. R., Powers, M. B., & Smits, J. A. J. (2004). Fear activation and distraction during the emotional processing of claustrophobic fear. *Journal of Behavior Therapy and Experimental Psychiatry, 35*, 219–232.

Tsao, J. C. I., & Craske, M. G. (2000). Timing of treatment and return of fear: Effects of massed, uniform-, and expanding-spaced exposure schedules. *Behavior Therapy, 31,* 479–497.

van Minnen, A., & Hagenaars, M. (2002). Fear activation and habituation patterns as early process predictors of response to prolonged exposure treatment in PTSD. *Journal of Traumatic Stress, 15,* 359–367.

Wolpe, J. (1958). *Psychotherapy by reciprocal inhibition.* Stanford, CA: Stanford University Press.

43 APPLICATIONS OF THE MATCHING LAW

John C. Borrero, Michelle A. Frank, and Nicole L. Hausman

At every moment of the day we are faced with the opportunity to choose between concurrently available alternatives. Thus, selection of one alternative when faced with an array of possible competing alternatives defines *choice* (Catania, 1998). Such choices may span the gamut from matters of grave clinical significance to those that are strictly mundane. For example, an adolescent may either assault a peer having been the subject of an inflammatory remark, or walk away from the peer and go to class (naturally, this is not a representative list of all potential alternative responses, but is strictly illustrative of two possible competing responses). Similarly, a child with intellectual disabilities may engage in self-injurious head hitting, or engage in cooperative play with a teacher's assistant. At a more mundane level, individuals must choose between oatmeal or toast for breakfast, for example, or which route to take to the office (McDowell, 1988; 1989). Because choice is ubiquitous in matters of everyday affairs, behavioral research on choice has flourished since the inception of the experimental analysis of behavior, and has become increasingly recognized as a relevant construct in clinical concerns of social significance (Fisher & Mazur, 1997). As will be illustrated next, a discussion of the matching law is inextricably tied to matters of choice.

The matching law, in its various formulations, is a quantification of the relationship between response rate and specific reinforcement parameters, most often, reinforcer rate. For example, in what is commonly recognized as the first formulation of this relationship Herrnstein (1961) exposed the key pecking of pigeons to concurrent variable-interval (VI) schedules of reinforcement (grain). In one situation, pigeons were given a choice between pecking the left key, which was correlated with a VI 75-s schedule of

grain presentation, and pecking the right key, which was correlated with a VI 270-s schedule of grain presentation. Herrnstein then expressed the resulting data as the relationship between relative response rate and relative reinforcement as follows:

$$\frac{B_1}{B_1 + B_2} = \frac{R_1}{R_1 + R_2} \qquad \text{(Equation 1)}$$

where B_1 and B_2 represent responding emitted to the left key, and the right key respectively, and R_1 and R_2 represent reinforcement rates associated with B_1 and B_2, respectively. Because of the disparity in reinforcement schedule values, Equation (1) predicts, *ceteris paribus*, that nearly four times as much responding will be allocated to the left key relative to the right key, using the schedule values described previously. When various pairs of VI schedules are arranged, a rather orderly, linear relationship emerges. Otherwise stated, relative rates of responding (i.e., how much of one response occurs relative to the other response) tend to track, or "match" relative rates of reinforcement. Numerous variations of Equation 1 have been constructed since Herrnstein's initial formulation (McDowell, 2005); however, a comprehensive summary of those equations is beyond the scope of this chapter (notable, however, is the work of Baum, 1974). What Equation 1 shows however, is that the relative rate of each of two responses will be determined by the relative rates of reinforcement associated with those responses.

Although initially assessed in the nonhuman operant laboratory, conceptualizations of behavior as choice are directly amenable to matters of clinical import, and thus in principle, applicable to evaluations from a matching perspective. We turn next to representative literature on the application of the matching law to applied matters.

APPLICATIONS

Three broad topical areas have consumed the majority of applied research on matching. These include: (1) evaluations of severe problem behavior (and appropriate alternative behavior) exhibited by persons with intellectual disabilities, (2) evaluations of communicative behavior exhibited by typically developing adults, and (3) evaluations of response allocation to concurrently available academic tasks by typically developing children, persons with learning difficulties, and persons with emotional disturbances.

Evaluations of Severe Problem Behavior

Severe problem behavior, including self-injurious behavior (SIB), property destruction, and aggression are common behavioral phenotypes exhibited by persons with intellectual disabilities (Bodfish & Lewis, 2002). The severity of such responses often places the person exhibiting such behavior, or persons in the immediate environment, in very real danger. The prevalence of SIB, for example, among individuals diagnosed with an autism spectrum disorder may range from 20% to upwards of 70% of the population (Dominick, Ornstein-Davis, Lainhart, Tager-Flusberg, & Folstein, 2007). As such, evaluations of response allocation (e.g., completing academic tasks or engaging in severe problem behavior) may be quite informative in both describing and explaining occurrences of such behavior.

Prior works by McDowell (1981) and Martens and Houk (1989) demonstrated that a matching account of behavior-environment relations effectively characterized SIB (McDowell) as well as disruptive classroom behavior and academic task completion (Martens & Houk). However, McDowell and Martens and Houk applied variations of Equation 1 that are beyond the scope of this chapter. In part using Equation 1 J. C. Borrero and Vollmer (2002) assessed severe problem behavior exhibited by 4 individuals diagnosed with intellectual disabilities, during naturally occurring interactions with their primary caregivers. The researchers first observed participants interacting with their caregivers and recorded data on occurrences of severe problem behavior (e.g., SIB), appropriate alternative behavior (e.g., vocal requests for tangible items), and potential reinforcers (e.g., provision of tangible items). Thus, instances of SIB were conceptualized as one response alternative (B_1 as expressed in Equation 1) and instances of appropriate alternative behavior were conceptualized as another response alternative (B_2 as expressed in Equation 1). Following descriptive observations, the researchers then conducted functional analyses of each participant's problem behavior using procedures similar to those described by Iwata, Dorsey, Slifer, Bauman, and Richman (1982/1994). The purpose of conducting functional analyses was to experimentally identify reinforcers for problem behavior. For example, for one participant, problem behavior was reinforced by provision of tangible items. Therefore, when descriptive data were assessed, instances of problem behavior that were contiguous with access to tangible items (10-s) were considered reinforced (R_1 in Equation 1) and instances of appropriate alternative behavior that were contiguous with access to tangible items were considered reinforced (R_2 in Equation 1). When results were aggregated across all participants, strong correlations were reported, suggesting that Equation 1 provided a comprehensive account of response allocation.

Noteworthy however, is the finding that response allocation may be differentially influenced by various reinforcement parameters. For example, rate of reinforcement, delay to reinforcement, quality of reinforcement, and magnitude of reinforcement have all been shown to influence response allocation (Borrero, Vollmer, Borrero, & Bourret, 2005; Neef, Mace, & Shade, 1993). A more recent study by Sy, Borrero, and Borrero (in press) demonstrated that the relative response allocation (between problem behavior and appropriate alternative behavior) of one participant was more sensitive to the duration of reinforcement, rather than its rate. For example, if rate of reinforcement is equal for two different responses (e.g., 1 response contingent reinforcer per min) the duration of each could vary (e.g., one response produces 3-s reinforcer access while the other produces 30-s reinforcer access). Clearly, in such cases one must look to variables other than reinforcer rate when responding for one alternative occurs at differentially higher rates.

The studies just described support the utility of the matching law as applied to evaluations of severe problem behavior in nonexperimentally manipulated contexts (e.g., the researchers did not program reinforcement rates). It is often assumed that response allocation occurs in accordance with the matching law, and again, the prior descriptive studies bolster this contention. However, the extent to which relative occurrences of problem behavior and appropriate communicative behavior match relative rates of reinforcement has only recently been assessed under experimentally manipulated reinforcement schedules. Borrero et al. (2008) arranged concurrent VI schedules for problem behavior and appropriate behavior, respectively. Reinforcers for problem behavior (as identified via functional analysis) were then delivered according to independent VI schedules, and response allocation was assessed. Although coefficients of determination, across participants, ranged from very low to very high, the work of Borrero et al. represents the first experimental evaluation of matching as applied to persons with severe problem behavior who exhibit severe problem behavior.

Evaluations of Communicative Behavior

Studies of human social interaction have suggested that conversational patterns are also applicable to evaluations of matching. For example, Dishion, Spracklen, Andrews, and Patterson (1996) demonstrated that the content of delinquent adolescent boys' conversations was well described by Equation 1. Specifically, the researchers found that when discussion of delinquent behavior or rule breaking occurred (B_1 in Equation 1), those responses were more likely to be followed by peer approval (laughing, or R_1 in Equation 1), as compared to content that involved rule following (e.g., discussions of school work that did not involve rule breaking, or B_2 in Equation 1). Building off of the seminal experimental work of Greenspoon

(1955), a handful of studies have evaluated how typical adults allocate their attention (orientation) to two peers. In the first of these studies, Conger and Killeen (1974) assessed how participants allocated their responding between two confederates, each of whom delivered statements of agreement or approval (e.g., "I agree with that point") according to independent VI schedules. In a period of only 30 min, Conger and Killeen showed that participants attended to confederates in a manner that was consistent with relative rates of reinforcement provided by the confederates. In two similar studies, Pierce, Epling, and Greer (1981) and J. C. Borrero et al. (2007) both reported response allocation that was also well described by relative reinforcement rates. As applied to evaluations of communicative behavior, the matching law has demonstrated, in purely practical terms, that we will allocate our attention and our conversation in a way that optimizes reinforcement.

Evaluations of Academic Behavior

In terms of academic behavior, matching evaluations have typically involved a choice between identical academic materials associated with differing independent VI schedules. For example, Mace, Neef, Shade, and Mauro (1994) arranged identical arithmetic problems on different colored cards for three adolescents identified as having learning difficulties. Reinforcers (nickels) were arranged on concurrent VI schedules (e.g., VI 20 s VI 240 s), and response allocation, in terms of the time spent working on either stack of arithmetic problems, was assessed. As predicted by the matching law, students allocated their relative responding in accord with relative reinforcement rates (all producing moderate to strong correlations). However, several additional procedures were required. For example, after stable responding under the first pair of VI schedules was obtained, the experimenters demonstrated the pattern of response allocation that would result in maximum amount of reinforcement (i.e., modeled efficient responding for the participants). Further, digital timers were used to count down time remaining in the interval. For example, when one schedule was associated with the VI 20-s schedule, the timer indicated the remaining time in the interval. When the timer reached zero, and a response occurred, a reinforcer was delivered. Although such procedures are not the norm in traditional matching research, the report by Mace et al. is very informative because it demonstrated some potential limits of the matching relation for socially significant human behavior. That is to say, for such a relation to hold, additional procedural manipulations may be required. However, research of the sort conducted by Mace et al. may be more representative of stimulus control research rather than schedule control (e.g., matching).

CONSIDERATIONS

While the matching relation has proven to be a rather robust one in a variety of applied contexts, some considerations are in order. First, evaluations of matching should not be conducted for the purposes of identifying reinforcers. For example, if behavior is frequently followed by a particular environmental event (e.g., attention from peers or adults), one may be inclined to presume that the event is a reinforcer. However, such events may merely be correlated with the occurrence of behavior and say nothing about the causal mechanisms (e.g., Borrero & Vollmer, 2002; Sy et al., in press). Second, unlike similar research conducted in the nonhuman animal laboratory, human behavior in uncontrolled environments is often associated with choice between asymmetrical outcomes, and the behavior itself often differs in topography. For example, a head hit differs in form from a vocal request for parental attention. Similarly, the outcomes associated with head hitting and vocal requests for attention may also differ along several dimensions (e.g., head hits may produce very high quality attention of relatively long duration, while appropriate requests may be met with low quality attention and relatively longer delays to reinforcement). As such, consideration should be given to the interplay of reinforcement parameters. Third, the responses just described are ones for which social contingencies are operative (effective). For example, the findings reported by Dishion et al. (1996) are predicated on the notion that participant behavior is sensitive to, and more importantly, reinforced by peer approval. In cases for which (problem) behavior is insensitive to socially mediated consequences, accounts of the matching relation are more difficult to interpret (e.g., St. Peter et al., 2005). For example, an adult with intellectual disabilities may exhibit stereotypic behavior because of propreoceptive properties of behavior, independent of any external consequences. In which case, the matter of quantifying the rate of reinforcement for such behavior becomes more difficult (using Equation 1). Alternative formulations of the matching relation do however account for the reinforcing value of consequences produced by the very act of engaging in a particular response (Herrnstein, 1970).

STEP-BY-STEP PROCDURES

When conducting either descriptive or experimental evaluations of matching, the first step is to identify reinforcers for responding. When severe problem behavior is the subject of study, this should be accomplished via the functional analysis method of behavioral assessment described by Iwata et al. (1982/1994). Evaluations of response allocation involving the presentation of events that have *not* been shown to function as reinforcers are moot (i.e., the matching relation is only relevant when reinforcers are known). Next, reinforcement schedules should be arranged for two or more alternatives (e.g., problem behavior and appropriate communicative behavior, or academic engagement with simple addition problems and academic engagement with long division problems). The matching relation is most informative when concurrent VI schedules are arranged (also note that the previously described matching studies all involved concurrent VI schedules). Computerized programming of VI schedules may be accomplished as described by Hantula (1991) and Bancroft and Bourret (2008). Because evaluations of choice (or more specifically, preference) are less informative when preference for either alternative is equal (i.e., the person switches between simple addition problems and long division problems equally), a programmed changeover delay (COD) will reduce the likelihood of stereotypic switching between alternatives. A COD may be arranged such that responses to one alternative are not reinforced if a response to the other alternative occurred within the prior x-s. A COD of 2 to 5 s is common, and also decreases the probability of potential chaining of behavior (Borrero et al., 2008; Mace et al., 1994).

After conducting the first experimental session, the rate of each response should be determined, as well as the rate of reinforcement associated with each response. For example, if a child completes 20 addition problems and 10 division problems during a 10 min study session, the rate of responding (expressed as responses per min) for addition problems would be 2 (20 problems completed divided by 10 min), while the rate of responding for division problems would 1 (10 problems completed divided by 10 min). Next, the rate of reinforcement associated with each response should be assessed for each alternative. For example, if completion of addition problems were reinforced according to a VI 30-s schedule and completion of division problems were reinforced according to a VI 60-s schedule, reinforcement rate for this academic work session might be 1.8 per min for addition problems and 0.8 per min for division problems. Next, these values would be plugged into Equation 1, as follows,

$$\frac{2}{2+1} \approx \frac{1.8}{1.8+.8}$$

Based on these results, perfect matching is not obtained (and in fact is infrequently observed, see Baum, 1974), however, relative response rate (0.67 rpm) rather closely approximates relative reinforcement rate, in this example (0.69). With the calculations for one experimental work session completed, data can be presented by way of scatter plot. Figure 43.1 depicts a hypothetical scatter plot on which the relation just assessed is plotted (as an open circle) as well as several additional data points (expressed as open triangles for which the analyses were not previously described).

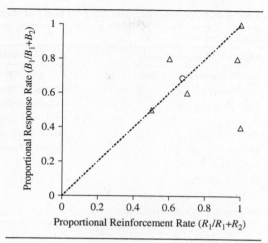

FIGURE 43.1 Hypothetical data illustrating a method of depicting matching data. Data resulting in the open circle are described in text. Data resulting in open triangles are not described in text, but illustrate a more complete assessment of the matching relation. Data that fall closer to the dashed line (representing perfect matching) illustrate a stronger relationship between relative response rate and relative reinforcement rate. Those that fall further from the dashed line illustrate larger deviations of relative response rate from relative reinforcement rates.

FOCUS ON APPLIED IMPLICATIONS

While the implications for evaluations of the matching relation are many, this section will focus on four potential applications. These include: (1) evaluations of treatment integrity, (2) evaluations of reinforcement parameters, (3) alternative interpretations of treatment effectiveness, and (4) pre- and posttraining evaluations of response allocation. A set of guidelines for evaluations of the matching relation is provided in Table 43.1.

Evaluations of Treatment Integrity

Even in the most highly controlled contexts (e.g., inpatient hospital care, one-to-one supervision in a classroom), implementation of treatment with perfect integrity is unlikely. *Treatment integrity* refers to the extent to which the independent variable (reinforcement schedules in the context of matching research) is implemented as prescribed. When extended to the

TABLE 43.1   Applied Evaluations of the Matching Relation

Topical Areas

Severe Problem Behavior	Communicative Behavior	Academic Behavior
C. S. W. Borrero et al. (2008)	J. C. Borrero et al. (2007)	Mace, Neef, Shade, & Mauro (1994)
J. C. Borrero & Vollmer (2002)	Conger & Killeen (1974)	Mace, Neef, Shade, & Mauro (1996)
Hoch & Symons (2007)	Dishion, Spracklen, Andrews, & Patterson (1996)	Martens (1992)
McDowell (1981)	Pierce, Epling, & Greer (1981)	Martens, Halperin, & Rummel (1990)
Martens & Houk (1989)	Synder & Patterson (1995)	Martens, Lochner, & Kelly (1992)
Oliver, Hall, & Nixon (1999)		Neef, Mace, Shea, & Shade (1992)
St. Peter et al. (2005)		Reed & Martens (in press)
Sy, Borrero, & Borrero (in press)		
Symons, Hoch, Dahl, & McComas (2003)		

home, or situations in which one-to-one supervision is not possible, the probability of treatment integrity failures increases considerably. For example, an intervention in which instances of problem behavior are never reinforced, and appropriate alternative behavior is always reinforced, may prove to be effective in highly controlled contexts. However, in application, it is unlikely that parents, teachers, or other primary caregivers would be able to completely eliminate reinforcers for problem behavior (e.g., if attention has been shown to reinforce problem behavior, and the target child is in the act of physically assaulting another child, then attention [physical intervention] must occur to ensure the safety of the subject of the assault). Experimental evaluations of treatment integrity have shown however that interventions may remain effective when implemented with less than perfect integrity (Vollmer, Roane, Ringdahl, & Marcus, 1999). Evaluations of the matching relation may too inform such analyses. For example, when the rate of reinforcement for problem behavior approximates a VI 30-s schedule, and the rate of reinforcement for appropriate behavior approximates a VI 10-s schedule, problem behavior may continue to occur, in accord with the relative reinforcement rates. However, if the rate of reinforcement for problem behavior increases (i.e., is thinned) to a VI 120 s schedule, while the rate of reinforcement for appropriate behavior remains VI 10 s, deviations from matching may occur such that the emission of problem behavior becomes increasingly less likely.

Evaluations of Reinforcement Parameters

Related to the notion of treatment integrity is the way in which reinforcers are arranged when responses *must* be reinforced. In keeping with the prior example, if one individual is in the process of physically assaulting another, and attention has been shown to reinforce physical aggression, then caregivers are at a loss: one must intervene. However, the existing literature on the various parameters of reinforcement suggests that maintenance of appropriate behavior and suppression of problem behavior is still possible. More specifically, when degradation of treatment integrity occurs, caregivers and clinicians may bolster other parameters of reinforcement such that choice still favors the appropriate response. For example, if an instance of severe problem behavior is reinforced caregivers and clinicians may simply increase the quality, magnitude (duration), or rate of reinforcement for appropriate alternative behavior. In which case, despite the fact that problem behavior was reinforced, appropriate behavior remains the relatively "better" alternative.

(Alternative) Interpretations of Treatment Effectiveness

As the matching law suggests, response allocation is affected not only by contingent reinforcement but also by other reinforcement available in one's environment (McDowell, 1989). For example, common interventions such as differential reinforcement of alternative behavior (DRA) and noncontingent reinforcement can be interpreted from a matching perspective and have implications for decelerative effects on problem behavior (McDowell, 1988). One such strategy has already been discussed: DRA, or provision of reinforcers contingent on appropriate alternative behavior. Another strategy to decrease problem behavior is to increase the level of noncontingent, or free, reinforcement in the environment. McDowell (1981) illustrated the effectiveness of these strategies to decrease the oppositional behavior of an adult male with mental retardation. A token economy was arranged in which tokens were delivered for behavior that was unrelated to target behavior, which resulted in a dramatic decrease in problem behavior. According to a matching account of behavior, such interventions are effective because they result in an increase in the total amount of reinforcement in the environment thus decreasing problem behavior, even if the contingencies in place for problem behavior remain the same. These same sorts of strategies can also be used to increase appropriate behavior. For example, one could decrease the amount of reinforcement provided for a concurrently available alternative response or decrease the amount of free reinforcement in the environment. Both interventions are designed to decrease the amount of reinforcement currently available in one's environment thus increasing the likelihood of the occurrence of the appropriate, targeted behavior.

Additionally, it has been suggested that for interventions to be maximally effective, a choice between reinforcers that are substitutable or exchangeable for one another should be arranged (Myerson & Hale, 1984). This is an important notion for clinicians to understand because it suggests that when developing treatments designed to decrease problem behavior, reinforcers arranged for appropriate behavior should function as substitutes for the reinforcers provided for problem behavior. One should note, however, that qualitatively different stimuli can still function as substitutes and, therefore, reinforcers should be identified on an individual basis. Thus, one may provide a reinforcer that is qualitatively different (yet still highly reinforcing) contingent on either the absence of problem behavior or for the occurrence of an appropriate behavior. This reinforcer should be one that the individual cannot obtain contingent upon problem behavior. For example, one might provide a bit of highly preferred food following compliance with academic tasks rather than a break that the child could also access by emitting problem behavior.

Evaluations of Caregiver Training

As some of the work described previously suggests, individuals have been shown to emit problem behavior and appropriate alternative behavior in ways that are largely consistent with the matching law. For example, if prior to seeking treatment a child exhibits relatively more problem behavior than appropriate behavior, the likely explanatory mechanism is to be found in some aspect of the reinforcement contingency (e.g., relative rate or duration of reinforcement favors problem behavior). Again, when relative rates of responding "match" relative rates of reinforcement, an orderly and linear function results. After identifying and evaluating an intervention designed to decrease problem behavior (and increase appropriate alternative behavior), how might such changes impact the matching relation? Let us assume that prior to caregiver training, problem behavior (in the natural environment) is reinforced on a schedule that approximates a VI 10-s schedule (6 reinforcers per min), while appropriate alternative behavior is reinforced on a VI 60-s (1 reinforcer per min) schedule. Let us assume further that problem behavior occurs at a rate of 30 rpm and that appropriate alternative behavior occurs at a rate of 5 rpm. By plugging these data into Equation 1, we find that relative rate of responding approximates relative rates of reinforcement associated with problem and appropriate behavior.

$$\frac{30}{30+5} \approx \frac{6}{6+1}$$

During training however, caregivers are taught to withhold reinforcers for problem

TABLE 43.2   Key Elements of Matching Analyses

Step	Description
1. Identify reinforcers for behavior	Conduct a preference assessment (e.g., Fisher et al., 1992) followed by a reinforcer assessment to demonstrate that events presented contingent on target behavior function as reinforcers. Alternatively, one can conduct a functional analysis of problem behavior (Iwata et al., 1982/1994) to identify reinforcers.
2. Arrange two or more concurrently available schedules	For a minimum of two responses, arrange concurrently available reinforcement schedules.
3. Select schedule type	The most commonly evaluated schedule for matching research is the VI schedule. Thus, concurrent VI schedules are recommended.
4. Program a changeover delay (COD)	In order to decrease the likelihood of sequential switching between alternatives, ensure that responses on one alternative do not have an effect immediately following a change from one schedule to another.
5. Data preparation	Rates of responding and rates of reinforcement (events per unit time) for each alternative should be determined.
6. Data presentation	Matching data are typically presented in graphic form, as a scatter plot. The behavior proportion (or ratio) is expressed as a function of the reinforcement proportion (or ratio). Behavior is expressed on the y-axis and reinforcement is expressed on the x-axis. Also see Figure 43.1.

behavior and increase the relative rate of reinforcement for appropriate alternative behavior. As noted previously however, problems with treatment integrity likely abound, and on some occasions, caregivers may inadvertently reinforce problem behavior, or must intervene due to the severity of problem behavior. If relative rates of reinforcement were merely reversed (after caregiver training), an orderly relationship is retained, however the relative rates of reinforcement, post caregiver training, favor the appropriate alternative response, as illustrated below.

$$\frac{5}{5+30} \approx \frac{1}{1+6}$$

Although reinforcers are not completely eliminated in the above example, carrying out such a standard in the natural environment is highly unlikely. With well-programmed reinforcement parameters however, caregivers may "stack the deck" in favor of appropriate alternative behavior.

SUMMARY

The matching relation was originally demonstrated in the nonhuman animal laboratory. Recently however, the relevance of choice and conceptualizations of matching have been become apparent for a range of clinical concerns (See Table 43.2). Applications of the matching law to matters of clinical importance have focused on evaluations of severe problem behavior exhibited by individuals with intellectual disabilities, communication exhibited by typically developing adults, and response allocation among concurrently available academic tasks. While evaluations of the matching law per se, are not suggestive of particular interventions, such evaluations can suggest the boundaries at which interventions may maintain effectiveness.

References

Bancroft, S. L., & Bourret, J. C. (2008). Generating variable and random schedules of reinforcement using Microsoft Excel™ macros. *Journal of Applied Behavior Analysis, 41*, 227–235.

Baum, W. M. (1974). On two types of deviation from the matching law: Bias and undermatching. *Journal of the Experimental Analysis of Behavior, 22*, 231–242.

Bodfish, J. W., & Lewis, M. H. (2002). Self-injury and comorbid behaviors in developmental, neurological, psychiatric, and genetic disorders. In S. R. Schroeder, M. L. Oster-Granite, & T. Thompson (Eds.), *Self-injurious behavior: Gene-brain-behavior relationships* (pp. 23–39). Washington, DC: American Psychological Association.

Borrero, C. S. W., Vollmer, T. R., Borrero, J. C., & Bourret, J. C. (2005). A method for evaluating parameters of reinforcement during parent-child interactions. *Research in Developmental Disabilities, 26*, 577–592.

Borrero, C. S. W., Vollmer, T. R., Borrero, J. C., Bourret, J. C., Sloman, K. N., Samaha, A. L., et al. (2008). Concurrent reinforcement schedules for problem behavior and appropriate behavior: Experimental applications of the matching law. Under review.

Borrero, J. C., Crisolo, S. S., Tu, Q., Rieland, W. A., Ross, N. A., Francisco, M. T., et al. (2007). An application of the matching law to social dynamics. *Journal of Applied Behavior Analysis, 40*, 589–601.

Borrero, J. C., & Vollmer, T. R. (2002). An application of the matching law to severe problem behavior. *Journal of Applied Behavior Analysis, 35*, 13–27.

Catania, A. C. (1998). *Learning* (4th ed.). Upper Saddle River, NJ: Prentice Hall.

Conger, R., & Killeen, P. (1974). Use of concurrent operants in small group research: A demonstration. *Pacific Sociological Review, 17*, 399–416.

Dishion, T. J., Spracklen, K. M., Andrews, D. W., & Patterson, G. R. (1996). Deviancy training in male adolescent friendships. *Behavior Therapy, 27*, 373–390.

Dominick, K. C., Ornstein Davis, N., Lainhart, J., Tager-Flusberg, H., & Folstein, S. (2007). Atypical behaviors in children with autism and children with a history of language impairment. *Research in Developmental Disabilities, 28*, 145–162.

Fisher, W., Piazza, C. C., Bowman, L. G., Hagopian, L. P., Owens, J. C., & Slevin, I. (1992). A comparison of two approaches for identifying reinforcers for persons with severe and profound disabilities. *Journal of Applied Behavior Analysis, 25*, 491–498.

Fisher, W. W., & Mazur, J. E. (1997). Basic and applied research on choice responding. *Journal of Applied Behavior Analysis, 30*, 387–410.

Greenspoon, J. (1955). The reinforcing effect of two spoken sounds on the frequency of two responses. *American Journal of Psychology, 68*, 409–416.

Hantula, D. A. (1991). A simple BASIC program to generate values for variable-interval schedules of reinforcement. *Journal of Applied Behavior Analysis, 24*, 799–801.

Herrnstein, R. J. (1961). Relative and absolute strength of response as a function of frequency of reinforcement. *Journal of the Experimental Analysis of Behavior, 4*, 267–272.

Herrnstein, R. J. (1970). On the law of effect. *Journal of the Experimental Analysis of Behavior, 13*, 243–266.

Hoch, J., & Symons, F. J. (2007). Matching analysis of socially appropriate and destructive behavior in developmental disabilities. *Research in Developmental Disabilities, 28*, 238–248.

Iwata, B. A., Dorsey, M. F., Slifer, K. J., Bauman, K. E., & Richman, G. S. (1994). Toward a functional analysis of self-injury. *Journal of Applied Behavior Analysis, 27*, 197–209. (Reprinted from *Analysis and Intervention in Developmental Disabilities, 2*, 3–20, 1982).

Mace, F. C., Neef, N. A., Shade, D., & Mauro, B. C. (1994). Limited matching on concurrent schedule reinforcement of academic behavior. *Journal of Applied Behavior Analysis, 27*, 585–596.

Mace, F. C., Neef, N. A., Shade, D., & Mauro, B. C. (1996). Effects of problem difficulty and reinforcer quality on time allocated to concurrent arithmetic problems. *Journal of Applied Behavior Analysis, 29*, 11–24.

Martens, B. K. (1992). Contingency and choice: The implications of matching theory for classroom instruction. *Journal of Behavioral Education, 2*, 121–137.

Martens, B. K., Halperin, S., & Rummel, J. E. (1990). Matching theory applied to contingent teacher attention. *Behavioral Assessment, 12*, 139–155.

Martens, B. K., & Houk, J. L. (1989). The application of Herrnstein's law of effect to disruptive and on-task behavior of a retarded adolescent girl. *Journal of the Experimental Analysis of Behavior, 51*, 17–27.

Martens, B. K., Lochner, D. G., & Kelly, S. Q. (1992). The effects of variable-interval reinforcement on academic engagement: A demonstration of matching theory. *Journal of Applied Behavior Analysis, 25*, 143–151.

McDowell, J. J. (1981). On the validity and utility of Herrnstein's hyperbola in applied behavior analysis. In C. M. Bradshaw, E. Szabadi, & C. F. Lowe (Eds.), *Quantification of steady-state operant behavior* (pp. 311–324). Amsterdam: Elsevier/North-Holland.

McDowell, J. J. (1988). Matching theory in natural human environments. *The Behavior Analyst, 11*, 95–109.

McDowell, J. J. (1989). Two modern developments in matching theory. *The Behavior Analyst, 12*, 153–166.

McDowell, J. J. (2005). On the classic and modern theories of matching. *Journal of the Experimental Analysis of Behavior, 84*, 111–127.

Myerson, J. M., & Hale, S. (1984). Practical implications of the matching law. *Journal of Applied Behavior Analysis, 17*, 367–380.

Neef, N. A., Mace, F. C., & Shade, D. (1993). Impulsivity in students with serious emotional disturbance: The interactive effects of reinforcer rate, delay, and quality. *Journal of Applied Behavior Analysis, 26*, 37–52.

Neef, N. A., Mace, F. C., Shea, M. C., & Shade, D. (1992). Effects of reinforcer rate and reinforcer quality on time allocation: Extensions of matching theory to educational settings. *Journal of Applied Behavior Analysis, 25,* 691–699.

Oliver, C., Hall, S., & Nixon, J. (1999). A molecular to molar analysis of communicative and problem behaviors. *Research in Developmental Disabilities, 20,* 197–213.

Pierce, W. D., Epling, W. F., & Greer, S. M. (1981). Human communication and the matching law. In C. M. Bradshaw, E. Szabadi, & C. F. Lowe (Eds.), *Quantification of steady-state operant behavior* (pp. 345–348). Amsterdam: Elsevier/North-Holland.

Reed, D. D., & Martens, B. K. (in press). Sensitivity and bias under conditions of equal and unequal academic task difficulty. *Journal of Applied Behavior Analysis.*

Snyder, J. J., & Patterson, G. R. (1995). Individual differences in social aggression: A test of a reinforcement model of socialization in the natural environment. *Behavior Therapy, 26,* 371–391.

St. Peter, C. C., Vollmer, T. R., Bourret, J. C., Borrero, C. S. W., Sloman, K. M., & Rapp, J. T. (2005). On the role of attention in naturally occurring matching relations. *Journal of Applied Behavior Analysis, 38,* 429–443.

Sy, J. R., Borrero, J. C., & Borrero, C. S. W. (in press). Computational evaluations of matching and problem behavior. *Journal of Applied Behavior Analysis.*

Symons, F. J., Hoch, J., Dahl, N. A., & McComas, J. J. (2003). Sequential and matching analyses of self-injurious behavior: A case of overmatching in the natural environment. *Journal of Applied Behavior Analysis, 36,* 267–270.

Vollmer, T. R., Roane, H. S., Ringdahl, J. E., & Marcus, B. A. (1999). Evaluating treatment challenges with differential reinforcement of alternative behavior. *Journal of Applied Behavior Analysis, 32,* 9–23.

44 MINDFULNESS PRACTICE

Sona Dimidjian and Marsha M. Linehan

In recent years, the practice of mindfulness has been increasingly applied to the clinical treatment of both physical and mental health problems. Although mindfulness practice has its roots in Eastern meditative and Western Christian contemplative traditions, the contemporary clinical use of mindfulness has focused largely on the core characteristics of mindfulness, independent of its spiritual origin and background. In this context, mindfulness is often understood as awareness simply of what is, at the level of direct and immediate experience, separate from concepts, category, and expectations. It is a way of living awake, with your eyes wide open. Mindfulness as a practice is the repetitive acts of directing your attention to only one thing. And that one thing is the one moment you are alive. The conceptualization and definition of mindfulness have been a topic of recent attention (Baer, 2003; Bishop et al., 2004; Brown, Ryan, & Creswell, 2007; Fletcher & Hayes, 2005). As a set of skills, mindfulness practice has been described as the intentional process of observing, describing, and participating in reality nonjudgmentally, in the moment, and with effectiveness (i.e., using skillful means) (Linehan, 1993a). Mindfulness is thus the practice of willingness to be alive to the moment and radical acceptance of the entirety of moment. Mindfulness has as its goal only mindfulness. At the same time, it is the window to freedom, wisdom, and joy.

There are many ways of teaching and practicing mindfulness; in fact, methods of teaching and practicing mindfulness in the spiritual traditions noted above have been evolving for centuries. Recent years have witnessed an explosion of interest in the clinical application of mindfulness and a rapidly expanding set of treatments that are based on the practice of mindfulness. In fact, a recent edited volume included mindfulness-based treatments for a range of clinical problems including depression, generalized anxiety disorder, eating disorders, chronically mental illness, borderline personality disorder, cancer, chronic pain, relationship distress, intimate partner violence, and stress (Baer, 2006). Many of these approaches, however, are quite early in their development and have not been extensively tested. In addition, emerging work is being done on the use of mindfulness-based interventions for substance abuse problems (Marlatt 1994; Bowen et al., 2006; Witkiewitz & Marlatt, 2004; Witkiewitz, Marlatt, & Walker, 2005). There exist three treatment models that employ the use of mindfulness strategies and that have been subjected to considerable empirical scrutiny; these include mindfulness-based stress reduction (MBSR), the closely related mindfulness-based cognitive therapy (MBCT), and dialectical behavior therapy (DBT)[1]. Because MBSR, MBCT, and DBT have been most extensively investigated, this chapter draws from these models to provide a basic background in the clinical use of mindfulness and to highlight a general step-by-step procedure comprised of common elements found in each of the various models.

PRIMARY MINDFULNESS STRATEGIES AND THEIR EMPIRICAL STATUS

Kabat-Zinn was the first to propose an empirically supported clinical application of

---

1. Although there is significant overlap between mindfulness and acceptance interventions, acceptance based models that do not principally employ mindfulness as core practices (e.g., Acceptance and Commitment Therapy, Integrative Couple Therapy).

mindfulness practice (Kabat-Zinn, 1990). This model, MBSR, was initially used for the treatment of chronic pain and was later applied to a diverse array of disorders. Segal, Williams, and Teasdale (2002) proposed an adaptation of Kabat-Zinn's model, MBCT, for use in the prevention of depressive relapse. Both MBSR and MBCT use a similar structure, which consists of an 8-week program of group sessions. Both models emphasize the importance of regular, formal mindfulness practices, which include sitting meditation, walking meditation, body scan meditation, and yoga. Clients are asked to commit to daily periods of formal practice, ranging between 30 and 45 minutes, as homework. Informal practice is also a focus of the program, as clients practice bringing mindfulness to daily activities such as eating, driving, washing the dishes, talking on the phone, etc. MBSR also includes a 1-day-long mindfulness practice session during the course, and MBCT integrates use of some cognitive and behavioral strategies.

Linehan (1993a, 1993b) pioneered the use of mindfulness strategies in the treatment of borderline personality disorder. Linehan's model, DBT, employs mindfulness strategies as part of a larger package of cognitive behavioral interventions. In contrast to other models, Linehan's DBT model does not teach formal mediation practices; instead, it breaks down the meditation process into its component parts; it thus teaches clients the psychological and behavioral skills comprise most Eastern meditative and Western contemplative practices. Most DBT mindfulness exercises emphasize opportunities for using the mindfulness skills in everyday activities and situations. The specific mindfulness skills taught in DBT include "what skills" (i.e., observing, describing, and participating) and "how" skills (i.e., nonjudgmentally, one-mindfully, and effectively). The mindfulness skills are a core module of the treatment and are woven into a range of treatment procedures used in DBT. For instance, they are taught as "the vehicles for balancing 'emotion mind' and 'reasonable mind' to achieve 'wise mind'" (Linehan, 1993b, 63) and as elements of emotion regulation and distress tolerance. Mindfulness skills are taught as part of the weekly DBT skills groups and are also emphasized in individual therapy sessions. As homework, clients also monitor their daily use of the mindfulness skills on a written diary card. Although the role of mindfulness interventions has been investigated across a broad range of clinical problems, many of the studies conducted to date have been uncontrolled. For instance, studies on MBSR in the treatment of the following disorders demonstrate promise, but all have lacked random assignment to control groups: chronic pain (Kabat-Zinn, 1982; Kabat-Zinn et al., 1985; Kabat-Zinn et al., 1987; Randolph et al. 1999); fibromyalgia (Kaplan, Goldenberg, & Galvin-Nadeau, 1993); anxiety and panic disorder (Kabat-Zinn et al., 1992; Miller, Fletcher, & Kabat-Zinn, 1995); mood and stress symptoms among cancer patients (Carlson, Ursuliak, Goodey, Angen, & Speca, 2001); binge eating disorder (Kristeller & Hallett, 1999); and multiple sclerosis (Mills & Allen, 2000).

The few controlled trials that have been conducted do suggest that MBSR is efficacious in the treatment of psoriasis (Kabat-Zinn et al., 1998) and mood disturbance and stress symptoms among cancer patients (Speca, Carlson, Goodey, & Angen, 2000). Two controlled trials found MBCT to be efficacious in preventing relapse among recovered depressed patients with multiple recurrences of prior depression (Teasdale et al., 2000; Ma & Teasdale, 2004). Recent preliminary studies have also suggested that MBCT may have promise as an acute phase treatment for depression (Kenny & Williams, 2007). There have been a number of randomized controlled trials of DBT (cf. Koerner & Dimeff, 2000), including a recent trial that compared DBT and treatment-by-expert in the reduction of suicidal behavior among patients with borderline personality disorder (Linehan et al., 2006).

In addition to the methodological problems discussed above, it should also be noted that the practice of mindfulness is a component of the larger treatment packages that have been empirically tested; in each case other cognitive, behavioral, and/or psychoeducational interventions are also included. Therefore, no studies have independently investigated the role of mindfulness per se.

WHO MIGHT BENEFIT FROM MINDFULNESS STRATEGIES AND CONTRAINDICATIONS OF THE TREATMENT

The research conducted to date suggests that mindfulness as a clinical intervention may have promise across a broad range of clinical problems; however, randomized controlled clinical trials are needed to document its efficacy. Although there is no evidence to date for any particular contraindications to the use of mindfulness interventions, investigators have suggested a number of cautions. Teasdale et al. (2000) caution therapists against using MBCT with clients currently in an acute depressive episode; however, as noted above, recent data suggest that some acutely depressed patients may benefit from MBCT (Kenny & Williams, 2007). Linehan (1994) also notes that extended formal practice is often not indicated for many seriously disturbed clients and instead suggests the use the component skills listed above and/or more abbreviated periods of formal practice (e.g., a few minutes).

OTHER FACTORS TO CONSIDER IN DECIDING WHETHER TO USE MINDFULNESS STRATEGIES

One of the key questions under discussion among treatment developers is whether therapists/instructors should be required to have their own mindfulness practice (Dimidjian, Epstein, Linehan, MacPherson, & Segal, 2001). The MBSR and MBCT approaches require that therapists be engaged in a daily formal practice (i.e., sitting meditation, yoga) as part of the model (Kabat-Zinn, 1990; Segal, Williams, & Teasdale, 2002). It is argued that this prerequisite ensures both that therapists will teach from an experiential as well as an intellectual knowledge base and that they will have direct understanding of the effort and discipline required of clients. In contrast, other models such as DBT do not prescribe a formal mindfulness practice for DBT therapists, though some mindfulness activities are required. For instance, formal mindfulness is practiced at the outset of every consultation team meeting, which is a requisite part of DBT, and therapists are required to practice particular mindfulness exercises prior to using them with clients. In this sense, although DBT therapists are not required to have a personal formal practice, they are members of a formal community of therapists learning mindfulness. The importance of having a mindfulness teacher, either in person or through books, has also been discussed.

Unfortunately, there is no empirical data to date that validates the importance of a therapist's personal practice for competent clinical practice; thus, the degree to which a therapist maintains a formal practice will, in part, be guided by the particular model used. For therapists interested in integrating mindfulness strategies as part of other treatment regimens, it will, at a minimum, be important to consider one's own degree of understanding and familiarity with mindfulness practices.

Another important consideration is the question: "Is mindfulness practice a means to an end or an end in itself?" In the spiritual traditions from which they are derived, an essential quality of mindfulness practice is the act of non-striving or non-attachment to outcome, and the models discussed above specifically emphasize this quality of mindfulness. Individuals seeking clinical care, however, are often expressly interested in a particular outcome (e.g., feeling better, less depressed, etc.). Therapists using mindfulness clinically must balance this inherent tension between the "end in itself" quality of mindfulness and the goal-directed quality of clinical care.

HOW DOES MINDFULNESS PRACTICE WORK?

There is no definitive evidence regarding mechanisms of change in the clinical use of mindfulness, though a number of theoretical models have been discussed (Baer, 2003; Warren Brown, Ryan, & Creswell, 2007; Lynch, Chapman, Rosenthal, Kuo, & Linehan, 2006). Specific hypothesized mechanisms include relaxation (Benson, 1984), metacognitive change (cf. Teasdale, Segal, & Williams, 1995), and replacement of a "negative addiction" with a "positive addiction" (Marlatt, 1994). It has also been suggested that the process of change in the clinical use of mindfulness parallels that of the clinical use of exposure interventions (Kabat-Zinn, 1982; Kabat-Zinn et al., 1992; Linehan, 1993a, b) and acceptance interventions (Linehan, 1993a, 1993b, 1994; Marlatt, 1994). Mindfulness practice may also work by enhancing the use of other cognitive and behavioral procedures, such as problem solving (Linehan, 1993a). Finally, recent studies have documented a range of biological correlates of MBSR (see, e.g., Davidson et al., 2003; Farb et al., 2007). A range of studies have also documented the physiological effects of meditation among nonclinical populations (Brefczynski-Lewis, Lutz, Schaefer, Levinson, & Davidson, 2007; Lazar et al., 2005; Lutz, Greischar, Rawlings, Ricard, & Davidson 2004). It is therefore likely that some of the clinical benefits of mindfulness practice may be mediated by such effects. It is also probable that mindfulness does not operate via one single pathway but that its effects are mediated by numerous processes; clearly, further investigation of mechanisms of change will be an important next step for empirical inquiry.

STEP-BY-STEP GUIDELINES FOR THE CLINICAL USE OF MINDFULNESS PRACTICE

Although the primary clinical models utilizing mindfulness strategies are unique in many respects, they also share basic common elements. These common elements are distilled here as a set of seven steps to employ in the clinical application of mindfulness practice (see Table 44.1). This guideline is offered to acquaint the reader with the practice of mindfulness; however, clinicians should be cautioned to recall that these steps have not been empirically tested independent of the larger models from which they are derived.

Step 1: Embodiment or Modeling

Embodiment or modeling of mindfulness consists of acting with mindfulness in one's implementation of the intervention model. MBSR and MBCT place heavy emphasis on the importance of embodying mindfulness in one's teaching, both through leading the specific meditation practices as well as guiding the process of

TABLE 44.1 Seven Major Steps of the Clinical Use of Mindfulness Practice

1. Embodiment/Modeling
2. Preparation
   - Select a target activity/stimuli for mindfulness practice.
   - Determine how long it will be practiced.
   - Complete personal preparation.
3. Instruction
   - Introduce client to the rationale and goals of mindfulness practice.
   - Introduce to the client the main characteristics of mindfulness.
   - Instruct the client on the specific target practice.
4. In-Session Practice
   - Lead and participate with the client in the selected practice activity.
5. Sharing
   - Elicit description from the client of his/her direct experience of the practice.
   - Elicit commentary about the practice from the client.
6. Feedback
   - Provide corrective feedback, weaving in information outlined in step 3 as indicated.
7. Homework
   - Review homework in manner consistent with procedures outlined in steps 5 and 6.

[i] Although there is significant overlap between mindfulness and acceptance interventions, acceptance based models that do not principally employ mindfulness as core practices (e.g., Acceptance and Commitment Therapy, Integrative Couple Therapy).

inquiry after meditation practices. DBT places a strong emphasis on the importance of modeling and specific strategies such as being radically genuine, non-judgmental, and awake to client in-session behavior. In all of these ways, the therapist's understanding of mindfulness is a key element and forms an essential foundation for the six remaining steps.

Step 2: Preparation

Preparation consists of three main parts. First, the therapist must decide what activity the client will practice. It is important to recall that mindfulness is not a particular activity (e.g., sitting quietly with crossed legs on a cushion), it is the quality of awareness that one brings to any activity, to any internal or external stimuli. Therefore, the activities or experiences that can serve as targets for mindfulness practice are endless. Awareness of breathing is perhaps most commonly associated with mindfulness (and it is a core element of most traditions and clinical models), but other possibilities for mindfulness practice abound, including: eating, walking, physical movement in yoga or dancing, laughing, singing, listening, seeing, driving, answering the telephone, and so forth.

Second, the therapist must decide how long the client will practice. Among the models discussed in this chapter, the duration of practice varies greatly, ranging from a single minute of practice to ten days. Duration of practice also varies across different interventions within one model; for instance, MBCT assigns 3-minute "breathing space" practices as well as 45-minute sitting meditations. At present, no empirical data exist to guide the selection of target activity and/or practice duration; therefore, therapists should be guided by the sequencing guidelines of the treatment model employed and/or their assessment of the individual needs, motivation, and capabilities of their clients.

Third, it is important for therapists to prepare personally for the use of mindfulness strategies. At a minimum, it is important for therapists to practice the target activity that will be used before teaching it to one's clients. Beyond this, the extent of personal preparation suggested varies across the primary models, as noted above. There is consensus, however, as noted above, on the importance of modeling or embodying mindfulness in one's interactions with the client. Toward this end, Segal, Williams, and Teasdale advise therapists to take the time necessary to begin sessions, not hurriedly, but with a balance of "openness and 'groundedness'" (2002, p. 84).

Step 3: Instruction and Orientation

There are three levels of instruction and orientation that the therapist must provide: (1) instruction on the goals and/or rationale of mindfulness practice, (2) instruction on the key characteristics of mindfulness and (3) instruction on the selected practice activity.

The first level of instruction requires the therapist to provide a rationale to clients for the use of mindfulness interventions. Although this should be specifically tailored to the client's presenting problems, most models incorporating mindfulness interventions also emphasize the general goal of helping the client to access a sense of wisdom and a corresponding experience of decreased struggle or suffering. In DBT, this is referred to as "wise mind" (Linehan, 1993a, b); MBCT refers to "inherent wisdom" (Segal, Williams, & Teasdale, 2002).

The second level of instruction involves the introduction of mindfulness and its key characteristics. Although each model uses slightly different language, there is considerable conceptual overlap in the key qualities of mindfulness that are emphasized. A brief summary of these qualities is outlined below. Consistent with the DBT conceptualization of mindfulness (Linehan, 1993a), the first three qualities refer to activities that one does when practicing mindfulness; the next three refer to the style in which the first three activities are undertaken.

Noticing/Observing/Bringing Awareness

This is one of the core characteristics of what one does when practicing mindfulness. It is paying attention to direct experience, at the level of pure sensation, without concepts or categories. Therapists can explain that, most often, we move without awareness from the level of direct experience and sensation to conceptual description (and often from there quickly to judgment). For instance, we hear sounds from the tree above and think, "Ah, a bird, what a lovely song." Noticing, however, is hearing the bird's song as *just the elements of sound* (e.g., timbre, pitch, pace, melody, etc.) without classifying or categorizing the experience of hearing as "bird" (or judging it to be "lovely").

Labeling/Noting/Describing

This refers to the activity of observing and then adding a descriptive label to the experience. Again, specific examples will be helpful in explaining this characteristic. For instance, if one is practicing mindfulness of washing the dishes and thinks, "I forgot to pay the phone bill!" labeling/noting/describing would be to say simply, "thinking" or "remembering" or "a thought went through my mind." If pain in the shoulder arises, labeling/noting/describing would be to attend to the specific sensation and say, for instance, "tightness." It is important to understand and convey that labeling occurs at the level of process, and thus avoids getting stuck in content. Thus, labeling/noting/describing allows one to step back from experience with awareness, to "decenter" (Segal, Williams, & Teasale, 2002). It is this act of mindfulness that gives rise to the direct experience of "I am not my emotions," "Thoughts are not facts," and so on.

Participating

This refers to throwing oneself fully into an activity or experience. It is becoming one with experience without reservation; it is characterized by spontaneity. This quality is an important one for clients to learn, but it is also a critical quality for therapist to bring to the teaching of mindfulness.

Nonjudgmentally/with Acceptance and Allowing

These refer to three closely related and central aspects of mindfulness practice. Judgment is the act of labeling things as good or bad. Most often, we live with great attachment to that which we judge as "good" great aversion to that which we judge as "bad." Nonjudging is bringing a gentle, open, and noncritical attitude to experience. It is "assuming the stance of an impartial witness to your own experience" (Kabat-Zinn, 1990, 33). Nonjudging also facilitates letting go or becoming nonattached, which means not trying to hold onto that which is "good" or push away that which is "bad" (e.g., difficult, painful, boring, etc.). Nonjudging is also a form of accepting. Accepting is seeing what is. It is not trying to be or get anywhere or anything else; it is not trying to be more relaxed, more joyful, less in pain, more enlightened, and the like. It is ceasing efforts to control or to make things other than they are.

It is important to explain to clients that we practice nonjudging/accepting/allowing with all aspects of mindfulness practice—even the act of judging (e.g., don't judge judging!). Asking clients to focus on the "facts" (e.g., who, what, when, and where) can be a helpful way of practicing nonjudgment (Linehan, 1993b). Therapists may also need to clarify that nonjudging does not mean replacing negative judgments with positive judgments. Non-judging means not

making judgments at all, as opposed to being "pollyannaish." It is also important to explain that non-judging and accepting can be very difficult to do; in fact, Linehan (1993a, b) uses the term *radical acceptance* to connote "that the acceptance has to come from deep within and has to be complete" (102). Therapists may need to address perceived obstacles to accepting; these often include thinking that acceptance confers approval and/or that acceptance will foreclose future opportunities for change (Linehan, 1993b; Kabat-Zinn, 1990). In DBT, the skills of "turning the mind" (or actively choosing to accept) and "willingness" as opposed to "willfulness" are presented as paths toward acceptance.

Effectively

This refers to the quality of mindfulness that has as its chief emphasis "what works." Mindfulness is not concerned with opinions or ideas about "right" or "wrong." A mindful approach is one that is concerned with being effective, one that easily abandons "being right" in favor of "being effective." This quality stems from the notion of "using skillful means" found in most Eastern meditative traditions.

In the Moment/with Beginner's Mind

Being in the moment refers to being in *this* moment without reference to past or future; only this moment exists. Being in the moment also is the opposite of doing one thing while thinking about something else or attempting to do several activities at once. Kabat-Zinn (1990, 35) explains the quality of beginner's mind, "No moment is the same as any other. Each is unique and contains unique possibilities. Beginner's mind reminds us of this simple truth."

It should be noted that the presentation of the key characteristics is rarely completed in a single presentation. Instead, certain characteristics may be emphasized in the instructions for specific mindfulness practices and/or woven into the process of sharing and feedback. In fact, the style of instruction varies considerably across models. MBSR and MBCT place a heavy emphasis on experiential learning and the process of discovery; thus, the role of didactic instruction is minimized. In contrast, group leaders help to guide clients through a process of inquiry to a new experience and understanding. In contrast, the skills training context of DBT places a heavy emphasis on didactic instruction and mindfulness skills and practices are taught in a manner consistent with a traditional classroom environment. DBT places a similarly heavy emphasis on client's direct experiential practice in sessions; however, the therapist's style is commonly more didactic in nature. Across all approaches, stories, metaphors, poetry, and concrete examples from clients' own lives are often useful methods of conveying the key characteristics of mindfulness.

At the third level of instruction, the therapist needs to instruct the client in the specific in-session or at-home practice activity. The instructions should be delivered before the practice and may also be repeated, in full or part, at several points during the practice. Instructions should be clear, specific, and simple. It is also common to begin many mindfulness instructions with an invitation to focus on body position or posture; specific instructions about whether to open or close the eyes should also be included if relevant to the activity. Instructions should also include information about the length of the practice and how the beginning and end will be identified; ringing a mindfulness bell may be useful for this purpose.

It is also often helpful, depending on the client's level of skill, to anticipate and provide instruction on common difficulties that may arise. Chief among these is the experience of wandering attention. Therefore, the therapist may anticipate the wandering of attention to thoughts (e.g., "I can't do this," "I forgot to put money in the parking meter," etc.), strong emotions (e.g., boredom, frustration, hopelessness, excitement, anxiety, etc.), physical sensations (e.g., itch on your left foot, soreness in your shoulders, hearing noises in the hall, etc.), and/or action urges (e.g., the urge to end the practice, to distract, etc.). In each case, the therapist should reassure the client that the wandering of attention is normal and even inevitable for most practitioners of mindfulness. The therapist can also explain that the wandering of attention does not indicate that the client is doing the practice "wrong;" in contrast, responding to the wandering of attention is, itself, part of the practice of mindfulness. The instruction is simply to observe that attention

has wandered and to bring it gently, without judgment, back to the target activity.

Step 4: In-Session Practice

Mindfulness is not something that can be taught (or learned) simply by talking about it. Mindfulness is an experientially based skill that needs to be developed over repeated trials of practice. Therefore, in-session practice is critical, as such practice provides the chief context for teaching and learning. Step three is, thus, leading the selected practice. In addition, it is important for the therapist to engage in the target practice with the client. Doing the practice with the client models the mindful behavior, decreases client self-consciousness (Marlatt & Kristeller, 1998), and helps to ensure that the therapist teaches from an immediate "moment-to-moment experience" (Segal, Williams, & Teasdale, 2002, 89).

Step 5: Sharing

After the target activity has been completed, the therapist asks the client to share his/her experience, including any difficulties encountered. Segal, Williams, and Teasdale (2002) emphasize the importance of using open-ended questions and an attitude of curiosity in this process. In this way, the activity of sharing may itself present opportunities for further mindfulness practice. For instance, if clients report their experience with judgmental language (e.g., "I tried to be mindful of walking, but I did a terrible job."), therapists can guide them to describe their experience without judgmental terms, thereby creating an opportunity for practicing non-judging (e.g., "I intended to be mindful of walking, but my mind kept wandering to other things."). MBCT formalizes this distinction by asking clients first "to describe their actual experience during the practice" and later to provide "comments on their experiences" (Segal, Williams, & Teasdale, 2002, 89).

Step 6: Feedback

Although this step is discussed as a separate step for heuristic purposes, in actuality, client sharing and feedback are often closely intertwined.

In fact, the careful weaving of client sharing and therapist feedback presents one of the most powerful opportunities for the therapist to teach mindfulness. Therapists are typically able to address obstacles to learning most effectively when instruction is linked to immediate and specific client experiences. Again, as previously noted, in MBSR and MBCT, providing feedback often occurs in the form of asking questions about clients' experiences, whereas in DBT, feedback may be of a more direct, corrective nature.

A number of difficulties are frequently addressed during feedback. For instance, being "distracted" (e.g., by thoughts, noises, emotions, urges, physical sensations, etc.) is a very common experience that clients describe during sharing. It is often helpful in providing feedback to remind clients that the wandering of one's mind from the target activity is not a sign of failure, but part and parcel of the practice. Clients often report, "I couldn't do it" following a mindfulness practice. To this, therapists can inquire, "Were you aware of "not doing it"? Frequently the response is "yes." At this point, therapists can explain, "You did it!," and again explain that the practice is to simply be aware of *whatever* arises during the practice.

Feelings of frustration or discouragement (and corresponding self-judgment) may also be common. Clients may feel frustrated that they do not see immediate results in reaching their therapeutic goals (e.g., "It didn't work; I don't feel any better."). Clients may think that being mindful is too difficult and feel frustrated with the need to practice what is seemingly such a simple activity again and again. In response to both of these concerns, therapists can highlight the inherent dialectic of mindfulness practice between goal orientation and letting go. Therapists can also remind clients that repeated practice is also an inherent part of learning mindfulness. Clients should be cautioned at the outset that mindfulness rarely "just happens." It is simple, but not easy. As in the learning of all new skills, it requires rehearsal and over-learning to master. It thus demands intention, concentration, commitment, and discipline. It requires effort even when one may not feel like exerting effort. MBCT and MBSR both explain to clients, "You don't have to like it; you just have

to do it" (Kabat-Zinn, 1990; Segal, Williams, & Teasdale, 2002). It also requires repeated practice and a corresponding attitude of patience. It will often feel like one is starting over, again and again. Often, reference to stories and metaphors that illustrate other skills that require repeated practice and the ineffectiveness of self-judgment and criticism in the process can be useful.

Step 7: Homework

All models utilizing mindfulness strategies emphasize at-home practice. As in all cognitive and behavioral therapies, a heavy emphasis is placed on the generalization of skills learned in sessions and the role of homework toward this end. Specific homework practices can be structured as part of the treatment program, as in MBSR and MBCT, which use a combination of formal and informal practices as well as instruction via CDs. Homework can also be individually tailored to particular clients, as in DBT. In general, homework assignments should be clear and specific, and potential obstacles to completion should be anticipated and discussed. The next session should include a review of homework that is conducted in a manner consistent with the guidelines above for sharing and feedback discussed above.

Further Reading

Kabat-Zinn, J. (1990). *Full catastrophe living: Using the wisdom of your body and mind to face stress, pain, and illness.* New York: Dell Publishing.

Linehan, M. M. (1993). *Cognitive-behavioral treatment of borderline personality disorder.* New York: Guilford Press.

Linehan, M. M. (1993). *Skills training manual for treating borderline personality disorder.* New York: Guilford.

Segal, Z., Williams, J. M. G., and Teasdale, J. D. (2002). *Mindfulness-based cognitive therapy for depression: A new approach to preventing relapse.* New York: Guilford.

References

Austin, J. H. (1998). *Zen and the brain: Toward an understanding of meditation and consciousness.* Cambridge, MA: MIT Press.

Baer, R. A. (2006). *Mindfulness-based treatment approaches.* Oxford, UK: Elsevier.

Baer, R.A. (2003). Mindfulness training as a clinical intervention: A conceptual and empirical review. *Clinical Psychology: Science and Practice, 10,* 125–143.

Benson, H. (1984). *Beyond the relaxation response: How to harness the healing power of your personal beliefs.* New York: Times Books.

Bishop, S. R., Lau, M., Shapiro, S., Carlson, L., Anderson, N. D., Carmody, J., et al. (2004). Mindfulness: A proposed operational definition. *Clinical Psychology: Science and Practice, 11,* 230–241.

Bowen, S., Witkiewitz, K., Dillworth, T., Chawla, N., Simpson, T., Ostafin, B., et al. (2006). Mindfulness meditation and substance use in an incarcerated population. *Psychology of Addictive Behaviors, 20,* 343–347.

Brefczynski-Lewis, J. A., Lutz, A., Schaefer, H. S., Levinson, D. B., & Davidson, R. J. (2007). Neural correlates of attentional expertise in long-term meditation practitioners. *Proceedings of the Nabreaktional Academy of Science, 104,* 11483–11488.

Brown, K. W., Ryan, R. M., & Creswell, J. D. (2007). Mindfulness: Theoretical foundations and evidence for its salutary effects. *Psychological Inquiry, 18,* 1–26.

Carlson, L. E., Ursuliak, Z., Goodey, E., Angen, M., & Speca, M. (2001). The effects of a mindfulness meditation-based stress reduction program on mood and symptoms of stress in cancer outpatients: 6-month follow-up results. *Supportive Care in Cancer, 9,* 112–123.

Davidson, R. J., Kabat-Zinn, J., Schumacher, J., Rosenkranz, M., Muller, D., Santorelli, S. F., et al. (2003). Alterations in brain and immune function produced by mindfulness meditation. *Psychosomatic Medicine, 65,* 564–570.

Dimidjian, S., Epstein, R., Linehan, M. M., MacPherson, L., & Segal, Z. (2001). The clinical application of mindfulness practice. Panel discussion conducted at the Association for the Advancement of Behavior Therapy 35th Annual Convention, Philadelphia.

Epstein, R. M. (1999). Mindful practice. *Journal of the American Medical Association, 282,* 833–839.

Farb, N., Segal, Z. V., Mayberg, H., Bean, J., McKeon, D., Fatima, Z., et al. (2007). Attending to the present: mindfulness meditation reveals distinct neural modes of self-reference. *Social Cognitive and Affective Neuroscience,* 1–10.

Fletcher, L., & Hayes, S. C. (2005). Relational frame theory, acceptance and commitment therapy, and a functional analytic definition of mindfulness. *Journal of Rational-Emotive & Cognitive-Behavior Therapy, 23,* 315–336.

Kabat-Zinn, J. (1990). *Full catastrophe living: Using the wisdom of your body and mind to face stress, pain, and illness.* New York: Dell.

Kabat-Zinn, J. (1982). An outpatient program in behavioral medicine for chronic pain patients based on the practice of mindfulness meditation: Theoretical considerations and preliminary results. *General Hospital Psychiatry, 4,* 33–47.

Kabat-Zinn, J., Massion, A. O., Kristeller, J., Peterson, L. G., Fletcher, K. E., Pbert, L., et al. (1992). Effectiveness of a meditation-based stress reduction program in the treatment of anxiety disorders. *American Journal of Psychiatry, 149,* 936–943.

Kabat-Zinn, J., Lipworth, L., & Burney, R. (1985). The clinical use of mindfulness meditation for the self-regulation of chronic pain. *Journal of Behavioral Medicine, 8,* 163–190.

Kabat-Zinn, J., Lipworth, L., Burney, R., & Sellers, W. (1987). Four-year follow-up of a meditation-based program for the self-regulation of chronic pain: Treatment outcomes and compliance. *Clinical Journal of Pain, 2,* 159–173.

Kabat-Zinn, J., Wheeler, E., Light, T., Skillings, Z., Scharf, M. J., Cropley, T. G., et al. (1998). Influence of a mindfulness meditation-based stress reduction intervention on rates of skin clearing in patients with moderate to severe psoriasis undergoing phototherapy (UVB) and photochemotherapy (PUVA). *Psychosomatic Medicine, 50,* 625–632.

Kaplan, K. H., Goldenberg, D. L., & Galvin-Nadeau, M. (1993). The impact of a meditation-based stress reduction program on fibromyalgia. *General Hospital Psychiatry, 15,* 284–289.

Kenny, M. A., & Williams, J. M. G. (2007). Treatment-resistant depressed patients show a good response to mindfulness-based cognitive therapy. *Behaviour Research and Therapy, 45,* 617–625.

Koerner, K., & Dimeff, L. (2000). Further data on dialectical behavior therapy. *Clinical Psychology: Science and Practice, 7,* 104–112.

Kristeller, J. L., & Hallett, C. B. (1999). An exploratory study of a meditation-based intervention for binge eating disorder. *Journal of Health Psychology, 4,* 357–363.

Lazar, S. W, Kerr, C. E., Wasserman, R. H., Gray, J. R., Greve, D. N., Treadway, M. T., et al. (2005). Meditation experience is associated with increased cortical thickness. *NeuroReport, 16*(17), 1893–1897.

Linehan, M. M. (1994). Acceptance and change: The central dialectic in psychotherapy. In S. C. Hayes, N. S. Jacobson, V. M. Follette, and M. J. Dougher (Eds.), *Acceptance and change: Content and context in psychotherapy* (pp. 73–86). Reno, NV: Context Press.

Linehan, M. M. (1993a). *Cognitive-behavioral treatment of borderline personality disorder.* New York: Guilford.

Linehan, M. M. (1993b). *Skills training manual for treating borderline personality disorder.* New York: Guilford.

Linehan, M. M., Comtois, K. A., Murray, A. M., Brown, M. Z., Gallop, R. J., Heard, H. L., et al.

(2006). Two-year randomized controlled trial and follow-up of dialectical behavior therapy vs therapy by experts for suicidal behaviors and borderline personality disorder. *Archives of General Psychiatry, 63,* 757–766.

Lutz, A., Greischar, L. L., Rawlings, N. B., Ricard, M., & Davidson, R. J. (2004). Long-term meditators self-induced high-amplitude gamma synchrony during mental practice. *Proceedings of the National Academy of Sciences, USA, 101,* 16369–16373.

Lynch, T. R., Chapman, A. L., Rosenthal, M. Z., Kuo, J. R., & Linehan, M. M. (2006). Mechanisms of change in dialectical behavior therapy: Theoretical and empirical observations. *Journal of Clinical Psychology, 62,* 459–480.

Ma, S. H., & Teasdale, J. D. (2004). Mindfulness-based cognitive therapy for depression: Replication and exploration of differential relapse prevention effects. *Journal of Consulting and Clinical Psychology, 72,* 31–40.

Marlatt, G. A. (1994). Addiction and acceptance. In S. C. Hayes, N. S. Jacobson, V. M. Follette, and M. J. Dougher (Eds.), *Acceptance and change: Content and context in psychotherapy* (pp. 175–197). Reno, NV: Context Press.

Marlatt, G. A., & Kristeller, J. A. (1998). Mindfulness and meditation. In W. R. Miller (Ed.), *Integrating spirituality in treatment: Resources for practitioners* (pp. 67–84). Washington, D.C.: APA Books.

Miller, J. J., Fletcher, K., & Kabat-Zinn, J. (1995). Three-year follow-up and clinical implications of a mindfulness meditation-based stress reduction intervention in the treatment of anxiety disorders. *General Hospital Psychiatry, 17,* 192–200.

Mills, N., & Allen, J. (2000). Mindfulness of movement as a coping strategy in multiple sclerosis: A pilot study. *General Hospital Psychiatry, 22,* 425–431.

Randolph, P. D., Caldera, Y. M., Tacone, A. M., & Greak, M. L. (1999). The long-term combined effects of medical treatment and a mindfulness-based behavioral program for the multidisciplinary management of chronic pain in west Texas. *Pain Digest, 9,* 103–112.

Segal, Z., Williams, J. M. G., and Teasdale, J. D. (2002). *Mindfulness-based cognitive therapy for depression: A new approach to preventing relapse.* New York: Guilford.

Speca, M., Carlson, L. E., Goodey, E., & Angen, M. (2000). A randomized, wait-list controlled clinical trial: The effect of a mindfulness meditation-based stress reduction program on mood and symptoms of stress in cancer outpatients. *Psychosomatic Medicine, 62,* 613–622.

Teasdale, J. D., Segal, Z. V., Williams, J. M., Ridgeway, V. A., Soulsby, J. M., Lau, M. A. (2000). Prevention of relapse/recurrence in major depression by mindfulness-based cognitive therapy. *Journal of Consulting and Clinical Psychology, 68,* 615–623.

Teasdale, J. D., Segal, Z., & Williams, J. M. G. (1995). How does cognitive therapy prevent depressive relapse and why should attentional control (mindfulness) training help? *Behaviour Research and Therapy, 33,* 25–39.

Witkiewitz, K., & Marlatt, G. A. (2004). Relapse prevention for alcohol and drug problems: That was Zen, this is Tao. *American Psychologist, 59*(4), 224–235.

Witkiewitz, K., Marlatt, G. A., & Walker, D. D. (2005). Mindfulness-based relapse prevention for alcohol use disorders: The meditative tortoise wins the race. *Journal of Cognitive Psychotherapy, 19,* 221–228.

45 MODERATE DRINKING TRAINING FOR PROBLEM DRINKERS

Frederick Rotgers

Ever since D. L. Davies (1962) published case reports of alcoholics who moderated their alcohol consumption, continuing controversy in the alcohol treatment field has centered on whether a return to moderate drinking is an appropriate treatment goal for problem drinkers. Fueled more by untested clinical lore than by data, those on the abstinence-only side of the controversy have largely ignored the substantial body of research demonstrating that many problem drinkers moderate their drinking to safe levels following treatment rather than becoming completely abstinent, and supporting the efficacy of moderation training for a large segment of problem drinkers (Heather & Robertson, 1997; Heather et al., 2000; Walters, 2000). In fact, this literature is now so extensive that Heather et al. described behavioral self-control training (one form of moderation-focused treatment) as "probably the most researched single treatment modality in the alcohol problems field with over 30 controlled trials devoted to it" (2000, p. 562), adding that it is "supported by the second-largest number of positive studies of any treatment modality in the literature" (p. 562).

In some ways, the controversy over moderation is surprising. The idea that many problem drinkers may be able to moderate successfully, and that personal commitment to moderation may be a critical determinant of outcome, is hardly new. In fact, acknowledgment of the possibility of moderate drinking outcomes for some problem drinkers, as well as a personal "experiment" that an individual may use to determine if moderation is possible for that individual, both appear in the "Big Book" of Alcoholics Anonymous.

It is not yet clear who is most likely to benefit from moderation training approaches but reviews of the literature suggest that most problem drinkers can derive some benefit, even those who demonstrate moderate to severe dependence on alcohol (Heather et al., 2000; Rosenberg, 1993; Walters, 2000). Research shows that allowing problem drinkers who enter treatment to select their own drinking goal enhances both retention and outcome (Ojehagen & Berglund, 1989; Sanchez-Craig & Lei, 1986) even though most problem drinkers who enter treatment choose abstinence over moderation (Rotgers, 1996). Considering the extensive research base, moderation approaches should now be a part of the overall armamentarium of treatment approaches available to clinicians working with problem drinkers.

MODERATION TRAINING APPROACHES

Two types of moderation training programs have been reported in the literature. The most common, and the one to be discussed in detail here, is based on principles of cognitive behavioral therapy and largely involves self-control training (Dimeff, Baer, Kivlahan, & Marlatt, 1999; Miller & Munoz, 1982; Sanchez-Craig, 1995; Sobell & Sobell, 1996). The other approach to moderation training is based on the principles of cue exposure treatment (Heather et al., 2000), but it will not be treated in detail here since there are few data supporting the efficacy of this approach as compared to self-control training.

Four manualized approaches to moderation training have received substantial empirical support: *behavioral self-control training* (BSCT;

Miller & Munoz, 1982); *Saying When,* now known as *DrinkWise* (Sanchez-Craig, 1995); and *guided self-change* (GSC; Sobell & Sobell, 1996). All three are aimed at adults, rely heavily on client-guided (self-help) methodologies, and are typically of short duration, at least with respect to formal therapist involvement. A fourth program, the *Brief Alcohol Screening and Intervention for College Students* (BASICS; Dimeff et al., 1999) is aimed at college students whose drinking places them at high risk for alcohol-related consequences. A support group based loosely on principles of moderation training, Moderation Management (MM), has been found by one study to be attracting many problem drinkers who would otherwise not seek formal intervention (Humphreys & Klaw, 2001; Kishline, 1994; Rotgers & Kishline, 1999). Self-help materials based on a combination of MM principles and BSCT are also becoming available (Rotgers, Kern, & Hoeltzel, 2002).

All of these programs are brief in duration (as few as three sessions, but typically no more than six) and highly client driven. They all differ from traditional approaches to the treatment of problem drinkers in that the main goal is not to stop drinking (although some clients may choose this as their goal), but to reduce the harm and negative consequences associated with the client's particular drinking behavior. As such, all of these programs can be considered "harm-reduction" programs in which the goal is not necessarily to eliminate substance use, but rather to enhance client health and well-being even though substance use continues (Marlatt, 1998).

KEY ELEMENTS OF MODERATION TRAINING

Moderation training approaches share several common elements. These elements are outlined in Table 45.1. The context for delivering this material varies with the specific approach, but moderation training programs can be administered with only limited therapist assistance via books or other materials. For example, BSCT is now available in a computerized version that can be administered with or without therapist assistance (Hester & Delaney, 1997).

TABLE 45.1 Key Elements of Moderation Training for Problem Drinkers

- Self-assessment and self-monitoring of drinking behavior or urges to drink
- Initial period of 2–4 weeks abstinence
- Normative feedback
- Goal setting
- Development and implementation of behavioral coping strategies
- Maintenance planning and lifestyle changes

Self-Assessment

Prior to actual initiation of change efforts, clients are urged to do an objective self-assessment of their drinking (quantity and frequency), its effect on their lives, the extent to which changing their drinking will likely result in difficulty coping with situations and emotions for which drinking was a primary coping strategy, and identification of situations in which drinking is more or less likely to be excessive. Some programs recommend that the client initiate a short (30 days or less) period of abstinence following a period of self-monitoring of drinking behavior. The period of abstinence is designed to allow physiological recovery from the effects of alcohol, reduce tolerance to the effects of alcohol, and provide an opportunity for continued self-assessment of the role alcohol plays in day-to-day coping. When abstinence is initiated immediately, self-monitoring is focused on urges and temptations to drink and situations in which they occur (Sanchez-Craig, 1995).

Of critical importance during the initial abstinence period, or period of self-monitoring of drinking if abstinence is eschewed, is the identification of situations (including both emotional and cognitive states and environments) in which the client is likely to overdrink (i.e., exceed safe drinking limits). Identification of these high-risk situations is critical further along in treatment when the client, either by himself or herself or in conjunction with the therapist, will develop a set of coping strategies for managing drinking in those situations. Self-monitoring of urges and temptations to drink assists in this process.

Normative Feedback

Most drinkers have little idea of what "normal" or "safe" drinking practices consist, and tend to view their own drinking as the same as or less than that of the average drinker. Normative feedback usually takes one or both of two forms: education about empirically derived "safe" drinking limits (Sanchez-Craig, Wilkinson, & Davila, 1995) or feedback from the therapist as to how the individual's reported drinking patterns compare with those of peers (Dimeff et al., 1999). For example, clients might be taught the empirically derived safe drinking limits of no more than 4 standard drinks daily for men, no more than 3 standard drinks daily for women, and no more than 16 and 12 standard drinks weekly for men and women respectively (Sanchez-Craig et al., 1995).

Normative feedback may also be provided in the form of education with respect to the relationship between alcohol consumption and blood alcohol content (BAC). As with general norms about drinking patterns and safe drinking limits, clients typically have little awareness of how many drinks they can consume and still remain below safe BAC levels (e.g., for operating a motor vehicle).

Goal Setting

Formal and explicit goal setting is a component of all of the well-developed moderation training programs. Clients set goals for maximum numbers of drinks per drinking day, number of abstinent days (always a part of an effective moderation program), and maximum numbers of drinks per week. Goals may also be formulated in terms of maximum BAC to be achieved during a given week. Finally, goals may be formulated with respect to drinking situations that the client may wish to avoid, or in which the client may decide to remain abstinent due to a heightened risk of overdrinking in those situations (e.g., drinks after work with coworkers).

All moderation programs accept abstinence as a legitimate outcome goal for clients who choose it. Based as they are in the philosophy of "harm reduction" (Marlatt, 1998), all moderation programs encourage movement toward the healthiest possible life circumstances a given client is willing to pursue. For many clients, this may mean abstaining from alcohol altogether for a specified period of time, or indefinitely.

Behavioral Strategy Development and Implementation

Once self-assessment and goal setting are completed, the next step in effective moderation is to develop specific strategies and techniques for coping with situations in which the client is at high risk to drink more than is safe. These strategies can be focused on either intrapersonal or extrapersonal (contextual) factors and should be made explicit and clear using an "if–then" strategy specification format. Various programs categorize the stages of strategy development and implementation differently, but all urge clients to develop strategies that are as behaviorally specific, and as easy to implement, as possible.

While the number and types of strategies available to clients to cope effectively with high-risk situations is large (and probably as varied as clients themselves) and limited only by client and therapist ingenuity, an example of a set of strategies and their focus will be helpful. A client might adopt a strategy of counting drinks by shifting coins from one pocket to another with each drink (focus on the drinking behavior itself), or might ensure that he or she doesn't drink alcohol to quench thirst; develop a pattern of pacing drinks over time; decide to not drink when angry, depressed, or anxious; and learn assertive drink refusal skills for use in situations in which the client feels strong social pressure to overdrink.

Maintenance of Behavior Change

All moderation programs contain an explicit focus on maintaining changes made during treatment. Specifically, developing healthy alternatives to drinking, continuing to monitor drinking even when the client feels he or she has achieved moderation successfully, changing social networks to include nondrinking peers, and addressing other psychological problems that may have contributed to overdrinking are all recommended components of moderation training programs.

WHO IS LIKELY TO BENEFIT FROM MODERATION TRAINING?

The research on moderation approaches initially suggested that persons who were younger, female, socially stable, had shorter problem drinking histories, and had lower levels of dependence on alcohol were most likely to maintain moderate drinking levels following treatment (Rosenberg, 1993). Recent literature reviews have begun to conclude that even some alcohol-dependent persons may be able to moderate successfully. Walters (2000) found that some dependent drinkers may benefit from BSCT, and that it is effective for dependent drinkers as is abstinence-focused treatment. Similarly, Heather et al. (2000) found that more severely dependent drinkers in their sample actually responded better to moderation approaches on a variety of indicators than did less dependent drinkers.

It appears that client commitment to moderation as a goal, coupled with a willingness to carry out the behavioral procedures needed to achieve moderation, are the two most important initial indicators of possible success in moderation training. However, at present there is no touchstone available to determine with certainly which clients will succeed and which will not.

THE RISKS OF MODERATION

Moderation training has its failures. Oddly, the clinical lore often seems to lay the failure of abstinence-based treatments at the feet of clients (they were "in denial" and thus "unmotivated") and those of moderation treatments at the feet of the therapists who use them. Overall, having moderation training as an alternative treatment augments the success of treatment.

A major concern voiced by opponents of moderation is that failure will lead to increased hazard to the client, who probably should have stopped drinking altogether. Abstinence-only advocates are concerned that the mere availability of moderation approaches will tempt people who have successfully achieved prolonged abstinence to attempt to resume drinking, but no empirical evidence supports this contention. Similarly, there is a concern that most drinkers will choose moderation over abstinence if a choice is offered, when the data show the exact opposite to be true (Rotgers, 1996). Furthermore, several studies suggest that when clients are permitted to select and to change their drinking goals during treatment, the typical shift of goal is from moderation to abstinence (Ojehagen & Berglund, 1989; Parker, Winstead, Willi, & Fisher, 1979). Thus, moderation training, systematically applied with therapist assistance, in a therapeutic climate of experimental observation of outcomes, can become a significant stepping stone to abstinence for many clients.

Some in the alcohol-treatment field assert (see, e.g., Maltzman, 1987) that most people with drinking problems who enter treatment have made many prior, unsuccessful attempts to moderate their drinking and thus that moderation training is contraindicated as a waste of treatment resources. Moderation training, however, is a specific, systematic technology. It should not be confused with unsystematic attempts to moderate drinking. Furthermore, there are data showing that any a priori assumption about drinking goals is dangerous, since therapist preselection of such a goal, be it abstinence or moderation, is associated with poorer outcomes (Sanchez-Craig & Lei, 1986). Offering moderation training as an option in treatment, and allowing the client to choose whether to pursue it based on objective feedback of assessment results (as in Miller's "Drinker's Check Up" procedure; Miller & Sovereign, 1989) can enhance treatment retention and improve outcome.

CONCLUSION

Despite the objections of many traditionally oriented treatment providers in the alcohol field, moderation training for problem drinkers has garnered a significant level of empirical support. Moderation training is an important component of empirically based treatment for alcohol problems.

References

Davies, D. L. (1962). Normal drinking by recovered alcohol addicts. *Quarterly Journal of Studies on Alcohol, 23,* 94–104.

Dimeff, L. A., Baer, J. S., Kivlahan, D. R., & Marlatt, G. A. (1999). *Brief Alcohol Screening and Intervention for College Students (BASICS): A harm reduction approach.* New York: Guilford.

Heather, N., Brodie, J., Wale, S., Wilkinson, G., Luce, A., Webb, E., & McCarthy, S. (2000). A randomized controlled trial of moderation-oriented cue exposure. *Journal of Studies on Alcohol, 61,* 561–570.

Heather, N., & Robertson, I. (1997). *Problem drinking* (3rd ed.). Oxford, UK: Oxford University Press.

Hester, R. K., & Delaney, H. D. (1997). Behavioral Self-Control Program for Windows: Results of a controlled clinical trial. *Journal of Consulting and Clinical Psychology, 65,* 686–693.

Humphreys, K., & Klaw, E. (2001). Can targeting non-dependent problem drinkers and providing Internet-based services expand access to assistance for alcohol problems? A study of the Moderation Management self-help/mutual aid organization. *Journal of Studies on Alcohol, 62,* 528–532.

Kishline, A. (1994). *Moderate drinking: The moderation management guide for people who want to reduce their drinking.* New York: Crown.

Maltzmann, I. (1987). Controlled drinking and the treatment of alcoholism. *Journal of the American Medical Association, 257,* 927.

Marlatt, G. A. (Ed.). (1998). *Harm reduction: Pragmatic strategies for managing high-risk behaviors.* New York: Guilford.

Miller, W. R., & Munoz, R. F. (1982). *How to control your drinking: A practical guide to responsible drinking* (rev. ed.). Albuquerque: University of New Mexico Press.

Miller, W. R., & Sovereign, G. (1989). The check-up: A model for early intervention in addictive behaviors. In T. Loberg, W. R. Miller, P. E. Nathan, & G. A. Marlatt (Eds.), *Addictive behaviors: Prevention and early intervention.* Amsterdam: Swets & Zeitlinger.

Ojehagen, A., & Berglund, M. (1989). Changes of drinking goals in a two-year out-patient alcoholic treatment program. *Addictive Behaviors, 14,* 1–9.

Parker, M., Winstead, D., Willi, F., & Fisher, P. (1979) Patient autonomy in alcohol rehabilitation: I. Literature review. *International Journal of the Addictions, 14,* 1015–1022.

Rosenberg, H. (1993). Prediction of controlled drinking by alcoholics and problem drinkers. *Psychological Bulletin, 113,* 129–139.

Rotgers, F. (1996). It's time to truly broaden the base of treatment for alcohol problems: Empowering clients with respect to drinking goals as a first step. *The Counselor, 14,* 33–36.

Rotgers, F., Kern, M. F., & Hoeltzel, R. (2002). *Responsible drinking: A moderation management approach for problem drinkers.* Oakland, CA: New Harbinger.

Rotgers, F., & Kishline, A. (1999). Moderation Management®: A support group for persons who want to reduce their drinking, but not necessarily abstain. *International Journal of Self Help and Self Care, 1,* 145–158.

Sanchez-Craig, M. (1995). *DrinkWise: How to quit drinking or cut down.* Toronto: Center for Addiction and Mental Health.

Sanchez-Craig, M., & Lei, H. (1986). Disadvantages of imposing the goal of abstinence on problem drinkers: An empirical study. *British Journal of Addiction, 81,* 505–512.

Sanchez-Craig, M., Wilkinson, D. A., & Davila, R. (1995). Empirically based guidelines for moderate drinking: One-year results from three studies with problem drinkers. *American Journal of Public Health, 85,* 823–828.

Sobell, L. C., & Sobell, M. R. (1996). *Problem drinkers: Guided self-change treatment.* New York: Guilford.

Walters, G. D. (2000). Behavioral self-control training for problem drinkers: A meta-analysis of randomized control studies. *Behavior Therapy, 31,* 135–149.

46 MULTIMODAL BEHAVIOR THERAPY

Arnold A. Lazarus

CONTEXT

When follow-ups on a variety of clients who had received standard behavior therapy revealed that many were apt to suffer setbacks within 6 months to a year (Lazarus, 1971), investigations into the reasons behind this lack of durability revealed that treatment omissions (leaving several response deficits untreated) lay behind most of the relapses. The treatment repertoire advocated by Wolpe (1958) and by Wolpe and Lazarus (1966) glossed over or completely disregarded many cognitive variables, sensory responses, mental images, and interpersonal factors. Thus, agoraphobic clients received relaxation training, imaginal and *in vivo* desensitization, and between-session homework assignments to consolidate and augment whatever gains ensued. Virtually no attention was paid to cognitive mediation (e.g., negative automatic thoughts, dichotomous reasoning, unrealistic expectations, and other self-defeating beliefs). Similarly, interpersonal processes (other than unassertive behaviors) were given short shrift (e.g., marital discord, familial tensions, the impact of authority figures, or sibling rivalry). Unaddressed and untreated, these issues, when triggered, retained the power to undermine whatever treatment gains had accrued.

ENTER COGNITIVE RESTRUCTURING AND MORE

The fact that Lazarus (1971) included an entire chapter on cognitive restructuring was met with strong disfavor by the mainstream behavior therapists, who regarded it as a regressive return to "mentalism." Nevertheless, by the mid-1970s, cognitive behavior therapy had replaced behavior therapy as the accepted designation, and the field became trimodal—emphasizing affect, behavior, and cognition (A-B-C). This remains true to this day. Nevertheless, Lazarus (1976, 1989, 1997, 2000) has contended that equal weight should be given to imagery, sensation, interpersonal relationships, and biological considerations thus operating from a seven-point multimodal perspective (behavior, affect, sensation, imagery, cognition, interpersonal relationships, and drugs/biological factors).

Using the easy-to-remember mnemonic acronym BASIC ID (taken from the initial letters of the foregoing modalities), the multimodal framework emphasizes the discrete and interactive impact of these seven modalities. (The D modality underscores that prescription drugs are the most commonly used biological intervention, but nonetheless one must not lose sight of the entire medical panoply.) Whenever feasible, multimodal therapists will employ empirically supported techniques, or refer out to an expert, when necessary, to implement a specific procedure. The aim, however, is to think in BASIC ID terms to ensure thorough and comprehensive assessment and treatment coverage.

WHO MIGHT BENEFIT FROM THIS APPROACH

Most clients are likely to show positive gains when receiving a broad-spectrum treatment in which salient issues are addressed. For example, a Dutch psychologist, Kwee (1984), organized a multimodal treatment outcome study on 84 hospitalized patients suffering from obsessive–compulsive disorders and extensive phobias, 90% of whom had received prior treatment without success. Over 70% of these patients had suffered from their disorders for more than 4 years. Multimodal treatment regimens resulted in substantial recoveries and durable 9-month follow-ups. This was confirmed and amplified by Kwee and Kwee-Taams (1994).

In Scotland, Williams (1988) in a carefully controlled outcome study compared multimodal assessment and treatment with less integrative approaches in helping children with learning disabilities. Clear data emerged in support of the multimodal procedures.

Follow-up studies that have been conducted since 1973 have consistently suggested that durable outcomes are in direct proportion to the number of modalities deliberately traversed (see Lazarus, 1989, 1997). Although there is obviously a point of diminishing returns, it is a multimodal maxim that the more someone learns in therapy, the less likely he or she is to relapse. To reiterate, it appears that lacunae or gaps in people's coping responses were responsible for many relapses.

CONTRAINDICATIONS

People in crisis require the therapist to focus immediately on the precipitating circumstances and events. There is often simply no time to dwell on the vicissitudes and nuances of the BASIC ID. These cases have need of instantaneous relief from their untoward anxiety and depression. Less acute issues and much less dramatic problem areas may call for unimodal or bimodal interventions. For example, clients in a smoking cessation group, in terms of treatment adherence, are likely to respond better to structured methods of habit control than to a broad band of assessments and interventions. And when dealing with frankly psychotic (e.g., schizophrenic) individuals, or those who are in the manic state of a bipolar disorder, the first inroad should probably consist of supportive treatment and biopsychiatric interventions. When appropriate medications have taken effect, a multimodal treatment program may then be instituted to remedy excesses and deficits that may precipitate or aggravate the patient's initial or major complaints.

THEORY AND MECHANISM

The BASIC ID or multimodal framework rests on a broad social and cognitive learning theory (e.g., Bandura, 1977, 1986; Rotter, 1954) because its tenets are open to verification or disproof. Instead of postulating putative unconscious forces, social learning theory rests on testable developmental factors (e.g., modeling, observational learning, the acquisition of expectancies, operant and respondent conditioning, and various self-regulatory mechanisms). It must be emphasized that while drawing on effective methods from any discipline, the multimodal therapist does not embrace divergent theories but remains consistently within social–cognitive learning theory. The virtues of technical eclecticism (Lazarus, 1967, 1992; Lazarus, Beutler, & Norcross, 1992) over the dangers of theoretical integration have been emphasized in several publications (e.g., Lazarus, 1986, 1989, 1995; Lazarus & Beutler, 1993). The major criticism of theoretical integration is that it inevitably tries to blend incompatible notions and only breeds confusion (Lazarus, 2008 b).

TWO SPECIFIC MULTIMODAL PROCEDURES

Whereas multimodal therapists draw on the entire range of empirically supported methods, two procedures—bridging and tracking—are unique to this approach.

Bridging

Let's assume that a therapist is interested in a client's emotional responses to an event, saying, "How did you feel when your husband drank so much that he passed out at the party?" Instead of discussing her feelings, the client responds with defensive and irrelevant intellectualizations. "Well, it's not as if this happens every time we go out." The therapist persists: "Nevertheless, were you upset, or angry, or embarrassed?" The client, still avoiding the question, says that her husband works extremely hard and often looks for a release on the weekends.

It is likely to be counterproductive to confront the client and point out that she is evading the question and seems reluctant to face her true feelings. In situations of this kind, bridging is usually effective. First, the therapist deliberately tunes in to the client's preferred modality—in this case, the cognitive domain. Thus, the therapist explores the cognitive content. "So you see it as a simple need to relax and let go of tensions that arise during the week at work. Please tell me more." In this way, after perhaps a 5- to 10-minute discourse, the therapist endeavors to branch off into other directions that seem more productive. "Tell me, while we have been discussing these matters, have you noticed any sensations anywhere in your body?" This sudden switch from cognition to sensation may begin to elicit more pertinent information (given the assumption that in this instance, sensory inputs are probably less threatening than affective material). The client may refer to some sensations of tension or bodily discomfort, at which point the therapist may ask her to focus on them, often with a hypnotic overlay: "Will you please close your eyes, and now feel that neck tension. [Pause.] Now relax deeply for a few moments, breathe easily and gently, in and out, in and out, just letting yourself feel calm and peaceful." The feelings of tension, their associated images and cognitions, may then be examined. One may then venture to bridge into affect. "Beneath the sensations, can you find any strong feelings or emotions? Perhaps they are lurking in the background." At this juncture it is not unusual for clients to give voice to their feelings. "I am in touch with anger, fear, and sadness." When the therapist begins where the client is and then bridges into a different modality, most clients then seem to be willing to traverse the more emotionally charged areas they had been avoiding.

Tracking the Firing Order

A fairly reliable pattern may be discerned in the way that many people generate negative affect. Some dwell first on unpleasant sensations (palpitations, shortness of breath, tremors), followed by aversive images (pictures of disastrous events), to which they attach negative cognitions (ideas about catastrophic illness), leading to maladaptive behavior (withdrawal and avoidance). This S-I-C-B firing order (sensation, imagery, cognition, behavior) may require a different treatment strategy from that employed with, say, a C-I-S-B sequence, an I-C-B-S, or yet

a different firing order. Clinical findings suggest that it is often best to apply treatment techniques in accordance with a client's specific chain reaction. A rapid way of determining someone's firing order is to have him or her in an altered state of consciousness—deeply relaxed with eyes closed—contemplating untoward events and then describing their reactions.

ILLUSTRATIVE CASE

A brief case history should elucidate the procedural niceties of the points alluded to previously.

Leon, 26, a single white male, was in an executive training program with a large corporation. He was raised in an affluent suburb, did well at school, and graduated from college, but had tended to be rather obsessive–compulsive, prone to bouts of depression, and conflicted about his career options. After an initial session that consisted of the usual exploration of the client's current situation, some background information, and an inquiry into antecedent events and their consequences, Leon was asked to complete a Multimodal Life History Questionnaire (Lazarus & Lazarus, 1991) and bring it with him to the next session. Clients who comply tend to facilitate their treatment trajectory because the questionnaire enables the therapist rapidly to determine the salient issues across the client's BASIC ID. Leon said that he was feeling too depressed to concentrate on answering the questionnaire; therefore, the therapist conducted a multimodal assessment.

A STEP-BY-STEP INQUIRY

B: What is Leon doing that is getting in the way of his happiness or personal fulfillment (self-defeating actions, maladaptive behaviors)? What does he need to increase and decrease? What should he stop doing and start doing?

A: What emotions (affective reactions) are predominant? Are we dealing with anger, anxiety, depression, or combinations thereof, and to what extent (e.g., irritation vs. rage; sadness vs. profound melancholy)? What appears to generate these negative affects—certain cognitions, images, interpersonal conflicts? And how does Leon respond (behave) when feeling a certain way? We discussed what impact various behaviors had on his affect and vice versa, and how this influenced each of the other modalities.

S: We discussed Leon's specific sensory complaints (e.g., tension, chronic lower back discomfort) as well as the feelings, thoughts, and behaviors that were connected to these negative sensations. Leon was also asked to comment on positive sensations (e.g., visual, auditory, tactile, olfactory, and gustatory delights). This included sensual and sexual elements.

I: Leon was asked to describe some of his main fantasies. He was asked to describe his "self-image." (It became evident that he harbored several images of failure.)

C: We explored Leon's main attitudes, values, beliefs, and opinions, and looked into his predominant shoulds, oughts, and musts. (It was clear that he was too hard on himself and embraced a perfectionistic viewpoint that was bound to prove frustrating and disappointing.)

I: Interpersonally, we discussed his significant others; what he wanted, desired, and expected to receive from them; and what he, in turn, gave to them. (He was inclined to avoid confrontations and often felt shortchanged and resentful.)

D: Despite his minor aches and pains, Leon appeared to be in good health and was health conscious. There were no untoward issues pertaining to his diet, weight, sleep, exercise, or alcohol and drug use.

The foregoing pointed immediately to three issues that called for correction:

1. His images of failure had to be altered to images of coping and succeeding.
2. His perfectionism needed to be changed to a generalized antiperfectionistic philosophy of life.
3. His interpersonal reticence called for an assertive modus vivendi wherein he would easily discuss his feelings and not harbor resentments.

To achieve these ends, the techniques selected were standard methods—positive and coping imagery exercises, disputing irrational cognitions, and assertiveness training.

This straightforward case has been presented to demonstrate how the multimodal behavior therapy approach provided a template (the BASIC ID) that pointed to three discrete but interrelated components that became the main treatment foci. In a sense, the term multimodal behavior therapy is a misnomer because while the assessment is multimodal, the treatment is cognitive behavioral and draws, whenever possible, on empirically supported methods. The main claim is that by assessing clients across the BASIC ID one is less apt to overlook subtle but important problems that call for correction, and the overall problem identification process is significantly expedited.

References

Bandura, A. (1977). *Social learning theory*. Englewood Cliffs, NJ: Prentice Hall.

Bandura, A. (1986). Social foundations of thought and action: A social cognitive theory. Englewood Cliffs, NJ: Prentice Hall.

Kwee, M. G. T. (1984). *Klinische multimodale gedragstherapie [Clinical multimodal behavior therapy]*. Lisse, Holland: Swets & Zeitlinger.

Kwee, M. G. T., & Kwee-Taams, M. K. (1994). *Klinishegedragstherapie in Nederland & vlaanderen [Clinical behavior therapy in the Netherlands and other countries]*. Delft, Holland: Eubron.

Lazarus, A. A. (1967). In support of technical eclecticism. *Psychological Reports, 21*, 415–416.

Lazarus, A. A. (1971). *Behavior therapy and beyond*. New York: McGraw-Hill.

Lazarus, A. A. (1976). *Multimodal behavior therapy*. New York: Springer.

Lazarus, A. A. (1986). Multimodal therapy. In J. C. Norcross (Ed.), *Handbook of eclectic psychotherapy* (pp. 65–93). New York: Brunner/Mazel.

Lazarus, A.A. (1989). *The practice of multimodal therapy*. Baltimore: Johns Hopkins University Press.

Lazarus, A. A. (1992). Multimodal therapy: Technical eclecticism with minimal integration. In J. C. Norcross & M. R. Goldfried (Eds.), *Handbook of psychotherapy integration* (pp. 231–263). New York: Basic Books.

Lazarus, A. A. (1995). Different types of eclecticism and integration: Let's be aware of the dangers. *Journal of Psychotherapy Integration, 5*, 27–39.

Lazarus, A.A. (1997). *Brief but comprehensive psychotherapy: The multimodal way*. New York: Springer.

Lazarus, A. A. (2008a). Multimodal therapy. In R. J. Corsini & D. Wedding (Eds.), *Current psychotherapies* (8th ed., pp. 368–401). Belmont, CA: Thompson.

Lazarus, A. A. (2008 b). Technical eclecticism and multimodal therapy. In Lebow J. L. (Ed.), *Twenty-first century psychotherapies: Contemporary approaches to theory and practice* (pp. 424–452). Hoboken, NJ: John Wiley & Sons.

Lazarus, A. A., & Beutler, L. E. (1993). On technical eclecticism. *Journal of Counseling and Development*, 71, 381–385.

Lazarus, A. A., Beutler, L. E., & Norcross, J. C. (1992). The future of technical eclecticism. *Psychotherapy*, 29, 11–20.

Lazarus, A. A., & Lazarus, C. N. (1991). *Multimodal life history inventory*. Champaign, IL: Research Press.

Rotter, J. B. (1954). *Social learning and clinical psychology*. Englewood Cliffs, NJ: Prentice Hall.

Williams, T. A. (1988). A multimodal approach to assessment and intervention with children with learning disabilities. Unpublished doctoral dissertation, Department of Psychology, University of Glasgow.

Wolpe, J. (1958). *Psychotherapy by reciprocal inhibition*. Stanford, CA: Stanford University Press.

Wolpe, J., & Lazarus, A. A. (1966). *Behavior therapy techniques*. New York: Pergamon Press.

47

POSITIVE PSYCHOLOGY: A BEHAVIORAL CONCEPTUALIZATION AND APPLICATION TO CONTEMPORARY BEHAVIOR THERAPY

Alyssa H. Kalata and Amy E. Naugle

Positive psychology is an emerging subfield within the broader field of psychology that is concerned primarily with the study of how individuals, families, communities, and institutions achieve optimal levels of functioning under normal circumstances (Gable & Haidt, 2005; Seligman & Csikzentmihalyi, 2000). Positive psychology is typically concerned with three main areas of inquiry: (1) positive emotion and/or positive subjective experience (e.g., happiness, hope, flow, well-being), (2) positive individual traits, strengths, virtues, and/or characteristics (e.g., creativity, wisdom, bravery, kindness, leadership, spirituality, patience, humor), and (3) positive institutions and/or groups and the characteristics associated with them (e.g., altruism, responsibility, work ethic, civility) (Bacon, 2005; Duckworth, Steen, & Seligman, 2005; Harris, Thorensen, & Lopez, 2007; Seligman & Csikzentmihalyi, 2000; Seligman, Steen, Park, & Peterson, 2005; Sheldon & King, 2001). These areas of study are fairly unique within the field of psychology, in that they do not focus on psychological dysfunction and the elimination of symptoms, nor are they framed from the perspective of the medical model (Cowen & Kilmer, 2002; Seligman, et al., 2005).

Although the definition of positive psychology seems relatively clear, concern has been expressed that the definition of positive psychology is in fact inconsistent and overly broad. Definitions of positive psychology have included a variety of terms and phrases, such as *assets, strengths, well-being, positive character traits, potentials, motives, capabilities, positive emotions, virtues,* and *positive institutions.* This inconsistency of terminology has made it unclear as to whether positive psychology represents a unitary construct or a variety of different constructs, an issue that has yet to be resolved by proponents of the positive psychology movement (Mollen, Ethington, & Ridley, 2006). Also unclear is the degree to which the concepts in positive psychology are transcendent versus contextual (Mollen, Ethington, & Ridley, 2006). Further commentary is needed regarding the extent to which these concepts are applicable across cultures and across generations within cultures.

THE HISTORICAL ROOTS OF POSITIVE PSYCHOLOGY

The Greek Influence

Much debate also exists regarding the specific point at which positive psychology emerged. The earliest historical antecedents of positive psychology could be attributed to the works of Aristotle, Plato, and Socrates (Duckworth, et al. 2005, Seligman & Csikzentmihalyi, 2000). Aristotle gave disproportionate amount of attention to the nature and value of pleasure, in comparison to his other areas of inquiry (Kraut, 2008). This notable amount of attention given to the topic perhaps reflects the extent to which Aristotle believed pleasure was to be valued. In his writings, Aristotle stated that he believed pleasure to one of the highest goods and had in fact stated that it was the highest good in some of his earlier works (Kraut, 2008). Of further note, Aristotle believed that pleasure was an activity, such that the experience of doing something could be experienced as pleasant, rather than merely the completion or outcome of an activity (Kraut, 2008). Plato devoted time to discussing the pursuit of the beautiful and the good, the attainment of which he believed led to happiness (Frede, 2007). He believed that part of this pursuit involved continual self-restoration and self-improvement, in response to the state of constant change within the world (Frede, 2007). Finally, although Socrates left no written works, his perspective is presumably represented in the works of Plato, who discussed and defined a number of virtues, including courage, temperance, reverence, wisdom, justice, and beauty from the perspective of Socrates (Woodruff, 2005). It is hypothesized that Socrates believed ethical virtue to be essential to the health of the soul (Woodruff, 2005).

Early Developments in Psychology

William James, considered to be one of the founders of psychology, was the first individual in the field of psychology to devote attention to topics relating to positive psychology in his work (Gable & Haidt, 2005). In 1902, James published *The Varieties of Religious Experience: A Study in Human Nature*, a text in which he devoted two lectures to the "religion of healthy-mindedness." In these lectures, James discussed the nature of happiness and the relationship of happiness and religious thought, in addition to providing some thoughts about ways in which happiness can be achieved. Psychology continued to develop rapidly through the earlier part of twentieth century and by the 1920s and 1930s, the field had been narrowed to primarily three topics of focus: (1) curing mental illness, (2) helping individuals live more productive and fulfilling lives, and (3) nurturing individuals with notable amounts of talent (Seligman & Csikzentmihalyi, 2000). In addition to work on curing mental illness, other common areas of study at this time included giftedness, marital happiness, effective parenting, and the search for and discovery of meaning of life (Seligman & Csikzentmihalyi, 2000). While curing mental illness has continued to be a primary focal point in psychology over

the course of its history, helping individuals to live more productive and fulfilling lives and nurturing individuals with large amounts of talent have become less common areas of inquiry.

Counseling Psychology

Paralleling the development of the field of psychology was the development of counseling psychology, a subdiscipline of psychology with an applied focus. The development of counseling psychology has some of its origin in the area of vocational counseling, which began to emerge in the early twentieth century. Early vocational counseling focused on identifying and increasing individual strengths and resources (Lopez, Magyar-Moe, Petersen, Ryder, Krieshok, O'Byrne, Lichtenberg, & Fry, 2006). Like early vocational counseling, early counseling psychology considered increasing personal and social resources of individuals to be important, in addition to "hygiology," or the study of the normal qualities of people (Lopez et al., 2006). Modern counseling psychology continues to value a focus on increasing the strengths and resources of individuals, which some authors have argued makes it difficult to differentiate from the current positive psychology movement.

Humanistic Psychology

As psychology in general, vocational counseling, and counseling psychology continued to develop, two additional fields emerged in the 1950s that also served as important historical antecedents to positive psychology. Humanistic psychology is a phenomenological approach to the understanding of human existence that places emphasis on defining the "good life," identifying contexts under which optimal human performance can occur, and identifying the conditions under which growth can be encouraged and enhanced (Duckworth et al., 2005, Lopez et al., 2006). In addition to these general themes, specific work by Carl Jung on personal and spiritual wholeness, Gordon Allport on positive human characteristics, Abraham Maslow on self-actualization and healthy individuals, Henry Murray on positive experiences and admirable traits, and Rollo May on human growth all could be argued to have influenced positive psychology as it is today (Duckworth et al., 2005; Gable & Haidt, 2005; Seligman et al., 2005; Taylor, 2001). During this same time period, the primary prevention and wellness enhancement movement was also beginning to develop. Marie Jahoda's *Current Concepts of Mental Health* was published in 1958 and outlined what she believed to be the six components of positive mental health (Cowen & Kilmer, 2002; Duckworth et al., 2005; Seligman et al., 2005). This provided the foundation for subsequent work in the area, which focused primarily on practices to prevent psychological dysfunction, although more contemporary work has also focused on enhancing well-being in addition to preventing dysfunction (Cowen & Kilmer, 2002).

CURRENT PERSPECTIVES IN THE POSITIVE PSYCHOLOGY MOVEMENT

In response to the somewhat heated debate about the influences and origins of positive psychology, Martin Seligman responded with his perspective about what he believes to be the origin of positive psychology. He noted that positive psychologists do not believe that they "invented" the subfield of positive psychology, independent of the aforementioned historical antecedents (Seligman et al., 2005). Instead, he argues that positive psychologists have united many separate lines of research and theory occurring across disciplines, have worked to create an overarching conceptual structure, and have more heavily emphasized the importance of rigorous, scientific study of areas pertaining to positive psychological thought (Duckworth et al., 2005; Seligman et al., 2005). Using this understanding of the origin of positive psychology, it could be argued that Seligman's election as president of the American Psychological Association in 1998 represents the origin of positive psychology. Since 1998, the First Positive Psychology Summit in 1999 and the issue of the American Psychologist devoted entirely to positive psychology in 2000 are considered to be two critical events in the recognition of contemporary positive psychology (Bacon, 2005; Simonton & Baumeister, 2005).

In the decade since positive psychology was first identified as a subfield of psychology, numerous books have been published, meetings have been held, centers have been developed, and graduate courses have been created (Seligman et al., 2005).

The development of positive psychotherapy has received far less scrutiny and attention than the development of positive psychology. The development of positive psychotherapy draws its origins from the time of Buddha, who spoke of ways to eliminate or reduce suffering through self-improvement (Seligman et al., 2005). The more contemporary human potential movement, which espoused achievement of human potentials as the key to building a life characterized by happiness and fulfillment, is also believed to have played an important role in providing a foundation for positive psychotherapy (Seligman et al., 2005). Most authors identify the official beginning of positive psychotherapy as occurring in 1988, when Michael Fordyce developed a therapy that focused on increasing activity and socialization, improving relationships, engaging in meaningful activities, and prioritizing happiness (Seligman et al., 2005; Seligman, Rashid, & Parks, 2006). A form of positive psychotherapy created by Seligman and colleagues has since been tested with positive results, although further testing is needed (Seligman et al., 2006).

BEHAVIORISM AND POSITIVE PSYCHOLOGY: COMMON FACTORS

Although positive psychology has begun to develop as a unique subfield within psychology, it continues to share much in common with the subfields and disciplines that have served as its historical antecedents. Furthermore, it shares much in common with other subfields of psychology that did not serve as historical antecedents, one of which is behavioral psychology. Behavioral psychology is a subfield of psychology that is concerned with both the overt and covert behaviors of organisms and the factors that influence these behaviors. Positive psychology and behavioral psychology share three important characteristics with each other.

A Constuctive Approach

First, both positive psychology and behavioral psychology take constructive, rather than eliminative, approaches to psychological health. Much of clinical psychology has traditionally focused primary on reducing symptoms of psychological distress and eliminating behavior problems, rather than focusing on increasing positive experiences and personal strengths (Follette, Linnerooth, & Ruckstuhl, 2001). Although reducing unpleasant psychological symptoms and eliminating behavior problems has helped numerous individuals, in many circumstances the mere absence of psychological symptoms or behavior problems does not entirely constitute a desired clinical outcome (Follette et al., 2001). Most individuals do not merely desire the absence of pain, sadness, anger, anxiety, and suffering; they also want lives characterized by joy, happiness, satisfaction, contentment, meaning, and purpose. It is a shared goal of positive psychology and behavioral psychology to help individuals build lives that are marked by these characteristics. In clinical behavior analysis, the area of behavioral psychology that focuses on applied clinical work, this constructivist framework is applied through the use of current client behavioral repertoires as building blocks for more adaptive repertoires. Using this approach to psychotherapy, the current client behavioral repertoires are built upon and enhanced, such that clients develop more adaptive repertoires that serve the same function as their current maladaptive behaviors (Follette et al., 2001). Many authors have argued that approaches that focus on increasing client strengths and other outcomes that are more explicitly positive in nature may actually be the most efficacious way to reduce psychological dysfunction (Cowen & Kilmer, 2002; Ellis & Ryan, 2005; Seligman & Csikzentmihalyi, 2000). Many hypotheses exist for why a constructivist approach may be the most efficacious way to reduce psychological dysfunction. From a behavioral standpoint, attempting to eliminate problem behaviors without providing clients with more adaptive repertoires often results in the client engaging in further problem behavior that serves the same

function. For example, a man who engages in problematic violations of his wife's privacy (e.g., reading her private journal) will likely engage in other behaviors serving the same function of getting information about his wife (e.g., checking her phone log, reading her e-mail) if his initial problem behaviors are somehow blocked (e.g., his wife hides or destroys her journal), unless he is taught more adaptive behaviors that serve the same function (e.g., appropriate communication skills to use with his wife).

A second hypothesis is that focusing on strengths may increase the likelihood of compliance with therapy, perhaps because of the reinforcing nature of the content of sessions, which in turn leads to the achievement of goals and therapy, and in some cases decreases in negative targets (Harris et al., 2007). Although it may seem as though positive psychology and behavioral psychology advocate for a solely constructivist approach to addressing psychological dysfunction and problematic behaviors, the intention of both subfields is to supplement current approaches to the treatment of psychological dysfunction, rather than replace them entirely. As Duckworth and colleagues (2005) state, these "build-what's-strong" approaches to therapy can serve as useful supplements to the "fix-what's-wrong" approaches that currently dominate the field.

Behavioral Flexibility

The second way in which positive psychology and behavioral psychology are similar is that they both focus on increasing behavioral flexibility. Behavioral flexibility, in this context, refers to the ability of an individual to apply an adaptive behavioral repertoire effectively in a variety of contexts and under a variety of different circumstances. Positive psychology makes explicit efforts to ensure that individuals are able to behave effectively in many different contexts (Follette et al., 2001). Similarly, a key focal point in behavioral psychology pertains to the generalization of skills learned in therapy to a variety of contexts outside of the therapeutic setting. Assessments in behavioral psychology almost always include strategies that examine clients' behavior outside of sessions, whether through the use of forms tracking their behavior throughout the day or through in person observations conducted by the therapist or a colleague of the therapist (e.g., school observations). Tasks that clients are assigned to do outside of therapy also explicitly target behavioral flexibility. A client who has difficulties with interpersonal communication will be asked to apply the skills learned and practiced in therapy with friends, coworkers, and family members outside of therapy sessions, just as a client with agoraphobia will be asked to complete tasks that involve him or her leaving the house. Both positive psychology and behavioral psychology recognize that therapy is only minimally useful if the skills taught in therapy are not applied outside of session.

The Importance of a Reinforcing Environment

The final way in which positive psychology and behavioral psychology are similar is in their emphasis on the use of positive reinforcement and the creation of reinforcing environments. Both positive psychology and behavioral psychology involve interventions in which selective attention and reinforcement are given when clients exhibit prosocial and adaptive behavioral repertoires. This is perhaps most commonly observed in work conducted with families and children although contemporary behavior therapies, such as Functional Analytic Psychotherapy, also commonly use this technique. In behavioral psychology, the goal is to strengthen adaptive behavior; reinforcement is almost always tried first when trying to alter a behavior, with punishment typically being used in instances in which reinforcement contingencies have not been effective. Both positive psychology and behavioral psychology also emphasize the modification of environments as an intervention to increase and sustain positive behavioral changes (Follette et al., 2001). Environments tend to shape people more than people tend to shape their environments, so as such it is important for clinicians to be aware of circumstances in which environmental changes can be made to help create and sustain positive behavioral changes (Linley, 2006). Finally, extending beyond clinical interventions, other authors have advocated

for increased reciprocal positive reinforcement in society more generally, as it has the potential to impact society in a desirable fashion (Catania, 2001).

CONTEMPORARY BEHAVIORAL THERAPIES AND POSITIVE PSYCHOLOGY

Positive psychology also shares much in common with evidence-based practice and contemporary cognitive behavioral interventions. Cognitive behavioral therapy, as a therapeutic approach, has a number of broad goals that can be found across each of the more specific cognitive behavioral therapies and techniques. These goals include increasing participation in valued activities or activities that are consistent with one's short- and long-term goals, increasing the degree to which one is focused on and mindful of these activities while doing them, decreasing avoidance through approach behaviors and the development of more adaptive repertoires, and developing more adaptive behavioral skills. In general, cognitive behavioral therapy is about building a life worth living, rather than merely eliminating symptoms. These overarching goals of cognitive behavioral therapy are all consistent with the goals of positive psychology. In addition, the goals in positive psychotherapy of increasing the amount of time one experiences the "pleasant life" (which involves experiencing positive emotions about the past, present, and future and developing skills to increase the intensity and duration of these emotions), the "engaged life" (which involves absorption in ones work, relationships, and leisure activities), and the "meaningful life" (which involves applying one's strengths to something bigger than oneself and finding meaning in one's life) are all consistent with the goals of cognitive behavioral therapy.

Four specific contemporary behavioral and cognitive behavioral interventions with varying degrees of empirical support have emerged in recent years: (1) behavioral activation (BA), (2) dialectical behavior therapy (DBT), (3) functional analytic psychotherapy (FAP), and (4) acceptance and commitment therapy (ACT). Although each of these therapies takes a unique approach, themes of both cognitive behavioral therapy and positive psychology can be observed throughout each of them.

Behavioral Activation

In many respects, BA is the antithesis to an eliminative, symptom-focused approach. BA involves building positive experiences through engaging in activities that make one feel pleasure, mastery, or both. Positive experiences that are intended to simply evoke positive emotions in the moment address the hedonistic aspects of positive psychology. Scheduling pleasant events is one of the primary features of BA, in which individuals specifically schedule time to engage in activities that they currently enjoy, or have enjoyed in the past. This component of BA addresses the "pleasant life," discussed by Seligman and colleagues (2006), as it helps to evoke positive emotions in the present, which in turn often leads to an increase in the intensity and duration of positive emotions experienced over the course of time. Another key component of BA involves scheduling activities that lead to one experiencing a sense of mastery. Frequently, these activities address issues of long-term happiness and building a life worth living. This component of BA relates more closely to the "engaged life" discussed by Seligman and colleagues (2006), as doing things that make one feel masterful often involves identifying one's strengths and applying them. In addition to building in positive experiences, BA approaches also have clients identify circumstances in which they are engaging in avoidance patterns. Once these patterns are identified, adaptive behaviors that can be engaged in instead of the avoidance pattern are determined, and clients are asked to use these adaptive behaviors in future situations during which they want to engage in avoidance. Finally, BA typically includes a problem-solving component, during which clients learn more effective systems to address problems as they arise. All of these strategies emphasize the constructivist approach of BA, in that BA addresses both pleasant emotions in the moment, as well as developing more adaptive behavioral repertoires to build strengths that increase the likelihood of future positive experiences.

Dialectical Behavior Therapy

The focus of DBT, "building a life worth living," is also very consistent with a positive psychology approach. Although DBT does focus on the elimination of problematic behaviors, it does so in the context of giving patients an extensive repertoire of behavioral skills to utilize in developing a more adaptive repertoire. DBT involves four primary sets of skills: (1) core mindfulness, (2) interpersonal effectiveness, (3) emotion regulation, and (4) distress tolerance. Each of these sets of skills involves specific interventions that are very similar to many of the interventions utilized in positive psychotherapy.

The core mindfulness skills in DBT play an important role in all the other skills that are learned, in that they teach clients to become fully aware of their experiences, to participate fully in these experiences, and to do so in a non-judgmental manner. The core mindfulness module helps clients to become aware of their emotional states and to diminish the amount of time they spend struggling to either push their emotions away or hold on to their emotions. In positive psychotherapy, the "good versus bad memories" exercise involves having clients willingly feel anger and bitterness they have been holding on to and also involves discussion about the effect of holding on to these emotions (Seligman, et al., 2006). This exercise fits well within the core mindfulness exercises of DBT that involve having clients learn to become aware of their emotions and experience them as they are, without struggling to push the emotions away or keep them around for an extended period of time.

The interpersonal effectiveness module helps clients to learn skills to make requests of others or skillfully turn down requests that are made of them, to communicate in a manner that is likely to maintain or increase the quality of their relationships, and to communicate in a manner that does not compromise their self-respect. One of the positive psychotherapy exercises, "love and attachment," focuses on teaching clients to respond actively and constructively to positive events by others (Seligman, et al., 2006). This skill is very similar to the GIVE skill in DBT, which encourages clients to be gentle, act interested, validate, and use an easy manner when having interpersonal interactions. Although the GIVE skill in DBT is intended more for use in conflicts and the "love and attachment" exercise is more intended for use in everyday conversation, both of the skills involve teaching clients to develop more effective interpersonal repertoires that involve actively listening to a conversational partner.

The emotion regulation module in DBT involves having clients learn to identify their emotions, the function these emotions serve, ways to decrease emotional vulnerability, ways to increase positive emotions, and how to reduce painful emotions through mindfulness and opposite action. This module takes a constructivist approach to reducing painful emotions and increasing pleasant emotions, through having clients attend to their basic needs (e.g., eating, sleep, exercise), become involved in activities that give them a sense of mastery, through working on short- and long-term goals, through awareness of positive experiences, and through directly engaging in adaptive behaviors that are opposite to those behaviors they may have urges to engage in. Examples of homework assignments one might encounter in positive psychotherapy, include having clients incorporate activities that make them feel pleasant in the moment (e.g., a daily walk), that make them feel competent over a longer period of time (e.g., taking a computer class), and that encourage clients to be mindful of pleasant experiences or sensations throughout the day (e.g., noticing beautiful things throughout the day). All of these exercises are similar to those that would be assigned for homework during the emotion regulation module of DBT.

Finally, the distress tolerance module of DBT focuses on activities that clients can engage in during times of distress. These include self-soothing through the use of the five senses, using imagery, engaging in relaxing or pleasant activities, helping or doing nice things for others, and finding meaning in adversity. Many exercises in positive psychotherapy are similar to those presented in the distress tolerance module of DBT. As an example, the "gift of time" exercise involves applying one's strengths to serve something bigger than

oneself. This exercise is similar to those in DBT that encourage clients to contribute to others and to find meaning. Extending beyond positive psychotherapy, the skills learned in DBT also apply to the broader concepts of the "pleasant life," the "engaged life," and the "meaningful life" discussed in positive psychology, as the skills help clients to find ways to increase the number of pleasant experiences they have, to help them become more mindful of their experiences, and to build lives that are imbued with meaning.

The very structure of DBT is one that emphasizes a progression toward building a life worth living. While the first two stages of DBT focus on eliminating symptoms in the context of building skills, the later stages focus much more heavily on topics relevant to positive psychology. Stage three of DBT focuses on increasing respect for self and achieving individual goals and stage four of DBT focuses on resolving lingering feelings of incompleteness and finding freedom and joy. Both of these stages move far beyond merely eliminating symptoms of problem behaviors.

Functional Analytic Psychotherapy

FAP involves working with individuals to develop a more adaptive social repertoire that ultimately helps them to have meaningful, well-functioning social relationships, often with the by-product of an increase in meaningfulness and joy in their lives. This goal is accomplished in part through natural, contingent reinforcement provided by therapists during sessions. Therapists taking a FAP approach look for three primary behaviors, all variations of "clinically relevant behaviors" (CRBs) on the part of the client: (1) CRB1s, which are problem behaviors that the client engages in during session that are also likely problematic outside of session, (2) CRB2s, which are improvements in client behavior that are observed during session, and (3) CRB3s, which are client descriptions of the variables that affect their behavior (Callaghan, Naugle, & Follette, 1996). Therapists respond contingently to each of these behaviors immediately after they have occurred in session. With CRB1s, the therapist provides immediate feedback about how the behavior of the client has impacted him or her. The therapist then works to shape responses that are described as CRB2s and CRB3s, through eliciting and reinforcing more adaptive behaviors. The very nature of FAP is consistent with that of positive psychology, in that the focus is on building more effective repertoires and abilities, rather than simply eliminating psychological distress. As discussed previously, some of the exercises in positive psychotherapy focus on helping individuals to develop interpersonal repertoires that are likely to help them to have more meaningful and fulfilling relationships with others, making FAP and positive psychotherapy very similar in this respect. Also consistent with positive psychology, the mechanism through which more adaptive interpersonal repertoires are developed in FAP is through natural reinforcement and extinction procedures on the part of the therapist, versus more punitive, aversive consequences. This approach is also consistent with that of positive psychology, which highlights the use of positive reinforcement as one particular mechanism of change. Furthermore, this approach is believed to assist in generalization, in that the therapeutic relationship and responses made within it are approached like a relationship outside of the therapeutic context.

Acceptance and Commitment Therapy

ACT, like all of the aforementioned contemporary behavior therapies, also involves helping individuals to develop abilities and strengths, rather than merely eliminating symptoms and problems. ACT is so similar to positive psychological approaches that some authors have stated that ACT is actually considered to be a form of positive psychology (Duckworth, et al, 2005). ACT in particular seeks to decrease experiential avoidance, in part through the constructivist approach of helping individuals to live their lives in an engaged, values-consistent manner (Follette, et al., 2001). This involves first learning mindfulness and acceptance skills, which are later applied in the process of values-based living. Values-based living involves having individuals identify their values in a number of different domains (e.g., intimate relationships,

career or employment, recreation or leisure) and then identify the degree to which they value these domains and the degree to which they are living consistently or inconsistently with them. Once this information is gathered, specific short- and long-term goals are identified to help the individuals begin to live more consistently with their values. This approach is very consistent with the focus on living the "engaged life" and the "meaningful life" that are essential components of positive psychotherapy. Furthermore, in both ACT and positive psychology approaches, an emphasis is placed on both the processes and the outcomes in life, in that efforts are made to make both positive experiences (Follette, et al, 2001). In ACT, values are identified to provide a "compass" for one's life, rather than a concrete endpoint. In this respect, the pleasure of the process, living consistently with one's values, is emphasized. However, goals are also identified in ACT, which provide specific and achievable outcomes that can be celebrated. Finally, in ACT, it is emphasized that the focus of treatment is not explicitly to eliminate pain and suffering. ACT approaches explicitly focus on ending the struggle with painful emotions and psychological symptoms and instead focus on devoting the energy from that struggle toward values-based living. In this respect, the ACT approach represents the essence of positive psychology.

CRITICISMS OF POSITIVE PSYCHOLOGY

While positive psychology has much to offer and already shares much in common with behavioral psychology and evidence-based practices, many authors have offered a number of critiques of positive psychology and have suggested some areas for growth within the discipline. First, many authors have expressed concern that positive psychology has failed to adequately identify its connections to earlier work done in a variety of subfields within the broader field of psychology, such as counseling psychology and vocational psychology, as well as work in other disciplines, such as primary prevention and wellness enhancement (Cowen & Kilmer, 2002; Linley, 2006; Lopez et al., 2006; Mollen, Ethington, & Ridley, 2006; Rich, 2003). More recent works in the positive psychology area (e.g., Duckworth et al., 2005) have addressed this issue and acknowledged that positive psychology is not the first discipline to study the primary topics of positive psychology scientifically. However, the future of positive psychology may depend in part on the willingness of the discipline to acknowledge both its historical antecedents to a greater degree and to work to establish connections with other disciplines.

Second, some authors have noted that positive psychology in its present form lacks a cohesive, guiding theoretical framework (Cowen & Kilmer, 2002). In order for a subfield of psychology to progress as a science, it must have a clearly articulated and coherent theoretical model to guide the development of the science. The perceived lack of consistency or agreement among proponents of the positive psychology movement regarding terminology and constructs is largely what fuels this criticism.

Third, many authors have noted that positive psychology has neglected a number of different populations and areas. Particular concern has been expressed that positive psychology focuses primarily on adulthood, without giving a great deal of attention to childhood and adolescence (Cowen & Kilmer, 2003). Rich (2003) notes that the literature available on adolescence has focused almost entirely on problem behaviors, such as suicide, pregnancy, delinquency, violence, and substance abuse, rather than topics that are addressed in the positive psychology literature. However, Gable and Haidt (2005) note that in more recent years, an increased amount of attention has been given to the positive psychology of youth and adolescence, as an entire issue of the *Journal of Youth and Adolescence* from 2003 focused on this precise topic. Other authors have expressed concern that positive psychology may be prescribing a vision of a unitary "good life" that may not be applicable to the values and morals of all cultures, or even of all individuals (La Torre, 2007; Lopez et al., 2006; Rich 2003). The need for positive psychology to become aware of the ways in which it is bound and influenced by western European and American norms has been noted (Linley, 2006). Finally, authors have noted that additional attention to positive institutions and communities is needed (Gable & Haidt, 2005).

Fourth, some authors have argued that positive psychology is continuing to operate within the medical model from which the movement has been making efforts to break away (Joseph & Linley, 2006; La Torre, 2007). These authors have noted that much of the work in positive psychology continues to operate from a dichotomous model of human experience, rather than a continuum approach, one of the hallmark traits of the medical model. In addition, the categorical approach taken by the "un-DSM" of positive psychology, *Character Strengths and Virtues: A Handbook of Classification*, continues to keep positive psychology more closely aligned with the medical model. On the other hand, the pervasiveness of the medical model within positive psychology may be the result of the movement's attempt to gain credibility through operating within the current zeitgeist.

Finally, concern has been expressed that positive psychology has not addressed ways in which it can be applied in the daily work of counselors, who work in settings that are time limited, restricted by insurance companies and financial constraints, and that are pathology oriented (Harris, et al., 2007). The degree to which positive psychology will permeate the field of psychology depends in part on its ability to find ways to become relevant and useful in these contexts.

CONCLUSION

Positive psychology has grown considerably since its inception in 1998 and optimism that it will continue to grow has increased as proponents of the positive psychology movement have acknowledged the subfield's historical predecessors and have made connections with existing fields within psychology. Positive psychology shares many common factors with behaviorism and contemporary behavior therapies and potential areas of collaboration are becoming increasingly apparent. As positive psychology continues to develop a conceptual framework and increase its body of empirical literature, it is likely that the relevance of the positive psychology movement to clinical practice and other areas of psychology will become increasingly apparent.

References

Bacon, S. F. (2005). Positive psychology's two cultures. *Review of General Psychology, 9*(2), 181–192.

Callaghan, G. M., Naugle, A. E., & Follette, W. C. (1996). Useful constructions of the client–therapist relationship. *Psychotherapy, 33*(3), 381–390.

Catania, A. C. (2001). Positive psychology and positive reinforcement. *American Psychologist, 56*(1), 86-87.

Cowen, E. L. & Kilmer, R. P. (2002). Positive psychology: Some plusses and some open issues. *Journal of Community Psychology, 30*(4), 449–460.

Duckworth, A. L., Steen, T. A., & Seligman, M. E. P. (2005). Positive psychology in clinical practice. *Annual Review of Clinical Psychology, 1,* 629–651.

Ellis, R., & Ryan, J. A. (2005). Emotional intelligence and positive psychology: Therapist tools for training/coaching clients to move beyond emotional relief. *Annals of the American Psychotherapy Association, 8*(3), 42–43.

Follette, W. C., Linnerooth, P. J. N., & Ruckstuhl, L. E. (2001). Positive psychology: A clinical behavior analytic perspective. *Journal of Humanistic Psychology, 41*(1), 102–134.

Frede, D. *Plato's Ethics: An Overview*. Retrieved March 4, 2008, from the Stanford Encyclopedia of Philosophy http://plato.stanford.edu/entries/plato-ethics/.

Gable, S. L. & Haidt, J. (2005). What (and why) is positive psychology? *Review of General Psychology, 9*(2), 103–110.

Harris, A. H. S., Thorensen, C. E., & Lopez, S. J. (2007). Integrating positive psychology into counseling: why and (when appropriate) how. *Journal of Counseling & Development, 85,* 3–13.

James, W. (1902). *The varieties of religious experience: A study in human nature*. Retrieved March 5, 2008, from Project Gutenberg. www.gutenberg.org/dirs/etext96/varre10.txt.

Joseph, S., & Linley, P. A. (2006). Positive psychology versus the medical model? *American Psychologist, 61*(4), 332–333.

Kraut, R. (2008). *Aristotle's ethics*. Retrieved March 4, 2008, from the Stanford Encyclopedia of Philosophy http://plato.stanford.edu/entries/aristotle-ethics/.

La Torre, M. A. (2007). Positive psychology: is there too much of a push? *Perspectives in Psychiatric Care, 43*(3), 151–153.

Linley, A. P. (2006). Counseling psychology's positive psychological agenda: a model for integration and inspiration. *The Counseling Psychologist, 34*(2), 313–322.

Lopez, S. J. & Magyar-Moe, J. L. (2006). A positive psychology that matters. *The Counseling Psychologist, 34*(2), 323–330.

Lopez, S. J., Magyar-Moe, J. L., Petersen, S. E., Ryder, J. A., Krieshok, T. S., O'Byrne, K. K., et al. (2006). Counseling psychology's focus on positive aspects of human functioning. *The Counseling Psychologist, 34*(2), 205–227.

Mollen, D., Ethington, L. L., & Ridley, C. R. (2006). Positive psychology: considerations and implications for counseling psychology. *The Counseling Psychologist, 34*(2), 304–312.

Rich, G. J. (2003). The positive psychology of youth and adolescence. *Journal of Youth and Adolescence, 32*(1), 1–3.

Seligman, M. E. P., & Csikszentmihalyi, M. (2000). Positive psychology: An introduction. *American Psychologist, 55*(1), 5–14.

Seligman, M. E. P., Rashid, T., & Parks, A. C. (2006). Positive psychotherapy. *American Psychologist, 61*(8), 772–788.

Seligman, M. E. P., Steen, T. A., Park, N., & Peterson, C. (2005). Positive psychology progress: Empirical validation of interventions. *American Psychologist, 60*(5), 410–421.

Sheldon, K. M. & King, L. (2001). Why positive psychology is necessary. *American Psychologist, 56*(3), 216–217.

Simonton, D. K. & Baumeister, R. F. (2005). Positive psychology at the summit. *Review of General Psychology, 9*(2), 99–102.

Taylor, E. (2001). Positive psychology and humanistic psychology: a reply to Seligman. *Journal of Humanistic Psychology, 41*(1), 13–29.

Woodruff, P. (2005). *Plato's Shorter Ethical Works*. Retrieved March 4, 2008, from the Stanford Encyclopedia of Philosophy, http://plato.stanford.edu/entries/plato-ethics-shorter/.

48 MOTIVATIONAL INTERVIEWING

Eric R. Levensky, Brian C. Kersh,
Lavina L. Cavasos, and J. Annette Brooks

A particular challenge clinicians often face when attempting to help clients make significant behavioral changes (e.g., stop smoking or using drugs or alcohol, start engaging in medication adherence, proper diet, or exercise), is getting the clients motivated to make these changes and committed to a particular course of therapeutic action. This challenge arises because behavioral changes of this nature are difficult to achieve, and client motivation is considered to be an important ingredient in producing such changes (Garfield, 1994; Miller, 1985).

Motivational interviewing (MI; Miller & Rollnick, 2002; Arkowitz, Westra, Miller & Rollnick, 2008; Rollnick, Miller & Butler, 2007) is a psychosocial intervention described by its developers as, "a directive, client-centered counseling style for eliciting behavior change by helping clients to explore and resolve ambivalence" (Rollnick & Miller (1995, p. 326). Originally developed for the treatment of alcohol abuse, MI has become a widely used treatment for a variety of substance use disorders, and has also been adapted to promote behavior change in a number of other areas, including treatment adherence, HIV risk, exercise, diet, and gambling. These adaptations have ranged from as brief as 5–15-minute interventions in medical settings to multiple-session interventions in traditional mental health settings (see Miller & Rollnick, 2002; Arkowitz, Westra, Miller & Rollnick, 2008; Rollnick, Miller & Butler, 2007 for reviews of this literature).

RESEARCH ON THE EFFICACY OF MI

Outcome evaluations of MI have been conducted across a range of adaptations of the approach (see Burke, Arkowitz, & Menchola, 2003; Dunn, Deroo, & Rivara, 2001; Hettema, Steele, & Miller, 2005; Lawendowski, 1998; Miller, 1996; Rollnick & Miller, 1995; and Rollnick, Miller, & Butler, 2007, for reviews of this literature). These evaluations have most often examined the efficacy of MI as an intervention for problem drinking, and have generally found MI to produce significant reductions in alcohol use, as well as increased participation in treatment (Dunn, Deroo, & Rivara, 2001; Hettema, Steele, & Miller, 2005). Motivational Interviewing has also been shown to be effective as a relatively brief intervention. For example, the multisite Project MATCH (Project MATCH Research Group, 1997) found that a 4-session version of MI was as effective as were more intensive (12-session) cognitive behavioral and 12-step treatments for problems drinkers.

In recent years, MI has garnered support for its efficacy in other domains of health behavior change. Hettema, Steele, and Miller (2005) conducted a systematic meta-analysis of 72 randomized clinical trials of adaptations of MI for the behavioral domains of alcohol abuse (31 studies), illicit drug abuse (14 studies), smoking (6 studies), HIV risk reduction (5 studies), treatment adherence (5 studies), diet/exercise (4 studies), water purification to promote health (4 studies), gambling (1 study), intimate relationships (1 study), and eating disorders (1 study). These authors found significant support for the efficacy of MI across these studies, with an average effect size of 0.77 immediately following treatment and 0.30 at follow-ups of about 1 year. Given that the average effect size for standard cognitive-behavioral therapies for substance abuse disorders is 0.30 immediately following treatment (Dutra et al., 2008), the outcomes of MI are quite promising.

Several other findings in the Hettema, Steele, and Miller study were particularly noteworthy. First, the effect sizes for MI tended to be larger in studies conducted with primarily ethnic minority samples. Second, a trend existed indicating that effect sizes were significantly lower in studies that used a manual-guided version of MI, suggesting that clinicians may deliver the treatment more effectively when they are free to act in accordance with their own and the client's individual differences. Third, MI seems to work particularly well with most addictive behaviors with the exception of tobacco use, which had low overall effect sizes. More recent research in the use of MI for smoking cessation, however, has produced some promising preliminary results (Rollnick, Miller & Butler, 2007).

WHO MIGHT BENEFIT FROM MI?

MI has been shown to be effective across a wide variety of health-behavior change domains. Theoretically, the basic principles and techniques of MI are applicable to any type of behavior change targets. What is required in successfully adapting MI to a new behavioral domain is faithfully applying the "spirit" (see later discussion) of MI when applying the techniques and strategies of the approach (Rollnick & Miller, 1995).

MI has also been shown to be effective in working with individuals from a wide range of nations and populations (Arkowitz & Miller, 2008). As noted previously, MI studies in the United States have demonstrated larger effect sizes on average for ethnic minority groups relative to Anglo/Caucasian samples. Given the approach's emphasis on the *client's* values, goals, and perspectives, as opposed to those of the clinician or majority culture, it is not surprising that MI may be a particularly culturally sensitive approach and that it would be effective across population domains, including age, gender, and sexual orientation, as well as ethnicity.

THEORETICAL UNDERPINNINGS OF MI

MI is well rooted in the transtheoretical model of change (Prochaska & DiClemente 1982;

Prochaska, DiClemente, & Norcross, 1992). This model explains behavior change as a process in which individuals pass through a series of five stages of change:

1. The *precontemplation* stage, during which the client does not believe that the behavior is a problem and is not intending to change the behavior in the near future
2. The *contemplation* stage, during which the client is considering changing the behavior but is ambivalent about doing so
3. The *preparation* stage, during which the client has decided to change the behavior and has a specific plan for doing so in the near future
4. The *action* stage, during which the client has actually made a behavioral change
5. The *maintenance* stage, during which the client takes actions to avoid a behavioral relapse

The transtheoretical model assumes that behavior change is a cyclical process, and that people tend to relapse and progress through the stages several times before successfully maintaining change. This model is an important component to MI in that it orients the clinician to first understand the client's current level of readiness to change, and then to work accordingly at facilitating the client's successful movement through these stages. This idea of working with clients "where they're at" in terms of readiness for change is crucial in MI. Of particular focus is helping clients move successfully through the contemplation and preparation stages.

To date, research on MI has not definitively identified the causal mechanisms of the approach. Initially, Miller & Rollnick (1991) suggested that MI produced behavioral change by creating an uncomfortable discrepancy for clients between how they would like to be living their lives (i.e., their values and goals) and how the clients are currently living (e.g., consequences of behavioral problem). These authors proposed that clients are motivated to reduce this uncomfortable discrepancy and, in the context of a directive, reflective, supportive, and nonconfrontational therapeutic interaction, do so by making behavioral changes that are consistent with their life goals and values.

Although this concept of discrepancy between values and behaviors remains important in the practice of MI, current views regarding the causal mechanisms of MI place less emphasis on this aspect as a sole agent of change.

Arkowitz, Miller, Westra, and Rollnick (2008) describe three hypothesized mechanisms to account for the efficacy of MI: the *directive*, *relational*, and *conflict resolution* hypotheses. The *directive* hypothesis emphasizes the role of client language and the importance of clinician behaviors with regard to eliciting "change talk" (i.e., client statements regarding desire, ability, need, reason, and/or commitment to change). This hypothesis stresses the value of clinician behaviors that reduce resistance and "counterchange talk" (i.e., arguments against change) and that evoke and reinforce change talk. The directive hypothesis is underscored by Miller and Rollnick (2002) and is supported by research regarding the impact of client talk on subsequent behavior change (Miller, Benefield, & Tonigan, 1993; Amrhein, Miller, Yahne, Palmer, & Fulcher, 2003; Moyers et al., 2007).

The *relational* hypothesis focuses primarily on the therapeutic relationship itself rather than on clinician behaviors that direct clients toward a particular goal. This perspective emphasizes the importance of the non-directive, client-centered atmosphere described by Carl Rogers, and suggests that this atmosphere alone is sufficient for producing healthy client change (Arkowitz, Miller, Westra, & Rollnick, 2008).

According to the *conflict resolution* hypothesis, it is crucial that, during the therapy session, clients explore *both* sides of their ambivalence regarding a particular behavioral change. That is, clinicians elicit arguments for as well as against change in a client-centered atmosphere, which promotes resolution of ambivalence. The conflict resolution hypothesis differs from the directive hypothesis in that it emphasizes the evocation of counterchange arguments, and differs from the relational hypothesis in that it stresses a more directive approach. Although these three perspectives hypothesize different mechanisms to account for the efficacy of MI, all share the assumption that clinician behaviors greatly impact client motivation. More research is needed to better understand the causal mechanisms of MI.

THE PRACTICE OF MOTIVATIONAL INTERVIEWING

The purpose of this chapter is to describe MI such that clinicians can come to understand the basic principles and techniques of this approach. Motivational Interviewing can be a rather technically complex intervention, and a comprehensive description of its techniques is beyond the scope of this chapter. However, it is hoped that the information provided here will serve as a useful primer. Readers are encouraged to refer to the more comprehensive descriptions of MI techniques listed in the "Further Reading" section at the conclusion of this chapter.

Rollnick & Miller (1995) propose that essential to the effective delivery of MI is that clinicians understand and act in accordance with the spirit of the approach, rather than merely applying the strategies and techniques that make up the treatment. A useful way to convey this spirit of MI is to contrast it with the assumptions and practices of other common approaches to promoting behavior change. Miller and Rollnick (1991) contrast important elements (e.g., principles, strategies, and techniques) of MI with key elements of *confrontation-of-denial*, *skills training*, and *nondirective* approaches to behavior change. These contrasting elements are presented here in Table 48.1. Several fundamental aspects of the MI spirit illustrated in this table are that (1) ambivalence is a normal part of the change process, (2) clinicians must be nonconfrontational and must meet clients "where they're are at" motivationally, (3) clinicians build intrinsic motivation by systematically eliciting the client's own reasons for change (i.e., change talk), (4) collaboration and client autonomy must be explicit and fostered, and (5) clients already have what is needed to make changes.

Basic Principles

As previously stated, MI is more of a principal-based stylistic approach clinicians can take to producing behavior change than a

TABLE 48.1   Contrasts between Motivational Interviewing and Other Common Methods of Producing Behavior Change

Confrontation-of-Denial Approach	Motivational Interviewing Approach
Heavy emphasis on acceptance of self as having a problem; acceptance of diagnosis seen as essential for change	De-emphasis on labels; acceptance of "alcoholism" or other labels seen as unnecessary for change to occur
Emphasis on personality pathology, which reduces personal choice, judgement, and control	Emphasis on personal choice and responsibility for deciding future behavior
Therapist presents perceived evidence of problems in an attempt to convince the client to accept the diagnosis	Therapist conducts objective evaluation, but focuses on eliciting the client's own concerns
Resistance is seen as "denial," a trait characteristic requiring confrontation	Resistance is seen as an interpersonal behavior pattern influenced by the therapist's behavior
Resistance is met with argumentation and correction	Resistance is met with reflection
Goals of treatment and strategies for change are prescribed for the client by the therapist; client is seen as "in denial" and incapable of making sound decisions	Treatment goals and change strategies are negotiated between client and therapist, based on data and acceptability; client's involvement in and acceptance of goals are seen as vital

Skill-Training Approach	Motivational Interviewing Approach
Assumes that the client is motivated; no direct strategies are used for building motivation	Employs specific principles and strategies for building client motivation for change
Seeks to identify and modify maladaptive cognitions	Explores and reflects client perceptions without labeling or "correcting" them
Prescribes specific coping strategies	Elicits possible change strategies from the client and significant others
Teaches coping behaviors through instruction, modeling, directed practice, and feedback	Responsibility for change methods is left with the client; no training, modeling, or practice
Specific problem-solving strategies are taught	Natural problem-solving processes are elicited from the client and significant others

Nondirective Approach	Motivational Interviewing Approach
Allows the client to determine the content and direction of counseling	Systematically directs the client toward motivation for change
Avoids injecting the counselor's own advice and feedback	Offers the counselor's own advice and feedback where appropriate
Empathetic reflection is used noncontingently	Empathetic reflection is used selectively, to reinforce certain processes
Explores the client's conflicts and emotions as they exist currently	Seeks to create and amplify the client's discrepancy in order to enhance motivation for change

Source: Reprinted, with permission, from Miller, W. R., & Rollnick, S. (1991). *Motivational interviewing: Preparing people for change.* New York: Guilford.

specific set of techniques clinician use in therapy. Miller and Rollnick (1991, 2002) provide four basic principles to guide the clinician as he or she applies the spirit of MI to the therapy session.

1. *Express empathy.* The clinician communicates understanding and acceptance of the client's feelings and perspectives, including difficulties with, and ambivalence about, change.
2. *Develop discrepancy.* The clinician facilitates the client's awareness of discrepancies between his or her current behavior and stated personal goals and values. MI assumes that for

change to take place, the *client* must present the arguments for change, not the clinician.

3. *Roll with resistance.* The clinician avoids argumentation, and instead uses the momentum of client resistance to foster change by inviting the client to consider new points of view and by enlisting the client to be an active participant in the process of change. (Please refer to the "Responding to Resistance" section).
4. *Support self-efficacy.* The clinician enhances the client's confidence in his or her ability to engage in the necessary change-related behaviors. MI assumes that client autonomy

in choosing if and how to change, and the clinician's expressed belief in the client's abilities are key elements in producing change.

Basic Method

The principles of MI can be instantiated in a number of different ways, depending on change targets, setting, population, and resources. A wide variety of MI adaptations are described in detail in Miller & Rollnick (2002), Arkowitz, Westra, Miller & Rollnick (2008), and Rollnick, Miller & Butler (2007). The basic method of MI is described here.

The essential task of the clinician in MI is to engage in behaviors that will enhance clients' intrinsic motivation to make behavioral changes. Motivational Interviewing provides clinicians with a set of specific therapeutic behaviors thought to produce this motivation through helping the client to identify and resolve his or her ambivalence about change. These behaviors center around eliciting and reinforcing client change talk, and include asking open-ended questions, listening reflectively, responding to resistance in a nonconfrontational manner, affirming the client, and summarizing. Each of these is described in the following sections.

Eliciting Change Talk

As discussed previously, MI assumes that most often clients have personal goals and values connected to their health-related behaviors; that clients may at times have little motivation to change, but that motivation is malleable; and that the way in which clinicians interact with clients relative to a particular health behavior change target can influence motivation for behavior change. These assumptions are grounded in concept that is fundamental to the practice of MI: *ambivalence*. Ambivalence is thought of as a state in which clients have compelling reasons for both changing their behavior and not changing it. An example of such ambivalence would be an individual wanting to stop smoking to increase the quality of his health and spousal relationship *and* not wanting to stop because in doing so he would lose the stress-reduction and weight control benefits of cigarette use. In MI, the clinician works to "tip the scale" of this ambivalence in

favor of change by eliciting from the client a discussion of the pros of change relative to the cons of change. The clinician does this not by presenting arguments to the client for the existence of a problem or for the need for change, but rather by having the *client* generate these arguments. Specifically, the clinician attempts to elicit *change talk* from the client by encouraging him or her to discuss the behavior of interest and its consequences in the context of the client's personal values and goals. Rollnick, Miller, and Butler (2007) describe several classes of such client change talk, which make up the acronym "DARN-CT":

- *Desire:* Statements that describe the client's preferences for change
- *Ability:* Statements that validate a client's ability to change
- *Reasons:* Statements that are arguments and reasons a client has for change
- *Need:* Statements that communicate the client's feelings of obligation to change
- *Commitment:* Statements that assert an intention to change
- *Taking steps:* Statements about actions taken toward behavior change

A method frequently used by the clinician in eliciting change talk is to ask the client questions regarding the problem behavior (or the lack of behavior) and its consequences. An important distinction here is that, whenever possible, the MI clinician asks *open-ended* questions, as opposed to *closed-ended*. The basic difference between these is that an open-ended question allows the client to elaborate, whereas a closed-ended question merits only a "yes" or "no" response. An example of a closed-ended question would be, "Do you plan on drinking less this weekend?" This same basic question could be communicated in an open-ended manner by the clinician asking, "What are your plans with regard to drinking this weekend?" Other examples of open-ended questions focused on eliciting change talk include the following:

- What specifically do you want to change [desire]?

- What makes you believe that you could take your medications as prescribed [ability]?
- What are some of your concerns about your diet [reasons]?
- Why is it important for you to quit drinking [need]?
- How likely is it that you will make the changes in your diet you talked about today [commitment]?
- What steps have you already taken toward changing your drinking patterns [taking steps]?

In MI, the clinician follows these open-ended questions up with reflective statements focused on specific content of the client's change talk. These reflections are intended to prompt the client to make additional change talk statements or to elaborate on change-talk statements. For example, in response to the open-ended question, "What are some of your concerns about your diet?" a client may respond, "Well, I know that my blood sugars are too high most of the time, and I know that it's not healthy." A reflective follow-up statement from the clinician might be, "You are concerned that frequent high blood sugars may be adding to your health problems." Further open-ended questions about the client's goals for the future and the impact of the problem behavior on the client's ability to reach these goals are also often asked, and are followed up with reflections.

Reflective Listening

As exemplified earlier, reflective listening is used in conjunction with open-ended questions as a primary means for eliciting and promoting change talk. At its most basic level, reflective listening entails the clinician's restating the exact content of what the client has said. In the practice of MI, however, other more complex iterations of the technique are also used, and include summarizing or paraphrasing, selectively stating back only portions of what was said, and "mind reading" or, based on an educated guess, reflecting back meaning or reactions not explicitly stated by the client. Two common types of reflections in MI are "continuing the paragraph" and "double sided" reflections. Continuing the

paragraph involves the clinician's providing the next statement for the client using added content that may facilitate further change talk. For example, a clinician may respond to a client's change talk, "The extra weight cannot be good for my knees," with the reflection, "You are concerned that the extra weight may be exacerbating your arthritis." Double-sided reflections involve the communication of both sides of the ambivalence, or reflecting back the client's stated pros *and* cons of change. Double-sided reflection can be especially useful when responding to client resistance (please refer to the next section, "Responding to Resistance," for more detailed discussion.)

An important feature of clinician reflections is that they are communicated as statements, and not as questions. Therefore, the MI clinician is careful not to provide a reflection in a tone that sounds like a question (i.e., inflection at the end of the sentence). The difference can seem subtle, but a statement is thought to be less likely to evoke client resistance because it does not tend to imply disagreement or judgment, or require an answer, and is more likely to elicit further discussion and elaboration on the part of the client. Reflective statements are thought to facilitate change talk and reduce resistance by making the client feel understood and accepted, facilitating the development and strengthening of discrepancy, prompting the client to further discuss and understand ambivalence, and ensuring that the clinician is accurately understanding what the client is saying (Miller, Zweben, DiClemente, & Rychtarik, 1992).

Reflective listening is fundamental to the practice of MI in that it is the primary therapeutic technique used by the clinician. Miller and Rollnick (2002) found that in traditional therapy sessions, clinician questions for the client outnumber reflections by a ratio of 10 to 1, respectively. In contrast, clinicians skilled in the practice of MI tend to average a question-to-reflection ratio of 1 to 3. Although sometimes mistaken for a passive process, reflective listening is quite unique and directive—the clinician chooses what and how to reflect, and by doing so greatly influences the direction and momentum of the conversation.

Responding to Resistance

As is the case with many treatment approaches, in MI client resistance is thought of as any behavior that interferes with behavior change and/or interferes with the therapeutic process. The manner in which the clinician conceptualizes and responds to resistance is considered to be a distinguishing feature of MI. Traditionally, resistance has been conceptualized as an innate characteristic or trait of the client—often viewed negatively, if not pathologically. In MI, however, resistance is thought to arise naturally from certain types of clinician–client interactions. Specifically, resistance is thought to arise from the clinician's misjudgment of the client's readiness to change, and the client subsequently feeling invalidated or misunderstood. In MI a client's readiness is thought to fluctuate throughout the change process. Accordingly, MI assumes that the clinician must be sensitive to and respond appropriately to the client's state of readiness, and that client resistance is a natural consequence of the clinician failing to respond in this way. Although sometimes tempting, the MI clinician never responds to client resistance in a confrontational manner (arguing, persuading, pathologizing, etc.). Rather, the clinician responds to resistance with specific types of reflection, which, as discussed above, are thought to reduce resistance and promote change talk. These types of reflections including simple reflection, double-sided reflection, amplified reflection, reframing, and coming alongside.

Simple reflection and reframing are well known to most clinicians. Double-sided reflection, amplified reflection, and coming alongside warrant further explication. Double-sided reflection permits an effective, nonconfrontational response to resistance because it replicates the client's ambivalence without judgment. For example, the clinician may respond to the client statement, "I know I need to eat better, but food is my only remaining pleasure," with, "You can see some benefit to eating better, and you are worried that doing so will leave you nothing to enjoy in life." The use of *and* instead of *but* as the connector here serves an important function of validating both sides of the ambivalence without judgment or preference.

Amplified reflections restate client statements against change, but in a more extreme fashion, often prompting a retreat from the initial statement and eliciting client discussion of the other side of his or her ambivalence. Clinician tone is important here, as any hint of sarcasm or disingenuousness can result in increased client resistance. Therefore, amplified reflections are delivered in a supportive, matter-of-fact tone. These principles are exemplified in the following exchange:

> *Client:* I have been drinking for 20 years and my liver is fine.
> *Clinician:* You have been drinking for a long time and see no reason for stopping.
> *Client:* I wouldn't say *no* reason; my wife would be happier.

In coming alongside, the clinician allies with client resistance and *genuinely* argues against change. This response is conceptualized as a special case of amplified reflection (Miller & Rollnick, 2002). In the past Miller and Rollnick (1991) have referred to this approach as *paradoxical*, but have since discontinued use of that term, as it is often confused with the paradoxical approach of "outsmarting" or "duping" the client (Miller & Rollnick 2002). Coming alongside the client as her or she argues for change permits the clinician to remain aligned with the client while eliciting change talk and, as such, is considered to be well in keeping with the spirit of MI. An example of coming alongside is illustrated in the following exchange between clinician and client:

> *Client:* Keeping a food log is a waste of time.
> *Clinician:* It is true that keeping track of carbohydrates is time-consuming and difficult. It may be that your schedule does not allow for this level of focus on health.
> *Client:* Well, if I really wanted to, I probably could figure out a way to make it happen.

Affirming and Supporting the Client

Affirming and supporting the client are clinician behaviors frequently used in the practice of MI. Affirming involves the clinician making statements that communicate encouragement and appreciation for the client. The function of affirming the client is to validate the client for his or her efforts, reinforce engagement in the therapeutic process, and enhance the therapeutic relationship. Examples of affirming clinician statements include "Thank you for sharing that with me" and "I really appreciate how hard you have worked on exercising this week."

Supporting the client is expressed through statements that communicate acceptance and respect, usually within the context of showing empathy and understanding for the client's circumstances. An example of a supportive understanding is, "You have had a really rough week, and it has been hard for you to focus on healthy eating." Affirming and supporting statements can be made throughout the therapeutic process; however, clinician genuineness and sincerity are critical to their effective delivery.

Summarizing

The clinician periodically summarizes what the client has said during the session, as a means of reinforcing change talk and increasing motivation. Rollnick, Miller, and Butler (2007) describe this process as picking the "flowers" (change talk) out of the "weeds" (statements against change, or irrelevant statements) and giving them back to the client in a bouquet. The summary also includes other important elements of the client's ambivalence; however, the emphasis is on change talk. Summarizing is particularly useful at the end of a session to reinforce important points that have been made; however, it can be used any time during the session anytime the client provides substantial amount of content.

Moving Toward Change

Throughout the motivational interviewing session, the clinician monitors the client's motivation for change. When the client appears to be highly motivated for change (i.e., client is in the preparation or action stage), the clinician uses open ended questions, reflective listening, and affirming and supportive statements to facilitate the client in discussing specific steps he or she will take next towards making the specific behavioral changes of interest. It is critical, however,

that the clinician does not move from building motivation to attempting to discuss a specific plan for change until the client is sufficiently motivated to do so.

Assessing Readiness to Change

Miller & Rollnick (1991, p. 115) suggest several factors the clinician can look for as signs that the client is motivated for change:

- The client is less resistant (e.g., stops arguing, denying the problem, and raising objections).
- The client appears more resolved (e.g., peaceful and settled).
- The client engages in change talk (i.e., asserting need or desire for change, affirming ability to change, asking about how to change, stating a commitment for change, imagining life with behavior change, etc.).
- The client makes attempts at behavior change or takes steps to prepare for change (e.g., smokes slightly fewer cigarettes, looks into a membership at the gym, etc.).

Although these behaviors can indicate a client's readiness to move on to the change-planning phase, it is important to note that readiness to change is not a fixed client trait, but rather, is an ever-fluctuating state. Therefore, it is often necessary for the clinician to take a step back and use the techniques described in the previous section when client resistance is observed.

Discussing a Plan

When the clinician has determined that the client is sufficiently motivated to change, the clinician begins to facilitate the client's movement to a specific course of action. The key here is that the clinician helps the *client* to suggest a course of action. A common method for transitioning from building client motivation for change to facilitating the client in developing a plan for change is the clinician providing a summary statement of the client's most relevant change talk, and then to ask, "So, what do you think you will do now?," or "What do you think is your next step?" The clinician then responds with further reflections, open-ended questions, and affirmations aimed at strengthening the client's commitment and of self-efficacy to taking change-related steps.

Providing Information

A fundamental assumption in MI is that clients generally have the ability to make changes once they are sufficiently motivated to do so, and do not need clinicians' advice on *how* to make these changes. The clinician, however, does provide clear and accurate information when the client requests it. If the client asks for advice, the clinician provides it as suggestions that the client can choose to "take or leave," rather than as prescriptions for what he or she should do. When possible, the clinician provides the client with several suggestions as opposed to just one.

When a clinician determines that providing specific information is critical to the client's success in making the desired changes, the clinician uses the "ask–provide–ask" method. In using this method, the clinician first *asks* the client what he or she already knows about the topic of interest. If the client appears to be in need of additional information, clinician asks for permission to impart it, and if the client is agreeable to this, the clinician *provides* the information without judgment. As a final step, the clinician *asks* the client to discuss his or her thoughts or reactions to the information provided, and then responds to the client's replies with reflections, open-ended questions, affirmations, and summarization.

CONCLUSION

MI is a directive, yet nonconfrontational, counseling approach to increasing clients' motivation to make behavioral changes. This approach assumes that clients have difficulty making such changes because they have compelling reasons for both changing and not changing. MI provides clinicians with a set of guiding principles and specific techniques for helping clients to identify factors that contribute to their normal ambivalence about change, and to resolve this ambivalence in a manner that produces healthy behavioral change. The therapeutic principles that guide MI are aimed primarily at increasing client "change talk," and include expressing empathy, developing a discrepancy, rolling with resistance, and supporting self-efficacy. These principles are instantiated through the techniques of asking open-ended questions, listening reflectively, "rolling" with resistance rather than responding with confrontation and argumentation, affirming and supporting the client, and providing summaries of client statements regarding change. A growing body of research has shown MI to be efficacious across a wide range of populations and behavioral domains.

Further Reading

Arkowitz, H., & Miller, W. R. (2008). Learning, applying, and extending motivational interviewing. In H. Arkowitz, H. A. Westra, W. R. Miller, & S. Rollnick (Eds.), *Motivational interviewing in the treatment of psychological problems* (pp. 1–25). New York: Guilford.

Arkowitz, H., Westra, H. A., Miller, W. R. & Rollnick, S. (2008). *Motivational interviewing in the treatment of psychological problems.* New York: Guilford.

Miller, W. R., & Rollnick, S. (2002). *Motivational interviewing: Preparing people for change* (2nd ed.). New York: Guilford.

Miller, W. R., Zweben, A. DiClemente, C. C., & Rychtarik, R. G. (1992). *Motivational enhancement therapy manual: A clinical research guide for clinicians treating individuals with alcohol abuse and dependence* (Project MATCH Monograph Series, Vol. 2). Rockville, MD: National Institute on Alcohol Abuse and Alcoholism.

Rollnick, S., Mason, P., & Butler, C (2000). *Health behavior change: A guide for practitioners.* Edinburgh, Scotland: Churchill/Livingstone.

Rollnick, S., & Miller, B. (1995). What is motivational interviewing? *Behavioural & Cognitive Psychotherapy, 23,* 325–334.

Rollnick, S., Miller, W. R., & Butler, C. (2007). *Motivational interviewing in health care: Helping patients change behavior.* New York: Guilford.

Web site: www.motivationalinterview.org

References

Amrhein, P. C., Miller, W. R., Yahne, C. E., Palmer, M., Fulcher, L. (2003). Client commitment language during motivational interviewing predicts drug use outcomes. *Journal of Consulting and Clinical Psychology, 71,* 862–878.

Arkowitz, H., & Miller, W. R. (2008). Learning, applying, and extending motivational interviewing. In H. Arkowitz, H. A. Westra, W. R. Miller, & S. Rollnick (Eds.), *Motivational interviewing in the treatment of psychological problems* (pp. 1–25). New York: Guilford.

Arkowitz, H., Westra, H. A., Miller, W. R., & Rollnick, S. (2008). *Motivational interviewing in the treatment of psychological problems*. New York: Guilford.

Arkowitz, H., Miller, W. R., & Westra, H. A. (2008). Motivational interviewing in the treatment of psychological problems: Conclusions and future directions. In H. Arkowitz, H. A. Westra, W. R. Miller, & S. Rollnick (Eds.), *Motivational interviewing in the treatment of psychological problems* (pp. 324–342). New York: Guilford.

Bien, T. H., Miller, W. R., Tonigan, J. S. (1993). Brief interventions for alcohol problems: A review. *Addiction, 88,* 315–336.

Burke, B., Arkowitz, H. & Menchola, M. (2003). The efficacy of motivational interviewing: A meta-analysis of controlled clinical trials. *Journal of Consulting and Clinical Psychology, 71,* 843–861.

Dunn, C., Deroo, L., & Rivara, F. (2001). The use of brief interventions adapted from motivational interviewing across behavior domains: A systematic review. *Addiction, 96*(12), 1725–1742.

Dutra, L., Stathopoulou, G., Basden, S. L., Leyro, T. M., Powers, M. B. & Otto, M. W. (2008). A meta-analytic review of psychosocial interventions for substance use disorders. *American Journal of Psychiatry, 165*(2), 179–187.

Garfield, S. L. (1994). Research on client variables in psychotherapy. In A. E. Bergin & S. L. Garfield (Eds.), *Handbook of psychotherapy and behavior change* (4th ed., pp. 190–228). New York: John Wiley & Sons.

Hettema, J., Steele, J. & Miller, W. R. (2005). Motivational interviewing. *Annual Review of Clinical Psychology, 1,* 91–111.

Lawendowski, L. A. (1998). A motivational intervention for adolescent smokers. *Preventative Medicine, 27,* A39–A46.

Miller, W. R. (1985). Motivation for treatment: A review with special emphasis on alcoholism. *Psychological Bulletin, 9,* 84–107.

Miller, W. R. (1996). Motivational interviewing: Research, practice, and puzzles. *Addictive Behaviors, 21*(6), 835–842.

Miller, W. R., Benefield R. G., & Tonigan, J. S. (1993). Enhancing motivation for change in problem drinking: A controlled comparison of two therapist styles. *Journal of Consulting and Clinical Psychology, 61,* 455–461.

Miller, W. R., & Rollnick, S. (1991). *Motivational interviewing: Preparing people for change.* New York: Guilford.

Miller, W.R., & Rollnick, S. (2002). *Motivational interviewing: Preparing people for change* (2nd ed.). New York: Guilford.

Miller, W. R., & Sanchez, V. C. (1993). Motivating young adults for treatment in lifestyle change. In G. Howard (Ed.), *Issues in alcohol use and misuse by young adults* (pp. 55–82). Notre Dame, IN: University of Notre Dame Press.

Miller, W. R., Zweben, A., DiClemente, C. C., & Rychtarik, R. G. (1992). Motivational enhancement therapy manual: A clinical research guide for therapists treating individuals with alcohol abuse and dependence (Project MATCH Monograph Series, Vol. 2). Rockville, MD: National Institute on Alcohol Abuse and Alcoholism.

Moyers, T. B., Martin, T., Christopher, P. J., Houck, J. M., Tonigan, J. S., & Amrhein, P. C. (2007). Client language as a mediator of motivational interviewing efficacy: Where is the evidence? *Alcoholism: Clinical and Experimental Research, 31*(suppl 10), 40–47.

Prochaska, J., & DiClemente, C. (1982). Transtheoretical therapy: Towards a more integrative model of change. *Psychotherapy: Theory Research and Practice, 19,* 279–288.

Prochaska, J., DiClemente, C., & Norcross, J. (1992). In search of how people change: Applications to addictive behaviors. *American Psychologist, 47,* 1102–1114.

Project MATCH Research Group (1997). Matching alcohol treatment to client heterogeneity: Project MATCH post-treatment drinking outcomes. *Journal of Studies on Alcohol, 58,* 7–29.

Rollnick, S & Allison, J. (2001). Motivational interviewing. In N. Heather, T. J. Peters, & T. Stockwell (Eds.), *International handbook of alcohol dependence and problems* (pp. 593–603). New York: John Wiley & Sons.

Rollnick, S., Heather, N, & Bell, A. (1992). Negotiating behaviour change in medical settings: The development of brief motivational interviewing. *Journal of Mental Health, 1,* 25–37.

Rollnick, S., Mason, P., & Butler, C. (2000). *Health behavior change: A guide for practitioners.* Edinburgh, Scotland: Churchill/Livingstone.

Rollnick, S., & Miller, B. (1995). What is motivational interviewing? *Behavioural & Cognitive Psychotherapy, 23,* 325–334.

Rollnick, S., Miller, W. R., & Butler, C. (2007). *Motivational interviewing in health care: Helping patients change behavior.* New York: Guilford.

49 NONCONTINGENT REINFORCEMENT AS A TREATMENT FOR PROBLEM BEHAVIOR

Timothy R. Vollmer and Carrie S. W. Borrero

Noncontingent reinforcement (NCR) involves the time-based presentation of reinforcers. This treatment is used most often to reduce the frequency of operant behavior problems including self-injury (e.g., Goh, Iwata, & DeLeon, 2000; Lindberg et al. 2003; Vollmer, Iwata, Zarcone, Smith, & Mazaleski, 1993) aggression (e.g., Hagopian, Bruzek, Bowman, & Jennett, 2007), mouthing (e.g., Roane, Kelly, & Fisher, 2003), and disruptive behavior (e.g., Fisher et al., 2000). In time-based schedules, reinforcers are delivered on fixed-time (FT) or variable-time (VT) arrangements. Time schedules should not be confused with interval schedules. *Interval schedules*, such as fixed interval (FI) and variable interval (VI), are response-dependent schedules—they require a response in order for reinforcers to be delivered. On the other hand, time schedules (FT, VT) require no response; the reinforcers are delivered freely, regardless of whether or not a target behavior has occurred. Although the use of free reinforcers as a clinical intervention may seem counterintuitive at first blush, the procedure makes good sense upon closer inspection. Dozens of studies now support the clinical utility of NCR (see Carr et al., 2000, for a comprehensive review; see Table 49.1).

It is widely recognized that many severe behavior problems are maintained by inadvertent social reinforcement. For example, a child might engage in self-injurious behavior (SIB) because SIB produces attention from adult care providers (Iwata, Dorsey, Slifer, Bauman, & Richman, 1982/1994). By providing reinforcement independent of behavior, as in NCR, a dependency no longer exists between problem behavior and a known reinforcer. For example, the care provider might provide attention once every 5 minutes instead of providing attention following SIB (Vollmer et al., 1993). Thus, because the reinforcer is made available freely and frequently, the motivation to engage in problem behavior is reduced. In addition, the problem behavior no longer directly produces the reinforcer, so NCR contains extinction-like features.

Advantages of NCR include reduced negative side effects in comparison to extinction (Vollmer, et al., 1998) and differential reinforcement (Vollmer et al., 1993), and ease of implementation in comparison to differential reinforcement. In clinical practice, the procedure is most commonly used as one component of a larger treatment package.

CONTRAINDICATIONS OF THE TECHNIQUE

The NCR procedure, in isolation, may not be the most appropriate intervention for individuals whose behavioral repertoire does not include appropriate alternative behavior. There is nothing explicit in the procedure for reinforcing adaptive alternative behavior. However, some studies have shown that NCR can be combined with differential reinforcement to teach adaptive skills, such as communication (Goh, Iwata, & Kahng, 1999; and Marcus & Vollmer, 1995). In other words, NCR should be viewed as one potential component of a larger treatment package that would include procedures for teaching adaptive skills.

Also, the successful application of NCR often requires good information about the operant function of the behavior problem. If an adequate functional analysis has not been or cannot be conducted, it is possible that NCR will be less effective. NCR is often implemented as a treatment for problem behavior following functional

TABLE 49.1   Evidenced-Based Applications

Problem Behavior	Examples
Self-injurious behavior	Hagopian et al. (2004); Lindberg et al. (2003)
Aggression	Baker, Hanley, & Mathews (2006); Gouboth, Wilder, & Booher (2007)
Disruption/property destruction	O'Callaghan, Allen, Powell & Salama (2006); Rasmussen & O'Neill (2006)
Food refusal	Reed et al. (2004); Wilder, Normand & Atwell (2005)
Rumination	Lyons, Rube, Luiselli & DiGennaro (2007); Wilder, Draper, Williams, & Higbee (1997)
Mouthing	Carr et al. (2002); Roane, Kelly, & Fisher (2003)
Tantrum behavior	Britton et al. (2000);
Pica	Goh, Iwata, & DeLeon (1999); Mace & Knight (1986)
Stereotypy	Rapp (2006); Rapp (2007)
Inappropriate talk/vocalizations	Falcomata et al. (2004); Hagopian, LeBlanc, & Maglieri (2000)
Elopement	Kodak, Grow, & Northup (2004); Tarbox, Wallace, & Williams (2003)

analyses. Little is known about the efficacy of the procedure in the absence of a functional analysis.

Although generally considered an easy-to-implement procedure, NCR can be labor intensive at the beginning of treatment. Most of the published studies showing positive effects involved rich schedules of reinforcement (e.g., continuous reinforcement) when treatment is first introduced. If a parent, teacher, or therapist does not have adequate resources to implement the procedure intensively at the outset, it may not be as effective. However, the schedule of reinforcement actually becomes very easy to implement once the schedule is thinned to something more manageable, such as FT 5 min.

Finally, if the behavior problem occurs at extremely high rates, the procedure may result in accidental reinforcement (Vollmer, Ringdahl, Roane, & Marcus, 1997). This happens because the delivery of the reinforcer continues to occur contiguously with the occurrence of behavior. Thus, the dependency between problem behavior and reinforcement is eliminated in fact, but a reinforcement contingency remains in place incidentally. There is a method to circumvent this problem, and that method will be discussed later in this chapter.

CONSIDERATIONS

The most important consideration in developing NCR treatments is to understand the operant function of the behavior prior to treatment.

Understanding the operant function is best accomplished via functional analysis (Iwata et al., 1982/1994). It is outside the scope of this chapter to fully explain functional analysis procedures; however, it should be noted that a functional analysis involves systematically introducing particular consequences, such as attention, escape from instructional activity, and tangible items (e.g., toys, food) following occurrences of problem behavior. By intentionally presenting these consequences, the assessor can evaluate whether such events serve as reinforcers for problem behavior. Because functional analyses can require specialized skills and resources, at times a reasonable clinical judgment can be made about the operant function by conducting naturalistic observations of the behavior. In short, there must be some hypothesis about the reinforcers maintaining the problem behavior so that those reinforcers may be presented noncontingently during treatment. For example, if the problem behavior is maintained by (reinforced by) escape from instructional activity, escape can be presented on an FT schedule so that it is no longer contingent upon the occurrence of problem behavior (e.g., Vollmer, Marcus, & Ringdahl, 1995).

Although NCR is most commonly implemented by delivering the reinforcer identified via functional analysis, potent positive reinforcers of any sort can sometimes be used as a treatment, or as a component of a treatment package, even if they do not match the reinforcers maintaining problem behavior (e.g., Reed et al., 2004). For example, by using potent tangible reinforcers such as food, demanding instructional situations may become less aversive to the individual receiving treatment, and, therefore, he or she may be less inclined to engage in escape behavior (Lalli et al., 1999). Also, through use of potent tangible reinforcers, behavior maintained by either attention or access to tangible items can be reduced because the individual is given something else to do (Fischer, Iwata, & Mazaleski, 1997). Most parents will recognize this sort of effect if they have ever given their toddler a favorite toy while they (the parents) finish some housework or pay bills (i.e., the non-contingent toy effectively competes with adult attention as reinforcement). Finally, because many behavior problems are maintained by automatic reinforcement (i.e., that is, they are not socially reinforced), NCR in the form of attention, toys, or leisure activities can be used as a means of environmental enrichment. Research shows that environmental enrichment can decrease automatically reinforced behavior, presumably because it provides alternative sources of reinforcement (e.g., Horner, 1980).

The main reasons that one might select NCR as a treatment include the following: (1) its effects typically occur rapidly; (2) it has been shown to produce fewer negative side effects than differential reinforcement of other behavior (DRO) and extinction; and (3) it is ultimately very simple to conduct. Most studies show that NCR effects are virtually immediate, insofar as the effects are evident within one experimental session (e.g., Hagopian, Fisher, & Legacy, 1994). Also, in one study, extinction-induced aggression was considerably lower in NCR versus DRO (Vollmer, et al., 1993). In another study (Vollmer, et al., 1998), extinction bursts were not seen with NCR but were consistently observed when a therapist implemented traditional extinction (i.e., when the therapist withheld the reinforcer that was maintaining problem behavior). The NCR procedure is ultimately easy to implement because the care provider does not need to see every instance of problem behavior in order to know when to deliver or not to deliver reinforcers. However, in DRO a therapist must reset a timer every time

the problem behavior occurs. In NCR, the reinforcer is delivered at a set point in time no matter whether the problem behavior has occurred.

HOW DOES THE TECHNIQUE WORK?

Two processes, extinction and satiation, may be responsible for the decrease in responding observed during NCR. The decrease may be a result of *extinction* because the reinforcer is no longer delivered contingent on a response. *Satiation* may contribute to the effects because the reinforcer is made available freely and frequently (e.g., Why bang your head to get attention when you are already getting lots of attention?). Another way to consider the effects of NCR is to examine the very nature of reinforcement. In NCR, the probability of obtaining a reinforcer is no greater given the occurrence of behavior than it would be given the nonoccurrence of behavior. Hence, a reinforcement effect is not expected and, therefore, the frequency of the target response should be reduced (Catania, 1998).

STEP-BY-STEP PROCEDURES

Functional Analysis (Assessment)

When designing an intervention for problem behavior, it is important to first identify the functional reinforcer for that behavior (see Table 49.2). A functional analysis of problem behavior can be conducted using procedures similar to those described by Iwata et al. (1982/1994). Conditions are arranged to test hypotheses about the reinforcer(s) maintaining problem behavior. Common test conditions include *attention, escape, tangible, alone,* and *play.* Typical functional analysis sessions last anywhere from 5 to 15 min, and several sessions of each condition should be conducted, usually in a multielement format (where sessions from each condition alternate either randomly or in some pre-designed order). In the *attention* condition, the "therapist" acts as if his or her attention is diverted to some task such as reading or chatting with someone else. Problem behavior produces attention from the therapist. The purpose of the *attention* condition

TABLE 49.2   Key Elements of NCR

Step	Description
Functional analysis	Identify reinforcers maintaining problem behavior.
Implementing a rich NCR schedule	Provide continuous (ideally) reinforcement for rapid suppression.
Thinning the NCR schedule	Use gradual increments.

is to test whether attention reinforces problem behavior. In the *escape* condition, the therapist presents instructional demands to the participant. Problem behavior produces a brief break from the instructional activity (usually about 15–30 seconds). The purpose of the *escape* condition is to test whether escape reinforces problem behavior. In the *tangible* condition, the therapist "takes a turn" with some tangible item such as a toy, food, or beverage. Problem behavior produces access to the tangible item for about 30 s. The purpose of the *tangible* condition is to test whether tangible items reinforce problem behavior. In the *alone* condition (usually used for self-injury or stereotypic behavior), there are no programmed contingencies for problem behavior. The purpose is to see if behavior persists even when the participant is alone. If so, the behavior is probably not socially reinforced (i.e., it is automatically reinforced). In the *play* condition, the participant receives a great deal of stimulation and attention, and no instructional demands are presented. Usually, low levels of problem

behavior are observed in this condition, so it is used as point of comparison for the other condition. Overall, the idea of a functional analysis is to see which condition (or conditions) produces the highest levels of problem behavior.

A hypothetical functional analysis outcome is presented in Figure 49.1. In this example, responses per minute of disruptive behavior (*y* axis) are graphed session by session (*x* axis). Disruption occurs only in the attention session. Results of this sort suggest that disruptive behavior is reinforced by attention. In this hypothetical case, attention should be used as the reinforcer during NCR (Vollmer et al., 1993). Alternatively, during times when noncontingent attention cannot be delivered, a highly preferred toy or leisure item could be made available noncontingently (Fischer et al., 1997).

If it is not practical to conduct the sort of functional analysis just described, the practitioner should at the very least conduct direct observations in the natural environment. These observations should be used to formulate a "best

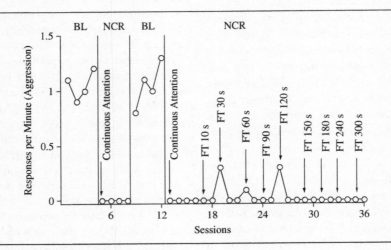

FIGURE 49.1   Hypothetical functional analysis outcome.

guess" about the reinforcers maintaining problem behavior.

NCR (First Variation)

After conducting the functional analysis, present the reinforcer known to maintain problem behavior on a very rich schedule. Ideally, the participant would have continuous access to the reinforcer. Thus, the participant has continuous access to attention, escape, or the tangible item, depending upon which reinforcer was shown to maintain problem behavior. This is a good starting point for very dangerous behavior because continuous access to the reinforcer usually produces an immediate suppression of behavior.

NCR (Second Variation)

After conducting the functional analysis, present a very potent tangible or social reinforcer during the context associated with problem behavior. For example, as treatment for escape behavior, juice could be made available continuously during instructional activity in order to reduce the aversiveness of instructional activity. Similarly, as treatment for attention-maintained behavior, a favorite toy could be made available to a child continuously when the adult must divert his or her attention (e.g., to pay bills, to talk on the telephone).

Schedule Thinning

Continuous access to reinforcement is sometimes both impractical (e.g., when the adult is busy) and undesirable (e.g., when a student should be engaged with school work). Thus, the schedule of access to the reinforcer must be thinned systematically (e.g., Kahng, Iwata, DeLeon, & Wallace, 2000). A timer is useful for ensuring that reinforcement is delivered according to the schedule. Initially, reinforcement is provided on a rich schedule and faded to a thinner schedule as problem behavior remains at low rates. In order to thin the schedule, it is helpful to specify a criterion for fading out reinforcement. For example, clinicians may decide that two consecutive sessions with one or fewer instances of problem behavior is a sufficient criterion to slightly thin out the schedule of reinforcement.

Usually, the schedule is thinned incrementally, such as in 10-s units, until a more manageable schedule, such as FT 5 min, is obtained. In addition, it is important to thin the NCR schedule gradually. If an increase in problem behavior is observed when the schedule is thinned, it may be necessary to increase the schedule by smaller increments. An example of NCR schedule thinning is illustrated in Figure 49.2. Initially, continuous reinforcement is provided, resulting in a decrease in responding to zero. Eventually, the schedule is faded so that attention is provided

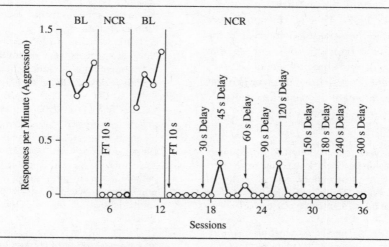

FIGURE 49.2 Examples of NCR schedule thinning.

every 5 min (FT 5 min) while problem behavior levels remain low.

If the behavior seems to inadvertently contact reinforcers, a momentary omission contingency can be established (Lindberg, Iwata, Kahng, & DeLeon, 1999). In short, a brief omission contingency changes the schedule from noncontingent to contingent on omission of behavior, but the brevity of the omission interval makes the procedure very similar to NCR while reducing the possibility of accidental reinforcement.

WHEN NCR DOES NOT DECREASE PROBLEM BEHAVIOR

If high rates of problem behavior persist, consider the following possibilities: (1) the reinforcers maintaining problem behavior were not properly identified, (2) the NCR schedule was thinned too rapidly, or (3) the behavior is being reinforced inadvertently because of contiguous coupling, albeit incidental, with the reinforcer. To address (1), additional functional analyses or naturalistic observations should be conducted to ensure that all of the reinforcers maintaining problem behavior were identified. Frequently, problem behavior is reinforced by more than one type of consequence (e.g., Smith, Iwata, Vollmer, & Zarcone, 1993). To address (2), thin the schedule in smaller increments; perhaps using half the increments selected initially. To address (3), introduce a *momentary omission contingency* (Vollmer et al., 1997). That is, do not deliver the reinforcer at the scheduled interval if the problem behavior happens to occur at that moment. This will avoid the problem of accidental reinforcement because the reinforcer is never delivered at the moment the behavior occurs.

Further Reading

Iwata, B. A., Dorsey, M. F., Slifer, K. J., Bauman, K. E., & Richman, G. S. (1994). Toward a functional analysis of self-injury. *Journal of Applied Behavior Analysis, 27,* 197–209. (Reprinted from *Analysis and Intervention in Developmental Disabilities, 2,* 3–20, 1982).

Vollmer, T. R. (1999). Time-based schedules as treatment for severe behavior disorders. *Mexican Journal of Behavior Analysis, 25,* 85–103.

Vollmer, T. R., Iwata, B. A., Zarcone, J. R., Smith, R. G., & Mazaleski, J. L. (1993). The role of attention in the treatment of attention-maintained self-injurious behavior: Noncontingent reinforcement and differential reinforcement of other behavior. *Journal of Applied Behavior Analysis, 26,* 9–21.

References

Baker, J. C., Hanley, G. P., & Mathews, R. M. (2006). Staff-administered functional analysis and treatment of aggression by an elder with dementia. *Journal of Applied Behavior Analysis, 39,* 469–474.

Britton, L. N., Carr, J. E., Kallum, K. K., Dozier, C. L., & Weil, T. M. (2000). A variation of noncontingent reinforcement in the treatment of aberrant behavior. *Research in Developmental Disabilities, 21,* 425–435.

Carr, J. E., Coriaty, S., Wilder, D. A., Gaunt, B. T., Dozier, C. L., Britton, L. N., et al. (2000). A review of "noncontingent" reinforcement as treatment for the aberrant behavior of individuals with developmental disabilities. *Research in Developmental Disabilities, 21,* 377–391.

Carr, J. E., Dozier, C. L., Patel, M. R., Nicolson-Adams, A., & Martin, N. (2002). Treatment of automatically reinforced object mouthing with noncontingent reinforcement and response blocking: Experimental analysis and social validation. *Research in Developmental Disabilities, 23,* 37–44.

Catania, A. C. (1998). *Learning* (interim 4th ed.). Cornwall-on-Hudson, NY: Sloan Publishing.

Falcomata, T. S., Roane, H. S., Hovanetz, A. N., Kettering, T. L., & Keeney, K. M. (2004). An evaluation of response cost in the treatment of inappropriate vocalizations maintained by automatic reinforcement. *Journal of Applied Behavior Analysis, 37,* 83–87.

Fischer, S. M., Iwata, B. A., & Mazaleski, J. L. (1997). Noncontingent delivery of arbitrary reinforcers as treatment for self-injurious behavior. *Journal of Applied Behavior Analysis, 30,* 239–249.

Fisher, W. W., O'Connor, J. T., Kurtz, P. F., DeLeon, I. G., & Gotjen, D. L. (2000). The effects of noncontingent delivery of high- and low-preference stimuli on attention maintained destructive behavior. *Journal of Applied Behavior Analysis, 33,* 79–83.

Goh, H., Iwata, B. A., & DeLeon, I. G. (2000). Competition between noncontingent and contingent reinforcement schedules during response acquisition. *Journal of Applied Behavior Analysis, 33,* 195–205.

Goh, H., Iwata, B. A., & Kahng, S. (1999). Multicomponent assessment and treatment of cigarette pica. *Journal of Applied Behavior Analysis, 32,* 297–316.

Gouboth, D., Wilder, D. A., Booher, J. The effects of signaling stimulus presentation during noncontingent reinforcement. *Journal of Applied Behavior Analysis, 40,* 725–730.

Hagopian, L. P., Bruzek, J. L., Bowman, L. G., & Jennett, H. K. (2007). Assessment and treatment of problem behavior occasioned by interruption of free-operant behavior. *Journal of Applied Behavior Analysis, 40,* 89–103.

Hagopian, L. P., Fisher, W. W., & Legacy, S. M. (1994). Schedule effects of noncontingent reinforcement on attention-maintained destructive behavior in identical quadruplets. *Journal of Applied Behavior Analysis, 27,* 317–325.

Hagopian, L. P., LeBlanc, L. A., & Maglieri, K. A. (2000). Noncontingent attention for the treatment of excessive medical complaints in a medically fragile man with mental retardation. *Research in Developmental Disabilities, 21,* 215–221.

Hagopian, L. P., Toole. L. M., Long, E. S., Bowman, L. G., & Lieving, G. A. (2004). A comparison of dense-to-lean and fixed lean schedules of alternative reinforcement and extinction. *Journal of Applied Behavior Analysis, 37,* 323–338.

Horner, R. D. (1980). The effects of an environmental enrichment program on the behavior of institutionalized profoundly retarded children. *Journal of Applied Behavior Analysis, 13,* 473–491.

Iwata, B. A., Dorsey, M. F., Slifer, K. J., Bauman, K. E., & Richman, G. S. (1994). Toward a functional analysis of self-injury. *Journal of Applied Behavior Analysis, 27,* 197–209. (Reprinted from *Analysis and Intervention in Developmental Disabilities, 2,* 3–20, 1982).

Kahng, S., Iwata, B. A., DeLeon, I. G., & Wallace, M. D. (2000). A comparison of procedures for programming noncontingent reinforcement schedules. *Journal of Applied Behavior Analysis, 33,* 223–231.

Kodak, T., Grow, L., & Northup, J. (2004). Functional analysis and treatment of elopement for a child with attention deficit hyperactivity disorder. *Journal of Applied Behavior Analysis, 37,* 229–232.

Lalli, J. S., Vollmer, T. R., Progar, P. R., Wright, C., Borrero, J., Daniel, D., et al. (1999). Competition between positive and negative reinforcement in the treatment of escape behavior. *Journal of Applied Behavior Analysis, 32,* 285–296.

Lindberg, J. S., Iwata, B. A., Kahng, S. W., DeLeon, I. G. (1999). DRO contingencies: An evaluation of variable-momentary schedules. *Journal of Applied Behavior Analysis, 32,* 123–136.

Lindberg, J. S., Iwata, B. A., Roscoe, E. M., Worsdell, A. S., & Hanley, G. P. (2003). Treatment efficacy of noncontingent reinforcement during brief and extended applications. *Journal of Applied Behavior Analysis, 36,* 1–19.

Lyons, E. A., Rue, H. C., Luiselli, J. K., & DiGennaro, F. D. (2007). Brief functional analysis and supplemental feeding for postmeal rumination in children with developmental disabilities. *Journal of Applied Behavior Analysis, 40,* 743–747.

Mace, F. C., & Knight, D. (1986). Functional analysis and treatment of severe pica. *Journal of Applied Behavior Analysis, 19,* 411–416.

Marcus, B. A., & Vollmer, T. R. (1995). Effects of differential negative reinforcement on disruption and compliance. *Journal of Applied Behavior Analysis, 28,* 229–230.

O'Callaghan, P. M., Allen, K. D., Powell, S. & Salama, F. (2006). The efficacy of noncontingent escape for decreasing children's disruptive behavior during restorative dental treatment. *Journal of Applied Behavior Analysis, 39,* 161–171.

Rapp, J. T. (2006). Toward an empirical method for identifying matched stimulation for automatically reinforced behavior: A preliminary investigation. *Journal of Applied Behavior Analysis, 39,* 137–140.

Rapp, J. T. (2007). Further evaluation of methods to identify matched stimulation. *Journal of Applied Behavior Analysis, 40,* 73–88.

Rasmussen, K. & O'Neill, R. E. (2006). The effects of fixed-time reinforcement schedules on problem behavior of children with emotional and behavioral disorders in a day-treatment classroom setting. *Journal of Applied Behavior Analysis, 39,* 453–457.

Reed, G. K., Piazza, C. C., Patel, M. R., Layer, S. A. Bachmeyer, M. H., et al. (2004). On the relative contributions of noncontingent reinforcement and escape extinction in the treatment of food refusal. *Journal of Applied Behavior Analysis, 37,* 27–41.

Roane, H. S., Kelly, M. L., & Fisher, W. W. (2003). The effects of noncontingent access to food on the rate of hand mouthing across three settings. *Journal of Applied Behavior Analysis, 36,* 579–582.

Smith, R. G., Iwata, B. A., Vollmer, T. R., & Zarcone, J. R. (1993). Experimental analysis and treatment of multiply controlled self-injury. *Journal of Applied Behavior Analysis, 26,* 183–196.

Tarbox, R. S. E., Wallace, M., & Williams, L. (2003). Assessment and treatment of elopement: A replication and extension. *Journal of Applied Behavior Analysis, 36,* 239–244.

Vollmer, T. R., Iwata, B. A., Zarcone, J. R., Smith, R. G., & Mazaleski, J. L. (1993). The role of attention in the treatment of attention-maintained self-injurious behavior: Noncontingent reinforcement and differential reinforcement of other behavior. *Journal of Applied Behavior Analysis, 26,* 9–21.

Vollmer, T. R., Marcus, B. A., & Ringdahl, J. E. (1995). Noncontingent escape as treatment for self-injurious behavior maintained by negative reinforcement. *Journal of Applied Behavior Analysis, 28*, 15–26.

Vollmer, T. R., Progar, P. R., Lalli, J. S., Van Camp, C. M., Sierp, B. J., Wright, C. S., et al. (1998). Fixed-time schedules attenuate extinction-induced phenomena in the treatment of severe aberrant behavior. *Journal of Applied Behavior Analysis, 31*, 529–542.

Vollmer, T. R., Ringdahl, J. E., Roane, H., S., & Marcus, B. A. (1997). Negative side effects of noncontingent reinforcement. *Journal of Applied Behavior Analysis, 30*, 161–164.

Wilder, D. A., Draper, R., Williams, W. L., & Higbee, T. S. (1997). A comparison of noncontingent reinforcement, other competing stimulation, and liquid scheduling for the treatment of rumination. *Behavioral Interventions, 12*, 55–64.

Wilder, D. A., Normand, M., & Atwell, J. (2005). Noncontingent reinforcement as treatment for food refusal and associated self-injury. *Journal of Applied Behavior Analysis, 38*, 549–553.

50   PAIN MANAGEMENT

Robert J. Gatchel and Richard C. Robinson

Research over the past three decades has clearly demonstrated the central importance of psychosocial factors in the experience of chronic pain and disability (Flor & Turk, 1984; W. Fordyce, 1976; Katon, Egan, & Miller, 1985; Sternbach, 1974). As early as 1959, Engel (1959) argued that pain is a psychological phenomenon. He also described a constellation of personality characteristics that he hypothesized placed individuals at risk for developing chronic pain. These characteristics included the following: a history of defeat, significant guilt, unsatisfied aggressive impulses, and a propensity to develop pain in response to a real or imagined loss. However, more recent research has focused on the cognitive error of catastrophizing as a central issue for patients with chronic pain (Edwards, Bingham, Bathon, & Haythornthwaite, 2006). Gatchel and Epker (1999) have provided a comprehensive review of many of the psychosocial risk factors, and have refuted the notion that there is one particular "pain-prone personality."

Melzack and Wall's (1965) *gate control theory of pain* further allowed for the incorporation of psychological factors in the role of pain perception. Specifically, these researchers theorized that neurophysiological nerve cells, located in the dorsal horns, served as a gate-like mechanism for pain in signals and allowed for modulating from various sources. Thus, the gate control theory integrated peripheral stimuli and cortical variables, and purported a model that could explain the impact that mood states may have on pain perception. Expanding upon this, the *biopsychosocial model* proposed by Engel combined social factors with the psychological and physiological components of pain (Engel, 1977). Turk and Rudy (1987) elaborated upon these previous models for pain patients by incorporating cognitive, affective, psychosocial, behavioral, and physiological elements. Their research suggested that, as suffering

increases, psychosocial factors play an increasingly significant role in the experience of pain.

Patients with chronic pain disorders often present with psychological difficulties that can be both a consequence of their pain condition and can contribute to their pain, suffering and disability. Therefore, clinicians are often addressing chronic pain and a wide array of painful feelings and distressing thoughts that accompany this condition. For example, Kinney, Gatchel, Polatin, Fogarty, and Mayer (1993) reported higher rates of depression, substance abuse and personality disorders in patients with chronic low back pain (CLBP) than the general population. Polatin and colleagues (1993) also attempted to explore the complex relationship between psychopathology and pain. Using the Structured Clinical Interview for the *Diagnostic and Statistical Manual of Mental Disorders, 3rd ed., Revised*, they found that of 200 CLBP patients, 77% met lifetime diagnostic criteria for psychiatric disturbances. The most common diagnoses included depression, substance abuse, and anxiety disorders. Futhermore, 51% of the patients met criteria for a personality disorder, which is substantially higher than rates found in the general population. Likewise, Gatchel, Polatin, Mayer and Garcy (1994) examined 152 CLBP patients prior to undergoing an intensive 3-week interdisciplinary treatment program, and found that 90% of the CLBP patients met criteria for a lifetime Axis I diagnosis. Consistent with their previous research, the most prevalent diagnoses found were depression and substance abuse (Gatchel et al., 1994).

Gatchel (1996) clarified this complex relationship among pain, psychopathology, and personality by theorizing and studying the progression from acute to chronic pain. The psychosocial changes that occur as a person progresses from acute to chronic pain is referred to as a "layering of behavioral/psychological problems over the original nociception of the pain experience itself" (p. 34). This model is based on a three-stage progression, from acute to subacute to chronic disability, as a result of an identifiable injury. Stage 1 takes into account the resulting emotional reactions (e.g., fear, anxiety, and worry) that arise as a consequence of perceived pain. Stage 2 begins when the pain lasts past a reasonable acute time period. It is at this stage that the development or exacerbation of existing psychological and behavioral problems occurs. Gatchel hypothesizes that the form these difficulties take depends on the premorbid personality and psychological characteristics of the individual (i.e., a diathesis), as well as current socioeconomic and environmental stressors. For instance, an individual with a tendency to become depressed may develop a depressive disorder in response to the economic and social *stress* of being unable to work as a result of pain (Gatchel & Turk, 1996). Such a diathesis–stress model has also been expanded upon by others investigating predisoposing factors to pain (e.g., Weisberg, Vittengle, Clark, Gatchel, & Garen, 2000). This complex interaction of physical and psychosocioeconomic factors leads to stage 3 of the model: As the patient's life begins center around the pain as a result of the chronic nature of the problem, the patient adopts the sick role. By adopting the sick role, the patient is excused from normal responsibilities and social obligations, which may serve to reinforce maladaptive behaviors.

KEY CONCEPTUAL FACTORS

Physical Deconditioning

Physical deconditioning, that results from the progressive lack of use of the body, generally accompanies patients during their progression toward chronic disability. It often co-occurs with increased emotional distress. The combined interaction of the symptoms negatively impacts the emotional well-being and self-esteem of an individual (Gatchel & Turk, 1996).

Catastrophizing

As mentioned, the importance of catastrophizing in patients with chronic pain and disability has gained acceptance (Edwards et al., 2006). Catastrophizing involves thinking in an exaggerated, negative fashion about events and stimuli. This can occur in individuals with pain as it applies to their pain or their ability to cope with their pain (Sullivan, Stanish, Waite, Sullivan, & Tripp, 1998). For instance, individuals with thoughts such as "I will never get the slightest bit better" or "I'll never be happy again, because of this pain" are engaging in catastrophizing. However, it should be noted that this catastrophic thinking occurs automatically and often just outside a person's awareness. In an excellent study examining this variable, Butler, Damarin, Beaulieu, Schwebel, and Thorn (1989) evaluated cognitive strategies and postoperative pain in general surgical patients and found that increased catastrophizing was associated with higher levels of postoperative pain intensity. Main and Waddell (1991) also found a strong relationship between catastrophizing and depressive symptoms in a sample of low back pain patients. Furthermore, of the cognitive variables investigated by Main and Wadell, catastrophizing was evaluated to have the "greatest potential for understanding current low back symptoms" (p. 287). Fortunately, cognitive errors, including catastrophizing, are amenable to, and especially suited for, cognitive behavioral interventions.

Pain versus Hurt

When patients engage in an activity that produces pain, they are likely to associate the pain with the initial injury or "hurt." This associative learning can contribute to individuals' fearing and avoiding pain and possible pain-producing situations. Unfortunately, pain often accompanies physical reconditioning and may be necessary in order to resume normal responsibilities and social obligations. Therefore, patients must extinguish the association between hurt and harm and learn that hurt and harm are not the same (Fordyce, 1988). In fact, Vlaeyen, Kole-Snijders, Rooteveel, Rusesink, & Heuts (1995) and Vlaeyen & Linton (2000) developed the *fear-avoidance model* for patients with CLBP. The model proposes that the way in which an individual interprets and thinks about their pain initially may lead to maintenance of their pain. When individuals engage in catastrophizing cognitions about their pain, they are hypothesized to be at greater risk of avoiding behavior, such as exercising needed for recovery and increase fear and hypervigilance. This is in contrast to the individual who has less threatening cognitions dealing with their pain, and thus more likely to engage in a normal range of activities. Leeuw and colleagues (2007) provide an excellent review of this topic and conclude that increasing evidence supports this model. They state, "As predicted from the vast literature on fear and anxiety, pain-related fear is associated with catastrophic misinterpretations of pain, hypervigilance, increased escape and avoidance behaviors, as well as with intensified pain intensity and functional disability" (p. 87).

Coping

The ways in which an individual manages and copes with the stressors associated with pain is an important element to understand when approaching patients with pain from a cognitive behavioral perspective. The assessment of coping style can inform the clinician on how best to instruct patients on more adaptive coping skills. The Multidimensional Pain Inventory (MPI), developed by Kerns, Turk and Rudy (1985), is one of the most widely used measures in the pain area. The MPI is a brief self-report instrument that examines a patient's perception of pain and coping ability. The MPI helps to identify a patient's coping style and can guide the implementation of pain reduction interventions. Turk and Rudy (1988) identified three coping styles based on a cluster analysis on the MPI scales with a heterogeneous group of chronic pain patients: *dysfunctional* (43%), *interpersonally distressed* (28%), and *adaptive copers* (29.5%). The dysfunctional group members indicated that their pain, and the interference caused by their pain, was extreme. Patients in the interpersonally distressed group reported a lack of support, concern, and understanding from their family members and significant others. In contrast, individuals in the adaptive copers group reported higher levels of activity and perceived life control, as well as lower levels

of pain intensity, perceived interference from the pain in their life, and affective distress.

COGNITIVE BEHAVIORAL THERAPY FOR CHRONIC PAIN

Turk and Gatchel (2002) succinctly describe five aims of cognitive behavior therapy (CBT) for patients with chronic pain. The *first goal* is to help patients alter their perceptions and cognitions of their pain, from something that is unmanageable to something that they can learn to manage. The *second goal* is to educate patients about CBT and how it will provide them with the tools they need to manage their pain. The *third goal* is to alter the individuals' perception of themselves, from someone who is passive to someone who is actively and intentionally engaged in managing themselves and impacting their environment. The *fourth goal* is to instruct patients on how to become aware of, and develop, an understanding of the interaction among their thoughts, feelings, behaviors, and physical functioning. Finally, the *fifth goal* is to instruct patients in more adaptive ways to manage their pain that can be used in a multiple settings.

With these goals in mind, treatment is made up of four major components: (1) reconceptualization; (2) skills acquisition; (3) skills consolidation; and (4) generalization and maintenance (Turk & Gatchel, 2002). Each of the procedures that accompany these components will be briefly reviewed.

Reconceptualization

The reconceptualization of chronic pain consists of two components: (1) recognizing maladaptive thoughts; and (2) challenging and restructuring the automatic cognitions into more adaptive thoughts (a process termed *cognitive restructuring*). Using a pain diary that asks patients to record their pain, thoughts and feelings is a useful way of identifying maladaptive thoughts such as "The pain is killing me" or "If it hurts, I must be making it worse."

Once common negative automatic thoughts have been identified, the therapist and the patient can work collaboratively to challenge the thoughts. The systematic exploration to previously unexamined assumptions allows the patients to develop more objective, problem-solving, and therefore adaptive thoughts. For instance, a patient who thinks to herself "I'll never travel again" can examine that thought objectively. It may be that the patient can travel, but that the physical cost of the pain would be unacceptable. However, with relaxation training, the cost of the pain could be decreased so that traveling is not something to be feared. Notice that the thought is not simply converted to a positive, Pollyanaish thought, but to one that is more objective, active, and adaptive. Alteration of perceptions and longstanding beliefs slowly occur when patients practice more adaptive coping thoughts in the context of their daily activity. When positive changes occur, the therapist continuously directs the patients' attention to the positive changes in an attempt to increase self-efficacy and reinforce the adaptive behavior in which the patient is engaging.

Skills Acquisition

Skills acquired in CBT for chronic pain can be roughly divided into self-regulatory skills and stress-management skills. *Self-regulatory skills* are techniques that allow patients to alter their physiological functioning in a manner that can decrease their pain, such as reducing muscle tension or autonomic arousal. The most common self-regulatory skills are relaxation training, distraction, self-hypnosis, and biofeed-back. *Stress management skills* entail teaching effective communication, planning, and time management strategies, as well as providing patients with a systematic approach to problem solving. It is important to note that the skills listed do not differ from the skills used in other CBT protocols that have been described in this volume.

Two skills that are listed that may not be as recognizable to other CBT clinicians are attention diversion and pacing. With regard to attention diversion, also referred to as distraction techniques, the goal is to help the patient focus on other thoughts or feelings that are unrelated to his or her pain. One can easily imagine

different distraction techniques, such as reading, conversing with a friend, or watching television.

Pacing is a deceptively simple-sounding concept that, in practice, can be challenging for patients without proper guidance and practice. The notion is that patients with chronic pain will eventually need to begin to exercise safely and engage in physical activity. The goal of pacing is for individuals to learn that, when physically active, it is important to set reasonable goals, rather than engaging in activity until the pain leads to exhaustions or emotional distress. For instance, if a patient can mow the yard for 30 min before his or her back begins to hurt, the patient may be instructed to mow the yard for 15 min increments.

Skills Consolidation

In the skills consolidation phase, patients continue to practice, develop and strengthen new skills they have acquired. Having the patient practice with the therapist in session, as well as beginning to have the patient more fully integrate the skill in his or her environment outside therapy, becomes increasingly important. Practitioners of CBT will often have patients imagine using the skills in different potentially problematic situations, or may role-play with the patient various different problems that may occur.

Generalization and Maintenance

CBT for chronic pain should not be thought of as a one-time treatment that leads to a definitive cure. It provides people with the tools to manage their pain, so that it has an appreciable impact on their ability to enjoy those things in their lives that the patients perceive as important. For CBT to be truly effective, patients must continue to practice even when they have completed their course of therapy. Follow-up appointments at 3- to 6-month intervals, or on an as-needed basis, ensure that the patient's gains are maintained and reinforce the progress he or she has made. It should be noted that Marlatt and Gordon (1985) have written extensively on the issue of relapse prevention, and their ideas are easily translatable to pain patients. That is to say, preparing the patients for inevitable setbacks does not make them more likely to occur. Instead, patients learn to reframe a setback as a temporary, manageable, and typical part of recovery. If a patient's pain flares up and the patient has stopped practicing his or her relaxation skills, then the patient is well prepared to engage in objective examination of any irrational negative thoughts. Patients can begin to take the necessary steps to retrain their bodies to relax without interference from thoughts that the situation is "hopeless."

A SESSION-BY-SESSION GUIDE TO A TYPICAL COURSE OF TREATMENT

In this section we have compiled a prototypical 12-week course of CBT for a chronic pain patient.

Assessment

A multimodal assessment should occur prior to the patient's starting treatment. During the assessment process, it is also critical to explain to patients that you are interested in all the ways that pain has impacted their lives, and that you are not trying to prove that their pain is fake or that they are "crazy" for having pain that has not resolved.

Session 1

As with all CBT protocols, the first session is used to establish rapport and provide the rationale for the procedures to be employed. The general concepts noted earlier (e.g., the gate control theory of pain) are explained and the idea that learnable skills can be of aid is introduced. Typically, the session concludes with the instruction in diaphragmatic breathing and assignment of homework, including daily pain diaries and material about managing pain.

Session 2

Each subsequent session begins with a review of the last sessions, and a review of the homework. In Session 2, self-regulatory techniques and their rationale are presented. Self-regulatory techniques such as progressive muscle relaxation, guided imagery, mindfulness meditation, or self-hypnosis can be used.

Session 3

This session focuses on how to identify and incorporate relaxation training in everyday situations that produce stress (as identified by review of the pain diary). The patient is asked to schedule brief relaxation periods prior to those particularly stressful situations.

Session 4

The rationale for distraction techniques is provided to the patient. Three distraction techniques are taught: (1) focusing on physical surroundings; (2) counting backward slowly; and (3) focusing on auditory stimuli. An example of each technique is provided, and the patient is asked to practice.

Session 5

The rationale for pleasant activity scheduling is provided to the patient. Examples are described to the patient, and possible barriers to engaging in the pleasant activity are reviewed.

Session 6

A step-by-step pleasant activity scheduling plan is introduced. These steps include creating a balance between unpleasant and pleasant behaviors, planning ahead, setting specific goals, rewarding oneself for achieving goals, and checking one's progress toward one's overall goals.

Session 7

The rationale for cognitive therapy is provided in this session. Patients are taught about irrational negative thoughts. Homework is assigned to help patients recognize when they are having these irrational, negative thoughts.

Session 8

Instructions are provided for changing irrational thoughts and self-instructional training. Patients are taught methods to change irrational thoughts, such as developing more rational alternative thoughts. The question "What evidence do you have for that?" is repeatedly posed to patients. Self-statements to deal with pain are also taught to the patient. Self-statements are broken down into four categories, including preparing, beginning, during, and after. These statements include, "I may have to move a little slower, but I can still go shopping," or "My pain is flaring up, but it will soon pass."

Session 9

Methods for improving assertiveness are introduced in this session. A plan to improve social skills and assertiveness is developed with the patient and includes developing a personal problem list, monitoring assertiveness, practice with assertive imagery, transfer from imaginary to real life, and evaluating progress.

Session 10

A rationale is provided for using newly developed social skills. Points that are stressed during this session often include the fact that it is important to have the opportunity to interact with other people, and that inadequate reward occurs when social activities are no longer rewarding.

Session 11

Strategies for maintaining treatment gains are reviewed in this session. Points that are stressed during this session include: reviewing material already covered; review of what has been achieved; integrating what has been learned and incorporated into life; monitoring level of pain and tension on a regular basis; and examining possible "pitfalls" and solutions to them.

Session 12

The major theme of this session is "making a life plan." Points that are stressed during this session include: maintaining one's gains; planning effectively; and spelling out long-term goals.

EVIDENCE-BASED APPLICATIONS

The National Institutes of Health developed a consensus statement regarding the application and effectiveness of behavioral medicine techniques for pain (National Institute of Health Technology Assessment Panel, 1995). Overall, the panel participating in the technology assessment conference found strong evidence supporting the use of relaxation training in alleviating chronic pain and moderate evidence

supporting the use of cognitive behavioral therapy. However, as discussed, relaxation training is used as a self-regulatory tool within the context of cognitive-behavioral therapy treatment. More recently, Ostelo and colleagues (2005) conducted a systematic review and found evidence that the combination of respondent cognitive therapy and progressive muscle relaxation is more effective than wait-list control for short-term pain relief in patients with low back pain. Evidence also has been found for the effectiveness of cognitive therapy for migraine headaches, arthritis pain, and cancer pain (Blanchard et al., 1990; Lake, 2001; Keefe, Abernethy, & Campbell, 2005; Keefe et al., 2005; Tatrow & Montgomery, 2006).

CONCLUSION

CBT for chronic pain incorporates techniques that are common for any CBT intervention. The slight adjustments to treatment involve educating patients about how psychosocial factors influence their pain. In addition, activity pacing and distraction are other techniques that are frequently used with chronic pain patients. Unfortunately, chronic pain has a ripple effect, and very few areas of a person's life are not impacted when his or her pain is severe enough, and when it has lasted for an extended period of time. However, the techniques learned in CBT have a ripple effect as well, and they frequently impact areas of a person's life that are outside the treatment's immediate focus. Of course, it is also extremely important that therapists working with chronic pain patients have a thorough understanding of the biopsychosocial approach to pain assessment and treatment because of the complex interaction among physical, psychological and socioeconomic factors that are underlying pathophysiology and pain behaviors (cf. Gatchel, 2005; Gatchel & Turk, 1996).

References

Blanchard, E. B., Appelbaum, K. A., Radnitz, C. L., Morrill, B., Michultka, D., Kirsch, C., et al. (1990). A controlled evaluation of thermal biofeedback and thermal biofeedback combined with cognitive therapy in the treatment of vascular headache.

Journal of Consulting & Clinical Psychology, 58(2), 216–224.

Butler, R. W., Damarin, F. L., Beaulieu, C., Schwebel, A. L., & Thorn, B. E. (1989). Assessing cognitive coping strategies for acute postsurgical. *Pain,* 139–153.

Edwards, R., Bingham, C. O., Bathon, J., & Haythornthwaite, J. A. (2006). Catastrophizing and pain in arthritis, fibromyalgia, and other rheumatic diseases. *Arthritis and Rheumatism, 55*(2), 325–332.

Engel, G. L. (1959). "Psychogenic" pain and the pain-prone patient. *American Journal of Medicine,* 899–918.

Engel, G. L. (1977). The need for a new medical model: A challenge for biomedicine. *Science, 196* (4286), 129–136.

Flor, H., & Turk, D. C. (1984). Etiological theories and treatments for chronic back pain: I. Somatic models and interventions. *Pain, 19,* 105–121.

Fordyce, W. (1976). *Behavioral methods of control of chronic Pain and Illness.* St. Louis: Mosby.

Fordyce, W. E. (1988). Pain and suffering: A reappraisal. *American Psychologist, 43,* 276–283.

Gatchel, R. J. (2005). *Clinical essentials of pain management.* Washington, DC: American Psychological Association Press.

Gatchel, R. J. (1996). Psychological disorders and chronic pain: Cause and effect relationships. In R. J. Gatchel & D. C. Turk (Eds.), *Psychological approaches to pain management: A practitioner's handbook* (pp. 33–52). New York: Guilford.

Gatchel, R. J., & Epker, J. T. (1999). Psychosocial predictors of chronic pain and response to treatment. In R. J. Gatchel & D. C. Turk (Eds.), *Psychosocial factors in pain: Critical perspectives* (pp. 412–434). New York: Guilford Publications, Inc.

Gatchel, R. J., Polatin, P. B., Mayer, T. G., & Garcy, P. D. (1994). Psychopathology and the rehabilitation of patients with chronic low back pain disability. *Archives of Physical Medicine and Rehabilitation, 75,* 666–670.

Gatchel, R. J., & Turk, D. C. (1996). *Psychological approaches to pain management: A practitioner's handbook.* New York: Guilford.

Katon, W., Egan, K., & Miller, D. (1985). Chronic pain: Lifetime psychiatric diagnoses and family history. *American Journal of Psychiatry, 142,* 1156–1160.

Keefe, F. J., Abernethy, A. P., & Campbell, L. (2005). Psychological approaches to understanding and treating disease-related pain. *Annual Review of Psychology, 56,* 601–630.

Kerns, R. D., Turk, D. C., & Rudy, T. E. (1985). The West Haven–Yale Multidimensional Pain Inventory. *Pain, 23,* 345–356.

Kinney, R. K., Gatchel, R. J., Polatin, P. B., Fogarty, W. J., & Mayer, T. G. (1993). Prevalence of psychopathology in acute and chronic low back pain patients. *Journal of Occupational Rehabilitation, 1993,* 95–103.

Lake, A. E. III. (2001). Behavioral and nonpharmacologic treatments of headache. *Medical Clinics of North America, 85*(4), 1055–1075.

Leeuw, M., Goossens, M. E. J. B., Linton, S. J., Crombez, G., Boersma, K., & Vlaeyen, J. W. (2007). The fear-avoidance model of musculoskeletal pain: current state of scientific evidence. *Journal of Behavioral Medicine, 30*(1), 77–94.

Main, C. J., & Waddell, G. (1991). A comparison of cognitive measures in low back pain: Statistical structure and clinical validity at initial assessment. *Pain, 56,* 287–298.

Marlatt, G. A., & Gordon, W. H. (1985). Relapse prevention: Introduction and overview of the model. *British Journal of Addiction, 79,* 261–273.

Melzack, R., & Wall, P. D. (1965). Pain mechanisms: A new theory. *Science, 50,* 971–979.

National Institute of Health Technology Assessment Panel, N. (1995, October 16, 18, 1995). *Integration of behavioral and relaxation approaches into treatment of chronic pain and insomnia.* Paper presented at the National Institute of Health Technology Assessment Conference.

Ostelo, R. W., van Tulder, M. W., Vlaeyen, J. W., Linton, S. J., Morley, S. J., & Assendelft, W. J. (2005). Behavioural treatment for chronic low-back pain. [update of Cochrane Database Syst. Rev. 2000; (2):CD002014; PMID: 10796459]. *Cochrane Database of Systematic Reviews, 1.*

Polatin, P. B., Kinney, R., Gatchel, R. J., Lillo, E., & Mayer, T. G. (1993). Psychiatric illness and chronic low back pain: The mind and the spine—which goes first? *Spine, 18,* 66–71.

Sternbach, R. A. (1974). *Pain Patients: Traits and Treatment.* New York: Academic Press.

Sullivan, M. J., Stanish, W., Waite, H., Sullivan, M., & Tripp, D. A. (1998). Catastophizing, pain and disability in patients with soft-tissue injury. *Pain, 77,* 253–260.

Tatrow, K., & Montgomery, G. H. (2006). Cognitive behavioral therapy techniques for distress and pain in breast cancer patients: A meta-analysis. *Journal of Behavioral Medicine, 29*(1), 17–27.

Turk, D., & Rudy, T. (1988). Toward an empirically derived taxonomy of chronic pain patients: Integration of psychological assessment data. *Journal of Consulting & Clinical Psychology, 56,* 233–238.

Turk, D. C., & Gatchel, R. J. (Eds.). (2002). *Psychological approaches to pain management: A practitioner's handbook* (2nd ed.). New York: Guilford.

Turk, D. C., & Rudy, T. E. (1987). Towards a comprehensive assessment of chronic pain patients. *Behavioral Research and Therapy, 25,* 237–249.

Vlaeyen, J. W., & Linton, S. J. (2000). Fear-avoidance and its consequences in chronic muscoloskeletal pain: A state of the art. *Pain, 85*, 317–332.

Vlaeyen, J. W. S., Kole-Snijders, Rooteveel, A., Rusesink, R., & Heuts, P. (1995). The role of fear of movement/(re)injury in pain disability. *Journal of Occupational Rehabilitation, 5*, 235–252.

Weisberg, J. N., Vittengle, J. R., Clark, L. A., Gatchel, R. J., & Garen, A. A. (2000). Personality and pain: Summary and future directions. In R. J. Gatchel & J. N. Weisberg (Eds.), *Personality Characteristics of Patients with Pain*. Washington, D.C.: American Psychological Association.

51 PARENT TRAINING*

Kevin J. Moore and Gerald R. Patterson

Behavioral treatment for out-of-control children began in the late 1960s. It particularly emphasized the idea that the problem did not reside in the child; rather, it was in the social environment. Changing the aggressive child meant changing the environment that he or she lived in. The strategy that emerged was focused on training the parents (family members) to alter the contingencies they provided for both deviant and prosocial child behaviors.

Four different groups contributed to the development of these new procedures. Bijou played a key role during the early stages through his influence first on Hawkins and later on the Kansas parent trainers such as A. Christensen. Bijou also supported the Eugene, Oregon, group that included Eyeberg, Johnson, Patterson, and Reid. A third group at the Portland, Oregon, Medical School centered around Hanf, who produced such outstanding students as Forehand, Webster-Stratton, and Barkley. The fourth group, in Tennessee, consisted of Wahler and, for example, such productive students as Dumas. The general procedures that eventually became parent training (PT) were worked out over a series of meetings and exchanges of papers during the late 1960s and early 1970s.

* We would like to thank Peter Sprengelmeyer for reading a draft of this chapter and providing useful suggestions. Support for this chapter was provided by Grants No. R37 MH 37940 and RO1 MH 54257 from the Antisocial and Other Personality Disorders Program, Prevention, Early Intervention, and Epidemiology Branch, National Institute of Mental Health (NIMH), U.S. Public Health Service (PHS); RO1 HD 34511 from the Center for Research for Mothers and Children, National Institute of Child Health and Human Development, U.S. PHS; RO1 MH 60195 and RO1 MH 38318 from the Child and Adolescent Treatment and Preventive Intervention Research Branch, DSIR, NIMH, U.S. PHS; and P30 MH 46690 from the Prevention and Behavioral Medicine Research Branch, NIMH, U.S. PHS.

THEORY

Observational data collected in homes and classrooms suggested that children's aggression was surprisingly functional (i.e., it worked; Patterson, Littman, & Bricker, 1967). Similarly, family interactions in homes showed that coercive child behaviors were very effective in manipulating aversive exchanges among family members. Also, these families provided little, if any, support for prosocial child behaviors. The parents were observed to be ineffective in such parenting practices as discipline (limit setting), encouragement (contingent positive), monitoring, involvement, and family problem solving. It was assumed that the parenting practices controlled the contingencies.

It was 25 years before it was possible to show that observation-based measures of the relative rate of reinforcement for coercive behaviors predicted children's observed rates of deviant behavior a week later (Snyder & Patterson, 1995). In another study, the relative rate of reinforcement observed in family interaction predicted the future likelihood of police arrest and out-of-home placement (Snyder, Schrepferman, & St. Peter, 1997).

The findings from several longitudinal studies strongly supported the assumed relationship between parenting skills and antisocial behavior (Forgatch, Patterson, & Ray, 1996; Patterson, Reid, & Dishion, 1992). Structural equation models were used to examine these relationships. Multimethod and multiagent indicators specified both the parenting practices and child outcomes. Now, 20 years later, parenting practices are widely accepted as being causally related to child antisocial outcomes.

More recent research literature emphasizes the important role played by positive reinforcers supplied by deviant peers for deviant behavior (Patterson, Dishion, & Yoerger, 2000). The programmatic studies by Dishion and his colleagues showed that the relative rate of reinforcement for deviant talk predicted criminal activity several years later (Dishion, Spracklen, Andrews, & Patterson, 1996). The influence of deviant peers seems to begin in the elementary grades with marked acceleration during early adolescence. The outcome seems to be reflected primarily in covert forms of antisocial behavior.

Furthermore, findings from many longitudinal studies have shown reliable correlations between early-onset delinquency (arrest prior to age 14) and later criminal careers. The data also showed that this trajectory may begin as early as age 2 or 3 years (Patterson, 1996; Shaw, Keenan, & Vondra, 1994).

Thus, the contingency or social learning theory stipulates that prevention should begin at an early age and should involve procedures that improve parenting practices. The outcomes should include both reduced rates of antisocial behavior and reduced contacts with deviant peers.

INTERVENTION

In the early 1970s and 1980s, a series of small-scale studies employed randomized trials and observation data to test the hypothesis that training in parenting skills was associated with significant reductions in observed deviant child behavior (Bry, 1982; Patterson, Chamberlain, & Reid, 1982; Walter & Gilmore, 1973; Wiltz & Patterson, 1974). The strongest evidence for the effectiveness of PT with younger antisocial children is to be found in the programmatic studies by Webster-Stratton (1984, 1990) and Webster-Stratton and Hammond (1997). There is now a sufficient number of randomized trial studies to merit systematic reviews of this literature. Reviewers consistently conclude that interventions based on PT procedures produce reliable reductions in antisocial behavior (Kazdin, 1997; Kazdin & Weisz, 1998; Serketich & Dumas, 1996; Southam-Gerow & Kendall, 1997).

Cases referred for treatment typically require an average of 20 hours of professional time (including telephone calls and school visits). The procedures seem more effective with younger children 4–8 years old, as compared to older and adolescent children. Findings show that treatment failures are more likely for socially disadvantaged families and those with extremely depressed or antisocial parents. Parent training as a stand-alone treatment may be less effective for adolescent chronic delinquents. Studies that have attempted to treat these families using only PT have either met with no success (Henggeler, Melton, Brondino, Scherer, & Hanley, 1997), had limited success (Bank, Marlowe, Reid, Patterson, & Weinrott, 1991), or display such serious design flaws that their results are not interpretable. Alternatively, the Treatment Foster Care procedure put forward by Chamberlain and colleagues (Chamberlain & Moore, 1998; Chamberlain & Reid, 1998) trains carefully selected foster parents to use PT concepts. They are effective with chronic offending adolescents. As the adolescent adapts to the highly structured environment, the child is returned to his or her home for brief periods, and the biological parents are trained to use PT procedures. The randomized trial shows significant reductions in police referrals for the members of the experimental group. Additional studies are now under way.

PARENT TRAINING PROCEDURES

Behavioral PT's primary treatment targets are to decrease coercive child behavior, primarily child noncompliance, and to increase the relative rates of reinforcement for prosocial behaviors. There are several reasons for having noncompliance be a main treatment target:

- Child noncompliance is the most frequent referral complaint.
- Noncompliance is involved in the largest percentage of negative parent–child interactions.
- Children with compliance problems often teach parents, teachers, and siblings and peers not to attempt interactions with them where cooperation is the preferred behavior.

- Noncompliant children are often noncompliant across settings (e.g., home, school, neighborhood).
- The category of noncompliance subsumes most of the behaviors of the children with disruptive behavior who are referred for treatment. Common noncompliant referral behaviors include arguing, teasing, yelling, whining, complaining, temper tantrums, talking back, profanity, running off, noncompletion of chores, lying, stealing, ignoring directives or requests, not engaging in or completing homework assignments, physically resisting, destroying property, screaming, defiance, and disrupting others' activities.

The steps of PT are as follows:

1. Observing and defining behavior
2. Use of reinforcement to encourage prosocial behavior, including the use of shaping to teach new behavioral repertoires (e.g., the skilled use of contingency management systems or token economies)
3. The use of mild punishment (e.g., time-out from reinforcement, loss of privileges, and small work chores), the reduction of verbal reprimands, and the use of unambiguous directives
4. Generalization of the skills to school-related behaviors, including homework, to other community-based settings (e.g., the use of time-out procedures in public places and monitoring the child's whereabouts) and to anticipate future behavioral problems or developmental transitions (or both) where parenting practices are likely to need adjustment and new skills developed (e.g., entering middle school and the increasing freedom from direct adult observation and increasing peer involvement that accompanies these types of childhood transitions)

As part of the consent for treatment procedures, parents are instructed in the basic social learning principles about how children learn to act in particular ways. Parents are taught that they are the primary socializing agent of their children, that they have the most power and opportunity to change the problematic behavior of their children, and that children learn though

encouragement and limit setting. Parents are taught that encouragement teaches children what they should do and limit setting teaches children what they should not do. Parents are also instructed in the "coercion cycle" (discussed earlier) and told that a primary focus of the training will be learning skills and strategies to avoid these problematic coercive cycles.

After consent is obtained, there is a clinical interview with one or both parents, direct observation and coding of parent–child interactions in the home and in the clinic, and the collection by phone three to five times per week of a Parent Daily Report (PDR; a list of 12 to 31 problem behaviors; Forehand & McMahon, 1981; Patterson, Reid, Jones, & Conger, 1975). This idealized observational assessment, particularly when it occurs in the home, is not always cost efficient or logistically possible (Forehand & McMahon). Fortunately, studies have demonstrated that both clinic-based observational assessment and the PDR are related at high enough levels to observed behavior in the home to be clinically sufficient for the assessment and clinical monitoring of targeted behaviors (e.g., Patterson, 1982; Patterson & Fleischman, 1979; Patterson, Reid, Jones, & Conger, 1975; Peed, Roberts, & Forehand, 1977).

Once the PDR has been collected, the parent or parents are asked to rate the endorsed items so that the two to four most troublesome behaviors are clearly identified. At the same time, the prosocial opposites of these behaviors are identified, and operational definitions are developed. Most of the time, an initial prosocial target behavior will be compliance to adult directives, and we usually label this "minding" versus "not minding." If the child is old enough, a chore is another behavior that is added to the data collection chart. Parents are then taught how to observe and collect data on the child's performance of these behaviors.

During this first step, we also currently recommend that one or more of the common broadband childhood assessment instruments (e.g., Child Behavior Checklist [CBC-L], Achenbach, 1991; Behavioral Assessment System for Children [BASC], Reynolds & Kamphaus, 1994) be administered to parents and, when appropriate, to teachers. Even though these instruments have their limitations, they allow PT clinicians to gain efficient knowledge of comorbidity, cross-setting behavioral problems, or problem areas that might become the focus of treatment once a reasonable level of compliance is established.

In addition to the components delineated previously, we have found that phone contacts help parents both initiate and develop consistency in the use of PT intervention procedures (particularly early in the intervention process). During these phone contacts, clinicians help parents problem-solve implementation roadblocks and provide encouragement and reinforcement for parents' initial attempts to apply the intervention procedures. To summarize this first step, the main clinical objectives are to collect assessment information in order to identify target behaviors and their social–environmental contexts; to develop a baseline, and to begin to help the parents parse the behavioral stream into less global, more concrete, and smaller interactional segments. The baseline data are also used to help ascertain change as the rest of the intervention steps are systematically taught to and applied by the parents.

Teaching parents to observe, pinpoint, and track their children's behavior is important because it helps them to see the interactional sequences that are involved in the development and maintenance of both positive and problematic child behaviors. It also begins to teach parents that they will be directly involved in the treatment process, and it moves the parents away from mentalistic conceptualizations of why their children perform either antisocial or prosocial behaviors. The initial tracking chart usually includes only two problem behaviors and their prosocial opposites (e.g., not minding vs. minding).

The next step involves teaching parents how to use contingent positive reinforcement to encourage appropriate behavior and to teach new prosocial behaviors. As part of this step, the clinician works with the parents to develop a written contingency plan for how the performance of developmentally appropriate prosocial behaviors will be reinforced. Usually, the criteria for the child's access to the reinforcer are specified and added to the tracking chart. The concept of reinforcement is carefully defined for the parents, and the powerful effects that attention (as a reinforcer) can have in the development and maintenance of problem behavior is discussed. Parents are then taught to place the majority of their attention on the prosocial behaviors they want their child to perform through the use of contingent praise, social reinforcement, and a contingency system. Examples of these contingency systems are readily available and range from very simple minding or not minding charts for very young children (Forehand & McMahon, 1981; Patterson, 1975; Webster-Stratton, 2000) to sophisticated token economies for older children and adolescents (e.g., Barkley, Edwards, & Robin, 1998; Chamberlain & Mihalic, 1998; Patterson & Forgatch, 1987).

During this step, two additional skills are emphasized: (1) teaching the parents not to use verbal reprimands (nattering) and (2) teaching the use of clear and unambiguous directives (e.g., "Please take out the garbage by 5:30," vs. "Would you take the garbage out when you have a chance?"). In order to shape the parental behavioral repertoires emphasized in this step, and in other steps of behavioral PT, role-playing, modeling (live and videotaped), and *in vivo* feedback are clinical techniques used extensively.

In addition to these concepts and strategies, we have found it clinically useful to teach parents who lack them to develop parent–child routines they can use during critical periods of the day that have been identified as periods where bursts of child problem behaviors occur (Goodenough, 1931, as cited in Patterson, 1982). Behavioral problems do not occur at a consistent rate throughout the day but rather occur in bursts. Diurnal variations strongly suggest that these bursts occur at predictable times throughout the day. The periods of day were 7:30 AM, 11:30 AM, 5:30 PM, and 8:30 PM, and correspond to the times of the day when three things are occurring: (1) transitions, including biological state transitions, are taking place; (2) compliance demands are occurring at high frequency; and (3) parents are multitasking such things as meals and their own transitions. It is our experience, both as parents and as parent trainers, that if predictable routines (including encouragement and limit-setting procedures) can be established and reinforced during these times of the day, parents can significantly reduce rates of problematic child behavior and household stress and tension.

During this step, the clinician's task is to help parents to become competent in the use of a daily contingency management system where appropriate behavior and compliance are consistently reinforced. For most families, this system is just an expansion of the tracking chart, where incentives or privileges are earned contingent on the child's earning a certain number of points, stickers, or smiley faces for appropriate behavior. A rule of thumb that we use is that the child should be earning the agreed-upon incentive or privilege 70%–75% of the time. If not, the criterion is too high and needs to be adjusted. If age appropriate for the child, parents are also taught how to negotiate with their child for behavioral changes using individual contingency contracts. These contracts are sometimes used as an adjunct to an ongoing contingency system or as a stand-alone strategy.

The next step is teaching parents to use effective limit-setting techniques. This step is taught after parents have become firm with the use of positive reinforcement and incentives. It is important to note that it is our clinical experience and that of others (e.g., Barkley, 1987; Forehand & McMahon, 1981) that if limit-setting techniques and skills are taught before parents are firm with the reinforcement and encouragement techniques, they will drop out of treatment prematurely. With regard to limit setting, a primary goal of the clinician is to teach parents that limit setting is a teaching method and not a method whereby pain and suffering are necessary for children to learn to behave. Thus, parents are taught that limit setting works best when it is applied immediately and consistently, is used early in a sequence of problem behavior or episode of noncompliance, and is of short duration.

The primary limit-setting techniques that are taught to parents in this step are the use of time-out from reinforcement, privilege removal, and small work chores. It is commonly necessary in this step first to help the parents develop a clear set of 5–10 house rules that are behaviorally defined, written down, and posted. There are many examples of time-out procedures

(e.g., Barkley, 1987; Becker, 1971; Christopherson, 1990; Forehand & McMahon, 1981; Patterson, 1975b) and clinicians using PT procedures must become familiar with and highly competent in the use of this procedure, including the use of backup consequences if time-out is refused. For training clinicians and parents to become competent with this skill, we like to use the procedure and description of its application contained in Patterson (1975a) because it is thorough and offers enough examples of how to manage common child and adult behaviors that have been shown to be problematic to the effectiveness of this technique.

In addition, the effectiveness of time-out (see Chapter 55) is enhanced by a social environment that is affectively upbeat and where there is a consistent probability of the child's receiving positive reinforcement. Although many skills taught in the previous steps help parents to develop a reasonably positive family environment, in families that have children with high rates of noncompliance, the development of a positive environment often needs to be explicitly taught. Christopherson (1990) presents a useful strategy for teaching parents this set of skills that he has called "Time In."

The other primary limit-setting skill that parents are taught to use is response-cost techniques, such as loss of privileges. This technique has a wide range of application. For example, response cost can be part of the contingency system whereby the child does not obtain enough points or tokens to gain access to privileges, such as later bedtime, riding his or her bike, or watching television. Parents are also taught how to remove access to privileges for refusing to go to a time-out and breaking rules. As children age, we also teach parents to use small, 5- to 10-minute work chores (e.g., emptying a dishwasher, wiping down a mirror, etc.) as limit-setting consequences.

During the last step of PT, parents are taught that their contingency program needs to be "worked" (e.g., changed, progress assessed, some behaviors dropped and others added, etc.) so that the parents are more likely to develop and generalize the parenting skills to new behaviors and situations. This final stage then involves generalizing the skills developed to

486 GENERAL PRINCIPLES OF COGNITIVE BEHAVIOR THERAPY

monitoring the child's educational performance (see Chapter 22), time away from home (e.g., monitoring friends, whereabouts, etc.), and the management of the child's behavior in other public settings. During this step, parents are taught how to tie home and school together by getting information concerning school performance and behavior. This is done primarily through the use of a school card that goes between home and school on a daily basis. The use of a school card is usually tied into the daily contingency management system being used in the home, whereby the child earns or loses points based on teacher-reported performance and behavior. Depending on the particular circumstances and skill level of the parents, it is sometimes necessary for the clinician to go to a school meeting with the parents to establish the school card system. Parents are also taught to anticipate and manage problem behaviors that occur in public places, including how to use time-out in public places. For example, time-out may not be appropriate, and parents are taught how to place a child in time-out immediately upon returning home. Throughout this stage, parent trainers remain alert for behaviors that the parents can generalize their skills to include, encouraging parents to continue to identify behaviors they want to change, to record the effectiveness of their interventions on these behaviors, and to fine tune their home and school contingency programs.

CAVEAT

Even though on the surface PT appears to be an easy set of skills to develop in clinicians and teach to parents, our experience over the past 30 years strongly suggests the opposite. That is, considerable clinical acumen ("soft clinical skills"; Patterson & Chamberlain, 1988) is necessary to effectively treat children and families within a behavioral PT approach, and this is particularly true for clinic-referred children and their families. We strongly recommend that clinicians attempting to use this treatment method for the first time have significant training and supervision by clinicians experienced in the use of these techniques.

References

Achenbach, T. M. (1991). Child Behavior Checklist—Cross-Informant Version (available from Thomas Achenbach, PhD, Child and Adolescent Psychiatry, Department of Psychiatry, University of Vermont, 5 South Prospect Street, Burlington, VT, 05401).

Bank, L., Marlowe, J. H., Reid, J. B., Patterson, G. R., & Weinrott, M. R. (1991). A comparative evaluation of PT for families of chronic delinquents. *Journal of Abnormal Child Psychology, 19,* 15–33.

Barkley, R. A. (1987). *Defiant children: A clinician's manual for parent training.* New York: Guilford Press.

Barkley, R. A., Edwards, G. H., & Robin, A. L. (1999). *Defiant teens: A clinician's manual for assessment and family intervention.* New York: Guilford.

Becker, W. C. (1971). *Parents are teachers: A child management program.* Champaign, IL: Research Press.

Bry, B. H. (1982). Reducing the incidence of adolescent problems through prevention/intervention: One and five year follow-up. *American Journal of Community Psychology, 10,* 265–276.

Chamberlain, P., & Mihalic, S. F. (1998). Multidimensional treatment foster care. In D. S. Elliott (Series Ed.), *Book eight: Blueprints for violence prevention.* Boulder, CO: Institute of Behavioral Science, University of Colorado.

Chamberlain, P., & Moore, K. J. (1998). A clinical model for parenting juvenile offenders: A comparison of group care versus family care. *Clinical Psychology and Psychiatry, 3,* 375–386.

Chamberlain, P., & Reid, J. B. (1998). Comparison of two community alternatives to incarceration for chronic juvenile offenders. *Journal of Consulting and Clinical Psychology, 66,* 624–633.

Christopherson, E. R. (1990). *Beyond discipline: Parenting that lasts a lifetime.* Kansas City: Westport Publishers.

Dishion, T. J., Spracklen, K. M., Andrews, D. W., & Patterson, G.R. (1996). Deviancy training in male adolescent friendships. *Behavior Therapy, 27,* 373–390.

Forehand, R., & McMahon, R. J. (1981). *Helping the noncompliant child: A clinician's guide to parent training.* New York: Guilford.

Forgatch, M. S., Patterson, G. R., & Ray, J. A. (1996). Divorce and boys' adjustment problems: Two paths with a single model. In E. M. Hetherington & E.A. Blechman (Eds.), *Stress, coping, and resiliency in children and families* (pp. 67–105). Mahwah, NJ: Lawrence Erlbaum.

Goodnough, F. L. (1931). *Anger in young children.* Minneapolis: University of Minnesota Press.

Henggeler, S. W., Melton, G. B., Brondino, M. J., Scherer, D. G., & Hanley, J. H. (1997). Multisystemic therapy with violent and chronic juvenile offenders and their families: The roles of treatment fidelity in successful dissemination. *Journal of Consulting and Clinical Psychology, 65,* 821–833.

Kazdin, A. E. (1997). Parent management training: Evidence, outcomes, and issues. *Journal of the American Academy of Child and Adolescent Psychiatry, 36,* 1349–1356.

Kazdin, A. E., & Weisz, J. R. (1998). Identifying and developing empirically supported child and adolescent treatments. *Journal of Consulting and Clinical Psychology, 66,* 19–36.

Patterson, G. R. (1975a). *Families: Applications of social learning to family life.* Champaign, IL: Research Press.

Patterson, G. R. (1975b). Multiple evaluations of a parent training program. In T. Thompson (Ed.), *Applications of behavior modification: Proceedings of the first international symposium on behavior modification* (pp. 299–322). New York: Academic Press.

Patterson, G. R. (1982). *A social learning approach: Vol. 3. Coercive family process.* Eugene, OR: Castalia.

Patterson, G. R. (1996). Some characteristics of a developmental theory for early onset delinquency. In M. F. Lenzenweger & J. J. Haugaard (Eds.), *Frontiers of developmental psychopathology* (pp. 81–124). New York: Oxford University Press.

Patterson, G. R., & Chamberlain, P. (1988). Treatment process: A problem at three levels. In L. C. Wynne (Ed.), *State of the art in family therapy research: Controversies and recommendations* (pp. 189–223). New York: Family Process Press.

Patterson, G. R., Chamberlain, P., & Reid, J. B. (1982). A comparative evaluation of parent training procedures. *Behavior Therapy, 13,* 638–651.

Patterson, G. R., Dishion, T. J., & Yoerger, K. (2000). Adolescent growth in new forms of problem behavior: Macro- and micro-peer dynamics. *Prevention Science, 1,* 3–13.

Patterson, G. R., & Fleischman, M. J. (1979). Maintenance of treatment effects: Some considerations concerning family systems and follow-up data. *Behavior Therapy, 10,* 168–185.

Patterson, G. R., & Forgatch, M. S. (1987). *Parents and adolescents living together, part 1: The basics.* Eugene, OR: Castalia.

Patterson, G. R., Littman, R. A., & Bricker, W. (1967). Assertive behavior in children: A step towards a theory of aggression. *Monographs of the Society for Research in Child Development, 32*(5), 1–43.

Patterson, G. R., Reid, J. B., & Dishion, T. J. (1992). *A social interactional approach: Vol. 4. Antisocial boys.* Eugene, OR: Castalia.

Patterson, G. R., Reid, J. B., Jones, R. R., & Conger, R. E. (1975). *A social learning approach: I. Families with aggressive children.* Eugene, OR: Castalia.

Peed, S., Roberts, M., & Forehand, R. (1977). Evaluation of the effectiveness of a standardized parent training program in altering the interaction of mothers and their non-compliant children. *Behavior Modification, 1,* 323–350.

Reynolds, C., & Kamphaus, R. (1994). Behavioral Assessment System for Children (available from American Guidance Service, 4201 Woodland Road, Circle Pines, MN, 55014).

Serketich, W. J., & Dumas, J. E. (1996). The effectiveness of behavioral parent training to modify antisocial behavior in children: A meta-analysis. *Behavior Therapy, 27,* 171–186.

Shaw, D. S., Keenan, K., & Vondra, J. I. (1994). Developmental precursors of externalizing behavior: Ages 1 to 3. *Developmental Psychology, 30,* 355–364.

Snyder, J. J., & Patterson, G. R. (1995). Individual differences in social aggression: A test of a reinforcement model of socialization in the natural environment. *Behavior Therapy, 26,* 371–391.

Snyder, J., Schrepferman, L., & St. Peter, C. (1997). Origins of antisocial behavior: Negative reinforcement and affect dysregulation of behavior as socialization mechanisms in family interaction. *Behavior Modification, 21,* 187–215.

Southam-Gerow, M. A., & Kendall, P. C. (1997). Parent-focused and cognitive-behavioral treatments of antisocial youth. In D. Stoff, J. Breiling, & J.D. Maser (Eds.), *Handbook of antisocial behavior* (pp. 384–394). New York: John Wiley & Sons.

Walter, H., & Gilmore, S. K. (1973). Placebo versus social learning effects in parent training procedures designed to alter the behaviors of aggressive boys. *Behavior Therapy, 4,* 361–371.

Webster-Stratton, C. (1984). Randomized trial of two parent training programs for families with conduct-disordered children. *Journal of Consulting and Clinical Psychology, 52,* 666–678.

Webster-Stratton, C. (1990). Long-term follow-up of families with young conduct problem children: From preschool to grade school. *Journal of Clinical Child Psychology, 19,* 144–149.

Webster-Stratton, C. (2000). *The incredible years training series.* Washington, DC: U.S. Department of Justice, Office of Justice Programs, Office of Juvenile Justice and Delinquency Prevention. (GPO no. 0718-A-09, Document # J 32.10:IN 2).

Webster-Stratton, C., & Hammond, M. (1997). Treating children with early-onset conduct problems: A comparison of child and parent training interventions. *Journal of Consulting and Clinical Psychology, 65,* 93–109.

Wiltz, N. A., Jr., & Patterson, G. R. (1974). An evaluation of parent training procedures designed to alter inappropriate aggressive behavior of boys. *Behavior Therapy, 5,* 215–221.

52 SELF-EFFICACY INTERVENTIONS: GUIDED MASTERY THERAPY

Walter D. Scott and Daniel Cervone

Research on perceived self-efficacy dates to the 1970s, its origin being the landmark paper of Bandura (1977). Bandura had observed that participant modeling treatments for phobics seemed to engender psychological change that was widespread. Therapy altered not only clients' autonomic arousal to threats, but their sense of self. Bandura reasoned that these self-perceptions might not be epiphenomenal, but causal. The basic tenet of self-efficacy theory (Bandura, 1977) was that people's appraisals of their capabilities to execute actions to cope with challenging environments are proximal determinants of affective arousal, cognitive processing, motivation, and behavior.

The publication of Bandura's theory was hailed as an "important event" (Rachman, 1978, p. 137), one that promised to "sustain and nourish ... a better understanding and more effective treatment of psychological disorders" (Wilson, 1978, p. 227). In the subsequent years, extensive lines of both correlational and experimental research has verified that self-efficacy perceptions causally contribute to human development, adjustment, and achievement (Bandura, 1997; Cervone & Scott, 1995; Stankovic & Luthans, 1998). In addition, in the treatment of anxiety, we have found that targeting self-efficacy can lead to more effective cognitive behavioral interventions (Williams, 1990).

Self-efficacy theory is not a single construct theory. Rather, it should be understood as one component of the broader social cognitive theory of personality functioning (Bandura, 1986; also see Cervone & Shoda, 1999). In social cognitive analyses, personality and individual differences are analyzed in terms of cognitive and affective mechanisms through which people interpret events, develop skills, reflect on themselves, and plan courses of action. Self-efficacy processes, then, are just one in a spectrum of social-cognitive determinants of experience and behavior. Efficacy beliefs, however, take on particular significance because they both directly influence behavior and influence other psychological variables of significance. For example, the goals people adopt of tasks are based partly on their subjective appraisals of their efficacy for performance. Efficacy beliefs affect skill development in that people who doubt their capabilities may fail to undertake activities that inherently build skills. Research on perceived self-efficacy converges with other lines of work involving control beliefs (e.g., Skinner, 1995) in showing that subjective perceptions of personal control and efficacy contribute to personal development.

The established links between self-efficacy perceptions and emotion and action suggest, of course, that perceived self-efficacy is a valuable target for therapeutic change. People who come to believe that they can master challenges may experience less anticipatory anxiety and engage in activities in a more vigorous, persistent, and ultimately successful manner. The challenge, then, is to identify types of psychosocial interventions that might boost self-efficacy perceptions.

Self-efficacy theory (Bandura, 1977, 1997) is particularly valuable in this regard, in that it analyzes not only the consequences of high versus low self-efficacy beliefs but their causes. Bandura (1977) has provided a taxonomy of the types of experiences that can alter efficacy beliefs. These include people's subjective interpretations of their emotional and physiological states; exposure to verbal persuasion; observation of others' success and failure (i.e., modeling); and first-hand, enactive performance experiences. The last of these is generally found to be the most reliable.

In guided mastery therapy, the primary goal of the therapist is to foster a subjective sense of mastery or self-efficacy. This approach has been applied mainly to the treatment of simple phobias and agoraphobia (Williams, 1992). For these conditions, guided mastery therapy has been found to boost self-referent beliefs and eradicate avoidant behavior more rapidly and more powerfully than do other performance-based treatments such as exposure therapies and systematic desensitization (Williams, 1990, 1995; Williams & Cervone, 1998). Research on simple phobias (Bandura, Adams, & Beyer, 1977) and agoraphobia (Williams, Dooseman, & Kleifield, 1984) reveals that guided mastery interventions enable clients to perform the vast majority of behavioral acts that they had originally been incapable of performing.

WHO MIGHT BENEFIT FROM THIS TECHNIQUE?

So far guided mastery treatment has been developed and evaluated for a diversity of phobias, including agoraphobia, social phobia, and simple phobias. For each of these conditions, there is strong support for the effectiveness of guided mastery therapy (see Bandura, 1997; Williams, 1992). Although guided mastery therapy has not yet been applied or evaluated outside anxiety problems, the role of self-efficacy beliefs in mood disorders, substance abuse, health habits, stress reduction, and athletic performance has been clearly documented (Bandura, 1997). Therefore, we would expect that mastery-based interventions targeting self-efficacy beliefs in these domains would be effective as well.

CONTRAINDICATIONS OF THE TREATMENT

The effectiveness of guided mastery therapy depends on the client's ability to attribute personal mastery as the reason for behavioral success. To the extent that other factors interfere with this cognitive process, which is critical, the success of guided mastery interventions is likely to be limited. For instance, guided mastery interventions may be inappropriate for clients who have elected psychotropic medication as a long-term component of their treatment regimen. Ingesting psychotropic medications provides a compelling and competing attribution

for performance success. Other more obvious contraindications include psychosis, which impairs both the ability to execute performances to one's full potential and to make meaningful mastery attributions. Finally, it is important to note that we currently know very little about how frequently occurring co-morbid conditions impact the effectiveness of guided mastery approaches to phobias. For instance, phobic disorders often co-occur with mood disorders. In such cases, although perhaps not contraindicated, special care is likely to be required in the delivery of guided mastery therapy (e.g., increasing motivation to attempt activity exercises, carefully attending to and challenging dysfunctional attributional processes, to name a few).

HOW DOES THE TECHNIQUE WORK?

Guided mastery therapy works by enhancing people's self-efficacy. Research using diverse methodologies, including structured questionnaires and thought-sampling techniques, suggest that thoughts about personal efficacy are the key mediator of behavior and behavioral change in successful agoraphobia and simple phobia treatment interventions (Bandura, 1997; Williams, Kinney, Harap, & Liebmann, 1997; but cf. Hoffart, 1995, 1998). Even when alternative cognitive mediators, such as anticipatory anxiety, outcome expectations, and perceived danger, are statistically controlled, self-efficacy perceptions continue to predict reductions in anxiety and phobic behaviors. Indeed, self-efficacy appraisals have been found to be superior even to past treatment behavior in predicting treatment outcome.

STEP-BY-STEP PROCEDURES

The key focus for guided mastery therapy is therefore to provide an enabling environment in which the client is able to achieve a high degree of self-efficacy for the relevant performance domain. Behavioral success does not automatically stamp in a sense of confidence. Nor does the sheer amount of time that one is exposed to the feared stimuli. Rather, the successful reduction of fear and avoidance requires that the "exposure" exercises lead to a sense of confidence that one can competently cope with the feared object. Therefore, the therapist must ensure that people not only expose themselves to the feared stimulus, nor that they only experience objective success, but that they subjectively attribute their exposure and success to their own effort and skills. Although exposure and guided mastery approaches share some features, this key distinction of guided mastery therapy regarding the importance of quickly instilling mastery perceptions leads to a number of therapeutic innovations.

In the guided mastery approach, the therapist takes a more active helping role so that they are able to rapidly promote performance success and attributions of mastery. In addition to providing support and encouragement, a number of strategies are utilized to facilitate mastery. Many of these interventions are conducted outside the therapy office and in field settings. Early on in treatment, the therapist utilizes a variety of modeling interventions to demonstrate the feared activity for the client. Various modeling strategies are employed, including enactive modeling, symbolic modeling, and joint participation of the therapist with the client in the activity. These modeling strategies are pursued with the goal of enabling the client to perform at a high level as quickly as possible. Then the activity is broken down into graded, manageable subtasks that the client can perform alone with a good probability of success. Tasks can be made easier in a number of ways to insure mastery. Exposure time can be reduced. Protective performance aids may be utilized. And modeling can be used at difficult points. However, when the client feels a high degree of efficacy, all of these aids are withdrawn. In addition, any safety rituals or aids that the client uses to cope with the performance are identified. The therapist then has the client execute the performance without relying on coping strategies so that a robust and generalized sense of self-efficacy is obtained. The final stage involves identifying self-directed mastery experiments that the client pursues outside of therapy. We will now review these guided mastery interventions in more detail.

Modeling

Modeling is used extensively in guided mastery therapy. In enactive modeling, the therapist behaviorally demonstrates the relevant performance. In symbolic modeling, the therapist offers verbal guidance or displays the relevant performance using video or film. Early in treatment, both enactive and symbolic modeling procedures are used to provide some guidance to clients in performing the specific feared task. They are also used throughout treatment to fine-tune performances and to assist clients with more challenging aspects of performance. In both forms of modeling, the therapist should strive to enact or specify very specific activities, usually the most problematic aspects of the performance.

Participant modeling is another modeling technique employed by guided mastery therapists. This involves the therapist performing the feared activity with the client. Joint performance of an activity with a therapist has several advantages. First, the therapist can provide a reassuring presence. Studies have shown that this type of presence itself can reduce anxiety reactions. In addition, participant modeling is extremely useful for correcting problematic aspects of a client's performance. When people are in the midst of performing a feared activity, they are usually quite attentive to such corrective modeling interventions.

Often in these participant modeling situations, the therapist employs a combination of both enactive and symbolic modeling strategies. For instance, the following enactive and symbolic modeling instructions might be offered to a height phobic as he or she attempts to lean over a rail looking down several stories:

> *Therapist:* Try to touch the railing here with your left hand. Good, you can touch it with your fingertips, so now see if you can touch it with the palm of the hand, like this [therapist models performance with client]. That's fine, now try to see if you can touch it with the palm of the hand, like this [again therapist models performance with client]. Very good, now can you also grab the railing with your right hand? That's a little difficult just now, so instead just touch it with

your fingers. Good, now try to grasp it. Don't hold your breath; you can do this and breathe at the same time. Ok, can you grab it with both hands? Great, now you have to get your legs and body closer to the rail. Try to move your left foot a little closer and straighten your legs if you can. Square your shoulders with the railing. All right, you're doing very well (Williams, 1990, pp. 101–102).

Graded Task Performance

Robust beliefs in personal efficacy are most instilled through firsthand mastery experiences (Bandura, 1997). The personal experience of mastery is difficult to deny, even among individuals who typically doubt their performance capabilities. Consequently, after modeling, guided mastery therapists utilize graded task assignments. These procedures are quite similar to the graded task performance techniques described elsewhere (e.g., Beck, Rush, Shaw, & Emery, 1979) with some distinctive components. The basic idea is to get clients attempting to perform those performances they fear. However, to the client, the entire performance is feared and appears overwhelming. Therefore, the therapist breaks the performance down into subtasks that the client perceives as more manageable.

In the guided mastery approach, the therapist should strive to identify subtasks that the client believes can be accomplished with extra effort and persistence. Using a self-efficacy scale with the standard anchors of 0–100, this translates into performance subtasks that the client generally rates in the range of 20–50. To increase client's efficacy levels, participant modeling can be used extensively. After accomplishing a subtask, clients typically experience a significant increase in self-efficacy, which leads to greater persistence and effort on subsequent subtasks. Graded task assignment continues until the entire performance sequence is mastered.

Special attention is given to those situations in which clients fail to adequately perform a given subtask. In these cases, the therapist guides clients so that they attribute the failed performance to the size of the task demand. Then an easier subtask is selected. To boost client's efficacy sufficiently so that they attempt the easier performance with good effort and persistence, the therapist can employ more extensive enactive, symbolic, and participant modeling techniques. Finally, on some occasions, the client's major difficulty with a performance may lie with a specific skill required as part of the entire performance. In such cases, the therapist can have the client focus on and master that particular skill prior to proceeding to the overall performance.

In defining subtasks, the therapist utilizes a number of strategies for manipulating the difficulty of the performance so that it is within the client's perceived ability level. One strategy involves graduating the amount of time that participants engage in the performance. For instance, an initial subtask might have a height phobic hold the rail and look over a balcony for a period of 5 seconds. Once this subtask is mastered, the duration can be increased to first 10 seconds, next 30 seconds, then 1 minute, and so on.

Another strategy involves providing a number of protective mastery aids to enable the client to achieve performance mastery. Often, these are direct physical aids provided by the therapist. For instance, a therapist might hold the client's arm as he walks over a feared bridge. A dog might be restrained with a leash as a dog phobic makes his or her initial approach. Of course, each of these protective aids is gradually withdrawn once these performances are mastered so that a robust, flexible, and more generalized sense of mastery is developed. However, these protective aids are useful initially for enabling the client to quickly attain a high level of performance and mastery. The more severe the phobia, the more these protective aids are utilized.

Identify and Remove Safety Rituals and Aids

Clients often use a number of safety rituals to cope with feared activities. For instance, clients may tense themselves to cope with approaching a high balcony. They may drive only in the slow lane to deal with their fear of driving in traffic. They may negotiate a grocery store by following a specific and circumscribed path. Although such coping strategies may help the client to cope with these fears, they limit the development of a sense of mastery that is both robust and resilient. The problem is that without these aids, clients doubt their abilities. And these self-doubts limit their ability to perform.

In guided mastery therapy, explicit attention is given to the presence of such coping aids. Clients are asked to tell the therapist about any special techniques, behaviors, or rituals that they use to help themselves to cope with the feared performance. Then the therapist encourages the client to perform the task without relying on these safety rituals and aids. The goal is to promote a robust sense of efficacy that will last and that will generalize outside the treatment setting. Unless such safety rituals and aids are identified, and the client is given full opportunities to perform the activity without relying on them, it is likely that any therapeutic gains will be highly specific and highly transient.

Self-Directed Mastery Experiments

The final phase of guided mastery therapy has the client functioning essentially as his or her own guided mastery therapist. The client is taught the principles of guided mastery therapy and works collaboratively with the therapist to identify homework assignments. These homework assignments are designed with the goal of increasing both the proficiency and the flexibility of the previously feared performance. By proficiency, assignments are executed outside therapy in which the client performs without relying on aids or special rituals. By flexibility, activities are chosen which requires the client to perform the task in a variety of different ways. Although the therapist helps to specify these assignments initially, the client executes them outside the therapy context, either with a significant other or alone. The goal is for the client to continue applying these guided mastery therapy principles independently after formal therapy has concluded.

References

Bandura, A. (1977). Self-efficacy: Toward a unifying theory of behavioral change. *Psychological Review, 84,* 191–215.

Bandura, A. (1986). *Social foundations of thought and action.* Englewood Cliffs, NJ: Prentice Hall.

Bandura, A. (1997). *Self-efficacy: The exercise of control.* New York: Freeman.

Bandura, A., Adams, N. E., & Beyer, J. (1977). Cognitive processes mediating behavior change. *Journal of Personality and Social Psychology, 35,* 125–139.

Beck, A. T., Rush, A. J., Shaw, B. F., & Emery, G. (1977). *Cognitive therapy of depression.* New York: Guilford.

Cervone, D., & Scott, W. D. (1995). Self-efficacy theory of behavioral change. In W. O'Donohue & L. Krasner (Eds.), *Theories of behavior therapy* (pp. 349–383). Washington, DC: American Psychological Association.

Cervone, D., & Shoda, Y. (1999). Social-cognitive theories and the coherence of personality. In D. Cervone & Y. Shoda (Eds.), *The coherence of personality: Social–cognitive bases of consistency, variability, and organization* (pp. 3–33). New York: Guilford.

Hoffart, A. (1995). A comparison of cognitive and guided mastery therapy of agoraphobia. *Behaviour Research and Therapy, 33,* 423–434.

Hoffart, A. (1998). Cognitive and guided mastery therapy of agoraphobia: Long-term outcome and mechanisms of change. *Cognitive Therapy and Research, 22,* 195–207.

Rachman, S. (1978). Perceived self-efficacy: Editorial introduction. *Advances in Behaviour Research and Therapy, 1,* 137.

Skinner, E. A. (1995). *Perceived control, motivation, and coping.* Thousand Oaks, CA: Sage.

Stajkovic, A. D., & Luthans, F. (1998). Social cognitive theory and self-efficacy: Going beyond traditional motivational and behavioral approaches. *Organizational Dynamics, 26,* 62–74.

Williams, S. L. (1990). Guided mastery treatment of agoraphobia: Beyond stimulus exposure. In M. Hersen, R. M. Eisler, & P. M. Miller (Eds.), *Progress in behavior modification* (Vol. 26, pp. 89–121). Newbury Park, CA: Sage.

Williams, S. L. (1992). Perceived self-efficacy and phobic disability. In R. Schwarzer (Ed.), *Self-efficacy: Thought control of action.* Washington, DC: Hemisphere Publishing Corporation.

Williams, S. L. (1995). Self-efficacy, anxiety, and phobic disorders. In J. E. Maddux (Ed.), *Self-efficacy, adaptation, and adjustment: Theory, research, and application* (pp. 69–107). New York: Plenum.

Williams, S. L., & Cervone, D. (1998). Social cognitive theory. In D. Barone, M. Hersen, & V. B. Van Hasselt (Eds.), *Advanced personality* (pp. 173–207). New York: Plenum.

Williams, S. L., Dooseman, G., & Kleifield, E. (1984). Comparative effectiveness of guided mastery and exposure treatments for intractable phobias. *Journal of Consulting and Clinical Psychology, 52,* 505–518.

Williams, S. L., Kinney, P. J., Harap, S. T., & Liebmann, M. (1997). Thoughts of agoraphobic people during scary tasks. *Journal of Abnormal Psychology, 106,* 511–520.

Wilson, G. T. (1978). The importance of being theoretical: A commentary on Bandura's Self-efficacy: Towards a unifying theory of behavioral change. *Advances in Behaviour Research and Therapy, 1,* 137.

53 POSITIVE ATTENTION

Stephen R. Boggs and Sheila M. Eyberg

Positive attention (PA) is a technique in which one person gives verbal or nonverbal attention to another person for the purpose of increasing the frequency or duration of the other person's ongoing or immediately preceding behavior. This chapter discusses PA in the context of child behavior therapy, in which caregivers (usually parents) are taught to respond to positive child behavior with positive social feedback. From a behavior analytic perspective, determining whether attention is "positive" for a particular child and equating it with positive reinforcement would require a functional assessment of its effect on the frequency or duration of the behavior preceding the positive attention. For purposes of this chapter, however, we define PA as a general class of positive verbal and non-verbal adult responses intended as social reinforcers for positive child behavior. Praise is an example of verbal PA and is perhaps the most common form of PA discussed in parent training. Hugging a child is an example of nonverbal PA.

Early research on PA, conducted largely in school settings, supported its utility in increasing children's cooperative play (Hart, Reynolds, Baer, Brawley, & Harris, 1968), study behavior (Hall, Lund, & Jackson, 1968), attention to task (Kazdin, 1973; Kazdin & Klock, 1973), compliance (Goetz, Holmberg, & LeBlanc, 1975), and cleanliness behavior (Miller, Brickman, & Bolen, 1975). In parent training programs, PA is often used in conjunction with active ignoring of negative child behaviors. Active ignoring requires the parent to withdraw all attention, positive or negative, during the time the child is engaging in negative behavior. By responding with PA to a child's positive behaviors and ignoring the child's negative behaviors, the parent creates a situation of *differential social attention*, which teaches the child how to obtain parental

attention in ways that result in increasingly positive interactions between parent and child. When parental PA is directed specifically to a behavior (e.g., using an inside voice) that is incompatible with a targeted negative behavior (e.g., yelling in the house), the negative behavior may decrease in frequency as it is replaced with the more rewarding positive behavior (see chapter on differential reinforcement of other behavior, this volume).

ADVANTAGES OF THE TECHNIQUE

One advantage of PA in parent training is its easy accessibility as a social reinforcer in the natural environment. It is a convenient behavior management technique for parents in almost any situation. A second advantage of PA is that behaviors sustained by social reinforcers (such as PA) are more likely to generalize across situations than tangible reinforcers, because similar social reinforcers are more likely than tangible reinforcers to occur across situations (e.g., from home to classroom). A third advantage is that PA is generally considered by parents to be the most acceptable method of behavior management (Jones, Eyberg, Adams, & Boggs, 1998). However, in certain cultural groups, such as among Mexican Americans (Borrego, Ibanez, Spendlar, & Pemberton, 2007), PA in the form of differential social attention may be less acceptable than other behavior management strategies.

LIMITATIONS OF THE TECHNIQUE

Some early studies questioned the effectiveness of differential social attention for reducing child disruptive behavior. For example, a study by Herbert et al. (1973) reported that in four of six children, differential parental attention led to increased negative behavior lasting over many sessions and replicated in a reversal design. In a subsequent series of studies, Roberts (1985) concluded that maternal praise may not serve a reinforcing function for compliance among noncompliant children. A 1987 review of the literature on parental PA reached the similar conclusion that rewards alone may not be sufficient for reliable behavior change in noncompliant children (Forehand, 1987).

Today, positive attention alone—or even in combination with active ignoring—is widely recognized as insufficient for treating children with disruptive behavior disorders. The utility of PA is in its potential for increasing behavior. Families of children with significant behavior disorders come to parent training with a constellation of negative behaviors that must be *decreased*. To decrease negative behaviors, PA may be helpful by increasing incompatible, positive behaviors that serve similar functions for the child and may therefore replace the negative behaviors. However, for children with disruptive behavior disorders, techniques designed to decrease negative behaviors directly, such as timeout (see chapter on time out, this volume), are generally necessary in addition to PA. For these children, PA may primarily serve an affective function that increases their willingness to engage in more positive behavior (see Kochanska, Forman, Aksan, & Dunbar, 2005).

WHO MIGHT BENEFIT FROM POSITIVE ATTENTION?

The childhood disorders catalogued in the *Diagnostic and Statistical Manual of Mental Disorders*, 4th ed. (American Psychiatric Association, 1994) are, by definition, associated with functional impairments in cognitive, social, or emotional developmental tasks. The effectiveness of interventions for these disorders may be increased by inclusion of PA designed to increase the frequency (practice) of specific functional behaviors (skills) responsive to social consequences. PA is an established component of most of the evidence-based psychosocial treatments for children and adolescents with

anxiety (Silverman, Pina, & Viswesvaran, 2008), depression, (David-Ferdon & Kaslow, 2008), attention deficit/hyperactivity disorder (Pelham & Fabiano, 2008), and disruptive behavior (Eyberg, Nelson, & Boggs, 2008).

HOW DOES POSITIVE ATTENTION WORK?

We have referred to PA as positive verbal or nonverbal behavior that parents use intentionally in response to child behavior for the purpose of increasing the likelihood that the child will repeat that positive behavior more frequently or for longer duration in the future. For almost all children, parental attention—whether intentional or not—is an effective and powerful positive reinforcement. Nevertheless, the effectiveness of PA may be influenced by a number of contextual variables, such as the form of the PA. For example, one study found that kindergartners who received process praise (e.g., "You must have tried really hard") showed more persistence than children who received person praise (e.g., "You are a good girl") for working on a puzzle (Kamins & Dweck, 1999). Another study found that positive touch (i.e., tickling), but not verbal praise, served as positive reinforcement for behavior change in a child with developmental delays, demonstrating that different forms of PA may not be functionally equivalent within individual children (Piazza et al., 1999).

POSITIVE ATTENTION IN PARENT–CHILD INTERACTION THERAPY

In this section, we illustrate the application of PA in parent–child interaction therapy (PCIT; Eyberg & Boggs, 1998; Butler & Eyberg, 2006), an evidence-based treatment for young children with disruptive behavior and their parents. Parents in PCIT learn two basic patterns of parent–child interaction that together represent an authoritative parenting style. Therapists first teach the child-directed interaction (CDI), which combines PA and active ignoring skills (differential social attention) to increase positive child behaviors and strengthen the parent–child bond. The CDI serves as the foundation for the discipline skills parents learn in the parent-directed interaction (PDI), in the second phase of treatment. In the PDI, parents learn to give effective commands when needed, and to follow-through consistently with labeled praise for compliance and time-out from positive reinforcement/PA for noncompliance.

The specific PA skills used in PCIT are taught to parents in the first session of CDI, a didactic session that parents attend without their child. Therapists explain the behavioral principles underlying PA and active ignoring, and how these techniques work in tandem to change the frequency of broad classes of positive and negative child behavior. In subsequent sessions, therapists shape the effective use of these skills during observations of parent–child interactions.

FUNCTIONAL ANALYSIS IN PCIT

Effective coaching of the rapidly occurring positive and negative behaviors of the parent and child during their interactions requires continuous, moment-by-moment functional analyses of their behaviors. Functional analysis is a detailed assessment of the antecedent and consequent parent behaviors that shape and maintain the child behaviors, as well as the antecedent and consequent child behaviors that shape and maintain the parent behaviors (see Chapter 32). Although the clinical setting offers substantially less control of the specific antecedent and consequent events surrounding behaviors than would a laboratory setting, the reinforcing function of certain forms of PA (e.g., parental praise of child behavior, therapist praise of parental behavior) has for most individuals been established empirically and clinically over many years. These forms of PA are therefore structured into treatment, and the functional analysis involves ongoing therapist and parent observations that fine-tune and informally assess the effectiveness of the individual applications of PA that are used in treatment.

STEP-BY-STEP PROCEDURES

In the first PCIT session, therapists teach parents specific PA skills used in the CDI that,

for most children, are highly positively reinforcing (described in detail later). Therapists also teach parents not to use commands, questions, or criticism during the CDI because these behaviors are intrusive and may negatively affect the positive quality of child-led play. In this didactic session, therapists teach the parents each CDI skill by (1) defining it with examples of positive behaviors observed in their child; (2) explaining the particular value of giving PA for "positive opposites" (positive behaviors that are incompatible with the child's negative behaviors); and (3) describing additional functions that PA might serve for their child (e.g., describing how a PA skill might be used to improve the speech of a language-delayed child). Therapists work to engage parents in the discussion of each CDI skill. Therapists then model the skills used together and have the parents role-play the skills, with the therapist in the role of their child. Parents are asked to practice the CDI at home with their child 5 minutes each day between sessions. The subsequent CDI "coaching" sessions include the child and begin with a 5-minute observation of the parent-child interaction to assess (code) parent progress in learning the skills and to inform therapist coaching during the session.

Therapists typically code and coach the parents' PCIT skills remotely from an observation room through microphone transmission to an earpiece worn by parents while the parents practice the skills alone with their child in the playroom. With two parents, each takes a turn being coached while the other parent observes from the observation room. Below we highlight some of the strategies therapists use in teaching the PA skills to the parents. In PCIT, these skills are called the PRIDE skills, to help parents remember the skills that increase positive behavior—*P*raise, *R*eflection, *I*mitation, *D*escription, and *E*nthusiasm.

Praise

Praise is described as giving a compliment to the child that labels for the child exactly what he or she did that was positive, so the child can learn to repeat that behavior to receive praise again (e.g., "You're doing a nice job of driving the cars quietly"). By praising specific behaviors, parents increase the frequency of those behaviors. Praise also leads to increased self-esteem and adds warmth to the interaction. A useful exercise to help some parents learn to use praise strategically is to provide them a list of praise stems (e.g., "I like how you are _____"; "You're getting really good at _____"; "Thank you so much for _____") and ask them to practice finishing the sentences with positive opposites that would be helpful for their child, such as "I like how you are staying in your chair while we work on this puzzle." During coaching sessions, the therapist points out each time the child repeats behaviors that the parents have earlier praised, to increase parent self-efficacy and lead to further praise by the parent.

Reflection

Reflection is described as repeating or paraphrasing what the child says. A reflection rewards the child for talking to the parent appropriately and demonstrates that the parent is paying attention to what the child says. In addition, reflecting the child's words may improve the child's speech and language when the parent restates the child's ideas in a clearer way than the child expressed them. For example, if the child said, "You don't got that red thing on there," the parent might reflect, "Yes, I don't have the chimney on the house yet." For parents, the most difficult part of learning to reflect is learning not to ask questions in response to their child's verbalizations, such as, "The red one?" Questions have the potential to be perceived by a child as critical. During coaching sessions, parents are encouraged to reflect everything their child says (unless it is inappropriate). The resulting increase in parent–child conversation is an important method of improving the child's social skills.

Imitation

Imitation involves watching the child's activity and engaging in similar behaviors with similar toys, next to the child. As therapy progresses, an oppositional child will gradually allow the parent to play with the same toys (e.g., build on the same house or draw a picture together). Therapists explain how imitating the child's

activity not only conveys approval and leads the child to seek increased positive parent–child interactions, but also tends to increase the child's imitation of the parent (Roberts, 1981).

Parents of disruptive children often do not know how to play with their child. These parents find it helpful to learn they can simply do the same thing their child is doing (unless the child's behavior is negative). Through imitation, parents can teach their child turn-taking and other important social skills that may be lacking. During coaching, therapists help parents maintain attention on the child's activity during imitation and gradually shape interactive play as the child becomes less angry and more trusting of the parent–child relationship.

Behavior Description

A behavior description is a statement that describes what the child is doing (e.g., "You're pouring it slowly so it doesn't spill"). The therapist explains how behavior descriptions convey approval of the child's activities. During coaching, therapists gradually guide parents to become thoughtful in selecting which aspect of their child's behavior to describe, because that selection will be the aspect of behavior likely to increase. Thus, the parent of a child with low frustration tolerance, would be encouraged to describe persistence whenever it occurs (e.g., "You're sticking with it until you find where it fits," rather than simply, "You're trying to find where it fits"). Parents are also coached to describe acceptable behaviors actually occurring, and to resist any temptation to describe how the child could do something "better." For example, even though a parent might want their child to build their block tower straighter, the parent would be coached to ignore straightness and instead describe something they find acceptable (e.g., "You are building a colorful tower"). Any time that parents begin to express disapproval of any behavior, even subtly in expression or tone of voice, the therapist would quickly coach them to ignore. If that behavior was actually an acceptable child behavior, the therapist would try to understand the parent's response and perhaps intervene. For example, with an intolerant parent, the therapist might attempt to reframe age appropriate child behavior during coaching. For example, during another block tower interaction, the therapist might say, "His tower's a little wobbly, but pretty good for his age. Describe the colors he's choosing for his tower."

Enthusiasm

Enthusiasm in CDI is a quality expressing strong interest or enjoyment in the interaction manifested largely by vocal intonation or facial expression. Parents are encouraged to express enthusiasm during the CDI to increase the positivity and warmth in the interaction. Positive words delivered with bland or apathetic emotional tone are unlikely to function as social reinforcers, particularly with young children. Parents may initially feel uncomfortable expressing enthusiasm when playing with their child, although it becomes more natural as parents become more proficient in using the verbal PA skills. Therapists point out positive child responses to parental enthusiasm that occur during coaching. Enthusiasm is also likely to decrease the depressed mood seen in many parents of children with disruptive behavior disorders. For depressed parents, in particular, the therapist will model enthusiasm with the child and during coaching will provide feedback about the child's positive response whenever the parent expresses PA with enthusiasm.

Active Ignoring

In conjunction with PA for positive child behavior, active ignoring is used to reduce negative attention-seeking behaviors such as yelling, sassing, whining, and playing roughly with toys. The first time a parent must ignore negative behavior during coaching, the therapist directs the parent to explain to the child that the parent will not pay attention to the child during playtime unless the child plays nicely. During any subsequent child misbehavior, the parent must avoid giving the child any attention (e.g., laughing, frowning, reprimanding). Initially, when coaching parents to ignore, the therapist talks nonstop for the duration of child misbehavior, explaining, empathizing, and praising the parent's ignoring.

The therapist's constant talk is intended in large part to distract the parent and thereby help the parent to continue to ignore until the child's negative behavior stops. Immediately when the child engages in nonnegative behavior the therapist coaches the parent to resume giving PA for whatever the child is doing. This contrast in parent behavior highlights for the child the difference in parental attention to positive versus negative behavior.

Achieving Parental Competence in Using Positive Attention

One of the keys to achieving parent competence in PA is the regular coding of the parents' PA skills and allowing parents to review a graph charting their progress in each skill and to compare their performance to the performance criteria that will indicate their mastery of the CDI. Behavioral coding of the PA skills during parent–child interactions at the beginning of each treatment session also enables therapists to determine the particular PA skills to emphasize in coaching during the session. A second key to achieving parental competence in PA is the active, directive coaching of the parents' PA skills during interactions with their child during treatment sessions. Coaching provides immediate feedback to parents on their skills. It also enables therapists to observe the effects of specific forms of PA on specific problem behaviors and to intervene on the spot. A final key to success is the structuring of treatment as performance based rather than time limited. Families in PCIT do not move to the second phase of treatment until the CDI skills are mastered, and they continue in treatment until parents have mastered both the CDI and PDI skills and their child's behavior is well within normal limits (i.e., at least one-half standard deviation of the normative mean on a parent rating scale of disruptive behavior).

Treatment research with families of children with disruptive behavior disorders has consistently shown significant decreases in maternal report of parenting stress, dysfunctional parenting practices, and disruptive child behavior after the CDI phase of PCIT alone (e.g., Harwood & Eyberg, 2006). Findings such as these provide strong support for the therapeutic value of PA, at least when combined with active ignoring of child disruptive behaviors.

References

American Psychiatric Association. (1994). *Diagnostic and Statistical Manual of Mental Disorders* (4th ed.). Washington, DC: American Psychiatric Association.

Borrego, J., Ibanez, E. S., Spendlar, S. J., & Pemberton, J. (2007). Treatment acceptability among Mexican-American parents. *Behavior Therapy, 38*, 218–227.

Butler, A. M., & Eyberg, S. M. (2006). Parent–child interaction therapy and ethnic minority families. In *Vulnerable Children and Youth, 1*, 246–255.

David-Ferndon, C., & Kaslow, N. J. (2008). Evidence-based psychosocial treatments for child and adolescent depression. *Journal of Clinical Child and Adolescent Psychology, 37*, 62-104.

Eyberg, S. M., & Boggs, S. R. (1998). Parent–child interaction therapy for oppositional preschoolers. In C. E. Schaefer & J. M. Briesmeister (Eds.), *Handbook of parent training: Parents as co-therapists for children's behavior problems* (2nd ed.) (pp. 61–97). New York: John Wiley & Sons.

Eyberg, S. M., Nelson, M. M., & Boggs, S. R. (2008). Evidence-based treatments for child and adolescent disruptive behavior disorders. *Journal of Clinical Child and Adolescent Psychology, 37*, 215-237.

Forehand, R. (1987). Parental positive reinforcement with deviant children: Does it make a difference? *Child & Family Behavior Therapy, 8*, 19–25.

Goetz, E. M., Holmberg, M. C., & LeBlanc, J. M. (1975). Differential reinforcement of other behavior and noncontingent reinforcement as control procedures during the modification of a preschooler's compliance. *Journal of Applied Behavior Analysis, 8*, 77–82.

Hall, R. V., Lund, D., & Jackson, D. (1968). Effects of teacher attention on study behavior. *Journal of Applied Behavior Analysis, 1*, 1–12.

Hart, B. M., Reynolds, N. J., Baer, D. M., Brawley, E. R., & Harris, F. R. (1968). Effect of contingent and non-contingent social reinforcement on the cooperative play of a preschool child. *Journal of Applied Behavior Analysis, 1*, 73–76.

Harwood, M. D., & Eyberg, S. M. (2006). Child-directed interaction: Prediction of change in impaired mother–child functioning. *Journal of Abnormal Child Psychology. 34*, 335–347.

Herbert, E. W., Pinkston, E. M., Hayden, M. L, Sajwaj, T. E., Pinkston, S., Cordua, G., & Jackson, C. (1973). Adverse effects of differential parental attention. *Journal of Applied Behavior Analysis, 6*, 15–30.

Jones, M. L., Eyberg, S.M., Adams, C. D., & Boggs, S. R. (1998). Treatment acceptability of behavioral interventions for children: An assessment by mothers of children with disruptive behavior disorders. *Child & Family Behavior Therapy, 20*, 15–26.

Kamins, M. L., & Dweck, C. S. (1999). Person versus process praise and criticism: Implications for contingent self-worth and coping. *Developmental Psychology, 35*, 835–847.

Kazdin, A. E. (1973). The effects of vicarious reinforcement on attentive behavior in the classroom. *Journal of Applied Behavior Analysis, 6*, 71–78.

Kazdin, A. E., & Klock, J. (1973). The effect of nonverbal teacher approval on student attentive behavior. *Journal of Applied Behavior Analysis, 6*, 643–654.

Kochanska, G., Forman, D. R., Aksan, N., & Dunbar, S. B. (2005). Pathways to conscience: Early mother–child mutually responsive orientation and children's moral emotion, conduct, and cognition. *Journal of Child Psychology and Psychiatry, 46*, 19–34.

Miller, R. L., Brickman, P., & Bolen, D. (1975). Attribution versus persuasion as a means for modifying behavior. *Journal of Personality and Social Psychology, 31*, 430–441.

Pelham, W. E., & Fabiano, G. A. (2008). Evidence-based psychosocial treatments for attention-deficit/hyperactivity disorder. *Journal of Clinical Child and Adolescent Psychology, 37*, 184-214.

Piazza, C. C., Bowman, L. G., Contrucci, S. A., Delia, M. D., Adelinis, J. D., & Goh, H. L. (1999). An evaluation of the properties of attention as reinforcement for destructive and appropriate behavior. *Journal of Applied Behavioral Analysis, 32*, 437–449.

Roberts, M. C. (1981). Toward a reconceptualization of the reciprocal imitation phenomenon: Two experiments. *Journal of Research in Personality, 15*, 447–459.

Roberts, M. W. (1985). Praising child compliance: Reinforcement or ritual? *Journal of Abnormal Child Psychology, 13*, 611–629.

Silverman, W. K., Pina, A. A., & Viswesvaran, C. (2008). Evidence-based psychosocial treatments for phobic and anxiety disorders in children and adolescents: A review and meta-analysis. *Journal of Clinical Child and Adolescent Psychology, 37*, 105-130.

54 PROBLEM-SOLVING THERAPY

Arthur M. Nezu, Christine Maguth Nezu, and Mary McMurran

Problem-solving therapy (PST) is an evidenced-based, cognitive-behavioral clinical intervention, that fosters the adoption and effective application of adaptive problem-solving attitudes and skills. The general aim of PST is to reduce psychopathology, enhance psychological and behavioral functioning, and to optimize one's overall quality of life. Originally outlined by D'Zurilla and Goldfried (1971), the theory and practice of PST has been refined and revised over the years by D'Zurilla, Nezu, and their associates (D'Zurilla & Nezu, 2007; D'Zurilla, Nezu, & Maydeu-Olivares, 2002; Nezu, 2004; Nezu, Nezu, & D'Zurilla, 2007; Nezu, Nezu, Friedman, Faddis, & Houts, 1998). Based on scores of randomized controlled trials (RCT) conducted by researchers around the world over the past several decades, PST has proven to be an effective treatment for a highly diverse population of adolescents and adults with a wide range of psychological, behavioral, and health disorders.

SOCIAL PROBLEM SOLVING

PST is based heavily on research linking the psychosocial construct of social problem solving (SPS) to both psychopathology (Nezu, Wilkins, & Nezu, 2004) and positive psychology variables (Chang, Downey, & Salata, 2004). SPS is the cognitive-behavioral process by which individuals attempt to identify or discover adaptive means of coping with the wide variety and range of stressful problems, both acute and chronic, encountered during the course of everyday living. More specifically, SPS reflects the process whereby people direct their coping efforts at altering the problematic nature of the situation itself and/or their reactions to such problems.

Rather than describing a singular type of coping behavior or activity, SPS represents the multidimensional meta-process of idiographically identifying and selecting various coping responses to implement in order to adequately address the unique features of a given stressful situation at a given time.

According to contemporary SPS theory, problem-solving outcomes are conceptualized as being largely determined by two general, but partially independent, dimensions: (a) problem orientation, and (b) problem-solving style. *Problem orientation* (PO) is the set of relatively stable cognitive-affective schemas that represent a person's generalized beliefs, attitudes, and emotional reactions about problems in living and one's ability to successfully cope with such problems. One's problem orientation can be either positive or negative. A *positive problem orientation* involves the tendency to (1) appraise problems as challenges, (2) be optimistic in believing that problems are solvable, (3) perceive one's own ability to solve problems as strong, (4) believe that successful problem solving involves time and effort, and (5) be willing to attempt to cope with the problem rather than avoid it.

Conversely, a *negative problem orientation* is one that involves the tendency to (1) view problems as threats, (2) expect problems to be unsolvable, (3) doubt one's own ability to solve problems successfully, and (4) become particularly frustrated and upset when faced with problems or confronted with negative emotions. As implied by its description, problem orientation serves a motivational function. For example, a positive orientation can engender positive affect and approach motivation, which in turn can facilitate later adaptive problem-solving efforts (e.g., willingness to attend to difficult situations rather than avoid them). Conversely, a negative orientation can foster negative affect (e.g., depressive symptoms and avoidance motivation), which can later serve to inhibit subsequent problem-solving attempts.

The second major dimension, *problem-solving style*, refers to the core cognitive-behavioral activities that people engage in when attempting to cope with problems in living. There are three differing styles that have been identified—one of which is adaptive, whereas the remaining two reflect maladaptive ways of coping. *Rational problem solving* is the constructive problem-solving style that involves the systematic and planful application of specific skills, each of which makes a distinct contribution toward the discovery of an adaptive solution or coping response. This style encompasses four specific skills:

1. Defining a problem (i.e., delineating a realistic problem-solving goal and identifying those obstacles that prevent one from reaching them)
2. Generating alternative solution ideas (i.e., producing a range of possible solution strategies using various brainstorming principles)
3. Decision making (i.e., predicting the likely consequences of the differing solution ideas in order to conduct a cost-benefit analysis that informs the decision-making process)
4. Implementing and evaluating the solution plan (i.e., monitoring and evaluating the consequences after a solution is carried out and determining whether one's problem-solving efforts have been successful or needs to continue).

In contrast, the two other problem-solving styles are dysfunctional or maladaptive in nature. In general, both styles can lead to ineffective or unsuccessful problem resolution. In fact, they are likely to worsen existing problems or even create new ones. An *impulsivity/carelessness style* involves the generalized response pattern characterized by impulsive, hurried, and careless attempts at problem resolution. Although the individual high on this dimension actively attempts to apply various strategies to address problems, such attempts are narrow, hurried, and incomplete.

For example, a person with this style is likely to consider only a few solution alternatives, often impulsively implementing the first idea that comes to mind. In addition, the narrow range of options and their consequences are scanned quickly, carelessly, and unsystematically.

Avoidance is a second general maladaptive problem-solving style, this one characterized by procrastination, passivity, and overdependence on others to provide solutions. Individuals high on this dimension generally avoid problems rather than confronting them "head on," wait for problems to resolve themselves, and attempt to shift the responsibility for solving one's problems to other people.

In essence, through psychoeducation, guided discussion, interactive problem-solving exercises, and motivational homework assignments, PST helps individuals to (1) adopt a more realistically optimistic view of coping; (2) better understand the role of negative emotions and how they impact coping effectiveness; and (3) create, implement, and monitor a solution action plan geared to reduce psychological distress and enhance well-being.

EVIDENCED-BASED APPLICATIONS

In the literature, PST has been effectively applied as the sole intervention to a wide range of psychological problems including depression, generalized anxiety disorder, suicidal ideation and behaviors, deficit social skills of persons with schizophrenia, emotional problems of primary care patients, social phobia, sexual offending, behavioral problems of adults with mental retardation, substance abuse, behavioral disorders of children, and impaired social functioning of adults with personality disorders. It has been used to reduce negative symptomatology and improve the quality of life of patients with various medical problems, such as cancer, hypertension, obesity, back pain, cardiovascular disease, head injury, diabetes, and arthritis. PST has also been combined with other cognitive-behavioral strategies for the treatment of borderline personality disorder, marital and family problems, HIV/AIDS risk behaviors (e.g., unsafe sex), and parent–adolescent conflict. PST has been applied as a maintenance strategy to enhance the effects of other treatment approaches. It has also been found to enhance the ability of individuals to serve as effective caregivers of persons with cancer, Alzheimer's disease, dementia, spinal cord injury, and strokes. PST has been used to enhance "normal" individuals' coping and stress management skills, to decrease "vocational indecision," and to enhance social skills among shy young adolescents. PST alone, and as a component of broader "thinking-skills" interventions, has been used to good effect in the treatment of offending behavior in prisoners and probationers worldwide (McMurran & McGuire, 2005).

CONTRAINDICATIONS

Because PST has been found to help individuals representing both a wide array of cognitive abilities (e.g., ranging from intellectually "normal" adults to persons with mild to moderate mental retardation) and psychological difficulties (e.g., ranging from "normal college students" to adults with schizophrenia), it would appear that few contraindications for this intervention exist at present.

EVIDENCE FOR THE EFFICACY OF PST

With regard to the conceptual underpinnings of PST, a large number of studies have found problem-solving effectiveness and psychological distress and dysfunction to be significantly related. Such converging findings have emerged from investigations using varying research designs and differing measures of SPS. For example, various studies have looked at simple correlations between measures of distress and problem solving, whereas others have focused on differences in problem solving between reliably diagnosed patient samples (e.g., major depressive disorder, posttraumatic stress disorder) and appropriate control groups. Further, additional studies have found SPS to be both a mediator and moderator of the relationship between stress and psychological distress.

As noted above, PST has been successfully applied to a wide range of clinical populations and psychological problems. Both qualitative and quantitative reviews of the outcome literature underscore its efficacy. For example, Malouff, Thorsteinsson, and Schutte (2007) recently published a meta-analysis of 32 RCTs of PST as applied across a variety of mental and physical health problems. In essence, PST was found to be (1) equally as effective as other psychosocial treatments, and (2) significantly more effective than either no treatment or attention placebo conditions. Moreover, these authors found significant moderators of treatment outcome to be whether the PST protocol being evaluated included training in problem orientation, whether homework was assigned, or whether a developer of PST helped conduct the investigation. In addition, focusing exclusively on PST for depression, Cuijpers, van Straten, and Warmerdam (2007) recently published a meta-analysis of 13 RCTs, and concluded that PST for this specific disorder is effective, a conclusion similarly reached by Bell and D'Zurilla (2007), who conducted a meta-analysis of 20 RCTs of PST for depression. A recent RCT found PST to be effective in improving the social functioning of adults with personality disorders (Huband, McMurran, Evans, & Duggan, 2007), whereby PST has been commended as having the potential to greatly improve the capability of mental health professionals to work with this population.

STEP-BY-STEP GUIDE

Although PST involves teaching individuals specific skills, similar to other CBT approaches, it should be conducted within a *therapeutic context*. Because PST does focus on skill building, it can easily be misunderstood by the novice therapist that it only entails a "teaching" process. However, it is important for the problem-solving therapist to be careful not to (1) conduct PST in a mechanistic manner, (2) focus only on skills training and not on the patient's emotional experiences, (3) deliver a "canned" treatment that does not address the unique strengths, weaknesses, and experiences of a given patient, and (4) assume that PST focuses only on superficial problems, rather than on more complex interpersonal, psychological, existential, and spiritual issues (if warranted). Thus, in addition to teaching the client certain techniques to better cope with problems, effective PST requires the therapist to be competent in a variety of other assessment and intervention strategies, such as fostering a positive therapeutic relationship, assessing for complex clinical problems, modeling, behavioral rehearsal, assigning homework tasks, and appropriately providing corrective feedback.

Structurally, PST training can be broken into three major foci: (1) training in problem orientation; (2) training in the four specific rational problem-solving skills (i.e., problem definition and formulation, generation of alternatives, decision making, solution verification), and (3) practice of these skills across a variety of real-life problems. However, as noted in D'Zurilla and Nezu (2007), PST can be implemented in a variety of ways. For example, the guidelines provided in the next section actually depict how PST might be conducted in a sequential fashion, such as that implemented in various treatment outcome studies. In clinical settings, however, PST should be applied based on a comprehensive assessment of a given individual's (couple's, family's) problem-solving strengths and weaknesses. As such, not all training components may be necessary to include across all patients.

Training in Problem Orientation

The goal of training in this problem-solving component is to foster adoption or facilitation of a positive problem orientation. Obstacles to adopting such a perspective include (1) poor self-efficacy beliefs, (2) negative thinking, and (3) negative emotions (i.e., a strong negative problem orientation).

A clinical strategy included in PST to help enhance patients' optimism or sense of self-efficacy is *visualization*. This is used to help individuals create the experience of successful problem resolution in their "mind's eye" in order to vicariously experience the reinforcement to be gained. Visualization in this context requests clients to close their eyes and imagine that they have successfully solved a current problem. The focus is on the end point—that is, not on "how one got to the goal," but rather "focusing on the feelings of having reached the goal." The central aim of this strategy is to have patients create and "experience" their own positive consequences related to solving a problem as a motivational step towards enhanced self-efficacy. In essence, this technique helps create a visual image of "the light at the end of the tunnel."

To help overcome *negative thinking*, various cognitive restructuring and reframing strategies can be used, including those advocated in more "formal" cognitive therapy. One technique focuses on the "A-B-C method of constructive thinking." With this approach, clients are taught to view emotional reactions from the "A-B-C" perspective, where A = activating event (such as a problem), B = beliefs about the event (including what people say to themselves), and C = emotional and behavioral consequences. In other words, how individuals *feel and act* often are products of how they *think*. Using a current problem, the PST therapist can use this procedure to diagnose negative self-talk and thoughts that are likely to lead to distressing emotions for a given patient. Such cognitions often include highly evaluative words, such as *should* and *must*; "catastrophic" words used to describe non-life-threatening events; and phrases that tend to be overgeneralizations (e.g., "*Nobody* understands me!"). By examining one's self-talk, the patient can learn to separate realistic statements (e.g., "I wish ... ") from maladaptive ones (e.g., "I must have ... ") as they pertain to problems in living. The patient can also be given a list of positive self-statements that can be used to substitute for or help dispute the negative self-talk (as in the *reverse-advocacy role-play* strategy described next).

According to the *reverse advocacy role-play* strategy, the PST therapist pretends to adopt a particular belief about problems and asks the patient to provide reasons why that belief is irrational, illogical, incorrect, or maladaptive. Such beliefs might include the following statements: "Problems are not common to everyone; if I have a problem, that means I'm crazy," "There must be a perfect solution to this problem," "I'll never be the same again." At times when the patient has difficulty generating arguments against the therapist's position, the counselor then adopts a more extreme form of the belief, such as "no matter how long it takes, I will continue to try and find the perfect solution to my problem." This procedure is intended to help individuals identify alternative ways of thinking and then to dispute or contradict previously held negative beliefs with more adaptive perspectives.

To help overcome negative emotions, patients are taught to interpret such negative feelings as *cues* that a problem exists. In other words, rather than labeling one's negative emotions as "the problem," they are helped to conceptualize such emotions as a "signal" that a problem exists and then to observe what is occurring in their environment in order to recognize the "real problem" that is causing such emotions. Once such feelings as depression, anger, muscle tension, nausea, or anxiety arise, the patient is then instructed to use the mnemonic *"STOP and THINK"* as a means of inhibiting avoidance or impulsive problem-solving behavior. The "think" aspect of this phrase refers to the use of the various rational problem-solving skills. In addition, PST emphasizes that combining emotions and rational thinking (rather than relying solely on only one of these areas) leads to "wisdom," which represents effective real-life problem solving. Accurately labeling a problem *as* a problem serves to inhibit the tendency to act impulsively or automatically in reaction to such situations. It also facilitates the tendency to approach or confront problems, rather than to avoid them.

Training in Rational Problem Solving

Problem Definition

This first rational problem-solving skill can be likened to "mapping" a guide for the remainder of the problem-solving process. The major focus of this task is to better understand the nature of the problem and to set clearly defined and reasonable goals. In other words, locating a specific destination on a map makes it easier to find the best route to get there. Training in problem definition focuses on the following tasks—gathering necessary additional information about a problem, using clear language, separating facts from assumptions, setting realistic problem-solving goals, and identifying those factors that exist that prevent one from reaching such goals.

Generating Alternatives

When generating alternative solutions to a problem, PST encourages broad-based, creative, and flexible thinking. In essence, clients are taught various brainstorming strategies (e.g., "the more the better," "defer judgment of ideas until a comprehensive list is created," "think of a *variety* of ideas"). Using such guides helps to increase the likelihood that the most effective solution ideas will be ultimately identified or discovered.

Decision Making

Once a list of alternative options has been generated, the individual is taught to systematically evaluate the potential for each solution to meet the defined goal(s). Training in this skill helps individuals to use the following criteria to conduct a cost-benefit analysis based on the utility of each alternative solution—the likelihood that the solution will meet the defined goal, the likelihood that the person responsible for solving the problem can actually carry out the solution plan optimally, personal and social consequences, and short- and long-term effects.

Solution Verification

This last rational problem-solving task involves monitoring and evaluating the consequences of the actual outcome after a solution plan is carried out. In addition, PST encourages clients to practice carrying out the solution as a means of enhancing the probability that it will be carried out in its optimal form. At times, it may be advisable for the PST counselor to include training in various other skills if relevant (e.g., communication skills, assertiveness skills, interpersonal skills). Once the plan is underway, the patient is encouraged to monitor the actual results. Using this information allows individuals to evaluate the results by comparing the actual outcome with their expectations or predictions about the outcome. Depending on the results, individuals are then guided to either troubleshoot where in the problem-solving process they need to extend additional effort toward if the problem is not adequately resolved or to engage in self-reinforcement if the problem is solved.

Supervised Practice

After the majority of "training" has occurred, the remainder of PST should be devoted to practicing the newly acquired skills and applying them to a variety of stressful problems. Beyond actually solving such problems, continuous in-session practice serves three additional purposes—the patient can receive "professional" feedback from the therapist, increased facility with the overall PST model can decrease the amount of time and effort necessary to apply the various problem-solving tasks with each new problem, and practice fosters relapse prevention.

In addition to focusing on resolving and coping with current problems, these practice sessions should also allow for "future forecasting," whereby individuals are encouraged to look to the future and anticipate where potential problems might arise in order to apply such skills in a preventive manner (e.g., anticipated geographic move, request for promotion, contemplating raising a family). Continuous application of these skills is encouraged, for as the poet Emily Dickinson stated—"Low at my problem bending, another problem comes."

References

Bell, A. C., & D'Zurilla, T. J. (2007). *Problem-solving therapy for depression: A meta-analysis*. Manuscript submitted for publication. State University of New York at Stony Brook.

Chang, E. C., Downey, C. A., & Salata, J. L. (2004). Social problem solving and positive psychological functioning: Looking at the positive side of problem solving. In E. C. Chang, T. J. D'Zurilla, & L. J. Sanna (Eds.), *Social problem solving: Theory, research, and training*. Washington, DC: American Psychological Association.

Cuijpers, P., van Straten, A., & Warmerdam, L. (2007). Problem solving therapies for depression: A meta-analysis. *European Psychiatry, 22,* 9–15.

D'Zurilla, T. J., & Goldfried, M. R. (1971). Problem solving and behavior modification. *Journal of Abnormal Psychology, 78,* 107–126.

D'Zurilla, T. J., & Nezu, A. M. (2007). *Problem-solving therapy: A positive approach to clinical intervention* (3rd ed.). New York: Springer Publishing Co.

D'Zurilla, T. J., Nezu, A. M., & Maydeu-Olivares, A. (2002). *Manual for the Social Problem-Solving Inventory-Revised*. North Tonawanda, NY: Multi-Health Systems.

Huband, N., McMurran, M., Evans, C., & Duggan, C. (2007). Social problem solving plus psychoeducation for adults with personality disorder: A pragmatic randomised controlled trial. *British Journal of Psychiatry, 190,* 307–313.

McMurran, M., & McGuire, J. (Eds.). (2005). *Social problem solving and offending: Evidence, evaluation and evolution*. Chichester, UK: John Wiley & Sons.

Malouff, J. M., Thorsteinsson, E. B., & Schutte, N. S. (2007). The efficacy of problem solving therapy in reducing mental and physical health problems: A meta-analysis. *Clinical Psychology Review, 27,* 46–57.

Nezu, A. M. (2004). Problem solving and behavior therapy revisited. *Behavior Therapy, 35,* 1–33.

Nezu, A. M., Nezu, C. M., & D'Zurilla, T. J. (2007). *Solving life's problems: A 5-step guide to enhanced well-being*. New York: SpringerPublsihing Co.

Nezu, A. M., Nezu, C. M., Friedman, S. H., Faddis, S., & Houts, P. S. (1998). *Helping cancer patients cope: A problem-solving approach*. Washington, DC: American Psychological Association.

Nezu, A. M., Wilkins, V. M., & Nezu, C. M. (2004). Social problem solving, stress, and negative affective conditions. In E. C. Chang, T. J. D'Zurilla, & L. J. Sanna (Eds.), *Social problem solving: Theory, research, and training* (pp. 49–65). Washington, DC: American Psychological Association.

55 PUNISHMENT

David P. Wacker, Jay Harding, Wendy Berg, Linda J. Cooper-Brown, and Anjali Barretto

Behavioral reduction procedures, such as punishment (e.g., Azrin & Holz, 1966; Iwata, 1988) and extinction (Iwata, Pace, Cowdery, & Miltenberger, 1998; Lerman & Iwata, 1996) have been discussed extensively in the literature. Punishment can be defined on the basis of its application (Catania, 1998), its operations (Catania, 1998), and its functional relationship to the target behavior (Iwata, Pace, Dorsey, et al., 1994). Relative to application, we can describe how a behavior resulted in punishment (e.g., tantrums led to a reprimand or placement in a "time-out" area). Relative to operations, we can describe the effect of punishment on behavior (e.g., time-out reduced the child's tantrums). Relative to function, we can describe how a punishment procedure was matched (Iwata, Pace, Dorsey, et al., 1994) to the reinforcer maintaining problem behavior (time-out from parental attention reduced the child's attention-maintained tantrum behavior). As discussed by Catania (1998), the differences in these definitions relate to how explicitly we are describing the response-consequence relation. At the application level, we are describing a sequence of events. At the operations level, we are describing the effects of a consequence on behavior. At the functional relations level, we are explaining why those effects occurred.

These levels of definition, from application to operation to function, provide increased clarity in clinical situations. For example, the statement that time-out should be used by parents for tantrum behavior requires inferences about the function of the behavior (e.g., that the tantrums are maintained by positive reinforcement) and that the specific application (the specified manner in which it is applied) will reduce the rate of tantrums. These inferences,

if left untested, can create confusion and over-generalization regarding the treatment and can result in counter-therapeutic effects. Confusion can occur, for example, if a parent implements a treatment as specified but target behavior remains unchanged. It is now unclear what adjustments to the treatment are needed because the difficulty may be the specific application of the treatment or that the treatment itself is not punishing. This lack of effect on behavior may lead the parent to make overgeneralizations about the treatment (e.g., "Time-out does not work for tantrums") or about the behavior (e.g., "My child's tantrums do not respond to punishment."). These types of overgeneralizations may hamper future attempts at treatment. Countertherapeutic treatments can occur when the application of treatment reinforces target behavior. Countertherapeutic treatments occur for several reasons, with at least some related to the function of the child's problem behavior. For example, if tantrums are maintained by negative reinforcement in the form of escape from demands or avoidance of a care provider, then removal to a time-out area may reinforce or strengthen the problem behavior (i.e., may function as a negative reinforcer). By specifying the applications and operations of the procedure and the functions of the target behavior, we can avoid a wide range of clinical problems.

THE OPERATION OF PUNISHMENT

According to Azrin and Holz (1966), *punishment* is defined as the delivery of a consequence of behavior that reduces the future probability of the behavior. This generic or minimal (Azrin & Holz, 1966) definition leaves much unspecified but adequately describes the operation of punishment. To determine when or under what conditions a given application will be effective, we also need to specify the relation of punishment to ongoing reinforcement (Catania, 1998), including the function of target behavior (Iwata, Dorsey, Slifer, Bauman, & Richman, 1982/1994). The relation of punishment to reinforcement identifies the range of applications (procedural variability) that will be effective. Ideally, reinforcement would be delivered only for a wide range of appropriate behavior but never for problem behavior. In this case, punishment may not need to be a critical component of the treatment package. In other cases, problem behavior will continue to be strengthened by the delivery of reinforcement, and punishment may need to be applied at a more intense (e.g., more consistent, more immediate) level.

THE FUNCTION OF PROBLEM BEHAVIOR

The function of problem behavior identifies the functional class of punishment applications that is likely to be most effective. Thus, if problem behavior occurs to gain adult attention, then consequences that reduce the presence of attention are likely to be effective, and consequences that increase the amount of attention are contraindicated. Punishment techniques, like extinction and reinforcement techniques, must be specified in relation to the function of target behavior. For this reason, it is important to identify the function of problem behavior prior to the selection of treatment. When the function (maintaining reinforcer) is known, then that reinforcer can be withheld (via extinction or punishment) contingent on problem behavior and provided contingently for adaptive behavior.

EFFECTIVENESS OF PUNISHMENT

The effectiveness of punishment has been reported in both the basic and the applied literatures for over 30 years (Azrin & Holz, 1966; Lerman & Vorndran, 2002). When combined with reinforcement and extinction procedures, punishment can have immediate and substantial effects on target behaviors that do not respond

to reinforcement treatments (e.g., Hagopian, Fisher, Sullivan, Acquisto, & LeBlanc, 1998; Wacker et al., 1990). Surprisingly few negative side effects have been reported in the applied literature, perhaps because reductive procedures are almost always combined with reinforcement procedures (Lerman & Iwata, 1994), and very few examples of corporal punishment are reported in the applied literature. Thus, the decision to use punishment often is based more on practical (e.g., the need to quickly reduce a target behavior) and emotional (e.g., a care provider's perceptions about a particular application) considerations than on its overall merits. (See Alberto & Troutman, 1999, and Miltenberger, 2001, for a more comprehensive discussion of common applications of punishment and the ethical issues related to the use of punishment.) We agree with Iwata (1988), who characterized the use of punishment as a default treatment. By *default treatment*, Iwata was referring to punishment as evolving from a failure to produce desired behavior via reinforcement procedures. Punishment is often needed when we either have failed to identify reinforcers or are unable to control the delivery of those reinforcers sufficiently to increase alternative, adaptive behaviors (Fisher et al., 1994). When the selection of punishment procedures is based on the function of problem behavior and is related to ongoing reinforcement for both problem and alternative behavior, punishment procedures can be highly effective in suppressing behavior.

When it has been determined that a punishment procedure is warranted, several factors related to the delivery of the punisher will influence its effectiveness in suppressing behavior (Miltenberger, 20021). In general, the effectiveness of punishment will be enhanced if the punisher follows problem behavior immediately and is contingent on the target behavior (follows every occurrence of problem behavior). Of equal importance is that alternative, adaptive behavior is reinforced in an immediate and contingent manner.

IDENTIFYING FUNCTIONAL TREATMENTS

In most cases, identifying the function of target behavior is a two-step process. First, we conduct a descriptive assessment based on interview, survey, or observation. This assessment, which is a type of antecedent–behavior–consequence (A-B-C) assessment (Bijou, Peterson, & Ault, 1968), is used to formulate hypotheses about the reinforcers maintaining target behavior and the consistency with which those reinforcers are delivered. We then formally test the hypotheses via either an extended (Iwata et al., 1982/1994) or a brief (Northup et al., 1991) functional analysis, depending on the setting: extended in homes and brief in outpatient clinics. Based on the results of these assessments, we provide a selection of intervention options to care providers that always includes differential reinforcement and may include punishment.

CASE EXAMPLES

In the following three case examples, we provide a summary of this approach in two settings (home and outpatient clinics) with two subgroups of young children (with and without developmental disabilities) and with different functions (positive and negative reinforcement) of target behavior.

Case Example of Korey

The Behavioral Pediatrics Clinic (Cooper et al., 1992) is an outpatient clinic that serves children ranging in age from 12 months to 9 years who are referred for behavioral concerns. A behavioral assessment is conducted as follows:

1. Initial information is obtained via school records, a parent questionnaire, behavior rating scales, and records from local service providers (e.g., counselors, social workers).
2. A phone call is made to the parents several days before the appointment to conduct an A-B-C interview. Based on the records and interview, hypotheses are formed regarding the variables maintaining target behavior.
3. A brief functional analysis is conducted by the parent with coaching from clinic staff.
4. A treatment plan is developed, and the parent practices the treatment in clinic.

Korey was a 2-year-old boy with overall development within normal limits. Problem behaviors included self-injury (biting himself, scratching his face), aggression (biting, hitting his mother), tantrums, and noncompliance with requests. We hypothesized that Korey's problem behavior was maintained by positive reinforcement (attention from his mother).

During the brief functional analysis, Korey was observed interacting with his mother via a video camera mounted in the examination room. Prior to each analysis condition, Korey's mother briefly left the examination room, and she was given instructions regarding the activities to present to Korey and the consequences to provide for his appropriate and problem behaviors. Each condition lasted 5 minutes.

Problem behavior occurred only in the attention condition, not when Korey was playing or "working" with his mother. During the attention condition, Korey's mother was instructed to read a magazine while seated in a chair away from Korey. She was instructed to ignore him while he played but to provide attention (e.g., "Don't do that") when he engaged in target behavior. His target behavior quickly diminished when he was provided with noncontingent attention and escalated when attention was contingent on target behavior.

We recommended a treatment package that consisted of a positive reinforcement component to increase appropriate behavior and a punishment component to reduce target behavior. The positive reinforcement component consisted of functional communication training (Carr & Durand, 1985; see Chapter 33, this volume) Korey was taught to say "please" to gain access to his mother's attention. The punishment component consisted of a brief, nonexclusionary time-out from reinforcement for episodes of problem behavior. Korey's mother looked away from him until problem behavior did not occur for several seconds. Immediately following time-out, Korey's mother provided opportunities for Korey to gain her attention using appropriate communication. Thus, the emphasis was on teaching and reinforcing appropriate communication to increase adaptive behavior, and punishment was used to augment the positive reinforcement component.

Case Example of Annie

The Biobehavioral Outpatient Service (Northup et al., 1991) is a weekly multidisciplinary clinic for persons with developmental disabilities who engage in severe problem behaviors such as self-injury, aggression, and destruction. The same assessment steps used in the Behavioral Pediatrics Clinic are used in this clinic.

Annie was a 2-year-old girl with severe developmental delays who received all nutrition via a gastric tube. Annie was referred for assessment and treatment of self-injury (head banging and hand biting), aggression (scratching and hitting), and tantrums. Annie's mother reported that these behaviors occurred primarily during demands such as diaper changes, tube feedings, and so on. Our hypothesis was that problem behavior was maintained by escape from demands. Annie also had very limited play skills, and when she was given a toy, she often threw it or tossed it aside. The primary goals of intervention were to decrease problem behavior and to increase adaptive behavior (e.g., communication and play skills).

A brief functional analysis was conducted to test the effects of gaining adult attention and escaping nonpreferred activities as possible reinforcers for engaging in more severe forms (self-injury and aggression) of the target behavior. No problem behavior occurred during the test for attention but did occur throughout the escape condition. Milder problem behavior also occurred during free play when Annie threw her toys. These results suggested that severe problem behavior was maintained by escape from demands.

A functional communication training (FCT) package was developed for Annie that included three components: (1) reinforcement, (2) escape extinction, and (3) response cost. Each treatment session began with Annie's mother presenting a demand to Annie. Reinforcement involved teaching Annie to press a microswitch that played a prerecorded message to request a break from the demand. Pressing the microswitch was an appropriate response that Annie could use to escape task demands for a brief period (e.g., 20–30 seconds). Problem behavior within the context of demands resulted in escape extinction; the demand remained in place and toys were withheld until the appropriate response occurred. The purpose of escape extinction was to prevent Annie from gaining access to the reinforcer (escape) by engaging in problem behavior. If Annie engaged in problem behavior (e.g., threw her toys) during the break, a response cost was implemented. Response cost involved the immediate removal of the toys (loss of potential positive reinforcers) and presentation of the task demand (loss of negative reinforcer).

Case Example of Jon

Jon was a participant in a National Institutes of Health research project (Wacker, Berg, & Harding, 2000) that provides in-home behavioral assessment and treatment to young children with developmental and behavioral disorders. Jon was 2 years 11 months old and was diagnosed with disruptive behavior disorder (not otherwise specified) and expressive language delays. Severe problem behaviors included aggression (e.g., biting, hitting, kicking, and pinching), property destruction (e.g., throwing items), and noncompliance. All assessment and treatment procedures were conducted in Jon's home on a weekly to monthly basis for 1 hour.

A behavioral assessment was conducted as follows:

1. Jon's mother recorded episodes of problem behavior during 30-minute intervals throughout the day for 1 week on an ABC recording form.
2. Following completion of this written record, Jon's parents were interviewed to clarify concerns and to formulate initial hypotheses regarding environmental events that might be related to the occurrence of problem behavior.
3. Problem behavior was hypothesized to be related to a variety of social contexts (attention, tangibles, and demands).
4. An extended functional analysis was conducted across multiple test conditions during 5-minute sessions over a 2-week period.

The results showed that problem behavior was elevated during attention, tangible, and escape conditions, but remained at zero or near-zero levels during the free-play condition. The occurrence of more severe problem behavior occurred at consistently high levels only during the escape condition. Thus, Jon's problem behavior appeared to be maintained by multiple social functions, with severe problem behavior most likely to occur during demands.

Treatment consisted of functional communication training to teach Jon to follow his mother's instructions and to mand appropriately when he wanted a break from tasks to play with his mother and preferred toys. Jon's treatment was matched to the results of his functional analysis, which indicated that his problem behavior was maintained by both escape from demands (negative reinforcement) and access to attention and preferred toys (positive reinforcement). An investigator modeled the procedures initially, provided prescriptive feedback to Jon's mother during subsequent sessions on a weekly basis for 3 months, and then provided feedback on a monthly basis for an additional 3 months.

During treatment probes, Jon had access to preferred toys and his mother's attention for 1 minute before she presented him with the task. His mother then used hierarchical prompts to guide Jon in completing the task. First, his mother provided a verbal prompt (e.g., "Put the red block on top of the green block."). Then she modeled the behavior. If Jon completed the task, his mother provided praise. She then produced a picture card with the word *play* printed on it, and said, "Tell me what you want to do." Initially, Jon's mother used hand-over-hand guidance to assist Jon in touching the card to request "play." This physical guidance was always accompanied by his mother saying the word *play* ("Oh, you want to *play*. Thank you for telling me."). After touching the card, Jon was allowed to play with his mother and preferred toys for 1 minute, at which time his mother gave him a new task. Thus, Jon received positive reinforcement (attention and toys) for complying with his mother's request and for communicating appropriately.

If Jon engaged in mild problem behavior (e.g., whined or said "no"), his mother kept the task in front of Jon and reminded him to "do your work and then you can play." This form of escape extinction procedure was often successful in obtaining Jon's completion of the request and, thus, in gaining an opportunity for Jon to mand for preferred toys. However, if Jon's behavior became more severe, his mother implemented a nonexclusionary time-out procedure blended with escape extinction. Jon was given no verbal attention and was not allowed to have any toys. Thus, in this treatment package, each function of Jon's problem behavior was matched to a treatment component, with one component involving punishment.

SUMMARY

In each case example, the combination of reinforcement for adaptive behavior (i.e., mands) and punishment for problem behavior produced rapid reductions in problem behavior and

---

TABLE 55.1   Key Elements of Function-Based Punishment Procedures

1. Conduct a descriptive assessment that identifies possible antecedent–response and response–reinforcer relations. One example is to conduct an ABC assessment via interview, recording form, or direct observation.
2. Conduct a brief or extended functional analysis to identify the function of target behavior.
3. Match all treatment components (reinforcement, extinction, punishment) to the hypothesized (descriptive) or identified (functional analysis) function of behavior. Make sure that the treatment package is internally consistent, meaning that all components are compatible.
4. Base the use of punishment on care provider preference. Some care providers have strong opinions (both pro and con) regarding the use of punishment applications. If no preference is indicated, we usually begin treatment with extinction and reinforcement components and then use punishment as a default technique.
5. Base the application of punishment on descriptive information obtained about the probability of ongoing reinforcement for problem behavior and the availability of alternative responses that can receive reinforcement.

gains in adaptive responding. In the third case example, treatment effects were also maintained over several months. This function-based approach to treatment increases the likelihood of developing an effective treatment plan while reducing the inadvertent reinforcement of problem behaviors. The key elements of applying punishment procedures that are matched to the function of target behavior are provided in Table 55.1.

Further Reading

The following articles provide empirical demonstrations of the effects of punishment across a wide range of behaviors (self-injury, aggression, noncompliance), function (positive, negative, and automatic reinforcement), and settings (home, school, outpatient, and inpatient).

Cooper, L., Wacker, D., Thursby, D., Plagmann, L., Harding, J., Millard, T., et al. (1992). Analysis of the effects of task preferences, task demands, and adult attention on child behavior in outpatient and classroom settings. *Journal of Applied Behavior Analysis, 25*, 823–840.

Fisher, W. W., Piazza, C. C., Bowman, L. G., Kurtz, P. F., Sherer, M. R., & Lachman, S. R. (1994). A preliminary evaluation of empirically derived consequences for the treatment of pica. *Journal of Applied Behavior Analysis, 27*, 447–457.

Fisher, W. W., Piazza, C. C., Cataldo, M. F., Harrell, R., Jefferson, G., & Conner, R. (1993). Functional communication training with and without extinction and punishment. *Journal of Applied Behavior Analysis, 26*, 23–36.

Hagopian, L. P., Fisher, W. W., Sullivan, M. T., Acquisto, J., & LeBlanc, L. A. (1998). Effectiveness of functional communication training with and without extinction and punishment. *Journal of Applied Behavior Analysis, 31*, 211–235.

Kennedy, C. H., & Souza, G. (1995). Functional analysis and treatment of eye poking. *Journal of Applied Behavior Analysis, 7*, 521–528.

Thompson, R. H., Iwata, B. A., Conners, J., & Roscoe, E. M. (1999). Effects of reinforcement for alternative behavior during punishment of self-injury. *Journal of Applied Behavior Analysis, 32*, 317–328.

References

Alberto, P. A., & Troutman, A. C. (1999). *Applied behavior analysis for teachers* (5th ed.). Columbus, OH: Prentice Hall.

Azrin, N. H., & Holz, W. C. (1966). Punishment. In W. K. Honig (Ed.), *Operant behavior: Areas of research and application* (pp. 380–447). New York: Appleton-Century-Crofts.

Bijou, S. W., Peterson, R. F., & Ault, M. H. (1968). A method to integrate descriptive and experimental field studies at the level of data and empirical concepts. *Journal of Applied Behavior Analysis, 1*, 175–191.

Carr, E. G., & Durand, V. M. (1985). Reducing behavior problems through functional communication training. *Journal of Applied Behavior Analysis, 18*, 111–126.

Catania, A. C. (1998). Consequences of responding: Aversive control. In *Learning* (4th ed., pp. 88–110). Upper Saddle River, NJ: Prentice Hall.

Cooper, L., Wacker, D., Thursby, D., Plagmann, L., Harding, J., Millard, T., et al. (1992). Analysis of the effects of task preferences, task demands, and adult attention on child behavior in outpatient and classroom settings. *Journal of Applied Behavior Analysis, 25*, 823–840.

Fisher, W. W., Piazza, C. C., Bowman, L. G., Kurtz, P. F., Sherer, M. R., & Lachman, S. R. (1994). A preliminary evaluation of empirically derived consequences for the treatment of pica. *Journal of Applied Behavior Analysis, 27*, 447–457.

Hagopian, L. P., Fisher, W. W., Sullivan, M. T., Acquisto, J., & LeBlanc, L. A. (1998). Effectiveness of functional communication training with and without extinction and punishment. *Journal of Applied Behavior Analysis, 31*, 211–235.

Iwata, B. A. (1988). The development and adoption of controversial default technologies. *Behavior Analyst, 11*, 149–157.

Iwata, B. A., Dorsey, M. F., Slifer, K. J., Bauman, K. E., & Richman, G. S. (1982/1994). Toward a functional analysis of self-injury. *Journal of Applied Behavior Analysis, 27*, 197–209. (Reprinted from Analysis and Intervention in Developmental Disabilities, 2, 2–30, 1982.)

Iwata, B. A., Pace, G. M., Cowdery, G. E., & Miltenberger, R. G. (1994). What makes extinction work: An analysis of procedural form and function. *Journal of Applied Behavior Analysis, 27*, 131–144.

Iwata, B. A., Pace, G. M., Dorsey, M. F., Zarcone, J. R., Vollmer, T. R., Smith, R. G., et al. (1994). The functions of self-injurious behavior: An experimental–epidemiological analysis. *Journal of Applied Behavior Analysis, 27*, 215–240.

Lerman, D. C., & Iwata, B. A. (1996). Developing a technology for the use of operant extinction in clinical settings: An examination of basic and applied research. *Journal of Applied Behavior Analysis, 29*, 345–382.

Lerman, D. C., & Vorndran, C. M. (2002). On the status of knowledge for using punishment: Implications for treating behavior disorders. *Journal of Applied Behavior Analysis, 35,* 431–464.

Miltenberger, R. G. (2001). *Behavior modification: Principles and procedures* (2nd ed.). Belmont, CA: Wadsworth/Thomson Learning.

Northup, J., Wacker, D., Sasso, G., Steege, M., Cigrand, K., Cook, J., & DeRaad, A. (1991). A brief functional analysis of aggressive and alternative behavior in an outclinic setting. *Journal of Applied Behavior Analysis, 24,* 509–522.

Wacker, D. P., Berg, W. K., & Harding, J. (2000). Functional communication training augmented with choices. Washington, DC: Department of Health and Human Services, National Institute of Child Health and Human Development.

Wacker, D., Steege, M., Northup, J., Sasso, G., Berg, W., Reimers, T., et al. (1990). A component analysis of functional communication training across three topographies of severe behavior problems. *Journal of Applied Behavior Analysis, 23,* 417–429.

56 RAPID SMOKING

Elizabeth V. Gifford and Deacon Shoenberger

Recent reports estimate that about 20% of adults over 18, or 44 million Americans, are smokers (Centers for Disease Control and Prevention [CDC], 2008). Ninety-five percent of them report a desire to quit (Fisher, Haire-Joshu, Morgan, Rehberg, & Rost, 1990). Many smokers who indicate a desire to quit actually attempt quitting, as evidenced by the CDC's (1993) report that 46% of adult daily smokers made a serious quit attempt (quitting for 1 day) in the previous year. These efforts are generally unsuccessful, as less than 6% of those surveyed were able to maintain abstinence for a single month (CDC, 1993), and only 2.5% were permanently successful.

Smoking-related mortality is responsible for approximately 20% of all deaths in the United States (CDC, 1993). Smoking is the single largest preventable cause of death in this country (CDC, 2000). In 1990 alone, the CDCP estimates that smoking resulted in 5,048,740 years of potential life lost (2002). Quitting smoking is a matter of life and death. Thus, there are few interventions behavioral clinicians can perform that will have a more meaningful impact on the lives of their patients. Indeed, clinicians are constantly seeking successful interventions for their cigarette-smoking clients. For those who have tried and failed to quit using other methods (see United States Department of Health and Human Services [USDHHS], 2000, for complete practice guidelines), rapid smoking is a powerful procedure with a well-supported track record.

The theoretical background for rapid smoking is well established. *Rapid smoking therapy* is an aversive conditioning procedure through which the pairing of gustatory cues with aversive internal consequences (e.g., nausea) is thought to produce conditioned responding. For example, after aversive conditioning patients experience increases in heart rate when exposed to the taste of cigarettes posttreatment (Zelman, Brandon, Jorenby, & Baker, 1992). This conditioned responding is thought to result in long-lasting taste aversion to cigarettes (Tiffany, Martin, & Baker, 1986).

Aversion treatment for smoking was developed in response to reported successful treatment of alcoholism (Bandura, 1969; Cautela, 1967) and sexual deviance (Feldman & MacCulloch, 1965) with aversive conditioning techniques. Wilde (1964) was the first to generalize these techniques to the treatment of smoking, using an apparatus that blew warm, smoky air into smokers' faces as they smoked. Further research eventually refined the technique to allow for the use of cigarettes themselves as the aversive stimulus (Resnick, 1968; Lichtenstein, Harris, Birchler, Wahl, & Schmal, 1973). Other methods of aversion therapy include rapid puffing (without inhaling), smoke holding, and smoke satiation; however, these modified versions are not as effective (see Schwartz, 1987).

Initial studies of rapid smoking as a therapeutic intervention for smoking cessation were performed in the mid-1960s. Early studies reported 60%–70% long-term follow-up abstinence rates when using rapid smoking techniques alone. For example, Resnick (1968) reported that instructing college students to smoke at a rate 2 to 3 times that of their normal rate for 1 week prior to a quit attempt resulted in 63% abstinence at 4-month follow-up as compared to 20% abstinence in controls.

One of the most prolific researchers into the efficacy of rapid smoking as an effective intervention for smoking cessation has been Ed Lichtenstein. Lichtenstein and colleagues performed numerous evaluations of rapid smoking in the early 1970s with extremely successful outcomes, showing 6-month follow-up abstinence rates of 60%–70% (Schmal, Lichten-stein, & Harris, 1972; Lichtenstein et al., 1973; Lichtenstein & Rodrigues, 1977). As stated previously, these researchers also presented data suggesting that complicated mechanisms were not necessary to induce an aversive response to smoking. Early research using an apparatus similar to that used by Wilde (1964) showed no difference between groups treated with the smoke-blowing procedure in combination with rapid smoking and those treatment solely with a rapid smoking protocol (both groups maintained 60% abstinence at 6-month follow-up). These findings provided justification for rapid smoking protocols using cigarettes as the aversive stimulus as an effective stand-alone intervention (Lichtenstein et al., 1973).

Most of the research studies that demon-strated rapid smoking's efficacy predate current standards for smoking cessation research. For example, many of these studies were small and used patients' self-report of smoking outcomes without biochemical confirmation. Later research has also demonstrated successful outcomes; for example, Hall, Sachs, Hall, and Renowitz (1984) found 50% quit rates at 2-year follow-up, using biochemical verification of participant's self-reports (however, the number of participants, $n = 18$, was small).

Other, even more recent outcome studies of rapid smoking have not matched the abstinence rates of the first studies on rapid smoking (although the outcomes are similar to those of other treatments). For example, Fiore and colleagues (2000) report quit rates of 19%–20% at 1-year follow-up in a meta-analysis of recent (1990s) research on rapid smoking. There could be a number of reasons for the differences in outcome, but it is important to note that these studies did not use the original methods used by Lichtenstein and colleagues. Later studies of rapid smoking have restricted or controlled the number of sessions, utilized group instead of individual treatment, added additional components, or had clients undergo rapid smoking treatment at home (Hall, et al., 1984). One conclusion is that rapid smoking is most effective when conducted according to the full-scale original research protocols. Indeed, basic behavioral principles suggest that conditioning must be thoroughly accomplished for treatment effects to hold, and it is quite possible that modified protocols either fail to achieve conditioning or produce an attenuated version.

Though deviations from the original method may have resulted in less impressive outcomes, in many cases rapid smoking has been successfully combined with other techniques. In recent studies rapid smoking protocols have generally been imbedded in multicomponent programs, particularly in combination with behavioral counseling (Erickson, Tiffany, Martin, & Baker, 1983). In a study examining outcomes of varying levels of rapid smoking and coping skills training, Tiffany and colleagues (1986) found that subjects who received full-scale rapid smok-ing in combination with full-scale coping skills training were more likely to remain abstinent at 6-month follow-up than subjects treated with reduced variations of the two components. This study showed 6-month follow-up abstinence rates of 59% for the full-scale treatment subjects, consistent with outcomes of the original research.

Similarly, Barber (2001) found rapid smoking to be effective when used in combination with a hypnotic intervention, as 39 of 43 patients reported abstinence at 6-month and 3-year follow-up. These and other studies (Zelman et al., 1992) provide evidence for the effectiveness of rapid smoking protocols in combination with other psychosocial strategies, though again, research using the original methods used by Lichtenstein and colleagues appears to have provided the most successful outcomes. Quite recently, Stitzer and colleagues found that rapid smoking is efficacious at reducing cravings in individuals relapsing to smoking at posttreatment, although these immediate reductions in craving did not predict reductions in smoking (Houtsmuller & Stitzer, 1999). However, this study used a different population (people relapsing immediately after treatment), and again, the protocols differed substantially from those previously developed by Lichtenstein or Hall and their colleagues.

WHO MIGHT BENEFIT FROM THIS TECHNIQUE

Rapid smoking has been shown to be safe for healthy subjects, but it is also associated with some risk. Rapid smoking calls for the ingestion of large amounts of nicotine in a short period of time in order to induce mild nicotine intoxication and concomitant aversive conditioning. Rapid smoking does present the potentially fatal risk of nicotine toxicity, though research has shown the incidence to by extremely rare (see Lichtenstein, in Hauser, 1974). Nonetheless, it is essential to evaluate the health of the patient and all current medications before beginning a rapid smoking treatment. Because of the challenging nature of the protocol, rapid smoking is recommended after multiple other treatment efforts have failed. These initial treatment efforts should include front-line treatments such as cognitive behavioral therapy and nicotine replacement therapy.

CONTRAINDICATIONS

For patients on medication or with any medical issues, it is advised that rapid smoking be undertaken by a physician or under medical supervision (Hall & Hall, 1987). Rapid smoking should always be under the supervision of an experienced clinician and with particular emphasis on cessation of smoking before loss of consciousness or vomiting. It is important to note that the unique risk factors associated with rapid smoking therapy constitute a serious potential danger to pregnant women.

OTHER FACTORS IN DECIDING WHETHER TO USE RAPID SMOKING

Because rapid smoking has been shown to elevate heart rate and blood pressure and to increase respiratory rate (Hall, Sachs, & Hall, 1979), there has been particular concern about the efficacy and safety of rapid smoking in patients with various cardiovascular diseases. Hall and colleagues (1984) found that rapid smoking could be safely conducted without medical monitoring in smokers with mild to moderate cardiopulmonary disease. These researchers determined

that abnormal heart rate elevations during rapid smoking were less frequent than abnormal heart rate elevations during exercise or sexual intercourse, and that blood nicotine levels were well below lethal levels. While this study provides encouraging results, the authors caution that smokers with cardiovascular disease should consult a physician when engaging in rapid smoking therapy if they are taking certain medications (including beta blockers, digoxin, or diuretics), if they have congestive heart failure, if they have an artificial pacemaker, if they have difficulty breathing while performing daily activities and while sleeping, and if they wheeze when breathing. According to Hall and Hall (1987):

> Cautious therapists may not wish to carry out rapid smoking on patients with cardiopulmonary disease unless the therapist is in a medical setting. The probability of a recurrent myocardial infarction in this population is greater no matter what the patient's activity. If enough patients with cardiac disease underwent rapid smoking, by chance alone a small percentage would have a heart attack during treatment. (Sachs, Hall, Pechack, & Fitzgerald, 1979, p. 311)

A physician should evaluate any patient presenting with one or more risk factors for serious cardiovascular disease before engaging in rapid smoking therapy.

HOW DOES THE TECHNIQUE WORK?

As mentioned previously, aversive cessation techniques rely on basic associative conditioning: Replace the pleasurable associations of smoking with overwhelmingly negative associations. The success of this procedure therefore depends on the perceived noxiousness of the experience. These negative sensations must be maintained at high levels within and across multiple sessions. Both provider and patient need to be highly motivated and explicitly willing to tolerate an unpleasant and possibly distressing experience (empathically uncomfortable and distressing in the case of the provider). As in any smoking treatment, a strong relationship with the client enhances the likelihood of completing treatment.

Providing the patient with a rationale and a detailed description of possible and expected symptoms is extremely important in rapid smoking procedures. An accurate description of the aversiveness of the procedure is required both for informed consent and because the patient's full attention on the noxious symptoms is required for conditioning. Rapid smoking is highly effective if and only if conditioning is accomplished. Patients should be informed that they will experience notable discomfort that may include nausea, light-headedness, burning throat or eyes, tingling of the extremities, and headache. They should be warned that vomiting and fainting are possible, though they should stop smoking before these occur. The most difficult hurdle in rapid smoking is completing treatment. This should be discussed openly with the patient, and strategies to facilitate adherence (i.e., what are the possible barriers and how would they solve them?) should be incorporated into the treatment plan.

Along with the rapid smoking procedure, cognitive behavioral or supportive counseling (or both) for smoking cessation is recommended. At a minimum, the following steps should occur. First, patients should discuss their upcoming quit attempt with the people in their lives and attempts to elicit support. Their quit date is first day of rapid smoking. Failing success in eliciting active support, the clients should attempt to elicit agreement not to smoke in the house or in their presence, and not to offer them cigarettes. Second, patients should be informed that drinking alcohol is highly linked to relapse, and cessation from alcohol is strongly recommended. Third, additional individualized risk factors should be discussed in detail: Where does the patient smoke now? When? Which situations are triggers? Which feelings? Strategies for coping with these high-risk feelings and situations should be discussed, and patients should be encouraged to (1) alter the triggers (e.g., cleaning out and putting candy in the ashtray in the car, not keeping cigarettes anywhere in the house, throwing away all their ashtrays, etc.), (2) develop coping strategies for when these situations are not avoidable (e.g., relaxation exercises, breathing, distraction, thinking about their grandchildren, etc.), and (3) escape

from high-risk situations whenever possible (see Antonuccio, 1993, for a useful patient handbook and description). A minimum of two to three sessions should occur before the intensive rapid smoking protocol is implemented.

STEP-BY-STEP PROCEDURES

The following protocol comes from Hall and Hall (1987). After the therapist has fully informed the patient, developed the plan, established a high level of rapport, and provided initial support or coping skills training, the rapid smoking phase of treatment begins. Rapid smoking requires some preparation, including recording a looped tape with 6-second cues for inhaling and developing a checklist of negative symptoms for the patient to fill out during rest sessions. An emesis basin should also be present, both in case of vomiting and as a prop to enhance the suggestion of aversive levels of nausea (R. Hall, personal communication, May 2002). Patients should bring one pack of cigarettes and matches, after having removed all other cigarettes from their home environments.

The setting in which the procedure will take place is important. Because the aversive sensations must be fully experienced, patients should be explicitly discouraged from using distraction (some patients can distract so successfully that they do not experience the rapid smoking as aversive; R. Hall, personal communication, May 2002). The setting should provide as few distracting stimuli as possible. It is preferable to perform the procedure indoors in a closed and uninteresting room, with patients facing a blank wall. Even where public health regulations refuse to allow patients to smoke indoors, outdoor settings should be arranged to offer as little distractions as possible (e.g., in a loading-area doorway facing the cement wall).

As rapid smoking commences, patients are instructed to inhale the smoke from their regular brand of cigarette every 6 seconds until they feel unable to continue. They should be encouraged to continue to the point that they feel they are about to vomit or become severely light-headed. While they are rapid smoking, the practitioner should regularly encourage them to concentrate on the aversive symptoms they are experiencing as a result of smoking. Once they reach the point that they can no longer tolerate another inhalation, they are permitted to rest briefly (approximately 5 minutes), during which time they should fill out the sheet detailing their aversive symptoms. This serves as another means of maintaining focus on the unpleasant symptoms, as well as a way for the clinician to monitor their experience. Even during the rest period, the therapist should continue to point out the relationship between these symptoms and smoking. After the rest period, the patient should resume on the same schedule of one puff per 6 seconds. A minimum of two trials must occur during each session and more are advisable if patients can tolerate them. At the end of the final trial, they should report experiencing maximum levels of unpleasantness (i.e., a 10 on a 10-point scale).

After their final rest, they should be asked to sit and close their eyes and recall the unpleasant aspects of the experience they just went through. While recalling the sensations, they should attempt to focus on amplifying and intensifying the negative experience and feelings. After they return home, if they experience the urge to smoke, they should be encouraged to recall the aversive experiences as much as possible in order to help them resist the urges. Please note that R. Hall recommends that patients refrain from driving themselves home after a session, as some have reported feeling "foggy" afterward (Hall & Hall, 1987, p. 312).

According to Hall and Hall (1987), patients must agree not to smoke between sessions. Although they will not want to smoke immediately after the first session, cravings will probably return after the first session and patients should be told to expect this. The sessions should be spaced as closely as possible on an intensive schedule. For example, if beginning on a Monday, sessions should continue on Tuesday, Wednesday, Friday, and the following Monday. After the first five meetings patients may select the intervals between sessions; these intervals should be based on the amount of time they feel confident they can remain quit. Most studies have limited the number of sessions to 12 for no

scientific reason, though it is unusual for patients to want to continue to participate for this long.

CONCLUSION

Rapid smoking is a powerful treatment for smoking cessation, perhaps the most powerful psychosocial treatment currently available. A recent meta-analysis evaluating psychosocial treatments identified that odds ratios and quit rates were higher for rapid smoking than for any other treatment: 2.0 (1.1, 3.5) and 19.9 (11.2, 29.0), respectively (USDHHS, 2000). Nonetheless, in recent years it has been infrequently practiced (USDHHS). This is probably due to the fact that, by definition, rapid smoking is an aversive procedure for both patients and practitioners. If the treatment is to be successful, the conditioning experience must be difficult.

The counterpoint to the difficulty of the protocol is the urgency of the need for powerful smoking cessation treatments. The truth about the current state of smoking treatment is that the best we have to offer is usually not enough. Smoking is a life-or-death matter for those who will acquire cancer of the lung, kidney, pancreas, larynx, or cervix; chronic lung and heart disease; or pneumonia; and for the children of smoking mothers. For those who have repeatedly tried and failed to quit smoking, rapid smoking may be their best last chance.

EVIDENCE-BASED APPLICATIONS

Following is a brief list of problems for which aversive conditioning techniques have been shown to be effective:

- Alcoholism (Bandura, 1969; Cautela, 1967)
- Self-injurious behavior (Barnard, Christophersen, & Wolf, 1976)
- Aggressive or dangerous behavior (Foxx, 2003)
- Chronic pain (Schneider, Palomba, & Flor, 2004)
- Gambling (Lesieur & Blume, 1991)
- Sexual problems (Marks, Gelder, & Bancroft, 1970)

Further Reading

Hall, S. M., & Hall, R. G. (1987). Treatment of cigarette smoking. In J. A. Blumenthal & D. C. McKee (Eds.), *Applications in behavioral medicine and health psychology: A clinician's resource book* (pp. 301–323). Sarasota, FL: Professional Resource Exchange.

Fiore, M. C., Bailey, W. C., Cohen, S. J., Dorfman, S. F., Goldstein, M. G., Gritz, E. R., et al. (2000). *Treating tobacco use and dependence: Clinical practice guideline.* Public Health Service, Rockville, MD: U.S. Department of Health and Human Services.

References

Antonuccio, D. O. (1993). *Butt out, the smoker's book: A compassionate guide to helping yourself quit smoking, with or without a partner.* Saratoga, CA: R & E Publishers.

Bandura, A. (1969). *Principles of behavior modification.* New York: Holt, Rinehart, & Winston.

Barber, J. (2001). Freedom from smoking: Integrating hypnotic methods and rapid smoking to facilitate smoking cessation. *International Journal of Clinical and Experimental Hypnosis, 49,* 257–265.

Barnard, J. D., Christophersen, E. R., & Wolf, M. M. (1976). Parent-mediated treatment of children's self-injurious behavior using overcorrection. *Journal of Pediatric Psychology, 3,* 56–61.

Cautela, J. R. (1967). Covert sensitization. *Psychological Record, 20,* 459–468.

Centers for Disease Control and Prevention. (1993). Cigarette smoking–attributable mortality and years of potential life lost: United States, 1990. *Morbidity and Mortality Weekly Report, 45,* 588–590.

Centers for Disease Control and Prevention. (2000). State-specific prevalence of current cigarette smoking among adults and the proportion of adults who work in a smoke-free environment: United States, 1999. *Morbidity and Mortality Weekly Report, 49,* 978–982.

Centers for Disease Control and Prevention. (2002). MMWR: Cigarette smoking-attributable mortality and years of potential life lost: United States, 1990. *Morbidity and Mortality Weekly Report, 48,* 993–996.

Centers for Disease Control and Prevention. (2008). *Early release of selected estimates based on data from the January–September 2007 National Health Interview Survey: Current smoking.*

Erickson, L. M., Tiffany, S. T., Martin, E. M., & Baker, T. B. (1983). Aversive smoking therapies: A conditioning analysis of therapeutic effectiveness. *Behavior Research and Therapy, 21,* 595–611.

Feldman, M. P., & MacCulloch, M. J. (1965). The application of anticipatory avoidance learning to the treatment of homosexuality: I. Theory, techniques, and preliminary results. *Behavior Research and Therapy, 2,* 165–183.

Fiore, M. C., Bailey, W. C., Cohen, S. J., Dorfman, S. F., Goldstein, M. G., Gritz, E. R., et al. (2000). *Treating tobacco use and dependence: Clinical practice guideline.* Public Health Service, Rockville, MD: U.S. Department of Health and Human Services.

Fisher, E. B., Haire-Joshu, D., Morgan, G. D., Rehberg, H., & Rost, K. (1990). Smoking and smoking cessation. *American Review of Respiratory Disorders, 142,* 702–720.

Foxx, R. M. (2003). The treatment of dangerous behavior. *Behavioral Interventions, 18,* 1–21.

Hall, S. M. & Hall, R. G. (1987). Treatment of cigarette smoking. In J. A. Blumenthal & D. C. McKee (Eds.), *Applications in behavioral medicine and health psychology: A clinician's resource book* (pp. 301–323). Sarasota, FL: Professional Resource Exchange.

Hall, R. G., Sachs, D. P. L., & Hall, S. M. (1979). Medical risk and therapeutic effectiveness of rapid smoking. *Behavior Therapy, 10,* 249–259.

Hall, R. G., Sachs, D. P. L., Hall, S. M., & Benowitz, N.L. (1984). Two-year efficacy and safety of rapid smoking therapy in patients with cardiac and pulmonary disease. *Journal of Consulting and Clinical Psychology, 52,* 574–581.

Hauser, R. (1974). Rapid smoking as a technique of behavior modification: Caution in selection of subjects. *Journal of Consulting and Clinical Psychology, 42,* 625–626.

Houtsmuller, E. J., & Stitzer, M. L. (1999). Manipulation of cigarette smoking through rapid smoking: Efficacy and effects on smoking behavior. *Psychopharmacology, 142,* 149–157.

Lesieur, H. R., & Blume, S. B. (1991). Evaluation of patients treated for pathological gambling in a combined alcohol, substance abuse and pathological gambling treatment unit using the Addiction Severity Index. *Addiction, 86,* 1017–1028.

Lichtenstein, E., Harris, D. E., Birchler, G. R., Wahl, J. M., & Schmal, D. P. (1973). Comparison of rapid smoking, warm, smoky air, and attention placebo in the modification of smoking behavior. *Journal of Consulting and Clinical Psychology, 40,* 92–98.

Lichtenstein, E., & Rodrigues, M. P. (1977). Long-term effects of rapid smoking treatment for dependent smokers. *Addictive Behaviors, 2,* 109–112.

Marks, I. M., Gelder, M. G., & Bancroft, J. H. (1970). Sexual deviants two years after electric aversion therapy. *British Journal of Psychiatry, 117,* 173–185.

Resnick, J. H. (1968). Effects of stimulus satiation on the overlearned maladaptive response of cigarette smoking. *Journal of Consulting and Clinical Psychology, 32,* 500–505.

Sachs, D. P., Hall, R. G., Pechacek, T. F., & Fitzgerald, J. (1979). Classification of risk–benefit issues in rapid smoking. *Journal of Consulting and Clinical Psychology, 47,* 1053–1060.

Schmal, D. P., Lichtenstein, E., & Harris, D. E. (1972). Successful treatment of habitual smokers with warm, smoky air and rapid smoking. *Journal of Consulting and Clinical Psychology, 38,* 105–111.

Schneider, C., Palomba, D., & Flor, H. (2004). Pavlovian conditioning of muscular responses in chronic pain patients: Central and peripheral correlates. *Pain, 112,* 239–247.

Schwartz, J. L. (1987). *Review and evaluation of smoking cessation methods: The United States and Canada, 1978–1985.* National Cancer Institute: U.S. Department of Health and Human Services, Public Health Service, National Institutes of Health, 1987. NIH Publication No. 87-2940.

Tiffany, S. T., Martin, E. M., & Baker, T. B. (1986). Treatments for cigarette smoking: An evaluation of the contributions of aversion and counseling procedures. *Behavior Research and Therapy, 24,* 437–452.

U.S. Department of Health and Human Services (2000). *Reducing tobacco use: A report of the Surgeon General (Rep. No. 29).* Atlanta, GA: Author.

Wilde, G. J. S. (1964). Behavior therapy for addicted cigarette smokers. *Behavior Research and Therapy, 2,* 107–110.

Zelman, D. C., Brandon, T. H., Jorenby, D. E., & Baker, T. B. (1992). Measures of affect and nicotine dependence predict differential response to smoking cessation treatments. *Journal of Consulting and Clinical Psychology, 60,* 943–952.

57 RELAPSE PREVENTION

Kirk A. B. Newring, Tamara M. Loverich, Cathi D. Harris, and Jennifer Wheeler

Relapse prevention (RP) is a cognitive-behavioral intervention that was originally developed as a post-treatment maintenance enhancement for addictive behaviors such as alcohol use, drug use, and cigarette smoking (Marlatt & George, 1984; Marlatt & Gordon, 1980, 1985). RP has since been modified for application to other behavioral problems, including eating disorders and sexual offending. RP was developed as a response to a common problem for many individuals who had undergone successful treatment for substance abuse (e.g. became "clean and sober" in the context of a 28-day inpatient hospitalization); a relapse to their pretreatment level of substance use (Hunt, Barnett, & Branch, 1971). Successful treatment of an addictive behavior connotes that someone has stopped using the substance, and has made a commitment to continued abstinence. RP was developed to help individuals maintain the effects of treatment by teaching strategies to avoid, manage, and escape (or a combination thereof) situations that will threaten the commitment to abstinence. RP was not conceived as an alternative to primary treatment interventions, but as a supplemental tool that would make a variety of treatments, particularly for addictive behaviors, more effective. RP is aimed at helping clients to readily recall and utilize treatment information when it is needed, subsequent to the termination of formal treatment.

WHO MIGHT BENEFIT

With regard to the stages of change (cf. Tierney & McCabe, 2005), RP focuses on the "maintenance" phase of treatment. The purpose of RP is to help individuals maintain the gains made in their primary treatment, which is arguably the most difficult challenge for any client. Many clients are able to reduce unwanted behaviors with the full support of daily or weekly therapy sessions; however, when treatment is inevitably terminated, the likelihood of returning to the behaviors skyrockets. Without the structure and accountability of therapy, and the support of a therapist or group, treatment gains are likely to wane over time. RP provides a posttreatment strategy to help individuals in maintaining their treatment gains, and avoid the return to pretreatment levels of the maladaptive behavior.

In the short period of time since its introduction, RP has evolved in numerous directions. It has long been applied for a variety of treatment targets, typically for problems often viewed as issues of "self-control" such as alcohol abuse, nicotine use, and eating-related difficulties (overeating, self-restriction). RP has also been popularly applied to target undercontrolled sexuality (e.g., sexual offending, sexual "addiction" and sexual harassment). In many venues, it is used as it was originally designed—that is, as a booster treatment. However, in the field of sexual offending, RP has been and continues to be applied as a full program of treatment, although it is not the treatment package recommended by the subfield's guiding body, the Association for the Treatment of Sexual Abusers (ATSA). RP also continues to be a maintenance program for a variety of other interventions, including cognitive behavioral therapy (CBT) for depression and anxiety, and substance abuse.

INDICATIONS/CONTRAINDICATIONS

RP should not be used in areas in which there is little theoretical or empirically based support for its utility, or in areas where there may be an existing treatment with empirical support. For example, while RP may serve as a useful booster for obsessive–compulsive disorder, exposure and response prevention should be the primary intervention. Likewise, teaching avoidance strategies might be contraindicated for other anxiety disorders, such as agoraphobia. For these problems, the clients typically already have a relapse prevention plan in place for the avoidance, management, and escape from feared stimuli or situations. However, and this point highlights some of the confusing aspects of RP, in terms of avoidance-based maladaptive coping, there may be utility in applying a RP analysis of cues, triggers, cognitive distortions, and high risk situations to inform exposure-based interventions (e.g., family conflict as a cue that leads to a high-risk situation of isolation for the agoraphobic).

RP is most useful when aspects of the environment are strongly associated with the behavior of interest such as holiday dinners and purging for a client with bulimia. RP's strength is making explicit the contextual cues that spur resumption of the behavior due to a history of conditioned association and reinforcement. When a behavior appears to be primarily organic in origin, such as an endogenous depressive disorder, RP is not the obvious maintenance option.

OTHER FACTORS TO CONSIDER

RP should also be avoided in cases in which the client's ability to recall historical data, or verbally process new information is impaired (e.g., mental retardation, developmental delay, organic injury, etc.) due to RP's heavy reliance on verbal processing. There may be other media through which RP instruction could occur, though the effectiveness of alternative approaches has not been thoroughly evaluated. While significant numbers of developmentally delayed sex offenders are receiving treatment, RP is often a small element in a comprehensive treatment program (cf. Haaven and Coleman in Laws, Hudson, and Ward 2000). When utilizing RP with special populations the therapist must be aware that alterations are needed in both language and assigned exercises. Failure to do so may result in

a decrease in motivation significantly impacting the therapeutic process and outcome.

THEORETICAL BASES

Behaviorism is the foundation of RP. The approach assumes that it is faulty or absent learning of effective and harmless coping strategies that is the source of behavioral difficulties. Overlearned and harmful conditioned responses interfere with effective functioning. Alan Marlatt and Judith Gordon developed RP to address their concerns over the loss of treatment gains after clients discontinued treatment. Many clients that responded to a variety of treatments for addictive behaviors could expect to reach abstinence, only to fail to maintain their gains following the cessation of treatment. Thus, an important assumption of RP evolved: The effects of a treatment that is designed to moderate or eliminate an undesirable behavior should not be expected to endure beyond the termination of treatment without additional intervention.

Most psychological treatments, particularly cognitive behaviorally–based approaches, typically involve an intense but limited period of time during which clients are brought into contact with new influences or experiences, information, and contextual components that aid in creating changes in their behaviors. The context of therapy promotes accountability and a regular "dose" of treatment given reliably over a period of time. After the client has reached his treatment goals and treatment is terminated, the client must learn to implement the skills and knowledge learned in a new context into an old context with little or no assistance. There are reasons to presume that once treatment is discontinued, a problem will reemerge as time passes. Factors such as returning to the old environment that elicited and previously maintained the problem behavior, forgetting the skills techniques and information taught during therapy, the challenges in programming for generalization from the treatment environment to the home environment, and a decrease in motivation may all lead to a return to pretreatment levels of the problem behavior. Clients often enter environments in which their demonstration of treatment gains may be punished. Generalizing the skills to varied situations poses a significant challenge and many treatment failures are the result. Research has demonstrated that within one year of ending treatment over 80 percent of clients resume the undesired behavior (treatment failure), and two-thirds of relapses would occur in the first 3 months after treatment cessation (Hunt, et al., 1971).

Marlatt and colleagues believed that treatment failures could be analyzed in order to discover internal and external variables that increased risk for relapse. They further reasoned that factors such as situations, mood states, cognitions, and individualized risk factors could be identified and targeted to receive ongoing attention following treatment. The RP model proposes that at the conclusion of treatment a client feels self-efficacious about eliminating the unwanted behavior, and that this perception of self-efficacy stems from learned and practiced skills. Over time, the client contacts internal and external risk factors and high-risk situations (HRSs) that threaten the client's self-control, and consequently his perception of self-efficacy. If the client has adaptive coping skills to adequately address the internal and external challenges to her control and can access them, she will not relapse. However, if her skills are not sufficient to meet the challenge, a lapse or relapse may occur (this will be described in greater detail below). In response to a resumption of the target behavior at some level, the client either increases attempts to implement adaptive coping skills, or fails to cope effectively and engages in the undesirable behavior because it provides immediate gratification. The model supposes that the targets of intervention are cognitions and behaviors, collectively referred to as coping skills. Accordingly, RP employs cognitive behavioral techniques to improve the retention, accessibility, and implementation of adaptive coping responses following the termination of treatment.

TREATMENT COMPONENTS

Laws (1995) outlined the key principal components that serve as the foundation of RP. They are:

- Identification of a maladaptive behavior
- A process of change defined by commitment and motivation
- Behavioral change and maintenance of behavior change
- Identification of lapses (a single instance of the maladaptive behavior) and relapses (a complete violation of the self-imposed abstinence rules)
- Lifestyle balance between obligatory and self-selected behaviors
- Recognition of the idiographic aspects of the maladaptive behavior
- Recognizing and planning behavioral responses for high-risk situations

In practice, RP identifies pathways to HRSs and how to effectively cope with pathway elements and HRSs in order to prevent or stop the unwanted target behavior. The goals of identification and effective coping are met through predicting and anticipating high-risk situations, identifying and challenging cognitive distortions, seemingly irrelevant decisions, and the abstinence violation effect, and combating the problem of immediate gratification through contingency management. Therapists using RP as a model in which a full treatment program is embedded also include skills training components, such as social skills and coping skills interventions. It is hypothesized that some clients may not have learned the requisite skills to cope effectively in some situations. Therefore, skills training often supplements RP. For other problems, functional assessment may indicate other skill deficits or behavioral excesses that work to maintain the maladaptive coping response that is the target of RP. Adjunctive treatment techniques are often employed within an extended RP framework to address these needs.

PROCEDURES

When implementing relapse prevention the client is first assisted in identifying his HRSs, and the thoughts, feelings, and behaviors that give rise to the HRS. In the RP model, the problem behavior is seen as one element of a pattern (behavioral chain/maladaptive life cycle) in which an often distal trigger or cue sets a chain of internal and external behaviors in motion. Cognitive distortions, seemingly irrelevant decisions, the problem of immediate gratification, and abstinence violation effect work to "speed the client along" toward a high-risk situation. HRSs are determined by an analysis of past displays of the undesirable behavior and accounts of tempting situations.

Step 1: Identification of Lapses and Relapses

- Lapses are occurrences of the problem behavior in the context of a behavior reduction or elimination plan, (e.g., a cigarette for the tobacco-cessation client).

- Relapse is the return to baseline levels or pretreatment levels of the occurrence of the problem behavior (e.g., returning to a pack-a-day habit for the tobacco-cessation client).

- The "acceptability" of lapses and relapses is dependent on the behavior[2] (e.g., sexual offenders may have more consequences for a relapse than a smoker has).

- The analysis of harm requires an idiographic assessment of the client's problem behavior (it), what it is, what it looks like, how it works for the client (functional assessment) and how the client and support group will recognize it as it happens.

- There is no set limit to the time required for this, or other intervention tasks. This aspect of RP is one of the features that make it a somewhat nebulous amalgam of techniques difficult to encapsulate as a uniform intervention.

In addition to identifying the high-risk elements of the behavior chain, the client is assisted in employing appropriate self-control responses (interventions), which are acquired through treatment. These interventions can be implemented at any point in the behavior chain, ideally before the client reaches a high-risk situation at the end of the chain. Appropriate self-control responses are those behaviors that lead to avoidance of, management in, escape from and debriefing after being faced with an HRS. Typically, the client will prepare avoid, escape and control responses in anticipation of contacting the fairly inevitable HRS. For example, if a sexual offender finds himself fantasizing about a young child he may, through treatment, learn to avoid triggers that lead to those thoughts, "urge surf" during the fantasy, distract himself to interrupt (escape from) the deviant fantasy and then journal about the event to perhaps modify his response strategies for the future.

High-Risk Situations

This component involves the ideographic assessment of HRSs. The client and clinician work together to identify the situations in which the client has previously engaged in problematic behavior and those situations in which the client is likely to engage in problematic behavior in the future. One technique often used requires the client to describe the thoughts, feelings and behaviors that occurred before, during, and after each relevant instance of the undesired behavior. This data set can then be used to discern repeated elements that can be identified as precursors of HRSs and reinforcers of losses of control. The client will be asked to generate a list of situations that are low risk, and what aspects of those situations differentiate them from high-risk situations. For more concrete thinking styles, some clients will have difficulty generalizing from geographical HRSs to emotional, cognitive, or physiological HRSs. The treatment focus is to train the client to recognize themes and commonalties in their HRSs so that they can generalize the ability to assess level of risk in novel circumstances. The therapist works with the client to ensure that the client is realistic in his or her assessment of the level of risk in a variety of hypothetical situations.

Step 2: Identification of High-Risk Situations

- Analyze all relevant previous significant occurrences of the problem behavior in terms of thoughts, feelings, and behaviors before (triggers), during, and after these occurrences. This can be done by constructing a 3×3 grid.

- Look for similarities across affect, cognitions and behaviors that tend to co-occur reliably with the problem behavior.

- For example, a common emotion that occurs before an act of sexual offending is "feeling discounted." For that client, any situation in which they have, or would be likely to feel discounted would be considered a high-risk situation.

- High-risk situations can be internal (affect, cognitions), external (victim types, locations) or interactive (given certain internal conditions, external conditions may make an occurrence of the problem behavior more likely).

- Work with the client to identify and monitor the before–during–afters of any high-risk situations encountered while in treatment to assist in generalization for aftercare.

- Develop a dynamic problem chain, the chain of behaviors that probabilistically lead to lapse or relapse, (e.g., what emotional and cognitive setting events set up what decisions and behaviors that place the client in a situation in which he is likely to lapse or relapse).

- Interventions (described later) focus on the avoidance, management, escape from, and debriefing after high-risk situations.

Cognitive Distortions

Another component of RP is identifying and challenging cognitive distortions, self-statements that provide permission to the client for engaging in offensive behaviors. Cognitive distortions function to bring the client from trigger or cue to a high-risk situation, lapse and potentially relapse. Clients typically view these statements as both accurate representations of the world and adequate justifications for engaging in the unwanted behavior. Examples of cognitive distortions can be seen in Steen's (2001) *The Adult Relapse Prevention Workbook*, as well as the Brunswig and O'Donohue (2002) *Relapse Prevention for Sexual Harassers* and Sbraga and O'Donohue's (2004) *Sex Addiction Workbook*. Some common cognitive distortions are victim blaming, entitlement, minimizing, rationalizing, projection, magnification, victim stance ("poor me"), catastrophizing, overgeneralizing, all-or-nothing thinking, negative bias, positive bias, and personalization. Jenkins-Hall (1989, in Laws, 1989) describes the steps for changing cognitive distortions as: identification of the thoughts that lead to maladaptive behavior, analyzing the validity and utility of the thoughts, and an intervention designed to change the cognitive distortions into more adaptive cognitions. The therapist first assists the client in developing alternative interpretations for his initial thoughts. The client is then asked to evaluate if the past thinking made it easier to commit the problematic behavior and begins to develop skills to analyze the logic behind certain types of thinking. Finally, the client is assisted in disputing and challenging his thoughts in therapy and generalizing these skills to his natural environment. In essence the client is taught to actively think and analyze his thoughts. With respect to RP, clients are assisted in examining how cognitive distortions affect the prevention of relapses and are aided in challenging their thinking as it relates to the above elements of RP. SIDs/SUDs, the PIG, and the AVE function similarly for many clients and are described next.

Step 3: Identify and Track Disinhibitors

Cognitive Distortions, Sids, Ave, And Pig

- Identify the relevant cognitive distortions and SIDs with your client.

- Homework: Assign the client the task of monitoring the occurrences of the cognitive distortions and SIDs encountered on a daily basis.

- Use techniques such analyzing the validity and utility of the thoughts, develop alternative interpretations, directing the client to dispute and challenge their own thoughts, and other similar Rational Emotive Behavior Therapy (REBT), Cognitive Behavior Therapy (CBT), and Cognitive Therapy (CT) techniques.

- Address the PIG through decision matrices and decisional balances.

- As a result of the PIG analysis, make the client acutely aware of the long term consequences of continuing the behavior, thereby putting her in touch with what she wants for her life, which typically transcends being comfortable in immediate situations.

- Discuss the AVE, as a peril predicted can be addressed more thoughtfully than an unanticipated threat to stability.

SIDs/SUDs

Seeming irrelevant decisions (SIDs) (also called seeming unimportant decisions or SUDs) are those behaviors that might not lead directly to a HRS, but are early in the chain of decisions that increase the likelihood the client will place himself in an HRS. For example, if the client reports that he is more likely to engage in the problematic behavior after drinking, an SID would be agreeing to attend a luncheon with a coworker who is known to drink alcohol heavily at lunch. Lunching with the coworker is not the HRS. However, the introduction of alcohol is likely to increase the potential of the individual finding himself in a HRS.

In addressing SIDs, the therapist works with the client to determine the types of decisions that lead to HRSs. Once the client can identify many potential SIDs the client learns and practices

effective coping strategies or interventions. The therapist works with the client to ensure that the generated solutions and skills are adaptive, adequate, appropriate, and numerous because there are times when a particular response may be restricted by the environment. Clients should have several tools ready for any given HRS. In addition, therapists may also role-play situations with the client to allow the client a chance to practice their intervention skills in a hypothetical HRS.

PIG

PIG refers to "the problem of immediate gratification." In essence, individuals acting in such a way as to receive immediate positive consequences will often suffer larger, more aversive consequences at a later date. However, there is a disconnect between pursuing the immediate positive (or negative) reinforcement and considering future aversive consequences of doing so. Sexual offenders offer a good example. Many will offend against a victim to immediately gratify or reduce negative feelings or experiences giving little thought to the long-term consequences of such behavior. Offending, or the problematic behavior, is a "quick fix" to feeling better. Some research has demonstrated that the PIG may be a significant predictor of self-reported likelihood to sexually recidivate (Wheeler, 2003).

Psychoeducational approaches that teach the client how to create a decision matrix are often employed to combat the PIG. The therapist assists the client in developing a matrix, which is a concise, written representation of the positive and negative outcomes for engaging or not engaging in the problematic behavior (cf. Brunswig & O'Donohue, 2002), and then assigning probabilities (0.0 to 1.0) of that outcome actually occurring. This is done in both an immediate and short-term frame of reference. The therapist challenges any unrealistic or improbable outcomes until the client is able to generate more realistic ones. The therapist then directs the client to analyze past situations in which they engaged in the problematic behavior, and to compare the immediate gratifications against the long-term consequences. Clients are then encouraged to utilize this decision matrix when encountering novel situations. Many sessions may be dedicated to role-playing situations to habituate this process. Moreover, many clients carry a small version of the decision matrix with them to have it available in case they contact an HRS and freeze. The reader should be cautioned that utilizing complicated exercises like this are not appropriate for some special populations.

AVE

The abstinence violation effect (AVE) occurs when a client fails to cope effectively in a high-risk situation, lapses, and views the lapse as so severe, that he may as well enjoy the immediate pleasure of a full relapse. The reasoning recognizes a small failure, focuses on it as evidence that behavioral control is not possible, and indulges the desire for the immediate positive reinforcement that comes with enacting the problem behavior. For example, the overeater may have an AVE when expressing, "one slice of cheesecake is a lapse and I have failed, so I may as well go all out, and have the rest of the cheesecake." The individual's belief is that since she has violated the rule of abstinence, she "may as well" get the most out of the lapse resulting in relapse.[1]

Treatment of the AVE involves describing and predicting it, and working with the client to learn alternative coping skills for when a lapse occurs, such that she is more confident in responding appropriately to lapses or an any point in the behavior chain. This also affords an opportunity for the client to anticipate the AVE and include interventions for the AVE as a part of the relapse prevention plan. This is done through practice sessions in which the client and therapist identify lapse situations and practice the implementation of intervention skills. It must be emphasized to the client that lapses are to be expected, and can be handled if planned for in advance. Clients who recognize that lapses are normal and expected

may be less likely to use a minor instance of the behavior in a rationale to relapse.

---

1. Note that the AVE is difficult to define in the case of sexual offending, due to the semantic redesignation of the terms *lapse* and *relapse* for sexual offending. For discussion see Wheeler, George, & Marlatt, 2003; Wheeler, George, & Stephens, 2006).

Step 4: Alternative Behaviors

- Build upon the self-monitoring effect by having the client keep track of occurrences of SIDs, cognitive distortions, HRSs, lapses, and AVE.

- Use psychoeducation, modeling, role-play, and contingency management to instruct or enhance alternative behaviors that may meet the intended function of the problem behavior (e.g., for the social skills deficient sexual harasser using inappropriate verbal behavior to enlist social attention, provide instruction and practice pro-social conversation skills).

- Teach or enhance distress tolerance skills for "hanging in there" when presented with a "want" to engage in the problem behavior or to reduce the aversive qualities of the withdrawal symptoms for not engaging in the problem behavior.

- Use psychoeducation to instruct or enhance interventions for each intermediary step in the behavioral chains described above. For example, work with the client to have practical and useful interventions for triggers, SIDs and cognitive distortions, and the avoidance, management (distress tolerance), escape and debriefing of HRSs. Intervention can occur at any point in the behavioral chain, and the earlier in the chain the better to prevent a relapse.

- The creation of a relapse prevention plan is a dynamic and iterative process in which the triggers, distortions, HRSs and interventions are planned for, documented, and debriefed on after their occurrence. While some clients have often presented voluminous plans (one has even presented his in a collection of three-ring binders!) the plan that can accompany the client everywhere will be more likely used.

- The relapse prevention plan is dynamic and should be revisited and revised as the client continues the self-exploration process.

Planning for Lapses and Utilizing a Support Group

As indicated earlier, clients should be informed that lapses are to be expected and can be handled when they are anticipated. To plan for lapses the client should know how she would handle and intervene in situations in which she feels at risk for engaging in the problematic behavior. This is referred to as the development of a relapse prevention plan. The client will need to have a plan that outlines strategies for avoiding, managing, escaping, and debriefing HRSs, recognizing and intervening in cognitive distortions, SIDs/SUDs, the PIG, and the AVE, for seeking help from an identified support group should the need arise after therapy, and modifying the relapse prevention plan based on feedback, successes and failures of the plan. One way to do this is for the client to learn and practice all of the requisite skills beforehand and continually review and update her relapse prevention plan. In addition, the client can be assisted in developing cue cards, which can be used to refresh and prompt the client on their relapse prevention strategies as needed.

Maintenance and Aftercare

Eventually, there is a gradual reduction of the role of therapy and therapist in the client's life. To enhance the gains made in therapy, as well as assist the client in the implementation of her relapse prevention plan, sessions are ideally faded from biweekly, to monthly, then bimonthly in order to provide the client time and opportunity to generalize new skills with support, accountability, and assistance in revising the RP plan if necessary. As many of the problems

addressed with RP are enduring behavior problems, practitioners employing RP typically inform their clients that the clients will struggle with the problem indefinitely, and they will likely never be "cured." To combat skills drift and assist in the maintenance of problem-free behavior, sessions may continue annually for years. The purpose of these sessions is to act as boosters to the primary therapy and to assist the client in updating and reviewing the relapse prevention plan with the knowledge gained through experience. New triggers for old behaviors inevitably appear. Constant revision keeps the relapse prevention plan fresh and useful.

As with any therapeutic intervention, therapists are obligated to design a plan for long term success. Relapse prevention is no exception. While the goal of RP is the prevention of the occurrence of problematic behavior, the client's lifestyle must also be addressed for the most effective process of change. The RP model speculates that lifestyle imbalance, that is, a lack of balance between positive and negative activities, is a major contributor to succumbing to potential losses of control. Therefore, the development of positive addictions or positive alternative behaviors is also emphasized. Positive alternatives are healthy behaviors and hobbies, (e.g., reading, bowling, fly fishing) in which the client can engage without experiencing adverse consequences. It is crucial that the therapist work with the client to avoid recommending triggers previously paired with the behavior (e.g., bowling for the smoker who smoked while bowling) as those alternatives may work as conditioned cues for the problem behavior. Prior to the fading of sessions, the therapist assists the client in approach planning which entails identifying and getting involved in enjoyable alternative activities that support the developed relapse prevention plan.

Step 5: Relapse Prevention

- Relapse prevention is a variety of cognitive behavioral techniques designed to maintain the longevity of addiction and self-control treatment gains.

- RP involves identifying the thoughts, feelings, and behaviors that lead to high-risk situations and coping effectively with them in order to prevent or stop a loss of self-control.

- Identifying and managing high-risk situations, cognitive distortions, seemingly unimportant decisions, the problem of immediate gratification, the abstinence violation effect, and lifestyle imbalances are core points of intervention.

- RP necessitates learning, practicing, and implementing difficult control skills throughout a lifetime. An evolving relapse prevention plan supports the generalizability of these efforts over time and changing contexts.

Relapse Prevention Research

In the second edition of *Relapse Prevention*, Marlatt and Donovan (2005) include chapters addressing relapse prevention for alcohol and drug problems, diverse populations, smoking, stimulant dependence, opioid dependence, cannabis abuse and dependence, abuse of club drugs, hallucinogens, inhalants and steroids, eating disorders and obesity, gambling disorders, sexual offenders, and sexually risky behaviors. Each of these chapters reviews the relevant literature on relapse prevention as applied in these domains.

Marlatt and Witkiewitz (2005) review the major tenets, meta-analysis, and the treatment outcome literature of the nearly 30-year history of relapse prevention techniques and approaches in the treatment of alcohol and drug problems. Their review spans from 1978 to the 2005 publication of the second edition of *Relapse Prevention*. They note that studies have evaluated the effectiveness and efficacy of relapse prevention approaches for problems such as: substance use disorders, depression, sexual offending, obesity, obsessive–compulsive disorder, schizophrenia, bipolar disorder, and panic disorder. They also make reference to the 24 randomized clinical trials (RCTs) utilizing RP or coping skills training, including evaluations of research on smoking, alcohol, marijuana, and cocaine addiction. According to the authors, additional research has evaluated the impact of RP approaches and techniques on the treatment of polysubstance abuse as well as problem gambling. In their review, Marlatt and Witkiewitz note that the stronger findings in support of RP for alcohol abuse and dependence may be in part related to the differences among alcohol abuse and the nature, course, and etiology for other problems for which it has been applied.

At the time of their review (Marlatt & Witkiewitz, 2005) an RCT on the use of relapse prevention as a primary treatment for sexual offenders was also published. Marques, Weideranders, Day, Nelson, and van Ommeren, (2005) reported that RP as a primary treatment did not appear to impact recidivism in an RCT program evaluation project. In their report Marques et al. noted several limitations to the study that may have impacted the researchers' ability to understand if RP was effective in reducing sex offending recidivism in a state hospital population. Since its publication, much has been made of the meaning of this finding in the sex offender research and treatment fields. More recently, Marshall and Marshall (2007) review the limitations of using the RCT approach for a treatment such as RP with a population such as sexual offenders.

Taken together, the research on relapse prevention, as a whole, is supportive for the use of relapse prevention the way it was designed and developed; as an adjunctive treatment meant to aid in maintaining treatment gains. The further afield treatment providers have shifted from its origins, the less beneficial RP may be.

Limitations and Future Directions

One problem that RP has faced in the last 3 decades is the potential for misapplication or other misuse. RP was designed as an adjunct to a primary treatment approach. A few key assumptions accompany the theoretical utility of RP to help maintain posttreatment gains. First, RP presumes that the individual has stopped the problem behavior, and has made a commitment to abstain from the problem behavior in the future. Second, RP supposes that the individual has a belief that he or she is able to successfully maintain his or her treatment gains. Violations of these assumptions, or other modifications to the original RP model, consequently may impact its effectiveness. For example, a randomized clinical trial of RP to target sexual offense behavior did not provide empirical support for RP as a primary treatment approach for this behavior (Marques, et al., 2005). This result is not surprising, given that RP was not designed as a primary treatment approach, and given that modifications were made to the original RP model that may not have "translated" well in its application to this population (see Wheeler, George, & Marlatt, 2006; Wheeler, George, & Stephens, 2005). Other models have been proposed recently as primary treatment approaches to target sexual offense behavior (e.g., Ward & Hudson, 2000; Ward & Marshal, 2004; Wheeler, George, & Stoner, 2005). A hypothesis yet to be tested is whether RP can enhance the ability of these approaches to help individuals maintain treatment gains.

Another problem faced by RP is the potential for overemphasis on "abstinence" as the only acceptable positive measure of treatment outcome. More recently, "harm reduction" (HR) has emerged as another way of evaluating the potential and actual success of interventions and prevention strategies. HR is a controversial philosophy, also derived from the field of addictive behaviors. Historically, substance abuse treatment programs required that clients remain abstinent in order to receive treatment services. Accordingly, individuals who experienced lapses or relapses often found themselves essentially abandoned by their treatment providers. Due to the persistence of relapse, substance abuse treatment providers began to consider approaches to "damage control"—that is, taking steps to minimize the damage caused by a relapse. As a public health alternative to the moral and medical/disease models of addictions, the HR philosophy suggests a more pragmatic focus on the consequences or effects of the addictive behavior rather than on the behavior itself (Marlatt, 1996, 1998). Examples of HR

interventions in the substance abuse field include reducing the damage associated with the route of drug administration (e.g., from injecting to smoking), the relative dangerousness of the drug (e.g., from heroin to methadone), and using clean needles. From an HR perspective, outcomes are considered in terms of whether harm is reduced and, if so, by how much (Stoner & George, 2000). In the addictions field, cognitive behavioral approaches such as RP are consistent with a movement away from the medical/disease model of "addiction," to pragmatically reducing and managing maladaptive behavior.

Several authors have presented mindfulness and meditation as possible avenues to enhance RP (Marlatt &, Witkiewitz, 2005). Increasing the client's mindfulness of the presence or likelihood of triggers, HRS, cognitive distortions and other core features of RP is intended to increase the likelihood that the client will be aware of the opportunity to intervene, and of the potential benefits of intervening. Wheeler, George, and Stoner, (2005) have proposed a model of including dialectical behavior therapy, including core mindfulness skills, for the treatment of sexual offenders. Mindfulness-based interventions have also been proposed for the treatment of depression. It is likely that future iterations of RP will include aspects of mindfulness.

FINAL COMMENTS

Relapse prevention was designed as an elegant booster shot. It was not intended to be a stand-alone treatment for any of the problems for which it has been used. There seems to be some recognition in the fields in which it is used that alone, it is not an adequate treatment. It does not naturally address change; it addresses the maintenance of change. RP is consequently logically supplemented by other cognitive and behavioral techniques that are hypothetically linked to, or have demonstrated efficacy in treating the problem behavior (e.g., Chapter 37, Harm Reduction, this volume). Therefore, each incarnation of the approach is customized to the problem at hand, and as a result, a RP program is often difficult to identify by its techniques. We have presented the stripped-down model that is unlikely to be encountered. However, it is important to recognize these core elements, particularly as efforts turn to empirically validating the use of RP for its variety of uses. Comparison of treatment programs that are identified as RP programs, but which include many different elements, almost ensures the obfuscation of its effectiveness in treating problems of self-control.

Future Reading

Brunswig, K. A. & O'Donohue, W. (2002). *Relapse prevention for sexual harassers.* New York: Kluwer Academic/Plenum Publishers.

Laws, D. R., Hudson, S. M., & Ward, T. (Eds.) (2000). *Remaking relapse prevention with sex offenders: A sourcebook.* Thousand Oaks: Sage.

Marlatt, G. A., & Gordon, J. R. (Eds.) (1985). *Relapse prevention.* New York: Guilford.

Marlatt, G. A., & Donovan, D. M. (Eds.) (2005). *Relapse prevention: Maintenance strategies in the treatment of addictive behaviors* (2nd ed.). New York: Guilford.

References

Brunswig, K. A., & O'Donohue, W. (2002). *Relapse prevention for sexual harassers.* New York: Kluwer Academic/Plenum Publishers.

George, W. H., & Marlatt, G. A. (1989). Introduction. In D. R. Laws (Ed.), *Relapse prevention with sex offenders* (pp. 1–31). New York: Guilford.

Hunt, W. A., Barnett, L. W., & Branch, L. G. (1971). Relapse rates in addiction programs. *Journal of Clinical Psychology, 27,* 455–456.

Jenkins-Hall, K. A. (1989). The decision matrix. In D. R. Laws (Ed.), *Relapse prevention with sex offenders* (pp. 159–166). New York: Guilford.

Laws, D. R., Hudson, S. M., & Ward, T. (Eds.) (2000). *Remaking relapse prevention with sex offenders: A sourcebook.* Thousand Oaks: Sage.

Laws, D. R. (Ed.) (1989). *Relapse prevention with sex offenders.* New York: Guilford.

Laws, D. R. (1995). A theory of relapse prevention. In O'Donohue, W., & Krasner, L. (Eds.). *Theories of behavior therapy: Exploring behavior change* (pp. 445–474). Washington DC: American Psychological Association.

Marlatt, G. A., & Donovan, D. M. (Eds.) (2005). *Relapse prevention: Maintenance strategies in the treatment of addictive behaviors* (2nd ed.). New York: Guilford.

Marlatt, G. A., & Gordon, J. R. (Eds.) (1985). *Relapse prevention.* New York: Guilford.

Marlatt, G. A. (1998). Harm reduction: Pragmatic strategies for managing high-risk behaviors. New York: Guilford.

Marlatt, G. A. & Witkiewitz, K. (2005). Relapse prevention for alcohol and drug problems. In Marlatt, G. A. & Donovan, D. M. (Eds.) (2005) *Relapse prevention: Maintenance strategies in the treatment of addictive behaviors* (2nd ed.). New York: Guilford.

Marques, J. K., Weideranders, M., Day, D., Nelson, C., & van Ommeren, A. (2005). Effects of a relapse prevention program on sexual recidivism: Final results from California's Sex Offender Treatment and Evaluation Project (SOTEP). *Sexual Abuse: A Journal of Research and Treatment, 17,* 79–107.

Marshall, W. L., & Marshall, L. E. (2007). The utility of random controlled trials for evaluating sex offender treatment: The gold standard or an inappropriate strategy? *Sexual Abuse: A Journal of Research and Treatment, 19,* 175–191.

Pithers, W. D., Marques, J. K., Gibat, C. C., & Marlatt, G. A. (1983). Relapse prevention with sexual aggressives: A self-control model of treatment and maintenance of change. In J. G. Greer & I. R. Stuart (Eds.), *The sexual aggressor* (pp. 124–239). New York: Van Nostrand Reinhold.

Sandberg, G. G., & Marlatt, G. A. (1991). Relapse prevention. In D. A. Gravlo & R. I. Shader (Eds.), *Clinical manual of dependence.* Washington, DC: American Psychiatric Press.

Sbraga, T. P., & O'Donohue, W. T. (2004). *The sex addiction workbook.* Oakland, CA: New Harbinger Press.

Steen, C. (2001). *The adult relapse prevention workbook.* Brandon, VT: Safer Society Press.

Tierney, D. W., & McCabe, M. P. (2005). The utility of the trans-theoretical model of behavior change in the treatment of sex offenders. *Sex Abuse: A Journal of Research and Treatment, 17*(2), 153–170.

Ward, T., & Hudson, S. (1996). Relapse prevention: A critical analysis. *Sexual Abuse: A Journal of Research and Treatment, 8,* 177–199.

Ward, T., & Hudson, S. M. (2000). A self-regulation model of the relapse prevention process. In D. R. Laws, S. M. Hudson, & T. Ward (Eds.), *Remaking relapse prevention with sex offenders: A source book* (pp. 79–101). Thousand Oaks, CA: Sage.

Ward, T., Hudson, S. M., & Marshall, W. L. (1994). The abstinence violation effect in child molesters. *Behavior Research and Therapy, 32,* 431–437.

Ward, T., & Marshall, W. L. (2004). Good lives, etiology and the rehabilitation of sex offenders: A bridging theory. *Journal of Sexual Aggression, 10,* 153–169.

Wheeler, J. G. (2003). The abstinence violation effect in a sample of incarcerated sexual offenders: A reconsideration of the terms lapse and relapse. *Dissertation Abstracts International: Section B: The Sciences & Engineering, 63,* 3946.

Wheeler, J. G., George, W. H., & Marlatt, G. A. (2006). Relapse prevention for sexual offenders: Considerations for the abstinence violation effect. *Sexual*

Abuse: Journal of Research and Treatment, 18(3), 233–248.

Wheeler, J. G., George, W. H., & Stephens, K. (2005). Assessment of sexual offenders: A model for integrating dynamic risk assessment and relapse prevention approaches. In D. M. Donavan & G. A. Marlatt (Eds.), *Assessment of addictive behaviors* (2nd ed., pp. 392-424). New York: Guilford.

Wheeler, J.G., George, W. H., & Stoner, S. A. (2005). Enhancing the relapse prevention model for sex offenders: Adding recidivism risk reduction therapy (3RT) to target offenders' dynamic risk needs. In G. A. Marlatt & D. M. Donavan (Eds.), *Relapse prevention* (2nd ed). New York: Guilford.

58 RELAXATION

Kyle E. Ferguson and Rachel E. Sgambati

Relaxation comes in many forms. Yoga, meditation, diaphragmatic breathing (see Chapter 14), hypnosis, guided imagery, Tai Chi, and Lamaze are common examples. In the empirical literature one review examined 12 scientific journals representing a nine-year span (1970–1979) and revealed 26 distinct referenced approaches (Hillenberg & Collins, 1982). Sleep disturbance, headache, hypertension, asthma, problematic alcohol use, hyperactivity, and various forms of anxiety were some of the problems targeted for intervention. Accordingly, relaxation is not monolithic, both in the techniques employed and the problem areas for which it is applied. Due to its widespread use, some go so far as to call relaxation the "aspirin" of behavioral medicine (Russo, Bird, & Masek, 1980).

This chapter opens with a discussion of several key developments in relaxation training. Of these, a specific type of training method called behavioral relaxation training and assessment is discussed at length (BRT; Poppen, 1988, 1998; Raymer & Poppen, 1985). Who might benefit from this form of training, contraindications of its use, and purported mechanisms underlying the technique are dealt with first. The remainder of the chapter provides step-by-step guidelines in teaching BRT to clients.

KEY DEVELOPMENTS IN RELAXATION TRAINING

Progressive Relaxation

Edmund Jacobson pioneered relaxation training early in the twentieth century, while working on his dissertation at Harvard University (Carlson & Bernstein, 1995). For his dissertation, Jacobson examined the effects of relaxation on the startle response. These fledgling ideas eventually culminated into two classic texts, one titled *You Must Relax* (1934) written for the layperson, and *Progressive Relaxation* (1938) written for a professional audience.

Progressive relaxation involves a muscular tense-release procedure targeting dozens of muscle groups. It generally requires 30–50 sessions and several hours of daily practice over many days to master the technique. The following are the three principal components of progressive relaxation training:

(1) The subject relaxes a group, for instance, the muscles that bend the right arm ... (2) He learns one after the other ... With each new group he simultaneously relaxes such parts as have received practice previously. (3) As he practices from day to day ... he progresses toward a habit of repose ... a state in which quiet is automatically maintained. (Jacobson, 1934, p. 54)

By *quiet*, Jacobson is referring to reductions in neuromuscular tension, verifiable electromyographically (EMG) (Jacobson, 1938), and "quieting the nerves"—automatically shutting off mental activity, including worry (Jacobson, 1934, p. 33ff.). And the extent to which clients achieve "quiescence," usually leads to beneficial health outcomes. Reportedly, Jacobson (1938, p. 417ff.) successfully treated insomnia, anxiety, stuttering, asthma, facial spasms, tremor, functional tachycardia (rapid heartbeat), and a host of other disorders using progressive relaxation. Indeed, his success in treating such intractable conditions paved the way for empirically driven relaxation techniques.

Systematic Desensitization

Wolpe adopted and streamlined progressive relaxation as a method of counterconditioning "neurotic-anxiety response habits" (1990, p. 150;

see "Systematic Desensitization" in the present volume). The muscular tense–release procedure, even after being abbreviated, induced a state of deep relaxation as clients progressed through a fear hierarchy, from less fearful to more fearful mental imagery. Wolpe (1958) called this procedure systematic desensitization. Insofar as clients remained in a deep state of relaxation, it was believed to reciprocally inhibit and thus weaken learned anxiety habits (Wolpe, 1976). Ultimately, through this manner of systematic counterconditioning the anxiety response would no longer be elicited in the presence of "stronger" feared stimuli, as exposure increased over time.

Systematic desensitization was a milestone in the advancement of behavior therapy, and, collaterally, streamlining Jacobson's labor intensive technique also marked a key development (O'Donohue et al., 2001). Wolpe's abbreviated and more practical version of progressive relaxation made this technique accessible to a wider audience. Wolpe's (1985) version took about four to six sessions versus 30–40, and required only 15 minutes at any given time, not hours. Moreover, clients could achieve a level of mastery practicing only 15–20 minutes daily for far fewer days. Although data were not taken, one can assume that the requirement of several hours of daily practice using the technique originally conceived by Jacobson would have drastically lower patient compliance.

Standardization of Progressive Relaxation

Another milestone in behavior therapy was the standardization of relaxation training. In 1973 Bernstein and Borkovec published a manual on progressive relaxation training, standardizing relevant aspects of the training situation. Among other points, physical properties of the "consultation room" (e.g., low ambient noise, proper lighting, etc.; p. 17), the client's chair (e.g., well-padded recliner providing complete support; p. 17), and detailed therapist's scripts (e.g., rationale and training scripts; p. 19ff.) were included in the manual. The manual even went so far as to describe to the reader "what words or phrases to avoid" (e.g., " . . . it is best to delete any reference which might possibly cause the

client anxiety or embarrassment"; p. 52) and to alert him or her about clients' "strange or unfamiliar feelings" (p. 49ff.) that sometime manifest during training (Bernstein & Borkovec, 1973). As far as the basic procedure is concerned, the following is the training sequence by which clients are taught to tense and release the various muscle groups (p. 25):

1. Dominant hand and forearm
2. Dominant biceps
3. Nondominant hand and forearm
4. Nondominant biceps
5. Forehead
6. Upper cheeks and nose
7. Lower cheeks and jaws
8. Neck and throat
9. Chest, shoulders, and upper back
10. Abdominal or stomach region
11. Dominant thigh
12. Dominant calf
13. Dominant foot
14. Nondominant thigh
15. Nondominant calf
16. Nondominant foot

Since the publication of Bernstein and Borkovec's manual there has been scores of studies that used their standardized procedures (see Carlson & Hoyle, 1993, for a recent review). And, as an extension of Jacobson's earlier work, this standardized protocol has been used in treating a variety of different psychological and stress-related conditions. The disorders targeted for intervention were simply those for which "tension" played a major role in clients' presenting complaints (e.g., benign headaches, insomnia, gastrointestinal disorders).

Behavioral Relaxation Training and Assessment

Many clients have difficulties with progressive relaxation. On one hand, there are those for whom tensing is contraindicated. Clients with lower back pain, tension headaches, myofacial pain, temporomandibular disorder (TMD), and arthritis are cases in point. When muscles are sore and possibly spasming from splinting or bracing, tensing those affected areas can trigger shooting pain over and above clients' extant pain (e.g., throbbing, burning, tingling, pounding, etc.). On the other hand, some clients simply cannot "let go" once they have tensed a particular muscle group. Both of these limitations of progressive muscle relaxation led to the development of behavioral relaxation training and assessment (BRT; Poppen, 1998).

Work in BRT began in the early 1980s. While attempting to teach progressive relaxation to "pre-delinquent boys," Roger Poppen and his graduate student Don Schilling found that their clients were able to tense the various muscle groups though they had difficulties releasing that tension (Poppen, personal communication with the first author, June 21, 1997). As a solution to this problem Schilling directly taught some of the relaxed postures that were to result from the tense–release cycle of progressive relaxation—he simply had the boys try to "look relaxed" (Poppen, 1998, p. 40). As it turned out the boys not only looked relaxed but reported feelings of relaxation while emitting the behaviors. Out of these observations, Schilling and Poppen (1983) derived a list of 10 specific relaxed behaviors and developed an assessment instrument to evaluate clients' proficiency in these, called the Behavioral Relaxation Scale (BRS). The behaviors and activities included in the BRS are: body, head, eyes, mouth, throat, shoulders, hands, feet, breathing, and quiet (i.e., no vocalizations or respiratory sounds) (Schilling & Poppen, 1983). More details of this assessment device will be taken up later in the chapter. These 10 items are the core targets for BRT (Raymer & Poppen, 1985; Poppen, 1988, 1998).

Since its inception nearly two decades ago, BRT has been used in managing a variety of different problems, including chronic headache (Michultka, Poppen, & Blanchard, 1988), recurrent seizures (Kiesel, Lutzker, & Campbell, 1989), ataxic tremor (Guercio, Chittum, & McMorrow, 1997), anxiety (Lindsay, Fee, Michie, & Heap, 1994), and aggression (Lundervold, 1986). Its primary assessment instrument, the BRS, has been validated (Poppen & Maurer, 1982; Norton, Holm, & McSherry II, 1997) and the effects of BRT have been shown to generalize outside of training settings (Poppen, Hanson, & Ip, 1988). BRT can be taught individually or in a group format (see Lindsay & Baty, 1989). And,

most important, nearly all clients, even those with severe intellectual or mental disabilities (e.g., mental retardation/developmental disabilities, acquired brain injuries, schizophrenia, hyperactivity disorder, dementia) can learn the techniques without undue effort (Poppen, 1998).

WHO MIGHT BENEFIT FROM THIS TECHNIQUE?

Relaxation training is seldom used on its own. It is usually combined with other procedures (e.g., biofeedback) and employed as part of a treatment package (e.g., stress management programs). Clients most likely to benefit from relaxation training are those for whom cognitive, autonomic, or muscular over-arousal has become maladaptive—to the point of interfering with therapeutic progress or compromising their quality of life. Relaxation training may also be useful in:

- *Preparing patients for surgery*. Patients are usually anxious when they have to undergo invasive medical and surgical procedures (Horne, Vatmanidis, & Careri, 1994). When combined with preoperative psychoeducational programs, relaxation training has been associated with fewer postoperative hospital days, reduced postsurgical complications, and a reduction in medication use (Ludwick-Rosenthal & Neufeld, 1988).
- *Teaching clients how to cope with chronic pain*. Long after an injury has healed, individuals with chronic pain often try to avoid experiencing pain by way of bracing and tensing the surrounding areas of the injury site. This coping style, however, actually exacerbates pain due to overtaxing the skeletal–muscular system (Hanson & Gerber, 1990). Relaxation training can be used as a coping strategy to break this muscle–tension–pain cycle (Linton, 1994; Poppen, Hanson, & Ip, 1988).
- *Reducing the frequency of migraine attacks*. Migraine is linked to arousal of the sympathetic branch of the autonomic nervous system (Sacks, 1992). Clients who are taught (via relaxation training) to regularly warm their hands to approximately 95°F tend to have fewer migraine attacks relative to clients

who fail to meet or exceed this therapeutic threshold (Blanchard, 1992). Relaxation works best as a prophylactic through preventing the initial vasoconstrictive reaction, not as an abortive strategy.

CONTRAINDICATIONS OF THE TREATMENT

While relaxation has produced beneficial outcomes for most clients, there is a minority of people for whom relaxation elicits negative reactions. Called relaxation-induced anxiety (RIA) it has been documented in the literature using several forms of relaxation training including meditation, biofeedback, and progressive relaxation (Heide & Borkovec, 1983). Anecdotally, several of the reported negative side effects are intense restlessness, trembling, pounding heart, shivering, and profuse perspiration (Carrington, 1977). In one study, Edinger and Jacobson (1982) sent out a mail survey to 116 behavior therapists that used relaxation training. Of 17,542 of their clients, it was estimated that approximately 3.5% experienced negative side effects of relaxation—"intrusive thoughts" and "fear of losing control" being the most common reactions—"disturbing sensory experiences" and "depersonalization" being some of the least common (Edinger & Jacobson, 1982, p. 138). Chronically tense or anxious clients are particularly prone to RIA (Heide & Borkovec, 1984).

Mark and Nancy Schwartz (1995, p. 292) recommend the following as a means of minimizing the effects of RIA:

1. Inform clients that they might experience thoughts and sensations that seem unusual or bizarre. Tell them that these are normal signs of relaxation and to let these happen.
2. Especially for those clients who appear anxious, let them know that they should expect intrusive thoughts early on, and that this is normal.
3. Relaxation should be discussed in the context of increased control rather than diminished control.
4. Explain to clients that people usually become better at relaxation when they exert less effort rather than more effort—avoid using

words like *try*—relaxation is "letting go" (See Hayes and Wilson's, 1994, p. 297, "polygraph metaphor," a thought experiment demonstrating that one cannot force relaxation).
5. The therapist should use a different form of relaxation should the above recommendations fail. When using a bodily focus type (e.g., progressive relaxation), switch to a cognitive approach (e.g., autogenic training). Conversely, when using a cognitive focus type, switch to a bodily approach. *Seldom do clients continue experiencing RIA after switching to a different form of relaxation.*

HOW DOES THE TECHNIQUE WORK?

Discrimination Training

There are two primary goals in relaxation training. The first goal is teaching clients how to discriminate between feelings of relaxation and psychophysiological arousal. This is achieved by having clients notice the sensations as they systematically relax targeted areas of their bodies. Ideally, once clients become proficient in this discrimination skill set they will be able to recognize when they are and are not relaxed, outside of the therapeutic context. And insofar as clients become "aware" of relaxation- or stress-related internal cues, they are more likely to let themselves relax when approaching stressful situations (coping response), or, more distally, use relaxation as a preventive measure (e.g., working it into their daily routines). Of course, in the absence of generalization probes or generalization training one would not know for certain whether these skills extend beyond the therapist's office (see Stokes & Baer, 1977, classic article detailing generalization strategies).

Self-Control Training

The second goal of relaxation training is teaching clients how to evoke the "relaxation response" as a means of self-control (Benson, 1975; Kazdin, 1989). The relaxation response, among other things (cognitive behavioral processes), is activating the parasympathetic branch of the autonomic nervous system (ANS).

Parasympathetic activation is concerned with "slowing down the organism"—it is "restorative in nature" (Asteria, 1985, p. 38). With parasympathetic activation there is a slowing of heart rate (and myocardial responsiveness), increased blood flow to the extremities, pupilary constriction, and better delivery of respiratory gases throughout the body (Benson, 1975).

Because the autonomic system works in an all-or-nothing manner when the parasympathetic branch is activated (or most of the system is activated), it suppresses sympathetic arousal (Asteria, 1985). Sympathetic arousal triggers "the fight-or-flight response" or what Selye called the "alarm reaction" (1974, p. 38ff.). Contrary to the functions of the parasympathetic branch, activating the sympathetic branch "speeds up the organism"; heart rate increases along with metabolism, and end organs not required in protecting the organism are suppressed (e.g., digestive system) (Asteria, 1985). Chronic sympathetic arousal is believed to play a role in: cardiovascular disease, gastrointestinal/genitourinary problems, compromised immune functioning, panic disorder, generalized disorder, social phobia, posttraumatic stress disorder, among many others (Sullivan, Kent, Coplan, 2000).

With that as background, let us turn next to a discussion of the procedures used in teaching BRT to clients.

STEP-BY-STEP PROCEDURES

Step 1: Setting

The training room should be quiet and "calm"—try eliminating as many distractions as possible (Benson, 1975, p. 159). A small fan usually produces enough "white noise" to mask conversations outside, the sound of footsteps in the hallway, and so on. Also turn off the ringer on the telephone.

Use a recliner, one that provides total support for most clients (Bernstein & Borkovec, 1973). Make adjustments accordingly to accommodate clients' body types. For example, if clients are of smaller stature, in which case the recliner is too big, use pillows to provide additional support (e.g., under the knees and elbows). These adjustments are almost always necessary when working with small children. Clients of larger stature (e.g., over 6 feet tall) may require an ottoman, should the recliner fail to support their feet.

Client should dress comfortably, in loose-fitting clothing. Have clients remove their glasses, watches, bracelets, and the like. Clients should be neither too hot nor cold in the training milieu. Use a space heater or gentle fan if the room is too cold or hot, respectively.

Step 2: Rationale

Providing a good rationale is an important strategy in motivating clients (also in increasing treatment compliance; Schwartz, 1995b). In presenting the rationale:

1. Review clients' problematic behavior.
2. Discuss how relaxation is a better functional alternative (e.g., as a coping strategy to reduce tension-arousal).
3. Provide an overview of the procedures (without being too specific, thus "contaminating" the initial assessment) and what clients should expect while learning the techniques (Poppen, 1998, pp. 71–72; include M. Schwartz & N. Schwartz's [1995, p. 292], recommendations mentioned earlier).
4. Emphasize the fact that the therapist serves mainly as a "coach" in relaxation training—most of the benefit comes from clients practicing on their own.
5. The ultimate aim of relaxation training is teaching self-management—it is the therapist's goal (as far as relaxation training is concerned) to become obsolete as soon as clients become proficient in this area.

Discuss the rationale using language commensurate with clients' education and/or intellectual functioning.

Sample Relaxation Rationale Script

... [R]elaxation training consists of learning to sequentially ... relax various groups of muscles all through the body, while at the same time paying very close and careful attention to the feelings of ... relaxation ... in addition to teaching you how to relax, I will also be encouraging you to learn to recognize and pinpoint tension and relaxation as they appear in everyday situations.... You should understand quite clearly that learning relaxation skills is very much like learning any other kind of skill such as swimming, or golfing, or riding a bicycle; thus in order for you to get better at relaxing you will have to practice doing it just as you would have to practice other skills. It is very important that you realize that ... relaxation training involves learning on your part; there is nothing magical about the procedures. I will not be doing anything *to* you; I will merely be introducing you to the technique and directing your attention to various aspects of it, such as the presence of certain feelings in the muscles. Thus, without your active cooperation and regular practicing of the things you will learn today, the procedures are of little use.... The goal of ... relaxation training is to help you learn to reduce muscle tension in your body far below your adaptation level at any time you wish to do so.... Do you have any questions about what I've said so far? (Answer any questions about the rationale behind relaxation training but defer questions about specific procedures until after you have covered the material to follow (Bernstein & Borkovec, 1973, pp. 19–20; italics in original).

Step 3: Assessment

Before commencing with the initial assessment, have clients sit quietly for a few minutes. After allowing clients to get acclimated, using the behavioral relaxation scale form (BRS; see Table 58.1), ask clients to rate their "state" or "degree" of relaxation. Use the following rating scale[1] (*always show clients the scale when assessing*

---

1. Another self-report measure that is especially useful when employing systematic desensitization or exposure and response prevention is the "subjective unit of disturbance" (SUD) scale (Wolpe & Lazarus, 1966, p. 73). Have the client think of the most distressing experience in his or her life. This event is assigned the number 100. Next, have the client think of the most relaxing experience in his or her life. This event is assigned the number 0. The remaining items in the fear hierarchy are then assigned numbers that fall somewhere along this continuum (i.e., between 0 and 100).

their self-report—never rely on clients' memory of the items):

Self-Report Rating Scale (Poppen, 1998, p. 182).

1. Feeling deeply and completely relaxed throughout my entire body
2. Feeling very relaxed and calm
3. Feeling more relaxed than usual
4. Feeling relaxed as in my normal resting state
5. Feeling tension in some parts of my body
6. Feeling generally tense throughout my body
7. Feeling extremely tense and upset throughout my body

Subsequent to taking clients' self-report measures, instruct them to "relax on their own" for the next few minutes while the trainer "sees how they relax." Avoid using language that suggests that clients' performance is being evaluated during the initial assessment. Use the BRS form to measure the 10 behaviors and activities already mentioned. A detailed description of these will be taken up shortly.

Assessment observation periods should be no less than 5 minutes, total. Observation periods are broken down into 1-minute blocks. On the BRS form these columns are labeled 1–10. Each block is further broken down into three intervals: a 30-second interval to measure breathing, a 15-second interval to observe the nine behaviors on the BRS, and the remaining 15 seconds to record responses (Poppen, 1998, p. 49).

Breathing

Baseline breathing rate is taken during the first assessment. The baseline breathing rate is the standard by which further breathing rates are evaluated (Poppen, 1998, p. 53). Once commencing with the first observational block, ideally using a stopwatch that does not beep, begin counting breaths when the client inhales. One breath equals an inhalation–exhalation cycle. Stop counting breaths after the initial 30 seconds for each observation block. If the client is exhaling at that point, count the breath, even if he or she has not fully exhaled—do not count it as a breath if the client is inhaling. Ignore all other behavior during the breathing interval. Mark an "X" in the box corresponding to breathing on

TABLE 58.1 The Behavioral Relaxation Scale Score Sheet

	1	2	3	4	5	6	7	8	9	10	Total
Breathing	− +	− +	− +	− +	− +	− +	− +	− +	− +	− +	
Quiet	− +	− +	− +	− +	− +	− +	− +	− +	− +	− +	
Body	− +	− +	− +	− +	− +	− +	− +	− +	− +	− +	
Head	− +	− +	− +	− +	− +	− +	− +	− +	− +	− +	
Eyes	− +	− +	− +	− +	− +	− +	− +	− +	− +	− +	
Mouth	− +	− +	− +	− +	− +	− +	− +	− +	− +	− +	
Throat	− +	− +	− +	− +	− +	− +	− +	− +	− +	− +	
Shoulders	− +	− +	− +	− +	− +	− +	− +	− +	− +	− +	
Hands	− +	− +	− +	− +	− +	− +	− +	− +	− +	− +	
Feet	− +	− +	− +	− +	− +	− +	− +	− +	− +	− +	
										Score %	

Breathing Baseline: _____   Overall Assessment: (−) = Unrelaxed (+) = Relaxed
Preobservation Self-Rating:
Relaxation: 1 2 3 4 5 6 7
Post-Observation Self-Rating:
Relaxation: 1 2 3 4 5 6 7

Reproduced from Poppen, 1998; permission granted by the author.

the BRS whenever breathing is interrupted with a snort, sneeze, sniffle, sigh, yawn, or cough, and the like.

In calculating the baseline breathing rate, add up the overall frequency of breathing responses and divide by the number of observational blocks—always round up decimals. Do not include those intervals in which breathing was interrupted. On subsequent training days breathing rates are calculated the same way. And should those rates fall below the baseline rate then these are considered "relaxed". During the recording interval, for the 15 seconds remaining in the observation block write in the breathing frequency and circle the "+" or "−" denoting "relaxed," "unrelaxed" breathing, respectively. *Of course, the therapist does not indicate whether breathing is relaxed or unrelaxed during the initial assessment.* A "+" or "−" also denotes "relaxed," "unrelaxed" postures for the remaining items.

During the next 15 seconds, scan the client's body, observing the remaining nine postures/behaviors. Again, as with the breathing interval, hold off recording responses until the final 15 seconds of the observation block. Below are the scoring criteria for the remaining items, indicated on the BRS.

Quiet

- *Relaxed:* The client is not making any sounds.
- *Unrelaxed:* The client makes noise such as talking, humming, burping, giggling, grunting, snorting, sneezing, snoring, sniffling, sighing, whistling, yawning, and coughing, and so on.

Body

- *Relaxed:* The shoulders, hips, and feet are in alignment, around midline (Poppen, 1998, p. 43). The body is supported by the recliner with no movement. Chest or abdominal movement resulting from breathing is, however, acceptable.
- *Unrelaxed:* (1) movement of the torso or shifting one's body weight; (2) shoulders, hips, and feet are out of alignment; (3) moving the limbs (e.g., knee jerk)—excluding the hands and feet, these are scored separately; (4) the back, legs, and/or buttocks are not supported by the recliner.

Head

- *Relaxed:* The head is supported by the chair, lying still. The nose is in midline with the body. The chin does not drop into the chest or point up. *If one were to fasten a piece of string to the person's nose and attach it to the floor, the string would bisect the sternum and belly button.*

- *Unrelaxed:* (1) The head is not supported by the chair; (2) the head is moving; (3) the nose is out of midline; (4) the head is tilted up, down, or to the left or right.

Eyes

- *Relaxed:* The eyelids are closed. The lids have a smooth appearance and the eyes are still.
- *Unrelaxed:* (1) The eyelids are open; (2) the lids are wrinkled from squeezing the lids together; (3) the eyes or lids are moving.

Mouth

- *Relaxed*: The teeth are apart by about 1/3 to 1 inch. There is no movement in the jaw region and the tongue is lying still.
- *Unrelaxed*: (1) The teeth or lips are together; (2) the teeth are more than an inch apart; (3) the jaw or tongue is moving; (4) the client is smiling or yawning.

Throat

- *Relaxed:* The throat is not moving. Have the client breathe in through the nose and out the mouth to prevent the throat from drying (eliciting swallowing). Should the client have problems with this breathing pattern, have him or her lightly press the tip of the tongue behind the top front teeth. This will impede airflow through the mouth.
- *Unrelaxed:* The throat or muscles in the neck are moving.

Shoulders

- *Relaxed:* Shoulders are rounded (from "letting go" of tension) and do not lean to one side or the other. Taking breathing into consideration, there is no additional movement.
- *Unrelaxed:* (1) Shoulder movement not attributable to breathing; (2) one shoulder is higher than the other; (3) shoulders are "shrugged," thus losing their rounded appearance.

Hands

- *Relaxed:* The hands are resting still in the lap or arms of the chair, palms down—fingers in a "clawlike" fashion. The fingers are resting on the pads, slightly splayed, and there is a small arch under the palm. A pencil should pass easily under the apex of the arch without touching the hand.
- *Unrelaxed:* (1) The hands or fingers are moving; (2) the hands are not supported or are otherwise out of position; (3) the fingers are curled into a fist; (4) the palms are flat.

Feet

- *Relaxed:* While the legs are comfortably straight, lying still, roughly shoulder-width apart, with a slight bend at the knee, the feet fall limp to either side creating a 60° to 90° angle between them.
- *Unrelaxed:* (1) movement of the feet, including the toes; (2) legs are crossed or knees are pulled towards the chest; (3) feet create more or less than a 60° to 90° angle.

Step 4: Behavioral Relaxation Training

BRT sessions usually take roughly a half hour, including assessment and training (Poppen, 1998, p. 72). BRT entails teaching clients the 10 behaviors on the BRS form. Although the 10 items may appear a lot for clients to take in, most clients can learn behavioral relaxation during the first session.

Each item on the BRS is taught by first (1) labeling the posture (or activity); followed by (2) a description of what it is and what it is not (i.e., relaxed and unrelaxed postures); next, the therapist provides a (3) demonstration of relaxed and unrelaxed postures (modeling; "Let me demonstrate how you relax your hand ... this is how you aren't supposed to relax your hand ... "); ask the client to (4) imitate the relaxed posture; provide (5) corrective feedback when necessary (e.g., "Not quite right, like this ... ")—*use manual guidance when clients are not responding to verbal instruction, but only as a last resort* (Poppen, 1998, p. 74). Each item is introduced successively, one at a time—building upon the mastery of previous skills. Once clients are in the correct posture instruct them to "notice the sensations as they relax" that body part or are engaged in one of the relaxed activities (e.g., quiet and breathing).

If a client is working on the fifth item and "loses" the second, for example, provide corrective feedback for the posture that "fell" out of relaxation. Accordingly, corrective feedback is always based on cumulative performance. Work through each of the items in the following order: breathing,[2] body, head, shoulders, mouth, throat, hands, and feet.

Step 5: Ongoing Assessment

Following the first day of BRT, at the beginning of each subsequent session have clients relax using their newly acquired relaxation skills. Assess performance using the same procedures as in the initial assessment (Step 3). After 5 minutes of observation, provide corrective feedback if the therapist notices unrelaxed behavior.

Data gathered from ongoing evaluations reflect the extent to which clients practice these skills at other times, outside of the therapist's office (an indirect measure of generalization). Should clients perform poorly on the BRS, they may not be practicing on their own. Given that home practice is so crucial to relaxation training, always address this issue when clients are not adhering to the program. Contingency contracting works well in reestablishing clients' motivation, even for seemingly "intractable cases" (see Chapter 21).

FURTHER CONSIDERATIONS

- Monitor the intake of vasoactive foods and beverages (e.g., caffeine, tyramine, monosodium glutamate, alcohol), as these are known to aggravate and trigger some physical symptoms—especially for those individuals who suffer from migraine and Raynaud's disease (Block & Schwartz, 1995).

---

2. Teach diaphragmatic breathing (see Chapter 14). Begin by discussing the difference between this approach and thoracic breathing; with an emphasis on how the former is far more efficient at increasing oxygen intake and regulating arousal states. One therapeutic standard is slowing respiration to approximately 6–8 breaths per minute (3–4 during the 30-second BRS assessment interval); this is about half the rate of what is typical for most people (Schwartz, 1995a, p. 249).

- Graphing performance helps reinforce the notion that many clients can quickly attain a high level of mastery. Most importantly, clients are more likely to employ these skills when they feel confident in their abilities.
- Audiotape sessions to increase compliance and conserve time (see Schwartz, 1995c, for full details in making relaxation tapes).
- Assign homework, asking clients to try out as many of the postures as possible in a variety of different situations. For example, while seated in a classroom students can relax their mouth and throat, remain quiet, engage in diaphragmatic breathing, relax their shoulders and head, and position their nonwriting hand in a "clawlike" manner (see Poppen, 1998, pp. 88–91, for modified BRT, called "upright relaxation training (URT)" and "mini-relaxation"). The more practice clients get in applying and adapting these skills to new settings, the greater the generalization gradient (Stokes, & Baer, 1977).
- Another generalization strategy is to train clients in "cue-controlled relaxation" (Smith, 1990, p. 76). Cue-controlled relaxation involves pairing a word or two-word phrase (e.g., "calm" or "let go") with the relaxation response. Simply have the client repeat this word while becoming increasingly relaxed. After frequent pairings of the word with relaxation, the client will eventually be able to evoke the relaxation response by saying the word alone. For example, if the client is getting upset while standing in a checkout line, sitting in the dentist's chair, or while on an airplane about to take off, have him or her quietly say the cue word (while emitting as many of the 10 BRT behaviors as possible). Of course, for the word or phrase to remain "powerful" in evoking the relaxation response, the client must continue pairing it with relaxation—otherwise, the word or phrase loses its influence.

References

Asteria, M. F. (1985). *The physiology of stress*. New York: Human Sciences Press.

Benson, H. (1975). *The relaxation response*. New York: Avon Books.

Bernstein, D. A., & Borkovec, T. D. (1973). *Progressive relaxation training: A manual for the helping professions*. Champaign, IL: Research Press.

Blanchard, E. B. (1992). Psychological treatment of benign headache disorders. *Journal of Consulting and Clinical Psychology, 60*, 537–551.

Block, K. I., & Schwartz, M. S. (1995). Dietary considerations: Rationale, issues, substances, evaluation, and patient education. In M. S. Schwartz and Associates (Eds.), *Biofeedback: A practitioner's guide* (2nd ed.) (pp. 211–247). New York: Guilford.

Carrington, P. (1977). *Freedom in meditation*. New York: Doubleday-Anchor.

Carlson, C. R., & Berstein, D. A. (1995). Relaxation skills training: Abbreviated progressive relaxation. In W. T. O'Donohue & L. Krasner (Eds.), *Handbook of psychological skills: Clinical techniques and applications* (pp. 20–35). Boston: Allyn and Bacon.

Edinger, J. D., & Jacobson, R. (1982). Incidence and significance of relaxation treatment side-effects. *Behavior Therapist, 5*, 137–138.

Guercio, J., Chittum, R., & McMorrow, M. (1997). Self-management in the treatment of ataxia: A case study in reducing ataxic tremor through relaxation and biofeedback. *Brain Injury, 11*, 353–362.

Hansen, R. W., & Gerber, K. E. (1990). Coping with chronic pain: A guide to patient self-management. New York: Guilford.

Hayes, S. C., & Wilson, K. G. (1994). Acceptance and commitment therapy: Altering the verbal support for experiential avoidance. *Behavior Therapist, 17*, 289–303.

Heide, F. J., & Borkovec, P. D. (1983). Relaxation-induced anxiety: Paradoxical anxiety due to relaxation training. *Journal of Consulting and Clinical Psychology, 51*, 171–182.

Heide, F. J., & Borkovec, P. D. (1984). Relaxation-induced anxiety: Mechanisms and theoretical implications. *Behaviour Research and Therapy, 22*, 1–12.

Hillenberg, J. B., & Collins, F. L. Jr. (1982). A procedural analysis and review of relaxation training research. *Behaviour Research and Therapy, 20*, 251–260.

Horne, D. J., Vatmanidis, P., & Careri, A. (1994). Preparing patients for invasive medical and surgical procedures: II. Using psychological interventions with adults and children. *Behavioral Medicine, 20*, 15–21.

Jacobson, E. (1934). You must relax: A practical method of reducing the strains of modern living. New York: McGraw-Hill.

Jacobson, E. (1938). Progressive relaxation: A psychological and clinical investigation of muscular states and their significance in psychological and medical practice. Chicago: University of Chicago Press.

Kazdin, A. E. (1989). Behavior modification in applied settings (4th ed.). Pacific Grove, CA: Brooks/Cole Publishing Company.

Kiesel, K. B., Lutzker, J. R., & Campbell, R. V. (1989). Behavioral relaxation training to reduce hyperventilation and seizures in a profoundly retarded epileptic child. *Journal of the Multihandicapped Person, 2*, 179–190.

Lindsay, W. R., & Baty, F. J. (1989). Group relaxation training with adults who are mentally handicapped. *Behavioural Psychotherapy, 17*, 43–51.

Lindsay, W. R., Fee, M., Michie, A., & Heap, I. (1994). The effects of cue control relaxation on adults with severe mental retardation. *Research in Developmental Disabilities, 15*, 425–437.

Linton, S. J. (1994). Chronic back pain: Integrating psychological and physical therapy. *Behavioral Medicine, 20*, 101–104.

Ludwick-Rosenthal, R., & Neufeld, R. W. J. (1988). Stress management during noxious medical procedures: An evaluative review of outcome studies. *Psychological Bulletin, 104*, 326–342.

Lundervold, D. (1986). The effects of behavioral relaxation and self-instruction training: A case study. *Rehabilitation Counseling Bulletin, 30*, 124–128.

Michultka, D., Poppen, R., & Blanchard, E. B. (1988). Relaxation training as a treatment for chronic headaches in an individual having severe developmental disabilities. *Biofeedback and Self-Regulation, 13*, 257–266.

Norton, M., Holm, J. E., & McSherry, W. C., II. (1997). Behavioral assessment of relaxation: The validity of a behavioral rating scale. *Journal of Behavior Therapy and Experimental Psychiatry, 28*, 129–137.

O'Donohue, W. T., Henderson, D. A., Hayes, S. C., Fisher, J. E., & Hayes, L. J. (2001). A history of the behavioral therapies. In *A history of the behavioral therapies: Founders' personal histories* (pp. xi–xxii). Reno, NV: Context Press.

Poppen, R. (1988). Behavioral relaxation training and assessment. New York: Pergamon.

Poppen, R. (1998). *Behavioral relaxation training and assessment* (2nd ed.). Thousand Oaks, CA: Sage Publications.

Poppen, R., Hanson, H., & Ip, S. V. (1988). Generalization of EMG biofeedback training. *Biofeedback and Self-Regulation, 13*, 235–243.

Poppen, R., & Maurer, J. (1982). Electromyographic analysis of relaxed postures. *Biofeedback and Self-Regulation, 7*, 491–498.

Raymer, R. H., & Poppen, R. (1995). Behavioral relaxation training with hyperactive children. *Journal of Behavior Therapy and Experimental Psychiatry, 16*, 309–316.

Russo, D. C., Bird, B. L., & Masek, B. J. (1980). Assessment issues in behavioral medicine. *Psychopathology and Behavioral Assessment, 2,* 1–18.

Sacks, O. (1992). *Migraine* (revised and expanded). Berkeley: University of California Press.

Schilling, D. J., & Poppen, R. (1983). Behavioral relaxation training and assessment. *Journal of Behavior Therapy and Experimental Psychiatry, 14,* 99–107.

Schwartz, M. S. (1995a). Breathing therapies. In M. S. Schwartz and Associates (Eds.), *Biofeedback: A practitioner's guide* (2nd ed.) (pp. 248–287). New York: Guilford.

Schwartz, M. S. (1995b). Compliance. In M. S. Schwartz and Associates (Eds.), *Biofeedback: A practitioner's guide* (2nd ed.) (pp. 184–207). New York: Guilford.

Schwartz, M. S. (1995c). The use of audiotapes for patient education and relaxation. In M. S. Schwartz and Associates (Eds.), *Biofeedback: A practitioner's guide* (2nd ed.) (pp. 301–310). New York: Guilford.

Schwartz, M. S., & Schwartz, N. M. (1995). Problems with relaxation and biofeedback: Assisted relaxation and guidelines for management. In M. S. Schwartz and Associates (Eds.), *Biofeedback:*

A practitioner's guide (2nd ed.) (pp. 288–300). New York: Guilford.

Selye, H. (1974). *Stress without distress.* New York: J. B. Lippincott.

Smith, J. C. (1990). *Cognitive-behavioral relaxation training: A new system of strategies for assessment and treatment.* New York: Springer.

Stokes, T. F., & Baer, D. M. (1977). An implicit technology of generalization. *Journal of Applied Behavior Analysis, 10,* 349–367.

Sullivan, G. M., Kent, J. M., & Coplan, J. D. (2000). The neurobiology of stress and anxiety. In D. I. Mostofsky & D. H. Barlow (Eds.), *The management of stress and anxiety in medical disorders* (pp. 15–35). Boston: Allyn and Bacon.

Wolpe, J. (1958). *Psychotherapy by reciprocal inhibition.* Stanford, CA: Stanford University Press.

Wolpe, J. (1976). *Theme and variations: A behavior therapy casebook.* New York: Pergamon Press.

Wolpe, J. (1990). *The practice of behavior therapy* (4th ed.). New York: Pergamon Press.

Wolpe, J., & Lazarus, A. A. (1966). *Behavior therapy techniques: A guide to the treatment of the neuroses.* New York: Pergamon Press.

59 RESPONSE PREVENTION

Martin E. Franklin, Deborah A. Ledley, and Edna B. Foa

Response (ritual) prevention (RP) is an intervention of behavior therapy conceptualized as blocking avoidance or escape from feared situations. As such, it often goes hand in hand another behavioral intervention, exposure (see relevant chapters in this volume). Exposure involves confronting situations, objects, and thoughts that evoke anxiety or distress because they are unrealistically associated with danger. By encouraging the individual to remain in the feared situation without engaging in compulsions or other forms of avoidance, response prevention allows the realization that the fear is unrealistic. This conceptualization has guided animal studies where fear extinction was achieved by blocking escape behavior (e.g., Baum, 1970), as well as the application of response prevention to the clinical problems.

In its clinical application, exposure and response (or ritual) prevention (EX/RP) is most closely associated with the treatment of obsessive–compulsive disorder (OCD), although it has been applied to the treatment of other disorders including hypochondriasis (e.g., Visser & Bouman, 2001), body dysmorphic disorder (e.g., McKay, Todaro, Neziroglu & Campisi, 1997), eating disorders (e.g., Bulik, Sullivan, Carter, McIntosh & Joyce, 1998), substance use disorders (see Lee & Oei, 1994), and Tourette's syndrome (Vedellen et al., 2004). Given the long history of the use of EX/RP for OCD (and empirical studies of it), we will focus on this particular application in this chapter.

EX/RP was first used by Meyer (1966) who titled his first publication on this treatment approach "Modification of Expectations in Cases with Obsessional Rituals," thus implying that cognitive changes underlies the treatment. In a series of experiments, Rachman and his colleagues (see Rachman & Hodgson, 1980)

demonstrated that exposure to cues which trigger obsessions increase anxiety and discomfort and that ritualistic behavior led to a decrease in anxiety and discomfort. When patients were exposed to obsessional cues, but were prevented from engaging in rituals, anxiety and discomfort decreased over time. When patients were then exposed to their obsessional cues again, the urge to ritualize had decreased as compared to the previous trial. This decrease in urge to ritualize did not occur if patients continued to engage in rituals in response to obsessional cues. These tenets form the premise of EX/RP—patients are exposed to cues that lead to obsessions and are asked to refrain from engaging in rituals in order to learn that their anxiety will come down on its own and that their feared consequences do not occur. In other words, EX/RP serves to disconfirm beliefs, not only about anxiety itself, but also about what will happen if rituals are not performed.

Foa and colleagues (1984) demonstrated the importance of using *both* exposure and ritual prevention in the treatment of OCD. In this study, patients with OCD were randomly assigned to receive either exposure alone, ritual prevention alone, or combined EX/RP. The component treatments seemed to have unique effects on OCD symptoms—ritual prevention led to reduction in compulsions and exposure led to reduction in the anxiety response to feared stimuli. Not surprisingly then, the combined treatment was found to be superior to the component treatments, with patients in this group showing the greatest reductions in both anxiety and compulsions. Following from these studies, exposure and response prevention has continued to be the treatment of choice for OCD with much evidence accrued for its efficacy and durability (see Franklin & Foa, 2007). Recent research indicates the efficacy of EX/RP both alone and in combination with pharmacotherapy in adults (e.g., Foa et al., 2005) and in youth (e.g., POTS Team, 2004). However, the Foa et al. study with adults suggests no advantage to using combined medication and EX/RP in the treatment of OCD over EX/RP monotherapy (see also Foa, Franklin, & Moser, 2002), whereas the pediatric study did find an overall advantage to combined treatment over the monotherapies.

WHO MIGHT BENEFIT FROM THIS TECHNIQUE?

The efficacy of EX/RP for OCD has been demonstrated in children/adolescents (see Piacentini, March, & Franklin, 2006), adults (see Franklin & Foa, 2007) and older adults (see Carmin, Pollard & Ownby, 1999). EX/RP seems to work equally well in strictly controlled randomized clinical trials and in more "real-world" outpatient, fee-for-service clinics (Franklin et al., 2000; Valderhaug et al., 2007; Warren & Thomas, 2001).

An important question is whether comorbidity negatively impacts treatment outcome. The presence of personality disorders is predictive of poor outcome in EX/RP (AuBuchon & Malatesta, 1994; Fals-Stewart & Lucente, 1993). In terms of Axis I disorders, comorbid major depression has garnered the most research attention. Abramowitz and colleagues (Abramowitz & Foa, 2000; Abramowitz, Franklin, Street, Kozak & Foa, 2000) failed to find a linear relationship between level of depression and treatment outcome in OCD. Depression only had an impact on treatment at high levels of severity—patients with Beck Depression Inventory (BDI) scores greater than 30 were less likely to be treatment responders than patients with lower BDI scores. It is important to note though that even these severely depressed patients showed clinically significant reductions in OCD symptoms following EX/RP.

CONTRAINDICATIONS OF THE TREATMENT

Although Axis II comorbidity and very high levels of depression seem to be predictive of poorer outcome in EX/RP, we do not regularly exclude patients with Axis II disorders or with major depression from our treatment program. A few caveats should be kept in mind, however, when making this decision. First, the OCD should be the primary diagnosis. In other words, if an Axis II disorder or depression is considered to be more severe than the OCD, these other conditions should be attended to first. This is particularly important when suicidality is part of the clinical picture.

OTHER FACTORS IN DECIDING WHETHER TO USE RESPONSE PREVENTION

Two other issues should be considered when determining a patient's suitability for EX/RP. First, the presence of positive and negative symptoms of thought disorder should be assessed carefully. While many patients with OCD have quite odd and unusual thoughts, this should not be taken as an indication that the problem is a thought disorder, and not OCD. To ensure the correct diagnosis, therapists should get a clear sense that patients know that their intrusive thoughts are a product of their own minds. EX/RP is contraindicated in patients who do not have a clear sense of the origins of their thoughts.

The second issue to attend to is whether patients' intrusive thoughts are indeed distressing and unwanted. This is of greatest concern with patients who present with intrusive sexual thoughts or intrusive thoughts about harming self or others. EX/RP is contraindicated in patients who seem to exert control over their thoughts (e.g., a patient who is angry at his boss and is purposefully thinking about ways of harming him) and in those who experience pleasure in response to them (e.g., a person who gets aroused from thoughts of incest). People with such thoughts would not be considered to have OCD. Patients with OCD who have aggressive and sexual thoughts experience them as unwanted, intrusive, and terribly distressing.

HOW DOES THE TECHNIQUE WORK?

EX/RP is based on the theory that obsessions and compulsions are maintained through avoidance of situations, objects, and thoughts that

TABLE 59.1 Keys to Ritual Prevention

1. The first step should always be detailed information gathering and treatment planning.
2. Optimal compliance with ritual prevention begins with a clear understanding of its rationale. Therapist should be clear to convey this rationale to patients and, perhaps especially with younger clients, should evaluate whether the patient indeed fully grasps the importance of ritual prevention in bringing about the reduction in the frequency and intensity of obsessions.
3. Use self-monitoring to help with information gathering, and later in treatment, to keep track of RP violations.
4. Give clear instructions for RP. Complete ritual prevention early in treatment might not be realistic. Focus on a specific OCD symptom cluster (e.g., tackle washing before checking) or work gradually on decreasing particular rituals (e.g., with a patient who wears three sets of rubber gloves when going to the bathroom, ask him to first try wearing just two, then one, and then none at all).
5. As treatment continues, complete RP should be more strongly encouraged.
6. When ritual violations occur, re-expose (e.g., if the patient washes after touching something contaminated, have him touch the contaminated object again and refrain from washing).
7. Help clients be mindful of their motivation for doing the treatment.

evoke distress due to their presumed association with danger. The treatment involves exposure to cues that lead to obsessions, while concomitantly refraining from rituals. The goal is to help patients to learn that their anxiety will come down on its own and that their feared consequences will not occur (see Table 59.1).

STEP-BY-STEP PROCEDURES

Information Gathering

The first step in implementing ritual prevention is for both the clinician and the patient is to identify the functional relationship between obsessions and compulsions. In conceptualizing OCD, clinicians must have a clear sense of the distinction between obsessions and compulsions; for most patients, however, this distinction is often unclear and perhaps not even something they have thought about previously. Accordingly, a good place to start is to provide definitions for *obsessions* and *compulsions*.

Obsessions are intrusive thoughts, images, or impulses that keep coming back to people and that do not make sense. An important point to get across to patients is that obsessions cause distress. Clearly, when people experience distress, they are motivated to get rid of it and this is where compulsions enter the OCD picture. Compulsions are behaviors or mental acts which people feel driven to perform and have difficulty resisting. Compulsions are meant to alleviate the distress brought on by obsessional thoughts and/or to prevent bad things from

happening (e.g., patients with contamination obsessions wash their hands to prevent themselves from getting ill).

It is important to emphasize to patients that compulsions can either be overt behaviors, like hand-washing, or mental acts, like saying a prayer or counting up to a certain number. Some patients (and clinicians) do not recognize mental acts as compulsions, which can be highly problematic in treatment. The goal of treatment is to refrain from rituals, but *not* to stop obsessions. Attempting to push obsessions out of one's mind can actually have a paradoxical effect, increasing the frequency with which the thought subsequently occurs (see Abramowitz, Tolin & Street, 2001). Thoughts are not inherently problematic. Rather, it is what people do with their thoughts that maintain OCD symptoms over time.

Another key to the assessment process is identifying avoidance behaviors. While rituals are certainly meant to alleviate anxiety, they can also be time consuming and embarrassing. People with OCD will sometimes attempt to avoid triggers that initiate the cycle of obsessions and compulsions. For example, a person who fears getting contaminated by food might never eat outside their own home and a person who is worried about catching their house on fire by leaving the stove on might avoid ever turning the stove on in the first place. Getting a clear picture of avoidance patterns is also crucial to good treatment planning since EX/RP will include exposure to cues that are being avoided and subsequent ritual prevention.

The process of information gathering is rounded out by having patients engage in self-monitoring. By increasing awareness, the process of self-monitoring gives patients a sense of the cues that trigger obsessions and how much time is being taken up by rituals in a typical day. It also helps patients to identify rituals of which they might not have even been aware.

Implementing Ritual Prevention

In our current treatment protocol, we spend 2 sessions on information gathering and then progress on to 15 sessions of exposure and ritual prevention. Sessions last for 2 hours to allow time for effective exposures. While we offer an intensive treatment program (daily sessions for 17 days in a row), less frequent visits (once or twice weekly) have been found equally effective over the long term (Abramowitz, Foa, & Franklin, 2003; Storch et al., 2007).

It is completely unrealistic to simply tell patients to stop engaging in rituals. If it were so simple to stop, they would have done so on their own. The best way to explain ritual prevention to patients is to place emphasis on the CB model of OCD and on the functional relationship between obsessions and compulsions. Patients should understand that the goal of EX/RP is to learn that anxiety decreases on its own without having to resort to rituals and that feared consequences are unlikely to happen. It is important to make clear that as long as patients acquiesce to that urge, the obsessional thoughts will be maintained over time. Given that obsessive thoughts are a source of distress, knowing that the thoughts should become less frequent and intense can be very motivating for patients. Of course, most patients also relish the idea of not having to engage in compulsions—even though this idea can be quite frightening. It can be very useful to spend some time with patients picturing a life without OCD. Many will voice a desire to spend more time doing pleasurable things and less time doing rituals.

One of the most commonly asked questions that we are asked about EX/RP is whether complete ritual prevention is required right from the beginning of treatment. It is our sense that this goal is unrealistic for most patients. For some OCD patients, rituals occupy their entire day and it would be near impossible for them to simply stop engaging in all rituals from one day to the next. Even with less pervasive rituals, some patients will refuse to do complete RP even if they understand the rationale for it. Rather than lose patients, it is sometimes appropriate to implement RP more gradually. Early success experiences can then be used to encourage more complete RP as treatment continues.

Another commonly asked question is how to institute ritual prevention in people who have rituals in many different areas (e.g., washing, symmetry, checking). Some patients might be able to handle doing widespread ritual prevention right away. Others might be less overwhelmed if they can start with one focused area. In making this decision early on in treatment, clinicians should be mindful of the importance of giving their patients success experiences. If an overwhelming assignment is given early on in treatment, patients might feel as if they have failed and might see the prospect of living life without OCD as impossible. It is certainly better to initially assign a manageable ritual prevention task and use the success of that experience as a motivator for working on more difficult OCD symptoms. As therapy continues, it is essential that patients understand the principle of generalization. Particularly for complicated cases, there will not be time in therapy to individually tackle each OC symptom. Rather, patients should see that the principles of exposure and ritual prevention can be applied to all OC symptoms and they must become comfortable working on difficult symptoms on their own. This is important in terms of long-term maintenance of gains since once therapy ends, patients might experience recurrences of OC symptoms and might also develop new concerns. It is essential that they be able to apply the principles of EX/RP at these challenging times regardless of the nature of the symptoms.

Although clinicians should certainly be realistically flexible about ritual prevention, they should clearly communicate to patients that complete ritual prevention is the goal of treatment and that they should develop a commitment to living life without OCD. It is important to recognize though that the vast majority of patients will inevitably violate ritual prevention rules and that they should be encouraged to view these violations as learning experiences, rather than as failures. This is particularly true early in treatment. When patients do engage in rituals, they should make a note of what happened and try to develop an awareness of what triggered the ritual. This knowledge can then be used to design subsequent exposures that specifically target these problematic areas.

As clinicians discuss the issue of ritual prevention violations with patients, it is essential that they establish a tone in the therapeutic relationship that encourages honesty and mutual respect, regardless of whether the patient has ritualized or not. Patients should not feel that they need to hide violations. Rather, they should be encouraged to be open with the clinician about such occurrences and work collaboratively with the clinician to reduce the likelihood that violations will continue to occur in the future.

As therapy progresses, ritual prevention violations should become less frequent and clinicians should be more firm about the importance of this progression. When patients do engage in rituals, they should know to immediately re-expose themselves to the cue that triggered the urge to ritualize. For example, when a person with contamination fears washes their hands after touching something they perceive to be contaminated, they should touch the object again and try again to resist the urge to ritualize. If that proves too difficult, the patient should select something from their hierarchy that is less anxiety provoking but would still prompt obsessional distress and expose to that item to ensure that the prior compulsion is not negatively reinforced via significant anxiety reduction.

Knowing When to Terminate EX/RP

Finally, clinicians need to consider when it is optimal to terminate OCD treatment. It is usually unrealistic to keep patients in treatment until they have *no* OCD symptoms. An important component of treatment is to help patients realize that they might continue to have some intrusive thoughts and urges to ritualize. The emphasis in the latter stages of treatment should therefore be placed not on whether obsessions and urges

are still present, but on how patients handle these challenges when they do arise. Patients will likely be ready to discontinue treatment when they recognize the importance of not suppressing obsessive thoughts and are able to refrain from ritualizing the great majority of the time. When they do slip, they should know to reexpose. Furthermore, as we mentioned earlier, it is important that patients know what to do if an old symptom starts to cause problems again or if a new concern arises. In short, we should feel confident sending patients away if they have the skills to be their own clinicians. As treatment progresses, it is essential to make patients comfortable in that role. Patients should take a more active role in designing exposures and if they come in to sessions with questions about how to deal with a challenging situation, they should be encouraged to try to devise strategies on their own first before the clinician offers suggestions.

Techniques for Dealing with Client Avoidance

Some patients are very resistant to exposure and ritual prevention. Given that this is the crux of the treatment, such resistance can put the therapy at a deadlock. Throughout this chapter, we have given some advice on making EX/RP palatable to patients, including doing gradual RP and not being punitive about ritual prevention violations. Setting a collaborative tone in the therapeutic relationship where both clinician and patient are working together to fight OCD (rather than the patient fighting the clinician) is absolutely essential to successful treatment.

Another excellent way to deal with resistance is to ask patients to articulate what they are afraid of. Often, they report being nervous about their feared consequences. It is best at these times to return to the model and to reiterate the rationale for EX/RP. It can also be comforting for patients to know that clinicians will not assign exercises that they would not do themselves. In fact, it is good clinical practice to do exposures along with the patient, particularly early in treatment. Finally, it can also be helpful to discuss with patients how they see their lives without OCD. The desire to return to work or to make more friends at school or to take up a previously enjoyed hobby can serve as excellent motivation for doing difficult tasks.

One potential pitfall of returning to the model is that some patients will not accept the veracity of the treatment model. In this case, the patient's doubt can be reframed as a hypothesis to be tested. The clinician should allow the patient to feel doubt, but should encourage the patient to test out his belief that EX/RP will not work by giving it a good try. Clinicians can be supportive of the treatment approach by explaining that they have seen it work for many other patients, while being sympathetic to the patient's concerns that it might not work in his particular case.

Some patients are very compliant during treatment sessions, but have a difficult time applying what they have learned outside of therapy. Many patients resist doing homework because they feel too anxious doing it without the support of the clinician. In this case, they can arrange for telephone contact with the clinician or secure the help of a trusted friend or family member. This support should gradually be faded to be sure that patients are not using other people as safety signals. This is simply another form of avoidance that will perpetuate the OCD over time. This concern should also be considered during treatment sessions. If it seems that the clinician is playing some sort of safety role, exposures can gradually be done without the clinician present.

Despite our best efforts, some patients simply refuse to engage in EX/RP. It might be that the cost of doing rituals fails to outweigh the benefit of not doing them. Simply put, patients sometimes come to treatment when they are not ready to change. When this is the case, it is often better to invite patients to come back to treatment when they are ready, rather than to have them stay in treatment and not have a success experience. Another option is to suggest that patients explore whether medication reduces their anxiety enough to make EX/RP seem more palatable.

References

Abramowitz, J. S., & Foa, E. B. (2000). Does major depressive disorder influence outcome of exposure and response prevention for OCD? *Behavior Therapy, 31*, 795–800.

Abramowitz, J. S., Foa, E. B., & Franklin, M. E. (2003). Exposure and ritual prevention for obsessive-compulsive disorder: Effects of intensive versus twice-weekly sessions. *Journal of Consulting & Clinical Psychology, 71*, 394–398.

Abramowitz, J. S., Franklin, M. E., Street, G. P., Kozak, M. J. & Foa, E. B. (2000). Effects of comorbid depression on response to treatment for obsessive-compulsive disorder. *Behavior Therapy, 31*, 517–528.

Abramowitz, J. S., Tolin, D. F. & Street, G. P. (2001). Paradoxical effects of thought suppression: A meta-analysis of controlled studies. *Clinical Psychology Review, 21*(5), 683–703.

AuBuchon, P. G. & Malatesta, V. J. (1994). Obsessive compulsive patients with comorbid personality disorder: Associated problems and response to a comprehensive behavior therapy. *Journal of Clinical Psychiatry, 55*, 448–453.

Baum, M. (1970). Extinction of avoidance responding through response prevention (flooding). *Psychological Bulletin, 74*, 276–284.

Bulik, C. M., Sullivan, P. F., Carter, F. A., McIntosh, V. V. & Joyce, P. R. (1998). The role of exposure with response prevention in the cognitive-behavioural therapy for bulimia nervosa. *Psychological Medicine, 28*, 611–623.

Carmin, C. N., Pollard, A. C., & Ownby, R. L. (1999). Cognitive behavioral treatment of older adults with obsessive–compulsive disorder. *Cognitive and Behavioral Practice, 6*, 110–119.

Fals-Stewart, W., & Lucente, S. (1993). An MCMI cluster typology of obsessive-compulsives: A measure of personality characteristics and its relationship to treatment participation, compliance and outcome in behavior therapy. *Journal of Psychiatric Research, 27*, 139–154.

Foa, E. B., Franklin, M. E., & Moser, J. (2002). Context in the clinic: How well do CBT and medications work in combination? *Biological Psychiatry, 51*, 989–997.

Foa, E. B., Liebowitz, M. R., Kozak, M. J., Davies, S. O., Campeas, R., Franklin, M. E., ed. (2005). Treatment of obsessive compulsive disorder by exposure and ritual prevention, clomipramine, and their combination: A randomized, placebo-controlled trial. *American Journal of Psychiatry, 162*, 151–161.

Foa, E. B., Steketee, G., Grayson, J. B., Turner, R. M., & Latimer, P. R. (1984). Deliberate exposure and blocking of obsessive-compulsive rituals: Immediate and long-term effects. *Behavior Therapy, 15*, 450–472.

Franklin, M. E., Abramowitz, J. S., Kozak, M. J., Levitt, J. T., & Foa, E. B. (2000). Effectiveness of exposure and ritual prevention for obsessive-compulsive disorder: Randomized compared with nonrandomized samples. *Journal of Consulting and Clinical Psychology, 68*, 594–602.

Franklin, M. E., & Foa, E. B. (2007). Cognitive-behavioral treatment of obsessive compulsive disorder. In P. Nathan & J. Gorman (Eds.). *A guide to treatments that work* (3rd ed.). New York: Oxford University Press.

Lee, N. K. & Oei, T. P. (1993). Exposure and response prevention in anxiety disorders: Implications for treatment and relapse prevention in problem drinkers. *Clinical Psychology Review, 13*, 619–632.

McKay, D., Todaro, J., Neziroglu, F. & Campisi, T. (1997). Body dysmorphic disorder: A preliminary investigation of treatment and maintenance using exposure with response prevention. *Behaviour Research and Therapy, 35*, 67–70.

Meyer, V. (1966). Modification of expectations in cases with obsessional rituals. *Behaviour Research and Therapy, 4*, 273–280.

Mowrer, O. H. (1947). On the dual nature of learning: A re-interpretation of "conditioning" and "problem-solving." *Harvard Educational Review, 17*, 102–148.

Mowrer, O. H. (1960). *Learning theory and behavior.* New York: Wiley.

Piacentini, J. C., March, J. S., & Franklin, M. E. (2006). Cognitive-behavioral therapy for youngsters with obsessive-compulsive disorder. In P. C. Kendall (Ed.), *Child and adolescent therapy, third edition: Cognitive-behavioral procedures* (pp. 297–321). New York: Guilford.

Pediatric OCD Treatment Study Team (2004). Cognitive–behavioral therapy, sertraline, and their combination for children and adolescents with obsessive–compulsive disorder: A randomized controlled trial. *Journal of the American Medical Association, 292*, 1969–1976.

Rachman, S. J., & Hodgson, R. J. (1980). *Obsessions and compulsions.* Englewood Cliffs, NJ: Prentice Hall.

Storch, E. A., Geffken, G. R., Merlo, L. J., Mann, G., Duke, D., Munson, M., et al. (2007). Family-based cognitive-behavioral therapy for pediatric obsessive-compulsive disorder: Comparison of intensive and weekly approaches. *Journal of the American Academy of Child & Adolescent Psychiatry, 46*(4), 469–478.

Valderhaug, R., Larsson, B., Gotestam, K. G., & Piacentini, J. (2007). An open clinical trial of cognitive–behaviour therapy in children and adolescents with obsessive–compulsive disorder administered in regular outpatient clinics. *Behaviour Research and Therapy, 45*, 577–589.

Verdellen, C. W. J., Keijsers, G. P. J., Cath, D. C., & Hoogduin, C. A. L. (2004). Exposure with response prevention versus habit reversal in Tourette's syndrome: A controlled study. *Behaviour Research and Therapy, 42*, 501–511.

Visser, S., & Bouman, T. K. (2001). The treatment of hypochondriasis: Exposure plus response prevention vs. cognitive therapy. *Behaviour Research and Therapy, 39*, 423–442.

Warren, R., & Thomas, J. C. (2001). Cognitive–behavior therapy of obsessive–compulsive disorder in private practice: An effectiveness study. *Journal of Anxiety Disorders, 15*, 277–285.

60   SATIATION THERAPY

Crissa Draper

Satiation therapy is currently used mainly in the treatment of sexual offenders or sexually deviant behavior. The therapy is rooted in behavioral principles, and may better be understood as "over-satiation." The concept is to provide a desired or reinforcing maladaptive stimulus to an excessive degree, with the idea that this may make the stimulus aversive, uninteresting, or boring in its abundance, thus losing the previously reinforcing qualities. Satiation therapy was based on ideas in the 1930s (Dunlap, 1932; Guthrie, 1935), and began more formally in the 1960s. It has since been used for a myriad of behavioral problems. One case study of effective use of satiation therapy was conducted in an inpatient setting, in which a patient was hoarding towels (Ayllon, 1963). Instead of taking the towels away, the staff began to intermittently bring towels to the patient throughout the day, increasing in number to an eventual 60 towels a day. After several weeks, the client began removing towels from her room, and during the next 12 months, the mean number of towels in her room was 1–5 per week (compared to the 20 towels per week pretreatment). Glaister and colleagues implemented satiation therapy to treat the feared auditory hallucinations in a case study in an inpatient setting (Glaister, 1985). The hallucinations occurred at a rate of 23 times per hour pretreatment, and after 16 months of repeating the content of the hallucinations, the rate lowered virtually zero. The rating of how demanding the voice was also declined throughout the sessions. Treatment goals were maintained for 5 years. Obsessive thoughts have also been successfully treated in case studies through satiation therapy (Beech & Vaughan, 1978). In this study, a woman with intrusive thoughts that she might harm her daughter was asked to orally repeat the phrase, "Something that I have done will cause harm to my daughter." After 800 repetitions, she no longer found the thought disturbing. Several of these and other applications, however, have been largely usurped by the use of the similar therapy of exposure training (see Chapter 38).

Beginning in the late 1970s, satiation therapy was used to treat sexual deviants; currently, satiation therapy is mainly used as a part of a treatment package for sexually deviant fantasies and behaviors. Several forms of satiation therapy have been used to treat sexual deviance. As Marshall and Lippens noted, "boredom seems to be a common enough occurrence especially in sexually dissatisfied people, and it appears that a loss of initial interest follows prolonged exposure to pornography" (Marshall & Lippens, 1977). This provided the basis for satiation therapy, in which patients are coached to take the fantasies that—while problematic—are reinforcing in some way to the patients, and make them lose their reinforcing qualities by becoming boring. Traditionally, patients were asked to verbally repeat their own sexually deviant fantasies for some time after ejaculating through masturbation, when the fantasies would no longer be desirable. In order to allow patients more privacy, verbal satiation has also been used, for which clients are asked to verbally repeat the fantasy for a given time (generally 30 minutes) over many sessions, without the use of masturbation. When used for sexual deviance, satiation therapy is generally but one component of a larger cognitive behavioral treatment package. Satiation therapy combined with directed masturbation is generally referred to as masturbatory reconditioning. Directed masturbation, or orgasmic reconditioning, provides patients with an alternate fantasy, and is accomplished by initially switching from the patient's deviant fantasy to an appropriate fantasy just before ejaculation.

As this pattern is established, the client is asked to switch to appropriate fantasies further and further from ejaculation, until the appropriate fantasies have eventually completely taken over. This combination provides both a new fantasy repertoire that is reinforced, as well as eliminating the previous reinforcement from the deviant fantasy. The masturbatory reconditioning package is sometimes used with other components as well, including cognitive restructuring, victim empathy training, sexual education, and social skills training (Marquis, 1970; Marshall & Laws, 2003). As is the unfortunate but understandable trend with a sexual deviant population, no large-scale or group design studies have been conducted for satiation therapy. However, many case studies, within-group studies, and single-subject designs have shown the therapy to be effective for reducing deviant sexual arousal. (Forget, 1991; Johnston, Hudson, & Marshall, 1992; Marshall, 1979; Marshall & Barbaree, 1988; Marshall & Lippens, 1977). An early success was a case study conducted by Marshall and Lippens in 1977, in which a male inmate had experienced previous failure with aversive therapy (in which a painful shock was paired with the patient's rape and fetish fantasies) combined with orgasmic reconditioning (Marshall & Lippens, 1977). In this case, the satiation treatment consisted of masturbating to deviant fantasies to the point of arousal (secluded in a separate room with only a microphone connecting him to the therapist), and then continuing to describe the deviant fantasies until the conclusion of the 1.5-hour session. The patient showed remarkable improvement. Pretreatment percentage deviant content in fantasies was 100%. After aversive reconditioning, this was reduced to 80%. During the satiation therapy treatment phase, deviant fantasies made up only 15% of his fantasies, and at follow-up, the patient's fantasies were 0% deviant (100% appropriate). While this study provided significant results in fantasy reduction, it did not have the control to demonstrate change in deviant behavior. Marshall expanded this line of research with two additional case studies, this time demonstrating control over the deviant behavior (Marshall, 1979). Both were male heterosexual pedophiles. In both cases, penile tumescence assessments were used in

order to verify self-report. One patient showed additional fetishistic fantasies around shoes and underwear and was treated for two separate age groups of children, as these were deemed to be different fantasies, as well as for the fetishistic fantasies.

In both cases, patients were instructed to continually masturbate to deviant fantasies for a full hour session (again while in a secluded room). They were given microphone headsets with which to verbally describe the fantasies. The treatment also included an element of orgasmic reconditioning, by having the therapist supply verbal descriptions of appropriate sexual activities. The second case was conducted with a multiple baseline design, with pretreatment baseline followed by self-esteem training, then aversive therapy, then baseline, then satiation therapy. Both cases showed significant improvement, and the multiple baselines case showed significant improvements in the reduction of deviant fantasies, as well as in the increase of appropriate fantasies. Follow-up showed maintained treatment goals in both cases. Many case studies have since emerged using similar versions of satiation therapy or the masturbatory reconditioning package (Marshall & Laws, 2003). However, because of the uncomfortable nature of treatment, Laws and colleagues formulated verbal satiation as an alternate form of satiation therapy, which was built on the same principles, but allowed patients the comfort of repeating the fantasies for half-hour sessions without masturbation. In 5 of 6 cases studied in this way, significant improvements were found (Laws, 1995). Verbal satiation has received some empirical support, although it is largely based on reports of unpublished data (Jenkins-Hall, 1990; Laws, 1995; Laws, Osborn, O'Neil, & Avery-Clark, 1987).

LIMITS OF SATIATION THERAPY

Several issues surround the use of satiation therapy for sexual deviance. One is the eventual need for the implementation of the voice-operated relay system in the headset. This device sends out a high-intensity tone in the event that there is a given amount of silence (generally 5 seconds), and was deemed necessary due to the propensity for patients to become bored or sleepy during the therapy. Another issue is that of self-report. As with any therapy for sexual deviance, it should be taken into account that these patients are often not entirely forthcoming about these problems; they generally don't seek treatment until they have been caught, and they may not give any information or details about the fantasies or deviant behaviors that are accurate. Therefore, additional penile tumescence measures are recommended. It should also be noted that there is no "cure" for sexual deviance. This is not to say that the behaviors cannot be treated, but follow-up sessions should be maintained even after the behavior has stopped, and stimulus control should remain a concern as well.

Possibilities here include relapse prevention (see Chapter 57). Additionally, the newer self-regulation model is a follow-up option (Ward, Hudson, & Keenan, 1998).

WHO MIGHT BENEFIT FROM THIS TECHNIQUE?

While the majority of empirical data for satiation therapy has been for pedophilia and rapist populations, it has also been used for other sexually deviant behaviors, including exhibitionism and fetishes (Marshall, 1979; Marshall & Fernandez, 2003). It has also been found effective in OCD spectrum behaviors, however this should be considered a second line of defense, used only after considering or trying exposure.

CONTRAINDICATIONS

The ability to concentrate on a particular topic for an extended period of time is essential for satiation therapy. Additionally, motivation may be an issue. Patients with sexually deviant fantasies may feel shame and guilt about their fantasies, and may not want to share them. Other patients may not be interested in changing these fantasies. It is likely that patients using masturbatory satiation will feel some discomfort around this, which may create a barrier to motivation. Additionally, while the therapy has been used successfully in rapist populations, it should be pointed out

that this is not necessarily a measure of success. Satiation therapy only treats sexual arousal from deviant fantasies, and does not interact with other pathways that might lead to sexually deviant behavior. For example, it has been pointed out that rape is "an enactment of physical coercion *and* sexual arousal" (Marshall & Laws, 2003, p. 132; italics added).

HOW DOES SATIATION THERAPY WORK?

There are discrepancies as to the exact mechanisms of change. Some consider satiation therapy to be a form of aversive therapy, while others consider it a therapy to block and eventually remove reinforcement. Whether conceptualized as positive or negative, the therapy is in short a behavioral punisher, which reduces future occurrences of the deviant fantasy behavior. It has been hypothesized that fantasy and masturbation activities "reciprocally reinforce each other so one is unlikely to be found without the other" (Laws, 1995). Research has suggested that aversive control may lead to temporary behavioral suppression, but not likely behavior change, because new repertoires must first be supplied for the individual to have an alternate behavior in place. Orgasmic reconditioning provides this new repertoire, and when used in conjunction with satiation therapy, patients are trained to recondition the paired reinforcement of deviant stimuli and pleasurable sensations with the paired punishment of either a lack of pleasurable sensation, or a negative sensation such as boredom, while simultaneously pairing appropriate stimuli and pleasurable sensations, allowing for a both positive and negative behavior change.

STEP-BY-STEP TECHNIQUE

The following procedure is for the less intrusive and more accessible verbal satiation therapy (Bowers, 2003). (For procedures on masturbatory satiation, see Marshall, 1979.)

1. *Consent.* Consent should include a detailed description of the procedure and the rationale

for treatment. Explain to clients that deviant thoughts may originally increase, but will decline with repetition, and should significantly decrease by the completion of treatment. Additionally, it should be discussed that satiation therapy—like other treatments for sexually deviant behavior—should not be considered a cure. It should instead be conceptualized as the first leap towards a different lifestyle, but therapy and self-management should continue throughout life.

2. *Structure*. No studies have been conducted to determine the optimum number of sessions or time of sessions, but it is important to remember that in this treatment, it is better to err on the side of too long. Traditionally, verbal satiation sessions last about 30 minutes, and occur three times per week. Treatment effects are often seen in 3–4 weeks; however, treatment should continue until the patient consistently shows behaviors consistent with fatigue or boredom. If possible, penile tumescence measures can be used to monitor progress.

3. *Specifics and apparatus*. Fantasies should be verbalized with few or no breaks or pauses. It is common for patients to become bored or tired during treatment, and they may even fall asleep. This shows positive treatment gains, but should be interrupted while treatment continues, so as to not allow the patient to avoid the boredom associated with the fantasy. Therapists can listen to the verbalization and prompt patients if these pauses occur. If possible, the use of voice-operated relay (VOR) headsets can take on the role of prompting the patient. VOR headsets can be set to detect five seconds of silence, and then emit a high-pitched tone in the headset, which can prompt the client to continue (Laws, 1995). VOR headsets limit the need for constant monitoring from the therapist, however content should still be monitored to ensure that it is consistent with treatment goals. Audio-taping can also be used to later code patient adherence. While they can be difficult and expensive to administer, penile tumescence assessments, such as the plethysmograph or strain gauge, should be used when possible to monitor progress. These could be outsourced if they are not available in the treating facility.

4. *Self-management and relapse prevention*. As with any treatment program for sexual deviance, therapy is an ongoing life process. Stimulus control will have to be a permanent change in the patient's life (e.g., someone who has engaged in child molestation should never again be alone with children). This idea may be upsetting to some clients. It may be helpful to discuss the role of treatment and life change in the patient's personal values, and to compare managing sexually deviant behavior to something like managing overeating, where it's more obvious that it's an ongoing life change. The client should commit to self management or the self-regulation model is a follow-up option (Ward et al., 1998), and the therapist should integrate relapse prevention (see Chapter 57).

Further Reading

Laws, D. R. (1995). Verbal satiation: Notes on procedure, with speculations on its mechanism of effect. *Sexual Abuse: Journal of Research and Treatment, 7*(2), 155–166.

Marshall, W. L. (1979). Satiation therapy: A procedure for reducing deviant sexual arousal. *Journal of Applied Behavior Analysis, 12*(3), 377–389.

Laws, D. R., & Marshall, W. L. (2003). A brief history of behavioral and cognitive behavioral approaches to sexual offenders: Part 1. Early developments. *Sexual Abuse: Journal of Research and Treatment, 15*(2), 75–92.

Marshall, W. L., & Laws, D. R. (2003). A brief history of behavioral and cognitive behavioral approaches to sexual offender treatment: Part 2. The modern era. *Sexual Abuse: Journal of Research and Treatment, 15*(2), 93–120.

References

Ayllon, T. (1963). Intensive treatment of psychotic behaviour by stimulus satiation and food reinforcement. *Behaviour Research and Therapy, 1*(1), 53–61.

Beech, H. R., & Vaughan, M. (1978). *Behavioural treatment of obsessional states*. Chichester, UK: John Wiley & Sons.

Bowers, A. H. (2003). Satiation therapy. In W. T. O'Donohue, J. E. Fisher & S. C. Hayes (Eds.), *Cognitive behaivor therapy: Applying empirically supported techniques in your practice*. Hoboken, NJ: John Wiley & Sons.

Dunlap, K. (1932). *Habits, their making and unmaking.* New York: Liveright.

Forget, J. (1991). L'élimination d'un comportement de ramassage de détritus par une technique de satiété. *Science et Comportement, 21*(1), 40–48.

Glaister, B. (1985). A case of auditory hallucination treated by satiation. *Behaviour Research and Therapy, 23*(2), 213–215.

Guthrie, E. R. (1935). *The psychology of learning.* New York: Harper.

Jenkins-Hall, K. (1990). Final Report. Grant No. R01MH42035. Prevention of relapse in sex offenders. Rockville, MD: National Institute of Mental Health.

Johnston, P., Hudson, S. M., & Marshall, W. L. (1992). The effects of masturbatory reconditioning with nonfamilial child molesters. *Behaviour Research and Therapy, 30*(5), 559–561.

Laws, D. R. (1995). Verbal satiation: Notes on procedure, with speculations on its mechanism of effect. *Sexual Abuse: Journal of Research and Treatment, 7*(2), 155–166.

Laws, D. R., Osborn, C. A., O'Neil, J. A., & Avery-Clark, C. A. (1987). A verbal satiation procedure to alter sexual arousal in sexual deviates: Unpublished raw data.

Marquis, J. N. (1970). Orgasmic reconditioning: Changing sexual object choice through controlling masturbation fantasies. *Journal of Behavior Therapy and Experimental Psychiatry, 1*, 263–271.

Marshall, W. L. (1979). Satiation therapy: A procedure for reducing deviant sexual arousal. *Journal of Applied Behavior Analysis, 12*(3), 377–389.

Marshall, W. L., & Barbaree, H. E. (1988). An outpatient treatment program for child molesters. *Annals of the New York Academy of Sciences, 528*, 205–214.

Marshall, W. L., & Fernandez, Y. M. (2003). Sexual preferences are they useful in the assessment and treatment of sexual offenders? *Aggression and Violent Behavior, 8*(2), 131–143.

Marshall, W. L., & Laws, D. R. (2003). A brief history of behavioral and cognitive behavioral approaches to sexual offender treatment: Part 2. The modern era. *Sexual Abuse: Journal of Research and Treatment, 15*(2), 93–120.

Marshall, W. L., & Lippens, K. (1977). The clinical value of boredom: A procedure for reducing inappropriate sexual interests. *Journal of Nervous and Mental Disease, 165*(4), 283–287.

Ward, T., Hudson, S. M., & Keenan, T. (1998). A self-regulation model of the sexual offense process. *Sexual Abuse: Journal of Research and Treatment, 10*(2), 141–157.

61 IDENTIFYING AND MODIFYING MALADAPTIVE SCHEMAS

Cory F. Newman

One of the central, identifying features of the cognitive theory of emotional disorders is its emphasis on the psychological significance of the client's beliefs about themselves, their personal world (e.g., other people), and the future (the "cognitive triad," in the words of A.T. Beck, 1976). As Aaron T. Beck formulated and developed cognitive therapy in the 1960s and 1970s, he postulated that much of the client's emotional distress—especially with regard to dysphoria and excessive anxiety—had to do with the problematic, inflexible ways they interpreted the events of their lives. Thus, even if the objective facts of the clients' lives were largely favorable, they may be prone to underestimate their resources and blessings, and to overestimate their losses and threats to well-being (e.g., A.T. Beck, Rush, Shaw, & Emery, 1979; A.T. Beck, Emery, & Greenberg, 1985). In other words, even those individuals who behaved in such a way that they could elicit a good deal of positive reinforcement in everyday life, by dint of the negatively biased ways in which they would construe their experience, would not optimally incorporate their successes into their cognitive triad, thus setting themselves up for needless sadness, worry, low self-esteem, and other threats to a higher quality of life.

For those clients whose life situations were sufficiently aversive that others would agree that there were significant reasons to be dysphoric or anxious, the clients' negative beliefs were hypothesized to inhibit them from actively trying to improve their lot, owing to pervasive, ongoing feelings of helplessness and hopelessness (Alloy, Peterson, Abramson, & Seligman, 1984; A.T. Beck, 1976; A.T. Beck, Riskind, Brown, & Steer, 1988). Further, if life events were to become more favorable, an attributional style that did not allow the clients to take personal credit for such good fortune would continue to keep them low in self-esteem, and self-efficacy, and thus at continued vulnerability to emotional disorders (Hollon, DeRubeis, & Seligman, 1992).

Various hypotheses have been put forth about the source of these dysfunctional thought processes, including modeling the cognitive style of emotionally troubled primary caregivers, and adverse life experiences, especially early life traumas and retraumatization (such as in the case of more severe personality disorders; see Layden, Newman, Freeman, & Morse, 1993; Young, Klosko, & Weishaar, 2003). The problem worsens when individuals with dysfunctional thinking styles cognitively filter out (or minimize) information that would otherwise contradict their negative beliefs. Thus, they come to trust their biased perceptions and beliefs more than they trust their ongoing life experiences, and the negative schemas stubbornly remain in place. Cognitive therapy endeavors to loosen and modify such troublesome schemas. (Note: The term schemas often denotes the most basic, core dysfunctional beliefs that clients accept as fundamental truths in their lives. As this chapter focuses on changing clients' beliefs, including those deep enough to be termed schemas, the terms beliefs and schemas will be used interchangeably).

One of the earliest attempts by A.T. Beck and his colleagues to identify and measure the maladaptive beliefs hypothesized to be the most common culprits in clinical depression and anxiety disorders was their development of the Dysfunctional Attitudes Scale (DAS; Weissman & Beck, 1978). With this self-report questionnaire, clients were asked to endorse their degree of agreement (on a 7-point, Likert-type scale) with a wide range of beliefs, the extremes of which were hypothesized to be indicative of cognitive vulnerability to depression and anxiety. Sample items included the following:

- People will think less of me if I make a mistake.
- If I fail at work, then I am a failure as a person.
- I am nothing if a person I love does not love me.

There is evidence with unipolar depressive clients that changes in such negative beliefs are associated with positive outcome in treatment, as well as the reduction of symptomatic relapses in the future (Evans et al., 1992; Hollon et al., 1992; Parks & Hollon, 1988). Further, major improvements in clients' mood during the course of cognitive therapy have been found to follow sessions in which they made measurable cognitive changes (Tang & DeRubeis, 1999; Tang, Beberman, DeRubeis, & Pham, 2005).

As cognitive therapy began to expand its application to additional clinical populations—most notably personality disorders (Beck, Freeman, Davis, & Associates, 2004; Layden et al., 1993; Young et al., 2003)—new measures were developed to tap into the dysfunctional beliefs and schemas that were hypothesized to be salient for clients with longstanding, cross-situational disturbance. For example, the Personality Beliefs Questionnaire (PBQ; Beck, Butler, Brown, Dahlsgaard, Newman, & Beck, 2001) is a self-report measure that uses a Likert-type scale and comprises a clinically derived set of beliefs hypothesized to correspond to specific personality disorders. For example, the item, "If I ignore a problem, it will go away," is hypothesized to reflect a part of the cognitive style of clients who would meet the criteria outlined by the fourth edition of the *Diagnostic and Statistical Manual of Mental Disorders* (*DSM-IV*; American Psychiatric Association, 1994) for avoidant personality disorder. In fact, research on this instrument indicates that clients with personality disorders preferentially endorse PBQ items theoretically linked to their specific diagnosis (Beck et al., 2001).

Additionally, the Young Schema Questionnaire (YSQ: see Schmidt, Joiner, Young, & Telch, 1995) uses a similar self-report, Likert-type scale format as the PBQ, but for the purpose of identifying which of its 15 factor-analyzed schemas clients load on most heavily. These schemas include "mistrust," "defectiveness," "abandonment," "entitlement," and others, and they are hypothesized to be most prevalent in clients with the most severe personality disorders. A sample item is, "It is only a matter of time before someone betrays me" (mistrust schema). More recently, Young et al. (2003) have introduced the concept of "schema modes" (clusters of schemas or coping responses that tend to be triggered together), most notably relevant in clients with borderline personality disorder, but applicable to other clients as well. In order to test the utility of this concept, a Schema Mode Questionnaire has been developed and subjected to empirical investigation (e.g., Arntz, Klokman, & Sieswerda, 2005).

A study conducted in the Netherlands (Spinhoven, Bockting, Kremers, Schene, & Williams, 2007), used the YSQ in conjunction with the DAS, along with a measure of autobiographical recall (the autobiographical memory test [AMT]; Williams & Broadbent, 1986). The investigators tested the hypothesis that dysfunctional, overgeneralized memory may arise from the cognitive matching of present task cues with dysfunctional attitudes or schemas. In a population of clients with recurrent major depression, as well as a population of clients who were diagnosed with borderline personality disorder, the clients retrieved significantly fewer, specific autobiographical memories in respond to cue words that matched highly endorsed schemas.

In another study from the Netherlands, a 34-item self-report questionnaire was developed for the assessment of key emotions and cognitive assumptions hypothesized to be characteristic of borderline personality disorder (the Questionnaire of Thoughts and Feelings [QTF]; Renneberg, Schmidt-Rathjens, Hippin, Backenstrass, & Fydrich, 2005). The measure was found to possess good psychometric properties, as well as good sensitivity to client changes on a wide range of other well-established assessment measures over time. Future research on the above questionnaires will indicate their utility in identifying clients' schemas and personality disorders, highlighting targets for cognitive intervention, and measuring changes in beliefs and schemas as a result of treatment.

More recently, a volume has been published that is dedicated to explicating the theoretical, empirical, and clinical bases of schema work across a wide range of specific disorders, including chronic depression, posttraumatic stress disorder, substance use disorders, eating disorders, and psychosis (Riso, du Toit, Stein, & Young, 2007). The contributors to this volume place special emphasis on the role of assessing and understanding the client's hypothesized schemas as an important part of the case formulation.

The major steps in changing cognitive schemas include:

- Helping clients to self-monitor their thinking styles so as to better understand their active role in creating their life views and emotions
- Teaching clients the cognitive skills (e.g., self-applied Socratic questioning, rational responding) to be more flexible and adaptive in their attributional style, problem-solving skills, and hopefulness, and to modify and even abandon old ways of thinking
- To create new behavioral repertoires and activities that would actively counteract their previously held (perhaps now outdated) maladaptive beliefs, and that would be more consistent with a broader, more flexible and constructive way of viewing oneself, one's world, and the future
- Utilizing experiential exercises such as guided imagery and role-playing to address schemas in a constructive way while they are emotionally charged (i.e., "hot" cognitions)

WHO MIGHT BENEFIT FROM THIS TECHNIQUE?

Any client can benefit from learning the skills of evaluating, testing, and reformulating their own thinking styles so that they become more functional in terms of good problem solving, self-efficacy, and hopefulness. In fact, therapists themselves often are encouraged in their training and supervision to practice these methods (see Bennett-Levy, 2006), both as a way to empathize with their clients' trial-and-error learning

process, and as a way to perform spot-checks on their own potentially problematic thinking styles (e.g., testing the belief that "If one of my clients has a depressive setback, it means that I have failed as a therapist").

However, the skills of self-monitoring, testing, and modifying one's beliefs can be particularly beneficial for clients who demonstrate one or both of the following clinical problems:

1. Those who have difficulty incorporating positive experiences into their overarching views of themselves, their lives, and their futures.
2. Those whose behavioral repertoire is based on faulty assumptions of personal failure and interpersonal rejection, such that they systematically inhibit themselves from trying to advance their lives, and expect (and then perhaps elicit) uncaring or conflictual interactions with others.

Clients such as those who exhibit these problems can improve their lives in an enduring way by learning to pay attention to, and to create, productive and constructive ways to use their time (without undue fear of failure), and to relate to others (without undue fear or mistrust).

CONTRAINDICATIONS

The drawbacks of the treatment fall into two categories, and they are readily avoided if the therapists are alert and diligent. The first category has to do with a suboptimal therapeutic relationship, and the second has to do with an incomplete or inaccurate case conceptualization.

Insufficient Rapport and/or Accurate Empathy

Regarding the first point, it is inadvisable for therapists to be too heavy-handed in their attempts to persuade clients to change their long-held beliefs. Cognitive therapy is a collaborative and compassionate therapy (see Gilbert & Leahy, 2007); thus it is contraindicated to apply undue pressure on clients to relinquish their viewpoints. Therapists must demonstrate respect for the clients' ways of construing their worlds. Thus, when therapists suggest that clients consider testing the objectivity and functionality of their thinking, they would do well to point out how the clients may benefit from this self-reflective skill, especially in the long run. It is very important for therapists to try to understand how it is that the clients have developed their beliefs, and how they are maintained. In doing so, therapists will be able to give sincere validation for their clients' ways of viewing their lives, as a prelude to trying to work together to find a better way to view them.

Similarly, the process of cognitive therapy loses its effectiveness and appeal if it is reduced to an arid, intellectual debate. The therapeutic relationship needs to involve empathy, warmth, and a little bit of appropriate humor. It is also important to insert some creativity into the process (cf. Rosen, 2000), so that there is stimulation and life in the therapeutic dialogue. These qualities in the therapeutic alliance help to ease the sometimes difficult and unfamiliar process of identifying and modifying maladaptive beliefs.

Inadequate Case Formulation

The second problem has to do with the therapist's insufficient attention to the client's unique phenomenology, including the client's personal history, current life situation (and its contingencies), and cultural factors. If therapists take a one-size-fits-all approach, such as by insisting that all clients need to relinquish a given belief, they will miss important, idiographic nuances that are vital to the understanding of the client. Thus, the therapist's interventions will seem off the mark, and the process of treatment will suffer (see Beck, 1995; Needleman, 1999; Persons, 1989; Tarrier, 2006).

STEP-BY-STEP PROCEDURES

The changing of dysfunctional schemas is neither a quick nor simple procedure. Accomplishing this difficult but worthy goal requires a combination of techniques, proffered in the spirit of a positive therapeutic alliance, and a well-formulated case conceptualization. Focusing on the clients' distant past experiences related to the formation and maintenance of their schemas will likely

be an important part of this process (Weertman & Arntz, 2007). There are a number of ways that cognitive therapists can help their clients in changing harmful beliefs into more healthy ones. Some of these methods are based on the structured, standard repertoire as demonstrated by Beck et al. (1979), and Beck (1995), such as the use of the daily thought records (DTRs). Other techniques stem from the principles inherent in using DTRs, but may require some flexibility, and creativity (e.g., see Young et al., 2003, for gestalt-like "reparenting" exercises).

The following are some of the most commonly used techniques, often used as a package over numerous sessions. Although the sequence of usage is by no means etched in stone, the following methods are presented as representing a reasonable progression.

Let Emotions Be the Cue to Start the Process

It is very useful to demonstrate how clients' problematic moods can provide them with valuable information about their thought process. Specifically, clients are asked to notice their episodes of excessive anger, despair, fear, and the like, and to choose not to accept them at face value. Rather, clients are instructed to ask themselves, "What could be going through my mind right now that could be triggering or worsening how I'm feeling right now?" Clients are taught to write down their hypotheses.

Sometimes clients have a difficult time with this process, saying that they do not know what they are thinking coincidental to their upset. Therapists respond by saying, "You do not need to know *for certain*. It is sufficient if you take some educated guesses." If clients still demur, therapists can provide clients with a multiple-choice list of reasonable thoughts, and the client is asked, "Which of these thoughts rings a bell with you? Which of these *could* represent the way you view the situation?" At this point, it is usually possible to write down a list of plausible thoughts.

Many of these thoughts will hang together thematically. Patterns will emerge, such as expectations of abandonment, or mistrust of others, or the conviction of being unlovable, or certainty of being a failure, among other schemas. Further, therapists can utilize the clients' responses from questionnaires such as the DAS, PBQ, and YSQ to identify schemas that will need to be targets for intervention.

One of the most compelling ways clients can identify their schemas is by learning to spot when their emotional buttons, so to speak, have been pushed. In other words, therapists inform their clients that there will be times when their emotional reactions seem greatly disproportionate to the situation (at least in retrospect). Other people may say to the clients that they are being hypersensitive or overreacting. Clients are taught that, rather than feeling angry or ashamed about this, they should ask themselves the question, "What *schema* just got activated?" For example, a woman became suicidal after getting what she thought was a bad haircut (see Layden et al., 1993). When the client asked herself this question, she concluded that she expected that her boyfriend would now leave her, thus activating both her "defectiveness" and "abandonment" schemas. This self-assessment paved the way for some cognitive modifications, along with emotional deescalation.

Use Socratic Questions

Clients learn that they are prone to have systematic biases in the way they perceive and interpret their experiences. Thus, they are encouraged to question their own reactions—not in a self-denigrating way, but rather in a spirit of self-enhancing inquiry. Therapists use Socratic questions throughout the course of therapy in order to highlight the clients' need to reevaluate their schemas. Additionally, clients are taught a standard series of Socratic questions they can use themselves, usually as part of their efforts to generate "rational responses" on their DTRs (see Beck, 1995).

Therapist-Generated Socratic Questions

Given that one of the main characteristics of dysfunctional schemas is their rigidity, it is unproductive for therapists to try to argue their clients out of their beliefs. If clients believe that "There is no point in getting close to others, because they will always leave me and I'll be devastated," the therapists will make little headway if they simply exhort the clients to believe that people will *not* always abandon them, and they will *not* always be devastated. Instead, therapists use open-ended, Socratic questions, with the goal of helping clients expand their ability to consider other ways of looking at the situation. Therapists should take the following, general approaches in order to maximize this method:

1. Listen carefully to all of the clients' statements that (in passing) go against their own beliefs, and compile a mental or written list of such utterances.
2. Ask clients for examples from their own life experience that seem to offer evidence against a rote acceptance of their negative schemas.
3. If clients can succeed in generating such examples, ask the clients to reconcile this with their belief, and to consider the possibility that there may be exceptions to the rule that need to be considered.
4. If the clients cannot offer such examples from their personal history, the therapist can tactfully report from the list they have generated (see step 1), as evidence for modifying the belief.

Further, it should be noted that examples of ongoing, positive interactions in the therapeutic relationship often are excellent examples of data that go against client's most pernicious schemas, most notably "mistrust" and "defectiveness."

Clients' Socratic Questions for Themselves

Clients are also taught to use the following Socratic (or *guided discovery*) questions for themselves, often as part of their between-sessions homework. After they have identified some of the thoughts and deeper schemas that may be responsible for their dysphoria or excessive anxiety, clients are asked to subject them to the following questions (adapted from Beck, 1995):

1. What other plausible perspective(s) can I take about this matter?
2. What factual evidence supports or refutes my beliefs?
3. What are the pros and cons of continuing to see things the way I see them, and what are the pros and cons of trying to see things differently?

4. What constructive action can I take to deal with my beliefs or schemas?
5. What sincere advice would I give to a good friend with the same beliefs?

Again, this exercise, performed repetitively across many situations and beliefs, has the power to loosen old, dysfunctional beliefs, and perhaps to prime them to be modified by new, more hopeful experiences.

Behavioral Experiments

Purely verbal techniques sometimes lack sufficient experiential power to provide clients with the necessary "aha!" reaction that can help them see things in a new and better way. Thus, behavioral experiments are used in order to provide *in vivo* evidence in support of the revised, more functional (i.e., less extreme, more flexible) beliefs.

In-Session Role-Playing

Here, therapists ask clients to adopt the role of someone who sees life options outside the confines of the negative schemas, while the therapist takes the role of the supporter of the maladaptive schemas. The challenge is to stay in the role, and to perform the negative part of the dialogue with respect—not as a caricature of the client. After the role-playing exercise is completed, the client is asked for feedback on the experience. Many repetitions of this process may be needed over the course of a number of sessions.

Homework between Sessions

In order to generalize the above process to the client's natural environment, clients are asked to test their beliefs between sessions. For example, the client who believes that everyone will abandon her may be asked to telephone three friends, or perhaps even to invite one or more to lunch (or another activity). Although the client may predict that she will be ignored, rejected, or stood up, she is encouraged nonetheless to take the chance of joining her friends and to pay close attention to *what actually happens*. If it happens that the client reports that her negative beliefs have been borne out, the therapist will turn the client's attention to a post-hoc evaluation of what

may have gone wrong, so as to make behavioral corrections in the future. More often than not, the outcome will go against the client's beliefs, but she will have a difficult time relinquishing the beliefs anyway. This is a standard outcome, because beliefs are difficult to change with any one intervention. Multiple interventions, with numerous repetitions, are required.

Imagery Reconstruction

A full description of imagery reconstruction techniques is beyond the scope of this chapter; however, its importance warrants mention. Combining aspects of relaxation, guided imagery, and rational re-evaluation of past experiences salient to the client's schemas, imagery reconstruction is a highly evocative technique that should be used judiciously, and with care. The rationale for this procedure includes the need for clients to be in an emotional state relevant to the activation of their schemas in order to best entertain alternative views to the schema, as well as the importance of revisiting key historical events that may have to do with the etiology of the schema.

For example, a client who believes he is a flawed and defective person owing to his experiences of childhood sexual abuse may be very resistant to changing this belief through standard methods of rational reevaluation in the here and now. However, in the context of a trusting therapeutic relationship, and under the calming influence of a relaxation induction, he may be more receptive to an imaginal revisiting of the scene of the abuse. The therapist guides the procedure cautiously and caringly, and the client's beliefs (pertinent to the memory) are elicited. The client is asked to talk to himself as he remembers himself at the critical time in question, to give support and offer alternative, compassionate, rational reinterpretations about his perceived defectiveness. Similar methods are described in Foa and Rothbaum (1998), Layden et al. (1993), Resick & Schnicke (1993), and Young et al. (2003). See Table 61.1 for a summary of procedures.

EVIDENCE-BASED APPLICATIONS

By and large, the study of schema change has been conducted in the context of clinical trials

TABLE 61.1 Summary of Procedures

1. Use instruments such as the DAS, PBQ, and YSQ to identify problematic schemas, or assess them in response to clients' emotional reactions that are greatly disproportionate to the situation (an indicator of schema activation).
2. Provide the clients with validation and accurate empathy, based on a well-constructed case conceptualization. Focusing on distant past experiences germane to the development of the clients' schema will likely be part of this process.
3. Teach the clients to use their magnified, problematic emotional response as cues to ask themselves what they are thinking, and what schemas may have been activated.
4. Use Socratic questions to "loosen" the beliefs or schemas, and teach the clients to use these questions for themselves. Look closely at evidence from life experiences.
5. Use behavioral enactments, both in the form of in-session role-playing and between-session experiments, so clients gain experience in acting on new beliefs.
6. In cases of early life traumas that have etiological significance, use a combination of relaxation, guided imagery, and rational re-evaluation to counteract the negative beliefs and schemas that the clients have derived from these salient, historical experiences.
7. Be prepared to have to use combinations of these techniques, numerous times, over the course of many sessions.

involving forms of cognitive therapy specifically applied to challenging populations (e.g., clients with chronic depression, personality disorders). In these studies, dependent measures have included the traditional assessment of mood scores on various, well-validated inventories, ratings of global adaptive functioning, diagnostic changes (i.e., do the clients no longer meet criteria for the disorder with which they began the trial?), and other important indicators of psychological wellness. In addition to these, measures of client beliefs and schemas have been employed as well, so as to examine the theory-specific benefits of a treatment geared to address and change clients' core, maladaptive ways of thinking.

For example, in a multisite study in the United Kingdom, Davidson et al. (2006) compared cognitive behavioral therapy plus treatment as usual (CBT + TAU) with TAU alone in a clinical trial for clients with borderline personality disorder. At the one year assessment the CBT + TAU group had greater improvement than the TAU group in symptom distress, and at two years showed greater improvement in state anxiety, dysfunctional core beliefs (as measured by the YSQ), as well as significantly reduced suicidal behaviors. An uncontrolled trial (Brown, Newman, Charlesworth, Crits-Christoph, & Beck, 2004) found that cognitive therapy (CT) for BPD was associated with significant and clinically important improvements on measures of depression, hopelessness, suicide ideation, number of borderline symptoms (as

per *Diagnostic and Statistical Manual of Mental Disorders* criteria), and dysfunctional beliefs (as measured by the PBQ) at the end of treatment and at 6-month follow-up. A single-case series trial of six clients tested the effectiveness of Young's schema-focused therapy for borderline personality disorder (Nordahl & Nysaeter, 2005). Assessments from baseline to 1-year follow-up showed large effect sizes, clinically meaningful improvements in five clients, and a remission of the borderline diagnosis in three clients. In a multicenter, randomized trial, Giesen-Bloo et al. (2006) compared the effectiveness of schema-focused CT (SFCT; Young et al., 2003) with the psychodynamically based transference-focused psychotherapy (TFP) in clients with borderline personality disorder. Over the course of three years of treatment, survival analyses demonstrated that significantly more SFT clients recovered, or showed reliable improvement. In addition, ratings of the quality of the therapeutic relationship—from both the therapists and clients—were higher in SFCT than in TFP (Spinhoven, Giesen-Bloo, van Dyck, Kooiman, & Arntz, 2007).

Empirical tests of schema-related interventions for additional disorders are reviewed extensively in Riso et al. (2007). Such clinical disturbances as chronic depression, posttraumatic stress disorder, substance abuse, eating disorders, psychotic disorder, and couples problems are also reviewed in the context of schema processes and schema changes in this comprehensive volume.

Further Reading

James, I. A., Southam, L., & Blackburn, I. M. (2004). Schemas revisited. *Clinical Psychology and Psychotherapy, 11*, 369–377.

Riso, L. P., Froman, S. E., Raouf, M., Gable, P., Maddux, R. E., Turini-Santorelli, N., et al. (2006). The long-term stability of early maladaptive *schemas. Cognitive Therapy and Research, 30*(4), 515–529.

Waller, G., Shah, R., Ohanian, V., & Elliott, P. (2001). Core beliefs in bulimia nervosa and depression: The discriminant validity of Young's Schema Questionnaire. *Behavior Therapy, 32*(1), 139–153.

References

Alloy, L. B., Peterson, C., Abramson, L. Y., & Seligman, M. E. P. (1984). Attributional style and the generality of learned helplessness. *Journal of Personality and Social Psychology, 46*(3), 681–687.

American Psychiatric Association (1994). *Diagnostic and statistical manual of mental disorders* (4th ed.). Washington, D.C.: Author.

Arntz, A., Klokman, J., & Sieswerda, S. (2005). An experimental test of the schema mode model of borderline personality disorder. *Journal of Behavior Therapy and Experimental Psychiatry: Special Issue: Cognition and emotion in borderline personality disorder, 36*(3), 226–239.

Beck, A. T. (1976). *Cognitive therapy and the emotional disorders.* New York: International Universities Press.

Beck, A. T., Butler, A. C., Brown, G. K., Dahlsgaard, K. K., Newman, C. F., & Beck, J. S. (2001). Dysfunctional beliefs discriminate personality disorders. *Behaviour Research and Therapy, 39*(10), 1213–1225.

Beck, A. T., Emery, G., & Greenberg, R. L. (1985). *Anxiety disorders and phobias: A cognitive perspective.* New York: Basic Books.

Beck, A. T., Freeman, A., Davis, D. D., & Associates (2004). *Cognitive therapy of personality disorders* (2nd ed.). New York: Guilford.

Beck, A. T., Riskind, J. H., Brown, G., & Steer, R. A. (1988). Levels of hopelessness in DSM-III disorders: A partial test of content specificity in depression. *Cognitive Therapy and Research, 12*(5), 459–469.

Beck, A. T., Rush, A. J., Shaw, B., & Emery, G. (1979). *Cognitive therapy of depression.* New York: Guilford.

Beck, J. S. (1995). *Cognitive therapy: Basics and beyond.* New York: Guilford.

Bennett-Levy, J. (2006). Therapist skills: A cognitive model of their acquisition and refinement. *Behavioural and Cognitive Psychotherapy, 34*(1), 57–78.

Brown, G. K., Newman, C. F., Charlesworth, S. E., Crits-Christoph, P., & Beck, A. T. (2004). An open trial of cognitive therapy for borderline personality disorder. *Journal of Personality Disorders, 18*(3), 257–271.

Davidson, K., Norrie, J., Tyrer, P., Gumley, A., Tata, P., Murray, H., & Palmer, S. (2006). The effectiveness of cognitive-behaviour therapy for borderline personality disorder: Results from the BOSCOT trial. *Journal of Personality Disorders, 20*(5), 450–465.

Evans, M. D., Hollon, S. D., DeRubeis, R. J., Piasecki, J. M., Grove, W. M., Garvey, M. J., et al. (1992). Differential relapse following cognitive therapy and pharmacology for depression. *Archives of General Psychiatry, 49*, 802–808.

Foa, E. B., & Rothbaum, B. O. (1998). *Treating the trauma of rape: Cognitive-behavioral therapy for PTSD.* New York: Guilford.

Giesen-Bloo, J., van Dyck, R., Spinhoven, P., van Tilburg, W., Dirksen, C., van Asselt, T., Kremers, I., Nadort, M., & Arntz, A. (2006). Outpatient psychotherapy for borderline personality disorder: Randomized trial of schema-focused therapy vs. transference-focused psychotherapy. *Archives of General Psychiatry, 63*(6), 649–658.

Gilbert, P., & Leahy, R. L. (Eds.) (2007). *The therapeutic relationship in the cognitive-behavioral psychotherapies.* London: Routledge-Brunner.

Greenberger, D., & Padesky, C. (1995). *Mind over mood.* New York: Guilford.

Hollon, S. D., DeRubeis, R. J., & Seligman, M. E. P. (1992). Cognitive therapy and the prevention of depression. *Applied and Preventive Psychiatry, 95*, 52–59.

Layden, M. A., Newman, C. F., Freeman, A., & Morse, S. B. (1993). *Cognitive therapy of borderline personality disorder.* Boston, MA: Allyn and Bacon.

Needleman, L. (1999). *Cognitive case conceptualization: A guide for practitioners.* Mahwah, NJ: Lawrence Erlbaum.

Nordahl, H. M., & Nysaeter, T. E. (2005). Schema therapy for patients with borderline personality disorder: A single case series. *Journal of Behavior Therapy and Experimental Psychiatry. Special Issue: Cognition and emotion in borderline personality disorder, 36*(3), 254–264.

Parks, C. W., Jr., & Hollon, S. D. (1988). Cognitive assessment. In A. S. Bellack & M. Hersen (Eds.), *Behavioral assessment: A practical handbook* (3rd ed.) (pp. 161–212). Elmsford, NY: Pergamon Press.

Persons, J. (1989). *Cognitive therapy in practice: A case formulation approach.* New York: W.W. Norton.

Renneberg, B., Schmidt-Rathjens, C., Hippin, R., Backenstrass, M., & Fydrich, T. (2005). Cognitive characteristics of patients with borderline personality disorder. *Journal of Behavior Therapy and*

Experimental Psychiatry: Special Issue: Cognition and Emotion in Borderline Personality Disorder, 36(3), 173–182.

Resick, P. A., & Schnicke, M. K. (1993). *Cognitive processing therapy for rape victims: A treatment manual.* London: Sage.

Riso, L. P., du Toit, P. L., Stein, D. J., & Young, J. E. (2007). *Cognitive schemas and core beliefs in psychological problems: A scientist-practitioner guide.* Washington, DC: American Psychological Association.

Rosen, H. (2000). The creative evolution of the theoretical foundation for cognitive therapy. *Journal of Cognitive Psychotherapy: An International Quarterly, 14*(2), 123–134.

Schmidt, N. B., Joiner, T. E., Jr., Young, J. E., & Telch, M. J. (1995). The Schema Questionnaire: Investigation of psychometric properties and the hierarchical structure of a measure of maladaptive schemas. *Cognitive Therapy and Research, 19*(3), 295–321.

Spinhoven, P., Bockting, C. L. H., Kremers, I. P., Schene, A. H., & Williams, J. M. G. (2007). The endorsement of dysfunctional attitudes is associated with an impaired retrieval of specific autobiographical memories in response to matching cues. *Memory, 15*(3), 324–338.

Spinhoven, P., Giesen-Bloo, J., van Dyck, R., Kooiman, K., & Arntz, A. (2007). The therapeutic alliance in schema focused therapy and transference-focused psychotherapy for borderline personality disorder. *Journal of Consulting and Clinical Psychology, 75*(1), 104–115.

Tang, T. Z., Beberman, R., DeRubeis, R. J., & Pham, T. (2005). Cognitive changes, critical sessions, and sudden gains in cognitive-behavioral therapy for depression. *Journal of Consulting and Clinical Psychology, 73*(1), 168–172.

Tang, T. Z., & DeRubeis, R. J. (1999). Sudden gains and critical sessions in cognitive–behavioral therapy for depression. *Journal of Consulting and Clinical Psychology, 67*(6), 894–904.

Tarrier, N. (2006). *Case formulation in cognitive–behavioral therapy: The treatment of challenging and complex cases.* New York: Routledge/Taylor & Francis.

Weertman, A., & Arntz, A. (2007). Effectiveness of treatment of childhood memories in cognitive therapy for personality disorders: A controlled study contrasting methods focusing. *Behaviour Research & Therapy, 45*(9), 2133–2143.

Weissman, A. N., & Beck, A. T. (1978). Development and validation of the Dysfunctional Attitudes Scale: A preliminary investigation. Paper presented at the Annual Meeting of the American Educational Research Association, Toronto, Canada.

Williams, J. M. G., & Broadbent, K. (1986). Autobiographical memory in suicide attempters. *Journal of Abnormal Psychology, 95*(2), 144–149.

Young, J. E., Klosko, J. S., & Weishaar, M. E. (2003). *Schema therapy: A practitioner's guide.* New York: Guilford.

62 SELF-MANAGEMENT

Lynn P. Rehm and Jennifer H. Adams

HOW DOES IT WORK?

The self-control model of depression (Rehm, 1977) was developed to integrate both cognitive and behavioral models of depression, provide a model to serve as a framework for depression research, and to serve as a structure for a therapy program that targets specific behavioral and cognitive deficits present in many individuals with depression (Rehm, 1985).

Kanfer's self-control model states that behavior directed toward long-term outcomes can be characterized as a three-stage feedback loop. When people want to change their behavior for a long-term outcome, they begin by self-monitoring the behavior; they compare this observed behavior to a standard in self-evaluation; and, based on the evaluation, they may reward or punish themselves in the self-reinforcement phase. The model assumes that people influence their own behavior as they might influence another person's behavior by applying contingent rewards or punishments.

Rehm's (1977) depression model suggests that people who are depressed or who are prone to depression have difficulty organizing their behavior around long-term goals, and that this difficulty can be described in terms of one or more of six deficits in self-control skills. These deficits include (1) selective attention to negative rather than positive information; (2) selective attention to immediate consequences of behaviors, as opposed to long-term consequences; (3) unrealistically high performance standards; (4) the use of a depressogenic attributional style—that is, the tendency to attribute failures to internal influences and successes to external influences or chance (see Chapter 9, "Attribution Change," in this volume); (5) the use of excessive self-punishment; and (6) the use of inadequate contingent self-reward to strengthen behavior toward long-term goals. When external reinforcements are absent, are lost, or are insufficient to maintain effortful behavior toward a goal, people with good self-control skills can manage their behavior to regain progress toward the same or a new goal. People who are prone to depression are at the mercy of external rewards and punishments and have difficulty maintaining behavior in their absence.

Self-management therapy (SMT) is a structured, manualized, cognitive-behavioral, group-format program for the treatment of depression that targets each of the skill deficits just identified. The program can be thought of in three ways. First, it is a program that systematically targets self-control components of depression and intervenes in each. Second, it is a program that teaches basic self-control skills in the context of depression. Third, in teaching self-control skills, the program can be thought of as teaching positive *self-esteem*. Self-esteem can be conceptualized not as a trait, but as a set of skills that people use to work toward goals.

Developed in a group therapy format, SMT has been successfully utilized with individuals as well. The group format, however, may impart additional benefits to the participants that are not available as part of the individual therapy experience. For example, the sharing of personal issues and concerns enables the participants to see that they are not alone in their experiences. Furthermore, the group members often provide support for one another, provide coping models, and challenge one another to meet their therapy-related goals (Rehm, 1985).

Self-management therapy, as it is currently implemented, is a 14-week program that meets for 1-1/2 hours each week. Twelve topic areas are discussed across the 14 weeks, with two additional weeks built in to allow for further review of topics as determined by the needs of the group members. Each session includes core elements, including a psychoeducational presentation, a discussion of the issues involved, written exercises, and weekly homework assignments. After the first session, each session begins with a review of the previous week's homework. The material and exercises are meant to target both the general deficits exhibited by many people with symptoms of depression, and the more specific concerns of the individual clients (Rehm, 1985).

EVIDENCE FOR THE EFFECTIVENESS OF SELF-MANAGEMENT THERAPY

Results of therapy outcome studies indicate that SMT is superior in reducing the severity, frequency, and duration of complaints common in those who meet the criteria for depression as compared to nonspecific therapies and to no-treatment and wait-list control conditions, and is equal to or superior to other forms of cognitive behavioral therapy for depression (see Rehm, 1990, for a review). SMT has been investigated in a number of studies with adult outpatients by Rehm and his colleagues (Fuchs & Rehm, 1977; Kornblith, Rehm, O'Hara, & Lamparski, 1983; Rehm, Fuchs, Roth, Kornblith, & Romano, 1979; Rehm, Kaslow, & Rabin, 1987; Rehm et al., 1981) and by other psychotherapy researchers (Fleming & Thornton, 1980; Roth, Bielski, Jones, Parker, & Osborn, 1982; Rude, 1986; Thomas, Petry, & Goldman, 1987; Tressler & Tucker, 1980). The SMT program has been adapted for a variety of age ranges and populations, including renal dialysis patients (Rogers, Kerns, Rehm, Hendler, & Harkness, 1982), veterans with comorbid Post-Traumatic Stress Disorder (PTSD; Dunn, et al., 2007); psychiatric inpatients (Kornblith & Greenwald, 1982), psychiatric day-treatment patients (van den Hout, Arntz, & Kunkels, 1995), battered women (Bailey, Rehm, Martin, Holton, & Le, 1994), rural women with disabilities (Robinson-Whelen, et.al., 2007) and both the elderly (Rokke, Tomhave, & Jocic, 1999, 2000) and children (Rehm & Sharp, 1996; Reynolds & Coats, 1986; Stark, Reynolds, & Kaslow, 1987).

INDICATIONS AND CONTRAINDICATIONS

SMT has been successfully employed with a wide variety of depressed patients. Participants must have a degree of motivation to complete a program that lasts 3 to 4 months and that includes homework. Dropouts are more common among people who seek treatment during an acute crisis. The program has been run with individuals having mild to severe levels of depression. Very severe depression may make it difficult for people to sustain the effort necessary for participation. Doing homework requires literacy, although we have had illiterate prisoners in the program who have kept self-monitoring logs as simple marks.

TOPIC-BY-TOPIC PROCEDURES

The following is an overview of the program. Interested therapists are encouraged to contact the first author to request a copy of the comprehensive therapist manual, which includes a step-by-step guide to each session, participant handouts, and visual aids (Rehm, 2001).

Topic I: Introduction, Depression, and Overall Rationale

At the start of the first session, the group leader reviews the parameters of group therapy and issues of confidentiality. Participants are given a binder in which they keep weekly handouts, in-session exercises, homework assignments, and the homework itself. By the end of the program they have assembled a set of materials that they may consult later to continue or to redo the program on their own.

Early in the first session, participants are asked to introduce themselves and say a few words about why they are seeking help and about their lives. The therapist guides this process by pointing out similarities among participants' concerns and encouraging discussion among participants. After these introductions, the therapist transitions into a presentation on the nature of depression. The therapist reviews the symptoms of depression in the categories of emotional, physical, cognitive, and behavioral symptoms. The therapist discusses the various forms and courses of depression.

The therapist then presents an overview and rationale for the therapy, emphasizing the psychoeducational nature of the group and the role of homework in the therapy process. The first homework assignment is to ask participants to monitor their moods daily, using a simple rating scale of 1 to 10 in which 1 represents the person's most depressed day ever and 10 represents his or her best day ever. It is stressed that the homework assignments are integral to the program, and will be reviewed each week.

Topic II: Self-Monitoring Positive Activities and Self-Statements

The first part of each session from this point on is devoted to reviewing the content of the previous session and the homework. Participants are encouraged to talk about any difficulties they may have had doing the assignment, and whether they noticed any pattern to their moods over the previous week. Participants are often surprised at the variability they see in their moods from one day to the next, which contrasts with their belief that every day is the same. The primary focus of this session is to present the idea that mood is influenced by behavior and thinking. Engaging in positive and rewarding activities is linked to positive mood and engaging in negative and punishing behavior is linked to negative mood. Thoughts that represent positive interpretations and evaluations of events lead to positive mood, whereas thoughts that involve pessimistic interpretations of events lead to negative mood. The concept that follows from this is that individuals can influence their own mood by their activities and by the thoughts they have about those activities. Mood cannot be influenced directly, but is influenced indirectly through changing behavior and thoughts. Mood can also be influenced biologically, as with antidepressant medications, but depression is not simply a biological process, despite much media attention to brain chemistry. It is important to acknowledge that the relationship is reciprocal. Mood also influences activity and thinking, in that being depressed leads to inactivity and negative thoughts. Attention plays

a role in the development and maintenance of depression, in that persons who are depressed tend to selectively attend to negative events to the relative exclusion of positive events. The result is predominantly negative thoughts. The homework assignment that follows from these ideas it to record positive behaviors and thoughts (i.e., thought statements that have positive content relative to oneself) in the daily self-monitoring log, along with the day's mood. The therapist emphasizes the importance of recording all positive events and self-statements, even those that might seem trivial to the participant. Participants are given a list of potential positive activities and thoughts as a list of prompts to be reviewed if they are not noticing positive events each day.

Topic III: Mood and Events

At the following session the relationship between mood, on the one hand, and activities and thoughts, on the other, is reviewed along with the homework. Participants are asked whether there seemed to be a relationship between mood and activity; which activities most influenced mood; and whether they recorded any positive thoughts. The central activity of the session is an exercise in which participants graph their moods for the week and then, on the same graph, enter the number of positive activities and thoughts they had each day. In most cases the graphed lines are roughly parallel with common peaks and valleys. The graph demonstrates from the participants' own logs the relationship between events and daily mood. This is often very persuasive in convincing participants that they can get a handle on their moods by changing behavior and thoughts. For homework, participants continue to monitor their positive activities, positive thoughts, and moods.

Topic IV: Immediate versus Delayed Consequences

After completing the check-in procedures the therapist builds upon the ideas from the previous week by suggesting that all activities can have both positive and negative consequences, both immediately and after a delay. Working out may lead to feeling good, but also to stiffness.

It may be uncomfortable immediately in the short term, but will lead to better health as a delayed, long-term outcome. Paper-and-pencil exercises are used to illustrate these ideas and to have participants practice identifying positive and negative, short- and long-term consequences of personal decisions, and the positive and negative thoughts that might be derived from each. When people are depressed they tend to focus on immediate consequences of their behavior and have difficulty thinking about the longer-term consequences. When a person is depressed it is particularly difficult to do things that have a long-term positive consequence, but are immediately boring or difficult. Homework for this session is to continue the self-monitoring assignment, and to identify and record at least one activity each day that represents engaging in a behavior that is difficult in the short term but has a high payoff in the long term. When such activities occur, each participant is also to record a positive thought reflecting the long-term consequence (e.g., "I will have a good result on my next cholesterol test because I am exercising").

Topic V: Attributions for Positive Events

After completing check-in procedures, the therapist presents the idea of a depressogenic attributional style. In this session the focus is on attributions for positive events. Depressed people tend to make attributions for positive events that are external, stable, and specific, rather than internal, stable, and specific. Essentially, depressed people tend not to take credit for personal successes and positive experiences and instead see them as caused by external, unreliable, and specific factors. Taking credit for a positive experience occurs when it is attributed to internal causes that represent stable, general characteristics of the person. These ideas are illustrated by a sequence of examples presented by the therapist. The homework assignment is to continue to monitor positive events and mood, and to attempt to write at least one positive self-statement about a positive event that reflects an internal, stable, and specific attribution on a daily basis.

Topic VI: Causes of Negative Events or Failures

The primary goal of this session is to discuss depressogenic attributions made for negative events. People who are depressed tend to make internal, stable, and general attributions about negative events. The therapist's presentation is parallel to that for the previous topic. Examples are used to elicit depressed attributions for negative events and then to generate alternative explanations for the negative-event examples that are more external, unstable, and specific in nature. It is important to point out that attributions of causality are not entirely arbitrary, and that sometimes people do cause negative events. However, most events can be thought of as having multiple causes, and there are usually external causes for negative events as well. We are not encouraging people to take credit for everything positive that happens to them, nor to deny responsibility for any negative event. Instead, we are encouraging a more balanced and realistic view to replace the typically pessimistic view of most depressed people. For homework, participants are to continue monitoring positive events and mood, and to record at least one positive (external, unstable, and specific) self-statement about a negative event each day (e.g., "My friend didn't call today because she was too busy at work. I am sure that she will call me tomorrow").

Topic VII: Goal Setting

The presentation in this session is based upon the idea that difficulty in goal-setting and attainment is another facet of the development and maintenance of depression. Goals organize behavior, and lack of goal setting, or setting goals that are vague or unrealistic, is often characteristic of people who are depressed. Depressed persons often feel hopeless about achieving goals and focus on their distance from the goal rather than on steps that can be taken toward a goal. A goal-setting exercise in this session teaches basic behavioral ideas about goal setting. Goals should be stated positively (e.g., "I want to increase ... "); they should be within the person's control and be realistically attainable; and, they should be concrete (it should be clear when the goal has been reached). Goals may be of short range (e.g., "Get groceries today"), medium range (e.g., "Complete my last semester in college"), or long range (e.g., "Save to buy sailboat"). Participants are asked to define a medium-range goal that they would like to work on over the next few weeks. Once the goal is defined, the participant writes sub-goals or specific behaviors that contribute to reaching the overall goal. For homework, each participant continues to monitor events and mood, and makes an effort to accomplish sub-goals that are then recorded as positive events. The idea is to practice working toward delayed consequences and paying attention to progress toward the goal. Participants may also redefine their goals or develop a second goal to work on.

Topic VIII: Rewards for Motivation

Goal setting is a central part of the program and discussion of progress and obstacles make up the beginning of subsequent sessions. After this discussion, the therapist talks about how rewards and punishments influence behavior and how people may administer rewards and punishments to themselves (e.g., "patting yourself on the back" or "kicking yourself"). The way we talk to ourselves can function as self-administered reward or punishment. Part of depression is little use of contingent self-administered reward to facilitate progress toward goals, and excessive use of self-punishment that inhibits progress toward goals. The goal of this session is to assist participants in creating a self-reward menu in order to enhance their ability to self-reward when engaging in positive behaviors. In this session the focus is on overt or tangible rewards. Participants are helped to develop a list that includes rewards that are (1) enjoyable, (2) of various magnitudes, and (3) freely available. Rewards may be either material in nature (e.g., a new book) or activities that are pleasant (e.g., going to a movie). For homework, in addition to monitoring behaviors and moods, participants are instructed to utilize their rewards contingently as motivators for engaging in behaviors related to their more difficult sub-goals. Self-rewards are also positive activities to be recorded on the self-monitoring logs.

Topic IX: Rewards as Self-Statements

The goal of this session is to build upon the concepts of the previous week, and to introduce the idea of positive self-statements as rewards. Participants identify verbal self-rewards that (1) focus on accomplishments, (2) serve to strengthen a desirable behavior, and (3) allow for the development of positive self-evaluation and self-esteem. Participants are to modify the types of phrases they might use to praise others so that they can be said to themselves (e.g., "I did a great job!"). Participants write at least five self-statements that could serve as motivators for goal-directed behavior. For homework, in addition to monitoring behaviors and mood, participants should utilize positive self-statements as rewards for sub-goal behaviors and note the use of these self-statements on their self-monitoring logs. The intent is to have the depressed participant practice acknowledging progress toward a goal with a clear, positive self-statement.

Topic X: Assets List

A negative self-image is a component of depression. A negative view of oneself derives from the habit of attending to the negative, making negative attributions for positive and negative events, not seeing progress toward goals, and thus talking to oneself in primarily negative ways. *Self-image* can be thought of as the accumulated set of self-statements that the person makes each day. Since the program has the participants focus on positive events, positive delayed outcomes, nondepressed attributions, progress toward goals, and, positive self-statements, participants may now be ready to acknowledge their positive characteristics or traits—that is, the accumulation of positive observations about themselves. With these ideas in mind, the exercise in this session is to develop an assets list. Participants are asked to identify and write down at least five positive general statements that they can make about themselves (e.g., "I am loyal to my friends," or "I am good at carpentry"). Depressed people often find this process difficult and qualify or discount their positive qualities. Participants may almost need to be given permission to say out loud that they do have some positive qualities. The homework assignment associated with this topic is to note positive activities that are instances of their general positive statements about themselves and to record these thoughts on the log. They are also to add to their assets lists as they observe other positive qualities in themselves.

Topic XI: Review and Continuation

The goal of the final sessions are to help group participants assimilate and implement the knowledge that they have gained over the course of the group in order to facilitate long-term gains in functioning. In our earlier research trials of this program, participant feedback indicated that they felt they learned a lot but then were sent out on their own to use the program. We now add several sessions of review at the end of the program. These extra sessions can also provide for more flexibility in earlier parts of the program—if the therapist wants to spend an extra session on a topic, one fewer review session can be used while keeping the program a fixed length. These review sessions begin with a review of homework and discussion of what each person is doing regarding his or her goals. It is helpful for group members to share with one another strategies that they found particularly helpful in completing the different homework exercises, or to encourage group members to ask for assistance from one another in developing strategies to deal with particularly problematic issues. The therapist reviews each participant's progress and provides feedback with a review of various topics covered in the program that might be relevant. During the final session, participants are encouraged to continue to utilize their self-management skills in order to maintain the progress made during the group and to monitor their behaviors, self-statements, and mood. Participants are given extra copies of the self-monitoring log and other worksheets so that they may continue to work on the exercises on their own.

Further Reading

Rehm, L. P.(1977). A self-control model of depression. *Behavior Therapy, 8, 787–804.*

Rehm, L. P. (1985). A self-management therapy program for depression. *International Journal of Mental Health,* 13(3/4), 34–53.

Rehm, L. P. (1990). Cognitive and behavioral theories. In B. B. Wolman & G. Stricker (Eds.), *Depressive Disorder: Facts, theories, and treatment methods* (pp. 64–91). New York: Wiley.

Rehm, L. P., Wagner, A., & Tyndall, C. (2001). Mood disorders. In P. B. Sutker & H. E. Adams (Eds.), *Comprehensive handbook of psychopathology* (3rd ed., pp. 277–308). New York: Plenum Press.

References

Bailey, S., Rehm, L. P., Martin, H., Holton, H., & Le, N. (1994, April). *Self-management therapy for battered, depressed women.* Poster presented at the annual meeting of the Southwestern Psychological Association, Tulsa, OK.

Barlow, J. (1986). *A group treatment for depression in the elderly.* Unpublished doctoral dissertation, University of Houston, Houston, TX.

Dunn, N. J., Rehm, L. P., Schillaci, J., Souchek, J., Mehta, P., Ashton, C. M., Yanasak, E., & Hamilton, J. D. (2007). A randomized trial of self-management and psychoeducational group therapies for comorbid chronic posttraumatic stress disorder and depressive disorder. *Journal of Traumatic Stress,* 20(3), 221–237.

Fleming, B. M., & Thornton, D. W. (1980). Coping skills as a component in the short-term treatment of depression. *Journal of Consulting and Clinical Psychology,* 48, 652–655.

Fuchs, C. Z., & Rehm, L. P. (1977). A self-control behavior therapy program for depression. *Journal of Consulting and Clinical Psychology,* 45, 206–215.

Kornblith, S. J., & Greenwald, D. (1982, November). *Self-control therapy with depressed inpatients.* Paper presented at the meeting of the Association for the Advancement of Behavior Therapy, Los Angeles, CA.

Kornblith, S. K., Rehm, L. P., O'Hara, M. W., & Lamparski, D. M. (1983). The contribution of self-reinforcement training and behavioral assignments to the efficacy of self-control therapy for depression. *Cognitive Therapy and Research,* 7, 499–527.

Rehm, L. P. (1977). A self-control model of depression. *Behavior Therapy,* 8, 787–804.

Rehm, L. P. (1985). A self-management therapy program for depression. *International Journal of Mental Health,* 13(3/4), 34–53.

Rehm, L. P. (1990). Cognitive and behavioral theories. In B. B. Wolman & G. Stricker (Eds.), *Depressive Disorder: Facts, theories, and treatment methods* (pp. 64–91). New York: Wiley.

Rehm, L. P., Fuchs, C. Z., Roth, D. M., Kornblith, S. J., & Romano, J. (1979). A comparison of self-control and social skills treatments of depression. *Behavior Therapy, 10*, 429- 442.

Rehm, L. P., Kaslow, N. J., & Rabin, A. S. (1987). Cognitive and behavioral targets in a self-control behavior therapy program for depression. *Journal of Consulting and Clinical Psychology, 55*, 60-67.

Rehm, L. P., Kornblith, S. J., O'Hara, M. W., Lamparski, D. M., Romano, J. M., & Volkin, J. I. (1981). An evaluation of major components in a self-control therapy program for depression. *Behavior Modification, 5*, 459-490.

Rehm, L. P., & Sharp, R. N. (1996). Strategies in the treatment of childhood depression. In M. Reinecke, F. M. Dattilio, & A. Freeman (Eds.), *Comprehensive casebook on cognitive behavior therapy with adolescents* (pp. 103–123). New York: Guilford Press.

Rehm, L. P., Wagner, A., & Tyndall, C. (2001). Mood disorders. In P. B. Sutker & H. E. Adams (Eds.), *Comprehensive handbook of psychopathology* (3rd ed., pp. 277–308). New York: Plenum Press.

Reynolds, W. M., & Coats, K. I. (1986). A comparison of cognitive-behavioral therapy and relaxation training for the treatment of depression in adolescents. *Journal of Consulting and Clinical Psychology. 54*(5), 653–60.

Robinson-Whelen, S., Hughes, R. B., Taylor, H. B., Hall, J. W., & Rehm, L. P. (2007). Depression self-management program for rural women with physical disabilities. *Rehabilitation Psychology, 52*, 254–262.

Rogers, P. A., Kerns, R., Rehm, L. P., Hendler, E. D., & Harkness, L. (1982, August). *Depression mitigation in hemo-dialysands: A function of self-control training*. Paper presented at the meeting of the American Psychological Association, Washington, DC.

Rokke, P. D., Tomhave, J. A., & Jocic, Z. (1999). The role of client choice and target selection in self-management therapy for depression in older adults. *Psychology of Aging, 14*(1), 155–169.

Rokke, P. D., Tomhave, J. A., & Jocic, Z. (2000). Self-management therapy and educational group therapy for depressed elders. Cognitive Therapy and Research, 24(1), 99–119.

Roth, D., Bielski, R., Jones, M., Parker, W., & Osborn, G. (1982). A comparison of self-control therapy and combined self-control therapy and antidepressant medication in the treatment of depression. *Behavior Therapy, 13*, 133–144.

Rude, S. S. (1986). Relative benefits of assertion or cognitive self-control treatment for depression as a function of proficiency in each domain. *Journal of Consulting and Clinical Psychology, 54*, 390–394.

Stark, K. D., Reynolds, W. M., & Kaslow, N. J. (1987). A comparison of the relative efficacy of self-control therapy and a behavioral problem-solving therapy for depression in children. *Journal of Abnormal Child Psychology, 15*(1), 91–113.

Thomas, J. R., Petry, R. A., & Goldman, J. (1987). Comparison of cognitive and behavioral self-control treatments of depression. *Psychological Reports, 60*, 975–982.

Tressler, D. P., & Tucker, R. D. (1980, November). *The comparative effects of self-evaluation and self-reinforcement training in the treatment of depression*. Paper presented at the annual meeting of the Association for the Advancement of Behavior Therapy, New York, NY.

van den Hout, J. H., Arntz, A., & Kunkels, F. H. (1995). Efficacy of a self-control therapy program in a psychiatric day-treatment center. *Acta Psychiatrika Scandinavia, 92*(1), 25–9.

63 SAFETY TRAINING/VIOLENCE PREVENTION USING THE SAFECARE PARENT TRAINING MODEL

Daniel J. Whitaker, Dan Crimmins, Anna Edwards, and John R. Lutzker

OVERVIEW

Violence is omnipresent in American life. It is regularly featured on the news and in popular media such as movies, television, music, and video games. Though there are various forms of violence including violence between intimate partners, gang violence, and self-directed violence, one particularly impactful and onerous forms of violence is child maltreatment. Child maltreatment encompasses several forms of violence including physical abuse, sexual abuse, and several forms of neglect including physical, educational, and emotional. The impacts of child maltreatment include a variety of negative emotional, cognitive, and behavioral consequences (Putnam, 2003) and may also involve long-term health consequences as well (Felitti et al., 1998). Experiencing child maltreatment has also been linked to later perpetration or victimization of various forms of violence, including crime and violent offenses (Widom, 1989), partner violence (White & Widom, 2003), sex offending (Salter et al., 2003), and self-directed violence (Fergusson, Woodward, & Horwood, 2000). Addressing child maltreatment as form of violence may have broad implications for addressing a range of violence types.

WHO MIGHT BENEFIT FROM SAFECARE?

The SafeCare® program is a structured behavioral training protocol for parents with the goal of reducing and/or preventing both physical abuse and neglect of children. Research has identified a number of characteristics that place parents at increased risk for child maltreatment including poverty, stress, marital discord, low social support, and cognitive deficits such as poor problem-solving skills and knowledge deficits about parenting (Black, Heyman, & Smith Slep, 2001; Schumacher, Slep, & Heyman, 2001). Conversely, there are a number of factors associated with lower rates of child maltreatment including parental employment, adequate housing, access to health care and social services, supportive communities, supportive and stable family relationships, and parental skills in setting household rules and monitoring children. SafeCare is one of several evidence-based programs that specifically seek to reduce risk factors and promote protective factors related to child maltreatment.

The SafeCare program has been utilized in a range of settings and with a range of types of families including: families involved in the child protective service systems with substantiated cases of abuse or neglect; families at risk for abuse/neglect, but not yet substantiated; families whose children are on the autism spectrum; families whose children have developmental disabilities.

CONTRAINDICATIONS FOR SAFECARE

The SafeCare model was developed for parents with substantiated or suspected cases physical abuse and/or neglect. SafeCare should not be used for all forms of maltreatment, in particular sexual abuse with a perpetrating parent. One of the goals of the SafeCare program is to strengthen the bonds between parent and child. In cases of sexual abuse by a parent or caregiver, the goal may be to weaken the bonds between the caregiver and child. SafeCare was also developed and intended for parents of children between birth and age 5 (or at most age 7). The safety and parent training protocols, for example, are geared toward the need of younger children and are not optimal for parents with older children. SafeCare is also a very structured protocol, and is used in child welfare service systems. Implementing SafeCare in a service system is not a simple matter. Training of service providers alone is not sufficient. Fixsen and colleagues (Fixsen, Naoom, Blasé, Friedman, & Wallace, 2005) describe the stages of implementation of evidenced-based programs and the core components needed to ensure that a model is implemented properly. Simple training of service system providers is unlikely to result in sustained implementation of the SafeCare model. Without pretraining buy-in, ongoing coaching, and systemic support for Safe-Care, implementation is likely to be at incomplete and possibly ineffective.

HOW DOES SAFECARE WORK?

SafeCare is a behaviorally based parent training program with three modules addressing three aspects of parenting behavior: safety, health, and parent–child interaction (Lutzker & Bigelow, 2002). SafeCare also provides parents with broad problem solving skills that can be used in a variety of situations. The modules grew out of an ecobehavioral approach to child maltreatment prevention that used behavioral principles to address the social ecologies of abusive families (Lutzker, Frame, & Rice, 1982). Principles such as behavioral rehearsal, demonstration of mastery criteria via observation, demonstration of skills across settings, and the collection of data to examine behavioral implementation of skills as well as generalization are a crucial part of the SafeCare model. The goals of the SafeCare modules are to teach skills that can be generalized to a variety of settings. Each module uses the same structured teaching format: explaining the rationale for the targeted behavior, a demon-

stration of skills by the counselor, termed a *home visitor* as SafeCare is generally conducted in the home, practicing of skills by the parent, observation and data collection of the parent behavior by the home visitor, feedback from the home visitor (positive and corrective), further demonstration by the parent, and finally, demonstration of skills to mastery criteria. SafeCare is virtually always conducted in family homes in order to promote generalization of skills to real-world settings. All SafeCare modules begin with an assessment phase. This is to help the home visitor better understand the problem situations for parent-child interaction training, the problem areas for safety training, and the parents' current knowledge regarding health information. Also, consistent with behavioral principles, the collection of data via an assessment assists the home visitor and the parent in gauging progress.

The development and testing of the SafeCare program has been demonstrated in a large number of single-case studies as well as group-design studies. The three SafeCare modules have been shown in separate studies to result in change of their targeted behaviors (Bigelow & Lutzker, 2000; Cordon, Lutzker, Bigelow, & Doctor, 1998; Gershater-Molko, Lutzker, & Wesch, 2003; Tertinger, Greene, & Lutzker, 1984), as well as generalization of skills across time, settings, and behaviors (Huynen, Lutzker, Bigelow, Touchette, & Campbell, 1996). Two quasi-experimental group design studies have shown that families receiving SafeCare have less initial occurrences of child maltreatment or recidivism than families receiving other services (Gershater-Molko, Lutzker, & Wesch, 2002; Wesch & Lutzker, 1991).

STEP-BY-STEP PROCEDURES FOR SAFECARE

Each of the three SafeCare modules begins with an assessment and proceeds to behaviorally based parent training. Modules need not conducted in a specific order, with the order being determined in part by parental interest in one module's content versus another's. Each module is planned to include five 90-minute sessions, but can be completed in fewer sessions (if parents are relatively skilled in the topic and meet mastery criteria) or may take longer (if parents require additional training to meet mastery criteria).

Parent–Child Interactions

The module on improving parent-child interactions includes two separate protocols—one for infants and the second for toddlers and older children. The protocol for toddlers and older children is termed *planned activities training*.

- The assessment phase includes the home visitor and parent completing a checklist documenting daily activities, which assesses that level of difficulty parents have with their children in various situations. The assessment continues with observations of parents during two activities they rated as difficult times with their children, as well as observed play situations.
- Training begins with the home visitor describing the steps in planned activities training and providing a rationale to parents for those steps. The steps are:

  1. Prepare in advance for the activity.
  2. Explain the activity to the child.
  3. Explain the rules to the child.
  4. Explain the consequences for misbehavior.
  5. Give the child choices about aspects of the activity.
  6. Talk about what you are doing while doing the activity.
  7. Use good interaction skills.
  8. Ignore minor misbehavior.
  9. Give feedback to the child on his or her behavior.
  10. Provide rewards or consequences to the child.

- Training across the five session of the parent–child interactions module focuses initially on play sessions, and then on activities identified in the planned activities training checklist.
- Finally, parents must demonstrate mastery of the skills taught in parent–child interactions module, performing the correct steps 85% of the time on five successive trials for mastery.

Safety and Cleanliness

The broad goal of the safety and cleanliness module is to make the home environment safer for children. Using the training methods described above, the protocol involves looking through the house to identify and modify areas that are unsafe, hazardous, or unclean. Several types of hazards are identified including poisons, firearms, sharp objects, choking hazards, and others.

Climbing and reach hazards are assessed based on the height of the tallest child in the home. Cleanliness is defined by areas that are unclean or unnecessarily cluttered with out-of-place objects. Sessions within the safety module follow the same describe–model–practice–feedback procedure as described earlier, and the specifics are as follows:

- The assessment phase begins with the completion of the Home Accident Prevention Inventory–Revised (HAPI-R). This scale involves counting the number of accessible hazards, and rating the extent of filth and clutter. These counts are later used to gauge progress in reducing hazards and filth in the home. The HAPI-R contains explicit guidelines for what is considered a hazard, an unclean area, and a cluttered area.
- Training begins in the room that is judged to have the greatest number of hazards and filth. The home visitor describes the training procedures to the client and provides a rationale and guidelines for addressing hazards, filth, and clutter. The parent and home visitor work together to address these concerns in one particular room or area. For subsequent sessions, parents are asked to maintain the

room in a safe and clean manner and then additional rooms are addressed. Responsibility for identifying safety and cleanliness concerns is gradually shifted to the parent. The home visitor and parent rate each room using the HAPI-R and parents are given feedback on the change in safety hazards.

Health

The goals of the health module are to teach parents critical skills in terms of recognizing when children are ill or injured, making decisions about where and when to seek treatment, and communicating with health care providers. Parents are taught to recognize common symptoms of childhood illnesses; they are also taught to consult health reference materials to gather more information. Parents are then taught decision rules for when to go to the emergency room, when to call a physician, and when to treat children's illnesses or injuries at home. Finally, parents are taught how to care for sick children at home and how to keep health records. As with all SafeCare modules, the describe–model–practice–feedback procedure is followed in the health module.

- The health assessment begins with three role play scenarios in which the symptoms are described and the parent must judge whether to treat at home, call the physician, or take the child to the emergency room. The home visitor scores the parents responses using a structured checklist.
- Training sessions consist of a series of role plays prompted by health scenarios. The home visitor uses validated scenarios to train the parent to assess the situation (e.g., properly take temperature), decide on the proper action (treat at home, call physician, or go to the emergency room), and perform that action.
- Parents are taught to use a health recording chart to record the child's symptoms and treatments. Parents are also given a health manual as a reference.

IMPLEMENTATION OF SAFECARE

SafeCare was designed to be implemented in the community by community-based providers. As such training and implementation of SafeCare requires attention ensure that providers are trained to a mastery criteria and implement SafeCare as intended, that is, with fidelity. As noted, SafeCare has been successfully implemented with community providers (Gershater-Molko et al., 2002). Training of providers to implement SafeCare, conducted by certified SafeCare Trainer, employs the same describe–model–practice–feedback sequence described above. Trainees are shown the SafeCare skills in each module, allowed to practice, given positive and corrective feedback by the trainer, and must demonstrate mastery of skills to a specified criterion. Perhaps more importantly, providers implementation of SafeCare is monitored closely initially (by certified SafeCare coaches), and implementation of SafeCare requires an ongoing commitment to maintaining model fidelity through observation and feedback of provider behavior. Thus, SafeCare attempts to follow the best practices in implementation research (Fixsen et al., 2005) to ensure an impact on the reduction of child maltreatment.

References

Bigelow, K. M., & Lutzker, J. R. (2000). Training parents reported for or at risk for child abuse and neglect to identify and treat their children's illnesses. *Journal of Family Violence, 15*(4), 311–330.

Black, D. A., Heyman, R. E., & Smith Slep, A. M. (2001). Risk factors for child physical abuse. *Aggression and Violent Behavior, 6*(2–3), 121–188.

Cordon, I. M., Lutzker, J. R., Bigelow, K. M., & Doctor, R. M. (1998). Evaluating Spanish protocols for teaching bonding, home safety, and health care skills to a mother reported for child abuse. *Journal of Behavior Therapy and Experimental Psychiatry, 29*(1), 41–54.

Felitti, V. J., Anda, R. F., Nordenberg, D., Williamson, D. F., Spitz, A. M., Edwards, V., et al. (1998). Relationship of childhood abuse and household dysfunction to many of the leading causes of death in adults: The Adverse Childhood Experiences (ACE) Study. *American Journal of Preventive Medicine, 14*(4), 245–258.

Fergusson, D. M., Woodward, L. J., & Horwood, L. J. (2000). Risk factors and life processes associated with the onset of suicidal behaviour during adolescence and early adulthood. *Psychological Medicine, 30*(1), 23–39.

Fixsen, D. L., Naoom, S. F., Blasé, K. A., Friedman, R. M., & Wallace, F. (2005). *Implementation research: A synthesis of the literature.* Tampa: University of South Florida, Louis de la Parte Florida Mental Health Institute, the National Implementation Research Network.

Gershater-Molko, R. M., Lutzker, J. R., & Wesch, D. (2002). Using recidivism to evaluate Project Safe-Care: Teaching bonding, safety, and health care skills to parents. *Child Maltreatment, 7*(3), 277.

Gershater-Molko, R. M., Lutzker, J. R., & Wesch, D. (2003). Project SafeCare: Improving health, safety, and parenting skills in families reported for, and at-risk for child maltreatment. *Journal of Family Violence, 18*(6), 377–386.

Huynen, K. B., Lutzker, J. R., Bigelow, K. M., Touchette, P. E., & Campbell, R. V. (1996). Planned activities training for mothers of children with developmental disabilities: Community generalization and follow-up. *Behavior Modification, 20*(4), 406.

Lutzker, J. R., & Bigelow, K. M. (2002). *Reducing child maltreatment: A guidebook for parent services.* New York: Guilford.

Lutzker, J. R., Frame, R. E., & Rice, J. M. (1982). Project 12-ways: An ecobehavioral approach to the treatment and prevention of child abuse and neglect. *Education and Treatment of Children, 5,* 141–155.

Putnam, F. W. (2003). Ten-year research update review: Child sexual abuse. *Journal of the American Academy of Child and Adolescent Psychiatry, 42*(3), 269–278.

Salter, D., McMillan, D., Richards, M., Talbot, T., Hodges, J., Bentovim, A., et al. (2003). Development of sexually abusive behaviour in sexually victimised males: A longitudinal study. *The Lancet, 361* (9356), 471–476.

Schumacher, J. A., Slep, A. M. S., & Heyman, R. E. (2001). Risk factors for child neglect. *Aggression and Violent Behavior, 6*(2–3), 231–254.

Tertinger, D. A., Greene, B. F., & Lutzker, J. R. (1984). Home safety: Development and validation of one component of an ecobehavioral treatment program for abused and neglected children. *Journal of Applied Behavior Analysis, 17*(2), 159–174.

Wesch, D., & Lutzker, J. R. (1991). A comprehensive 5-year evaluation of project 12-ways: An ecobehavioral program for treating and preventing child abuse and neglect. *Journal of Family Violence, 6*(1), 17–35.

White, H. R., & Widom, C. S. (2003). Intimate partner violence among abused and neglected children in young adulthood: The mediating effects of early aggression, antisocial personality, hostility and alcohol problems. *Aggressive Behavior, 29*(4), 332–345.

Widom, C. S. (1989). Child abuse, neglect, and adult behavior: Research design and findings on criminality, violence, and child abuse. *American Journal of Orthopsychiatry, 59*(3), 355–367.

SELF-MONITORING
AS A TREATMENT VEHICLE

Kathryn L. Humphreys, Brian P. Marx,
and Jennifer M. Lexington

Self-monitoring, with its origins in behavioral assessment, is used by clients to maintain a record of identified problem behaviors. In this technique, clients are instructed to keep a log of the frequency and severity of a problem behavior and the situational circumstances in which that behavior occurs. Such information may inform clinicians about the antecedents and consequences of a client's noted problem behaviors as well as the extent to which behavior changes during treatment. Although self-monitoring was originally used to help determine the exact nature of a client's problem and to track a client's progress within a prescribed treatment, observers of this practice began to note that clients' behaviors changed when engaging in self-monitoring, often shifting in the direction of the desired outcome. This observation led to the widespread use of self-monitoring as a treatment modality.

Evidence supporting the use of self-monitoring as a treatment strategy began to accumulate in the early 1970s. Despite a more recent decline in research on this topic (Korotitsch & Nelson-Gray, 1999), many clinicians continue to use self-monitoring as a treatment strategy. In fact, one study found that a majority of behavior therapists reported using self-monitoring with many of their clients as an intervention (Elliott, Miltenberger, Kaster-Bundgaard, & Lumley, 1996).

The act of self-observation has powerful effects on an individual's perception of their own behavior (e.g. clients frequently admit that they did not realize, prior to recording the frequency of a behavior, just how often they engaged in the behavior). Such detailed information regarding a behavior may help the client to recognize the sheer magnitude of the behavior, or how much of an effect it had on their daily activities prior to self-monitoring. Such feedback could serve as a "wake-up call" to the client, who may become intrinsically motivated to "correct" the problem.

Additionally, clients learn when and in what situations the identified behavior is likely to occur and can use this knowledge to help identify situations or aspects of situations to be more cognizant of or avoid altogether in the future. It may be that the act of monitoring one's own behavior helps clients to understand the control they have over their behaviors. This may be particularly salient to those who are instructed to self-monitor *before* an event occurs. Rozensky (1974) found that clients who were instructed to record their cigarette smoking before the event occurred ceased smoking altogether.

Self-monitoring may also work by providing either reinforcing or aversive contingencies for the behavior of concern. For example, a client attempting to decrease the frequency of a given behavior (e.g., eating) may become encouraged (or discouraged) by the frequency rates recorded during self-monitoring and view such decreases (or increases) in problem behavior as a measure of their success in therapy. Bornstein et al. (1986) elaborated on the benefits of using self-monitoring as an assessment and treatment tool. He pointed out that this practice implicitly calls attention to the client's ability to control the behavior, provides constant feedback to the client, and is a more complete record of behavior than most other methods.

McFall (1970) demonstrated that college students who monitored their desire to smoke decreased both the number of cigarettes consumed and the time spent smoking cigarettes. In a case study of a 25-year-old woman with obsessive thoughts surrounding breast and stomach cancer, Frederickson (1975) found that when the client simply monitored the frequency of her ruminative thoughts, they decreased rapidly from 13 to 2 per day. When asked to monitor her thoughts in a more detailed fashion (i.e., when the thoughts occurred, their specific content, etc.), the thoughts abated entirely, with no evidence of recurrence up to four months posttreatment. The use of self-monitoring was found to decrease suicidal ideation in a group of severely suicidal college students (Clum & Curtin, 1993). These studies, among others, suggest that self-monitoring may be a useful treatment technique for a variety of behavioral and psychological difficulties.

The success of self-monitoring as an intervention has encouraged clinicians to incorporate the procedure into other methods of treatment. For example, Beck, Rush, Shaw, and Emery (1979) and Lewinsohn, Anotonuccio, Steinmetz, and Teri (1984) incorporated self-monitoring techniques into their treatments for depression. Beck et al.'s multiple column technique encourages the client to report as much information as possible regarding increases in dysphoria. This included the date of the occurrence of depressive mood, a description of the situation associated with the occurrence, the client's emotional reaction to the situation, the thoughts that occurred between the situation and emotional reaction, and finally, a more adaptive positive interpretation of the situation.

WHO MIGHT BENEFIT FROM THIS TECHNIQUE?

In general, self-monitoring has wide applicability and is appropriate for both adults and children with a variety of psychopathology (see Table 64.1 for a noncomprehensive list of disorders in which self-monitoring has received empirical support as a treatment vehicle). Buxton, Williamson, Absher, and Warner (1985) used the procedure to graph caloric intake among individuals who overeat. Others have used the procedure to monitor daily intake of food and output of energy (in the form of exercise) in obese individuals (Coates & Thoresen, 1981; Gormally & Rardin, 1981), monitor nicotine content consumed in smokers (Abrams & Wilson, 1979; Shiffman, 1988), monitor drinking and blood alcohol levels in problem drinkers (Alden, 1988; Flegal, 1991; Sobell, Bogardis, Schuller, Leo, & Sobell, 1989), and monitor

TABLE 64.1 Common Problems in which the use of Self-Monitoring Is Empirically Supported

Academic/Conduct Problems	Addictive Behaviors	Anxiety and Depression	Disordered Eating	Physical Health Problems	Psychosis
Academic/on-task behavior (Green, 1982)	Alcohol use (Sobell & Sobell, 1973)	Ruminative thinking (Frederickson, 1975)	Weight loss/management (Germann et al., 2007)	Type II diabetes (Wing, Epstein, Norwalk, & Scott, 1988)	Hallucinations (Rutner & Bugle, 1969)
Academic performance in those with ADHD (Harris, Friedlander Saddler, Frizzelle, & Graham, 2005)	Cigarette smoking (McFall, 1970; Rozensky, 1974)	Depression (Beck et al., 1979)	Objective Bulimic Episodes (Hildebrandt & Latner, 2006)	Pain (Kerns, Finn, & Haythornthwaite, 1988)	Paranoid ideation (Williams, 1976)
	Amphetamine abuse (Hay, Hay, & Angle, 1977)	Suicidal ideation (Clum & Curtin, 1993)		Insomnia (Jason, 1975)	
		Internalizing disorders in children (Beidel et al., 1991)			
		Anxiety (Basoglu et al., 1992)			

academic behaviors in increasing academic performance and decreasing procrastination in individuals with low academic achievement (Green, 1982). Self-monitoring has also been used to examine and restructure maladaptive cognitions and monitor situations in which perceived level of anxiety increases (Basoglu, Marks, & Sengun, 1992; Hiebert & Fox, 1981; Rapee, Craske, & Barlow, 1990) and monitor emotional reactions to situational contexts among depressed individuals (Beck et al., 1979; Jarrett & Nelson, 1987).

Self-monitoring has been used successfully to address internalizing disorders in children (Beidel, Neil, & Lederer, 1991; Stark, Reynolds, & Kaslow, 1987). Also, recent studies on weight loss in obese children have found that those who consistently self-monitor lost more weight than those who were less consistent (Germann, Kirschenbaum, & Rich, 2007; Kirschenbaum, Gernmann, & Rich, 2005). These studies also emphasized the importance of parental involvement, as children of parents who self-monitored their own eating and exercise lost more weight than those whose parents did not.

VARIABLES RELATED TO THE EFFECTIVENESS OF SELF-MONITORING

Self-monitoring is a relatively time intensive task, one which requires a good deal of motivation on the part of the client. It may be less effective for individuals who either have chaotic schedules or who have been entered into treatment by someone other than themselves (e.g., court mandated therapy). Self-monitoring may not be indicated for all clients, especially those not willing or able to put in time or effort. However, for those who may have trouble with certain aspects of the intervention method, the therapist can adapt the self-monitoring task to better suit the individual, thereby increasing motivation as well as the likelihood of engaging in the task. For example, adapting the type of log that is required to a client's ability to self-monitor (e.g., for children, providing them with a structured log sheet which requires only that they mark off when certain events occur) and their particular problems/pathology (e.g., for obsessive clients, limiting the amount of time/detail that should be put into the task) may serve to address some of the client's difficulties with self-monitoring.

Instructing the client to call in or email with progress reports in-between sessions may also increase the effectiveness of treatment. In a study in which participants aimed to increase their number of workouts during a 12-week session, individuals who were instructed to call the researchers with their workout progress were significantly more likely to workout than those in the experimental condition who also self-monitored, but did not call to inform anyone of their progress (Shepich, Slowiak, & Keniston, 2007). Table 64.2 provides optimal conditions and examples for increasing the success of self-monitoring.

TABLE 64.2   Variables Affecting the Reactivity of Self-Monitoring

Variables Affecting Reactivity	Optimal Conditions for Enhanced Reactivity
Target behavior valence	Positively valenced behaviors increase in frequency while negatively valenced behaviors decrease in frequency.
Motivation	The client is highly motivated to change the target behavior.
Topography of target behavior	The target behavior is overt motoric.
Schedule of recording	Each occurrence of the target behavior is self-monitored.
Concurrent response requirements	A single target behavior is self-monitored.
Timing of recording	Recordings are made just before the occurrence of the target response.
Goal setting, feedback, and reinforcement	Goals for changes in the target behavior are clearly specified, and reinforcement contingent on behavior change is provided.
Nature of recording device	Some studies have indicated that an obtrusive recording device enhances reactivity.

Source: Reproduced, with permission, from Korotitsch & Nelson-Gray (1999).

FACTORS TO CONSIDER IN DECIDING WHETHER TO USE SELF-MONITORING

If a therapist questions whether the client will provide invalid responding, whether intentional or unintentional, he or she may reconsider the use of self-monitoring. Clients who have a history of deceit may be more likely to be dishonest in their self reports. Some clients may be prone to forget to self-monitor for period of time and spontaneously "fill in" the blanks from that time. A verbal commitment or behavioral contract may help to increase the completeness or truthfulness of self-monitoring reports. For clients who may be less motivated, clinicians might consider involving them extensively in the analysis of the information gleaned from behavior logs, with the hope of making the client feel as though he or she has an active role in therapy, thereby increasing motivation. Additionally, problems with self-monitoring might occur in cases where the targeted behavior is difficult to quantify. Even if the client makes an honest effort to record the behavior, they could fail to notice or misidentify some instances, for a variety of reasons (see Bornstein et al., 1986).

Self-monitoring may not be appropriate for clients who present with particular types of problems. For example, Hollon and Kendall (1981) noted that depressed clients may fail to engage in self-monitoring because they find the task overwhelming or may not believe that such strategies can provide any help. Hollon and Kendall also noted caution in using the procedure with anxious clients who might balk at examining distressing cognitions and emotions in depth. Clients may not want to know the extent of the problem, and may resist efforts to specifically examine and target a behavior they hope to avoid confronting.

Although reactivity, or a change in the behavior being monitored, is the goal of the intervention, there are some cases in which the problem behavior may worsen rather than improve as a result of self-monitoring. Korotisch and Nelson-Gray (1999) have suggested that the use of self-monitoring in individuals who aim to reduce obsessive thoughts could in fact cause the client to focus more on the obsessional thoughts than before self-monitoring began. Hollon and Kendall (1981) noted that clients who are monitoring negative affect may, in turn, increase the frequency and/or duration of the negative mood state. In such cases, it is recommended that the clinician examine what in particular about the monitoring process is inciting such reactions in the client and incorporate this information into treatment. For example, depressed clients may report that focusing on their dysphoric state increases hopelessness. More specifically, a depressed client might report that the act of writing about a present dysphoric state incurs memories of previous depressive episodes and extensive rumination over past misfortunes, which may all come together as a formidable reminder that, despite attempts to alleviate it, the depression will always return. In such situations, the clinician should use such information to adapt both self-monitoring and cognitive restructuring procedures (e.g., encouraging the client to focus on the present, record the present behavior and cognitions and avoid rumination over prior events).

STEP-BY-STEP PROCEDURES

There are six steps involved in self-monitoring (see Table 64.3): presentation of the rationale underlying self-monitoring, discrimination of the target response, recording the target response, charting/graphing the target response, displaying the data collected, and analyzing the data collected (Thoresen & Mahoney, 1974). The step-by-step list provided in the table is merely a guide for how to conduct a self-monitoring procedure with a client and should be altered to reflect the client's specific targeted problem and special needs.

Presentation of Rationale to Client

It is essential that the client understand the reasons behind using self-monitoring as a therapeutic device. The clinician should explain that self-monitoring is a tool that the client can use on his or her own, one which will provide information regarding target behaviors to both the clinician and the client. The client should be made aware that self-monitoring may require

TABLE 64.3   Steps of Self-Monitoring

Step 1. Presentation of Rationale to Client
- Why is self-monitoring a good choice for this client and how will it be beneficial?
- Is the client's motivation great enough to input the effort required?

Step 2. Discrimination of Target Response
- What behavior is the client most intent on changing?
- How is the behavior operationalized?
- Is the client capable of discrimination (guided practice required)?

Step 3. Recording the Target Response
- Does the client understand the concept of *systematic* recording?
- Will the recording precede or follow the behavior?
- What method will the client utilize in recording (diary, structured log sheet, wrist counter, etc.)?

Step 4. Charting/Graphing the Target Response
- Can the client chart their progress on a weekly basis?

Step 5. Displaying the Data Collected
- Can the client display their progress charts in a public area as both personal and environmental reinforcement?

Step 6. Analyzing the Data Collected
- How does the client's collected data compare with goals set prior to treatment?
- How does the client feel about the progress to date (encouragement is essential)?

significant effort and that extent of his or her involvement (i.e., how much they put into the monitoring) will likely determine how effective the treatment will be. The client should also be informed that observable change via self-monitoring is gradual and that he or she should not be discouraged if rapid change is not seen immediately.

Recording the Target Response

There are a number of things to consider in recording the target response. The most important point for the client to understand is the need for systematic recording. Instructions must be clearly delineated such that the client knows when, where, and how to record responses. For instance, in a treatment program for individuals suffering from bulimia, Agras and Apple (1997) instructed participants to record several aspects of bulimic episodes. This included the volume and type of food consumed, the time and place, anything that may have influenced the event, as well as the details about the purging episode.

As mentioned earlier, a decision should be made regarding whether the client should record an instance of behavior prior to engaging in the behavior (e.g., when the client has the urge to smoke or eat) or shortly after the behavior

has been completed. Typically, prebehavior recording should be implemented in cases where the client is attempting to decrease an undesired behavior (such as smoking or overeating), whereas postbehavior recording may be more beneficial in cases where a client is trying to increase a desired behavior (such as asserting oneself). Regardless of whether the recording is made before or after the behavior, self-monitoring is likely to be more effective when the recording occurs as temporally close to the behavior as possible. Delayed recording of behaviors has been shown to diminish the effectiveness of self-monitoring (Kanfer, 1980).

Another important decision in recording is the method the client will use, a factor largely determined by the nature of the target behavior and what elements about that behavior the client is hoping to change. If a client wants to monitor the frequency of a behavior that is typically of short duration, a wrist counter can be worn and the client can simply use the counter to record each instance of the behavior. If a client wants to monitor both the frequency and duration of a behavior, a stopwatch can be used in conjunction with a journal. Diaries are frequently employed in self-monitoring, particularly in situations where the target behavior is being monitored in great detail. In such cases, an individual can record all instances of the behavior in the diary, as well as any supplemental information, such as emotions and cognitions surrounding the target behavior. Daily log sheets can be employed in self-monitoring and are most useful if structured in a logical, systematic, easy to use fashion. Whatever method is decided upon, it is imperative that the client is comfortable with the system and that all questions are addressed prior to implementing the system in vivo. If therapists are unsure whether a client will have trouble with any aspect of the self-monitoring procedure, they should arrange for a training sessions in which clients can practice recording their targeted behavior.

There is some evidence that the more obtrusive the monitoring device, the more accurate the recording will be. Obtrusiveness can be defined in terms of size or the inability to ignore the device. Amato Zech, Hoff, and Doepke (2006) implemented the use of a vibrating electronic beeper called the MotivAider, in a study to increase on-task behavior among special education students. Use of this tool resulted in a mean increase of on-task behavior from 55% to more than 90%. Results of this study support the use of devices to provide cues to the client to self-monitor.

Charting/Graphing the Target Response

Once the client has collected data for a given time period, the information obtained regarding target behaviors can be translated into a chart or graph. A typical presentation is a line graph comparing aspects about the target behavior (e.g., frequency, duration) across days or weeks. For example, a client monitoring eating behavior could examine the number of calories they consumed every day over the course of a week, graphing the number of calories on the vertical axis and the day of the week on the horizontal axis. Similarly, the same client conceivably would also be monitoring the amount of time they spent exercising, graphing the duration of exercise on the vertical axis and the days of the week on the horizontal. Clients who are monitoring a number of behaviors are likely to be reinforced if all graphs yield consistent results, demonstrating behavior change in the desired

direction, yet not overly discouraged if some graphs demonstrate improvement, while others evidence a need to work on different areas. Displaying the client's graph in a public area is likely to serve a dual purpose. It can provide the client with a personal reminder of their hard work as well as serve as a reinforcer for behavior change. Additionally, displaying the chart in a public arena increases the possibility of reinforcement from others, such as a family member who may notice the improvement documented in the graph.

Analyzing the Data Collected

Feedback is an integral aspect of the self-monitoring technique. More specifically, self-monitoring is likely to be beneficial to the client both as a personal progress monitor and reinforcer; however, the clinician can aide in the proper interpretation of various aspects of the data. For example, clients who do not see immediate, monumental improvement may become rapidly discouraged. It is the clinician's job to explain that the process of change often takes a long period of time and that constant improvement at every session (depicted as a perfect linear graph with a steep slope) is rare. Rather, seemingly minor improvements early on can be viewed as monumental in their own right, while mistakes or relapses do not imply that treatment is doomed to failure. Clients should bring their data to weekly sessions with the clinician for analysis, feedback, and encouragement. The clinician should analyze and discuss the results with the client, comparing data collected to the goals agreed upon by both clinician and client prior to the initiation of treatment. Clients should also be encouraged to make such comparisons on their own outside the therapy sessions in order to further facilitate treatment.

Conclusions

There is empirical evidence supporting the use of self-monitoring as a treatment for a number of behavioral and psychological problems in both children and adults. Self-monitoring can be easy to use and tailored to a client's specific needs and abilities. The practice of self-monitoring may help individuals realize the control they have over their problem behaviors and to identify and be prepared for situations in which the behaviors most often arise. Although self-monitoring can be useful as an intervention, it is likely best paired with another form of treatment for more serious disorders. In these cases, the initial reactivity to self-monitoring may provide reinforcement for clients looking for signs of progress early in the treatment regimen. The self-monitoring logs can also continue to play a valuable role in assessing treatment progress over time.

Further Reading

Bornstein, P. H., Hamilton, S. B., & Bornstein, M. T. (1986). Self-monitoring procedures. In A. R. Ciminero, K. S. Calhoun, & H. E. Adams (Eds.), *Handbook of behavioral assessment* (2nd ed.). New York: John Wiley & Sons.

Cormier, W. H., & Cormier, L. S. (1991). Self-Management strategies: Self-Monitoring, stimulus control, and self-reward. In Cormier, W. H., & Cormier, L.S., *Interviewing strategies for helpers: Fundamental skills and behavioral interventions* (pp. 518–549). Pacific Grove, CA: Brooks/Cole.

Korotitsch, W., & Nelson-Gray, R. (1999). An overview of self-monitoring research in assessment and treatment. *Psychological Assessment, 11,* 415–425.

References

Abrams D. B., & Wilson, G. T. (1979). Self-monitoring and reactivity in the modification of cigarette smoking. *Journal of Consulting and Clinical Psychology, 47,* 243–251.

Agras, W. S., & Apple, R. F. (1997). *Overcoming eating disorders: Therapist guide.* New York: Graywind Publications.

Alden, L. E. (1988). Behavioral self-management controlled-drinking strategies in a context of secondary prevention. *Journal of Consulting and Clinical Psychology, 56,* 280–286.

Amato Zech, N., Hoff, K., & Doepke, K. (2006). Increasing on-task behavior in the classroom: Extension of self-monitoring strategies. *Psychology in the Schools, 43,* 211–221.

Basoglu, M., Marks, L., & Sengun, S. (1992). A prospective study of panic and anxiety in agoraphobia with panic disorder. *British Journal of Psychiatry, 160,* 57–64.

Beck, A. T., Rush, A. J, Shaw, B. F., & Emery, G. (1979). *Cognitive therapy of depression.* New York: Guilford.

Beidel, D. C., Neal, A. M., & Lederer, A. S. (1991). The feasibility and validity of a daily diary for the assessment of anxiety disorders in children. *Behavior Therapy, 22,* 505–517.

Bornstein, P. H., Hamilton, S. B., & Bornstein, M. T. (1986). Self-monitoring procedures. In A. R. Ciminero, K. S. Calhoun, & H. E. Adams (Eds.), *Handbook of behavioral assessment* (2nd ed.). New York: John Wiley & Sons.

Buxton, A., Williamson, D. A., Absher, N., & Warner, M. (1985). Self-management of nutrition. *Addictive Behaviors, 10,* 383–396.

Clum, G. A., & Curtin, L. (1993). Validity and reactivity of a system of self-monitoring suicide ideation. *Journal of Psychology and Behavioral Assessment, 15,* 375–385.

Coates, T. J., & Thoresen, C. E. (1981). Behavior and weight changes in three obese adolescents. *Behavior Therapy, 12,* 383–399.

Cormier, W. H., & Cormier, L. S. (1991). Self-management strategies: Self-monitoring, stimulus control, and self-reward. *Interviewing strategies for helpers: Fundamental skills and behavioral interventions* (pp. 518–549). Pacific Grove, CA: Brooks/Cole.

Elliot, A. J., Miltenberger, R. G., Kaster-Bundgaard, J., & Lumley, V. (1996). A national survey of assessment and therapy used by behavior therapists. *Cognitive and Behavioral Practice, 3,* 107–125.

Flegal, K. M. (1991). Agreement between two dietary methods in reported intake of beer, wine, and liquor. *Journal of Studies on Alcohol, 52,* 174–179.

Frederickson, L. W. (1975). Treatment of ruminative thinking by self-monitoring. *Journal of Behavior Therapy and Experimental Psychiatry, 6,* 258–259.

Germann, J., Kirschenbaum, D., & Rich, B. (2007). Child and parental self-monitoring as determinants of success in the treatment of morbid obesity in low-income minority children. *Journal of Pediatric Psychology, 32,* 111–121.

Gormally, J., & Rardin, D. (1981). Weight loss and maintenance and changes in diet and exercise for behavioral counseling and nutrition education. *Journal of Counseling Psychology, 28,* 295–304.

Green, L. (1982). Minority students' self-control of procrastination. *Journal of Counseling Psychology, 29,* 636–644.

Harris, K., Friedlander, B., Saddler, B., Frizzelle, R., & Graham, S. (2005). Self-monitoring of attention versus self-monitoring of academic performance: Effects among students with ADHD in the general education classroom. *The Journal of Special Education, 39,* 145–156.

Hay, L. R., Hay, W. M., & Angle, H. V. (1977). The reactivity of self-recording: A case report of a drug abuser. *Behavior Therapy, 8,* 1004–1007.

Hiebert, B., & Fox, E. E. (1981). Reactive effects of self-monitoring anxiety. *Journal of Counseling Psychology, 28,* 187–193.

Hildebrandt, T., & Latner, J. (2006). Effect of Self-Monitoring on Binge Eating: Treatment Response or "Binge Drift"? *European Eating Disorders Review, 14,* 17–22.

Hollon, S. D., & Kendall, P. C. (1981). In vivo assessment techniques for cognitive-behavioral processes. In P. C. Kendall & S. D. Hollon (Eds.), *Assessment strategies for cognitive–behavioral interventions* (pp. 319–362). New York: Academic Press.

Jarrett, R. B., & Nelson, R. O. (1987). Mechanisms of change in cognitive therapy of depression. *Behavior Therapy, 18,* 227–241.

Jason, L. (1975). Rapid improvement in insomnia following self-monitoring. *Journal of Behavior Therapy and Experimental Psychiatry, 6,* 349–350.

Kanfer, F. H. (1980). Self-management methods. In F. H. Kanfer & A. P. Goldstein (Eds.), *Helping people change* (2nd ed.) (pp. 334–389). New York: Pergamon Press.

Kerns, R. D., Finn, P., & Haythornthwaite, J. (1988). Self-monitored pain intensity: Psychometric properties and clinical utility. *Journal of Behavioral Medicine, 11,* 71–82.

Kirschenbaum, D., Germann, J., & Rich, B. (2005). Treatment of morbid obesity in low-income adolescents: Effects of parental self-monitoring. *Obesity Research, 13,* 1527–1529.

Korotitsch, W., & Nelson-Gray, R. (1999). An overview of self-monitoring research in assessment and treatment. *Psychological Assessment, 11,* 415–425.

Lewinsohn, P. M., Antonuccio, D. O., Steinmetz, J. L., & Teri, L. (1984). *The coping with depression course.* Eugene, OR: Castalia.

McFall, R. M. (1970). Effects of self-monitoring on normal smoking behavior. *Journal of Consulting and Clinical Psychology, 35,* 135–142.

Rapee, R. M., Craske, M. G., & Barlow, D. H. (1990). Subject described fears of panic attacks using a new self-monitoring form. *Journal of Anxiety Disorders, 4,* 171–181.

Rozensky, R. H. (1974). The effect of timing of self-monitoring behavior on reducing cigarette consumption. *Journal of Behavior Therapy and Experimental Psychiatry, 5,* 301–303.

Rutner, I. T., & Bugle, C. (1969). An experimental procedure for the modification of psychotic behavior. *Journal of Consulting and Clinical Psychology, 33,* 651–653.

Shepich, J., Slowiak, J., & Keniston, A. (2007). Do subsidization and monitoring enhance adherence to prescribed exercise? *American Journal of Health Promotion, 22,* 2–5.

Shiffman, S. (1988). Smoking behavior: Behavioral assessment. In D. M. Donovan & G. A. Marlatt (Eds.), *Assessment of addictive behaviors* (pp. 139–188). New York: Guilford.

Sobell, M. B., Bogardis, J., Schuller, R., Leo, G. I., & Sobell, L. C. (1989). Is self-monitoring of alcohol consumption reactive? *Behavioral Assessment, 11,* 447–458.

Sobell, L. C., & Sobell, M. B. (1973). A self-feedback technique to monitor drinking behaviors in alcoholics. *Behaviour Research and Therapy, 11,* 237–238.

Stark, K. D., Reynolds, W. M., & Kaslow, M. J. (1987). A comparison of the relative efficacy of self-control therapy and a behavioral problem-solving therapy for depression in children. *Journal of Abnormal Child Psychology, 15,* 91–113.

Thoresen, C. E., & Mahoney M. J. (1974). *Behavioral self-control.* New York: Holt, Rinehart and Winston.

Williams, J. E. (1976). Self-monitoring of paranoid behavior. *Behavior Therapy, 7,* 562.

Wing, R. R., Epstein, L. H., Norwalk, M. P., & Scott, N. (1988). Self-regulation in the treatment of Type II diabetes. *Behavior Therapy, 19,* 11–23.

65 SENSATE FOCUS

Lisa Regev and Joel Schmidt

INTRODUCTION

Historically, sensate focus has been a principal component in the treatment for many of the sexual dysfunctions. Masters and Johnson (1970) developed this technique to address performance anxiety, which was seen as the underlying mechanism of many sexual problems. When utilizing sensate focus, the couple is guided through a series of exercises that become progressively more anxiety provoking, analogous to the anxiety-mastering techniques proposed by Wolpe (1958) and Lazarus (1963). Prototypically, the couple begins with exercises imposing the least demand for sexual performance, such as nonsexual caressing while clothed, and moves through a hierarchy of increasingly demanding sexual activities over the course of treatment, eventually resulting in intercourse. During each of these exercises, they are taught to focus on the sensations they experience as their partner touches them, rather than engage in "spectatoring" (focusing on the adequacy of their performance). The receiver of sensate focus is also instructed to communicate specifically about the more and less enjoyable aspects of the interaction.

Sensate focus begins with a ban on intercourse until the exercises are successfully completed (Masters & Johnson, 1970). This serves two possible functions. One is to eliminate the anxiety-provoking thought that engaging in sensual touching may lead to intercourse, which is the sexual activity often associated with performance anxiety. By banning intercourse, both partners can focus on the sensation instead of worrying about what will happen next. Another benefit is that it allows the couple to start from scratch in building positive sexual experiences, rather than repeating problematic learned sexual patterns.

Sensate focus is one component within multi-component treatments for several sexual dysfunctions (Wincze & Carey, 2001). Other common ingredients of sex therapy include psychoeducation, relaxation training, communication training, and directed practice (e.g., directed masturbation for female orgasmic disorder, squeeze technique for premature ejaculation, or insertion of graduated vaginal dilators for vaginismus).

WHO MIGHT BENEFIT FROM SENSATE FOCUS?

Sensate focus is a central treatment component for individuals presenting with arousal disorders (male erectile disorder and female sexual arousal disorder). Performance anxiety is hypothesized to play a predominant role in preventing arousal. By teaching couples to focus on their bodily sensations without the demand for sex, they are presumably more likely to become aroused (Masters & Johnson, 1970).

Sensate focus contributes to the treatment of other sexual problems as well. It is used in conjunction with other treatment components to alleviate problems of desire and orgasm (e.g., Heiman & LoPiccolo, 1988; Zeiss & Zeiss, 1978). It has also been used as one component in preventing relationship distress among premarital couples in the Prevention and Relationship Enhancement Program (PREP; Markman, Blumberg, & Stanley, 1993).

CONTRAINDICATIONS

Sex therapy is generally contraindicated when the problem is due to organic causes. Prior to initiating sex therapy, it is important to rule out possible physiological causes for the problem, including pharmacological side effects (e.g., antidepressants, antihypertensives, anxiolytics, antiulcer medications, street drugs, and alcohol) and medical conditions (e.g., diabetes, hypogonadism, cancer, and menopause). Most sexual problems that result primarily from medication use are reversible once the drug is discontinued. In some cases, changing the dose or class of drug can reverse the sexual problem as well (Crenshaw & Goldberg, 1996). Individuals who suffer chronic medical illnesses that impact sexual functioning may benefit from sex therapy, particularly if they are willing to pursue more modest treatment goals (Schover, 2000). For example, sensate focus may facilitate improved sensual pleasure and intimacy with a partner even if sexual functioning (i.e., physiological arousal and/or intercourse) cannot be improved.

OTHER FACTORS IN DECIDING WHETHER TO USE SENSATE FOCUS

Prior to beginning sex therapy, it is important to assess factors that may impede progress. For example, Sexual Aversion Disorder resulting from a sexual trauma may be difficult to treat without first treating the trauma (Kaplan, 1995). Hypoactive sexual desire disorder resulting from severe marital discord may be difficult to treat without first attending to general relationship functioning. Sex therapy relies on trust, emotional intimacy, attraction, and communication. However, a history of sexual trauma or marital discord should not be assumed to preclude sex therapy. Enhancing a couple's sexual relationship may help establish intimacy and communication (Regev, O'Donohue, & Avina, 2003). Clinical judgment plays a central role in determining appropriate action in these cases.

HOW DOES SENSATE FOCUS WORK?

Masters and Johnson (1970) speculated that performance anxiety interferes with arousal, whereby the fear of sexual inadequacy leads individuals to continually monitor their arousal at the expense of focusing on the pleasurable

experience. Barlow (1986) explicated a model of sexual arousal in which people with sexual dysfunctions tend to experience more negative affect, underreport levels of arousal, and focus more on the consequences of negative sexual performance than individuals without sexual dysfunctions (Beck & Barlow, 1986; Heiman & Rowland, 1983). Sensate focus is designed to mitigate this excessive evaluation of the sexual experience by providing an alternative focus.

Sensate focus (in conjunction with a ban on intercourse) teaches individuals who suffer from arousal problems to focus on the pleasurable sensations of sexual contact, without worrying about their ability to perform. It is hypothesized that refocusing them on erotic cues will facilitate arousal and possibly orgasm. Additionally, by teaching individuals to focus on their sensations, men learn to identify their "point of inevitability" when learning to control their ejaculatory latency (see Chapter 68) and women learn to identify their pleasure points when learning to reach orgasm (see Chapter 26).

For individuals presenting with low desire, sensate focus may work for different reasons. For example, it requires couples to extend foreplay and reduce the demand for sex. By engaging in prolonged foreplay without the ultimate goal (and pressure) of intercourse, some couples rediscover sexual enjoyment and hence, increased desire to engage in sexual activity. Another reason is that sensate focus teaches couples to communicate their sexual preferences as they engage in the exercises. It is no longer taboo to talk about what does and does not feel good sexually. Instead, it is a required aspect of the treatment. This newly developed skill in communicating sexual preferences is hypothesized to result in improved sexual interactions overall, which may lead to more desire to engage in sexual activity. Additionally, sensate focus provides another venue for couples to engage in an intimate form of pleasant events. The exercises require couples to set aside time to be together intimately, which would be expected to enhance their general relationship functioning and their desire to be together. Additional research is needed to help clarify the process by which sensate focus works.

EVIDENCE FOR THE EFFECTIVENESS OF SENSATE FOCUS

The Masters and Johnson approach to treating sexual problems (which includes sensate focus, among other components) has been found to be generally effective (Clement & Schmidt, 1983; Everaerd & Dekker, 1985; Hartman & Daly, 1983; Matthews, et al., 1976). Thus, sensate focus is one element within a multicomponent treatment that has empirical support. However, future research is needed to further clarify the unique contribution of sensate focus to this treatment effectiveness.

When treating primary female orgasmic disorder, sensate focus and ban on intercourse significantly increased women's level of enjoyment of sexual activity (Fichten, Libman, & Brender, 1983). However, women were more likely to gain orgasmic capacity when directed masturbation was also included as a treatment component (Riley & Riley, 1978). This treatment package has also been used to effectively treat low desire in women (Hurlbert, White, Powell, & Apt, 1993). Incorporating sensate focus in a relationship distress prevention program proved effective in preventing sexual dissatisfaction 3 years later (Markman, Floyd, Stanley, & Storaasli, 1988).

Masters and Johnson's (1970) intensive 2-week training required couples to abstain from sex for a few days. However, the prescribed ban on intercourse has not been uniformly accepted. Lipsius (1987) argued that rigidly adhering to the ban on intercourse in the extended treatment format may have detrimental effects, such as loss of spontaneity and erotic feelings, because the ban may last several weeks or even months. Instead, he proposed a more moderate prohibition, where couples are encouraged to refrain from intercourse. However, spontaneous sex is not forbidden. Communication of sexual preferences was found to be effective whether intercourse was banned or not (Takefman & Brender, 1984). Instead of banning intercourse during treatment with sensate focus, Riley and Riley (1978) instructed that intercourse should take place only after extended foreplay.

STEP-BY-STEP PROCEDURES

The following procedures are most typically utilized when treating couples with sensate focus (see Table 65.1). This discussion will focus on treating a couple presenting with male erectile disorder. However, this procedure may be adapted to be used for females or males (homosexual or heterosexual) presenting with a variety of sexual problems (as noted above). Generally speaking, sessions last approximately 1 hour, once per week. Sessions consist of psychoeducation and instruction on exercises to be completed at home. Bibliotherapy with minimal therapist contact (varying from 10 min per week to four sessions over a 3-month period) has also been found to be effective when treating premature ejaculation and female orgasmic disorder (van Lankveld, 1998).

Ban on Intercourse

The first step in sensate focus usually involves contracting with the couple to abstain from attempting sexual intercourse until they are instructed otherwise (but, see discussion above regarding alternatives to the intercourse ban). The duration of the ban is typically a few weeks. Couples are provided the following rationale: Sexual problems often stem from distracting thoughts during sexual activity or pressure to perform sexually. By banning intercourse, they will learn to focus on pleasurable sensations without worrying about the need to perform adequately.

Sensate Focus I

Following the intercourse-ban contract, the couple is instructed to engage in relatively low-anxiety exercises. The exact form of the homework exercises will require negotiation and will vary from couple to couple. Usually, the couple is instructed to caress each other's bodies, excluding the breasts and genitals. However, some couples may begin with more basic exercises, such as holding hands or hugging in bed in the dark. It is important to stress that the exercises should take place in a relaxed atmosphere and at a relaxed pace.

TABLE 65.1   Sensate Focus Step-by-Step Procedures

Step	Details
Ban on intercourse	
Negotiate form, number and initiation of exercises	
Sensate focus I (example)	Induce relaxation (e.g., by taking a warm bath).
	Partners take turns caressing each other without touching breasts or genitals.
	Focus attention on sensations of caressing or being caressed.
	Communicate what feels good.
Sensate focus II (example)	Induce relaxation (e.g., by taking a warm bath).
	Partners take turns caressing each other including touching breasts or genitals.
	Focus attention on sensations of caressing or being caressed.
	Communicate what feels good.
	If they become aroused (e.g., erection), pause until arousal subsides.
Sensate focus III (example)	Induce relaxation (e.g., by taking a warm bath).
	Partners take turns caressing each other including touching breasts or genitals.
	Engage in intercourse without thrusting.
	Focus attention on sensations of caressing or being caressed.
	Communicate what feels good.
	If they are about to reach orgasm, pause until arousal subsides.
Resume engaging in intercourse	Continue to focus on sensations.
	Continue to communicate what feels good.
Self-monitor	Problem-solve treatment noncompliance.
	Modify progression of treatment based on couple's needs.

Success is unlikely if either of the partners feel rushed or distracted by other tasks.

An example of sensate focus I: The male is instructed to sensually caress the woman's back, while he concentrates on how it feels to touch her and the woman concentrates on how it feels to be touched. An emphasis is placed on the importance of each person focusing on his or her own sensations. They are instructed to notice distracting thoughts and refocus their attention to their sensations. The woman is also instructed to communicate which touches feel good and to pay particular attention to sensitive spots. She is to guide his caresses through communication, while avoiding talking too much, as it can distract them from focusing on their sensations. She is then instructed to lie on her back as he caresses her top to bottom, excluding her breasts and vagina. Again, they are to focus on their sensations as he caresses her. Once he has completed caressing her, she is to complete the same exercise caressing him, without caressing his penis.

The specifics of the exercise should be negotiated prior to initiation. This includes the exact form of the exercise, who will initiate, and the number of times they will practice the exercise prior to the next session. Four to seven times per week is typical—presumably, the more they practice, the faster they progress.

Sensate Focus II

Once the couple completes sensate focus I without feeling anxious (usually after 2 weeks), they progress to sensate focus II. This exercise is the same as that in sensate focus I but also includes stimulation of breasts and genitals. Couples are reminded that arousal is not the goal and that they are not to stimulate each other to the point of orgasm. In fact, if they do become aroused at this stage, they are to pause their caresses until the arousal subsides (e.g., if a man becomes erect while his partner caresses his penis, she is to pause her caresses until he becomes flaccid again). This emphasizes the notion that arousal is not the goal. Instead, both partners are to focus on the sensations and prevent their thoughts from wandering.

Sensate Focus III

Once couples complete sensate focus II without feeling anxious, they progress to sensate focus III. In this exercise, couples also engage in vaginal containment, whereby they are instructed to manually insert his flaccid penis into her vagina. Again, if he becomes aroused, they are to pause the exercise until his erection subsides. They are to continue to focus on the sensations of touching and being touched. Once they successfully complete sensate focus III and no longer feel anxious while engaging in the exercises, the ban on sexual intercourse is lifted. For couples presenting with an arousal disorder, the problem may be resolved at this point. For other sexual problems, these exercises are part of a larger treatment package.

Self-Monitoring

During the course of treatment, couples are asked to self-monitor their sexual activity (defined broadly) on a daily basis. For example, couples may be asked to identify the sexual activities they engaged in and rate their levels of enjoyment, anxiety, communication of preferences, and ability to focus on their bodily sensations. This provides information about treatment adherence, readiness to move to the next level of exercises, and possible barriers to progress. More specifically, it helps identify ways in which exercises should be modified and tailored to the couple's needs.

HOW TO AVOID COMMON PROBLEMS

Couples practicing sensate focus may encounter a number of problems. Common problems include couples' failure to comprehend the task, nonadherence or partial adherence to the treatment protocol, and an inability to focus on their sensations. When practicing sensate focus, it is imperative that couples understand how sensate focus works. Generally, this may

require repeated explanations. Specifically, it should be explained that (1) sensate focus requires couples to take small steps towards achieving the long-term goal of a more satisfying sexual relationship and (2) at this stage, they are asked to focus on their sensations. This may be challenging, as couples may be more interested in focusing on performance. It should be emphasized that sessions will not focus on erections or orgasms during these exercises.

When couples fail to adhere to the treatment, the barriers to completion should be explored. One common barrier occurs when couples are so anxious about engaging in particular sexual exercises that they find reasons to avoid them. In this case, it is possible that a particular exercise is too high on the couple's hierarchy of anxiety-provoking activities. Encouraging the couple to identify a less anxiety-provoking activity and incorporating it as the next step may be helpful in resolving this problem. Along these lines, careful attention should be paid so as not to explicitly or implicitly over-emphasize the goal of reaching a certain level of technical performance at the expense of a pleasurable, intimate human interaction. Otherwise, the therapist my unwittingly endorse widely held but harmful beliefs about the ultimate importance of achieving culturally sanctioned sexual functioning parameters as discussed by McCarthy and McCarthy (1998).

Another barrier may be an underlying desire discrepancy between partners. It is typical for couples to present for sex therapy because one partner desires more frequent sexual activity than the other, which may pose a problem when attempting to negotiate sexual activity. For example, the low-desire partner may be motivated to maintain the low-frequency status quo. In contrast, the high-desire partner may be frustrated with the idea of slowing down the sexual activity between them, as prescribed by sensate focus. Such partners often complain that they already do not engage in sufficiently frequent sexual activity and they feel frustrated that therapy involves a further reduction in activity. In these situations, reaching a common ground is critical and may require teaching basic communication and problem-solving skills.

A third barrier to adherence may involve competing time demands and/or inconsistent motivations. Many couples have busy schedules that involve work, family, and community obligations. Often, finding a time that promotes a relaxed and comfortable sexual atmosphere is difficult. Time management and negotiation skills training may be of benefit. In addition, motivation in the therapy room does not always translate into actually finding the time and energy to complete tasks at home. In these situations, it may be helpful to explore the couple's motivational ambivalence as discussed in Chapter 48.

Couples frequently report difficulty maintaining focus on their bodily sensations during this exercise. When this occurs, it is helpful to reassure the couple that staying focused can be difficult, especially at first. They should also be instructed to notice their distraction without self-criticism and return their attention to their sensations. This process is analogous to the process outlined in Chapter 44.

Further Reading

Leiblum, S. R. (Ed.). (2006). *Principles and practice of sex therapy* (4th ed.). New York: Guilford.

O'Donohue, W., & Geer, J. H. (Eds.) (1993). *Handbook of sexual dysfunctions: Assessment and treatment.* Boston: Allyn and Bacon.

Wincze, J. P., & Carey, M. P. (2001). *Sexual dysfunction: A guide for assessment and treatment* (2nd ed.). New York: Guilford.

References

Barlow, D. H. (1986). Causes of sexual dysfunction: The role of anxiety and cognitive interference. *Journal of Consulting and Clinical Psychology, 54,* 140–148.

Beck, J. G., & Barlow, D. H. (1986). The effects of anxiety patterns in erectile dysfunction. *Behaviour Research and Therapy, 24*(1), 19–26.

Clement, U., & Schmidt, G. (1983). The outcome of couple therapy for sexual dysfunctions using three different formats. *Journal of Sex and Marital Therapy, 9,* 67–78.

Crenshaw, T. L., & Goldberg, J. P. (1996). *Sexual pharmacology: Drugs that affect sexual function.* New York: Norton.

Everaerd, W., & Dekker, J. (1985). Treatment of male sexual dysfunction: Sex therapy compared with systematic desensitization and rational emotive therapy. *Behaviour Research and Therapy, 22,* 114–124.

Fichten, C. S., Libman, E., & Brender, W. (1983). Methodological issues in the study of sex therapy: Effective components in the treatment of secondary orgasmic dysfunction. *Journal of Sex and Marital Therapy, 9*(3), 191–202.

Hartman, L. M., & Daly, E. M. (1983). Relationship factors in the treatment of sexual dysfunction. *Behaviour Research and Therapy, 21,* 153–160.

Heiman, J., & LoPiccolo, J. (1988). *Becoming orgasmic: A sexual and personal growth program for women* (2nd ed.). New York: Simon & Schuster.

Heiman, J. R., & Rowland, D. L. (1983). Affective and physiological sexual response patterns: The effects of instructions on sexually functional and dysfunctional men. *Journal of Psychosomatic Research, 27*(2), 105–116.

Hurlbert, D. F., White, L. C., Powell, R. D., & Apt, C. (1993). Orgasm consistency training in the treatment of women reporting hypoactive sexual desire: An outcome comparison of women-only groups and couples-only groups. *Journal of Behavior Therapy and Experimental Psychiatry, 24,* 3–13.

Kaplan, H. S. (1995). Sexual aversion disorder: The case of the phobic virgin, or an abused child grows up. In R. Rosen and S. Leiblum (Eds.), *Case studies in sex therapy* (pp. 65–80). New York: Guilford.

Lazarus, A. (1963). The treatment of chronic frigidity by systematic desensitization. *Journal of Nervousness and Mental Diseases, 136,* 272–278.

Lipsius, S. H. (1987). Prescribing sensate focus without proscribing intercourse. *Journal of Sex and Marital Therapy, 13*(2), 106–116.

Markman, H. J., Blumberg, S. L., & Stanley, S. M. (1993). Prevention and relationship enhancement program: Consultant's manual. Unpublished treatment manual.

Markman, H. J., Floyd, F. J., Stanley, S. M., & Storaasli, R. D., (1988). Prevention of marital distress: A longitudinal investigation. *Journal of Consulting and Clinical Psychology, 56,* 210–217.

Masters, W., & Johnson, V. (1970). *Human sexual inadequacy.* Boston: Little, Brown.

Matthews, A., Bancroft, J., Whitehead, A., Hackmann, A., Julier, D., Bancroft, J., Gath, D., & Shaw, P. (1976). The behavioral treatment of sexual inadequacy: A comparative study. *Behaviour Research and Therapy, 14,* 427–436.

McCarthy, B. W., & McCarthy, E. J. (1998). *Male sexual awareness: Increasing sexual satisfaction.* New York: Carroll & Graf.

Regev, L. G., O'Donohue, W. T., & Avina, C. (2003). Treating couples with sexual dysfunction. In D. Snyder & M. Whisman (Eds.), *Treating difficult couples: Helping clients with coexisting mental and relationship disorders.* New York: Guilford.

Riley, A. J., & Riley, E. J. (1978). A controlled study to evaluate directed masturbation in the management of primary orgasmic failure in women. *British Journal of Psychiatry, 133,* 404–409.

Schover, L. R. (2000). Sexual problems in chronic illness. In S. Leiblum & R. Rosen (Eds.), *Principles and practice of sex therapy* (3rd ed., pp. 398–422). New York: Guilford.

Takefman, J., & Brender, W (1984). An analysis of the effectiveness of two components in the treatment of erectile dysfunction. *Archives of Sexual Behavior, 13*(4), 321–340.

van Lankveld, J. J. D. M. (1998). Bibliotherapy in the treatment of sexual dysfunctions: A meta-analysis. *Journal of Consulting and Clinical Psychology, 66,* 702–708.

Wincze, J. P., & Carey, M. P. (2001). *Sexual dysfunction: A guide for assessment and treatment* (2nd ed.). New York: Guilford.

Wolpe, J. (1958). *Psychotherapy by reciprocal inhibition.* Stanford, CA: Stanford University Press.

Zeiss, R. A., & Zeiss, A. M. (1978). *Prolong your pleasure.* New York: Pocket Books.

66   SHAPING

Kyle E. Ferguson and Kim Christiansen

Behavioral repertoires are not always effective when applied to new environments or even their current environments should conditions change. A skill set acquired under one set of conditions does not necessarily generalize to other settings, even when those settings bear a number of similarities. In other circumstances, the "natural contingencies" following a behavior can rapidly "shape up" or refine those skills until a person's repertoire becomes maximally effective (Ferster & Skinner, 1957). Colloquially, the person gets "acclimated" to his or her new surroundings with minimal effort. This can be seen when a person begins a new job or a child transfers to a new school and "fits right in" almost immediately.

Sometimes making the adjustment to a new environment is more difficult and takes more time, especially in the case of special populations (e.g., cognitively impaired elderly, children with developmental disabilities, and survivors of acquired brain injury). In these populations, the natural contingencies often fail to bring appropriate responding under environmental control, and, in the absence of direct instruction, reinforcement becomes less likely and punishment more likely. These individuals may continue to experience difficulty adapting to their new roles regardless of how hard they try. These individuals simply lack the requisite skills required to successfully function in these environments. When the appropriate response class (i.e., different behaviors producing similar outcomes) is absent from a person's repertoire the class of responding must be shaped by contingencies carefully arranged by other people, the contingencies must be programmed (Skinner, 1966).

This chapter begins with a technical definition of shaping. Clinical case examples that use the shaping technique are considered next, followed by a discussion of who is likely to benefit from shaping, contraindications of the technique, other factors to consider when deciding whether or not to use shaping, and purported learning mechanisms underlying this approach. Step-by-step guidelines in using the technique of shaping are included at the end of the chapter.

DEFINITION OF SHAPING

Shaping is the differential reinforcement of successive approximations towards desired performance (Holland & Skinner, 1961; Martin & Pear, 1978; Miltenberger, 2001; Skinner, 1953). It should be noted that the term "reinforcement" means one of two things as used in the definition of shaping. The term *reinforcement* is the *procedure* of presenting a reinforcing consequence after the target behavior occurs. The procedural definition concerns what the therapist does in response to what the client does. The other meaning of the term denotes an increase in the rate of behavior (responding over time) as a *function* of its consequences (e.g., smiling when a person makes eye contact increases the duration of eye contact; Pierce & Epling, 1999). The functional definition pertains to what the client is doing.

The term *differential reinforcement* suggests that the "reinforcer" be delivered "in a different way" based on the current level of performance. Initially, the criterion is set low. Any behavior that resembles the desired performance, even if it bears only a slight resemblance, is reinforced. Insofar as the current behavior increases over baseline levels (i.e., prior to implementing reinforcement), and the behavior maintains a steady rate for several minutes (longer, for more complex behaviors), the criterion can then be raised. At a more stringent level, the reinforcer is only delivered when the individual emits behavior that meets or exceeds this new level of performance. Again, after a steady state of performance is achieved at this new criterion, the criterion can then be increased. This process of gradually increasing performance criteria is repeated until the target behavior is emitted.

If many demonstrations of differential reinforcement of successive approximations were graphed, it would look similar to Figure 66.1. The data would organize into stepwise patterns, like an ascending flight of stairs, alternating between the conditions of extinction (the effects of withholding reinforcement) and reinforcement.

CASE EXAMPLES

During the 1950s and 1960s many psychologists began applying the behavioral principles discovered in the learning laboratory to real-life settings. Although these empirical regularities were based largely on work with nonhuman subjects, extending this technology to applied settings often produced dramatic clinical outcomes. Most notably, this technology of modifying behavior worked extremely well with those with extremely limited repertoires (e.g., mental retardation and serious mental illness), whereas other approaches, namely, psychoanalytic and humanistic therapies, were of no use.

In a classic study, Haughton and Ayllon (1965) examined the development of unusual and repetitive behaviors that appeared "meaningless" to casual observers (p. 94). Their subject was a 54-year-old women diagnosed with schizophrenia. She had been hospitalized for over 20 years. Using cigarettes as reinforcement, they shaped an arbitrary (and meaningless) response—"holding a broom while in an upright posture" (Haughton and Ayllon, 1965, p. 96). To evoke this behavior, the researchers had one staff hand the woman the broom while another handed her a cigarette. In just a few days their subject "developed a stereotyped behavior of pacing while holding the broom" (Haughton and Ayllon, 1965, p. 96).

Haughton and Ayllon's study demonstrates how abnormal behavior might develop through learning mechanisms. The study also demonstrates the danger in ignoring environmental contingencies. The following quotation depicts the clinical impressions of one of two psychiatrists (naïve to the study):

> Dr. B's evaluation of the patient ... Her constant and compulsive pacing holding a broom in the manner she does could be seen as a ritualistic procedure, a magical action ... Symbolism is a

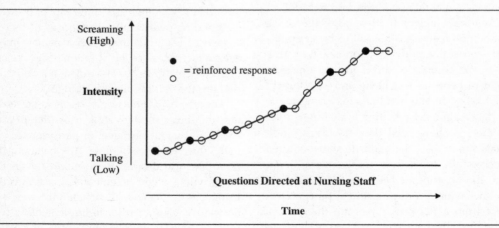

FIGURE 66.1 A Functional Relationship between Reinforcer Delivery on the Part of Nursing Home Staff and Topographical Characteristics of Client Communicative Behavior.
The abscissa (x-axis) depicts perseverative questioning directed at nursing staff. Questions that resulted in reinforcement are represented by black circles. Questions that resulted in extinction (withholding of the reinforcer) are represented by white (open) circles. The ordinate (y-axis) depicts a continuum of communicative intensity from "talking" on one extreme (low) to "screaming" on the other (high).

predominant mode of expression of deep seated unfulfilled desires and instinctual impulses. By magic, she controls others, cosmic powers are at her disposal and inanimate objects become living creatures (Haughton & Ayllon, 1965, p. 97).

Another classic study was conducted by Wolf, Risley, and Mees (1964). After having undergone cataract surgery their subject, a young boy with autism, was required to wear glasses but refused to put them on. This, of course, posed two problems. While not wearing his glasses made it almost impossible to see (first problem), what made matters worse was the fact that failing to wear his glasses increased the risk of developing irreversible blindness (caused by retinal cell degeneration) (second problem).

To encourage the boy to wear glasses, Wolf and his colleagues differentially reinforced closer approximations to the desired response (i.e., wearing them) using an edible reinforcer (i.e., food). During the initial stages of the shaping process responses that only remotely approximated final performance were reinforced. These behaviors included simply touching the glasses and handling them.

Criteria for performance were increased a little at a time. Earlier behaviors that resulted in reinforcement were put on extinction (no reinforcer followed responding), while more behavior was required from the boy to obtain the reinforcer. For example, he had to bring the glasses within the proximity of his face before obtaining the reinforcer. Ultimately, the criterion was increased to the point of putting the glasses on. To summarize the outcome of the Wolf et al. study, the boy eventually learned to put the glasses on and became comfortable wearing them for extended periods of time.

In another case example, Jackson and Wallace (1974) used the principle of differential reinforcement in shaping the vocal intensity of a socially withdrawn 15-year-old girl diagnosed with mental retardation. Additionally, she had a condition known as aphonia (insufficient volume). As a means of shaping effective performance, namely, increasing the volume of her voice, the clinicians used a voice-operated relay along with a decibel meter to accurately set performance criteria, provide continuous feedback, and automatically dispense the token reinforcer (exchangeable for books, beauty aids, photo albums, etc.).

Initially, criterion was set low with respect to the complexity of the words she was required to read (100 monosyllabic words) and the volume with which the words were read (i.e., the relay device was set for maximum sensitivity). After emitting responses above the device's threshold, with a "hit" rate of approximately 80%, the sensitivity on the machine was decreased slightly. Hence, the subject was required to speak louder to activate the reinforcer mechanism. Once her speech was shaped to "normal" intensity, they targeted word complexity next. Namely, she was required to read polysyllabic words (one to five syllables). Eventually, criteria and reinforcer density were increased to five or six polysyllabic words spoken per token. These words, of course, were emitted within the range of normal volume.

It took about 100 sessions to reach target criteria, which translated into several months of training. To summarize the outcome of this study, relative to baseline performance where the subject's voice wasn't any louder than background noise (the sound of an overhead fan), the volume of her voice was eventually shaped to that required for normal conversation. Remarkably, in part due to this intervention, the subject went from the special classroom to the regular classroom, and ultimately became gainfully employed as a waitress.

WHO MIGHT BENEFIT FROM THIS TECHNIQUE?

Shaping is a versatile technique that can be used with any population, by itself, or as a component of a treatment package. The following list provides examples of published controlled studies using this technique:

- Increasing reading fluency and comprehension in 11- to 18-year-old boys with emotional disabilities (Miller & Polk, 1994)
- Teaching a problem-solving repertoire to adults with acquired brain injury (Foxx et al., 1988)
- A toilet training program for clients with mental retardation and developmental disabilities (Foxx & Azrin, 1973)

- An early detection and prevention of breast cancer program (Saunders, Pilgram, & Pennypacker, 1986)
- A program targeting children with autism that increases social behavior, teaches children to speak, and eliminates self-stimulation (Lovaas, 1977)
- Assertiveness training targeting adults with chronic schizophrenia (Bloomfield, 1973)
- Overcoming learned nonuse that develops after a stroke (Taub et al., 1993)
- Teaching motor skills to preschool children (Hardiman et al., 1975)
- Differentially reinforcing higher rates of speaking with a chronically depressed individual (Robinson & Lewinsohn, 1973)
- Reducing tremor caused by an acquired brain injury (Guercio, Ferguson, & McMorrow, 2001)

CONTRAINDICATIONS

Shaping is not contraindicated for most clients when used by therapists who are knowledgeable about the principles of learning. One of the dangers in using shaping by therapists who are not knowledgeable is inadvertently shaping harmful behavior. After all, reinforcement increases the probability of any behavior that enters into the contingency. Accordingly, therapists must be careful not to deliver reinforcement right after the occurrence of behavior that threatens the safety of the client or others.

OTHER FACTORS TO CONSIDER WHEN DECIDING WHETHER TO USE THIS TECHNIQUE

The first question to ask in deciding whether to use a shaping program is: Are performance problems related to a skill deficiency or do problems lie in the person's environment (Mager & Pipe, 1984)? Hypothetically, if someone offered the client $10,000 to engage in the activity, would he or she be able to perform the behavior? If not, chances are the problem is related to a skill's deficit.

In determining whether shaping is the best approach to take in ameliorating a skill's deficit, we need to ask ourselves: was the individual ever able to perform the activity? If so, the client needs refresher training, not shaping. In these circumstances, modeling the behavior or telling the client what to do (instructional control) are usually all that is required (Miltenberger, 2001). Does the client have sufficient opportunities to practice the skill? If not, employ booster sessions coupled with corrective feedback. Are environmental prompts called for? If so, checklists, posted signs, and reminders might alleviate the problem. Both of these, namely, increasing opportunities for practice or ameliorating deficient antecedent control (prompts), obviate shaping.

After ruling out rationales for alternative treatments, the next step is to consider environmental factors related to performance, before turning to a shaping program. Technically, do the prevailing contingencies of reinforcement have the power to influence the target behavior (Pierce & Epling, 1999)?

Performance deficits could also be caused by deficient contingencies, thus obviating the need for shaping. The first question to ask about the prevailing contingencies is whether performance is punishing (Mager & Pipe, 1984). If so, it is necessary to decrease or eliminate punishment. The second question to ask is: Is nonperformance reinforcing? If so, why? Perhaps, behavior incompatible with the target response ("nonperformance") should be extinguished or prevented in some way. Does the social milieu hinder effective performance (not all work environments are task oriented)? If so, shaping an individual's behavior might be a waste of time if the problem is a "faulty system" (in which case staff training might be in order).

Finally, if the target behavior is not in the person's repertoire, there is reason to believe that the person cannot emit the behavior in spite of reinforcing contingencies, and other training strategies (e.g., modeling, prompting, instructional control) would be less effective, then shaping should be employed.

HOW DOES THE TECHNIQUE WORK?

Shaping is conceptualized within an evolutionary framework (environmental selectionism) (Skinner, 1990; Staddon & Simmelhag, 1971). While natural selection is the mechanism responsible for the evolution of species, contingencies of reinforcement (reinforcement and punishment) are the mechanism responsible for variations in operant behavior (Skinner, 1987).

Emitted behavior always varies topographically—no two responses are *exactly* the same. When responding appears virtually identical from one moment to the next, what we are actually witnessing is "average performance" within certain parameters or dimensions (Baum, 1994, pp. 64–65). For example, when we hear a familiar voice say "hello" it varies each time in volume (e.g., louder if the speaker is farther away), pitch (e.g., a lower pitch when the person has a cold), speed (e.g., the speaker is in a hurry), and clarity (e.g., the person has food in his or her mouth), and so on.

Taking our "hello" example, if these data were graphed along some response dimension (e.g., pitch), it would likely result in a distribution similar to the one shown in Figure 66.2 (in this case, a normal distribution). Shaping works by reinforcing responses that vary toward one end of the response continuum. In this example the therapist sets the criterion a little higher than average. This, of course, places the behavior below the criterion on extinction (no reinforcement follows responding). Extinction produces increased variability in performance (Galbicka, 1994). Thus, the new reinforcement contingency is designed to "select" or "capture" extinction-induced behavior that meets or exceeds the criterion.

Once performance stabilizes, and thus forms a new distribution (Distribution 2), the criterion is again increased and a new distribution is formed (Distribution 3). When responding stabilizes around this new criterion (Distribution 3), the criterion is increased again (Distribution 4).

STEP-BY-STEP PROCEDURES

All effective shaping programs are comprised of the following components: (1) selecting a

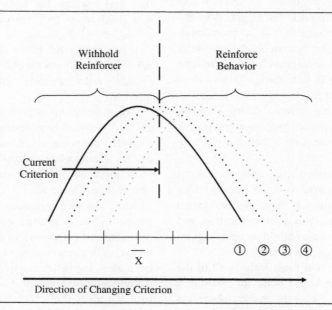

FIGURE 66.2   As Criteria are Gradually Increased, Distributions of Responses Centered around New Means Shift to the Right.
②, ③, and ④ denote the changing distributions (Modeled after Baum's, 1994, Figure 4.3, p. 65; and Galbicka, 1994, Figures 1 and 2, pp. 742–3).

target behavior, (2) assessing the current level of performance, (3) selecting the initial behavior, (4) selecting a reliable reinforcer, and (5) differentially reinforcing successive approximations (Alberto & Troutman, 1990; Baldwin & Baldwin, 1981; Cooper, Heron, & Heward, 1987; Foxx, 1982; Martin & Pear, 1978; Miltenberger, 2001; Sulzer-Azaroff & Mayer, 1991; Sundel & Sundel, 1993). The reader should note that these steps are arranged in a linear fashion.

Step 1: Select a Target Behavior

The first step in developing a shaping program is to specify the instructional goal or, precisely, the target behavior (Sulzer-Azaroff & Mayer, 1991). For a behavioral target to be workable, it must be described in an *objective*, *clear*, and *complete* manner (Barlow & Hersen, 1984; Hawkins & Dobes, 1977).

An *objective* description refers only to the observable aspects of the target response. In other words, what does the target behavior look, sound, or feel like? For example, if eye contact is the target, are eyes of both the client and other person in alignment for over 20 seconds? If speech volume is the target, does the speaker talk loud enough so that a person standing 10 feet away can hear what he or she is saying? While there is obvious flexibility in how the target behavior is described, objective definitions never reflect the intent of the person or internal processes (e.g., internal drive). Descriptions referring to internal processes are simply unreliable and in most cases impossible to verify objectively.

A *clear* definition must be unambiguous, short and to the point (parsimonious). Ideally, after reading the description of the behavioral target any person with a ninth-grade education and unfamiliar with the case should be able to point the target out when it is occurring.

A *complete* definition must include all of the critical parts of the target behavior. Including all of its essential elements enables observers to discern when the target behavior begins and ends. Consider how one might treat someone with extreme claustrophobia, who has to use the elevator every day. Going from one floor

to at least the next floor might be the behavioral target. This definition would be considered complete because it entails approaching the elevator, pressing the up or down button, getting on, pressing the button for the next floor, etc. Observers can easily discern whether the client actually rides the elevator successfully by waiting in front of the elevator on the destination floor.

Step 2: Assess the Current Level of Performance

Once the target behavior has been defined, the next step is to develop a method of measuring performance. Effective shaping programs use direct observational methods.

Direct observational methods are highly accurate and relatively simple to use. General points to consider in using a direct observational system are: when will behavior be observed, duration of the observation interval (e.g., in 1-minute blocks or using spot checks), and what specific response dimensions are targeted (i.e., frequency, duration, topography, and/or intensity; Bloom, Fischer, & Orme, 1995). Regarding the first point, target behavior should be observed at times that best capture the behavior. For example, if a child tends to "tantrum" on the way to school, then observing the child on the way to school will most likely capture the tantrum behavior. Observing the child at other times will probably not adequately capture the behavior of interest.

The observation interval depends on the target of interest. More discrete behaviors (with a clearly definable beginning and end) would call for shorter observational intervals, whereas more involved activities would involve longer observational intervals.

More discrete behaviors lend themselves to frequency (i.e., counting the number of responses or using rate, frequency/time) and intensity measures (e.g., measuring voice tone with a decibel meter). For behaviors that are less transitory, durational measurement strategies that best capture the most important temporal dimensions of behavior should be used (e.g., how long a child can sit in his or her desk before getting up) (see Bloom, Fischer, & Orme, 1995, p.127ff. for details).

Step 3: Select the Initial Behavior

After deciding what measurement strategies to employ, the next step is to set the initial criterion or behavioral target. The best way of identifying where to begin is by observing the individual under natural conditions, in the context in which the target behavior ought to occur (Foxx, 1982). If this is not feasible, the therapist should make an attempt at approximating what he or she believes to be the most crucial variables of the natural conditions, in a more convenient milieu (e.g., in the therapist's office).

In any event, under natural or analog conditions, try identifying what behaviors bear any resemblance to final performance. These are the behaviors the therapist will be targeting in ensuing steps, monitoring, reinforcing, and so on. This will be taken up in Step 6.

Step 4: Select Reliable Reinforcers

We move next to selecting reliable (positive) reinforcers. A reinforcer is any stimulus or event that increases the probability of the behavior that produces it (Pierce & Epling, 1999). Said differently, for a stimulus or event to function as a reinforcer there must be an observable change in performance; namely, an increase in response frequency. In contrast, when an event reliably follows behavior and no change in frequency is noted or there is a reduction in the behavior, then the event does not function as a reinforcer.

Identifying powerful reinforcers are crucial to the shaping program (Miltenberger, 2001; see the chapter on stimulus preference assessment in this volume). Powerful reinforcers will help maintain a high level of motivation in the client (Foxx, 1982). Select reinforcers that can be delivered immediately. Also, choose reinforcers for which the client does not readily satiate (i.e., gets bored with or loses interest).

If clients are higher functioning verbally, the therapist can simply ask them about their preferences. However, in spite of what the client says, it is best to briefly test the potential reinforcers to verify whether they produce the intended effects. If they work as reinforcers, use them. If they do not work, continue the search. For clients who are lower functioning, it is also a good idea to

ask them as well, to promote their investment in treatment.

Reinforcers usually differ between people, and the same reinforcer does not increase the frequency of responding all of the time with the same individual. Take meat for example. Although meat reinforces the behavior of someone who enjoys the taste of meat, meat will not reinforce the behavior of a vegetarian under most conditions (unless the person is starving). By contrast, "Tofurky" may reinforce the purchasing behavior of the vegetarian most of the time, though not always. For instance, the vegetarian probably will not stock up on Tofurky several hours after eating a big Thanksgiving meal, where Tofurky is the centerpiece.

It follows, therefore, that the greater the number of items on the reinforcer "menu," the less likely satiation will become a problem. Before proceeding to Step 6, be sure to have a well stocked "armamentarium" of reinforcers. Should any fail to function as reinforcing stimuli, employ another that has demonstrated efficacy and is readily available.

Step 5: Differentially Reinforce Successive Approximations

After completing Steps 1–4, we are now ready to begin shaping the client's behavior. Begin with the initial behavior as identified in Step 3 (Miltenberger, 2001). Deliver the reinforcer contingently every time the client emits the initial behavior. The reinforcer-to-response ratio should be 1:1. Technically, this is called a continuous reinforcement schedule (CRF) or fixed ratio (FR) schedule. These terms are used interchangeably throughout the shaping literature (Ferster & Skinner, 1957).

Once reliable performance has been achieved,[1] increase the criterion ever so slightly (again using a CRF schedule). The next approximation should require just a little more effort from the

---

1. If the target behavior can be "shaped up" in one session "reliable" performance might consist of a steady rate maintained for several minutes. If the target behavior will take more than one session, as a rule of thumb, begin each ensuing session with the average criterion for performance derived from the previous session.

client. Bear in mind that if the therapist raises the criterion too high, "ratio strain" can occur (Pierce & Epling, 1999). Simply, the client becomes frustrated and gives up trying. On the other end of the continuum once a person has clearly mastered an approximation, move on to the next criterion quickly (Miltenberger, 2001).

While reinforcing responding at the next approximation, the therapist will undoubtedly see earlier behavior emerge. Do not reinforce "old" behavior—these behaviors must be placed on extinction (i.e., no reinforcer follows responding). Only reinforce behavior that meets or exceeds the current criterion[2]. Continue using differential reinforcement of successive approximations, alternating between conditions of reinforcement (CRF schedule) and extinction. Eventually, the target behavior will be reached and the behavioral program can shift from behavioral acquisition to maintenance.

To ensure that responding is maintained after completing the program, the client must be gradually "weaned" off of the reinforcer-rich FR1 schedule (Sulzer-Azaroff & Mayer, 1991). By degrees, begin thinning out the FR1 schedule to an FR3 schedule (3 responses per reinforcer) or variable ratio 3 schedule, VR3 (on average every third response produces the reinforcer). Once behavior is emitted reliably, thin the reinforcer density again to yet a leaner schedule of reinforcement, and so on (e.g., FR6, FR9, FR12, etc.). Don't rush this aspect of the program, for fear of losing the target behavior.

CONCLUSION

Employ shaping when the appropriate response class is missing from a client's repertoire and other more parsimonious interventions can be ruled out. How long it takes to shape a new behavior and the extent to which such programs are successful depends on whether the program is principle-driven (not technique-driven). Functionally oriented, principle-driven programs are solidly based on the principles of learning. Effective shaping programs are tailored for specific presenting problems. In other words, the program adjusts continuously in accordance with the client's current level of performance.

References

Alberto, P. A., & Troutman, A. C. (1986). *Applied behavior analysis for teachers: Influencing student performance* (2nd ed.). Columbus, OH: Charles E. Merrill.

Baldwin, J. D., & Baldwin, J. I. (1986). *Behavior principles in everyday life* (2nd ed.). Englewood Cliffs, NJ: Prentice Hall.

Barlow, D. H., & Hersen, M. (1984). *Single case experimental designs: Strategies for studying behavior change* (2nd ed.). New York: Pergamon Press.

Baum, W. M. (1994). *Understanding behaviorism: Science, behavior, and culture.* New York: HarperCollins.

Bloom, M., Fischer, J., & Orme, J. G. (1995). *Evaluating practice: Guidelines for the accountable professional* (2nd ed.). Boston: Allyn and Bacon.

Bloomfield, H. H. (1973). Assertiveness training in an outpatient group of chronic schizophrenics: A preliminary report. *Behavior Therapy, 4,* 277–281.

Cooper, J. O., Heron, T. E., & Heward, W. L. (1987). *Applied behavior analysis.* Columbus, OH: Merrill.

Ferster, C. B., & Skinner, B. F. (1957). *Schedules of reinforcement.* New York: Appleton-Century-Crofts.

Foxx, R. M. (1982). *Increasing behaviors of persons with severe retardation and autism.* Champaign, IL: Research Press.

Foxx, R. M., & Azrin, N. H. (1973). *Toilet training the retarded: A rapid program for day and nighttime independent toileting.* Champaign, IL: Research Press.

Foxx, R. M., Marchand-Martella, N. E., Martella, R. C., Braunling-McMorrow, D., & McMorrow, M. J. (1988). Teaching a problem-solving strategy to closed head-injured adults. *Behavioral Residential Treatment, 3,* 193–210.

Galbicka, G. (1994). Shaping in the 21st century: Moving percentile schedules into applied settings. *Journal of Applied Behavior Analysis, 27,* 739–760.

Guercio, J. M., Ferguson, K. E., McMorrow, M. J. (2001). Increasing functional communication through relaxation and neuromuscular feedback. *Brain Injury, 15,* 1073–1082.

Hardiman, S. A., Goetz, E. M., Reuter, K. E., & LeBlanc, J. M. (1975). Primis, contingent attention, and training: Effects on child's motor behavior. *Journal of Applied Behavior Analysis, 8,* 399–409.

Haughton, E., & Ayllon, T. (1965). Production and elimination of symptomatic behavior. In L. Ullmann

---

2. The exception to this rule is when a client has a run of failures at a given criterion. When this occurs you must lower the criterion and establish a run of successes before returning to the previously unsuccessful level. Establishing a behavioral momentum by backing up should push the client over such hurdles.

& L. Krasner (Eds.), *Case studies in behavior modification* (pp. 94–98). New York: Holt, Rinehart & Winston.

Hawkins, R. P., & Dobes, R. W. (1977). Behavioral definitions in applied behavior analysis: Explicit or implicit. In B. C. Etzel, J. M. LeBlanc, & D. M. Baer (Eds.), *New directions in behavioral research: Theory, methods, and applications. In honor of Sidney W. Bijou* (pp. 167–188). Hillsdale, NJ: Lawrence Erlbaum.

Holland, J. G., & Skinner, B. F. (1961). *The analysis of behavior: A program for self-instruction.* New York: McGraw-Hill.

Jackson, D. A., & Wallace, R. F. (1974). The modification and generalization of voice loudness in a fifteen-year-old retarded girl. *Journal of Applied Behavior Analysis, 7,* 461–471.

Lovaas, O. I. (1977). *The autistic child: Language development through behavior modification.* New York: Irvington.

Mager, R. F., & Pipe, P. (1984). *Analyzing performance problems or you really oughta wanna* (2nd ed.). Belmont, CA: Pitman.

Martin, G., & Pear, J. (1978). *Behavior modification: What it is and how to do it.* Englewood Cliffs, NJ: Prentice Hall.

Miller, B. L., Hou, C., Goldberg, M., & Mena, I. (1999). Anterior temporal lobes: Social brain. In B. L. Miller & J. L. Cummings (Eds.), *The human frontal lobes* (pp. 557–567). New York: Guilford.

Miller, A. D., Polk, A. L. (1994). Repeated readings and precision teaching: Increasing reading fluency and comprehension in sixth through twelfth grade boys with emotional disabilities. *Journal of Precision Teaching, 1,* 46–66.

Miltenberger, R. G. (2001). *Behavior modification: Principles and procedures* (2nd ed.). Belmont, CA: Wadsworth.

Pierce, W. D., & W. F. Epling. (1999). *Behavior analysis and learning* (2nd ed.). Upper Saddle River, NJ: Prentice Hall.

Robinson, J. C., Lewinsohn, P. M. (1973). Behavior modification of speech characteristics in a chronically depressed man. *Behavior Therapy, 4,* 150–152.

Saunders, K. J., Pilgram, C. A., & Pennypacker, H. S. (1986). Increased proficiency of research in breast cancer self-examination. *Cancer, 58,* 2531–2537.

Skinner, B. F. (1953). *Science and human behavior.* New York: Macmillan.

Skinner, B. F. (1957). *Verbal behavior.* New York: Appleton-Century-Crofts.

Skinner, B. F. (1966). The phylogeny and ontogeny of behavior. *Science, 153,* 1205–1213.

Skinner, B. F. (1987). *Upon further reflection.* Englewood Cliffs, NJ: Prentice Hall.

Skinner, B. F. (1990). Can psychology be a science of the mind? *American Psychologist, 45,* 1206–1210.

Staddon, J. E. R., & Simmelhag, V. L. (1971). The "superstition" experiment: A reexamination of its implications for the principles of adaptive behavior. *Psychological Review, 78,* 3–43.

Sulzer-Azaroff, B., & Mayer, G. R. (1991). *Behavior analysis for lasting change.* New York: Harcourt Brace College Publishers.

Sundel, S. S., & Sundel, M. (1993). *Behavior modification in the human services* (3rd ed.). Newbury Park, CA: Sage.

Taub, E., Miller, N. E., Novack, T. A., Cook, E. W., III, Fleming, W. D., Nepomuceno, C. S., Connell, J. S., & Crago, J. E. (1993). Technique to improve chronic motor deficit after stroke. *Archives of Physical Medicine and Rehabilitation, 74,* 347–354.

Wolf, M. N., Risley, T. R., & Mees, H. (1964). Application of operant conditioning procedures to the behavior problems of an autistic child. *Behaviour Research and Therapy, 1,* 305–312.

67 SOCIAL SKILLS TRAINING

Chris Segrin

Social skills training is a widely applied and effective treatment for a range of psychosocial problems that include depression, anxiety, schizophrenia, loneliness, and marital distress to name but a few. Perhaps one reason for the ubiquity of this technique in clinical contexts is that it is actually a collection of techniques aimed at improving the quality of people's interpersonal communication and relationships. For this reason, social skills training can take a variety of specific forms that can be tailored to the particular needs of the client.

Social skills involve the ability to communicate with other people in a fashion that is both appropriate and effective. Appropriateness indicates that the social behavior does not violate social and relational norms. Socially skilled behaviors are instrumentally effective; that is, they allow the actor to successfully achieve his or her goals in social situations. Socially skilled behavioral performances are a complex amalgamation of declarative and procedural knowledge, motivation, ability to select among multiple behavioral response options, and at a most basic level, the ability to enact a particular social behavior.

Social skills training as a primary therapy for psychosocial problems or as an adjunct to other techniques has a long history with an efficacious track record. A number of narrative and meta-analytic reviews (e.g., Brady, 1984; Corrigan, 1991; Erwin, 1994; Taylor, 1996; Kopelowicz, Liberman, & Zarate, 2006) show that social skills training is effective at increasing clients' social skills and at reducing their psychiatric symptoms. Most empirical tests indicate that social skills training is as effective in treating psychosocial problems as most other therapeutic techniques that are in vogue. Furthermore, clients often adhere to social skills training therapies more readily than some other therapies that have higher dropout rates. Social skills training also appears to be more effective in outpatient compared to inpatient settings (Corrigan, 1991).

WHO WILL BENEFIT FROM SOCIAL SKILLS TRAINING?

Social skills training is well-suited to clients who are experiencing a psychosocial problem that is at least partly caused or exacerbated by interpersonal difficulties. These difficulties might include, for example, martial distress, low frequency dating, a lack of close friends, insufficient social support, trouble initiating new relationships, strained relationships with coworkers, or impoverished social networks. Similarly, social skills training may be an effective adjunct to other therapeutic techniques when the psychosocial problem has collateral deleterious effects on clients' interpersonal relationships. For example, an individual with alcoholism is likely to experience troubled interpersonal relationships, regardless of what "caused" the problem drinking. Social skills training may be helpful for improving the quality of clients' communication with significant others and may help them to more effectively marshal social support in their time of distress. Because the majority of people who are afflicted with a psychosocial problem will have some interpersonal difficulties (Segrin, 2001), whether etiologic or consequential, social skills training has a very broad based applicability and utility. An especially attractive feature of social skills training is that it can be easily tailored to suit the client's particular needs. For instance, an adolescent who is having difficulty making new friends, but otherwise has satisfying interactions and relationships with family members and school teachers, might participate in a social skills training regime that is focused exclusively on how to effectively initiate conversation, invite others to participate in shared activities, show interest in other people, and so on.

CONTRAINDICATIONS

Notwithstanding the broad applicability of social skills training for treating many psychosocial problems, there are certain circumstances that will limit the effectiveness of the technique. Because social skills training relies heavily on learning processes, clients with profound learning disabilities are unlikely to benefit from more sophisticated forms of social skills training. Related prerequisites for social skills training include the ability to pay attention to the therapist/trainer for at least 15–90 minutes at a time, the ability to understand and follow instructions for appropriate and effective behaviors, and most importantly, a motivation to learn new, and improve or correct existing, social behaviors (Liberman, DeRisi, & Mueser, 1989). For this reason, clients with severe attention deficits or gross thought disorders may not respond as readily to social skills training. Also, those with low motivation to enhance their interpersonal relationships, such as people with antisocial personalities or catatonia are unlikely to reap immediate benefits for social skills training. In such cases, psychotic symptoms, attention deficits, or maladaptive personalities need to first be brought under control or addressed, after which social skills training may be more effective.

OTHER FACTORS IN DECIDING WHETHER TO USE SOCIAL SKILLS TRAINING

This technique demands a significant degree of skill on the part of the trainer. Social skills training has historically been offered by individuals whose backgrounds are as varied as the problems to which the technique is applied. More powerful effects for social skills training have been documented in those cases where the trainer was a practicing psychologist as opposed to, say, a schoolteacher (Erwin, 1994). The decision to employ social skills training in the treatment of a psychosocial problem requires a frank and candid self-appraisal on the part of the practitioner. Ideally, the trainer would possess strong social skills and have a strong background in the rationale and application of the technique.

HOW DOES SOCIAL SKILLS TRAINING WORK?

The theoretical rational behind social skills training can be described at two levels. In the most general sense, the technique is predicated on the assumption that improvements in people's social relationships will translate directly and immediately into improved quality of life. By teaching clients how to improve their social skills, it is believed that they will be able to have more satisfying, effective, and enjoyable interactions with other people. As inherently social animals, most people are predisposed to respond positively to such outcomes. What is particularly powerful about this assumption is that it is generally thought to operate regardless of whether the client's actual problem was caused by troubled interpersonal relationships. Even in cases where a psychosocial problem appears more attributable to biological, cognitive, or environmental issues, there will be salutary effects pursuant to improving interpersonal communication and relationships through social skills training.

At a more specific level, the causal mechanisms underlying social skills training are essentially learning principles. In essence, the technique teaches clients new behaviors or appropriate modifications of existing behaviors. The new behaviors are aimed at producing positive reinforcement and diminishing the probability of punishing responses from the social environment. Indeed, this is how Libet and Lewinsohn (1973) actually define *social skill*. By emitting a greater proportion of behaviors that are positively reinforced by others (and a smaller proportion of behaviors that produce punishing responses from others) after social skills training, the client's overall sense of happiness, self-worth, and satisfaction is increased. There is also strong evidence to suggest that social skills training contributes to improved psychosocial functioning by reducing anxiety in social situations (Stravynski, Grey, & Elie, 1987).

STEP-BY-STEP PROCEDURES

As noted earlier, social skills training is actually a collection of techniques. Not all training programs utilize every one of these techniques, but the better developed and more successful programs use most of them (see for example Becker, Heimberg, & Bellack, 1987; Bellack, Mueser, Gingerich, & Agresta, 2004; Kopelowicz, Corrigan, Schade, & Liberman, 1995; Liberman et al., 1989). Many of the techniques presented in Table 67.1 can be successfully implemented in individual or group settings.

Assessment

Social skills training must start with an assessment phase. As social skills training is a nonspecific technique, decisions invariably have to be made about what types of social skills to focus on during the training. Given the extensive and complex nature of social interaction skills, it is unwise to assume that all people in need of social skills training need the same type of intervention. To proceed otherwise would create the potential for spending resources teaching skills that clients already possess, and missing skill areas in which clients genuinely need improvement.

The assessment of social skills can be carried out by a variety of methods (see Becker & Heimberg, 1988; Meier & Hope, 1998 for reviews). One very popular and cost efficient method is the use of *self-report instruments*. There are numerous popular and psychometrically sound instruments for assessing social skills as a traitlike entity such as the Social Skills Inventory (Riggio, 1986, 1989), or for assessing social skills in particular interpersonal domains, such as the Interpersonal Competence Questionnaire (Buhrmester, Furman, Wittenberg, & Reis, 1988). There are an abundance of additional self-report instruments for assessing particular components or aspects of social skills such as the Conflict Resolution Inventory (McFall & Lillesand, 1971) or the Dating and Assertion Questionnaire (Levenson & Gottman, 1978). In addition to self-reports, social skills can be effectively assessed through *behavioral observations*. While this ideally entails observation in naturalistic contexts, the use of staged role-plays with therapists and assistants has proven to be a useful mechanism for observing clients' enactment of skilled and unskilled social behaviors. A third method for the assessment of social skills involves the use of *third-party observers*. These might be spouses, teachers, parents, roommates, or friends of the client who can provide some information about how he or she behaves in various social situations. Ideally, the initial assessment phase in social skills training would employ the technique of triangulation by using multiple methods for assessing clients' social skills. The results of these assessments will then dictate the focal points of subsequent training.

TABLE 67.1   Key Elements of Social Skills Training

---

1. Assessment: Determine the specific area of the client's social skills deficits through self-reports, behavioral observations, and/or third party assessments.
2. Direct Instruction/Coaching: Teach and explain the basis of effective and appropriate social behaviors to the client along with specific suggestions for how to enact such behaviors.
3. Modeling: Show the client models enacting appropriate social behaviors, and receiving positive reinforcements for doing so. The modeling of inappropriate behaviors along with critiques and explanations may also be helpful.
4. Role-Playing: Encourage the client to practice certain social behaviors in a controlled environment, typically with the therapist and perhaps an assistant. Provide feedback to the client immediately after enacting the role-plays.
5. Homework Assignments: Instruct the client to enact certain social behaviors in the "real world." Start with easy behaviors and graduate to more complex ones. Debrief in the following session.

Direct Instruction/Coaching

Once a determination has been made concerning appropriate targets for intervention via social skills training, a reasonable starting point would involve offering instructions on how to interact more effectively with other people. This can be achieved in a lecture format, small group discussion, more casual one-on-one conversation, and even through videotapes and written manuals. Social skills training is often commenced with instructions about how to effectively use various communication behaviors, complete with a rationale for how and why the behaviors function as they do. Without any coaching or direct instruction there is a risk that clients will learn the behavior without also learning the reason for using it, and without learning when and why to use it. Explanation of how and why different behaviors are effective and appropriate is vital at this stage.

An example of direct instruction or coaching might involve explaining the importance of showing interest in other people. The social skills trainer might start by stating that when we show interest and pay attention to our conversational partners that makes them feel valued. Further, most people respond very positively to others who make them feel worthwhile, valued, and cared for. This later information provides an explanation for how and why "showing interest in others" works, and how it can be functional. In direct instruction and coaching the trainer must explain how to enact the behaviors and how they work to create rewarding social interactions and relationships. So the therapist might offer suggestions for how to show interest in other people such as asking, "How's it going today?" and then following up with another inquiry or a positive response to what the other person has to say. Similarly, the therapist might suggest that the client ask questions such as, "How was your weekend?" or "What have you been up to lately?" Of course, it would be important to work on developing these conversation starters in more extended interactions in which the client responds appropriately to the discourse of his or her partner. These suggestions would be coupled with discussions and explanations of their effect on other people (e.g., making them feel valued, letting them know that other people care about them, and so on).

Modeling

Modeling figures prominently among the mechanisms by which humans acquire new behaviors (Bandura, 1977). Capitalizing on this phenomenon, most social skills trainers are inclined to include modeling as an important part of the overall training package. In fact, Liberman et al. (1989) argued that "the most effective way to teach complex social behavior is through modeling and imitation" (p. 102). Modeling can be presented either on videotape or in live depiction. The purpose of modeling is to demonstrate the effective, and sometimes ineffective, use of certain behaviors. People who have difficulty saying and doing certain things when in the presence of others are sometimes more comfortable doing so after seeing someone else perform the behavior first. For this reason modeling is an important and effective component of many social skills training programs.

There are several steps that social skills trainers can take to increase the likelihood of successful modeling and acquisition of new behaviors by the trainee (Bandura, 1977; Smith, 1982; Trower, 1995). First, multiple models demonstrating the same behavior, or the same model repeating the demonstration, will increase the potential for learning the behavior. Multiple models challenge the idea that only rare and super-capable people can perform the behavior. Second, the more similar the model is to the client, in terms of sex, age, and other characteristics, the more likely the trainee is to imitate that model. Models that are similar to the target individual implicitly send the message that "people like us can perform this behavior." Third, models who are rewarded for their actions are more likely to be imitated. If the modeling can build in interaction with a second actor or confederate who rewards the model, the modeling process will be more effective. This is the cornerstone of observational learning: When models are rewarded for performing a behavior, observers are more likely to enact that behavior.

Modeling works because it gives people a template or guide for their own behavior.

Bandura refers to this as "making the unobservable observable" (Badura, 1986, p. 66). People cannot observe their own behavior. However, the observation of others' behavior gives people a mental picture of how the behavior can and should be performed. The primary outcome of successful modeling is the production of perceived *response efficacy*. This is the feeling that "this task can be accomplished" or "there are things that can be done to solve this problem or accomplish this goal." Response efficacy is an important component in reducing anxiety in social situations. When people have no sense of response efficacy they may feel that the situation is hopeless and simply avoid it all together. The use of models that are similar to the self also contributes to perceived *self-efficacy*. This is the feeling that "*I* can accomplish this task," or "there are things that *I* can do to solve this problem or accomplish this goal." Modeling is an important source of perceived self-efficacy (Bandura, 1986, 1999).

Role-Playing

After appropriate behaviors have been clearly modeled, the next step often involves having the client enact the behavior in the context of a role-play. Coaching and modeling are passive techniques in which trainees absorb information presented by others. However, role-playing is literally an interactive learning technique that calls for production and practice of actual behavior. The purpose of role playing is to have clients practice the desired behaviors in a controlled setting where they can be observed and from which feedback and reinforcement can be offered.

Typically, role-plays are set up with a description of a fictitious scene that resembles the problematic situation in which new behaviors are desired. For example, in their social skills training with alcoholics, Foy and his colleagues had subjects role-play drink refusal (Foy, Miller, Eisler, & O'Toole, 1976). The scene was set up as follows: "You are at your brother's house. It is a special occasion and your whole family and several friends are there. Your brother says, 'How about a beer?'" (p. 1341). The therapist who

played the role of the brother would also counter refusals from the subjects with statements such as, "One drink won't hurt you." Clients were instructed to act as if they were actually in that situation.

The effective use of role-playing in social skills training must include more than the simple production and practice of behavior on the part of the trainee. It is vital that the trainer provide a detailed critique and abundant positive reinforcement for appropriate and desired behaviors. It is recommended that clients rerun the scene, performing it several times in order to produce the desired response (Liberman et al., 1989). Clients should be reminded that it is okay if things do not go well on the first try. The use of rewards for successful role-playing is predicated on the assumption that the behaviors that are positively reinforced are more likely to be repeated, hopefully in contexts outside of the training environment. It is essential that there be proportionally more positive reinforcement than negative criticism (Trower, Bryant, & Argyle, 1978). The reward inherent in positive feedback can intensify motivation and effort. Negative criticism, on the other hand, can be discouraging if it is abundant and may inhibit subsequent attempts at performing the behavior. Trower et al. also note that feedback must emphasize effect rather than appearance. For example, it is better to tell a trainee that "You made me feel like you did not know what you were talking about" rather than "you looked confused." The emphasis on effect over appearance is predicted on the assumption that "skilled" behavior is ultimately a social perception that has to be created in others. Feedback following role-plays should also be detailed and specific, with a commentary on particular behaviors such as posture, vocal tone, eye contact, specific utterances, and so forth. Sometimes in group contexts, other clients are requested to offer feedback (a useful technique for getting them to practice social perception skills). One reason why role plays are such a useful part of social skills training is because they allow the client to practice the desired behaviors in a controlled setting, while also allowing the trainer to make observations and assessments of the client's progress.

Homework Assignments

Homework assignments call for *in vivo* practice of targeted behaviors. Homework assignments are not for the debutante in social skills training. Without successful training and verification of primary social skills through the techniques discussed above, homework assignments can set the client up for disaster. Of all the social skills training techniques, homework assignments require the highest level of existing skill on the part of the trainee. At the same time they have perhaps the highest potential for payoff in that the client puts into actual practice the skills learned in the training setting.

Homework assignments that are commonly employed in social skills training include things like asking directions from a bus driver, going to a business and asking for a job application, and calling up a friend and making a lunch date. Typically, homework assignments are graduated by difficulty, and "easier" tasks are assigned first. For example, a client might be asked to solicit information from the bus driver first, and then to make a lunch date with a friend after successfully completing other "easy" homework assignments.

Like role-plays, homework assignments often benefit from a "debriefing" during which the client and trainer discuss and critique the performances. Here again, the use of praise and positive reinforcement is often used to enhance the effectiveness of the learning process. It has also been recommended that trainers appropriately prepare clients for the possibility of failures in future homework assignments (Liberman et al., 1989) and explain how people cannot realistically expect success in all of their social interactions. The goal of social skills training is simply to increase the probability of success in social interactions.

The adept trainer will capitalize on problems or failures that arise in the context of these homework assignments in order to highlight what went wrong and how it can be corrected. This "learn from your mistakes" approach can be an effective component of homework assignments, so long as these interpersonal failures are not disproportionately represented in the trainee's experiences. Again, supportive feedback and encouragement are an important part of the analysis of interpersonal failures, if the trainee's motivation level and self-esteem are to be maintained.

Follow-up

A thorough social skills training program must involve some form of follow-up. Social skills, like most other skills, will decay unless practiced somewhat diligently. There is little reason to believe that social skills training can be successfully accomplished via one-shot training procedures that teach skills, and then send people out into the world with no follow-up. It is essential to monitor clients' successes and failures, with attempts to fine-tune their performances. Follow-up training may occur weeks or months after completion of the primary training regime, and often begins with a reassessment of clients' social skills. Depending on the outcome of these reassessments, the trainer may offer "refresher" training procedures that could involve more coaching, role-plays, and homework assignments, for those areas that are still in need of improvement.

EXAMPLES OF EVIDENCE-BASED APPLICATIONS

Alcoholism/Substance Dependence

Eriksen, L., Björnstad, S., & Götestam, K. G. (1986). Social skills training in groups for alcoholics: One-year treatment outcome for groups and individuals. *Addictive Behaviors, 11*, 309–329.

Monti, P. M., Abrams, D. B., Binkoff, J. A., Zwick, W. R., Liepman, M. R., Nirenberg, T. D., & Rohsenow, D. J. (1990). Communication skills training, communication skills training with family and cognitive behavioral mood management training for alcoholics. *Journal of Studies on Alcohol, 51*, 263–270.

Monti, P. M., & O'Leary, T. A. (1999). Coping and social skills training for alcohol and cocaine dependence. *Psychiatric Clinics of North America, 22*, 447–470.

Attention-Deficit-Hyperactivity Disorder

Frankel, F., Myatt, R., Cantwell, D. P., & Feinberg, D. T. (1997). Parent assisted transfer of children's social skills training: Effects on children with and without attention-deficit hyperactivity disorder. *Journal of the American Academy of Child and Adolescent Psychiatry, 36,* 1056–1064.

Gol, D., & Jarus, T. (2005). Effect of a social skills training group on everyday activities of children with attention deficit hyperactivity disorder. *Developmental Medicine and Child Neurology, 47,* 539–545.

Pfiffner, L. J., & McBurnett, K. (1997). Social skills training with parent generalization: Treatment effects for children with attention deficit disorder. *Journal of Consulting and Clinical Psychology, 65,* 749–757.

Bullying

DeRosier, M. E. (2004). Building relationships and combating bullying: Effectiveness of a school-based social skills group intervention. *Journal of Clinical Child and Adolescent Psychology, 33,* 196–201.

Depression

Bellack, A. S., Hersen, M., & Himmelhoch, J. M. (1981). Social skills training compared with pharmacotherapy and psychotherapy in the treatment of unipolar depression. *American Journal of Psychiatry, 138,* 1562–1567.

Bellack, A. S., Hersen, M., & Himmelhoch, J. M. (1983). Social skills training for unipolar depression. *Psychotherapy in Private Practice, 1,* 9–13.

Bellack, A. S., Hersen, M., & Himmelhoch, J. M. (1983). A comparison of social-skills training, pharmacotherapy, and psychotherapy for depression. *Behaviour Research and Therapy, 21,* 101–107.

Schizophrenia

Benton, M. K., & Schroeder, H. E. (1990). Social skills training with schizophrenics: A meta-analytic evaluation. *Journal of Consulting and Clinical Psychology, 58,* 741–747.

Granholm, E., McQuaid, J. R., McClure, F. S., Link, P. C., Perivoliotis, D., Gottlieb, J. D., Patterson, T. L., & Jeste, D. V. (2007). Randomized controlled trial of cognitive behavioral social skills training for older people with schizophrenia: 12-month follow-up. *Journal of Clinical Psychiatry, 68,* 730–737.

Kurtz, M. H., & Mueser, K. T. (2008). A meta-analysis of controlled research on social skills training for schizophrenia. *Journal of Consulting and Clinical Psychology, 76,* 491–504.

Further Reading

Bellack, A. S., & Hersen, M. (Eds.). (1979). *Research and practice of social skills training.* New York: Plenum Press.

Liberman, R. P., DeRisi, W. J., & Mueser, K. T. (1989). *Social skills training for psychiatric patients.* New York: Pergamon Press.

Segrin, C., & Givertz, M. (20003). Methods of social skills training and development. In J. O. Greene & B. R. Burleson (Eds.), *Handbook of communication and social interaction skills* (pp. 135–176). Mahwah, NJ: Lawrence Erlbaum.

References

Bandura, A. (1977). *Social learning theory.* Englewood Cliffs, NJ: Prentice Hall.

Bandura, A. (1986). *Social foundations of thought and action.* Englewood Cliffs, NJ: Prentice Hall.

Becker, R. E., & Heimberg, R. G. (1988). Assessment of social skills. In A. S. Bellack & M. Hersen (Eds.) *Behavioral assessment: A practical handbook* (3rd ed.) (pp. 365–395). New York: Pergamon.

Becker, R. E., Heimberg, R. G., & Bellack, A. S. (1987). *Social skills training treatment for depression.* New York: Pergamon Press.

Bellack, A. S., Mueser, K. T., Gingerich, S., & Agresta, J. (2004). *Social skills training for schizophrenia* (2nd ed.). New York: Guilford Press.

Brady, J. P. (1984). Social skills training for psychiatric patients, II: Clinical outcome studies. *American Journal of Psychiatry, 141,* 491–498.

Buhrmester, D., Furman, W., Wittenberg, M. T., & Reis, H. T. (1988). Five domains of interpersonal competence in peer relationships. *Journal of Personality and Social Psychology, 55,* 991–1008.

Corrigan, P. W. (1991). Social skills training in adult psychiatric populations: A meta-analysis. *Journal* of *Behavior Therapy and Experimental Psychiatry, 22,* 203–210.

Erwin, P. G. (1994). Effectiveness of social skills training with children: A meta-analytic study. *Counselling Psychology Quarterly, 7,* 305–310.

Kopelowicz, A., Corrigan, P. W., Schade, M., & Liberman, R. P. (1998). Social skills training. In K. T. Mueser & N. Tarrier (Eds.), *Handbook of social functioning in schizophrenia* (pp. 307–326). Boston, MA: Allyn and Bacon.

Kopelowicz., A., Liberman, R. P., & Zarate, R. (2006). Recent advances in social skills training for schizophrenia. *Schizophrenia Bulletin, 32,* S12–S23.

Levenson, R. W., & Gottman, J. M. (1978). Toward the assessment of social competence. *Journal of Consulting and Clinical Psychology, 46,* 453–462.

Liberman, R. P., DeRisi, W. J., & Mueser, K. T. (1989). *Social skills training for psychiatric patients.* New York: Pergamon Press.

Libet, J., & Lewinsohn, P. M. (1973). The concept of social skill with special reference to the behavior of depressed persons. *Journal of Consulting and Clinical Psychology, 40,* 304–312.

McFall, R. M., & Lillesand, D. B. (1971). Behavioral rehearsal with modeling and coaching in assertion training. *Journal of Abnormal Psychology, 77,* 313–323.

Riggio, R. E. (1986). Assessment of basic social skills. *Journal of Personality and Social Psychology, 51,* 649–660.

Riggio, R. E. (1989). *Social skills inventory manual.* Palo Alto, CA: Consulting Psychologists Press.

Segrin, C. (2001). *Interpersonal processes in psychological problems.* New York: Guilford.

Smith, M. J. (1982). *Persuasion and human action.* Belmont, CA: Wadsworth.

Stravynski, A., Grey, S., & Elie, R. (1987). Outline of the therapeutic process in social skills training with socially dysfunctional adults. *Journal of Consulting and Clinical Psychology, 55,* 224–228.

Taylor, S. (1996). Meta-analysis of cognitive-behavioral treatment for social phobia. *Journal of Behavior Therapy and Experimental Psychiatry, 27,* 1–9.

Trower, P. (1995). Adult social skills: State of the art and future direction. W. O'Donohue & L. Krasner (Eds.), *Handbook of psychological skills training: Clinical techniques and applications* (pp. 54–80). Boston, MA: Allyn and Bacon.

Trower, P., Bryant, B., & Argyle, A. (1978). *Social skills and mental health.* Pittsburgh: University of Pittsburgh Press.

68

SQUEEZE TECHNIQUE FOR THE TREATMENT OF PREMATURE EJACULATION

Claudia Avina

The squeeze technique was derived from Seman's (1956) stop–start technique and popularized by Masters and Johnson (1970). Both treatments require that males masturbate just prior to ejaculation and resume once the urge to ejaculate has dissipated. The difference between the two treatments is that in the squeeze technique the male or his partner is required to squeeze the head of his penis to decrease his urge to ejaculate while in the stop–start technique he is simply required to suspend sexual stimulation until his urge has decreased.

Masters and Johnson (1970) reported a remarkable posttreatment success rate of 97.8% for the squeeze technique in a sample of 186 men suffering from premature ejaculation over a span of 11 years. At the 5-year follow-up, a 2.7% failure rate was reported. To date, the dramatic results reported by Masters and Johnson (1970) have not been replicated in other studies (O'Donohue, Letourneau, & Geer, 1993). One obvious methodological difference between more recent studies and the work by Masters and Johnson is the inconsistency in outcome criteria. Masters and Johnson used the criterion of achieving partner satisfaction in 50% of coital attempts while others have compared posttreatment ejaculatory latency to baseline (Lowe & Mikulas, 1975). It has been suggested that the vagueness of the treatment criterion used by Masters and Johnson may have inflated their results (O'Donohue et al., 1993). The work by Masters and Johnson has also been criticized for a lack of scientific rigor (O'Donohue et al., 1993; Zilbergeld & Evans, 1980).

Evaluating the effectiveness of the squeeze technique is problematic because treatment outcome studies commonly have either used mixed samples, used the squeeze technique in combination with other sex therapy approaches (Heiman & LoPiccolo, 1983; LoPiccolo, Heiman, Hogan, & Roberts, 1985), or failed to specify actual treatment practices (LoPiccolo et al., 1985; Trudel & Proulx, 1987). In addition, the squeeze technique and the stop-start technique have been employed jointly or as equivalent treatments (Golden, Price, Heinrich, & Lobitz, 1978; Zeiss, 1978). The squeeze technique has also been used as part of a larger treatment package that involves other potentially active interventions such as CBT (Carey, 1998; Yulis, 1976) or systematic desensitization (Ince, 1973).

Empirical studies evaluating treatment outcomes with homogeneous samples of premature ejaculators and where the squeeze technique was one component of treatment have generally found significant improvements in ejaculatory latency (Lowe & Mikulas, 1975; Trudel & Proulx, 1987; Zeiss, 1978). The treatment packages in these studies were commonly composed of the squeeze technique, the stop–start technique, and sensate focus or communication skills. Lowe and Mikulas (1975) evaluated statistical differences between baseline and posttreatment latency, whereas Trudel and Proulx (1987) and Zeiss (1978) measured whether males met a criterion latency of more than 5 minutes. Golden and colleagues (1978) reported no significant differences of ejaculatory latency between the treatment and control group but did find that males in the treatment group were more satisfied with their orgasmic ability.

Treatment outcome studies using samples presenting with multiple sexual dysfunctions provide results that are difficult to interpret due to the practice of reporting improvements in sexual functioning for the entire treatment group (Clement & Schmidt, 1983; Everaerd & Dekker, 1985). It is difficult to discern how specific treatments impact specific problems. Studies that report improvements for premature ejaculation do so in terms of changes in length of foreplay and intercourse but not actual ejaculatory latency (Hartman & Daly, 1983; Heiman & LoPiccolo, 1983). Also, the small sample of men suffering from premature ejaculation (ranging from 2 to 21 subjects) in each of these studies provides inadequate evidence to make generalizations about treatment outcomes (Clement & Schmidt, 1983; Everaerd & Dekker, 1985; Hartman & Daly, 1983; Heiman & LoPiccolo, 1983; LoPiccolo et al., 1985).

The squeeze technique continues to be recommended as the psychological treatment for premature ejaculation (Masters & Johnson, 1993; O'Donohue et al., 1993; Segraves & Althof, 1998). The lack of satisfactory data on the effectiveness of the squeeze technique can be more adequately accounted for by the lack of rigorous research than by deficiencies in the intervention. Yet, it is not clearly understood why the squeeze technique works. It has been proposed that the squeeze technique may work because the procedure creates response extinction through a process of counterconditioning, teaches men to monitor arousal levels, and/or provides a greater frequency of sexual activity (LoPiccolo & Stock, 1986).

WHO MIGHT BENEFIT FROM THIS TREATMENT?

As a treatment that helps individuals gain ejaculatory control, the squeeze technique will benefit males suffering from premature ejaculation. The *Diagnostic and Statistical Manual of Mental Disorders* (4th ed., Text Revision, or *DSM-IV-TR*; American Psychiatric Association, 2000) diagnostic criteria define premature ejaculation as ejaculation resulting from minimal stimulation

and before the person wishes it to occur (p. 554). In light of social pressure that the man is responsible for long-lasting intercourse, it is very likely that healthy sexual functioning males will experience ejaculation before they wish it to happen. The recognition of premature ejaculation as a disorder should occur when there exists a consistent pattern of ejaculating quickly in the context of little stimulation, the pattern persists, and this behavior causes marked distress or interpersonal difficulty. The squeeze technique may be most appropriate for males who ejaculate too quickly because the behavior is a conditioned response (i.e., ending sexual activity quickly in order to avoid being discovered) or for males who lack a learning history of controlled ejaculatory latency during intercourse (i.e., ejaculating outside the vagina as a means of birth control or limited opportunities to engage in coitus).

CONTRAINDICATIONS

The squeeze technique is appropriate for males who suffer from a lack of ejaculatory control. However, currently there is no accepted standard for normal functioning in this domain as the range of normative ejaculatory latency is fairly broad (O'Donohue et al., 1993). Recommended criteria include the lack of ability to control ejaculation for a sufficient amount of time to achieve partner satisfaction in at least 50% of coital attempts (Masters & Johnson, 1970) or ejaculating before a specified time criterion ranging from 1 to 10 minutes (Metz, Pryor, Nesvacil, Abuzzahab, & Koznar, 1997). The squeeze technique is expected to teach men ejaculatory control for approximately 15–20 minutes of sexual stimulation. The intervention may not be appropriate for males who can already control ejaculation for this length of time but still complain that they are ejaculating before the desired time or that they have not achieved sexual satisfaction with their partners. In these cases it may be more appropriate to provide psychoeducation about sexual functioning or to assess for problems in the sexual interactions between client and partner.

The problem of insufficient ejaculatory control may be a result of psychological factors, organic factors, or a combination. A medical evaluation should be consistently employed when a client complains of problems in sexual functioning. Administering the squeeze technique is not appropriate and potentially iatrogenic for individuals suffering from premature ejaculation that is largely due to a medical condition such as diabetes, prostatitis, urethritis, and urological disorders, or to organic factors such as trauma to the sympathetic nervous system and pelvic fractures (Athanasiadis, 1998).

OTHER FACTORS IN DECIDING WHETHER TO USE THE SQUEEZE TECHNIQUE

It is very possible that comorbid problems will exist in males suffering from premature ejaculation. These individuals may be suffering from a different sexual dysfunction related to desire or arousal, as well as some other mental disorder such as major depression or panic disorder. In these instances, treatment providers should ascertain temporal order of the disorders when assessing the onset, context, and etiology of each sexual dysfunction or other disorder. One concern is that clients with underlying psychopathology may respond poorly to sex therapy (e.g., the squeeze technique) (Avina, O'Donohue, & Regev, 1997). Another important issue is deciding on the appropriate treatment when premature ejaculation is the result of another disorder. Treatment providers must decide whether to (1) treat other mental disorders prior to implementing the squeeze technique, (2) implement the squeeze technique simultaneously with some other treatment, (3) treat only the other mental disorder, or (4) implement only the squeeze technique.

Although there does not appear to be a relationship between marital satisfaction and sexual dysfunction, except for problems of desire (Morokoff & Gillilland, 1993), it is not uncommon for committed partners to seek services for problems in sexual functioning (Heiman, Gladue, Roberts, & LoPiccolo, 1986; LoPiccolo et al., 1985; Masters & Johnson, 1970; Snyder & Berg, 1983). Sexual partners can experience anger, inadequate communication, distrust, or low levels of emotional closeness. Individuals in a committed relationship could also experience a fear of pregnancy, fear of losing control, or fear of contracting a sexually transmitted disease. Any one of these aspects could be detrimental to an individual's sexual functioning as they interfere with one's willingness and comfort in engaging in sexual intimacy. Avoidant and distant behaviors on behalf of the individual experiencing these factors may result in his or her partner's feeling insecure about his or her ability to sexually satisfy the other individual or distrustful of the individual's commitment to the relationship. The decision to implement the squeeze technique in the face of relationship problems should be made by determining the temporal order of the relationship and sexual difficulties, willingness of the couple to work on the diagnosed problem or problems, and the treatment that will likely lead to the most efficient and comprehensive positive outcomes (Jacobson & Margolin, 1979).

CLINICAL APPLICATION OF THE SQUEEZE TECHNIQUE

The squeeze technique can be employed by an individual or by his partner if his partner is willing to participate. The treatment involves providing psychoeducation about the ejaculatory process and a procedure for helping the individual gain ejaculatory control. Specifically, the treatment provider educates the individual about the two stages of ejaculation involving involuntary contractions by the prostate gland and the discharge of seminal fluid (Masters & Johnson, 1970). This information is used to help the individual recognize different levels of arousal.

The individual is instructed to masturbate until a full erection is achieved and just prior to ejaculation. Moreover, the individual is expected to monitor their arousal in order to recognize when they have reached this point. The individual is further instructed to stop masturbating at this point and squeeze the head of his penis with enough force that his urge to ejaculate halts almost immediately. Squeezing of the head of the penis is achieved using two fingers on the top and the thumb on the bottom of the coronal ridge (the dorsal side and frenulum of the penis) for approximately 3–4 seconds. Stimulation should resume about 10–30 seconds after the head of the penis has been released and once the urge to ejaculate has completely subsided. This process should be repeated at least three times prior to ejaculation. It is recommended that the client continue these exercises until he can delay his ejaculation for 15–20 minutes.

The individual's partner can be incorporated into this treatment by having the partner instead of the client carry out the manual stimulation and/or squeezing of the head of the client's penis. In order for the partner to carry out the technique successfully, the client will have to notify his partner when he is at the point just prior to ejaculation. It is important that client–partner communication indicating when the male is at this point be clear, readily received, and acted on (McCarthy, 1989).

The squeeze technique may also include behavioral exercises between the client and his partner involving penile intromission once ejaculatory control is achieved with masturbation exercises. The couple is instructed to manually stimulate the penis until a full erection is achieved and then allow insertion of the penis without movement or pelvic thrusting. The client is instructed to concentrate on the sensations produced by this activity. When the client feels that he is about to ejaculate, the penis should be removed, the squeeze technique should be employed, and the penis should be reinserted. Similar to masturbation or manual stimulation exercises, this process should be repeated at least three times before ejaculation. As the client begins to gain ejaculatory control during intromission without movement, he will be instructed to begin using pelvic thrusting. Once ejaculatory control is achieved during intromission, his partner will be instructed to begin using thrusting movements and the couple will be instructed to repeat the process of using the squeeze technique at least three times prior to ejaculation. The goal of the technique is to allow the male to gain ejaculatory control for 15–20 minutes during intercourse (see Table 68.1).

Masters and Johnson (1970) have suggested that after treatment is completed, the couple should use the squeeze technique at least once

TABLE 68.1 Steps in the Clinical Application of the Technique

- Individual homework sessions should last approximately 15 to 20 minutes.
- Apply the squeeze technique 3–4 times before ejaculating.
- Begin employing the squeeze technique with manual stimulation first.
- After achieving prolonged latency with manual stimulation exercises, proceed to intromission without thrusting.
- After achieving prolonged latency with intromission without thrusting, proceed to intromission with thrusting.
- Continue employing technique once a month for 6–12 months following treatment.

a week with intercourse, maintain a regular frequency of intercourse (this will depend on the individual couple's preferences), and utilize the exercises using manual stimulation/masturbation and the squeeze technique for one 15–20—minute session once a month. It is recommended that ejaculatory control exercises continue for 6–12 months following treatment. It is also recommended that the squeeze technique be employed when there is a sufficient period of time where sexual activity allowing for controlled ejaculation is present (a few weeks).

One final caveat should be highlighted regarding the expected success of this treatment. While the squeeze technique is administered in order to teach men ejaculatory latency, the goal should not be the length of latency but rather on the sexual pleasure experienced by the client and his partner (McConaghy, 1993; Wincze & Carey, 1991). Ejaculatory control is considered one component in achieving sexual satisfaction. Treatment providers should remain cognizant of other repertoire deficits in the client or his partner that may hinder sexual satisfaction and apply appropriate interventions as needed.

CURRENT APPLICATIONS OF THIS TREATMENT

Despite the issues identified above including the methodological problems of empirical studies and the lack of clarity regarding the working mechanism(s) of the intervention, research examining and evaluating the squeeze technique has seemingly discontinued in the past two decades. Yet, it continues to be recommended as a standard component of sex therapy when premature ejaculation is one of the primary identified problems (Zilbergeld & Kilmann, 1984). Because of the nature of the intervention, it is delivered with great specificity. It does not lend itself to be used across psychological diagnoses. The most modern practice is the use of psychiatric medications such as antidepressants and selective serotonin reuptake inhibitors (Ginsberg, 2004; Richardson, 2005; Waldinger, 2001) to achieve effects similar to those offered by the squeeze technique. The administration of drug treatment alone should be conducted cautiously as premature ejaculation often exists as one of a complex interaction of relationship problems (Rosen, 1995). In this respect, the squeeze technique may allow the clinician greater flexibility to adapt it to relationship issues given that it involves partner participation in the interruption of intercourse and thus, necessitates foundational relationship skills. Moreover, the competent use of the squeeze technique is one in which all contributing relationship factors are addressed within the application of the treatment. The treatment provider should take great care in identifying and targeting how relationship dynamics will influence and be influenced by the use of this technique.

Further Reading

Zeiss, R. A., & Zeiss, A. M. (1978). *Prolong your pleasure*. New York: Pocket Books.
Masters, W., & Johnson, V. (1970). *Human sexual inadequacy*. Boston: Little, Brown.

References

American Psychiatric Association (2000). Diagnostic and statistical manual of mental disorders (4th ed., Text Revision). Washington, DC: American Psychiatric Association.
Athanasiadis, L. (1998). Premature ejaculation: Is it a biogenic or a psychogenic disorder? *Sexual and Marital Therapy, 13,* 241–255.
Avina, C., O'Donohue, W., & Regev, L. (2007). Psychological and behavioral counseling in the management of male sexual dysfunction. In F. Kandeel (Ed.), *Male Sexual Dysfunction: Pathophysiology and treatment*. New York: Marcel Dekker.
Carey, M. P. (1998). Cognitive-behavioral treatment of sexual dysfunctions. In V. E. Caballo (Ed.), *International handbook of cognitive and behavioural treatment for psychological disorders* (pp. 251–280). Kidlington, UK: Elsevier Science.
Clement, U., & Schmidt, G. (1983). The outcome of couple therapy for sexual dysfunctions using three different formats. *Journal of Sex and Marital Therapy, 9,* 67–78.
Everaerd, W., & Dekker, J. (1985). Treatment of male sexual dysfunction: Sex therapy compared with systematic desensitization and rational emotive therapy. *Behaviour Research and Therapy, 22,* 114–124.
Ginsbeg, D. L. (2004). Gabapentin treatment of premature ejaculation. *Primary Psychiatry, 11,* 20–24.
Golden, J. S., Price, S., Heinrich, A. G., & Lobitz, W. C. (1978). Group vs. couple treatment of sexual dysfunctions. *Archives of Sexual Behavior, 7,* 593–602.
Hartman, L. M., & Daly, E. M. (1983). Relationship factors in the treatment of sexual dysfunction. *Behaviour Research and Therapy, 21,* 253–260.
Heiman, J. R., Gladue, B. A., Roberts, C. W., & LoPiccolo, J. (1986). Historical and current factors discriminating sexually functional from sexually dysfunctional married couples. *Journal of Marital and Family Therapy, 12,* 163–174.
Heiman, J. R., & LoPiccolo, J. (1983). Clinical outcome of sex therapy. *Archives of General Psychiatry, 140,* 94–101.
Ince, L. P. (1973). Behavior modification of sexual disorders. *American Journal of Psychotherapy, 27,* 446–451.
Jacobson, N. S., & Margolin, G. (1979). Marital therapy: Strategies based on social learning and behavior exchange principles. New York: Brunner/Mazel.
LoPiccolo, J., Heiman, J. R., Hogan, D. R., & Roberts, C. W. (1985). Effectiveness of single therapists versus cotherapy teams in sex therapy. *Journal of Consulting and Clinical Psychology, 53,* 287–294.
LoPiccolo, J., & Stock, W. E. (1986). Treatment of sexual dysfunction. *Journal of Consulting and Clinical Psychology, 54,* 158–167.
Lowe, J. C., & Mikulas, W. L. (1975). Use of written material in learning self-control of premature ejaculation. *Psychological Reports, 37,* 295–298.
Masters, W., & Johnson, V. *Human sexual inadequacy*. Boston: Little, Brown.
McCarthy, B. W. (1989). Cognitive-behavioral strategies and techniques in the treatment of early ejaculation. In S. R. Leiblum & R. C. Rosen (Eds.). *Priniciples and practice of sex therapy* (2nd ed., pp. 141–167).
Metz, M. E., Pryor, J. L., Nesvacil, L. J., Abuzzahab, F., Sr., & Koznar, J. (1997). Premature ejaculation:

A psychophysiological review. *Journal of Sex and Marital Therapy, 23,* 3–23.

O'Donohue, W., Letourneau, E., & Geer, J. H. (1993). Premature ejaculation. In W. O'Donohue & J. H. Geer (Eds). *Handbook of sexual dysfunctions: Assessment and treatment* (pp. 303–334). Needham Heights, MA: Allyn and Bacon.

Richardson, D. (1995). Pharmacological treatment for premature ejaculation. *International Journal of STD & AIDS, 16,* 709–711.

Rosen, R. C. (1995). A case of premature ejaculation: Too little, too late? In R. C. Rosen & S. R. Leiblum (Eds.), *Case studies in sex therapy* (pp. 279–294). New York: Guilford.

Segraves, R. T., & Althof, S. (1998). Psychotherapy and pharmacotherapy of sexual dysfunctions. In P. E. Nathan & J. M. Gorman (Eds.), *A guide to treatments that work* (pp. 447–471). New York: Oxford University Press.

Seman, J. H. (1956). Premature ejaculation: A new approach. *Southern Medical Journal, 49,* 353–358.

Snyder, D. K., & Berg, P. (1983). Determinants of sexual dissatisfaction in sexually distressed couples. *Archives of Sexual Behavior, 12,* 237–246.

Trudel, G., & Proulx, S. (1987). Treatment of premature ejaculation by bibliotherapy: An experimental study. *Sexual and Marital Therapy, 2,* 163–167.

Waldinger, M. Antidepressants and ejaculation: A double-blind, randomized, placebo-controlled, fixed-dose study with paroxetine, sertraline, and nefazodone. *Journal of Clinical Psychopharmacology, 21,* 293–297.

Yulis, S. (1976). Generalization of therapeutic gain in the treatment of premature ejaculation. *Behavior Therapy, 7,* 355–358.

Zeiss, R. A., (1978). Self-directed treatment for premature ejaculation. *Journal of Consulting and Clinical Psychology, 46,* 1234–1241.

Zilbergeld, R. B., & Evans, M. (1980). The inadequacy of Masters and Johnson. *Psychology Today, 14,* 29–43.

Zilbergeld, B., & Kilmann, P. R. (1985). The scope and effectiveness of sex therapy. *Psychotherapy, 21,* 319–326.

69 STIMULUS CONTROL

Alan Poling and Scott T. Gaynor

Stimulus control is present when a change in a particular property of a stimulus produces a change in behavior, such as an increase in the rate of occurrence of a particular response. In a general sense, a stimulus is a physical event. Changes in stimuli can be discrete, as when a particular person is either present or absent, or continuous, as when the intensity of a siren increases as a police car approaches. For example, the probability of a heroin abuser making a request for the drug might be greater when a pusher was present than when he or she was absent, or the probability of a driver with a marijuana cigarette smoking the joint might decrease directly with the loudness of the siren. In the first case, stimulus control is *excitatory*. That is, a particular response is more likely to occur in the presence of a designated stimulus than in its absence. *Inhibitory* stimulus control, where a particular response is less likely to occur in the presence of a particular stimulus than in its absence, is evident in the second example.

Stimulus control does not refer to a particular therapeutic technique. Rather, the term describes relationships between antecedent stimuli and subsequent behaviors. Such relationships, which can be established through classical or operant conditioning, are of quintessential importance in cognitive behavior therapy. Many behavioral problems are to some extent stimulus control problems. For example, phobias involve exaggerated fear responses engendered by specific stimuli (e.g., spiders, crowds) or by thinking about those stimuli. Sexual fetishes are defined by sexual arousal educed by encountering or thinking about stimuli that do not evoke sexual arousal in most people. Reading problems are present when someone fails to react appropriately (e.g., make certain sounds) when presented with configurations of letters that constitute words. In fact, it is difficult to envision a behavior disorder that

does not involve some degree of inappropriate stimulus control.

A great deal of research has examined various aspects of stimulus control and interest in the topic appears to have increased over time. For instance, a recent (January 14, 2008) search of the Scopus database yielded 45,259 publications in which "stimulus control" appeared in the title, abstract, or list of key words. Table 69.1 shows that the number of publications in each 10-year block increased progressively from 1968–1977 through 1998–2007. A great deal of information is available regarding the development and maintenance of stimulus control and its relevance to normal and pathological behavior in humans and other animals. The balance of this chapter is based on, but cannot do justice to, this information.

STIMULUS CONTROL AND CLASSICAL CONDITIONING

Not surprisingly, establishing, abolishing, or otherwise altering stimulus control is an important aspect of treating a wide range of behavior disorders. One general way in which stimulus control can be established or altered is through classical (or respondent) conditioning. In the context of classical conditioning, stimulus control is exercised by unconditional stimuli (USs), which reflexively elicit unconditional responses (URs). Stimulus control is also exercised by conditional stimuli (CSs), which are previously neutral stimuli that gain the capacity to elicit conditional responses (CRs) by virtue of being paired with USs in a particular way. In essence, for classical conditioning to occur, the probability of the US occurring must be higher shortly after presentation of the CS than at any other time. Most therapeutic applications that involve respondent

TABLE 69.1 Number of Publications Involving "Stimulus Control".

	Years				
	1900–1967	1968–1977	1978–1987	1988–1997	1998–2007
Number Cited	137	2,646	6,693	13,214	22,569

conditioning entail altering stimulus control by a clinically relevant CS.

For example, CRs elicited by stimuli (CSs) that reliably precede delivery of any of a number of abused drugs (e.g., alcohol, cocaine, heroin), which serve as USs, can function as establishing operations (EOs) that increase the reinforcing effectiveness of the drug and increase the likelihood of behaviors that historically have produced it (see Laraway, Snycerski, Michael, & Poling, 2003, for a discussion of behavior analytic approaches to motivation and related terminology). The CRs also contribute to subjective "urges" or "cravings" for the drug. In this case, classical conditioning interacts with operant conditioning to contribute to drug use and abuse—EOs, established by classical conditioning, affect drug seeking and drug taking, which is operantly conditioned behavior (i.e., behavior primarily controlled by its consequences). For instance, the sight of a syringe by an intravenous heroin user may increase the momentary reinforcing effectiveness of heroin for that person and cause her or him to call someone from whom the drug has previously been obtained. This can occur even if the person has not used heroin for a protracted period and is not physically dependent on the drug.

The importance of classical conditioning in the genesis and treatment of drug abuse is emphasized in cue exposure therapy, which has gained considerable popularity in the past decade (e.g., Cunningham, 1998; Drummond, Tifany, Glautier, & Remington, 1995). An important part of cue exposure therapy is exposing the client to stimuli that historically preceded drug delivery (CSs) under conditions where the drug (US) is not delivered. For example, a person who abuses alcohol would repeatedly see, hold, and smell her or his preferred adult beverage without taking a drink. With sufficient exposures, the capacity of the sight, smell, and feel of the beverage to elicit CRs that function as

EOs would be abolished through the process of respondent extinction. The same process would be used to deal with the effects of other pre-drug stimuli, such as thinking about having a drink or entering a bar. The specific CSs that need to be dealt with will vary across clients and, as Cunningham (1998) points out, knowledge of how stimulus control of CRs is established and abolished is necessary to develop effective therapies. He notes that removal of drug-related CSs, arranging extinction in multiple contexts, conditioned inhibition training, extinction reminder training, alternative outcome training, and outcome devaluation training can be useful adjuncts to respondent extinction. Each of these training procedures alters stimulus control in the context of classical conditioning.

STIMULUS CONTROL AND OPERANT CONDITIONING

Stimulus control also can be established (or altered) in the context of operant conditioning. One way to accomplish this is by arranging different consequences for a particular kind of behavior in the presence and absence of a stimulus (or stimulus class). That is, a particular response is reinforced in the presence of one stimulus, called a discriminative stimulus (S^D), and is not reinforced in the presence of another stimulus, called an S-delta (S^Δ). Under these conditions, the S^D comes to exercise excitatory stimulus control over responding. If conditions are arranged so that a particular stimulus (an S^D for punishment) is predictably correlated with punishment, inhibitory stimulus control will be established.

Behavior therapists sometimes arrange differential reinforcement to establish appropriate stimulus-controlled behavior in their clients, especially in educational settings. Using a discrete-trials procedure to teach young people with autism to label objects accurately is a good example of this strategy. Here, on each trial, one of several possible objects would be presented to the child and he or she would be asked to label the object (e.g., the therapist might ask "What is that?"). A correct response (e.g., saying "apple" when an apple was presented) would be reinforced (e.g., by delivering food or praise), whereas an incorrect response (e.g., saying "ball" when an apple was presented) would be followed by corrective feedback. If necessary, prompts would be provided to initiate responding (e.g., the therapist would tell the student, "Say apple"). With repeated trials, accurate labeling would be established. Lovaas and his colleagues (e.g., McEachin, Smith, & Lovaas, 1993) have provided substantial evidence that early and extensive exposure to discrete-trials training programs greatly benefits people with autism.

In using any differential reinforcement procedure to establish stimulus control, it is essential that participants learn to respond to relevant stimulus features (e.g., to the shape, not the color or size of the letter "A") and that an appropriate degree of stimulus generalization is established. Stimulus generalization occurs when a novel stimulus evokes behavior similar to that controlled by an established S^D. In general, the degree to which the novel stimulus is physically similar to the S^D determines the degree of stimulus generalization. However, discrimination training using S^Δs with features similar to the S^D can dramatically influence generalization.

In some cases, multiple physical dimensions define an S^D. For example, no single physical attribute defines the animals we call "dogs" or allows a person to label novel animals as "dogs" or "not dogs" with accuracy. In such cases, accurate labeling is established by presenting multiple examples and non-examples of a class of stimuli (e.g., "dogs" and "not dogs") and arranging differential reinforcement in the presence of the two types of stimuli (e.g., reinforcing saying "dog" only when an example of this class of stimuli was presented). Such arrangements are used to develop concepts, which may be viewed as complex S^Ds.

In many clinical situations, functional assessment will reveal S^Ds that evoke inappropriate behaviors. For instance, delinquent behavior typically occurs more frequently in the presence of certain peers, who are S^Ds for such behavior, than in their absence. It is not surprising that teens with conduct disorders are often encouraged in therapy sessions to change peer groups. Avoiding contact with S^Ds that engender inappropriate responding, like avoiding exposure to CSs that have similar effects, can be a valuable component of therapy. In many instances, it is not possible to change naturally occurring contingencies of reinforcement, but it may be possible to teach a client to stay away from people who, or situations that, historically supported, and may continue to support, undesirable actions.

Altering a client's motivation to obtain the kind of reinforcer previously available in the presence of a particular S^D is another technique of potential therapeutic value. For instance, methadone maintenance may reduce the momentary reinforcing value of heroin and make it less likely that a person will engage in drug-seeking behaviors in a situation where such behaviors historically had been successful in producing the drug. Behavior therapists historically have not focused a great deal of attention on treatments that alter motivational variables, but interest in such treatments has increased in recent years (e.g., Iwata, Smith, & Michael, 2000).

RULES AND STIMULUS CONTROL

A second general way in which stimulus control can be established in the context of operant conditioning is by providing verbal humans with rules, which are statements that specify relations among stimuli and responses. Rules can establish inhibitory or excitatory stimulus control, even though there is no actual history of differential reinforcement in their presence of those stimuli. Therefore, they are not S^Ds, but they can function similarly. Moreover, rules can diminish sensitivity to consequences, thereby making it difficult to establish stimulus control. Thus, rules appear relevant to understanding and treating many psychopathological conditions (Hayes & Ju, 1998).

Hayes and his colleagues have developed a therapeutic approach, acceptance and commitment therapy (ACT), which is intended to overcome unhealthy forms of rule-governed behavior (Hayes, Strosahl, & Wilson, 1999). Special emphasis is placed on dealing with problematic derived stimulus equivalence relations. Derived stimulus equivalence occurs when a person learns, by direct experience with the stimuli or through other people's verbal descriptions, that stimulus B goes with A (A → B) and C goes with B (B → C). As a result of learning that A → B and B → C, symmetrical (A ← B, B ← C) and transitive relations (A ←→ C) automatically emerge, although they were not specifically trained or described. The result is that stimuli A, B and C become functionally equivalent. That is, they control the same responses. Such derived stimulus relations may be useful in understanding how many types of avoidance behavior emerge and are maintained despite the absence of a direct history of aversive consequences occurring in the presence of the avoided stimulus. For instance, imagine a child who has a history involving direct experiences with injections from a hypodermic needle, which the child found to be painful (i.e., the child would avoid it if possible). The child now overhears that "An insect bite is like a shot with a needle." Hearing such a statement will now endow the conceptual stimulus class of insects with similar stimulus functions as a needle. That is, the child may now respond in the presence of an insect with a classically conditioned response (increased heart rate) and operant escape response (running away), even though the insect may in fact be harmless and the child lacks any direct experience with insect bites. Although it is beyond our purposes to describe ACT, it is worth noting that the approach shows promise for reducing control by derived stimulus relations that occasion a variety of problematic avoidance responses.

Verbal interactions between a therapist and a client frequently are intended to alter the rules that the client generates and follows. Such interactions can be a valuable therapeutic technique, but it is important to realize that these activities are themselves influenced by their consequences. If there is nothing in a client's everyday social or nonsocial environment to support (i.e., reinforce) appropriate rule-governed behavior, then such behavior probably will not endure over long periods. In some cases, naturally occurring consequences in the client's everyday environment are sufficient to support appropriate behaviors that emerge. In other cases, however, contrived consequences may be needed. A significant problem in providing treatment for outpatients is arranging such consequences.

STIMULUS CONTROL BY THE CONSEQUENCES OF BEHAVIOR

Although stimulus control by definition involves relationships between antecedent events and behavior, the consequences of one's behavior in a social setting frequently serve as discriminative stimuli for subsequent responding. Reacting appropriately to such stimuli is an important part of daily social interactions. Imagine an adolescent girl from an authoritarian household where social praise is rarely provided for any kind of behavior, while social displeasure is readily displayed following most attempts at conversation or other social gestures. Such an environment essentially trains the teen to discriminate stimuli (e.g., facial features) that signal the availability of aversive social consequences (and to withhold behaviors that historically have produced such consequences), but gives her little exposure to stimuli associated with a high likelihood of affiliation. This type of history leaves her "primed" to discover that others also disapprove of her, but unlikely to recognize and react appropriately to signs of approval and liking from others. Therefore, she is unlikely to react appropriately in social settings.

If the teen has a fairly well-developed repertoire of social skills, a reasonable therapeutic goal would be to facilitate the development of control of social approach responses by stimuli indicative of social affiliation and liking (smiles, greetings, invitations) and to decrease excessive sensitivity to potential signs of social displeasure.

One might pursue this goal by focusing on instances of behavior that occur in the therapy session. For instance, does the teen ever misinterpret the therapist's actions as signs of disappointment or displeasure? If so, this can be made an immediate focus of the therapy. For instance, the therapist can clarify the variables controlling his or her facial expressions (e.g., such as being in deep concentration) and block the client's escape and avoidance responses. Similarly, the therapist can help the teen recognize instances when he or she is showing genuine signs of interest, warmth, and caring in the therapy session, emphasize the fact that these signs are to be valued, and are indicative of appropriate behavior by the client. In essence, when such procedures are used, the therapist provides corrective differential reinforcement *in vivo*—during the therapy session (Kohlenberg & Tsai, 1991).

As noted previously, however, therapists often attempt to engender changes in stimulus control through verbal means. For instance, the therapist may describe the client's tendency to see only the negative (be under the control of stimuli that have signaled social punishment) and explain how this might have evolved and be maintained in the current environment. Then, the therapist might recommend a technique for changing stimulus control. For instance, the client may be taught social skills for initiating and maintaining conversations. As part of the skills training process, potential S^Ds (e.g., when another person says "hello" to you, makes eye contact, or is smiling) and S^Δs (e.g., when the other person looks preoccupied, is in a rush, or is looking away) are described to the client. During the session the therapist and client may then conduct role-playing exercises to practice identification of relevant stimulus conditions for initiating a conversation. For "homework," the therapist might recommend that the client conduct a "behavioral experiment," where she is told to initiate conversations with several same-age peers who are not strongly negative towards her and then rate the success of her efforts. This strategy is intended to place the client in situations in the natural social environment where reinforcing consequences for appropriate reactions to social stimuli are likely to be provided.

TREATING INSOMNIA THROUGH STIMULUS CONTROL

An excellent example of the use of stimulus control clinically is in the treatment of insomnia. Stimulus control therapy for insomnia (SCT) is an empirically-supported intervention (Morin et al., 2006) that has received the highest level of recommendation from the American Academy of Sleep Medicine (Morgenthaler et al., 2006). In SCT the client is instructed to: (1) get up at a set rise time, (2) avoid naps, (3) go to bed only when sleepy, (4) use the bed only for sleeping, and (5) leave the bed (and bedroom) after 15 minutes of sleeplessness, returning again when sleepy, and repeating as necessary (Morin, Davidson, & Savard, 2005). The first three recommendations are related to the establishing operation of sleep deprivation (or, more colloquially, tiredness). That is, adherence to these stipulations helps to create optimum preconditions for sleep to occur upon entering the bed. Points 4 and 5 address stimulus control linked to classical and operant conditioning.

For the chronic insomniac, the bed and stimuli surrounding getting into bed do not reliably signal that entering the bed and closing one's eyes will lead directly to the onset of sleep. Instead, these stimuli have become S^Ds for punishment (signals for a negative outcome) and CSs that elicit arousal, rather than calm. Over time, following steps four and five helps to (re)establish a close link between the bed (and stimuli linked to getting into bed) and sleep onset. In addition, following these steps contributes to a disruption and reduction in negative cognitions and worry about insomnia that often accompanies lying in bed awake. Finally, it should be noted that the guidelines for SCT are usually presented as instructions; that is, as rules to follow, and are provided in the context of psychoeducation about sleep. This approach can reduce control by ineffective verbal rules that some insomniacs may have developed, which can unwittingly contribute to faulty stimulus control and insomnia (e.g., incorrect ideas related to the benefits of napping or sleeping until one naturally wakes up, or that one is at least resting when lying sleepless in bed).

HOW TO IMPLEMENT STIMULUS CONTROL PROCEDURES

Recognizing that essentially all learned behavior is under some degree of stimulus control is important in conceptualizing any behavioral problem and in designing a treatment for that problem. With respect to stimulus control, it is helpful to distinguish: (1) behavior that is undesirable regardless of the antecedent stimuli that influence it (e.g., a person with autism engaging in self-injury), (2) behavior that is undesirable because it is under the control of inappropriate stimuli (e.g., a person with a closed head injury approaching and greeting strangers on the street), and (3) behavior that is stimulus controlled and desirable, but absent from the client's repertoire (e.g., a child with a learning disability failing to voice the appropriate sounds when shown letters of the alphabet).

The examples of developing appropriate social reactions and of treating insomnia illustrate a number of points that should be kept in mind if the problem at hand involves the absence of appropriate stimulus-controlled behavior (3 above). First, for an S^D to control behavior reliably, appropriate EOs must be arranged to ensure that the event whose availability is correlated with the presence of the S^D is effective as a reinforcer. Second, stimulus dimensions that define the S^D and S^Δ should be described to verbal clients. Third, the consequences of target behaviors in the presence of the S^D and S^Δ should be described to such clients. Rules that specify relations between stimuli and responses may help to foster appropriate behavior. Fourth, artificially arranging differential reinforcement in the presence of the S^D and S^Δ may be necessary to establish appropriate stimulus control. Typically, each instance of appropriate behavior in the presence of the S^D is reinforced initially, with the schedule becoming more intermittent over time until real-life conditions are approximated. Fifth, when the S^D and S^Δ comprise classes of stimuli, which is usually the case in clinical situations, it is important to provide multiple examples and nonexamples of members of each class. Sixth, if individual members of the classes differ in salience, begin training with an S^D and S^Δ that are maximally different from one another. Once stimulus control is well established, training can be extended to S^Ds and S^Δs that are more alike. Seventh, care must be taken to ensure that stimulus control established in a contrived

setting can be carried over into everyday life. Such generalization cannot be assumed to occur automatically, and training especially designed to produce it often is required.

If the problem at hand involves control of behavior by inappropriate stimuli (2 above), strategies should be simultaneously put in place to establish control by appropriate stimuli, as discussed in the immediately preceding paragraph, as well as to weaken control by the inappropriate stimuli. To weaken control by inappropriate stimuli, first consider whether it is feasible to arrange abolishing operations that eliminate the reinforcing effectiveness of the consequences that maintain the behavior in question in the situation of concern. If so, this is a simple and reasonable tack to take. Second, in all cases, provide verbal clients with rules describing the inappropriate stimuli and the appropriative alternative stimuli and the short- and long-term consequences of responding to those stimuli. Third, if possible, arrange extinction for responding to the inappropriate S^Ds. This may have to be done in contrived circumstances (e.g., in therapy sessions), rather than in the client's everyday environment. Fourth, if required (e.g., because operant extinction cannot be arranged), arrange procedures such as response cost or overcorrection to weaken responses occasioned by the inappropriate stimuli. Again, this may have to be done in contrived circumstances. Fifth, if behavior is under the control of a class of inappropriate S^Ds (e.g., strangers on the street), be sure to provide sufficient examples and nonexamples of the class to determine that all members of the class fail to control the response in question. Sixth, following any treatment in contrived circumstances, arrange procedures to increase the likelihood that treatment gains extend to the situations of clinical concern and check to ensure that this actually occurs.

The general strategies described in the immediately foregoing paragraph can also be used to eliminate the capacity of S^Ds to evoke behaviors that are inappropriate, regardless of the antecedent stimuli that influence them (1 above). If such behaviors are evoked by CSs, arranging respondent extinction (i.e., eliminating the predictive CS–US pairing) is an effective strategy for eliminating stimulus control by those CSs.

TABLE 69.2   Key Points to Stimulus Control

1. Stimulus control is present when a change in a particular property of a stimulus produces a change in a given response, such as an increase in the probability of its occurrence.
2. Inappropriate stimulus control contributes to the genesis and maintenance of a wide range of behavior disorders.
3. Establishing, abolishing, or otherwise altering stimulus control is an important aspect of cognitive behavior therapy. Many therapeutic techniques affect stimulus control, although their actions may not commonly be construed in this way.
4. Stimulus control can be established or altered through classical or operant conditioning.
5. Differential reinforcement is a powerful technique for establishing or altering stimulus control in the context of operant conditioning. Verbal rules, which specify relations among stimuli and responses, also can establish or alter stimulus control.

Of course, altering stimulus control by CSs may require additional considerations. Stimulus control is a large and complex topic that cannot be adequately covered in a short chapter such as this. A short chapter can, however, make the case that stimulus control is germane to the genesis and treatment of almost all forms of behavior disorders, and we have attempted to do so here. More detailed analyzes, like those provided in the listed references, extend that case and offer detailed suggestions for therapists. Table 69.2 provides a useful summary of the main points of stimulus control.

References

Cunningham, C. L. (1998). Drug conditioning and drug-seeking behavior. In W. O'Donohue (Ed.) (1998). *Learning and behavior therapy* (pp. 518–544). Boston: Allyn and Bacon.

Drumond, D. C., Tiffany, S. T., Glautier, S., & Remington, B. (Eds.) (1995). *Addictive behavior: Cue exposure therapy and practice.* Chichester, UK: Wiley.

Hayes, S. C. & Ju, W. (1998). Rule-governed behavior. In W. O'Donohue (Ed.), *Learning and behavior therapy* (pp. 374–391). Boston: Allyn and Bacon.

Hayes, S. C., Strosahl, K. & Wilson, K. G. (1999). *Acceptance and commitment therapy: An experiential approach to behavior change.* New York: Guilford.

Iwata, B. A., Smith, R. G., & Michael, J. (2000). Current research on the influence of establishing operations on behavior in applied settings. *Journal of Applied Behavior Analysis, 33,* 411–418.

Kohlenberg, R. J. & Tsai, M. (1991). *Functional analytic psychotherapy: Creating intense and curative therapeutic relationships.* New York: Plenum Press.

Laraway, S., Snycerski, S., Michael, J., & Poling, A. (2003). Motivating operations and terms to describe them: Some further refinements. *Journal of Applied Behavior Analysis, 36,* 407–414.

McEachin, J. J., Smith, T., & Lovaas, O. I. (1993). Long-term treatment outcome for children with autism who received early intensive behavioral treatment. *American Journal on Mental Retardation, 97,* 359–372.

Morgenthaler, T., Kramer, M., Alessi, C., Friedman, L., Boehlecke, B., Brown, T., et al. (2006). Practice parameters for the psychological and behavioral treatment of insomnia: an update. *Sleep, 29,* 1415–1419.

Morin, C. M., Bootzin, R. R., Buysse, D. J., Edinger, J. D., Espie, C. A., & Lichstein K. L. (2006). Psychological and behavioral treatment of insomnia: Update of the recent evidence (1998–2004). *Sleep, 29,* 1398–414.

Morin, C. M., Davidson, J. R., & Savard, J. (2005). Behavioral treatment of insomnia (pp. 160–164). In M. Hersen and J. Rosqvist (Eds.), *Encyclopedia of behavior modification and cognitive behavior therapy volume one: Adult clinical applications* (pp. 160–164). Thousand Oaks, CA: Sage Publications.

Jane E. Fisher, Jeffrey A. Buchanan, and Stacey Cherup-Leslie

Stimulus preference assessment techniques are used for empirically identifying functional reinforcers in persons with limited verbal repertoires. In addition, they can also be effective for assessing preferred activities within programs designed to reduce depression through behavioral activation (see Chapter 10) in persons with developmental or cognitive disabilities.

The concept of stimulus preference assessment was originally developed by Pace, Ivancic, Edwards, Iwata, and Page (1985) for the purpose of identifying functional reinforcers in individuals with severe developmental disabilities. Stimulus preference assessment techniques emerged through recognition of the limitations in accuracy of nonempirical approaches to identifying functional reinforcers (e.g., those based on pleasant activity menus or caregiver report). The procedures are now commonly used for identifying preferred tangible, edible, olfactory, auditory, and leisure stimuli in persons with developmental disabilities (Horrocks & Higbee, 2008). They are now increasingly employed with other populations including older adults with cognitive impairment (Fisher, Buchanan, & Hadden, 2008; LeBlanc, Cherup, Feliciano, & Sidener, 2006), persons diagnosed with schizophrenia (Wilder, Wilson, Ellsworth, & Heering, 2003), and adolescents with emotional–behavioral disorders (Paramore & Higbee, 2005).

Since first described by Pace and colleagues (1985), several variations of stimulus preference assessment procedures have been reported in the literature (e.g., DeLeon & Iwata, 1996; Fisher et al., 1992; Horrocks & Higbee, 2008; Tessing, Napolitano, McAdam, DiCesare, & Axelrod, 2006). The basic procedure involves identifying a sample of potentially preferred stimuli for a particular client (e.g., based on the report of caregivers or informal observation) and then sequentially presenting the stimuli to the client singly, in pairs, or in groups while systematically recording the duration or frequency of the clients' touching or orienting to each stimulus. A hierarchy of preference is then generated based on the duration or frequency of the client's response to each stimulus. The client's preference is inferred based on the level of response, with more preferred stimuli being associated with higher levels of responding. Following the development of the stimulus preference hierarchy, the contingent presentation of the stimuli ranked as highly preferred can be implemented to determine whether there is an increase in the target response indicating that the preferred stimuli are functional reinforcers (e.g., Graff, Gibson, & Galiatsatos, 2006). Variations in stimulus preference assessment procedure are described in the following sections.

ADVANTAGES OF THE TECHNIQUE

An important advantage of stimulus preference assessment procedures is that they involve *direct* sampling of a client's choice–behavior and the functional relationship between preferred stimuli and a target response. A second advantage involves their applicability for use with persons with limited verbal or physical repertoires for communicating preferences as the procedures do not require a verbal or complex physical response (e.g., visual orientation to a stimulus can be used as the preference response for a client who is unable to speak or manipulate an object). Finally, there is significant empirical support for their utility in identifying functional reinforcers for use in interventions designed to strengthen adaptive responses in populations with limited repertoires. Training caregivers in the logic and procedures of stimulus preference assessment may increase access to reinforcers in persons with severe disabilities. This feature is particularly appealing when individuals are residing in relatively impoverished environments (e.g., nursing homes and other institutions) (Fisher et al., 2008) or when caregivers' have a history of responding to complex verbal constructions by a client who has recently experienced significant declines in the ability to communicate (e.g., as is the case when a client has a degenerative form of dementia).

WHO MIGHT BENEFIT FROM STIMULUS PREFERENCE ASSESSMENT?

Stimulus preference assessment procedures have been found to be effective for efficiently identifying functional reinforcers in individuals with limited verbal abilities who cannot express their preferences through other forms of communication including clients with developmental disabilities (e.g., Fischer, Iwata, & Mazaleski, 1997; Fisher et al., 1992; Horrocks & Higbee, 2008), persons diagnosed with schizophrenia (Wilder, Ellsworth, White, & Schock, 2003) and elderly persons with dementia (LeBlanc et al., 2006).

HOW DOES THE TECHNIQUE WORK?

Several variations of stimulus preference assessment procedures are described in the literature. These include single-stimulus presentations, paired stimulus/forced choice presentations, and multiple-stimulus presentation assessments.

Single-Stimulus Method

The single-stimulus (SS) method was initially described by Pace and colleagues (1985). The SS assessment involves the following steps:

1. A list of potentially preferred stimuli is generated. It is generally recommended that the menu of items include stimuli that provide sensory, auditory, visual, olfactory, gustatory, and/or thermal stimulation.

2. A single item is presented to the individual. In some studies, the individual is prompted to attend to the stimulus (e.g., Spevack, Yu, Lee, & Martin, 2006).

3. Record whether the individual approaches the stimulus or not within 5 seconds. "Approach" is usually defined as moving toward the object/event with the hand or body within 5 seconds of the stimulus being presented (Pace et al., 1985). This definition is sometimes referred to as "active approach" because it requires a somewhat effortful physical response. With more physically impaired populations that might have difficulties making these more effortful approach responses, it may be useful to record "passive approaches" as well. Passive approach is defined as looking at or turning toward a stimulus, smiling, or laughing (Spevack et al., 2006).

4. If the individual approaches the stimulus within 5 seconds, allow the individual to have 5 additional seconds of access to the stimulus.

5. If the individual does not approach the stimulus, prompt the individual to sample the stimulus (e.g., turn on music box, rub stuffed animal on individual's hand) and then repeat the trial. If the stimulus is approached, allow 5 seconds of access to the stimulus. If the item is not approached, remove the stimulus.

6. Repeat this procedure with all stimuli. Stimuli should be presented in a random order. It is generally recommended that each stimulus be presented a total of 10 times. For example, if you have 12 items, a total of 120 presentations/trials are necessary to complete the procedure. These trials can be completed over a series of sessions and do not have to be done all at one time. The number of trials done per session can vary depending on the cooperation and stamina of the individual.

7. Calculate the percentage of times an item was approached. An item that is approached more than 80% of the time is considered highly preferred.

Caveat: It is noteworthy that the SS procedure can be time consuming and may therefore be less effective for persons easily fatigued.

Paired-Stimulus Procedure

The paired stimulus (PS) procedure for conduct-ing stimulus preference assessments was first described by Fisher and colleagues (1992) and is sometimes referred to as *forced choice assessment*. A PS assessment can be conducted using the following steps:

1. A list of potentially preferred stimuli is generated. Generally, this list is constructed by interviewing caregivers familiar with the client or through informal direct observation of the client in the natural environment. The number of stimuli chosen depends on several factors, such as how many stimuli caregivers can identify, the accessibility of the identified stimuli, and the amount of time available to conduct the assessment (the more items chosen, the longer the assessment will take).
2. Construct a recording form that includes a list of all pairs of stimuli to be presented. All stim-uli should be paired with every other stimulus once, and the order of pairings should be ran-domized. For example, if there are a total of 5 stimuli, there should be a total of 10 pairs of stimulus presentations. In addition, the posi-tioning of each stimulus should be counter balanced such that each stimulus is presented on the client's left- and right-handed sides an equal number of times in order to control for placement effects.
3. Prior to beginning the procedure, allow the client to sample each stimulus for 30 seconds.
4. Place two stimuli from the list generated in step 1 in front of the client. The literature rec-ommends that items should be spaced about 0.7 m apart and both should be close enough to the client so he or she can touch or grab the stimuli.
5. When the client approaches one of the stim-uli, provide the client access to the chosen stimulus for a brief period of time (i.e., about 5 seconds) and remove the other stimulus. An approach response may include touch-ing the stimulus, gesturing to the stimulus, making eye contact, or making positive state-ments about the stimulus. Any attempts to grab both stimuli simultaneously should be blocked. Also, if the client does not approach

either stimulus, allow access to each stimulus for 5 seconds and then repeat the paired pre-sentation. If no approach response occurs, the trial is terminated.
6. Continue this process until all pairings have been presented to the client.
7. Calculate the percentage of time each stimulus was chosen when presented.
8. Organize data into a rank-ordered list of stim-uli from most preferred to least preferred. The literature suggests that stimuli chosen at least 80% of the time are considered highly preferred and may be useful in treatment pro-grams for strengthening behavior.

Caveats in applying the PS procedure: One poten-tial difficulty with the PS procedure is that an individual may make an initial approach response to one of the stimuli only to quickly switch to the other stimuli. For example, an indi-vidual is presented a baby doll and a music box. The individual initially orients to the music box, but then reaches to pick up the baby doll and holds it. In this example the music box is technically considered "chosen" because it was approached (i.e., looked at) first. However, it could be argued that the baby doll is actually preferred because the individual switched their attention away from the music box and physi-cally contacted the doll. There are two options when this occurs. One is to simply repeat the trial. This option is less desirable if the individ-ual switches attention frequently during trials because many trials will need to be repeated and simply repeating trials may not actually solve the problem. The second option is to provide access to both stimuli for a longer period of time (e.g., 20 seconds) and measure allocation of atten-tion to each stimulus. This can be done by having observers use two stopwatches to measure the amount of time allocated to each stimulus (both watches can be activated if the person is attend-ing to both stimuli). This procedural variation allows the individual more time to sample both items and switch their attention amongst the two items. Using the above example, the indi-vidual may spend the first 2 seconds looking at the music box, but then spends the remaining 18 seconds of the trial holding the baby doll. Using the traditional PS procedure, the music box would be considered preferred, but when the procedure is altered to provide more time to chose, it is clear the baby doll is preferred. This procedural variation is desirable when the individual frequently shifts attention during PS trials as described above or when the individual simply needs more time to make a choice due to severe cognitive and/or physical impairments. This variation, however, can take significantly longer, particularly when there are many items (more than 10) being tested.

Multiple Stimulus without Replacement

The multiple stimulus without replacement (MSWO) procedure was first described by DeLeonand Iwata (1996). An MSWO assessment can be conducted using the following steps:

1. As with PS assessment procedures, the MSWO procedures begin by generating a list of potentially preferred stimuli based on caregiver reports or informal observation. The literature suggests that up to seven items can be used in a MSWO procedure. Using more than seven items may present practical difficulties in having enough space so that the client can have equal access to all stimuli simultaneously, particularly if some of the stimuli are large.
2. Construct a data sheet listing all stimuli.
3. Place all items in a straight line in random order. Items should be about 5 cm apart (farther apart if the items are larger).
4. Seat the client approximately 0.3 m from the stimulus array.
5. Instruct the client to select one of the items. Allow the client 30 seconds to make a selection.
6. Once the client selects an item, allow access to the stimulus for 30 seconds (or to completely consume the item if it is food or a beverage). Then, either remove the item from the immediate area or do not replace the item (if the item is edible). DeLeon and Iwata (1996) used physical contact with a stimulus as their definition of a selection. However, this definition can be expanded to include responses such as looking at, gesturing toward, touching, eating, or talking about the item.

7. Before the next trial, the remaining items should be rotated by taking the item at the left end and moving it to the right end. Then, shift all other stimuli to the left so that they are equally spaced on the table.
8. Continue this procedure until all items are selected. If during any trial the client does not select an item in the 30 seconds allowed, the procedure should be terminated and all other items recorded as "not selected."
9. The original study by DeLeon and Iwata (1996) suggested that the entire procedure should be repeated five times to provide adequate data concerning preferences and for identifying functional reinforcers. However, a study by Carr, Nicolson, and Higbee (2000) suggests that functional reinforcers can be identified if the procedures are repeated only three times. This shortened version of the MSWO procedure described by Carr and associates can be completed in less than 1 hour.
10. Calculate the percentage of times each stimulus was chosen during trials in which it was presented.
11. Create a rank-ordered list of stimuli from most preferred to least preferred. It should be noted that a multiple-stimulus assessment procedure with replacement has been used in the research literature (e.g., Windsor, Piche, & Locke, 1994). Although, it has been found that this procedure is less time consuming than the PS or MSWO procedures, there is a risk of false negatives (DeLeon & Iwata, 1996). False negatives are likely due to the fact that highly preferred items are chosen repeatedly because they are replaced after being chosen.

EVIDENCE FOR THE EFFECTIVENESS OF STIMULUS PREFERENCE ASSESSMENT

Empirical evidence suggests that the SS, PS, and MSWO procedures successfully identify functional reinforcers. The SS procedure has been found to identify functional reinforcers in individuals with profound intellectual disabilities (Pace et al., 1985). In general, those items ranked highest tend to serve as more effective reinforcers than those items ranked lowest (Pace et al., 1985; Spevack et al., 2006).

In evaluating the PS assessment procedure, Piazza and colleagues (1996) found that contingent presentation of stimuli ranked as highly preferred (i.e., ranked in the top 4 of 16 stimuli) during a PS assessment increased target responses (such as sitting in a chair or standing in a square) more effectively than those stimuli that were of middle or low preference. Fisher and colleagues (1992) also provide evidence that stimuli frequently chosen during a PS assessment could be used to strengthen behaviors such as in sitting in a chair or standing in a square. DeLeon and Iwata (1996) provide evidence that the MSWO procedure also identifies functional reinforcers. These authors found that highly preferred items presented contingently upon target behaviors (e.g., placing blocks in a bucket, pressing a response panel) produced higher rates of responding when compared to baseline levels of responding. Other studies have found that preferred stimuli can be used to reduce disruptive behaviors. For example, Fischer and colleagues (1997) presented a preferred stimulus (i.e., food) on a time-based schedule to two developmentally disabled individuals displaying self-injurious behavior. Although food was empirically determined not to function as a reinforcer for self-injurious behavior, noncontingent presentation of food produced reductions in this behavior. In addition, other studies have used different versions of stimulus preference assessment to reduce self-injurious behavior and destructive behaviors such as physical and verbal aggression (e.g., Fisher, O'Conner, Kurtz, DeLeon, & Gotjen, 2000; Ringdahl, Vollmer, Marcus, & Roane, 1997).

WHEN TO CHOOSE ONE PROCEDURE OVER ANOTHER

As mentioned earlier, the SS procedure generally takes much longer than either the PS or MSWO procedures and so may be impractical in applied settings. Both the PS and MSWO procedures, however, require some movement from the individual in order to make choices. Therefore, it is recommended that the SS procedure be used when individuals suffer from both severe cognitive and physical impairments that make active approach responses (e.g., pointing, moving hand toward objects, turning head or body more than a few inches) difficult to execute.

Further Reading

DeLeon, I. G., & Iwata, B. A. (1996). Evaluation of a multiple-stimulus presentation format for assessing reinforcer preferences. *Journal of Applied Behavior Analysis, 29*, 519–533.

Fisher, W., Piazza, C. C., Bowman, L. G., Hagopian, L. P., Owens, J. C., & Slevin, I. (1992). A comparison of two approaches for identifying reinforcers for persons with severe and profound disabilities. *Journal of Applied Behavior Analysis, 25*, 491–498.

Piazza, C. C., Fisher, W. W., Hagopian, L. P., Bowman, L. G., & Toole, L. (1996). Using a choice assessment to predict reinforcers' effectiveness. *Journal of Applied Behavior Analysis, 29*, 1–9.

References

Carr, J. E., Nicolson, A. C., & Higbee, T. S. (2000). Evaluation of a brief multiple-stimulus preference assessment in a naturalistic context. *Journal of Applied Behavior Analysis, 33*, 353–357.

Fischer, S. M., Iwata, B. A., & Mazaleski, J. L. (1997). Noncontingent delivery of arbitrary reinforcers as treatment for self-injurious behavior. *Journal of Applied Behavior Analysis, 30*, 239–249.

Fisher, J. E., & Buchanan, J. A., & Hadden, J. (2008). Presentation of preferred stimuli as an intervention for escape-maintained aggression in a person with dementia. Under editorial review.

Fisher, W. W., O'Conner, J. T., Kurtz, P. E, DeLeon, I. G., & Gotjen, D. L. (2000). The effects of noncontingent delivery of high- and low-preference stimuli on attention-maintained destructive behavior. *Journal of Applied Behavior Analysis, 33*, 79–83.

Graff, R. B., Gibson, L., & Galiatsatos, G. T. (2006). The impact of high- and low-preference stimuli on vocational and academic performances of youths with severe disabilities. *Journal of Applied Behavior Analysis, 39*, 131–135.

Horrocks, E. & Higbee, T. S. (2008). An evaluation of a stimulus preference assessment of auditory stimuli for adolescents with developmental disabilities. *Research in Developmental Disabilities, 29*, 11–20.

LeBlanc, L. A., Cherup, S. M., Feliciano, L., & Sidener, T. M. (2006). Using choice-making opportunities to increase activity engagement in individuals with dementia. *American Journal of Alzheimer's Disease and Other Dementias, 21*, 318–325.

Pace, G. M., Ivancic, M. T., Edwards, G. L., Iwata, B. A., & Page, T. J. (1985). Assessment of stimulus preference and reinforcer value with profoundly retarded individuals. *Journal of Applied Behavior Analysis, 18*, 249–255.

Paramore, N. W. & Higbee, T. S. (2005). An evaluation of a brief multiple-stimulus preference assessment with adolescents with emotional–behavioral disorders in an educational setting. *Journal of Applied Behavior Analysis, 38*, 399–403.

Ringdahl, J. E., Vollmer, T. R., Marcus, B. A., & Roane, H. S. (1997). An analogue evaluation of environmental enrichment: The role of stimulus preference. *Journal of Applied Behavior Analysis, 30*, 203–216.

Spevack, S., Yu, C. T., Lee, M. S., & Martin, G. L. (2006). Sensitivity of passive approach during preference and reinforcer assessments for children with severe and profound intellectual disabilities, and minimal movement. *Behavioral Interventions, 21*, 165–175.

Tessing, J. L., Napolitano, D. A., McAdam, D. B., DiCesare, A., Axelrod, S (2006). The effects of providing access to stimuli following choice making during vocal preference assessments. *Journal of Applied Behavior Analysis, 39*, 501-506.

Wilder, D. A., Ellsworth, C., White, H., & Schock, K. (2003). A comparison of stimulus preference assessment methods in adults with schizophrenia. *Behavioral Interventions, 18*, 151-160.

Wilder, D. A., Wilson, P., Ellsworth, C., & Heering, P. W. (2003). A comparison of verbal and tangible stimulus preference assessment methods in adults with schizophrenia. *Behavioral Interventions, 18*, 191–198.

Windsor, J., Piche, L. M., & Locke, P. A. (1994). Preference testing: A comparison of two presentation methods. *Research in Developmental Disabilities, 15*, 439–455.

71 STRESS INOCULATION TRAINING

Donald Meichenbaum

We live in stressful times—whether it is war, the threat of terrorist attacks, natural disasters, or the hassles of daily life. Such stressors may come in the form of personal threats, uncertainties about the future, or loss, both material and spiritual, there is a need to bolster coping effectiveness. Stress inoculation training (SIT), which was developed in the 1980s as a form of cognitive behavioral interventions (see Meichenbaum 1985, 1993, 2007), has been employed successfully in helping individuals cope with various forms of stress including:

1. Acute time-limited stressors such as medical examinations and surgery
2. Stress sequences that follow the exposure to traumatic events such as rape or that require transitional adjustment due to the stress of job loss
3. Chronic intermittent stressors such as competitive athletic performance and ongoing evaluations
4. Chronic continual stressors such as the experience of medical conditions (e.g., chronic and intermittent pain) and psychiatric disorders (e.g., anxiety and anger-related disorders), as well as the exposure to persistent occupational dangers such as police work, combat, nursing and teaching

In short, SIT has been employed on both a preventative and treatment basis with a broad array of individuals who have experienced stress responses.

WHO MIGHT BENEFIT FROM SIT?

A recent computer literature search revealed some 200 studies that have used SIT with varied populations. On a preventative basis, SIT has been used successfully with such populations as surgical patients, patients undergoing stressful medical examinations, hemodialysis and various stressful occupational groups (flight attendants, soldiers, police, fire fighters, nurses, teachers, oil rig workers, step parents, parents of children who have cancer, staff workers who work with developmentally delayed individuals, and foreign students who have to deal with the stress of adjustment). On a treatment basis, SIT has been employed with medical patients including patients with various forms of pain disorders, hypertension, cancer, ulcers, burns, AIDS, genital herpes, individuals with traumatic brain injury and childhood asthma. With psychiatric patients, SIT has been used successfully with individuals who have anger-control problems (children, adolescents, adults), anxiety disorders (performance anxiety, dental anxiety, phobias and PTSD such as rape victims and victims of sexual abuse), individuals with addictive disorders, and those with chronic psychiatric disorders. (For literature reviews see Maag & Kotlash, 1994; Meichenbaum, 1996, 2001, 2007; Saunders et al., 1996, as well as Google SIT).

CONTRAINDICATIONS

Based on a review of the literature and on 25 years experience with SIT, there are no populations for whom SIT has been contraindicated. Rather, the ways in which SIT should be applied varies with each population, with the nature of the stress being experienced, and with the length of treatment. Foa and her colleagues (1999) raise a cautionary note about SIT being insufficient in the treatment of rape victims. They found that with rape victims, gradual exposure-based treatment procedures were found to be more efficacious than SIT over a follow-up period. Thus, when the nature of exposure to the stressor is traumatic and explicit, specific interventions that focus on the impact and meaning of such stressful events may be an important addition to the SIT procedures or exposure-based interventions should be the primary focus of the treatment.

HOW DOES SIT WORK?

SIT is a broad-based cognitive behavioral intervention that employs multicomponent training that is arranged in flexible interlocking phases. The three phases include:

1. A conceptual educational phase
2. A skills acquisition and consolidation phase
3. An application phase

SIT provides a set of procedural guidelines to be individually tailored to both the needs and characteristics of each client/trainee and to the specific form of stress that is being experienced. SIT follows a set of general principles and the flexible application of accompanying clinical procedures, rather than being a set of canned interventions. See the step-by-step procedural guidelines below.

The treatment goals of SIT are to bolster the client's coping repertoire (intra- and interpersonal skills) and their confidence in being able to apply their coping skills in a flexible fashion that meets the appraised demands of the stressful situation. Stressors come in a variety of forms. Sometimes stressors lend themselves to change and can be altered or avoided; while other stressors are *not* changeable (e.g., irreversible loss, incurable illness) (Meichenbaum, 2006a).

SIT recognizes that some stressful situations do *not* lend themselves to direct-action problem-solving efforts, since solutions are not always readily attainable. In such instances, an emotionally palliative set of coping responses— such as acceptance, perspective taking, reframing, attention diversion, adaptive affective expression, and humor may be employed. SIT highlights that there are no "correct" ways to cope. What coping efforts may work in one

situation, or at one time, may not be applicable at other times.

A central concept underlying SIT is that of "inoculation" which has been borrowed analogously from medicine and from social–psychological research on attitude change. The central notion is that bolstering an individual's repertoire of coping responses to milder stressors can serve to build skills and confidence in handling more demanding stressors. By means of gradual exposure, imagery rehearsal, in clinic and in situ rehearsal, a sense of mastery can be nurtured.

SIT adopts both a transactional view of stress, as well as a strengths-based approach. From a transactional perspective, SIT highlights that in many instances the ability to cope most effectively with stress requires the need to alter, avoid, or minimize the effects of stressors by better managing the stress-engendering environment. For example, in dealing with medical stressors, SIT trainers can teach patients a variety of coping techniques, but they can also work to alter the ways in which doctors and hospital staff interact with patients. With athletes, the focus of SIT may be on influencing the ways coaches relate to athletes, as well as teaching athletes to cope with performance anxiety. With rape victims, the focus of SIT is not only on helping individuals to cope with the aftermath of trauma exposure, but also on learning how to alter the environmental stressors that reduce the impact of secondary victimization. Examples of the transactional nature of SIT were illustrated by Wernick (1983) who demonstrated the benefits of providing SIT to nurses who work on burn units in reducing the stress of burn patients, and by Cohen, Mannarino & Deblinger, (2006) and Deblinger and Heflin (1996) who demonstrated the benefits of using cognitive behavioral stress reduction procedures with the nonoffending parents of sexually abused children. Stress occurs in a context, and SIT therapists need to embrace such an ecologically sensitive treatment approach. See Meichenbaum and Jaremko (1983) for further examples of such transactional-based treatment approaches.

Second, SIT highlights that exposure to stressful events has the potential of making individuals, groups, and communities stronger and more resilient. There is a need to help individuals and groups access and employ natural occurring intra- and interpersonal coping resources and social supports. SIT helps individuals deal with safety issues and the immediate and long-term sequelae of stress exposure. Other SIT treatment goals include the need to help individuals transform their distress and "emotional pain" into something meaningful that gives comfort and purpose to their lives. Issues of relapse prevention and ways to avoid revictimization also receive major attention (Meichenbaum, 1996, 2006b, 2008). SIT builds upon and supplements these coping efforts.

STEP-BY-STEP PROCEDURES

One of the strengths of SIT is its flexibility. SIT has been carried out with individuals, couples, small and large groups. The length of the SIT intervention has varied, being as short as 20 minutes for preparing patients for surgery to 40 sessions with psychiatric patients and with patients with chronic medical conditions. In most instances, SIT consists of some 8–15 sessions, plus booster and follow-through sessions conducted over a 3–12-month period.

A PROCEDURAL FLOW CHART OF STRESS INOCULATION TRAINING

Phase 1: Conceptualization–educational
Phase 2: Skills acquisition, consolidation, and rehearsal
Phase 3: Application and follow-through

Phase 1: Conceptual–Educational

- In a collaborative fashion, identify the determinants of the presenting clinical problem or the individual's stress concerns by means of (1) interview with the client and significant others; (2) the client's use of an imagery-based reconstruction of a prototypical stressful incident; (3) psychosocial and behavioral assessments. Help the client to transform his description from global terms into behaviorally specific terms and learn how to disaggregate global stressors.

- Elicit the client's "story" or narrative accounts of stress and coping and collaboratively help the client identify coping strengths and resources. Help the client to appreciate the differences between changeable and unchangeable aspects of stressful situations and to collaboratively identify short-term, intermediate, and long-term treatment goals.

- Have the client engage in self-monitoring in order to better appreciate how he may inadvertently, unwittingly and unknowingly contribute to how stress reactions build and to better appreciate the interconnections between his feelings, thoughts, behaviors and reactions of others.

- Ascertain the degree to which coping difficulties arise from coping skills deficits, or whether such difficulties are the result of performance failures (e.g., maladaptive beliefs, feelings of low self-efficacy, negative ideation, secondary gains).

- Collaboratively develop a conceptualization of stress that highlights that stress reactions go through different "phases" (namely, preparing for the stressor, confronting the stressful situations, handling feelings of being overwhelmed, and reflecting on how his coping efforts went—sometimes they went well and sometimes not so effectively). The specific reconceptualization that is developed will vary depending upon the nature of the stressor.

- Debunk any myths concerning stress and coping.

Phase 2: Skills Acquisition, Consolidation, and Rehearsal

- Tailor coping skills training to the specific population and to the length of training.

- Ascertain the client's preferred mode of coping and how these coping efforts can be employed in the current situation. Consider what factors are blocking such coping efforts.

- Train problem-focused instrumental coping skills that are directed at the modification, avoidance, and minimization of the impact of stressors (e.g., problem-solving, assertive training, using social supports).

- Train emotionally focused coping skills (e.g., acceptance skills, perspective taking, emotion regulation, cognitive reframing).
- Have clients rehearse skills by means of imagery and behavioral practice.
- Build in generalization procedures. Consider possible barriers to using coping behaviors and ways to anticipate and address these possible obstacles.

Phase 3: Application and Follow-through

- Encourage the application of coping skills to gradually more demanding stressful situations.
- Use relapse prevention procedures.
- Bolster the client's self-efficacy. Ensure that the client "takes credit" for improvement and offers self-attributions for change.
- Gradually phase out treatment and include booster and follow-through sessions.
- Involve significant others in the intervention plan.
- Have the client coach someone with a similar stressful situation. Put the client in a consultative role.
- Help the client restructure and reappraise environmental stressors, and when possible, alter them either individually or with the help of others.

Further Reading

Meichenbaum, D. (1985). *Stress inoculation training.* Elmsford, NY: Pergamon Press.

Meichenbaum, D. (1996). *Treating adults with post-traumatic stress disorder.* Clearwater, FL: Institute Press.

Meichenbaum, D. (2001). *Treating individuals with anger-control problems and aggressive behaviors.* Clearwater, FL: Institute Press.

Meichenbaum, D. (2007). Stress inoculation training: A preventative and treatment approach. In P. M. Lehrer, R. L. Woolfolk, & W. E. Sime (Eds.), *Principles and practice of stress management* (3rd ed.). (pp. 497–518). New York: Guilford.

Meichenbaum, D., & Deffenbacher, J. L. (1988). Stress inoculation training. *Counseling Psychologist, 16,* 69–90.

Also see the following Websites: *www.melissainstitute.org* and *www.musc.edu/tfcbt*, for examples of cognitive behavioral stress management interventions.

References

Cohen, J. A., Mannarino, A. P. & Deblinger, E. (2006). *Treating trauma and traumatic grief in children and adolescents.* New York: Guilford.

Deblinger, E., & Heflin, A. H. (1996). *Treating sexually abused children and their nonoffending parents: A cognitive-behavioral approach.* Thousand Oaks, CA: Sage.

Foa, E. B., Dancu, C., Hembree, E. A., Jaycox, L. H., Meadows, E. A., & Street, G. D. (1999). A comparison of exposure therapy, stress inoculation training and their combination for reducing posttraumatic stress disorder in female assault victims. *Journal of Consulting and Clinical Psychology, 67,* 194–200.

Maag, J., & Kotlash, J. (1994). Review of stress inoculation training with children and adolescents: Issues and recommendations. *Behavior Modification, 18,* 443–469.

Meichenbaum, D., & Jaremko, M. E. (Eds.). (1993). *Stress reduction and prevention.* New York: Plenum Press.

Meichenbaum, D. (1993). Stress inoculation training: A 20-year update. In R. L. Woolfolk and P. M. Lehrer (Eds.), *Principles and practices of stress management* (pp. 373–406).

Meichenbaum, D. (2006a). Trauma and suicide. In T. Ellis (Ed.), *Cognition and suicide: Theory, research and practice.* Washington, DC: American Psychological Association.

Meichenbaum, D. (2006b). Resilience and posttraumatic growth: A constructive narrative perspective. In L. Calhoun & R. Tedeschi (Eds.), *Handbook of posttraumatic growth: Research and practice.* Mahwah, NJ: Lawrence Erlbaum.

Meichenbaum, D. (2007). Stress inoculation training: A preventative and treatment approach. In R. L. Woolfolk, & P. M. Lehrer (Eds.), *Principles and practice of stress management* (pp. 497–518). New York: Guilford.

Meichenbaum, D. (2008). Bolstering resilience: Benefiting from lessons learned. In D. Brom, P., Horenczyk & E. Ford (Eds.), *Treating traumatized children: Risk, resilience and recovery.* New York: Routledge.

Saunders, T. Driskell, J. E., Johnston, J. H., & Salas, E. (1996). The effect of stress inoculation training on anxiety and performance. *Journal of Occupational Psychology, 1,* 170–186.

Wernick, R. L. (1983). Stress inoculation in the management of clinical pain: Applications to burn pain. In D. Meichenbaum and M. E. Jaremko, (Eds.), *Stress reduction and prevention* (pp. 191–218). New York: Plenum Press.

Victoria E. Mercer

While we all know intuitively what stress is, the term *stress* is not terribly useful for scientists due the subjective nature of the phenomenon it describes. In 1936 Hans Selye adopted the term stress from physics and engineering and applied it to the physiological response of an organism to any demand for change. In the First Annual Report on Stress in 1951 a critic of the term used verbatim citations from Selye's own writings to demonstrate confusions around the word stating that, "Stress in addition to being itself, was also the cause of itself, and the result of itself" (Rosch, 2007). Selye attempted to resolve the continuing confusion by developing the concept of the stressor as stimulus and an organisms' response to the stimulus as stress. Stated differently, each situation has an associated stressor, stress response, and stress outcome.

Today, stress is conceptualized as developing through an interplay of biological, psychological, and social–environmental factors. This biopsychosocial model of stress provides us with a comprehensive theoretical understanding of the phenomena as well as the three major foci for assessment and treatment.

- *Biological factors:* Research on the biological factors associated with stress began when Selye (1950) developed the three-stage general adaptation syndrome to describe an organism's response to a stressor. When a severe physical demand is placed upon an organism it mobilizes resources and attempts to eliminate the stressor (alarm), if the stressor persists the organism adapts and becomes more resistant to disease or illness (resistance). However, with chronic exposure to the stressor there is a gradual deterioration in functioning that eventually results in illness and death (exhaustion).

The biological factors influencing one's response to and experience of stress are largely explained by the functioning of the endocrine hormones involved in the hypothalamic– pituitary axis (Auerbach & Gramling, 1998). Research demonstrates that when individuals are exposed to high level of stress hormones it can result in decreased immunity and eventual development of chronic illness (Kiecolt-Glaser & Glaser, 1987). Stress influences both the physiological process that leads to an illness as well as the psychological and behavioral processes that lead to illness behavior. However, while stress has been found to play a role in the development of illnesses such as cancer, coronary diseases, and ulcers, it cannot be said to be the single cause (Auerbach & Gramling, 1998).

- *Psychological factors:* Given the idiosyncratic nature of the stress response, psychological research has focused on identifying and explaining people's cognitive and behavioral response to stressors. Early research on the psychological effect of stress discovered that the controllability of the stressor correlates with health outcomes (Weiss, 1970). In situations where the organism has less control there are more severe health outcomes. Psychological research has also focused on how different emotion and problem-focused coping skills correlate with an individual's resilience to stress (Beck, 1967; Ellis, 1973).
- *Social–environmental factors:* Whether an individual experiences negative events such as numerous daily hassles (e.g., losing keys, being stuck in traffic) or more major chronic stressors (e.g., moving away to go to school, living with an illness) all events elicit a stress

response. Furthermore, even a positive event such as a wedding or buying a home is a significant source of positive stress known as eustress. Social relationships can act as stressors (e.g., strain in a relationship or at work) and or as a source of support against stress (e.g., emotional and or instrumental support).

Just as each individual experiences stress ideographically there is no stress management technique that is a panacea. Numerous techniques exist to help individuals reduce or eliminate the stressors in their lives. For this reason stress management interventions are highly variable and are operationalized in a number of different ways (Ong, Linden, & Young, 2004). Peer-reviewed studies demonstrate the empirical validity of common techniques used as components of stress management interventions (Lehrer & Woolfolk, 1993). However, there is no standardized stress management treatment manual that would ensure the inclusion of such an intervention on the APA Division 12's list of empirically validated treatments.

WHO MIGHT BENEFIT FROM THIS TECHNIQUE?

Stress management interventions may be used as primary or secondary interventions depending on a client's presenting problem(s) and the setting in which the intervention is being delivered. Any individual experiencing difficulties coping with the stressors in their lives, or individuals anticipated exposure to a stressful event, may benefit from a stress management intervention.

CONTRAINDICATIONS

There are no specific contraindications for stress management interventions. This being said, a clinician should assess each client's physical and mental health and use this information judiciously when determining the type of arousal reduction and lifestyle change techniques to incorporate. If a clinician has concerns over determining such parameters, the client's physician should be consulted when developing an individual's behavioral plan.

OTHER FACTORS IN DECIDING WHETHER TO USE STRESS MANAGEMENT

If any acute comorbid mental or physical health problems are revealed during assessment, these should be given priority and treated with an appropriate empirically validated treatment before employing stress management interventions. However, it should be noted that stress management interventions may be very beneficial in conjunction with such treatments and can be easily integrated into an individuals' primary treatment plan.

HOW DOES THE TECHNIQUE WORK?

As noted earlier, stress management interventions use a collection of different techniques. Not all programs use all techniques, but the better-developed interventions use components of arousal reduction, cognitive behavioral skills training, and some focus on improving relevant systematic and lifestyle issues (Lehrer & Woolfolk, 1993; Ong, Linden, & Young, 2004). Individuals use arousal reduction techniques to improve their physiological response to stress and cognitive behavioral techniques to cope better with current and future stressors. Clients often commit to changing systematic variables to reduce exposure to stressors and commit to other positive lifestyle changes (e.g., diet and exercise) in order to improve their general quality of life. All of these components are bundled into parsimonious individual behavioral plans.

Typical stress management interventions include small-group treatment, 6–19 sessions in length that average 10–15 hours of client exposure to treatment (Ong, Linden, & Young, 2004). Generally, stress management interventions include teaching the clients six different techniques, which means that clients only spend 1–2 hours on each technique, providing exposure to alternative behaviors and some skill acquisition rather than mastery of any one technique.

STEP-BY-STEP PROCEDURES

Assessment

Stress management interventions must start with an assessment phase. Whether assessed by self-report during the clinical interview or by pencil-and-paper measures it is important to comprehensively assess the health, daily responsibilities, family and social functioning, and coping repertoires of each individual. This information is central to developing a comprehensive behavioral plan.

- *Self-report measures of health*: Given the relationship between stress and health mentioned earlier, it is vital to thoroughly assess an individual's general health and health behaviors. The presence of health-promoting and -reducing behaviors (e.g., poor diet, substance use, lack of exercise) may compromise an individual's ability to cope with stress. These health-compromising behaviors may be demonstrative of existing maladaptive coping strategies (e.g., drinking alcohol to get to sleep) that may act as barriers to successful treatment. Common measures with good psychometric properties include the Sickness Impact Profile (SIP; Bergner, Bobbitt, Kressel, et al., 1976) and the Short Form-36 Health Survey (SF-36; McHorney, Ware, & Raczek, 1993). Two stress measures that include health-related items are the Perceived Stress Scale (PSS; Cohen, Kamarck, & Mermelstein, 1983), the Derogatis Stress Profile (DSP; Derogatis, 1987).

- *Self-report measures of daily responsibilities*: It is important to assess the client's encounter of hassles across different domains of responsibility (e.g., family obligations, occupational tasks, home responsibilities) and their satisfaction with their level of functioning across these domains. Instruments that assess stressors present (statistical or perceived) and an individuals functioning include the Daily Hassles Scale (DeLongis, Folkman, & Lazarus, 1988), the Derogatis Stress Profile (DSP; Derogatis, 1987), the Life Experiences Survey (LES; Sarason, Johnson, & Siegel, 1978), the Perceived Stress Scale (PSS; Cohen, Kamarck, & Mermelstein, 1983), and the Recent Life Changes Questionnaire (RLCQ; Miller & Rahe, 1997). These measures are easy to administer and have documented reliability and validity information available (Shaw, Dinsdale, & Patterson, 2000).

- *Self-report measures of family and social functioning*: As mentioned earlier, family and social support must be assessed in order to ascertain what areas provide support and what areas are themselves sources of stress. Some stress measures assess the domain of family and occupations stress including the Derogatis Stress Profile (DSP; Derogatis, 1987), the Life Experiences Survey (LES; Sarason, Johnson, & Siegel, 1978), and the Recent Life Changes Questionnaire (RLCQ; Miller & Rahe, 1997). The clinician may want to use a measure designed to assess family functioning specifically, such as the Family Assessment Device (FAD; Epstein, Baldwin, & Bishop, 1983) or to assess dyadic relationships such as the Dyadic Adjustment Scale (DAS; Spanier, 1979).

- *Self-report measures of coping strategies*: The clinician must assess both adaptive and maladaptive coping thoughts and behaviors. One commonly used self-report measure of individual's coping repertoires and patterns is the Ways of Coping Scale (Folkman & Lazarus, 1980). The information gained from pencil-and-paper measures or from narrative reports can be used to tailor a behavioral plan that will be most functional for each client.

Didactic Psychoeducation

The clinician must present the client with an explanation of the biopsychosocial model of stress. This ought to include describing the interplay between the biological, psychological, and social-environmental components of stress. Selye's general adaptation syndrome should be taught along with information on the body's physiological (short- and long-term) response to stress. It is key that the client understands the connection between exposure to a stressor, the body's immune response, and the potential to develop chronic health problems.

Create a Behavioral Plan

The behavioral plan for each client should include at least one stress-reducing lifestyle change, one adaptive coping behavior and one adaptive coping statement. As with behavioral plans in general, the information should be very specific and concrete in order to address barriers and increase motivation for change, as well as ensure the client experience opportunities for mastery of new behavior. The plan should be incorporated into the client's environment in a prominent and useful way (e.g., post plan on fridge). The plan is viewed as a work in progress and should be reviewed and modified as necessary throughout the client's participation in the stress management intervention.

Arousal Reduction Strategies

Clients are taught to practice some relaxation technique. The following list is not exhaustive and is provided to demonstrate the variety of arousal reduction techniques available to a clinician:

- *Passive relaxation:* Using verbal suggestions or pleasant imagery the client is asked to focus their attention on the physical sensations of warmth and relaxation. Clients can be given a written script or an auditory recording to use at home.
- *Progressive muscle relaxation:* The client is asked to find a comfortable position and sequentially tighten and relax muscle groups while focusing on the associated physical sensations. Clients usually start with 16 different muscle groups, graduating to 7 and finally 4 larger groupings (Jacobsen, 1938; Bernstein & Borkovec, 1973).
- *Meditation:* There are two broad categories of meditation techniques: concentrative techniques that focus attention on single stimulus like a word such as "relax" or an image, and nonconcentrative techniques that encourage openness and expansion of attention (Auerbach & Gramling, 1998).
- *Mindfulness meditation:* Mindfulness practices as pioneered by Kabat-Zinn (1990) have been used to reduce stress in a number of different clinical populations and settings (Mackenzie,

Carlson, & Munoz, 2007; Agee, 2007; Shigaki, Glass, & Schopp, 2006; Schensstrom, Ronnberg, & Bodlund, 2006). The practice consists of focusing the mind on something specific (like breath) with intention. The client is instructed in techniques to attend to the present moment and let go of the past and the future. Kabat-Zinn (1990) recommends practicing mindful meditation through body scans, sitting meditation, walking meditation, or body movement such as yoga for 45 minutes every day. Clients often find that practicing short mindful meditations, such as a 3-minute breathing space, can be revitalizing and relaxing (Segal, Williams, & Teasdale, 2002).
- *Biofeedback:* The client achieves relaxation of physiological sensations such as headache or muscle tension through attention and control of peripheral temperature or muscle tension (Peek, 1995).
- *Guided Imagery:* The client is instructed to find an image that is associated with a feeling of well being and peace and hold that image in their mind. The client may generate his or her own image or can be prompted to try some commonly used images such as a mountain stream with rushing water or walking on a beach at sunset.

Cognitive Behavioral Approaches

Many stress management clients feel overwhelmed and demoralized by life events. Clients who are impeded by their negative thoughts and beliefs about their ability to cope with life stressors may benefit from cognitive behavioral techniques. Cognitive behavioral techniques are used to teach clients skills for identifying and controlling stress and the effects of stress on their body. Clients are encouraged to develop positive expectations about their ability to cope with stressful activities and life events as well as to adopt a sense of self-control.

The techniques addressed in this chapter are the most common components of stress management interventions and are broken down into behavioral skills including problem-focused and emotion-focused coping skills, cognitive restructuring, systematic and lifestyle changes (Ong, Linden, & Young, 2004).

Clients are taught behavioral skills that assist with eliminating or avoiding the stressor or with reducing the emotional impact of the stressor. Information on the client's coping repertoires and functioning will have been gathered during the assessment phase. If the individual identifies many maladaptive coping behaviors (e.g., "When I get overwhelmed I stop doing anything," or "When I get stressed out I yell at my spouse.") these must be addressed in group and the individual should be taught adaptive coping alternatives. Coping behaviors should be individualized based on the client's preferences and needs. For example, the coping behavior of distraction will be employed differently for stressors in the workplace than stressors in the home and while one group member may find breathing exercises very helpful, another will say they do not help at all.

Problem-focused coping skills

- *Time management:* Many clients are overwhelmed by the quantity of demands put upon them and either procrastinate or avoid tasks due to inability to manage their time appropriately. Clients are taught to schedule, prioritize, and breakdown larger tasks into smaller units in order to reduce the stress associated with managing their time.
- *Assertiveness training:* For individuals who experience stress from difficulties with interpersonal communication, assertiveness training can be helpful. Clients are taught the difference between being assertive, nonassertive, and aggressive. Assertiveness training provides clients with skills to express their wishes effectively without being disrespectful or aggressive toward the other party.
- *Self-monitoring of stress intensity:* The clinician will find during assessment that some individuals are unable to generate the environmental triggers that act as stressors or are unable to identify their bodies physiological response to stress (e.g., "I feel my stomach clench. I start to sweat.") For these individuals it can be helpful complete self-monitoring of their stress intensity as associated with antecedents and consequences. The

information gathered from self-monitoring can then be used within the intervention to enhance an individual's behavioral plan (e.g., "When I feel my stress level rise to a 5, I will do deep breathing for 2 minutes").

Emotion-Focused Coping Skills

- *Breathing:* Diaphragmatic breathing is often useful for clients who identify tightness in their chest, or respiratory distress as a response to stress. Clients are encouraged to engage in deep, regular breaths from their diaphragm for a minimum of 2 minutes when exposed to a stressor or before entering into a situation that induces stress.
- *Distraction:* If excessive worry or rumination is causing stress for a client then distraction may be an appropriate technique to reduce their stress response. Techniques may focus on visual, auditory, or tactile stimulation to distract from a stressor or stress response. It is important that the clinician identifies and addresses inappropriate distraction, such as if a client is distracting as a means of procrastination and actually making the situation more stressful.
- *Time-out:* If the stressful activity or situation must be completed but can be left for a period of time the client may reduce stress by removing themselves and doing something else in a time out. It is important that the patient indicate what they will be doing during the time out on their behavioral plan. The alternate activity should be stress reducing not an additional source of stress (e.g., I will take a walk during my study time, rather than, I will pay my bills during my time out from studying).
- *Systematic desensitization:* Once a client has the skills to implement a desensitization hierarchy and practice relaxation techniques to manage the consequential anxiety, self-directed desensitization can be a useful technique for patients in their daily lives (Rosenbaum & Merbaum, 1984). Clients should learn standard therapist-directed desensitization and the therapist should ensure patient mastery before they are encouraged to use the technique on their own.

Cognitive Restructuring

Distorted thoughts and irrational beliefs must be addressed and specific alternative adaptive thoughts or coping statements should be included in a client's behavioral plan. Clients are taught the ABC model of thinking and emotion (Ellis, 1973) and are introduced to the common cognitive distortions and irrational beliefs that may impact their emotional reactions to stressful events (Beck, 1967; Burns 1990). It is important to provide the Clients with a handout demonstrating the ABCs of thinking and clarify how these distortions and irrational beliefs increase their stress level. As mentioned previously, if a client has trouble identifying a distorted thought or irrational belief and is unable to generate the consequences of these thoughts on their stress level they can be provided with a thought tracking and stress intensity monitoring diary card. The therapist can include space for the patient to then rewrite the distorted thought or belief as an adaptive coping statement. The statements can be generic such as "I've been through this before and things turned out ok," "I can handle this—I've handled things like this before," or more specific to the patient's individual distorted thought or belief. The focus of restructuring is to alter people's belief systems or improve the clarity of their logical interpretations of a stressful experience. The outcome should be to reduce uncertainty and enhance people's sense of control thereby reducing people's overall level of stress.

Systematic Approaches

In some clients' lives stress is managed appropriately but they are simply exposed to overwhelmingly high levels of social–environmental stress. If efforts have been made to reduce the impact of the stressor and this is insufficient, then it may be the case that the clinician needs to coach the client on generating strategies to change or modify their environment in order to eliminate or avoid contact with the stressor. Some sources of social or environmental stress come from a patient's family, others from occupational or community issues. Upon assessing the stressors present in the individual's environment it should be determined whether the system can be modified to reduce or eliminate the sources of stress. If the stressor cannot be eliminated (e.g., caring for an ill family member), the client should be given skills to manage the emotional impact of the situation.

Lifestyle Changes

Changing a client's lifestyle habits to be less stressful include addressing issues as varied as developing healthy eating habits (e.g., eat a well-balanced diet by reducing or eliminating consumption of sugar, processed foods, alcohol and caffeine); developing regular patterns of physical activity (ideally 30 minutes three times per week); getting enough sleep (improve sleep hygiene or address comorbid anxiety issues); and implementing components of a pleasant events schedule. These lifestyle changes should be tailored to the individual patients preferences and included in concrete terms in their behavioral plan.

EVIDENCED-BASED APPLICATIONS

Stress management techniques have been found effective with a number of problems, including:

- Sports and peak performance (Jones & Hardy, 1990; Schilling & Gubelmann, 1995)
- Emotional and behavioral disorders, including: anxiety (Lee, Ahn, & Lee, 2007; Toneatto & Nguyen, 2007), depression (Carrico, Antoni, & Weaver, 2005; Manber, Allen, & Morris, 2002), substance use disorders (Back, Gentilin, & Brady, 2007; Miley, 2001)
- Somatic disorders, including: oncology (Mackenzie, Carlson, & Munoz, 2007; McLean & Jones, 2007); coronary health issues (Daubenmier, Weidner, & Sumner, 2007; Langosch, Budde, & Linden, 2007); asthma (Lehrer, Feldman, Giardino, Song, & Schmaling, 2002); persistent and chronic pain (Bogart, McDaniel, Dunn, et al., 2007; Hughes, Robinson-Whelen, Taylor, & Hall, 2006)
- School refusal and academic problems (Briones, 2007; Hori & Akihito, 2007; Krag, van Breukelen, & Lamberts, 2007; Redwood & Pollack, 2007);
- Caregiver stress (Lopez, Crespo, & Zarit, 2007; Long, Krisztal, Rabinowitz, et al., 2004);

- Occupational and workplace issues (Page-Pressley, 2007; Davison, 2007: Ruwaard, Lange, Bouwman, Broeksteeg, & Schrieken, 2007)

CONCLUSION

This chapter presents an approach to using evidence based cognitive behavioral strategies as components of an effective stress management intervention. Given the high rates of reported stress and the high levels of comorbidity with other mental and physical health issues, it is hoped that these stress management techniques will improve clients' biological, psychological, and social–environmental quality of life.

References

Agee, J. D. (2007). Stress reduction in a community sample: A comparison of mindfulness and progressive muscle relaxation. *Dissertation Abstracts International: Section B: The Sciences and Engineering, 67*(8-B), 4697.

Auerbach, S. M., & Gramling, S. E. (1998). *Stress management: Psychological foundations.* Upper Saddle River, New Jersey: Prentice Hall.

Back, S. E., Gentilin, S., & Brady, K. T. (2007). Cognitive–behavioral stress management for individuals with substance use disorders: A pilot study. *Journal of Nervous and Mental Disease, 195*(8), 662–668.

Beck, A. T. (1967). *Depression: Causes and Treatment.* Philadelphia: University of Pennsylvania Press.

Bergner, M., Bobbitt, R. A., Kressel, S., Pollard, W. E., Gilson, B. S., & Morris, J. R. (1976). The Sickness Impact Profile: Conceptual formulation and methodology for the development of a health status measure. *International Journal of Health Sciences, 6,* 393–415.

Bernstein, D. A., & Borkovec, T. D. (1973). *Progressive relaxation training: A manual for the helping professions.* Champaign, Illinois: Research Press.

Bogart, R. K., McDaniel, R. J., Dunn, W. J., Hunter, C., Peterson, A. L., & Wright, E. E. (2007). Efficacy of group cognitive behavior therapy for the treatment of masticatory myofascial pain. *Military Medicine, 172*(2), 169–174.

Briones, J. (2007). A stress management and coping skills classroom guidance program for elementary school students. *Dissertation Abstracts International Section A: Humanities and Social Sciences, 68*(4-A), 1337.

Burns, D. (1990). *Feeling good handbook.* New York: NAL/Dutton.

Carrico, A. W., Antoni, M. H., & Weaver, K. E. (2005). Cognitive-behavioural stress management with HIV-positive homosexual men: Mechanisms of sustained reductions in depressive symptoms. *Chronic Illness, 1*(3), 207–215.

Cohen, S., Kamarck, T., & Mermelstein, R. (1983). A global measure of perceived stress. *Journal of Health and Social Behavior, 24,* 385–396.

Daubenmier, J. J., Weidner, G., & Sumner, M. D. (2007). The contribution of changes in diet, exercise, and stress management to changes in coronary risk in women and men in the multisite cardiac lifestyle intervention program. *Annals of Behavioral Medicine, 33*(1), 57–68.

Davison, K. M. (2007). Teacher resilience promotion: A pilot program study. *Dissertation Abstracts International: Section B: The Sciences and Engineering, 67*(9-B), 5395.

DeLongis, A., Folkman, S., & Lazarus, R. S. (1988). The impact of daily stress on health and mood: Psychological and social resources as mediators. *Journal of Personality and Social Psychology, 54,* 486–495.

Derogatis, L. R., (1987). Derogatis Stress Profile (DSP): Quantification of psychological stress. *Advances in Psychosomatic Medicine, 17,* 30–54.

Ellis. A. (1973). *Humanistic psychotherapy: The rational-emotive approach.* New York: Julian Press.

Epstein, N. B., Baldwin, L. M., & Bishop, D. S. (1983). The McMaster Family Assessment Device. *Journal of Marital and Family Therapy, 9,* 171–180.

Folkman, S., & Lazarus, R. S. (1980). An analysis of coping in a middle-aged community sample. *Journal of Health and Social Behavior, 21,* 219–239.

Hori, M., & Shimazu, A. (2007). A stress management program for university students. *Japanese Journal of Psychology, 78*(3), 284–289.

Hughes, R. B., Robinson-Whelen, S., Taylor, H. B., & Hall, J. W. (2006). Stress self-management: An intervention for women with physical disabilities. *Women's Health Issues, 16*(6), 389–399.

Jacobsen, E. (1938). *Progressive relaxation.* Chicago: University of Chicago.

Jones, J. G., & Hardy, L. (1990). *Stress and performance in sport.* Oxford, England: John Wiley & Sons.

Kabat-Zinn, J. (1990). *Full catastrophe living: Using the wisdom of your body and mind to face stress, pain, and illness.* New York: Delta Trade Paperbacks.

Kraag, G., van Breukelen, G., & Lamberts, P. (2007). Process evaluation of "learn young, learn fair": A stress management programme for 5th and 6th graders. *School Psychology International, 28*(2), 206–219.

Langosch, W., Budde, H. G., & Linden, W. (2007). Psychological Interventions for Coronary Heart Disease: Stress Management, Relaxation, and Ornish Groups. In J. Jordan, B. Bardé, & A. M. Zeiher, (Eds.), *Contributions toward evidence-based psychocardiology: A systematic review of the literature* (pp. 231–254). Washington, DC: American Psychological Association.

Lee, S. H., Ahn, S. C., & Lee, Y. J. (2007). Effectiveness of a meditation-based stress management program as an adjunct to pharmacotherapy in patients with anxiety disorder. *Journal of Psychosomatic Research, 62*(2), 189–195.

Lehrer, P., Feldman, J., Giardino, N., Song, H., & Schmaling, K. (2002). Psychological aspects of asthma. *Journal of Consulting and Clinical Psychology, 70*(3), 691–711.

Lehrer, P. M., & Woolfolk, R. L. (1993). *Principles and practices of stress management* (2nd ed.). New York: Guilford.

Long, C., Krisztal, E., Rabinowitz, Y., Gillispie, Z., Oportot, M., Tse, C., et al. (2004). Caregiver stress and physical health: The case for stress management therapy. *Clinical Psychologist, 8*(1), 22–28.

López, J., Crespo, M., & Zarit, S. H. (2007). Assessment of the efficacy of a stress management program for informal caregivers of dependent older adults. *The Gerontologist, 47*(2), 205–214.

Mackenzie, M. J., Carlson, L. E., & Munoz, M. (2007). A qualitative study of self-perceived effects of mindfulness-based stress reduction (MBSR) in a psychosocial oncology setting. *Stress and Health: Journal of the International Society for the Investigation of Stress, 23*(1), 59–69.

Manber, R., Allen, J. J. B., & Morris, M. M. (2002). Alternative treatments for depression: Empirical support and relevance to women. *Journal of Clinical Psychiatry, 63*(7), 628–640.

McHorney, C.A., Ware, J. E., Jr., & Raczek, A.E. (1993). The MOS 36-Item Short-Form Health Survey (SF-36): II. Pscyhometric and clinical tests of validity in measuring physical and mental health constructs. *Medical Care, 31*, 247–263.

McLean, L. M., & Jones, J. M. (2007). A review of distress and its management in couples facing end-of-life cancer. *Psycho-Oncology, 16*(7), 603–616.

Meichenbaum, D. (1993). Stress inoculation training: A 20-year update. In R. L. Woolfolk & P. M. Lehrer (Eds.), *Principles and practices of stress management* (2nd ed.) (pp. 373–406). New York: Guilford,.

Miley, W. M. (2001). Use of abnormal and health psychology as topics in a classroom format to reduce alcohol and other drug abuse among college students at risk. *Psychological Reports, 89*(3), 728–730.

Miller, M. A., & Rahe, R. H. (1997). Life changes scaling for the 1990s. *Journal of Psychosomatic Research, 43*(3), 279–292.

Ong, L., Linden, W., & Young, S. (2004). Stress management. What is it? *Journal of Psychosomatic Research, 56*, 133–137.

Page-Pressley, S. (2007). The effects of childcare provider training on stress reduction and behavioral-based management. *Dissertation Abstracts International: Section B: The Sciences and Engineering, 67*(8-B), 4696.

Peek, C. J. (1995). A Primer of Biofeedback Instrumentation. In M. S. Schwartz (Ed.), *Biofeedback: A Practitioner's Guide* (2nd ed.) New York: Guilford, pp. 47–48.

Redwood, S. K., & Pollak, M. H. (2007). Student-led stress management program for first-year medical students. *Teaching and Learning in Medicine, 19*(1), 42–46.

Rosch, P. J. (2007). *Reminiscences of Hans Selye, and the birth of "stress".* The American Institute of Stress. Retrieved December 30, 2007, from www.stress.org/hans.htm.

Rosenbaum, M., & Merbaum, M. (1984). Self-control of anxiety and depression. An evaluative review of treatments. In C. M. Franks (Ed.), *New developments in behavior therapy: From research to clinical application* (pp. 105–154). New York: Haworth Press.

Ruwaard, J., Lange, A., Bouwman, M., Broeksteeg, J., & Schrieken, B. (2007). E-mailed standardized cognitive behavioural treatment of work-related stress: A randomized controlled trial. *Cognitive Behaviour Therapy, 36*(3), 179–192.

Sarason, I. G., Johnson, J. H., & Siegel, J. M. (1978). Assessing the impact of life changes: Development of the Life Experiences Survey. *Journal of Consulting and Clinical Psychology, 46*(5), 932–946.

Schenström, A., Rönnberg, S., & Bodlund, O. (2006). Mindfulness-based cognitive attitude training for primary care staff: A pilot study. *Complementary Health Practice Review, 11*(3), 144–152.

Schilling, G., & Gubelmann, H. (1995). Enhancing performance with mental training. In S. J. H. Biddle (Ed.), *European Perspectives on Exercise and Sport Psychology* (pp. 179–192). Champaign, IL: Human Kinetics Publishers.

Segal, Z. V., Williams, J. M. G., & Teasdale, J. D. (2002). *Mindfulness-based cognitive therapy for depression.* New York: Guilford.

Selye, H. (1936). A syndrome produced by diverse nocuous agents. *Nature, 138*, 32.

Selye, H. (1950). *Stress* (1st ed.). Montreal: Acta.

Shaw, W. S., Dimsdale, J. E., & Patterson, T. L. (2000). Stress and life events measures. In A. J. Rush (Ed.), *Handbook of Psychiatric Measures* (pp. 221–239). Washington, DC: American Psychiatric Association,.

Shigaki, C. L., Glass, B., & Schopp, L. H. (2006). Mindfulness-based stress reduction in medical settings. *Journal of Clinical Psychology in Medical Settings, 13*(3), 209–216.

Spanier, G. B. (1979). The measurement of marital quality. *Journal of Sex and Marital Therapy, 5*(3), 288–300.

Toneatto, T., & Nguyen, L. (2007). Does mindfulness meditation improve anxiety and mood symptoms? A review of the controlled research. *Canadian Journal of Psychiatry, 52*(4), 260–266.

73 SYSTEMATIC DESENSITIZATION

Lara S. Head and Alan M. Gross

Systematic desensitization is an effective therapeutic treatment in the reduction of maladaptive anxiety (Wolpe, 1990). It is the process by which a person is induced into a deeply relaxed state and is presented with a series of graduated anxiety-evoking situations using imaginal, also known as in vitro, exposure. When anxiety is experienced during exposure, the image is terminated and a relaxed state is induced. With continued exposure to each situation, the person's level of anxiety weakens progressively, until the person no longer experiences anxiety in response to the aversive stimuli (Wolpe, 1958; 1990).

TYPES OF SYSTEMATIC DESENSITIZATION

In vivo desensitization

Similar to imaginal exposure in terms of procedure, *in vivo* desensitization utilizes a hierarchy of real-life anxiety-evoking situations that are presented to the client. While both are effective in isolation, imaginal and *in vivo* desensitization are often used together to facilitate transfer of skills. The client first successfully responds to anxiety-evoking situations using imaginal exposure and then confronts similar situations in a real-life setting (Wolpe, 1990).

Group Desensitization

Based on Wolpe's procedures, systematic desensitization using imaginal exposure is presented to a group of individuals with common anxiety-related difficulties. Administration of hierarchy items is typically determined by the progress rate of the slowest participating group member. Group desensitization can be especially useful for therapists treating multiple clients with similar phobias, allowing for cost- and time-effective intervention (Lazarus, 1961).

Self-Control Desensitization

Founded on Davison's counterconditioning model, the self-control desensitization process is regarded as a "behavioral rehearsal" procedure in which the client learns how to cope with anxiety during a series of anxiety-evoking situations using imaginal exposure. Rather than attempting to reduce anxiety caused by a specific scenario, the primary focus is to assist the client in identifying the physiological cues that indicate anxiety and then using the cues to help the client initiate relaxation to reduce the tension (Davison, 1968; Goldfried, 1971).

Exposure Therapy

Exposure therapy extracts the exposure element of Wolpe's systematic desensitization procedures and suggests that exposure to fear signals is the key mechanism for change (Marks, 1975; McNally, 2007). Four types of exposure therapy have been proposed based on the level of intensity in exposure (e.g., gradual or intense) and whether the fear signals are based on real or imagined stimuli (Taylor, 2002), with gradual in vivo exposure being the preferred technique (Marks, 1978). Many clinicians have adopted exposure therapy as an alternative to traditional systematic desensitization techniques, with focus given exclusively to providing sufficient exposure as the sole mode of treatment for fear reduction (McGlynn et al., 2004; McNally, 2007).

EVIDENCED-BASED APPLICATIONS

Systematic desensitization is among the most empirically supported psychotherapeutic treatments available (Tryon, 2005). However, how it is utilized in the clinical setting has changed over time as the fundamental mechanisms to the technique's success have been further explored (McNally, 2007; Tryon, 2005). Rather than being utilized in its classic format as Wolpe originally described, clinicians are more frequently integrating its basic elements of exposure to aversive cues as a component of more comprehensive cognitive/behavioral therapeutic programs to treat a variety of issues (McGlynn, Smitherman, & Gothard, 2004; McNally, 2007; Tryon, 2005).

Anxiety/Obsessive–Compulsive Disorder/Phobia

Systematic desensitization is most commonly used in the treatment of anxiety and is considered one of the first empirically supported treatments established using behavioral principles in an outpatient mental health setting (McNally, 2007; St. Onge, 1995; McGlynn, Mealiea, & Landau, 1981). It can be administered individually or in a group setting with equally effective results (Lazurus, 1961; Wolpe, 1990). While useful with persons experiencing generalized anxiety, systematic desensitization is most commonly used in treating persons with phobia where specific anxiety-evoking stimuli such as animals, insects, water, airplanes, and closed spaces have been identified.

Fear reduction using *in vivo* exposure is considered the preferred approach to treating individuals with specific phobias (McNally, 2007). Ideal systematic desensitization candidates have three or fewer phobias, demonstrate anxiety that is not the result of a lack of knowledge or skill regarding the stimuli, are able to demonstrate anxiety in response to imaginal exposure to anxiety-evoking stimuli, and with relaxation training, are able to successfully relax (St. Onge, 1995). In addition, clients must also be able to develop a well-defined hierarchy of anxiety-evoking situations (Wolpe, 1990).

In vivo desensitization is effective with all age groups but has proven most beneficial in the treatment of children with phobias or anxiety disorders. Children often do not have the visualization capabilities to implement imaginal exposure effectively (Ultee, Griffioen, & Schellekens, 1982). Systematic desensitization has also been used to treat patients with obsessive–compulsive

disorder (OCD) and patients with agoraphobia (Foa, Steketee, & Ascher, 1980).

Recently, developments in the study of anxiety disorders have suggested that neuroscience may play a role in understanding the underlying mechanisms for anxiety (McNally, 2007). Interventions that promote the development of inhibitory associations to suppress the fear-conditioned response and that promote fear extinction are being investigated such as using N-methyl-D-aspartate (NMDA) glutamatergic agonists to facilitate fear extinction (McNally, 2007, p. 755). Such insights may prove beneficial in understanding how to incorporate systematic desensitization as part of an individual's therapeutic program. Therapists should evaluate each individual's symptoms for effective use of systematic desensitization; other empirically supported treatments may be more appropriate given the client's primary problem.

Posttraumatic Stress Disorder

More recently, systematic desensitization has been utilized with a number of special populations exhibiting a variety of aversive responses to various stimuli. Among individuals with acute stress disorder or posttraumatic stress disorder (PTSD), exposure to trauma, including the increasing number of military veterans reporting trauma resulting from combat exposure, both short and long-term imaginal exposure treatment has demonstrated improvement in the reported severity and frequency of PTSD symptoms, level of anxiety and depression, and reported overall psychological well-being (Van Minnen & Foa, 2006). Its use and success has also been reported when administered as a group desensitization technique in response to acute traumatic stress generated such as a result of the September 11, 2001, attacks on the Pentagon in Washington, D.C. (Waldrep & Waits, 2002).

Developmental Disabilities

Individuals with autism often demonstrate hypersensitivity and other unusually aversive responses to common stimuli such as different foods, clothing textures, and sounds. Further, difficulties with (e.g. from one activity to another) can result in significant levels of anxiety. While these behaviors are commonly associated with individuals with an autism spectrum disorder, aversive responses to common stimuli, transition issues, and other daily living activities are often seen among individuals with other developmental disabilities, particularly those with varying degrees of associated intellectual disability. Systematic desensitization has been successful in reducing anxiety and other fear related responses. Graduated exposure has been paired with differential reinforcement, social attention, and modeling to facilitate use of skin care products (Ellis, Ala'i-Rosales, Glenn, Rosales-Ruiz, & Greenspoon, 2006), decrease hypersensitivity to auditory stimuli such as vacuum cleaners and toilet flushing (Koegel, Openden, & Koegel, 2004), and eliminate specific phobic responses to water (Davis, Kurtz, Garner, & Carman, 2007; Rapp, Vollmer, & Hovantez, 2005), and heights (Davis et al., 2007).

Medication and Procedure Compliance

Systematic desensitization is also effective among children in pediatric settings in facilitating compliance and adherence to various medical procedures and treatments. Many children will be uncooperative and avoidant of medical procedures because of the fear and other aversive responses they experience, thereby potentially creating undue obstacles to their recovery. Psychoeducation, visual imagery, and other cognitive behavioral techniques are frequently utilized in the clinical setting to reduce anxiety prior to surgery or other invasive medical procedures. By contrast, systematic desensitization can be used to assist with treatments that require frequent blood drawings, a procedure often complicated by children with needle phobias (Zambanini & Feher, 1997).

Among children and adults with developmental disabilities, systematic desensitization has increased compliance during dental procedures in individuals with intellectual disabilities ranging from mild to profound (Conyers, et al., 2004; Altabet, 2002). Further, it has been effective in treating specific phobias associated with medical procedures including needle use with children with autism (Ricciardi & Luiselli, 2006; Shabani & Fisher, 2006) and pill swallowing among children with autism and attention-deficit hyperactivity disorder (Beck, Cataldo, Slifer, Pulbrook, & Guhman, 2005). Among individuals with developmental disabilities, systematic desensitization techniques can prevent use of more resistive procedures, (e.g., sedation, general anesthesia, and physical restraint, to facilitate treatment compliance), and techniques that may prolong and further aggravate the individual's fear response (Shabani & Fisher, 2006).

CONTRAINDICATIONS

Three common difficulties are frequently cited as reasons a client may be unsuccessful in the systematic desensitization process: difficulty relaxing, poorly developed hierarchies, and difficulty visualizing images (Wolpe, 1990). If a client is unable to relax, additional practice may be needed. If the client feels uncomfortable being observed, adjustments can be made to the relaxation script as well as to the room arrangement to help the client feel more comfortable (Foa, et al., 1980). In terms of hierarchies, if the appropriate fears and anxieties are not addressed, the client may report little anxiety during exposure. Hierarchy revision may be needed to identify the appropriate anxiety-evoking stimuli. Or, if the client reports significant gaps in the anxiety levels of subsequent item presentations, hierarchy revision is needed to identify less-anxiety-evoking items. Finally, clients must be able to visualize each item presentation clearly, and with adequate detail. If visualization difficulties occur, visualization training can be provided (Wolpe, 1990).

HOW DOES THE TECHNIQUE WORK?

Developed by Joesph Wolpe (1958), systematic desensitization was based on the principle of "reciprocal inhibition" (Wolpe, 1958, p.71). Wolpe suggested that "If a response antagonistic to anxiety can be made to occur in the presence of anxiety-evoking stimuli so that it is accompanied by a complete or partial suppression of the anxiety response, the bond between these stimuli and the anxiety response will be weakened" (Wolpe, 1958, p. 71). While other responses incompatible with anxiety have been used, deep muscle relaxation remains the most commonly used and convenient anxiety inhibitor (Wolpe, 1961).

Contrary to Wolpe's suggestion that the effectiveness of systematic desensitization can be accounted for by reciprocal inhibition, Davison asserts that systematic desensitization is a counterconditioning process (Davison, 1968). Rather than inhibiting anxiety as Wolpe proposed, the presence of anxiety triggers physiological and behavioral cues that are used to prompt the implementation of replacement behaviors. Using this counterconditioning model, Goldfried (1971) developed self-control desensitization in which a person learns to cope with anxiety by recognizing bodily tension cues and using them to initiate relaxation in response to typically anxiety-evoking situations. Goldfried suggested that with practice, not only does the anxiety-evoking situation become less aversive, the person also learns to generalize these coping skills to other forms of anxiety.

Other theories have also been proposed as explanations for the success of systematic desensitization. Lader and Mathews (1968) suggested that desensitization procedures result in habituation to the aversive stimuli. Anxiety is alleviated by increasing the frequency of sympathetic responses to aversive stimuli, which in turn encourages habituation. Wilson and Davison's (1971) theory involving extinction posited that exposure to the stimuli (imagined or real life) not followed by the anxiety reinforcing element leads to extinction of fear responses. Wilkins' (1971) cognitive-social reinforcement theory attributed systematic desensitization's success to five different elements: therapist expectations of improvement, positive reinforcement of client effort, concrete evidence of improvement, client-control of aversive stimuli, and consistent focus on systematic desensitization as a learning process (McGlynn, et al., 1981). More recently, Tryon (2005) asserted that desensitization works based on a connectionist network learning theory. Therapeutic change occurs when an individual's

neural synaptic networks seek consonance, or dissonance reduction. As individuals develop dissonance in response to each exposure experience, connection or synaptic weights are continually modified through the learning process to accept a preferred behavioral response.

STEP-BY-STEP PROCEDURES: TRADITIONAL SYSTEMATIC DESENSITIZATION

Determining when to use systematic desensitization depends upon the individual and the problems being experienced. A complete behavioral analysis is suggested to identify anxiety-evoking stimuli and to determine the appropriateness of the anxiety given the actual level of danger (Wolpe, 1976; St. Onge, 1995). Consideration should also be given to ensure that no "cognitive misconceptions" exist (Foa, et al., 1980, p. 40). If anxiety occurs as a result of a lack of knowledge about the situation or object, then correct information should be given and the client's level of anxiety reassessed. Phobic patients are typically aware that the fear they are experiencing in response to a particular object or situation is illogical (Foa, et al., 1980). Once systematic desensitization has been determined as an appropriate therapeutic treatment for the client, a three-step process unfolds:

1. Relaxation training
2. Development of graduated anxiety hierarchies
3. Presentation of hierarchy items while the client is in a deeply relaxed state (Wolpe, 1990)

Step 1: Relaxation Training

Instruction in relaxation training involves teaching the client how to reduce tension in the body using a systematic procedure and assisting the client in its implementation (Wolpe, 1990). Relaxation provides the client with the necessary antagonist that will serve to inhibit anxiety (Wolpe, 1958). In addition, relaxation serves as a calming mechanism, allowing the client to participate more readily in the imaginal exposure process by increasing the clarity of images sought (Levin & Gross, 1985). Relaxation training typically lasts approximately five to seven sessions, but more time may be needed depending upon the individual. The primary goal is "differential relaxation" in which the client is able to relax completely muscles that are not being used during a given situation and reduce all unnecessary tension in pertinent muscles to a minimal degree (Wolpe, 1958, p. 135). Instruction focuses on teaching the client to recognize muscle tension by contracting and flexing muscles and then releasing that tension while focusing on the difference in body tension before and after muscle contraction (Wolpe, 1990). Different muscle groupings can be addressed during separate sessions using the following sequence: session 1—arms; session 2—head; session 3—mouth; session 4—neck and shoulders; session 5—back, abdomen, and chest muscles; session 6—lower body. However, relaxation training can be conducted in fewer sessions, according to the therapist's preference and client's progress.

During relaxation training, the client should be able to sit comfortably and concentrate with few distractions. Closing eyes is encouraged but not a necessity. The therapist should speak softly when explaining instructions and presenting hierarchy items (St. Onge, 1995). The following relaxation script is provided for session one (St. Onge, 1995).

1. Take a deep breath, hold it (about 10 seconds). Hold it. Now, let go, feeling the release.
2. Stick your arms out and make a tight fist. Really tight. Feel the tension in your hands; notice the discomfort. I am going to count to three, and when I say 'three', drop your arms and hands. One ... Two ... Three ... Relax ... Just let go ... Notice the difference.
3. Raise your arms again, and bend your fingers back toward your body. Hold it. Now drop your arms and hands; just let go. Notice the sensations; feel the difference; feel the comfort.
4. Tense your forearms and upper arms by pressing your elbows down against the chair. Feel the tightness ... Hold it. Now, relax. The muscles are letting go; your arms may even be getting warmer. Let your forearms really

rest on a chair (or lap). Let go even more. [It is the act of relaxing these additional fibers that will bring about the greatest emotional effect.] Let the whole arm go limp, soft. Good (St. Onge, 1995, pp. 100–101)

Each relaxation step lasts approximately 10 seconds with 10–15 second pauses between each step. The entire relaxation process typically lasts about 25 minutes (St. Onge, 1995). Subjective units of discomfort (SUD) ratings (0–100 range) should be taken at the end of each relaxation session to determine the level of relaxation. Once the client is able to relax to a point of zero or near zero and an anxiety hierarchy has been developed, hierarchy item presentation can begin (Wolpe, 1990).

Step 2: Anxiety Hierarchy Development

Step two in the process of systematic desensitization is the formulation of a hierarchy of anxiety-evoking situations (Wolpe, 1990). Construction can be done concurrently with relaxation training and should be a collaborative effort on the part of the patient and therapist. Using information gathered from the client's history, clinical interview, as well as any number of anxiety assessment tools, the therapist and client first identify a series of situations that cause the client maladaptive levels of anxiety. Daily logs completed by the client that record common behaviors and activities can be utilized to assist in item identification (Goldstein & Foa, 1980). Therapists can also use their personal observations of the client's behavior to determine additional anxiety-evoking scenarios that could be included in the hierarchy (Goldfried & Davison, 1994). Each situation should be specific and include sufficient detail to facilitate visualization (Goldfried & Davison, 1994). While many of the situations will have been previously experienced by the client, previous exposure is not a prerequisite. Situations must however, be circumstances that would cause the client anxiety (Wolpe, 1990). Hierarchies typically include 10–20 items (St. Onge, 1995).

Once a list of situations has been devised, the client ranks the scenarios in order of aversiveness, with the most anxiety-evoking situation located at the top of the hierarchy (Wolpe, 1990). While some clients will construct only one hierarchy, many clients will be experiencing anxiety in response to a number of different stimuli. In these cases, multiple hierarchies may need to be constructed, each addressing related situations (Wolpe, 1990).

Step 3: Imaginal Exposure

Imaginal exposure is the final step in the systematic desensitization process. The client has been taught how to relax, has identified a series of anxiety-evoking situations, and is now ready to confront them. Each imaginal exposure session begins and ends with the client in a relaxed state. The client should report a SUD rating of 10 or less before beginning scene presentation (Wolpe, 1990).

Using verbal descriptions given by the client during the assessment process, a neutral scene is first presented by the therapist to serve as a "control"; it allows the therapist to assess the client's capacity to visualize clearly and determine if any obstacles exist that will hamper visualization (Wolpe, 1990, p. 172). The neutral scene, typically pleasurable in nature, will be utilized whenever the client experiences anxiety during the exposure process and can be returned to during relaxation periods. A signal, such as raising the index finger, should be used by the client to indicate that the scene image is clear. Once a clear image has been obtained, the client continues visualizing the scene for approximately 10 seconds at which point the client is then asked to stop visualizing and a SUD rating is taken. The client is then returned to a relaxed state, with a reported SUD rating of 10 or less (Wolpe, 1990). The following script is provided (Wolpe, 1990).

First I am going to help you to relax. When you are relaxed I will ask you to imagine certain scenes. Each time a scene becomes clear to you in your mind, let me know by raising your index finger ... [Begin relaxation process] ... Now you are feeling relaxed and calm. Imagine that you are sitting beside a clear blue lake. The sun is shining and a slight breeze is blowing. You feel so comfortable and relaxed. Fluffy white clouds are moving slowly overhead. [Watch the client for raised index finger,

when indicated, allow visualization to continue for approximately 10 seconds] ... Stop the scene. On a scale of 1 to 100, what is your SUDs rating?

The first hierarchy item is then presented in a similar fashion, using verbal descriptions of the anxiety-evoking situations. The client signals the therapist when the scene has been visualized clearly. Visualization continues for approximately five to seven seconds at which point the client is asked to terminate the scene, a SUD rating is taken, and the client is returned to a relaxed state. Additional presentations of the same scene continue until the SUD rating following visualization is zero (Wolpe, 1990). Once a client has reported a zero SUD rating in response to a hierarchy item, the therapist can move on to the next item. Those scenes anticipated to create significant levels of anxiety can be initially presented for shorter periods of time such as two to three seconds, with subsequent presentations of the same item increasing in length until the client tolerates a 5–7-second exposure period. The context of the image may also dictate the time length of visualization, with simple tasks requiring less exposure time (Wolpe, 1990).

During a typical 30-minute exposure session, a client may be presented as many as three to four scene presentations, each ultimately yielding a zero SUD rating. However, the number of items addressed in a single session and over the course of treatment will vary depending upon the progress of the client through the hierarchy. Each new session should begin with the most recent item to receive a zero SUD rating or any item that was not previously given a zero SUD rating. Some reoccurrence of anxiety previously reported as zero can occur. If so, the item should be presented again until the client reports a zero anxiety level. The number of scene presentations will increase as the client's level of anxiety increases (Wolpe, 1990).

Following each session and especially during relaxation training, homework should be encouraged. This may include continued practice of relaxation techniques or *in vivo* exposure. Audio and videotapes can be prepared by the therapist and given to the client to assist in these activities. However, the client should not attempt imaginal or *in vivo* exposure of a new hierarchy item without the therapist present (St. Onge, 1995).

KEY ELEMENTS OF SYSTEMATIC DESENSITIZATION

1. Relaxation training
2. Development of graduated anxiety hierarchies
3. Imaginal exposure—presentation of hierarchy items while the client is in a deeply relaxed state

Further Reading

Tryon, W. W. (2005). Possible mechanism for why desensitization and exposure therapy work. *Clinical Psychology Review, 25*, 67–95.

Wolpe, J. (1961). The systematic desensitization treatment of neuroses. *Journal of Nervous and Mental Disease, 132*, 189–203.

Wolpe, J. (1990). *The practice of behavior therapy* (4th ed.). New York: Pergamon Press.

References

Altabet, S. (2002). Decreasing dental resistance among individuals with severe and profound mental retardation. *Journal of Developmental and Physical Disabilities, 14*, 297–305.

Beck, M. H., Cataldo, M., Slifer, K. J., Pulbrook, V., & Guhman, J. K. (2005). Teaching children with attention deficit hyperactivity disorder (ADHD) and autistic disorder (AD) how to swallow pills. *Clinical Pediatrics, 44*, 515–526.

Conyers, D., Miltenberger, R. G., Peterson, B., Gubin, A., Jurgens, M., Selders, A., et al. (2004). An evaluation of in vivo desensitization and video modeling to increase compliance with dental procedures in persons with mental retardation. *Journal of Applied Behavior Analysis, 37*, 233–238.

Davis, T. E., Kurtz, P. F., Gardner, A. W., & Carman, N. B. (2007). Cognitive–behavioral treatment for specific phobias with a child demonstrating severe problem behavior and developmental delays. *Research in Developmental Disabilities, 28*, 546–558.

Davison, G. C. (1968). Systematic desensitization as a counter-conditioning process. *Journal of Abnormal Psychology, 73*, 91–99.

Ellis, E. M., Ala'i-Rosales, S. S., Glenn, S.S., Rosales-Ruiz, J., & Greenspoon, J. (2006). The effects of graduated exposure, modeling, and contingent social attention on tolerance to skin care products with two children with autism. *Research in Developmental Disabilities, 27*, 585–598.

Foa, E. B., Steketee, G. S., & Ascher, L. M. (1980). Systematic desensitization. In E. B. Foa & A. Goldstein (Eds.), *Handbook of behavioral interventions: A clinical guide* (pp. 38–91). New York: John Wiley & Sons.

Goldfried, M. R. (1971). Systematic desensitization as training in self-control. *Journal of Consulting and Clinical Psychology, 37*, 228–234.

Goldfried, M. R., & Davison, G. C. (1994). *Clinical behavior therapy* (exp.). New York: John Wiley & Sons.

Koegel, R. L., Openden, D., & Koegel, L. K. (2004). A systematic desensitization paradigm to treat hypersensitivity to auditory stimuli in children with autism in family contexts. *Research and Practice for Persons with Severe Disabilities, 29*, 122–134.

Lazarus, A. A. (1961). Group therapy of phobic disorders by systematic desensitization. *Journal of Abnormal and Social Psychology, 63*, 504–510.

Levin, R. B., & Gross, A. M. (1985). The role of relaxation in systematic desensitization. *Behavior Research and Therapy, 23*, 187–196.

Marks, I. (1975). Behavior treatments of phobic and obsessive compulsive disorders: A critical appraisal. In M. Hersen, R. M. Eisler, & P. M. Miller (Eds.), *Progress in Behavior Modification, vol. 1*. New York: Academic Press.

Marks, I. (1978). Behavioral psychotherapy of adult neurosis. In S. L. Garfield & A. E. Bergin (Eds.), *Handbook of psychotherapy and behavior change: Am empirical analysis* (2nd ed.) (pp. 493–547). New York: John Wiley & Sons.

McGlynn, F. D., Mealiea, W. L., Jr., & Landau, D. L. (1981). The current status of systematic desensitization. *Clinical Psychology Review, 1*, 149–179.

McGlynn, F. D., Smitherman, T. A., & Gothard, K. D. (2004). Comment on the status of systematic desensitization. *Behavior Modification, 28*, 194–205.

McNally, R. J. (2007). Mechanism of exposure therapy: How neuroscience can improve psychological treatments for anxiety disorders. *Clinical Psychology Review, 27*, 750–759.

Rapp, J. T., Vollmer, T. R., & Hovanetz, A. N. (2005). Evaluation and treatment of swimming pool avoidance exhibited by an adolescent girl with autism. *Behavior Therapy, 36*, 101–105.

St. Onge, S. (1995). Systematic desensitization. In M. Ballou (Ed.), *Psychological interventions: A guide to strategies* (pp. 95–115). Westport, CT: Praeger.

Ricciardi, J. & Luiselli, J. (2006). Shaping approach responses as intervention for specific phobia in a child with autism. *Journal of Applied Behavior Analysis, 39*, 445–448.

Shabani, D. B. & Fisher, W. W. (2006). Stimulus fading and differential reinforcement for the treatment of needle phobia in a youth with autism. *Journal of Applied Behavior Analysis, 39,* 449–552.

Taylor, S. (2002). Systematic desensitization. In M. Hersen, & W. Sledge (Eds.), *Encyclopedia of Psychotherapy, vol. 2* (pp. 755–759). New York: Elsevier Science.

Tryon, W. W. (2005). Possible mechanism for why desensitization and exposure therapy work. *Clinical Psychology Review, 25,* 67–95.

Ultee, C.A., Griffioen, D., & Schellekens, J. (1982). The reduction of anxiety in children: A comparison of the effects of systematic desensitization *in vitro* and systematic desensitization *in vivo. Behavior Research and Therapy, 20,* 61–67.

Van Minnen, A., & Foa, E. B. (2006). The effect of imaginal exposure length on outcome of treatment for PTSD. *Journal of Traumatic Stress, 19,* 427–438.

Waldrep, D. & Waits, W. (2002). Returning to the pentagon: The use of mass desensitization following the September 11, 2001 attack. *Military Medicine, 167,* 58–59.

Wolpe, J. (1958). *Psychotherapy by reciprocal inhibition.* Stanford, CA: Stanford University Press.

Wolpe, J. (1961). The systematic desensitization treatment of neuroses. *Journal of Nervous and Mental Disease, 132,* 189–203.

Wolpe, J. (1976). *Theme and variations: A behavior therapy casebook.* New York: Pergamon Press.

Wolpe, J. (1990). *The practice of behavior therapy* (4th ed.). New York: Pergamon Press.

Zambanini, A., & Feher, M. D. (1997). Needle phobia in type I diabetes mellitus. *Diabetic Medicine, 14,* 321–323.

Gerald C. Davison, Jennifer L. Best, and Marat Zanov

As your eyes glance over the text contained within the covers of this book, what thoughts are going through your mind? Is there an underlying theme to your cognitions? Are extraneous thoughts intruding as you read? Perhaps you are conscientiously poring over these pages with the sole purpose of extracting as much meaning from the text as possible. Perhaps something on a given page brings to mind a patient you are working with. Maybe you are silently talking back to the text, interjecting a running commentary or critique of what you are reading—or maybe you are reading more passively, with most of your mental resources devoted to thoughts such as what you had for lunch this afternoon, or reviewing the list of tasks you must finish in preparation for an upcoming professional conference.

With the advent of the cognitively centered Zeitgeist within behavior therapy in the late 1960s (Bandura, 1969; Beck, 1967; Davison & Valins, 1969; Ellis, 1962; Mahoney, 1974; Mischel, 1968) came a burgeoning of methods for describing and analyzing the content of thought. These approaches fell primarily into two broad categories: endorsement techniques and production techniques (see Glass, 1993, for a review).

Endorsement techniques include self-report questionnaires such as the Fear of Negative Evaluation Scale (FNE; Watson & Friend, 1969) and the Irrational Beliefs Test (IBT; Jones, 1968). Questionnaires contain a series of preassigned, experimenter-defined or theory-driven statements. Participants are requested to endorse which items best apply and to what degree they reflect current, past or future thoughts, beliefs, and attitudes. Though endorsement methods require very little time and effort and though they easily facilitate standardization procedures and the development of norms, they also constrain participants to define aspects of their thinking in terms of already established, a priori formulations.

Production methods include think aloud (e.g., Genest & Turk, 1981), thought-sampling (e.g., Hurlbut, 1979; Klinger, 1978), thought-listing (e.g., Cacioppo & Petty, 1981), and video-mediated recall (e.g., Schwartz & Garamoni, 1986) protocols. Each of these procedures involves the participants either verbally reporting or creating a written record of what they are thinking or feeling. These more open-ended approaches allow study participants the freedom to describe their reactions rather than, as in endorsement methods, confine their response to predetermined categories. Subsequently, the verbal productions are content-analyzed for the variables of interest.

Production methods tend to vary with respect to the context of recording (e.g., in an experimentally contrived laboratory situation versus in the participants' natural, day-to-day environments). Another point of divergence for production techniques is the type of stimulus medium (e.g., fictional or imaginal interpersonal vignettes presented via headphones or video monitor) used in the investigations (Glass, 1993).

Other important dimensions in the several cognitive assessment paradigms include the proximity of measurement to events of interest and the context dependence of thought recording. Endorsement measures typically rely on the individual's memory, with participants having to mentally survey their stores of retrospective accounts for thoughts and behaviors. Such measures of cognitive assessment also usually attempt to abstract general (vs. situationally diverse), enduring, emotional, cognitive, or behavioral tendencies. Production methods, in contrast, are often designed to characterize thinking in relation to specific situations relatively close to or concurrent with the experimental manipulation or task presented. For many thought-sampling studies, however, cognitions are randomly sampled throughout the day over several days (e.g., see Hurlbut, 1997, for a review). Thus events are naturally occurring as opposed to experimentally defined.

We turn now to a discussion of one type of production method, commonly referred to as think-aloud.

THINK-ALOUD METHODS OF COGNITIVE ASSESSMENT

Think aloud paradigms in particular have been a useful means of collecting thoughts in a variety of task situations and with various participant groups (see Davison, Vogel, & Coffman (1997); Genest et al., 1981, and Kendall & Hollon, 1981, for detailed reviews). Some of the earliest think-aloud studies were focused on determining the underlying mechanisms and thought processes associated with different aspects of academic performance among students at different age levels. Their findings may have important implications for designing effective prevention along with remediation interventions for students with learning disabilities.

For example, Randall and colleagues studied metacognitive processing in college students while performing a think-aloud task as they read (Randall, Fairbanks, & Kennedy, 1986). Researchers wanted to learn more about how students attended to their own reading behaviors while actually reading. Reading comprehension difficulties were highlighted from the transcribed protocol analyses of the think-aloud data (e.g., how word substitutions affected interpretation of the material).

Another group of researchers used a think-aloud approach to examine cognition and metacognition among gifted, learning disabled, and average-performing middle school children while solving a series of math problems (Montague & Applegate, 1993). Verbalized self-talk while completing three mathematical word problems of increasing difficulty distinguished among the groups. In general, learning-disabled

students tended to exhibit qualitatively different strategic processes during the task.

In addition to the study of learning disabilities, think-aloud methods have been employed extensively within the mental health literature. Think-aloud methodologies have been useful in the study of emotional reactions to social rejection (Craighead, Kimball, & Rehak, 1979); test anxiety in elementary school children (Fox, Houston, & Pittner, 1983); dysphoric college students (Conway, Howell, & Giannopoulos, 1991; Mayo & Tanaka-Matsumi, 1996); math-anxious college students (Blackwell, Galassi, Galassi, & Watson, 1985); adults with fear of snakes (Eifert & Lauterbach, 1987); and anxious elementary school children (Lodge, Tripp, & Harte, 2000).

The rest of this chapter will very briefly introduce readers to a specific think-aloud paradigm that has been used in several investigations of interest to cognitive-behavioral theorists, scientists, and practitioners.

THE "ARTICULATED THOUGHTS IN SIMULATED SITUATIONS" THINK-ALOUD COGNITIVE ASSESSMENT PARADIGM

Among the think aloud techniques mentioned previously in this chapter is the *articulated thoughts in simulated situations (ATSS)* think-aloud approach of Davison and associates (Davison, Robins, & Johnson, 1983). ATSS is described as a research paradigm rather than as a specific procedure or assessment instrument because the various parameters of ATSS can take different forms depending on the purposes and practicalities of a particular experimental situation.

There are several basic features that define the ATSS paradigm. ATSS involves presenting study participants with multisegmented vignettes or scenarios. During the course of a simulated situation, individuals think out loud at specified points interspersed between brief segments of the story. Participants are requested to pretend that the experimental scene is actually happening to them in the laboratory. Their think-aloud reports are transcribed for later content analysis.

The following are typical instructions for ATSS as we have employed it so far:

> In this study we are interested in the kinds of thoughts people have when they are in certain situations. Often, when people are going about their daily affairs, interacting with others, and so forth, they have a kind of internal monologue going through their heads, a constant stream of thoughts of feelings that reflect their reactions to something that is happening.
>
> What we'd like you to do is play a part in a couple of situations we have taped. Your part will involve listening to situations and tuning in to what is running through your mind, and then saying these thoughts out loud. The tapes are divided into seven segments. At the end of each segment, there will be a tone, followed by a pause of 30 seconds, during which time we would like you to say out loud whatever is going though your mind. Say as much as you can until you hear another tone. Of course, there are no right or wrong answers, so please just say whatever comes to mind, without judging whether it seems appropriate or not. The more you can tell us the better.
>
> Try to imagine as clearly as you can that it is really you in the situation right now. Note that your task is not to speak back to any one of the recorded voices as though you were having a conversation with one of them. Rather, you should tune in to your own thoughts and say them out loud. The microphones in front of you will enable us to record your comments.

One scene in which the participant overhears two pretend acquaintances criticizing him or her includes the following segments:

> *First acquaintance:* He certainly did make a fool of himself over what he said about religion. I just find that kind of opinion very closed-minded and unaware. You have to be blind to the facts of the universe to believe that. [30-second pause for subject's response]
>
> *Second acquaintance:* What really bugs me is the way he expresses himself. He never seems to stop and think, but just blurts out the first thing that comes into his head. [30-second pause for subject's response]

ATSS data are content analyzed using a priori defined codes for the cognitive constructs under investigation. Continuous frequency counts or categorical present–absent counts comprise the traditional data reduction methods employed in ATSS studies.

There are distinct features that set ATSS apart from other think-aloud approaches as an experimental tool. First, ATSS has traditionally provided participants with imagined, recorded encounters versus scenarios shown on videotape [1] or in response to actual experimental tasks, such as contending with a series of math problems. This feature of ATSS permits participants to envision particularly meaningful images instead of having experimenter-generated images as the stimuli. It further provides not only the unique opportunity to study the interplay of thoughts, emotions, and behavioral intentions in situations that commonly occur; but also facilitates the chance to examine these interrelationships in unusual or rare events that might not be ethical or even possible to expose persons to *in vivo*.

Second, unlike think-aloud approaches that are truly online and therefore may interrupt task performance and attention, ATSS is pseudo-online. Participants alternate between hearing segments of the scenario unfold and verbalizing their thoughts. Third, ATSS relies less heavily on the memory of the participant than do think-aloud methods that require participants to think out loud directly after the entire experimental manipulation (e.g., after completing a problem set). Thoughts instead are articulated in response to smaller bits of information than if a vignette were presented to participants in full before they were instructed to think aloud. Thus, one can sample very nearly in the moment of experience instead of relying on participants' recollections of thinking during a prior experience.

---

1.   The ATSS *paradigm* per se does not preclude other modes of presentation of the complex social stimulus—for example, videotape or even virtual reality. Thus far in our lab and in independent research settings, however, audiorecorded presentations have been quite effective.

In order for readers to obtain some idea of the breadth of ATSS investigations, results from selected studies employing ATSS methodology are briefly listed here. Those interested in a more detailed review of ATSS research are referred to three ATSS review papers (Davison, Navarre, & Vogel, 1995; Davison, Vogel, & Coffman, 1997; Zanov, & Davison, 2008) and to the specific studies themselves.

- The articulated thoughts of participants hearing the criticisms of two pretend acquaintances or the negative comments of a pretend teaching assistant about their term papers were more irrational than was their thinking aloud to a neutral scenario (Davison, Feldman, & Osborn, 1984; Davison & Zighelboim, 1987).
- Depressed patients from a psychiatric clinic and outpatients with other psychological disorders listened to a recording that described an outdoor barbecue, one that they had supposedly planned and on which it had rained. The articulated thoughts of the depressed participants were more distorted, as predicted by Beck's (1967) cognitive theory of depression, than those of the other nondepressed outpatients (White, Davison, Haaga, & White, 1992).
- Socially anxious therapy patients articulated thoughts of greater irrational content (in line with Ellis' 1962 theory) than did nonanxious control participants (Bates, Campbell, & Burgess, 1990; Davison & Zighelboim, 1987).
- Men with borderline hypertension and Type A behavior pattern verbalized more hostile thoughts than did men with Type B personality (Weinstein, Davison, DeQuattro, & Allen, 1986) and responded to social criticism with less self-supportive cognitions (Williams, Davison, Nezami, & DeQuattro, 1992).
- Recent ex-smokers who relapsed within 3 months following ATSS demonstrated a greater tendency to articulate thoughts about smoking without prompting (Haaga, 1987) and expressed fewer negative expectations associated with smoking than did those who remained abstinent at 3-month follow-up (Haaga, 1988).

- In a study that directly compared ATSS articulations to overt behavior, Davison, Haaga, Rosenbaum, Dolezal, and Weinstein (1991) found that verbalized expressions of positive self-efficacy were inversely related to behaviorally indexed speech anxiety; that is, the more anxiously participants behaved on a timed behavioral-checklist measure of public-speaking anxiety, the less capable they felt themselves to be while articulating thoughts in a stressful simulated speech-giving situation.
- In a treatment outcome study comparing progressive muscle relaxation (PMR) and health education to health education alone, men with borderline hypertension articulated fewer hostile expressions at posttreatment in the PMR condition than in the health education condition (Davison, Williams, Nezami, Bice, & DeQuattro, 1991).
- An ATSS investigation of martially violent men found that ATSS variables distinguished between levels of marital aggression better than did questionnaire measures of dysfunctional thinking (Eckhardt, Barbour, & Davison, 1998). Marital violence was associated with, for example, more articulated hostile attributions, illogical thought content (e.g., dichotomous thinking), and demandingness and with fewer anger control statements than the men who were not martially violent.
- In reaction to personal criticism and jealousy-evoking situations, Eckhardt, Jamison, and Watts (2002) found that college-age males with a history of acting violently against their present dating partner were more verbally aggressive than nonviolent daters. The latter group was also more likely to use anger-control statements, which turned out to be a better predictor of group membership than self-report measures of irrational thinking and cognitive biases (Eckhardt & Jamison, 2002).
- An ATSS study examining attitudes toward homosexuals and anti-gay hate crimes demonstrated that anti-gay attitudes predicted more articulated disapproval of the victim and support for the perpetrator during the hate crime scenario than in the non-hate crime condition (Rayburn & Davison, 2003).

- Immediate and delayed reactions to parental conflict in college-age adults were evaluated in an ATSS investigation by Duggan, O'Brien, and Kennedy (2001). Compared to those without a history of violent physical aggression between their parents, individuals with such history were more likely to predict negative outcomes of the ATSS-simulated conflict between a husband and a wife. The latter group also reported greater experienced and perpetrated verbal and physical aggression in their own dating relationships, suggesting that witnessing one's own parental discord might be a diathesis for aggressive behaviors in their own personal relationships.
- Rayburn, Jaycox, McCaffrey, Ulloa, Zander-Cottugno, Marshall, and Shelley (in press) compared teenagers' gender-specific reactions to violent dating situations. Boys and girls generally differed in that the boys were more likely to confront the involved parties and even physically aggress against the male perpetrator. However, if the perpetrator was the participant's acquaintance, they were less willing to get involved in the simulated altercation. Additionally, dating violence was perceived as more serious and received more disapproval if the perpetrator was a male. In contrast, the violent actions of a female were more likely to be justified.

CONCLUSION

Think-aloud typically provides an open-ended online response format, examines the potential contextual or situational influence on cognitive and emotional processing, and strives for ecological validity in stimulus design. Think-aloud techniques also exhibit notable convergent, predictive, and construct validity when pitted against, for example, self-report measures (e.g., see Davison et al., 1997).

On the other hand, a principal criticism of the think-aloud method (as well as other production methods) is the issue of reliability or replicability of findings. Although researchers allow participants to verbalize extensively what is on their minds, the data are analyzed with experimenter-defined, a priori codes for the information-processing variables of interest. Coded categories are rarely repeated in a large number of studies, either within or across research laboratories. Experimenter-devised codes for describing cognitive, affective and behavioral processes may not be the most accurate representation of how the actual participants conceptualize their own thinking. However, despite their limitations, think-aloud techniques, and in particular ATSS, have clearly been demonstrated to be useful for studying cognitive, behavioral, and affective reactions in a wide range of academic and social situations.

References

Bandura, A. (1969). *Principles of behavior modification.* New York: Holt, Rinehart, & Winston.

Barlow, D. H. (1993). *Clinical handbook of psychological disorders* (2nd ed.). New York: Guilford Press.

Bates, G. W., Campbell, T. M., & Burgess, P. M. (1990). Assessment of articulated thoughts in social anxiety: Modification of the ATSS procedure. *British Journal of Clinical Psychology, 29,* 91–98.

Beck, A. T. (1967). Depression: Clinical, experimental, and theoretical aspects. New York: Harper & Row.

Blackwell, R. T., Galassi, J. P., Galassi, M. D., & Watson, T. E. (1985). Are cognitive assessment methods equal? A comparison of think-aloud and thought-listing. *Cognitive Therapy and Research, 9,* 399–413.

Cacioppo, J. T., & Petty, R. E. (1981). Social psychological procedures for cognitive response assessment: The thought-listing technique. In T. V. Merluzzi, C. R. Glass, & M. Genest (Eds.), *Cognitive assessment* (pp. 309–342). New York: Guilford.

Conway, M., Howell, A., & Giannopoulos C. (1991). Dysphoria and thought suppression. *Cognitive Therapy and Research, 15,* 153–166.

Craighead, W. E., Kimball, W. H., & Rehak, P. J. (1979). Mood changes, physiological response, and self-statements during social rejection imagery. *Journal of Consulting and Clinical Psychology, 47,* 385–396.

Davison, G. C., Feldman, P. M., & Osborn, C. E. (1984). Articulated thoughts, irrational beliefs, and fear of negative evaluation. *Cognitive Therapy and Research, 8,* 349–362.

Davison, G. C., Haaga, D. A., Rosenbaum, J., Dolezal, S. L., & Weinstein, K. A. (1991). Assessment of self-efficacy in articulated thoughts: "States of mind" analysis and association with speech anxious behavior. *Journal of Cognitive Psychotherapy: An International Quarterly, 5,* 83–93.

Davison, G. C., Williams, M. F. Nezami, E., Bice, T. L., & DeQuattro, V. (1991). Relaxation, reduction in angry articulated thoughts, and improvements in borderline essential hypertension and heart rate of. *Journal Behavioral Medicine, 14,* 453–468.

Davison, G. C., Navarre, S. G., & Vogel, R. S. (1995). The articulated thoughts in simulated situation paradigm: A think-aloud approach to cognitive assessment. *Current Directions in Psychological Science, 4,* 29–33.

Davison, G. C., Robins, C., & Johnson, M. K. (1983). Articulated thoughts during simulated situations: A paradigm for studying cognition in emotion and behavior. *Cognitive Therapy Research, 7,* 17–40.

Davison, G. C., Vogel, R. S., & Coffman, S. G. (1997). Think-aloud approaches to cognitive assessment and the articulated thoughts in simulated situations paradigm. *Journal of Consulting and Clinical Psychology, 65,* 950–958.

Davison, G. C., & Zighelboim, V. (1987). Irrational beliefs in the articulated thoughts of college students with social anxiety. *Journal of Rational-Emotive Therapy, 5,* 238–254.

Duggan, S., O'Brien, M., & Kennedy, J. K. (2001). Young adults' immediate and delayed reactions to simulated marital conflicts: Implications for intergenerational patterns of violence in intimate relationships. *Journal of consulting and clinical psychology, 69*(1), 13–24.

Eckhardt, C. I., Barbour, K. A., & Davison, G. C., (1998). Articulated thoughts of maritally violent and nonviolent men during anger arousal. *Journal of Consulting and Clinical Psychology, 66,* 259–269.

Eckhardt, C., & Jamison, T. R. (2002). Articulated thoughts of male dating violence perpetrators during anger arousal. *Cognitive Therapy and Research, 26*(3), 289–308.

Eckhardt, C., Jamison, T. R., & Watts, K. (2002). Anger experience and expression among male dating violence perpetrators during anger arousal. *Journal of Interpersonal Violence, 17*(10), 1102–1114.

Eifert, G. H., & Lauterbach, W. (1987). Relationships between overt behavior to a fear stimulus and self-verbalizations measured by different assessment strategies. *Cognitive Therapy and Research, 11,* 169–183.

Ellis, A. (1962). *Reason and emotion in psychotherapy,* Secaucus, NJ: Lyle Stuart.

Fox, J. E., Houston, B. K., & Pittner, M. S. (1983). Trait anxiety and children's cognitive behaviors in an evaluative situation. *Cognition Therapy and Research, 7,* 149-154.

Genest, M., & Turk, D. C. (1981). Think-aloud approaches to cognitive assessment. In T. V. Merluzzi, C. R. Glass, & M. Genest (Eds.), *Cognitive assessment.* New York: Guilford.

Glass, C. R. (1993). A little more about cognitive assessment. *Journal of Counseling and Development, 71,* 546–548.

Haaga, D. A. (1987). *Smoking schemata revealed in articulated thoughts predicts early response relapse from smoking cessation.* Paper presented at the 21st Annual Convention of the Association for Advancement of Behavior Therapy, Boston.

Haaga, D. A. (1988). *Cognitive aspects of the relapse prevention model in the prediction of smoking relapse.* Paper presented at the 22nd Annual Convention of the Association for Advancement of Behavior, New York.

Hurlburt, R. T. (1979). Random sampling of cognitions and behavior. *Journal of Research in Personality, 13,* 103–111.

Hurlburt, R. T. (1997). Randomly sampling thinking in the natural environment. *Journal of Consulting and Clinical Psychology. 65,* 941–949.

Jones, R. G. (1968). A factored measure of Ellis's irrational belief system with personality and maladjustment correlates. Unpublished doctoral dissertation, Texas Technological College, Lubbock.

Kendall, P. C., & Hollon, S. D. (1981). Assessing self-referent speech: Methods in the measurement of self-statements. In P. C. Kendall & S. D. Hollon (Eds.), *Assessment strategies for cognitive-behavioral interventions.* New York: Academic Press.

Klinger, E. (1978). Modes of normal conscious flow. In K. S. Pope & J. L. Singer (Eds.), *The stream of consciousness: Scientific investigations into the flow of human experience* (pp. 225–258). New York: Plenum.

Lodge, J. L, Tripp, G., Harte, D. K. (2000). Think-aloud, thought-listing, and video-mediated recall procedures in the assessment of children's self-talk. *Cognitive Therapy and Research, 24,* 399–418.

Mahoney, M. J. (1974). *Cognition and behavior modification.* Cambridge, MA: Ballinger.

Mayo, V. D., & Tanaka-Matsumi, J. (1996). Think-aloud statements and solutions of dysphoric persons on a social problem-solving task. *Cognitive Therapy and Research, 20,* 97–113.

Mischel, W. (1968). *Personality and assessment.* New York: Wiley.

Montague, M., & Applegate, B. (1993). Middle school students' mathematical problem solving: An analysis of think-aloud protocols. *Learning Disability Quarterly, 16,* 19–32.

Randall, A., Fairbanks, M. M., & Kennedy, M. L. (1986). Using think-aloud protocols diagnostically with college readers. *Reading Research and Instruction, 25,* 240–253.

Rayburn, N., & Davison, G. C. (2003). Articulated thoughts about anti-gay hate crimes. *Cognitive Therapy and Research, 23,* 431–447.

Rayburn, N. R., Jaycox, L. H., McCaffrey, D. F., Ulloa, E. C., Zander-Cotugno, M., Marshall, G. N., & Shelley, G. A. (in press). Reactions to dating violence among Latino teenagers: An experiment utilizing the Articulated Thoughts in Simulated Situations Paradigm. *Journal of Adolescence*.

Schwartz, R. M. & Garamoni, G. L. (1986). A structural model of positive and negative states of mind; Asymmetry in the internal dialogue. *Advances in cognitive-behavioral research and therapy, 5,* 1–62.

Watson, D., & Friend, R. (1969). Measurement of social-evaluative anxiety. *Journal of Consulting and Clinical Psychology, 33,* 87-104.

Weinstein, K. A., Davison, G. C., DeQuattro, V., & Allen, J. W. (1986). *Type A behavior and cognitions; Is hostility the bad actor?* Paper presented at the 94th Annual Convention of the American Psychological Association, Washington, DC.

White, J., Davison. G. C., Haaga, D. A. F., & White, K. (1992). Cognitive bias in the articulated thoughts of depressed and nondepressed psychiatric patients. *Journal of Nervous and Mental Disease, 180,* 77–81.

Williams, M. E., Davison, G. C., Nezami, E., & DeQuattro, V. I., (1992). Articulated thoughts of Type A and B individuals in response to social criticism. *Cognitive Therapy and Research, 16,* 19–30.

Zanov, M. V., & Davison, G. C. (2008). Getting into the black box: Cognitive assessment and 25 years of the articulated thoughts in simulated situations (ATSS) paradigm. Manuscript in preparation.

75 TIME-OUT, TIME-IN, AND TASK-BASED GROUNDING

Patrick C. Friman

INTRODUCTION

There appear to have been no significant research based changes in the time-out (TO) literature since the first edition of this book. This is unsurprising given the size of that literature. TO is still the most commonly used child disciplinary tactic directly derived from behavioral science in the United States—and it has a body of well established research findings to match. Therefore this chapter will closely resemble the one in the previous edition with two notable differences. The first involves an expansion of the section on evidence of effectiveness. The second involves the inclusion of an extension of TO, a TO type procedure referred to as task-based grounding (TBG).

TO is an abbreviation of a longer label—time-out from positive reinforcement—first reported in basic science reports on animals in the 1950s (e.g., Ferster, 1958). As a procedure, TO involved either placing experimental animals in chambers devoid of access to activities with known reinforcing (i.e., motivating) properties (e.g., drinking, eating, wheel running, etc.) or eliminating such access in chambers where the animals had already been placed. In these basic experiments TO proved to be an extraordinarily powerful procedure with two particularly salient effects: (1) reducing the likelihood of future occurrences of the behavior that led to its administration; and (2) increasing the reinforcing properties of events that were eliminated or denied during TO. In more colloquial terms, TO reduced an experimental animal's interest in some behaviors while simultaneously increasing its interest in others.

The basic science reports on TO attracted the attention of applied researchers and, in the early 1960s, the first reports showing the beneficial effects of TO on child misbehavior appeared and the dissemination of this now universally used procedure began (e.g., Wolf, Risley, & Mees, 1964). At present, a professional or popular book on child management techniques that does not include a section on TO would be hard to find (e.g., Christophersen, 1997; McMahon & Forehand, 2003). Unfortunately for readers searching for an optimal method for using TO, more variability than uniformity is found across the multitude of published descriptions. This paper provides a synthesis of the published studies and descriptions, with special emphasis on teaching parents to use TO with children at home. Also included is a table detailing steps to follow when prescribing TO (see Table 75.1).

UNDERLYING PROCESSES

The fundamental process underlying the utility of TO involves how children derive meaning from the teeming multitude of events that compose their day-to-day life, how they learn to exhibit appropriate and inappropriate behavior, or more generally, how they learn. Research on learning by several of the most eminent behavioral scientists of the twentieth century (e.g., Bandura, Bijou, Skinner, Thorndike, Watson) shows that child learning largely results from the emergence of functional relations between what children do, what happened before they did it, and the change or contrast in experience generated by what they have done. Said slightly differently, child learning occurs as a function of repetition followed by changes or contrast in child experience. Pleasant or preferred changes lead children to continue the

TABLE 75.1   Steps to Prescribing Time-Out

1. Determine whether TO is an appropriate approach to discipline or whether it is contraindicated (e.g., because of illness, impoverished home life, potential for abuse, etc).
2. Help parents generate a variety of ways to establish time for their child.
3. Help parents identify the most typical child behaviors for which TO will be used.
4. Help parents identify a variety of places for TO to be used (e.g., chair, corner, front step).
5. Review with parents the importance of consistent use of TO.
6. Instruct parents in the actual use of time out including:
   What is said to the child before TO (e.g., specific and brief).
   What is said to the child during TO (i.e., nothing).
   What is said to the child after he/she has become calm and quiet (e.g., are you ready to get up now?).
   What to do if the child leaves time out before time is up.
   What do when TO is over (e.g., practice desired behavior).
7. Instruct parents when to contact therapist for additional help (e.g., if something unusual happens or if no results are produced).

behavior that produced the changes and unpleasant or nonpreferred lead them to discontinue it. An important corollary of this position is that the number of repetitions necessary for children to make meaningful connections is governed by the amount of the experiential contrast that follows what they do. The more contrast, the fewer repetitions necessary for learning a meaningful relationship between a behavior, its antecedents, and its experiential consequences.

A major class of experientially unpleasant events for children involves those in which very little happens. In other words children do not like situations in which nothing of interest is occurring and avoidance of such situations motivates a substantive portion of their behavior. From a theoretical perspective nothing is hard to define. From an empirical perspective it can be hard to document. But from a procedural perspective experiences involving nothing, not much, or very little can be arranged and related arrangements compose the first important dimension of effective TO. The second (and equally) important dimension of TO involves a severe restriction on the child's capacity to make something happen or to change the experience of nothing into an experience of something interesting. In other words, situations in which there is nothing going on and little or nothing that can be done about it are aversive for children. After placing a child in a situation with nothing going on (i.e., in TO), the next step is to narrow the range of responses that result in escape from TO to include only appropriate behavior (e.g., quiet acceptance).

In addition to reducing the likelihood of behavior it follows (because children will avoid it), TO also increases the reinforcing properties of events that were denied during its implementation, the primary one of which for children is parental attention. Thus, immediately following TO, parents are in possession of a powerful commodity (i.e., attention) that can be used to teach their child appropriate alternatives to the behavior that led to TO.

EVIDENCE OF EFFECTIVENESS

The widespread use of TO in American culture is matched by a long and large line of relevant research with initial basic experiments beginning in the 1950s (e.g., Ferster, 1958) and initial applied experiments beginning shortly thereafter (e.g., Wolf et al., 1964). A particularly informative early review traced the systematic replication of TO as it evolved from a basic science preparation to a regularly reported treatment application (Johnston & Pennypacker, 1980). The voluminous applied research that occurred during that period and since shows that TO is an effective method for managing a broad range of misbehavior in children. A much-abbreviated sample of empirically documented successes includes routine misbehavior (e.g., Mathews, Friman, Barone, Ross, & Christophersen, 1987), disruptive behavior disorders (Kavale, Forness, & Walker, 1999) and clinically exotic habits (e.g., trichotillomania; Blum, Barone, & Friman, 1994). TO is also a primary component in the most widely used and empirically supported multi-component approaches for managing defiance, noncompliance, opposition, and disruption in young children. As an example, it is a key component in parent–child interaction therapy (PCIT). The title of a review of PCIT published a decade ago is indicative of the size of the body of relevant research: "Effective psychosocial treatments of conduct-disordered children and adolescents: 29 years, 82 studies, 5,272 kids" (Brestan & Eyberg, 1998). Furthermore, PCIT is only one of several well-researched multicomponent treatment packages that employ TO. A sample of others includes Kazdin's Parent Management Training (e.g., Kazdin, 2005), McMahon & Forehand's program for noncompliant children (e.g., McMahon & Forehand, 2003), Barkley's approach to defiant children (e.g., Barkley, 1998), Patterson's parent training program (e.g., Patterson, Chamberlain, Reid, 1982), Christophersen's behavioral pediatric program (e.g., Christophersen, 1982), and Webster-Stratton's program for oppositional children (e.g., Reid, Webster-Stratton, & Hammond, 2003).

CONTRAINDICATIONS

From a conceptual perspective, TO appears to be a generically effective, basically harmless reductive procedure because it merely involves strategic diminishment of preferred events. From a procedural perspective, however, TO can be complicated and it is contraindicated in some cases. Chief among them are those involving the possibility of self-harm or the probability of excessive stimulation if children are left unattended. TO is also not appropriate for children whose lives are impoverished in terms of human contact, marked by neglect, abuse, or inappropriate out-of-home placement, or who are ill. Additionally, TO is not appropriate for children whose misbehavior is motivated primarily by social avoidance. TO can be useful to establish a "cooling off" period for older children (i.e., older than 7 years) faced with disciplinary action, but probably should not be the only disciplinary method employed.

THE ROLE OF TIME-IN

As indicated, the fundamental basis for the utility of TO is that children learn through repetition with experiential contrast and thus, in order for TO to be effective, children must be in situations the removal from which generates nonpreferred contrast. If nothing preferred was occurring prior to a TO, the possibility for experiential contrast during a subsequent TO is reduced and thus the possibility of learning following TO is also reduced. Conversely, if engagement, fun, and/or affection is abundant prior to a TO, the possibility for nonpreferred experiential contrast during a subsequent TO is increased and correspondingly the possibility of learning following TO is also increased. Therefore, prior to using TO, it is necessary to establish a high degree or level of time-in (TI) (Solnick, Rincover, & Peterson, 1977). Heuristically, TI can be thought of as the functional opposite of TO. TO is a procedure that minimizes preferred experience and is used in response to inappropriate child behavior. TI is a procedure that maximizes preferred experience (e.g., physical affection, parental participation in child activities, etc.) and is used in response to appropriate child behavior. There are many ways to establish TI, several of which are described below:

- *Physical affection.* The general goal of TI is to increase children's enjoyment of their own life. At the simplest level of application, TI involves the provision of frequent and consistent physical affection when children are engaged in acceptable behavior. One way to prescribe this is to instruct parents to increase the number of times they touch their child affectionately by at least 50 discrete times a day. This does not mean that parents have to extensively hold and cuddle their child, rather it merely means that whenever children are within reach parents should reach out and provide one or two seconds of physical affection (e.g., by patting them on the shoulder, ruffling their hair, etc.) Frequent touching is particularly beneficial when children are involved in boring, effortful, onerous, or distracting activities. Additionally, physical

affection with children can be more powerful if it is supplied nonverbally. Questioning, commenting, or even praising, although
enhanced by being paired with physical affection, can diminish the central message carried
by the affection itself (e.g., I love you).

- *Let them help.* Children may not like to do their
own chores but they often do like to help as
parents work on parent projects. With a little
creativity, a parent can readily arrange for
their child to provide some real or apparent
assistance with whatever task the parent is
currently engaged (e.g., sweep small corner of
kitchen, hold the dustpan, turn on the garden
hose, etc.). Allowing children to help can be
rewarding for children because it suggests
they can make valuable contributions to the
parent and it also sets the occasion for parents
to acknowledge and praise the help provided.

- *Catch them being good.* Even flagrantly misbehaving children exhibit some appropriate
behavior yet, for a variety of reasons (e.g., a
high rate of misbehavior obscures it) adults
often fail to acknowledge much it. Training
parents to be at least as observant of and
positively responsive to appropriate behavior, as they are observant of and critical
towards inappropriate behavior, will naturally increase the amount of TI a child's life
(e.g., Christophersen, 1997).

- *Second and third hand compliments.* Sometimes direct compliments have limited
potency because their delivery is ineffective
(e.g., insincere) or their meaning has been
contaminated by the parent-child interactions
that preceded them (e.g., praise following a
power struggle may suggest the child has
lost). However, when compliments about the
child are shared with a second person and
then are either overheard or delivered to the
child by the other person, they can be a very
effective means of increasing TI (e.g., Ervin,
Miller, & Friman, 1996).

- *Special time.* One way to ensure a modicum
of TI is to have parents provide each of
their children a small amount of special time
(e.g., 5–15 minutes) that the child determines
how to use (e.g., piggy back rides, talking).
The time should be delivered every day the

children and parents are home together (i.e.,
even on days when children have misbe-
haved).

- *Miscellaneous.* There are many other ways of
establishing TI (e.g., games, family meetings,
outings, etc.) and they are limited only by
the imagination of the therapist and parent
and by the resources in the home. Although
it is not necessary for parents to conduct
a TI procedure immediately prior to a TO,
the therapist should ensure that parents are
frequently using TI procedures prior to prescribing TO.

USING TO

Where?

The central difficulty for the therapist teaching
parents about TO is to communicate that it is a
condition, not a location. Thus, although a bar-
ren locked room can provide TO, it is entirely
unnecessary (and usually inhumane) to use one
for that purpose. The key components of TO are
major reductions in children's access to preferred
events and their methods for changing the situation. The most preferred events in a child's life
are social contact with others and engagement
with entertaining objects (e.g., toys, games, television) and thus these are the preferred events to
which access is curtailed in TO. Confining children to their room can accomplish these goals but
so too can confining them to a seated position
anywhere in the home (e.g., chair in the dining
room) or out of the home (e.g., bench while at
the park). Relying solely on bedrooms can inconvenience parents (e.g., when bedrooms are on
a different floor than the location of the infraction) whereas the goal of TO is to strategically
inconvenience misbehaving children. Children
confined to their rooms may also find ways to
amuse themselves and thus diminish the nonpreferred aspect of their TO. Also, if children
are in their rooms crying out or yelling with no
response from the parent, the children may not
know whether they are being ignored or just not
being heard. When children are crying out and
yelling and their parents are well within visual
and auditory range, it is clear to the children
that they are being ignored and this knowledge

activates the second functional dimension of TO, a dramatic limitation on the children's capacity to control the situation. Thus the bedroom can be used as a backup for TO but probably should not be the primary location for its implementation. Generally, an adult-sized chair located near but not within the center of activities in the house is best. Larger chairs are more difficult for children to leave and thus reduce child attempts at escape. Locating the chair near central activities makes parental vigilance easier and makes what the child has temporarily lost more apparent.

What If Children Refuse to Go to TO?

This problem can be avoided by physically guiding children to TO rather than instructing them to go. Using an instruction sets the occasion for defiance or noncompliance whereas using guidance obviates these concerns. Use of guidance is also a clear demonstration that the parent has taken control of the interaction.

For What Behavior?

Parental discipline of children is the primary method by which children are acculturated and trained to exhibit civilized conduct. Most children do not automatically or spontaneously generate the behaviors that compose such conduct. Rather they emit approximations in response to the unfolding events of their lives. Shaping these approximations into fully expressed exemplars of civilized conduct requires teaching, the success of which is dependent on response repetition followed by experiential contrast. TO provides the kind of contrast that teaches children that the behavior that preceded its administration is unacceptable. TO also increases the value of parental attention, denied during TO, which increases a parent's subsequent capacity to reinforce appropriate child behavior. Therefore, TO should be used for any behaviors that parents feel are unacceptable, or more generally, for any instance where the parents may be tempted to raise their hand or voice to their child. To make matters simpler, unacceptable child behaviors can be divided into three categories: dangerous, defiant, and disruptive behavior. As a general rule, TO should always follow dangerous

and/or defiant behavior. Because disruption is an inevitable dimension of child behavior, however, much of it can be ignored. But disruption can also either be a target for TO or the target of a command (e.g., "go in your room and do that") compliance with which should be followed by praise and noncompliance with which should be followed by TO.

What to Say before and during TO

Although language is the primary tool most adults use to teach children, absent the experiential changes discussed here it actually is not very powerful, especially for young children. In the act of discipline involving TO, therefore, it is best to say very little. A rule of thumb is to use one or two words for every year of child life to label the infraction and then take the child to TO and say no more.

How Long Should TO Last?

Clinic lore and a variety of child behavior manuals assert TO should last one minute for every year of child age. This rule was the product of efficiency, not empirical research. That is, it was easy to remember but it has not been empirically evaluated. Generally, exit from TO should be contingent upon child behavior, not the passage of time. Departure from TO is typically a highly preferred event and thus it has power to strengthen the behavior preceding it. Therefore, departure should be allowed when the child has accepted TO as indicated by the exhibition of quiet and composed behavior (i.e., behaviors such as crying, pleading, and bargaining have stopped). A version of the clinic lore assertion can then be used. Specifically, once children in TO are quiet and composed they should not be required to remain there any longer than one minute for every year of age. Acceptance can be tested merely by asking the child if they would like to get out of TO. If they say "yes" in an acceptable tone of voice, departure is allowed. If they say "no," nothing at all, or anything that is tonally or semantically unacceptable, TO should continue.

Clinic lore also asserts timers should be used. They are unnecessary but if used one critical rule should be borne in mind. The timer is for the parent, not the child. That is, the timer is to be used to remind parents how long their child has been in TO, not to show children in TO the rate at which time is passing. While in TO children would typically prefer to know that rate, but in TO preferences are held to a minimum and thus the timer is not used for them.

What to Do about Misbehavior in TO

Children will inevitably misbehave while in TO, especially in the early stages of teaching it to them. The cardinal rule is that adult responses to children in TO are always *nonverbal*. Between the instruction to go to TO and the parental inquiry about whether the child would like to leave TO, adults should say *nothing*. All misbehavior exhibited while children remain in TO should be ignored and this includes profanity, insults, removing clothes, and even spitting. There are two reasons for ignoring this rule. First, TO involves a severe restriction on child preferences and children angry about being placed in TO would prefer that their parent respond to them, so this preference should not be granted. Second, TO increases the reinforcing properties of events denied during its administration, one of which is parent response to the child. Thus if the parent responds to gross misbehavior during TO, even if the parental response is negative, there is a heightened probability that behavior will be exhibited in the future (i.e., learned).

Perhaps the most difficult challenge involves children that repeatedly leave TO prior to being granted permission to do so. The simplest method for contending with these unexcused departures is simply to physically (and nonverbally) return children to TO repeatedly until they surrender to the process. There are also several mild forms of physical restraint that can be used. One involves using a chair with sides (arms) for TO and placing an arm across the sides and near or against the child's lap in a fashion that approximates a seat belt. Another involves using a chair with a gap in the backside through which a parent can grasp the back of a child's pants and gently hold when escape is attempted. Or the child's bedroom can be used as a backup TO location when children are highly resistant.

What to Do after TO

Contrary to clinic lore and most child behavior manuals, it is unnecessary and usually unproductive to lecture children on what they did that led to TO (Blum, Williams, & Friman, 1995). As indicated above, messages about discipline should be very brief. Additionally, the assertion that such messages should be revisited thoroughly after TO is based on the widely held but mistaken assumption that children primarily learn from what they hear or are told. Consistent with our assertion that children learn through repetition with experiential contrast, following TO, children should be given multiple opportunities to practice acceptable alternatives to the behaviors that led to TO. The easiest form of practice is to issue several simple commands and to praise and appreciate any child compliance and conversely, to use another TO as a consequence for noncompliance. If defiance or noncompliance led to TO, a related instruction should inaugurate the practice session. The reasons for using parental instructions for post-TO practice are straightforward. Diminished instructional control is a major component of most child misbehavior and practice complying with simple parental instructions followed by appropriate consequences strengthens this critical skill. Additionally, a parent's ability to effectively teach children to follow instructions is increased after TO due to the increased value of parental attention resulting from the TO.

TASK-BASED GROUNDING: A RECENT EXTENSION OF TO

Although TO is, when used with tactical and strategic effectiveness, a very effective first line of defense against child behavior problems, it does have limitations, the most significant of which is limited utility for older children. The limited utility of TO for older children leads parents to seek other methods for managing their children's behavior problems.

The most frequently used alternative involves extended withdrawal of privileges and freedoms, the colloquial term for which is 'grounding'. Virtually by definition, the procedure is time-based and its most common form consists of restricting the localities to which the child is allowed access for a specific period of time (e.g., day, week, month). For example, parents might ground their children by restricting them to the house for a week (except for school) following inappropriate behavior. Unfortunately, time based grounding has an inherent limitation that violates some primary principles of learning. A major one is that release criteria merely involve the passage of time and not the performance of appropriate behavior. Thus there is no clear incentive for prosocial performance during the time-based restriction. If prosocial behavior does not lead to termination of grounding (i.e., escape-based incentive for performing prosocial behavior is established) coercive behavior (e.g., defiance, pouting, and/or aggressive behaviors) often emerges. It is as if grounded children believe they can make parents or the household at large uncomfortable enough, they may achieve early release—an outcome that is pleasant and preferred and that could inadvertently strengthen coercive behaviors.

An alternative approach, one that is more consistent with the principles of learning, combines the customary elements of grounding (e.g., restriction of freedoms) with performance-based release criteria. This approach, called task-based grounding (TBG) has been developed for older children (i.e., ages 7–16). The advantage of TBG over time-based grounding is that the children determine by their behavior how long they will be restricted. To start the procedure require that parents make up a list of jobs that are not essential to the running of the house—jobs that if left undone for an extended period of time would produce minimal inconvenience for the household. Some examples include cleaning the garage floor, washing windows (every large window would be one job), cleaning windows on parental or household cars, cleaning grout, washing baseboards, or seasonal outdoor tasks such as weeding (unless being outdoors is a highly preferred activity)—there are numerous other examples. These jobs should then be described on note or recipe cards and arranged in a deck. When children misbehave, they are then given cards and told that until the jobs written on the cards are completed, they will be grounded. Being grounded means being restricted from all recreational activities that are not part of an organized educational program (e.g., soccer team). While at home, grounded children are not allowed access to electronics for any form of recreation or entertainment (e.g., no TV). In essence, they are allowed to do only their assigned jobs or their homework. Violating the rules or exhibiting additional misbehavior should lead to room based TO and/or additional job cards. Parents are instructed not to nag, remind, or lecture; rather they are instructed to let the TBG condition motivate the children to do the jobs and gain their freedom. The number of jobs is determined by the parental view of the gravity of the child offense. For example, bickering in the car after an unheeded instruction to stop might lead to one job for each bickerer. Major violations of curfew or sneaking out of the house would lead to many jobs. A final point is that jobs are not complete until the parent is completely satisfied.

The ubiquity of time-based grounding contrasts sharply with a paucity of research on the effectiveness of its use. In fact, a literature search yielded no published research directly evaluating it or even research that directly evaluated withdrawal of privileges as an intervention for the behavior problems of typically developing children. There was, however, a relatively recent published description of TBG (Eaves, Sheperis, Blanchard, Baylot, & Doggett, 2005) as well as an evaluation showing that TBG reduced high rate behavior problems to near zero levels in a group of problematic children between the ages of 8 and 15 years (Richards, 2003).

CONCLUSION

Children learn through repetition with experiential contrast and thus good discipline will provide detectable contrast. Yelling or spanking can serve this purpose but there are multiple problems associated with their use. TO is much more subtle but it can serve the purpose very well if three conditions are met: (1) sources of social interaction and preferred child experiences are restricted; (2) the child's inappropriate attempts to terminate TO are ignored outright; and (3) the child's life was generally interesting and fun before TO was imposed. In other words, to be effective TO must minimize child preferences and must occur in a generalized context called TI. As children grow out of typical TO, usually around the age of seven or eight years, TBG can be substituted as an effective extension. Its ultimate effectiveness is also dependent upon the amount and quality of social and material resources (i.e., TI) that are available prior to and after instances of TBG have been implemented.

Further Reading

Barkley, R. (1998). *Your defiant child: Eight steps to better behavior*. New York: Guilford.

Blum, N., Williams, G., Friman, P. C., & Christophersen, E. R. (1995). Disciplining young children: The role of reason. *Pediatrics, 96,* 336–341.

Christophersen, E. R. (1997). *Little people*. Kansas City, KS: Overland Press.

Christophersen, E. R. (1982). Incorporating behavioral pediatrics into primary care. *Pediatric Clinics of North America, 29,* 261–295.

Friman, P. C., & Blum, N. J. (2003). Behavioral pediatrics: Therapy for child behavior problems presenting in primary care. Hersen, M., and Sledge, W. (Eds.), *Encyclopedia of psychotherapy* (pp. 379–399). New York: Academic Press.

Kazdin, A. E. (2005). Parent management training: *Treatment for oppositional aggressive and antisocial behavior in children and adolescents*. New York: Oxford University.

McMahon, R. J., & Forehand, R. L. (2003). *Helping the noncompliant child: Family based treatment for oppositional behavior* (2nd ed.). New York: Guilford.

References

Blum, N. J., Barone, V. J., & Friman, P. C. (1993). A simplified behavioral treatment for trichotillomania in the young child. *Pediatrics, 91,* 993–995.

Brestan, E. V., & Eyberg, S. M. (1998). Effective psychosocial treatments of conduct-disordered children and adolescents: 29 years, 82 studies, 5,272 kids. *Journal of Clinical Child Psychology, 24,* 180–189.

Eaves, S. H., Sheperis, C. J., Blanchard, T., Baylot, L., & Doggett, A. (2005). Teaching time out and job card grounding procedures to parents: A primer for family counselors. *The Family Journal, 13,* 252–258.

Ervin, R., Miller, P., & Friman, P. C. (1996). Feed the hungry bee: Using positive peer reports to improve the social interactions and acceptance of a socially rejected girl in residential placement. *Journal of Applied Behavior Analysis, 29,* 251–253.

Ferster, C.B. (1958). Control of behavior in chimpanzees and pigeons by time out from positive reinforcement. *Psychological Monographs, 72* (8, Whole No. 461).

Kavale, K. A., Forness, S. R., & Walker, H. M. (1999). Interventions of oppositional defiant disorder and conduct disorder in the schools. In H. C. Quay and A. E. Hogan (Eds.), *Handbook of disruptive behavior disorders* (pp. 441–454). New York: Kluwer.

Johnston, J. M., & Pennypacker, H. S. (1980). *Strategies and tactics of human behavioral research*. Hillsdale, NJ: Lawrence Erlbaum.

Mathews, J. R., Friman, P. C., Barone, J. V., Ross, L. V., & Christophersen, E. R. (1987). Decreasing dangerous infant behavior through parent instruction. *Journal of Applied Behavior Analysis, 20,* 165–170.

Patterson, G. R., Chamberlain, P. & Reid, J. B. (1982). Comparative evaluation of a parent training program. *Behavior Therapy, 13,* 638–650.

Reid, J. M., Webster-Stratton, C., & Hammond, M. (2003). Follow-Up of children who received the Incredible Years Intervention for Oppositional-Defiant Disorder: Maintenance and prediction of a 2-year outcome. *Behavior Therapy, 34,* 471–491.

Solnick, J. V., Rincover, A., & Peterson, C. R. (1977). Some determinants of the reinforcing and punishing effects of timeout. *Journal of Applied Behavior Analysis, 10,* 415–424. Wolf, M. M., Risley, T. & Mees, H. Application of operant conditioning procedures to the behavior problems of an autistic child. *Behavior Research & Therapy, 1,* 305–312.

76 GUIDELINES FOR DEVELOPING AND MANAGING A TOKEN ECONOMY

Patrick M. Ghezzi, Ginger R. Wilson,
Rachel S. F. Tarbox, and Kenneth R. MacAleese

It was Ayllon & Azrin's (1965, 1968) pioneering work in the 1960s with psychiatric patients at Anna State Hospital in Illinois that gave birth to the token economy. Volumes of research articles, literature reviews, books and book chapters have since been published on the topic.

Our purpose for this chapter is to offer a set of *guidelines* for practitioners to follow when designing and managing a token economy for an individual or group of individuals. We underscore "guidelines" to call attention to the fact that as with any other deliberate, systematic behavior management technique, a token economy is always tailored for a particular individual, whether alone or in a group. There is no "one size fits all" token economy, and for that reason we encourage practitioners to use the guidelines as starting points for managing behavior in their own token economy.

WHO MIGHT BENEFIT FROM A TOKEN ECONOMY?

All modern textbooks on applied behavior analysis (e.g., Cooper, Heron, & Cooper, 2007; Miltenberger, 2006) give examples of the benefits of a token economy with people as diverse as the intellectually and developmentally disabled, drug and alcohol abusers, prisoners, geriatric patients, students, classroom teachers, and outpatient children and adults. Similarly, the settings in which token economies have been applied range from hospitals, prisons, and community mental health facilities to day care centers, classrooms, nursing homes and households.

In theory, there is no limit to the number of participants in a token economy. Nor is there any limit, in theory, to the number of behaviors that may be targeted for change. There are practical limits, however, that each practitioner must consider in the light of his or her own unique circumstances.

FACTORS IN DECIDING WHETHER TO USE A TOKEN ECONOMY

Most of us know how an economy works. We know that our pay depends on performing the tasks our jobs entail, that our pay is money, typically, and that we can exchange the money we earn for whatever goods and services are attractive, available and affordable to us. These relations between tasks, receiving payment for performing them, and using money to buy things is at the center of all modern economic systems. They are also at the center of a token economy.

While knowing how an economy works is one's own life may be necessary, it is insufficient preparation for designing and managing an economy for someone else. For starters, what will the person be paid to do, and when and where will they do it? What will they be paid, and how and when will they get paid? What can they buy with their pay, and how much will it cost them for whatever it is they want to buy? These are just a few of the many and often vexing questions that must be answered, both when designing a token economy and while managing one over time.

As with any economic system, a token economy affects people in powerful and sometimes unexpected ways. People may become irritated or angry over what they have to do, when, where, and why they have to do it, how much they

663

get paid and how much things cost. Some may even try to sabotage the economy by counterfeiting, stealing, or trading tokens. The people responsible for designing and managing a token economy must be alert to problems of this sort and must be willing and able to change tasks, alter pay rates, adjust costs, or tighten security as needed to ensure a smooth running system that ultimately benefits the individual(s) who participate in it.

The fact that a token economy requires a great deal of planning, monitoring, and modifying discourages many professionals from using it as a means to manage an individual's behavior. That is a good reaction, for the most part, because behavior can ordinarily be managed in much easier ways. The child who seldom helps around the house may need nothing more than timely encouragement or an occasional reward for taking out the trash, feeding the dog, or watering the plants. If that fails to increase helping around the house, then perhaps more consistent or sincere encouragement or more frequent or attractive rewards are needed. The point is that it is always best to manage behavior simply, naturally, and conveniently. A token economy has none of those characteristics, and thus should be regarded as a treatment option only when other, less cumbersome and intrusive interventions have failed to produce the desired results.

GUIDELINES

Following are eight guidelines for designing and managing a token economy. Keep in mind that the guidelines are starting points, and that each one must be tailored to an individual's specific circumstances, whether alone or in a group.

Define the Target Behavior(s)

It is important to clarify exactly what behavior is, and what it is not. In the simplest terms, behavior is what a person says or does. What a person says or does is stated as verbs or action words. Saying "please," "thank-you," and "excuse me" are actions, as are kicking, running, climbing, and reading. A person does not say or do "bad attitudes," "laziness," or "stubbornness." Terms of that sort must be translated into the observable behaviors to which they refer.

One approach to defining behavior in this way is to think in terms of what a person says or does that leads someone to say, for example, that the person is "lazy," "stubborn," or has a "bad attitude." The lazy child may be so called because he seldom takes out the trash, feeds the dog, or mows the lawn. The stubborn teenager may refuse to clean her room or obey her curfew, while the student with a bad attitude may never study or complete his homework assignments.

The reason for defining behavior is straightforward: The sole purpose of designing and maintaining a token economy is to change an individual's behavior. Knowing exactly what behavior(s) will be targeted for change is critical to that purpose. Clear, concise and easy-to-understand definitions are preferred over vague or ambiguous definitions or definitions that are subject to change or interpretation. Indeed, arguments over whether or not a behavior has occurred ordinarily centers on imprecise or capricious definitions. Disputes may be avoided by making sure that everyone agrees on what does and does not constitute the target behavior(s). When disputes occur, be prepared to clarify, refine, or revise the definition of the target behavior in question.

Some token economies have a penalty component, technically termed a *response cost*. It is essentially a punishing consequence for inappropriate or undesirable behavior: When the offending behavior occurs, reinforcers —the "tokens" in a token economy—are taken away immediately. The intended effect is to reduce or eliminate future occurrences of the behavior to which the response cost penalty applies. Needless to say, the inappropriate or undesirable behavior(s) targeted for reduction or elimination in this way must be clearly and unambiguously defined. (Restrictions on the length of this chapter prevent us from any further discussion of response cost. The context is here, however, for the careful reader to see how response cost might be used—and abused—in a token economy.)

Specify the Setting(s)

Because a person's behavior is always a matter of time and place, it is important to be clear on exactly when and where the token economy will and will not operate. The teacher who uses a token economy to increase the rate at which her student solves simple subtraction problems may restrict the economy to a certain activity, arithmetic, and probably to a certain place, a desk, and perhaps as well to a certain time of the day, say, morning. The teacher may decide to expand or constrict the time and place that the token economy operates, and may even suspend the token economy for a while, for example, to see how accurate her student performs on his subtraction problems without the token economy in place. Whatever the case may be, make sure to specify the time and place that the token economy will and will not operate.

Select Tokens

The "tokens" in a token economy are just that—tokens. Technically, they are "conditioned reinforcers" that are to a token economy what money is to an economy more generally. The best tokens are durable, inexpensive to make or buy, and easy to store, handle, and dispense.

A token economy can be an easy mark for counterfeiters and other saboteurs. It is always good practice to make it impossible for unauthorized persons to duplicate tokens. Points or stars on a sheet of paper, poker chips and the like should be used with caution, as these and similar other "tokens" are fairly easy to find, make, or copy. It is also good practice to preempt a related problem, stealing tokens. This can be prevented by using tokens, for example, that are color-coded by days of the week or that bear the name or initials of the person to whom they belong. If subversive activities occur, then consequences must be in place to discourage the person(s) responsible from making the same or a similar mistake in the future. Steps must be taken as well to prevent others from undermining the token economy.

Identify Backups

By themselves, tokens, like money, have no value. Tokens gain in value, as does money, when they can be used to buy an assortment of things and activities. The things and activities that tokens buy are called "backup reinforcers" or simply "backups."

It is vital to the success of a token economy to back up the tokens with tangible things and activities. The challenge is to identify exactly what those things and activities are for a given individual. Fortunately, there are ways to do that, with each way more or less tailored for the individual (s) for whom the token economy is created. For example, with typically developing children and adults, it may be sufficient simply to ask them what they would like to work toward. With children and adults with delays or deficiencies in their behavior development, it may be necessary to interview their parent or caregiver (see Fisher, Piazza, Bowman, & Almari, 1996) or to conduct what is termed a *stimulus preference assessment* (DeLeon & Iwata, 1996).

Whatever the method used to identify backups, keep in mind, first, that a person will ordinarily work for tokens in exchange for the things that they normally enjoy doing such as snacking, watching television, listening to music, or talking on the phone, and second, that a person will work hardest for the things that they do not ordinarily do but would enjoy doing such as staying up late, going to the movies, spending the night with a friend, or using the family car.

Determine a Schedule of Token Reinforcement

The matter of determining a schedule of token reinforcement raises two questions: (1) How many tokens should be given for appropriate or desirable behavior? and (2) How often should tokens be given? The answer to the first question is, "It depends." That is, the amount of tokens a person earns by performing any one of a number of target behaviors depends on the relative merit or importance that is attached to each behavior. This is a personal judgment, one that is ordinarily made by those who design and manage the token economy.

As to how often tokens should be given, the general rule is that the more frequent a behavior occurs, the fewer tokens earned. The reciprocal rule—less frequent behavior earns more tokens—also applies. It is also important to make sure that the person earns enough tokens to make it "worth his while" in terms of being able to exchange tokens for backups.

In the early phases of the token economy, it is best to present tokens immediately following each and every occurrence of a target behavior. However, sometimes a target behavior should occur only under certain circumstances. The parents of a child who identify "taking out the trash" as a target behavior may find that their child takes out the trash several times a day without regard to how much trash is in the container. Avoiding those sorts of problems is usually a matter of specifying the conditions under which tokens may and may not be earned.

The practice of giving tokens for all occurrences of a target behavior may eventually be relaxed. By this we mean that once a target behavior is occurring regularly and appropriately, tokens may be given intermittently, say, after every third or fourth instance of the behavior (ratio or "response-based" token reinforcement) or after every minute or so of continuously performing the behavior (interval or "time-based" token reinforcement). The main advantage of this practice follows from the finding that intermittently reinforced behavior is more durable and persistent than is behavior that is always or continuously reinforced. Put another way, it is possible, and often desirable, to get a person to do more with less frequent or fewer reinforcements.

The move from continuous to intermittent token reinforcement must be made with care. "Lean" the schedule slowly or gradually, and be alert for undesirable changes in either or both the quantity and quality of the target behavior. Parents may move their child too quickly, for example, from earning one token for every five minutes spent studying to earning one token for every 30 minutes spent studying. Under the strain of suddenly having to work longer or harder for the same token amount, the child may become inattentive or careless, or may simply stop studying altogether. Gradual increases in the amount of time or the number of times a target behavior occurs before a token is earned

should prevent that sort of undesirable change from occurring.

Giving tokens on an intermittent basis has the practical advantage of having to keep only a relatively small number of tokens on hand to dispense. It has the advantage, too, of keeping the number of tokens that a person earns or can save relatively low. This becomes important when faced with the challenge of making sure that tokens retain their value.

Tokens may lose their value when there are too many or too few tokens in circulation. When a person earns as many or more tokens than are needed to exchange for a backup, there is no reason for him to continue working and earning additional tokens. Likewise, when a person cannot earn the tokens that are needed to exchange for a backup, there is no reason for her to continue or to even begin to work for it. These problems relate, respectively, to the admonition that there are no "millionaires" or "impoverished" persons in a token economy. Preventing or remediating problems of this sort is often a matter of establishing an appropriate exchange rate for the token economy.

Establish an Exchange Rate

The exchange rate in a token economy specifies exactly how many tokens are needed to buy exactly how much or how many of the things and activities that constitute the backups. Determining the cost in tokens of each back-up is therefore an integral and ongoing part of a token economy.

One way to establish an exchange rate is to begin by determining the maximum number of tokens that a person can earn say, in one day. With that figure in hand, set the cost for each back-up according these guidelines:

1. The most preferred or highly valued back-up(s) should be expensive, but not so expensive that the person will never earn enough tokens for an exchange.
2. The least preferred or lowest valued backup(s) should be inexpensive, but not so inexpensive that the person can quickly or easily earn enough tokens for an exchange.
3. Moderately preferred or valued backup(s) should be at the median, neither too expensive nor too inexpensive.

To illustrate how an exchange rate might be established, suppose that Janice, a typically developing pre-adolescent, can earn a maximum of four tokens each day for performing four after-dinner kitchen chores. If Janice's most preferred backup for the moment is a one-night weekend sleepover at her girlfriend's house, then the cost for that backup might be set at four tokens, meaning that she must to do all four of her chores in one day in exchange for spending the night at her friend's house. A backup with momentarily less value, say, a ride to school one morning, might cost one token, meaning that she must do at least one of her four chores in a day, for instance, loading and starting the dishwasher. With this rate, the number of tokens Janice earns is proportional both to the amount of work she must do to earn tokens and to the cost of the backups.

Establish a Place and Time to Exchange Tokens

It is important to be clear on the time and place that tokens can be exchanged for backups. As to time, exchanges should occur frequently in the early stages of the token economy, where the rules of the system are being learned and the reinforcing value of the tokens in relation to their backups are being established. Later stages may enforce less frequent exchanges.

Increasing the time between earning tokens and exchanging them for backups is often a worthy goal, one that capitalizes on the increase in the value of the backups that ordinarily occurs when a person has infrequent access to them. The main advantage of this practice is that it encourages a person to continue earning tokens between exchanges. An added benefit is that as tokens are being earned between exchanges, praise, attention, approval and other consequences that typically or naturally accompany or follow the target behavior(s) may acquire reinforcing properties. Providing natural consequences in addition to tokens is especially important when preparing a person to return to a token-free environment.

A convenient place or location where a person can go to exchange tokens for backups must also be determined. The arrangement may be formal or informal. A "store" at the back of a classroom displaying backups and their prices and staffed at set times by the teacher's aide who collects tokens, dispenses backups, and records exchanges is a far more formal arrangement than, say, a parent who sits down with her two children in the living room to handle the day's exchanges. Whether formal or informal, it is important to decide where exchanges will take place, and, wherever that place may be, to have the backups, and their costs, available and in plain sight.

Keep Records

At a minimum, objective records should be kept continuously on (1) the number of tokens earned by a person for each and every target behavior, (2) the number of tokens a person exchanges at any one time, (3) exactly what backups were purchased, and when, and (4) the token cost of the backups. Records of which target behaviors are on what schedule of token reinforcement should also be kept. Records pertaining to other aspects of the token economy should be kept as well, as needed, to ensure that the token economy is being properly and efficiently administered and most important, to ensure that the token economy is maximally effective in producing and maintaining significant behavioral gains.

Table 76.1 contains the eight guidelines for designing and managing a token economy. Use the table as a checklist, making sure that each guideline is in place for the duration of the token economy.

TABLE 76.1 Guidelines for Designing and Managing a Token Economy

1. Define the behaviors targeted for change in clear, concise, unambiguous actions words.
2. Specify the setting(s) in which the token economy will and will not operate.
3. Select tokens that are durable, inexpensive, easy to handle and store, and hard to forge.
4. Identify backups that are effective for each person.
5. Determine a schedule of token reinforcement for each target behavior.
6. Establish an exchange rate for tokens and back-ups.
7. Decide when and where tokens may be exchanged for backups.
8. Keep continuous records on tokens earned and exchanges made by each person.

Further Reading

We recommend studying the research on the token economy, both while designing a token economy and while managing one over time. In addition to the surveys presented in modern textbooks in applied behavior analysis, books by Ayllon and Azrin (1968), Kazdin (1977), and Leitenberg (1976) are especially helpful resources. These books also contain a wealth of references to specific applications of a token economy, for example, to children in a classroom setting. Research on specific populations and settings are invaluable sources for guidance on how practitioners can best design and manage a token economy to suit their own and their clients' particular circumstances.

References

Ayllon, T., & Azrin, N. H. (1965). The measurement and reinforcement of behavior of psychotics. *Journal of the Experimental Analysis of Behavior, 8*, 357–383.

Ayllon, T., & Azrin, N. H. (1968). *The token economy: A motivational system for therapy and rehabilitation.* New York: Appleton-Century-Crofts.

Cooper, J. O., Heron, T. E., & Heward, W. L. (2007). *Applied behavior analysis* (2nd ed.). Upper Saddle River, NJ: Pearson Education.

DeLeon, I. G., & Iwata, B. A. (1996). Evaluation of a multiple-stimulus presentation format for assessing reinforcer preferences. *Journal of Applied Behavior Analysis, 29*, 519–533.

Fisher, W. W., Piazza, C. C., Bowman, L. G., & Almari, A. (1996). Integrating caregiver report with a systematic choice assessment to enhance reinforcer identification. *American Journal on Mental Retardation, 31*, 15–25.

Kazdin, A. E. (1977). *The token economy: A review and evaluation.* New York: Plenum.

Kazdin, A. E. (1982). The token economy: An evaluative review. *Journal of Applied Behavior Analysis, 15*, 431–445.

Miltenberger, R. G. (2006). *Behavior modification: Principles and procedures.* Belmont, CA: Wadsworth.

Leitenberg, H. (1976). *Handbook of behavior modification and behavior therapy.* Englewood Cliffs, NJ: Prentice Hall.

77 URGE SURFING

Andy Lloyd

Of the many barriers to a productive and healthy life that people face, urge control may be one of the most daunting (Baumeister, Heatherton & Tice, 1994). Giving in to temptation, whether it is to drugs, irresponsible spending, or infidelity, can have broad negative implications for clients. Many skills have been developed to address such problems within the domain of addictions and habit control. Abstinence-based approaches (e.g., Alcoholics Anonymous), relapse prevention techniques, and urge management techniques (Marlatt & Gordon, 1985) are widely used with clients suffering from addictions. This chapter focuses on urge management, in particular, the skill known as urge surfing. Urge surfing has been demonstrated to be an effective component of cognitive behavioral treatment packages (Copeland, Swift, Roffman, & Stephens, 2001). Teaching the client how to urge surf can play an instrumental role in the client's ability to resist the temptations the urge is directed toward (e.g., drinking, smoking, infidelity, etc.).

Urge surfing is a cognitively based urge management technique. In general, urge surfing involves teaching the client a collection of closely related strategies to cope with and overcome urges to behave in ways (e.g., to smoke) that are counter to their therapeutic goals. Clients are taught to treat urges as though they were like waves in the ocean. Urges come on, grow in intensity, and eventually subside just like ocean waves. Moreover, like waves, urges tend to be brief. They do not grow and grow until the client has to do something before they will go away. Urges go away on their own. The only way that urges get stronger is to give in to them. The more an individual acquiesces to urges, the more frequent and strong they may become. Each time an urge is resisted through urge surfing,

the urge has been beaten and subsequent urges become less frequent and less intense.

Although urge surfing has elements that can be understood as being avoidance based, it is fundamentally an acceptance strategy. Urge surfing can be viewed as an avoidance skill when the client is most successful with the distraction components of the skill. Clients who are skilled at thinking about something else when an urge strikes, or at engaging in an incompatible behavior when the urge strikes (Azrin & Nunn, 1977), may successfully ride out the urge without fully experiencing its severity. To do this is to avoid fully experiencing the urge. Despite this observation, urge surfing is fundamentally an acceptance skill (see Hayes, Strosahl, & Wilson, 1999, for an example of a prominent acceptance-based intervention strategy). Urge surfing does not combat the urge in order to make it go away. Rather, clients are taught how to fully experience the urge in a different way—that is, to experience the urge for what it is: brief, nonlethal, of relatively predictable course, and most important, defeatable.

CLINICAL POPULATIONS

Urge surfing has been widely used with clients suffering from alcohol and drug dependencies (Copeland, Swift, Roffman, & Stephens, 2001), but its principles could easily be applied to other clinical domains where self-control skills are relevant (e.g., sexual behavior, financial excesses, etc.). It is typically used as a component of larger treatment packages (e.g., Copeland et al.), but there is no clear reason to believe that it could not be used as a stand-alone skill applied to a wide variety of client problems involving the detrimental effects of urges. The skill is readily understandable when delivered along with the ocean-wave metaphor and it can easily be taught within the confines of a 50-minute therapy session.

People tend to be their weakest in the face of urges during periods of negative emotional arousal (Prochaska, Norcross, & DiClemente, 1994). These times are referred to as high-risk situations. Despite positive therapeutic gains (e.g., abstinence from smoking for many days or weeks), clients are likely to struggle with urges and may experience a lapse or relapse. A lapse is defined as an individual, circumscribed event that runs counter to the goal of abstinence. A person who "breaks down" and smokes a cigarette after 2 months of abstinence, but does not pick up the habit again, is said to have experienced a lapse. A relapse is defined as a more robust return to the behavior that the client wants to abstain from. A person who gradually starts to smoke again following a period of abstinence has experienced a relapse. Approximately 35% of relapses take place during periods of negative emotional arousal (Prochaska, Norcross, & DiClemente). It is during such situations that urges seem to get the best of us. Clients are more prepared to face these urges utilizing their newly developed urge-surfing skills if they are aware that they are in high-risk situations. Prochaske and colleagues also found that certain cognitive errors lead to relapse:

- Overconfidence (e.g., "I'll have no problem quitting smoking. I've gone a day without cigarettes and it will be a breeze from here on out.")
- Inappropriate self-testing (e.g., "If I keep a pack of cigarettes with me at all times, then I can truly prove I am strong enough to quit.")
- Self-blaming (e.g., "My drinking ran my family away and ruined my job. It has already ruined my life. What do I have to gain from quitting now?")

These attitudes set the client up for failure in a number of ways. First, by thinking that they've beaten the habit, clients are setting themselves up for a potentially severe letdown when they experience urges for that habit. Second, clients are unnecessarily placing themselves in high-risk (or "trigger") situations by testing themselves with access to cigarettes, alcohol, and so on. Finally, clients are admitting to failure before they even try to quit by selectively focusing on the costs already incurred by the habit they are trying to break. Therapists need to be aware of these and similar thoughts being expressed by clients so that they can be dealt with constructively.

In addition to the beliefs just expressed, Chiauzzi (1989) identified several personality traits that may contribute to client relapse:

- Perfectionism (e.g., the client may not be able to handle small setbacks and failures while struggling with the addiction)
- Dependency (e.g., the client may return to the apparent comfort of the habit when others are pushing him or her to change)
- Passive–aggressiveness (e.g., the client may blame others and drive them away)
- Self-centeredness (e.g., the client may not be willing to admit that he or she has a problem that needs to be dealt with)
- Rebelliousness (e.g., the client may resent or resist those who offer help)

URGE SURFING STEP-BY-STEP

There are four basic steps to urge surfing. Although more or less emphasis can be placed on each of the steps, it is important to cover each one of them at least briefly. The basic components of urge surfing can be taught within a single session. Once the skill is taught, the client can then continue to self-monitor his or her urges, or the skill can be further developed by spending session time discussing the client's urges and his or her reactions to them. The four basic steps to urge surfing are:

1. Describing the skill of urge surfing
2. Assessing the client's high-risk urge situations with him or her
3. Developing a clear understanding of how the client experiences his or her urges
4. Challenging the client's irrational assumptions that typically occur during the urge

Each of these four steps will be described in detail so that the skill of urge surfing can be taught by the practitioner who reads this chapter.

Step 1: Describing Urge Surfing

For the client who is suffering, and giving in to, his or her urges, it is important to begin by emphasizing that urges are natural biological reactions to an addiction or strong habit. There is nothing wrong or bad about experiencing urges, and their presence does not point to a character flaw or weakness on the part of the client. More or less time can be spent normalizing the presence of urges and validating the uncomfortable feelings they bring about.

Next, the therapist should spend time describing both the costs associated with giving in to the urges and the basic phenomenology of urges. One cost associated with giving in to urges is that the urges don't go away, and they may become more frequent and even intense. Another, more evident, cost associated with giving in to urges involves the very behaviors the client is working to reduce (e.g., drug dependence and its costs to quality of life). Every time the client gives in to the urge to, say, smoke a cigarette, he or she is not living in a valued way. These points should be explained to the client in commonsense terms.

Experiencing an urge is an aversive condition. If this were not the case, then few people would have difficulty overcoming urges. Again, it is important to validate the client's claims regarding the difficulty of dealing with the urges. This creates a context within which rapport can develop. For a client who is struggling with urges, any therapist comment to the effect that "Your urges aren't that bad, and you should be able to easily deal with them" may contribute to the client's belief that he or she is just too weak to handle the urges. Such negative self-efficacy beliefs may already be implicated in the client's difficulty with urges, and it is counter to the goals of urge surfing to contribute in any way toward such beliefs.

Although urges can be difficult to withstand, it should be stressed to the client that urges are like waves. Instead of getting worse as time goes by, urges actually gradually decrease in intensity.

It is in this way that urges are like waves and the client can view him- or herself riding out the wave. Urges typically last only a few minutes, and rarely more than 10 minutes. People tend to give in to their urges before they ever get a chance to experience their gradual decrease in intensity. In the experience of some people, urges simply do not go away until they are defeated, so to speak, when the individual gives in to them. These individuals are giving in to the urges right away. This is another reason that it is important to validate the client's experiences with urges. For many clients, the very idea that urges subside after time is simply untenable because they have experienced so many urges without ever noticing this phenomenon.

Step 2: Assessing High-Risk Urge Situations

It is important to identify the situations that typically trigger urges for the client. This step facilitates a discussion of urges, affording client and therapist the opportunity to clear up any questions and confusion regarding the client's urges. Have the client develop a list of urge triggers. A client who is trying to quit smoking cigarettes, for example, may experience urges after meals, while driving or drinking, or when with friends who smoke. Developing an urge trigger list may help the client to avoid such situations. Drawing the client's attention to trigger situations can help him or her avoid making seemingly irrelevant decisions (SIDs) that lead him or her into the situations in the first place.

After a list of trigger situations has been developed, the therapist should help the client develop an easy-to-remember and simple list of strategies to avoid trigger situations, or to distract when such situations are unavoidable.

Step 3: Experiencing Urges

Have the client create a detailed description of how he or she experiences urges. This can be done in session or *in vivo*. While experiencing an urge the client should sit in a comfortable position with feet flat on the floor, take some deep breaths, turn his or her attention inward, and focus on where in the body the urge is being experienced. The urge may be experienced in the chest, the stomach, or just about anywhere else in the body. Have the client simply notice the urge as it is experienced. Does it stay in one area of the body or does it move around to different places?

Have the client describe the urge in as many terms as possible. For example, does the urge feel like a tingling sensation, a burning sensation, maybe a pressure? If the urge feels like a pressure, then what kind of pressure? Is it a constant pressure, like a vice is being closed, or is it a pulsating pressure, like a heartbeat? If the urge changes body locations, have the client describe what it feels like when it changes. Instruct the client to use descriptive words while he or she attends to the urge as it grows in intensity and then slowly goes away. This is urge surfing.

Two important goals have been accomplished at this point, and you will likely want to discuss these with the client. First, the client has successfully urge surfed. That is, the client has resisted an urge even though the urge was confronted directly. By describing the urge, where it is felt, how it changes, and so on, the client has fully experienced the urge without having given in to it. One of the experiential differences between the way that urges were previously experienced and how they are experienced by the client while urge surfing might be attributable to an experiential shift from what Mischel (1996) referred to as "hot" to "cold" thoughts.

Hot thoughts are thoughts that focus on desirable qualities of objects such as the sweet, sugary taste associated with eating a cookie or the relaxing, euphoric state brought about by smoking a cigarette. Hot thoughts are consummative thoughts. Cold thoughts, however, are thoughts that focus on the neutral, purely descriptive qualities of objects, such as the round shape and brown color of a cookie, and the sticklike shape and cost of a cigarette. Cold thoughts are nonconsummative thoughts. In this sense, when a client urge surfs he or she can be said to be thinking about the desired object in a different way.

Some clients may express surprise at how easily they resisted the urge in this way, and even more surprise at just how quickly the urge subsided. For some clients this experience will mark the first time that they can recall having experienced an urge going away naturally because they

had previously "defeated" their urges by giving in to them. The purpose of urge surfing is to teach the client to experience the urge directly and wait it out. By focusing on the physical sensations of the urge and keeping track of how these sensations change and gradually subside over time, the client is attending to the cold aspects of the urge rather than the hot aspects of the desired object. The more the client practices this skill, the more evidence, in the form of personal experience, the client will have to support the claim that urges are, in fact, brief and capable of being dealt with.

Step 4: Challenging Irrational Thoughts

After the client has successfully engaged in urge surfing for a short time, it might be necessary to check in with him or her to determine what kinds of thoughts are accompanying the urges. It is important to remind the client that giving in to urges only makes them stronger. It is like starting a storm at sea that makes the waves more frequent and strong. To defeat the urges the client has to surf them out.

Ask the client to report whether the urges are successfully being surfed and, if so, how they may be changing in duration, frequency, and intensity. The client may experience a moderate increase along any one of these three dimensions if he or she has never maintained abstinence from the behavior or substance they are trying to abstain from. If this happens, the client may start to question his or her dedication to abstinence or ability to abstain, or may even the claim that the urges will eventually subside. These thoughts need to be dealt with because they can provide an obstacle to the client's abstinence. A number of approaches can be used to maintain client compliance with the therapeutic goals:

- Discuss the client's original decision to abstain from using.
- Discuss the benefits of abstaining.
- Remind the client that he or she has successfully surfed an urge and that it can be done again, maybe even with less difficulty.
- Remind the client that the urges only get stronger when they are given in to.

Sometimes this is not enough. Clients may express skepticism regarding their potential success. Maybe the client believes that his or her experience is far worse than the normal person's experience at dealing with urges, saying that, for example, "For them it was easy, but I am really hooked." If this is the case, then straightforward cognitive restructuring procedures can be applied.

The client can be asked to provide evidence that he or she really is more hooked than other addicts. Discussing the fact that other addicts who have successfully quit had to go through the same difficult situations can help reorient the client to his or her original valued therapy goals.

Clients may complain that the urges are just too horrible to endure despite what others may have gone through to kick the habit. Again, the therapist can challenge such statements by asking, "And what's so bad about a few minutes of discomfort?" The therapist can also simply have the client create a pro-and-con list for the habit. Likely, the only pro on the list will be the avoidance of the uncomfortable urges that come with it.

References

Azrin, N. H., & Nunn, R. G. (1977). *Habit control in a day (stuttering, nail biting, and other nervous habits).* New York: Pocket Books.

Baumeister, R. F., Heatherton, T. F., & Tice, D. M. (1994). *Losing control: How and why people fail at self-regulation.* New York: Academic Press.

Chiauzzi, E. (1989). Breaking the patterns that lead to relapse. *Psychology Today* (December), 18–19.

Copeland, J., Swift, W., Roffman, R., & Stephens, R. (2001). A randomized controlled trial of brief cognitive–behavioral interventions for cannabis use disorder. *Journal of Substance Abuse Treatment, 21*(2), 55–64.

Hayes, S. C., Strosahl, K. D., & Wilson, K. G. (1999). *Acceptance and commitment therapy: An experiential approach to behavioral change.* New York: Guilford.

Larimer, M. E., Palmer, R. S., & Marlatt, G. A. (1999). Relapse prevention: An overview of Marlatt's cognitive–behavioral model. *Alcohol Research and Health, 23*(2), 151–160.

Marlatt, G. A., & Gordon, J. R. (1985). *Relapse prevention.* New York: Guilford.

Mischel, W. (1996). From good intentions to willpower. In P. M. Gollwitzer & J. A. Bargh (Eds.), *The psychology of action: Linking cognition and motivation to behavior* (pp. 197–218). New York: Guilford.

Prochaska, J. O., Norcross, J. C., & DiClemente, C. C. (1994). *Changing for good.* New York: William Morrow.

78 VALIDATION PRINCIPLES AND STRATEGIES

Kelly Koerner and Marsha M. Linehan

Empathy is the platform for all therapeutic intervention (Bohart & Greenberg, 1997). A related but distinct concept also important in psychotherapy is validation. Whereas empathy is the accurate understanding of the world from the client's perspective, *validation* is the active communication that the client's perspective makes sense (i.e., is correct). To validate means to confirm, authenticate, corroborate, substantiate, ratify, or verify. To validate, the therapist actively seeks out and communicates to the client how a response makes sense by being relevant, meaningful, justifiable, correct, or effective. Validating an emotion, thought, or action requires *empathy*, an understanding of the particular or unique significance of the context from the other person's perspective. However, validation adds to this the communication that the emotion, thought, or action is a valid response. Were the client to ask, "Can this be true?" empathy would be understanding the "this" whereas validation would be communicating "yes."

WHO MIGHT BENEFIT FROM VALIDATION?

All clients may benefit from validation, but validation may be essential for the success of change-oriented strategies with those who are particularly emotionally sensitive and prone to emotional dysregulation (Linehan, 1993). It may also be especially beneficial in working with disoriented elderly individuals (Feil, 1992). Precise and specific validation may be most indicated when much of the client's responding is dysfunctional or disoriented but where the therapist's corrective feedback about this may produce a client who is less collaborative and open to learning and, in effect, more dysfunctional.

In general, validation is used to balance change, increase verbal and nonverbal communication, prevent or decrease withdrawal, provide feedback and strengthen self-validation, strengthen clinical progress, and strengthen the therapeutic relationship. Feil (1992) suggests that with the old-old, validation can also be used to help the individual justify continuing to live. In nearly all situations, the therapist may usefully validate that the client's problems are important, that a task is difficult, that emotional pain or a sense of being out of control is justifiable, and that there is wisdom in the client's ultimate goals, even if not by the particular means he or she is currently using. Similarly, it is often useful for the therapist to validate the client's views about life problems and beliefs about how changes can or should be made. Unless the client believes that the therapist truly understands the dilemma (e.g., exactly how painful, difficult to change, or important a problem is) he or she will not trust that the therapist's solutions are appropriate or adequate, and collaboration and consequently the therapist's ability to help the client change will be limited.

However, helping clients change often requires invalidating, rather than validating, the client's important self-constructs, emotional avoidance, and other responses incongruent with achieving his or her long-term goals. When the client says, "I can't stand this emotional pain," the therapist's interventions are versions of, "Yes, you can," which encourages the experience and acceptance of painful emotions without avoidance or maladaptive responses to emotional pain. Yet, it is a normal psychological process for emotional arousal to occur when significant goals are blocked and important self-constructs are disconfirmed. When feedback is inconsistent with important self-constructs, consequent arousal and the sense of being out of control result in both failure to process new information and intense effort to gain control.

Therefore, helping clients change often requires intervening in a manner that modulates emotional arousal so that work on the therapeutic task continues. The therapist must simultaneously align with the client's goals and self-constructs without reinforcing dysfunctional behavior, without evoking such emotional reactivity that the therapeutic task is derailed, and without dropping a focus on needed change. Validation strategies add needed balance to change procedures. Validation is a therapeutic "yes, but," when combined with change strategies so that the therapist simultaneously communicates why something could not be otherwise yet must change. When the client says, "I can't stand it!" the therapist says "Yes, I know the pain is excruciating and seems unendurable, but I think we can go a little bit further."

Validation is also used to balance pathologizing that both clients and therapists are prone to do. Clients often have learned to treat their own valid responses as invalid (as stupid, weak, defective, or bad). Similarly, therapists also have learned to view normal responses as pathological. Validation strategies balance this by requiring the therapist to search for the strengths, normality, or effectiveness inherent in the client's responses whenever possible and by teaching the client to self-validate. Even patently invalid behavior may be valid in terms of being effective. Cutting one's arms in response to overwhelming emotional distress makes sense given that it often produces relief from unbearable emotions: It is an effective emotion regulation strategy.

WHAT TO VALIDATE

Validate the valid. Note that

> ... validation means the acknowledgement of that which is valid. It does not mean the "making" of something valid. Nor does it mean validating that which is invalid. The therapist observes, experiences and affirms but does not create validity. That which is valid preexists the therapeutic action. (Linehan, 1997, p. 356)

Validation functions as reinforcement—what you validate you will see more of.

To determine how a response is valid (or invalid), consider three ways it could be valid (Linehan, 1997). A response is valid if it is (1) relevant and meaningful; (2) well-grounded or justifiable in terms of facts, logical inference, or generally accepted authority; or (3) an appropriate or effective means to obtain one's ultimate goals. In other words, something can be valid in terms of current context (i.e., empirical facts, consensual agreement), antecedents (i.e., previous events), or consequences (i.e., effective for immediate or ultimate goals). During a psychotherapy session, it is invalid to fall asleep, refuse to talk, or change topics whenever problem solving is broached. The behavior is not relevant to the therapeutic task at hand. When a client says she hates herself, hatred might be both relevant and justifiable if the person violated her own important values (e.g., had deliberately harmed another person out of anger). The response of self-hatred may be relevant and justifiable, yet at the same time ineffective because it is incompatible with the balanced problem solving required to keep oneself from doing the hateful behavior again. Or say, for example, you've forgotten some fact that is important to a client without being aware you have done so. As the conversation continues, the client becomes overly cheery and stops saying anything of substance about the topic. When you wonder aloud about the change in mood and depth of the conversation, the client airily dismisses your concern. The client's response may be valid in terms of past learning history (understandable if her cultural background prohibits drawing attention to another's failings or directly expressing irritation about them) or current circumstances (if your tone is defensive or accusatory and it's logical to infer you won't be open to the feedback). But her response may be simultaneously invalid in that it may be ineffective to her long-term goals if her response fails to prompt any examination or correction in your behavior that hurt her feelings or if you need the fact in order to be most helpful to her. In short, look at context, antecedents, and consequences of the response. Does the response make sense in light of empirical facts, previous events, current context, logic, or consensual agreement? Is it compatible with the client's long-term goals? If yes, then the behavior is valid.

All behavior is valid in some way. Coming to a party at 5:00 P.M. that doesn't start until 8:00 P.M. may be invalid in that it is based on an incorrect belief about when the party starts, but it would be a valid response to an incorrectly stated invitation for 5:00 P.M. Even extremely dysfunctional behavior may be valid in terms of historically making sense—all of the factors needed for the behavior to develop have occurred: therefore, how could the behavior be other than it is?

CONTRAINDICATIONS

The only true contraindication is that therapists should not validate invalid behavior. That is, the therapist does not want to validate responses that are dysfunctional and incompatible with progress toward the agreed-upon therapeutic goals. Because validation by definition functions as reinforcement, the therapist should be aware of what he or she is implicitly or explicitly validating and respond differentially to valid and invalid responses. Particularly with clients who are highly sensitive to emotional cues (e.g., individuals who tend to respond in an angry or extremely despairing manner to perceived threat), the therapist may become more and more careful in what he or she says in order to avoid setting off the client's reaction. But this means that the client does not change. In fact, emotional sensitivity and intensity (e.g., anger or despair) are inadvertently made more likely (negatively reinforced) as the therapist withdraws a focus on change. In other words, the client's emotional response may gradually shape the therapist out of using effective change-oriented strategies that increase painful emotions. Validation can provide the balm for both therapist and client to negotiate through change procedures.

HOW DOES THE TECHNIQUE WORK?

Validation likely works via a number of processes. Validation appears to soothe and reduce negative emotional arousal, whether measured physiologically or via self-report (Shenk &

Fruzzetti, in press). Validation may also make important changes in interaction patterns that impact more distal outcomes. For example, in work with couples, validation can be taught to one partner, and the subsequent increased validation leads to increased self-disclosure and expression of the other partner. Such increases in validation predict improvements in couple and individual distress. In fact, validating and invalidating behaviors may be more explanatory than negativity in understanding couple distress. Process research on Motivational Interviewing (Miller & Rollnick, 2002) suggests that therapist behaviors that are validating impact client "change talk" and thereby impact the likelihood of behavioral change such as drinking outcomes (Moyers, et al., 2007). Validation may function as self-verification. A compelling series of research studies by Swann and his colleagues (Swann, 1984, 1987, 1992, 1997; Swann & Ely, 1984; Swann, Griffin, Predmore, & Gaines, 1987; Swann, Hixon, Stein-Seroussi, & Gilbert, 1990; Swann, Pelham, & Chidester, 1988; Swann & Read, 1981a, 1981b; Swann & Schroeder, 1995; Swann, Stein-Seroussi, & Giesler, 1992) suggests that verification of one's self-view, all other things being equal, will serve as a general reinforcer for most individuals. People will work to obtain feedback, even if negative, that is consistent with important self-constructs and views (a process called *self-verification*). It is a normal psychological process for emotional arousal to occur when significant goals are blocked and important self-constructs are disconfirmed. When feedback is inconsistent with important self-constructs, consequent arousal and the sense of being out of control result in both failure to process new information and intense effort to gain control. Validation, on the other hand, reduces arousal and the sense of being out of control and thereby increases learning and collaboration.

In contrast, it may be that the most important function of validation is that it communicates to the individual that he or she is understood and that this sense of being understood is critical to trusting a therapist sufficiently to collaborate. From this viewpoint, it is not the nonverification of the individual's self-constructs that is so important but rather the misunderstanding of the problems, needs, goals, and capabilities of the client. Whichever position is borne out by future research, both offer insight into the function of validation in psychotherapy.

EVIDENCE FOR THE EFFECTIVENESS OF VALIDATION

Moyers et al. (2007) cited above provides some of the first support for a causal chain between therapists' validating behavior and clinical outcomes. The work by Fruzzetti and colleagues indicates that the addition of validation training for partners or family members has a similar positive impact. For example, validation predicts long term improvements in individual distress, even after accounting for the couple's level of distress and criticism. A family training intervention that emphasizes validation (ref) has x impacts. Further research is needed in this area.

STEP-BY-STEP PROCEDURES

Step 1: Know Thy Client

Know thy client—and know thy psychopathology and normal psychology literatures. Be aware of what is valid and invalid for the specific client. Does the response move the client toward his or her immediate or ultimate goals? If so, the response is valid. Remember that a response can be both valid and invalid simultaneously. Constantly be aware of the client's current emotional arousal and how this is affecting the ability to process new information, and balance change and validation accordingly.

Step 2: Validate the Valid, Invalidate the Invalid

Be specific about what you are validating. For example, a case manager who has come to ignore repeated requests by a client to become his own payee because the client typically injudiciously spends the money, hears another impassioned request but ignores it completely as if it were irrelevant. Dismissiveness invalidates both the valid and invalid aspects of the request. Differential responding would require validating the

valid (the wisdom of the ultimate goal of independence) while invalidating the invalid (e.g., insisting that an adequate plan to correct the mishandling of money be in place before making the change). The same behavior can be both valid and invalid. Of course, the case manager's ignoring of the requests is also both valid and invalid: valid in the sense of being justifiable based on the client's mishandling of money, but invalid to the extent that it ignores the client's normative desire to control his own money and work toward greater independence.

To validate emotional responses, encourage emotional expression, teach emotion observation and labeling, read the client's emotions, and directly validate emotions (e.g., "feeling sad makes sense"). To validate behavioral responses, teach behavioral observation and labeling skills. Identify self-imposed demands or unrealistic standards for acceptable behavior and use of guilt, self-berating, or other punishment strategies (identify the *should*). Counter the *should* (i.e., communicate that all behavior is understandable in principle). Accept the *should* (i.e., respond to the client's behavior nonjudgmentally and discover whether there is truth to the *should* when phrased as "should in order to . . ."). Validate the client's disappointment in his or her own behavior. To validate cognitive responses, elicit and reflect thoughts and assumptions, find the "kernel of truth" in the client's cognitions, acknowledge the client's intuitive ability to know what is wise or correct, and respect the client's values. To validate the person's ability to attain desired goals, assume the best, encourage, focus on strengths, contradict or modulate external criticism, and be realistic in assessment of capabilities. To invalidate the invalid, be descriptive and nonjudgmental, articulating how the response does not make sense either in terms of antecedents or consequences.

Step 3: Validate at the Highest Possible Level

Remember that actions speak louder than words. Linehan (1997) has described six levels of validation. While all levels are important, higher levels are viewed as more important and at times crucial.

At each level, do not rely solely on explicit verbal validation. Acting and responding as if the client's responses are valid is often both required and more powerful than verbal validation. In other words, if you were trapped at a fourth-floor window of a burning building, and a firefighter showed interest, accurately reflected your distress, understood better than you your terror, and genuinely communicated how it made sense with both your learning history and current circumstances for you to be on the verge of a panic attack, it would still be insufficient! Putting the fire out is what you need and this functional validation, responding to the client's experience as valid (and therefore compelling), is essential. Verbal validation alone, when in fact functional validation is required, is one of the most therapist-like of errors. Avoid it.

- *Level 1: Listen with complete awareness, be awake.* Listen and observe in an unbiased manner, communicate that the client's responses are valid by listening without prejudging. For example, the case manager hears the client's request to become his own payee without construing it solely in terms of the mismanagement of money.
- *Level 2: Accurately reflect the client's communication.* Communicate understanding by repeating or rephrasing, using words close to the client's own without added interpretation.
- *Level 3: Articulate unverbalized emotions, thoughts, or behavior patterns.* Perceptively understand what is not stated but meant without the client's having to explain things.
- *Level 4: Describe how the client's behavior makes sense in terms of past learning history or biology.* Identify the probable factors that caused the client's response. For example, to a client who constantly seeks reassurance that therapy "is going okay," the therapist might validate by saying, "Given the unpredictability of your parents, it makes sense to have the feeling of waiting for the other shoe to drop and seek reassurance."
- *Level 5: Actively search for the ways that the client's behavior makes sense in the current circumstances and communicate this.* Find the ways

a response is currently valid, whenever possible, and remember not to rely only on verbal validation. For example, say you were walking to a movie theater with a friend who'd been raped in an alley, you proposed that you take a shortcut through an alley so that you wouldn't be late for the movie, and your friend said she did not want to because she was afraid. Saying, "Of course you're afraid, you were raped in an alley, how insensitive of me" would be a Level-4 validation. Saying, "Of course you are afraid, alleys are dangerous, let's walk around" would be a Level-5 validation. When you can find a Level-5 validation (and search like a fiend for it), use it rather than a Level 4. So, for example, with the client seeking reassurance, the therapist might search for ways that he or she is communicating ambivalence or in some other way cueing the client's response, so that seeking reassurance is sensible, even if the history of unpredictable parents were known. Validating in terms of the past when in fact there are aspects in the current situation prompting the response is experienced as extremely invalidating. For example, if a client is angry that his therapist is rigid about adjusting the therapy payment in the face of his unexpected layoff and difficulty finding new work (and in fact the therapist is decidedly and unreasonably inflexible), it is to be expected that the client would become angrier if the therapist attempted to validate by beginning with how the client's response is understandable given how withholding and rigid his father was.

- *Level 6: Be radically genuine.* Act in a manner that communicates respect for the client as a person and an equal, more than the person as client or disorder. Play to the person's strengths rather than to fragility, in a manner comparable to how you'd offer help to a treasured colleague or loved one. Whereas levels 1 to 5 represent sequential steps in validation of a kind, Level 6 represents both changes in level as well as in kind, in which the therapist validates the individual

1. **Know thy client.** Know what responses are normative, abnormal, and in line with the client's ultimate therapeutic goals.
2. **Validate the valid; invalidate the invalid.** Be specific, precise, and differentially respond to strengthen emotional, behavioral, and cognitive responses in line with the client's ultimate therapeutic goals.
3. **Validate at the highest possible level. Remember, actions speak louder than words.** Listen with complete awareness; accurately reflect; articulate the unverbalized; describe how responses make sense in terms of the past or preferably current circumstances. Be radically genuine.
4. **Actively validate early in therapy; fade to normal levels over time.**

FIGURE 78.1 Keys to Validation

rather than any particular response or behavioral pattern. As Rogers has described this radically genuine stance:

> He is without front or façade, openly being the feelings and attitudes which at the moment are flowing in him. It involves the element of self-awareness, meaning that the feelings the therapist is experiencing are available to his awareness, and also that he is able to live these feelings, to be them in the relationship, and able to communicate them if appropriate. It means that he comes in to a direct personal encounter with his client, meeting him on a person-to-person basis. It means he is being himself, not denying himself. (Rogers & Truax, 1967, p. 101).

Step 4: Actively Validate Early in Therapy; Fade to Normal Levels of Validation over Time

Finally, while empathy and functional validation should remain high throughout therapy, the active verbal validation to provide corrective feedback or balance pathologizing should be faded from an initially high level to normative level. (For a summary of the steps of validation, see Figure 78.1).

Further Reading

Linehan, M. M. (1993). Validation. In *Cognitive behavioral therapy for Borderline Personality Disorder* (pp. 221–249). New York: Guilford Press.
Linehan, M. M. (1997). Validation and psychotherapy. In A. Bohart & L. Greenberg (Eds.), *Empathy reconsidered: New directions in psychotherapy*

(pp. 353–392). Washington, DC: American Psychiatric Association.

References

Bohart, A., & Greenberg, L. (Eds.). (1997). *Empathy reconsidered: New directions in psychotherapy.* Washington, DC: American Psychiatric Association.
Feil, N. (1992). *Validation: The Feil method.* Ohio: Edward Feil.
Fruzzetti, A. E. (2000). *The role of validation in individual psychopathology, relationship quality, and treatment.* Symposium paper presented at the 34th annual convention of the Association for the Advancement of Behavior Therapy, New Orleans, LA.
Fruzzetti, A. E., & Mosco, E. (2006) Dialectical behavior therapy adapted for couples and families: A pilot group intervention for couples (Unpublished manuscript).
Fruzzetti, A. E., & Rubio, A. (1998). *Observing intimacy: Self-disclosure and validation reciprocity and its impact on relationship and individual well-being.* Symposium paper presented at the 32nd annual convention of the Association for the Advancement of Behavior Therapy, Washington, DC.
Greenberg, L. S. & Paivio, S. C. (1997). *Working with emotions in psychotherapy.* New York: Guilford Press.
Linehan, M. M. (1993). Validation. In *Cognitive behavioral therapy for Borderline Personality Disorder* (pp. 221–249). New York: Guilford Press.
Linehan, M. M. (1997). Validation and psychotherapy. In A. Bohart & L. Greenberg (Eds.), *Empathy reconsidered: New directions in psychotherapy* (pp. 353–392). Washington, DC: American Psychiatric Association.
Miller, W. R., & Rollnick, S. (1991). *Motivational interviewing: Preparing people for change.* New York: Guilford.
Moyers, T. B., Martin, T., Christopher, P. J., Houck, J. M., Tonigan, J. S., & Amrhein, P. C. (2007). Client language as a mediator of motivational interviewing efficacy: Where is the evidence? *Alcoholism: Clinical and Experimental Research, 31* (suppl 3), 40s–47s.
Rogers, C. R., & Truax, C. B. (1967). The therapeutic conditions antecedent to change: A theoretical view. In C. R. Rogers (Ed.), *The therapeutic relationship and its impact* (pp. 97–108). Madison: University of Wisconsin Press.
Shenk, C., & Fruzzetti, A. E. (in press). The impact of validating and invalidating behavior on emotional arousal.
Swann, W. B. (1984). Quest for accuracy in person perception: A matter of pragmatics. *Psychological Review, 91,* 457–477.

Swann, W. B. (1987). Identity negotiation: Where two roads meet. *Journal of Personality and Social Psychology, 53,* 1038–1051.

Swann, W. B. (1992). Seeking "truth," finding despair: Some unhappy consequences of a negative self-concept. *Current Directions in Psychological Science, 1,* 15–18.

Swann, W. B. (1997). The trouble with change: Self-verification and allegiance to the self. *Psychological Science, 8,* 177–180.

Swann, W. B., & Ely, R. J. (1984). A battle of wills: Self-verification versus behavioral confirmation. *Journal of Personality and Social Psychology, 46,* 1287–1302.

Swann, W. B., Griffin, J., Predmore, S. C, & Gaines, B. (1987). The cognitive-affective crossfire: When self-consistency confronts self-enhancement. *Journal of Personality and Social Psychology, 52,* 881–889.

Swann, W. B., Hixon, J. G., Stein-Seroussi, A., & Gilbert, D. T. (1990). The fleeting gleam of praise: Cognitive processes underlying behavioral reactions to self-relevant feedback. *Journal of Personality and Social Psychology, 59,* 17–26.

Swann, W. B., Pelham, B. W., & Chidester, T. R. (1988). Change through paradox: Using self-verification to alter beliefs. *Journal of Personality and Social Psychology, 54,* 268–273.

Swann, W. B. & Predmore, S. C. (1985). Intimates as agents of social support: Sources of consolation or despair? *Journal of Personality and Social Psychology, 49,* 1609–1617.

Swann, W. B., & Read, S. J. (1981a). Acquiring self-knowledge: The search for feedback that fits. *Journal of Personality and Social Psychology, 41,* 1119–1128.

Swann, W. B., & Read, S. J. (1981b). Self-verification processes: How we sustain our self-conceptions. *Journal of Experimental and Social Psychology, 17,* 351–372.

Swann, W. B., & Schroeder, D. G. (1995). The search for beauty and truth: A framework for understanding reactions to evaluations. *Personality and Social Psychology Bulletin, 21,* 1307–1318

Swann, W. B., Stein-Seroussi, A., & Giesler, R. B. (1992). Why people self-verify. *Journal of Personality and Social Psychology, 62,* 392–401.

79 VALUES CLARIFICATION

Michael P. Twohig and Jesse M. Crosby

Changing behavior can be difficult, especially when there is a lack of motivation or the target behavior presents a formidable challenge. Values clarification is an intervention strategy that seeks to increase motivation by linking behavior change to areas of life that clients find meaningful, thereby increasing the reinforcing value of engaging in target actions.

The term *values* has been used in different contexts within psychology, but in this context values refer to areas in life that a person cares about and is willing to work towards. Every person values different areas of life, and these areas are valued to varying degrees. For instance, many people care about family, spirituality, and/or social causes, but this is not the case for everyone. Also, values should not be confused with the manner in which an individual behaves. People do not always behave consistently with their values, but they can still value an area even if they are not behaving consistently with it. For example, many people value helping the poor, but spend very little time acting on this value. Clarification of values aims to foster more value-consistent behavior.

Values are different than goals. Values can never be achieved (e.g., someone who values being a good parent will always have more opportunities to do so); whereas goals are attainable steps that are guided by values (e.g., a goal of spending more time with one's children is part of the value of being a good parent). Often therapy focuses on goals and sometimes loses sight of values; while in actuality the ultimate purpose of therapy is to increase quality of life and overall functioning of the client—which are values-based activities. For example, a goal in the treatment of obsessive compulsive disorder (OCD) is the reduction of compulsions, but reductions in compulsions are not the larger purpose of therapy. The larger focus of therapy is

to help the client return to work, spend time with family, or live a more meaningful life, all of which are guided by values. Values clarification can both enhance a client's motivation to engage in therapy and provide therapeutic direction. Using the treatment of OCD as an example again, exposure exercises can be done in the service of one's values by tying completion of the exercises to an increased ability to engage in activities that are important to the client (e.g., completion of exposures will make activities with the client's family easier). Values can have a more immediate impact by making the exposures part of a valued activity (e.g., having a client with contamination obsessions take their partner out to dinner and not engaging in compulsions so that he can enjoy the event).

Clients are often so focused on symptom reduction that they have abandoned any hope of moving forward in life until their symptoms are eliminated. This intervention shifts the focus from symptom reduction to valued living by helping the client define the concept of values, identify their own values, and use behavioral strategies to act in accordance with their chosen values. Values clarification is an important component of acceptance and commitment therapy (ACT; Hayes, Strosahl, & Wilson, 1999) and is similar in process to motivational interviewing (Miller & Rollnick, 2002). This chapter will describe the values clarification intervention as it is used in ACT.

WHO MIGHT BENEFIT FROM VALUES CLARIFICATION?

Any person can benefit from evaluating the consistency between their values and the manner in which they are currently behaving, but therapeutically, values clarification procedures are most likely to be used with clients who are not fully engaging in treatment, resistant to treatment, or having difficulties changing behavior. Values clarification is used to motivate behavior change or provide direction for change. Thus, individuals who are not capable of the target behavior or do not have the skills in their repertoire are not good candidates. Values clarification can be helpful to motivate skills acquisition, but the clarification of values is not the most appropriate intervention for someone who lacks the skills to perform the behavior. For example, if someone's social phobia is largely caused by a lack of social skills, then social skills training is most appropriate. If anxiety in social situations is the issue, then motivation to confront anxiety would be a useful component of therapy.

CONTRAINDICATIONS

There are three concerns that can arise in values clarification: (1) The client's reported values are unduly influenced by external pressures, (2) the client has difficulty selecting values, or (3) the values that are selected are highly inconsistent with the therapist's values or ethical guidelines.

There are many external pressures on the selection of values including, but not limited to, peer and family, media, and therapist pressures. Some external influence on the selection of values should be expected, but values that are selected because of too much pressure from external sources are unlikely to be useful for guiding behavior. For example, a client who reports being a successful professional as an important value may be doing so because of societal pressures to be successful. The therapist needs to closely monitor the motivation for value selection and assist the client in selecting and pursuing honest values.

Sometimes a client will have difficulty identifying meaningful values. There are many causes for this, but this is more common with people whose behavior is under aversive control or largely done in the service of external reinforcement. Additionally, people who are referred for treatment rather than self-referred often lack motivation to participate. In cases such as these,

focusing on smaller and more immediate values can serve as an initial motivator to participate in treatment and as treatment progresses, values can be readdressed and more long-term values can be clarified. For example, a client diagnosed with substance dependence who is court referred for treatment may have very little motivation to participate in treatment. In this situation, the value of "being free" can serve to motivate participation, and larger values relating to family, occupation, and so forth can be addressed later in therapy.

In general, the therapist should accept the client's values in a nonjudgmental manner, but there are some cases where the client's values are highly inconsistent with the therapist's values or ethical guidelines. In situations such as these, this inconsistency could be interpreted as a sign that the client's value may be the result of an external pressure or some other source of concern. For instance, if the client's value involves harming others, the therapist should discuss the motivation for this value, because it may not truly be the client's value. It is a clinical concern if the client wants the therapist's assistance in pursuing a value that is highly inconsistent with the therapist's values or ethical guidelines. In most cases, the therapist can usually find a way to work with the client, but if no solution can be found the client should be referred to alternative services.

HOW DOES VALUES CLARIFICATION WORK?

Values clarification is based on the assumption that the significance of values can influence behavior by providing a way to connect immediate acts with long-term consequences. In other words, personal values provide a purpose for the behavior (Pepper, 1947). The identification and clarification of values can provide a stronger purpose for immediate behavior change because it links a difficult behavior with a desired long-term outcome. For example, exposure therapy is the most empirically supported treatment for anxiety disorders, but fostering full participation can be difficult. Linking the person's chosen values with the exposure shifts the focus from the immediate negative consequences to long-term valued living (Wilson & Murrell, 2004). This can easily be accomplished by saying something like, "touching this garbage can [for contamination-type OCD] and experiencing the anxiety is similar to the anxiety you feel hugging your daughter. Doing this exercise is a step toward being with your family."

STEP-BY-STEP PROCEDURES

Values clarification procedures can be broken down into a series of steps for easier implementation. When familiarity with these procedures increases, one will find it easy to increase motivation by linking therapy procedures to valued ends without working through all of the following steps. Nonetheless, the following steps are useful for conducting a full session on values clarification.

Values clarification can be broken down into the following seven steps:

1. Creating distance from social rules
2. Defining values as a concept
3. Defining personal values
4. Choosing values
5. Determining the consistency of current actions and values
6. Choosing immediate goals that are consistent with values
7. Behaving in accordance with goals and values

Much of this description overlaps with the *Values Homework* described in Hayes et al. (1999).

Creating Distance from Social Rules

Behavior is under many sources of control. The type of employment chosen may be for financial compensation, benefits, prestige, ease of the job, hours worked, enjoyment, or the meaning and importance of the work. In most cases it is the combination of many of these areas that helps us select our occupations. The exact reasons that different areas are important to each of us are hard to determine, but there is a distinction between choices that are made based on rules of how we should behave and choices made

freely based on the process of natural learning. Values chosen based on social rules will likely be less effective at maintaining behavior than values that are naturally important to the client. Naturally important values are more reinforcing.

The first step in values clarification is to help the client distinguish between choices based on rules of the way things "should be" and choices that are freely made. For example, how many people would attend college or graduate school if nobody ever knew you had done so? A question such as this illuminates the social approval that partially supports the decision to attend college or graduate school. The amount that income affects college attendance could similarly be illuminated by asking, "Would you attend college if it did not increase your income?" No particular type of motivation is more appropriate than any other, but awareness of the source of the motivation can help foster choices that are more in line with the client's values rather than social pressures. For example, if the client finds that she is only attending college to please her parents or that she has chosen a career only to make more money, she may decide not to pursue this value or might benefit from finding the true value behind schooling. Clients should be able to freely choose between options even when there are external factors influencing the decision. Clarification of the sources of influence allows for choices that are more guided by values.

Defining Values as a Concept

The term *values* has many different meanings in psychology. In this context it refers to areas of life that are important to the client. Values can never be achieved; one can always more fully pursue a value, and at any point it has been well pursued, there are additional opportunities to work on that value. For example, the value of being a good parent can never be achieved; one can always be a better parent and there will always be additional opportunities to do so. Values are different than goals; goals are steps that are consistent with values. Even though society may put greater emphasis on some values over others, in therapy, the importance of particular values is chosen by the client and not judged by the therapist (unless the therapist believes the value was not chosen freely). The client is welcome to value or not value any area that she chooses. Values can be described to the client in the following fashion:

> Values are areas of life that you really care about. A value can never be achieved like a goal; it can only be worked towards. For example, someone who values being a good parent will never achieve the status of "good parent." Once the parent has done well, such as helping the child do well in school, there will be additional opportunities to be a good parent. Helping the child do well in school is a good example of a goal. Goals are useful as steps in the service of values. Values are often compared to a lighthouse in a storm. The light tells the sailor which way to steer the ship, just as values are useful for telling you which direction to go in life. You get to pick your values. There are no right or wrong choices here—these are not my [the therapist's], your parent's, or your friend's values—and you are welcome to change them at any time.

Defining Personal Values

There are an infinite number of areas of life that people can value, and each value means something different to each person. In many cases, people pursue values without thinking about what the value means to them or how they would really like to behave. In some cases the same value may have different functions for different people, (e.g., someone may be a doctor because it pays well and someone else may be a doctor to help the sick, or someone can value both at the same time). This phase of values training aims to help clarify what the person cares about in a number of areas in life.

Table 79.1 helps clients identify and clarify their values in nine major areas of life. This list is not exhaustive, but includes areas that many people find important. In this phase of values clarification, clients are asked to think about, discuss, and write about what they care about in the areas listed in the table. Clients are taught to select what they really care about in each area—as though nobody would see what is

written. The client is also welcome to write that she has no value in a particular area. This list is then discussed with the therapist.

Choosing Values

The issue of choice is purposefully included in the discussion of values. Choice is defined as a selection amongst alternatives that is not necessarily done for reasons. Reasons are avoided because there are always reasons for or against any selection and the client can get bogged down in whether or not pursuing a value is the "correct" decision. Whereas, a choice can be made while the client is uncertain if the choice is "correct," or choices can be made that are inconsistent with reasons. The impact of rules, social pressures, and pressures from the therapist (as well as many other pressures) needs to be decreased because they get in the way of value selection and the pursuit of values. For example, a client might value romantic relationships, but could reason himself out of pursuing one because he could "get hurt." The client is taught to simply *choose* to pursue that value regardless of the reasons for or against it.

Choosing values is conducted after they are defined so there is clarity to the choice being made. In this phase of values clarification the client declares that the values listed are indeed his and ranks the level of importance that is associated with each value. As described by Hayes et al. (1999), each one of these areas is ranked on a scale of 1 to 10 (where 1 = not at all important, and 10 = very important). Again, clients are reminded that they are welcome to rate the areas however they choose. Therapists should try to create a therapeutic context where clients feel welcome to be honest about their values.

Determining Consistency of Values and Current Actions

After clients have defined their values and rated the importance of each area, they assess the consistency between their current actions and their corresponding values. Clients are asked to look at how they defined each of the values and then rate how consistent their current actions are with their values on a scale of 1 to 10 (where 1 = not

TABLE 79.1 Values Clarification Exercise

Area	Description
Intimate Relationships	What kind of person would you like to be in the relationship? What would the relationship be like? What is your role in the relationship?
Family Relationships	Describe the type of brother/sister, son/daughter, father/mother you would like to be. What would the relationship be like? How would you want to treat others?
Social Relationships	What does it mean to be a good friend? What kind of friends do you want? How would you treat your friends? What is an ideal friendship like for you?
Career and Employment	What type of work would you like to do? Why does it appeal to you? What kind or worker would you like to be? What kind of relationships would you like to have with your coworkers or your employer?
Personal Growth and Development	What do you want to be able to do? What do you want to be like? Would you like to pursue a formal education? Specialized training? An informal education? Why does this appeal to you?
Recreation and Leisure	What type of hobbies, sports, or leisure activities would you like to be involved in? Why do these things appeal to you?
Spirituality	What does spirituality mean to you? (It doesn't have to be any kind of organized religion.) Is this an important part of life for you? What would it be like?
Citizenship	What is your role in the community? What groups would you like to be a part of? What volunteer work would you do? What appeals to you in these areas?
Health	What do you value in your physical health? What issues are important to you (e.g., sleep, diet, exercise)?

at all consistent and 10 = completely consistent). The function of this phase of therapy is not to make clients feel like failures, but to motivate and clarify areas that would likely benefit from additional attention. If the client rates a value as very high, but rates his behavioral consistency with that value as very low, then a treatment target is clarified. Areas where the client is behaving consistently with her values are less of a treatment target.

Choosing Immediate Goals that Are Consistent with Values

Based on the results from the previous step, clients are assisted in defining goals that are consistent with their values. Immediate goals are usually set in areas where clients are behaving inconsistently with values. There are an infinite number of ways that behavior can be altered to be more consistent with the stated value, and the link from each value to the specific goal should be clarified for the client.

In this phase of values clarification just about any method of behavior therapy or behavior change procedures are acceptable, as long as they are done in the service of the client's values. A very commonly used procedure is to break

down values into manageable steps of increasing difficulty. For example, if a parent values being a good mother—defined as being there for her son and supporting his growth—this might involve the following steps: (1) signing her son up for an activity he has wanted to participate in, (2) helping him with homework for 20 minutes each night, and (3) taking him out to do something enjoyable. These are all actions that would be considered consistent with the client's value of being a good parent.

Behaving in Accordance with One's Values

The final step involves behaving in accordance with these values. This is done in the form of specific exercises that are agreed upon in session and also as opportunities present themselves outside of session. The client should state an action that would be consistent with a value and engage in it between sessions. The idea is that a commitment to engage in the behavior is made prior to engaging in it and that the client is responsible for achieving it between sessions. After the client begins completing tasks with little difficulty, the need to commit to the tasks can be removed and the value itself can provide the motivation to engage in the tasks.

EVIDENCE-BASED APPLICATIONS

Values clarification is part of the larger treatment package of ACT. It is part of the choice to live life according to one's desires with the presence of painful emotions or uncomfortable experiences (Hayes et al., 1999). As such, the evidence in support of values clarification is contained in the literature that supports ACT. Evidence has been found in support of ACT for the treatment of a wide range of psychological problems including social phobia, agoraphobia, stress, smoking, diabetes management, substance abuse, depression, psychosis, chronic pain, bipolar disorder, and trichotillomania (Hayes, Luoma, Bond, Masuda, & Lillis, 2006; Hayes, Masuda, Bissett, Luoma, & Guerrero, 2004). Additionally, empirical support exists for the use of values based ACT interventions for chronic pain (Dahl, Wilson, & Nilsson, 2004) and epilepsy (Lundgren, Dahl, Melin, & Kies, 2006).

Motivational interviewing also includes a values-based component in which the therapist works to identify a discrepancy between the client's present behavior and important personal goals or values (Miller & Rollnick, 2002). The literature supports the application of motivational interviewing to problems such as substance use, gambling, eating disorders, and dieting and exercise (Hettema, Steele, & Miller, 2005).

SUMMARY

Values clarification is a useful process for behaviors that are difficult to change or for clients who lack motivation to participate in therapy. Values clarification links therapy goals to areas of life that the client finds important, and as a result there is an increase in motivation to make therapeutically significant changes. Additionally, this process can provide direction for treatment and help maintain outcomes achieved in therapy. There are multiple procedures that can be used to clarify values ranging from brief comments to session-long analyses. Procedures that focus on values clarification are receiving increased attention in the field of psychology.

Further Reading

Hayes, S. C., Strosahl, K. D., & Wilson, K. G. (1999). *Acceptance and commitment therapy: An experiential approach to behavior change.* New York: Guilford.

Luoma, J. B., Hayes, S. C., & Walser, R. D. (2007). *Learning ACT: An acceptance & commitment therapy skills-training manual for therapists.* Oakland, CA: New Harbinger/Reno, NV: Context Press.

Twohig, M. P., & Hayes, S. C. (2008). ACT verbatim for depression and anxiety: Annotated transcripts for learning Acceptance and Commitment Therapy. Oakland, CA: New Harbinger/Reno, NV: Context Press.

Wilson, K. G., & Murrell, A. R. (2004). Values work in acceptance and commitment therapy. In S. C. Hayes, V. M. Follette, & M. M. Linehan (Eds.), *Mindfulness and acceptance* (pp. 120–151). New York: Guilford.

References

Dahl, J., Wilson, K. G., & Nilsson, A. (2004). Acceptance and commitment therapy and the treatment of persons at risk for long-term disability resulting from stress and pain symptoms: A preliminary randomized trial. *Behavior Therapy, 35,* 785–801.

Hayes, S. C., Luoma, J. B., Bond, F. W., Masuda, A., & Lillis, J. (2006). Acceptance and Commitment Therapy: Model processes and outcomes. *Behaviour Research and Therapy, 44,* 1–25.

Hayes, S. C., Masuda, A., Bissett, R., Luoma, J., & Guerrero, L. F. (2004). DBT, FAP, and ACT: How empirically oriented are the new behavior therapy technologies? *Behavior Therapy, 35,* 35–54.

Hayes, S. C., Strosahl, K. D., & Wilson, K. G. (1999). *Acceptance and commitment therapy: An experiential approach to behavior change.* New York: Guilford.

Hettema, J., Steele, J., & Miller, W. R. (2005). Motivational interviewing. *Annual Review of Clinical Psychology, 1,* 91–111.

Lundgren, T., Dahl, J., Melin, L., & Kies, B. (2006). Evaluation of acceptance and commitment therapy for drug refractory epilepsy: A randomized controlled trial in South Africa—a pilot study. *Epilepsia, 47,* 2173–2179.

Miller, W. R., & Rollnick, S. (2002). *Motivational Interviewing: Preparing people for change.* New York: Guilford.

Pepper, S. C. (1947). *A digest of purposive values.* Berkeley, CA: University of California Press.

Wilson, K. G., & Murrell, A. R. (2004). *Values work in acceptance and commitment therapy.* In S. C. Hayes, V. M. Follette, & M. M. Linehan (Eds.), Mindfulness and acceptance (pp. 120–151). New York: Guilford.

AUTHOR INDEX

Ruckstuhl, L. E., 448, 449, 452
Rude, S. S., 565
Rudy, T., 473, 475
Rudy, T. E., 473, 475
Ruef, A. M., 300
Rummel, C., 216
Rusch, F. R., 328–330, 332
Ruscio, A. M., 15, 166
Rusesink, R., 474
Rush, A. G., 194, 196
Rush, A. J., 46, 77, 82, 83, 86, 88–90, 92, 133, 134,
    335, 339, 491, 555, 556, 558, 577, 578
Rush, J. A., 358
Rush, K. S., 312
Russell, D. W., 69
Russo, D. C., 532
Ruth, W. J., 151
Ruwaard, J., 637
Ryan, C., 245, 247–249
Ryan, J. A., 448
Ryan, R. M., 111, 276, 425, 427
Rychtarik, R. G., 353, 460
Ryden, A. M., 381
Ryder, J. A., 446, 452, 453
Ryon, N. B., 55

Sachs, D. P. L., 514, 515
Sackett, C. F., 182
Sacks, O., 534
Saelens, B. E., 217, 218
Safran, J. D., 275, 277
Safren, S. A., 73
Sahler, O. J., 120
Sajwaj, T. E., 494
Salas, E., 627
Salata, J. L., 500
Salkovskis, P. M., 92
Salter, A., 1, 2, 5, 189, 407
Salter, D., 571
Salters-Pedneault, K., 81, 94
Samaha, A. L., 417, 419
Sampson, W. S., 388
Sanchez-Craig, M., 435–438
Sanford, S., 390
Sanislow, C. A. III, 56
Sank, L. I., 335
Sanna, L. J., 120
Sanson-Fisher, R., 336
Santorelli, S. F., 428
Santoro, S. O., 78

Sarason, I. G., 633
Saslow, G., 35
Sasso, G., 310, 507–509
Sassu, K. A., 223
Sateia, M., 382, 390
Saudargas, R. A., 151
Saunders, K. J., 594
Saunders, T., 627
Savard, J., 381, 390, 618
Sawalani, G., 53
Sayette, M. A., 78
Sbraga, T. P., 524
Schade, M., 602
Schaefer, H. S., 428
Scharf, M. J., 426, 428
Schaub, A., 336
Schellekens, J., 641
Schene, A. H., 556
Scherer, D. G., 482
Schillaci, J., 565
Schilling, D. J., 534
Schilling, G., 636
Schlatter, M., 272
Schmal, D. P., 513, 514
Schmaling, K., 636
Schmaling, K. B., 57, 92, 138, 194, 195, 204,
    351–353
Schmidt, G., 586, 609
Schmidt, G. W., 217
Schmidt, N. B., 399–401
Schmidt-Rathjens, C., 556
Schnülle, J., 272
Schneider, D. J., 236
Schneider, R. H., 115
Schnelle, J. F., 221
Schnicke, M. K., 79, 560
Schober, R., 360
Schock, K., 622
Schoeder, B., 306
Schoenfeld, D., 116
Scholing, A., 92, 306
Schopp, L. H., 634
Schover, L. R., 585
Schrank, F. A., 158, 159
Schrieken, B., 637
Schroeder, D. G., 676
Schroeder, S. R., 250
Schry, R., 116
Schuller, R., 577
Schulz, R., 336, 337

SUBJECT INDEX

Spielman insomnia model, 382, 383
Spinning exercise in IE, 400
Sports, DRL in, 243
Squeeze technique, 608
    evaluating, 608
    partner in, 611
Standard behavioral treatment of insomnia, 385
Standard eight-session behavioral intervention,
        for insomnia, 387
State-Trait Anger Expression Inventory-2
        (STAXI-2), 115
stimulus, 199
Stimulus control
    excitatory, 614
    inhibitory, 614
stimulus control strategies, 280
Stimulus control therapy, for insomnia, 386
Stimulus mode of conditioned stimulus
        presentation, 374
Stimulus preference assessment, 621
    advantages, 621
    beneficiaries, 622
    effectiveness of, 624
    multiple stimulus without replacement, 624
    paired-stimulus procedure, 623
    procedure, choosing, 625
    single stimulus method, 622
    working of, 622
Stop–start technique, 608
Stress, 631
    biological factors, 631
    psychological factors, 631
    social-environmental factors, 631
Stress inoculation training, 627
    beneficiaries, 627
    contraindications, 627
    for stress forms, 627
    procedural flow chart, 629
        application and follow-through, 630
        conceptual-educational, 629
        consolidation, 629
        rehearsal, 629
        skills acquisition, 629
    step-by-step procedures, 629
    treatment goals, 628
    working of, 628
Stress management intervention, 631
    arousal reduction strategies, 634
    assessment procedure, 633
    behavioral plan creation, 634

beneficiaries, 632
cognitive behavioral approaches, 634
cognitive restructuring, 636
contraindications, 632
deciding factors, 632
didactic psychoeducation, 633
emotion-focused coping skills, 635
evidence-based applications, 636
lifestyle changes and, 636
problem-focused coping skills, 635
step-by-step procedures, 633
systematic approaches, 636
working of, 632
Stress management skills, in chronic pain CBT,
        476
Structural equation modeling, 54
Structuring time, in harm reduction, 354
Substance use interventions, 217
Support (Therapist, Social), in homework
        assignment, 366
Symbolic modeling in self-efficacy
        interventions, 490
Systematic desensitization, 11, 635, 640
    anxiety hierarchy development, 644
    contraindications, 642
    evidence-based applications, 640
        anxiety/OCD/phobia, 641
        developmental disabilities, 641
        medication and procedure compliance,
            642
        posttraumatic stress disorder, 641
    imaginal exposure, 645
    in relaxation training, 532
    key elements, 646
    relaxation training, 643
    step-by-step procedures, 643
    types, 640
        exposure therapy, 640
        group desensitization, 640
        in vivo desensitization, 640
        self-control desensitization, 640
    working of, 642

Tangible condition, NCR, 468
Tapering, in harm reduction, 354
task analysis, in response chaining, 148
Task-based grounding, 655, 660
teaching situations creations in FCT, 323
Tension-releasing exercises, for anger control,
        116